P9-DFN-237

THE HANDBOOK OF SECOND LANGUAGE ACQUISITION

Blackwell Handbooks in Linguistics

This outstanding multi-volume series covers all the major subdisciplines within linguistics today and, when complete, will offer a comprehensive survey of linguistics as a whole.

Already published:

The Handbook of Child Language
Edited by Paul Fletcher and Brian MacWhinney

The Handbook of Phonological Theory
Edited by John A. Goldsmith

The Handbook of Contemporary Semantic Theory
Edited by Shalom Lappin

The Handbook of Sociolinguistics
Edited by Florian Coulmas

The Handbook of Phonetic Sciences
Edited by William J. Hardcastle and John Laver

The Handbook of Morphology
Edited by Andrew Spencer and Arnold Zwicky

The Handbook of Japanese Linguistics
Edited by Natsuko Tsujimura

The Handbook of Linguistics
Edited by Mark Aronoff and Janie Rees-Miller

The Handbook of Contemporary Syntactic Theory
Edited by Mark Baltin and Chris Collins

The Handbook of Discourse Analysis
Edited by Deborah Schiffrin, Deborah Tannen, and Heidi E. Hamilton

The Handbook of Language Variation and Change
Edited by J. K. Chambers, Peter Trudgill, and Natalie Schilling-Estes

The Handbook of Historical Linguistics
Edited by Brian D. Joseph and Richard D. Janda

The Handbook of Language and Gender
Edited by Janet Holmes and Miriam Meyerhoff

The Handbook of Second Language Acquisition
Edited by Catherine Doughty and Michael H. Long

The Handbook of Second Language Acquisition

EDITED BY

Catherine J. Doughty and Michael H. Long

350 Main Street, Malden, MA 02148-5018, USA
108 Cowley Road, Oxford OX4 1JF, UK
550 Swanston Street, Carlton South, Melbourne, Victoria 3053, Australia
Kurfürstendamm 57, 10707 Berlin, Germany

First published 2003 by Blackwell Publishing Ltd

Library of Congress Cataloging-in-Publication Data

The handbook of second language acquisition / edited by Catherine J. Doughty and Michael H. Long.
p. cm. – (Blackwell handbooks in linguistics ; 14)
Includes bibliographical references and index.
ISBN 0-631-21754-1 (hardcover : alk. paper)
1. Second language acquisition. I. Doughty, Catherine. II. Long, Michael H. III. Series.

P118.2 .H363 2003
418–dc21 2002154756

A catalogue record for this title is available from the British Library.

Set in 10/12pt Palatino
by Graphicraft Limited, Hong Kong
Printed and bound in the United Kingdom
by TJ International, Padstow, Cornwall

For further information on
Blackwell Publishing, visit our website:
http://www.blackwellpublishing.com

Contents

Contributors

Niclas Abrahamsson
Stockholm University

Craig Chaudron
University of Hawai'i

Robert M. DeKeyser
University of Pittsburg

Zoltán Dörnyei
University of Nottingham

Catherine J. Doughty
University of Hawai'i

Nick C. Ellis
Bangor University of Wales

Susan M. Gass
Michigan State University

Kevin Gregg
Momoyama Gakuin/St Andrew's University

Jan H. Hulstijn
University of Amsterdam

Kenneth Hyltenstam
Stockholm University

Judith F. Kroll
Pennsylvania State University

Michael H. Long
University of Hawai'i

Sarah Nielsen
Las Positas College

John Norris
Northern Arizona University

Terence Odlin
Ohio State University

William O'Grady
University of Hawai'i

Lourdes Ortega
Northern Arizona University

Manfred Pienemann
Paderborn University

Peter Robinson
Aoyama Gakuin University

Suzanne Romaine
Merton College, University of Oxford

Norman Segalowitz
Concordia University

Jeff Siegel
University of New England, Armadale, and University of Hawai'i

Peter Skehan
King's College, London

Antonella Sorace
University of Edinburgh

Gretchen Sunderman
University of Illinois at Urbana-Champaign

Karen Ann Watson-Gegeo
University of California, Davis

Lydia White
McGill University

Acknowledgments

The editors gratefully acknowledge the following, who provided valuable reviews of one or more of the chapters: Alan Beretta, Craig Chaudron, Richard Cameron, Robert DeKeyser, Susan Gass, Kevin Gregg, Jan Hulstijn, Georgette Ioup, Peter Robinson, Dick Schmidt, Bonnie Schwartz, Larry Selinker, Mary Tiles, Michael Ullman, Jessica Williams, Lydia White, Kate Wolfe-Quintero, and several individuals who prefer to remain anonymous. The support and efficiency of Steve Smith, Sarah Coleman, and Fiona Sewell at Blackwell Publishing were greatly appreciated.

I Overview

1 The Scope of Inquiry and Goals of SLA

CATHERINE J. DOUGHTY AND
MICHAEL H. LONG

1 The Scope of Inquiry

The scope of second language acquisition (SLA) is broad. It encompasses basic and applied work on the acquisition and loss of second (third, etc.) languages and dialects by children and adults, learning naturalistically and/or with the aid of formal instruction, as individuals or in groups, in foreign, second language, and lingua franca settings (see, e.g., R. Ellis, 1994; Gass and Selinker, 2001; Gregg, 1994; Jordens and Lalleman, 1988; W. Klein, 1986; Larsen-Freeman, 1991; Larsen-Freeman and Long, 1991; Ritchie and Bhatia, 1996; Towell and Hawkins, 1994). Research methods employed run the gamut from naturalistic observation in field settings, through descriptive and quasi-experimental studies of language learning in classrooms or via distance education, to experimental laboratory work and computer simulations.

Researchers enter SLA with graduate training in a variety of fields, including linguistics, applied linguistics, psychology, communication, foreign language education, educational psychology, and anthropology, as well as, increasingly, in SLA per se, and bring with them a wide range of theoretical and methodological allegiances. The 1980s and 1990s witnessed a steady increase in sophistication in the choice of data-collection procedures and analyses employed, some of them original to SLA researchers (see, e.g., Birdsong, 1989; Chaudron, this volume; Doughty and Long, 2000; Faerch and Kasper, 1987; Sorace, 1996; Tarone, Gass, and Cohen, 1994), and also in the ways SLA is measured (Bachman and Cohen, 1998; Norris and Ortega, this volume). However, longitudinal studies of children (e.g., Huebner, 1983a, 1983b; F. Klein, 1981; Sato, 1990; Watson-Gegeo, 1992) and adults (e.g., Iwashita, 2001; Liceras, Maxwell, Laguardia, Fernandez, Fernandez, and Diaz, 1997; Schmidt, 1983) are distressingly rare; the vast majority of SLA studies are cross-sectional, with serious resulting limitations on the conclusions that can be drawn on some important issues. Theory proliferation remains a weakness, too, but the experience of more mature disciplines in overcoming this and related teething problems is gradually being brought to bear (see, e.g., Beretta, 1991; Beretta and Crookes, 1993; Crookes, 1992; Gregg, 1993, 1996, 2000, this volume; Gregg, Long, Jordan, and Beretta, 1997; Jordan, 2002; Long, 1990a, 1993, forthcoming a).[1]

As reflected in the contributions to this volume (see also Robinson, 2001), much current SLA research and theorizing shares a strongly cognitive orientation, while varying from nativist, both special (linguistic) and general, to various kinds of functional, emergentist, and connectionist positions. The focus is firmly on identifying the nature and sources of the underlying L2 knowledge system, and on explaining developmental success and failure. Performance data are inevitably the researchers' mainstay, but understanding underlying competence, not the external verbal behavior that depends on that competence, is the ultimate goal. Researchers recognize that SLA takes place in a social context, of course, and accept that it can be influenced by that context, both micro and macro. However, they also recognize that language learning, like any other learning, is ultimately a matter of change in an individual's internal mental state. As such, research on SLA is increasingly viewed as a branch of cognitive science.

2 The Goals: Why Study SLA?

Second language acquisition – naturalistic, instructed, or both – has long been a common activity for a majority of the human species and is becoming ever more vital as second languages themselves increase in importance. In many parts of the world, monolingualism, not bilingualism or multilingualism, is the marked case. The 300–400 million people whose native language is English, for example, are greatly outnumbered by the 1–2 billion people for whom it is an official second language. Countless children grow up in societies where they are exposed to one language in the home, sometimes two, another when they travel to a nearby town to attend primary or secondary school, and a third or fourth if they move to a larger city or another province for tertiary education or for work.

Where literacy training or even education altogether is simply unavailable in a group's native language, or where there are just too many languages to make it economically viable to offer either in all of them, as is the case in Papua New Guinea and elsewhere in the Pacific (Siegel, 1996, 1997, 1999, this volume), some federal and state governments and departments of education mandate use of a regional lingua franca or of an official national language as the medium of instruction. Such situations are sometimes recognized in state constitutions, and occasionally even in an official federal language policy, as in Australia (Lo Bianco, 1987); all mean that SLA is required of students, and often of their teachers, as well.

Elsewhere, a local *variety* of a language may be actively suppressed or stigmatized, sometimes even by people who speak it natively themselves, resulting in a need for widespread second *dialect* acquisition (SDA) for educational, employment, and other purposes. Examples include Hawai'i Creole English (Reynolds, 1999; Sato, 1985, 1989; Wong, 1999), Aboriginal English in Australia (Eades, 1992; Haig, 2001; Malcolm, 1994), and African-American Vernacular English in the USA (Long, 1999; Morgan, 1999; Rickford, 2000). In such cases, a supposedly "standard" variety may be prescribed in educational settings, despite the difficulty of defining a *spoken* standard objectively, and despite the notorious track record of attempts to legislate language change. The prescribed varieties are second languages or dialects for the students, and as in part of the Solomon Islands (Watson-Gegeo, 1992; Watson-Gegeo and Nielsen, this volume), once again, sometimes for their teachers, too, with a predictably negative effect on educational achievement. In a more positive development, while language death throughout the world continues at an alarming pace, increasing numbers of children in some countries attend various kinds of additive bilingual, additive bidialectal, or immersion programs designed to promote first language maintenance, SLA, or cultural revitalization (see, e.g., Fishman, 2001; Huebner and Davis, 1999; Philipson, 2000; Sato, 1989; Warner, 2001).

SLA and SDA are not just common experiences for the world's children, of course. More and more adults are becoming second language or second dialect learners voluntarily for the purposes of international travel, higher education, and marriage. For increasing numbers of others, the experience is thrust upon them. Involuntary SLA may take the fairly harmless form of satisfying a school or university foreign language requirement, but regrettably often it has more sinister causes. Each year, tens of millions of people are obliged to learn a second language or another variety of their own language because they are members of an oppressed ethnolinguistic minority, because forced to migrate across linguistic borders in a desperate search for work, or worse, due to war, drought, famine, religious persecution, or ethnic cleansing. Whatever they are seeking or fleeing, almost all refugees and migrants need to reach at least a basic threshold proficiency level in a second language simply to survive in their new environment. Most require far more than that, however, if they wish to succeed in their new environment or to become members of the new culture. States and citizens, scholars and laypersons alike recognize that learning a society's language is a key part of both acculturation and socialization. Finally, less visibly, economic globalization and progressively more insidious cultural homogenization affect most people, knowingly or not, and each is transmitted through national languages within countries and through just a few languages, especially English at present, at the international level.

Any experience that touches so many people is worthy of serious study, especially when success or failure can so fundamentally affect life chances. However, the obvious *social* importance of second language acquisition (SLA) is by no means the only reason for researchers' interest, and for many, not the primary reason or not a reason at all. As a widespread, highly complex, uniquely human, cognitive process, language learning of all kinds merits careful study for *what it can reveal about the nature of the human mind and intelligence*. Thus, a good deal of what might be termed "basic research" goes on in SLA without regard for its potential applications or social utility.

In linguistics and psychology, for example, data on SLA are potentially useful for testing theories as different from one another as grammatical nativism (see, e.g., Eubank, 1991; Gregg, 1989; Liceras, 1986; Pankhurst, Sharwood-Smith, and Van Buren, 1988; Schwartz, 1992; White, 1989; and chapters by Gregg, Sorace, and White, this volume), general nativism (see, e.g., Eckman, 1996a; O'Grady, 2001a, 2001b, this volume; Wolfe-Quintero, 1996), various types of functionalism (see, e.g., Andersen, 1984; Eckman, 1996b; Mitchell and Miles, 1998, pp. 100–20; Rutherford, 1984; Sato, 1988, 1990; Tomlin, 1990), and emergentism and connectionism (see, e.g., Ellis, this volume; Gasser, 1990; MacWhinney, 2001). Research on basic processes in SLA draws upon and contributes to work on such core topics in cognitive psychology and linguistics as implicit and explicit learning (e.g., DeKeyser, this volume; N. Ellis, 1993, 1994; Robinson, 1997), incidental and intentional learning (e.g., Hulstijn, 2001, this volume; Robinson, 1996), automaticity (e.g., DeKeyser, 2001; Segalowitz, this volume), attention and memory (e.g., N. Ellis, 2001; Robinson, this volume; Schmidt, 1995; Tomlin and Villa, 1994), individual differences (e.g., Segalowitz, 1997; Dörnyei and Skehan, this volume), variation (e.g., Bayley and Preston, 1996; R. Ellis, 1999; Johnston, 1999; Preston, 1989, 1996; Romaine, this volume; Tarone, 1988; Williams, 1988; Young, 1990; Zobl, 1984), language processing (e.g., Clahsen, 1987; Doughty, this volume; Harrington, 2001; Pienemann, 1998, this volume), and the linguistic environment for language learning (e.g., Doughty, 2000; Gass, this volume; Hatch, 1978; Long, 1996; Pica, 1992), as well as at least two putative psychological processes claimed to distinguish first from second language acquisition, that is, cross-linguistic influence (see, e.g., Andersen, 1983a; Gass, 1996; Gass and Selinker, 1983; Jordens, 1994; Kasper, 1992; Kellerman, 1984; Kellerman and Sharwood-Smith, 1986; Odlin, 1989, this volume; Ringbom, 1987; Selinker, 1969) and fossilization (see, e.g., Kellerman, 1989; Long, this volume; Selinker, 1972; Selinker and Lakshmanan, 1992). SLA data are also potentially useful for explicating relationships between language and thought; for example, through exploring claims concerning semantic and cultural universals (see, e.g., Dietrich, Klein, and Noyau, 1995), or relationships between language development and cognitive development (Curtiss, 1982) – confounded in children, but not in SLA by adults. There is also a rich tradition of comparisons among SLA, pidginization, and creolization (see, e.g., Adamson, 1988; Andersen, 1983b; Andersen and Shirai, 1996; Bickerton, 1984; Meisel, 1983; Schumann, 1978; Valdman and Phillips, 1975).

In neuroscience, SLA data can help show where and how the brain stores and retrieves linguistic knowledge (see, e.g., Green, 2002; Obler and Hannigan, 1996; Ullman, 2002); which areas are implicated in acquisition (see, e.g., Schumann, 1998); how the brain adapts to additional burdens, such as bilingualism (see, e.g., Albert and Obler, 1978; Jacobs, 1988; Kroll, Michael, and Sankaranarayanan, 1998; Kroll and Sunderman, this volume), or trauma resulting in bilingual or multilingual aphasia (see, e.g., Galloway, 1981; Paradis,

1990); and whether the brain is progressively more limited in handling any of those tasks. In what has become one of the most active areas of work in recent years, SLA researchers seek to determine whether observed differences in the success of children and adults with second languages is because the brain is subject to maturational constraints in the form of sensitive periods for language learning (see, e.g., Birdsong, 1999; Bongaerts, Mennen, and van der Slik, 2000; DeKeyser, 2000; Flege, Yeni-Komshian, and Liu, 1999; Hyltenstam and Abrahamsson, this volume; Ioup, Boustagui, El Tigi, and Moselle, 1994; Long, 1990b, forthcoming b; Schachter, 1996).

Basic research sometimes yields unexpected practical applications, and that may turn out to be true of basic SLA research, too. Much work in SLA, however, has clear applications or potential applications from the start. The most obvious of these is second (including foreign) language teaching (see, e.g., Doughty, 1991, this volume; Doughty and Williams, 1998; N. Ellis and Laporte, 1997; R. Ellis, 1989; de Graaff, 1997; Lightbown and Spada, 1999; Long, 1988; Norris and Ortega, 2000; Pica, 1983; Pienemann, 1989; Sharwood-Smith, 1993), since SLA researchers study the process language teaching is designed to facilitate.[2] For bilingual, immersion, and second dialect education, second language literacy programs, and whole educational systems delivered through the medium of a second language, SLA research findings offer guidance on numerous issues. Examples include the optimal timing of L1 maintenance and L2 development programs, the linguistic modification of teaching materials, the role of implicit and explicit negative feedback on language error, and language and content achievement testing.

SLA research findings are also potentially very relevant for populations with special language-learning needs. These include certain abnormal populations, such as Alzheimer's patients (see, e.g., Hyltenstam and Stroud, 1993) and Down syndrome children, where research questions concerning so-called (first) "language intervention" programs are often quite similar to those of interest for (second) "language teaching" (see, e.g., Mahoney, 1975; Rosenberg, 1982). Other examples are groups, such as immigrant children, for whom it is crucial that educators not confuse second language problems with learning disabilities (see, e.g., Cummins, 1984); bilinguals undergoing primary language loss (Seliger, 1996; Seliger and Vago, 1991; Weltens, De Bot, and van Els, 1986); and deaf and hearing individuals learning a sign language, such as American Sign Language (ASL), as a first or second language, respectively (see, e.g., Berent, 1996; Mayberry, 1993; Strong, 1988). In all these cases, as Bley-Vroman (1990) pointed out, researchers are interested in explaining not only how success is achieved, but why – in stark contrast with almost uniformly successful child first language acquisition – at least partial failure is so common in SLA.

NOTES

1 A seminar on theory change in SLA, with readings from the history, philosophy, and sociology of science and the sociology of knowledge, is now regularly offered as an elective for M.A. and Ph.D. students in the University of Hawai'i's Department of Second Language Studies. The importance of such a "big picture" methodology course in basic training for SLA researchers – arguably at least as great as that of the potentially endless series of "grassroots" courses in quantitative and qualitative research methods and statistics that are now routine – will likely become more widely recognized over time.

2 The utility of some work in SLA for this purpose does not mean that SLA is the only important source of information, and certainly not that a theory of SLA should be passed off as a theory of language teaching. Nor, conversely, does it mean, as has occasionally been suggested, that SLA theories should be evaluated by their relevance to the classroom.

REFERENCES

Adamson, H. D. 1988: *Variation Theory and Second Language Acquisition*. Washington, DC: Georgetown University Press.

Albert, M. L. and Obler, L. 1978: *The Bilingual Brain: Neuropsychological and Neurolinguistic Aspects of Bilingualism*. San Diego: Academic Press.

Andersen, R. W. 1983a: Transfer to somewhere. In S. M. Gass and L. Selinker (eds), *Language Transfer in Language Learning*. Rowley, MA: Newbury House, 177–201.

Andersen, R. W. 1983b: *Pidginization and Creolization as Language Acquisition*. Rowley, MA: Newbury House.

Andersen, R. W. 1984: The one to one principle of interlanguage construction. *Language Learning*, 34 (4), 77–95.

Andersen, R. W. and Shirai, Y. 1996: The primacy of aspect in first and second language acquisition: the pidgin–creole connection. In W. R. Ritchie and T. J. Bhatia (eds), *Handbook of Second Language Acquisition*. San Diego: Academic Press, 527–70.

Bachman, L. and Cohen, A. D. 1998: *Interfaces between Second Language Acquisition and Language Testing Research*. Cambridge: Cambridge University Press.

Bayley, R. and Preston, D. R. (eds) 1996: *Second Language Acquisition and Linguistic Variation*. Philadelphia: John Benjamins.

Berent, G. P. 1996: The acquisition of English syntax by deaf learners. In W. R. Ritchie and T. J. Bhatia (eds), *Handbook of Second Language Acquisition*. San Diego: Academic Press, 469–506.

Beretta, A. 1991: Theory construction in SLA. Complementarity and opposition. *Studies in Second Language Acquisition*, 13 (4), 493–512.

Beretta, A. and Crookes, G. 1993: Cognitive and social determinants in the context of discovery in SLA. *Applied Linguistics*, 14 (3), 250–75.

Bickerton, D. 1984: The language bioprogram hypothesis and second language acquisition. In W. E. Rutherford (ed.), *Language*

Universals and Second Language Acquisition. Amsterdam and Philadelphia: John Benjamins, 141–61.

Birdsong, D. 1989: *Metalinguistic Performance and Interlinguistic Competence*. Berlin and New York: Springer Verlag.

Birdsong, D. (ed.) 1999: *Second Language Acquisition and the Critical Period Hypothesis*. Mahwah, NJ: Lawrence Erlbaum Associates.

Bley-Vroman, R. 1990: The logical problem of foreign language learning. *Linguistic Analysis*, 20 (1–2), 3–49.

Bongaerts, T., Mennen, S., and van der Slik, F. 2000: Authenticity of pronunciation in naturalistic second language acquisition. The case of very advanced late learners of Dutch as a second language. *Studia Linguistica*, 54, 298–308.

Clahsen, H. 1987: Connecting theories of language processing and (second) language acquisition. In C. Pfaff (ed.), *First and Second Language Acquisition Processes*. Cambridge, MA: Newbury House, 103–16.

Crookes, G. 1992: Theory format and SLA theory. *Studies in Second Language Acquisition*, 14 (4), 425–49.

Cummins, J. 1984: *Bilingualism and Special Education: Issues on Assessment and Pedagogy*. Clevedon: Multilingual Matters.

Curtiss, S. 1982: Developmental dissociation of language and cognition. In L. K. Obler and L. Menn (eds), *Exceptional Language and Linguistics*. New York: Academic Press, 285–312.

DeKeyser, R. 2000: The robustness of critical period effects in second language acquisition. *Studies in Second Language Acquisition*, 22 (4), 493–533.

DeKeyser, R. 2001: Automaticity and automatization. In P. Robinson (ed.), *Cognition and Second Language Instruction*. Cambridge: Cambridge University Press, 125–51.

Dietrich, R., Klein, W., and Noyau, C. 1995: *The Acquisition of Temporality in a Second Language*. Amsterdam and Philadelphia: John Benjamins.

Doughty, C. J. 1991: Second language instruction does make a difference: evidence from an empirical study of SL relativization. *Studies in Second Language Acquisition*, 13 (4), 431–69.

Doughty, C. J. 2000: Negotiating the L2 linguistic environment. *University of Hawai'i Working Papers in ESL*, 18 (2), 47–83.

Doughty, C. J. and Long, M. H. 2000: Eliciting second language speech data. In L. Menn and N. Bernstein Ratner (eds), *Methods for Studying Language Production*. Mahwah, NJ: Lawrence Erlbaum Associates, 149–77.

Doughty, C. J. and Williams, J. 1998: *Focus on Form in Classroom Second Language Acquisition*. Cambridge: Cambridge University Press.

Eades, D. 1992: *Aboriginal English and the Law: Communicating with Aboriginal English-Speaking Clients: A Handbook for Legal Practitioners*. Brisbane: Queensland Law Society.

Eckman, F. R. 1996a: On evaluating arguments for special nativism in second language acquisition theory. *Second Language Research*, 12 (4), 335–73.

Eckman, F. R. 1996b: A functional-typological approach to second language acquisition theory. In W. C. Ritchie and T. K. Bhatia (eds), *Handbook of Second Language Acquisition*. San Diego: Academic Press, 195–211.

Ellis, N. 1993: Rules and instances in foreign language learning: interactions of explicit and implicit knowledge. *European Journal of Cognitive Psychology*, 5, 289–318.

Ellis, N. 1994: *Implicit and Explicit Learning of Languages*. New York: Academic Press.

Ellis, N. 2001: Memory for language. In P. Robinson (ed.), *Cognition and Second Language Instruction*. Cambridge: Cambridge University Press, 33–68.

Ellis, N. and Laporte, N. 1997: Contexts of acquisition: effects of formal instruction and naturalistic exposure on second language acquisition. In A. M. de Groot and J. F. Kroll (eds), *Tutorials in Bilingualism: Psycholinguistic Perspectives*. Mahwah, NJ: Lawrence Erlbaum Associates, 53–83.

Ellis, R. 1989: Are classroom and naturalistic acquisition the same? A study of classroom acquisition of German word order rules. *Studies in Second Language Acquisition*, 11 (3), 305–28.

Ellis, R. 1994: *The Study of Second Language Acquisition*. Oxford: Oxford University Press.

Ellis, R. 1999: Item versus system learning: explaining free variation. *Applied Linguistics*, 20 (4), 460–80.

Eubank, L. 1991: Introduction: Universal Grammar in the second language. In L. Eubank (ed.), *Point Counterpoint: Universal Grammar in the Second Language*. Amsterdam and Philadelphia: John Benjamins, 1–48.

Faerch, C. and Kasper, G. (ed.) 1987: *Introspection in Second Language Research*. Clevedon: Multilingual Matters.

Fishman, J. A. 2001: *Can Threatened Languages be Saved?* Clevedon: Multilingual Matters.

Flege, J. E., Yeni-Komshian, G. H., and Liu, S. 1999: Age constraints on second-language acquisition. *Journal of Memory and Language*, 41, 78–104.

Galloway, L. M. 1981: The convolutions of second language: a theoretical article with a critical review and some new hypotheses towards a neuropsychological model of bilingualism and second language performance. *Language Learning*, 31 (2), 439–64.

Gass, S. M. 1996: Second language acquisition and linguistic theory: the role of language transfer. In W. R. Ritchie and T. J. Bhatia (eds), *Handbook of Second Language Acquisition*. San Diego: Academic Press, 317–45.

Gass, S. M. and Selinker, L. (eds) 1983: *Language Transfer in Language Learning*. Rowley, MA: Newbury House.

Gass, S. M. and Selinker, L. 2001: *Second Language Acquisition: An Introductory Course*. Second edition. Mahwah, NJ: Lawrence Erlbaum Associates.

Gasser, M. 1990: Connectionism and universals of second language acquisition. *Studies in Second Language Acquisition*, 12 (2), 179–99.

Graaff, R. de 1997: The eXperanto experiment: effects of explicit instruction on second language acquisition. *Studies in Second Language Acquisition*, 19 (2), 249–76.

Green, D. W. (ed.) 2002: The cognitive neuroscience of bilingualism. *Bilingualism: Language and Cognition*, 4 (2), 101–201.

Gregg, K. R. 1989: Second language acquisition theory: the case for a generative perspective. In S. M. Gass and J. Schachter (eds), *Linguistic Perspectives on Second Language Acquisition*. Cambridge: Cambridge University Press, 15–40.

Gregg, K. R. 1993: Taking explanation seriously; or, Let a couple of flowers bloom. *Applied Linguistics*, 14 (3), 276–94.

Gregg, K. R. 1994: Second language acquisition: history and theory. *Encyclopedia of Language and Linguistics*. Second edition. Oxford: Pergamon, 3720–6.

Gregg, K. R. 1996: The logical and developmental problems of second language acquisition. In W. R. Ritchie and T. J. Bhatia (eds), *Handbook of*

Second Language Acquisition. San Diego: Academic Press, 49–81.

Gregg, K. R. 2000: A theory for every occasion: postmodernism and SLA. *Second Language Research*, 16 (4), 343–59.

Gregg, K. R., Long, M. H., Jordan, G., and Beretta, A. 1997: Rationality and its discontents in SLA. *Applied Linguistics*, 17 (1), 63–83.

Haig, Y. 2001: Teacher perceptions of student speech. Ph.D. dissertation. Edith Cowan University.

Harrington, M. 2001: Sentence processing. In P. Robinson (ed.), *Cognition and Second Language Instruction*. Cambridge: Cambridge University Press, 91–124.

Hatch, E. M. 1978: Discourse analysis and second language acquisition. In E. M. Hatch (ed.), *Second Language Acquisition: A Book of Readings*. Rowley, MA: Newbury House, 401–35.

Huebner, T. 1983a: *A Longitudinal Analysis of the Acquisition of English*. Ann Arbor, MI: Karoma.

Huebner, T. 1983b: Linguistic systems and linguistic change in an interlanguage. *Studies in Second Language Acquisition*, 6 (1), 33–53.

Huebner, T. and Davis, K. A. 1999: *Sociopolitical Perspectives on Language Policy and Planning in the USA*. Amsterdam and Philadelphia: John Benjamins.

Hulstijn, J. H. 2001: Intentional and incidental second language learning: a reappraisal of elaboration, rehearsal and automaticity. In P. Robinson (ed.), *Cognition and Second Language Instruction*. Cambridge: Cambridge University Press, 258–86.

Hyltenstam, K. and Stroud, C. 1993: Second language regression in Alzheimer's dementia. In K. Hyltenstam and A. Viberg (eds), *Progression and Regression in Language: Sociocultural, Neuropsychological and Linguistic Perspectives*. Cambridge: Cambridge University Press, 222–42.

Ioup, G., Boustagui, E., El Tigi, M., and Moselle, M. 1994: Reexamining the critical period hypothesis: a case study of successful adult SLA in a naturalistic environment. *Studies in Second Language Acquisition*, 16 (1), 73–98.

Iwashita, N. 2001: The role of task-based conversation in the acquisition of Japanese grammar and vocabulary. Ph.D. thesis. University of Melbourne, Department of Linguistics and Applied Linguistics.

Jacobs, B. 1988: Neurobiological differentiation in primary and secondary language acquisition. *Studies in Second Language Acquisition*, 10 (3), 303–37.

Johnston, M. 1999: System and variation in interlanguage development. Unpublished Ph.D. dissertation. Canberra: Australian National University.

Jordan, G. 2002: Theory construction in SLA. Ph.D. dissertation. London University, Institute of Education.

Jordens, P. 1994: The cognitive function of case marking in German as a native and a foreign language. In S. M. Gass and L. Selinker (eds), *Language Transfer in Language Learning*. Second edition. Amsterdam and Philadelphia: John Benjamins, 138–75.

Jordens, P. and Lalleman, J. (eds) 1988: *Language Development*. Dordrecht: Foris.

Kasper, G. 1992: Pragmatic transfer. *Second Language Research*, 8 (3), 203–31.

Kellerman, E. 1984: The empirical evidence for the influence of the L1 in interlanguage. In A. Davies, C. Criper, and A. Howatt (eds), *Interlanguage*. Edinburgh: Edinburgh University Press, 98–122.

Kellerman, E. 1989: The imperfect conditional. In K. Hyltenstam and L. K. Obler (eds), *Bilingualism Across the Lifespan: Aspects of Acquisition, Maturity, and Loss*. Cambridge: Cambridge University Press, 87–115.

Kellerman, E. and Sharwood-Smith, M. (eds) 1986: *Cross-Linguistic Influence in Second Language Acquisition*. New York: Pergamon.

Klein, F. 1981: The acquisition of English in Hawai'i by Korean adolescent immigrants: a longitudinal study of verbal auxiliary agreement. Ph.D. dissertation. University of Hawai'i, Department of Linguistics.

Klein, W. 1986: *Second Language Acquisition*. Cambridge: Cambridge University Press.

Kroll, J. F., Michael, E., and Sankaranarayanan, A. 1998: A model of bilingual representation and its implications for second language acquisition. In A. F. Healy and L. E. Bourne, Jr (eds), *Foreign Language Learning: Psycholinguistic Studies on Training and Retention*. Mahwah, NJ: Lawrence Erlbaum Associates, 365–95.

Larsen-Freeman, D. 1991: Second language acquisition research: staking out the territory. *TESOL Quarterly*, 25 (2), 315–50.

Larsen-Freeman, D. and Long, M. H. 1991: *An Introduction to Second Language Acquisition Research*. London: Longman.

Liceras, J. 1986: *Linguistic Theory and Second Language Acquisition*. Tubingen: Gubter Narr.

Liceras, J. M., Maxwell, D., Laguardia, B., Fernández, Z., Fernández, R., and Diaz, L. 1997: A longitudinal study of Spanish non-native grammars: beyond parameters. In A. T. Pérez-Leroux and W. Glass (eds), *Contemporary Perspectives on the Acquisition of Spanish. Vol. 1: Developing Grammars*. Somerville, MA: Cascadilla Press, 99–132.

Lightbown, P. M. and Spada, N. 1999: *How Languages are Learned*. Revised edition. Oxford: Oxford University Press.

Lo Bianco, J. 1987: *National Policy on Languages*. Canberra: Australian Government Publishing Service.

Long, M. H. 1988: Instructed interlanguage development. In L. M. Beebe (ed.), *Issues in Second Language Acquisition: Multiple Perspectives*. Cambridge, MA: Newbury House, 115–41.

Long, M. H. 1990a: The least a second language acquisition theory needs to explain. *TESOL Quarterly*, 24 (4), 649–66.

Long, M. H. 1990b: Maturational constraints on language development. *Studies in Second Language Acquisition*, 12 (3), 251–85.

Long, M. H. 1993: Assessment strategies for second language acquisition theories. *Applied Linguistics*, 14 (3), 225–49.

Long, M. H. 1996: The role of the linguistic environment in second language acquisition. In W. R. Ritchie and T. J. Bhatia (eds), *Handbook of Second Language Acquisition*. San Diego: Academic Press, 413–68.

Long, M. H. 1998: SLA: breaking the siege. *University of Hawai'i Working Papers in ESL*, 17 (1), 79–129. Also to appear in M. H. Long, *Problems in SLA*. Mahwah, NJ: Lawrence Erlbaum Associates.

Long, M. H. 1999: Ebonics, language and power. In F. L. Pincus and H. J. Ehrlich (eds), *Race and Ethnic Conflict: Contending Views on Prejudice, Discrimination, and Ethnoviolence*. Second edition. Westview/HarperCollins, 331–45.

Long, M. H. forthcoming a: Theory change in SLA. In M. H. Long, *Problems in SLA*. Mahwah, NJ: Lawrence Erlbaum Associates.

Long, M. H. forthcoming b: Age differences and the sensitive periods controversy in SLA. In M. H. Long, *Problems in SLA*. Mahwah, NJ: Lawrence Erlbaum Associates.

Long, M. H. and Robinson, P. 1998: Focus on form: theory, research and practice. In C. J. Doughty and J. Williams (eds), *Focus on Form in Classroom Second Language Acquisition*. Cambridge: Cambridge University Press, 15–41.

MacWhinney, B. 2001: The Competition Model: the input, the context and the brain. In P. Robinson (ed.), *Cognition and Second Language Instruction*. Cambridge: Cambridge University Press, 69–90.

Mahoney, G. 1975: Ethnological approach to delayed language acquisition. *American Journal of Mental Deficiency*, 80, 139–48.

Malcolm, I. 1994: Aboriginal English inside and outside the classroom. *Australian Review of Applied Linguistics*, 17 (1), 147–80.

Mayberry, R. 1993: First-language acquisition after childhood differs from second-language acquisition: the case of American Sign Language. *Journal of Speech and Hearing Research*, 36, 1258–70.

Meisel, J. M. 1983: Strategies of second language acquisition: more than one kind of simplification. In R. W. Andersen (ed.), *Pidginization and Creolization as Second Language Acquisition*. Rowley, MA: Newbury House, 120–57.

Mitchell, R. and Miles, F. 1998: Functional/pragmatic perspectives on second language learning. In R. Mitchell and F. Miles (eds), *Second Language Learning Theories*. London: Arnold, 100–20.

Morgan, M. 1999: US language planning and policies for social dialect speakers. In T. Huebner and K. A. Davies (eds), *Sociopolitical Perspectives on Language Policy and Planning in the USA*. Amsterdam and Philadelphia: John Benjamins, 173–91.

Norris, J. and Ortega, L. 2000: Effectiveness of instruction: a research synthesis and quantitative meta-analysis. *Language Learning*, 50 (3), 417–528.

Obler, L. and Hannigan, S. 1996: Neurolinguistics of second language acquisition and use. In W. R. Ritchie and T. J. Bhatia (eds), *Handbook of Second Language Acquisition*. San Diego: Academic Press, 509–23.

Odlin, T. 1989: *Language Transfer*. Cambridge: Cambridge University Press.

O'Grady, W. 2001a: Language acquisition and language loss. Ms. University of Hawai'i, Department of Linguistics.

O'Grady, W. 2001b: An emergentist approach to syntax. Ms. University of Hawai'i, Department of Linguistics.

Pankhurst, J., Sharwood-Smith, M., and Van Buren, P. 1988: *Learnability and Second Languages: A Book of Readings*. Dordrecht: Foris.

Paradis, M. 1990: Bilingual and polyglot aphasia. In F. Boller and J. Grafman (eds), *Handbook of Neuropsychology. Vol. 2*. New York: Elsevier, 117–40.

Philipson, R. (ed.) 2000: *Rights to Language: Equity, Power, and Education*. Mahwah, NJ: Lawrence Erlbaum Associates.

Pica, T. 1983: Adult acquisition of English as a second language under different conditions of exposure. *Language Learning*, 33 (4), 465–97.

Pica, T. 1992: The textual outcomes of native speaker/non-native speaker negotiation: what do they reveal about second language learning? In C. Kramsch and S. McConnell-Ginet (eds), *Text and Context: Cross-Disciplinary Perspectives on Language Study*. Lexington, MA: D. C. Heath, 198–237.

Pienemann, M. 1989: Is language teachable? *Applied Linguistics*, 10 (1), 52–79.

Pienemann, M. 1998: *Language Processing and Second Language Development:*

Processability Theory. Amsterdam and Philadelphia: John Benjamins.

Preston, D. R. 1989: *Sociolinguistics and Second Language Acquisition*. Oxford: Blackwell.

Preston, D. R. 1996: Variationist linguistics and second language acquisition. In W. C. Ritchie and T. K. Bhatia (eds), *Handbook of Second Language Acquisition*. San Diego: Academic Press, 229–65.

Reynolds, S. B. 1999: Mutual intelligibility? Comprehension problems between American Standard English and Hawai'i Creole English in Hawai'i's public schools. In J. R. Rickford and S. Romaine (eds), *Creole Genesis, Attitudes and Discourse*. Amsterdam and Philadelphia: John Benjamins, 303–19.

Rickford, J. R. 2000: *African American Vernacular English: Features, Evolution, Educational Implications*. Oxford: Blackwell.

Ringbom, H. 1987: *The Role of the First Language in Foreign Language Learning*. Clevedon: Multilingual Matters.

Ritchie, W. R. and Bhatia, T. J. (eds) 1996: *Handbook of Second Language Acquisition*. San Diego: Academic Press.

Robinson, P. 1996: Learning simple and complex second language rules under implicit, incidental, rule-search and instructed conditions. *Studies in Second Language Acquisition*, 18 (1), 27–67.

Robinson, P. 1997: Individual differences and the fundamental similarity of implicit and explicit adult second language learning. *Language Learning*, 47 (1), 45–99.

Robinson, P. (ed.) 2001: *Cognition and Second Language Instruction*. Cambridge: Cambridge University Press.

Rosenberg, S. 1982: The language of the mentally retarded: development processes and intervention. In S. Rosenberg (ed.), *Handbook of Applied Psycholinguistics: Major Thrusts of Research and Theory*. Hillsdale, NJ: Lawrence Erlbaum Associates, 329–92.

Rutherford, W. E. (ed.) 1984: *Language Universals and Second Language Acquisition*. Amsterdam and Philadelphia: John Benjamins.

Sato, C. J. 1985: Linguistic inequality in Hawai'i: the post-creole dilemma. In N. Wolfson and J. Manes (eds), *Language of Inequality*. Berlin: Mouton, 255–72.

Sato, C. J. 1988: Origins of complex syntax in interlanguage development. *Studies in Second Language Acquisition*, 10 (3), 371–95.

Sato, C. J. 1989: A non-standard approach to Standard English. *TESOL Quarterly*, 23 (2), 259–82.

Sato, C. J. 1990: *The Syntax of Conversation in Interlanguage Development*. Tubingen: Gunter Narr.

Schachter, J. 1996: Maturation and the issue of UG in L2 acquisition. In W. R. Ritchie and T. J. Bhatia (eds), *Handbook of Second Language Acquisition*. San Diego: Academic Press, 159–93.

Schmidt, R. W. 1983: Interaction, acculturation and the acquisition of communicative competence. In N. Wolfson and E. Judd (eds), *Sociolinguistics and Second Language Acquisition*. Rowley, MA: Newbury House, 137–74.

Schmidt, R. W. (ed.) 1995: *Attention and Awareness in Foreign Language Learning*. Honolulu: University of Hawai'i Press.

Schumann, J. H. 1978: *The Pidginization Process: A Model for Second Language Acquisition*. Rowley, MA: Newbury House.

Schumann, J. H. 1998: The neurobiology of affect in language. *Language Learning*, 48: Supplement 1.

Schwartz, B. D. 1992: Testing between UG-based and problem-solving models of L2A: developmental sequence data. *Language Acquisition*, 2 (1), 1–19.

Segalowitz, N. 1997: Individual differences in second language acquisition. In A. M. de Groot and J. F. Kroll (eds), *Tutorials in Bilingualism: Psycholinguistic Perspectives*. Mahwah, NJ: Lawrence Erlbaum Associates, 85–112.

Seliger, H. W. 1996: Primary language attrition in the context of bilingualism. In W. R. Ritchie and T. J. Bhatia (eds), *Handbook of Second Language Acquisition*. San Diego: Academic Press, 605–26.

Seliger, H. W. and Vago, R. M. (eds) 1991: *First Language Attrition*. Cambridge: Cambridge University Press.

Selinker, L. 1969: Language transfer. *General Linguistics*, 9, 67–92.

Selinker, L. 1972: Interlanguage. *International Review of Applied Linguistics*, 10 (3), 209–31.

Selinker, L. and Lakshmanan, U. 1992: Language transfer and fossilization: the multiple effects principle. In S. M. Gass and L. Selinker (eds), *Language Transfer in Language Learning*. Amsterdam and Philadelphia: John Benjamins, 97–116.

Sharwood-Smith, M. 1993: Input enhancement in instructed SLA: theoretical bases. *Studies in Second Language Acquisition*, 15 (2), 165–79.

Siegel, J. 1996: *Vernacular Education in the South Pacific*. International Development Issues No. 45. Canberra: Australian Agency for International Development.

Siegel, J. 1997: Using a pidgin language in formal education: help or hindrance? *Applied Linguistics*, 18, 86–100.

Siegel, J. 1999: Creole and minority dialects in education: an overview. *Journal of Multilingual and Multicultural Development*, 20, 508–31.

Sorace, A. 1996: The use of acceptability judgments in second language acquisition research. In W. R. Ritchie and T. J. Bhatia (eds), *Handbook of Second Language Acquisition*. San Diego: Academic Press, 375–409.

Strong, M. (ed.) 1988: *Language Learning and Deafness*. Cambridge: Cambridge University Press.

Tarone, E. E. 1988: *Variation and Second Language Acquisition*. London: Edward Arnold.

Tarone, E. E., Gass, S. M., and Cohen, A. D. 1994: *Research Methodology in Second-Language Acquisition*. Hillsdale, NJ: Lawrence Erlbaum Associates.

Tomlin, R. S. 1990: Functionalism in second language acquisition. *Studies in Second Language Acquisition*, 12 (2), 155–77.

Tomlin, R. and Villa, V. 1994: Attention in cognitive science and second language acquisition. *Studies in Second Language Acquisition*, 16 (2), 183–203.

Towell, R. and Hawkins, R. 1994: *Approaches to Second Language Acquisition*. Clevedon: Multilingual Matters.

Ullman, M. T. 2002: The neural basis of lexicon and grammar in first and second language: the declarative/procedural model. *Bilingualism: Language and Cognition*, 4 (2), 105–22.

Valdman, A. and Phillips, J. 1975: Pidginization, creolization and the elaboration of learner systems. *Studies in Second Language Acquisition*, 1 (1), 21–40.

Warner, N. 2001: Küi ka mäna'ai: children acquire traits of those who raise them. Plenary: Pacific Second Language Research Forum. University of Hawai'i, October 6.

Watson-Gegeo, K. A. 1992: Thick explanation in the ethnographic study of child socialization: a longitudinal study of the problem of schooling for

Kwara'ae (Solomon Islands) children. In W. A. Corsaro and P. J. Miller (eds), *Interpretative Approaches to Children's Socialization*. San Francisco: Jossey-Bass, 51–66.

Weltens, B., De Bot, K., and van Els, T. (eds) 1986: *Language Attrition in Progress*. Dordrecht: Foris.

White, L. 1989: *Universal Grammar and Second Language Acquisition*. Amsterdam and Philadelphia: John Benjamins.

Williams, J. 1988: Zero anaphora in second language acquisition: a comparison among three varieties of English. *Studies in Second Language Acquisition*, 10 (3), 339–70.

Wolfe-Quintero, K. 1996: Nativism does not equal Universal Grammar. *Second Language Research*, 12 (4), 335–73.

Wong, L. 1999: Language varieties and language policy: the appreciation of Pidgin. In T. Huebner and K. A. Davies (eds), *Sociopolitical Perspectives on Language Policy and Planning in the USA*. Amsterdam and Philadelphia: John Benjamins, 205–22.

Young, R. 1990: *Variation in Interlanguage Morphology*. Amsterdam and Philadelphia: John Benjamins.

Zobl, H. 1984: The Wave Model of linguistic change and the naturalness of interlanguage. *Studies in Second Language Acquisition*, 6 (2), 160–85.

II Capacity and Representation

2 On the Nature of Interlanguage Representation: Universal Grammar in the Second Language

LYDIA WHITE

1 Introduction

In the late 1960s and early 1970s, several researchers pointed out that the language of second language (L2) learners is systematic and that learner errors are not random mistakes but evidence of rule-governed behavior (Adjémian, 1976; Corder, 1967; Nemser, 1971; Selinker, 1972). From this developed the conception of "interlanguage," the proposal that L2 learners have internalized a mental grammar, a natural language system that can be described in terms of linguistic rules and principles. The current generative linguistic focus on interlanguage representation can be seen as a direct descendent of the original interlanguage hypothesis. Explicit claims are made about the nature of interlanguage competence, the issues being the extent to which interlanguage grammars are like other grammars, as well as the role of Universal Grammar (UG).

The question of whether UG mediates L2 acquisition, and to what extent, has been much debated since the early 1980s. This question stems from a particular perspective on linguistic universals and from particular assumptions about the nature of linguistic competence. In the generative tradition, it is assumed that grammars are mental representations, and that universal principles constrain these representations. Linguistic universals are as they are because of properties of the human mind, and grammars (hence, languages) are as they are because of these universal principles.

The first decade of research on the role of UG in L2 acquisition concentrated on so-called "access," exploring whether UG remains available in non-primary acquisition. The issue of UG access relates to fundamental questions such as: what are natural language grammars like? What is the nature of linguistic competence? How is it acquired? UG is proposed as a partial answer, at least in the case of the first language (L1) grammar, the assumption being that language acquisition is impossible in the absence of specific innate linguistic principles which place constraints on grammars, restricting the "hypothesis space," or, in other words, severely limiting the range of possibilities that the language acquirer has to entertain. In L2 acquisition research, then, the issue is whether interlanguage representations are also constrained by UG.

2 UG and the Logical Problem of Language Acquisition

UG is proposed as part of an innate biologically endowed language faculty (e.g., Chomsky, 1965, 1981; Pinker, 1994). It places limitations on grammars, constraining their form (the inventory of possible grammatical categories in the broadest sense, i.e., syntactic, semantic, phonological), as well as how they operate (the computational system, principles that the grammar is subject to). UG includes invariant principles, as well as parameters which allow for variation. While theories like Government-Binding (GB) (Chomsky, 1981), Minimalism (Chomsky, 1995), or Optimality Theory (Archangeli and Langendoen, 1997) differ as to how universal principles and parameters are formalized, within these approaches there is a consensus that certain properties of language are too abstract, subtle, and complex to be acquired in the absence of innate and specifically linguistic constraints on grammars.

UG is postulated as an explanation of how it is that learners come to know properties of grammar that go far beyond the input, how they know that certain things are not possible, why grammars are of one sort rather than another. The claim is that such properties do not have to be learned. Proposals for an innate UG are motivated by the observation that, at least in the case of L1 acquisition, there is a mismatch between the primary linguistic data (PLD), namely the utterances a child is exposed to, and the abstract, subtle, and complex knowledge that the child acquires. In other words, the input (the PLD) underdetermines the output (the grammar). This is known as the problem of the *poverty of the stimulus* or the *logical problem of language acquisition*.

As an example of a proposed principle of UG which accounts for knowledge too subtle to be learned solely from input, we will consider the Overt Pronoun Constraint (OPC) (Montalbetti, 1983), a constraint which has recently received attention in L2 acquisition research. The OPC states that in null argument languages (languages allowing both null and overt pronouns), an overt pronoun cannot receive a bound variable interpretation, that is, it cannot have a quantified expression (such as *everyone, someone, no one*) or a wh-phrase (*who, which*) as its antecedent.[1] This constraint holds true of null argument languages in general, including languages unrelated to each other, such as Spanish and Japanese.

Consider the sentences in (1) from English, a language requiring overt subjects. In particular, we are concerned with the coreference possibilities (indicated by subscripts) between the pronominal subject of the lower clause and its potential antecedent in the main clause:

(1) a. Everyone$_i$ thought [he$_i$ would win]
b. Who$_i$ thought [he$_i$ would win]?
c. John$_i$ thought [he$_i$ would be late]

In (1a), the pronoun *he* can be bound to the quantifier *everyone*. On this interpretation, every person in the room thinks himself or herself a likely winner: *he*, then, does not refer to a particular individual. This is known as a *bound variable interpretation*. Similarly, in (1b) the pronoun can be bound to the wh-phrase *who* without referring to a particular individual. In (1c), on the other hand, the pronoun refers to a particular person in the main clause, namely *John*. (In addition, in all three cases, disjoint reference is possible, with the pronoun in the lower clause referring to some other person in the discourse – this interpretation is not of concern here.)

In null argument languages, the situation regarding quantified antecedents is somewhat different. On the one hand, an embedded null subject can take either a quantified or a referential antecedent (or it can be disjoint in reference from other NPs in the sentence), just like overt pronouns in English. This is illustrated in (2) for Japanese:[2]

(2) a. Dare$_i$ ga [$\varnothing_i$ kuruma o katta to] itta no?
Who NOM car ACC bought that said Q
Who$_i$ said that (he$_i$) bought a car?
b. Tanaka-san$_i$ wa [$\varnothing_i$ kaisya de itiban da to] itte-iru
Tanaka-Mr TOP company in best is that saying-is
Mr Tanaka$_i$ is saying that (he$_i$) is the best in the company

On the other hand, overt pronouns are more restricted than either null pronouns in null argument languages or overt pronouns in languages requiring overt arguments. In particular, an overt pronoun may not have a quantified antecedent, as in (3a), whereas it can have a sentence-internal referential antecedent, as in (3b):

(3) a. *Dare$_i$ ga [kare$_i$ ga kuruma o katta to] itta no?
Who NOM he NOM car ACC bought that said Q
Who$_i$ said that he$_i$ bought a car?
b. Tanaka-san$_i$ wa [kare$_i$ ga kaisya de itiban da to] itte-iru
Tanaka-Mr TOP he NOM company in best is that saying-is
Mr Tanaka$_i$ is saying that he$_i$ is the best in the company

The differences between null argument languages like Japanese and languages that do not permit null arguments like English are summarized in table 2.1.

At issue, then, is how the L1 acquirer of a language like Japanese discovers the restriction on overt pronouns with respect to quantified antecedents. This case constitutes a clear poverty-of-the-stimulus situation. The phenomenon in question is very subtle. In many cases, overt and null pronouns will appear in the same syntactic contexts (although sometimes under different pragmatic

Table 2.1 Antecedents for pronouns in null and overt argument languages

	Null argument languages		*Overt argument languages*
	Null subjects	*Overt subjects*	*Overt subjects*
Referential antecedents	Yes	Yes	Yes
Quantified antecedents	Yes	No	Yes

and discourse conditions), so it is unlikely that the absence of overt pronouns with quantified antecedents would be detected. It is also highly unlikely that L1 acquirers produce utterances incorrectly using overt pronouns with quantified antecedents and are then provided with negative evidence on this point. How, then, could an L1 acquirer of a language like Japanese discover this property? The argument is that the knowledge is built in, in the form of a principle of UG, the OPC; it does not have to be learned at all.

3 UG and the Logical Problem of L2 Acquisition

Assuming a logical problem of L1 acquisition, hence motivating UG, people have asked whether the same holds true of L2; that is, whether there is a mismatch between the input that L2 learners are exposed to and the unconscious knowledge that they attain (Bley-Vroman, 1990; Schwartz and Sprouse, 2000; White, 1985). In the case of L2 acquisition, it is important to distinguish between (i) the logical problem and (ii) UG availability. The first issue is whether L2 learners attain unconscious knowledge (a mental representation) that goes beyond the L2 input. (There would be no logical problem at all, if L2 learners turned out not to achieve knowledge that goes beyond the input.) The second issue is whether such knowledge (if found) is achieved by means of UG. These are not in fact the same question, although they are often collapsed, since the way to determine whether UG principles and parameters constrain interlanguage representations is similar to the way to assess whether there is a logical problem of L2 acquisition. However, it is conceivable that there is a logical problem of L2 acquisition, with L2 learners achieving far more than could have come from the input alone, and that their achievement is to be explained by postulating a reliance on the L1 grammar rather than a still-functioning UG (Bley-Vroman, 1990; Schachter, 1988).

The strongest case for the operation of UG in L2 acquisition, then, is if learners demonstrate knowledge of subtle and abstract properties which could not have been learned from L2 input alone or from input plus general learning principles (not specifically linguistic) or on the basis of explicit instruction or from the L1 grammar. In such cases, not only is there a logical problem of L2 acquisition but also UG remains the only way to account for the knowledge in question. To demonstrate an L2 logical problem, hence the likelihood of involvement of UG, researchers have sought out genuine L2 poverty of the stimulus cases, in which both of the following hold (White, 1989b, 1990):

i The phenomenon in question is underdetermined by the L2 input. That is, it must not be something that could have been acquired by simple observation of the L2 input, as an effect of input frequency, or on the basis of instruction, analogical reasoning, etc.
ii The phenomenon in question works differently in the L1 and the L2. If L2 learners show evidence of subtle and abstract knowledge, we want to exclude the possibility that such knowledge is obtained solely via the L1 grammar.

However, the requirement that L1 and L2 differ in the relevant respects becomes harder and harder to achieve, in that many properties of UG will of necessity manifest themselves in the L1 in some form (Dekydtspotter, Sprouse, and Anderson, 1998; Hale, 1996). Nevertheless, if the L1 and L2 differ in terms of surface properties, then transfer can be ruled out, at least at this level, as an explanation of successful acquisition.

In the first decade of work on SLA from a UG perspective (starting in the early 1980s), research focused mainly on whether or not UG is available to L2 learners, and in what form. The UG question seemed relatively straightforward (and relatively global): is UG available (or accessible) to L2 learners? The assumption was that if you can show that a particular UG principle operates/does not operate then this generalizes to other principles, hence to UG availability/non-availability in general. Researchers looked for evidence that L2 learners could (or could not) apply principles of UG, and set or reset parameters, as well as investigating the extent to which the L1 was involved, in the form of L1 parameter settings in interlanguage grammars. Hypotheses varied as to whether learners had no access, partial (indirect) access, or full (direct) access to UG, and there were differing views on the role of the L1 grammar. But although the issues were phrased in terms of access to UG, the question was then, and remains, whether interlanguage representations show evidence of being constrained by principles of UG; that is, whether interlanguage grammars are restricted in the same way as the grammars of native speakers are restricted.

As a recent example of research which takes into account the logical problem of L2 acquisition and looks for evidence as to whether a principle of UG constrains the interlanguage representation, consider Kanno's (1997) investigation of the operation of the OPC in the grammars of L2 learners of Japanese (see box 2.1). Using a coreference judgment task, Kanno shows that L2 learners demonstrate subtle knowledge of the restriction on overt pronouns, correctly

Box 2.1 The Overt Pronoun Constraint (OPC) (Kanno, 1997)

Research question: Do adult L2 learners observe principles of UG which are not operative in their L1? In particular, do English-speaking learners of Japanese observe the OPC?

Overt Pronoun Constraint (OPC) (Montalbetti, 1983): In null argument languages, an overt pronoun cannot receive a bound variable interpretation.

L2 logical problem:

i There appears to be nothing in the L2 input to signal the difference between overt and null pronominals with respect to quantified antecedents. It is unlikely that the absence of overt pronouns with quantified antecedents would be detected. This issue is not explicitly taught and not discussed in L2 textbooks.
ii Knowledge of the restriction on overt pronouns in Japanese is not available from the L1 English. In English, overt pronouns can receive a bound variable interpretation, contrary to Japanese.

Methodology:
Subjects: 28 intermediate-level English-speaking adult learners of Japanese. Control group of 20 adult native speakers of Japanese.

Task: Coreference judgment task, involving 20 biclausal sentences (4 sentence types, 5 tokens of each). Each sentence had a pronoun subject (overt or null) in the lower clause, and a potential antecedent (quantified or referential) in the main clause. Participants had to indicate whether the subject of the embedded clause could refer to the same person as the subject of the main clause or whether it referred to someone else.

Results: Native speakers and L2 learners differentiated in their treatment of overt pronouns depending on the type of antecedent involved (quantified or referential), as well as differentiating between overt and null pronominals in these contexts (see table 2.2), supporting the claim that the OPC is being observed. Native speakers overwhelmingly rejected quantified antecedents for overt pronouns (2 percent), while accepting them in the case of null subjects (83 percent). They indicated that null subjects can always take a sentence-internal referential antecedent (100 percent), whereas for overt pronouns an internal referential antecedent was accepted at about 50 percent (both an internal and an external referent are possible). The L2 learners showed a remarkably similar pattern of results and their responses did not differ significantly from the controls.

Conclusion: Adult L2 acquirers of Japanese observe the OPC, suggesting that interlanguage grammars are constrained by UG.

Table 2.2 Acceptances of antecedents by subject type (percentages)

	Native speakers (n = 20)		*L2 learners (n = 28)*	
	Quantified antecedent	*Referential antecedent*	*Quantified antecedent*	*Referential antecedent*
Null subject	83.0	100.0	78.5	81.5
kare ("he")	2.0	47.0	13.0	42.0

disallowing quantified antecedents in cases like (3a). Kanno's test sentences are carefully constructed to control for use of both types of pronoun (overt and null) in the context of both kinds of antecedent (referential and quantified). This allows her to eliminate the possibility that L2 learners simply prohibit overt pronouns from taking sentence-internal antecedents in general, as well as the possibility that they reject quantified antecedents altogether. In addition to considering group results, Kanno shows that subjects largely behave consistently with respect to the OPC when analyzed individually. Such individual analyses are crucial, since the hypothesis is that UG constrains the grammars of individuals, and group results may conceal individual variation.

The knowledge demonstrated by these L2 learners of Japanese could not have come from the L1 English, where overt pronouns do take quantified antecedents; it is knowledge that is underdetermined by the L2 input, where null and overt pronouns allow similar antecedents in many cases. The distinction between permissible antecedents for overt and null pronouns is not taught in L2 Japanese textbooks or classes. It seems unlikely that there are relevant surface patterns in the L2 input that could be noticed by the learner, leading to this result. Nevertheless, L2 learners demonstrate knowledge of the restriction, suggesting that L2 representations must be constrained by UG. Similar results have been reported for L2 Spanish by Pérez-Leroux and Glass (1997); that is, adult English-speaking learners of Spanish also observe the OPC.

4 The Comparative Fallacy

So far, we have considered the case of learners who acquire subtle knowledge of the constraint on antecedents for pronouns (the OPC). Here, then, properties of the L2 assumed to stem from UG are manifested in the interlanguage grammar. The interlanguage grammar and the L2 grammar converge in this respect, as suggested by Kanno's results. But what if interlanguage representations fail to demonstrate certain L2 properties? What if the interlanguage and the L2 diverge? Does this necessarily imply lack of UG? This was, in fact, the interpretation taken (implicitly or explicitly) by a number of researchers in the 1980s.

Some researchers were quite explicit in their assumption that one should compare L2 learners and native speakers with respect to UG properties, the native speaker of the L2 providing a reference point for assessing UG availability. If L2 learners rendered judgments (or otherwise behaved) like native speakers with respect to some principle or parameter of UG, then they were deemed to have access to UG; on the other hand, if they differed in their judgments from native speakers, then their grammars were assumed not to be constrained by UG. For example, in Schachter's (1989, 1990) investigations of constraints on wh-movement, this was the underlying rationale for claiming the non-operation of UG. Schachter found that, compared to native speakers, L2 learners of English of certain L1 backgrounds were very inaccurate in their judgments on illicit wh-movement out of structures such as embedded questions and relative clauses; hence, Schachter argued, L2 learners do not have access to UG principles independently of the L1.

The problem with this kind of approach to UG in L2 acquisition is that it presupposes that the interlanguage representation must converge on the grammar of native speakers of the L2, that the endstate grammar of a second language learner must be identical to that of a native speaker. But this is a misconception (Cook, 1997; Schwartz, 1993, 1998b; White, 1996). An interlanguage grammar which diverges from the L2 grammar can nevertheless fall within the bounds laid down by UG. If we are going to take the issue of representation seriously, we need to consider Bley-Vroman's *comparative fallacy*. Bley-Vroman (1983) warned that "work on the linguistic description of learners' languages can be seriously hindered or sidetracked by a concern with the target language" (p. 2) and argued that "the learner's system is worthy of study in its own right, not just as a degenerate form of the target system" (p. 4).

A number of researchers pointed out quite early on the need to consider interlanguage grammars in their own right with respect to principles and parameters of UG, arguing that one should not compare L2 learners to native speakers of the L2 but instead consider whether interlanguage grammars are natural language systems (e.g., duPlessis et al., 1987; Finer and Broselow, 1986; Liceras, 1983; Martohardjono and Gair, 1993; Schwartz and Sprouse, 1994; White, 1992b). These authors have shown that L2 learners may arrive at representations which indeed account for the L2 input, though not in the same way as the grammar of a native speaker. The issue, then, is whether the interlanguage representation is a *possible* grammar, not whether it is identical to the L2 grammar. For example, with respect to the violations of constraints on wh-movement that Schachter (1989, 1990) reports, Martohardjono and Gair (1993), White (1992b), and, more recently, Hawkins and Chan (1997) argue that L2 learners have a different analysis for the phenomenon in question, whereby structures involving a fronted wh-phrase are derived without movement (based on properties of the L1 grammar), explaining the apparent lack of movement constraints.

A related kind of misleading comparison involves the use of control groups in experimental tasks. There is often an (implicit) expectation that L2 speakers should not differ significantly from native speakers with respect to performance on sentences testing for UG properties. Suppose that on a grammaticality judgment task native speakers accept sentences violating some principle of UG at less than 5 percent and accept corresponding grammatical sentences at over 95 percent. In order to demonstrate "access" to this principle, it is not necessary for L2 speakers to perform at the same level. Rather, the issue is whether the interlanguage grammar shows evidence of certain distinctions: does learners' performance on grammatical sentences differ significantly from their performance on ungrammatical sentences (cf. Grimshaw and Rosen, 1990, for related comments on L1 acquisition)? Do L2 learners distinguish between different kinds of ungrammatical sentences (see Martohardjono, 1993)? If certain sentence types are treated significantly differently from other sentence types, this suggests that the interlanguage grammar represents the relevant distinction (whatever it may be), even if the degree to which L2 learners observe it in performance differs from that of native speakers. To return to Kanno's study on the OPC, the importance of her results lies not in the fact that the L2 learners did not differ significantly from the native speakers, but rather in the fact that the L2 learners showed a significant difference in their acceptances of quantified antecedents depending on pronoun type, suggesting that their grammars make the relevant distinction between licit and illicit antecedents.

It is not the case, however, that one should never compare L2 speakers to native speakers of the L2 as far as properties of the grammar are concerned.[3] There are legitimate reasons for asking whether the L2 learner has in fact acquired properties of the L2. After all, the learner is exposed to L2 input in some form, and the L2 is a natural language. What is problematic is when certain conclusions are drawn based on failure to perform exactly like native speakers. Failure to acquire L2 properties may nevertheless involve acquiring properties different from the L1, properties of other natural languages, properties that are underdetermined by the L2 input. Such failure does not necessarily entail lack of UG.

5 UG "Access" and Terminological Confusions

Earlier approaches to UG in L2 acquisition revealed a somewhat ambivalent attitude to the L1. Perhaps because the strongest case for UG can be made if one can eliminate the L1 as a potential source of UG-like knowledge, some researchers felt that evidence of the influence of the L1 grammar on the interlanguage representation would somehow weaken the case for UG. Nowhere is this more evident than in the terminological confusions and disagreements that arose over terms like *direct access* to UG. *Direct access* for some researchers was taken to mean that L2 learners arrive at UG properties independently of their L1 (e.g., Cook, 1988). For others (e.g., Thomas, 1991b), it meant the instantiation of any legitimate parameter setting (L1, L2, Ln). Similar problems have arisen with the term *full access*, which at some point replaced *direct access*. Epstein, Flynn, and Martohardjono (1996) restrict the term *full access* to the position that UG operates independently of the L1 representation, whereas Schwartz and Sprouse (1996) do not so restrict it.

Part of the problem is that terms like *direct/full* or *indirect/partial access* are too global. In addition, in some cases at least, an overly simplistic and misleading dichotomy between UG and the L1 is adopted. Since the L1 is a natural language, there is no a priori justification for assuming that a representation based on the L1 implies lack of UG constraints on the interlanguage grammar.

What is required is a greater focus on the nature of the representations that L2 learners achieve. It may not always be appropriate to dwell explicitly on the UG access question. But by looking in detail at the nature of interlanguage representation, we in fact remain committed to this issue, since evidence of an interlanguage grammar that does not fall within the hypothesis space sanctioned by UG is evidence that UG does not fully constrain interlanguage grammars.

6 Interlanguage Representation: Convergence, Divergence, or Impairment

In the 1990s, the UG debate shifted from a consideration of the broad access question to a detailed consideration of the nature of interlanguage representation. Specific grammatical properties have been investigated and claims have been made as to how they are represented. It is largely presupposed that the interlanguage grammar and the grammars of native speakers of the L2 will diverge in some respects, at least initially and possibly also finally (see Flynn, 1996, for a contrary view). Of interest, then, is the nature of that divergence: is it indicative of a representation that is nevertheless constrained by UG (cf. Sorace, 1993) or is it suggestive of some kind of impairment to the grammar, such that the interlanguage representation is in some sense defective? If interlanguage representations were to show properties not found elsewhere in natural languages, this would suggest that they are not UG-constrained, at least in some domains (see Thomas, 1991a, and Klein, 1995).

The focus on representation manifests itself particularly clearly in proposals relating to the L2 initial state. Theories about the initial state are theories about the representation that L2 learners start out with, the representations that they initially use to make sense of the L2 input.

6.1 *Example: strong features and verb movement*

Since proposals regarding initial and subsequent interlanguage grammars often dwell, in one way or another, on functional categories, we will consider an example here to illustrate the kinds of properties that researchers have investigated in recent years. Functional categories, such as inflection (I), complementizer (C), and determiner (D), have certain formal features associated with them (tense, agreement, case, number, person, gender, etc.). These features vary as to strength (strong vs. weak). Functional categories are seen as the locus of parametric variation (e.g., Borer, 1984; Chomsky, 1995), which can be found at the level of the categories themselves (not all categories are realized in all languages), at the level of formal features (the features of a particular functional category may vary from language to language), and at the level of feature strength (a particular feature can be strong in one language and weak in another).

Here we will consider properties relating to functional projections above the verb phrase (VP). Finite verbs have features (tense, agreement) which have to be checked against corresponding features in I (Chomsky, 1995).[4] If features in I are strong, the finite verb raises overtly to check its features, as in the French

(4a). If features are weak, overt movement does not take place, as in the English (4b):[5]

(4)

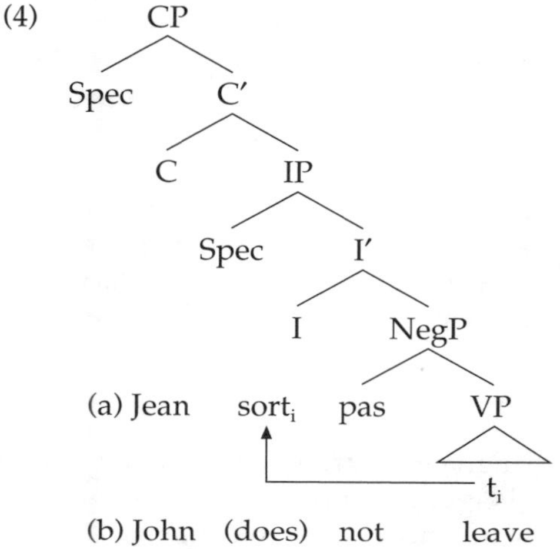

Feature strength results in a number of syntactic consequences related to word order. In languages such as French, where features in I are strong, there are alternations between the positions of finite and non-finite verbs, since non-finite verbs have no features to check, hence do not raise.[6] Comparing French to a language with weak features, like English, there are word order differences between the two with respect to where the finite verb is found (Emonds, 1978; Pollock, 1989). The difference between finite and non-finite verbs in French is illustrated in (5); the differences between finite verbs in French and English are illustrated in (6) and (7). In these examples, we consider only the position of the verb with respect to negation and adverbs, but there is a variety of other verb placement facts which are subsumed under this analysis (see Pollock, 1989):

(5) a. ne sortez pas
(ne) leave-2PP not
b. pas sortir
not leave-INF
'don't go out'

(6) a. Marie n'aime pas Jean
Mary likes not John
b. Marie voit rarement Jean
Mary sees rarely John

(7) a. Mary does not like John
b. *Mary likes not John
c. Mary rarely sees John
d. *Mary sees rarely John

In French, finite lexical verbs appear to the left of the negative *pas* while non-finite verbs appear to the right (compare (5a) and (5b)). English and French contrast with respect to the position of the finite verb in relation to negation and adverbs (compare (6) and (7)). In English, lexical verbs appear to the right of negation (7a) and adverbs (7c) and cannot precede them (7b, 7d), in contrast to French (6a, 6b). A range of word order differences between the two languages are thus accounted for by one parametric difference between them, namely the strength of features in I.

In the next section, we will use the example of verb movement to illustrate some of the representational issues that are currently being pursued. It should be noted, however, that not all of the theories to be discussed in fact have made claims specifically about verb placement.

6.2 Initial state

Proposals concerning the initial interlanguage representation can broadly be classified into two types: (i) the interlanguage representation conforms to properties of natural language (though not necessarily the L2); or (ii) the interlanguage representation differs from adult natural languages in fundamental respects (which, however, may not be permanent). Into the first category falls the Full Transfer/Full Access (FTFA) Hypothesis of Schwartz and Sprouse (1994, 1996). I will also consider Epstein et al.'s (1996) Full Access Hypothesis in this category. Although the Full Access Hypothesis is not, strictly speaking, a hypothesis about the initial state (Epstein et al., 1996, p. 750), it nevertheless has clear implications for the nature of the earliest grammar. The second category includes the Minimal Trees Hypothesis of Vainikka and Young-Scholten (1994, 1996), as well as Eubank's (1993/4, 1994) claim that initially features are neither strong nor weak but rather "inert" or "valueless."

Schwartz and Sprouse (1994, 1996) propose that the L1 grammar constitutes the interlanguage initial state. In other words, faced with L2 input that must be accounted for, learners adopt the representation that they already have. Schwartz and Sprouse (1994) originally presented this proposal in the context of an analysis of the acquisition of German word order by a native speaker of Turkish. Schwartz and Sprouse (1996) and Schwartz (1998a) extend the analysis to French-speaking learners of English, arguing, following White (1991a, 1991c, 1992a), that the initial interlanguage grammar includes strong features, because this is the case in the L1 French. In consequence, verbs are incorrectly placed with respect to adverbs, as White found. However, a potential problem for FTFA is that while White's (1992a) subjects had considerable problems with adverb placement, producing and accepting forms like (7d), they did not have equivalent problems with negation, correctly recognizing the impossibility of (7b).[7]

According to FTFA, the interlanguage representation is necessarily different from the grammar of native speakers of the L2, at least initially; it is nevertheless

UG constrained, exemplifying functional categories and features, as well as syntactic properties that derive from feature strength. The interlanguage representation may or may not converge on the L2 grammar in later stages of development. When the L1 representation is unable to accommodate the L2 input, the learner has recourse to options made available through UG. Once the L2 input reveals an analysis to be inappropriate, there is restructuring of the interlanguage representation. For example, in the case of verb raising, there are properties of the L2 input that could signal the need to change from strong to weak feature values: the presence of *do*-support in negatives (7a) shows that finite lexical verbs in English do not raise (Schwartz, 1987; White, 1992a). Thus, convergence might be expected in this case.

In contrast to FTFA, Epstein et al. (1996, p. 751) and Flynn (1996) claim the L1 grammar is not implicated in the initial interlanguage representation. The implicit logic of their argumentation suggests that UG must be the initial state[8] and that the early grammar in principle has available all functional categories, features, and feature values, from UG, so that an appropriate representation for the L2 can be constructed without recourse to categories or features from the L1. As far as representation of functional categories is concerned, there is no development on such an account: the L2 categories are in place from early on; because they are appropriate, there is no need for subsequent restructuring of the grammar.

In terms of our example, this would mean that a French-speaking learner of English should assume weak features initially, hence would make no word order errors, contrary to fact, at least as far as adverb placement is concerned (White, 1991a, 1991c). Similarly, an English-speaking learner of French should assume strong features, hence exhibiting verb raising. Again, there is research that suggests that this is not inevitable. White (1989a, 1991b) reports that English-speaking children learning French fail to consistently accept verb raising in a variety of tasks. Hawkins, Towell, and Bazergui (1993) suggest that intermediate proficiency adult English-speaking learners of French fail to reset from the weak L1 feature strength to the strong value required by the L2.

Although Schwartz and Sprouse (1996) and Epstein et al. (1996) differ radically in their claims about the involvement of the L1 grammar, they share the assumption that the interlanguage representation shows a full complement of functional categories, drawn either from the L1 or from UG. In other words, the interlanguage representation is a grammar sanctioned by UG, both in the initial state and subsequently.

Other theories posit a greater degree of divergence between what is found in the interlanguage grammar and what is found in the grammars of adult native speakers. Vainikka and Young-Scholten (1994, 1996) propose the Minimal Trees Hypothesis, whereby the initial state lacks functional categories altogether, only lexical categories (N, V, P, etc.) being found. Lexical categories are assumed to be drawn from the L1 grammar, hence to exhibit the same properties as the L1 with respect to headedness, for example. Thus, this theory shares with FTFA the assumption that L1 properties are found in the initial representation. However, as far as functional categories are concerned, Vainikka and Young-Scholten (1994, 1996) assume no transfer at all.

Vainikka and Young-Scholten's (1994) proposals are based on an examination of spontaneous production data from adult learners of German whose L1s are Turkish and Korean. The evidence that they adduce is largely morphological: in early production data from adult learners of German, inflectional morphology is lacking. This leads them to conclude that the corresponding abstract categories are lacking in the interlanguage grammar. (See Sprouse, 1998, and Lardiere, 2000, for arguments against assuming such a close relationship between surface morphology and abstract syntactic categories.) In addition, Vainikka and Young-Scholten (1994) claim that the early grammar lacks word orders that would be the result of movement of the finite verb to a functional projection. In terms of our example, the prediction of Minimal Trees is that French-speaking learners of English should *not* produce errors like (7d), since these are the result of verb movement from V to I (motivated by strong features) (Schwartz, 1998b; Schwartz and Sprouse, 1996). If the functional category I is altogether absent and there is only a VP projection, there is nowhere for the verb to move to. Hence, the only interlanguage word order should be the order that is in fact correct for English, namely (7c), contrary to fact. (See Vainikka and Young-Scholten, 1996, 1998, for discussion.)

Further evidence against Minimal Trees is provided by Grondin and White (1996), who examine spontaneous production data from two English-speaking children learning French. Grondin and White show that there is both morphological and syntactic evidence in favor of an IP projection in early stages. For example, the children show an alternation in verb placement with respect to negation: finite verbs precede *pas* whereas non-finite verbs follow it, suggesting movement of the finite verb to I; this is inconsistent with Minimal Trees, which postulates no I in the early grammar. However, as Vainikka and Young-Scholten (1996) point out, these data may not be truly representative of the initial state, since the children had several months of exposure to the L2 prior to beginning to speak.

In some sense, the Minimal Trees Hypothesis might be seen as implying a defective interlanguage grammar (Lardiere, 2000), since it postulates a period during which the representation lacks functional categories, which are otherwise presumed to be a necessary characteristic of natural language grammars. However, this impairment is assumed to be temporary, with functional categories developing gradually until, eventually, all functional categories appropriate for the L2 are acquired. Furthermore, Vainikka and Young-Scholten (1994, 1996) take the position that gradual emergence of functional categories is also characteristic of L1 acquisition (Clahsen, Eisenbeiss, and Vainikka, 1994); thus, for them, L2 acquisition in this domain is similar to L1.

The final initial state proposal to be considered here also implies that interlanguage grammars are in some sense defective. Eubank (1993/4, 1994) shares with Schwartz and Sprouse (1994, 1996) the assumption that the L1 grammar constitutes a major part of the initial state: L1 lexical categories and functional categories are assumed to be present. However, Eubank maintains that the initial representation lacks fully specified feature values, at least some interlanguage features being unspecified or "inert." In Eubank (1993/4) and subsequently (e.g., Eubank and Grace, 1998) the focus is specifically on feature strength: while features are strong or weak in natural language grammars, they are argued to be neither in the interlanguage, suggesting an impairment in this domain. According to Eubank, a consequence of inertness is that finite verbs will vary optionally between raised and unraised positions; this will be true regardless of what language is being acquired as the L2 and regardless of the situation in the L1. In the case of French-speaking learners of English, then, variable word orders are expected, that is, both (7c) and (7d). The same would be expected of English-speaking learners of French. In support, Eubank (1993/4) points to White's (1991a, 1991c) results on the position of the verb with respect to the adverb, where there was some evidence of variability, with francophone subjects allowing word orders like not only (7d) but also (7c). However, Yuan (2000) shows that French-speaking and English-speaking learners of Chinese (a language with weak features, hence lacking verb movement) are very accurate in positioning verbs in Chinese, even at the beginner level, showing no evidence of optional verb placement.

In fact, Eubank's assumption that raising of finite verbs will be optional appears to be a stipulation which does not follow from any particular theory of feature strength: if features have no strength, there is nothing to motivate verb raising, since this requires a strong feature value (Robertson and Sorace, 1999; Schwartz, 1998b). Prévost and White (2000) provide evidence that finite verbs in adult L2 French and German fail to appear in non-finite positions (i.e., unraised); instead, they occur almost exclusively in positions appropriate for finite verbs, suggesting that inertness cannot be involved.

In its early instantiation, Eubank's proposal was not unlike (indeed, was modeled on) similar proposals that features in L1 acquisition are initially underspecified (e.g., Hyams, 1996; Wexler, 1994). Although a grammar with underspecified features is in some sense defective, underspecification in L1 is assumed to be a temporary property. Similarly, Eubank originally assumed inertness to be a passing phase in the interlanguage representation, with L2 feature strength ultimately attainable.

6.3 *Beyond the initial state*

Initial state theories necessarily have implications for the nature of representation during the course of development, as well as for endstate representation (that is, the steady state interlanguage grammar). According to FTFA, while the L1 grammar forms the interlanguage initial state, restructuring takes place in response to L2 input; hence, convergence on the relevant L2 properties is possible, though not guaranteed, since in some cases the L1 grammar may appear to accommodate the L2 input adequately and thus change will not be triggered. Divergent outcomes, then, would not be surprising, but the interlanguage representation is nevertheless assumed to be UG-constrained.

There are researchers who agree with Schwartz and Sprouse that the L1 grammar is the initial state but who maintain that at least some (and possibly all) L1 features and feature values remain in the interlanguage representation, L2 features or feature values not being acquirable (Hawkins, 1998; Hawkins and Chan, 1997; Liceras, Maxwell, Laguardia, Fernández, and Fernández, 1997; Smith and Tsimpli, 1995). This means that development in the form of restructuring toward a more appropriate functional structure for the L2 is not expected.

On Epstein et al.'s proposal, there is no reason to expect change or development in the domain of functional categories for a different reason, since all categories (including L2 categories) are present from early stages. Convergence on the L2 grammar, then, is guaranteed (Flynn, 1996, p. 150). The only kind of development to be expected is in the surface instantiation of abstract categories in the language-particular morphology of the L2. The Minimal Trees Hypothesis also appears to predict eventual convergence on the L2 functional properties, as L2 functional categories are gradually added, in response to the L2 input.

Whether predicting ultimate divergence from or convergence on the L2 grammar, the above researchers agree that the interlanguage representation does not suffer from any essential long-term impairment, that it ends up with characteristics of a natural language, be it the L1, the L2, or some other language. This contrasts with recent proposals that the interlanguage representation suffers from a permanent deficit, rendering it unlike natural languages, hence not fully UG-constrained.

In recent work, Beck (1998) has suggested that inert feature values are a permanent phenomenon, a proposal also adopted by Eubank in later work (e.g., Eubank and Grace, 1998). In other words, the interlanguage representation is assumed to be defective not just initially and temporarily but permanently. In terms of our example, this means that variable word orders in the case of English-speaking learners of French or French-speaking learners of English are predicted to be found even in the endstate. The results of Yuan (2000), mentioned above, argue against this claim: Yuan demonstrates that L2 learners can indeed reset feature strength to the value appropriate for the L2, even when the L1 value is different (as is the case for the French-speaking learners of Chinese), and that there is no variability in word order at any level of proficiency.

Meisel (1997) proposes more global impairment to functional (and other) properties. He argues that interlanguage grammars are of an essentially different nature from those found in L1 acquisition. He points to differences between L1 and L2 acquisition: in L1 acquisition, the position of the verb is determined by finiteness (compare (5a) and (5b)), whereas, according to Meisel, in L2 acquisition it is not. Prévost and White (2000) provide counter-arguments and data that show that verb placement is not as free as Meisel suggests.

In order to investigate the nature of the interlanguage representation in the functional domain, some of the researchers discussed above have considered both morphological properties (namely whether inflection is present or absent, accurate or faulty) and syntactic ones (whether there are alternations suggestive of verb movement to higher functional projections). Thus, Vainikka and Young-Scholten (1994) argued that the early interlanguage exhibits both a lack of verbal morphology and a lack of word orders indicating movement; Eubank (1993/4) argued that syntactic optionality is associated with absence of inflection; Meisel (1997) argued that both interlanguage morphology and interlanguage verb placement are variable.

But what is one to conclude if syntactic reflexes of feature strength are demonstrably present and morphological ones are lacking or not robustly present? If the interlanguage contains a full complement of functional categories, it might seem somewhat mysterious that L2 learners reveal problems in the domain of morphology associated with functional categories, such as verb inflection. If functional categories are in place, and in place early, why should L2 learners have problems with morphology? Yet it is well known that they exhibit variability in their use of inflection, with tense and agreement morphology sometimes present and sometimes absent in L2 production.

This issue is addressed by Lardiere (1998a, 1998b), who provides a case study of an adult L2 English speaker, Patty, whose L1 is Chinese and whose interlanguage grammar is clearly at its endstate. Patty reveals a lack of consistency in her use of English inflectional morphology: tense marking on verbs in spontaneous production is at about 35 percent, while 3rd person singular agreement is less than 17 percent. At the same time, Patty shows full command of a variety of syntactic phenomena which suggest that tense and agreement are represented in her grammar, with appropriate weak values. For example, Patty shows 100 percent correct incidence of nominative case assignment (nominative case being checked in I, hence implicating this functional category) and complete knowledge of the fact that English verbs do not raise. In other words, she shows no variability in verb placement with respect to adverbs or negation. Word orders like (7b) and (7d) are never found; rather she consistently produces orders like (7a) and (7c), suggesting that verbal features are appropriately weak. According to Eubank and Grace (1998), if interlanguage grammars have permanently inert features, then learners with an L1 with weak features, such as Chinese, learning an L2 also with weak features, like English, should allow optional verb movement. However, Lardiere shows that Patty's interlanguage grammar disallows verb movement and that her problems are not due to any deficit in functional features as such. Even in the absence of appropriate inflectional morphology, functional categories and their feature specifications are present in the grammar and function in ways appropriate for the L2. In this case, then, the underlying grammar does in fact converge on the native grammar, though the surface morphology is divergent, in the sense that it is often absent.

Lardiere argues that this divergence reflects a problem in mapping from abstract categories to their particular surface morphological manifestations. This problem in surface mapping is very different from the impairment to the grammar implied by inert features. In the former case, abstract properties are present and the grammar shows reflexes of feature strength, such as appropriate case marking and word order. There is nothing in UG that says that past tense in English must be realized by a morpheme /*-ed*/ or that agreement must manifest itself as /*-s*/ in the 3rd person singular. Yet it is this realization that is problematic, rather than the syntactic consequences of tense or agreement.

To conclude this section, while the issues are by no means resolved, it seems clear that we have left behind the more general, global question (is there access to UG?) and are now probing quite intricate properties of the interlanguage representation, in order to understand the nature of the grammar that the learner creates to account for the L2. (Of course, the issue of UG involvement is still central, since a grammar constrained by UG will be different in nature from one that is not.) Interesting conceptual questions are being raised: does it make sense to think of an interlanguage representation as being defective in one domain (morphological mapping) but not another (syntax); does it make sense to think of some features being impaired but not others? If the interlanguage representation indeed draws on a variety of knowledge sources (UG, the L1, etc.), how do these come together?

7 Beyond Representation

UG is a theory relevant to the issue of linguistic competence, a theory as to the nature of grammatical representation. Although UG provides constraints on possible grammars in the course of acquisition, it is not, of itself, a theory of acquisition. This point is often misunderstood, perhaps because of terms like "Language Acquisition Device" (LAD) (Chomsky, 1965), which many people in the past equated with UG. It would be more accurate to think of UG as a component within an LAD or as part of a language faculty. A theory of language acquisition will also have to include learning principles, processing principles, triggering algorithms, etc.

In other words, in addition to a theory of constraints on interlanguage representation, we need a theory of how that representation is acquired, a theory of development (whether we are talking about L1 or L2 acquisition). A number of researchers have pointed out that theories of acquisition must explain both the representational problem (what L2 learners come to know) and the developmental problem (how they attain this knowledge) (e.g., Carroll, 1996; Felix, 1987; Gregg, 1996; Klein and Martohardjono, 1999). Most research looking at the operation of UG in second language acquisition has focused on the nature of the L2 learner's grammar, looking for evidence for or against the involvement of principles and parameters of UG, and exploring the nature of the initial state and subsequent grammars. These are representational issues, as we have seen.

Even if one looks for UG-based properties in learner grammars at various points in time, this is a question of representation rather than development. A representational theory is not the same as a developmental one; there is clearly a need for both and room for both. A representational theory makes claims about what learner grammars are like (a grammar at time X conforms to property X and at time Y to property Y) but does not seek to explain how or why grammars develop in a particular way. We should bear in mind that UG itself is not a learning theory; it can only interact with other theories that try to explain development.

To account for grammar change (i.e., development), one needs a theory of how the L2 input interacts with the existing grammar, what properties of the input act as triggers for change, what properties force changes to the current representation, what might drive stages of acquisition. Some L2 learnability work has looked into these kinds of questions (the role of positive and negative evidence, learning principles, proposals that grammar change is failure driven, possible triggers in the input, etc.) (e.g., Schwartz and Sprouse, 1994; Trahey and White, 1993; White, 1991a). However, this is an area where much remains to be done.

Another issue is relevant in this context. In the field of second language acquisition, there is often a confusion between competence (in the sense of underlying linguistic representation) and performance (use of that representation to understand and produce language). People often look at L2 performance, note that it differs from that of native speakers, and argue that this demonstrates essential defects in competence, or lack of UG (the comparative fallacy again). But it is in fact possible that L2 learners' underlying competence is to some extent hidden by performance factors, such as the demands of processing or parsing. Knowledge and use of knowledge do not always coincide. In recent years, there has been an increase in research which investigates how the interlanguage mental representation is accessed during processing, seeking to determine how the representation is used on-line and off-line and the extent to which processing pressures may mask competence (e.g., Juffs and Harrington, 1995; Schachter and Yip, 1990). Again, this is an area where more research is needed.

8 Conclusion

It is not the aim of UG-based theories of second language acquisition to account for all aspects of L2 development. These theories concentrate largely on the nature of unconscious interlanguage knowledge. I have argued that it is not necessary to show that the interlanguage representation is identical to the grammars of native speakers of the L2 in order to demonstrate that the representation is constrained by UG. The pursuit of interlanguage representation has led to a number of interesting and competing proposals: that interlanguage grammars are natural language grammars, constrained by UG (on some accounts, restricted to L1 properties, on other accounts not), versus that interlanguage grammars suffer from impairments (permanent, according to some researchers). The local impairment position contrasts with earlier views which assumed a more global deficit, in the form of a total inability to reset parameters (e.g., Clahsen and Muysken, 1989).

In conclusion, it is important to bear in mind that claims for UG operation in L2 acquisition are simply claims that interlanguage grammars will fall within a limited range, that the "hypothesis space" is specified by UG. As Dekydtspotter et al. (1998, p. 341, n. 1) point out: "Given that the sole 'role' of UG is to restrict the hypothesis space available to the language acquirer, *Full Restriction* might be a more perspicuous name than the standard *Full Access*." If we have to use such terms at all, this one has many advantages, since it focuses our attention on properties of the learner's representation, while at the same time reminding us that the restrictions come from UG.

NOTES

1 For a more recent treatment of this phenomenon, see Noguchi (1997).
2 The examples are drawn from Kanno (1997). The following abbreviations are used: NOM = nominative; ACC = accusative; TOP = topic.
3 Of course native speaker control groups should be included in experiments in order to make sure that the test instrument achieves what it is meant to test. This is a different matter.
4 For purposes of exposition, I ignore analyses that have tense (T) and agreement (Agr) heading their own projections (e.g., Pollock, 1989).
5 Where features are weak, feature checking is achieved by the mechanism of covert movement (Chomsky, 1995).
6 This is an oversimplification, which I will adopt for the sake of the argument. See Pollock (1989).
7 See White (1992a) and Schwartz and Sprouse (2000) for analyses that account for these data in a full transfer framework.
8 In fact, Epstein et al. (1996, p. 751) reject this possibility as well, so that it is impossible to determine their precise position on the initial state.

REFERENCES

Adjémian, C. 1976: On the nature of interlanguage systems. *Language Learning*, 26, 297–320.

Archangeli, D. and Langendoen, T. (eds) 1997: *Optimality Theory: An Overview*. Oxford: Blackwell.

Beck, M. 1998: L2 acquisition and obligatory head movement: English-speaking learners of German and the local impairment hypothesis. *Studies in Second Language Acquisition*, 20, 311–48.

Bley-Vroman, R. 1983: The comparative fallacy in interlanguage studies: the case of systematicity. *Language Learning*, 33, 1–17.

Bley-Vroman, R. 1990: The logical problem of foreign language learning. *Linguistic Analysis*, 20, 3–49.

Borer, H. 1984: *Parametric Syntax*. Dordrecht: Foris.

Carroll, S. 1996: Parameter-setting in second language acquisition: explanans and explanandum.

Behavioral and Brain Sciences, 19, 720–1.
Chomsky, N. 1965: *Aspects of the Theory of Syntax*. Cambridge, MA: MIT Press.
Chomsky, N. 1981: *Lectures on Government and Binding*. Dordrecht: Foris.
Chomsky, N. 1995: *The Minimalist Program*. Cambridge, MA: MIT Press.
Clahsen, H. and Muysken, P. 1989: The UG paradox in L2 acquisition. *Second Language Research*, 5, 1–29.
Clahsen, H., Eisenbeiss, S., and Vainikka, A. 1994: The seeds of structure: a syntactic analysis of the acquisition of Case marking. In T. Hoekstra and B. D. Schwartz (eds), *Language Acquisition Studies in Generative Grammar*. Amsterdam: John Benjamins, 85–118.
Cook, V. 1988: *Chomsky's Universal Grammar: An Introduction*. Oxford: Blackwell.
Cook, V. 1997: Monolingual bias in second language acquisition research. *Revista Canaria de Estudios Ingleses*, 34, 35–49.
Corder, S. P. 1967: The significance of learners' errors. *International Review of Applied Linguistics*, 5, 161–70.
Dekydtspotter, L., Sprouse, R., and Anderson, B. 1998: Interlanguage A-bar dependencies: binding construals, null prepositions and Universal Grammar. *Second Language Research*, 14, 341–58.
duPlessis, J., Solin, D., Travis, L., and White, L. 1987: UG or not UG, that is the question: a reply to Clahsen and Muysken. *Second Language Research*, 3, 56–75.
Emonds, J. 1978: The verbal complex V′–V in French. *Linguistic Inquiry*, 9, 151–75.
Epstein, S., Flynn, S., and Martohardjono, G. 1996: Second language acquisition: theoretical and experimental issues in contemporary research. *Brain and Behavioral Sciences*, 19, 677–758.
Eubank, L. 1993/4: On the transfer of parametric values in L2 development. *Language Acquisition*, 3, 183–208.
Eubank, L. 1994: Optionality and the initial state in L2 development. In T. Hoekstra and B. D. Schwartz (eds), *Language Acquisition Studies in Generative Grammar*. Amsterdam: John Benjamins, 369–88.
Eubank, L. and Grace, S. 1998: V-to-I and inflection in non-native grammars. In M. Beck (ed.), *Morphology and its Interface in L2 Knowledge*. Amsterdam: John Benjamins, 69–88.
Felix, S. 1987: *Cognition and Language Growth*. Dordrecht: Foris.
Finer, D. and Broselow, E. 1986: Second language acquisition of reflexive-binding. In S. Berman, J.-W. Choe, and J. McDonough (eds), *Proceedings of NELS 16*. Amherst, MA: Graduate Linguistics Students Association, 154–68.
Flynn, S. 1996: A parameter-setting approach to second language acquisition. In W. Ritchie and T. Bhatia (eds), *Handbook of Language Acquisition*. San Diego: Academic Press, 121–58.
Gregg, K. R. 1996: The logical and developmental problems of second language acquisition. In W. Ritchie and T. Bhatia (eds), *Handbook of Second Language Acquisition*. San Diego: Academic Press, 49–81.
Grimshaw, J. and Rosen, S. T. 1990: Knowledge and obedience: the developmental status of the binding theory. *Linguistic Inquiry*, 21, 187–222.
Grondin, N. and White, L. 1996: Functional categories in child L2 acquisition of French. *Language Acquisition*, 5, 1–34.
Hale, K. 1996: Can UG and the L1 be distinguished in L2 acquisition? *Behavioral and Brain Sciences*, 19, 728–30.
Hawkins, R. 1998: The inaccessibility of formal features of functional categories

in second language acquisition. Paper presented at the Pacific Second Language Research Forum. Tokyo, March.

Hawkins, R. and Chan, Y.-C. 1997: The partial availability of Universal Grammar in second language acquisition: the "failed features" hypothesis. *Second Language Research*, 13, 187–226.

Hawkins, R., Towell, R., and Bazergui, N. 1993: Universal Grammar and the acquisition of French verb movement by native speakers of English. *Second Language Research*, 9, 189–233.

Hyams, N. 1996: The underspecification of functional categories in early grammar. In H. Clahsen (ed.), *Generative Perspectives on Language Acquisition: Empirical Findings, Theoretical Considerations, Crosslinguistic Comparisons*. Amsterdam: John Benjamins, 91–127.

Juffs, A. and Harrington, M. 1995: Parsing effects in second language sentence processing: subject and object asymmetries in wh-extraction. *Studies in Second Language Acquisition*, 17, 483–516.

Kanno, K. 1997: The acquisition of null and overt pronominals in Japanese by English speakers. *Second Language Research*, 13, 265–87.

Klein, E. 1995: Evidence for a "wild" L2 grammar: when PPs rear their empty heads. *Applied Linguistics*, 16, 87–117.

Klein, E. and Martohardjono, G. 1999: Investigating second language grammars: some conceptual and methodological issues in generative SLA research. In E. Klein and G. Martohardjono (eds), *The Development of Second Language Grammars: A Generative Perspective*. Amsterdam: John Benjamins, 3–34.

Lardiere, D. 1998a: Case and tense in the "fossilized" steady state. *Second Language Research*, 14, 1–26.

Lardiere, D. 1998b: Dissociating syntax from morphology in a divergent end-state grammar. *Second Language Research*, 14, 359–75.

Lardiere, D. 2000: Mapping features to forms in second language acquisition. In J. Archibald (ed.), *Second Language Acquisition and Linguistic Theory*. Oxford: Blackwell, 102–29.

Liceras, J. 1983: Markedness, contrastive analysis and the acquisition of Spanish as a second language. Ph.D. thesis. University of Toronto.

Liceras, J., Maxwell, D., Laguardia, B., Fernández, Z., and Fernández, R. 1997: A longitudinal study of Spanish non-native grammars: beyond parameters. In A. T. Pérez-Leroux and W. Glass (eds), *Contemporary Perspectives on the Acquisition of Spanish. Vol. 1: Developing Grammars*. Somerville, MA: Cascadilla Press, 99–132.

Martohardjono, G. 1993: Wh-movement in the acquisition of a second language: a crosslinguistic study of three languages with and without movement. Ph.D. thesis. Cornell University.

Martohardjono, G. and Gair, J. 1993: Apparent UG inaccessibility in second language acquisition: misapplied principles or principled misapplications? In F. Eckman (ed.), *Confluence: Linguistics, L2 Acquisition and Speech Pathology*. Amsterdam: John Benjamins, 79–103.

Meisel, J. 1997: The acquisition of the syntax of negation in French and German: contrasting first and second language acquisition. *Second Language Research*, 13, 227–63.

Montalbetti, M. 1983: After binding: on the interpretation of pronouns. Ph.D. dissertation. MIT.

Nemser, W. 1971: Approximative systems of foreign language learners. *International Review of Applied Linguistics*, 9, 115–23.

Noguchi, T. 1997: Two types of pronouns and variable binding. *Language*, 73, 770–97.

Pérez-Leroux, A. T. and Glass, W. 1997: OPC effects in the L2 acquisition of Spanish. In A. T. Pérez-Leroux and W. Glass (eds), *Contemporary Perspectives on the Acquisition of Spanish. Vol. 1: Developing Grammars.* Somerville, MA: Cascadilla Press, 149–65.

Pinker, S. 1994: *The Language Instinct.* New York: William Morrow.

Pollock, J.-Y. 1989: Verb movement, Universal Grammar, and the structure of IP. *Linguistic Inquiry*, 20, 365–424.

Prévost, P. and White, L. 2000: Missing surface inflection or impairment in second language acquisition? Evidence from tense and agreement. *Second Language Research*, 16, 103–33.

Robertson, D. and Sorace, A. 1999: Losing the V2 constraint. In E. Klein and G. Martohardjono (eds), *The Development of Second Language Grammars: A Generative Approach.* Amsterdam: John Benjamins, 317–61.

Schachter, J. 1988: Second language acquisition and its relationship to Universal Grammar. *Applied Linguistics*, 9, 219–35.

Schachter, J. 1989: Testing a proposed universal. In S. Gass and J. Schachter (eds), *Linguistic Perspectives on Second Language Acquisition.* Cambridge: Cambridge University Press, 73–88.

Schachter, J. 1990: On the issue of completeness in second language acquisition. *Second Language Research*, 6, 93–124.

Schachter, J. and Yip, V. 1990: Grammaticality judgments: why does anyone object to subject extraction? *Studies in Second Language Acquisition*, 12, 379–92.

Schwartz, B. D. 1987: The modular basis of second language acquisition. Ph.D. dissertation. University of Southern California.

Schwartz, B. D. 1993: On explicit and negative data effecting and affecting competence and "linguistic behavior." *Studies in Second Language Acquisition*, 15, 147–63.

Schwartz, B. D. 1998a: On two hypotheses of "Transfer" in L2A: minimal trees and absolute L1 influence. In S. Flynn, G. Martohardjono, and W. O'Neil (eds), *The Generative Study of Second Language Acquisition.* Mahwah, NJ: Lawrence Erlbaum Associates, 35–59.

Schwartz, B. D. 1998b: The second language instinct. *Lingua*, 106, 133–60.

Schwartz, B. D. and Sprouse, R. 1994: Word order and nominative case in nonnative language acquisition: a longitudinal study of (L1 Turkish) German interlanguage. In T. Hoekstra and B. D. Schwartz (eds), *Language Acquisition Studies in Generative Grammar.* Amsterdam: John Benjamins, 317–68.

Schwartz, B. D. and Sprouse, R. 1996: L2 cognitive states and the full transfer/full access model. *Second Language Research*, 12, 40–72.

Schwartz, B. D. and Sprouse, R. 2000: When syntactic theories evolve: consequences for L2 acquisition research. In J. Archibald (ed.), *Second Language Acquisition and Linguistic Theory.* Oxford: Blackwell, 156–86.

Selinker, L. 1972: Interlanguage. *International Review of Applied Linguistics*, 10, 209–31.

Smith, N. and Tsimpli, I.-M. 1995: *The Mind of a Savant.* Oxford: Blackwell.

Sorace, A. 1993: Incomplete and divergent representations of unaccusativity in non-native grammars of Italian. *Second Language Research*, 9, 22–48.

Sprouse, R. 1998: Some notes on the relationship between inflectional morphology and parameter setting in first and second language acquisition. In M. Beck (ed.), *Morphology and the Interfaces in Second Language Knowledge.* Amsterdam: John Benjamins, 41–67.

Thomas, M. 1991a: Do second language learners have "rogue" grammars of anaphora? In L. Eubank (ed.), *Point Counterpoint: Universal Grammar in the Second Language*. Amsterdam: John Benjamins, 375–88.

Thomas, M. 1991b: Universal Grammar and the interpretation of reflexives in a second language. *Language*, 67, 211–39.

Trahey, M. and White, L. 1993: Positive evidence and preemption in the second language classroom. *Studies in Second Language Acquisition*, 15, 181–204.

Vainikka, A. and Young-Scholten, M. 1994: Direct access to X′-theory: evidence from Korean and Turkish adults learning German. In T. Hoekstra and B. D. Schwartz (eds), *Language Acquisition Studies in Generative Grammar*. Amsterdam: John Benjamins, 265–316.

Vainikka, A. and Young-Scholten, M. 1996: Gradual development of L2 phrase structure. *Second Language Research*, 12, 7–39.

Vainikka, A. and Young-Scholten, M. 1998: The initial state in the L2 acquisition of phrase structure. In S. Flynn, G. Martohardjono, and W. O'Neil (eds), *The Generative Study of Second Language Acquisition*. Mahwah, NJ: Lawrence Erlbaum Associates, 17–34.

Wexler, K. 1994: Optional infinitives, head movement and the economy of derivations. In D. Lightfoot and N. Hornstein (eds), *Verb Movement*. Cambridge: Cambridge University Press, 305–50.

White, L. 1985: Is there a logical problem of second language acquisition? *TESL Canada*, 2, 29–41.

White, L. 1989a: The principle of adjacency in second language acquisition: do L2 learners observe the subset principle? In S. Gass and J. Schachter (eds), *Linguistic Perspectives on Second Language Acquisition*. Cambridge: Cambridge University Press, 134–58.

White, L. 1989b: *Universal Grammar and Second Language Acquisition*. Amsterdam: John Benjamins.

White, L. 1990: Second language acquisition and universal grammar. *Studies in Second Language Acquisition*, 12, 121–33.

White, L. 1991a: Adverb placement in second language acquisition: some effects of positive and negative evidence in the classroom. *Second Language Research*, 7, 133–61.

White, L. 1991b: Argument structure in second language acquisition. *Journal of French Language Studies*, 1, 189–207.

White, L. 1991c: The verb-movement parameter in second language acquisition. *Language Acquisition*, 1, 337–60.

White, L. 1992a: Long and short verb movement in second language acquisition. *Canadian Journal of Linguistics*, 37, 273–86.

White, L. 1992b: Subjacency violations and empty categories in L2 acquisition. In H. Goodluck and M. Rochemont (eds), *Island Constraints*. Dordrecht: Kluwer, 445–64.

White, L. 1996: Universal grammar and second language acquisition: current trends and new directions. In W. Ritchie and T. Bhatia (eds), *Handbook of Language Acquisition*. New York: Academic Press, 85–120.

Yuan, B. 2000: Is thematic verb raising inevitable in the acquisition of a nonnative language? In C. Howell, S. Fish, and T. Keith-Lucas (eds), *Proceedings of the 24th Annual Boston University Conference on Language Development*. Somerville, MA: Cascadilla Press, 797–807.

3 The Radical Middle: Nativism without Universal Grammar

WILLIAM O'GRADY

1 Introduction

A phenomenon as puzzling and complex as language acquisition is no doubt worthy of the controversy that its study has engendered. Indeed, it would be unreasonable to expect a broad consensus on such a profoundly mysterious phenomenon after a mere 30 or 40 years of investigation, much of it focused on the acquisition of a single language.

Under these circumstances, the most that can perhaps be hoped for in the near term is some agreement on the research questions that need to be addressed and on the merits and shortcoming of the various explanatory ideas that are currently being pursued. In the longer term, of course, one hopes for a convergence of views, and even now there is some indication that this has begun in a limited way, as I will explain below. Nonetheless, for the time being at least, there is still ample room for disagreement on many important points.

The purpose of this chapter is to outline a view of language acquisition – both first and second – that is sometimes referred to as "general nativism." I will begin in the next section by offering an overview of this approach, including its principal claims and the major challenges that it faces. Section 3 outlines a general nativist theory of syntactic representations with respect to a well-established asymmetry in the development of relative clauses in the course of first and second language acquisition. Section 4 addresses the possible advantages of general nativism compared to other theories of language acquisition.

2 Defining General Nativism

There is a near-consensus within contemporary linguistics (which I will not question here) that language should be seen as a system of knowledge – a sort of "mental grammar" consisting of a lexicon that provides information about the linguistically relevant properties of words and a computational system that is responsible for the formation and interpretation of sentences.

The details of the computational system and even of the lexicon are the subject of ongoing dispute, of course, but there is substantial agreement on a number of points. For instance, it seems clear that the grammar for any human language must assign words to categories of the appropriate type (noun, verb, etc.), that it must provide a set of mechanisms for combining words into phrases and sentences with a particular internal architecture, and that it must impose constraints on phenomena such as "movement" and pronoun interpretation.

What makes matters especially interesting for theories of language acquisition is that grammars that include even these basic and relatively uncontroversial mechanisms are underdetermined by experience in significant ways. As far as we can tell, for instance, the input to the acquisition process (i.e., the speech of others) includes no direct information about the criteria for category membership, the architecture of syntactic representations, or the content of constraints on movement and pronoun interpretation. (For a general review, see O'Grady, 1997, pp. 249 ff.) How then can a language be acquired?

Theories of linguistic development typically address this problem by assuming that children are endowed with an "acquisition device" – an innate system that both guides and supplements the learner's interaction with experience. This much is accepted by a broad spectrum of researchers ranging from Slobin (e.g., 1985, p. 1158) to Chomsky (e.g., 1975, p. 13), but differences arise on one important point. In one class of acquisition theories, a significant portion of the grammar is taken to be "given in advance" by the acquisition device. This grammatical component of the inborn acquisition device is known as Universal Grammar, or UG – a system of categories and principles that is taken to determine many of the core properties of human language (see figure 3.1). Such theories are instances of what might be called "grammatical nativism," since they adopt the view that the innate endowment for language includes actual grammatical categories and principles. Elsewhere, I have referred to this view as "special nativism" (O'Grady, 1997, p. 307), because of its commitment to the existence of innate mechanisms with a specifically grammatical character (see also White, this volume).

Grammatical nativism contrasts with "general nativism," which posits an innate acquisition device but denies that it includes grammatical categories or principles per se. According to this view (which might also be labeled "cognitive nativism" or "emergentism," as is more common these days), the entire grammar is the product of the interaction of the acquisition device with experience; no grammatical knowledge is inborn (see figure 3.2) (see Ellis, this volume).

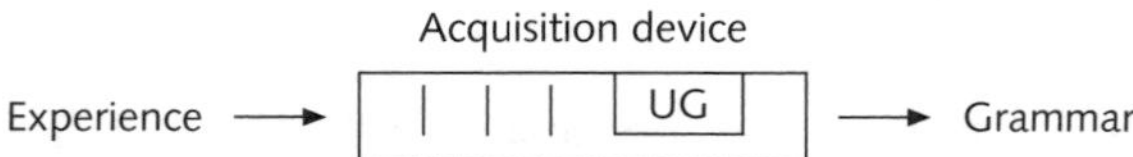

Figure 3.1 The UG-based acquisition device

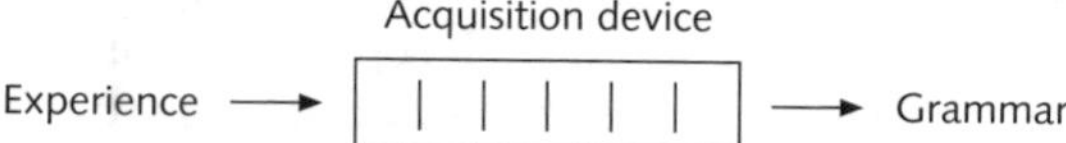

Figure 3.2 The general nativist acquisition device

Later in this chapter, I will suggest that there are some signs of convergence between general nativism and recent versions of grammatical nativism. For now, though, I would like to emphasize the profound historical difference between the two views. UG is not simply the name for whatever mechanisms happen to be involved in grammatical development. As I interpret the literature on grammatical nativism, proponents of the view that UG is part of the acquisition device subscribe to a very strong claim about its content and character – namely, that it is an *autonomous* system of *grammatical* categories and principles – autonomous in the sense that it is not reducible to non-linguistic notions and grammatical in the sense that it is primarily concerned with matters of well-formedness, not parsing or processing or other types of language-related cognition. (For detailed discussion, see Newmeyer, 1998.) All varieties of general nativism reject these assumptions, however much they may disagree on what the acquisition device actually does comprise.

Skepticism concerning UG is widespread in the field of language acquisition research. Relatively little of the literature on first language acquisition is couched within a UG framework, and the same seems to be true of the literature on second language acquisition as well. In addition to the huge amount of work that simply ignores UG, there is also a substantial and varied literature that explicitly rejects it in one form or another. This includes work by Martin Braine (1987), Dan Slobin (1985), Melissa Bowerman (1990), and Michael Tomasello (1995) (among many others) on first language acquisition and work by Eric Kellerman (Kellerman and Yoshioka, 1999), Fred Eckman (1996), Kate Wolfe-Quintero (1992, 1996), and others on second language acquisition. It should be noted, though, that there is no unified general nativist approach to language acquisition and certainly no agreement on the particular views that I outline in the remainder of this chapter.

As I see it, the principal limitation of most work on general nativism lies in its failure to develop a theory of learnability and development that is tied to an explicit and comprehensive theory of grammar (see also Gregg, 1996). Most non-UG work is quite casual in its approach to syntax: the phenomena whose acquisition is being investigated are typically analyzed informally and on a case-by-case basis, without reference to an overarching syntactic theory. By contrast, work in the special nativist tradition has not only put forward a theory of learnability (built around an inborn UG) but linked it to a far-reaching and explicit theory of grammar (transformational grammar in its various incarnations).

For reasons that I will discuss further below, the most promising theories of language posit explanatory principles that make reference to phonological, syntactic, and semantic *representations* of various sorts. Yet the vast majority of work on general nativism either makes no reference to such representations or adopts a very casual view as to their properties, typically avoiding any explicit proposal about their architecture or ontogeny.

A good illustration of this point comes from an important body of research on the acquisition of relative clauses by second language learners (e.g., Doughty, 1991; Eckman, Bell, and Nelson, 1988; Gass, 1979, 1980). This work has yielded a robust and interesting finding: subject relative clauses such as (1) are easier than direct object relatives such as (2) for second language learners. (The same seems to be true for first language acquisition, all other things being equal; see O'Grady, 1997, p. 179 for discussion.)

(1) *Subject relative:*
the truck that [_ pushed the car]

(2) *Object relative:*
the truck that [the car pushed _]

Further, it has been observed that this finding parallels an important generalization in syntactic typology dating back at least to Keenan and Comrie (1977): direct object relatives are more marked than subject relatives. (That is, some languages have only subject relatives, but any language with direct object relatives must also permit subject relatives.)

The developmental pattern and its relationship to Keenan and Comrie's typological generalization raise questions that force us to address the two principal explanatory challenges confronting contemporary linguistics:

i Why is language the way it is (e.g., why do all languages with direct object relatives also have subject relatives, but not vice versa)?
ii How is it acquired (e.g., why are subject relatives easier for language learners than direct object relatives)?

It is my position that neither of these questions can be answered without reference to hierarchically structured symbolic representations. On this view, then, the first priority for general nativism must be a theory of syntactic representations that includes a proposal about their composition and architecture.

3 A General Nativist Theory of Representations

In a number of recent publications (e.g., O'Grady, 1996, 1997, 1998), I have put forward the outlines of a general nativist theory of syntactic representations. As I see it, the key to such a theory lies in two propositions. First, syntactic categories, which are treated as purely formal elements in special nativism, must be reducible to a semantic base. I have made one proposal about precisely how

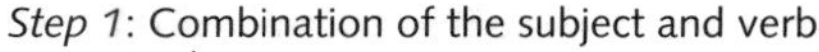

Figure 3.3 First step in the formation of the sentence *Mary speaks French*

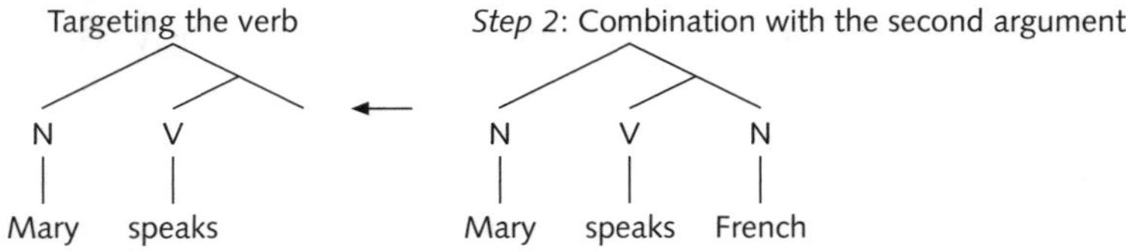

Figure 3.4 Second step in the formation of the sentence *Mary speaks French*

this might be achieved (O'Grady, 1997, 1998), and other ideas can be found in the literature on grammatical categories (e.g., Croft, 1991; Langacker, 1987).

Second, contra the view adopted within UG-based approaches to language acquisition, the computational principles that combine and arrange words to form phrases and sentences cannot be specifically grammatical in character (that is, there is no X-bar Schema, no Empty Category Principle, and so forth). How then do we account for the sorts of grammatical phenomena that have been the focus of so much linguistic research since the early 1960s?

In recent work on this matter (e.g., O'Grady, 2001b), I have proposed that the theory of sentence structure can and should be unified with the theory of sentence processing. As I see it, the processor itself has no specifically grammatical properties. Rather, its design reflects two more general computational features – a propensity to operate on pairs of elements (a characteristic of the arithmetical faculty as well)[1] and a propensity to combine functors with their arguments at the first opportunity (a storage-reducing strategy that I refer to simply as "efficiency"). The system operates in a linear manner (i.e., "from left to right"), giving the result depicted in figure 3.3 in the case of a simple transitive sentence such as *Mary speaks French.*

In the next step, the verb combines directly with its second argument, an operation that requires splitting the previously formed phrase in the manner depicted in figure 3.4. (Such an operation has long been assumed, at least implicitly, in the literature on sentence processing; see, e.g., Frazier, 1987, p. 561; Levelt, 1989, p. 242; Marcus, 1980, pp. 79–80.)

Syntactic representations in this type of efficiency-driven computational system have the familiar binary-branching design, with the subject higher than the direct object – but not as the result of an a priori grammatical blueprint such as the X-bar schema. Rather, their properties are in a sense epiphenomenal – the by-product of a sentence formation process that proceeds from left to right, combining a verb with its arguments one at a time at the first opportunity. Syntactic representations are thus nothing more than a residual record of how the computational system goes about combining words to form sentences.

The architecture of the proposed syntactic representations offers a promising account of why subject relatives are easier than direct object relatives. The key idea is that the relative difficulty (and, by extension, the developmental order) of structures that contain gaps is determined by the distance (calculated in terms of intervening nodes) between the gap and its filler (e.g., the nominal modified by the relative clause). As illustrated in (3) and (4), there is one such node in the case of subject relatives (i.e., S) and two in the case of object relatives (i.e., S and VP):[2]

(3) *Subject relative:*
the truck that [$_S$ _ pushed the car]

(4) *Direct Object relative:*
the truck that [$_S$ the car [$_{VP}$ pushed _]]

A problematic feature of English is that structural distance is confounded with linear distance: subject gaps are not only less deeply embedded than object gaps, they are also linearly closer to the head noun. In order to ensure that structural distance rather than linear distance is responsible for the contrast in the difficulty of relative clauses, it is necessary to consider the acquisition of languages such as Korean, in which the relative clause precedes the head. (The verbal suffixes in Korean simultaneously indicate both tense and clause type. RC = relative clause.)

(5) a. *Subject relative:*
[$_S$ _ namca-lul cohaha-nun] yeca
man-Acc like-RC.Prs woman
"the woman who likes the man"
structural distance: one node (S)
linear distance: two words
b. *Direct object relative:*
[$_S$ Namca-ka [$_{VP}$ _ cohaha-nun]] yeca
man-Nom like-RC.Prs woman
"the woman who the man likes"
structural distance: two nodes (VP and S)
linear distance: one word

If structural distance is the key factor, then the subject relative should be easier; on the other hand, if linear distance is the key factor, the direct object relative should be easier. O'Grady, Lee, and Choo (forthcoming) investigated this matter with the help of a comprehension task (see box 3.1), uncovering a strong and statistically significant preference for subject relative clauses.

Box 3.1 The acquisition of relative clauses in Korean as a second language (O'Grady et al., forthcoming)

Research questions: Is there a subject–object asymmetry in the acquisition of Korean relative clauses? If so, does it reflect a contrast in linear distance or in structural distance?

Methodology:
Subjects: 53 native English speakers studying Korean as a second language – 25 second-semester students at the University of Texas at Austin, 20 fourth-semester students at the same institution, and 8 fourth-semester students at the University of Hawai'i at Manoa.

Task: Picture selection, in accordance with the following instructions:

> Each page of this booklet contains a series of three pictures. As you go to each page, you will hear a tape-recorded voice describing a person or animal in one of the three pictures. Your job is simply to put a circle around the person or animal described in the sentence. (Do NOT put the circle around the entire box.)

Figure 3.5 presents a sample page from the questionnaire.

Figure 3.5 Sample test items

Subjects who correctly understand relative clauses should circle the right-hand figure in the third panel in response to a subject relative clause such as (ia) and the left-hand figure in the second panel in response to a direct object relative such as (ib):

(i) a. *Subject relative clause:*
[_ namca-lul cohaha-nun] yeca
man-Acc like-RC.Prs woman
'the woman who likes the man'

b. *Direct object relative clause:*
[namca-ka _ cohaha-nun] yeca
man-Nom like-RC.Prs woman
'the woman who the man likes'

Results: The subjects did far better on subject relative clauses than on direct object relatives, with scores of 73.2 percent correct on the former pattern compared to only 22.7 percent for the latter. This contrast is highly significant (F 30.59, $p = .0001$). Equally revealing is an asymmetry in reversal errors (i.e., the number of times a pattern of one type was misanalyzed as a pattern of the other type): direct object relatives were misunderstood as subject relatives 115 times while subject relatives were misanalyzed as direct object relatives only 26 times – a clear indication that subject relatives are the easier pattern.

Conclusion: Learners of Korean as a second language find subject relatives far easier than direct object relatives, which supports the claim that structural distance between a gap and its filler is the key factor in determining the relative difficulty of these patterns.

If the structural distance account is correct, we expect to find comparable asymmetries in the development of other gap-containing structures as well. *Wh*-questions are a case in point. As illustrated in (6) and (7), subject and object *wh*-questions exhibit a contrast that parallels the asymmetry found in relative clauses:

(6) *Subject wh-question:*
Who [$_S$ _ met Mary]?

(7) *Object wh-question:*
Who did [$_S$ Mary [$_{VP}$ meet _]]?

The relative difficulty of these two patterns has been studied for both first language acquisition (Yoshinaga, 1996) and second language acquisition (Kim, 1999) with the help of an elicited production task. Both studies revealed significantly better performance on subject *wh*-questions and a strong tendency for these patterns to be used in place of their direct object counterparts, but not vice versa.

By adopting a particular theory of syntactic representations, then, we are able to uncover a plausible computational explanation for why object relatives are more difficult than subject relatives for language learners and for why object wh-questions are harder than subject *wh*-questions. This is a potential step forward, not only because it helps explain the developmental facts, but also because it sheds light on the typological facts as well.

In particular, it makes sense to think that the cut-off points that languages adopt in defining the limits for relative clause formation are determined by the same measure of computational complexity that defines developmental difficulty. Thus, subject relatives – the computationally simplest structure – will be the most widespread typologically.[3] Moreover, any language that allows the computationally more difficult direct object relatives will also permit the simpler subject relatives. And so on.

This cannot be all there is to it, of course. Syntactic representations have properties other than just binarity, and syntactic principles make reference to more than just structural distance. The illustration given here omits many details in order to make the key point – which is that the best prospects for an explanatory general nativist theory of language lie in an approach that takes syntactic representations as its starting point. As we have just seen, reference to such representations allows us to make a proposal not only about how language is acquired (e.g., why subject relatives are acquired first) but also about why language is the way it is (e.g., why any language that allows object relatives must also allow subject relatives).

The parallels between first and second language acquisition that are manifested in the emergence of relative clauses lend credence to the idea that the two phenomena are fundamentally alike, at least in some respects. I believe that this is right, at least insofar as computational operations are concerned. The matter is hardly clear, though. Indeed, the facts are somewhat difficult to interpret: as Bley-Vroman (1994, p. 4) has observed, experimental work on computational principles in second language acquisition has yielded indecisive results – "better than chance, [but] far from perfect." Although this seems to suggest diminished access to the computational mechanisms underlying sentence formation, a less pessimistic view is adopted by Uziel (1993), who follows Grimshaw and Rosen (1990) in arguing that any indication that learners perform above the level of chance on contrasts involving computational principles should be interpreted as evidence for access to those principles – a not unreasonable proposal in light of the many extraneous factors (e.g., inattention, processing limitations, vocabulary deficits, nervousness, and so forth) that can interfere with performance in experimental settings. (See also White, this volume.)

If this is right, then performance on computational principles should improve as the effect of extraneous factors diminishes. There is already some indication that this is right: Kanno (1996) investigates the status of a computational principle that is responsible for the asymmetry in the admissibility of case drop in subject and direct object positions in Japanese (see section 4 for details). Because the contrast is manifested in very simple sentences, Kanno was able to elicit grammaticality judgments for sentences that were just two and three words long, thereby dramatically diminishing the potential effect of extraneous factors. Interestingly, she reports that adult learners of Japanese as a second language do not perform significantly differently from native speakers in assessing the relative acceptability of the two patterns.

Why then are adults such poor language learners? There are a number of possibilities, of course, two of which I find particularly interesting. First, it is evident that some parts of the language faculty fare less well than the computational system with the passage of time. For instance, the ability to distinguish among phonemic contrasts apparently begins to diminish by the age of 12 months (Werker, Lloyd, Pegg, and Polka, 1996), with the result that language acquisition after age six or so typically results in a foreign accent (Long, 1990, p. 266). There also appears to be a significant decline in learners' ability to exploit subtle semantic contrasts, including those underlying such familiar phenomena as the *the/a* contrast in English (Larsen-Freeman and Long, 1991, p. 89) or the *wa/ga* (topic/nominative) contrast in Japanese (Kuno, 1973, p. 37; Russel, 1985, p. 197). This suggests that the acquisition device comprises several autonomous components (at least a computational module, a perceptual module, and a conceptual module), each with its own maturational prospects and its own role to play in shaping the outcome of second language learning.

A second possibility, which focuses just on syntactic deficits (see, e.g., O'Grady, 2001a), is that the computational system, while intact, is underpowered in the case of adult language learners. The effects of this deficit are manifested in patterns which, for one reason or another, place extra demands on the computational system. One such pattern involves object relative clauses, which require the establishment of a link between a direct object gap and a structurally distant filler. As we have seen, both children and adults have trouble with these patterns compared to subject relative clauses. Interestingly, similar problems have been observed in agrammatic aphasics (e.g., Grodzinsky, 2000).

Another sort of pattern that may place an extra burden on the computational system involves double object datives such as (8), compared to their prepositional dative counterparts as in (9):

(8) *Double object dative:*
agent *goal* *theme*
The boy sent the donkey the horse.

(9) *Prepositional dative:*
agent *theme* *goal*
The boys sent the horse to the donkey.

As observed by Dik (1989), Langacker (1995, pp. 18–20), and Talmy (1988), among others, the word order employed in the prepositional pattern (agent–theme-goal) is iconic with the structure of the event, which involves the agent acting on the theme and then transferring it to the goal, giving the "action chain" (to employ Langacker's term) depicted in (10):

(10) agent → theme → goal

Interestingly, the double object dative, with its non-iconic agent–goal–theme order, is harder to comprehend, both for children in the early stages of language acquisition (Osgood and Zehler, 1981; Roeper, Lapointer, Bing, and Tavakolian, 1981; Waryas and Stremel, 1974) and for adult second language learners (Hawkins, 1987; Mazurkewich, 1984; White, 1987). And here again, agrammatic aphasics have been found to have difficulty with this pattern too (Caplan and Futter, 1986; Kolk and Weijts, 1996, p. 111; O'Grady and Lee, 2001).

All of this suggests that in the early stages of language acquisition (and perhaps in the case of agrammatism as well) the computational system may be too underpowered to reliably execute the more demanding tasks involved in natural language processing, including dealing with long-distance dependencies and non-iconic word order. Whereas children routinely overcome this deficit, its effects in the case of adults may be longer lasting, contributing to the pattern of partial attainment that is typical of second language learning.

4 The Advantages of General Nativism

In evaluating general nativism, it is useful to compare it with two well-known alternatives – UG-based special nativism, which posits inborn grammatical categories and principles, and connectionism, certain varieties of which deny the existence of traditional symbolic representations and principles altogether (e.g., Elman, Bates, Johnson, Karmiloff-Smith, Parisi, and Plunkett, 1996). Each approach has its own merits, of course, but it is nonetheless possible to identify considerations that justify continued pursuit of the general nativist research program.

The *potential* advantage of general nativism with respect to special nativism is obvious. All scientific work, including the special nativist research program, seeks the most general properties and principles possible. One does not posit a grammatical rule specifically for passivization if the properties of passive structures can be derived from a more general grammatical principle. And one does not posit a grammatical constraint if the phenomena that it accounts for can be derived from principles that are not specific to the language faculty. (For an identical view within grammatical nativism, see Lightfoot, 1982, p. 45.)

Interestingly, the pursuit of this very goal within the special nativist research program has led to a partial convergence of views with general nativism in recent years. As observed in O'Grady (1999), work within the "Minimalist Program" that has grown out of Government and Binding theory (e.g., Chomsky, 1995) suggests that UG as it was conventionally understood is being abandoned even by those traditionally committed to grammatical nativism in its strongest form. The latest generation of explanatory principles focuses on the notion of economy, demanding "short moves" (the "Minimal Link Condition") that take place only if necessary ("Last Resort") and are postponed for as long as possible ("Procrastinate") – in short, the sort of principles that one would expect to find in almost any computational system. (In fact, Fukui, 1996, has gone so far as to suggest that the economy principles of the Minimalist Program follow from the laws of physics!)[4]

A concrete example of this convergence of views can be seen in the treatment of gap-containing structures in the two varieties of nativism, where one can find parallel proposals for calculating relative complexity and markedness. As explained above, I have suggested that the relative ease of subject gaps compared to object gaps can be explained with reference to their distance from the "filler" (the head in the case of relative clauses, the wh-word in the case of questions). Working within the minimalist program, Collins (1994, p. 56) has put forward a virtually identical proposal: the cost of "movement operations" is determined by the number of nodes traversed.

In the final analysis, then, general and special varieties of nativism agree on the existence of an inborn acquisition device, of hierarchically structured symbolic representations, and of explanatory principles that refer to these representations. The principal difference between the two approaches revolves around the precise nature of these constructs, with disagreement centered on the question of whether the language faculty includes inborn categories and mechanisms that are narrowly grammatical in character. But even here, there is agreement that we should seek out the most general constructs that are consistent with a viable account of the properties of language and the facts of development. What remains to be determined is whether some of these constructs have the status necessary to justify continued adherence to the traditional conception of Universal Grammar.

At first glance at least, the type of general nativism advocated here shares much less common ground with connectionism. This is somewhat ironic since, in a sense, connectionism is an extreme form of general nativism. Indeed, some of its current proponents (e.g., Elizabeth Bates and Brian MacWhinney) were earlier associated with a more traditional general nativist perspective (e.g., Bates and MacWhinney, 1988), and Elman et al. (1996, p. 114) note that connectionism embodies aspects of Piaget's (general nativist) theory of the mind.

As I see it, the attractiveness of connectionism stems in large part from the fact that it takes the pursuit of generality so seriously, ultimately arriving at the strongest possible conclusion concerning the nature of the human language faculty – namely that it has no special properties of its own, grammatical or otherwise. This idea deserves to be taken seriously. Ultimately, though, the connectionist program must be evaluated in terms of the same criteria as apply to all theories of language: it must account both for how language is acquired and for why it is the way it is. To date, connectionist work seems to have concentrated almost exclusively on the former question. There have been impressive results in this area, but, for me at least, the challenge of explaining why language is the way it is has yet to be satisfactorily addressed. A simple example will help illustrate this point.

As is well known, many languages exhibit so-called "subject–verb" agreement: affixation on the verb records person and number features of the subject. For example:

(11)

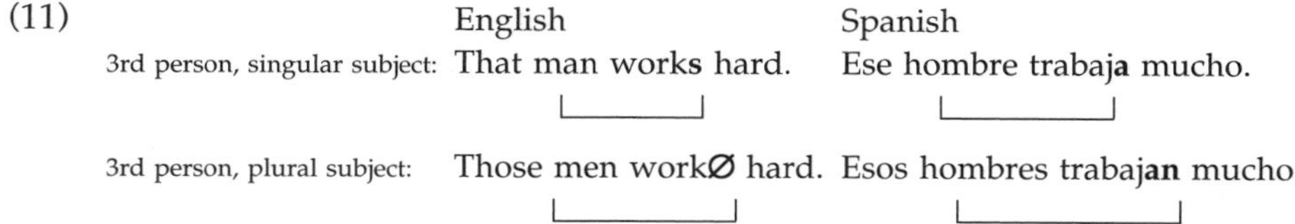

We know from the intriguing work of Elman (1993) and others that it is possible to build a connectionist net that can "learn" subject–verb agreement without reference to hierarchical syntactic representations per se. Moreover, on the face of it, it appears that such a proposal could count as an explanation for how at least this feature of language is acquired.

But there is another challenge here. This is because the same connectionist net could almost certainly "learn" a language – call it Lisheng – in which agreement is triggered by the direct object rather than the subject:

(12)

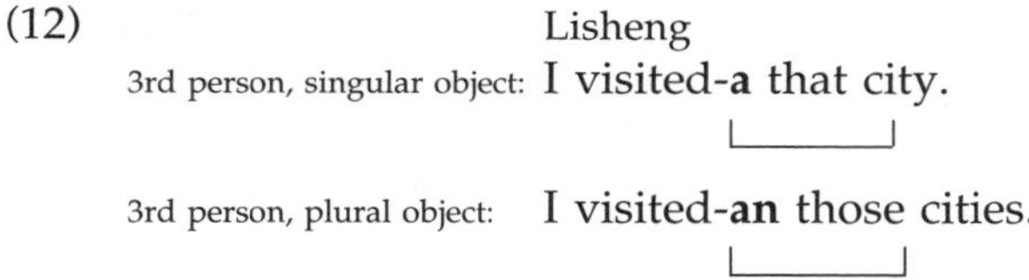

The problem is that there is apparently no such language: there are languages such as English and Spanish in which the verb agrees only with the subject and languages such as Swahili in which the verb agrees with both the subject and the direct object, but no languages in which the verb agrees only with the direct object (e.g., Croft, 1990, p. 106). Why should this be?

This asymmetry has a straightforward explanation in theories of language that make use of hierarchically structured syntactic representations: the need for agreement to mark a head–argument relation increases with the computational distance between the two elements. Since verbs are structurally closer to their direct objects than to their subjects in the sort of representation that I posit, it follows that the need for agreement is greater in the latter case. This is true not only for SOV languages such as Tamil, in which the subject is linearly more distant from the verb, but also for SVO languages such as English, in which the subject and direct object are both adjacent to the verb, and for VSO languages such as Irish, in which the subject is linearly closer to the verb than is the direct object (see figure 3.6).[5]

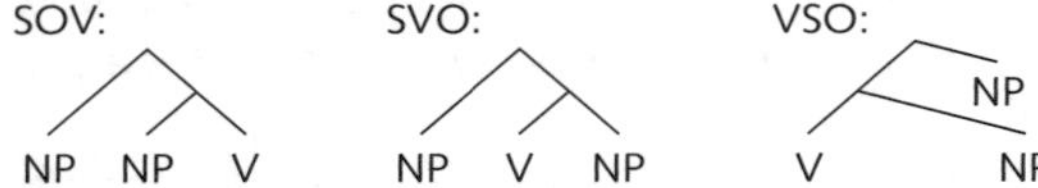

Figure 3.6 The subject–object asymmetry

Syntactic representations such as these shed light on other phenomena as well. For instance, it is surely no accident that in languages such as Japanese, case can be dropped from the direct object but not from the subject (Fukuda, 1993): the need for case presumably is greater on the more distant of the verb's arguments:

(13) a. *Case drop on the subject:*
*Dare gakusei-o nagutta-no?
who student-AC hit -Ques
'Who hit the student?'
b. *Case drop on the direct object:*
Gakusei-ga dare nagutta-no?
student-Nom who hit -Ques
'Who did the student hit?'

Explanations such as these are plainly based on processing considerations. As such, they are perfectly compatible with Elman et al.'s hint (1996, p. 386) that linguistic universals are perhaps attributable to processing mechanisms – an idea that they do not develop. Crucially, however, the specific processing factors that underlie agreement and case drop asymmetries come to light only when we consider symbolic representations with the defining properties of traditional syntactic structure – binary branching and a subject–object asymmetry. (Recall, though, that these architectural features are derived from general computational properties, not UG, in the approach that I adopt.) It remains to be seen how and whether the connectionist program deals with these issues.

In the course of proposing an account for why language is the way it is with respect to phenomena such as agreement and case drop, a theory based on traditional symbolic representations also takes us a good deal of the way toward understanding how language is acquired. In the case of agreement, for instance, it seems reasonable to suppose that the computational demands associated with keeping track of the structurally more distant verb–subject relation create a place in syntactic representations where agreement would be especially welcome.

Confounding factors make it difficult to test this prediction against developmental data, since subject agreement morphemes are more frequent than their object agreement counterparts and may occur in the more salient word-initial or word-final position (vs. word-medial position). Nonetheless, the developmental facts are at least suggestive.

In languages with both subject and object agreement, there seem to be only two developmental patterns: either subject agreement is learned before object agreement (the case in Sesotho, according to Demuth, 1992, p. 600), or the two types of agreement emerge simultaneously (this is apparently what happens in West Greenlandic (Fortescue and Olsen, 1992), K'iche' Maya (Pye, 1992), Walpiri (Bavin, 1992), and Georgian (Imedadze and Tuite, 1992). There appear to be no languages in which object agreement is acquired before subject agreement.

Turning now to case drop, if in fact the computational demands associated with keeping track of the more distant verb–subject relation make it worthwhile to retain case on the subject while permitting its suppression on the direct object, we would expect this contrast to be evident in the course of linguistic development. This seems to be right: Suzuki (1999) reports that children learning Japanese exhibit an overwhelming greater tendency to have a case marker on the subject than on the direct object, even though they sometimes use the wrong case form (see also Lakshmanan and Ozeki, 1996; Miyata, 1993). Moreover, as noted in the preceding section, Kanno (1996) reports that the same tendency is strongly manifested in adult second language learners, even when there is no relevant experience or instruction.

5 Conclusion

Reduced to its essentials, the study of language is centered on the investigation of two very fundamental questions – why language is the way it is, and how it is acquired. To date, the most detailed answer to these questions has come from proponents of grammatical nativism, who have put forward a theory that simultaneously addresses both questions: Universal Grammar determines the properties that any human language must have and, by virtue of being inborn, it helps explain the success and rapidity of the language acquisition process.

A defining feature of UG-based theories is their commitment to hierarchically structured symbolic representations. Not only are the key properties of language defined in terms of these representations, but the mechanisms determining a sentence's pronunciation and interpretation are thought to make crucial reference to them as well. On this view, then, the end point of the language acquisition process can be seen, in part at least, as the ability to associate such representations with the sentences of one's language.

At the other extreme, recent work in connectionism denies the existence of conventional syntactic representations, of Universal Grammar, and of an inborn acquisition device specifically for language. Language acquisition, it is claimed, is not fundamentally different from any other type of learning and can be accounted for by the same mechanisms as are required for interaction with the environment in general.

My own work has been exploring a radical idea of a different sort. As I have characterized it, general (or cognitive) nativism differs from connectionism in being committed to the existence of hierarchically structured symbolic representations as part of a theory of why language is the way it is and to the existence of an inborn acquisition device as part of a theory of how language is acquired. At the same time, it differs from grammatical nativism in not positing inborn categories or principles that are exclusively grammatical in character.

Differences as deep as these are unlikely to be resolved immediately, but the challenge is at least clear – we need a viable account both of the properties that define human language and of the acquisition of individual languages on the basis of very limited types of input. There is surely a place for the study of second language acquisition in all of this. At the very least, research on second language learning provides opportunities to observe the acquisition device functioning under conditions of duress – either because of extreme limitations on the available input (as in the case of classroom learning) or because one or more of its component modules have been compromised, or both. It is perhaps not too optimistic to think that the further study of this phenomenon will provide opportunities to extend and deepen our understanding of the acquisition device for human language.

NOTES

1 When we add three or more numbers (e.g., 7 + 4 + 8), we always proceed in a pair-wise fashion; no one is able to compute all the numbers in a single step.

2 As predicted, direct object relatives are known to be easier than indirect object relatives, in both first language acquisition (de Villiers, Tager Flusberb, Hakuata, and Cohen, 1979; Hildebrand, 1987) and second language acquisition (Gass, 1979; Wolfe-Quintero, 1992). However, depth of embedding cannot account for the relative preference for preposition stranding over "pied-piping" found in children learning English as a first language (e.g., McDaniel, McKee, and Bernstein, 1998) and, possibly, in second language learners too (White, 1989, pp. 122ff):

   i *Preposition stranding: three intervening nodes:*
   the man who [$_S$ you [$_{VP}$ talked [$_{PP}$ to _]]]

   ii *Pied-piping: two intervening nodes:*
   the man to whom [$_S$ you [$_{VP}$ talked _]]

   The obvious explanation for this contrast is simply that the pied-piped structure is all but non-existent in the input. But this raises the question of why English is this way, given the general tendency in human language to avoid preposition stranding. J. Hawkins (1999) makes an interesting proposal in this regard, but space does not permit further discussion of this matter here.

3 The same should be true of wh-questions as well, and there do in fact appear to be some languages in which only subjects undergo *wh*-movement (Cheng, 1991).

4 The Minimalist Program still falls well short of being general nativist, however. Chomsky (1995) makes a number of proposals with a strong special nativist character, including a property "P" that permits multiple

nominative patterns in Japanese by allowing a feature to remain active even after being checked and deleted (p. 286) and a parameter that licenses multiple subject constructions in Icelandic by permitting an unforced violation of Procrastinate (p. 375).

5 As illustrated in the syntactic representation for VSO languages, the computational system I adopt permits discontinuous constituents. For extensive discussion, see O'Grady (2001b).

REFERENCES

Bates, E. and MacWhinney, B. 1988: What is functionalism? *Papers and Reports on Child Language Development*, 27, 137–52.

Bavin, E. 1992: The acquisition of Walpiri. In D. Slobin (ed.), *The Crosslinguistic Study of Language Acquisition. Vol. 3*. Hillsdale, NJ: Lawrence Erlbaum Associates, 309–71.

Bley-Vroman, R. 1994: Updating the Fundamental Difference Hypothesis. Talk presented at the EuroSLA Convention, Aix-en-Provence.

Bowerman, M. 1990: Mapping thematic roles onto syntactic functions: are children helped by innate linking rules? *Linguistics*, 28, 1253–89.

Braine, M. 1987: What is learned in acquiring word classes – a step toward an acquisition theory. In B. MacWhinney (ed.), *Mechanisms of Language Acquisition*. Hillsdale, NJ: Lawrence Erlbaum Associates, 65–87.

Caplan, D. and Futter, C. 1986: Assignment of thematic roles to nouns in sentence comprehension by an agrammatic patient. *Brain and Language*, 27, 117–34.

Cheng, L. 1991: On the typology of wh-questions. Unpublished Ph.D. dissertation. MIT.

Chomsky, N. 1975: *Reflections on Language*. New York: Pantheon.

Chomsky, N. 1995: *The Minimalist Program*. Cambridge, MA: MIT.

Collins, C. 1994: Economy of derivation and the Generalized Proper Binding Condition. *Linguistic Inquiry*, 25, 45–61.

Croft, W. 1990: *Typology and Universals*. New York: Cambridge University Press.

Croft, W. 1991: *Syntactic Categories and Grammatical Relations: The Cognitive Organization of Information*. Chicago: University of Chicago Press.

Demuth, C. 1992: The acquisition of Sesotho. In D. Slobin (ed.), *The Crosslinguistic Study of Language Acquisition. Vol. 3*. Hillsdale, NJ: Lawrence Erlbaum Associates, 557–638.

Dik, S. 1989: *The Theory of Functional Grammar. Part I: The Structure of the Clause*. Dordrecht: Foris.

Doughty, C. 1991: Second language instruction does make a difference. *Studies in Second Language Acquisition*, 13, 431–69.

Eckman, F. 1996: On evaluating arguments for special nativism in second language acquisition theory. *Second Language Research*, 12, 398–419.

Eckman, F., Bell, L., and Nelson, D. 1988: On the generalization of relative clause instruction in the acquisition of English as a second language. *Applied Linguistics*, 9, 1–13.

Ellis, N. 1996: Sequencing in SLA: phonological memory, chunking and points of order. *Studies in Second Language Acquisition*, 18, 91–126.

Elman, J. 1993: Learning and development in neural networks: the importance of starting small. *Cognition*, 48, 71–99.

Elman, J., Bates, E., Johnson, M., Karmiloff-Smith, A., Parisi, D., and Plunkett, K. 1996: *Rethinking Innateness: A Connectionist Perspective on Development*. Cambridge, MA: MIT Press.

Fortescue, M. and Olsen, L. 1992: The acquisition of West Greenlandic. In D. Slobin (ed.), *The Crosslinguistic Study of Language Acquisition. Vol. 3*. Hillsdale, NJ: Lawrence Erlbaum Associates, 111–219.

Frazier, L. 1987: Sentence processing: a tutorial review. In M. Coltheart (ed.), *Attention and Performance XII: The Psychology of Reading*. Hillsdale, NJ: Lawrence Erlbaum Associates, 559–86.

Fukuda, M. 1993: Head government and case marker drop in Japanese. *Linguistic Inquiry*, 24, 168–72.

Fukui, N. 1996: On the nature of economy in language. *Ninti Kagaku [Cognitive Studies]*, 3, 51–71.

Gass, S. 1979: Language transfer and universal grammatical relations. *Language Learning*, 29, 327–44.

Gass, S. 1980: An investigation of syntactic transfer in adult second language learners. In R. Scarcella and S. Krashen (eds), *Research in Second Language Acquisition*. Rowley, MA: Newbury House, 132–41.

Gregg, K. 1996: The logical and developmental problems of second language acquisition. In W. Ritchie and T. Bhatia (eds), *Handbook of Second Language Acquisition*. San Diego: Academic Press, 49–81.

Grimshaw, J. and Rosen, S. 1990: Knowledge and obedience: the developmental status of the binding theory. *Linguistic Inquiry*, 21, 187–222.

Grodzinsky, Y. 2000: The neurology of syntax: language use without Broca's area. *Behavioral and Brain Sciences*, 23, 1–71.

Hawkins, J. 1999: Processing complexity and filler-gap dependencies across grammars. *Language*, 75, 244–85.

Hawkins, R. 1987: Markedness and the acquisition of the English dative alternation by L2 speakers. *Second Language Research*, 3, 20–55.

Hildebrand, J. 1987: The acquisition of preposition stranding. *Canadian Journal of Linguistics*, 32, 65–85.

Imedadze, N. and Tuite, K. 1992: The acquisition of Georgian. In D. Slobin (ed.), *The Crosslinguistic Study of Language Acquisition. Vol. 3*. Hillsdale, NJ: Lawrence Erlbaum Associates, 39–109.

Kanno, K. 1996: The status of a non-parametrized principle in the L2 initial state. *Language Acquisition: A Journal of Developmental Linguistics*, 5, 317–34.

Keenan, E. and Comrie, B. 1977: Noun phrase accessibility and Universal Grammar. *Linguistic Inquiry*, 8, 63–100.

Kellerman, E. and Yoshioka, K. 1999: Inter- and intra-population consistency: a comment on Kanno (1998). *Second Language Research*, 15, 101–9.

Kim, S. 1999: The subject–object asymmetry in the acquisition of wh-questions by Korean learners of English. Paper presented at the Hawaii Language Acquisition Workshop. Honolulu, Hawaii.

Kolk, H. and Weijts, M. 1996: Judgments of semantic anomaly in agrammatic patients: argument movement, syntactic complexity, and the use of heuristics. *Brain and Language*, 54, 86–135.

Kuno, S. 1973: *The Structure of the Japanese Language*. Cambridge, MA: MIT Press.

Lakshmanan, U. and Ozeki, M. 1996: The case of the missing particle: objective case assignment and scrambling in the early grammar of Japanese. In

A. Stringfellow, D. Cahana-Amitay, E. Hughes, and A. Zukowski (eds), *Proceedings of the 20th Annual Boston University Conference on Language Development.* Somerville, MA: Cascadilla Press, 431–42.

Langacker, R. 1987: Nouns and verbs. *Language*, 63, 53–95.

Langacker, R. 1995: Raising and transparency. *Language*, 71, 1–62.

Larsen-Freeman, D. and Long, M. 1991: *An Introduction to Second Language Acquisition Research.* New York: Longman.

Levelt, W. 1989: *Speaking: From Intention to Articulation.* Cambridge, MA: MIT Press.

Lightfoot, D. 1982: *The Language Lottery.* Cambridge, MA: MIT Press.

Long, M. 1990: Maturational constraints on language development. *Studies in Second Language Acquisition*, 12, 251–85.

Marcus, M. 1980: *A Theory of Syntactic Recognition for Natural Language.* Cambridge, MA: MIT Press.

Mazurkewich, I. 1984: The acquisition of the dative alternation: unlearning overgeneralizations. *Cognition*, 16, 261–83.

McDaniel, D., McKee, C., and Bernstein, J. 1998: How children's relatives solve a problem for minimalism. *Language*, 74, 308–34.

Miyata, H. 1993: The performance of the Japanese case particles in children's speech: with special reference to "ga" and "o." *MITA Working Papers in Psycholinguistics*, 3, 117–36.

Newmeyer, F. 1998: *Language Form and Language Function.* Cambridge, MA: MIT Press.

O'Grady, W. 1996: Language acquisition without Universal Grammar: a proposal for L2 learning. *Second Language Research*, 12, 374–97.

O'Grady, W. 1997: *Syntactic Development.* Chicago: University of Chicago Press.

O'Grady, W. 1998: The acquisition of syntactic representations: a general nativist approach. In W. Ritchie and T. Bhatia (eds), *Handbook of Language Acquisition.* San Diego: Academic Press, 157–93.

O'Grady, W. 1999: Toward a new nativism. *Studies in Second Language Acquisition*, 21, 621–33.

O'Grady, W. 2001a: Language acquisition and language deficits. Invited keynote address presented to the Japan Society for Language Sciences.

O'Grady, W. 2001b: Syntactic computation. Ms. University of Hawai'i, Department of Linguistics.

O'Grady, W. and Lee, W. 2001: The Isomorphic Mapping Hypothesis: evidence from Korean. To appear. *Brain and Cognition*, 46, 226–30.

O'Grady, W., Lee, M., and Choo, M. forthcoming: The acquisition of relative clauses in Korean as a second language. *Studies in Second Language Acquisition.*

Osgood, C. and Zehler, A. 1981: Acquisition of bi-transitive sentences: pre-linguistic determinants of language acquisition. *Journal of Child Language*, 8, 367–84.

Pye, C. 1992: The acquisition of K'iche' Maya. In D. Slobin (ed.), *The Crosslinguistic Study of Language Acquisition. Vol. 3.* Hillsdale, NJ: Lawrence Erlbaum Associates, 221–309.

Roeper, T., Lapointe, S., Bing, J., and Tavakolian, S. 1981: A lexical approach to language acquisition. In S. Tavakolian (ed.), *Language Acquisition and Linguistic Theory.* Cambridge, MA: MIT Press, 35–58.

Russel, R. 1985: An analysis of student errors in the use of Japanese *-wa* and *-ga*. *Papers in Linguistics*, 18, 197–221.

Slobin, D. 1985: Crosslinguistic evidence for the language-making capacity. In D. Slobin (ed.), *The Crosslinguistic Study of Language Acquisition. Vol. 2.*

Hillsdale, NJ: Lawrence Erlbaum Associates, 1157–256.

Suzuki, T. 1999: Two aspects of Japanese case in acquisition. Unpublished Ph.D. dissertation. University of Hawai'i at Manoa.

Talmy, L. 1988: Force dynamics in language and cognition. *Cognitive Science*, 12, 49–100.

Tomasello, M. 1995: Language is not an instinct. *Cognitive Development*, 10, 131–56.

Uziel, S. 1993: Resetting Universal Grammar parameters: evidence from second language acquisition of Subjacency and the Empty Category Principle. *Second Language Research*, 9, 49–83.

de Villiers, J., Tager Flusberb, H., Hakuata, K., and Cohen, M. 1979: Children's comprehension of relative clauses. *Journal of Psycholinguistic Research*, 8, 499–528.

Waryas, C. and Stremel, K. 1974: On the preferred form of the double object construction. *Journal of Psycholinguistic Research*, 3, 271–79.

Werker, J., Lloyd, V., Pegg, J., and Polka, L. 1996: Putting the baby in the bootstraps: toward a more complete understanding of the role of the input in infant speech processing. In J. Morgan and K. Demuth (eds), *Signal to Syntax*. Mahwah, NJ: Lawrence Erlbaum Associates, 427–47.

White, L. 1987: Markedness and second language acquisition: the question of transfer. *Studies in Second Language Acquisition*, 9, 261–85.

White, L. 1989: *Universal Grammar and Second Language Acquisition*. Philadelphia: John Benjamins.

Wolfe-Quintero, K. 1992: Learnability and the acquisition of extraction in relative clauses and *wh* questions. *Studies in Second Language Acquisition*, 14, 39–70.

Wolfe-Quintero, K. 1996: Nativism does not equal Universal Grammar. *Second Language Research*, 12, 335–73.

Yoshinaga, N. 1996: Wh-questions: a comparative study of their form and acquisition in English and Japanese. Ph.D. dissertation. University of Hawai'i at Manoa.

4 Constructions, Chunking, and Connectionism: The Emergence of Second Language Structure

NICK C. ELLIS

1 Introduction and Overview

Constructivist views of language acquisition hold that simple learning mechanisms operating in and across human systems for perception, motor action, and cognition while exposed to language data in a communicatively rich human social environment navigated by an organism eager to exploit the functionality of language are sufficient to drive the emergence of complex language representations. The various tribes of constructivism – that is, connectionists (Christiansen and Chater, 2001; Christiansen, Chater, and Seidenberg, 1999; Levy, Bairaktaris, Bullinaria, and Cairns, 1995; McClelland, Rumelhart, and the PDP Research Group, 1986; Plunkett, 1998), functional linguists (Bates and MacWhinney, 1981; MacWhinney and Bates, 1989), emergentists (Elman, Bates, Johnson, Karmiloff-Smith, Parisi, and Plunkett, 1996; MacWhinney, 1999a), cognitive linguists (Croft and Cruse, 1999; Lakoff, 1987; Langacker, 1987, 1991; Ungerer and Schmid, 1996), constructivist child language researchers (Slobin, 1997; Tomasello, 1992, 1995, 1998a, 2000), applied linguists influenced by chaos/complexity theory (Larsen-Freeman, 1997), and computational linguists who explore statistical approaches to grammar (Bod, 1998; Jurafsky, 1996) – all share a functional-developmental, usage-based perspective on language. They emphasize the linguistic sign as a set of mappings between phonological forms and conceptual meanings or communicative intentions; thus, their theories of language function, acquisition, and neurobiology attempt to unite speakers, syntax, and semantics, the signifiers and the signifieds. They hold that structural regularities of language emerge from learners' lifetime analysis of the distributional characteristics of the language input and, thus, that the knowledge of a speaker/hearer cannot be understood as an innate grammar, but rather as a statistical ensemble of language experiences that changes slightly every time a new utterance is processed. Consequently, they analyze language acquisition processes rather than the final state or the language acquisition device (see Sorace, this volume; White, this volume). They work within the broad remit of cognitive science, seeking functional and neurobiological descriptions of the learning processes which, through exposure to representative experience, result in change, development, and the emergence of linguistic representations.

Section 2 of this review describes cognitive linguistic theories of construction grammar. These focus on constructions as recurrent patterns of linguistic elements that serve some well-defined linguistic function. These may be at sentence level (such as the imperative, the ditransitive, the yes-no question) or below (the noun phrase, the prepositional phrase, etc.). Whereas Government-Binding Theory denied constructions, viewing them as epiphenomena resulting from the interaction of higher-level principles-and-parameters and lower-level lexicon, cognitive linguistics – construction grammar in particular (Croft, 2001; Goldberg, 1995) – has brought them back to the fore, suspecting instead that it is the higher-level systematicities that emerge from the interactions of constructions large and small. Section 3 concerns the development of constructions as complex chunks, as high-level schemata for abstract relations such as transitives, locatives, datives, or passives. An acquisition sequence – from formula, through low-scope pattern, to construction – is proposed as a useful starting point to investigate the emergence of constructions and the ways in which type and token frequency affect the productivity of patterns. Section 4 presents the psychological learning mechanisms which underpin this acquisition sequence. It describes generic associative learning mechanisms such as chunking which, when applied to the stream of language, provide a rich source of knowledge of sequential dependencies ranging from low-level binary chunks like bigrams, through phonotactics, lexis, and collocations, up to formulae and idioms. Although a very basic learning mechanism, chunking results in hierarchical representations and structure dependency.

Emergentists believe that many of the rule-like regularities that we see in language emerge from the mutual interactions of the billions of associations that are acquired during language usage. But such hypotheses require testing and formal analysis. Section 5 describes how connectionism provides a means of evaluating the effectiveness of the implementations of these ideas as simulations of language acquisition which are run using computer models consisting of many artificial neurons connected in parallel. Two models of the emergence of linguistic regularity are presented for detailed illustration. Other simulations show how analysis of sequential dependencies results in grammatically useful abstract linguistic representations. The broad scope of connectionist and other distributional approaches to language acquisition is briefly outlined. The review concludes by discussing some limitations of work to date and provides some suggestions for future progress.

2 Construction Grammar

This section outlines cognitive linguistic analyses of the interactions between human language, perception, and cognition, and then focuses on construction grammar (Croft, 2001; Fillmore and Kay, 1993; Goldberg, 1995; Langacker, 1987; Tomasello, 1998a, 1998b) as an approach for analyzing the ways in which particular language patterns cue particular processes of interpretation. If words are the atoms of language function, then construction grammar provides the molecular level of analysis.

2.1 *Cognitive linguistics*

Cognitive linguistics (Barlow and Kemmer, 2000; Croft and Cruse, 1999; Goldberg, 1995; Lakoff, 1987; Lakoff and Johnson, 1980; Langacker, 1987, 1991; Talmy, 1988; Ungerer and Schmid, 1996) provides detailed qualitative analyses of the ways in which language is grounded in human experience and in human embodiment, which represents the world in a very particular way. The meaning of the words of a given language, and how they can be used in combination, depends on the perception and categorization of the real world around us. Since we constantly observe and play an active role in this world, we know a great deal about the entities of which it consists, and this experience and familiarity is reflected in the nature of language. Ultimately, everything we know is organized and related in some meaningful way or other, and everything we perceive is affected by our perceptual apparatus and our perceptual history. Language reflects this embodiment and this experience.

The different degrees of salience or prominence of elements involved in situations that we wish to describe affect the selection of subject, object, adverbials, and other clause arrangement. Figure/ground segregation and perspective taking, processes of vision and attention, are mirrored in language and have systematic relations with syntactic structure. Thus, paradoxically, a theory of language must properly reflect the ways in which human vision and spatial representations are explored, manipulated, cropped and zoomed, and run in time like movies under attentional and scripted control (Kosslyn, 1983; Talmy, 1996a). In language production, what we express reflects which parts of an event attract our attention; depending on how we direct our attention, we can select and highlight different aspects of the frame, thus arriving at different linguistic expressions. The prominence of particular aspects of the scene and the perspective of the internal observer (i.e., the attentional focus of the speaker and the intended attentional focus of the listener) are key elements in determining regularities of association between elements of visuo-spatial experience and elements of phonological form. In language comprehension, abstract linguistic constructions (like simple locatives, datives, and passives) serve as a "zoom lens" for the listener, guiding their attention to a particular perspective on a scene while backgrounding other aspects (Goldberg, 1995).

Thus, cognitive linguistics describes the regularities of syntax as emergent from the cross-modal evidence that is collated during the learner's lifetime of using and comprehending language.

Cognitive linguistics was founded on the principle that language cognition cannot be separated from semantics and the rest of cognition. The next section shows how it similarly denies clear boundaries between the traditional linguistic separations of syntax, lexicon, phonology, and pragmatics.

2.2 Constructions

Traditional descriptive grammars focus on constructions, that is, recurrent patterns of linguistic elements that serve some well-defined linguistic function. As noted earlier, these may be at sentence level (such as the imperative, the ditransitive, the yes-no question) or below (the noun phrase, the prepositional phrase, etc.). The following summary of construction grammar, heavily influenced by Langacker (1987) and Croft and Cruse (1999), illustrates the key tenets.

A construction is a conventional linguistic unit, that is, part of the linguistic system, accepted as a convention in the speech community, and entrenched as grammatical knowledge in the speaker's mind. Constructions may (i) be complex, as in [Det Noun], or be simple, as in [Noun] (traditionally viewed as "syntax"); (ii) represent complex structure above the word level, as in [Adj Noun], or below the word level, as in [NounStem-PL] (traditionally viewed as "morphology"); or (c) be schematic, as in [Det Noun], or specific, as in [the United Kingdom], traditionally viewed as "lexicon." Hence, "morphology," "syntax," and "lexicon" are uniformly represented in a construction grammar, unlike both traditional grammar and generative grammar. Constructions are symbolic. In addition to specifying the properties of an utterance's defining morphological, syntactic, and lexical form, a construction also specifies the semantic, pragmatic, and/or discourse functions that are associated with it. Constructions form a structured inventory of speakers' knowledge of the conventions of their language (Langacker, 1987, pp. 63–6), usually described by construction grammarians in terms of a semantic network, where schematic constructions can be abstracted over the less schematic ones which are inferred inductively by the speaker in acquisition. This non-modular semantic network representation of grammar is shared by other theories such as Word Grammar (Hudson, 1984, 1990). A construction may provide a partial specification of the structure of an utterance. Hence, an utterance's structure is specified by a number of distinct constructions. Constructions are independently represented units in a speaker's mind. Any construction with unique, idiosyncratic formal or functional properties must be represented independently in order to capture speakers' knowledge of their language. However, absence of any unique property of a construction does not entail that it is not represented independently and simply derived from other, more general or schematic constructions. Frequency of occurrence may lead to independent representation of even "regular" constructional patterns. This usage-based perspective implies that the acquisition of grammar is the piecemeal learning of many thousands of constructions and the frequency-biased abstraction of regularities within them.

Many constructions are based on particular lexical items, ranging from simple (*Howzat!* in cricket) to complex (*Beauty is in the eye of the beholder*). The importance of such lexical units or idiomatic phrases is widely acknowledged in SLA research when discussing holophrases (Corder, 1973), prefabricated routines and patterns (Hakuta, 1974), formulaic speech (Wong Fillmore, 1976), memorized sentences and lexicalized stems (Pawley and Syder, 1983), formulae (R. Ellis, 1994), sequences in SLA (N. Ellis, 1996, 2002), discourse management (Dörnyei and Kormos, 1998; Tannen, 1987), register (Biber and Finegan, 1994), style (Brewster, 1999), and lexical patterns and collocational knowledge (Carter, 1998; Hoey, 1991; Lewis, 1993; Schmitt, 2000). According to Nattinger (1980, p. 341), "for a great deal of the time anyway, language production consists of piecing together the ready-made units appropriate for a particular situation and . . . comprehension relies on knowing which of these patterns to predict in these situations." As Pawley and Syder (1983, p. 192) put it:

> In the store of familiar collocations there are expressions for a wide range of familiar concepts and speech acts, and the speaker is able to retrieve these as wholes or as automatic chains from the long-term memory; by doing this he minimizes the amount of clause-internal encoding work to be done and frees himself to attend to other tasks in talk-exchange, including the planning of larger units of discourse.

But other constructions are more abstract. Goldberg (1995) focuses on complex argument structure constructions such as the ditransitive (*Pat faxed Bill the letter*), the caused motion (*Pat pushed the napkin off the table*), and the conative (*Sam kicked at Bill*). She holds that these abstract and complex constructions themselves carry meaning, independently of the particular words in the sentence. For example, even though the verb *kick* does not typically imply transfer of possession, it works in the ditransitive *Pat kicked Bill the football*, and even though one is hard pressed to interpret anything but an intransitive *sneeze*, the caused motion *Pat sneezed the napkin off the table* is equally good. These abstract argument structure constructions thus create an important top-down component to the process of linguistic communication. Such influences are powerful mechanisms for the creativity of language, possibly even as manifest in derivational phenomena such as denominal verbs (*They tabled the motion*) and deverbal nouns (*Drinking killed him*) (Tomasello, 1998b).

Constructions show prototype effects. For example, for ditransitive constructions there is the central sense of agent-successfully-causes-recipient-to-receive-patient (*Bill gave/handed/passed/threw/took her a book*), and various more peripheral meanings such as future-transfer (*Bill bequeathed/allocated/granted/reserved her a book*) and enabling-transfer (*Bill allowed/permitted her one book*). Prototype effects are fundamental characteristics of category formation, again blurring the boundaries between syntax and lexicon and other cognitive domains (N. Ellis, 2002).

3 Learning Constructions

If linguistic systems comprise a conspiracy of constructions, then language acquisition, L1 or L2, is the acquisition of constructions. There is nothing revolutionary in these ideas. Descriptive grammars (e.g., Biber, Johansson, Leech, Conrad, and Finegan, 1999; Quirk, Greenbaum, Leech, and Svartvik, 1985) are traditionally organized around form–function patterns; so are grammars which are designed to inform pedagogy (e.g., Celce-Murcia and Larsen-Freeman, 1983). But what about the processes of acquisition? To date, construction grammar has primarily concerned descriptions of adult competence, although language acquisition researchers, particularly those involved in child language, are now beginning to sketch out theories of the acquisition of constructions which involve a developmental sequence from formula, through low-scope pattern, to construction.

3.1 Formulae and idioms

Formulae are lexical chunks which result from memorizing the sequence of frequent collocations. Large stretches of language are adequately described by finite-state grammars, as collocational streams where patterns flow into each other. Sinclair (1991, p. 110), then director of the Cobuild project, the largest lexicographic analysis of the English language to date, summarized this in the principle of idiom:

> A language user has available to him or her a large number of semi-preconstructed phrases that constitute single choices, even though they might appear to be analyzable into segments. To some extent this may reflect the recurrence of similar situations in human affairs; it may illustrate a natural tendency to economy of effort; or it may be motivated in part by the exigencies of real-time conversation.

Rather than its being a somewhat minor feature compared with grammar, Sinclair suggests that, for normal texts, the first mode of analysis to be applied is the idiom principle, as most text is interpretable by this principle. Whereas most of the material that Sinclair was analyzing in the Bank of English was written text, comparisons of written and spoken corpora demonstrate that collocations are even more frequent in spoken language (Biber et al., 1999; Brazil, 1995; Leech, 2000). Parole is flat and Markovian because it is constructed "off the top of one's head," and there is no time to work it over. Utterances are constructed as intonation units which have the grammatical form of single clauses, although many others are parts of clauses, and they are often highly predictable in terms of their lexical concordance (Hopper, 1998). Language reception and production are mediated by learners' representations of chunks of language: "Suppose that, instead of shaping discourse according to rules, one really pulls old language from memory (particularly old language, with all its words in and everything), and then reshapes it to the current context: " 'Context shaping', as Bateson puts it, 'is just another term for grammar' " (Becker, 1983, p. 218).

Even for simple concrete lexis or formulae, acquisition is no unitary phenomenon. It involves the (typically) implicit learning of the sequence of sounds or letters in the word along with separable processes of explicit learning of perceptual reference (N. Ellis, 1994c, 2001). Yet however multifaceted and fascinating is the learning of words (Aitchison, 1987; Bloom, 2000; N. Ellis and Beaton, 1993a, 1993b; Miller, 1991; Ungerer and Schmid, 1996), lexical learning has generally been viewed as a phenomenon that can readily be understood in terms of basic processes of human cognition. Learning the form of formulae is simply the associative learning of sequences. It can readily be understood in terms of the process of chunking which will be described in section 4.

The mechanism of learning might be simple, but the product is a rich and diverse population of hundreds of thousands of lexical items and phrases. The store of familiar collocations of the native language speaker is very large indeed. The sheer number of words and their patterns variously explains why language learning takes so long, why it requires exposure to authentic sources, and why there is so much current interest in corpus linguistics in SLA (Biber, Conrad, and Reppen, 1998; Collins Cobuild, 1996; Hunston and Francis, 1996; McEnery and Wilson, 1996). Native-like competence and fluency demand such idiomaticity.

3.2 *Limited scope patterns*

The learning of abstract constructions is more intriguing. It begins with chunking and committing formulae to memory. But there is more. Synthesis precedes analysis. Once a collection of like examples is available in long-term memory, there is scope for implicit processes of analysis of their shared features and for the development of a more abstract summary schema, in the same way as prototypes emerge as the central tendency of other cognitive categories.

Consider first the development of slot-and-frame patterns. Braine (1976) proposed that the beginnings of L1 grammar acquisition involve the learning of the position of words in utterances (e.g., *More car, More truck*, etc. allow induction of the pattern "more + recurring element"). Maratsos (1982) extended this argument to show that adult-like knowledge of syntactic constructions (including both syntactic relations and part-of-speech categories like verb and noun) can also result from positional analysis without the influence of semantic categories like agent and action. He proposed that this learning takes place through the amassing of detailed information about the syntactic handling of particular lexical items, followed by discovery of how distributional privileges transfer among them. The productivity of distributional analyses resultant from connectionist learning of text corpora will be described in section 5.

It is important to acknowledge the emphases of such accounts on piecemeal learning of concrete exemplars. Longitudinal child-language acquisition data suggest that, to begin with, each word is treated as a semantic isolate in the sense that the ability to combine it with other words is not accompanied by a parallel ability with semantically related words. An early example was that of Bowerman (1976), who demonstrated that her daughter Eva acquired the *more* + *X* construction long before other semantically similar relational words like *again* and *all-gone* came to be used in the similar pivot position in two-word utterances. Pine and Lieven (Lieven, Pine, and Dresner Barnes, 1992; Pine and Lieven, 1993, 1997; Pine, Lieven, and Rowland, 1998) have since demonstrated widespread lexical specificity in L1 grammar development. Children's language between the ages of 2 and 3 years is much more "low-scope" than theories of generative grammar have argued. A high proportion of children's early multi-word speech is produced from a developing set of slot-and-frame patterns. These patterns are often based on chunks of one or two words or phrases and they have "slots" into which the child can place a variety of words, for instance subgroups of nouns or verbs (e.g., *I can't* + *Verb*; *where's* + *Noun* + *gone?*). Children are very productive with these patterns and both the number of patterns and their structure develop over time. But they are lexically specific. Pine and Lieven's analyses of recordings of 2–3-year-old children and their mothers measure the overlap between the words used in different slots in different utterances. For example, if a child has two patterns, *I can't* + *X* and *I don't* + *X*, Pine and Lieven measure whether the verbs used in the X slots come from the same group and whether they can use any other CAN- or DO-auxiliaries. There is typically very little or no overlap, an observation which supports the conclusion that (i) the patterns are not related through an underlying grammar (i.e., the child does not "know" that *can't* and *don't* are both auxiliaries or that the words that appear in the patterns all belong to a category of Verb); (ii) there is no evidence for abstract grammatical patterns in the 2–3-year-old child's speech; and (iii) that, in contrast, the children are picking up frequent patterns from what they hear around them, and only slowly making more abstract generalizations as the database of related utterances grows.

Tomasello (1992) proposed the Verb Island hypothesis, in which it is the early verbs and relational terms that are the individual islands of organization in young children's otherwise unorganized grammatical system – in the early stages the child learns about arguments and syntactic markings on a verb-by-verb basis, and ordering patterns and morphological markers learned for one verb do not immediately generalize to other verbs. Positional analysis of each verb island requires long-term representations of that verb's collocations, and, thus, this account of grammar acquisition implies vast amounts of long-term knowledge of word sequences. Only later are syntagmatic categories formed from abstracting regularities from this large dataset in conjunction with morphological marker cues (at least in case-marking languages). Goldberg (1995) argues that certain patterns are more likely to be made more salient in the input because they relate to certain fundamental perceptual primitives, and, thus, that the child's construction of grammar involves both the distributional analysis of the language stream and the analysis of contingent perceptual activity:

> Constructions which correspond to basic sentence types encode as their central senses event types that are basic to human experience . . . that of someone causing something, something moving, something being in a state, someone possessing something, something causing a change of state or location, something undergoing a change of state or location, and something having an effect on someone. (Goldberg, 1995, p. 39)

Goldberg and Sethuraman (1999) show how individual "pathbreaking" semantically prototypic verbs form the seed of verb-centered argument structure patterns. Generalizations of the verb-centered instances emerge gradually as the verb-centered categories themselves are analyzed into more abstract argument structure constructions. The verb is a better predictor of sentence meaning than any other word in the sentence. Nevertheless, children ultimately generalize to the level of constructions, because constructions are much better predictors of overall meaning. Although verbs thus predominate in seeding low-scope patterns and eventually more abstract generalizations, Pine et al. (1998) have shown that such islands are not exclusive to verbs, and that the theory should be extended to include limited patterns based on other lexical types such as bound morphemes, auxiliary verbs, and case-marking pronouns.

3.3 *Exemplar frequency and construction productivity*

The research reviewed thus far has focused on piecemeal learning, the emergence of syntactic generalizations, and the elements of language which seed such generalizations. There is another important strand in L1 construction-learning research that concerns how the frequency of patterns in the input affects acquisition. Usage-based linguistics holds that language use shapes grammar through frequent repetitions of usage, but there are separable effects of token frequency and type frequency. Token frequency is how often in the input particular words or specific phrases appear; type frequency, on the other hand, counts how many different lexical items a certain pattern or construction is applicable to. Type frequency refers to the number of distinct lexical items that can be substituted in a given slot in a construction, whether it is a word-level construction for inflection or a syntactic construction specifying the relation among words. The "regular" English past tense *-ed* has a very high type frequency because it applies to thousands of different types of verbs, whereas the vowel change exemplified in *swam* and *rang* has a much lower type frequency. Bybee (Bybee, 1995; Bybee and Thompson, 2000) shows how the productivity of a pattern (phonological, morphological, or syntactic) is a function of its type rather than its token frequency. In contrast, high token frequency promotes the entrenchment or conservation of irregular forms and idioms – the irregular forms only survive because they are very frequent.

Type frequency determines productivity because: (i) the more lexical items that are heard in a certain position in a construction, the less likely it is that the construction is associated with a particular lexical item, and the more likely it is that a general category is formed over the items that occur in that position; (ii) the more items the category must cover, the more general are its criterial features, and the more likely it is to extend to new items; and (iii) high type frequency ensures that a construction is used frequently, thus strengthening its representational schema and making it more accessible for further use with new items (Bybee and Thompson, 2000).

3.4 The same sequence for SLA?

To what degree might this proposed developmental sequence of syntactic acquisition apply in SLA? SLA is different from L1A in numerous respects, particularly with regard to:

i *mature conceptual development:*
  a in child language acquisition knowledge of the world and knowledge of language are developing simultaneously whereas adult SLA builds upon pre-existing conceptual knowledge;
  b adult learners have sophisticated formal operational means of thinking and can treat language as an object of explicit learning, that is, of conscious problem-solving and deduction, to a much greater degree than can children (N. Ellis, 1994a);

ii *language input:* the typical L1 pattern of acquisition results from naturalistic exposure in situations where caregivers naturally scaffold development (Tomasello and Brooks, 1999), whereas classroom environments for second or foreign language teaching can distort the patterns of exposure, of function, of medium, and of social interaction (N. Ellis and Laporte, 1997);

iii *transfer from L1:* adult SLA builds on pre-existing L1 knowledge (MacWhinney, 1992; Odlin, this volume), and, thus, for example, whereas a young child has lexically specific patterns and only later develops knowledge of abstract syntactic categories which guide more creative combinations and insertions into the slots of frames, adults have already acquired knowledge of these categories and their lexical membership for L1, and this knowledge may guide creative combination in their L2 interlanguage to variously good and bad effects. Nevertheless, unless there is evidence to the contrary, it is a reasonable default expectation that naturalistic SLA develops in broadly the same fashion as does L1 – from formulae, through low-scope patterns, to constructions – and that this development similarly reflects the influences of type and token frequencies in the input. (But see Doughty, this volume, for a discussion of how L1 and L2 processing procedures differ.)

There are lamentably few longitudinal acquisition data for SLA that are of sufficient detail to allow the charting of construction growth. Filling this lacuna and performing analyses of SLA which parallel those for L1A described in section 3.2 is an important research priority. But the available evidence does provide support for the assumption that constructions grow from formulae through low-scope patterns to more abstract schema. For a general summary, there are normative descriptions of stages of L2 proficiency that were drawn up in as atheoretical a way as possible by the American Council on the Teaching of Foreign Languages (ACTFL) (Higgs, 1984). These Oral Proficiency Guidelines include the following descriptions of novice and intermediate levels that emphasize the contributions of patterns and formulae to the development of later creativity:

> *Novice Low*: Oral production consists of isolated words and perhaps a few high-frequency phrases . . . *Novice High*: Able to satisfy partially the requirements of basic communicative exchanges by relying heavily on learned utterances but occasionally expanding these through simple recombinations of their elements . . . *Intermediate*: The intermediate level is characterized by an ability to create with the language by combining and recombining learned elements, though primarily in a reactive mode. (ACTFL, 1986, p. 18)

Thus, the ACTFL repeatedly stresses the constructive potential of collocations and chunks of language. This is impressive because the ACTFL guidelines were simply trying to describe SLA as objectively as possible – there was no initial theoretical focus on formulae – yet nonetheless the role of formulae became readily apparent in the acquisition process.

There are several relevant case studies of child SLA. Wong Fillmore (1976) presented the first extensive longitudinal study that focused on formulaic language in L2 acquisition. Her subject, Nora, acquired and overused a few formulaic expressions of a new structural type during one period, and then amassed a variety of similar forms during the next. Previously unanalyzed chunks became the foundations for creative construction (see also Vihman's, 1982, analyses of her young son Virve's SLA). Such observations of the formulaic beginnings of child L2 acquisition closely parallel those of Pine and Lieven for L1.

There are a few studies which focus on these processes in classroom-based SLA. R. Ellis (1984) described how three classroom learners acquired formulae which allowed them to meet their basic communicative needs in an ESL classroom, and how the particular formulae they acquired reflected input frequency – they were those which more often occurred in the social and organizational contexts that arose in the classroom environment. Weinert (1994) showed how English learners' early production of complex target-like German foreign language negation patterns came through the memorization of complex forms in confined linguistic contexts, and that some of these forms were used as a basis for extension of patterns. Myles, Hooper, and Mitchell (1998; Myles, Mitchell, and Hooper, 1999) describe the first two years of development of interrogatives in a classroom of anglophone French L2 beginners, longitudinally tracking the breakdown of formulaic chunks such as *comment t'appelles-tu?* (what's your name?), *comment s'appelle-t-il?* (what's his name?), and *où habites-tu?* (where do you live?), in particular the creative construction of new interrogatives by recombination of their parts, and the ways in which formulae fed the constructive process. Bolander (1989) analyzed the role of chunks in the acquisition of inversion in Swedish by Polish, Finnish, and Spanish immigrants enrolled in a 4-month intensive course in Swedish. In Swedish, the inversion of subject–verb after a sentence-initial non-subject is an obligatory rule. Bolander identified the majority of the inversion cases in her data as being of a chunk-like nature with a stereotyped reading such as *det kan man säga* (that can one say) and *det tycker jag* (so think I). Inversion in these sort of clauses is also frequent when the object is omitted as in *kan man säga* (can one say) and *tycker jag* (think I), and this pattern was also well integrated in the interlanguage of most of these learners. Bolander showed that the high accuracy on these stereotyped initial-object clauses generalized to produce a higher rate of correctness on clauses with non-stereotyped initial objects than was usual for other types of inversion clause in her data, and took this as evidence that creative language was developing out of familiar formulae.

Although there are many reviews which discuss the important role of formula use in SLA (e.g., Hakuta, 1974; Nattinger and DeCarrico, 1992; Towell and Hawkins, 1994; Weinert, 1995; Wray, 1992), there is clearly further need for larger-sampled SLA corpora which will allow detailed analysis of acquisition sequences. De Cock (1998) presents analyses of corpora of language-learner productions using automatic recurrent sequence extractions. These show that second language learners use formulae at least as much as native speakers and at times at significantly higher rates. There is much promise of such computer-based learner corpus studies (Granger, 1998), providing that sufficient care is taken to gather the necessarily intensive longitudinal learner data. There is also need to test the predictions of usage-based theories regarding the influences of type frequency and token frequency as they apply in SLA.

4 Psychological Accounts of Associative Learning

This section concerns the psychological learning mechanisms which underpin the acquisition of constructions. Constructivists believe that language is cut of the same cloth as other forms of learning. Although it differs importantly from other knowledge in its specific content and problem space, it is acquired using generic learning mechanisms. The Law of Contiguity, the most basic principle of association, pervades all aspects of the mental representation of language: "Objects once experienced together tend to become associated in the imagination, so that when any one of them is thought of, the others are likely to be thought of also, in the same order of sequence or coexistence as before" (James, 1890, p. 561).

4.1 *Chunking*

What's the next letter in a sentence beginning *T* . . . ? Native English speakers know it is much more likely to be *h* or a vowel than it is *z* or other consonants, and that it could not be *q*. But they are never taught this. What is the first word in that sentence? We are likely to opt for *the*, or *that*, rather than *thinks* or *theosophy*. If *The* . . . begins the sentence, how does it continue? "With an adjective or noun," might be the reply. And, if the sentences starts with *The cat* . . . , then what? And then again, how should we complete *The cat sat on the* . . . ? Fluent native speakers know a tremendous amount about the sequences of language at all grains. We know how letters tend to co-occur (common bigrams, trigrams, and other orthographic regularities). Likewise, we know the phonotactics of our tongue and its phrase structure regularities. We know thousands of concrete collocations, and we know abstract generalizations that derive from them. We have learned to chunk letters, sounds, morphemes, words, phrases, clauses, bits of co-occurring language at all levels. Psycholinguistic experiments show that we are tuned to these regularities in that we process faster and most easily language which accords with the expectations that have come from our unconscious analysis of the serial probabilities in our lifelong history of input (N. Ellis, 2002).

Furthermore, we learn these chunks from the very beginnings of learning a second language. N. Ellis, Lee, and Reber (1999) observed people reading their first 64 sentences of a foreign language. While they read, they saw the referent of each sentence, a simple action sequence involving colored geometrical shapes. For example, the sentence *miu-ra ko-gi pye-ri lon-da* was accompanied by a cartoon showing a square moving onto red circles. A linguistic description of this language might include the following facts: (i) that it is an SOV language; (ii) it has adjective–noun word order; (iii) grammatical number (singular/plural) agreement is obligatory, and in the form of matching suffix endings of a verb and its subject and of a noun and the adjective that modifies it; (iv) that the 64 sentences are all of the type: $[N]_{Subject}$ $[A\ N]_{Object}$ V; and (v) that lexis was selected from a very small set of eight words. But such explicit metalinguistic knowledge is not the stuff of early language acquisition. What did the learners make of it? To assess their intake, immediately after seeing each sentence, learners had to repeat as much as they could of it. How did their intake change over time? It gradually improved in all respects. With increasing exposure, performance incremented on diverse measures: the proportion of lexis correctly recalled, correct expression of the adjective–noun agreement, correct subject–verb agreement, totally correct sentence production, correct bigrams and trigrams, and, overall, conformity to the sequential probabilities of the language at letter, word, and phrase level. With other measures it was similarly apparent that there was steady acquisition of form–meaning links and of generalizable grammatical knowledge that allowed success on grammaticality judgment tests which were administered later (Ellis et al., 1999). To greater or lesser degree, these patterns, large and small, were being acquired simultaneously and collaboratively.

Acquisition of these sequential patterns is amenable to explanation in terms of psychological theories of chunking. The notion of chunking has been at the core of short-term memory research since Miller (1956) first proposed the term. While the chunk capacity of short-term memory (STM) is fairly constant at 7 ± 2 units, its information capacity can be increased by chunking, a useful representational process in that low-level features that co-occur can be organized together and thence referred to as an individual entity. Chunking underlies superior short-term memory for patterned phone numbers (e.g., *0800-123777*) or letter strings (e.g., *AGREEMENTS, FAMONUBITY*) than for more random sequences (e.g., *4957-632518, CXZDKLWQPM*), even though all strings contain the same number of items. We chunk chunks too, so *Ellis is wittering on about chunking again* is better recalled than *again wittering on is about Ellis chunking*, and, as shown by Epstein (1967) in a more rigorous but dreary fashion than Lewis Carroll's, *A vapy koobs desaked the citar molently um glox nerfs* is more readily read and remembered than *koobs vapy the desaked um glox citar nerfs a molently*:

> A chunk is a unit of memory organization, formed by bringing together a set of already formed elements (which, themselves, may be chunks) in memory and welding them together into a larger unit. Chunking implies the ability to build up such structures recursively, thus leading to a hierarchical organization of memory. Chunking appears to be a ubiquitous feature of human memory. (Newell, 1990, p. 7)

It operates at concrete and abstract levels, as we shall now see.

Sequences that are repeated across learning experiences become better remembered. Hebb (1961) demonstrated that, when people were asked to report back random nine-digit sequences in short-term memory task, if, unbeknownst to the participants, every third list of digits was repeated, memory for the repeated list improved over trials faster than memory for non-repeated lists. This pattern whereby repetitions of particular items in short-term memory result in permanent structural traces has since become known as the Hebb effect. It pervades learning in adulthood and infancy alike. Saffran, Aslin, and Newport (1996) demonstrated that 8-month-old infants exposed for only 2 minutes to unbroken strings of nonsense syllables (for example, *bidakupado*) are able to detect the difference between three-syllable sequences that appeared as a unit and sequences that also appeared in their learning set but in random order.

Chunks that are repeated across learning experiences also become better remembered. In early Project Grammarama experiments, Miller (1958) showed that learners' free recall of redundant (grammatical) items was superior to that of random items, and hypothesized that this was because they were "recoding" individual symbols into larger chunks which decreased the absolute number of units. *Structural patterns* that are repeated across learning experiences as well become better remembered. Reber (1967) showed that memory for grammatical "sentences" generated by a finite-state grammar improved across learning sets. More recent work reviewed by Manza and Reber (1997), Mathews and Roussel (1997), and others in Berry (1997) shows that learners can transfer knowledge from one instantiation to another, that is, learn an artificial grammar instantiated with one letter set (*GFBQT*) and transfer to strings instantiated in another (*HMVRZ*), so that if there are many letter strings which illustrate patterned sequences (e.g., *GFTQ, GGFTQ, GFQ*) in the learning set, the participants show faster learning of a second transfer grammar which mirrors these patterns (*HMZR, HHMZR, HMR*) than one which does not (*HMZR, VMHZZ, VZH*). Learners can also demonstrate cross-modal transfer, where the training set might be letters, as above, but the testing set comprises sequences of colors which, unbeknownst to the participant, follow the same underlying grammar. These effects argue for more abstract representations of tacit knowledge.

Hebb effects, Miller effects, and Reber effects all reflect the reciprocal interactions between short-term memory and long-term memory (LTM) which allow us to bootstrap our way into language. The "cycle of perception" (Neisser, 1976) is also the "cycle of learning," such that bottom-up and top-down processes are in constant interaction. Repetition of sequences in phonological STM results in their consolidation in phonological LTM as chunks. The cognitive system that stores long-term memories of phonological sequences is the same system responsible for perception of phonological sequences. Thus, the tuning of phonological LTM to regular sequences allows more ready perception of input which contains regular sequences. Regular sequences are thus perceived as chunks, and, as a result, language- (L1 or L2) experienced individuals' phonological STM for regular sequences is greater than for irregular ones. This common learning mechanism underpins language acquisition in phonological, orthographic, lexical, and syntactic domains.

But this analysis is limited to language form. What about language function? Learning to understand a language involves parsing the speech stream into chunks which reliably mark meaning. The learner does not care about theoretical analyses of language. From a functional perspective, the role of language is to communicate meanings, and the learner wants to acquire the label–meaning relations. Learners' attention to the evidence to which they are exposed soon demonstrates the recurring chunks of language (to use written examples, in English *e* follows *th* more often than *x* does, *the* is a common sequence, *the* [*space*] is frequent, *dog* follows *the* [*space*] more often than it does *book, how do you do?* occurs quite often, etc.). At some level of analysis, the patterns refer to meaning. It does not happen at the lower levels: *t* does not mean anything, nor does *th*, but *the* does, and *the dog* does better, and *how do you do?* does very well, thank you. In these cases the learner's goal is satisfied, and the fact that this chunk activates some meaning representations makes this sequence itself more salient in the input stream. When the learner comes upon these chunks again, they tend to stand out as units, and adjacent material is parsed accordingly (see Doughty, this volume, for a detailed discussion of this).

What is "meaning" in such an associative analysis? At its most concrete, it is the perceptual memories which underpin the conscious experience which a speaker wishes to describe and which, with luck, will be associated with sufficient strength in the hearer to activate a similar set of perceptual representations. These are the perceptual groundings from which abstract semantics emerge (Barsalou, 1999; Lakoff, 1987). Perceptual representations worth talking about are complex structural descriptions in their own right, with a qualifying hierarchical schematic structure (e.g., a room schema which nests within it a desk schema which in turn nests within it a drawer schema, and so on). These visuo-structural descriptions are also acquired by associative chunking mechanisms, operating in a neural system for representing the visual domain. When we describe the structural properties of objects and their interactions we do so from particular perspectives, attending to certain aspects and foregrounding them, sequencing events in particular orders, etc., and so we need procedures for spotlighting and sequencing perceptual memories with language. The most frequent and reliable cross-modal chunks, which structure regular associations between perception and language, are the constructions described in sections 2 and 3. Chunking, the bringing together of a set of already formed chunks in memory and welding them into a larger unit, is a basic associative learning process which can occur in and between all representational systems.

4.2 *Generic learning mechanisms*

Constructivists believe that generic, associative-learning mechanisms underpin all aspects of language acquisition. This is clearly a parsimonious assumption. But additionally, there are good reasons to be skeptical of theories of learning mechanisms specific to the domain of language, first because innate linguistic representations are neurologically implausible, and second because of the logical problem of how any such universals might come into play:

i Current theories of brain function, process and development, with their acknowledgement of plasticity and input-determined organization, do not readily allow for the inheritance of structures which might serve, for instance, as principles or parameters of UG (Elman et al., 1996; Quartz and Sejnowski, 1997).

ii Whether there are innate linguistic universals or not, there is still a logical problem of syntactic acquisition. Identifying the syntactic category of words must primarily be a matter of learning because the phonological strings associated with words of a language are clearly not universal. Once some identifications have been successfully made, it may be possible to use prior grammatical knowledge to facilitate further identifications. But the acquisition of relevant phrase structure grammar requires knowledge of syntactic word class in the first place. This is a classic bootstrapping problem (Redington and Chater, 1998). Thus, in early L1 acquisition there simply is no specialized working memory system involved in the assignment of syntactic structure. Instead there is a general-purpose phonological memory, a process which stores enough verbal information to permit the analysis of distributional regularities which eventually results in word-class information and phrase-structure constructions (see also Doughty, this volume).

4.3 *Trees from string: hierarchy and structure dependence*

I have emphasized how large stretches of spoken language are adequately described by finite-state grammars, as collocational streams where patterns flow into each other. As Bolinger (1976, p. 1) puts it, "[o]ur language does not expect us to build everything starting with lumber, nails and blueprint, but provides us with an incredibly large number of prefabs, which have the magical property of persisting even when we knock some of them apart and put them together in unpredictable ways." Nativelike competence is indexed as much by fluent idiomaticity as by grammatical creativity, and chunking is the mechanism of learning which underpins the acquisition and perception of these formulaic sequences.

But eventually language learners do become open-class, generative, and grammatically creative in their language productions. Their language operations become structure dependent. Any blueprint we might posit as a summary model of their abilities needs at least the power of phrase-structure grammars for successful analysis, and the resultant descriptions are hierarchical in structure. Rules of phrase-structure grammar such as (i) *Sentence* → *NP + VP*, (ii) *NP* → *D + N*, (iii) *VP* → *Verb + NP*, (iv) *N* → {*man, ball*}, etc., by "rewriting" yield labeled bracketed phrase-structures such as *Sentence* (*NP + VP* (*Verb + NP*)), which are more usually represented as tree diagrams that more clearly show the hierarchy. Can chunking help us in understanding the acquisition of these more abstract hierarchical constructions? Constructivists believe so. They view such rules for constituent analysis as top-down, a posteriori linguistic descriptions of a system that has emerged bottom-up from usage-based analysis of the strings themselves. Top-down or bottom-up, either way, bracketing is the link between hierarchical structure and string. Inductive accounts thus require a learning mechanism which provides bracketing, and that is exactly what chunking is.

We have seen how this works in the examples of slot-and-frame acquisition described in section 3.2. Once a child has chunks for *(Lulu)*, *(Teddy)*, *(The ball)*, *(Thomas the Tank)*, and the like, then the following utterances are parsed as bracketed, *(The ball's) (Gone)*, *(Teddy's) (Gone)*, *(Thomas the Tank's) (Gone)*, and subsequent analysis of these and other related exemplars results in the more abstract pattern *(X) (Gone)*, where, in subsequent utterances, the object is consistently put in preverbal position. But the slot-filler in this position is itself made up of chunks which also will be analyzed further, sometimes a bare noun, *(Salad) (Gone)*, *(Peter Pan) (Gone)*, sometimes a noun phrase, *((Funny) (Man)) (Gone)*; the branches of the hierarchy grow; and possible combinations are determined categorically rather than lexically. As Tomasello concludes in his account of epigenesis in his daughter Travis's early language acquisition:

> It is not until the child has produced or comprehended a number of sentences with a particular verb that she can construct a syntagmatic category of "*cutter*", for example. Not until she has done this with a number of verbs can she construct the more general syntagmatic category of agent or actor. Not until the child has constructed a number of sentences in which various words serve as various types of arguments for various predicates can she construct word classes such as noun or verb. Not until the child has constructed sentences with these more general categories can certain types of complex sentences be produced. (Tomasello, 1992, pp. 273–4; see also Tomasello, 2000, on "analogy-making" and "structure-combining").

Likewise, Bolander's (1989) analysis of the role of chunking in the acquisition of Swedish subject–verb inversion after a sentence-initial non-subject, described in section 3.4, provides a clear illustration of the role of chunking in the integration and differentiation of second language structure. In sum, although a very basic learning mechanism, chunking results in hierarchical representations and structure dependency. In constructivist usage-based accounts, phonology, lexis, and syntax develop hierarchically by repeated cycles of differentiation and integration of chunks of sequences (Studdert-Kennedy, 1991).

Language has no monopoly on hierarchical structure. Instead, because the formation of chunks, as stable intermediate structures, is the mechanism underlying the evolution and organization of many complex systems in biology, society, and physics, hierarchical structure and structure dependence are in fact a characteristic of the majority of complex systems which exist in nature (Simon, 1962). It is the norm that animal behavioral sequences, from the grooming of blowflies to the goal-directed behavior of cormorants, exhibit hierarchical structure, so much so that hierarchical organization has been proposed as a general principle for ethology (Dawkins, 1976). Human behavioral sequences are no different – slips of action exhibit structure dependence (Reason, 1979), just as do slips of the tongue (Fromkin, 1980).

4.4 *Emergentism*

The study of language demonstrates many complex and fascinating structural systematicities. Generative linguistics provides careful descriptions of these regularities that are necessary for a complete theory of language acquisition. But they are not sufficient because they do not explain how learners achieve the state of knowledge that can be described in this way. Indeed, many cognitive scientists believe that such linguistic descriptions are something very different from the mental representations that underpin performance, that there has, at times, been an unfortunate tendency to raise these "rules" from explanandum to explanans, and that, instead, the complexities of language are emergent phenomena (MacWhinney, 1999a, 1999b). Like many scientific descriptions, the regularities of generative grammar provide well-researched patterns in need of explanation. Meteorology has its rules and principles of the phenomena of the atmosphere which allow the prediction of weather. Geology has its rules and principles to describe and summarize the successive changes in the earth's crust. But these rules play no causal role in shifting even a grain of sand or a molecule of water. It is the interaction of water and rocks which smooths the irregularities and grinds the pebbles and sand. As with these other systems, emergentists believe that the complexity of language emerges from relatively simple developmental processes being exposed to a massive and complex environment. The interactions that constitute language are associations, billions of connections which co-exist within a neural system as organisms co-exist within an eco-system. And systematicities emerge as a result of their interactions and mutual constraints.

Bod (1998) describes experience-based, data-oriented parsing models of language which learn how to provide appropriate linguistic representations from an unlimited set of utterances by generalizing from examples of representations of previously occurring utterances. These probabilistic models operate by decomposing the given representations into fragments and recomposing those pieces to analyze new utterances. Bod (1998, ch. 5) shows that any systematic restriction of the fragments seems to jeopardize the statistical dependencies that are needed for predicting the appropriate structure of a sentence. This implies that the productive units of natural language cannot be defined in terms of a minimal set of rules, constraints, or principles, but rather need to be defined in terms of a large, redundant set of previously experienced structures with virtually no restriction on size or complexity – the behavior of the society of syntax is determined by the interactions and associations of all of its members. If communities are excised or if new individuals join, the ecology changes. This conclusion is supported in L1 acquisition by the findings of Bates and Goodman (1997) that syntactic proficiency is strongly correlated with vocabulary size. Total vocabulary at 20 months predicts grammatical status at 28 months, and grammar and vocabulary stay tightly coupled across the 16–30-month range.

The representational database for language is enormous. It is the history of our language input and the multifarious syntagmatic and paradigmatic associations that were forged in its processing. We not only have representations of chunks of language, but we also have knowledge of the likelihood of their occurrence, and the regularity with which they are associated with other corresponding mental events. N. Ellis (2002) reviews the evidence that, in the course of normal language comprehension and production, unconscious learning processes strengthen the activations of representations and associations that are used in language processing. These processes effectively count the relative frequencies of use of the language representations (at all levels), and they strengthen the weights of the associations between those that are contiguously activated. The result is that we are tuned to our language input. Thus, our language processing evidences regularity effects in the acquisition of orthographic, phonological, and morphological form. There are effects of bigram frequency in visual word identification, of phonotactic knowledge in speech segmentation, of spelling-to-sound correspondences in reading, and of cohort effects in spoken word recognition. There are effects of neighbors and the proportion of friends (items which share surface pattern cues and have the same interpretation) to enemies (items which share surface pattern but have different interpretations) in reading and spelling, morphology, and spoken word recognition (see Kroll and Sunderman, this volume). At higher levels, it can be shown that language comprehension is determined by the listeners' vast amount of statistical information about the behavior of lexical items in their language, and that, at least, for English, verbs provide some of the strongest constraints on the resolution of syntactic ambiguities. Comprehenders know the relative frequencies with which individual verbs appear in different tenses, in active vs. passive structures, and in intransitive vs. transitive structures, the typical kinds of subjects and objects that a verb takes, and many other such facts. Such information is acquired through experience with input that exhibits these distributional properties; it is not some idiosyncratic fact in the lexicon isolated from "core" grammatical information. Rather, it is relevant at all stages of lexical, syntactic, and discourse comprehension. Comprehenders tend to perceive the most probable syntactic and semantic analyses of a new utterance on the basis of frequencies of previously perceived utterance analyses. Language users tend to produce the most probable utterance for a given meaning on the basis of frequencies of utterance representations.

This research, the mainstay of psycholinguistics (Altman, 1997; Gernsbacher, 1994; Harley, 1995), shows that our language processing systems resonate to the frequencies of occurrence that are usual in language input. Most, if not all, of this tuning is the result of implicit rather than explicit learning (Doughty, this volume; N. Ellis, 1994a, 1994b; N. Ellis et al., 1999) – the on-line conscious experiences of language learning involve language understanding rather than counting. Fluent language users have had tens of thousands of hours on task. They have processed many millions of utterances involving tens of thousands of types presented as innumerable tokens. The evidence of language has ground on their perceptuo-motor and cognitive apparatus to result in complex competencies which can be described by formal theories of linguistics.

4.5 *Probabilistic parsing: chunks and their frequencies in language processing*

The use of this probabilistic knowledge, and the way it is combined for multiple cue sources, is fruitfully explored in the competition model (Bates and MacWhinney, 1987; MacWhinney, 1987, 1997a). This emphasizes lexical functionalism where syntactic patterns are controlled by lexical items. Lexical items provide cues to functional interpretations for sentence comprehension or production. Some cues are more reliable than others. The language learner's task is to work out which are the most valid predictors. The competition model is the paradigmatic example of constraint-satisfaction accounts of language processing.

Consider the particular cues that relate subject-marking forms to subject-related functions in the English sentence, *The learner chunks the words*. They are preverbal positioning (*learner* before *chunks*), verb agreement morphology (*chunks* agrees in number with *learner* rather than *words*), sentence initial positioning, and use of the article *the*. Case-marking languages, unlike English, might additionally include nominative and accusative cues in such sentences. The corresponding functional interpretations include actor, topicality, perspective, givenness, and definiteness. Competition model studies analyze a corpus of exemplar sentences which relate such cue combinations with their various functional interpretations, thus to determine the regularities of the ways in which a particular language expresses, for example, agency. They then demonstrate how well these probabilities determine (i) cue use when learners process that language, and (ii) cue acquisition – the ease of learning an inflection is determined by its cue validity, a function of how often an inflection occurs as a cue for a certain underlying function (cue availability) and how reliably it marks this function (cue reliability) (MacWhinney, 1997a).

There are many attractive features of the competition model. It developmentally models the cues, their frequency, reliability, and validity, as they are acquired from representative language input. The competition part of the model shows how Bayesian cue use can resolve in activation of a single interpretive hypothesis from an interaction of cues. It has been extensively tested to assess the cues, cue validity, and numerical cue strength order in many different languages. Finally, it goes a long way in predicting language transfer effects (MacWhinney, 1992). Recent competition model studies have simulated the natural language performance data using simple connectionist models relating lexical cues and functional interpretations for sentence comprehension or production. Section 5 illustrates one of these studies, Kempe and MacWhinney (1998), in detail.

The use of this probabilistic knowledge is also made clear in Natural Language Processing (NLP) analyses of sentence processing. Computational implementations of generative grammars which are large enough to cover a non-trivial subset of natural language assign to many sentences an extremely large number of alternative syntactic analyses, yet fluent humans perceive only one or two of these when faced with the same input. Such models may be judged successful if the defining criterion is that it describes the space of possible analyses that sentences may get, but the combinatorial explosion of syntactic analyses and corresponding semantic interpretations is very problematic if the criterion is rather to predict which analyses human comprehenders actually assign to natural language utterances (Bod, 1998; Church and Patil,

1982; Martin, Church, and Patil, 1981). The NLP community has moved to the use of stochastic grammars to overcome these problems (Bunt and Nijholt, 2000; Charniak, 1993). Examples include stochastic context-free grammar (Sampson, 1986), stochastic unification-based grammar (Briscoe, 1994), stochastic head-driven phrase-structure grammar (Brew, 1995), stochastic lexical-functional grammar (Kaplan, 1999), and data-oriented parsing (Bod, 1998).

Since the late 1960s, theories of grammar have increasingly put more syntax into the lexicon, and correspondingly less into rules. The result is that lexical specifications now include not only a listing of the particular constructions that the word can appear in, but also the relative likelihoods of their occurrence. In stochastic models of parsing using lexicalist grammars, these probabilities are used to determine the levels of activation of candidate lexical frames, with the network of candidate unification links being set up between those that are activated, the most probable being favored. This, combined with a unification-based parser based on competitive inhibition, where candidate links that are incompatible compete for inclusion in the final parse by sending each other inhibitory signals that reduce the competitor's attachment strength (Vosse and Kempen, 2000), promises a model of language processing that is both effective and psychologically plausible.

5 Connectionism

Constructivists believe that the complexity of language emerges from associative learning processes being exposed to a massive and complex environment. But belief in syntax or other language regularities as emergent phenomena, like belief in innate linguistic representations, is just a matter of trust unless there are clear process, algorithm, and hardware explanations. A detailed transition theory is needed. If language is not informationally encapsulated in its own module, if it is not privileged with its own special learning processes, then we must eventually show how generic learning mechanisms can result in complex and highly specific language representations. We need dynamic models of the acquisition of these representations and the emergence of structure. And we need processing models where the interpretation of particular utterances is the result of the mutual satisfaction of all of the available constraints. For these reasons, emergentists look to connectionism, since it provides a set of computational tools for exploring the conditions under which emergent properties arise.

Connectionism has various advantages for this purpose: neural inspiration; distributed representation and control; data-driven processing with prototypical representations emerging rather than being innately pre-specified; graceful degradation; emphasis on acquisition rather than static description; slow, incremental, non-linear, content- and structure-sensitive learning; blurring of the representation/learning distinction; graded, distributed, and non-static representations; generalization and transfer as natural products of learning; and, since the models must actually run, less scope for hand-waving (for introductions see Elman et al., 1996; McClelland et al., 1986; McLeod, Plunkett, and Rolls, 1998; Plunkett, 1998; Plunkett and Elman, 1997; Redington and Chater, 1998; Seidenberg, 1997).

Connectionist approaches to language acquisition investigate the representations that can result when simple associative learning mechanisms are exposed to complex language evidence. Connectionist theories are data-rich and process-light. Massively parallel systems of artificial neurons use simple learning processes to statistically abstract information from masses of input data. Lloyd Morgan's canon ("In no case may we interpret an action as the outcome of a higher psychical faculty if it can be interpreted as the outcome of one which stands lower in the psychological scale") is influential in connectionists' attributions of learning mechanisms:

> Implicit knowledge of language may be stored in connections among simple processing units organized in networks. While the behavior of such networks may be describable (at least approximately) as conforming to some system of rules, we suggest that an account of the fine structure of the phenomena of language use can best be formulated in models that make reference to the characteristics of the underlying networks. (Rumelhart and McClelland, 1987, p. 196)

Connectionist implementations are computer models consisting of many artificial neurons that are connected in parallel. Each neuron has an activation value associated with it, often being between 0 and 1. This is roughly analogous to the firing rate of a real neuron. Psychologically meaningful objects can then be represented as patterns of this activity across the set of artificial neurons. For example, in a model of vocabulary acquisition, one subpopulation of the units in the network might be used to represent picture detectors and another set the corresponding word forms. The units in the artificial network are typically multiply interconnected by associations with variable strengths or weights. These connections permit the level of activity in any one unit to influence the level of activity in all of the units that it is connected to (e.g., spreading activation). The connection strengths are then adjusted by a suitable learning algorithm in such a way that, when a particular pattern of activation appears across one population, it can lead to a desired pattern of activity arising on another set of units. These learning algorithms are intended to reflect basic mechanisms of neuronal learning, they are generic in that they are used for a wide variety of learning problems, and they do not encapsulate any aspects of cognitive learning mechanisms. The cognitive learning emerges from these neuronal mechanisms being exposed to large amounts of experience in a particular problem space. Thus, over the course of many presentations of many different picture–name pairs in our example simulation of vocabulary acquisition, if the connection strengths have been set appropriately by the learning algorithm, then it may be possible for units representing the detection of particular pictures to cause the units that represent the appropriate lexical labels for that stimulus to become activated. The network could then be said to have learned the appropriate verbal output for that picture stimulus.

There are various standard architectures of the models, each suited to particular types of classification. The most common has three layers: the input layer of units, the output layer, and an intervening layer of hidden units (so called because they are hidden from direct contact with the input or the output). An example is illustrated in figure 4.1 (see box 4.1 below). The presence of these hidden units enables more difficult input and output mappings to be learned than would be possible if the input units were directly connected to the output units (Elman et al., 1996; Rumelhart and McClelland, 1986). The most common learning algorithm is back propagation, in which, on each learning trial, the network compares its output with the target output, and any difference, or error, is propagated back to the hidden unit weights, and, in turn, to the input weights, in a way that reduces the error.

Some models use localist representations, where each separate unit might, for example, represent a word or picture detector. Other models use distributed representations where different words are represented by different patterns of activity over the same set of units (in the same way as different patterns of activation over the set of detectors in the retina encode the reflections of all of our different visual inputs). Localist representations are clearly more akin to the units of traditional symbolic computation and linguistic description. But not all of language processing is symbol manipulation. Many of the representations that conspire in the semantics from which language is inextricable, in vision, in motor action, in emotion, are analog representations. There are interesting interactions between all levels of representation (in reading, for example, from letter features through letters, syllables, morphemes, lexemes . . .). These different levels interact, and processing can be primed or facilitated by prior processing at subsymbolic or pre-categorical levels, thus demonstrating subsymbolic influences on language processing. These processes are readily modeled by distributed representations in connectionist models. But note well, non-exclusivity of symbolic representation is by no means a denial of symbolic processes in language. Frequency of chunk in the input, and regularity and consistency of associative mappings with other representational domains, result in the emergence of effectively localist, categorical units, especially, but by no means exclusively, at lexical grain. It may well be that symbolic representations are themselves an emergent phenomenon (Deacon, 1997; MacWhinney, 1997b).

Perhaps the most exciting aspect of connectionist models is that, in the course of processing particular exemplars, they often acquire knowledge of the underlying structural regularities in the whole problem space. They develop representations of categories and prototypes. They generalize from this knowledge. This is why they are so relevant to usage-based accounts of language acquisition. There are now many separate connectionist simulations of a wide range of linguistic phenomena including acquisition of morphology, phonological rules, novel word repetition, prosody, semantic structure, syntactic structure, etc. (see for reviews: Allen and Seidenberg, 1999; Christiansen and Chater, 2001; Christiansen et al., 1999; N. Ellis, 1998; Elman et al., 1996; Levy et al., 1995; MacWhinney and Leinbach, 1991; Plunkett, 1998; Redington and Chater, 1998). These simple, small-scale demonstrations repeatedly show that connectionist models can extract the regularities in each of these domains of language, and then operate in a rule-like (but not rule-governed) way. To the considerable degree that the processes of learning L1 and L2 are the same, these L1 simulations are relevant to SLA. The problem, of course, is determining this degree and its limits. Because ground is still being broken for first language, there has been rather less connectionist work directly concerning SLA, although the following provide useful illustrations: Broeder and Plunkett (1994), N. Ellis (2001), N. Ellis and Schmidt (1998), Gasser (1990), Kempe and MacWhinney (1998), Sokolik and Smith (1992), Taraban and Kempe (1999). I will concentrate on just two of these for detailed illustration.

Box 4.1 describes a model of the acquisition of regular and irregular inflectional morphology. There have been a number of compelling connectionist models of the acquisition of morphology. Rumelhart and McClelland (1986) presented the first connectionist model of the acquisition of morphology, in this case in the quasi-regular domain of the English past tense. The model generated U-shaped learning for irregular forms, like children tending to overgeneralize to produce past tense forms like *runned* and *drinked*. Yet there was no "rule" – "it is possible to imagine that the system simply stores a set of rote-associations between base and past-tense forms with novel responses generated by 'on-line' generalizations from the stored exemplars" (Rumelhart and McClelland, 1986, p. 267). This original past tense model was very influential. It laid the foundations for the connectionist approach to language research; it generated a large number of criticisms (Lachter and Bever, 1988; Pinker and Prince, 1988), some of which are undeniably valid; and, in turn, it spawned a number of revised and improved connectionist models of different aspects of the acquisition of the English past tense. These recent models have been successful in capturing the regularities that are present (i) in associating phonological form of lemma with phonological form of inflected form (Daugherty and Seidenberg, 1994; MacWhinney and Leinbach, 1991; Marchman, 1993; Plunkett and Marchman, 1991), and (ii) between referents (+past tense or +plural) and associated inflected perfect or plural forms (Cottrell and Plunkett, 1994; N. Ellis and Schmidt, 1998), closely simulating the error patterns, profiles of acquisition, differential difficulties, false-friends effects, reaction times for production, and interactions of regularity and frequency that are found in human learners, as well as acquiring a default case allowing generalization on "wug" tests, even in test cases of "minority default inflections," as are found in the German plural system (Hahn and Nakisa, 2000). Such findings strongly support the notion that acquisition of morphology is also a result of simple associative learning principles operating in a massively distributed system abstracting the regularities of association using optimal inference. Much of the information that is needed for syntax falls quite naturally out of simple sequence

Box 4.1 Connectionist simulations of longitudinal learning logs (N. Ellis and Schmidt, 1998)

Ellis and Schmidt (E & S) investigated the acquisition of a quasi-regular morphosyntactic domain by experimentally recording learners' language productions throughout learning, and then simulating acquisition using connectionist models exposed to the same language input. In fluent speakers, variables like frequency have much more observable an effect on the production of irregular items than of regular ones. Such observations underpin theories which hold that there are dual mechanisms involved in morphological inflection: regular items are computed procedurally by a suffixation rule in a grammatical processing module, while irregular items are retrieved from an associative memory. E & S gathered longitudinal acquisition data under precisely known circumstances to show how this pattern emerges as a natural result of associative learning, and, therefore, that frequency by regularity interactions does not implicate hybrid theories of morphosyntax. E & S further demonstrated that a simple connectionist model, as an implementation of associative learning, provided with the same language evidence, accurately simulated human SLA in this domain.

Alternative theoretical accounts:
Can human morphological abilities be understood in terms of associative processes, or is it necessary to postulate rule-based symbol processing systems underlying these grammatical skills?

Prasada, Pinker, and Snyder (1990) showed that when fluent English speakers see verb stems on a screen and are required to produce the past tense form, they take significantly less time for irregular verbs with high past tense frequencies (like *went*) than for irregular verbs with low past tense frequencies (like *slung*), even when stem frequencies are equated. However, there is no effect on latency of past tense frequency with regular verbs whose past tense is generated by adding *-ed*. Since frequency generally affects latency of retrieval from associative memory systems, this lack of frequency effect on regular forms has been taken as evidence that there must be symbol-manipulating syntactic mechanisms for language. Pinker's (1991) conclusion is that the language system responsible for morphological inflection is a hybrid: regular verbs (*walk–walked*) are computed by a suffixation rule in a neural system for grammatical processing, while irregular verbs (*run–ran*) are retrieved from an associative memory.

Rumelhart and McClelland (1986) pioneered an alternative connectionist approach to language acquisition by showing that a simple learning model reproduced, to a remarkable degree, the characteristics of young children learning the morphology of the past tense in English – the model generated the so-called U-shaped learning curve for irregular forms, it exhibited a tendency to overgeneralize, and, in the model, as in children, different past tense forms for the same word could co-exist at the same time. This original past tense model spawned a number of revised and improved connectionist models of different aspects of the acquisition of morphosyntax. According to such accounts, there are no "rules" of grammar. Instead, the systematicities of syntax emerge from the set of learned associations between language functions and base and past tense forms, with novel responses generated by "on-line" generalizations from stored exemplars.

Recording acquisition of a quasi-regular morphosyntactic system:
E & S argued that it is difficult to understand learning and development from observations like those of Prasada et al. (1990) of the final state, when we have no record of

the content of the learners' years of exposure to language or of the developmental course of their proficiencies. To understand learning, one must study learning.

E & S therefore recorded adult acquisition of second language morphology using an artificial language where frequency and regularity were factorially combined. Learners' accuracy and latency in producing artificial language names for single or multiple items was recorded after *each* exposure. Plurality was marked by a prefix: half of the items had a regular plural marker 'bu-' (e.g., *car* = 'garth,' *cars* = 'bugarth'), the remaining items had idiosyncratic affixes (e.g., *horse* = 'naig,' *horses* = 'zonaig'). Frequency was factorially crossed with regularity, with half of each set being presented five times more often.

The acquisition data for both accuracy and latency evidenced frequency effects for both regular and irregular forms early on in the acquisition process. However, as learning progresses, so the frequency effect for regular items diminishes, whilst it remains for irregular items. The results, illustrated in the left-hand lower panel of figure 4.1, thus converge on the end point described by Prasada et al. (1990), but they additionally show how this end point is reached – the convergence of the latencies for high- and low-frequency regular plural responses indexes the rate of acquisition of the schema for the regular form, and the attenuation of the frequency effect for regular items is a simple consequence of the power law of learning.

Connectionist modeling of acquisition:
E & S describe a simple connectionist model which is exposed to the same exemplars in the same order as the human subjects. The model, shown in the top panel of figure 4.1, had input nodes representing the different referents of the language and whether any particular stimulus was singular or plural. The output units represented the stem forms for the referents and the various affixes for marking plurality. The model learned to associate each input with its appropriate name, chunking appropriately each affix and stem. The model acquired some patterns more slowly than others. The simulations closely paralleled human learning (see the right-hand lower panel of figure 4.1), explaining 78 percent of the variance of the human correctness data. There are initially frequency effects on both the regular and irregular forms, but with increased exposure, so the frequency effect for regular forms is attenuated.

Further simulations demonstrated how varying the computational capacity of the model affects the rate of acquisition of default case, as indexed by successful performance on "wug" tests (*Q*.: Here is a wug, here is another, what have we got? *A*.: A "buwug."); the presence or absence of frequency effects for regular items; and ability to acquire irregular items. These findings illuminate the difficulties of children with specific language impairment and individual differences in L2 learner aptitude.

Conclusions:
The connectionist system duplicated the human "rule-like" behavior, yet there are no "rules" in a connectionist network. Rather, frequency–regularity interactions are a natural and necessary result of the associative ways in which connectionist models learn. These data serve to remind one that regular, rule-like behavior does not imply rule-generation. Instead regularity effects can stem from consistency: regular affixes are more habitual and frequent, since consistent items all involve pairings between plurality and the regular affix. Thus, regularity is frequency by another name. These data and simulations demonstrate that adult acquisition of these aspects of L2 morphology, at least, is tractable using simple associative learning principles.

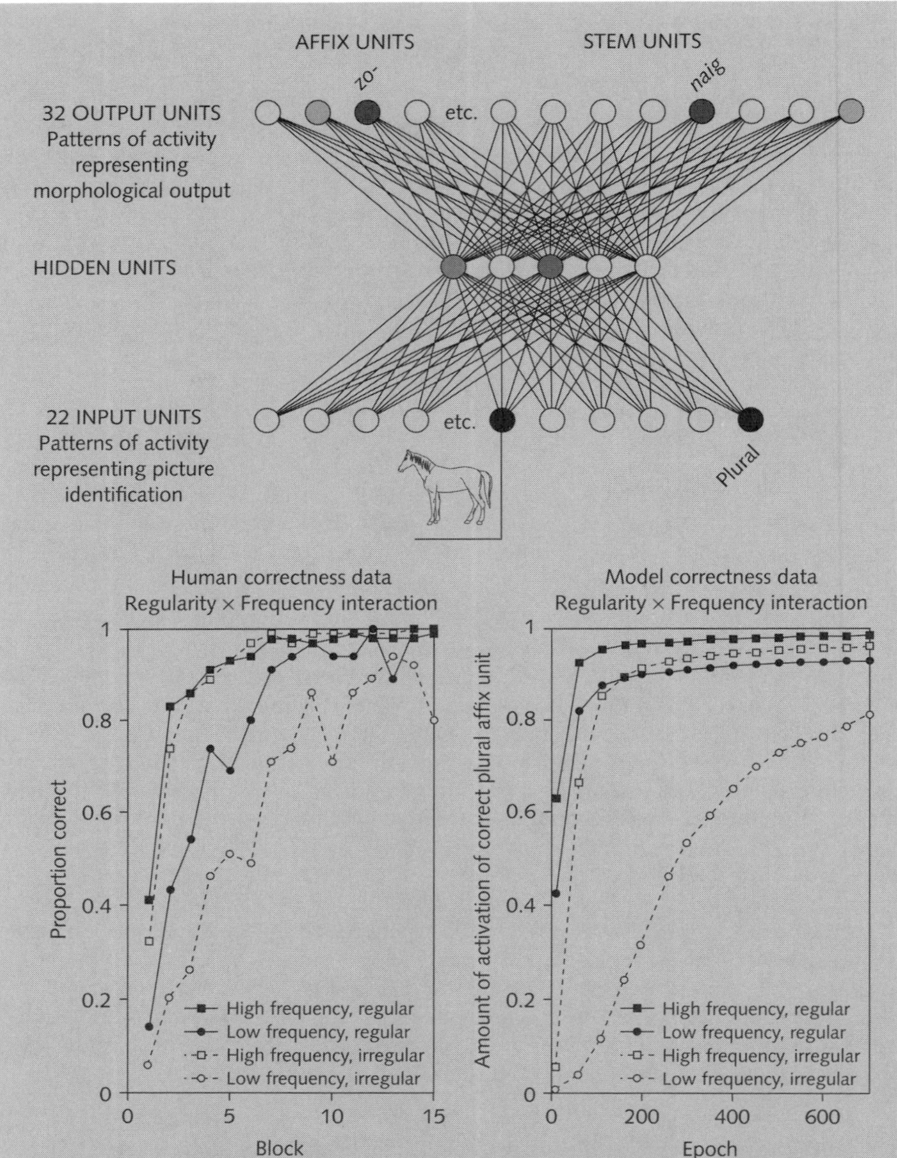

Figure 4.1 Human acquisition of high- and low-frequency, regular and irregular morphological inflections as a function of language exposure (lower left), a connectionist model for learning morphological inflection (top), and the acquisition functions of the model when exposed to the same pattern of language exemplars as the human learners (lower right).

Source: Adapted from Ellis and Schmidt (1998). Copyright 1998 by Psychology Press Ltd.

analysis and the patterns of association between patterns of sequences and patterns of referents.

The Ellis and Schmidt study in box 4.1 was selected for illustration because it clearly shows how this style of research strives to determine exactly what history of language exposure results in what learner competencies. Participants were taught an artificial second language in an experiment that measured their performance after each language experience so that their entire history of language input could be recorded. As shown in the detailed learning curves of figure 4.1, their resultant abilities in producing regular and irregular inflections of different frequencies of occurrence were assessed throughout learning. These results contradicted the findings of earlier studies which had restricted their observations to adult fluency. If we want to understand acquisition then we must study it directly. The study further demonstrated that a simple connectionist model, as an implementation of associative learning, when provided with the same relative frequencies of language evidence (something that was only possible because this history was determined in the experimental part of the study), accurately simulated human SLA in this domain.

The Kempe and MacWhinney study in box 4.2 again seeks to determine exactly what patterns are latent in learners' language input experience, but it assesses this in a different way. It illustrates the shared goals of connectionists and corpus linguists. Corpora of natural language are the only reliable sources of frequency-based data, and they provide the basis of a much more systematic approach to the analysis of language. For these reasons, we need large collections of representative language and the tools for analyzing these data. Corpus linguistics (Biber et al., 1998; McEnery and Wilson, 1996) bases its study of language on such examples of real-life performance data. Under normal circumstances, these natural language corpora provide the information that we need concerning the frequencies of different cues in language. However, Kempe and MacWhinney needed to estimate the language input to second language learners of German and Russian. In order to measure the validity of nominative and accusative cues in the two languages, they, therefore, analyzed a corpus of active transitive sentences from five textbooks widely used by learners of each language, and estimated the validity of these markers in the context of other surface cues such as word order, animacy of the nouns, and verb agreement. This showed that case marking in Russian is more complex than in German, but Russian case inflections are more reliable cues to sentence interpretation. Kempe and MacWhinney exploited the opposition of paradigm complexity and cue reliability in these two languages in order to contrast rule-based and associative theories of acquisition of morphology and to evaluate their predictions. Their connectionist model, as an implementation of associative learning and cue competition/constraint-satisfaction processing, was highly successful in predicting learners' relative acquisition rates.

Connectionist studies are important in that they directly show how language learning takes place through gradual strengthening of the associations between co-occurring elements of language, and how learning the distributional

Box 4.2 Connectionist learning from input corpus analysis (Kempe and MacWhinney, 1998)

Kempe and MacWhinney (K & M) investigated acquisition of the comprehension of morphological case marking by adult native speakers of English who were learning Russian or German as an L2. Their work compared acquisition of different languages using a fruitful combination of the methods of corpus analysis, psycholinguistic measurement of on-line performance, and connectionist simulations. Case marking in Russian is more complex than in German, but Russian case inflections are more reliable cues to sentence interpretation. K & M exploited the opposition of paradigm complexity and cue reliability in these two languages in order to contrast rule-based and associative theories of acquisition of morphology and to evaluate their predictions.

Alternative theoretical accounts:
Rule-based approaches to morphology view the learning of inflections as a process of discovering the grammatical dimensions underlying an inflectional paradigm (e.g., number, gender, person, case, or tense) through systematic hypothesis testing. According to such accounts, the more complex a paradigm, the longer it should take to learn.

Associative approaches to morphology view paradigms as epiphenomena that emerge from distributional characteristics of the language input. Learning takes place through gradual strengthening of the association between co-occurring elements of the language. According to these accounts, the ease of learning an inflection is determined by its cue validity, a function of how often an inflection occurs as a cue for a certain underlying function (cue availability) and how reliably it marks this function (cue reliability).

Quantifying paradigm complexity:
Complexity of paradigm in rule-based theories is determined by the number of dimensions, the number of cells, and the extent to which the cells in the paradigm are marked by unique inflections. Russian had more dimensions (animacy[2], number[2], gender[3], and case[6]) than German (number[2], gender[3], and case[4]). The crossings of these dimensions yields 72 cells in Russian, far more than the German system, which has only 24 cells. Average uniqueness of inflections is also lower in Russian. Russian is, thus, the more complex system by all three paradigm-based complexity measures. Rule-based accounts therefore predict that learners of German should do far better than learners of Russian in picking up case marking in the new language.

Quantifying cue validity using corpus analysis:
German and Russian differ in the extent to which they provide nominative and accusative markers as cues for agents and objects in sentences. In order to measure the validity of nominative and accusative cues in the two languages, K & M analyzed a corpus of active transitive sentences from five textbooks widely used by learners of each language, and estimated the validity of these markers in the context of other surface cues such as word order, animacy of the nouns, and verb agreement. Availability of a cue was computed as the total number of sentences in which a cue was present, divided by the total number of transitive sentences. Reliability of the cue

was the ratio of sentences in which the cue correctly signaled the agent, divided by the number of sentences in which the cue was present. Validity was the product of availability and reliability. These methods showed that the validity of case marking is much higher in Russian (.97) than in German (.56). Associative accounts therefore predict that learners of Russian, where case markers are readily available and reliable markers of thematic roles, should acquire case marking faster than learners of German.

Measuring acquisition as a function of exposure:
Learners of Russian and German were matched for language exposure on the basis of their knowledge of vocabulary, measured using a lexical decision task. Matching familiarity of learners of different languages is an accomplishment in itself (Kempe and MacWhinney, 1998).

As in other Competition Model studies, a computerized picture-choice task was used to probe the comprehension of L2 learners by varying the cues of case marking, noun configuration, and noun animacy, and determining the degree to which presence of a cue affected the accuracy and speed of learners' judgments of the agent of spoken sentences. As shown in figure 4.2a, the results demonstrated that learners of Russian used case marking at much earlier levels of language familiarity than learners of German.

Connectionist modeling of acquisition:
A small recurrent network (figure 4.2b) was used to model these cross-linguistic acquisition data. The four input units coded the following feature for each noun: animacy (±), nominative marking (±), accusative marking (±), and whether the input sentence is in English or in the L2. The input was restricted to the information for the first and second nouns of each sentence. In the output unit, an activation value of 1 was associated with the first noun as agent, 0 with second noun as agent. The network was first trained on a corpus of English transitive sentences where there was no case marking and the first noun was always the agent. Then it was trained on a representative sample of either Russian or German transitive sentences – essentially those same textbook sentences analyzed in the corpus analysis phase. The learning curves for this network's acquisition of Russian and German case marking are shown in figure 4.2c, where it is clear that, as in human learners, the network acquires the Russian system faster than the German one. The simulation data predicted 90 percent of the variance of the learner mean choice probabilities per pattern for Russian and 64 percent of the variance of the German choice data. It was also significantly successful in predicting on-line processing performance in terms of the human latency data.

Conclusions:
The match between simulation data and human performance supports the notion that adult SLA has a large associative component, and that the learning of inflectional morphology can be viewed as a gradual strengthening of the associations between co-occurring elements of language form and language function.

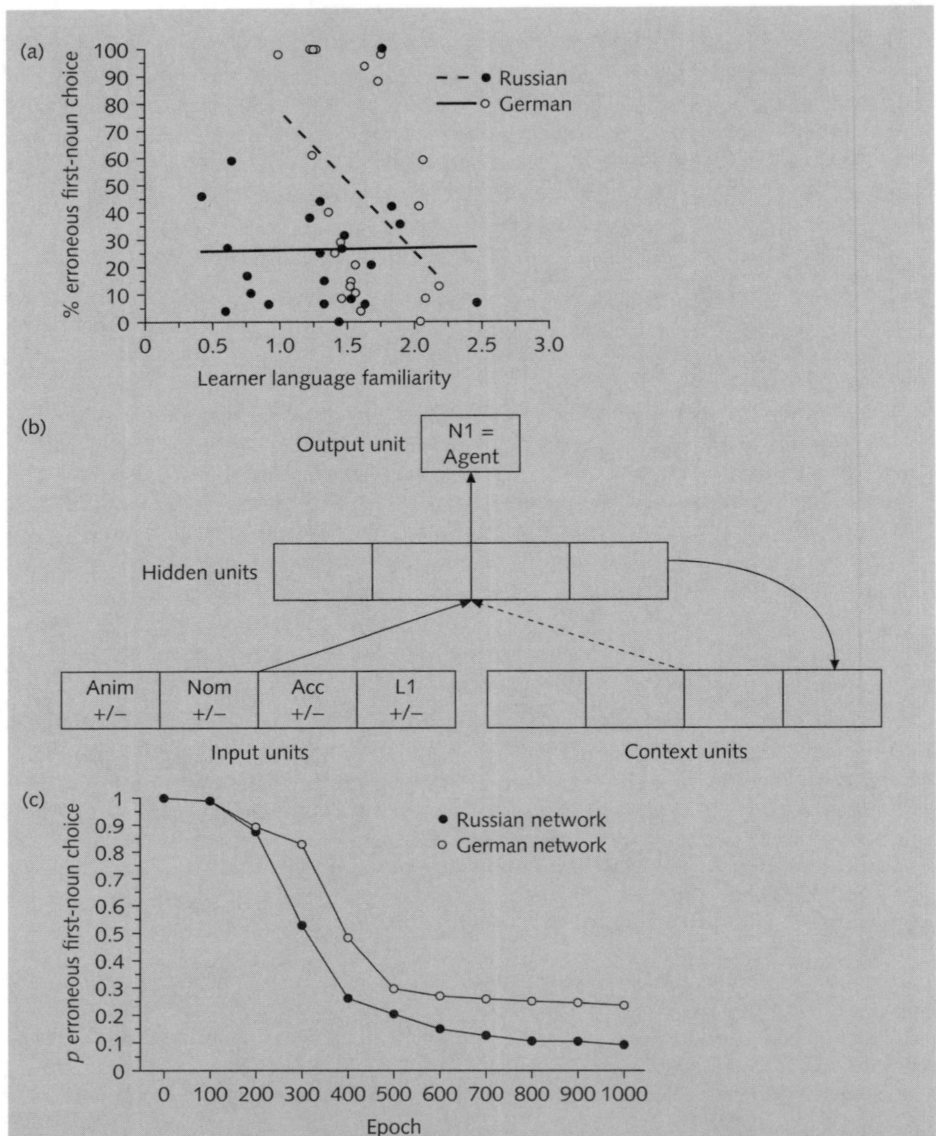

Figure 4.2 Acquisition data for Russian and German case marking, a connectionist model for learning case marking from representative language exposure, and the cross-linguistic acquisition functions for this model.

Source: Adapted from Kempe and MacWhinney (1998). Copyright 1998 by Cambridge University Press.

characteristics of the language input results in the emergence of rule-like, but not rule-governed, regularities. They are ways of looking at the effects of type and token frequency in the input and at how cue validity, a function of how often a surface form occurs as a cue for a certain underlying function (cue availability) and how reliably it marks this function (cue reliability), affects the emergence of regularities. Given that connectionist models have been used to understand various aspects of child language acquisition, the successful application of connectionism to SLA suggests that similar mechanisms operate in children and adults, and that language acquisition, in its essence, is the distributional analysis of form–function mappings in a neural network that attempts to satisfy simultaneously the constraints of all other constructions that are represented therein.

6 Current Limitations, Future Directions

"No discipline can concern itself in a productive way with the acquisition and utilization of a form of knowledge without being concerned with the nature of that system of knowledge" (Chomsky, 1977, p. 43). While this may be true, so is the emergentist counter that one cannot properly understand something without knowing how it came about. This brings us back to our opening stance. Constructivist views of language acquisition hold that simple learning mechanisms operating in and across human systems for perception, motor action, and cognition, while exposed to language data in a communicatively rich human social environment navigated by an organism eager to exploit the functionality of language, are sufficient to drive the emergence of complex language representations. The problem, though, is that just about every content word in this sentence is a research discipline in itself and that in our attempt to reunite speakers, syntax, and semantics, we have to be linguist, psychologist, physiologist, computational neuroscientist, and much more besides. At present there is far too little interdisciplinarity of research effort.

My sincere hope is that the material reviewed here convinces readers of the promise of these constructivist approaches to language acquisition. Clearly, there is much further to go. We need more-detailed longitudinal SLA corpora which will allow a proper tracking of the developmental sequences of constructions. We need more connectionist investigations of the emergence of linguistic structures from exemplars. Current connectionist models often use "test-tube" fragments of language and, thus, have low input representativeness. However good their contact with the data, more research is needed to explore the degrees to which these initial promising results can be scaled up to deal with the complexities of real language. Most connectionist work to date concerns L1 acquisition, and there needs to be far more work using this approach in SLA. If we wish to understand the emergence of language and we believe in the constraints of embodiment, then our models have to capture realistically the physical and psychological processes of perception, attention, and memory; the visual, motor, and other modalities which underpin conceptual knowledge; the limits of working memory; and all the rest.

There needs to be much more cross-talk between SLA and cognitive linguistic, child language, NLP, psycholinguistic, and connectionist research. The study of SLA must go forward within the broader remit of cognitive science. It is from these mutually supportive and naturally symbiotic interdisciplinary associations that eventually a more complete understanding of SLA will emerge.

ACKNOWLEDGMENT

Thanks to the Chester Language Development Group for feedback on a draft of this chapter and for pointing me at the right stuff in the first place.

REFERENCES

ACTFL 1986: *The ACTFL Proficiency Guidelines*. Yonkers, NY: American Council on the Teaching of Foreign Languages (ACTFL).

Aitchison, J. 1987: *Words in Mind*. Oxford: Blackwell.

Allen, J. and Seidenberg, M. S. 1999: The emergence of grammaticality in connectionist networks. In B. MacWhinney (ed.), *The Emergence of Language*. Mahwah, NJ: Lawrence Erlbaum Associates, 115–52.

Altman, G. T. M. 1997: *The Ascent of Babel: An Exploration of Language, Mind, and Understanding*. Oxford: Oxford University Press.

Barlow, M. and Kemmer, S. (eds) 2000: *Usage Based Models of Language*. Stanford, CA: CSLI Publications.

Barsalou, L. W. 1999: Perceptual symbol systems. *Behavioral and Brain Sciences*, 22, 577–609.

Bates, E. and Goodman, J. 1997: On the inseparability of grammar and the lexicon: evidence from acquisition, aphasia and real-time processing. *Language and Cognitive Processes*, 12, 507–86.

Bates, E. and MacWhinney, B. 1981: Second language acquisition from a functionalist perspective. In H. Winitz (ed.), *Native Language and Foreign Language Acquisition, Annals of the New York Academy of Sciences*, 379, 190–214.

Bates, E. and MacWhinney, B. 1987: Competition, variation, and language learning. In B. MacWhinney (ed.), *Mechanisms of Language Acquisition*. Hillsdale, NJ: Lawrence Erlbaum Associates, 157–93.

Becker, A. L. 1983: Toward a post-structuralist view of language learning: a short essay. *Language Learning*, 33, 217–20.

Berry, D. C. (ed.) 1997: *How implicit is implicit learning?* Oxford: Oxford University Press.

Biber, D. and Finegan, E. (eds) 1994: *Sociolinguistic Perspectives on Register*. New York: Oxford University Press.

Biber, D., Conrad, S., and Reppen, R. 1998: *Corpus Linguistics: Investigating Language Structure and Use*. Cambridge: Cambridge University Press.

Biber, B., Johansson, S., Leech, G., Conrad, S., and Finegan, E. 1999: *Longman Grammar of Spoken and Written English*. Harlow: Pearson Education.

Bloom, P. 2000: *How Children Learn the Meanings of Words*. Cambridge, MA: MIT Press.

Bock, J. 1986: Syntactic persistence in language production. *Cognitive Psychology*, 18, 355–87.

Bod, R. 1998: *Beyond Grammar: An Experience-Based Theory of Language*. Stanford, CA: CSLI Publications.

Bolander, M. 1989: Prefabs, patterns, and rules in interaction? Formulaic speech in adult learners' L2 Swedish. In K. Hyltenstam and L. K. Obler (eds), *Bilingualism across the Lifespan: Aspects of Acquisition, Maturity, and Loss*. Cambridge: Cambridge University Press, 73–86.

Bolinger, D. 1976: Meaning and memory. *Forum Linguisticum*, 1, 1–14.

Bowerman, M. 1976: Semantic factors in the acquisition of rules for word use and sentence construction. In D. Morehead and A. Morehead (eds), *Normal and Deficient Child Language*. Baltimore, MD: University Park Press, 99–180.

Braine, M. D. S. 1976: The ontogeny of English phrase structure: the first phase. In C. A. Ferguson and D. I. Slobin (eds), *Studies of Child Language Development*. New York: Holt, Rinehart and Winston, 407–20.

Brazil, D. 1995: *A Grammar of Speech*. Oxford: Oxford University Press.

Brent, M. R. 1999: Speech segmentation and word discovery: a computational perspective. *Trends in Cognitive Sciences*, 3, 294–301.

Bresnan, J. 1999: Linguistic theory at the turn of the century. Plenary presentation, 12th World Congress of Applied Linguistics. Tokyo, August 1–6.

Brew, C. 1995: Stochastic HPSG. *Proceedings of the European chapter of ACL '95*. Dublin, 83–99.

Brewster, J. 1999: Exploring gendered talk: some effects of interactional style. In A. Tosi and C. Leung (eds), *Rethinking Language Education*. London: CILT, 196–212.

Briscoe, T. 1994: Prospects for practical parsing of unrestricted text: robust statistical parsing techniques. In N. Oostdijk and P. de Haan (eds), *Corpus-Based Research into Language*. Amsterdam: Rodopi, 67–95.

Broeder, P. and Plunkett, K. 1994: Connectionism and second language acquisition. In N. Ellis (ed.), *Implicit and Explicit Learning of Languages*. London: Academic Press, 421–54.

Bunt, H. and Nijholt, A. 2000: *Advances in Probabilistic and Other Parsing Technologies*. Dordrecht: Kluwer Academic.

Bybee, J. 1995: Regular morphology and the lexicon. *Language and Cognitive Processes*, 10, 425–55.

Bybee, J. and Thompson, S. 2000: Three frequency effects in syntax. *Berkeley Linguistics Society*, 23, 65–85.

Carter, R. 1998: *Vocabulary: Applied Linguistic Perspectives*. Second edition. London: Routledge.

Celce-Murcia, M. and Larsen-Freeman, D. 1983: *The Grammar Book*. London: Newbury House.

Charniak, E. 1993: *Statistical Language Learning*. Cambridge, MA: MIT Press.

Chomsky, N. 1977: *Knowledge and Responsibility*. New York: Pantheon Books.

Christiansen, M. H. and Chater, N. 2001: Connectionist psycholinguistics: capturing the empirical data. *Trends in Cognitive Sciences*, 5, 82–8.

Christiansen, M. H., Allen, J., and Seidenberg, M. S. 1998: Learning to segment speech using multiple cues: a connectionist model. *Language and Cognitive Processes*, 13, 221–68.

Christiansen, M. H., Chater, N., and Seidenberg, M. S. (eds) 1999: Connectionist models of human language processing: progress and prospects. Special issue of *Cognitive Science*, 23, 415–634.

Church, K., and Patil, R. 1982: Coping with syntactic ambiguity or how to put the block in the box on the table. *Computational Linguistics*, 8, 139–49.

De Cock, S. 1998: A recurrent word combination approach to the study of formulae in the speech of native and non-native speakers of English. *International Journal of Corpus Linguistics*, 3, 59–80.

Collins Cobuild 1996: *Grammar Pattern 1: Verbs*. London: HarperCollins.

Corder, S. P. 1973: *Introducing Applied Linguistics*. Harmondsworth: Penguin.

Cottrell, G. and Plunkett, K. 1994: Acquiring the mapping from meaning to sounds. *Connection Science*, 6, 379–412.

Croft, W. 2001: *Radical Construction Grammar: Syntactic Theory in Typological Perspective*. Oxford: Oxford University Press.

Croft, W. and Cruse, A. 1999: Cognitive linguistics. Ms. University of Manchester.

Daugherty, K. G., and Seidenberg, M. S. 1994: Beyond rules and exceptions: a connectionist approach to inflectional morphology. In S. D. Lima, R. L. Corrigan, and G. K. Iverson (eds), *The Reality of Linguistic Rules*. Amsterdam: John Benjamins, 353–88.

Dawkins, R. 1976: Hierarchical organisation: a candidate principle for ethology. In P. P. G. Bateson and R. A. Hinde (eds), *Growing Points in Ethology*. Cambridge: Cambridge University Press, 7–54.

Deacon, T. W. 1997: *The Symbolic Species*. New York: Norton.

Dörnyei, Z. and Kormos, J. 1998: Problem-solving mechanisms in L2 communication: a psycholinguistic perspective. *Studies in Second Language Acquisition*, 20, 349–85.

Ellis, N. C. (ed.) 1994a: *Implicit and Explicit Learning of Languages*. London: Academic Press.

Ellis, N. C. 1994b: Implicit and explicit processes in language acquisition: an introduction. In N. Ellis (ed.), *Implicit and Explicit Learning of Languages*. London: Academic Press, 1–32.

Ellis, N. C. 1994c: Vocabulary acquisition: the implicit ins and outs of explicit cognitive mediation. In N. Ellis (ed.), *Implicit and Explicit Learning of Languages*. London: Academic Press, 211–82.

Ellis, N. C. 1996: Sequencing in SLA: phonological memory, chunking, and points of order. *Studies in Second Language Acquisition*, 18, 91–126.

Ellis, N. C. 1998: Emergentism, connectionism and language learning. *Language Learning*, 48, 631–64.

Ellis, N. C. 2001: Memory for language. In P. Robinson (ed.), *Cognition and Second Language Instruction*. Cambridge: Cambridge University Press.

Ellis, N. C. 2002: Frequency effects in language acquisition: a review with implications for theories of implicit and explicit language acquisition. *Studies in Second Language Acquisition*, 24, 143–88.

Ellis, N. C. and Beaton, A. 1993a: Factors affecting the learning of foreign language vocabulary: imagery keyword mediators and phonological short-term memory. *Quarterly Journal of Experimental Psychology*, 46A, 533–58.

Ellis, N. C. and Beaton, A. 1993b: Psycholinguistic determinants of foreign language vocabulary learning. *Language Learning*, 43, 559–617.

Ellis, N. C. and Laporte, N. 1997: Contexts of acquisition: effects of formal instruction and naturalistic exposure on second language acquisition. In A. M. B. de Groot and J. F. Kroll (eds), *Tutorials in Bilingualism: Psycholinguistic*

Perspectives. Hillsdale, NJ: Lawrence Erlbaum Associates, 53–83.

Ellis, N. C. and Schmidt, R. 1998: Rules or associations in the acquisition of morphology? The frequency by regularity interaction in human and PDP learning of morphosyntax. *Language and Cognitive Processes*, 13, 307–36.

Ellis, N. C., Lee, M. W., and Reber, A. R. 1999: Phonological working memory in artificial language acquisition. Ms. University of Wales, Bangor.

Ellis, R. 1984: Formulaic speech in early classroom second language development. In J. Handscome, R. Orem, and B. Taylor (eds), *On TESOL '83: The Question of Control*. Washington, DC: TESOL, 57–71.

Ellis, R. 1994: *The Study of Second Language Acquisition*. Oxford: Oxford University Press.

Elman, J. L., Bates, E. A., Johnson, M. H., Karmiloff-Smith, A., Parisi, D., and Plunkett, K. 1996: *Rethinking Innateness: A Connectionist Perspective on Development*. Cambridge, MA: MIT Press.

Epstein, W. 1967: The influence of syntactical structure on learning. In N. J. Slamecka (ed.), *Human Learning and Memory: Selected Readings*. New York: Oxford University Press, 391–5.

Fillmore, C. J. and Kay, P. 1993: *Construction Grammar Coursebook*. Berkeley, CA: University of California Press, chapters 1–11 (Reading Materials for Ling. X20).

Fromkin, V. A. 1980: *Errors in Linguistic Performance: Slips of the Tongue, Ear, Pen and Hand*. New York: Academic Press.

Gasser, M. 1990: Connectionism and universals of second language acquisition. *Studies in Second Language Acquisition*, 12, 179–99.

Gernsbacher, M. A. (ed.) 1994: *Handbook of Psycholinguistics*. San Diego: Academic Press.

Givón, T. 1998: The functional approach to language. In M. Tomasello (ed.), *The New Psychology of Language: Cognitive and Functional Approaches to Language Structure*. Mahwah, NJ: Lawrence Erlbaum Associates, 41–66.

Goldberg, A. E. 1995: *Constructions: A Construction Grammar Approach to Argument Structure*. Chicago: University of Chicago Press.

Goldberg, A. and Sethuraman, N. 1999: Learning argument structure generalizations. Ms. University of Illinois, Urbana-Champaign.

Granger, S. (ed.) 1998: *Learner English on Computer*. London: Longman.

Hahn, U. and Nakisa, R. C. 2000: German inflection: single or dual route? *Cognitive Psychology*, 41, 313–60.

Hakuta, K. 1974: Prefabricated patterns and the emergence of structure in second language acquisition. *Language Learning*, 24, 287–98.

Harley, T. A. 1995: *The Psychology of Language: From Data to Theory*. Hove: Lawrence Erlbaum Associates.

Hebb, D. O. 1961: Distinctive features of learning in the higher animal. In J. F. Delafresnaye (ed.), *Brain Mechanisms and Learning*. Oxford: Blackwell, 37–46.

Higgs, T. V. (ed.) 1984: *Teaching for Proficiency: The Organizing Principle*. Lincolnwood, IL: National Textbook Company.

Hoey, M. P. 1991: *Patterns of Lexis in Text*. Oxford: Oxford University Press.

Hopper, P. J. 1998: Emergent grammar. In M. Tomasello (ed.), *The New Psychology of Language: Cognitive and Functional Approaches to Language Structure*. Mahwah, NJ: Lawrence Erlbaum Associates, 155–76.

Hudson, R. 1984: *Word Grammar*. Oxford: Blackwell.

Hudson, R. 1990: *English Word Grammar*. Oxford: Blackwell.

Hunston, S. and Francis, G. 1996: *Pattern grammar: A corpus driven approach to the lexical grammar of English*. Amsterdam: John Benjamins.

James, W. 1890: *The Principles of Psychology*. New York: Holt.

Jurafsky, D. 1996: A probabilistic model of lexical and syntactic access and disambiguation. *Cognitive Science*, 20, 137–94.

Kaplan, R. M. 1999: Computational and theoretical linguistics. Plenary presentation, 12th World Congress of Applied Linguistics. Tokyo, August 1–6.

Kempe, V. and MacWhinney, B. 1998: The acquisition of case-marking by adult learners of Russian and German. *Studies in Second Language Acquisition*, 20, 543–87.

Kosslyn, S. 1983: *Ghosts in the Mind's Machine: Creating and Using Images in the Brain*. New York: Norton.

Lachter, J. and Bever, T. 1988: The relation between linguistic structure and associative theories of language learning: a constructive critique of some connectionist learning models. *Cognition*, 28, 195–247.

Lakoff, G. 1987: *Women, Fire, and Dangerous Things: What Categories Reveal about the Mind*. Chicago: University of Chicago Press.

Lakoff, G. and Johnson, M. 1980: *Metaphors We Live By*. Chicago: University of Chicago Press.

Langacker, R. W. 1987: *Foundations of Cognitive Grammar. Vol. 1: Theoretical Prerequisites*. Stanford, CA: Stanford University Press.

Langacker, R. W. 1991: *Foundations of Cognitive Grammar. Vol. 2: Descriptive Application*. Stanford, CA: Stanford University Press.

Larsen-Freeman, D. 1997: Chaos/complexity science and second language acquisition. *Applied Linguistics*, 18, 141–65.

Leech, L. 2000: Grammars of spoken English: new outcomes of corpus-oriented research. *Language Learning*, 50, 675–724.

Levy, J. P., Bairaktaris, D., Bullinaria, J. A., and Cairns, P. (eds) 1995: *Connectionist Models of Memory and Language*. London: UCL Press.

Lewis, M. 1993: *The Lexical Approach: The State of ELT and the Way Forward*. Hove: English Language Teaching Publications.

Lieven, E. V. M., Pine, J. M., and Dresner Barnes, H. 1992: Individual differences in early vocabulary development: redefining the referential–expressive dimension. *Journal of Child Language*, 19, 287–310.

MacWhinney, B. (ed.) 1987: *Mechanisms of Language Acquisition*. Hillsdale, NJ: Lawrence Erlbaum Associates.

MacWhinney, B. 1992: Transfer and competition in second language learning. In R. J. Harris (ed.), *Cognitive Processing in Bilinguals*. Amsterdam: North-Holland, 371–90.

MacWhinney, B. 1997a: Second language acquisition and the competition model. In A. M. B. de Groot and J. F. Kroll (eds), *Tutorials in Bilingualism: Psycholinguistic Perspectives*. Hillsdale, NJ: Lawrence Erlbaum Associates, 113–44.

MacWhinney, B. 1997b: Lexical connectionism. In P. Broeder and J. Murre (eds), *Cognitive Approaches to Language Learning*. Cambridge, MA: MIT Press.

MacWhinney, B. (ed.) 1999a: *The Emergence of Language*. Mahwah, NJ: Lawrence Erlbaum Associates.

MacWhinney, B. 1999b: The emergence of language from embodiment. In B. MacWhinney (ed.), *The Emergence of Language*. Mahwah, NJ: Lawrence Erlbaum Associates, 213–56.

MacWhinney, B. and Bates, E. (eds) 1989: *The Crosslinguistic Study of Sentence Processing*. New York: Cambridge University Press.

MacWhinney, B. and Leinbach, J. 1991: Implementations are not conceptualizations: revising the verb learning model. *Cognition*, 40, 121–57.

Manza, L. and Reber, A. S. 1997: Representing artificial grammars: transfer across stimulus forms and modalities. In D. C. Berry (ed.), *How Implicit is Implicit Learning?* Oxford: Oxford University Press, 73–106.

Maratsos, M. 1982: The child's construction of grammatical categories. In E. Wanner and L. R. Gleitman (eds), *Language Acquisition: The State of the Art*. Cambridge: Cambridge University Press, 240–66.

Marchman, V. A. 1993: Constraints on plasticity in a connectionist model of the English past tense. *Journal of Cognitive Neuroscience*, 5, 215–34.

Martin, W. K., Church, K., and Patil, R. 1981: *Preliminary Analysis of a Breadth-First Parsing Algorithm: Theoretical and Experimental Results*. Tech. Rep. MIT/LCS/TR 261. Cambridge, MA: MIT, Laboratory for Computer Science.

Mathews, R. C. and Roussel, L. G. 1997: Abstractness of implicit knowledge: a cognitive evolutionary perspective. In D. C. Berry (ed.), *How Implicit is Implicit Learning?* Oxford: Oxford University Press, 13–47.

McClelland, J. L. Rumelhart, D. E., and the PDP Research Group (eds) 1986: *Parallel Distributed Processing: Explorations in the Microstructure of Cognition. Vol. 2: Psychological and Biological Models*. Cambridge, MA: MIT Press.

McEnery, T. and Wilson, A. 1996: *Corpus Linguistics*. Edinburgh: Edinburgh University Press.

McLeod, P., Plunkett, K., and Rolls, E. T. 1998: *Introduction to Connectionist Modelling of Cognitive Processes*. Oxford: Blackwell.

Miller, G. A. 1956: The magical number seven, plus or minus two: some limits on our capacity for processing information. *Psychological Review*, 63, 81–97.

Miller, G. A. 1958: Free recall of redundant strings of letters. *Journal of Experimental Psychology*, 56, 485–91.

Miller, G. A. 1991: *The Science of Words*. New York: Scientific American Library.

Myles, F., Hooper, J., and Mitchell, R. 1998: Rote or rule? Exploring the role of formulaic language in classroom foreign language learning. *Language Learning*, 48, 323–64.

Myles, F., Mitchell, R., and Hooper, J. 1999: Interrogative chunks in French L2: a basis for creative construction. *Studies in Second Language Acquisition*, 21, 49–80.

Narayanan, S. 1997: Talking the talk is like walking the walk: a computational model of verb aspect. In *Proceedings of the Cognitive Science Conference 1997*. Pittsburgh, PA: Cognitive Science Society.

Nattinger, J. R. 1980: A lexical phrase grammar for ESL. *TESOL Quarterly*, 14, 337–44.

Nattinger, J. R. and DeCarrico, J. S. 1992: *Lexical Phrases and Language Teaching*. Oxford: Oxford University Press.

Neisser, U. 1976: *Cognition and Reality: Principles and Implications of Cognitive Psychology*. San Francisco: Freeman.

Newell, A. 1990: *Unified Theories of Cognition*. Cambridge, MA: Harvard University Press.

Pawley, A. and Syder, F. H. 1983: Two puzzles for linguistic theory: nativelike selection and nativelike fluency. In J. C. Richards and R. W. Schmidt (eds), *Language and Communication*. London: Longman, 191–225.

Pine, J. M. and Lieven, E. V. M. 1993: Reanalyzing rote-learned phrases: individual differences in the transition to multi-word speech. *Journal of Child Language*, 20, 551–71.

Pine, J. M. and Lieven, E. V. M. 1997: Slot and frame patterns in the development of the determiner category. *Applied Psycholinguistics*, 18, 123–38.

Pine, J. M., Lieven, E. V. M., and Rowland, C. F. 1998: Comparing different models of the development of the English verb category. *Linguistics*, 36, 807–30.

Pinker, S. 1991: Rules of language. *Science*, 253, 530–5.

Pinker, S. and Prince, A. 1988: On language and connectionism: analysis of a parallel distributed processing model of language acquisition. *Cognition*, 29, 195–247.

Plunkett, K. (ed.) 1998: *Language and Cognitive Processes*, 13. Special issue on connectionist models of language.

Plunkett, K. and Elman, J. L. 1997: *Exercises in Rethinking Innateness*. Cambridge, MA: MIT Press.

Plunkett, K. and Marchman, V. 1991: U-shaped learning and frequency effects in a multi-layered perceptron: implications for child language acquisition. *Cognition*, 38, 3–102.

Plunkett, K. and Marchman, V. 1993: From rote learning to system building: acquiring verb morphology in children and connectionist nets. *Cognition*, 48, 21–69.

Prasada, S., Pinker, S., and Snyder, W. 1990: Some evidence that irregular forms are retrieved from memory but regular forms are rule-governed. Paper presented at the Thirty First Meeting of the Psychonomic Society. New Orleans, November.

Quartz, S. R. and Sejnowski, T. J. 1997: The neural basis of cognitive development: a constructivist manifesto. *Behavioral and Brain Sciences*, 20, 537–56.

Quirk, R., Greenbaum, S., Leech, G., and Svartvik, J. 1985: *A Comprehensive Grammar of the English Language*. London: Longman.

Reason, J. T. 1979: Actions not as planned: the price of automatisation. In G. Underwood and R. Stevens (eds), *Aspects of Consciousness. Vol. 1: Psychological Issues*. London: Academic Press, 67–89.

Reber, A. S. 1967: Implicit learning of artificial grammars. *Journal of Verbal Learning and Verbal Behavior*, 77, 317–27.

Redington, M. and Chater, N. 1998: Connectionist and statistical approaches to language acquisition: a distributional perspective. *Language and Cognitive Processes*, 13, 129–92.

Rumelhart, D. and McClelland, J. 1986: On learning the past tense of English verbs. In D. E. Rumelhart and J. L. McClelland (eds), *Parallel Distributed Processing: Explorations in the Microstructure of Cognition. Vol. 2: Psychological and Biological Models*. Cambridge, MA: MIT Press, 272–326.

Rumelhart, D. E. and McClelland, J. L. 1987: Learning the past tense of English verbs: implicit rules or parallel distributed processes? In B. MacWhinney (ed.), *Mechanisms of Language Acquisition*. Hillsdale, NJ: Lawrence Erlbaum Associates, 195–248.

Saffran, J. R., Aslin, R. N., and Newport, E. L. 1996: Statistical learning by 8-month-old infants. *Science*, 274, 1926–8.

Sampson, G. 1986: A stochastic approach to parsing. In *Proceedings of COLING '86*. Bonn, 151–5.

Schmitt, N. 2000: *Vocabulary in Language Teaching*. Cambridge: Cambridge University Press.

Seidenberg, M. S. 1997: Language acquisition and use: learning and applying probabilistic constraints. *Science*, 275, 1599–603.

Simon, H. A. 1962: The architecture of complexity. *Proceedings of the American Philosophical Society*, 106, 467–82. Reprinted in H. A. Simon (1969), *The Sciences of the Artificial*. Cambridge, MA: MIT Press.

Simon, H. A. 1969: *The Sciences of the Artificial*. Cambridge, MA: MIT Press.

Sinclair, J. 1991: *Corpus, Concordance, Collocation*. Oxford: Oxford University Press.

Slobin, D. I. 1997: The origins of grammaticizable notions: beyond the individual mind. In D. I. Slobin (ed.), *The Crosslinguistic Study of Language Acquisition. Vol. 5*. Mahwah, NJ: Lawrence Erlbaum Associates, 265–323.

Sokolik, M. E. and Smith, M. 1992: Assignment of gender to French nouns in primary and second language acquisition: a connectionist model. *Second Language Research*, 8, 39–58.

Studdert-Kennedy, M. 1991: Language development from an evolutionary perspective. In N. A. Krasnegor, D. M. Rumbaugh, R. L. Schiefelbusch, and M. Studdert-Kennedy (eds), *Biological and Behavioral Determinants of Language Development*. Hillsdale, NJ: Lawrence Erlbaum Associates, 5–28.

Talmy, L. 1988: Force dynamics in language and cognition. *Cognitive Science*, 12, 49–100.

Talmy, L. 1996a: The windowing of attention in language. In M. Shibatani and S. Thompson (eds), *Grammatical Constructions: Their Form and Meaning*. Oxford: Oxford University Press, 235–87.

Talmy, L. 1996b: Fictive motion in language and "ception." In P. Bloom, M. Peterson, L. Nadel, and M. Garrett (eds), *Language and Space*. Cambridge, MA: MIT Press, 211–75.

Tanenhaus, M. and Trueswell, J. 1995: Sentence comprehension. In J. L. Miller and P. D. Eimas (eds), *Speech, Language and Communication*. New York: Academic Press, 217–62.

Tannen, D. 1987: Repetition and variation as spoken formulaicity in conversation. *Language*, 63, 574–605.

Taraban, R. and Kempe, V. 1999: Gender processing in native (L1) and non-native (L2) Russian speakers. *Applied Psycholinguistics*, 20, 119–48.

Tomasello, M. 1992: *First Verbs: A Case Study of Early Grammatical Development*. Cambridge: Cambridge University Press.

Tomasello, M. 1995: Language is not an instinct. *Cognitive Development*, 10, 131–56.

Tomasello, M. (ed.) 1998a: *The New Psychology of Language: Cognitive and Functional Approaches to Language Structure*. Mahwah, NJ: Lawrence Erlbaum Associates.

Tomasello, M. 1998b: The return of constructions: review of the book *Constructions: A Construction Grammar Approach to Argument Structure. Journal of Child Language*, 75, 431–47.

Tomasello, M. 2000: Do young children have adult syntactic competence? *Cognition*, 74, 209–53.

Tomasello, M. and Brooks, P. 1999: Early syntactic development: a construction grammar approach. In M. Barrett (ed.), *The Development of Language*. London: UCL Press, 116–90.

Towell, R. and Hawkins, R. 1994: *Approaches to Second Language Acquisition*. Clevedon: Multilingual Matters.

Ungerer, F. and Schmid, H. J. 1996: *An Introduction to Cognitive Linguistics*. Harlow: Addison Wesley Longman.

Vihman, M. 1982: Formulas in first and second language acquisition. In L. Obler and L. Menn (eds), *Exceptional Language and Linguistics*. San Diego: Academic Press, 261–84.

Vosse, T. and Kempen, G. 2000: Syntactic structure assembly in human parsing: a computational model based on competitive inhibition and a lexicalist grammar. *Cognition*, 75, 105–43.

Weinert, R. 1994: Some effects of a foreign language classroom on the development of German negation. *Applied Linguistics*, 15, 76–101.

Weinert, R. 1995: Formulaic language in SLA: a review. *Applied Linguistics*, 16, 180–205.

Wong-Fillmore, L. 1976: *The second time around*. Doctoral dissertation. Stanford University.

Wray, A. 1992: *The Focussing Hypothesis*. Amsterdam: John Benjamins.

5 Cognitive Processes in Second Language Learners and Bilinguals: The Development of Lexical and Conceptual Representations

JUDITH F. KROLL AND
GRETCHEN SUNDERMAN

1 Introduction

In the past decade there has been increasing interest on the part of cognitive psychologists and psycholinguists in characterizing the cognitive processes that support second language acquisition. One focus is to understand how cognitive systems are constrained by the context and timing of acquisition and to identify the source of these constraints (e.g., Birdsong, 1999; Hyltenstam and Abramsson, this volume; Long, 1990, 1993; MacWhinney, 1999). A second concerns the cognitive consequences of having two languages active in early childhood (e.g., Bialystok, 1997). A third addresses the representations, processes, and strategies that are used when skilled adult bilinguals read and speak words and process sentences in each of their two languages (e.g., Costa, Miozzo, and Caramazza, 1999; Dijkstra, Van Jaarsveld, and Ten Brinke, 1998; Dussias, 2001; Jared and Kroll, 2001). These strategies include processes that are a feature of monolingual performance as well as those that peculiarly reflect the specific demands of juggling two languages in a single mind (e.g., Green, 1998; Grosjean, 2001). It is this third focus that is the topic of our chapter. From a psycholinguistic perspective, understanding the basis of proficient bilingual performance reveals the cognitive processes that are necessarily recruited during second language acquisition as well.

We first review the recent psycholinguistic evidence on reading and speaking in two languages. In each section, we summarize studies on skilled bilingual performance and, where available, the corresponding data for second language learners. Our review will address issues of lexical acquisition and representation because it is this topic on which the greatest research efforts have been focused. In the course of the chapter we will also attempt to illustrate the methods that psycholinguists use to examine these issues. Within each section we also illustrate the manner in which psycholinguistic models of lexical representation and processing have been extended to accommodate the presence of two languages. Finally, we consider the implications of the recent psycholinguistic research for second language pedagogy.

2 Reading and Speaking Words in Two Languages

Early research on the bilingual lexicon investigated the question of whether the bilingual or second language learner possessed one or two lexicons for words in each language (for recent reviews see Gollan and Kroll, 2001; Francis, 1999). It eventually became clear that this question alone was too unconstrained to provide an adequate model of either the developing or proficient lexicon. For one thing, there was disagreement about what the lexicon itself might include and whether the conclusion that the lexicon was integrated or separated for words in two languages applied to all aspects of lexical representation or only to some. For example, an initial proposal was that lexical forms were represented separately but that words in the bilingual's two languages shared a common semantic system (e.g., Potter, So, Von Eckardt, and Feldman, 1984; Smith, 1997). However, subsequent research suggested that, at least under some circumstances, the representation of lexical forms may be integrated (e.g., Van Heuven, Dijkstra, and Grainger, 1998) and that although some core aspects of semantic representation may be similar across languages, differences in usage and context may limit the degree to which even the semantics are shared (e.g., De Groot, 1993; Pavlenko, 1999).

A second source of confusion in thinking about the number of lexicons in bilinguals was that assumptions about representation were typically confounded with assumptions about access. Van Heuven et al. (1998) point out that separate lexicon models tended to be associated with selective access whereas integrated models assumed non-selective access. In other words, models which assume separate lexical representations are likely to claim that it is possible to selectively activate words in one language only, whereas models which assume an integrated lexicon are likely to claim non-selective and parallel activation of word forms in both languages. Because the form of representation and the mode of access are potentially independent, a number of additional alternatives are logically possible, although rarely considered. For example, there might be separate lexicons, one for words in each language, but with non-selective access to both in parallel.

More recent research has addressed five questions that will serve to frame our review: (1) How are lexical forms in each language represented and activated during reading?; (2) Are semantic representations shared across the bilingual's two languages?; (3) On what basis are lexical and semantic representations connected for words and concepts in each language?; (4) How are words spoken in the second language when a more dominant alternative almost always exists in the first language?; and (5) How is the activation of lexical form and meaning controlled so that bilinguals recognize and speak words in the intended language?

2.1 *How are lexical forms in each language represented and activated during reading?*

Psycholinguists use a variety of tasks to investigate word recognition during reading. One of the most common is lexical decision, a paradigm in which a letter string is presented on a computer screen and the participant is simply asked to judge, as quickly as possible, whether it forms a real word. By manipulating the properties of the task and the properties of the letter string, it is possible to identify those aspects of lexical representation that are involved when words are identified and to examine the extent to which information in the bilingual's two languages interact during this process. For example, in a study by Van Heuven et al. (1998) proficient Dutch–English bilinguals performed lexical decision in each of their languages. The main question was whether the time to decide that a letter string was a word in either language would be influenced by the presence of orthographic neighbors in the other language. Past research on word recognition within a single language has shown that the time to recognize a word is influenced by the number and frequency of its neighbors (see Andrews, 1997, for a review). The question in the Van Heuven et al. study was whether the time for Dutch–English bilinguals to judge a string of letters as an English word would be affected by the presence of neighbors in both languages (e.g., for a Dutch–English bilingual the letter string *word* has the neighbors *work* and *wore* in English but also the neighbors *bord* and *worp* in Dutch). The results showed that even when only one of the bilingual's two languages was required for lexical decision, performance was influenced by the presence of neighbors in both languages, suggesting that access to the lexicon is non-selective and that the lexicon may be integrated, at least for languages that are similar, like Dutch and English.

Van Heuven et al. (1998) interpreted the presence of cross-language effects of lexical form as support for a bilingual version of the interactive activation model (McClelland and Rumelhart, 1981), or BIA (see also Dijkstra and Van Heuven, 1998; Dijkstra, Van Heuven, and Grainger, 1998). The main claim of the BIA model is that the bilingual's lexicon is integrated and that lexical access is non-selective, with candidates in both languages activated whenever the input shares features with alternatives in either language. The model (see figure 5.1) assumes that upon receiving some orthographic input, a set of letter

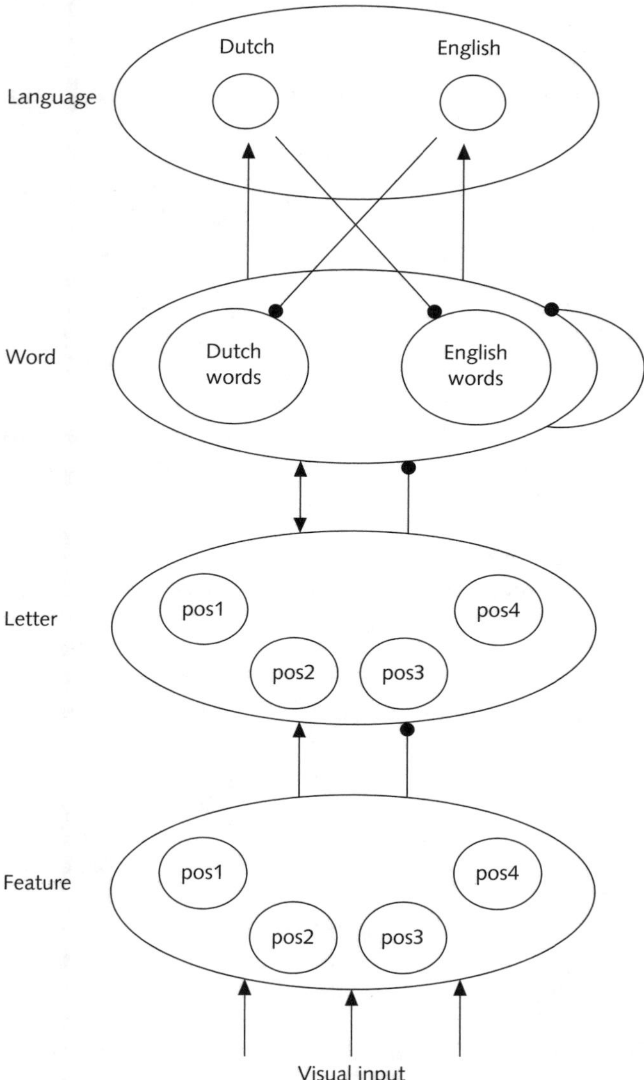

Figure 5.1 Bilingual interaction activation (BIA) model
Source: Adapted from Dijkstra, Van Heuven, and Grainger (1998)

and then word units is activated in parallel for words in both languages. Inhibitory connections then create competition among same and other-language alternatives. Unlike monolingual models, BIA includes an additional language node level so that it is possible to bias the activation of one language relative to the other. BIA has been implemented as a computer model and the subsequent simulations closely parallel the empirical results reported by Van Heuven et al.

Subsequent research has provided converging support for the conclusion that lexical access is non-selective and driven by the stimulus properties of the input, not by the intentions of the reader. For example, the time to recognize interlingual homographs or false friends (e.g., the word *room* in English, which also means "cream" in Dutch) is a function of the frequency of the alternative reading and relative activation of the non-target language (Dijkstra, Van Jaarsveld, and Ten Brinke, 1998). Bilinguals are slow to accept interlingual homographs as real words in their L2 when the L1 reading of the word is also active and must be ignored. Moreover, the activation of the alternative in the other language does not appear to be under the bilingual's control. Dijkstra, De Bruijn, Schriefers, and Ten Brinke (2000) recently showed that these effects are apparently immune to the effects of instructions. Other recent studies have shown that not only orthographic but also phonological features of the non-target language are activated during word recognition (e.g., Brysbaert, Van Dyck, and Van de Poel, 1999; Dijkstra, Grainger, and Van Heuven, 1999; Jared and Kroll, 2001).

The results we have reviewed are based primarily on the performance of highly skilled bilinguals. Remarkably little research has traced the development of lexical form activation across L2 acquisition. The few studies which have included comparisons of second language speakers who differ in their L2 proficiency suggest that the pattern of cross-language influence changes with level of skill in L2 (e.g., Bijeljac-Babic, Biardeau, and Grainger, 1997; Jared and Kroll, 2001; Talamas, Kroll, and Dufour, 1999). In general, there is more of an asymmetry at early stages of L2 acquisition with stronger effects from L1 to L2 than the reverse. However, when the activation of even a weak L2 is increased, it is possible to observe cross-language interactions that suggest that the processing mechanisms that characterize the fully formed lexicon of the proficient bilingual are in place.

A recent study by Jared and Kroll (2001) illustrates the change in the effect of L2 on L1 with increasing L2 proficiency (see box 5.1). Native English speakers named words aloud in English, their L1. The dependent measures were the time to begin to articulate the word and the corresponding accuracy. The words were chosen on the basis of the properties of their neighbors in English and in French, the L2 of these learners. Some words had enemies in English (i.e., words with similar orthography but distinct phonology), some had enemies in French, and others had no enemies. The question was whether native English speakers naming words in English would be affected by the presence of enemies in French. The results showed that when these speakers performed the naming task in English without prior activation of French, there were effects only of the English enemies, that is, no cross-language influence. However, when French was activated by requiring participants to name a block of French words aloud, there was then an effect of the French enemies on the time to name English words, but only for the most proficient L2 speakers. When the

Box 5.1 Illustrating psycholinguistic approaches to second language acquisition

Jared and Kroll (2001) examined the degree to which native speakers of English were influenced by their knowledge of French when reading words in English. According to a selective model of lexical access, reading words in one language alone, particularly when it is the first and dominant language (L1), should not be affected by the second language (L2). However, as the evidence we have reviewed suggests, there is a great deal of support for the alternative non-selective model, whereby lexical candidates in both languages are active during word recognition.

In this study, native English speakers who had been assessed to have relatively high or low levels of proficiency in French performed a simple word-naming task. A letter string was presented on a computer screen and participants simply had to pronounce the word aloud as quickly and as accurately as possible. The dependent measure was the speed of word naming.

Participants were pre-screened for their knowledge of French but then recruited to the experiment in English only. French was not mentioned when participants were recruited or during the first part of the experiment. They were simply asked to name a series of English words, presented one at a time, as quickly as possible. Following the first portion of the experiment, an interpolated French naming task was introduced. The interpolated task also involved simple naming but now the words to be pronounced aloud were French words. Following the French naming task, a final series of English words was presented and participants again were asked to name them aloud in English. The logic of the design was to assess English naming performance when participants were in a monolingual English mode, as best as could be established, and then to compare performance before and after French was activated explicitly.

To test whether word naming in L1 is influenced by L2, Jared and Kroll (2001) manipulated the types of English words that participants were asked to name. The English words varied according to whether they had enemies in English or French. An enemy is a word that is an orthographic neighbor of the target word but pronounced differently. For example, in English, the word "gave" is an enemy of the word "have" because although they are orthographic neighbors (they differ by only a single letter), they have distinct pronunciations.

Jared and Kroll included three types of English words that are listed below. Some words had no enemies in either language, some had enemies only in French, and others had enemies only in English:

1 No enemies: *stump, poke, drip*
2 French enemies: *strobe, pier, died*
3 English enemies: *steak, pear, dough*

If the phonology of French is activated when native English speakers are naming words in English, as the non-selective model supposes, then enemies in French as well as English would be expected to affect the time to name English words.

Jared and Kroll (2001) found that before the interpolated French naming task, neither less nor more proficient English–French bilinguals showed any effect of the presence of French enemies; only words with English enemies were named more slowly than the no-enemy controls. However, following the French naming task, the performance of the more proficient bilinguals was affected by the activation of French; they were slower to name English words when they had either English or French enemies relative to controls.

How does a non-selective model account for the absence of the cross-language effects in the first block of English word naming? These results are most consistent with a non-selective model in which it is assumed that the degree of cross-language interaction is a function of the relative activity of the non-target language. When the non-target language, French in this case, was not sufficiently active, there was little apparent influence on processing. However, once it became active, by virtue of explicitly requiring bilinguals to use French by naming words in French, or by the level of the bilingual's proficiency in French, or both, then regardless of the intention to name words in English only, there was an effect of the presence of competitors in both languages.

block of French words contained the enemies themselves (i.e., the French words that looked like but did not sound like the English words to be named), there were then inhibitory effects of French enemies on English naming for even the less skilled L2 speakers. These results converge closely with the findings for proficient bilinguals in that whether non-target words function as competitors during word recognition appears to depend on the degree to which both languages are active. When both languages are active, the system appears to be functionally non-selective with respect to language.

2.2 *Are semantic representations shared across the bilingual's two languages?*

The evidence reviewed above suggests that information about the lexical form of words in both of the bilingual's languages is active during word recognition. But what about meaning? It is perhaps surprising given the interest in issues of linguistic relativity (for recent reviews see Green, 1998; Pavlenko, 1999) that most models of bilingual representation and processing have assumed that words in each of the bilingual's languages access a common semantic code. For a number of reasons, the view that semantics are shared across languages has been dominant in the psycholinguistic literature. First, bilinguals are able to translate most words from one language to the other to a level that is at least functionally acceptable. Second, experiments using the semantic priming paradigm have shown that it is possible to observe priming across languages (e.g., Altarriba, 1990; Chen and Ng, 1989; Keatley, Spinks, and De Gelder, 1994; Meyer and Ruddy, 1974; Schwanenflugel and Rey, 1986; Tzelgov and Eben-Ezra, 1992). Third, semantically related words in both of the bilingual's languages tend to interfere with picture naming in either language (e.g., Costa et al., 1999; Hermans, 2000; Hermans, Bongaerts, de Bot, and Schreuder, 1998). If words in the two languages accessed fundamentally different representations,

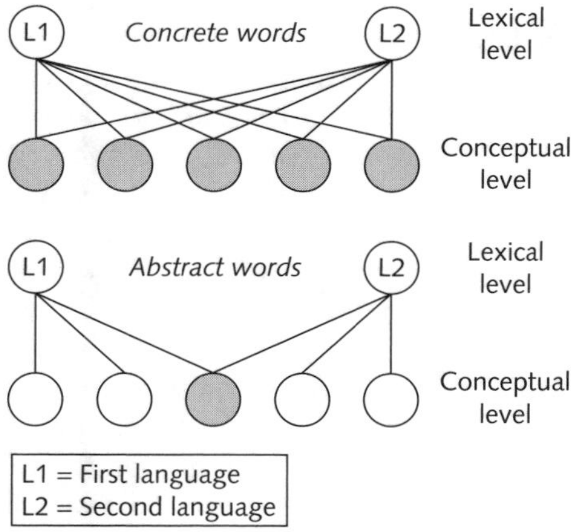

Figure 5.2 Distributed feature model
Source: Adapted from Van Hell and De Groot (1998)

then under the conditions of speeded timing in these tasks, we should not expect to see cross-language interactions. Fourth, models of lexical development suggest that during initial L2 acquisition, L1 semantics may be transferred to the new L2 word (e.g., Jiang, 2000). A note of caution in interpreting these findings is in order because much of the research on bilingual processing has used tasks limited to pictured objects and their names, thereby restricting the scope of the semantics to concrete nouns.

Recent developments in the realm of computational modeling have enabled a view of semantic representation that is graded so that concepts are not simply the same or different but differentiated in the degree to which they share types of semantic features (see McRae, de Sa, and Seidenberg, 1997, for an illustration of this approach in the monolingual domain). In the bilingual domain, De Groot and her colleagues (De Groot, 1992, 1993, 1995; De Groot, Dannenburg, and Van Hell, 1994; Van Hell, 1998; Van Hell and De Groot, 1998) proposed the distributed feature model shown in figure 5.2. The model represents concepts as constellations of activated semantic features. Across languages, the degree to which concepts are shared is hypothesized to be a function of word type, with more overlap for concrete than abstract nouns and for cognates than for non-cognate translations. The empirical results that support the model come from experiments on word translation. The time to translate words from one language to the other is generally faster for concrete words and cognates than for abstract words and non-cognates. To the extent that translation requires access to meaning, an issue that we will address in the next section, the time to perform translation will be fast when there is a high degree of overlap across languages and slow when there is a low degree of overlap.

A further qualification to the distributed feature model was described in a series of recent papers showing that ambiguity is also an important factor.

Schönpflug (1997) and Tokowicz and Kroll (forthcoming) examined the consequence of having more than a single translation equivalent for a given word. Words with more than a single dominant translation equivalent took longer to translate than words with only one, suggesting that both semantic alternatives were available and competing for selection. Tokowicz and Kroll also showed that at least for the English–Spanish bilinguals in their study, these effects were restricted to abstract words. Because abstract words are more likely to be ambiguous than concrete words, the initial demonstration of a concreteness effect in translation was likely to have been confounded with the number of available translation equivalents. This finding suggests that factors that influence the ease of computing a single meaning or the likelihood of having a set of semantic competitors available will determine bilingual performance, particularly when spoken production requires the selection of only a single candidate. Existing research does not allow a precise estimate of the manner in which each of these factors influences semantic processing within and across languages.

Like the work described above on lexical form activation in word recognition, the research on semantic access has focused largely on the performance of proficient bilinguals. A few studies have investigated changes in the ability to access semantics for L2 words with increasing L2 skill. Talamas et al. (1999) examined the ability of learners and proficient bilinguals to judge that two words were translation equivalents. In one condition of the experiment, the words were not translations of one another, but closely related semantically. For example, the English word *man* might be followed by the Spanish word *mujer* and the participant would be required to respond that they are not translation equivalents. Talamas et al. found that it took longer to reject these semantically related pairs than matched controls, but only for the proficient bilinguals; the learners did not appear to process the semantics directly. However, a pair-by-pair analysis based on the degree of semantic similarity between word pairs showed that the learners were sensitive to the semantics when pairs were very highly related. The results suggest that access to semantics for learners is a matter of degree.

The same general conclusion was reached in a study by Dufour and Kroll (1995) in which two groups of native English speakers, less and more proficient in French, performed a categorization task within and across the two languages. Participants saw a category prompt (e.g., *fruit*) and then an exemplar which was or was not a member of that category (e.g., *pear* or *table*). Their task was simply to decide whether the exemplar was a member of the category. Not surprisingly, Dufour and Kroll found that the less proficient French speakers were slower to respond in French than in English. However, they also found that the less proficient group was faster to respond in French when the category prompt was also in French than when it was in English. They hypothesized that the effect of the category prompt in English, the participants' L1, was to activate semantics too broadly for L2. Because the less proficient individuals were unlikely to know the names of all of the category members in French, the initial activation of the category in English may have increased the number of competitors from which the exemplar was selected. Dufour and Kroll proposed that learners do have access to semantics for L2 words, but only in a limited manner. In the next section we will return to the issue of how early in acquisition semantics are available directly for L2 words.

2.3 *On what basis are lexical and semantic representations connected for words and concepts in each language?*

Regardless of the commitment one makes to the architecture of lexical and semantic representations, a complete model of the lexicon must specify the manner in which lexical forms are mapped to their respective meanings. Potter et al. (1984) contrasted two alternatives for how these mappings might operate. According to the word association model, associations are formed between new L2 words and their corresponding translation equivalents in L1. L2 is therefore always mediated through L1. However, according to the concept mediation model, concepts can be accessed directly by and for L2 words, without L1 activation. To test the two models, Potter et al. contrasted the performance of a group of highly proficient Chinese–English bilinguals on picture naming and translation. If L2 is mediated via L1 as the word association model predicts, then word-to-word translation should bypass semantics and thereby be faster than picture naming, a task which cannot bypass conceptual access. However, if concepts can be accessed directly for L2 words as the concept mediation model predicts, then both translation and picture naming should require approximately the same amount of processing time to be performed. Potter et al. found no evidence that translation was faster than picture naming and therefore concluded in favor of the concept mediation alternative. Surprisingly, they found precisely the same pattern of results for a group of less proficient L2 speakers, suggesting that direct conceptual processing of L2 was in place very early in acquisition (for additional evidence for direct conceptual access for L2, even for learners at early phases of acquisition, see Altarriba and Mathis, 1997; Frenck-Mestre and Prince, 1997).

The conclusions of the Potter et al. (1984) study were subsequently challenged by a series of experiments (Chen and Leung, 1989; Kroll and Curley, 1988) which showed that individuals at very early stages of L2 acquisition were indeed faster to translate than to name pictures, consistently with the predictions of the word association model. The results for the more proficient bilinguals in each of these studies replicated the pattern reported by Potter et al., suggesting that early in acquisition there is reliance on word-to-word mappings across the two languages, but with increasing proficiency there is an increasing ability to conceptually mediate L2. The evidence for concept mediation for less proficient learners in the Potter et al. study can be understood as a reflection of the nature of the participants tested. Potter et al.'s less proficient bilinguals were native English-speaking high school students about to leave

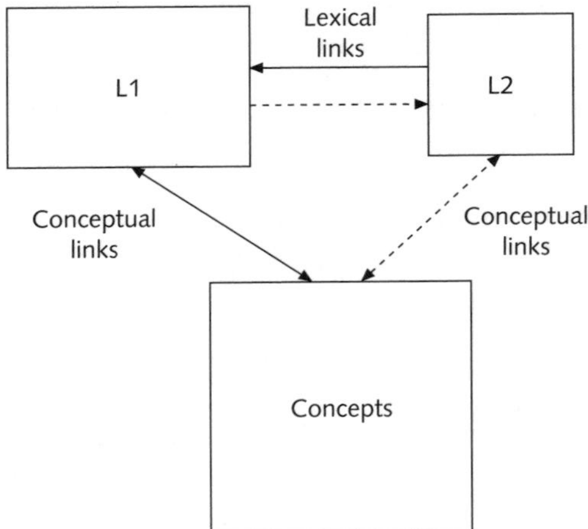

Figure 5.3 Revised hierarchical model
Source: Adapted from Kroll and Stewart (1994)

for a summer in France. It seems likely that they were highly motivated to learn French and therefore past a very early stage of L2 acquisition that characterizes more typical classroom learners. The less proficient participants in the subsequent studies were at an earlier stage of acquisition and therefore more likely to reveal the word association pattern.

How does the shift from word association to concept mediation occur? Kroll and Stewart (1994) proposed the revised hierarchical model (RHM) shown in figure 5.3 to account for the development of conceptual processing with increasing L2 skill. The model includes the direct lexical connections of the word association model in addition to the word-to-concept connections of the concept mediation model. However, unlike the earlier models, the RHM proposes differential weighting of the strength of the word-to-word and word-to-concept connections for L1 and L2. The model assumes that early in L2 acquisition, L2 words are associated with their L1 translations for the purpose of accessing the meaning that is already represented for those concepts. Thus strong lexical links map L2 to L1. At the lexical level, only weak activation of associative links from L1 to L2 is assumed. Initially, only word-to-word associations will link L2 to L1. With increasing L2 proficiency, direct conceptual connections from L2 words to semantics will begin to develop. However, for all but the most balanced bilinguals, the word-to-concept connections will be stronger for L1 than for L2. (For recent reviews of research based on the RHM, see also Kroll and De Groot, 1997; Kroll, Michael, and Sankaranarayanan, 1998; Kroll and Tokowicz, 2001.)

Kroll and Stewart (1994) tested two predictions of the RHM. First, if lexical associations link words in L2 to their translation equivalents in L1, then translation from L2 to L1 should be faster than translation from L1 to L2, because it reflects a more direct processing route. Second, if L1 words are more likely to activate semantics than L2 words, then translation from L1 to L2 should also be more likely to be influenced by the manipulation of semantic variables than translation from L2 to L1. Each of these predictions was examined in an experiment in which highly proficient, but L1 dominant, Dutch–English bilinguals translated words in both directions. The words were presented in lists that were organized by semantic category (e.g., all fruits or all vehicles) or randomly mixed. The results supported both predictions. Translation was faster from L2 to L1 than from L1 to L2, a phenomenon termed the *translation asymmetry*. Furthermore, only translation from L1 to L2 was affected by the context of a semantically organized list; there was no effect from L2 to L1.

More recent research has provided mixed support for the claims of the RHM. Sholl, Sankaranarayanan, and Kroll (1995) demonstrated that transfer from a picture-naming task to translation was differential for the two directions of translation, with priming from the conceptual picture-naming task only to translation from L1 to L2, the direction hypothesized to be conceptually mediated. This result provides strong support for the asymmetry assumed within the RHM. In contrast, in a study examining the effects of semantically related picture context on translation, La Heij, Kerling, and Van der Velden (1996) found semantic effects in both directions of translation, contrary to the claims of the RHM. Because La Heij et al.'s participants were Dutch–English bilinguals very similar to those used in the Kroll and Stewart (1994) study, it is unlikely that the nature of the participants' bilingualism or the nature of the two languages can account for the observed differences. (For further discussion of this issue, see Kroll and De Groot, 1997; Kroll and Tokowicz, 2001.)

Unlike the BIA or distributed feature models described in the previous sections, the RHM is explicitly a developmental model. It assumes that the connections between words and concepts in bilingual memory change with increasing proficiency in the L2. At early stages of acquisition, the cross-language lexical connections will be critical, whereas with greater L2 proficiency there will be increasingly direct semantic processing of L2. A clear prediction of the RHM is that translation from L2 to L1, the direction of translation hypothesized to operate by direct access to translation equivalents, should be in place early in acquisition, whereas L1 to L2 translation, the direction of translation hypothesized to require conceptual access, will be more difficult for learners to perform. If L2 is linked to L1 initially for the purpose of accessing meaning, then those connections should be the first available to the learner. A recent study by Kroll, Michael, Tokowicz, and Dufour (forthcoming) examined the developmental predictions of the RHM by having learners at different levels of L2 proficiency translate in each direction and name words in each language. The results supported the prediction that translation from L1 to L2, the route hypothesized to be conceptually mediated, changes more over the course of acquisition than translation from L2 to L1. Although learners' L2 vocabularies increase over time, they are capable of translating from L2 to L1 as quickly and almost as accurately as more proficient speakers. In contrast, translation from L1 to L2 is very slow and error prone for learners. The comparison with simple word naming (i.e., naming aloud) further demonstrates that the problem in L1 to L2 translation is not simply one of producing the L2 phonology. Learners are indeed slower to name words in L2 than in L1, but that difference is generally small relative to the magnitude of the translation asymmetry. Because learners at this stage appear able to access concepts for some L2 words (e.g., Dufour and Kroll, 1995; Talamas et al., 1999), the difficulty in performing L1 to L2 translation suggests that it is not access to concepts that is the central problem, but rather difficulty in lexicalizing concepts into L2 words. We take up this issue in the next section.

2.4 *How are words spoken in the second language when a more dominant alternative almost always exists in the first language?*

How do speakers of more than one language manage to speak their ideas in the intended language? Although even highly skilled bilinguals occasionally make speech errors (e.g., Poulisse, 1997, 1999) and have more tip-of-the-tongue experiences than monolinguals (e.g., Gollan and Silverberg, forthcoming), their speech is not typically marked by random language mixtures. Rather, bilinguals appear able to modulate their spoken production so that they speak in one language alone or code switch with another bilingual. How is this finely tuned control achieved? One possibility was proposed by Grosjean (1997, 2001), who suggested that bilinguals adjust the relative activation of their two languages along a continuum from a monolingual mode, in which one language is spoken primarily, to a bilingual mode, in which there is a high level of activation of both languages. However, it is not entirely clear what factors determine the control of language mode itself: hearing someone speak a language that is known, or processing contextual information in one language only, or anticipating that listeners also speak both of the speaker's languages?

The issue of how the intended language is selected prior to speaking is particularly problematic because a set of recent picture-naming studies suggests that lexical alternatives in both of the bilingual's languages may be active for some period of time prior to the selection of the word to be produced. The intention to speak in one language does not appear to be sufficient to achieve selective access to information in that language alone. A model of language production based on work by Poulisse and Bongaerts (1994) and Hermans (2000) is shown in figure 5.4. The model adapts monolingual production models (e.g., Levelt, 1989; Levelt, Roelofs, and Meyer, 1999) for the bilingual case (see also De Bot and Schreuder, 1993, for another example of a bilingual model of production). The figure illustrates the case in which a bilingual who speaks both English and Spanish is attempting to name the pictured object as *chair* in English. Three levels of representation are depicted. First, at the conceptual level, semantic features are activated corresponding to the meaning of the

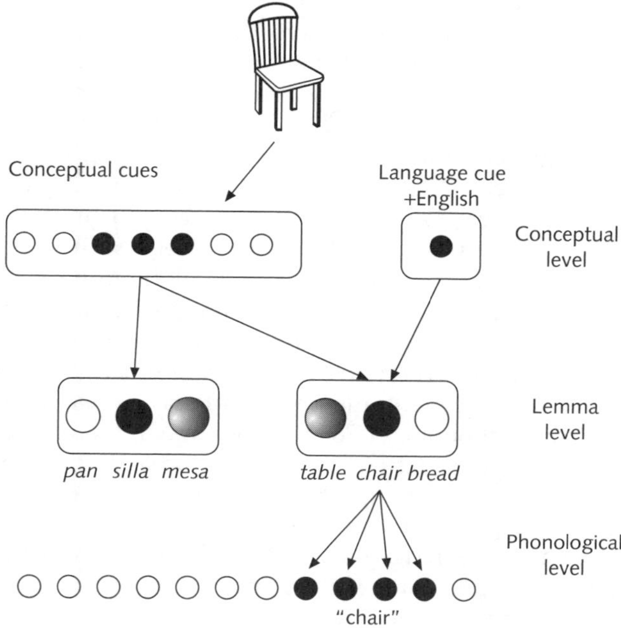

Figure 5.4 Models of bilingual language production
Source: Adapted from Poulisse and Bongaerts (1994); Hermans (2000)

pictured object. At the same level, there is also information about the intended language of the utterance, in this case English. At the next level, lemmas, or abstract lexical representations, are specified for each of the lexical alternatives in the two languages. At the lemma level, both language alternatives, *chair* in English and *silla* in Spanish, will be active to some degree as will lemmas that are semantically related to the meaning of the object, such as *table* in English and *mesa* in Spanish. Finally, at the phonological level, the form of the spoken utterance is specified. In the model depicted in figure 5.4, lexical access is assumed to be language non-selective through the level of the lemma. Notice that although both *chair* and *silla* are assumed to be available as abstract lexical representations, only the phonology of *chair* is actually specified.

Without going into much more detail about the workings of the model, one can appreciate immediately that the further into the production process alternatives in the non-target language are active, the more potential competition there will be across languages. What is the evidence for cross-language competition? To investigate this issue, research on language production has used the picture–word interference paradigm. A picture is presented briefly and preceded or followed by a word, presented visually or auditorily, after a variable time interval. The task is to name the picture and ignore the word. By manipulating the relation of the word distractor to the picture's name, it is possible to infer the nature of the processes that are active at a given point in planning the spoken utterance. In monolingual versions of the task, words that are semantically related to the picture's name generally produce interference and words that are related to the phonological form of the picture's name produce facilitation (e.g., Lupker, 1979, 1982; Rosinski, 1977; Starreveld and La Heij, 1995). Moreover, semantic effects tend to be greater early in the planning of an utterance and phonological effects tend to be observed late, although there is some debate about the precise timing of these processes (e.g., Levelt et al., 1991; Schriefers, Meyer, and Levelt, 1990; Starreveld, 2000; Starreveld and La Heij, 1995).

A recent set of monolingual production studies holds particularly important implications for bilinguals. Peterson and Savoy (1998) and Jescheniak and Schriefers (1998) showed that when an object has more than one name (i.e., it could be named by either of two close synonyms, such as *sofa* or *couch*), the unintended alternative appears to be active in the process of speech planning to the point of having specified its phonology. For a monolingual, there may be consequences of having a competitor active on only rare occasions, since few words have synonyms that are close enough to cause a delay in production. However, for a proficient bilingual, for whom most words have a translation equivalent in the other language, having a word in the other language ready to speak will have serious implications for the speed and accuracy of production unless one language alone can be selected.

The evidence on bilingual speakers suggests that the other-language alternative is available well into the process of planning to speak a word in one language alone. A series of cross-language picture–word interference studies (Costa et al., 1999; Hermans, 2000; Hermans et al., 1998) showed that production in one language is influenced by the presence of a distractor word in the other language. Semantically related distractor words produce interference in naming a picture even when the picture is named in one language and the distractor word appears in the other language. Like the example illustrated in figure 5.4, this result suggests that at the lemma level, alternatives in both languages compete for selection. In picture–word interference, when the word distractor is itself the name of the picture, there is facilitation of naming latencies relative to unrelated controls. Both Costa et al. (1999) and Hermans (2000) showed that there was also facilitation, although smaller in magnitude, when the distractor was the translation of the word to be produced. Furthermore, when the picture has a cognate name that is phonologically similar in the bilingual's two languages, there is facilitation of picture-naming latencies relative to non-cognate controls (Costa, Caramazza, and Sebastian-Galles, 2000; Kroll, Dijkstra, Janssen, and Schriefers, 2000). Because cognates are unlikely to share the same lemma (e.g., even similar sounding translation equivalents may differ on dimensions such as grammatical gender), the effect is likely to reflect the activation of shared phonology. Although there is some debate about the interpretation of these results with respect to the level at which the language is selected (see Costa et al., 1999, for a language-selective model based on these findings), the findings can be viewed as support for a model in which lexical alternatives in both languages are active, at least through the level of the lemma and possibly all the way to the phonology. The few studies of production in L2 learners also suggest that much of the difficulty that learners have in producing words in L2 is attributable to competition from more active L1 alternatives (Kroll et al., forthcoming).

Research on language production is at an early stage, so caution is warranted in drawing strong conclusions on the basis of the available evidence. Finding that lexical access appears to be language non-selective access in production is quite surprising given the top-down nature of processing in production tasks (see Kroll and Dijkstra, forthcoming, for a comparison of comprehension and production). It is also surprising given observations of fluent bilingual speech in context, where there is little suggestion of interference from the non-target language unless the speaker is intentionally code switching. Because most of the experimental evidence on language production has used picture-naming tasks, it is also likely that task-specific factors contribute to the observed results. It may be possible to select the language of production early in speech planning under some circumstances, for example when strong cues are present, but not in others (see Miller and Kroll, forthcoming, for an argument about selection in translation). However, what is very clear from the available evidence is that the intention to speak words in one language is not sufficient, in and of itself, to prevent the activation of words in the other language. In the next section we consider other ways in which control might be achieved.

2.5 *How is the activation of lexical form and meaning controlled so that bilinguals recognize and speak words in the intended language?*

The evidence we have reviewed provides a much more open picture of the bilingual lexicon than the early literature on this topic implied. Research on comprehension suggests that orthographic and phonological information about words in both languages is activated even when a bilingual is reading in one language alone. Likewise, research on production suggests that the translation equivalent and related words are active prior to speaking even when the bilingual intends to speak only in one of his or her two languages.

How is the activation and potential competition between candidates in the two languages modulated to achieve accurate comprehension and production? In past research, two general solutions have been proposed to explain how cross-language competition is resolved. One places the locus of selection and control within the functioning of the lexicon itself such that the factors that modulate the relative activation of words in each language determine the word that is selected (e.g., Dijkstra et al., 1998). The alternative is to assume that mechanisms external to the lexicon constrain the manner in which the output of lexical activity is utilized (e.g., Green, 1998; Thomas and Allport, 2000).

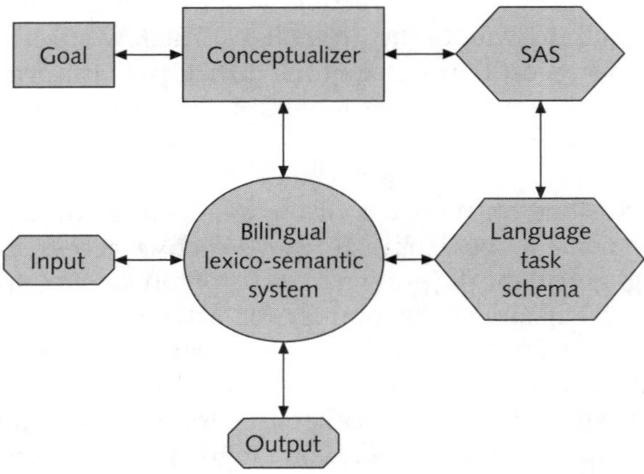

Figure 5.5 Inhibitory control model
Source: Adapted from Green (1998)

Green (1998) proposed the inhibitory control (IC) model to describe one way in which external regulation of the two languages might be achieved. The model, shown in figure 5.5, includes a set of mechanisms outside the lexical system itself that are hypothesized to work together with the output from the system to accomplish proficient performance. A full consideration of the workings of the model is beyond the scope of the present chapter (see Green, 1998, and associated commentaries for a more detailed discussion). In brief, the idea is that performance is determined by an interaction between a set of attentional mechanisms that serve to effect the goals associated with particular tasks and the activity within the bilingual lexicon that we have characterized in the preceding sections of this chapter. A focus within the IC model is to account for the ability of bilinguals to perform the intended task in the intended language. For example, when presented with a word to translate, how does a bilingual prevent himself or herself from naming the word aloud instead of translating it? According to the IC model, prior to the production of a spoken utterance, a conceptual representation is generated. This in turn activates the lexico-semantic system and also the supervisory attentional system or SAS. The SAS is hypothesized to control the activation of language task schemas.

To illustrate, the IC model offers an alternative interpretation of the translation asymmetry whereby translation is slower from L1 to L2 than from L2 to L1 (Kroll and Stewart, 1994). To translate from L1 to L2 it will be necessary to inhibit L1 lemmas in order to produce words in L2. Because L1 lemmas are assumed to be more active than L2 lemmas, they will require greater attentional resources to be suppressed so that L2 production can proceed. L1 to L2 translation will therefore be slower than L2 to L1 translation, not because the two routes to translation necessarily require different component processes, as the RHM proposed, but rather because the two translation tasks impose differential inhibitory demands.

An important source of evidence regarding inhibitory control comes from experiments on deliberate language switching. In a recent study, Meuter and Allport (1999) examined switching performance on a number-naming task in which the individual was instructed to name the number in one of their two languages depending on the color of the background on which the number appeared. They observed switch costs, with longer response times following language switches, but the switch costs were greater when bilinguals switched into their L1 than into their L2. The result may seem counter-intuitive, because we might think that L1 would always be more available. However, it can be understood in the context of models of inhibitory control, such as Green's (1998), in which it is assumed that more attentional resources are required to suppress the more active language. Switch costs are taken to be the consequence of having inhibited L1.

If inhibitory control is a central characteristic of bilingual language processing, then we need to expand our view of acquisition to include the development of control mechanisms in addition to the development of the lexicon and grammar. That is, L2 learners may need to acquire a new set of processing skills that fall outside the language itself to be able to effectively use both languages. In previous work we have argued that this may be a particularly difficult task for L2 learners who are restricted to classroom exposure because it will be difficult to acquire cues that are unique to the new L2 (Kroll et al., 1998; Kroll and Tokowicz, 2001). In immersion contexts, the availability of linguistic and non-linguistic information that specifically marks the use of L2 may facilitate this process.

Kroll et al. (1998) described a study that attempted to examine the manner in which cues might be used to inhibit L1 during L2 acquisition. A group of native English-speaking students who had no knowledge of Dutch or German were taught 40 Dutch words. In one study condition, the Dutch words were presented together with their English translations. In another study condition, they were presented with pictures of the objects that they named. For half of the pictures, the objects were shown in their normal orientation. For the remaining pictures, the objects were presented in a non-canonical orientation (e.g., upside down or to one side). Kroll et al. hypothesized that the non-canonical presentation of the objects might facilitate acquisition of the new Dutch name because it would slow down the process of retrieving the L1 name. At test, participants either named pictures in Dutch or translated English words into Dutch. The results showed a clear processing advantage for the Dutch words that had been learned by association with the non-canonical pictures. More surprising was the fact that this advantage held even when participants were tested on a translation task, in the absence of the picture itself. We would not suggest that having students in classroom settings slant their heads to one side might facilitate L2 vocabulary acquisition. More modestly, the results suggest that identifying factors that reduce the activity of L1 or uniquely cue L2 may facilitate learning.

3 Implications of Psycholinguistic Research for Second Language Pedagogy

As we have discussed in this chapter, recent research on language and cognitive processes in proficient bilinguals suggests that lexical and semantic information in L1 is activated during both comprehension and production in L2. If this is the case for skilled bilinguals, then we might logically assume that less skilled second language learners would be similarly affected, if not to a greater degree, by unintended L1 activation and might have a more difficult time controlling the cross-linguistic competition. As mentioned previously, there is little psycholinguistic research investigating cross-linguistic competition in second language learners. However, second language teaching methods have long been aware of cross-language competition and have been striving to minimize it.

In examining second language pedagogy, we find methods for teaching a second language that are predicated on notions of inhibiting L1 activation. For example, in today's communicative second language classroom, the use of the first language is typically avoided. Learners in a Spanish classroom are often told to think of that classroom as a "little Spain or Mexico." Spanish teachers, in an attempt to simulate this cultural oasis, go to great lengths to maintain Spanish in the class at all times. In teaching vocabulary, they use various techniques that avoid the L1, such as pictures, context, miming, and circumlocution, in an attempt to promote "form–meaning" connections for the learners in the L2. This process of making form–meaning connections is what Terrell (1986) terms "binding" (p. 214). He explains that binding is "the cognitive and affective mental process that occurs when an instructor insists that a new word ultimately be associated directly with its meaning and not with a translation" (p. 214). The use of the L1 is almost seen as detrimental to the learning process. Maintaining L2 at all times and keeping learners in the L2 mode is a critical component of the communicative second language classroom.

Historically, if we look at other second language teaching methods, we see similar assumptions regarding L1 emerge. For example, the Direct method (commonly known as the Berlitz method) assumed that learners would acquire language much like children, through direct association of words and phrases with objects and actions and an enormous amount of input. The native language was not used and translation was strictly forbidden. Definitions of new vocabulary were given via paraphrases in the target language. In the same vein, the overarching goal of the Audiolingual method of the 1950s was to develop in learners the same abilities that native speakers have, handling the language at an unconscious level. L1 was to be banned from the classroom and a "cultural island" was to be maintained. Essentially, one was to teach L2 without reference to L1.

In the 1960s Total Physical Response (TPR) was proposed (Asher, 1977). The underlying philosophy of TPR is that language comprehension should develop before any oral participation, as it does with children. It is based on the belief that skills can be acquired more rapidly if you involve the kinesthetic-sensory system. In fact, TPR is linked to the *trace theory* of memory (e.g., Katona, 1940), which claims that activities such as motor activity or verbal rehearsal will strengthen the memory connection and will then facilitate recall. Accordingly, this method uses oral commands of which students show their understanding by performing an action. The target language is the exclusive language of instruction. Asher describes TPR: "Understanding should be developed through movement of the student's body" (p. 4). "When you cast material in the imperative there is no translation" (p. 20). It was therefore assumed that by using the kinesthetic-sensory system, one could bypass the L1 linguistic system, thus facilitating acquisition.

In the 1970s the Natural approach (Terrell, 1986) emerged. This methodology was based on Krashen's (1982) theory of second language acquisition that made the strong claim that comprehensible input causes acquisition. The use of the L2 was then seen as the only tool for providing comprehensible input to the learners; L1 had no place in the Natural approach. Another method that avoided the L1 was *The Silent Way* (Gattegno, 1976), a method which used colored wooden sticks called Cuisenaire rods, language charts, and the L2 exclusively. This method seemed to be predicated on the notion of language control. In fact, Gattegno states "Throughout our oral work with rods and the visual diction on the charts, we have carefully avoided the use of the students' native language. We have even succeeded in blocking the native language so that the students relate to the new language directly" (p. 99). Clearly, controlling any cross-linguistic interference was a critical aspect of this approach.

The assumption that it is beneficial for foreign language learners to think as much as possible through the language they are learning is not new and not specific to any one teaching method. As early as 1966, Mario Pei, in his book *How to Learn Languages and What Languages to Learn*, gave students specific learning hints. He states, "Link the content of the foreign phrase to its mental concept rather than to its English translation. If possible, link it to a pictorial object or action. The trick is to link the thought concept not with your own language, but with the language you are learning" (p. 101). This assumption is still prevalent among teachers today.

These teaching methods, in the past and today, whether intended to or not, are based on ideas about language activation and control (i.e., use of only L2 in the classroom and avoidance of L1). While the evidence from the psycholinguistic literature overwhelmingly suggests that words are active simultaneously in the proficient bilingual, we know that it is not the case that skilled bilinguals often produce words in the "wrong" language. Therefore, as noted above, a regulatory mechanism must control cross-language competition in skilled bilinguals. However, we do know that beginning bilinguals in the second language classroom often produce words in the wrong language. The critical question then becomes how learners begin to modulate the cross-linguistic activation that is present in the system in a manner similar to proficient bilinguals, and why some learners are more successful at it than others.

There are many questions in second language pedagogy that could be answered by psycholinguistic research. For example, do certain learners struggle in communicative classrooms that use only the L2 because they fail to inhibit the L1 as easily as others? Is it the case that inhibition of cross-linguistic interference is a critical component of second language acquisition? Moreover, is the communicative second language classroom that essentially imposes a specific L2 language mode helping or hindering the development of cross-linguistic control? Are there processing costs when less proficient individuals are forced to assume a monolingual mode in L2? And, if so, are those initial processing costs beneficial for the development of an inhibitory control mechanism? Finally, is it simply the case that some learners, due to certain cognitive differences, are better able to generate internal strategies for suppressing L1 and processing L2?

The answers to these questions hold important implications for teaching methods and psycholinguistic models alike. Research on skilled bilingual lexical processing will help to inform our understanding of second language acquisition. If we begin to understand what it is that allows one to become a proficient bilingual, we can then re-evaluate our teaching methodologies and attempt to modify them to facilitate the developmental process. Similarly, many psycholinguistic models, such as the BIA model, address skilled bilingual processing but make no explicit claims about the nature of lexical competition during acquisition. Currently absent from the psycholinguistic literature is a comprehensive picture of how lexical activity changes and is controlled from early stages of learning through high levels of skilled performance. Second language learners can provide this much needed information. In future research we anticipate that the cognitive processes underlying the development of second language acquisition and the proficient use of two languages by bilinguals will be the focus of unified models that relate developmental processes to the skilled state.

ACKNOWLEDGMENT

The writing of this chapter was supported in part by NSF Grant BCS-9905850 to Judith F. Kroll. Correspondence concerning this article should be addressed to Judith F. Kroll, Department of Psychology, 641 Moore Building, The Pennsylvania State University, University Park, PA 16802, USA. Electronic mail may be sent to jfk7@psu.edu.

REFERENCES

Altarriba, J. 1990: Constraints on interlingual facilitation effects in priming in Spanish–English bilinguals. Dissertation. Vanderbilt University.

Altarriba, J. and Mathis, K. M. 1997: Conceptual and lexical development in second language acquisition. *Journal of Memory and Language*, 36, 550–68.

Andrews, S. 1997: The effect of orthographic similarity on lexical retrieval: resolving neighborhood conflicts. *Psychonomic Bulletin and Review*, 4, 439–61.

Asher, J. 1977: *Learning Another Language Through Actions: The Complete Teacher's Guidebook*. Los Gatos, CA: Sky Oaks Productions.

Bialystok, E. 1997: Effects of bilingualism and biliteracy on children's emerging concepts of print. *Developmental Psychology*, 33, 429–40.

Bijeljac-Babic, R., Biardeau, A., and Grainger, J. 1997: Masked orthographic priming in bilingual word recognition. *Memory and Cognition*, 25, 447–57.

Birdsong, D. 1999: *Second Language Acquisition and the Critical Period Hypothesis*, Mahwah, NJ: Lawrence Erlbaum Associates.

Brysbaert, M., Van Dyck, G., and Van de Poel, M. 1999: Visual word recognition in bilinguals: evidence from masked phonological priming. *Journal of Experimental Psychology: Human Perception and Performance*, 25, 137–48.

Chen, H.-C. and Leung, Y.-S. 1989: Patterns of lexical processing in a nonnative language. *Journal of Experimental Psychology: Learning, Memory, and Cognition*, 15, 316–25.

Chen, H.-C. and Ng, M.-L. 1989: Semantic facilitation and translation priming effects in Chinese–English bilinguals. *Memory and Cognition*, 17, 454–62.

Costa, A., Caramazza, A., and Sebastian-Galles, N. 2000: The cognate facilitation effect: implications for models of lexical access. *Journal of Experimental Psychology: Learning, Memory, and Cognition*, 26, 1283–96.

Costa, A., Miozzo, M., and Caramazza, A. 1999: Lexical selection in bilinguals: do words in the bilingual's two lexicons compete for selection? *Journal of Memory and Language*, 41, 365–97.

De Bot, K. and Schreuder, R. 1993: Word production and the bilingual lexicon. In R. Schreuder and B. Weltens (eds), *The Bilingual Lexicon*. Amsterdam: John Benjamins, 191–214.

De Groot, A. M. B. 1992: Determinants of word translation. *Journal of Experimental Psychology: Learning, Memory, and Cognition*, 18, 1001–18.

De Groot, A. M. B. 1993: Word-type effects in bilingual processing tasks: support for a mixed representational system. In R. Schreuder and B. Weltens (eds), *The Bilingual Lexicon*. Amsterdam: John Benjamins, 27–51.

De Groot, A. M. B. 1995: Determinants of bilingual lexicosemantic organization. *Computer Assisted Language Learning*, 8, 151–80.

De Groot, A. M. B., Dannenburg, L., and van Hell, J. G. 1994: Forward and backward word translation by bilinguals. *Journal of Memory and Language*, 33, 600–29.

Dijkstra, A. and Van Heuven, W. J. B. 1998: The BIA model and bilingual word recognition. In J. Grainger and A. Jacobs (eds), *Localist Connectionist Approaches to Human Cognition*. Hillsdale, NJ: Lawrence Erlbaum Associates, 189–225.

Dijkstra, A., Grainger, J., and Van Heuven, W. J. B. 1999: Recognition of cognates and interlingual homographs: the neglected role of phonology. *Journal of Memory and Language*, 41, 496–518.

Dijkstra, A., Van Heuven, W. J. B., and Grainger, J. 1998: Simulating competitor effects with the Bilingual Interactive Activation model. *Psychologica Belgica*, 38, 177–96.

Dijkstra, A., Van Jaarsveld, H., and Ten Brinke, S. 1998: Interlingual homograph recognition: effects of task demands and language intermixing. *Bilingualism: Language and Cognition*, 1, 51–66.

Dijkstra, A., De Bruijn, E., Schriefers, H., and Ten Brinke, S. 2000: More on interlingual homograph recognition: language intermixing versus explicitness of instruction. *Bilingualism: Language and Cognition*, 3, 69–78.

Dufour, R. and Kroll, J. F. 1995: Matching words to concepts in two languages: a test of the concept mediation model of bilingual representation. *Memory and Cognition*, 23, 166–80.

Dussias, P. 2001: Bilingual sentence parsing. In J. L. Nicol (ed.), *One Mind, Two Languages: Bilingual Language Processing*. Cambridge, MA: Blackwell, 159–76.

Francis, W. 1999: Cognitive integration of language and memory in bilinguals: semantic representation. *Psychological Bulletin*, 125, 193–222.

Frenck-Mestre, C. and Prince, P. 1997: Second language autonomy. *Journal of Memory and Language*, 37, 481–501.

Gattegno, C. 1976: *The Common Sense of Teaching Foreign Languages*. New York: Educational Solutions.

Gollan, T. and Kroll, J. F. 2001: Bilingual lexical access. In B. Rapp (ed.), *The Handbook of Cognitive Neuropsychology: What Deficits Reveal about the Human Mind*. Philadelphia, PA: Psychology Press, 321–45.

Gollan, T. and Silverberg, N. forthcoming: Tip-of-the-tongue states in Hebrew–English bilinguals. *Bilingualism: Language and Cognition*.

Green, D. W. 1998: Mental control of the bilingual lexico-semantic system. *Bilingualism: Language and Cognition*, 1, 67–81.

Grosjean, F. 1997: Processing mixed language: issues, findings, and models. In A. M. B. De Groot and J. F. Kroll (eds), *Tutorials in Bilingualism: Psycholinguistic Perspectives*. Mahwah, NJ: Lawrence Erlbaum Associates, 225–54.

Grosjean, F. 2001: The bilingual's language modes. In J. L. Nicol (ed.), *One Mind, Two Languages: Bilingual Language Processing*. Cambridge, MA: Blackwell, 1–22.

Hermans, D. 2000: Word production in a foreign language. Doctoral dissertation. University of Nijmegen.

Hermans, D., Bongaerts, T., De Bot, K., and Schreuder, R. 1998: Producing words in a foreign language: can speakers prevent interference from their first language? *Bilingualism: Language and Cognition*, 1, 213–29.

Jared, D. and Kroll, J. F. 2001: Do bilinguals activate phonological representations in one or both of their languages when naming words? *Journal of Memory and Language*, 44, 2–31.

Jescheniak, J. D. and Schriefers, K. I. 1998: Discrete serial versus cascading processing in lexical access in speech production: further evidence from the coactivation of near-synonyms. *Journal of Experimental Psychology: Learning, Memory, and Cognition*, 24, 1256–74.

Jiang, N. 2000: Lexical representation and development in a second language. *Applied Linguistics*, 21, 47–77.

Katona, G. 1940: *Organizing and Memorizing: Studies in the Psychology of Learning and Teaching*. New York: Columbia University Press.

Keatley, C., Spinks, J., and De Gelder, B. 1994: Asymmetrical semantic facilitation between languages. *Memory and Cognition*, 22, 70–84.

Krashen 1982: *Principles and Practices in Second Language Acquisition*. New York: Pergamon.

Kroll, J. F. and Curley, J. 1988: Lexical memory in novice bilinguals: the role of concepts in retrieving second language words. In M. Gruneberg, P. Morris, and R. Sykes (eds), *Practical Aspects of Memory. Vol. 2*. London: John Wiley, 389–95.

Kroll, J. F. and De Groot, A. M. B. 1997: Lexical and conceptual memory in the bilingual: mapping form to meaning in two languages. In A. M. B. De Groot and J. F. Kroll (eds), *Tutorials in Bilingualism: Psycholinguistic Perspectives*. Mahwah, NJ: Lawrence Erlbaum Associates, 169–99.

Kroll, J. F. and Dijkstra, A. forthcoming: The bilingual lexicon. In R. Kaplan (ed.), *Handbook of Applied Linguistics*. Oxford: Oxford University Press.

Kroll, J. F. and Stewart, E. 1994: Category interference in translation and picture naming: evidence for asymmetric connections between bilingual memory representations. *Journal of Memory and Language*, 33, 149–74.

Kroll, J. F. and Tokowicz, N. 2001: The development of conceptual representation for words in a second language. In J. L. Nicol (ed.), *One Mind, Two Languages: Bilingual Language Processing*. Cambridge, MA: Blackwell, 49–71.

Kroll, J. F., Michael, E., and Sankaranarayanan, A. 1998: A model of bilingual representation and its implications for second language acquisition. In A. F. Healy and L. E. Bourne (eds), *Foreign Language Learning: Psycholinguistic Experiments on Training and Retention*. Mahwah, NJ: Lawrence Erlbaum Associates, 365–95.

Kroll, J. F., Dijkstra, A., Janssen, N., and Schriefers, H. 2000: Selecting the language in which to speak: Experiments on lexical access in bilingual production. Paper presented at the 41st Annual Meeting of the Psychonomic Society. New Orleans, LA.

Kroll, J. F., Michael, E., Tokowicz, N., and Dufour, R. forthcoming: The development of lexical fluency in a second language.

La Heij, W., Kerling, R., and Van der Velden, E. 1996: Nonverbal context effects in forward and backward translation: evidence for concept mediation. *Journal of Memory and Language*, 35, 648–65.

Levelt, W. J. M. 1989: *Speaking: From Intention to Articulation*. Cambridge, MA: MIT Press.

Levelt, W. J. M., Roelofs, A., and Meyer, A. S. 1999: A theory of lexical access in speech production. *Behavioral and Brain Sciences*, 22, 1–75.

Levelt, W. J. M., Schriefers, H., Vorberg, D., Meyer, A. S., Pechman, T., and Havinga, J. 1991: The time course of lexical access in speech production: a study of picture naming. *Psychological Review*, 98, 122–42.

Long, M. H. 1990: Maturational constraints on language development. *Studies in Second Language Acquisition*, 12, 251–85.

Long, M. H. 1993: Second language acquisition as a function of age: substantive findings and methodological issues. In K. Hyltenstam and A. Viberg (eds), *Progression and Regression in Language*. Cambridge: Cambridge University Press, 196–221.

Lupker, S. J. 1979: The semantic nature of response competition in the picture–word interference task. *Memory and Cognition*, 7, 485–95.

Lupker, S. J. 1982: The role of phonetic and orthographic similarity in picture–word interference. *Canadian Journal of Psychology*, 36, 349–67.

MacWhinney, B. 1999: *The Emergence of Language*. Cambridge, MA: MIT Press.

McClelland, J. L. and Rumelhart, D. E. 1981: An interactive activation model of context effects in letter perception. Part 1: an account of basic findings. *Psychological Review*, 88, 375–405.

McRae, J., de Sa, V. R., and Seidenberg, M. S. 1997: On the nature and scope of featural representations of word meaning. *Journal of Experimental Psychology: General*, 126, 99–130.

Meuter, R. F. I. and Allport, A. 1999: Bilingual language switching in naming: asymmetrical costs of language selection. *Journal of Memory and Language*, 40, 25–40.

Meyer, D. E. and Ruddy, M. G. 1974: Bilingual word recognition: organization and retrieval of alternative lexical codes. Paper presented at the Eastern Psychological Association Meeting. Philadelphia, PA.

Miller, N. A. and Kroll, J. F. forthcoming: Stroop effects in bilingual translation.

Pavlenko, A. 1999: New approaches to concepts in bilingual memory. *Bilingualism: Language and Cognition*, 2, 209–30.

Pei, M. 1966: *How to Learn Languages and What Languages to Learn*. New York: Harper and Row.

Peterson, R. R. and Savoy, P. 1998: Lexical selection and phonological encoding during language production: evidence for cascaded processing. *Journal of Experimental Psychology: Learning, Memory, and Cognition*, 24, 539–57.

Potter, M. C., So, K.-F., Von Eckardt, B., and Feldman, L. B. 1984: Lexical and conceptual representation in beginning and more proficient bilinguals. *Journal of Verbal Learning and Verbal Behavior*, 23, 23–38.

Poulisse, N. 1997: Language production in bilinguals. In A. M. B. De Groot and J. F. Kroll (eds), *Tutorials in Bilingualism: Psycholinguistic Perspectives*. Mahwah, NJ: Lawrence Erlbaum Associates, 201–24.

Poulisse, N. 1999: *Slips of the Tongue. Speech Errors in First and Second Language Acquisition*. Amsterdam and Philadelphia: John Benjamins.

Poulisse, N. and Bongaerts, T. 1994: First language use in second language production. *Applied Linguistics*, 15, 36–57

Rosinski, R. R. 1977: Picture–word interference is semantically based. *Child Development*, 48, 643–7.

Sánchez-Casas, R. M., Davis, C. W., and García-Albea, J. E. 1992: Bilingual lexical processing: exploring the cognate–noncognate distinction. *European Journal of Cognitive Psychology*, 4, 293–310.

Schönpflug, U. 1997: Bilingualism and memory. Paper presented at the International Symposium on Bilingualism. Newcastle-upon-Tyne.

Schriefers, H., Meyer, A. S., and Levelt, W. J. M. 1990: Exploring the time-course of lexical access in production: picture–word interference studies. *Journal of Memory and Language*, 29, 86–102.

Schwanenflugel, P. J. and Rey, M. 1986: Interlingual semantic facilitation: evidence for a common representational system in the bilingual. *Journal of Memory and Language*, 25, 605–18.

Sholl, A., Sankaranarayanan, A., and Kroll, J. F. 1995: Transfer between picture naming and translation: a test of asymmetries in bilingual memory. *Psychological Science*, 6, 45–9.

Smith, M. C. 1997: How do bilinguals access lexical information? In A. M. B. De Groot and J. F. Kroll (eds), *Tutorials in Bilingualism: Psycholinguistic Perspectives*. Mahwah, NJ: Lawrence Erlbaum Associates, 145–68.

Starreveld, P. A. 2000: On the interpretation of onsets of auditory context effects in word production. *Journal of Memory and Language*, 42, 497–525.

Starreveld, P. A. and La Heij, W. 1995: Semantic interference, orthographic facilitation, and their interaction in naming tasks. *Journal of Experimental Psychology: Learning, Memory, and Cognition*, 21, 686–98.

Talamas, A., Kroll, J. F., and Dufour, R. 1999: From form to meaning: stages in the acquisition of second language vocabulary. *Bilingualism: Language and Cognition*, 2, 45–58.

Terrell, T. D. 1986: Acquisition in the natural approach: the binding/access framework. *Modern Language Journal*, 75, 52–63.

Thomas, M. S. C. and Allport, A. 2000: Language switching costs in bilingual visual word recognition. *Journal of Memory and Language*, 43, 44–66.

Tokowicz, N. and Kroll, J. F. forthcoming: Accessing meaning for words in two languages: the effects of concreteness and multiple translations in production.

Tzelgov, J. and Eben-Ezra, S. 1992: Components of the between-language semantic priming effect. *European Journal of Cognitive Psychology*, 4, 253–72.

Van Hell, J. G. 1998: Cross-language processing and bilingual memory organization. Doctoral dissertation. University of Amsterdam.

Van Hell, J. G. and De Groot, A. M. B. 1998: Conceptual representation in bilingual memory: effects of concreteness and cognate status in word association. *Bilingualism: Language and Cognition*, 1, 193–211.

Van Heuven, W. J. B., Dijkstra, A., and Grainger, J. 1998: Orthographic neighborhood effects in bilingual word recognition. *Journal of Memory and Language*, 39, 458–83.

6 Near-Nativeness

ANTONELLA SORACE

1 Introduction

One of the central questions in contemporary adult second language acquisition theory is whether, and to what extent, Universal Grammar (UG) still constrains the acquisition process: given that adults can rely on general cognitive abilities, it is at least conceivable that they may use them, instead of UG, in the task of learning a second language, particularly if UG, for maturational reasons, ceases to operate after a certain age. Indeed, this may appear intuitively plausible, given two obvious differences between first (L1) and second (L2) language acquisition: first, adult learners already know (at least) one other language: the *initial state* of the child and of the adult are not the same (e.g., Schwartz, 1998; Schwartz and Eubank, 1996; Schwartz and Sprouse, 1994); second, unlike children, who reach perfect mastery of whatever language they are exposed to, many adults after long periods of exposure to a second language display varying degrees of "imperfection" (by monolingual native standards), and even those who are capable of nativelike performance often have knowledge representations that differ considerably from those of native speakers (Sorace, 1993). So not only the initial state but also the *final state* of the child and of the adult learner are different.

But how different can the final state be? Research specifically focused on ultimate attainment can tell us what kind of "steady state" can be reached in non-primary language acquisition, whether such a state is quantitatively and/or qualitatively different from the monolingual steady state, and whether it is UG-constrained. The characteristics of the best attainable final state – that is, the competence of near-native speakers – are, in a sense, more revealing of UG constraints on L2 acquisition than those of other stages (see Borer, 1996, on this point). If it is found, for example, that intermediate grammars appear to violate UG, the argument can always be made that, given more input, or more time, or a better learning environment, the non-native grammar may in due course converge on the target. However, if adult learners have become virtually undistinguishable from native speakers, and continue to benefit from full exposure to the L2, they can be assumed to have progressed to the furthest attainable competence level: any differences between their grammar and the target grammar may be considered permanent, and any difference that embodies a UG violation may likewise be regarded as a permanent feature of this grammar.

The evidence from second language acquisition research is rather contradictory. On the one hand, adult second language acquisition is regarded as (i) incomplete, (ii) variable, and (iii) non-equipotential in comparison with L1 acquisition (see Bley-Vroman, 1990). We know that there are some age-related effects: generally speaking, starting young seems to confer some advantages, although it is by no means clear what the reasons are (Johnson and Newport, 1989; Long, 1990). On the other hand, we also know that there is a "logical problem" of second language acquisition; that properties that are not instantiated in the L1 and are not explicitly taught may be successfully acquired; and that interlanguages are, by and large, natural languages (i.e., they present no violations of Universal Grammar), although they may also be shaped by other cognitive principles (White, 1989, this volume).

Most research to date adopts as points of reference the monolingual native speaker and L1 acquisition by monolinguals. In addition, knowledge of the L1 is regarded as a factor that can have a determinant influence on L2 attainment but is itself unaffected by it. It will be suggested in this chapter that the majority of non-native speakers may develop a competence – *in both the L2 and the L1* – which differs, often in non-obvious ways, from the monolingual native's (Sorace, 1999, 2000a, 2000b). The phenomenon of optionality, which is the central focus of this chapter, is one such non-obvious difference that characterizes near-native grammars.

The chapter is structured as follows. Section 2 provides a short overview of research on ultimate attainment. Section 3 examines the phenomenon of optionality, exploring some of its implications for theories of generative grammar and comparing its manifestations in the development of child grammars and adult interlanguage grammars. Section 4 deals with constraints on optionality. Section 5 sketches out the effects of L2 ultimate attainment on the L1 grammar of the near-native speaker in terms of emerging optionality. Finally, section 6 draws some general conclusions.

2 Perspectives on Near-Nativeness and Empirical Evidence

Empirical studies of near-nativeness to date have focused on the "completeness vs. incompleteness" issue (see, e.g., Schachter, 1990). The reasoning guiding this research has been that if near-natives have the same knowledge as that exhibited by natives, the existence of UG constraints on L2 acquisition is confirmed; if, on the other hand, near-natives do not possess this knowledge, their competence is missing particular properties because it is not UG-constrained. This line of argument is fundamentally flawed because it does not consider the possibility of other UG-constrained final outcomes (see Sorace, 1996a; White, 1996). Furthermore, the assessment of near-nativeness has targeted isolated grammatical properties, rather than clusters of properties related to particular parameters. As Neeleman and Weerman (1997) maintain, success in the acquisition of what they call "construction-specific" parameters (i.e., parameters that are manifested only in one construction) is compatible both with a general learning strategies model and with a UG model, thus making it difficult to distinguish between the two. In contrast, success in the acquisition of parameters that are tied to a number of different constructions is unambiguously due to UG constraints, since such parameters entail a range of empirical consequences beyond the input to which the learner is exposed.

More generally, existing studies of near-nativeness support a variety of (often contradictory) conclusions, reflecting a lack of consensus over what counts as "UG-constrained behavior" and ultimately about what counts as "near-native." The following brief summary of the main studies carried out to date will highlight this multiplicity of views in the field.

2.1 *Studies of ultimate attainment*

The pioneering study by Coppieters (1987) tested near-native speakers of French from a variety of language backgrounds. The variables investigated included both semantic contrasts (e.g., tense/aspect distinctions) and syntactic conditions (cliticization and raising). The method used was a grammaticality judgment test. The results indicated significant differences between native and non-native norms. Interestingly, the most dramatic differences involved not so much syntactic as subtle semantic or interpretive knowledge.[1] This discrepancy is suggestive of crucial differences in near-native representations between purely syntactic aspects of the L2 grammar, which are nativelike, and syntax–semantics interface aspects, which may not be. As will be seen in section 4, recent research confirms the importance of this distinction. Inspiring as it was, however, Coppieters's study was criticized on methodological grounds, particularly because of the impressionistic criteria employed in the selection of near-native speakers.

Birdsong's (1992) study was a methodologically more rigorous replication of Coppieters's work. It also tested near-native speakers of French on various syntactic and semantic properties, including some of those investigated by Coppieters. Methods used ranged from grammaticality judgments to think-aloud procedures. Birdsong's results pointed to the opposite conclusion to Coppieters's: there are no significant differences between native and non-native norms in a number of individual near-natives, although such differences are there when natives and near-natives are compared as groups.

White and Genesee (1996) studied 42 near-native speakers of English from various language backgrounds (though the majority were Francophones). To counterbalance the frequent criticism of arbitrariness and subjectiveness in the criteria used to identify near-native speakers, they used more rigorous selection procedures (interviews, psychological tests, ratings by two native speakers). The area of grammar tested was island constraints on movement, particularly the Empty Category Principle and the Subjacency Principle, which prohibit extraction out of complex NPs, adjuncts, and subjects. The tests employed included grammaticality judgments and question formation, and reaction times were also recorded. Their results supported Birdsong's conclusion: no differences were found between the performance of natives and that of near-natives, but reaction times were shorter for native speakers. White and Genesee's suggestion is that near-native competence is (or can be) the same as native competence. However, their study is open to the objection that, at least for the majority of Francophone subjects, responses were due to a combination of L1 knowledge and metalinguistic awareness (Eubank and Gregg, 1999).

Johnson et al. (1996), arguing against Sorace (1988), suggested that one could in principle expect consistent results from two successive replications of the same test with L2 advanced learners because their competence is unlikely to have changed substantially in the meantime. Johnson et al. studied very advanced Chinese speakers of English in order to assess the degree of consistency between two successive administrations of the same (aural) acceptability judgment test. Results suggested that natives are consistent, but non-natives are not; their knowledge is indeterminate. However, these findings may have been affected by the uneven proficiency level of the learners tested (whose average length of residence in the US ranged from 5 to 12 years), and by the choice of an aural acceptability judgment test, which, because of its demands on on-line comprehension, may have imposed an additional burden on the subjects, creating a confounding effect.

In contrast with the other studies, Sorace (1993) demonstrates that final states may be incomplete, but may also be complete *and* systematically different from the target (see box 6.1). Her study targeted English and French near-native

Box 6.1 Clitic-climbing and auxiliary selection (Sorace, 1993)

Research question:

i Do near-native speakers of Italian acquire the constraints on auxiliary selection in restructuring constructions, specifically constructions with and without clitic-climbing?

ii Does the difference between L1 French (which has auxiliary choice in compound tenses and clitic pronouns, but no clitic-climbing) and L1 English (which has no auxiliary choice and no clitics) affect the knowledge attainable by near-native speakers of Italian with respect to these phenomena?

Restructuring constructions in Italian: In a complex predicate consisting of a main modal or aspectual verb followed by an embedded infinitive, a main verb generally taking *avere* 'have' can optionally take *essere* 'be' when the embedded verb requires *essere*.

Clitic-climbing (Rizzi, 1982; Burzio, 1986): In complex predicates consisting of a main modal or aspectual verb followed by an embedded infinitive, an unstressed clitic pronoun can be attached to the embedded verb or it can "climb" to the main verb. If the clitic remains attached to the embedded verb, the main verb can take either auxiliary *essere* or *avere*; if the clitic climbs to the main verb, auxiliary *essere* is obligatory.

Methodology:
Subjects: 24 L1 English near-native speakers of Italian; 20 L1 French near-native speakers of Italian; a control group of 36 adult native speakers of Italian.
Task: Timed grammaticality judgments of 48 sentences, collected by means of Magnitude Estimation (ME). With the ME technique, subjects assign numerical ratings to sentences presented in isolation. They are instructed to assign numbers so as to reflect their perception of the proportional acceptability of each sentence compared to the previous one.

Results: French-speaking subjects do not differ from the Italian controls with respect to clitic-climbing: their judgments on obligatory *essere* with clitic-climbing are nativelike. Their judgments on the optionality of auxiliary selection in the absence of clitic-climbing are different from those of Italians: they have a significant preference for *avere* both in sentences without clitics and in sentences where the clitic remains attached to the embedded verb. English subjects have indeterminate judgments (i.e., no pattern of clear acceptances or rejections) on both obligatory *essere*-selection with clitic-climbing and optional auxiliary selection in sentences without clitics/clitic-climbing. See table 6.1.

Conclusions: The learners' L1 affects ultimate attainment in L2 acquisition. French near-native speakers of Italian exhibit *divergence*, that is, determinate grammatical representations that are systematically different from those of native speakers. English near-natives show *incompleteness*, that is, the absence of representations for properties required by the L2.

Table 6.1 Mean acceptability scores on auxiliary choice in restructuring constructions

Auxiliary choice	*Italians*	*French near-natives*	*English near-natives*
No clitics:			
essere	9.260	3.824	7.231
avere	9.749	9.420	6.977
Clitic attached to embedded verb:			
essere	8.159	4.065	6.784
avere	8.779	7.841	6.211
Clitic-climbing:			
essere	8.587	8.525	6.286
**avere*	3.143	4.285	6.623

speakers of Italian, testing knowledge of (i) auxiliary choice with different semantic types of unaccusative verbs,[2] and (ii) auxiliary choice in syntactic phenomena related to restructuring (i.e., change of auxiliary, clitic-climbing).[3] Grammaticality judgments were elicited by means of magnitude-estimation techniques (Bard, Robertson, and Sorace, 1996; Sorace, 1996b). The results point not only to significant differences between natives and near-natives, but also to significant differences between English and French near-natives. Specifically, the English near-natives display *incompleteness*, that is, the absence of properties required by the L2, whereas the French near-natives exhibit *divergence*, namely representations of L2 properties that are consistently different from native representations. Both incomplete and divergent representations are affected by the L1 grammar, and both are UG-constrained (see White, 1996).

The interim conclusion to be drawn from this brief overview of research on near-nativeness is that an *overall* state of competence *identical* to that of monolingual speakers is difficult to attain in adult second language acquisition. However, what looks like incompleteness may on closer scrutiny turn out to be systematic divergence (Papp, 2000). The empirical question facing L2 research is exactly what constitutes divergence, what forms divergence can take, and which of these forms can or cannot be part of the make-up of a natural language grammar.

3 A Different Perspective on Near-Nativeness: Optionality

One type of divergence that has emerged from recent research on L2 final states is optionality. Pre-theoretically, optionality can be defined as the existence of two or more variants of a given construction that are identical in meaning and have a clear correspondence in form (Müller, 1999). Two examples from English are PP extraposition from NP, as in (1), and complementizer-drop, shown in (2):

(1) a. An article on second language acquisition came out last week
    b. An article came out last week on second language acquisition

(2) a. I think that Paul is very clever
    b. I think Paul is very clever

Optionality is well attested in both the mature and the developing grammatical competence. The question of interest is whether "stable" and "developmental" optionality are the same phenomenon; a related question is whether second language developmental optionality is a phenomenon of a different nature from that of developmental optionality in a first language. A positive answer to the first question would indicate that near-native grammars that exhibit optionality are natural language grammars.

The following two assumptions will be made:

i "Optionality" refers to a state of grammatical competence. It is, therefore, not the same as variation. Variation is not necessarily a manifestation of optionality; optionality at the level of underlying knowledge is neither a necessary nor a sufficient condition for variable performance. The optionality in auxiliary choice discussed in Sorace (1993), for example, often does not give rise to any variation in performance, probably because native Italian speakers have well-established routines that lead to access of only one option in production: so they may produce only *Maria ha voluto tornare a casa* 'Mary has wanted to go home,' even though they know that *Maria è voluta tornare a casa* is equally acceptable (see n. 3).
ii Alternating forms are almost never in free variation, but are acceptable/determinate to different degrees (i.e., the *strength of preference* for one variant over the other may change over time, particularly in the course of language development).

3.1 *Optionality in mature grammars*

The existence of (stable) optionality in native grammars is well documented. Examples analysed in the literature are scrambling in West Germanic, multiple *wh*-movement in Hungarian, *wh*-questions in French, auxiliary alternations under restructuring in Italian, singular concord in Belfast English, and phonologically overt agreement with object shift in French, among others (Henry, 1997; Müller, 1999). However, optionality is problematic for formal grammatical theory. The problems it poses are not just theory-internal: to the extent to which theories of generative grammar are assumed to account for the representation and acquisition of grammatical knowledge in the speaker's mind, their solutions will impinge on our understanding of optionality in language acquisition. It is, therefore, worth considering them in some detail.

There are two types of problems that optionality creates for grammatical theory: (i) economy and cost for the grammar, and (ii) learnability. Two solutions have been proposed:

- *Solution 1*: optional variants express the same meaning but belong to different grammars.
- *Solution 2*: optional variants belong to the same grammar but express different meanings.

Let us examine each problem, and the relevant possible solutions, in turn.

First, optionality is "costly" for the grammar. Contemporary formal models of grammars (e.g., Minimalism, Optimality Theory) are in fact essentially comparative: they assume a set of candidates competing for well-formedness and an evaluation metric based on economy principles. Only one candidate in each set emerges as the "optimal" winner: the others are assigned no grammatical status. Optionality, however, involves the coexistence of two (or more) optimal forms, one of which is usually "more grammatical" than the other, in a sense to be made precise.

All theories of generative grammar make some restricted allowance for optionality when the alternatives are equal in terms of economy of derivation. This is the way Fukui (1993), for example, analyses certain types of movement, such as rightward movement in English and scrambling in Japanese. The Minimalist framework (Chomsky, 1995) eliminates some of the mechanisms that could account for optionality in previous models: for example, the possibility of optional transformations.[4] All syntactic operations are obligatory. Solution 1 therefore becomes the only possible one: optional forms belong to different grammars. In this vein, Roeper (1999) suggests that "grammar" should receive a narrower, more local interpretation. Such a redefinition has profound implications for optionality, because it entails that speakers may have an indefinite number of mutually incompatible grammars as part of their competence, that is, every speaker, native or non-native, is "multilingual" (see also Cook's, 1991, proposal for "multi-competence"). This idea bears an obvious resemblance to the "double base" hypothesis (Kroch, 1989), according to which more than one grammar may underlie a single language. Optional forms belong to different grammars; therefore, optionality, as a visible manifestation of a state of diglossia, is not internal to the grammar. However, there is a difference: while the double base hypothesis has been proposed to account for optionality in diachronic change (see Lightfoot, 1999), Roeper regards the coexistence of multiple grammars, or "Universal Bilingualism," as an ordinary feature of grammatical competence.

Second, optionality poses a learnability problem. If language acquirers were free to entertain optional rules x and y, generating constructions a and b, where the target language has an obligatory rule x that generates a, they would need negative evidence to learn that y is incorrect. This is in fact the kind of problem that the Subset Principle addressed in the early literature (see Hyams, 2000; White, 1989).

Solution 2 involves attributing subtle semantic differences to the optional variants. Given that optionality is dependent on whether two or more alternatives are perfectly equivalent in terms of meaning, it is possible to show that optionality is more apparent than real (Adger, 1996; Grimshaw and Samek-Lodovici, 1995; Müller, 1999) if there are constraints on the distribution of optional forms, or if optional forms involve different semantic representations, and thus are not in competition with one another. The differences that are invoked to distinguish between optional variants are often related to pragmatic or functional notions, rather than truth conditions. Under this account, each optional form is the optimal derivation in its own candidate set.

Neither solution is wholly satisfactory. As for Universal Bilingualism, or the double base hypothesis, it is difficult to see how it could possibly be falsified. What evidence would unambiguously indicate that the speaker is using different grammars? As for "pseudo-optionality," the interpretive differences suggested are often so subtle that native speakers could not agree on them. However, both solutions to the optionality problems have been adopted to explain optionality that arises in the course of language development.

3.2 Developmental optionality

3.2.1 Optionality in child grammars

In first language acquisition, children go through stages of temporary optionality which allow for the coexistence of forms that are mutually exclusive in adult grammars. Optionality is attributed to different causes, depending on the theory of grammatical development adopted. There are essentially two views within generative grammar on the nature of developmental optionality: the "structure-building" approach and the "underspecification" approach.

Within the "structure-building" account proposed by, for example, Radford (1995, 1996), optionality arises because of maturational constraints that delay the appearance of functional categories in child grammars until the third year of age: during periods of transition between stages (i.e., from a VP grammar to an IP grammar, or from an IP grammar to a CP grammar), the child will often exhibit features of both the old and the new grammar, alternating between the two until the new grammar becomes categorical. At the same stage of development, children may produce both the sentence types in (3):

(3) a. Where did Daddy go?
    b. Where Daddy go?

There are different versions of the "underspecification" scenario. Under the "Continuity approach," the whole phrase structure characterizes child grammars from the beginning, but features may be temporarily underspecified: it is this underspecification that generates optionality (Hyams, 1996; Wexler, 1994). However, the term "underspecification" does not receive a uniform interpretation in current research. For Wexler (1994, 1998), it means the optional absence of a particular functional head (Tense or Agr). Underspecification in this sense is viewed as responsible for the alternation between finite and non-finite verbal forms that characterizes child grammars in a well-represented set of languages, including English, Dutch, German, and French. In a similar vein, Rizzi's (1994) "Truncation Hypothesis" assumes that child grammars may lack the principle "CP = root," so that the starting point of the child's projection is sometimes VP, sometimes IP, and sometimes CP. Hyams (1996), on the other hand, argues that functional nodes, in both the clausal and nominal domains, may be underspecified in the sense of "unindexed" – not part of syntactic chains that anchor the event or the referent. In recent work, Hoekstra and Hyams (1998) develop this analysis further, arguing that the lack of anchoring can be traced back specifically to the underspecification of the Number feature. In these underspecification scenarios, the child can, for example, optionally project either Agr or Tense, optionally choose CP as the root node (Rizzi, 1994), or optionally project Number. All these accounts of optionality are compatible with the idea that children's grammars are diglossic: that is, their developing grammatical competence consists of different grammars, each instantiating different UG options. In this sense "underspecification" could be interpreted as a general term to refer to the child's temporary inability to eliminate non-target grammars.

Whatever its cause, children in due course abandon optionality and retain the option allowed by the target grammar (unless the optionality is in the target grammar, in which case children acquire both options *and* the same pattern of distribution: see Henry, 1997). This process involves a gradual decrease in the use of the non-target option and a gradual increase in the use of the target option. For example, the abandonment of optionality of Tense or Agr involves a gradual increase in the proportion of finite sentences. The observed pattern of systematic changes in the preferences for one option over the other in the course of development is left unexplained by underspecification accounts (see Sorace, Heycock, and Shillcock, 1998, for discussion).

The general picture suggests that optionality tends to occur because of misunderstanding of interpretive conditions, which govern the interface between syntax and other domains. For normal L1 acquisition, Wexler (1998) explains the alternation of finite and non-finite forms by assuming an optional developmental constraint which prohibits the simultaneous presence of both Agreement and Tense; he hypothesizes that such a constraint is ultimately due to the child's temporary misunderstanding of the syntax–pragmatics interface conditions that – in the adult grammar – require the specification of both functional heads. Hoekstra and Hyams (1998) identify the lack of temporal anchoring in the child's grammar as a consequence of missing interface principles. A similar split between syntactic and interface features has been shown to be relevant for impaired acquisition. Tsimpli and Stavrakaki (1999) demonstrate the existence of a specific language impairment in the Determiner system which affects functional categories differentially, depending on whether they include "interpretable" (i.e., at the syntax–semantics interface) or "non-interpretable" (i.e., purely morphosyntactic) formal features: only the latter are impaired, but the former are spared. As will be shown in section 4, there is evidence that interpretive conditions are at the root of much L2 residual optionality in end-state grammars.

3.2.2 *Optionality in L2 acquisition*

In L2 acquisition, learners go through stages characterized by optionality; these have been particularly well documented for a range of phenomena related to X^0 movement (see Beck, 1998; Robertson and Sorace, 1999, for review). But L2 optionality is different from L1 optionality in at least three respects:

i L2 learners have the L1 as an additional source of optionality.
ii L2 optionality tends to persist at advanced competence levels.
iii Residual optionality is found at ultimate L2 attainment.

The persistence of optionality at advanced stages of development, including L2 end state, is a consequence of the fact that L2 learners may not be exposed to data that are robust and/or frequent enough to expunge one of the optional variants from the grammar. In the typical L2 end state characterized by optionality, optional variants are not in free variation: a steady state is reached in which the target option is strongly but not categorically preferred and the non-target option surfaces in some circumstances. L2 grammars exhibit a greater tolerance for optionality than native grammars.

Most examples of optionality discussed in the literature to date are related to optional verb movement. A substantial body of research has tried to provide an explanation for the long-lived alternations in adverb placement that characterize the second language production of French learners of English (Eubank, 1996; Schwartz and Gubala-Ryzak, 1992; Schwartz and Sprouse, 1996; White, 1990/1, 1992; etc.):

(4) a. Mary speaks very well English
    b. Mary speaks English very well

Robertson and Sorace (1999) show that advanced German learners of English retain a residual V2 constraint, occasionally producing sentences like (5a) instead of (5b):

(5) a. For many kids is living with their parents a nightmare
    b. For many kids living with their parents is a nightmare

A different example of end-state residual optionality, discussed in Sorace (1999), concerns the overproduction of overt referential subjects in the near-native Italian grammar of English-speaking learners, as in (6), and the placement of focused subjects in pre-verbal position, as in (7). Near-native speakers of L2 Italian optionally produce (6b) and (7b) in response to (6a) and (7a), whereas native Italian speakers would produce (6c) and (7c), respectively:

(6) a. Perchè Lucia non ha preso le chiavi?
    why Lucia not has taken the keys
    'Why didn't Lucia take her keys?'
  b. Perchè lei pensava di trovarti a casa
    because she thought of find-you at home
    'Because she thought she would find you at home'
  c. Perchè pensava di trovarti a casa
    because thought of find-you at home

(7) a. Che cosa è successo?
    what is happened
    'What happened?'
  b. Paola ha telefonato
    Paola has telephoned

c. Ha telefonato Paola
has telephoned Paola

In contrast, there is no corresponding optionality in the L2 grammar of Italian near-native speakers of English, that is, no tendency to use null subjects when an overt subject is required. Errors such as the one in (8b) are unattested:

(8) a. Why didn't Mary come to the party?
b. *Because ___ fell ill

It is worth stressing again that examples (4) to (7) are exceptions to a pattern of strong preference for the target variant, which, however, never reaches categorical status. The typical developmental pattern of optionality (see Robertson and Sorace, 1999, for detailed examples and discussion) is that, as in L1 acquisition, preferences for one option over the other change over time. Unlike child grammars, however, L2 grammars present a potentially permanent stage at which the target option is strongly, but not categorically, preferred, and the dispreferred non-target option is never completely expunged, but still surfaces in some circumstances. This stage may be difficult to capture without appropriate elicitation techniques, since advanced non-native speakers' metalinguistic knowledge would in most cases successfully prevent the expression of the non-target option (Sorace and Robertson, 2001).

The nature of optionality and the timing of its appearance can be interpreted differently, depending on the scope attributed to L1 transfer and on the cognitive mechanisms assumed to shape L2 development (see, e.g., Beck, 1998; Eubank, 1994, 1996). However, residual optionality in end-state grammars poses a conceptual problem for most current theories of L2 development.

As in the L1 acquisition literature, one can distinguish between the "structure-building" view of L2 development and the "underspecification" model. An example of the former is "Minimal Trees" (Vainikka and Young-Scholten, 1996), which predicts two kinds of optionality. In the early stages of L2 development, when learners are assumed to operate with a grammar devoid of functional categories, optionality should not occur. At a later stage, the acquisition of the underspecified functional projection FP causes unconstrained optionality of verb raising. As other functional projections are acquired, developmental optionality arises as a partial overlap of developmental stages; this prediction parallels that of the "structure-building" model of L1 acquisition; no optionality should arise at advanced stages.

In contrast with Minimal Trees (Eubank, 1996), the kind of optionality predicted by the "Valueless Features" position is a phenomenon characterizing only L2 acquisition. Optionality results from the fact that functional categories are transfered from the L1 and are therefore part of the initial state, but the features associated with functional heads are initially "inert." Optionality thus manifests itself from the very beginning of L2 development as unconstrained wavering between two options, and is predicted to disappear once learners have acquired the L2 morphological paradigm and therefore established the strong or weak value of the L2 features. Once again, optionality at ultimate attainment remains unexplained within this model.

Recently, a variant of this view has been proposed that assumes that adult L2 acquisition is characterized by a specific impairment affecting X^0 movement, specifically "that part of the feature matrix indicating the strength of inflection" (Beck, 1998, p. 317). This view, unlike Valueless Features, predicts that optionality never disappears because it is not a (L2-specific) developmental phenomenon, but rather the consequence of a permanent property of the interlanguage grammar. However, optionality is predicted to be unsystematic at all stages, including ultimate attainment. It is not clear what the etiology of this particular maturational change would be. Lardiere (1998), Prévost and White (2000), and Sprouse (1998) provide evidence for a dissociation between mastery of inflection, which can be poor, and mastery of the syntactic consequences of verb raising, which can be target-like. These findings lend support to the view that morphology and verb raising are not necessarily related, and that optionality may result from a "surface" difficulty with the morphological instantiation of syntactic features, rather than with the acquisition of abstract features themselves.

The position known as Full Transfer/Full Access (Schwartz, 1998; Schwartz and Sprouse, 1994) is the one that most naturally accounts for residual optionality. On the assumption that a copy of the L1 final state is the L2 initial state, developmental optionality is predicted as a result of the learner's wavering between the native and the target setting of the same syntactic parameter. Advanced optionality is the consequence of unsuccessful restructuring of the L2 grammar (and the related failure to expunge the L1 setting), most likely due to the absence of robust evidence. Protracted optionality is more likely to arise when the coexistence of the L1 and the L2 analyses is congruent with a natural language grammar (see, e.g., Hulk, 1991; for relevant arguments, see Schwartz, 1998); it is not clear, however, how the coexistence of optional variants is accounted for if such a correspondence is not satisfied.

4 Constraints on Optionality

The arguments reviewed so far suggest that optionality exists in both native and non-native grammars, but the cognitive mechanisms responsible for optionality are poorly understood. No model of grammar or language acquisition is able to predict precisely when optionality is likely to arise and when it becomes potentially permanent. Clearly there are constraints on optionality: it is a restricted phenomenon not only in native grammars, but also in non-native grammars, since many aspects of the L2 can be learned categorically. Moreover, optionality effects are often asymmetric: for example, the L2 grammar of Italian near-native speakers of English does not exhibit optional null subjects, as was shown in (8).

While only further empirical data specifically bearing on this question will provide an answer, some recent studies are suggestive. For L2 acquisition, it has been proposed that a test-bed for the existence of UG constraints on the learner's hypothesis space is knowledge of the interpretive conditions that operate at the syntax–semantics/pragmatics interface. Many such conditions are underdetermined by the input, and not amenable to classroom instruction: their presence in interlanguage grammars would therefore constitute evidence for UG. Some of these constraints can be successfully acquired by L2 learners. Dekydtspotter, Sprouse, and Anderson (1997), for example, argue that English learners of French are sensitive to the semantic distinctions governing the licensing of multiple postnominal genitives. It is likely, however, that knowledge of interface conditions is a primary candidate for advanced or emerging optionality.

Let us again consider the optionality exhibited by English near-native speakers of Italian with respect to null vs. overt subject pronouns. Recall that, overall, the distribution of overt pronominal subjects in the near-native Italian grammar is broader than in native Italian, while the distribution of null subjects is correspondingly more restricted. This asymmetry needs to be explained.

Let us assume that the existence of null subjects in a particular language is licensed by a purely syntactic feature.[5] Early descriptive research showed that the acquisition of the syntactic properties of null-subject grammars by speakers of a non-null-subject language is relatively unproblematic (Phinney, 1987; White, 1989). This is supported by the data in (5); null subjects, when they are produced, appear in the appropriate contexts, but overt subjects are sometimes produced in the wrong contexts.

However, it is syntax–semantics interface conditions which determine the distribution of null and overt subjects (Cardinaletti and Starke, 1994; Grimshaw and Samek-Lodovici, 1998; Montalbetti, 1984). In other work (Sorace, 2000a), I have argued that null pronouns are characterized by the absence of a feature that the corresponding overt pronoun has. The precise characterization of such a feature is a matter of debate: while at least in some cases it can be defined as Focus (see Cardinaletti and Starke, 1994, for arguments in favor of and against this assumption), in a broader sense it may be regarded as Topic Shift (for proposals in this direction, see Dimitriadis, 1996; Grimshaw and Samek-Lodovici, 1998). The important point that all proposals agree on is that the recoverability of null pronouns is dependent on the presence of an antecedent with topic status. Whenever this coreferentiality condition obtains, that is, when the feature [Topic Shift] is absent, null pronouns are chosen over overt pronouns: this is what happens in the native Italian grammar. In English, on the other hand, there are no pronouns that are obligatorily specified for [+Topic Shift]: all pronouns that can occur in [+Topic Shift] context can also occur in contexts without this feature.

This proposal predicts two effects in the near-native grammar of Italian. First, since the option of having null subjects is the result of the specification of purely syntactic features, this is acquired by L2 learners: the near-native grammar is, in all relevant respects, a null-subject grammar. Null subjects are possible, and occur in all (and only) the contexts in which they occur in the speech of native Italian speakers, that is, in [–Topic Shift] contexts.

Second, since the distribution of null and overt subjects is governed by interpretive conditions, it is vulnerable to optionality. Native proficiency in English involves mastery of a system in which there is no obligatory occurrence of [+Topic Shift] with any pronominal form. As a result, this possibility may never be completely acquired in the null subject L2 grammar: that is, the interpretive feature obligatorily associated with an overt subject pronoun remains optionally unspecified. The existing evidence (see Herschensohn, 2000; Liceras, 1989) is consistent with this prediction.

A similar argument can be made with regard to the distribution of pre-verbal and post-verbal subjects. It has been argued (see, e.g., Pinto, 1997) that so called "subject–verb inversion" in wide-focus clauses in Italian depends on the possibility of interpreting the verb as denoting a deictic event (with reference to the speaker). Such a deictic feature may be lexical (as in 9a), implicit (as in 9b), or explicit in the context (as in 9c); when the deictic interpretation is not possible, post-verbal subjects are ungrammatical (as shown in 9d–f):

(9) Che cosa e' successo? 'What happened?'

a.	E' entrato Paolo *is come in Paolo*	*interpreted as 'here' (where the speaker is)*
b.	Ha telefonato Mario *has telephoned Mario*	*interpreted as meaning that the telephone call came here*
c.	In questa casa ha vissuto un poeta famoso *in this house has lived a poet famous*	*deictic reference explicit*
d.	*E' impallidito Fabio *is gone pale Fabio*	*no deictic reference possible*
e.	*Ha vissuto un poeta famoso *has lived a poet famous*	*no deictic reference present*
f.	*Ha starnutito Gianni *has sneezed Gianni*	*no deictic reference possible*

The prediction is that these interpretive constraints on post-verbal indefinite subjects are not completely acquired in the near-native grammar. Because of the protracted influence of English, in which subjects obligatorily occupy the pre-verbal position regardless of the nature of the verb, there are asymmetric optionality effects in the grammar of near-native speakers of Italian: specifically, pre-verbal subjects will occasionally be overgeneralized in wide-focus contexts, regardless of whether the verb has a hidden or overt deictic component.

5 L1 Optionality as a Consequence of L2 Near-Nativeness

Recent research (Sorace, 1998, 1999) has begun to consider the effects of ultimate attainment on native syntactic competence. While a full discussion of attrition effects falls outside the scope of this chapter, it is worth mentioning some parallels between residual L2 optionality and optionality that emerges in the L1 as a result of prolonged exposure to a second language. There is evidence that native Italian speakers who have near-native competence in English display a similar pattern to that of near-native speakers of Italian: namely, they optionally extend overt subject pronouns and pre-verbal subjects to contexts that would require the use of a null pronoun or a post-verbal subject (see Sorace, 1998, 1999, for further evidence and discussion).

The cause of emerging L1 optionality is the same as that for L2 optionality: insufficient input (because of diminished exposure to the L1) and conflicting evidence (because of continued exposure to the L2). What this suggests is that *all* grammars, native or non-native, need continued exposure to *robust* input in order to be not only acquired, but also maintained.

Are L1 and L2 optionality related? This is ultimately an empirical question. There is at least preliminary evidence from experimental phonology that optionality in both the L1 and the L2 characterizes the grammatical competence of most, but not all, very advanced non-native speakers. In a series of experiments on the acquisition of intonation, Mennen (1998) discovered two possible types of ultimate attainment in Dutch near-native speakers of Greek: most of the subjects in this group do not establish the target Greek category for peak alignment, and also exhibit different Dutch alignment categories from Dutch monolinguals (although not a truly intermediate system as, e.g., Flege's, 1995, model would predict for L2 phonology). Only two subjects exhibit evidence of target-like attainment of Greek peak alignment, and at the same time evidence of essentially unaffected native Dutch alignment.

While it remains to be ascertained (beyond anectodal evidence) whether this dual pattern of ultimate attainment also occurs in the acquisition of L2 syntax, we could hypothesize that the truly successful L2 learners are the minority who manage to maximally differentiate the L1 rankings from the L2 rankings, so that there are no overlaps between them: these learners acquire native L2 competence and at the same time preserve their L1 intact. This outcome, while rare in adult language acquisition, is normal in bilingual first language acquisition (cf. Paradis and Genesee, 1996, 1997).

6 Conclusions

This chapter has focused on optionality as a phenomenon that tends to occur in L2 end-state grammars, and has characterized it as follows:

- Residual optionality is a type of divergence that characterizes non-native grammars at the ultimate attainment stage.
- Optionality is selective: it tends to affect interpretive interface aspects of grammar, or interface conditions on syntax.
- Optionality may involve a more widespread use of a mechanism that is found in mature grammars.
- Residual L2 optionality might be related to states of emerging optionality in the L1 grammar of near-native speakers.

Although the examples of residual optionality discussed in this chapter involve L1–L2 contrasts, and, therefore, suggest that transfer effects are present at all stages in L2 development, optionality may be caused by other factors: one is the input itself (see Papp, 2000), and the other is the relative markedness of features within the grammar (see Sorace, 1998, for examples). Further research is needed to deepen our understanding of optionality in native and non-native grammars. The elements at our disposal already confirm, however, that near-native grammars are different from monolingual grammars, but still fall within the range of options allowed by Universal Grammar.

NOTES

1 For example, near-native speakers gave idiosyncratic judgments on the difference between prenominal and postnominal adjectives in French (as in *une histoire triste* vs. *une triste histoire*), whereas the native speakers' judgments were remarkably uniform and stable.

2 Unaccusative and unergative verbs are sub-classes of intransitive verbs that have different syntactic and semantic properties. There is a vast literature on this topic: see Perlmutter (1978) for the original "Unaccusative Hypothesis" (UH) that posited the distinction; Burzio (1986) for a reformulation of the UH in Government-Binding terms; Van Valin (1990) and Dowty (1991) for a treatment of split intransitivity in purely semantic terms; and Levin and Rappaport Hovav (1995) for an analysis of the UH at the interface between syntax and semantics.

Auxiliary selection is considered as one of the main diagnostics of the distinction: in languages that have a choice of perfective auxiliary, unaccusative verbs tend to select 'be' and unergative verbs tend to select 'have' (but see Sorace, 2000, for a demonstration that auxiliary selection is affected by the aspectual characteristics of verbs).

3 The term "restructuring" was introduced by Rizzi (1982) within a Government-Binding theoretical framework to account for a set of syntactic processes in Italian that apply to some verbs taking infinitival complements. For example, some verbs which normally select auxiliary *avere* 'have' in perfective tenses can optionally take *essere* 'be' when the embedded verb selects *essere*, as shown in (i-b); with some verbs, an

unstressed pronoun that originates in the infinitival complement can be cliticized either to the main verb, as in (ii-b) or to the embedded verb, as in (ii-a). The former option is known as "clitic-climbing":

(i) a. Maria ha voluto tornare
Mary has wanted to go back
a casa
home
b. Maria è voluta tornare
Mary is wanted to go back
a casa
home
(ii) a. Paolo ha voluto venire a
Paolo has wanted to come to
salutarmi
greet me-CL
b. Paolo mi è /*ha voluto
Paolo me-CL is /has wanted
venire a salutare
to come to greet

Notice that the auxiliary selection under clitic-climbing is obligatorily *essere*. The "restructuring" rule posited by Rizzi, governed by a restricted class of main verbs, changes the structure of the phrase marker without changing its terminal string (see Burzio, 1986, for further refinements).

4 There are recent proposals within a Minimalist framework (e.g., Pettiward, 1997) that allow for optionality within the grammar, by associating it not with the possibility of occurrence of optional constructions, but rather with the timing of movement that generates them.

5 This feature can be identified as the phonological realization of phi-features (agreement features) and the strong D[eterminer] feature on the T[ense] head (see Alexiadou and Anagnostopoulou, 1998; Rizzi, 1986).

REFERENCES

Adger, D. 1996: Economy and optionality: interpretations of subjects in Italian. *Probus*, 8, 117–35.

Alexiadou, A. and Anagnostopoulou, E. 1998: Parametrizing Agr: word order, V-movement and EPP checking. *Natural Language and Linguistic Theory*, 16, 491–539.

Bard, E. G., Robertson, D., and Sorace, A. 1996: Magnitude estimation of linguistic acceptability. *Language*, 72 (1), 32–68.

Beck, M. 1998: L2 acquisition and obligatory head movement: English-speaking learners of German and the Local Impairment Hypothesis. *Studies in Second Language Acquisition*, 20, 311–48.

Birdsong, D. 1992: Ultimate attainment in second language acquisition. *Language*, 68, 706–55.

Bley-Vroman, R. 1990: The logical problem of second language learning. *Linguistic Analysis*, 20, 3–49.

Borer, H. 1996: Access to Universal Grammar: the real issues. *Brain and Behavioral Sciences*, 19, 718–20.

Burzio, L. 1986: *Italian Syntax: A Government-Binding Approach*. Dordrecht: Foris.

Cardinaletti, A. and Starke, M. 1994: The typology of structural deficiency. On the three grammatical classes. *Working Papers in Linguistics*, 4 (2). Centro Linguistico Interfacoltà, Università degli Studi di Venezia.

Chomsky, N. 1995: *The Minimalist Program*. Cambridge, MA: MIT Press.

Cook, V. 1991: The poverty-of-the-stimulus argument and multicompetence. *Second Language Research*, 7, 103–17.

Coppieters, R. 1987: Competence differences between native and fluent nonnative speakers. *Language*, 63, 544–73.

Dekydtspotter, L., Sprouse, R., and Anderson, B. 1997: The interpretive interface in L2 acquisition: the process–result distinction in English–French interlanguage grammars. *Language Acquisition*, 6, 297–332.

Dimitriadis, A. 1996: When pro-drop language don't: overt pronominal subjects and pragmatic inference. *Proceedings of the Chicago Linguistic Society*, 32.

Dowty, D. 1991: Thematic proto-roles and argument selection. *Language*, 67, 547–619.

Eubank, L. 1994: Optionality and the initial state in L2 development. In T. Hoekstra and B. Schwartz (eds), *Language Acquisition Studies in Generative Grammar*. Amsterdam: John Benjamins, 369–88.

Eubank, L. 1996: Negation in early German–English interlanguage: more valueless features in the L2 initial state. *Second Language Research*, 12, 73–106.

Eubank, L. and Gregg, K. 1999: Critical periods and (second) language acquisition: divide et impera. In D. Birdsong (ed.), *Second Language Acquisition and the Critical Period Hypothesis*. Mahwah, NJ: Lawrence Erlbaum Associates, 65–100.

Flege, J. E. 1995: Second language speech learning: theory, findings and problems. In W. Strange (ed.), *Speech Perception and Linguistic Experience: Issues at Crosslanguage Speech Research*. Timonium, MD: York Press, 233–77.

Fukui, N. 1993: Parameters and optionality. *Linguistic Inquiry*, 24, 399–420.

Grimshaw, J. and Samek-Lodovici, V. 1995: Optimal subjects. In J. N. Beckman, L. Walsh Dickey, and S. Urbanczyk (eds), *Papers in Optimality Theory*. Amherst, MA: University of Massachusetts Occasional Papers 18, 193–220.

Grimshaw, J. and Samek-Lodovici, V. 1998: Optimal subjects and subject universals. In P. Barbosa, D. Fox, P. Hangstrom, M. McGinnis, and D. Pesetsky (eds), *Is the Best Good Enough? Optimality and Competition in Syntax*. Cambridge, MA: MIT Press, 193–219.

Henry, A. 1997: Dialect variation, optionality, and the learnability guarantee. In A. Sorace, C. Heycock, and R. Shillcock (eds), *Proceedings of the GALA '97 Conference on Language Acquisition*. Edinburgh: University of Edinburgh, 62–7.

Herschensohn, J. 2000: *The Second Time Around: Minimalism and L2 Acquisition*. Amsterdam: John Benjamins.

Hoekstra, T. and Hyams, N. 1998: Aspects of root infinitives. *Lingua*, 156, 81–112.

Hulk, A. 1991: Parameter setting and the acquisition of word order in L2 French. *Second Language Research*, 7, 1–34.

Hyams, N. 1996: The underspecification of functional categories in early grammar. In H. Clahsen (ed.), *Generative Perspectives on Language Acquisition*. Amsterdam: John Benjamins, 91–128.

Hyams, N. 2000: Now you hear it, now you don't: the nature of optionality in child grammars. In *Proceedings of the 25th Boston University Conference on Language Development*. Somerville, MA: Cascadilla Press, 34–58.

Johnson, J. S. and Newport, E. L. 1989: Critical period effects in second language learning: the influence of maturational state on the acquisition of English as a second language. *Cognitive Psychology*, 21, 60–99.

Johnson, J. S., Shenkman, K. D., Newport, E. L., and Medin, D. L. 1996: Indeterminacy in the grammar of adult language learners. *Journal of Memory and Language*, 35, 335–52.

Kroch, A. 1989: Reflexes of grammar in patterns of language change. *Language Variation and Change*, 1, 199–244.

Lardiere, D. 1998: Dissociating syntax from morphology in a divergent L2 end state grammar. *Second Language Research*, 14, 359–75.

Levin, B. and Rappaport Hovav, M. 1995: *Unaccusativity: At the Syntax–Semantics Interface*. Cambridge, MA: MIT Press.

Liceras, J. 1989: On some properties of the "pro-drop" parameter: looking for missing subjects in non-native Spanish. In S. Gass and J. Schachter (eds), *Linguistic Perspectives on Second Language Acquisition*. Cambridge: Cambridge University Press, 109–33.

Lightfoot, D. 1999: *The Development of Language. Acquisition, Change, and Evolution*. Oxford: Blackwell.

Long, M. 1990: Maturational constraints on language development. *Studies in Second Language Acquisition*, 12, 251–86.

Montalbetti, M. 1984. After binding. Ph.D. dissertation. MIT.

Mennen, I. 1998: Second language acquisition of intonation: the case of peak alignment. *Proceedings of the Chicago Linguistic Society*, 34.

Müller, G. 1999: Optionality in Optimality-theoretic syntax. *Glot International*, 4, 3–8.

Neeleman, A. and Weerman, F. 1997: L1 and L2 word order acquisition. *Language Acquisition*, 6, 125–70.

Papp, S. 2000: Stable and developmental optionality in native and non-native Hungarian grammar. *Second Language Research*, 16, 173–200.

Paradis, J. and Genesee, F. 1996: Syntactic acquisition in bilingual children: autonomous or interdependent? *Studies in Second Language Acquisition*, 18, 1–25.

Paradis, J. and Genesee, F. 1997: On continuity and the emergence of functional categories in bilingual first-language acquisition. *Language Acquisition*, 6, 91–124.

Perlmutter, D. 1978: Impersonal passives and the Unaccusative Hypothesis. In *Proceedings of the Fourth Annual Meeting of the Berkeley Linguistic Society*. Berkeley: University of California, 157–89.

Pettiward, A. 1997: Movement and optionality in syntax. Dissertation. School of Oriental and African Studies, London.

Phinney, M. 1987: The pro-drop parameter in second language acquisition. In T. Roeper and E. Williams (eds), *Parameter Setting*. Dordrecht: Reidel, 221–38.

Pinto, M. 1997: *Licensing and Interpretation of Inverted Subjects in Italian*. Utrecht: Utrecht Instituut voor Linguistiek (UiL OTS).

Prévost, P. and White, L. 2000: Missing surface inflection or impairment in second language acquisition? Evidence from tense and agreement. *Second Language Research*, 16, 103–34.

Radford, A. 1995: Children: architects or brickies? In D. MacLaughlin and S. McEwen (eds), *Proceedings of BUCLD 19*. Somerville, MA: Cascadilla Press, 1–19.

Radford, A. 1996: Towards a structure-building model of acquisition. In H. Clahsen (ed.), *Generative Perspectives on Language Acquisition*. Amsterdam: John Benjamins, 43–90.

Rizzi, L. 1982: *Issues in Italian Syntax*. Dordrecht: Foris.

Rizzi, L. 1986: Null objects in Italian and the theory of pro. *Linguistic Inquiry*, 17, 501–55.

Rizzi, L. 1994: Early null subjects and root null subjects. In T. Hoekstra and B. Schwartz (eds), *Language Acquisition Studies in Generative Grammar*. Amsterdam: John Benjamins, 151–76.

Robertson, D. and Sorace, A. 1999: Losing the V2 constraint. In E. Klein and G. Martohardjono (eds), *The Development of Second Language Grammars. A Generative Approach*. Amsterdam: John Benjamins, 317–61.

Roeper, T. 1999: Universal bilingualism. *Bilingualism: Language and Cognition*, 2, 169–86.

Schachter, J. 1990: On the issue of completeness in second language acquisition. *Second Language Research*, 6, 93–124.

Schwartz, B. 1998: The second language instinct. *Lingua*, 156, 133–60.

Schwartz, B. and Eubank, L. 1996: What is the "L2 initial state"? *Second Language Research*, 12, 1–6.

Schwartz, B. and Gubala-Ryzak, M. 1992: Learnability and grammar reorganization in L2 A: against negative evidence causing the unlearning of verb movement. *Second Language Research*, 8, 1–38.

Schwartz, B. and Sprouse, R. 1994: Word order and nominative case in non-native language acquisition: a longitudinal study of (L1 Turkish) German interlanguage. In T. Hoekstra and B. Schwartz (eds), *Language Acquisition Studies in Generative Grammar*. Amsterdam: John Benjamins, 317–69.

Schwartz, B. and Sprouse, R. 1996: L2 cognitive states and the Full Transfer/ Full Access model. *Second Language Research*, 12, 40–72.

Sorace, A. 1988: Linguistic intuitions in interlanguage development: the problem of indeterminacy. In M. Sharwood-Smith, P. Van Buren, and J. Pankhurst (eds), *Learnability in Second Languages*. Dordrecht: Foris, 167–90.

Sorace, A. 1993: Incomplete vs. divergent representations of unaccusativity in near-native grammars of Italian. *Second Language Research*, 9, 22–47.

Sorace, A. 1996a: On gradience and optionality in non-native grammars. Commentary on D. Epstein et al., "Second language acquisition: theoretical and experimental issues in contemporary research." *Brain and Behavioral Sciences*, 19 (4), 741–2.

Sorace, A. 1996b: The use of acceptability judgments in second language acquisition research. In V. T. Bhatia and W. Ritchie (eds), *Handbook of Second Language Acquisition*. New York: Academic Press, 375–409.

Sorace, A. 1998: Near-nativeness, optionality and L1 attrition. In *Proceedings of the 12th International Symposium of Theoretical and Applied Linguistics. Vol. 1: Papers on Theoretical Linguistics*. Thessaloniki: Aristotle University of Thessaloniki, 17–35.

Sorace, A. 1999: Initial states, end-states, and residual optionality in L2 acquisition. In *Proceedings of the 23rd Boston University Conference on Language Development*. Somerville, MA: Cascadilla Press, 666–74.

Sorace, A. 2000a: Differential effects of attrition in the L1 syntax of L2 near-native speakers. In *Proceedings of the 24th Boston University Conference on Language Development*. Somerville, MA: Cascadilla Press, 719–25.

Sorace, A. 2000b: Syntactic optionality in non-native grammars. *Second Language Research*, 16, 93–102.

Sorace, A. 2000c: Gradients in auxiliary selection with intransitive verbs. *Language*, 76, 859–90.

Sorace, A. and Robertson, D. 2001: Measuring development and ultimate attainment in non-native grammars. In C. Elder et al. (eds), *Experimenting with*

Uncertainty. Cambridge: Cambridge University Press, 264–74.

Sorace, A., Heycock, C., and Shillcock, R. 1998: Trends and convergences in language acquisition research. *Lingua*, 156, 1–21.

Sprouse, R. 1998: Some notes on the relationship between inflectional morphology and parameter setting in first and second language acquisition. In M. Beck (ed.), *Morphology and its Interfaces in Second Language Knowledge*. Amsterdam: John Benjamins, 41–68.

Tsimpli, I. M. and Stavrakaki, S. 1999: The effects of a morphosyntactic deficit in the determiner system: the case of a Greek SLI child. *Lingua*, 103, 31–85.

Vainikka, A. and Young-Scholten, M. 1996: Gradual development of L2 phrase structure. *Second Language Research*, 12, 7–39.

Van Valin, R. D. 1990: Semantic parameters of split intransitivity. *Language*, 66, 221–60.

Wexler, K. 1994: Finiteness and head movement in early child grammars. In D. Lightfoot and N. Hornstein (eds), *Verb Movement*. Cambridge: Cambridge University Press, 305–50.

Wexler, K. 1998: Very early parameter setting and the Unique Checking Constraint: a new explanation of the optional infinitive stage. *Lingua*, 156, 23–80.

White, L. 1989: *Universal Grammar and Second Language Acquisition*. Amsterdam: John Benjamins.

White, L. 1990/1: The verb-movement parameter in second language acquisition. *Language Acquisition*, 1, 337–60.

White, L. 1992: On triggering data in L2 acquisition: a reply to Schwartz and Gubala-Ryzak. *Second Language Research*, 8, 93–119.

White, L. 1996: Universal grammar and second language acquisition: current trends and new directions. In T. V. Bhatia and R. Ritchie (eds), *Handbook of Second Language Acquisition*. New York: Academic Press, 85–120.

White, L. and Genesee, F. 1996: How native is near-native? The issue of age and ultimate attainment in the acquisition of a second language. *Second Language Research*, 12, 233–65.

III Environments for SLA

7 Language Socialization in SLA

KAREN ANN WATSON-GEGEO AND SARAH NIELSEN

1 Introduction

The rise of sociolinguistic and contextual approaches in L2 research over the past decade reflects a growing recognition that learning language is a more complex process than merely acquiring linguistic structures, and that language learning and use (if indeed the two can be separated) are shaped by sociopolitical processes (Hall, 1995; Losey, 1995; McKay and Wong, 1996; Zuengler, 1989). To date one sociocultural approach in SLA research, *language socialization* (LS), is represented by only a few studies. We believe, however, that among such approaches (see Siegel, this volume, for a discussion of sociocultural approaches), LS stands to contribute the most to an understanding of the cognitive, cultural, social, and political complexity of language learning.

Our purpose here is to lay out LS as a theoretical and methodological approach in L1 research and its implications for SLA research; to examine from an LS perspective certain key concepts often simplified in SLA and ESL research; to evaluate existing L2 socialization studies and their contributions; and to propose a research agenda for LS in SLA for the next decade.

2 Cognitive and Social Models in SLA: A Metatheoretical Perspective

In a 1997 issue of *Modern Language Journal,* Firth and Wagner called for "a significantly enhanced awareness of the contextual and interactional dimensions of language use" (p. 285) that would reconstitute all SLA research. At times their spirited critique almost appeared headed toward declaring that cognition is a minor consideration in language acquisition (e.g., "it is at least debatable whether there is such a thing as 'interlanguage,'" p. 294). Long (1997) (among others) countered that while studies of language use produce "theoretically interesting and socially beneficial results," SLA is about a cognitive process, the "acquisition of new knowledge" (emphasis removed). Long, Poulisse (1997), Gregg (1996), and other psycholinguists draw a sharp distinction between *acquisition* and *use*, one apparently (and rather surprisingly) supported by some socioculturalists. For example, Kasper (1997, p. 310) joined psycholinguists in arguing that acquisition is about "establishing new knowledge structures" and thus SLA should have an "essentially cognitivist" definition – thereby relegating sociocultural approaches to a supportive rather than formative role in the study of language learning.[1]

The framing of the debate between cognitivist and socioculturist camps (for want of better terms) in SLA is problematic on at least two counts. First, at a metatheoretical level, the camps are based on strongly contrastive ontologies or *world hypotheses* (Pepper, 1966): *mechanism* (a machine metaphor) for cognitivists, and *contextualism* (an act/event metaphor) for socioculturalists. The tendency to approach aspects of SLA as unconnected modules that virtually preclude arriving at an integrated theory (Hatch, Shirai, and Fantuzzi, 1990) is an example of how the mechanistic metaphor plays itself out in cognitivist SLA research. Metaphors both facilitate and constrain how we conceptualize language acquisition, and represent "truth" in opposing ways, as simple (an "elegant" theory being one that explains a phenomenon with the fewest variables) or as complex and messy (in the sense of the reality of experience, everyday practice, and the complicated process of learning). Neither of the two worldviews alone, we believe, will move SLA in the direction of a full understanding of language learning. (For further discussion of these philosophical issues and implications for research, see Carspecken, 1996; Diesing, 1971, 1991; Glaser and Strauss, 1967; Kaplan, 1964; Pepper, 1966; and especially Lakoff and Johnson, 1999.)

Secondly, theory in L1 acquisition seems ahead of SLA theory in recognizing, on the basis of both experimental and qualitative research, that cognition itself is constructed and shaped in the context of experience and through social interaction (Nelson, 1996). Such an integrative perspective is congruent with second-generation cognitive science research.

In sum, we agree with Kasper (1997) – although for reasons different from hers – that Firth and Wagner somewhat misconstrue the importance of contextual approaches for SLA research. The cognitive/social dichotomy widely taken for granted in SLA theory obscures the relationship between the knowledge about language that learners construct and the social, cultural, and political contexts in which acquisition takes place. Cognition *originates* in social interaction. Constructing new knowledge is therefore *both* a cognitive *and* a social process. SLA theory's need for just this sort of integrative perspective is one of the arguments for taking a language socialization approach in L2 research.

3 Language Socialization: Theory and Method

As a theoretical perspective, LS "grew out of concerns with the narrowness of the prevailing child language acquisition model of the late 1960s and 1970s,

[and] the recognition that language learning and enculturation are part of the same process" (Watson-Gegeo, 1992, p. 52). LS was grounded in the pioneering sociolinguistic and anthropological work on communicative and interactional competence by Hymes and Gumperz (Gumperz, 1982; Gumperz and Hymes, 1972; Hymes, 1972, 1980), and on child language acquisition and discourse by Ervin-Tripp (Ervin-Tripp and Mitchell-Kernan, 1977) and others (Cook-Gumperz, 1973, 1977; Heath, 1983; Philips, 1972; Schieffelin and Ochs, 1986; Watson, 1975). Its basic premise is that linguistic and cultural knowledge are *constructed* through each other, and that language-acquiring children or adults are active and selective agents in both processes (Schieffelin and Ochs, 1986).

With regard to the *impact of socialization on language*, a child's development of linguistic competence is an outcome of the language varieties he or she is encouraged implicitly if not explicitly to learn, and of the activities in which children routinely interact with others (Ochs and Schieffelin, 1995, p. 91). All activities in which children participate with adults and other children (whether in the family, community, or classroom) are by definition socially organized and embedded in cultural meaning systems. Thus children learn language in social, cultural, and political contexts that constrain the linguistic forms they hear and use, and also mark the social significance of these forms in various ways (e.g., the acquisition of pronoun forms in a language marking rank/status on the pronoun, i.e., honorifics [Agha, 1994]; or of differing syntactic patterns associated with formal and non-formal register in languages such as Kwara'ae [Watson-Gegeo and Gegeo, 1986a]). These points also apply to adult L2 learners because there is no context-free language learning, and all communicative contexts involve social, cultural, and political dimensions affecting which linguistic forms are available or taught and how they are represented. Yet in typical ESL studies, the influence of the classroom context is largely ignored. Some SLA researchers see classroom contexts as "unnatural" (Cummins, 1992; Krashen, 1985) even though schooling in most societies is a normal and pervasive feature of socialization. Although classrooms involve a distinct discourse register that may not be as rich as other contexts in a student's life, they are not inherently "unnatural."

The learning of language, cultural meanings, and social behavior is experienced by the language learner as a single, continuous (although not linear) process (Watson-Gegeo and Gegeo, 1995). Learners construct "a set of [linguistic and behavioral] practices that enable" them to communicate with and live among others in a given cultural setting (Schieffelin, 1990, p. 15). The social contexts in which learning takes place are variable, leading to systematic variation in learning. Moreover, "children who speak the same language (even as native speakers) do not necessarily take information from talk or texts in identical ways" (Schieffelin and Ochs, 1986, p. 170) due to their prior experiences and individual variation in language-learning strategies, etc. LS research has also found cross-cultural variation in the kinds of support and input caregivers provide for young children to assist their L1 learning (e.g., Demuth, 1983;

Miller, 1982; Ochs, 1986). However, in all societies studied so far, speakers accommodate to language-acquiring children in some fashion.

With regard to the *impact of language on socialization*, LS research has shown that children learn culture largely through participating in linguistically marked events, the structure, integrity, and characteristics of which they come to understand through verbal cues to such meanings. The acquisition of syntax, semantics, and discourse practices – including the organization of discourse – are especially fundamental to children's socialization in framing and structuring their development of both linguistic and cultural knowledge. From a cultural standpoint, "discourse practices provide a medium through which worldview and social activities are constituted" (Schieffelin, 1990, p. 20). In particular, language and discourse practices encode a cultural group's indigenous epistemology (Gegeo, 1994), which involves "cultural ways of conceptualizing and constructing knowledge about the human and natural worlds" (Gegeo and Watson-Gegeo, 1999). Second language classrooms exhibit and teach – with varying degrees of explicitness – a set of cultural and epistemological assumptions that may well differ from that of the L2 learner's native culture. Such differences have been well documented for linguistic and cultural minorities in a variety of settings (e.g., Boggs, 1985; Heath, 1983; Philips, 1983; Watson-Gegeo and Gegeo, 1994), and have often been shown to be problematic for child and adult second language or second dialect learners.

4 Cognitive Issues in LS

Schieffelin and Ochs base their distinction between language acquisition and socialization on Hymes's (1972) distinction between linguistic and communicative competence. Since the early 1990s, however, it has become clear that social identities, roles, discourse patterns, and other aspects of context all affect the process of L1 and L2 acquisition (including motivation [see Peirce, 1995a] and consciousness [Schmidt, 1990]). The interdependence of worldview and language (long a subject of intense study by anthropologists and linguists) has also been shown (Chaudhry, 1991; Ervin-Tripp, 1964; see Hill, 1992, for an extended discussion). All of these issues concern cognitive processes. As the foregoing discussion indicates, LS provides a perspective and set of strategies additional to experimental research for understanding cognitive processes in language learning because such processes are built and shaped through interaction in sociocultural contexts over time, and are recoverable from discourse data (see Watson-Gegeo, 1992). Here we sketch out some of the theoretical lines informing current LS research that view cognition as a social phenomenon.

The work of LS researchers on cognitive processes (Ochs, 1986; Watson-Gegeo, 1990; Watson-Gegeo and Gegeo, 1999) is supported and informed by recent advances in several lines of theoretical work in psychology and cognitive anthropology. Neo-Vygotskians (Rogoff, 1990; Wertsch, 1985) have built on

Vygotsky's (1962) argument that children develop higher-order cognitive functions, including linguistic skills, through social interaction with adults or more knowledgeable peers, eventually internalizing these skills and functioning independently. The most important interactions take place within a child's Zone of Proximal Development (ZPD), that is, slightly ahead of the learner's independent ability (Vygotsky, 1978, p. 86).[2]

What the learner constructs are representations of activities, events, and meanings. Drawing on schema/script theory (Schank and Abelson, 1977), her twenty years of naturalistic and experimental research on children's language development, and cross-cultural LS studies, Nelson (1996) argues that children's knowledge of language and the world develops in the everyday routines in which they participate and from which they construct "Mental Event Representations (MERs)," that is, thematic and script-like representations of behavior and events, some individual and others socially shared. In common with LS researchers, Nelson is concerned with both how children acquire language, and how language itself structures other kinds of cognitive development. Nelson agrees with Gibson's (1982) argument – an aspect of his "ecological realist approach," grounded in research on cognition in early infancy – that infants' perceptual, conceptual, and enactive systems are not simply innate, but "tuned" through experience to the sociocultural world in which they live. Gibson's work on perception has informed recent LS studies on the earliest stages of language development, that of focusing attention and moving from gesture to speech (e.g., Zukow-Goldring, 1996; Zukow-Goldring and Ferko, 1994). Nelson sees such "tuning" as involving the formation of MERs.

The application of Nelson's work for L2 socialization and SLA lies in the concept of MERs as cognitive structures built out of experience and the language-learning process. The construction of MERs is the building of new neuronal networks or links between networks, from the standpoint of cognitive science.

Nelson's (1996, p. 12) view that "Human minds are equipped to construct complicated 'mental models' that represent . . . the complexities of the social and cultural world" echoes cognitive anthropologists' work on culturally shared knowledge organized into cultural models (D'Andrade and Strauss, 1992; Holland and Quinn, 1987; Shore, 1996; Strauss and Quinn, 1997). Quinn and Holland (1987, p. 24) define cultural models as "prototypical event sequences in simplified worlds." Such models underlie most of what human beings do within cultural frames, including our academic notions about teaching and learning, our assumptions about what constitutes science and how language works, etc. They are also reflected in the metaphors we select to describe experience (Lakoff, 1984; Lakoff and Johnson, 1980). Children learn cultural models as they learn the language(s) that constitute their "native" repertoire. School "culture" typically reflects the sociopolitically dominant culture in a society, although much about school is not "native" to any cultural group (and is an outcome of institutional cultural history).

The issue of differing cultural models is highly salient not only for SLA theory, but also for the L2 classroom. In our own experience as teachers, competing and diverse cultural models at varying levels – for pedagogy, interaction, conversational inferencing and exchange, affect expression, epistemology (knowledge construction, worldview) – must be simultaneously dealt with by both instructor and students when teaching/learning a second language.

While Vygotsky focused on the individual child in interaction with peers and adults, the work of Lave and her collaborators has been more group-oriented, examining the development of learners' cognitive skills in the context of communities of practice (Chaiklin and Lave, 1993; Rogoff and Lave, 1984). Lave and Wenger (1993) are concerned with a particular form of participation in such communities, "legitimate peripheral participation." Building on the "radical shift [in the human sciences] from *invariant* structures to ones that are less rigid and more deeply adaptive," with structure "more the variable outcome of action than its invariant precondition" (Hanks, 1993, p. 17), Lave and Wenger emphasize the central importance of learners' access to participatory roles in expert performances of all knowledge skills, including language. The term "legitimate peripheral participation" describes the incorporation of learners into the activities of communities of practice, beginning as a legitimated (recognized) participant on the edges (periphery) of the activity, and moving through a series of increasingly expert roles as skills develop. Capacities and skills are therefore built by active participation in a variety of different roles associated with a given activity over a period of time, from peripheral to full participant. Lave and Wenger thus move beyond the Vygotskian notion of "internalization" into a more criticalist perspective on learning. As a theory of social practice related to the work of Giddens (1979) and Bourdieu (1977), their formulation speaks to the "relational interdependency of agent and world, activity, meaning, cognition, learning, and knowing," emphasizing the inherently socially "situated negotiation and renegotiation of meaning in the world" (Lave and Wenger, 1993, pp. 50–1).[3]

Lave and Wenger's theoretical framework helps us understand the complex sociocultural/cognitive process of L2 learning in classroom and community contexts, and how learners are brought into or excluded from various activities that shape language acquisition. They draw our attention to the importance of studying access, negotiation and renegotiation, and roles in L2 learners' movement from beginner to advanced L2 speaker status. These issues and processes have critical importance for linguistic minorities and immigrants, who may face social and political hostility or exclusion, and may react with resistance.

The theoretical perspectives briefly sketched here disagree on many points, and much further research is needed to develop anything like a unified theory. However, they all do agree on a fundamental premise: the necessity of understanding cognitive development – including language learning – through an integrated approach in which experience and sociocultural contexts play formative rather than secondary roles.

As Jacobs and Schumann (1992, p. 293) argue, proposed models of SLA must be "neurobiologically plausible." The foregoing perspectives are compatible in their broad outlines with recent brain research emphasizing the key role of experience and socialization in shaping cognitive development (e.g., Edelman, 1987; Harth, 1993). Connectionist models (Gasser, 1990; Rumelhart, McClelland, et al., 1986; Sokolik, 1990; see also Rivers, 1994; Schmidt, 1988) especially seem promising for further exploration, due to their emphasis on multiply connected networks, parallel distributed processing of information, and learning as the strengthening of connections through frequency. These models show the essential relationship between cognitive development and experience, and are congruent with notions like MER, cultural model, and legitimate peripheral participation.

5 Methodological Strategies in LS

Among discussions of ethnographic methods in ESL and SLA (Davis, 1995; Edge and Richards, 1998; Lazaraton, 1995; Peirce, 1995b; Ramanathan and Atkinson, 1999; Watson-Gegeo, 1988), only one (Watson-Gegeo, 1992) addresses an LS perspective. To understand the cognitive and social complexity of language learning, LS studies may combine ethnographic, sociolinguistic, discourse analytic, quantitative, and experimental methods, as needed. Studies should begin with careful ethnographic documentation of the process of learning language and culture in the learner's everyday and/or classroom settings. LS studies are longitudinal, following language development and socialization over a period of several months to a year or longer, with the analyst writing up results at significant points coinciding with identified developmental stages, or with the semester or school year in classroom studies. Interactional events are recorded on a schedule ranging from daily to bi-weekly for routine events, and an effort is also made to record non-routine and unplanned events. Infrequent events may be culturally loaded or marked, that is, carry important symbolic meaning and have a highly significant impact on learning. The LS ethnographer takes careful observational fieldnotes as recordings are being made. Some studies include recordings made in the researcher's absence, to help assess the effect of observer presence on interactions, and to capture interactions that might not take place in front of outsiders due to privacy or other concerns.

Audio- and videotaped recordings are indexed and transcribed, using one of several transcription schemes designed for psycholinguistic studies of language acquisition, or one or another form of discourse analysis. The way transcripts represent interaction is widely recognized as a theoretical as well as methodological issue. Choice of transcription layout, for example, may profoundly bias the analysis in terms of which speaker is seen to initiate an interaction, or how contributions by a language learner are interpreted with regard to contingency and other aspects of discourse organization (Edwards and Lampert, 1993; Gumperz and Berenz, 1993; Ochs, 1979). Participants in an analyzed interaction are also interviewed to disambiguate problematic utterances and exchanges, and to explore their understandings of the interaction at the time.

An adequate LS analysis requires examining events and behavior in light of both the history of relationships and other aspects of the immediate context (micro-context) and relevant sociocultural, historical, political, and other institutional processes (macro-context) (Watson-Gegeo and Gegeo, 1995, p. 61). This holistic approach meets the psycholinguistic criteria of ecologically valid research, and addresses the interaction of individual and social context in cognitive development of concern to Vygotsky, Nelson, and LS research generally. It also reveals the important interplay of structure and agency, in which knowledge systems and social systems are "both the medium and the outcome of the practices that constitute those systems" (Giddens, 1979, p. 69).

6 Language Socialization For and In SLA

What can LS bring to SLA research? As implied above, we believe that LS suggests a different view of learning, language, and cognition from more traditional SLA approaches. Here we examine each of these three constructs in turn, focusing on key concepts often essentialized and/or simplified by SLA and ESL researchers.

The view of *learning* offered by LS suggests a more complex model than input-output mechanistic theories advanced in much of the SLA literature. For that reason, an LS perspective can help resolve the modularity problem (mentioned earlier) by emphasizing and clarifying connections among language learning and teaching processes, including the role of interaction in language learning, and how learning and teaching are shaped by levels of sociocultural, political, and historical context.

For example, an LS perspective is consistent with many of the critiques – in *Beyond the Monitor Model* (Borasch and Vaughan James, 1994) and elsewhere – leveled at Krashen's (1985)[4] distinction between "acquisition" and "learning," rejecting the idea that acquisition occurs almost exclusively in "naturalistic" (non-school) settings and learning in "formal" (classroom) settings, and that as "learned" language is only accessible through conscious use of "the Monitor," it will never have the automaticity of acquired language. Rather, LS regards language learning as similar to other kinds of learning. Human beings may come endowed with certain species-specific predispositions to learn language, but all cognitive development is constructed in and profoundly shaped by sociocultural contexts, whether they be home, community, or school. Formative contextual factors for SLA include local "theories" of how learning occurs, the sorts of situations in which learners are allowed and/or expected to participate, the roles they can take, and the linguistic, sociolinguistic, and discoursal complexity of oral or written language forms to which they are exposed. Moreover, in virtually all societies some form of knowledge or skill is directly taught to adults and/or children, sometimes in highly formal, even ritualistic contexts that may exert a powerful effect on learning. Some SLA research shows that naturalistic and classroom learning results are identical (Ellis, 1989), and that instruction even accelerates learning, ultimately leading to higher levels of skills (Long, 1988). Other studies with an overtly LS perspective (cf. Willet, 1997) show the facilitative effects of routinized classroom speech in child SLA. Additional evidence comes from the Canadian French immersion programs (Long, 1996; Swain, 1981). Although students in these programs spent years in an environment Krashen would probably see as ideal for language acquisition, they failed to achieve nativelike proficiency in all aspects of their productive French skills. Finally, connectionist models of cognitive function (mentioned above) and second-generation cognitive science research seriously undermine the compartmentalized, serial processing suggested in Krashen's acquisition/learning dichotomy (Rivers, 1994, p. 73).

The view of *language* offered by LS goes beyond single, isolated and idealized utterances to focus on discourse practices. Language is seen as integrated into sociocultural behavior, and both the result and creator of context and structure. As with learning as a construct, an LS perspective can help SLA theory move beyond its traditional study of language in modular, individualistic terms.

Even when sociolinguistic concepts have been borrowed into SLA, for example, they have tended to be modularized in the way that Canale and Swain (1980) and Canale (1983) modularize Gumperz's notion of communicative competence into a series of discrete categories: grammatical, sociolinguistic, discourse, and strategic, with a strong emphasis on rules. Ellis and Roberts (1987, p. 19) rightfully point out Gumperz's (1984) argument that communicative competence is not about "rules," but about "creating conditions that make possible shared interpretation" (their wording). Thus Gumperz emphasizes the connection rather than the division between grammar and contextualization, in contrast to some SLA theorists who would like to divorce communicative competence from issues of acquiring language structure.

While Gumperz's formulation emphasizes conversational cooperation, helping to move our understanding of language beyond idealized notions, LS today is more in tune with Peirce's (1995a, p. 18) argument that SL learning studies should include "an understanding of the way rules of use are socially and historically constructed to support the interests of a dominant group within a given society." This formulation is especially relevant to L2 or FL classrooms, where certain social and linguistic identities and uses are rewarded (or discredited), and taught together with accompanying sociopolitical behaviors, values, expectations, and rights. Peirce's argument is that such matters affect the learner's motivation or investment in learning. But as Watson-Gegeo and Gegeo (1994) show, issues of power are central to the quality of the instruction itself – and thus to both language structure and language use – in English language instruction in Third World classrooms, such as in the Solomon Islands, where disadvantaged populations often experience poorly trained teachers with minimal English skills.

LS also alters our view of *cognition* to one recognizing that language and other forms of cognitive development and knowledge are constructed in and emerge through practice and interaction in specific historical, political, and sociocultural contexts. Thus, LS rejects the traditional SLA view that cognition happens solely "inside the head" of an individual. This perspective also implies that language and other types of cognitive development are likely formed in a bottom-up fashion rather than top-down, as more Chomskian-conceived models of language suggest.[5]

Formal strategies, such as routines and formulaic speech, which focus learners' attention (in the sense meant by Schmidt, 1990), are one example of how cognitive development involving language is formed bottom-up. Such strategies have been shown to be used by caregivers in many societies to guide children's L1 acquisition and facilitate their cognitive development. The LS and L1 acquisition literatures emphasize the role of formulaic speech and routines in children's linguistic and cognitive development. Formulaic speech is also a much studied topic in SLA, but here again researchers have tended to treat the concept narrowly. For Krashen and Scarcella (1978), "prefabricated routines" are short, fixed-format, and equated with automatic speech. The L1 (e.g., Peters, 1983) and LS literature (beginning with Watson, 1975) have shown routines to be variable, flexible, and graded according to a learner's linguistic and interactional competence (Watson-Gegeo and Gegeo, 1986b). Such grading is a major reason that routines function to scaffold language acquisition. In this respect, research on routines has helped to clarify how classroom discourse is its own register in comparison with caregiver–child discourse. L1 routines occurring outside classrooms do involve substitution into slots, but they also involve more, especially negotiation and creative manipulation by children as their skills increase. None of this is allowable in most classrooms, including L2 classrooms, probably because, as Pica (1987, p. 12) points out, attempts by students to restructure social interaction in the classroom "may be misinterpreted as challenges to the teacher" (emphasis removed).

As Weinert (1995) argues in her review of the research on formulaic language in SLA, linearly stored word sequences may in fact benefit learners in helping them to overcome cognitive constraints on acquisition. If this is true, then "it may be necessary to abandon the notion of a homogenous grammatical competence as separate from language use" (p. 199). In a recent study, Myles, Hooper, and Mitchell (1998) found that when pressed by communicative needs that went beyond classroom routines, the FL French learners they observed did not abandon the formulaic chunks they had previously depended on in classroom interactions. Instead, the learners seemed to analyze them, then use the analysis to construct required formal features, such as the pronoun system (p. 359). This finding adds to previous evidence that routines and other formulaic language are productive tools rather than fixed units in language learning.

An LS approach can also further our understanding of cognitive issues by providing a richer view of *context* than is currently the case in SLA research. Ellis and Roberts's (1987) approach to context, for example, claims to draw on Hymes (1974), but in fact follows Brown and Fraser's (1979) reductionist approach to Hymes's heuristic discussion of context, and also reduces the notion of macro- and micro-contexts as used by LS researchers. Roberts and Simonot (1987) want to "deepen" context beyond such narrow uses, but reduce context to three levels in their own analysis. Their formulation leaves out many historical and sociocultural dimensions that, although they may not always all be essential to a given analysis, should not be precluded in advance.

In contrast, in LS, "context refers to the whole set of relationships in which a phenomenon is situated" (Watson-Gegeo, 1992, p. 51), including macro-levels of institutional, social, political and cultural aspects, and micro-levels involving the immediate context of situation. The history of macro- and micro-dimensions, including interactants' individual experiences and the history of interaction with each other, are also important to the analysis. In this respect, LS study aims to go beyond thick description (Geertz, 1973) to *thick explanation*, which "takes into account all relevant and theoretically salient micro- and macro-contextual influences that stand in a systematic relationship to the behavior or events" (Watson-Gegeo, 1992, p. 54) to be explained, with systematic relationship as the key for setting boundaries (Diesing, 1971, pp. 137–41; DeWalt and Pelto, 1985), and with attention to data collection to the point of theoretical saturation (Glaser and Strauss, 1967). An LS approach agrees with Roberts and Simonot (1987, p. 135) that language and society are "parts of a dialectic process in which language both expresses but simultaneously constructs social systems and structures." However, SL research has yet to embody this notion in its analysis.

Similarly, as by definition everything is always in a context, LS rejects the notion that language or discourse can be "decontextualized" or even "context-reduced" (Cummins, 1992), and that a distinction can be drawn between a "natural" and a "classroom" teaching/learning situation on that basis. The language/discourse used in schools is contextualized as school language, and minority and SL children who are not familiar with that kind of contextualization (the linguistic forms appropriate to the classroom, literacy activities, and the social class-based values and assumptions they encode) may be at a disadvantage compared to students who come already familiar with school-contextualized language forms and use.

Finally, LS can contribute to SLA research by expanding its *methodological tool kit* to include, as we have seen, a wider range of approaches and techniques, and an emphasis on integrating fine-grained longitudinal studies of language development in classroom and non-classroom contexts.

7 Existing LS Studies in SLA: Contributions and Shortcomings

L2 socialization studies so far have been variable in focus and uneven in quality. The first major study was Wong Fillmore's (1976) dissertation on five 5–7-year-old Spanish-speaking children acquiring English without explicit instruction in a bilingual classroom setting. Wong Fillmore showed how these children used formulaic speech in conversation, analyzed the constituents of formulae to free them for productive use, and arrived at patterns and rules for constructing new utterances. Her study generated a continuing line of research on formulaic speech in SLA (for reviews see McLaughlin, 1984; Weinert, 1995). Since then only a handful of studies have self-identified as or been consistent with an LS framework (e.g., Harklau, 1994; He, 1997; Losey, 1995; Poole, 1992; Schecter and Bayley, 1997). Most studies have a variety of weaknesses, including the need to disambiguate cultural from situational effects, the need to interrogate key analytic concepts, unsupported interpretive leaps from data to cultural pattern, lack of contrastive examples where these are essential to assessing the quality of the analysis, and less than transparent procedures of data collection and/or analysis. The two most common problems are the lack of discourse examples to support the analysis, and failure to address cognitive implications in largely socioculturally based studies. These latter two points we make less as criticisms of prior work than as advisories of where L2 socialization research needs to go.

Among the better studies, Duff's (1995) research on nine history classrooms taught in English in a progressive Hungarian secondary school took place during a shift from a ritualized student recitation format to a more open oral reports format. She focuses on the interactions between one experienced teacher and her students in two classrooms, where all speakers are acquiring English. Duff finds that error correction, as well as linguistic form and historical content of student oral reports, are mutually constructed by participants. Her findings illustrate how scaffolded involvement and student feedback together ensure the use of appropriate, comprehensible English. But she provides no example of a recitation format, the contrasting model for student oral presentations, making it difficult to assess some of her claims.

Willet's (1997) year-long study examines the routines that support four ESL children's participation in a mainstream first-grade classroom at an international school. She finds that communicative and linguistic competence are jointly constructed by the children and teachers, but especially among the children themselves. Her analysis of how the social context shapes routines and interactional strategies has implications for language acquisition. The children practice and experiment linguistically in important ways, including using syntax to construct meaning rather than merely stringing prefabricated chunks together. Her work echoes and extends Wong Fillmore's original argument for the implications of children's analysis of formulaic chunks in L2 learning. However, Willet's examples need far more analysis than she offers. Her data include marvelous cases of paradigmatic substitutions and other processes that are directly relevant to cognitive processes in SL development and to the points she makes about prefabricated chunks. The data clearly show a very strong connection between social and cognitive dimensions of language learning, even though Willet's analysis does not address this issue. Willet also needs to show how her findings in many ways replicate those in several classroom ethnography studies in the educational research literature, with which SLA readers may not be familiar.

In a year-long ethnographic study of a 5-year-old Moroccan girl learning Italian in a nursery school, Pallotti (1996) examines features of the child's interlanguage development via lexical items and unanalyzed formulae, affect-marking suffixes, and "sentence producing tactics" (following Wong Fillmore, 1976). Only the latter are illustrated with discourse examples. Although her data are very thorough, Pallotti's otherwise excellent analysis exemplifies Tollefson's (1991, p. 38) concern that SLA research has "limited the term [context] to a narrow, neoclassical meaning, primarily verbalization patterned by 'strategies' of individual speakers within the 'context' of conversation" (in Pallotti's case, focused by Grice's conversational maxims). Pallotti recognizes that the nursery-school context of competition for the speaking floor shapes conversational strategies, but other aspects of context influential in language learning also need to be examined.

Four studies by Atkinson and Ramanathan (1995), Siegal (1996), Watson-Gegeo (1992), and Watson-Gegeo and Gegeo (1994) provide promising models for future LS research in SLA. Atkinson and Ramanathan (1995) compare the L1 and L2 language programs at the same university, examining attitudes and practices among teachers/administrators in teaching academic writing. Their study, which involves a great number of carefully analyzed data, finds that L1 and L2 students are taught different formal expectations for, and models of, writing. The L2 program promotes a deductive essay format, simplicity, and clarity, while the L1 program (into which ESL students are ultimately transitioned) emphasizes form dependent on rhetorical purpose, and preference for sophisticated, subtle thought and expression. Thus, the L1 program not only presupposes cultural knowledge ESL students lack, but holds expectations for writing they have not been taught. Presumably the researchers' next step will be to examine what happens in classrooms.

Siegal (1996) (see table 7.1) is an exemplary study focusing on the role of language learner subjectivity in the acquisition of sociolinguistic competence by a European woman learning Japanese in Japan. Siegal's sophisticated theoretical framing is matched by the thorough way in which she approaches data collection (some 150 hours of interactional and interview data) and analysis. She shows how power and positionality issues affect interactions between the white female student and her male Japanese language instructor. In imperfectly manipulating her interlanguage – including modality, honorifics, and topic control – to display politeness and create a voice for herself in Japanese, the student also creates examples of inappropriate language use. It appears that cognitively she may not have worked out which expectations take precedence, and this problem in turn affects the input to which she is exposed. We would have liked Siegal to more fully articulate the cognitive implications of her data, which we think are significant. It would also be useful to know how this woman's strategies and learning compare with others in the data set of 11 European women studying Japanese in Japan.

Table 7.1 Studies by Siegal (1996) and Watson-Gegeo (1992)

Study	*Focus*	*Data/Methods*	*Contributions*	*Weaknesses*
Siegal (1996)	Role of language learner subjectivity in the acquisition of sociolinguistic competence in L2 within a richly described social, cultural, and historical framework	Seven types of qualitative data collected, including 116 hours of audiotaped conversation and 42 hours of interview material	Shows how subject's incomplete control of modality, honorific language, topic control, and intonation in her L2 interferes with the production of sociolinguistically appropriate language; examines the influences of social positions and a "foreigner" identity within Japanese society on interactions between native and non-native speakers	Examines only one subject, although additional subjects exist in data set; could make analysis of cognitive issues more explicit
Watson-Gegeo (1992)	Theoretical and methodological piece which focuses on the relationship between sociopolitical processes and cognition in language education and on the detailing of a rigorous model for LS studies	Review of Watson-Gegeo and Gegeo's L1 child socialization work, which includes multi-year ethnographic and discourse analytic studies conducted in nine families' home and community contexts	Demonstrates the importance of macro-level factors (e.g., national and provincial institutions which affect materials, pedagogy, and parental schooling experiences) in developing a richer understanding of child language acquisition	Additional classroom data are needed

Watson-Gegeo and Gegeo (1994) examine how institutional factors constrain Solomon Islands teachers' use of cultural teaching strategies in four rural primary classrooms where the teacher is teaching English (a language neither the teacher nor students know) through English or Solomon Islands Pijin (a language rural children do not know). The authors conducted a multi-year study of rural children's LS in home and community contexts before carrying out ethnographic and discourse analytic studies in kindergarten through third grade classrooms. The focus of the article is on teacher practices, but the analysis has language-learning implications in the way lessons are performed, such that many incorrect morphological, lexical, and semantic choices are modeled or directly taught by the teachers, leaving students confused or bored. In a fifth, contrastive classroom, the teacher teaches English to an attentive and enthusiastic class through the students' first language, using a culturally derived pedagogy. In doing so, he successfully builds on their culturally shaped cognitive expectations and skills. The arguments Watson-Gegeo and Gegeo make are suggestive, but they need to be supported by a longitudinal study of students' L2 development and learning outcomes across classrooms using differing pedagogical practices.

Watson-Gegeo (1992) (see table 7.1) is a primarily theoretical and methodological piece (based partly on the above classroom study) making a strong case for the connection between cognitive and sociopolitical processes in language education, and laying out a rigorous model for LS methodology. To illustrate her concept of thick explanation, Watson-Gegeo reviews Watson-Gegeo and Gegeo's longitudinal L1 socialization study in nine families, which showed that contrary to other studies of disadvantaged rural populations, Kwara'ae (Solomon Islands) children grow up in linguistically and cognitively rich home environments parallel in many ways to those of white middle-class Americans, yet fail school in large numbers. A classroom discourse study revealed significant differences in values and language use between home and school, submersion of the children's first language by a restricted version of English, and many other problems. Yet these problems alone did not seem to explain why some of the children best prepared for school were failing. Watson-Gegeo and Gegeo examined the complex institutional factors at the national and provincial levels that shape classroom materials, teacher practices, and parental experiences with schooling. These macro-level factors fold back into children's LS in family contexts, because parents recount their own negative schooling experiences, fears for their children's school success, and doubt about the value of schooling to their children in culturally marked "shaping the mind" sessions central to Kwara'ae children's cognitive and social development. Watson-Gegeo concludes that the complexity of the Kwara'ae case demonstrates the need to go beyond single settings and immediate environmental influences in order to understand children's language acquisition.

Finally, it should be noted that LS researchers face difficult space constraints when they publish their work in the form of articles. Qualitative and discourse data sufficient to support theoretical claims effectively, much less thoroughly illustrate identified patterns in data, rarely fit into the 20-page format typically required by journals or edited volumes.

8 A Research Agenda for the Next Decade

We have argued that neither a strict cognitivist nor a strict socioculturalist position alone can fully illuminate the complexities inherent in SLA. Here we lay out some directions for LS research in the next decade that, if pursued, could result in LS studies making a major contribution to SLA theory. We are not arguing that all sociocultural research must focus on cognition, but rather that LS research has an important role to play in cognitive research generally and in SLA research specifically.

We recognize that the LS perspective is only now gaining attention in SLA, and that a great deal of basic research is needed. Nevertheless, given limited time and resources, certain areas of work especially suited to LS research are also most likely to be productive for SLA theory. In these areas, LS researchers can build on, deepen, and demonstrate the connections among findings from existing experimental studies, thereby helping to address the modularity problem referred to earlier. An example is research being done on interaction by Long, Doughty (1993) and others (see Gass, this volume; Long, 1996, for reviews), which does not explicitly include social factors in conceptions of cognition, but implicitly recognizes the importance of context. These studies usually omit an accounting of what came before and after a given interaction, as well as varying interactant roles, all of which may affect outcomes. A related area is formulaic speech, along the lines of Schmidt's (1983) study of Wes's use of memorized chunks in the world of work, service encounters, and ordinary conversational contexts. Although Wes continued to rely on formulae, of particular interest are L2 speakers who go beyond fixed-format chunks to productive acquisition, and who also learn the flexible and complex routines that structure so much of human interaction in any speech community. In these and other cases, an LS perspective allows for a richer look at the cognitive complexities inherent in L2 learners' necessarily being involved in the simultaneous processing of many levels of structure, meaning, and strategy in learning and communicating. Some factors include: the linguistic structure(s) being (imperfectly) acquired and the state of the learner's interlanguage at any given point; sociohistorical/political factors in the interactional moment within a given but imperfectly understood speaking situation; and the learner's strategies for accomplishing a communicative goal given what she or he understands at that moment about language, culture, and situation.

More generally, over the next decade, LS researchers should conduct rigorous studies clearly demonstrating how the social shapes the cognitive in L2 language learning, in both classroom and non-classroom environments. On the individual level, we need careful diary studies modeled on Schmidt's (1990) groundbreaking work on his own acquisition of Portuguese, paying specific attention to the interaction of sociocultural and cognitive factors. Individual or small-sample longitudinal studies of immigrant L2 learners from time of entry into the receiving country and/or its schools, following learners over several months to two to five years, would illuminate the L2 learning process. Such studies involve intensive data collection and analysis during the first and second year, and data sampling for two to three subsequent years. Some issues these studies might help resolve include to what extent L1 socialization carries over into L2 socialization (e.g., with regard to literacy skills); the importance of peer group influence in how learners create an understanding of a second language; and the role of interaction and different types of input in facilitating L2 learning. Rich case studies of small samples chosen for their diversity and similarity with regard to significant social factors (gender, age, previous language learning experience, etc.) are essential to identify the variety of ways learning occurs. Specifically, what do learner strategies as used in everyday contexts reveal about how learners are building cognitive models of language and culture?

Finally, we note that although there is a growing literature on L2 acquisition in German, Japanese, Chinese, French, Spanish, and a few other languages, SLA research is still overwhelmingly concerned with ESL/EFL, for a variety of reasons. LS studies of non-English speakers learning a non-English and especially a non-European second language might well illuminate and clarify (or possibly complicate) our current SLA assumptions and models – leading, no doubt, to a few surprises and some new insights.

NOTES

1 Kasper (1997, p. 311), however, emphasized in her reply to Firth and Wagner the importance of doing language socialization research: "language socialization theory has a particularly rich potential for SLA because it is inherently developmental and requires (rather than just allows) establishing links between culture, cognition, and language."

2 For an excellent refutation of the assumption in some quarters of second language research that Krashen's (1985) construct of *i + 1* can be equated with Vygotsky's notion of the Zone of Proximal Development, see Dunn and Lantolf (1998).

3 With regard to classroom teaching/learning, and taking physics as the example case, Lave and Wenger (1993, pp. 99–100) point out that the "actual reproducing community of practice, within which students learn about physics, is not the community of physicists but the community of schooled adults." They are not saying that direct teaching is useless for teaching skills, as some have argued in SLA research. Their point applies more specifically to the artificial nature of much classroom pedagogy together with assumptions about internalization of skills that are the raison d'etre of much educational research and pedagogy.

4 While some SLA theorists might feel we should omit any discussion of the monitor model here because it has been virtually discredited in whole or part, we have found that Krashen's ideas are still revered in many university departments, teacher training programs, and especially school systems. Hence our concern with including a language socialization critique of the Monitor Model.

5 For a careful deconstruction of Chomskian theory based on second-generation cognitive science, see Lakoff and Johnson (1999).

REFERENCES

Agha, A. 1994: Honorification. *Annual Review of Anthropology*, 23, 277–302.

Atkinson, D. and Ramanathan, V. 1995: Cultures of writing: an ethnographic comparison of L1 and L2 university writing/language programs. *TESOL Quarterly*, 29 (3), 539–68.

Boggs, S. T. 1985: *Speaking, Relating and Learning: A Study of Hawaiian Children at Home and at School*. Norwood, NJ: Ablex.

Borasch, R. M. and Vaughan James, C. (eds) 1994: *Beyond the Monitor Model*. Boston: Heinle and Heinle.

Bourdieu, P. 1977: *Outline of a Theory of Practice*. Cambridge: Cambridge University Press.

Brown, P. and Fraser, C. 1979: Speech as a marker of situation. In K. Scherer and H. Giles (eds), *Social Markers in Speech*. Cambridge: Cambridge University Press, 33–62.

Canale, M. 1983: From communicative competence to language pedagogy. In J. C. Richards and R. W. Schmidt (eds), *Language and Communication*. London: Longman, 2–27.

Canale, M. and Swain, M. 1980: Theoretical bases of communicative language teaching and testing. *Applied Linguistics*, 1 (1), 1–47.

Carspecken, P. F. 1996: Ontological models and research design. In P. F. Carspecken, *Critical Ethnography in Educational Research: A Theoretical and Practical Guide*. New York: Routledge, 23–42.

Chaiklin, S. and Lave, J. (eds) 1993: *Understanding Practice: Perspectives in Activity and Context*. Cambridge: Cambridge University Press.

Chaudhry, L. 1991: Portraits of South Asia bilingualism: multiple measures of dominance, interference, and the bilingual imagination. Master's thesis. Department of English as a Second Language, University of Hawai'i at Manoa.

Cook-Gumperz, J. 1973: *Social Control and Socialization*. London: Routledge and Kegan Paul.

Cook-Gumperz, J. 1977: Situated instructions: language socialization of school age children. In S. Ervin-Tripp and C. Mitchell-Kernan (eds), *Child Discourse*. New York: Academic Press, 103–21.

Cummins, J. 1992: Language proficiency, bilingualism, and academic achievement. In P. A. Richard-Amate and M. A. Snow (eds), *The Multicultural Classroom*. London: Longman, 16–26.

D'Andrade, R. G. and Strauss, C. (eds) 1992: *Human Motives and Cultural Models*. Cambridge: Cambridge University Press.

Davis, K. A. 1995: Qualitative theory and methods in applied linguistics research. *TESOL Quarterly*, 29 (3), 427–53.

Demuth, K. A. 1983: Aspects of Sesotho language acquisition. Ph.D. dissertation. University of Indiana.

DeWalt, B. R. and Pelto, P. J. (eds) 1985: *Micro and Macro Levels of Analysis in Anthropology: Issues in Theory and Research*. Boulder, CO: Westview Press.

Diesing, P. 1971: *Patterns of Discovery in the Social Sciences*. Chicago: Aldine.

Diesing, P. 1991: *How Does Social Science Work? Reflection on Practice*. Pittsburgh: University of Pittsburgh.

Doughty, C. 1993: Fine-tuning of feedback by competent speakers to language learners. In J. E. Alatis (ed.), *Georgetown University Round Table on Languages and Linguistics 1993*. Strategic Interaction and Language Acquisition: Theory, Practice, and Research. Washington, DC: Georgetown University Press, 96–108.

Duff, P. A. 1995: An ethnography of communication in immersion classrooms in Hungary. *TESOL Quarterly*, 29, 505–37.

Dunn, W. E. and Lantolf, J. P. 1998: Vygotsky's Zone of Proximal Development and Krashen's *i + 1*: incommensurable constructs; incommensurable theories. *Language Learning*, 48 (3), 411–42.

Edelman, G. 1987: *Neural Darwinism: The Theory of Neuronal Group Selection*. New York: Basic Books.

Edge, J. and Richards, K. 1998: May I see your warrant, please?: justifying outcomes in qualitative research. *Applied Linguistics*, 19 (3), 334–56.

Edwards, J. A. and Lampert, M. D. (eds) 1993: *Talking Data: Transcription and Coding in Discourse Analysis*. Hillsdale, NJ: Lawrence Erlbaum Associates.

Ellis, R. 1989: Are classroom and naturalistic acquisition the same? A study of classroom acquisition of German word order rules. *Studies in Second Language Acquisition*, 11, 305–28.

Ellis, R. and Roberts, C. 1987: Two approaches for investigating second language acquisition. In R. Ellis (ed.), *Second Language Acquisition in Context*. London: Prentice-Hall, 3–29.

Ervin-Tripp, S. 1964: Language and TAT content in bilinguals. *Journal of Abnormal and Social Psychology*, 68, 500–7.

Ervin-Tripp, S. and Mitchell-Kernan, C. (eds) 1977: *Child Discourse*. New York: Academic Press.

Firth, A. and Wagner, J. 1997: On discourse, communication, and (some) fundamental concepts in SLA research. *Modern Language Journal*, 8 (3), 285–330.

Gasser, M. 1990: Connectionism and universals of second language acquisition. *Studies in Second Language Acquisition*, 12, 179–99.

Geertz, C. 1973: *The Interpretation of Cultures*. New York: Basic Books.

Gegeo, D. W. 1994: *Kastom* and *bisnis*: toward integrating cultural knowledge into rural development. Ph.D. dissertation. Department of Political Science, University of Hawai'i at Manoa.

Gegeo, D. W. and Watson-Gegeo, K. A. 1999: Adult education, language change, and issues of identity and authenticity in Kwara'ae (Solomon Islands). *Anthropology and Education Quarterly*, 30 (1), 22–36.

Gibson, J. J. 1982: *Reasons for Realism: Selected Essays of James J. Gibson*, eds E. Reed and R. Jones. Hillsdale, NJ: Lawrence Erlbaum Associates.

Giddens, A. 1979: *Central Problems in Social Theory: Action, Structure, and Contradiction in Social Analysis*. Berkeley: University of California.

Glaser, B. and Strauss, A. 1967: *The Discovery of Grounded Theory*. Chicago: Aldine.

Gregg, K. 1996: The logical and developmental problems of second language acquisition. In W. R. Ritchie and T. Bhatia (eds), *Handbook of Second Language Acquisition*. San Diego: Academic Press, 49–81.

Gumperz, J. J. 1982: *Discourse Strategies*. Cambridge: Cambridge University Press.

Gumperz, J. J. 1984: *Communicative Competence Revisited*. Berkeley: University of California.

Gumperz, J. J. and Berenz, N. 1993: Transcribing conversational exchanges. In J. A. Edwards and M. D. Lampert (eds), *Talking Data: Transcription and Coding in Discourse Analysis*. Hillsdale, NJ: Lawrence Erlbaum Associates, 91–122.

Gumperz, J. J. and Hymes, D. (eds) 1972: *Directions in Sociolinguistics: The Ethnography of Communication*. New York: Holt, Rinehart, and Winston.

Hall, J. K. 1995: (Re)creating our worlds with worlds: a sociohistorical perspective on face-to-face interaction. *Applied Linguistics*, 10 (1), 206–32.

Hanks, W. F. 1993: Foreword. In J. Lave and E. Wenger, *Situated Learning: Legitimate Peripheral Participation*. Cambridge: Cambridge University Press, 13–24.

Harklau, L. 1994: ESL versus mainstream classes: contrasting L2 learning environments. *TESOL Quarterly*, 28 (2), 241–72.

Harth, E. 1993: *The Creative Loop: How the Brain Makes a Mind*. Reading, MA: Addison-Wesley.

Hatch, E., Shirai, Y., and Fantuzzi, C. 1990: The need for an integrated theory: connecting modules. *TESOL Quarterly*, 24 (4), 697–716.

He, A. W. 1997: Learning and being: identity construction in the classroom. In L. Bouton (ed.), *Pragmatics and Language Learning* 8. Urbana: University of Illinois, Urbana-Champagne, 201–22.

Heath, S. B. 1983: *Ways with Words: Language, Life and Work in Communities and Classrooms*. Cambridge: Cambridge University Press.

Hill, J. H. 1992: Language and world view. *Annual Review of Anthropology*, 21, 381–406.

Holland, D. and Quinn, N. (eds) 1987: *Cultural Models in Language and Thought*. New York: Cambridge University Press.

Hymes, D. 1972: On communicative competence. In J. B. Pride and J. Holmes (eds), *Sociolinguistics*. Harmondsworth: Penguin, 269–93.

Hymes, D. 1974: *Foundations in Sociolinguistics*. Philadelphia: University of Pennsylvania Press.

Hymes, D. 1980: *Language in Education: Ethnolinguistic Essays*. Washington, DC: Center for Applied Linguistics.

Jacobs, B. and Schumann, J. 1992: Language acquisition and the neurosciences: towards a more integrative perspective. *Applied Linguistics*, 13 (3), 282–301.

Kaplan, A. 1964: *The Conduct of Inquiry*. San Francisco: Chandler.

Kasper, G. 1997: "A" stands for acquisition: a response to Firth and Wagner. *Modern Language Journal*, 81 (3), 307–12.

Krashen, S. D. 1985: *The Input Hypothesis: Issues and Implications*. London: Longman.

Krashen, S. D. and Scarcella, R. 1978: On routines and patterns in language acquisition and performance. *Language Learning*, 28 (2), 283–300.

Lakoff, G. 1984: *Classifiers as Reflection of Mind: A Cognitive Approach to Prototype Theory*. Berkeley Cognitive Science Report No. 19. Berkeley: University of California Institute of Human Learning.

Lakoff, G. and Johnson, M. 1980: *Metaphors We Live By*. Chicago: University of Chicago Press.

Lakoff, G. and Johnson, M. 1999: *Philosophy in the Flesh: The Embodied*

Mind and its Challenge to Western Thought. New York: Basic Books.

Lave, J. and Wenger, E. 1993: *Situated Learning: Legitimate Peripheral Participation*. Cambridge: Cambridge University Press.

Lazaraton, A. 1995: Qualitative research in applied linguistics: a progress report. *TESOL Quarterly*, 29 (3), 455–72.

Long, M. H. 1988: Instructed interlanguage development. In L. Beebe (ed.), *Issues in Second Language Acquisition: Multiple Perspectives*. Rowley, MA: Newbury House, 77–100.

Long, M. H. 1996: The role of the linguistic environment in second language acquisition. In W. R. Ritchie and T. Bhatia (eds), *Handbook of Second Language Acquisition*. San Diego: Academic Press, 413–68.

Long, M. H. 1997: Construct validity in SLA research: a response to Firth and Wagner. *Modern Language Journal*, 81 (3), 318–23.

Losey, K. M. 1995: Gender and ethnicity as factors in the development of verbal skills in bilingual Mexican American women. *TESOL Quarterly*, 29 (4), 635–61.

McKay, S. L. and Wong, S.-L. C. 1996: Multiple discourse, multiple identities: investment and agency in second-language learning among Chinese adolescent immigrant students. *Harvard Educational Review*, 66, 577–608.

McLaughlin, B. 1984: *Second-Language Acquisition in Childhood. Volume 1: Preschool Children*. Second edition. Hillsdale, NJ: Lawrence Erlbaum Associates.

Miller, P. 1982: *Amy, Wendy and Beth: Learning Language in South Baltimore*. Austin: University of Texas Press.

Myles, F., Hooper, J., and Mitchell, R. 1998: Rote or rule? Exploring the role of formulaic language in foreign language learning. *Language Learning*, 48 (3), 323–63.

Nelson, K. 1996: *Language in Cognitive Development: The Emergence of the Mediated Mind*. New York: Cambridge University Press.

Ochs, E. 1979: Transcription as theory. In E. Ochs and B. B. Schieffelin (eds), *Developmental Pragmatics*. New York: Academic Press, 43–72.

Ochs, E. 1986: *Culture and Language Acquisition: Acquiring Communicative Competence in a Western Samoan Village*. New York: Cambridge University Press.

Ochs, E. and Schieffelin, B. B. 1995: The impact of language socialization on grammatical development. In P. Fletcher and B. MacWhinney (eds), *The Handbook of Child Language*. Oxford: Blackwell, 73–94.

Pallotti, G. 1996: Towards an ecology of second language acquisition: SLA as a socialization process. In E. Kellerman, B. Weltens, and T. Bongaerts (eds), *EuroSLA 6: A Selection of Papers*, 55, 121–34.

Peirce, B. N. 1995a: Social identity, investment, and language learning. *TESOL Quarterly*, 29 (1), 9–29.

Peirce, B. N. 1995b: The theory of methodology in qualitative research. *TESOL Quarterly*, 29 (3), 569–76.

Pepper, S. C. 1966: *World Hypotheses*. Berkeley: University of California.

Peters, A. 1983: *The Units of Language Acquisition*. Cambridge: Cambridge University Press.

Philips, S. U. 1972: Participant structures and communicative competence: Warm Springs children in community and classroom. In C. B. Cazden, V. P. John, and D. Hymes (eds), *Functions of Language in the Classroom*. New York: Teachers College Press, 370–94.

Philips, S. U. 1983: *The Invisible Culture: Communication in Classroom and Community on the Warm Springs Indian Reservation*. New York: Longman.

Pica, T. 1987: Interlanguage adjustments as an outcome of NS–NNS negotiated interaction. *Language Learning*, 38 (1), 45–73.

Poole, D. 1992: Language socialization in the second language classroom. *Language Learning*, 42, 593–616.

Poulisse, N. 1997: Some words in defense of the psycholinguistic approach: a response to Firth and Wagner. *Modern Language Journal*, 81 (3), 324–8.

Quinn, N. and Holland, D. 1987: Introduction. In D. Holland and N. Quinn (eds), *Cultural Models in Language and Thought*. New York: Cambridge University Press, 3–40.

Ramanathan, V. and Atkinson, D. 1999: Ethnographic approaches and methods in L2 writing research: a critical guide and review. *Applied Linguistics*, 14 (1), 1–43.

Rivers, W. 1994: Comprehension and production: the interactive duo. In R. M. Barasch and C. V. James (eds), *Beyond the Monitor Model: Comments on Current Theory and Practice in Second Language Acquisition*. Boston: Heinle and Heinle, 71–95.

Roberts, C. and Simonot, M. 1987: "This is my life": how language acquisition is interactionally accomplished. In R. Ellis (ed.), *Second Language Acquisition in Context*. London: Prentice-Hall, 133–48.

Rogoff, B. and Lave, J. (eds) 1984: *Everyday Cognition: Its Development in Social Context*. Cambridge, MA: Harvard University Press.

Rumelhart, D. E., McClelland, J. L., and the PDP Research Group 1986: *Parallel Distributed Processing*. Cambridge, MA: MIT Press.

Schank, R. and Abelson, R. 1977: *Scripts, Plans, Goals and Understanding: An Inquiry into Human Knowledge Structures*. Hillsdale, NJ: Lawrence Erlbaum Associates.

Schecter, S. R. and Bayley, R. 1997: Language socialization practices and cultural identity: case studies of Mexican-descent families in California and Texas. *TESOL Quarterly*, 31 (3), 513–41.

Schieffelin, B. B. 1990: *The Give and Take of Everyday Life: Language Socialization of Kaluli Children*. New York: Cambridge University Press.

Schieffelin, B. B. and Ochs, E. 1986: Language socialization. *Annual Review of Anthropology*, 15, 163–91.

Schmidt, R. 1983: Interaction, acculturation, and the acquisition of communicative competence: a case study of an adult. In N. Wolfson and E. Judd (eds), *Sociolinguistics and SLA*. Rowley, MA: Newbury House, 137–267.

Schmidt, R. 1988: The potential of PDP for SLA theory and research. *University of Hawai'i Working Papers in ESL*, 7, 55–66.

Schmidt, R. 1990: The role of consciousness in second language learning. *Applied Linguistics*, 11 (2), 129–58.

Shore, B. 1996: *Culture in Mind: Cognition, Culture, and the Problem of Meaning*. New York and London: Oxford University Press.

Siegal, M. 1996: The role of learner subjectivity in second language sociolinguistic competency: Western women learning Japanese. *Applied Linguistics*, 17, 356–82.

Sokolik, M. E. 1990: Learning without rules: PDP and a resolution of the adult language learning paradox. *TESOL Quarterly*, 24 (4), 685–96.

Strauss, C. and Quinn, N. 1997: *A Cognitive Theory of Cultural Meaning*. New York: Cambridge University Press.

Swain, M. 1981: Immersion education: applicability for nonvernacular teaching to vernacular speakers. *Studies in Second Language Aquisition*, 4 (1), 1–17.

Tollefson, J. W. 1991: *Planning Language, Planning Inequality: Language Policy in the Community*. New York and London: Longman.

Vygotsky, L. S. 1962: *Thought and Language*. Cambridge, MA: MIT Press.

Vygotsky, L. S. 1978: *Mind in Society*. Cambridge, MA: Harvard University Press.

Watson, K. A. 1975: Transferable communicative routines: strategies and group identity in two speech events. *Language in Society*, 4 (2), 53–72.

Watson-Gegeo, K. A. 1988: Ethnography in ESL: defining the essentials. *TESOL Quarterly*, 22, 575–92.

Watson-Gegeo, K. A. 1990: The social transfer of cognitive skills in Kwara'ae. *Quarterly Newsletter of the Laboratory of Comparative Human Cognition*, 12 (53), 86–90.

Watson-Gegeo, K. A. 1992: Thick explanation in the ethnographic study of child socialization: a longitudinal study of the problem of schooling for Kwara'ae (Solomon Islands) children. In W. A. Corsaro and P. J. Miller (eds), *Interpretive Approaches to Children's Socialization*. Special issue of *New Directions for Child Development*, 58, 51–66.

Watson-Gegeo, K. A. and Gegeo, D. W. 1986a: The social world of Kwara'ae children: acquisition of language and values. In J. Cook-Gumperz, W. Corsaro, and J. Streeck (eds), *Children's Worlds and Children's Language*. The Hague: Mouton, 109–28.

Watson-Gegeo, K. A. and Gegeo, D. W. 1986b: Calling-out and repeating routines in Kwara'ae children's language socialization. In B. B. Schieffelin and E. Ochs (eds), *Language Socialization Across Cultures*. London and New York: Cambridge University Press, 17–50.

Watson-Gegeo, K. A. and Gegeo, D. W. 1994: Keeping culture out of the classroom in rural Solomon Island schools: a critical analysis. *Educational Foundations*, 8 (2), 27–55.

Watson-Gegeo, K. A. and Gegeo, D. W. 1995: Understanding language and power in the Solomon Islands: methodological lessons for educational intervention. In J. W. Tollefson (ed.), *Power and Inequality in Language Education*. New York: Cambridge University Press, 59–72.

Watson-Gegeo, K. A. and Gegeo, D. W. 1999: (Re)modeling culture in Kwara'ae: the role of discourse in children's cognitive development. *Discourse Studies*, 1 (2), 241–60.

Weinert, R. 1995: The role of formulaic speech in second language acquisition: a review. *Applied Linguistics*, 16, 180–205.

Wertsch, J. V. 1985: *Vygotsky and the Social Formation of Mind*. New York: Cambridge University Press.

Willet, J. 1997: Becoming first graders in an L2: an ethnographic study of L2 socialization. *TESOL Quarterly*, 29 (3), 437–503.

Wong Fillmore, L. 1976: The second time around: cognitive and social strategies in second language acquisition. Ph.D. dissertation. University of California, Berkeley.

Zuengler, J. 1989: Identity and IL development and use. *Applied Linguistics*, 10 (1), 80–96.

Zukow-Goldring, P. G. 1996: Sensitive caregivers foster the comprehension of speech: when gestures speak louder than words. *Early Development and Parenting*, 5 (4), 195–211.

Zukow-Goldring, P. G. and Ferko, K. R. 1994: An ecological approach to the emergence of the lexicon: socializing attention. In V. P. John-Steiner, C. Panofsky, and L. Smith (eds), *Sociocultural Approaches to Language and Literacy: Interactionist Perspectives*. New York: Cambridge University Press, 170–90.

8 Social Context

JEFF SIEGEL

1 Introduction

This chapter examines the influence of the social context on SLA from four different angles. Section 2 describes the various sociolinguistic settings in which SLA occurs. Here we will see if the type of setting is relevant to the generalizations about SLA that have been made over the years. Section 3 looks at various ways of analysing social context and at SLA studies that take social contextual factors into account. Here we will look at particular sociostructural and interactional factors that are relevant to SLA. Section 4 outlines various types of educational programs. Here we will see how SLA attainment depends on the interaction of the type of program, the sociolinguistic setting, and various sociostructural factors. Section 5 considers the importance of the perceived sociolinguistic relationship between the L1 and L2 and covers the now neglected area of second dialect acquisition (SDA). Here we will explore whether there are significant differences between SDA and SLA. Thus, this chapter focuses on the broader social factors which may affect groups of learners, rather than on the more immediate situational factors which may affect individual learners.[1]

2 Sociolinguistic Settings for SLA

Various broad sociolinguistic settings for SLA can be distinguished on the basis of the functional roles and domains of use of the L1 and L2. Factors taken into account are whether the L2 has a widespread or restricted functional role in the society, whether it is spoken as a native language by a significant section of the population, and whether most of the society is monolingual or bilingual. Another significant sociolinguistic factor relevant to all settings is the particular variety of the L2 which provides the input (see table 8.1).

Table 8.1 Sociolinguistic settings for SLA

Setting	*Typical learners*	*L2*	*Examples*
Dominant L2	Speakers of minority languages (e.g., immigrants, swamped indigenous people)	Dominant or majority language	Turks learning German in Germany; Native Americans learning Spanish in Peru
External L2	Speakers of the dominant language	Foreign or distant language	Japanese learning English in Japan; English speakers in Western Canada learning French
Coexisting L2	Speakers in multilingual environments	Nearby language spoken by a large proportion of the population	German speakers learning French in Switzerland
Institutional L2	Speakers in multilingual environments	Indigenous or imported language with a wide range of official uses	English in India; Swahili in Tanzania; English in Samoa
Minority L2	Speakers of the dominant language	Language of minority group (indigenous or immigrant)	English speakers learning Welsh or Panjabi

In the *dominant L2* setting, the L2 is the native language of the majority of the population and used in all domains in everyday life, including the home, education, government, the legal system, business, and the media. This setting is sometimes called the "majority language context" (Ellis, 1994). It is found in countries such as the USA, Australia, France, and Japan. The L1 speakers are either immigrants, visitors, or indigenous peoples, such as Native Americans or Australian Aborigines, who have been swamped by L2-speaking invaders. They are expected to acquire the dominant language, either inside or outside the classroom, in order to take part in mainstream society.

In the *external L2* setting, a language not generally used for everyday communicative functions within the society is learned in the classroom by usually monolingual L1 speakers. This L2 may be a foreign language (such as Japanese in Australia), a language spoken in a distant part of the same country (such as French in Western Canada), or a world lingua franca (such as English in Korea).

In the third setting, the target is a *coexisting L2*, spoken in the immediate or nearby environment as the native language of a large proportion of the population – for example in border areas or in countries with two or more large language groups, as with French and German in Switzerland, and neighboring group languages in Papua New Guinea. The L1 and L2 are used in similar domains by their respective speakers and have similar status. Studies done in this setting have concentrated almost exclusively on classroom acquisition.

The vast majority of SLA studies have been conducted in these three types of sociolinguistic settings, of which the first two are basically monolingual. Furthermore, SLA research has almost always considered the target to be the standard dialect of the L2 – the variety codified in dictionaries and grammars, normally used in published expository writing, and taught in schools. The study of acquisition where the input includes varieties other than the standard has been neglected, despite the common knowledge that some learners acquire non-standard varieties of the L2 outside the classroom – for example, Caribbean immigrants in London. One exception is the work of Eisenstein (1986), who looked at learners exposed to standard English, New York non-standard English and African-American Vernacular English, and examined their preferences among these varieties and the effects of dialect intelligibility on SLA.

Other sociolinguistic settings exist but have been virtually ignored by SLA research. The first of these is the *institutional L2* setting, where the L2 is widely used in a number of domains and institutions, but for most of the population it is an additional language, rather than a native language. A large proportion of the society is typically bi- or multilingual, maintaining their L1 for use in the home and other domains, such as literature, but also acquiring the L2 for communicating with speakers of the other languages in the society and for official purposes in various institutions of government and education. This is sometimes called the "official language context" (Ellis, 1994). The L2 may be a former colonial language, such as English in Singapore and Fiji, or it may be one of the indigenous languages of the country, such as Bahasa Melayu in Malaysia and Swahili in Tanzania. In some societies, the institutional L2 is used in a more restricted set of domains – for example in official functions, but not for inter-group communication, as with English in Hong Kong, or mainly in education, as with English in Scandinavia and in some Pacific countries, such as Tonga and Samoa.

Research on the acquisition of English illustrates how the field of SLA has been limited to particular sociolinguistic settings. One of the most common classifications of social contexts in SLA is the distinction between the acquisition of English as a second language and as a foreign language, or the ESL/EFL dichotomy. But this classification fails to distinguish between English as second language when it is the dominant language in a basically monolingual setting and when it is an institutional language in a multilingual setting. This has been pointed out by scholars such as Judd (1987) and Nayar (1997), who have proposed alternative taxonomies. Furthermore, almost all studies of the acquisition of English have concentrated on learners in dominant L2 settings in Britain, the USA, Canada, Australia, and New Zealand. However, there are far more learners of English in institutional L2 settings in India, Pakistan, Sri Lanka, Singapore, Malaysia, the Philippines, Kenya, Nigeria, Papua New Guinea, Fiji, and other countries. (See Kachru, 1985.)

This has led to a rather skewed view of the nature of the L2 and its speakers. First, nearly all studies of the acquisition of English have concentrated on the standard varieties spoken in the dominant L2 settings. They have all but ignored the "indigenized varieties" of English (sometimes called "New Englishes") which have become established with their own norms in most of the institutional L2 settings and are the target languages of hundreds of millions of learners. Second, the benchmark for the acquisition of English is normally considered to be the language of native speakers who in dominant L2 contexts are typically monolingual. Yet the majority of users of English in the world are non-native speakers and bilingual. Sridhar and Sridhar (1986) describe several ways in which acquisition of indigenized varieties of English (IVEs) in institutional L2 settings differs from acquisition in other settings. First, with regard to the target, the goal is to be able to use the L2 effectively with other mostly non-native speakers, not with native speakers. Thus, the target is actually the particular non-native IVE of the country, such as Indian or Singapore English, not a native variety, such as British or American English. Second, most of the input comes from the IVE, not from a native variety, and most of it is obtained in the classroom or in interactions with other non-native speakers, not with native speakers. Third, learners use the English they acquire alongside the other languages of their verbal repertoires which are already used for particular functions. Thus they do not need to acquire English for as wide a range of functions as learners in dominant L2 settings have to.

Because of these factors, Sridhar and Sridhar (1986, p. 12) observe that "SLA theory has been counter-intuitive and limited in explanatory power with regard to a very substantial segment of the second language learner population." This is especially true with regard to the notions of interlanguage and interference or negative transfer. For example, as Kachru and Nelson (1996) point out, considering the "non-standard" features of indigenized varieties to be the result of L1 interference and fossilized interlanguage (see Selinker, 1972) relies on two assumptions: (i) learners in institutional L2 settings wish to emulate a particular dominant variety of standard English, and (ii) models of this variety are available in the environment. In most cases, however, both of these assumptions are unfounded. Sridhar and Sridhar (1986, p. 10) also emphasize the positive use of transfer in communication in bilingual IVE settings:

> Far from impeding intelligibility, transfer acts as the grease to make the wheels of bilingual communication turn smoothly. Given that transfer features are not idiosyncratic to learners but shared by speakers with the same substratal languages, they serve as effective simplification strategies, modes of acculturation

> . . . and as markers of membership in the community of speakers of a given indigenized variety.

With regard to actual research on IVEs, Lowenberg's work on Malaysian English (1986b, 1993) shows that lexical transfer serves not only as a compensatory acquisition strategy but as an enrichment strategy for adapting the language to its new sociocultural surroundings. Examples are the Malay words *gotong-royong* 'a form of communical cooperation' and *adat* 'a body of traditional law,' which are commonly transferred into English to refer to these unique cultural institutions of the Malay-speaking areas of Southeast Asia (1993, p. 44). Lowenberg (1986a) also observes that phonological transfer, especially in stress and intonation patterns, is often associated with group identity. In addition, he illustrates that generalization of rules in IVEs is different from overgeneralization in other SLA contexts in that it is actually an extension of what are extremely productive processes in the native varieties.

In a slightly different vein, Williams (1987) examines common features across a number of IVEs as a potential source of insight into SLA processes. She comes up with the following relevant speaker-oriented processes: economy of production, regularization, selection production of redundant markers, and hyperclarity (reduction of ambiguity and maximization of transparency). Perhaps the most detailed study of the acquisition of an IVE is that of Gupta (1994) on Singapore Colloquial English (SCE). Data come from tape-recordings of children in two families acquiring SCE in multilingual environments. The linguistic feature that she concentrates on, interrogatives, reveals an additive or sequential acquisition of structures in SCE which differs from the developmental patterns described for the acquisition of standard forms of English as a first and second language.

Finally, the other setting for SLA that has rarely been studied is the *minority L2* setting – where speakers of a dominant language learn a minority language, usually in naturalistic rather than classroom contexts (see table 8.1 above). The few studies that have been conducted have provided insights which question some of the assumptions made on the basis of research in other settings. One example is the study by Ben (M. B. H.) Rampton (1991, 1995) of minority language learning and use in England among an adolescent peer group made up of South Asians, Afro-Caribbeans, and White Anglos. He describes (1991, pp. 232–3) the latter two groups learning Panjabi in recreational settings through translation, elicitation, and even practice and revision. Rampton notes (p. 292) that this kind of formal instruction and form-focused activity in such a setting is a phenomenon not reported elsewhere. Rampton (1995, p. 292) also observes that rather than generating "situational anxiety," as L2 learning is assumed to do, the learning of Panjabi was a pleasurable experience for the youths involved.

Another assumption that is questioned by research in minority L2 settings is that SLA learners are stigmatized. While this may be true in dominant L2 settings, Rampton's research, as well Trosset's (1986) study of learning Welsh, a minority language in Britain, and Woolard's (1989, p. 76) observations on learning Catalan in Spain, reveal that learners of a minority L2 are often accorded prestige by speakers of the language (Rampton, 1995, p. 293). Trosset's (1986) study also highlights several aspects of language learning which are not usually considered in studies in other contexts, such as the importance of native speakers' perceptions of the learner and the learner's roles as both "consciousness raiser" and performer (p. 189).

To sum up, one shortcoming of the field of SLA is that generalizations have been made on the basis of research carried out in only a limited range of sociolinguistic settings and involving only standard varieties of language. The findings of the few studies done in alternative settings and with other varieties question the validity of these generalizations and illustrate the importance of considering sociolinguistic context in SLA.

3 Analysis of Social Context in SLA

Ways of analysing social context generally vary along three parameters: macro vs. micro, structural vs. interactional, and objective vs. subjective. Macro-analysis focuses on society as a whole and the characteristics of the various social groups which comprise it. With regard to SLA, it considers the relative size, status, and power of the L1 and L2 groups and the general domains of use of the L1 and L2. In contrast, micro-analysis pays attention to the behavior of individuals in particular situations which results from broader social factors. With regard to SLA, it examines specific activities involving L2 learning and use, the social relationships between particular L1 and L2 speakers, and the status and power of individual L2 learners and their interlocutors within social interactions.

The structural point of view sees power, prestige, and other specific aspects of social context as given, determined by the structure of the society and by the historical forces that shaped this structure. For example, a person's social identity is the result of the particular social group to which she or he belongs and the position of this group in society. SLA may be affected directly or indirectly by these sociostructural or sociohistorical factors. In contrast, the interactional point of view sees social context not as given, but as created in each specific situation by the interplay of several social factors. According to this view, a person has multiple social identities, and the one that emerges in a particular situation is determined not only by the person's group membership but by the social interaction. Social identities and relationships may be continuously changing and renegotiated as the interaction proceeds. The particular kind of language used both reflects and creates one's social position and identity in the interaction. It affects the interaction and, at the same time, the way the interaction proceeds affects the language that is used. In the same manner, rather than just the social context affecting SLA, there is a "reflexive" relationship between the two (Firth and Wagner, 1997), with second language learning and use also affecting the social context.

Finally, the objective perspective concentrates on the observable aspects of the social context, while the subjective perspective concentrates on individuals' perceptions of these aspects. For example, a person's social identity may be determined objectively by membership in a particular social group or by the characteristics of a particular social interaction, but subjectively by attitudes toward this and other groups or by perceptions of the social interaction. Also, while the objective perspective looks at the institutional associations of particular languages, the subjective perspective looks at symbolic associations.

Of SLA studies that have taken social context into account, the vast majority have involved macro-analysis and the structural point of view, with both objective and subjective perspectives represented. However, more studies using micro-analysis and the interactional approach have recently begun to appear.

We will begin by looking at macro SLA studies which examine the effects of particular sociostructural factors – most commonly the relative size, status, and power of the L1 and L2 groups. With regard to size, Gardner and Clément (1990) observe on the basis of studies with French and English in Canada that the relative proportion of the L2 group in the community is positively related to the extent of L2 acquisition, at least in classroom situations. But of course the presence of L2 speakers is not a necessary condition for SLA, as seen with the success of other Canadian programs (e.g., Genesee, 1987) in which other factors seem to be more important, such as the nature of the course and teacher, support from parents, and learners' attitudes. With regard to the relative political power of the learners' language group and the L2 group, different studies from Canada show that increased power and recognition of a group along with significant numbers affect the extent to which the language will be learned by other groups (Gardner and Clément, 1990).

The problem with considering sociostructural factors as determinants of SLA is that they may be confounded with other factors, such as the amount of contact between the L1 and the L2 group. For example, it seems that a low-status minority group will have more opportunities for contact with a high-status majority group than vice versa. However, as pointed out by Gardner and Clément (1990, p. 507), few researchers examining the minority/majority distinction have controlled systematically for the amount of contact. An exception is a study by Clément and Kruidenier (1983), who found that the variables of the relative status of the L1 and L2 groups and the amount of contact with the L2 have independent effects, at least with regard to *orientation* – that is, the underlying reasons for learning the L2.

This brings us to the social psychological approach and various models (discussed below) which seek to explain the individual characteristics that affect SLA, and sometimes how social context influences these characteristics. Within this approach, there are several perspectives which differ according to the variables they emphasize. These include the affective factors of motivation, self-confidence, and anxiety, as well as the degree of contact or interaction. We will start by looking briefly at motivation. (For more detailed discussion, see Crookes and Schmidt, 1991; Dörnyei, 1994; Dörnyei and Schmidt, 2001; Ellis,

1994, pp. 508–17; Gardner and Tremblay, 1994a, 1994b; Larsen-Freeman and Long, 1991, pp. 172–84). In the social psychological literature on SLA, motivation is usually thought of as the inclination to put in effort to achieve a desired goal – namely acquisition of the L2. As with many social psychological constructs, the motivation of subjects is determined by a combination of several factors, measured by using self-report questionnaires. Nearly all social psychological models of SLA distinguish two types of orientation which may affect motivation. *Integrative orientation* relates to the learner's wish to identify with the L2-speaking community, whereas *instrumental orientation* relates to the desire to learn the L2 for a particular purpose, such as getting a job or fulfilling some educational requirement (Belmechri and Hummel, 1998; Clément, Dörnyei, and Noels, 1994; Gardner and Lambert, 1959; Spolsky, 2000). Earlier social psychological research distinguished between two corresponding types of motivation – integrative and instrumental. Motivation is also influenced by the learner's attitudes toward the L2, its speakers and culture, toward the social and practical value of using the L2, and toward his or her own language and culture.

The results of early research on the effects of motivation and attitudes on SLA illustrate the importance of taking social context into account. Mainly on the basis of initial studies with English-speaking (majority) learners of French in Canada, it was claimed that integrative motivation is more important than instrumental motivation in determining L2 achievement (Gardner and Lambert, 1959). However, later studies (Gardner and Lambert, 1972; Lukmani, 1972; Oller, Baca, and Vigil, 1979; Shaw, 1981) found instrumental motivation to be more important for learners from minority language groups in dominant L2 settings (L1 French and Spanish speakers learning English in the USA) and for learners in institutional L2 settings (learners of English in India and the Philippines). Similarly with regard to attitudes, studies in dominant L2 settings in North America showed strong correlations between positive attitudes toward speakers of the L2 (English) and L2 achievement (see Larsen-Freeman and Long, 1991, p. 176). However, studies in external L2 settings (L2 English in Israel and Japan) showed weak or non-existent correlations (Chihara and Oller, 1978; Cooper and Fishman, 1977).

Leaving aside the problems of defining and operationalizing the notions of integrative motivation and positive attitudes (see Crookes and Schmidt, 1991; Dörnyei, 1994; Oller, 1981), we can explain these contradictory results by referring to the different functions and statuses of both the L1 and the L2 in the various sociolinguistic settings in which these studies took place. These sociostructural factors influence motivation and attitudes, as well as opportunities for contact between learners and L2 speakers, which, in turn, influence SLA (Clément and Kruidenier, 1983; Gardner, 1980). They also have an effect on other individual characteristics which may influence SLA, such as self-confidence (Clément, 1986).

Now let us turn to various models within the social psychological approach which take sociostructural factors into account (see table 8.2). The *socioeducational*

Table 8.2 The role of social context in four social psychological models of SLA

Model	*Acquisitional context/ sociolinguistic setting*	*Social contextual factors considered*	*Factors influenced*	*Key determinant of SLA*
Socioeducational	Classroom/external L2, dominant L2	"Social-cultural milieu" (prevailing attitude toward bilingualism of L2 group)	Integrative orientation; attitudes toward learning situation	Motivation
Acculturation	Naturalistic/ dominant L2	L1 group size, cohesiveness, etc.; L2 group dominance/ status; inter-group attitudes	Social distance, psychological distance	Acculturation (of learner to L2 group)
Social context	Classroom/dominant L2, coexisting L2	"Social milieux" (relative size of L1 and L2 groups)	Integrativeness, fear of assimilation, self-confidence	Motivation
Inter-group	Naturalistic/ dominant L2	Perceived ethnolinguistic vitality (relative size, status, support of L1 group); identification with L1 group; etc.	Integrative motivation, degree of insecurity	Social interaction

model (Gardner, 1983, 1985, 1988) attempts to explain how certain aspects of the social context are related to L2 proficiency through intervening variables such as motivation and anxiety. The model concentrates on L2 learning in the classroom. Although the model does not emphasize sociostructural factors such as size and status of the L1 and L2 groups, it does consider the *social-cultural milieu*, which includes the prevailing attitude toward bilingualism in the community – for example, whether bilingualism is valued, as in Canada, or whether it is considered an undesirable obstacle to assimilation, as in the USA. The social-cultural milieu influences individual factors, such as the degree of integrative orientation and attitudes toward the learning situation, which in turn determine the degree of motivation. This has a more direct relationship to various outcomes in one of two learning contexts – formal, in which case aptitude is also relevant, or informal. The outcomes are both linguistic (relating to the acquisition of L2 proficiency) and non-linguistic (relating to the re-evaluation of one's self-image and the acquisition of new social and cultural ideas). The model has been supported by empirical studies of English speakers in Canada learning French (for example, Gardner, 1985; Gardner, Lalonde, and Pierson, 1983; Gardner, Tremblay and Masgoret, 1997). It has been criticized on several fronts by Au (1988) and Dörnyei (1994), but defended by Gardner (1988) and Gardner and Tremblay (1994b).

Other social psychological models of SLA emphasize objective characteristics of the L1 and L2 social groups, and contact rather than motivation as the determinant of SLA proficiency. The *acculturation model* (Schumann, 1978a, 1978b, 1986) applies to naturalistic rather than classroom SLA in dominant L2 settings. The premise of the model is that the degree of L2 proficiency is proportional to the degree of acculturation by the learner to the L2 group. In other words, the acquisition of a second language is related to a more general modification of attitudes, knowledge, and behavior toward those of the group who speak that language.[2] According to the model, the extent of acculturation depends on the degree of *social distance* and *psychological distance* between learners and the L2 group. The greater the social and psychological distance, the less contact learners will have with the L2 and the less they will be open to the available input – thus, the lower the degree of SLA.

Social distance is determined by a set of factors characterizing the L1 group and the relationships it has with the L2 group. L1 group characteristics are size, cohesiveness, integration pattern, enclosure, and intended length of residence. Social distance will be greater when the L1 group is large and cohesive, wants to preserve its lifestyle and values, does not wish to assimilate, has its own social facilities, and intends to stay for a short time. Inter-group characteristics include social dominance and attitudes. Social distance will be greater when the L2 group is politically dominant and has higher status, and when the two groups have negative attitudes toward each other. Psychological distance is determined by individual factors, such as language and culture shock and motivation. If learners feel anxious, disoriented, and inhibited, and if they are not integratively motivated to learn the L2, then psychological distance will be greater. Thus, the sum of these social and individual factors indirectly determines the degree to which the L2 is acquired. In spite of being widely referred to in the SLA literature, the acculturation model has received only limited support in empirical studies. (For detailed conceptual and methodological critiques, see Larsen-Freeman and Long, 1991, pp. 251–66; McLaughlin, 1987, pp. 109–32.)

A major influence on other SLA models emphasizing social group characteristics has been speech accommodation theory (Beebe, 1988; Giles, 1977; Giles, Taylor, and Bourhis, 1973). According to this theory, people may adjust their speech to either reduce or accentuate linguistic differences with their interlocutors. Adjustment toward others is called *convergence* and away from others *divergence*. Convergence occurs when the speaker wants approval from people with similar beliefs, values, and attitudes. Divergence occurs when the speaker wants to assert distinctiveness from interlocutors from another social group.

Closely associated with speech accommodation is ethnolinguistic identity theory (Bourhis and Giles, 1977; Giles and Johnson, 1981, 1987), which draws on the work of Tajfel (1974, 1978) and considers language to be a salient marker of group membership and thus social identity. The key notion of this theory is *ethnolinguistic vitality* (Giles, Bourhis, and Taylor, 1977). This refers to the combination of factors which make a group behave distinctively and act collectively. The higher a group's ethnolinguistic vitality, the greater the chance of its continued existence as a distinct group. Ethnolinguistic vitality depends on three sets of factors: status (economic power and prestige), demographics (numbers relative to other groups and population trends), and institutional support (representation of members in formal and informal institutions). Clearly, then, this construct is largely determined by the sociostructural factors of size, status, and power.

In the *social context model* of SLA (Clément, 1980), the relative ethnolinguistic vitality of the L1 and L2 groups influences the strength of two opposing forces in the learner: *integrativeness* and *fear of assimilation*. Integrativeness, as we have seen, refers to the desire to become an accepted member of the L2 culture. Fear of assimilation is the fear that learning the second language will result in the loss of the first language and culture. The model distinguishes two different "social milieux": *unicultural,* where one language group is clearly the majority (that is, a dominant L2 setting), and *multicultural,* where the two language groups do not differ greatly in numbers (a coexisting L2 setting). The operation of the two opposing forces, integration and fear of assimilation, is considered to be the "primary motivational process" in the model. In a unicultural milieu, the net result of this process will directly determine the degree of motivation to learn the L2, which in turn determines the extent of the communicative competence acquired. However, in a multicultural milieu, this process is mediated by a "secondary motivational process" associated with self-confidence. More specifically, the balance between integrativeness and fear of assimilation influences the frequency and pleasantness of interaction with

L2 speakers, which affect the learners' confidence in their ability to use the L2. The level of this self-confidence then determines the degree of motivation to acquire the L2. This model has received some support from empirical studies (Clément, 1986; Clément and Kruidenier, 1985).

The *inter-group model* (Giles and Byrne, 1982) also emphasizes social group characteristics, but it focuses on the social identity of the individual members of the group and their subjective perceptions of characteristics such as ethnolinguistic vitality, rather than on any objective measurements. It applies to dominant L2 settings, and while motivation is an important factor, it considers interaction to be the main determinant of SLA proficiency. Giles and Byrne (1982) set out five conditions under which learners from the minority L1 group are most likely to acquire nativelike proficiency in the dominant L2. These are:

i learners' identification with the L1 group is weak and/or the L1 is not an important marker of group identity;
ii learners do not often compare themselves with the L2 group;
iii learners perceive the ethnolinguistic vitality of the L1 group as low;
iv learners perceive cultural and linguistic boundaries between the L1 and L2 groups as soft and open; and
v learners identify with and have status in other social groups, based on categories such as occupation, religion, or gender.

These conditions are related to low ethnolinguistic vitality and minimal insecurity, and they are associated with strong integrative motivation. This leads to anxiety-free social interaction and eventually long-term convergence with L2 speakers, resulting in high levels of L2 proficiency. Conversely, if the opposites of the five conditions apply, ethnolinguistic vitality and insecurity will be high, integrative motivation weak, interaction rare, and L2 proficiency low.

The inter-group model has been tested in only a few empirical studies (e.g., Giles and Johnson, 1987; B. J. Hall and Gudykunst, 1986) and these obtained mixed results. Sachdev and Bourhis (1991) emphasize the importance of applying the model to minority groups that have relatively low and subordinate status, as well as being outnumbered by the dominant group. A study of a subordinate minority group in London (Spanish speakers) by Kelly, Sachdev, Kottsieper, and Ingram (1993) found support for some aspects of the model – especially the inverse relationship between the degree of identification with the L1 group and the use or approval of the L2.

The social psychological models in general have been criticized on several fronts. Tollefson (1991, pp. 72–6) points out that these models imply that learners are free to make choices about when they interact with L2 speakers or whether they are motivated to integrate with the L2 culture. Thus, lack of L2 attainment can be blamed on the individual learner. This ignores the historical-structural factors that actually limit the "choices" learners can make and that determine the meaning of these "choices." These approaches do not pay enough attention to the sociohistorical factors of power and domination which have shaped factors they do consider, such as language prestige and cultural and linguistic boundaries. J. K. Hall (1995) calls for a sociohistorical approach to the study of SLA which takes into account the "sociocultural and/or sociopolitical authority" attached to conventionalized uses of language and the resources available to various users of the languages (p. 220). She criticizes the notions of interlanguage and fossilization, saying that the movement from the L1 to the L2 is not unilinear and that it depends on historical and sociocultural forces, not merely psychological abilities.

Rampton (1995) agrees that sociohistorical issues of authority and power have to be taken into account, but also points out the importance of a subjective examination of people's attitudes toward these issues and the symbolic associations of languages. With regard to methodology, Rampton (1991, p. 235) proposes a more "delicate" analysis of second language learning situations and learner statuses than is found in macro-analyses. Rather than using experimental methods and the collection of data prestructured through questionnaires, he advocates more holistic but detailed investigations through participant observation and ethnography (1995, pp. 291–2). Rampton also illustrates the value of the interactional point of view. He notes that the adolescents in his study (mentioned above) seem to be able to "negotiate the relationships between language and group membership" in their interactions (1995, p. 4) and he considers "the ways in which race and ethnicity are asserted, questioned and contested" in the learning and use of Panjabi, as well as Caribbean Creole and stylized South Asian English, in these interactions (p. 19).

Views similar to those of Tollefson, J. K. Hall, and Rampton are found in three recent articles which are specifically on SLA. Peirce (1995) proposes an approach which better integrates the learner and the social context and which takes into account the socially and historically constructed relationships between the learner and the L2. This approach is based on her longitudinal ethnographic study of five immigrant women in a dominant L2 setting (see box 8.1). It suggests that inequitable power relationships, rather than factors such as strong identification with the L1 group or low motivation, may limit opportunities for learners to interact with L2 speakers, and thus to practice the L2 outside the classroom.

Peirce's approach shifts not only to a micro- rather than macro-analysis of social context but also to an interactional rather than structural perspective. It takes the view that people have multiple and changing social identities, rather than the unitary static social identity of most social psychological models. Furthermore, Peirce introduces the concept of "investment," based on Bourdieu's (1977) idea of language as cultural capital, to capture the complex relationship between power, identity, and SLA. According to this concept, learners will invest effort in using and acquiring the L2 because of the returns they receive in resources such as friendship and education, as well as material gains. However, since learners have complex social identities and a variety of

Box 8.1 Peirce (1995)

Research questions: The author's basic research questions were (pp. 13–14):

> How are the opportunities for immigrant women in Canada to practice ESL socially structured outside the classroom? How do immigrant women respond to and act upon these social structures to create, use, or resist opportunities to practice English? To what extent should their actions be understood with reference to their investment in English and their changing social identities across time and space?

Underlying this research were the following assumptions:

i Language is not a neutral medium of communication; rather, it must be understood with reference to its social meaning (p. 13).
ii Both exposure to and practice in the target language are a necessary condition of SLA (p. 14).

Methodology: This qualitative longitudinal study focuses on the naturalistic language learning experiences of five immigrant women in their homes, workplaces, and communities (p. 14). The major source of data was diaries kept by participants for a six-month period, where participants kept records of their interactions with English-speaking Canadians and reflected on their learning experiences. The researcher also met regularly with the participants to share some diary entries and discuss their insights and concerns. Other sources of data were two detailed questionnaires administered before and after the study, personal and group interviews, and home visits (p. 14).

Findings: The conclusions of the research were:

i Affective factors such as motivation, introversion, and inhibition are not static, and may differ over time and space even within the same individual. These factors are socially constructed according to power relationships and other conditions.
ii Inequitable power relations may limit L2 learners' opportunities to practice the target language outside the classroom. However, "the decision to remain silent or the decision to speak may both constitute forms of resistance to inequitable social forces" (p. 20).
iii Language learners, like other people, have complex, non-static social identities which depend on both social structures and day-to-day social interaction. The efforts learners are willing to invest in acquiring the L2 are closely bound up with their changing social identities as well as the returns they expect to receive.

desires, the nature of their investment will always be changing. Thus, unlike integrative or instrumental motivation, investment is not a fixed individual attribute. In addition, when learners interact in the L2, they are continually renegotiating their own social identity. Therefore, investing in the L2 also involves investing in one's own constantly changing social identity (Peirce, 1995, pp. 17–18).

McKay and Wong (1996) expand on Peirce's approach, similarly drawing on a longitudinal ethnographic study of immigrants in a dominant L2 setting, but this time of four adolescents involved in classroom instruction. McKay and Wong conceive of the language learner from what they call a "contextualist perspective" – that is, a perspective which highlights the interrelationships between discourse and power in the social context of SLA.

Siegal (1996) examines a conversation between a New Zealand woman studying in Japan and her male Japanese professor. This is part of a larger longitudinal ethnographic study of the acquisition of sociolinguistic competence by several foreign women in Japan, based on language learning journals, interviews, observations, and tape-recorded interactions. The study demonstrates "the dynamic co-construction of identity and sociolinguistic proficiency within conversational interactions" (p. 356). The significant factors are the learner's conceptions of herself and her position in society, her views of the L2 language and culture, the constraints and resources in interactions which affect SLA, and the views of both the learner and the L2 society regarding sociolinguistic competency.

In general, research using micro-analysis and the interactional approach has provided some important insights into the role of social context in SLA. First, the attitudes of L1 speakers toward L2 learners and their proficiency may be just as significant as those of the L2 learners toward the L1 group, as shown by Trosset (1986), Rampton (1995), and Siegal (1996). As Rampton (1995, pp. 293–4) points out, communication difficulties may be caused not only by the learner's lack of L2 proficiency but also by the L1 interlocutor's assumptions about the L2 user's competence.

Second, a variety which differs from that of an idealized native speaker does not necessarily represent deficiency in L2 competence, as we have already seen for speakers of indigenized varieties of English. In addition to expressing a particular identity of the speaker, it may also be used to show solidarity with a peer group or to indicate attitudes toward society in general. For example, stylized South Asian English is used by the adolescents studied by Rampton (1995) not because of any lack of proficiency but for joking and ridiculing racist attitudes. As Firth and Wagner (1997, p. 292) observe, non-nativelike structures may be "deployed resourcefully and strategically to accomplish social and interactional ends." Furthermore, the decision not to use nativelike L2 forms or not to use the L2 at all may represent a form of resistance, which, alongside achievement and avoidance, is another kind of communication strategy (Rampton, 1991, p. 239). It follows, then, that in many situations nativelike proficiency is not the target of language learning. For example, in Rampton's study, Panjabi is a language learner variety for Anglo and Afro-Caribbean adolescents, and it is precisely this status that makes it suited for its use in inter-ethnic jocular abuse (1995, p. 175).

Third, the notions of the native speaker and nativelike proficiency are themselves questionable when one considers multiple and changing social identities and language abilities (Firth and Wagner, 1997; Rampton, 1995).

There are clearly many cases in which non-native speakers have greater proficiency in and allegiance to a language than have native speakers. In fact, Cook (1999) suggests that skilled L2 users, rather than native speakers, should be used as models in second language teaching.

Thus, once again we can see that the deficit view of L2 competence implicit in the notions of interlanguage, fossilization, and non-native speaker holds only in particular social contexts. SLA researchers need to examine both the functions of the L2 in social interaction and its symbolic associations before applying such notions.

4 Educational Programs

With regard to classroom SLA, the social context includes the type of educational program. This is the result of language policy decisions about the role of the L1 and L2 as a medium of instruction and subject of study. Programs differ according to whether or not the educational goal is *additive bilingualism* (Lambert, 1974) – where learners become active users of the L2 but also maintain their L1. Programs that do not promote additive bilingualism often result in *subtractive bilingualism* – where learners shift to the L2, which replaces their L1 – or in failure to acquire adequately the L2.

Many typologies of educational programs have been put forward (for example, Cummins, 1988; García, 1997; Skutnabb-Kangas, 1984, 1988). Here we will distinguish between *monolingual programs* – where only one language is used in the school as the medium of instruction – and *bilingual programs* – where two (or sometimes more than two) languages are used for instruction (see table 8.3). We will also consider how these programs correspond to the sociolinguistic settings described above.

Monolingual programs are of two types: L1 and L2. In L1 monolingual programs, the L1 is the medium of instruction and the L2 a subject of classroom study – for example, Australian high-school students learning Japanese. This is typically found in external L2 situations. In L2 monolingual programs, the L2 is the only medium of instruction, as found in *submersion* programs in dominant L2 settings. Children of immigrants or other minorities are placed in schools where the majority language is the language of education and teachers are monolingual in this language. Most submersion programs make no special allowances for the children who do not speak the L2. However, some have "pull-out" classes where children are withdrawn at times from the mainstream classroom for special instruction either in the L2 or in the children's L1. In other programs, sometimes called *sheltered* or *structured immersion*, L1-speaking children are taught entirely in the L2, but with specially designed materials to help them to learn it. (Such programs are sometimes preceded by a period of intensive instruction in the L2.)

L2 monolingual programs are also found in some *institutional* L2 settings, such as in the Solomon Islands and Vanuatu in the Pacific, where children's

Table 8.3 Types of educational programs

Program	*Description*	*Examples*
Monolingual: L1 monolingual	L1 is the only medium of instruction; L2 is taught as subject	English speakers learning German in Australia
L2 monolingual	L2 is the only medium of instruction:	
	Submersion programs (no support for L1 speakers)	Spanish-speaking immigrants learning English in California
	Sheltered or structured immersion programs (some support for L1 speakers)	
	Institutional L2 programs (some support for L1 speakers)	Paamese-speaking students learning English in Vanuatu
Bilingual:		
Transitional	L1 initial medium of instruction and language of initial literacy; later switch to L2	Fijian-speaking students learning English in Fiji
Immersion	L2 is the medium of instruction for all or most content areas; later switch to both L1 and L2	Some English-speaking students learning French in Canada
Continuing	Both the L1 and L2 are used as language of instruction throughout:	
	Mainstream programs (in coexisting L2 settings)	French and German in Switzerland
	Maintenance programs (for minority students in dominant L2 settings)	
	Dual-language (or two-way) programs (for both majority and minority students in dominant L2 settings)	Both Spanish and English used for instruction of mixed L1 Spanish and L1 English classes in the USA

education is entirely in English or French. However, these programs differ from the submersion programs in dominant L2 settings in three ways. First, the teachers are bi- or multilingual and know the children's L1 or the common language of wider communication (in these cases, Melanesian Pidgin). Second, the content and teaching materials are generally more culturally appropriate for the students. Third, the students are not competing with (or interacting with) native speakers of the L2.

Bilingual programs are of three types: *transitional* (L1 → L2), *immersion* (L2 → L1 + L2), and *continuing* (L1 + L2). In transitional programs, the students' L1 is the medium of instruction for the first few years of school and the language in which children are taught initial literacy. During this period, the L2 is taught as a subject. Eventually there is a changeover to the L2 as the medium of instruction. This may be abrupt, such as between grade 3 and 4, or gradual, with more and more content areas changing each year. Transitional programs are found in both dominant L2 and institutional L2 situations – for example, with Spanish-speaking students in the USA and with Fijian- and Hindi-speaking students learning English in Fiji.

Immersion programs are found in coexisting L2 or external L2 situations. The L2 is used as the medium of instruction for all or most content areas, usually beginning early in primary school. However, teachers are bilingual and the content is modified to make it more understandable to students. After the first few grades, there is a strong emphasis on development of the L1 and instruction is in both languages. The best-known immersion programs are in Canada, with French being used as the initial medium of instruction for English-speaking children. Intermediate or late immersion programs, beginning in grade 4 or 7, also exist, but they are more like transitional programs, except for the sociolinguistic context.

In continuing bilingual programs, both the L1 and L2 are used as the languages of instruction all through the school years. *Mainstream* continuing bilingual programs are found in coexisting L2 settings where the languages have relatively equal status. In dominant L2 settings, there are two types of continuing bilingual programs. *Maintenance* programs are only for minority students, who are separated from majority students. *Dual-language* or *two-way* programs are for both minority and majority students – for example, L1 Spanish minority students in the USA learning English and L1 English majority students learning Spanish. Since both languages are used for instruction, each group experiences some immersion in the L2.

A considerable amount of research has been done on the effectiveness of the various types of educational programs. (For summaries, see Cummins, 1988; García, 1997; Siegel, 1996; Thomas and Collier, 1997; World Bank, 1995.) Basically, the results show that bilingual programs are clearly better than monolingual programs with regard to both L2 attainment and overall academic achievement. In fact, monolingual submersion programs have negative effects on many children (Cummins, 1988, p. 161). The research also refutes the "time-on-task" hypothesis (Cummins, 1993), the belief that the more instructional time devoted to a language, the greater the achievement in that language. For example, in the Canadian immersion programs, it was feared that students' English would suffer because time was taken away for instruction in French. However, research has shown that these fears were unfounded (Swain and Lapkin, 1982). Also, the extensive research by Thomas and Collier (1997) has demonstrated that schooling in the L1 in continuing bilingual programs clearly reduces the amount of time taken to acquire academic proficiency in the L2, even though these programs take away from instruction time in the L2.

In interpreting these results, it is important to consider the interaction of the type of educational program, the sociolinguistic setting, and the sociostructural factors of size, status, and power of the L1 and L2 groups. For example, as Auerbach (1995, p. 25) has pointed out, L2 immersion programs are effective for learners from dominant, majority language groups, whose L1 is valued and supported at home and by society in general. However, transitional or continuing bilingual programs are more effective for subordinate, minority language groups, whose L1 is seen to be of little value and receives minimal support. Furthermore, the same type of program may lead to different outcomes in different settings. For example, in institutional L2 settings, transitional bilingual programs usually result in additive bilingualism, whereas in dominant L2 situations, they often result in subtractive bilingualism.

Finally, with regard to the policies themselves which determine the education settings for L2 learning, it must be remembered that they have been put in place by those in a position of power. Thus, the wider issues of power differential, racism, "linguicism" (Phillipson, 1988; Skutnabb-Kangas, 1988), and language rights (Hernández-Chávez, 1988) must also be considered when analyzing the results of research on different educational programs.[3]

The large body of research on the various education programs has had very little impact on the field of SLA, even though many of the findings are relevant to various models and theories. One area that has been dealt with is the research on immersion programs in external L2 settings. Long (1983) suggests that the success of these programs, in contrast to traditional foreign language teaching, lies in the fact that they focus on content rather than form – or, as Cummins (1988) points out, that they provide comprehensible L2 input. This supports the various forms of the input hypothesis (for example, Krashen, 1985). Presumably the reason for the lack of success of submersion programs, which also focus on content, is that in such programs the L2 input is not modified to make it comprehensible.

On the other hand, one area that has not been dealt with is the success of transitional and continuing bilingual programs in dominant L2 settings. These findings seem to contradict the predictions of the inter-group model described earlier. One would expect that the use of the L1 in formal education would lead to an increase in the ethnolinguistic vitality of the L1 group and to an increase in learners' identification with this group. According to the model, however, these factors would result in lower rather than higher levels of L2 proficiency.

A challenge to the field of SLA is to understand and explain the positive influence of schooling in the L1 on the acquisition of the L2. There are several possibilities, some of which have been considered, and some which have not. We will briefly consider three areas here: (i) positive influence on affective variables, (ii) the promotion of metalinguistic awareness, and (iii) the learning of relevant skills in L1.

First, most theories of SLA agree that the affective variables of learner motivation, attitudes, self-confidence, and so forth have some effect on L2 attainment. It may be that the use of the L1 in formal education results in positive values to these variables with regard to L2 learning. As Skutnabb-Kangas (1988, p. 29) points out, when the child's mother tongue is valued in the educational setting, it leads to low anxiety, high motivation, and high self-confidence, three factors which are closely related to successful programs. In Clément's social context model, for example, use of the L1 in the schools would be expected to reduce fear of assimilation and thus increase motivation to learn the L2.

Second, it may be that schooling in the L1, especially developing literacy skills, leads to greater metalinguistic awareness, which in turn benefits SLA. Studies of learner strategies and "good" language learners (summarized in Ellis, 1994) show the advantages of metalinguistic skills such as treating language as a system and attending to form.

The third possibility is that specific knowledge and skills learned in L1 schooling have a positive affect on L2 attainment. This is the view of Cummins (1981, 1988). According to his "interdependency principle" (1981) or "common underlying proficiency generalization" (1988), the combination of linguistic knowledge and literacy skills necessary for academic work, which Cummins originally called "cognitive/academic language proficiency" (CALP), is common across languages and once acquired in one language can be transferred to another. The greater attainment of L2 proficiency in bilingual compared to monolingual L2 programs is accounted for by the facts that CALP is easier to acquire in the L1 than in the L2, and that in bilingual programs, students are able to acquire these skills in the L1 and then transfer them to the L2.

5 Second Dialect Acquisition

When the sociolinguistic relationship between the L1 and the L2 is such that their speakers consider them to be varieties of the same language, the term "second dialect acquisition" (SDA) is often used, and we can talk of speakers of one dialect (D1) acquiring another dialect (D2). In sociolinguistics, dialects refer to varieties of a language which differ in vocabulary, pronunciation, and grammar and which are associated with particular geographic regions or social groups. While SDA most often refers to acquisition of the standard dialect, there are also instances when a non-standardized regional or social dialect is the target. A special case of SDA involves a pidgin or creole language and its lexifier (the language which provided the bulk of the vocabulary) – for example, Jamaican Creole and English. This occurs in societies where the general view is that the pidgin or creole is just a degenerate form of the lexifier rather than a separate language.

SLA and SDA are distinguished by several social factors, discussed below, and also by an important linguistic factor. The "language distance," or the degree of typological difference, between the typical L1 and L2 in SLA situations is greater than between the D1 and D2 in SDA situations. This has at least two significant implications for SDA. First, research has shown that the more similar varieties are, the more likely it is that transfer (or interference) will occur (Kellerman, 1977, 1979; Ringbom, 1978, 1987; Wode, 1976). Thus, as Lin points out (1965, p. 8): "The interference between two closely related dialects – such as a nonstandard dialect and standard English – is far greater than between two completely different languages." Second, because of the general similarities between the D1 and the D2, learners are often unaware of the specific differences between their own variety and the target (Cheshire, 1982, p. 55). Both of these points are quite relevant to SDA methodology, as will be shown later.

The greater similarity between first and second dialects than between first and second languages also poses some controversial questions relevant to acquisition studies. First, there is the question of the relative ease of acquisition. Escure (1997, p. 7) notes the popular consensus that SDA is easier than SLA. But Haugen (1964, p. 125) writes: "Bidialectalism may actually be harder to acquire than bilingualism. All scholars have agreed that it is harder to keep two similar languages apart than two very different ones." (See also Wolfram and Schilling-Estes, 1998, p. 297.) There have been no empirical studies to indicate which point of view may be correct. Second, because of the closeness of the D1 and D2, there is the psycholinguistic question of whether they are unified, partially overlapping, or separate linguistic systems (Reigel and Freedle, 1976). Although some recent research has been done in this area (e.g., De Bot, 1992; Woutersen, Cox, Weltens, and De Bot, 1994), this question remains unanswered.

The rest of this section discusses SDA, first in naturalistic, informal contexts and then in educational contexts. Since SDA is normally neglected in volumes on SLA, some background information is provided and studies done in the area are described. The main question to be considered is how SDA is similar to and/or different from SLA.

5.1 *Studies of SDA in naturalistic contexts*

The small amount of research on SDA in naturalistic contexts has been done almost entirely by sociolinguists and social dialectologists. Three types of SDA have been studied. The first is community dialect acquisition, when people who speak one dialect migrate to a region where another is spoken and acquire the informal dialect of their new community. The second is prestige dialect acquisition, when people acquire the prestige spoken variety of the language of their wider community in addition to the variety spoken by their own social group. Third is the much rarer situation involving the acquisition of a non-prestigious dialect (or pidgin or creole) by a speaker of a more prestigious dialect from outside the community.

First we will look at the work of three researchers who have dealt with community dialect acquisition. Payne (1980) studied the acquisition of the dialect spoken in a Philadelphia suburb by children whose families had moved there from "out-of-state" – that is, from other dialect areas. Data were obtained by interviewing children in peer pairs. Out of five phonetic variables studied, two were completely or partially acquired by all of the children and the other three by 80 percent or more. The factor that most influenced success of acquisition was age of arrival – those under 8 years old being most successful. Payne concludes that these variants were acquired so successfully because they could be added to the grammar by simple rule addition (p. 153). On the other hand, another variable, the short-*a* pattern, which cannot be incorporated into the grammar by simple rule addition, was not successfully acquired by any of the children born out-of-state. This leads to the conclusion that while children can add lower-level rules to their grammars up to the age of 14, they cannot "freely restructure and/or reorganize their grammars" (p. 175).

Trudgill (1986) uses speech accommodation theory to explain changes in dialects that are in contact with one another, and the formation of new dialects. As mentioned earlier, accommodation (or in particular, convergence) refers to individuals changing their speech (usually accent or some other salient dialectal feature) to become similar to that of their interlocutors in a particular social setting. Thus, it is normally a transitory phenomenon. But according to Trudgill (p. 40), if accommodation occurs frequently enough, the adoption of features from another dialect can become permanent. Thus, it appears that frequent accommodation can lead to second dialect acquisition. Although Trudgill does not deal specifically with SDA, it is clear that in some cases he equates the processes of long-term accommodation with those of dialect acquisition. As Chambers (1992, p. 676) notes, the boundary between long-term accommodation and acquisition is vague.

On the basis of several studies, Trudgill observes that adults first acquire the salient features of the segmental phonology of the target dialect, and follow a fixed "route" of acquisition. This route is determined by a combination of factors, some that delay accommodation of particular features (such as phonotactic constraints and homonymic clash) and others that accelerate it (such as comprehension difficulties and phonological naturalness) (Trudgill, 1986, p. 38). On the other hand, the route of acquisition is not so fixed for young children because they are not subject to the factors that delay accommodation. This conclusion is based on a longitudinal study of 7-year-old twins from England who moved to Australia for a year (Trudgill, 1982, referred to in Trudgill, 1986, pp. 28–31).

In discussing partial accommodation, Trudgill describes several phenomena which have parallels in SLA. First, there is *interdialect*, analogous to interlanguage, which refers to "situations where contact between two dialects leads to the development of forms that actually originally occurred in neither dialect" (p. 62). Then there is *hyperdialectalism* (p. 66), corresponding to overgeneralization in SLA and hypercorrection in sociolinguistics. Finally, there is *simplification* (pp. 102–7), but here it is more frequently regularization rather than the reduction found in SLA.

Chambers (1992, 1995) did research on second dialect acquisition among six Canadians who moved to Oxfordshire in southern England at ages ranging from 9 to 17. In two sets of interviews two years apart, he studied lexical and pronunciation variants in their speech, using methods from traditional social dialectology (asking subjects to identify objects pictured on cards). On the basis of his research and other studies, Chambers proposes several "principles" of dialect acquisition. The most relevant ones are as follows. First, pronunciation and phonological changes occur at a similar rate in the early stages of acquisition, but at a slower rate than lexical replacements, indicating that these may be separate processes. Second, lexical replacements occur rapidly in the early stages, but later slow down. Third, simple phonological rules are acquired earlier than complex ones. This principle is supported by Chambers's examination of medial *t*-voicing and vowel backing, by Payne's (1980) study mentioned above, and by two other studies cited by Chambers (pp. 684–6), one on the acquisition of the Limburg dialect in the Netherlands (Vousten and Bongaerts, 1990) and the other on the acquisition of London English by speakers of Jamaican Creole (Wells, 1973).

With regard to the acquisition of complex rules and new phonemes, Chambers found that two groups could be distinguished: early and later acquirers. Age was clearly a factor, with younger subjects being earlier acquirers. Chambers presents evidence from several studies which shows a sensitive period for the acquisition of complex phonological rules. He concludes: "A person seven or under will almost certainly acquire a new dialect perfectly, and a person 14 or over almost certainly will not. In between those ages, people will vary." This conclusion corresponds to findings with regard to a sensitive period in SLA (Long, 1990).

Kerswill (1994) studied morpholexical and phonological variables in the speech of adult Norwegian speakers of the rural Stril dialects who migrated to the city of Bergen. Data consisted of tape-recordings of in-depth interviews and conversations. Individual differences in the route of acquisition of the Bergen dialect were examined with regard to several social factors, including social status of the speaker, social integration and social network type, geographic origin, education, attitudes toward the Stril dialects, language use at work, gender, age, age of arrival in Bergen, and duration of stay. Kerswill found that morpholexical acquisition was more affected than phonological acquisition by a range of these factors, and that the patterns of the two types of acquisition differed in other ways as well. With regard to age, older speakers were more successful in acquiring morpholexical features but less so in acquiring phonological features, where the early movers had the higher scores (as in

Chambers's study). Another significant factor was whether similar phonological features existed in the first dialect. If this was the case, acquisition was possible even if speakers moved after the age of 17. Kerswill reports that at least one informant was truly bidialectal, having the two dialects as discrete codes, and being able to switch between them.

Moving on to prestige dialect acquisition, Labov (1964) describes the informal acquisition of the adult norms of standard English. This account is not based on any particular study, and it is not clear whether it should be considered SDA or a continuation of first language development involving the acquisition of additional styles or registers. Nevertheless, Labov outlines six stages: (i) acquisition of the basic grammar (ages 0–5); (ii) acquisition of the local vernacular spoken by the peer group (5–12); (iii) social perception of the significance of different dialect characteristics (early adolescence); (iv) stylistic variation, with some modification of speech toward the standard (first year of high school); (v) consistent use of the standard; and (vi) the full range of appropriate styles. He also mentions several obstacles to acquisition of the standard, including isolation, structural interference from the vernacular, and conflict between value systems of vernacular, and standard speakers.

Two studies focus on the acquisition of non-prestigious varieties.[4] Baugh (1992) analyses the African-American Vernacular English (AAVE) spoken by African-Americans whose first dialect is standard English and approximations of AAVE by some whites. These illustrate the phenomenon of *hypocorrection* – "linguistic over-compensation beyond the nonstandard linguistic target" (p. 317). This is a consequence of the covert prestige (Trudgill, 1983) of AAVE in the African-American community (see below). In SLA terms, this would be considered a form of overgeneralization. Winer (1985) examines her own acquisition of Trinidadian English Creole (TEC) in Trinidad, describing some of the unique characteristics of language learning in this situation. These include disbelief and resentment among some TEC speakers about her desire to learn the language, a lack of any written descriptions of the language, the belief among speakers that no rules exist in their "dialect," and the deceptive similarity between some features of TEC and English.

Before moving on to classroom SDA, we will look at the research of Escure (1997) on second dialects acquired in both naturalistic and educational contexts. She starts out by examining acrolectal varieties of Belize Creole, which she defines as non-native versions of the standard (in this case English) which are extensions of the speakers' repertoires used in formal contexts (p. 67). Escure believes that instead of acquiring the standard form of the lexifier as a second dialect, speakers have created highly variable acrolects through a complex process of incorporation and reinterpretation of features of both the lexifier language and the basic grammatical system of the creole (the basilect). This process involves the linguistic strategies of frequency variability, structural hypercorrection, and relexification (p. 76). Escure goes on to analyse second dialect texts of Putonghua (standard Beijing Mandarin Chinese) produced by speakers of other varieties of Chinese (Wuhan and Suzhou). Both the acrolects of Belize Creole and the second dialect versions of Putonghua differ from the first dialect as well as the "target" dialect (the standard) in some aspects of phonology and morphology; however, they do not differ pragmatically in informal discourse structure, using basically the same topic-marking strategies. With regard to persistence of first dialect features in second dialect varieties, Escure observes, like some of the scholars referred to earlier, that the notion of fossilization "fails to capture the dynamic, innovative, and – at least subconsciously – intentional use of old features to preserve a sociolinguistic identity distinct from the majority (usually dominant) group identity" (p. 275).

5.2 Studies of SDA in educational contexts

In SDA in educational contexts, the D2 is always the standard dialect used in the education system. We will look first at situations where the D1 is one of several regional dialects in the society, each with its own range of varieties, from vernacular to educated. In such situations, only a minority of people are native speakers of varieties close to the standard, and a large proportion of society is bidialectal. An example is in Germany with speakers of the Swabian dialect, spoken around Stuttgart, acquiring High German. Fishman and Lueders-Salmon (1972) describe how children are allowed to speak in the dialect in the classroom and never pushed to speak High German, and how the different functional roles of the two varieties are clearly recognized by teachers. Young-Scholten (1985) studied errors made by first and second grade Swabian-dialect-speaking children in Standard German. She found that 87 percent of phonological errors and 73 percent of morphological errors were interference-based rather than developmental. She attributes these high percentages to the similarity between the two varieties.

A similar situation is found in societies where there is classical diglossia (Ferguson, 1959) – that is, strict functional differentiation of two varieties of the same language in different domains. The D1 is used in informal contexts, such as conversation with family and friends, whereas the D2, which is learned in school, is used in formal domains such as writing and public speaking. Again, a large proportion of society is bidialectal. Stern (1988) describes SDA in such a situation in Switzerland with Swiss German (D1) and High German (D2). He observes that children discover phonological and morphological correspondences between their D1 and the D2 and perform transformations to comprehend and produce D2 forms. With regard to phonology, his observations correspond with the findings of the naturalistic SDA studies referred to above – that low-level rules, such as phonetic substitutions, are acquired easily while high-level rules, such as allophonic variation, are more difficult. Stern also notes that in areas where the D1 and D2 are similar, SDA is like a continuation of first language acquisition, with the development of new registers. But where the D1 and D2 diverge, "we observe typical second language acquisition processes, such as gradual approximation to the target form, simplification and regularization of irregular target structures and slow progress with large individual variation" (pp. 147–8).

A very different situation exists in societies where the powerful majority speak varieties linguistically very close to the standard and subordinate minorities speak ethnic, social, or regional varieties with marked differences from the standard. An important distinction between this kind of situation and the ones just described in Germany and Switzerland is that the D1 is not viewed as a separate variety, but is stigmatized as a corrupted or careless version of the standard. This dominant D2 setting is found, for example, in the USA with AAVE and in Australia with Aboriginal English. A similar situation exists with pidgins and creoles when the standard form of the lexifier is the language of education and government, even in places where the pidgin or creole is spoken by the majority of the population. This "lexifier L2" situation, as it is called by Craig (1998), is found, for example, in the Caribbean with Jamaican Creole and in Hawai'i with Hawai'i Creole English (HCE).

In contrast to teaching the D2 in places like Germany and Switzerland, teaching the D2 when it is the dominant dialect or lexifier language has traditionally taken place as if the students' D1 did not exist. Speakers of non-standard varieties were considered to be merely poor speakers of the standard language. In the 1960s, however, this began to change, at least in the USA and Britain, in the wake of the advances being made in sociolinguistics and social dialectology. First of all, work on social dialects, especially AAVE, demonstrated that they are legitimate, rule-governed varieties of language which differ in systematic ways from the standard (e.g., Labov, 1969). Second, it was assumed that the disadvantage in education and employment faced by social groups such as African-Americans was to a great extent due to the fact that they spoke a non-standard dialect. What seemed to be the obvious solution, as proposed mainly by sociolinguists, was to concentrate on teaching the standard dialect so that people could become bidialectal. The approach was to affirm the legitimacy of the first dialect while at the same time promoting additive bidialectalism (Alatis, 1973). This idea was soon embraced by the growing field of teaching English to speakers of other languages (TESOL) and came to be known as Standard English as a second dialect (SESD) (Harris, 1973). An extensive literature on SESD and the promotion of bidialectalism appeared in the 1960s and 1970s – for example, in the volumes edited by Aarons (1975); Aarons, Gordon, and Stewart (1969); Alatis (1969); Baratz and Shuy (1969); De Stefano (1973); Fasold and Shuy (1970); Fox (1973); Shuy, Davis, and Hogan (1964); and Stewart (1964a).

Stewart (1964b) used the term "quasi-foreign language" situation to refer to the learning of standard English by speakers of English-based pidgins and creoles and "radically nonstandard" dialects of English. Although these learners have native or near-native command of some aspects of the standard dialect, there are other areas where the learner's first dialect differs markedly from that of the standard, which warrant the use of foreign language teaching (FLT) procedures (Stewart, 1964b, p. 11). For the next 10 years, methodologies of FLT and later TESOL were advocated for teaching SESD (Carroll and Feigenbaum, 1967; Feigenbaum, 1969, 1970; Stewart, 1970). Following the audiolingual approach popular at that time, the emphasis was on habit formation and oral fluency, with teaching focused on particular grammatical structures. Contrastive analysis of the L1 and L2 (in this case D1 and D2) was done to determine which structures should be taught, and pattern practice and drills were used to teach them.

Those interested in SESD in the 1960s also looked to bilingual education programs for inspiration. Wolfram and Fasold (1969, p. 144) observed that if the goal of SESD was really additive bidialectalism, then the value of the students' first dialect would be affirmed by using it in the educational process – especially in reading materials. Stewart (1964b) also advocated using reading materials written in the students' dialect, pointing to the educational advantages of being able to learn to read in one's mother tongue and then transferring these skills to the target language. Since that time, the notion of "dialect readers" has been extremely controversial, with both educational and social arguments for and against. A reading program for AAVE using dialect readers was published, the *Bridge* series (Simpkins, Holt, and Simpkins, 1977), but it was not promoted because of negative reactions from parents and teachers. The potential benefits of dialect readers are still being discussed, not only for AAVE (Labov, 1995; Rickford and Rickford, 1995) but also for Chicano and Puerto Rican Spanish (Bixler-Márquez, 1988).[5]

Later, however, the problems of the uncritical use of FLT methods for students speaking stigmatized varieties became apparent and were pointed out by scholars, such as Allen (1969), Jagger and Cullinan (1974), Johnson (1969), Politzer (1973), and Shuy (1971). These had to do with both the ineffectiveness of the teaching methods themselves (Kochman, 1969) and significant differences between the SDA and FLT situations (as described below). As Shuy (1969, p. 83) noted, the assumption that FLT or TESOL techniques are valid for learning a second dialect was without any solid proof. Di Pietro (1973, p. 38–9) also noted that teachers should be wary of using such techniques in teaching SESD, and that much more research was needed to test their applicability. Such research has never been conducted, on teaching SESD or any other standard variety, such as prestige varieties of Spanish (Valdés, 1981, 1997; Valdés-Fallis, 1978). At any rate, as behaviorist views of language acquisition were abandoned in the 1970s, so were most of these FLT teaching methods, for both SDA and SLA. (An exception for SDA is Love, 1991.) Publications on SESD and bidialectalism became as rare as behaviorists. At the same time, SLA began to emerge as a distinct field of research, but with a few notable exceptions, namely Edwards and Giles (1984), Politzer (1993), and Sato (1985, 1989), second language researchers have not been concerned with the acquisition of dialects.

Some of the significant differences between the social contexts of learning another language and those of learning another dialect were pointed out by Stewart (1964b). In SLA, two different autonomous linguistic systems are easily recognized. The learners' first language often has its own dictionaries and grammars, just like the L2. But in SDA, because of similarities with the standard, the learners' first dialect is not recognized as a separate variety of language. This leads to both teachers and students thinking that there is only one legitimate language involved, and that the learners' dialect is just "sloppy speech" (Johnson, 1974, p. 154). Thus, the first dialect, unlike the first language, is almost always socially stigmatized.

On the other hand, the first dialect has its own covert prestige as a marker of the sociocultural group and a part of members' social identity. As Delpit (1990, p. 251) observes, children often have the ability to speak standard English, but choose "to identify with their community rather than with the school." Also, because of the ideology of correctness attached to standard dialects, students may fear that learning the standard means abandoning their dialect and thus risking being ostracized from their social group. (For an illuminating recent analysis, see Fordham, 1999.) Furthermore, a long history of racism and exploitation has led to antagonism between majority standard dialect speakers and minority non-standard dialect speakers. Thus, if a key factor in learning a language is identifying with its speakers, then we would not expect many people from minority groups to have the integrative motivation to learn the standard dialect. Even instrumental motivation would not apply; as Kochman (1969, p. 88) points out: "The Black child knows that he pays the social price for being Black, not because he does or does not speak standard dialect."

Because of these factors, there have been some strong reactions to the notions of teaching SESD and bidialectalism (e.g., Sledd, 1969, 1972), portraying them as yet another attempt to dominate and exploit minority groups. (For the opposite point of view, however, see Adler, 1987.) Proposals to use minority dialects in education have also been portrayed as attempts to institutionalize inequities, as reported by Di Pietro (1973, p. 38). This view was still quite evident in the reactions of many African-Americans to the Oakland Board of Education's 1996 resolution to make use of Ebonics (AAVE) to teach standard English. (For discussions of the Ebonics debate, see articles in the *Black Scholar*, 27 [1997]; Long, 1999; McWhorter, 1998; Perry and Delpit, 1998; Rickford, 1999; Rickford and Rickford, 2000) Although there are similar ghettoization arguments against bilingual education (see Snow, 1990), they are not as common as those against bidialectal education.

Other differences between SDA and SLA have been pointed out by Craig (1966, 1976, 1983, 1988) in relation to classroom contexts. In most foreign or second language learning situations, learners have little if any familiarity with the target language. But in situations where the standard dialect is the target, learners already recognize and produce some aspects of it as part of their linguistic repertoires. Also, unlike learners of a separate language, learners of the standard variety have no communicative reason to keep using the target (that is, the standard) in the classroom. It is easy for them to slip back into their own variety and still be understood. In addition, as mentioned above, because of the similarity between the D1 and the D2, the learner might not be aware of some of the differences that do exist. Thus, as Craig (1966, p. 58) observes, "the learner fails to perceive the new target element in the teaching situation."

But how significant are the differences between the D1 and the D2? Pandey (2000) used the Test of English as a Foreign Language (TOEFL) to measure the standard English proficiency of pre-college and first-year college students who were raised in the inner city and were basically monodialectal in AAVE. She found that their first-time performance on the TOEFL, particularly in the listening comprehension and grammar sections, was similar to that of low-level ESL/EFL students. According to the author (p. 89), these results support the validity of the Oakland School Board's Ebonics resolution, mentioned above, and the value of using ESL-based methods in teaching standard English to AAVE speakers. On the other hand, McWhorter (2000, p. 191) says that the reason African-American children do poorly in school is not because there is a gap between AAVE and standard English, but "because there is a psychological barrier between them and school in general." A lack of significant difference between the D1 and D2 would bring into question the need for the dialect readers described above. Scholars such as Politzer (1993) point out that differences between AAVE or Chicano Spanish and their respective written standard varieties may not be large enough to warrant the large-scale production of D1 reading materials. Goodman (1969), Venezky and Chapman (1973), and others suggested earlier that using standard dialect reading materials should not cause problems with reading acquisition if children are allowed to read as they speak. (See also Wiley, 1996, pp. 127–31.) However, as Wolfram (1994, p. 75) notes: "At this point, there are no carefully designed experimental studies that have examined this important research question."

Indeed, despite all the rhetoric, there is very little empirical research on the acquisition of dominant standard dialects and lexifiers in educational settings. What has been done focuses almost exclusively on the outcomes of various types of methodologies or programs, which can be divided into two broad areas: those that concentrate on teaching particular structures of the second (standard) dialect, and those that actually use the first dialect in the classroom. The two areas are analogous to the monolingual and bilingual settings of SLA described earlier.

Studies in the first area were done in the 1960s and 1970s when the FLT methods were in vogue, and used either pre-test/post-test or experimental design or both. In terms of the acquisition of particular targeted structures, some modestly successful results were reported – for example, by Hagerman (1970) and Lin (1965) for speakers of AAVE; Ching (1963), Crowley (1968), and Peterson, Chuck, and Coladarci (1969) for Hawai'i Creole English; and Craig (1967) for Jamaican Creole. On the other hand, Torrey (1972) reported only very limited positive results, and as mentioned above, this methodology was abandoned because of overall lack of success.

Studies in the second area are on three types of educational programs in which the first dialect is used in the classroom: instrumental, accommodation,

Table 8.4 Research on instrumental programs

Type of program	*Study*	*Location [variety]*
Bilingual	Murtagh (1982)	Australia [Kriol]
	Ravel and Thomas (1985)	Seychelles [Seselwa]
Initial literacy	Österberg (1961)	Sweden [regional dialect]
	Bull (1990)	Norway [regional dialects]
	Siegel (1997)	Papua New Guinea [Melanesian Pidgin]
"Dialect readers"	Leaverton (1973)	USA [AAVE]
	Simpkins and Simpkins (1981)	USA [AAVE]
	Kephart (1992)	Carriacou [Carriacou English Creole]

Table 8.5 Research on programs with an accommodation component

Level	*Study*	*Location [variety]*
Kindergarten-grade 3	Cullinan, Jagger, and Strickland (1974)	New York [AAVE]
Kindergarten-grade 4	Day (1989)	Hawai'i [HCE]
Grade 1	Piestrup (1973)	California [AAVE]
Grade 2	Rynkofs (1993)	Hawai'i [HCE]
High school	Campbell (1994)	USA inner city [AAVE]

and awareness (Siegel, 1999a). The overall aims of all three types of programs are additive bidialectalism and improving students' linguistic self-respect. In *instrumental* programs, the D1 is used as a medium of instruction to teach initial literacy, and content subjects such as mathematics, science, and health, as in transitional bilingual SLA programs (see table 8.4). In *accommodation* programs, the D1 is not a medium of instruction or subject of study, but it is accepted in the classroom; students are allowed and even encouraged to use their home varieties in speaking and sometimes writing (Wiley, 1996, p. 127) (see table 8.5). In *awareness* programs, the D1 is an object of study in the context of discussions about linguistic and cultural diversity and about the use of different varieties in different contexts. An additional goal is to make students aware of the grammatical and pragmatic differences between their own varieties and the standard using a contrastive approach (see table 8.6).

Table 8.6 Research on programs with an awareness component

Level	*Study*	*Location [variety]*
Primary	Actouka and Lai (1989)	Hawai'i [HCE]
	Harris-Wright (1999)	Georgia [AAVE]
High school	Afaga and Lai (1994)	Hawai'i [HCE]
College/university	Taylor (1989)	Illinois [AAVE]
	Hoover (1991)	California [AAVE]
Adult	Scherloh (1991)	Ohio [AAVE]

(See Berry and Hudson, 1997; Delpit, 1988; Rickford, 1999; Wolfram, Christian, and Adger, 1999.)

All the studies listed in tables 8.4–8.6 demonstrate that the use of the students' own varieties of language leads to higher scores in tests measuring reading and writing skills in standard English and to increases in overall academic achievement. (For summaries of these studies, see Siegel, 1999b.) In addition, there are reports of the success of similar programs in the Virgin Islands with Caribbean Creole speakers (Elsasser and Irvine, 1987), in Alaska with Native American speakers of "Village English" (Delpit, 1988), in North Carolina with speakers of Appalachian English and other dialects (Wolfram et al., 1999), and in Los Angeles with AAVE speakers (Los Angeles Unified School District and LeMoine, 1999). These results are thus analogous to those for bilingual programs reported earlier in this chapter.

In addition, two recent experimental studies on the acquisition of standard English by AAVE speakers appear to show some benefits of using the D1 in the classroom, but in two very different ways. Fogel and Ehri (2000) compared the effectiveness of three instructional treatments on improving the standard English writing of groups of AAVE-speaking third- and fourth-grade students, targeting six syntactic features which differ in the two varieties. They found that the most effective treatment was instruction which included guided practice in translating sentences from AAVE into standard English and then providing corrective feedback. Pandey (2000) studied the effectiveness of a six-week program using a "contrastive analysis" approach to teaching standard English as a second dialect (basically an awareness program). The subjects were the group of AAVE-speaking pre-college and first-year college students, mentioned above, whom she initially tested with the TOEFL. Pandey found that the approach led to more relaxed attitudes toward learning, increased bidialectal awareness, and marked improvement in performance on subsequent TOEFL tests.

Another challenge to the field of SLA is to understand and explain the positive influence of using the D1 in educational programs for the acquisition of the D2. The three possibilities discussed earlier to account for the advantages of using the L1 in education may also be relevant to the use of the D1.

However, the development of metalinguistic awareness and the acquisition of CALP would apply only to instrumental programs. On the other hand, the positive influence on affective variables is probably more significant in SDA, where the D1 is usually much more stigmatized than the L1 is in SLA. This would be supported by researchers such as Wolfram and Schilling-Estes (1998), who point out that "there is now some indication that students who feel more confident about their own vernacular dialect are more successful in learning the standard one" (p. 290).

A fourth possibility – one that is much more relevant to SDA than to SLA – is that using the D1 in educational programs makes learners aware of differences between the D2 and the D1 that they may not otherwise notice (see Siegel, 1999b). According to Schmidt's "noticing hypothesis" (1990, 1993), attention to target language (L2) forms is necessary for acquisition; these forms will not be acquired unless they are noticed. Because of the similarities between the D1 and D2, as discussed above, learners often do not notice differences between their dialect and the standard. However, it may be that looking at features of their own varieties in instrumental or awareness programs helps students to notice features of the standard that are different, which is the first step of acquisition.

As also noted above, because of D1–D2 similarities, interference errors are unlikely to affect communication. According to Politzer (1993, p. 53), such errors are "not likely to disappear without specific instructional effort and without being called to the learner's attention." A similar statement is found in the study of errors made by Swabian-dialect-speaking children learning High German, mentioned above (Young-Scholten, 1985, p. 11): "[T]hose errors due to interference from a crucially similar first language will tend to persist if the learner's attention is not drawn to these errors."

The awareness programs in particular draw attention to potential errors which may be caused by lack of recognition of differences. The methods they use are analogous to some advocated in the SLA literature. First there is *consciousness raising* (Ellis, 1997), where attention is drawn to particular grammatical features of the target but students are not expected to produce or practice them. Second, as noted by Menacker (1998), there is the *focus on form* approach (Doughty and Williams, 1998). In this approach, noticing particular target structures is induced by "briefly drawing students' attention to linguistic elements . . . *in context*, as they arise incidentally in lessons whose overriding focus is on meaning, or communication" (Long, 1998, p. 40). An important difference is that in awareness programs the focus on form is part of a lesson on language and dialect diversity, rather than a reaction to students' comprehension or production problems.

However, the major difference between awareness approaches to SDA and form-focused approaches to SLA is in the role of contrastive activities. While contrastive analysis has been all but abandoned in SLA methodology, it is becoming more common in teaching second dialects, especially in activities where students examine their language variety in order to discover its rule-governed features, and then compare these features with those of other varieties, including the standard. James (1996, p. 255) calls this activity "interfacing" and describes it as follows: "It involves juxtaposing or confronting D1 and D2 and helping the learner to notice the differences between them, sometimes subtle and sometimes gross. It is a modern development of contrastive analysis . . . which is now done by the learner himself rather than by the teacher." Of course this is most useful in SDA situations where the D1 and D2 are similar enough so that the differences that do exist do not normally affect communication. But it is interesting to note that the value of what James (1992) calls "contrastive consciousness raising" is also being recognized for the advanced stages of SLA, where the differences between the learner's interlanguage and the target language are also so small that they cause no communicative difficulty (see Swain, 1998).

To conclude this section, while there are indications of some of the factors that may affect ultimate attainment in a second dialect, very little is known about how second and especially standard dialects are acquired, or how similar the processes of SLA and SDA actually are. Valdés (1997, p. 24) sums up the situation: "Teachers of standard dialects who hoped to be guided by theories of L2 acquisition now have serious doubts about the parallels to be found between these two very different kinds of acquisition."

6 Conclusion

We have seen that different sociolinguistic settings, educational contexts, and relationships between the L1 and L2 may have an effect on SLA. The importance of various concepts developed over the years in SLA – such as interlanguage, fossilization, integrative and instrumental motivation, and the distinction between native and non-native speaker – are not necessarily generalizable to all social contexts. At the same time, other notions which are no longer considered important – such as L1 interference and contrastive language teaching – may have more significance in some contexts. However, of the studies that have taken social context into account, nearly all have examined only ultimate L2 proficiency. More longitudinal studies are needed with closely related as well as distant languages in order to find out about developmental patterns, rate of acquisition, learning strategies, and other aspects of SLA in different contexts.

With regard to the analysis of social context, the factors that affect ultimate L2 proficiency appear to be related to the learner's opportunities and desire to use the L2 for particular purposes in social interaction. For each situation, then, researchers need to consider the nature of these purposes and the use of the L2 in social interaction, and how these are determined by the structural and historical factors affecting both the L1 and L2 social groups and their languages. Researchers also need to understand the nature of the status, power, and social identity that may be asserted and negotiated by L2 learners in particular social interactions. Thus, more of the fine-grained ethnographic studies of interactional sociolinguistics and discourse analysis are needed in addition to the survey studies of social psychology and the experimental studies of psycholinguistics.

NOTES

1 Although the difference between naturalistic and classroom contexts of SLA is touched upon here, it is not a focus of the discussion, as it is covered in other chapters.

2 Another component of the model is the Pidginization Hypothesis, in which an analogy is made between early naturalistic SLA and pidginization. However, this will not be dealt with here.

3 For example, two years after the passing of Proposition 227, which virtually eliminated bilingual programs in California, Noonan (2000) reports "dramatic academic gains" for Spanish-speaking students in second grade. He concludes that this is evidence that "English immersion" (i.e., submersion) works better than bilingual instruction. However, it is well known from more extensive research (e.g., Thomas and Collier, 1997) that the positive effects of bilingual programs are most evident in the later primary years.

4 Hewitt (1986) and Rampton (1991, 1995) describe the use of Caribbean Creole by speakers of English in Britain but do not focus on acquisition.

5 Studies by Österberg (1961) and Bull (1990) with dialects of Swedish and Norwegian and by Leaverton (1973) and Simpkins and Simpkins (1981) with AAVE all showed positive effects of learning to read in the first dialect. However, in the most recent argument against dialect readers, McWhorter (1998, pp. 220–1) says that the Scandinavian studies are irrelevant to AAVE because the dialects concerned are so different from each other. He points out methodological problems with the Leaverton study, and mentions nine experimental studies which he says show that using dialect reading materials have no positive effect on AAVE students' reading scores. But a close look at these nine studies reveals methodological problems with all of them. Most importantly, the subjects were already used to reading in standard English, and not the dialect; factors of novelty and perceived inappropriateness of the dialect materials were not taken into account.

REFERENCES

Aarons, A. C. (ed.) 1975: *Issues in the Teaching of Standard English. Florida FL Reporter*, 12 (1 and 2).

Aarons, A. C., Gordon, B. Y., and Stewart, W. A. (eds) 1969: *Linguistic-Cultural Differences in*

American Education. Florida FL Reporter, 7 (1).

Actouka, M. and Lai, M. K. 1989: *Project Holopono, Evaluation Report, 1987–1988*. Honolulu: Curriculum Research and Development Group, College of Education, University of Hawai'i.

Adler, S. 1987: Bidialectalism? Mandatory or elective? *ASHA*, 29 (1), 41–4.

Afaga, L. B. and Lai, M. K. 1994: *Project Akamai, Evaluation Report, 1992–93, Year Four*. Honolulu: Curriculum Research and Development Group, College of Education, University of Hawai'i.

Alatis, J. E. (ed.) 1969: *Linguistics and the Teaching of Standard English*. Monograph Series on Language and Linguistics, no. 22. Washington, DC: Georgetown University Press.

Alatis, J. E. 1973: Teaching standard English as a second dialect: the unanswered questions, the successes, and the promise. In R. P. Fox (ed.), *Essays on Teaching English as a Second Dialect*. Urbana, IL: National Council of Teachers of English, 43–56.

Allen, V. F. 1969: Teaching standard English as a second dialect. *Florida FL Reporter*, 7 (1), 123–9, 164.

Au, S. 1988: A critical appraisal of Gardner's social-psychological theory of second language (L2) learning. *Language Learning*, 38, 75–100.

Auerbach, E. R. 1995: The politics of the ESL classroom: issues of power in pedagogical choices. In J. W. Tollefson (ed.), *Power and Inequality in Language Education*. Cambridge: Cambridge University Press, 9–33.

Baratz, J. C. and Shuy, R. W. (eds) 1969: *Teaching Black Children to Read*. Washington, DC: Center for Applied Linguistics.

Baugh, J. 1992: Hypocorrection: mistakes in production of vernacular African American English as a second dialect. *Language and Communication*, 12, 317–26.

Beebe, L. M. 1988: Five sociolinguistic approaches to second language acquisition. In L. M. Beebe (ed.), *Issues in Second Language Acquisition: Multiple Perspectives*. New York: Newbury House, 43–77.

Belmechri, F. and Hummel, K. M. 1998: Orientations and motivation in the acquisition of English as a second language among high school students in Quebec city. *Language Learning*, 48 (2), 219–44.

Berry, R. and Hudson, J. 1997: *Making the Jump: A Resource Book for Teachers of Aboriginal Students*. Broome: Catholic Education Office, Kimberley Region.

Bixler-Márquez, D. J. 1988: Dialects and initial reading options in bilingual education. In D. J. Bixler-Márquez and J. Ornstein-Galicia (eds), *Chicano Speech in the Bilingual Classroom*. New York: Peter Lang, 135–41.

Bourdieu, P. 1977: The economics of linguistic exchanges. *Social Science Information*, 16, 645–68.

Bourhis, R. Y. and Giles, H. 1977: The language of intergroup distinctiveness. In H. Giles (ed.), *Language, Ethnicity and Intergroup Relations*. London: Academic Press, 119–36.

Bull, T. 1990: Teaching school beginners to read and write in the vernacular. In E. H. Jahr and O. Lorentz (eds), *Tromsø Linguistics in the Eighties*. Tromsø Studies in Linguistics 11. Oslo: Novus Press, 69–84.

Campbell, E. D. 1994: Empowerment through bidialectalism. ERIC document no. ED 386 034.

Carroll, W. S. and Feigenbaum, I. 1967: Teaching a second dialect and some implications for TESOL. *TESOL Quarterly*, 1, 31–9.

Chambers, J. K. 1992: Dialect acquisition. *Language*, 68, 673–705.

Chambers, J. K. 1995: Acquisition of lexical and pronunciation variants. In

W. Viereck (ed.), *Verbandlugen des Internationalen Dialektologenkongresses Bamberg 1990. Band 4*. Stuttgart: Franz Steiner, 3–19.

Cheshire, J. 1982: Dialect features and linguistic conflict in schools. *Educational Review*, 14, 53–67.

Chihara, T. and Oller, J. W. 1978: Attitudes and attained proficiency in EFL: a sociolinguistic study of adult Japanese learners. *Language Learning*, 28, 55–68.

Ching, D. C. 1963: Effects of a six month remedial English program on oral, writing, and reading skills of third grade Hawaiian bilingual children. *Journal of Experimental Education*, 32 (2), 133–45.

Clément, R. 1980: Ethnicity, contact and communicative competence in a second language. In H. Giles, W. P. Robinson, and P. M. Smith (eds), *Language: Social Psychological Perspectives*. Oxford: Pergamon, 147–54.

Clément, R. 1986: Second language proficiency and acculturation: an investigation of the effects of language status and individual characteristics. *Journal of Language and Social Psychology*, 5, 271–90.

Clément, R. and Kruidenier, B. G. 1983: Orientations in second language acquisition: I. The effects of ethnicity, milieu and target language on their emergence. *Language Learning*, 33, 273–91.

Clément, R. and Kruidenier, B. G. 1985: Aptitude, attitude and motivation in second language proficiency: a test of Clément's model. *Journal of Language and Social Psychology*, 4, 21–37.

Clément, R., Dörnyei, Z., and Noels, K. A. 1994: Motivation, self-confidence, and group cohesion in the foreign language classroom. *Language Learning*, 44 (3), 417–48.

Cook, V. 1999: Going beyond the native speaker in language teaching. *TESOL Quarterly*, 33 (2), 185–209.

Cooper, R. L. and Fishman, J. A. 1977: A study of language attitudes. In J. A. Fishman, R. L. Cooper, and A. Conrad (eds), *The Spread of English: The Sociology of English as an Additional Language*. Rowley, MA: Newbury House, 239–76.

Craig, D. 1966: Teaching English to Jamaican Creole speakers: a model of a multi-dialect situation. *Language Learning*, 16 (1 and 2), 49–61.

Craig, D. 1967: Some early indications of learning a second dialect. *Language Learning*, 17 (3 and 4), 133–40.

Craig, D. 1976: Bidialectal education: Creole and standard in the West Indies. *International Journal of the Sociology of Language*, 8, 93–134.

Craig, D. 1983: Teaching standard English to nonstandard speakers: some methodological issues. *Journal of Negro Education*, 52 (1), 65–74.

Craig, D. 1988: Creole English and education in Jamaica. In C. B. Paulston (ed.), *International Handbook of Bilingualism and Bilingual Education*. New York: Greenwood, 297–312.

Craig, D. 1998: "Afta yu laan dem fi riid an rait dem Kriiyol, den wa muo?": Creole and the teaching of the lexifier language. Paper presented at the 3rd International Creole Workshop, Miami.

Crookes, G. and Schmidt, R. W. 1991: Motivation: reopening the research agenda. *Language Learning*, 41, 469–512.

Crowley, D. P. 1968: The Keaukaha model for mainstream dialect instruction. *Language Learning*, 18 (1 and 2), 125–38.

Cullinan, B. E., Jagger, A. M., and Strickland, D. S. 1974: Language expansion for Black children in the primary grades: a research report. *Young Children*, 24 (2), 98–112.

Cummins, J. 1981: The role of primary language development in promoting educational success for language minority students. In California State Department of Education (ed.),

Schooling and Language Minority Students: A Theoretical Framework. Los Angeles: National Evaluation, Dissemination and Assessment Center, 3–49.

Cummins, J. 1988: Second language acquisition within bilingual education programs. In L. M. Beebe (ed.), *Issues in Second Language Acquisition: Multiple Perspectives.* New York: Newbury House, 145–66.

Cummins, J. 1993: Bilingualism and second language learning. *Annual Review of Applied Linguistics*, 13, 51–70.

Day, R. R. 1989: The acquisition and maintenance of language by minority children. *Language Learning*, 29 (2), 295–303.

De Bot, K. 1992: A bilingual production model: Levelt's "Speaking" Model adapted. *Applied Linguistics*, 13, 1–24.

Delpit, L. D. 1988: The silenced dialogue: power and pedagogy in educating other people's children. *Harvard Educational Review*, 58 (3), 280–98.

Delpit, L. D. 1990: Language diversity and learning. In S. Hynds and D. L. Rubin (eds), *Perspectives on Talk and Learning.* Urbana, IL: National Council of Teachers of English, 247–66.

De Stefano, J. S. (ed.) 1973: *Language, Society, and Education: A Profile of Black English.* Worthington, OH: Charles A. Jones.

Di Pietro, R. J. 1973: Bilingualism and bidialectalism. In R. P. Fox (ed.), *Essays on Teaching English as a Second Dialect.* Urbana, IL: National Council of Teachers of English, 35–42.

Dörnyei, Z. 1994: Understanding L2 motivation: on with the challenge. *Modern Language Journal*, 78 (4), 515–23.

Dörnyei, Z. and Schmidt, R. 2001: *Motivation and Second Language Acquisition.* SLTCC Technical Report no. 23. Second Language Teaching and Curriculum Center, University of Hawai'i.

Doughty, C. and Williams, J. (eds) 1998: *Focus on Form in Classroom Second Language Acquisition.* Cambridge: Cambridge University Press.

Edwards, J. and Giles, H. 1984: Applications of the social psychology of language: sociolinguistics and education. In P. Trudgill (ed.), *Applied Sociolinguistics.* London: Academic Press, 119–58.

Eisenstein, M. 1986: Target language variation and second-language acquisition: learning English in New York City. *World Englishes*, 5 (1), 31–46.

Ellis, R. 1994: *The Study of Second Language Acquisition.* Oxford: Oxford University Press.

Ellis, R. 1997: *SLA Research and Language Teaching.* Oxford and New York: Oxford University Press.

Elsasser, N. and Irvine, P. 1987: English and Creole: the dialectics of choice in a college writing program. In I. Shor (ed.), *Freire for the Classroom: A Sourcebook for Literacy Teaching.* Portsmouth, MA: Boynton/Cook, 129–49.

Escure, G. 1997: *Creole and Dialect Continua: Standard Acquisition Processes in Belize and China.* Amsterdam: John Benjamins.

Fasold, R. W. and Shuy, R. W. (eds) 1970: *Teaching Standard English in the Inner City.* Washington, DC: Center for Applied Linguistics.

Feigenbaum, I. 1969: Using foreign language methodology to teach standard English: evaluation and adaptation. *Florida FL Reporter*, 7 (1), 116–22, 156–7.

Feigenbaum, I. 1970: The use of nonstandard English in teaching standard: contrast and comparison. In R. W. Fasold and R. W. Shuy (eds), *Teaching Standard English in the Inner City.* Washington, DC: Center for Applied Linguistics, 87–104.

Ferguson, C. A. 1959: Diglossia. *Word*, 15, 325–40.

Firth, A. and Wagner, J. 1997: On discourse, communication, and (some) fundamental concepts in SLA research. *Modern Language Journal*, 81, 285–300.

Fishman, J. A. and Lueders-Salmon, E. 1972: What has the sociology of language to say to the teacher? On teaching the standard variety to speakers of dialectal or sociolectal varieties. In C. B. Cazden, V. P. John, and D. Hymes (eds), *Functions of Language in the Classroom*. New York: Teachers College, Colombia University, 67–83.

Fogel, H. and Ehri, L. C. 2000: Teaching elementary students who speak Black English Vernacular to write in standard English: effects of dialect transformation practice. *Contemporary Educational Psychology*, 25, 212–35.

Fordham, S. 1999: Dissin' "the Standard": Ebonics and guerrilla warfare at Capital High. *Anthropology and Education Quarterly*, 30 (3), 272–93.

Fox, R. P. (ed.) 1973: *Essays on Teaching English as a Second Dialect*. Urbana, IL: National Council of Teachers of English.

García, O. 1997: Bilingual education. In F. Coulmas (ed.), *The Handbook of Sociolinguistics*. Oxford: Blackwell, 405–20.

Gardner, R. C. 1980: On the validity of affective variables in second language learning: conceptual, contextual and statistical considerations. *Language Learning*, 30, 255–70.

Gardner, R. C. 1983: Learning another language: a true social psychological experiment. *Journal of Language and Social Psychology*, 2, 219–40.

Gardner, R. C. 1985: *Social Psychology and Second Language Learning: The Role of Attitudes and Motivation*. London: Edward Arnold.

Gardner, R. C. 1988: The socio-educational model of second language learning: assumptions, findings and issues. *Language Learning*, 38, 101–26.

Gardner, R. C. and Clément, R. 1990: Social psychological perspectives on second language acquisition. In H. Giles and W. P. Robinson (eds), *Handbook of Language and Social Psychology*. Chichester: John Wiley, 495–517.

Gardner, R. C. and Lambert, W. E. 1959: Motivational variables in second language acquisition. *Canadian Journal of Psychology*, 13, 266–72.

Gardner, R. C. and Lambert, W. E. 1972: *Attitudes and Motivation in Second Language Learning*. Rowley, MA: Newbury House.

Gardner, R. C. and Tremblay, P. F. 1994a: On motivation: measurement and conceptual considerations. *Modern Language Journal*, 78 (3), 359–68.

Gardner, R. C. and Tremblay, P. F. 1994b: On motivation, research agendas, and theoretical frameworks. *Modern Language Journal*, 78 (4), 524–7.

Gardner, R. C., Lalonde, R. M., and Pierson, R. 1983: The socio-educational model of second language acquisition: an investigation using LISREL causal modelling. *Journal of Language and Social Psychology*, 2, 1–15.

Gardner, R. C., Tremblay, P. F., and Masgoret, A.-M. 1997: Towards a full model of second language learning: an empirical investigation. *Modern Language Journal*, 81 (3), 344–62.

Genesee, F. 1987: *Learning through Two Languages*. Cambridge, MA: Newbury House.

Giles, H. 1977: Social psychology and applied linguistics: towards an integrated approach. *ILT Review of Applied Linguistics*, 35, 27–42.

Giles, H. and Byrne, J. L. 1982: An intergroup approach to second language acquisition. *Journal of Multilingual and Multicultural Development*, 1, 17–40.

Giles, H. and Johnson, P. 1981: The role of language in ethnic group relations. In J. C. Turner and H. Giles (eds),

Intergroup Behaviour. Oxford: Blackwell, 199–243.

Giles, H. and Johnson, P. 1987: Ethnolinguistic identity theory. *International Journal of the Sociology of Language*, 68, 69–99.

Giles, H., Bourhis, R. Y., and Taylor, D. M. 1977: Toward a theory of language in ethnic group relations. In H. Giles (ed.), *Language, Ethnicity and Intergroup Relations*. New York: Academic Press, 307–48.

Giles, H., Taylor, D., and Bourhis, R. 1973: Towards a theory of interpersonal accommodation through speech: some Canadian data. *Language in Society*, 2, 177–92.

Goodman, K. S. 1969: Dialect barriers to reading comprehension. In J. C. Baratz and R. W. Shuy (eds), *Teaching Black Children to Read*. Washington, DC: Center for Applied Linguistics, 14–28.

Gupta, A. F. 1994: *The Step-Tongue: Children's English in Singapore*. Clevedon: Multilingual Matters.

Hagerman, B. P. 1970: *Teaching Standard English as a Second Dialect to Speakers of Nonstandard English in High School Business Education: Final Report*. ERIC document no. ED 038 639. Washington, DC: Department of Health, Education and Welfare, Office of Education, Bureau of Research.

Hall, B. J. and Gudykunst, W. B. 1986: The intergroup theory of second language ability. *Journal of Language and Social Psychology*, 5, 291–302.

Hall, J. K. 1995: (Re)creating our worlds with words: a sociohistorical perspective of face-to-face interaction. *Applied Linguistics*, 16, 206–32.

Harris, D. P. 1973: The future of ESOL: continuity or generation gap. In R. P. Fox (ed.), *Essays on Teaching English as a Second Dialect*. Urbana, IL: National Council of Teachers of English, 67–81.

Harris-Wright, K. 1999: Enhancing bidialectalism in urban African American students. In C. T. Adger, D. Christian, and O. Taylor (eds), *Making the Connection: Language and Academic Achievement among African American Students: Proceedings of a Conference of the Coalition on Diversity in Education*. McHenry, IL: Center for Applied Linguistics/Delta Systems, 53–60.

Haugen, E. 1964: Bilingualism and bidialectalism. In R. W. Shuy, A. L. Davis, and R. F. Hogan (eds), *Social Dialects and Language Learning*. Champaign, IL: National Council of Teachers of English, 123–6.

Hernández-Chávez, E. 1988: Language policy and language rights in the United States: issues in bilingualism. In T. Skutnabb-Kangas and J. Cummins (eds), *Minority Education: From Shame to Struggle*. Clevedon: Multilingual Matters, 45–56.

Hewitt, R. 1986: *White Talk Black Talk: Inter-Racial Friendships and Communication among Adolescents*. Cambridge: Cambridge University Press.

Hoover, M. R. 1991: Using the ethnography of African-American communication in teaching composition to bidialectal students. In M. E. McGroarty and C. J. Faltis (eds), *Languages in School and Society*. Contributions to the Sociology of Language 58. Berlin: Mouton de Gruyter, 465–85.

Jagger, A. M. and Cullinan, B. E. 1974: Teaching standard English to achieve bidialectalism: problems with current practices. *Florida FL Reporter*, 12 (1 and 2), 63–70.

James, C. 1992: Awareness, consciousness and language contrast. In C. Mair and M. Markus (eds), *New Departures in Contrastive Linguistics. Vol. 2*. Innsbrucker Beiträge zur Kulturwissenschaft, Anglistische Reihe Band 5. Innsbruck: Institüt für Anglistik, Universität Innsbruck, 183–98.

James, C. 1996: Mother tongue use in bilingual/bidialectal education: implication for Bruneian Duibahasa. *Journal of Multilingual and Multicultural Development*, 17, 248–57.

Johnson, K. R. 1969: Pedagogical problems of using second language techniques for teaching standard English to speakers of nonstandard Negro dialect. *Florida FL Reporter*, 7 (1), 75–8, 154.

Johnson, K. R. 1974: Teacher's attitude toward the nonstandard Negro dialect – let's change it. In J. S. de Stefano and S. E. Fox (eds), *Language and the Language Arts*. Boston: Little, Brown, 148–58.

Judd, E. L. 1987: Language policy, curriculum development, and TESOL instruction: a search for compatibility. In M. H. Long and J. C. Richards (eds), *Methodology in TESOL: A Book of Readings*. New York: Newbury House, 3–9.

Kachru, B. B. 1985: Standards, codification and sociolinguistic realism: the English language in the outer circle. In R. Quirk and H. Widdowson (eds), *English in the World: Teaching and Learning the Language and Literatures*. Cambridge: Cambridge University Press, 11–30.

Kachru, B. B. and Nelson, C. L. 1996: World Englishes. In S. L. McKay and N. H. Hornberger (eds), *Sociolinguistics and Language Teaching*. Cambridge: Cambridge University Press, 71–102.

Kellerman, E. 1977: Towards a characterization of the strategies of transfer in second language learning. *Interlanguage Studies Bulletin*, 2, 58–145.

Kellerman, E. 1979: Transfer and non-transfer: where are we now? *Studies in Second Language Acquisition*, 2, 37–57.

Kelly, C., Sachdev, I., Kottsieper, P. and Ingram, M. 1993: The role of social identity in second-language proficiency and use: testing the Intergroup Model. *Journal of Language and Social Psychology*, 12, 288–301.

Kephart, R. F. 1992: Reading creole English does not destroy your brain cells! In J. Siegel (ed.), *Pidgins, Creoles and Nonstandard Dialects in Education*. Occasional Paper no. 12. Melbourne: Applied Linguistics Association of Australia, 67–86.

Kerswill, P. 1994: *Dialects Converging: Rural Speech in Urban Norway*. Oxford: Clarendon Press.

Kochman, T. 1969: Social factors in the consideration of teaching standard English. *Florida FL Reporter*, 7 (1), 87–8, 157.

Krashen, S. 1985: *The Input Hypothesis: Issues and Implications*. New York: Longman.

Labov, W. 1964: Stages in the acquisition of Standard English. In R. W. Shuy, A. L. Davis, and R. F. Hogan (eds), *Social Dialects and Language Learning*. Champaign, IL: National Council of Teachers of English, 77–103.

Labov, W. 1969: The logic of nonstandard English. In J. E. Alatis (ed.), *Linguistics and the Teaching of Standard English*. Monograph Series on Language and Linguistics, no. 22. Washington, DC: Georgetown University Press, 1–24.

Labov, W. 1995: Can reading failure be reversed? A linguistic approach to the question. In V. L. Gadsden and D. A. Wagner (eds), *Literacy among African-American Youth*. Cresskill, NJ: Hampton Press, 39–68.

Lambert, W. E. 1974: Culture and language as factors in learning and education. In F. Aboud and R. D. Mead (eds), *Cultural Factors in Learning*. Bellingham: Western Washington State College, 105–19.

Larsen-Freeman, D. and Long, M. H. 1991: *An Introduction to Second Language Acquisition Research*. London: Longman.

Leaverton, L. 1973: Dialectal readers: rationale, use and value. In J. L. Laffey and R. Shuy (eds), *Language Differences: Do They Interfere?* Newark, DE: International Reading Association, 114–26.

Lin, S.-S. C. 1965: *Pattern Practice in the Teaching of Standard English to Students with a Non-Standard Dialect*. New York: Teachers College – Columbia University.

Long, M. H. 1983: Native speaker/non-native speaker conversation in the second language classroom. In M. A. Clarke and J. Handscombe (eds), *On TESOL '82: Pacific Perspectives in Language Learning and Teaching*. Washington, DC: TESOL, 207–25.

Long, M. H. 1990: Maturational constraints on language development. *Studies in Second Language Acquisition*, 12, 251–85.

Long, M. H. 1998: Focus on form in task-based language teaching. *University of Hawai'i Working Papers in English as a Second Language*, 16 (2), 35–49.

Long, M. H. 1999: Ebonics, language and power. In F. L. Pincus and H. J. Ehrlich (eds), *Race and Ethnic Conflict: Contending views on Prejudice, Discrimination, and Ethnoviolence*. Second edition. Westview and HarperCollins, 331–45.

Los Angeles Unified School District and LeMoine, N. 1999: *English for Your Success: Handbook of Successful Strategies for Educators*. Maywood, NJ: Peoples Publishing.

Love, T. A. 1991: *A Guide for Teaching Standard English to Black Dialect Speakers*. EDRS Document ED 340 248.

Lowenberg, P. H. 1986a: Non-native varieties of English: nativization, norms, and implications. *Studies in Second Language Acquisition*, 8 (1), 1–18.

Lowenberg, P. H. 1986b: Sociolinguistic context and second-language acquisition: acculturation and creativity in Malaysian English. *World Englishes*, 5 (1), 71–83.

Lowenberg, P. H. 1993: Language transfer and levels of meaning potential in Malaysian English. In J. E. Alatis (ed.), *Language, Communication and Social Meaning*. Georgetown University Round Table on Languages and Linguistics 1992. Washington, DC: Georgetown University Press, 41–55.

Lukmani, Y. M. 1972: Motivation to learn and language proficiency. *Language Learning*, 22, 261–73.

McKay, S. L. and Wong, S. C. 1996: Multiple discourses, multiple identities: investment and agency in second-language learning among Chinese adolescent immigrant students. *Harvard Educational Review*, 66, 577–608.

McLaughlin, B. 1987: *Theories of Second Language Learning*. London: Edward Arnold.

McWhorter, J. 1998: *The Word on the Street: Fact and Fable about American English*. New York and London: Plenum Trade.

McWhorter, J. 2000: *Losing the Race: Self-Sabotage in Black America*. New York: Free Press.

Menacker, T. 1998: Second language acquisition for languages with minimal distance. Ms. Department of English as a Second Language, University of Hawai'i.

Murtagh, E. J. 1982: Creole and English as languages of instruction in bilingual education with Aboriginal Australians: some research findings. *International Journal of the Sociology of Language*, 36, 15–33.

Nayar, P. B. 1997: ESL/EFL dichotomy today: language politics or pragmatics? *TESOL Quarterly*, 31, 9–37.

Noonan, K. 2000: Why we were wrong about bilingual education. *Learning English* [supplement to the *Guardian Weekly*], 24 October–1 November, 3.

Oller, J. W. 1981: Research on the measurement of affective variables: some remaining questions. In R. Andersen (ed.), *New Dimensions in Second Language Acquisition Research.* Rowley, MA: Newbury House, 14–27.

Oller, J. W., Baca, L., and Vigil, F. 1979: Attitudes and attained proficiency in ESL: a sociolinguistic study of Mexican Americans in the Southwest. *TESOL Quarterly*, 11, 173–83.

Österberg, T. 1961: *Bilingualism and the First School Language: An Educational Problem Illustrated by Results from a Swedish Language Area.* Umeå: Västernbottens Tryckeri.

Pandey, A. 2000: TOEFL to the test: are monodialectal AAL-speakers similar to ESL students? *World Englishes*, 19 (1), 89–106.

Payne, A. C. 1980: Factors controlling the acquisition of the Philadelphia dialect by out-of-state children. In W. Labov (ed.), *Locating Language in Time and Space.* New York: Academic Press, 143–78.

Peirce, B. N. 1995: Social identity, investment, and language learning. *TESOL Quarterly*, 29, 9–31.

Perry, T. and Delpit, L. (eds) 1998: *The Real Ebonics Debate: Power, Language, and the Education of African-American Children.* Boston: Beacon Press.

Peterson, R. O., Chuck, H. C., and Coladarci, A. P. 1969: *Teaching Standard English as a Second Dialect to Primary School Children in Hilo, Hawaii.* Final Report: Project no. 5-0692. Washington, DC: US Department of Health, Education, and Welfare, Office of Education, Bureau of Research.

Phillipson, R. 1988: Linguicism: structures and ideologies in linguistic imperialism. In T. Skutnabb-Kangas and J. Cummins (eds), *Minority Education: From Shame to Struggle.* Clevedon: Multilingual Matters, 339–58.

Piestrup, A. M. 1973: *Black Dialect Interference and Accommodation of Reading Instruction in First Grade.* Monographs of the Language-Behavior Research Laboratory no. 4. Berkeley: University of California.

Politzer, R. L. 1973: Problems in applying foreign language teaching methods to the teaching of standard English as a second dialect. In J. S. De Stefano (ed.), *Language, Society, and Education: A Profile of Black English.* Worthington, OH: Charles A. Jones, 238–50.

Politzer, R. L. 1993: A researcher's reflections on bridging dialect and second language learning: discussion of problems and solutions. In B. J. Merino, H. T. Trueba, and F. A. Samaniego (eds), *Language Culture and Learning: Teaching Spanish to Native Speakers of Spanish.* London: Falmer Press, 45–57.

Rampton, B. 1995: *Crossing: Language and Ethnicity among Adolescents.* London: Longman.

Rampton, M. B. H. 1991: Second language learners in a stratified multilingual setting. *Applied Linguistics*, 12, 229–48.

Ravel, J.-L. and Thomas, P. 1985: *État de la Réforme de l'Enseignement aux Seychelles 1981–1985.* Paris: Ministère des Relations Extérieures, Coopération et Développement.

Reigel, K. F. and Freedle, R. 1976: What does it take to be bilingual or bidialectal? In D. S. Harrison and T. Trabasso (eds), *Black English: A Seminar.* Hillsdale, NJ: Lawrence Erlbaum Associates, 25–44.

Rickford, J. R. 1999: *African American Vernacular English: Features, Evolution, Educational Implications.* Oxford: Blackwell.

Rickford, J. R. and Rickford, A. E. 1995: Dialect readers revisited. *Linguistics and Education*, 7, 107–28.

Rickford, J. R. and Rickford, R. J. 2000: *Spoken Soul: The Story of Black English*. New York: John Wiley.

Ringbom, H. 1978: The influence of the mother tongue on the translation of lexical items. *Interlanguage Studies Bulletin*, 3, 80–101.

Ringbom, H. 1987: *The Role of the First Language in Foreign Language Learning*. Clevedon: Multilingual Matters.

Rynkofs, J. T. 1993: Culturally responsive talk between a second grade teacher and Hawaiian children during writing workshop. Ph.D. dissertation. University of New Hampshire.

Sachdev, I. and Bourhis, R. Y. 1991: Power and status differentials in minority and majority group relations. *European Journal of Social Psychology*, 21, 1–24.

Sato, C. J. 1985: Linguistic inequality in Hawaii: the post-creole dilemma. In N. Wolfson and J. Manes (eds), *Language of Inequality*. Berlin: Mouton, 257–72.

Sato, C. J. 1989: A nonstandard approach to Standard English. *TESOL Quarterly*, 23, 259–82.

Scherloh, J. M. 1991: Teaching standard English usage: a dialect-based approach. *Adult Learning*, 2 (5), 20–2.

Schmidt, R. 1990: The role of consciousness in second language learning. *Applied Linguistics*, 11, 129–58.

Schmidt, R. 1993: Awareness and second language acquisition. *Annual Review of Applied Linguistics*, 13, 206–26.

Schumann, J. H. 1978a: The acculturation model for second language acquisition. In R. Gingras (ed.), *Second Language Acquisition and Foreign Language Teaching*. Arlington, VA: Center for Applied Linguistics, 27–50.

Schumann, J. H. 1978b: Social and psychological factors in second language acquisition. In J. Richards (ed.), *Understanding Second and Foreign Language Learning*. Rowley, MA: Newbury House, 163–78.

Schumann, J. H. 1986: Research in the acculturation model for second language acquisition. *Journal of Multilingual and Multicultural Development*, 7, 379–92.

Selinker, L. 1972: Interlanguage. *International Review of Applied Linguistics*, 10, 209–31.

Shaw, W. D. 1981: Asian student attitudes towards English. In L. E. Smith (ed.), *English for Cross-Cultural Communication*. London: Macmillan, 108–22.

Shuy, R. W. 1969: Bonnie and Clyde tactics in English teaching. *Florida FL Reporter*, 9 (1), 81–3, 160–1.

Shuy, R. W. 1971: Social dialects: teaching vs learning. *Florida FL Reporter*, 9 (1 and 2), 28–33, 55.

Shuy, R. W., Davis, A. L., and Hogan, R. F. (eds) 1964: *Social Dialects and Language Learning*. Champaign, IL: National Council of Teachers of English.

Siegal, M. 1996: The role of learner subjectivity in second language sociolinguistic competency: Western women learning Japanese. *Applied Linguistics*, 17, 356–82.

Siegel, J. 1996: *Vernacular Education in the South Pacific*. International Development Issues no. 45. Canberra: Australian Agency for International Development.

Siegel, J. 1997: Using a pidgin language in formal education: help or hindrance? *Applied Linguistics*, 18, 86–100.

Siegel, J. 1999a: Creole and minority dialects in education: an overview. *Journal of Multilingual and Multicultural Development*, 20, 508–31.

Siegel, J. 1999b: Stigmatized and standardized varieties in the classroom: interference or separation? *TESOL Quarterly*, 33 (4), 701–28.

Simpkins, G. A. and Simpkins, C. 1981: Cross-cultural approach to curriculum development. In G. Smitherman (ed.),

Black English and the Education of Black Children and Youth. Detroit: Center for Black Studies, Wayne State University, 221–40.

Simpkins, G. A., Holt, G., and Simpkins, C. 1977: *Bridge: A Cross-Cultural Reading Program*. Boston: Houghton Mifflin.

Skutnabb-Kangas, T. 1984: *Bilingualism or Not: The Education of Minorities*. Clevedon: Multilingual Matters.

Skutnabb-Kangas, T. 1988: Multilingualism and the education of minority children. In T. Skutnabb-Kangas and J. Cummins (eds), *Minority Education: From Shame to Struggle*. Clevedon: Multilingual Matters, 9–44.

Sledd, J. 1969: Bi-dialectalism: the linguistics of white supremacy. *English Journal*, 58, 1307–29.

Sledd, J. 1972: Doublespeak: dialectology in the service of Big Brother. *College English*, 33, 439–56.

Snow, C. E. 1990: Rationales for native language instruction: evidence from research. In A. M. Padilla, H. H. Fairchild, and C. M. Valdez (eds), *Bilingual Education: Issues and Strategies*. Newbury Park: Sage, 60–74.

Spolsky, B. 2000: Language motivation revisted. *Applied Linguistics*, 21 (2), 157–69.

Sridhar, K. K. and Sridhar, S. N. 1986: Bridging the paradigm gap: second language acquisition theory and indigenized varieties of English. *World Englishes*, 5 (1), 3–14.

Stern, O. 1988: Divergence and convergence of dialects and standard from the perspective of the language learner. In P. Auer and A. di Luzio (eds), *Variation and Convergence: Studies in Social Dialectology*. Berlin: Walter de Gruyer, 134–56.

Stewart, W. A. (ed.) 1964a: *Non-Standard Speech and the Teaching of English*. Washington, DC: Center for Applied Linguistics.

Stewart, W. A. 1964b: Urban Negro speech: sociolinguistic factors affecting English teaching. In R. W. Shuy, A. L. Davis, and R. F. Hogan (eds), *Social Dialects and Language Learning*. Champaign, IL: National Council of Teachers of English, 10–18.

Stewart, W. A. 1970: Foreign language teaching methods in quasi-foreign language situations. In R. W. Fasold and R. W. Shuy (eds), *Teaching Standard English in the Inner City*. Washington, DC: Center for Applied Linguistics, 1–19.

Swain, M. 1998: Focus on form through conscious reflection. In C. Doughty and J. Williams (eds), *Focus on Form in Classroom Second Language Acquisition*. Cambridge: Cambridge University Press, 64–81.

Swain, M. and Lapkin, S. 1982: *Evaluating Bilingual Education: A Canadian Example*. Clevedon: Multilingual Matters.

Tajfel, H. 1974: Social identity and intergroup behavior. *Social Science Information*, 13, 65–93.

Tajfel, H. (ed.) 1978: *Differentiation between Social Groups: Studies in the Social Psychology of Intergroup Relations*. London: Academic Press.

Taylor, H. 1989: *Standard English, Black English, and Bidialectalism: A Controversy*. New York: Peter Lang.

Thomas, W. P. and Collier, V. 1997: *School Effectiveness for Language Minority Students*. Washington, DC: National Clearinghouse for Bilingual Education.

Tollefson, J. W. 1991: *Planning Language, Planning Inequality: Language Policy in the Community*. London: Longman.

Torrey, J. 1972: *The Language of Black Children in the Early Grades*. New London: Connecticut College.

Trosset, C. S. 1986: The social identity of Welsh learners. *Language in Society*, 15, 165–92.

Trudgill, P. 1982: Linguistic accommodation: sociolinguistic observations on a sociopsychological theory. In C. Masek, R. Hendrick, and M. Miller (eds), *Papers from the Parasession on Language and Behavior: Chicago Linguistic Society (1981)*. Chicago: University of Chicago Press, 218–37.

Trudgill, P. 1983: *On Dialect*. New York: New York University Press.

Trudgill, P. 1986: *Dialects in Contact*. Oxford: Blackwell.

Valdés, G. 1981: Pedagogical implications of teaching Spanish to the Spanish-speaking in the United States. In G. Valdés, A. G. Loranzo, and R. García-Moya (eds), *Teaching Spanish to the Hispanic Bilingual: Issues, Aims and Methods*. New York: Teachers College Press, 3–20.

Valdés, G. 1997: The teaching of Spanish to bilingual Spanish-speaking students. In M. Cecilia and F. Alarcon (eds), *La Ensenanza del Español a Hispanohablantes*. Boston: Houghton Mifflin, 8–44.

Valdés-Fallis, G. 1978: A comprehensive approach to the teaching of Spanish to bilingual Spanish-speaking students. *Modern Language Journal*, 43 (3), 101–10.

Venezky, R. L. and Chapman, R. S. 1973: Is learning to read dialect bound? In J. L. Laffey and R. Shuy (eds), *Language Differences: Do They Interfere?* Newark, DE: International Reading Association, 62–9.

Vousten, R. and Bongaerts, T. 1990: Acquiring a dialect as L2: the case of the dialect of Venray in the Dutch province of Limburg. Paper presented at the International Congress of Dialectologists, Bamberg, Germany (published in W. Viereck (ed.) 1995, *Verbandlugen des Internationalen Dialektologenkongresses Bamberg 1990. Band 4*. Stuttgart: Franz Steiner, 299–313).

Wells, J. C. 1973: *Jamaican Pronunciation in London*. Publications of the Philological Society, 25. Oxford: Blackwell.

Wiley, T. G. 1996: *Literacy and Language Diversity in the United States*. Washington, DC, and McHenry, IL: Center for Applied Linguistics and Delta Systems.

Williams, J. 1987: Non-native varieties of English: a special case of language acquisition. *English World-Wide*, 8 (2), 161–99.

Winer, L. 1985: Trini Talk: learning an English-Creole as a second language. In I. F. Hancock (ed.), *Diversity and Development in English-Related Creoles*. Ann Arbor: Karoma, 44–67.

Wode, H. 1976: Developmental sequences in L2 acquisition. *Working Papers on Bilingualism*, 11, 1–31.

Wolfram, W. 1994: Bidialectal literacy in the United States. In D. Spener (ed.), *Adult Biliteracy in the United States*. Washington, DC, and McHenry, IL: Center for Applied Linguistics and Delta Systems, 71–88.

Wolfram, W. and Fasold, R. W. 1969: Toward reading materials for speakers of Black English: three linguistically appropriate passages. In J. C. Baratz and R. W. Shuy (eds), *Teaching Black Children to Read*. Washington, DC: Center for Applied Linguistics, 138–55.

Wolfram, W. and Schilling-Estes, N. 1998: *American English: Dialects and Variation*. Malden, MA: Blackwell.

Wolfram, W., Christian, D., and Adger, C. 1999: *Dialects in Schools and Communities*. Mahwah, NJ: Lawrence Erlbaum Associates.

Woolard, K. 1989: *Double Talk: Bilingualism and the Politics of Ethnicity in Catalonia*. Stanford: Stanford University Press.

World Bank 1995: *The Use of First and Second Languages in Education: A Review of International Experience*.

Draft for Discussion, February 1995. Pacific Islands Education Study, Basic Studies no. 2. Washington, DC: World Bank.

Woutersen, M., Cox, A., Weltens, B., and De Bot, K. 1994: Lexical aspects of standard dialect bilingualism. *Applied Psycholinguistics*, 15, 447–73.

Young-Scholten, M. 1985: Interference reconsidered: the role of similarity in second language acquisition. *Selecta*, 6, 6–12.

9 Input and Interaction

SUSAN M. GASS

Over the past few decades there have been many ways that scholars have approached the study of second language acquisition. This book, and hence this chapter on input and interaction, takes a cognitive science perspective on second language acquisition. The input and interaction approach takes as its starting point the assumption that language learning is stimulated by communicative pressure, and examines the relationship between communication and acquisition and the mechanisms (e.g., noticing, attention) that mediate between them. We begin with a discussion of the evidence requirements for learning. We then take an historical look at the study of input/interaction, and from there move to a review of recent research, followed by a consideration of how learning is fostered through interaction.

1 Language Learning Requirements: Input and Output

If we are to understand the role of input and output in second language learning, we need to know: (i) What kind of language is available to learners? (ii) What are the theoretical consequences of having such language information available? (iii) What is the significance of language use (output)? In other words, what do learners need in order to construct second language grammars? These issues are considered in the next sections. In particular, the focus is on the types of information that learners must have in order to construct L2 grammatical knowledge (sections 1.1 and 1.2) and what they need to do with the information in language use situations.

1.1 Nature vs. nurture

Two positions on how learning takes place have appeared in the literature: they are commonly referred to as nature and nurture.[1] The first refers to the possibility that learners (whether child first language learners or adult second language learners) come to the learning situation with innate knowledge about language; the second position claims that language development is inspired and conditioned by the environment, that is, the interactions in which learners engage.

The major question being addressed is: how can learners attain certain kinds of knowledge without being explicitly taught it or without being exposed to it in some direct way? The nature position is an innatist one that claims that learners (at least children) are born with a structure (Universal Grammar [UG]) that allows them to learn language. UG "is taken to be a characterization of the child's prelinguistic state" (Chomsky, 1981, p. 7).

With regard to input, the question to be asked is: how can children learn a complex set of abstractions when the input alone does not contain evidence of these abstractions? If the input does not provide the information necessary for the extraction of abstractions, there must be something in addition to the input that children use in grammar formation. UG is hypothesized to be an innate language faculty that limits the kinds of languages that can be created. While there is still considerable disagreement as to the nature of UG, there is widespread agreement among linguists that there is some sort of innately specified knowledge that children are born with; the position for L2 acquisition is much less clear (cf. Bley-Vroman, 1989, 1990; Clahsen, 1990; Clahsen and Muysken, 1986; O'Grady, 1996; Schachter, 1988, 1991; Wolfe-Quintero, 1996). The underlying theoretical need to posit an innate language faculty comes from the fact that there is no way to "retreat" from an overgeneralized grammar.[2] In sum, within this framework, the input provides language-specific information which interacts with whatever innate structure an individual (child or adult) brings to the language learning situation.

1.2 *Evidence types*

Traditionally, there are three types of evidence discussed in the literature on language learning (both first and second): positive evidence, negative evidence, and indirect negative evidence.[3] We will deal only with the first two.[4]

1.2.1 *Positive evidence*

Broadly speaking, positive evidence refers to the input and basically comprises the set of well-formed[5] sentences to which learners are exposed. In some SLA literature (particularly that dealing with instruction), positive evidence is referred to as models. These utterances are available from the spoken language (or visual language in the case of sign language) and/or from the written language. This is the most direct means that learners have available to them from which they can form linguistic hypotheses.

1.2.2 *Negative evidence*

Negative evidence refers to the type of information that is provided to learners concerning the incorrectness of an utterance. This might be in the form of explicit or implicit information. The following are examples of explicit and implicit negative evidence respectively:

(1) I seed the man.
    No, we say "I saw the man"

(2) From Mackey, Gass, and McDonough (2000):
    NNS: There's a basen of flowers on the bookshelf
    NS: a basin?
    NNS: base
    NS: a base?
    NNS: a base
    NS: oh, a vase
    NNS: vase

In the first example, the learner is receiving direct information about the ungrammaticality of what was said, whereas in the second example, ungrammaticality must be inferred. In the second example, it is, of course, possible that the learner will not understand that this is intended as a correction and may only think that the speaker really did not hear what was said, although as the interaction progresses, it becomes less and less likely that the "lack of understanding" explanation is an appropriate one.

As a summary of the two evidence types discussed thus far, Long (forthcoming) provides a useful taxonomy. Evidence can be positive or negative. If positive, it can be either authentic or modified. If modified, it can be simplified or elaborated. Negative evidence can also be of two types: pre-emptive (occurring before an actual error – as in a classroom context) or reactive. If reactive, it can be explicit or implicit. Explicit evidence is an overt correction. Implicit evidence can result in a communication breakdown or in a recast. Recasts, in turn, can be simple (a repetition) or elaborated (a change to a [generally grammatical] form).

1.2.3 The significance of evidence types

The distinction among types of evidence has theoretical ramifications for language acquisition. Positive evidence is the most obviously necessary requirement for learning. One must have exposure to the set of grammatical sentences in order for learning to take place. However, the role of negative evidence is less clear. In fact, for first language acquisition, the argument is that there is a need to posit an innate structure that allows acquisition to take place precisely because negative evidence is not available or, at least, is not consistently available. Therefore, without an innate structure, there would be no way to eliminate certain errors given the lack of availability of full information through positive evidence (see White, 1989, for a fuller discussion). For second language acquisition similar arguments have been made. In addition, Schwartz (1993) argues that only positive evidence contributes to the formation and restructuring of second language grammars. She does acknowledge a role for negative evidence although she questions the extent to which negative evidence can engage UG.

1.3 *Output*

A third component that has been argued to be required for successful second language learning is output. Swain (1985, 1995) and Swain and Lapkin (1995, 1998) discuss what Swain originally referred to as comprehensible output. Her argument for the need for output was based initially on observations of immersion programs in Canada and, most notably, dealt with the lack of target-like abilities of children who had spent years in such programs. She hypothesized that what was lacking was sufficient opportunities for language use. Language production moves learners from a primarily semantic use of language (as takes place in comprehension) to a syntactic use. In other words, through production, learners are forced to impose syntactic structure on their utterances. As Swain (1995, p. 128) states: "Output may stimulate learners to move from the semantic, open-ended nondeterministic, strategic processing prevalent in comprehension to the complete grammatical processing needed for accurate production. Output, thus, would seem to have a potentially significant role in the development of syntax and morphology." In addition to the argument of imposing syntactic structure on utterances, it is through production that one is able to receive feedback (either implicit or explicit), as has been shown earlier with the numerous examples of negotiation. But there are other ways in which production may be significant: (i) hypothesis testing and (ii) automaticity (cf. Gass, 1997; Swain, 1995).

While it may not always be obvious through an inspection of data alone, it is often the case that learners use a conversation precisely to test hypotheses. In a recent study in which learners were involved in interactions (videotaped) and then interviewed immediately following, Mackey et al. (2000) found evidence of an active hypothesis-testing mode. This is illustrated in (3):

(3) Hypothesis testing (INT = interviewer):
NNS: *poi un bicchiere*
then a glass
INT: *un che, come?*
a what, what?
NNS: *bicchiere*
glass

In comments provided through a stimulated recall session following this interaction, the NNS reported: "I was drawing a blank. Then I thought of a vase but then I thought that since there was no flowers, maybe it was just a big glass. So, then I thought I'll say it and see. Then, when she said '*come*' (what?), I knew that it was completely wrong." The comment "I'll say it and see" suggests that she was using the conversation as a way to see if a hypothesis was correct or incorrect.

The second significant function of production is to create greater automaticity. Automatic processes are those that have become routinized. Little effort is required to execute an automatic process (e.g., the steps involved in getting into a car and starting it are relatively automatized and require little thought). Automatic processes come about as a result of "consistent mapping of the same input to the same pattern of activation over many trials" (McLaughlin, 1987, p. 134). What this suggests is that a certain amount of practice is needed in order for language use to be routinized, that is, to take it from the labored production of early learners to the more fluent production of advanced second language speakers.

This section has dealt with requirements for learning; we next turn to an historical view of input showing how its usefulness has evolved from a behaviorist perspective (section 2) to today's cognitive approach to acquisition (section 3).

2 The Role of Input in Early Language Learning Studies

In the early part of the twentieth century, conceptualizations or theories of how languages were learned (both first and second) relied heavily on the input provided to the learner. This was particularly the case within the behaviorist period of language study, a research tradition that can reasonably be seen as falling outside of the "modern era" of language acquisition research.[6] Within the behaviorist orthodoxy, language acquisition was seen to rely entirely on the input that a child received because, within that framework, a child was seen to learn by imitation. Bloomfield (1933, p. 29) describes the then current view of language use as follows:

> The particular speech-sounds which people utter under particular stimuli, differ among different groups of men; mankind speaks many languages. A group of people who use the same system of speech-signals is a *speech-community*. Obviously, the value of language depends upon people's using it in the same way. Every member of the social group must upon suitable occasion utter the proper speech-sounds and, when he hears another utter these speech-sounds, must make the proper *response* [emphasis added].

He goes on to state with regard to children learning a language that: "Every child that is born into a group acquires these *habits* of speech and response in the first years of his life" (p. 29) (emphasis added). In this view language learning is heavily reliant on the concept of stimulus-response and the consequent concept of habit formation.

The same mechanistic view of language learning can be seen in some of the work focusing on second language acquisition in the mid-1900s. Fries (1957,

p. vii), recognizing the importance of basing pedagogical materials on principles of language learning, echoed the prevailing view of language learning – that of habit formation based on associations that stem from the input: "Learning a second language, therefore, constitutes a very different task from learning the first language. The basic problems arise not out of any essential difficulty in the features of the new language themselves but primarily out of the special 'set' created by the first language *habits*" (emphasis added). In these early approaches to understanding both first and second language acquisition, input was of paramount importance, since the input formed the basis of what was imitated and, therefore, the basis on which one created so-called language habits.

3 The Role of Input in Later Views of Language Learning

The important role of input has not diminished over the years; what has changed, however, is the conceptualization of how individuals process the input and how the input interacts with the mental capacities of those learning a language (first or second).

3.1 *The nature of input*

Within second language studies, the general function of input has been treated variably. In many approaches to SLA, input is seen as being a highly important factor in acquisition. However, in others, such as the Universal Grammar approach, input is relegated to a secondary role, interacting with an innate structure (and, in some versions, the L1) to effect acquisition. Table 9.1 (modified from Gass, 1997) provides a synoptic view of some of the major approaches to SLA over the years and the place of input within those approaches. The table specifies whether or not input must be of a specific type and attempts to specify the extent of the importance accorded to input. In the

Table 9.1 Overview of the role of input

	Focus is specific input?	*How important?*
Input/interaction	No	Very
Input Hypothesis (Krashen)	Yes ($i + 1$) Comprehensible input	Very
UG	Yes (related to specific parameter)	Depends
Information processing	No	Very

early 1970s, Ferguson (1971, 1975) began his investigations of special registers, for example "baby talk" – the language addressed to young children – and "foreigner talk" – the language addressed to non-proficient non-native speakers (NNS) of a language. His work was primarily descriptive and was aimed at an understanding of the similarities of these systems and, hence, the human capacity for language. (For a review of some of the features of "baby talk," see Cruttenden, 1994, and Pine, 1994, and for some of the features of "foreigner talk," see Gass, 1997, and Hatch, 1983.) In general, one observes linguistic modifications made by the more proficient speaker in all areas of language.[7] For example, speech tends to be slower (and even sometimes louder); intonation is often exaggerated; syntax tends to be simpler (e.g., two sentences instead of a single sentence with a relative clause); lexical items tend to be simpler (often reflecting the more frequently used words in a language). The descriptions that have been provided in the literature have, in general, been based on descriptions of such talk within western culture. One should not overlook the fact that important differences exist between talk addressed to non-proficient speakers in western cultures and similar talk in non-western cultures (see Bavin, 1992; Nwokah, 1987; Ochs, 1985; Schieffelin, 1985; much of this work is reviewed in Lieven, 1994, and, to a lesser extent, in Gass, 1997).

3.2 *The usefulness of modified input*

Most of the debate concerning the complex relationship between simplified speech and acquisition has appeared in the child language literature. Pine (1994) provides a synopsis. In general, he concludes, following work of Snow (1986), that the functions of child-directed speech may differ depending on the developmental stage of the child. At early stages of development, the major task confronting a child is to learn vocabulary and "simple semantic forms and pragmatic functions" (p. 24). It is likely that simplified speech is appropriate for this task. However, as the child's linguistic task becomes more complex and is focused on morphology and syntax, there is a need for more complex speech.

For second language learning, a similar situation obtains in terms of the variable nature of modified speech. Clearly, one function of modification is to make the language comprehensible, as is made evident in the modification sequence presented in (4a–f), below, from Kleifgen (1985). Kleifgen's data show instructions being given to a group of kindergarten children by their teacher. The class was a mixed class, consisting of English native-speaking (NS) children and non-native speakers of English with a range of proficiency levels. It is quite clear from the examples that the teacher is making modifications in order to ensure comprehension:

(4) Data from Kleifgen (1985):
 a Instructions to English NSs in a kindergarten class:
 These are babysitters taking care of babies. Draw a line from Q to q. From S to s and then trace.

b To a single NS of English:
  Now, Johnny, you have to make a great big pointed hat.
c To an intermediate-level native speaker of Urdu:
  No her hat is big. Pointed.
d To a low-intermediate-level native speaker of Arabic:
  See hat? Hat is big. Big and tall.
e To a beginning-level native speaker of Japanese:
  Big, big, big hat.
f To a beginning-level native speaker of Korean:
  Baby sitter. Baby.

These examples reveal the way the teacher adjusts her speech, most likely to ensure comprehension[8] on the part of all students; the data also illustrate the changing nature of input – the nature of the input reflects the perceived proficiency level of one's interlocutor.

Clearly, not all input serves the same learning purpose. For example, Parker and Chaudron (1987) found a greater correlation between comprehension of an elaborated passage and independent reading measures than between comprehension of a simplified passage and independent measures of reading. Yano, Long, and Ross (1994) also distinguished between simplified and elaborated input, finding no significant difference in learners' comprehension. They argue that it is the greater amount of semantic detail available in an elaborated text that allows learners to make inferences from the text. Traditionally simplified texts do not provide this richness.

3.3 *Input processing*

A crucial question in understanding the role of input relates to processing. VanPatten and his colleagues have been concerned with what they refer to as input processing (VanPatten, 1995, 1996; VanPatten and Cadierno, 1993a, 1993b; VanPatten and Sanz, 1995), which deals with presentation and timing of input. Their research, conducted within a pedagogical context, relies on the concept of attention to form and its role as a learner moves from input to intake and then to output. In VanPatten's studies, two instructional models were compared: (i) grammatical information (i.e., input) is presented to the learner and then practiced, and (ii) the input is presented before an internalized system begins to develop; in other words, there is an attempt to influence how the input will be processed and hence how an internalized system develops. The results of these studies suggest a positive effect for the second model of presentation over the first. In a replication[9] study of VanPatten and Cadierno (1993a), VanPatten and Oikkenon (1996) attempted to determine the extent to which explicit information provided during processing instruction was the source of the beneficial effect of processing. Their study involving learners of Spanish showed that it was the structured input activities and not the explicit information that resulted in the beneficial effects of instruction. In another replication study of VanPatten and Cadierno (1993a, 1993b), DeKeyser and Sokalski (1996) looked specifically at the effects of production versus comprehension activities. Their results (also based on data from learners of Spanish) do not support those of the original studies. In particular, they noted that practice at the level of input versus practice at the level of output differentially affected comprehension and production, with the former being better for comprehension and the latter for production, leading the researchers to suggest that the skills of comprehension and production are learned separately. Results also depended on the structure tested (conditionals and direct object clitics), further suggesting the complexity of studying input processing.

Similar work was conducted by Tomasello and Herron (1988, 1989).[10] They compared two groups of English learners of French. Their work dealt with retreating from overgeneralized errors. One group was presented with grammatical instruction, including exceptions to a rule; they then practiced those forms (as in group 1 of the VanPatten studies). The second group was not presented with the exceptions from the outset; rather, they were presented with a rule and were then induced to make an overgeneralized error, at which point correction occurred. The type of input that allowed corrective feedback to occur after the learner had made an error was more meaningful than input that attempted to prevent an error from occurring. In other words, allowing a natural process to occur and "interrupting" it has a greater likelihood of bringing the error to a learner's attention.

In sum, we have shown the variable nature of input, its possible functions, and finally, how it can be investigated with an eye to processing, in an effort to understand how learners actually take input and convert it into something meaningful as part of the process of grammar formation.

4 Interaction

In this section we provide descriptive background on interaction. As mentioned in section 3.1, some of the early work on input focused on the ways that proficient speakers (generally native speakers) modify their speech, presumably with the goal of making their speech comprehensible, to those with limited knowledge of the target language. Within that early tradition, consideration of an entire conversational structure was not an object of investigation.

4.1 Descriptions of interaction

Wagner-Gough and Hatch (1975) were among the first second language researchers to consider the role of conversation in the development of a second language. Their work was followed by pioneering work of Long (1980), who refined the notion of conversational structure, showing (at least quantitative) differences between NS/NNS conversations and NS/NS conversations. He proposed that there was more than just simple native speaker modification to consider; in addition, one needed to look at the interactional structure itself. When compared with interactional structures of NS/NS conversations, NS/NNS conversations showed a greater amount of interactional modification. Examples of these are provided below.

In confirmation checks, one conversational partner checks to make sure that they have correctly understood what his or her conversational partner has said:

(5) Confirmation check (from Mackey and Philp, 1998):
NNS: what are they (.) what do they do your picture?
→ NS: what are they doing in my picture?
NS: there's there's just a couple more things
NNS: a sorry? Couple?

With comprehension checks, speakers may have some idea that their conversational partner has not understood. They seek to determine whether this is the case or not:

(6) Comprehension check (from Varonis and Gass, 1985a):
NNS1: and your family have some ingress
NNS2: yes ah, OK OK
→ NNS1: more or less OK?

In (7), there is a recognized lack of comprehension and one party seeks to clarify:

(7) Clarification request (from Oliver, 1998):
NNS1: Where do I put-?
→ NNS2: What?
NNS1: The pl[a]nt
NNS2: The pl[a]nt
→ NNS: What's that pl[a]nt?

Other modification types also exist, for example, reformulations such as "or choice" questions, as in example (8), where the native speaker asks a question and upon an obvious sign of non-comprehension rephrases the question giving alternatives for the non-native speaker to choose from:

(8) From Varonis and Gass (1985b):
NS: What did you want? A service call?
NNS: uh 17 inch huh?
→ NS: What did you want a service call? or how much to repair a TV?

Other modifications include topic-focused questions, as in example (9):

(9) From Larsen-Freeman and Long (1991):
NS: When do you go to the uh Santa Monica?
→ You say you go fishing in Santa Monica, right?
NNS: Yeah
NS: When?

In (9), the NS takes the original questions, which include the concepts of fishing and the location of Santa Monica, and establishes them as the topic before proceeding to the crucial part of the question, "when?"

In (10) is an elaborated question in which the NS, probably recognizing that the NNS has had problem with "daily meals," exemplifies the term:

(10) Eavesdropped by Gass:
NS: Where do you eat your daily meals?
NNS: Daily meals?
→ NS: Lunch and dinner, where do you eat them?

and recasts, as in (11) (also in (5)). In this example, the NS "recasts" (see section 5.3) the ungrammatical NNS utterance as a grammatical sentence:

(11) From Philp (1999):
NNS: why he want this house?
→ NS: why does he want this house?

4.2 *The function of interaction: the Interaction Hypothesis*

The line of research that focuses on the interactional structure of conversation was developed in the following years by many researchers (see, e.g., Gass and Varonis, 1985, 1989; Long, 1981, 1983; Pica, 1987, 1988; Pica and Doughty, 1985; Pica, Doughty, and Young, 1986; Pica, Young, and Doughty, 1987; Varonis and Gass, 1985a). The emphasis is on the role which negotiated interaction between native and non-native speakers and between two NNSs[11] plays in the development of a second language. That early body of research as well as more recent work has taken as basic the notion that conversation is not only a medium of practice, but also the means by which learning takes place. In other words, conversational interaction in a second language forms the basis for the development of language rather than being only a forum for practice of specific language features. This has been most recently expressed by Long (1996, pp. 451–2) as the Interaction Hypothesis:

> *negotiation for meaning*, and especially negotiation work that triggers *interactional* adjustments by the NS or more competent interlocutor, facilitates acquisition because it connects input, internal learner capacities, particularly selective attention, and output in productive ways.

and:

> it is proposed that environmental contributions to acquisition are mediated by selective attention and the learner's developing L2 processing capacity, and that these resources are brought together most usefully, although not exclusively, during *negotiation for meaning*. Negative feedback obtained during negotiation work or elsewhere may be facilitative of L2 development, at least for vocabulary, morphology, and language-specific syntax, and essential for learning certain specifiable L1–L2 contrasts. (p. 414)

What is intended is that through focused negotiation work, the learner's attentional resources may be oriented to (i) a particular discrepancy between what she or he "knows" about the second language and what is reality vis-à-vis the target language, or (ii) an area of the second language about which the learner has little or no information. Learning may take place "during" the interaction, or negotiation may be an initial step in learning; it may serve as a priming device (Gass, 1997), thereby representing the setting of the stage for learning, rather than being a forum for actual learning. In (12), we see an example of recognition of a new lexical item as a result of negotiation of that word. This illustrates how the learner may have used the conversation as a resource to learn the new phrase *reading glasses*:

(12) From Mackey (1999):

	NS:	there's there's a pair of reading glasses above the plant
	NNS:	a what?
	NS:	glasses reading glasses to see the newspaper?
	NNS:	glassi?
	NS:	you wear them to see with, if you can't see. Reading glasses
→	NNS:	ahh ahh glasses to read you say reading glasses
	NS:	yeah

In the penultimate line, the NNS acknowledges the fact that the new word "reading glasses" came from the interaction and, in particular, as a consequence of the negotiation work. We return to the Interaction Hypothesis in section 5, where we present some of the recent empirical evidence relating specifically to the relationship between interaction and learning.

Example (13) illustrates "delayed" learning. Two NNSs were involved in a picture-description task. NNS1 is describing a part of the picture and initiates the description with an incorrectly pronounced word which NNS2 immediately questions. NNS1 most likely ponders the pronunciation problem, never again mispronouncing *cup*. To the contrary, after some time, she correctly pronounces *cup*. In other words, the negotiation itself made her aware of a problem; she was then able to listen for more input until she was able to figure out the correct pronunciation:

(13) From Gass and Varonis (1989):
NNS1: Uh holding the [k^p]
NNS2: Holding the cup?
NNS1: Hmm hmmm . . .
(seventeen turns later)
NNS2: Holding a cup
NNS1: Yes
NNS2: Coffee cup?
NNS1: Coffee? Oh yeah, tea, coffee cup, teacup.
NNS2: Hm hm.

It is important to point out that the Interaction Hypothesis is agnostic as to the role of UG. In other words, no claims are made about the ultimate source of syntax that a learner uses as he or she creates hypotheses. This will be returned to briefly in the concluding section of this chapter. Before turning to a discussion of what is involved in the relationship between interaction and learning, we present a brief background on the type of language information needed for learning.

5 Data as Evidence for the Interactionist Position

5.1 *Difficulties in determining learning*

In the preceding sections we discussed the concept of interaction, in particular focusing on the structure of conversations in which non-native speakers are involved. We noted that often the structure is such that there are multiple instances of what has been termed negotiation, as shown in (2). But, in that example, is there any evidence that anything other than "mimicking" is at play? We repeat the example here for the sake of convenience:

(14) From Mackey, Gass, and McDonough (2000):
NNS: There's a basen of flowers on the bookshelf
NS: a basin?
NNS: base
NS: a base?
NNS: a base
NS: oh, a vase
NNS: vase

Here, the NNS and the NS appear to be negotiating their way to a successful conclusion where the NS finally understands that the NNS is talking about a vase rather than a basin, but has the NNS really learned "vase," or is she only repeating the NS without true understanding? This is a perennial problem in determining the extent to which such exchanges result in learning (i.e., was the word "vase" learned?) or serve only as negotiation for meaning with no consequent learning. Hawkins (1985) questions whether apparent acknowledgment of understanding truly reflects understanding at all. She presents the following example taken from a game in which a NS and a NNS are trying to order parts of a story to make a coherent whole:

(15) From Hawkins (1985):

NS: Number two, . . . is . . . the man . . . look for help
NNS: Uh-huh, ((yes)) for help.
NS: Help, you know. . . . "Aah! Help" (shouts softly)
NNS: Uh-huh. ((yes))
NS: No *Up* . . . *HELP*.
→ NNS: Help
NS: Yeah . . . He asked, . . . he asked . . . a man . . . for . . . help.
→ NNS: . . . for help
NS: Yeah . . . he asked . . . the man . . . for telephone.

Within the interactionist tradition, one might be tempted to take the last two NNS responses *help, for help* as suggesting that the learner had indeed understood, and one might even be attempted to assume that the acknowledgment of comprehension signified an initial step in the learning process. However, through retrospective comments from the participants in this exchange, Hawkins showed that indeed no comprehension had taken place vis-à-vis the meaning of the word *help*; rather it is likely that the complex phenomenon of social relationships had led the NNS not to pursue the lack of understanding.[12]

Another instance might be useful in illustrating the difficulties in attributing cause to conversational production. Houck and Gass (1996) present the following example. A NS and a NNS were beginning a discussion about an assignment for an SLA class:

(16) From Houck and Gass (1996):

NS: Okay, so we're just gonna give our opinions about these. Uhm, do you have an overall opinion?
NNS: Do I have a overall (one)? Uhm. (longish pause – head movement and smile).

Again, within the interactionist tradition, this might be seen as a negotiation routine with the NNS perhaps questioning the meaning of "overall one." However, a closer examination of the data suggests that what was in actuality taking place was a difference in discourse style. The NNS (a native speaker of Japanese) appears to be thrown by the abruptness of the initial question. It is typical in Japanese discussions of this sort to have an initial exchange about procedures. On the other hand, Americans will typically begin with *OKAY*, as this speaker did, and then jump right in (Watanabe, 1993). As Houck and Gass argued, the problem was a global discourse one (as opposed to a language one) and the apparent negotiation for meaning was only reflective of the unexpectedness of the discourse opening.

5.2 *Linking interaction and learning*

In the preceding section we discussed some of the difficulties in determining the extent to which learning arises from conversation. However, there are true instances when learning appears to occur as a result of negotiation work. Gass and Varonis (1989) provided the example in (13) which suggests something beyond the immediate "echo" of an appropriate response. In other words, evidence of forms which were "corrected" through negotiation work appear later in a learner's production. As Gass and Varonis noted, these negotiated forms are incorporated into a learner's speech.

In the past few years, scholars have attempted to make the link between interaction and learning more explicit and direct. This is, of course, a difficult task, since one can rarely come to know the full extent of input to a learner or observe all of the interactions in which a particular learner participates. One of the earliest of such researchers was Sato (1986, 1990), who questioned a direct positive relationship between interaction and development. In her study of the acquisition of English by two Vietnamese children, she suggested that interaction did not foster development, at least in the specific area of morphosyntax that she was investigating (past tense marking). As she acknowledged, this might have been due to the particular structure investigated, since past tense marking is not crucial to an understanding of the time referent. Loschky (1994) investigated the effects of comprehensible input and interaction on vocabulary retention and comprehension. The results from his study were largely inconclusive. Negotiation had a positive effect on comprehension, but no such claim could be made for retention. Ellis, Tanaka, and Yamazaki (1994) also investigated the role of negotiation in vocabulary acquisition and word order. In that study, interactionally modified input yielded better comprehension rates and resulted in the acquisition of more new words.

Polio and Gass (1998) conducted a study similar to that of Gass and Varonis (1994), to be discussed below. NNSs had to describe where to place objects on a board. The extent to which the NSs were able to understand NNSs' descriptions was determined by how accurately the NS actually placed the object. Half of the NS/NNS dyads completed the task with no interaction and half completed it with interaction. Polio and Gass found a positive effect for negotiated interaction on production (measured by NS comprehension).

In an interesting analysis of the talk of eighth grade students in a French immersion program, Swain and Lapkin (1998) specifically argued, through the analysis of one particular dyad, that the talk itself mediates actual learning.

5.3 *What kind of interaction? Negotiation and recasts*

The question arises as to the efficacy of different types of feedback to learners. In this section, two types of feedback are considered: negotiation and recasts. The former have been dealt with extensively throughout this chapter; the latter refer to those instances in which an interlocutor rephrases an incorrect utterance with a corrected version, while maintaining the integrity of the original meaning. We will not detail the complexities of recasts here (are they partial recasts? full recasts? in response to a single error? in response to multiple errors?), but will present two examples which illustrate the form that they take. In (17), a recast with rising intonation, the auxiliary is added and the verbal morphology is corrected. In (18) the verb form is corrected (from future to subjunctive, required after *avant que*) without rising intonation:

(17) From Philp (1999, p. 92):
NNS: What doctor say?
NS: What is the doctor saying?

(18) From Lyster (1998, p. 58) (St = student; T3 = teacher):
St: Avant que quelqu'un le prendra
before someone it will take
'Before someone will take it'
T3: Avant que quelqu'un le prenne
before someone it takes
'Before someone takes it'

In recent years, there have been a number of studies in which recasts, as a form of implicit negative feedback, have been the focus. With regard to their effectiveness, the results are mixed. Lyster and Ranta (1997) collected data from grades 4–6 children in French immersion programs. Their research considered recasts by teachers following errors and, importantly, the reaction by the student (*uptake*, in their terminology) in the subsequent turn. They argue that uptake "reveals what the student attempts to do with the teacher's feedback" (p. 49). Their results showed that, despite the preponderance of recasts in their database, recasts were not particularly effective. Other types of feedback led more successfully to student-generated repair.

Using the same database reported on in the Lyster and Ranta (1997) study, Lyster (1998) divided recasts into four types depending on whether the recast was a declarative or interrogative and whether it sought confirmation of the original utterance or provided additional information. He found that there was some confusion between the corrective and approval functions of recasts. He argued that recasts may not be particularly useful in terms of corrective feedback, but they may be a way that teachers can move a lesson forward by focusing attention on lesson content rather than on language form.

Other studies do show a positive effect for recasts, while highlighting two main problems in research on recasts: (i) the concept of uptake, and (ii) the data to be included in an analysis.

Mackey and Philp (1998) point out that uptake, as defined by Lyster and Ranta, may be the wrong measure to use in determining effectiveness. Their data represent an attempt to go beyond the turn immediately following a recast. They make the point (cf. Gass, 1997; Gass and Varonis, 1994; Lightbown, 1998) that if one is to consider effectiveness (i.e., development/acquisition), then one should more appropriately measure delayed effects. In particular, they considered the effects of interaction with and without recasts on learners' knowledge of English questions. Their results showed that for more advanced learners, recasts plus negotiation were more beneficial than negotiation alone. This was the case even though there was not always evidence for a reaction by the learner in the subsequent turn.

Additional research that attempts to determine the role of recasts (in this case as opposed to models) is a study by Long, Inagaki, and Ortega (1998), who investigated (i) the acquisition of ordering of adjectives and a locative construction by English learners of Japanese, and (ii) the acquisition of topicalization and adverb placement by English learners of Spanish. Their results were mixed, inasmuch as only one of the learner groups (Spanish) showed greater learning following recasts as opposed to models. Further, these findings were true for adverb placement only.

A second problem, having to do with the data used for analysis, was noted by Oliver (1995). After a recast, there is frequently no opportunity for the original speaker to make a comment. This may be due to a topic shift, as in (19), or the inappropriateness of making a comment, because the recast had been in the form of a *yes/no* question and the appropriate response would not be a repetition, but a *yes/no* response:

(19) From Oliver (1995, p. 472):
NNS: a [c]lower tree.
NS: A flower tree. How tall is the trunk?

When the lack of opportunity/appropriacy is included, the percentage of "incorporated" recasts greatly increases. Lyster (1998) argued that the contexts of language use (child–child dyadic interactions in Oliver's research and teacher–student interactions in Lyster's own work) are different, and that, in fact, in classrooms the teacher often keeps the floor, thereby, as mentioned earlier, drawing attention to content and not to language form.

5.4 *The progression of research within the interactionist tradition: two examples*

Much of the research specifically intended to investigate the direct relationship between interaction and learning suffers from methodological difficulties in determining a cause and effect relationship. In what follows, we highlight two studies because they represent a progression in the kind of research that has been conducted (boxes 9.1 and 9.2). It is probably not a coincidence that their titles are similar, with the only crucial change in the last word (*production* in the Gass and Varonis title and *development* in the Mackey title).

These two studies were selected for their similarity in goals and, importantly, because they illustrate a progression in the development of this area of inquiry. In both studies, the researchers were concerned with the potential effects of interaction on language development. However, there are significant differences which, in a sense, reflect the development of the field. In the Gass and Varonis study, published five years prior to Mackey's work, the researchers dealt with a shorter time span (from the execution of the first board game to the execution of the second). In the Mackey study, the time period covered approximately five weeks – clearly a more persuasive snapshot of the learning effects of interaction. A second difference is in the measurement of learning. In the Gass and Varonis study, learning was operationalized in terms of comprehension and production, whereas the Mackey study attempted to measure particular learning effects through a pre-test/post-test design. The Gass and Varonis design was such that little specific information could be obtained on the change over time of particular grammatical structures. The goal was to gain an overall picture of the effects of interaction. Mackey's design, which focused specifically on question formation, was able to isolate certain developmental features of questions, enabling her to provide answers on the issue of development.

In sum, these two studies both address the same questions, albeit at a distance of five years, and both show the effects of interaction on production/learning.

5.5 *Conversation and learning requirements*

The interactionist position is one that accords an important role to conversation as a basis for second language learning. In section 1, we dealt with three requirements of learning (positive evidence [input], negative evidence [feedback], and output) and suggested the role that they might play in learning and the ways in which conversation is involved in their effectiveness.

But conversation is obviously not the only forum for language information for second language learners. In some ways conversation plays a (near) privileged role; in others it plays a significant, although not necessarily privileged role. Positive evidence, clearly a crucial part of the acquisition picture, is an example of the latter because conversation is only one of many ways of obtaining positive evidence (reading, listening to a lecture, and listening to television/radio are but some of the other ways). In this sense, for the purpose of obtaining positive evidence, conversation does not play a privileged role in acquisition. A more important role for conversation relates to the obtaining of negative evidence. Here conversation may have a more important role to play

Box 9.1 Gass and Varonis (1994)

Research questions:

i Does modified input result in better NNS comprehension and better production?
ii Does interaction yield better NNS comprehension and better L2 production?
iii Does interaction yield better NS comprehension?

Predictions:

i Modified input results in better NNS comprehension and better production.
ii Interaction yields better NNS comprehension and better L2 production.
iii Interaction yields better NS comprehension.

Participants:
Sixteen native speakers of English and 16 non-native speakers of English (various L1s).

Methodology:
Task: Each NS–NNS dyad completed two board-game tasks in which each participant had a board depicting an outdoor scene. On one, objects were permanently affixed. The other board had the same objects to the side. The individual with the permanently affixed board had to describe to his or her partner where to place the objects.

Groups: The 16 dyads were divided into two subgroups: a modified input group and an unmodified input group (see figure 9.1). The groups were differentiated by the type of input provided on the initial part of the task. These two subgroups of eight dyads were further subdivided into two more subgroups according to whether or not normal interaction was allowed on the first board description task. These four groups were further subdivided as to whether or not interaction was allowed on the second board description task.

Procedure: On the first board description task, the NS described to the NNS. These descriptions were "scripted" on the basis of prior data gathered differentiating between modified and unmodified input. On the second task, the NNS described a different board scene to the NS.

Operationalization:

i Comprehension by NNS = Accurate placement of objects by NNS on task one.
ii Comprehension by NS = Accurate placement of objects by NS on task two in interaction condition on task two.
iii Accurate production by NNS; accurate placement of objects by NS on task two in condition in which task one included interaction.

Results: Modified input yielded better NNS comprehension than unmodified input. Interaction yielded better NNS comprehension. Interaction did not yield better NS comprehension. Prior interaction yielded better L2 production. Prior input modification did not yield better L2 production.

Conclusion: Evidence of interaction having an effect on L2 production; no specific claims of learning.

Box 9.2 Mackey (1999)

Research questions:

i Does conversational interaction facilitate second language development?
ii Are the developmental outcomes related to the nature of the conversational interaction and the level of learner involvement?

Main prediction: Interaction focused on specific morphosyntactic structures will lead to an increase in production of structures at higher developmental levels.

Linguistic structure tested: Question formation (following Pienemann and Johnston [1987]).

Participants: Thirty-four adult ESL learners (various L1s) and 6 NSs.

Methodology:
Five groups:

i *Interactors (n = 7)*: NS/NNS pairs participated in a task-based activity in which interaction was allowed.
ii *Interactor Unreadies (n = 7)*: NS/NNS pairs participated in a task-based activity in which interaction was allowed. They differed from the "Interactor" group in that they were developmentally lower than it vis-à-vis English question formation.
iii *Observers (n = 7)*: NNS who only observed an interaction (but did not participate).
iv *Scripted (n = 6)*: NS/NNS pairs participated in the same task, but the input from the NSs was premodified.
v *Control (n = 7)*: no treatment.

Procedure: Seven sessions:

- pre-test;
- three treatment sessions (on the three days subsequent to the pre-test);
- three post-tests: (a) one on the day following the last treatment session, (b) one one week after (a), and (c) one three weeks after (b).

Results: The interactor groups combined ((i) and (ii)) showed greater improvement than the other groups and the increase was maintained. All groups increased the number of higher-level questions (see Pienemann and Johnston [1987]), but only the two "Interactor" groups and the "Scripted" group maintained the increase in all post-tests.

Conclusion: Interaction led to development. More active involvement led to greater development.

since there are fewer possibilities (and fewer opportunities) for obtaining information about incorrect forms or ungrammaticality. In other words, conversation may not be the only way of obtaining negative evidence, but other possibilities (e.g., teacher correction) are limited. Perhaps the most important

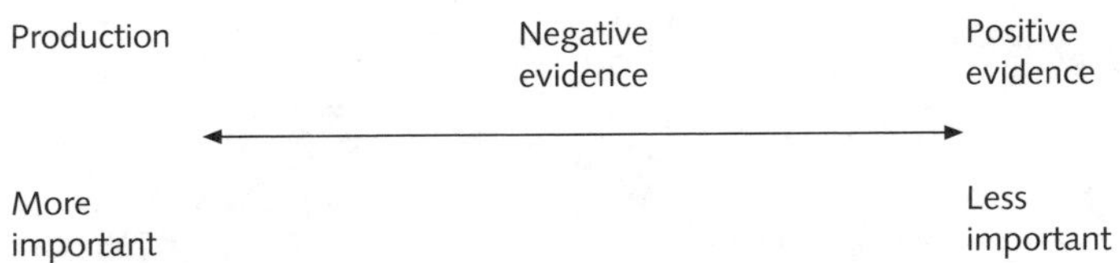

Figure 9.1 Conversation and language learning requirements

role for conversation can be found in production, particularly production where hypothesis testing and the increase of automaticity are involved. As mentioned in section 1.3, conversation is one of the few forums in which learners can reap those benefits assigned to production. Figure 9.1 illustrates the value of conversation relative to these three requirements of acquisition.

6 Attention

The two studies highlighted in section 5.4 and other similar ones (e.g., Philp, 1999) suggest that interaction and learning are related. This observation is an important one, but is in need of an explanation in order to advance our understanding of how learning takes place. That is, what happens during a negotiation event that allows learners to utilize the content of the negotiation to advance their own knowledge? Long's (1996) Interaction Hypothesis, given in section 4.2, suggests an important role for attention, as does Gass (1997, p. 132): "Attention, accomplished in part through negotiation, is one of the crucial mechanisms in this process."

We turn now to the concept of attention as a way of accounting for the creation of new knowledge and/or the modification (restructuring) of existing knowledge. In the recent history of SLA research, much emphasis has been placed on the concept of attention and the related notion of noticing (cf. Doughty, 2001, for an extended discussion of processing issues during focus on form instruction). Schmidt (1990, 1993a, 1993b, 1994) has argued that attention is essential to learning; that is, there is no learning without attention. While this strong claim is disputed (cf. Gass, 1997; Schachter et al., 1998), it is widely accepted that selective attention plays a major role in learning. Schmidt (1998, 2001) has modified his strong stance and acknowledges that learning may occur without learners being aware of learning, but he also claims that such learning does not play a significant role in the larger picture of second language learning. It is through interaction (e.g., negotiation, recasts) that a learner's attention is focused on a specific part of the language, specifically on those mismatches between target language forms and learner-language forms. Doughty (2001) points out that this assumes that these mismatches are indeed noticeable (cf. Truscott, 1998, for a discussion of attention, awareness, and noticing) and that, if they are noticeable and if a learner is to use these mismatches as a source for grammar restructuring, he or she must have the capacity to hold a representation of the TL utterance in memory while executing a comparison. Doughty provides three ways in which such a cognitive comparison could work (p. 18):

> 1) Representations of the input and output utterances are held in short term memory and compared there
> 2) Only a deeper (semantic) representation of the already-processed utterance is held in long-term memory, but it leaves useable traces in the short term memory against which new utterances may be compared; and
> 3) The memory of the utterance passes to long term memory but can readily be reactivated if there is any suspicion by the language processor that there is a mismatch between stored knowledge and incoming linguistic evidence.

There is anecdotal and empirical evidence in the literature that indeed learners are capable of noticing mismatches. Schmidt and Frota (1986) report on Schmidt's learning of Portuguese, in which he clearly documents his noticing of new forms. There is also anecdotal evidence that suggests that learners learn new forms as a result of conversation (see example (9) above). In an empirical investigation of just this issue, Mackey et al. (2000) provided data showing that learners do indeed recognize feedback through interaction, although it is not always the case that what is intended through negative feedback is what the learner perceives. Through stimulated recalls, Mackey et al. investigated three types of linguistic feedback (phonological, lexical, and morphosyntactic) in two groups of learners (English as a second language and Italian as a foreign language), and the perception of the feedback by the learners. In other words, Mackey et al.'s research question concerned the extent to which learners recognized feedback, and in the event that they did, whether they recognized it as intended. In (20–2), we present examples of each of these three areas of feedback, along with the stimulated recall comments:

(20) Morphosyntactic feedback (perceived as lexical feedback):

NNS: *c'è due tazzi*
There is two cups (m. pl.)
INT: *due tazz-come?*
Two cup- what?
NNS: *tazzi, dove si puó mettere té, come se dice questo?*
Cups (m. pl.), where one can put tea, how do you say this?
INT: *tazze?*
Cups (f. pl.)?
NNS: ok, *tazze*
Ok, cups (f. pl.)
RECALL: I wasn't sure if I learned the proper word at the beginning.

(21) Phonological feedback correctly perceived:

NNS:	vincino la tavolo è near the table is (the correct form is *vicino*)
INT:	vicino? near?
NNS:	la, lu tavolo the ? table
RECALL:	I was thinking . . . when she said *vicino* I was thinking, OK did I pronounce that right there?

(22) Lexical feedback correctly perceived:

NNS:	there is a library
NS:	a what?
NNS:	a place where you put books
NS:	a bookshelf?
NNS:	bok?
NS:	shelf
NNS:	bookshelf
RECALL:	That's not a good word she was thinking about library like we have here on campus, yeah.

While the results were not identical for the two groups of learners, it was generally the case that morphosyntactic feedback was not recognized as such (less than 25 percent by either group), whereas lexical and phonological feedback were more likely to be recognized as such. Phonological feedback was accurately recognized in 60 percent of the cases by the ESL group and 21 percent by the Italian group; lexical feedback was accurately recognized 83 percent of the time by the ESL group and 66 percent by the Italian group.

These results suggest that there may be a differential role for feedback in different linguistic areas,[13] as suggested by Pica (1994). It may be that morphosyntactic feedback is not noticed because, as is typical in a conversational context, individuals are focused on meaning, not on language form. Phonological and lexical errors can interfere with basic meaning and hence need to be attended to on the spot if shared meaning is to result; the morphosyntactic examples in the Mackey et al. study generally dealt with low-level, non-meaning-bearing elements.

7 The Theory of Contrast

Earlier in this chapter we dealt with the concept of negative evidence and the fact that corrective feedback cannot be relied upon in language learning (either first or second). In this section, we consider a broadened definition of negative evidence, one that relies heavily on conversational interaction. In so doing, we are not making the argument that negative evidence can indeed replace the need for an innate structure; rather, our point is simply that the concept of negative evidence and learners' ability to attend to corrective feedback needs to be broadened. We take the following definition from Saxton (1997), whose definition of negative evidence departs somewhat from the more general definition provided by Pinker (1989) and others. Saxton (1997, p. 145) defines negative evidence as follows: "Negative evidence occurs directly contingent on a child error (syntactic or morphosyntactic), and is characterized by an immediate contrast between the child error and a correct alternative to the error, as supplied by the child's interlocutor." This definition allows researchers to determine what the "corrective potential" of an utterance is vis-à-vis two factors: (i) the linguistic content of the response and (ii) the proximity of the response to an error (p. 145). It is not clear from this definition from whose perspective negative evidence is to be viewed. In fact, Saxton (p. 145) states that "there is ample evidence that negative evidence, as defined here, is supplied to the child." However, it is more important to view negative evidence from the perspective of the learner (child or adult second language learner) and to understand what learners are doing with the information that is provided.

Saxton (1997) proposes what he calls the "Direct Contrast Hypothesis." This is defined within the context of child language acquisition as follows:

> When the child produces an utterance containing an erroneous form, which is responded to immediately with an utterance containing the correct adult alternative to the erroneous form (i.e. when negative evidence is supplied), the child may perceive the adult form as being in *contrast* with the equivalent child form. Cognizance of a relevant contrast can then form the basis for perceiving the adult form as a correct alternative to the child form [emphasis in original]. (p. 155)

The fact that a correct and an incorrect form are adjacent is important in creating a conflict for the learner. The mere fact of a contrast or a conflict draws a learner's attention to a deviant form. The contrast can be highlighted as a result of recasts or through negotiation work. Saxton specifically tests two competing hypotheses, one nativist and one relying on Contrast Theory. The nativist hypothesis suggests that negative evidence, even when occurring adjacent to a child error, should be no more effective than positive evidence in bringing about language change. Contrast Theory says that the former will be more effective than the latter. Saxton's research with children suggests that Contrast Theory makes the correct prediction. Children reproduced correct forms more frequently when the correct form was embedded in negative as opposed to positive evidence. As with some of the SLA literature reported above, the correct form was seen in immediate responses; hence, there is no information about long-term effectiveness.

This is not unlike what has been dealt with in the SLA literature under the rubric of "noticing the gap," that is, noticing where learner production and target language forms differ. Conversation provides the means for the contrast to become apparent. The immediate juxtaposition of correct and erroneous forms may lead a learner to recognize that his or her own form is in fact erroneous. However, many problems remain, as Doughty (2001) points out. What is the function of working memory? What happens when learners take the next step, which undoubtedly (at least in the case of syntax or morphosyntax) involves some sort of analysis? Contrasts occurring within the context of conversation often do not have an immediate outcome. Research has not yet been successful at predicting when a single exposure – for example, through a negotiation sequence or a recast – will suffice to effect immediate learning and when it will not.

It is likely that there are limitations to what can and cannot be learned through the provision of negative evidence provided through conversation. One possibility is that surface-level phenomena can be learned, but abstractions cannot. This is consistent with Truscott's (1998) claim that competence is not affected by noticing. Negative evidence can probably not apply to long stretches of speech, given memory limitations (see Philp, 1999). But it may be effective with low-level phenomena, such as pronunciation or basic meanings of lexical items. Future research will need to determine the long-term effects of interaction on different parts of language (see Gass, Svetics, and Lemelin, forthcoming).

NOTES

1 See Pinker (1994, pp. 277–8), who takes the position that the nature/nurture argument is a false dichotomy. He makes the point that if wild children "had run out of the woods speaking Phrygian or ProtoWorld, who could they have talked to?" (p. 277). In other words, nature provides part of the answer and nurture provides another.

2 Within the behaviorist view, "errors" were eliminated by correction. When a child said something that contained an error, the so-called error was corrected and thereby eliminated. We now know that there are a number of reasons why this position is not sufficient to account for language learning. First, as (i) shows, children don't always focus on the correction (Cazden, 1972, p. 92):

(i) Child: My teacher holded the baby rabbits and we patted them.
Adult: Did you say your teacher held the baby rabbits?
Child: Yes.
Adult: What did you say she did?
Child: She holded the baby rabbits and we patted them.
Adult: Did you say she held them tightly?
Child: No, she holded them loosely.

Second, correction is not consistent. That is, the pressures of the moment may preclude a more proficient interlocutor from making all corrections. And, third, even when correction does occur, it is not always the case that the "correct" solution is provided.

3 All three of these evidence types are treated in the literatures on both first and second language acquisition. However, perhaps with the exception of positive evidence, they play a different role in first and second language acquisition. The comments in this section are restricted to the case of second language acquisition.

4 Indirect negative evidence will not be dealt with in this chapter because it is the least relevant in a discussion of interaction. It is, nonetheless, perhaps the most interesting of the types of evidence that learners can avail themselves of. Unfortunately, it is the least studied, perhaps because no theoretical arguments rest crucially on it. Chomsky (1981, pp. 8–9), in discussing evidence types, states:

> indirect negative evidence – a not unreasonable acquisition system can be devised with the operative principle that if certain structures or rules fail to be exemplified in relatively simple expressions, where they would be expected to be found, then a (possibly marked) option is selected excluding them in the grammar, so that a kind of "negative evidence" can be available even without corrections, adverse reactions, etc. There is good reason to believe that direct negative evidence is not necessary for language acquisition, but indirect negative evidence may be relevant.

As Plough (1994, p. 30) states, it is an "indirect means of letting the learner know that a feature is not possible because it is never present in the *expected* environment."

5 A discussion of the extent to which the input consists of well-formed sentences can be found in White (1989).

6 Snow (1994) places the beginnings of "modern child language research" to the 1964 publication of Brown and Bellugi.

7 While there have been some reports of ungrammatical speech to non-native speakers (particularly in high- to lower-status situations and to low proficiency learners; cf. Gass, 1997), in most cases non-native directed speech is grammatical albeit modified in the ways discussed in this section.

8 We do not intend to discuss the role of comprehension in any detail. It should be noted, however, that a minimal requirement of acquisition is that the language has been comprehended (see Gass, 1997, for a discussion of levels of comprehension) in the traditional sense of the word comprehension.

9 This and the DeKeyser and Sokalski study (1996, discussed below) are intended to be replication studies (see Polio and Gass, 1997, for further discussion of replication studies). However, there is a crucial difference that makes the results somewhat non-comparable – the participant population. In the VanPatten and Cadierno studies, participants were from second year university-level Spanish classes; in the DeKeyser and Sokalski study, they were from first year university-level Spanish classes; in the VanPatten and Oikkenon study (1996, discussed below), participants were from fourth semester high school Spanish classes.

10 See criticisms of this research by Beck and Eubank (1991) and the response by Tomasello and Herron (1991).

11 Most of the research in second language acquisition within this framework has considered dyads rather than large groups of conversational participants. This is, in some sense, an accident of research design, or more likely due to the ease with which dyadic conversational data can be gathered. This should not be taken to imply that conversations with more than two individuals do not serve the same purpose as dyadic conversations. It only means that larger groups engaged in conversations have not been investigated to any significant extent in the second language literature.

12 The burden of continuing a conversation with a non-proficient and non-understanding participant is often too great. Instead, participants opt out and either end the conversation or change the topic completely.

13 It must be recognized that reporting and noticing are not isomorphic. Because something is not reported does not necessarily mean that it has not been noticed. However, not reporting something when probed (as in Mackey et al., 2000) may be suggestive of its not being noticed.

REFERENCES

Bavin, E. 1992: The acquisition of Walpiri. In D. Slobin (ed.), *The Crosslinguistic Study of Language Acquisition*. Hillsdale, NJ: Lawrence Erlbaum Associates, 309–72.

Beck, M. and Eubank, L. 1991: Acquisition theory and experimental design: a critique of Tomasello and Herron. *Studies in Second Language Acquisition*, 13, 73–6.

Bley-Vroman, R. 1989: The logical problem of second language learning. In S. Gass and J. Schachter (eds), *Linguistic Perspectives on Second Language Acquisition*. Cambridge: Cambridge University Press, 41–68.

Bley-Vroman, R. 1990: The logical problem of foreign language learning. *Linguistic Analysis*, 20, 3–49.

Bloomfield, L. 1933: *Language*. New York: Holt, Rinehart, and Winston.

Brown, R. and Bellugi, U. 1964: Three processes in the child's acquisition of syntax. *Harvard Educational Review*, 34, 133–51.

Cazden, C. 1972: *Child Language and Education*. New York: Holt, Rinehart, and Winston.

Chomsky, N. 1981: *Lectures on Government and Binding*. Dordrecht: Foris.

Clahsen, H. 1990: The comparative study of first and second language acquisition. *Studies in Second Language Acquisition*, 12, 135–53.

Clahsen, H. and Muysken, P. 1986: The availability of universal grammar to adult and child learners – a study of the acquisition of German word order. *Second Language Research*, 2, 93–119.

Cruttenden, A. 1994: Phonetic and prosodic aspects of baby talk. In C. Gallaway and B. Richards (eds), *Input and Interaction in Language Acquisition*. Cambridge: Cambridge University Press, 135–52.

DeKeyser, R. and Sokalski, K. 1996: The differential role of comprehension and production practice. *Language Learning*, 46, 613–42.

Doughty, C. 2001: Cognitive underpinnings of focus on form. In P. Robinson (ed.), *Cognition and Second Language Instruction*. Cambridge: Cambridge University Press, 206–57.

Ellis, R., Tanaka, Y., and Yamazaki, A. 1994: Classroom interaction, comprehension, and the acquisition of L2 word meanings. *Language Learning*, 44, 449–91.

Ferguson, C. 1971: Absence of copula and the notion of simplicity: a study of normal speech, baby talk, foreigner talk and pidgins. In Dell Hymes (ed.), *Pidginization and Creolization of Languages*. Cambridge: Cambridge University Press, 141–50.

Ferguson, C. 1975: Towards a characterization of English foreigner talk. *Anthropological Linguistics*, 17, 1–14.

Fries, C. 1957: Preface to R. Lado's *Linguistics Across Cultures*. Ann Arbor: University of Michigan Press.

Gass, S. 1997: *Input, Interaction and the Second Language Learner*. Mahwah, NJ: Lawrence Erlbaum Associates.

Gass, S. and Varonis, E. 1985: Variation in native speaker speech modification to non-native speakers. *Studies in Second Language Acquisition*, 7, 37–57.

Gass, S. and Varonis, E. 1989: Incorporated repairs in NNS discourse. In M. Eisenstein (ed.), *The Dynamic Interlanguage*. New York: Plenum Press, 71–86.

Gass, S. and Varonis, E. 1994: Input, interaction and second language production. *Studies in Second Language Acquisition Research*, 16, 283–302.

Gass, S., Svetics, I., and Lemelin, S. forthcoming: The differential effects of attention on the acquisition of syntax, morphology, and lexicon.

Hatch, E. 1983: *Psycholinguistics: A Second Language Perspective*. Rowley, MA: Newbury House.

Hawkins, B. 1985: Is the appropriate response always so appropriate? In S. Gass and C. Madden (eds), *Input in Second Language Acquisition*. Rowley, MA: Newbury House, 162–78.

Houck, N. and Gass, S. 1996: The pragmatics of disagreement. Paper presented at the Sociolinguistics Colloquium, TESOL, Chicago, IL, March.

Kleifgen, J. 1985: Skilled variation in a kindergarten teacher's use of foreigner talk. In S. Gass and C. Madden (eds), *Input in Second Language Acquisition*. Rowley, MA: Newbury House, 59–68.

Larsen-Freeman, D. and Long, M. 1991: *An Introduction to Second Language Acquisition Research*. New York: Longman.

Lieven, E. 1994: Crosslinguistic and crosscultural aspects of language addressed to children. In C. Gallaway and B. Richards (eds), *Input and Interaction in Language Acquisition*. Cambridge: Cambridge University Press, 56–73.

Lightbown, P. 1998: The importance of timing in focus on form. In C. Doughty and J. Williams (eds), *Focus on Form in Classroom Second Language Acquisition*. Cambridge: Cambridge University Press, 177–96.

Long, M. 1980: Input, interaction, and second language acquisition. Doctoral dissertation. University of California, Los Angeles.

Long, M. 1981: Input, interaction, and second language acquisition. *Foreign Language Acquisition: Annals of the New York Academy of Sciences*, 379, 259–78.

Long, M. 1983: Linguistic and conversational adjustments to non-native speakers. *Studies in Second Language Acquisition*, 5, 177–93.

Long, M. 1996: The role of the linguistic environment in second language acquisition. In W. Ritchie and T. Bhatia (eds), *Handbook of Second Language Acquisition*. San Diego: Academic Press, 413–68.

Long, M. forthcoming: *Task-Based Language Teaching*. Oxford: Blackwell.

Long, M., Inagaki, S., and Ortega, L. 1998: The role of implicit negative feedback in SLA: models and recasts in Japanese and Spanish. *Modern Language Journal*, 82, 357–71.

Loschky, L. 1994: Comprehensible input and second language acquisition: what is the relationship? *Studies in Second Language Acquisition*, 16, 303–24.

Lyster, R. 1998: Recasts, repetition, and ambiguity in L2 classroom discourse. *Studies in Second Language Acquisition*, 20, 51–81.

Lyster, R. and Ranta, L. 1997: Corrective feedback and learner uptake: negotiation of form in communicative classrooms. *Studies in Second Language Acquisition*, 20, 37–66.

Mackey, A. 1999: Input, interaction and second language development. *Studies in Second Language Acquisition*, 21, 557–81.

Mackey, A. and Philp, J. 1998: Conversational interaction and second language development: recasts, responses, and red herrings. *Modern Language Journal*, 82, 338–56.

Mackey, A., Gass, S., and McDonough, K. 2000: How do learners perceive implicit negative feedback? *Studies in Second Language Acquisition*, 22, 471–97.

McLaughlin, B. 1987: *Theories of Second Language Learning*. London: Edward Arnold.

Nwokah, E. 1987: Maidese vs. motherese: is the language input of child and adult caregivers similar? *Language and Speech*, 30, 213–37.

Ochs, E. 1985: Variation and error: a sociolinguistic approach to language acquisition in Samoa. In D. Slobin (ed.), *The Crosslinguistic Study of Language Acquisition. Vol. 1*. Hillsdale, NJ: Lawrence Erlbaum Associates, 783–838.

O'Grady, W. 1996: Language acquisition without Universal Grammar: a general nativist proposal for learning. *Second Language Research*, 4, 374–97.

Oliver, R. 1995: Negative feedback in child NS–NNS conversation. *Studies in Second Language Acquisition*, 17, 459–81.

Oliver, R. 1998: Negotiation of meaning in child interactions. *Modern Language Journal*, 82, 372–86.

Parker, K. and Chaudron, C. 1987: The effects of linguistic simplifications and elaborative modifications on L2 comprehension. *University of Hawai'i Working Papers in English as a Second Language*, 6, 107–33.

Philp, J. 1999: Interaction, noticing and second language acquisition: an examination of learners' noticing of recasts in task-based interaction. Ph.D. dissertation. University of Tasmania.

Pica, T. 1987: Second language acquisition, social interaction, and the classroom. *Applied Linguistics*, 8, 3–21.

Pica, T. 1988: Interlanguage adjustments as an outcome of NS–NNS negotiated interaction. *Language Learning*, 38, 45–73.

Pica, T. 1994: Research on negotiation: what does it reveal about second-language learning conditions, processes, and outcomes? *Language Learning*, 44, 493–527.

Pica, T. and Doughty, C. 1985: Input and interaction in the communicative language classroom: a comparison of teacher-fronted and group activities. In S. Gass and C. Madden (eds), *Input in Second Language Acquisition*. Rowley, MA: Newbury House, 115–32.

Pica, T., Doughty, C., and Young, R. 1986: Making input comprehensible: do interactional modifications help? *ITL Review of Applied Linguistics*, 72, 1–25.

Pica, T., Young, R., and Doughty, C. 1987: The impact of interaction on comprehension. *TESOL Quarterly*, 21, 737–58.

Pine, J. 1994: The language of primary caregivers. In C. Gallaway and

B. Richards (eds), *Input and Interaction in Language Acquisition*. Cambridge: Cambridge University Press, 15–37.

Pinker, S. 1989: *Learnability and Cognition: The Acquisition of Argument Structure*. Cambridge, MA: MIT Press.

Pinker, S. 1994: *The Language Instinct*. New York: William Morrow.

Plough, I. 1994: A role for indirect negative evidence in second language acquisition. Ph.D. dissertation. Michigan State University.

Polio, C. and Gass, S. 1997: Replication and reporting: a commentary. *Studies in Second Language Acquisition*, 19, 499–508.

Polio, C. and Gass, S. 1998: The role of interaction in native speaker comprehension of nonnative speaker speech. *Modern Language Journal*, 82, 308–19.

Sato, C. 1986: Conversation and interlanguage development: rethinking the connection. In R. Day (ed.), *Talking to Learn: Conversation in Second Language Acquisition*. Rowley, MA: Newbury House, 23–45.

Sato, C. 1990: *The Syntax of Conversation in Interlanguage Development*. Tübingen: Gunter Narr Verlag.

Saxton, M. 1997: The contrast theory of negative input. *Journal of Child Language*, 24, 139–61.

Schachter, J. 1988: Second language acquisition and its relationship to Universal Grammar. *Applied Linguistics*, 9, 219–35.

Schachter, J. 1991: Issues in the accessibility debate: a reply to Felix. In L. Eubank (ed.), *Point Counterpoint: Universal Grammar in the Second Language*. Amsterdam: John Benjamins, 105–16.

Schachter, J., Rounds, P. L., Wright, S., and Smith, T. 1998: Comparing conditions for learning syntactic patterns: attention and awareness. Ms.

Schieffelin, B. 1985: The acquisition of Kaluli. In D. Slobin (ed.), *The Crosslinguistic Study of Language Acquisition. Vol. 1*. Hillsdale, NJ: Lawrence Erlbaum Associates, 525–94.

Schmidt, R. 1990: The role of consciousness in second language learning. *Applied Linguistics*, 11, 129–58.

Schmidt, R. 1993a: Consciousness, learning and interlanguage pragmatics. In G. Kasper and S. Blum-Kulka (eds), *Interlanguage Pragmatics*. New York: Oxford University Press, 21–42.

Schmidt, R. 1993b: Consciousness in second language learning: introduction. Paper presented at AILA 10th World Congress of Applied Linguistics, Amsterdam.

Schmidt, R. 1994: Implicit learning and the cognitive unconscious: of artificial grammars and SLA. In N. Ellis (ed.), *Implicit and Explicit Learning of Languages*. London: Academic Press, 165–209.

Schmidt, R. 1998: Attention. *University of Hawai'i Working Papers in ESL*, 15, 1–34.

Schmidt, R. 2001: Attention. In P. Robinson (ed.), *Cognition and Second Language Instruction*. Cambridge: Cambridge University Press, 3–32.

Schmidt, R. and Frota, S. 1986: Developing basic conversational ability in a second language: a case study of an adult learner of Portuguese. In R. Day (ed.), *Talking to Learn: Conversation in Second Language Acquisition*. Rowley, MA: Newbury House, 237–326.

Schwartz, B. 1993: On explicit and negative data effecting and affecting competence and linguistic behavior. *Studies in Second Language Acquisition*, 15, 147–63.

Snow, C. 1986: Conversations with children. In P. Fletcher and M. Garman (eds), *Language Acquisition: Studies in Second Language Development*. Second edition.

Cambridge: Cambridge University Press, 69–89.

Snow, C. 1994: Beginning from baby talk: twenty years of research on input and interaction. In C. Gallaway and B. Richards (eds), *Input and Interaction in Language Acquisition*. Cambridge: Cambridge University Press, 1–12.

Swain, M. 1985: Communicative competence: some roles of comprehensible input and comprehensible output in its development. In S. Gass and C. Madden (eds), *Input in Second Language Acquisition*. Rowley, MA: Newbury House, 235–53.

Swain, M. 1995: Three functions of output in second language learning. In G. Cook and B. Seidlhofer (eds), *Principle and Practice in Applied Linguistics: Studies in Honour of H. G. Widdowson*. Oxford: Oxford University Press, 125–44.

Swain, M. and Lapkin, S. 1995: Problems in output and the cognitive processes they generate: a step toward second language learning. *Applied Linguistics*, 16, 371–91.

Swain, M. and Lapkin, S. 1998: Interaction and second language learning: two adolescent French immersion students working together. *Modern Language Journal*, 82, 320–37.

Tomasello, M. and Herron, C. 1988: Down the garden path: inducing and correcting overgeneralization errors in the foreign language classroom. *Applied Psycholinguistics*, 9, 237–46.

Tomasello, M. and Herron, C. 1989: Feedback for language transfer errors: the garden path technique. *Studies in Second Language Acquisition*, 11, 385–95.

Tomasello, M. and Herron, C. 1991: Experiments in the real world: a reply to Beck and Eubank. *Studies in Second Language Acquisition*, 13, 513–17.

Truscott, J. 1998: Noticing in second language acquisition: a critical review. *Second Language Research*, 14, 103–35.

VanPatten, B. 1995: Input processing and second language acquisition: on the relationship between form and meaning. In P. Hashemipourk, R. Maldonado, and M. Van Naerssen (eds), *Festschrift in Honor of Tracy D. Terrell*. New York: McGraw-Hill, 170–83.

VanPatten, B. 1996: *Input Processing and Grammar Instruction: Theory and Research*. Norwood, NJ: Ablex.

VanPatten, B. and Cadierno, T. 1993a: Explicit instruction and input processing. *Studies in Second Language Acquisition*, 15, 225–43.

VanPatten, B. and Cadierno, T. 1993b: Input processing and second language acquisition: a role for instruction. *Modern Language Journal*, 77, 45–57.

VanPatten, B. and Oikkenon, S. 1996: Explanation versus structured input in processing instruction. *Studies in Second Language Acquisition*, 18, 495–510.

VanPatten, B. and Sanz, C. 1995: From input to output: processing instruction and communicative tasks. In F. Eckman, D. Highland, P. Lee, J. Mileham, and R. Weber (eds), *Second Language Acquisition Theory and Pedagogy*. Hillsdale, NJ: Lawrence Erlbaum Associates, 169–86.

Varonis, E. and Gass, S. 1985a: Non-native/non-native conversations: a model for negotiation of meaning. *Applied Linguistics*, 6, 71–90.

Varonis, E. and Gass, S. 1985b: Miscommunication in native/non-native conversation. *Language in Society*, 14, 327–43.

Wagner-Gough, J. and Hatch, E. 1975: The importance of input data in second language acquisition studies. *Language Learning*, 25, 297–307.

Watanabe, S. 1993: Cultural differences in framing: American and Japanese group discussions. In D. Tannen (ed.), *Framing in Discourse*. New York: Oxford University Press, 176–97.

White, L. 1989: *Universal Grammar and Second Language Acquisition*. Amsterdam: John Benjamins.

Wolfe-Quintero, K. 1996: Nativism does not equal Universal Grammar. *Second Language Research*, 12, 335–73.

Yano, Y., Long, M., and Ross, S. 1994: The effects of simplified and elaborated texts on foreign language reading comprehension. *Language Learning*, 44, 189–219.

10 Instructed SLA: Constraints, Compensation, and Enhancement

CATHERINE J. DOUGHTY

1 Introduction

The domain of this chapter is instructed SLA by adult (i.e., post-critical period) learners. We focus mainly on the development of L2 speech comprehension and production, leaving aside entirely the vexing complexities of the acquisition of L2 literacy. Post-critical period SLA is notorious for its difficulty, high degree of variation, and often very poor outcome (see Long, 1993; Hyltenstam and Abramsson, this volume). The primary aim of L2 instruction is to ameliorate, if not solve, these problems. But the potential for instruction to do so has always been contentious among SLA researchers.

The debate concerning the effectiveness of L2 instruction takes place at two fundamental levels. At the first level, SLA theorists address in absolute terms any potential at all for (even the best possible) instructional intervention in SLA. A small number of SLA researchers claim that instruction can have no effect beyond the provision of an environment conducive to SLA. At the second level of debate, a case is made for the benefits of instruction. Then, assuming the effectiveness and sometimes even the necessity of relevant and principled instruction, researchers investigate the comparative efficacy of different types. A fundamental question in this second line of research is whether adult SLA involves, in the main, implicit or explicit language processing, and the related question of whether the most effective instruction is implicit or explicit.

After reviewing the cases for and against L2 instruction, we will conclude that instruction is potentially effective, provided it is relevant to learners' needs. However, we will be forced to acknowledge that the evidence to date for either absolute or relative effectiveness of L2 instruction is tenuous at best, owing to improving, but still woefully inadequate, research methodology. Furthermore, since instructional procedures have often been operationalized in terms of declarative L2 knowledge, it is not clear that much of the evidence amassed to date is valid. Thus, an important aim of this chapter is to make recommendations for future empirical studies of instructed SLA of the psycholinguistically relevant kind. These will be studies investigating pedagogical procedures that appropriately engage SLA processes. Accordingly, we will examine how human processing mechanisms change as a consequence of primary language acquisition, and how implicit and explicit modes of complex learning interact. In the end, we will see that, for adult SLA, instruction is necessary to compensate for developmental changes that put adults at a cognitive disadvantage.

2 The Case Against L2 Instruction

Let us begin by considering the argument sometimes made against any kind of L2 instruction whatsoever. As evident in the following, in the early days of research on SLA, skepticism concerning L2 instructional intervention prevailed:

> foreign language learning under classroom conditions seems to partially follow the same set of natural processes that characterize other types of language acquisition . . . there seems to be a universal and common set of principles which are flexible enough and adaptable to the large number of conditions under which language learning may take place. These observations furthermore suggest that the possibility of manipulating and controlling the students' verbal behavior in the classroom is in fact quite limited. (Felix 1981, p. 109)

> the only contribution that classroom instruction can make is to provide comprehensible input that might not otherwise be available outside the classroom. (Krashen, 1985, pp. 33–4, and passim)

Two proposals, implicit in the above proscriptions, motivate what Long and Robinson (1998) have called the strong non-interventionist position: (i) that SLA is driven by the same Universal Grammar (UG) that guides first language acquisition, and (ii) that SLA, like first language acquisition, is entirely incidental. With regard to the first proposal, there are also competing views (see White, this volume). The full-transfer, full-access hypothesis (Schwartz, 1993; Schwartz and Sprouse, 1996) posits that first and second language acquisition involve the resetting of parameterized universal principles, triggered only by positive evidence (i.e., input), and that there is no role for negative evidence (e.g., instruction concerning what is not possible in the L2). The second UG account of SLA is one that allows for, or even requires, negative evidence, such as that provided by instruction, but the need for instruction is strictly limited to cases where triggering evidence is not sufficiently informative. More specifically, when the L2 is a proper subset of the L1 with respect to a certain aspect of language, L2 learners will have to retreat from the overly general hypothesis that emanates from their L1 (White, 1987, 1991), something which cannot be done on the basis of positive evidence alone. By the UG SLA accounts, then, instruction is either entirely or largely unnecessary.

The second proposal, more commonly known as the Input Hypothesis within Krashen's (1982, 1985) monitor theory of SLA, proscribes traditional instructional devices (grammar teaching, linguistic grading, error correction, etc.) due to the so-called "non-interface" concerning any potential relationship between learned and acquired knowledge (Krashen and Scarcella, 1978). Krashen (1982, 1985) has claimed that knowledge of consciously learned language is distinct in memorial representation from unconsciously acquired language, that only the latter type of knowledge can be deployed in spontaneous language use, and, furthermore, that there can be no interaction between these two independent knowledge systems (i.e., the so-called *learning/acquisition* distinction). The non-interface position states that *learned* knowledge can never become *acquired* knowledge. This claim has been given some credence by the all-too-common observation of two kinds of typical L2 classroom learner performance: fluent use, which appears to derive from intuitive knowledge, and more deliberate use, which clearly depends upon expressible knowledge. Until recently, language teachers have been persuaded by this view to adopt a laissez-faire approach to the development of accuracy in instructed SLA, concentrating only on providing opportunities for learners to process rich and comprehensible input (for discussion, see Doughty, 1998).

Following the arguments of Doughty and Williams (1998c), the position taken in this chapter is that both the no-negative-evidence and non-interface versions of the non-interventionist position are too extreme in their nearly complete prohibition on L2 instruction. Even if a UG explanation of SLA were to prevail, the elements of language that are governed solely by UG are limited. Much more of the L2 remains which is potentially acquired more efficiently provided instruction appropriately engages learners' cognitive processing ability (see also Doughty, 2001). Furthermore, while there can be no doubt that both spontaneous and more deliberate L2 performance exist, what type of knowledge underlies each, and whether there is any connection between the two during SLA and L2 use, are contentious issues that are far from settled in SLA, let alone any other domain of human cognition (Berry, 1997; Berry and Dienes, 1993; Stadler and Frensch, 1998).

There are further arguments that L2 instruction is likely to be necessary for some aspects of adult SLA. As has often been noted, the prognosis for adult second language acquisition is not nearly as good as that for child (first or second) language acquisition. Given adequate exposure, normal intelligence, and normal social conditions, children can be expected to learn the language(s) of their caregivers incidentally and fully, such that they are eventually indistinguishable from other native speakers of their speech community. In stark contrast, language acquisition by adults is guaranteed only to be variable both within and across individuals, most typically relatively unsuccessful, and always incomplete, such that non-native speakers can be invariably identified as such, provided judgments are made on adequate samples of performance (see Hyltenstam and Abrahamsson, this volume; Long, this volume). Thus, as will be discussed further in the next section, it appears that child language acquisition and adult SLA are not instances of the same phenomenon taking place at different points in the life span. Rather, they involve different or somehow altered cognitive processes, and, without instruction, adult SLA is more difficult, slower, and less successful. In sum, it is far too soon to announce a moratorium on L2 instruction. Rather, the position taken by Doughty and Williams (1998c) is the prudent one:

> we do not consider leaving learners to their own devices to be the best plan. Does this mean that practitioners should take up the opposite position that [instruction] is appropriate . . . for all learners all the time? We think not, and that, between the two poles, there are many ensuing pedagogical decisions to be made. At the outset, it must be said that it is not the case that adult second language acquisition cannot take place in the absence of instruction . . . ; for many learners, clearly much of it can. However, our interest is not limited to what is merely possible, but extends to a determination of what would comprise the most *effective* and *efficient* instructional plan given the normal constraints of acquiring a second language in the classroom. (p. 197, emphasis added)

3 The Case For Instructed SLA

What evidence is there that L2 instruction is efficient and effective? In comparison with other fields, work on instructed SLA is still in its infancy. Nonetheless, the past decade has witnessed a virtual explosion of interest in instructed SLA research of all types (Lightbown, 2000), and of experimental or quasi-experimental effects-of-instruction studies, in particular (Doughty and Williams, 1998a, 1998b). Furthermore, there is every reason to be optimistic about continued progress, given the increasing number of researchers interested in classroom language learning who are also sufficiently trained in SLA theory and research methodology (see Chaudron, this volume; Norris and Ortega, this volume, for discussions of L2 research methodology). The discussion will now turn to a consideration of the evidence for the benefits of instruction in adult SLA.

3.1 Overall effectiveness of L2 instruction

The question of whether second language instruction makes a difference was first posed in earnest by Long (1983), who attempted a preliminary answer to this question by reviewing the handful of empirical studies which directly tested Krashen's then influential claim of a learning/acquisition distinction (outlined above in the case against L2 instruction). In those early studies, only very global comparisons were made, for instance between the L2 proficiency of subjects who either had or had not attended L2 classes, or who had done both in varying combinations. Such studies yielded instruction vs. exposure comparisons or independent assessments of five types (see table 10.1). In general, the findings indicated that, for those for whom the classroom is the

Table 10.1 The advantage for instruction over exposure (principal findings of Long's, 1983, review)

Type of comparison	*Findings*	*Interpretation*
1 The relative utility of equal amounts of instruction and exposure	Four studies showed no differences	Instruction beneficial for those for whom classroom is the only opportunity for exposure
2 The relative utility of varying amounts of instruction and exposure when the sum total of both is equal	Two studies with ambiguous findings	None possible
3 Varying amounts of instruction when the amount of exposure is held constant	Two studies showed that more instruction led to more SLA	Either more instruction is beneficial, or more instruction merely serves as more exposure
4 Varying amounts of exposure when the amount of instruction is held constant	Three studies showed variable results. One study was matched to the type of study in type 3 and showed that fewer subjects with more exposure scored higher on proficiency measures	Taken together, the results of studies of types 3 and 4 support the benefits of instruction *per se*
5 Independent effects of varying amounts of both instruction and exposure when the sum total of both also varies	Of four studies of this type, all showed a benefit for instruction, and three showed a benefit for exposure. The strength of the relationship was greater for instruction than for exposure	Taken together, the results of studies of types 4 and 5 support the benefits of instruction

only opportunity for exposure to L2 input, "instruction" is beneficial. When differing amounts of instruction were added on to a fixed amount of exposure, positive outcomes were interpreted to mean either that more instruction is beneficial *or* that more instruction merely serves as more L2 exposure. However, when differing amounts of exposure were added on to a fixed amount of instruction, these findings, taken together with instruction-plus-exposure findings, favored the benefits of the L2 instruction *per se*. Finally, although very few in number, when studies independently varied the amounts of instruction and L2 exposure, positive outcomes, taken together with all of the other findings, lent credence to this interpretation.

While Long concluded that second language instruction does make a difference, his work was more noteworthy for having identified a number of weaknesses in the prevailing research methodology, and for having inspired the ensuing line of empirical effects-of-instruction research, than for the trustworthiness of the reviewed findings. In particular, since the studies themselves did not directly make the appropriate comparisons, considerable reanalysis and reinterpretation of findings was needed to overcome design flaws even to be able to tease out this preliminary indication of an advantage for L2 instruction over naturalistic exposure. There were at least three fundamental problems. First, the comparisons between instruction and exposure were too global: it was not known whether instruction and exposure constituted different opportunities for SLA, let alone what specific SLA processes, cognitive or otherwise, might have taken place during the course of the investigations. Second, there were no direct comparisons of either instruction or exposure conditions with true control groups; and third, neither the type of instruction nor any specific aspect of SLA were operationalized in the study variables. Without any information on the type of L2 instruction *per se* and the relevant SLA processes, study findings were always open to the interpretation that a null finding was due to poor quality or mismatched instruction.

Several years later, Long (1988) reconsidered the question of whether instruction makes a difference, but this time within four operationalized domains of SLA. By now, these domains are well known, if not entirely understood: (i) SLA processes; (ii) SLA route; (iii) SLA rate; and (iv) level of ultimate SL attainment. Table 10.2 provides a synopsis of early research findings within these domains.

SLA processes include, for instance, transfer, generalization, elaboration, stabilization, destabilization, noticing, omission, and oversuppliance (see chapters by DeKeyser, Hulstijn, Long, Odlin, Romaine, and Segalowitz, this volume; Hulstijn, forthcoming). Even now, the proportion of studies that investigate SLA processes in instructed settings is very small. The general findings were that, while instructed and untutored populations of learners follow similar paths in SLA (see below), the processes observed differ. For instance, although morphemes emerge in roughly the same order for both groups, naturalistic learners tend to omit obligatory morphemes at lower proficiency levels, whereas classroom learners tend to oversupply them (Pica, 1983), presumably as a consequence of instruction.

Table 10.2 Effects of instruction within domains of SLA (categories from Long, 1988)

Domain of SLA	*Findings*	*Interpretation*
SLA processes	Both similarities and differences exist in naturalistic and classroom SLA	These must be understood in order to enhance SLA
SLA route	Routes of development have been identified for negation, questions, and word order. Instruction on non-contiguous stages was ineffective	Where development hinges upon processing constraints, stages cannot be skipped, even with instruction. L2 learners must be psycholinguistically ready for instruction
SLA rate	At least four studies show a rate advantage for instructed learners	Taken together with the SLA route findings, appropriately timed instruction can speed SLA
Level of ultimate SL attainment	Instructed learners advance further down markedness hierarchies than untutored subjects	Instruction may be necessary to bring L2 learners closer to nativelike competence (for instance through provision of enhanced input or feedback)

In the second domain, SLA route, developmental sequences (i.e., fixed series of stages) have been identified in, for example, the acquisition of negation, interrogatives, relativization, and word order. Progress through the routes can be affected by the L1 in complex ways (e.g., speed-up or delay) (Zobl, 1982) or by instruction (Doughty, 1991; Pienemann, 1989), but only in terms of sub-stages or rate of passage. In other words, stages are not skipped, and the route itself cannot be altered (Pienemann, 1989), a phenomenon known as developmental readiness. Despite this constraint, evidence continues to accumulate that the rate of instructed SLA is faster than that of naturalistic SLA. However, it is sometimes the case that what is learned quickly is forgotten equally fast (Lightbown, 1983). This may depend upon the mode of learning that is evoked by the L2 instruction, an issue to which we return in a later section.

In the final domain discussed by Long, level of ultimate attainment in the L2, three studies indicated that, perhaps owing to the different types of input to which naturalistic and instructed learners are exposed, or to negative feedback, instructed learners make more progress toward the target language. For example, when learners are provided with input that includes marked examples (where markedness refers to infrequency) of systems that enter into implicational hierarchies (e.g., relativization), they are able to acquire both the marked and unmarked aspects of the system (Doughty, 1988; Eckman, Bell, and Nelson, 1988; Gass, 1982). Uninstructed learners, who may never gain access to marked input, tend to acquire only the unmarked elements in the system hierarchies (Pavesi, 1986).

By the 1990s, the evidence in the four domains of SLA, although scant, formed the basis of an assumption that L2 instruction is effective. Research interest then turned to the question of the type of instruction most facilitative of SLA. Like early investigations of the benefits of instruction versus exposure in SLA, initial comparisons of the relative effectiveness of types of instruction were too global. Typically in such studies, two "methods" of instruction were pitted against one another, and the findings were always the same: no difference (see, e.g., Smith, 1970). This was because, as has been found to be the case in general education research, the variable of instructional method is actually a composite one (Clark, 1985), and, even if a method has an overall description (see, e.g., Richards and Rodgers, 1986), any particular implementation by a teacher is subject to significant variation. Furthermore, many typical teaching practices are each components of a range of so-called methods, and it may, in fact, be those specific L2 pedagogical procedures that are responsible for observed effects (and, hence, which cancel each other out when different methods employing the same critical techniques are compared). Thus, "method" is not the appropriate level of analysis in type-of-instruction studies (Long, 1980).

The problem of overly general comparisons of input, exposure, and instructional conditions meant that, when interpreting research findings, no direct link between learning outcomes and instructional treatments could be made. To remedy this, Doughty (1988) identified three crucial elements of experimental design that needed to be present in effects-of-instruction research: (i) a specific learning target must be identified (i.e., some aspect of the L2); (ii) the instructional treatment must be psycholinguistically appropriate (i.e., take into account constraints discussed in section 4, and attempt the relevant compensation or enhancement that may be necessary); and (iii) specific gains in the L2 must be evaluated with respect to the target of instruction (e.g., by including a control group).

Furthermore, because of the difficulty noted earlier regarding interpretation of results obtained after a period of unspecified instruction unknown to, and hence not analyzable by, the researcher, effects-of-instruction designs must specify that treatments be documented in some fashion (e.g., through video- or audio-recording or via computer delivery of treatments). In this way, at some point later in the investigation, the nature of the treatment can be examined in conjunction with the findings. For instance, to explain similar gains made by both instructional groups in a study of the development of relative clauses in English as a second language, Doughty pointed to the coding features of both computer-delivered treatments, which might have drawn the subjects' attention to the target of instruction in the same psycholinguistically relevant way (i.e., promoting salience of the elements in the input). In addition to facilitating the interpretation of study findings, the documentation of instructional treatments must be reported in detail if systematic replication is to become a regular practice in research on instructed SLA.

Following these guidelines *in vivo* is by no means a simple matter, and by 1997, some SLA researchers were arguing that to conduct SLA research was "almost impossible in 'normal' classrooms with real L2 learners" (Hulstijn, 1997, pp. 131–2), and, hence, they recommended that the investigation of SLA issues primarily be pursued under laboratory conditions. This proposal, however, raises the issue of ecological validity, since L2 instruction most often takes place in classrooms.

3.2 *Relative effectiveness of different types and categories of L2 instruction*

The most recent review of empirical studies that attempts to determine the overall effectiveness of L2 instruction, as well as the relative effectiveness of types of instruction, is also by far the most rigorous. In a statistical meta-analysis[1] of the burgeoning literature published between 1980 and 1998, Norris and Ortega (2000)[2] identified 250 potentially relevant studies from the published applied SLA literature. Although they noted a publishing bias in the research pool,[3] it is nonetheless clear that the state of instructed SLA research is more robust now than it was 20 years ago when Long published the first review.

Norris and Ortega's investigation included a careful assessment of the components of instructed SLA research methodology that, as noted above, had been identified as utterly lacking in precision (e.g., operationalization of instructional treatments and consideration of appropriate research design), as well as a host of new considerations (e.g., comparison of instructional treatment types, influence of measures, and duration and durability of instructional treatments).[4] Unfortunately, only 77 studies of the original pool of 250 studies survived the initial screening for inclusion in the coding phase of the meta-analysis (i.e., that they be quasi-experimental or experimental in design; that the independent variable be reasonably well operationalized in the report; and that L2 features be targeted). Furthermore, of those, only 49 studies reported sufficient statistical information to be included in the final round of the meta-analysis. Thus, despite the increase in sheer quantity of work and improvement in operationalizing variables, it must be admitted that the state of the instructed SLA research is still far less robust than is required for the findings reported to be considered truly trustworthy. For this reason, a clear understanding of the findings of the meta-analysis and their interpretations are important for an assessment of the state of the science of instructed SLA, and to delineate directions for future research.

Rather than at the level of "method," the operationalization of instructional treatments is now considered best analyzed psycholinguistically in terms of input-processing enhancements that facilitate L2 learners' extracting forms and mapping them to meaning and function. The general issues are whether an explicit or implicit approach to instruction is best, and to what extent and in what ways learner attention should be directed to the elements of language involved in mapping. Explicit instruction includes all types in which rules are explained to learners, or when learners are directed to find rules by attending to forms (see also DeKeyser, this volume). Conversely, implicit instruction makes no overt reference to rules or forms. During either explicit or implicit instruction, attention may be directed to language forms in isolation, during the processing of meaning, or not at all. These types of attention can be understood as forming a tripartite contrast. Long offers the following definitions of *focus on form*: "focus on form . . . overtly draws students' attention to linguistic elements as they arise incidentally in lessons whose overriding focus is on meaning or communication" (Long, 1991, pp. 45–6); and "focus on form involves . . . an occasional shift in attention to linguistic code features – by the teacher and/or one or more students – triggered by perceived problems with comprehension or production" (Long and Robinson, 1998, p. 23). Doughty and Williams (1998b) contrast focus on form and the other two foci in Long's original discussion of options in language teaching (Long, 1988, 1991, 2000), namely *focus on meaning* and *focus on forms*, in the following way:

> focus on formS and focus on form are *not* polar opposites in the way that "form" and "meaning" have often been considered to be. Rather, a focus on form *entails* a focus on formal elements of language, whereas focus on formS is *limited to* such a focus, and focus on meaning *excludes* it. Most important, it should be kept in mind that the fundamental assumption of focus-on-form instruction is that meaning and use must already be evident to the learner at the time that attention is drawn to the linguistic apparatus needed to get the meaning across. (Doughty and Williams, 1998b, p. 4)[5]

Particular pedagogical procedures can be ranged along a continuum describing degree of obtrusiveness of attention to form during instruction, as shown in the taxonomy displayed in figure 10.1 (Doughty and Williams, 1998c).

Building upon DeKeyser's (1995) definition of explicit instruction, Long's tripartite distinction among *focus on forms, meaning,* and *form,* and Doughty and Williams's continuum of degree of intrusiveness of the pedagogical intervention on the processing of meaning, Norris and Ortega (2000) set out to classify each instructional type in the studies they reviewed as implicit or explicit, and as focusing on meaning only, forms only, or form. In practice, deciphering operationalizations of L2 instruction has continued to prove difficult.

Unobtrusive ←——— **Attention to form** ———→ **Obtrusive**

Input flood	X						
Task-essential language	X						
Input enhancement		X					
Negotiation		X					
Recast			X				
Output enhancement			X				
Interaction enhancement				X			
Input processing					X		
Dictogloss						X	
Consciousness-raising tasks						X	
Garden path							X

Figure 10.1 A taxonomy of degree of obtrusiveness
Source: Doughty and Williams (1998c, p. 258)

Although initially guided by these constructs, Norris and Ortega (2000) ultimately had to resort to extrapolating the operational definitions for coding the type-of-instruction variable from the studies themselves, a problem to which we will return (see table 10.3). In sum, attention is said to be directed to meaning via exposure to L2 targets or experience with L2 tasks, but without explicit attempts to effect shifts of learner attention. Attention to both forms and meaning can occur in any of the six ways listed under the heading of "focus on form." These include both psycholinguistic and task-inherent means of promoting form–meaning connections. Finally, we see that when the first four types of focus-on-form conditions did not apply, and when the learners' attention nonetheless was focused in some particular way on a specific structure targeted for investigation, this was considered focus on forms.

Table 10.4 lists the 20 or so different pedagogical procedures employed, alone or in combination, in the instructional treatments of the studies analyzed, and groups them according to the categories of implicit/explicit approach and type of attention to meaning, to form–meaning connections, and to forms in isolation.

Of the many important comparisons that were made by Norris and Ortega, the following are of greatest interest here: (i) overall effectiveness of instruction in comparison with exposure; (ii) relative effectiveness of implicit and explicit types of instruction; and (iii) relative effectiveness of attention to meaning, form–meaning connections, or forms. The major findings of the meta-analysis concerning the five instructional type variables (two describing degree of explicitness of instruction, and three levels of obtrusiveness of attention to form) are displayed in table 10.5. Leaving aside for the moment the case of meaning-only groups (meaning-only treatments were considered to be

Table 10.3 Operationalizing the construct of L2 instruction (adapted from Norris and Ortega, 2000)

Instructional type	*Operationalization, as derived from study descriptions*
Explicit	+ Rule explanation (deductive/metalinguistic), *or* + direction to attend to forms and arrive at rules (explicit induction)
Implicit	– Rule explanation, *and* – direction to attend to forms
Focus on meaning	Exposure to L2 targets or experience with L2 tasks, *but* no attempts to effect shifts of learner attention
Focus on form	Integration of forms and meaning, *any of*: (a) designing tasks that promote engagement with meaning prior to form (b) seeking task essentialness/naturalness of L2 forms (c) ensuring unobtrusiveness (d) documenting L2 mental processes (e.g., "noticing") (e) selecting target forms by analysis of learner needs (f) considering IL constraints
Focus on forms	None of (a)–(d) above apply, *and* learner attention was nevertheless focused in some particular way on the particular structure targeted for learning

a type of classroom exposure, and hence, along with control groups, were classified as comparison, not instructed, groups), the general findings of the overall and relative effectiveness of L2 instruction and instructional types can be summarized as follows. Once again, as had been the case in the two earlier comparisons of the effectiveness of L2 instruction with simple exposure or with meaning-driven communication (Long, 1983, 1988), the answer to the overall research question is in the affirmative: second language instruction makes a difference, and, furthermore, the difference is substantial (effect size $d = 0.96$, where 0.80 is considered a large effect).

With regard to differences among instructional types (see table 10.5), the clearest finding (and, according to Norris and Ortega, the only trustworthy one) is an apparent advantage for explicit over implicit types of L2 instruction. Moreover, combining the nature of the instruction with the degree of obtrusiveness of attention to form in the pedagogical procedures employed, the findings are as follows: Explicit focus on form (large effect) > Explicit focus on forms (large effect) > Implicit focus on form (medium effect) > Implicit focus

Table 10.4 Distribution of pedagogical procedures in the type-of-instruction studies (adapted from Norris and Ortega, 2000)

Focus on form	*Focus on forms*
Implicit (30% of the instructional types):	
18% of the instructional types:	11% of the instructional types:
form-experimental (anagram)	corrective models
input enhancement	pre-emptive modeling
input flood	traditional implicit
recasts	
other implicit	
Explicit (70% of the instructional types):	
26% of the instructional types:	45% of the instructional types:
compound focus on form (enhancement + feedback)	rule-oriented forms-focused
consciousness-raising	garden path
processing instruction	input practice
metalinguistic task essentialness (cross-word)	metalinguistic feedback
rule-oriented focus on form	output practice
	traditional explicit (e.g., rule explanation)

on forms (small effect).[6] In the 20 or so different pedagogical procedures utilized in these types of instruction (table 10.4), it was not possible to discern any patterns of effectiveness, mainly because of the lack of sufficient replication studies. In sum, Norris and Ortega (2000) interpret the results of their meta-analysis to mean that: "L2 instruction can be characterized as effective in its own right, at least as operationalized and measured within the domain" (p. 480).

Another clear finding in this phase of the meta-analysis was that, where a comparison could be made between instructed groups and control (true) or comparison (defined as non-focused exposure) groups, the control/comparison groups experienced 18 percent pre-test to post-test gains (see also Doughty, 1991; Hulstijn, 1997). Moreover, although instructed subjects experienced greater improvement, the nature of interlanguage change exhibited by instructed subjects was variable, whereas that exhibited by control/comparison subjects was more homogeneous. However, at delayed post-testing (in studies where this was carried out), instructed groups both maintained a modest advantage in gains over control/comparison groups, and were more homogeneous. These findings can be interpreted in a number of ways. The most plausible explanations concerning the progress made by groups not receiving targeted instruction are (i) the already-demonstrated rate advantage for instruction (i.e., uninstructed subjects improve, but instructed subjects improve more, hence they are faster), and (ii) test effect. These possibilities have not yet been

Table 10.5 Type of instruction effects (results of Norris and Ortega's, 2000, meta-analysis)

Type of treatment	*Findings*	*Interpretation*
Control/comparison groups	18% gain	Any of practice effect, effect of exposure, maturation
All instructional types (vs. all comparison groups)	49 studies examined (98 treatments) Large effect size, but only 70% include a comparison group (e.g., exposure or control)	"As operationalized thus far in the domain, L2 instruction is effective" (Norris and Ortega, 2000)
All explicit	Large effect size	Explicit > Implicit
All implicit	Medium effect size	
All focus on form	Large effect size	(FonF > FonFs)
All focus on forms	Large effect size	1 FonF explicit
Implicit focus on form	Medium effect size	2 FonFs explicit
Explicit focus on form	Large effect size	3 FonF implicit
Implicit focus on forms	Small effect size	4 FonFs implicit
Explicit focus on forms	Large effect size	

Note: FonF = focus on form; FonFs = focus on forms.

systematically teased apart. Individual variation in effects of instruction shown by subjects in experimental treatment groups could have been due to true individual differences factors (e.g., aptitude for language learning), or to mismatches between cognitive learning style and instructional type. Again, such factors have not routinely been included in the design of instructed SLA studies, although they have figured prominently in the very recent SLA literature (see Robinson, 2002; Dörnyei and Skehan, this volume). That the individual variation has disappeared by the time of the delayed post-test is also in need of explanation. Given that the delayed post-test interval is typically quite short (four weeks on average), it might be expected that the effects of instruction demonstrated would not remain after a longer period of time, either because control subjects have caught up (a common finding), or because the particular type of instruction favored in this set of studies leads to the type of knowledge that is easily forgotten, as discussed in section 3.1.

Finally, by virtue of somewhat improved reporting in the published literature, Norris and Ortega were able to revisit the question of the differential effects of exposure and instruction originally raised by Long (1983). In the more recent published studies, exposure is operationalized as pure exposure or experience with L2 tasks without any focus on form or forms, or some minimal amount of both. Results are straightforward: the effect of instruction in comparison with exposure is still substantial, but smaller than when instructed subjects are compared with true controls. This finding is consistent with the rate advantage for instruction already discussed.

3.3 *Problems of research bias*

To interpret the relative effectiveness findings properly, we must revisit the operationalizations of instructional treatments in the studies in the instructed SLA research base, and, crucially, we must note the accumulation of research bias reported by Norris and Ortega. Table 10.3 above reveals that the operational definitions of types of instruction unfortunately comprise a rather convoluted set of features, which, as noted earlier, simply reflects the state of the current research. Norris and Ortega reported that coding the types of instruction using these categories involved a high degree of inference in comparison with other variables examined in the meta-analysis. To illustrate, consider the definition of *focus on forms* extracted from table 10.3: "None of (a)–(d) above [i.e., features defining focus on form] apply, *and* learner attention was nevertheless focused in some particular way on the particular structure targeted for learning." More importantly, perhaps, a strong bias was identified concerning the number of comparisons within each approach to L2 instruction: within the 49 studies, there were 98 distinct instructional treatments, owing to some studies comparing two or more types of treatment with a control or an exposure-only group. Of these, 70 percent were explicit in approach, and 30 percent implicit. With regard to attention to form, 56 percent were focus-on-forms type, and 44 percent were classified as focus on form. The bias also reveals itself in the hybrid classifications: of the focus-on-forms type treatments, 80 percent were explicit in approach, and of the focus-on-form type treatments, 58 percent were explicit in approach. Figure 10.2 illustrates the over-representation in the

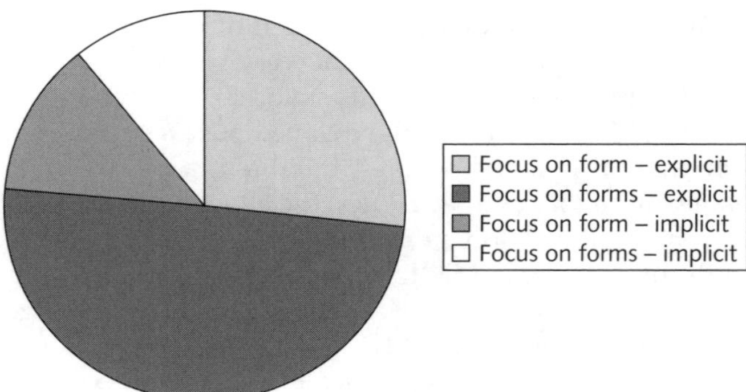

Figure 10.2 Type of L2 instruction: attention to form and degree of explicitness ($n = 98$)

sample of explicit approaches to L2 instruction, in particular the favoring of explicit focus-on-forms procedures above all others.

It must be emphasized that, given the completely decontextualized nature of explicit focus on forms, this type of instruction promotes a mode of learning that is arguably unrelated to SLA, instructed or otherwise, in that the outcome is merely the accumulation of metalinguistic knowledge about language.

A final bias in the design of effects-of-instruction studies concerns the duration of the instructional treatment. Norris and Ortega report four lengths of duration: brief (< 1 hour), short (1–2 hours), medium (3–6 hours), and long (> 7 hours). The typical period of instruction was 1–4 hours. One study provided 50 hours of instruction, but this was rare (and also involved instruction on a large number of L2 features). The only real difference found among these durations was that between "short" and "medium"-length treatments, with shorter treatments of two hours or less being more effective. Instruction that is intensive but only of short duration is well known to be the most vulnerable to rapid forgetting (Lightbown, 1983).

In addition to problems of study design and conceptualization of L2 instructional types, there is an enormous problem concerning validity of outcome measures. This problem has at least three dimensions: (i) a bias in favor of testing explicit, declarative knowledge (which is not surprising, given the pedagogical procedure bias just discussed); (ii) insensitivity to interlanguage change; and (iii) a lack of concern with the reliability of the measures used. We will elaborate on only the first two here, except to note that just 16 percent of the studies included in the meta-analysis reported reliability estimates for the dependent measures (see Norris and Ortega, this volume, for a detailed discussion of reliability issues).

The 49 studies of instructed SLA employed 182 measures (studies typically measuring outcomes in more than one way), which were coded by Norris and Ortega according to the type of L2 knowledge that was tapped by the measure, as shown in table 10.6. Most striking is that approximately 90 percent of the type-of-instruction studies implemented discrete-point or declarative knowledge-based measures (i.e., the first three categories in table 10.6), rather than requiring any real deployment of L2 knowledge under anything like spontaneous conditions (i.e., only the last category in table 10.6). This constitutes an extreme bias in the response type, as illustrated in figure 10.3. Norris and Ortega (2000, p. 486) concluded that "[g]enerally, the observed instructional effectiveness within primary research to date has been based much more extensively on the application of explicit declarative knowledge under controlled conditions, without much requirement for fluent spontaneous speech."

A detailed consideration of the 182 measures in type-of-instruction studies reveals that the problem of type of L2 knowledge assessed is even more severe than might be surmised from Norris and Ortega's interpretation. The essential difficulty is that most of the outcome measures do not appear to be measuring L2 ability in any valid sense (see this chapter's appendix for a detailed list of measures used in the type-of-instruction studies). Fundamentally, whereas it

Table 10.6 The measurement bias toward declarative knowledge (definitions from Norris and Ortega, 2000, p. 440)

Outcome measure	*Directions to subjects*	*Example*
Metalinguistic judgment	Evaluate the appropriateness or grammaticality of L2 targets as used in item prompts	Grammaticality judgments
Selected responses	Choose the correct response from a range of alternatives	Multiple choice in verbal morphology
Constrained, constructed responses	Produce the target form(s) under highly controlled circumstances, where the use of the appropriate form was essential for grammatical accuracy	Sentence-combination with relative clauses
Freely constructed responses	Produce language with relatively few constraints and with meaningful responses or communication as the goal for L2 production	Written composition

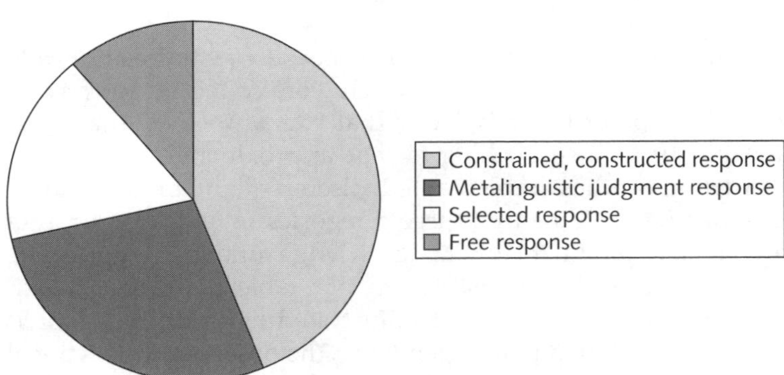

Figure 10.3 Response type in measures (n = 182)

is well established that completely unconstrained data collection is not likely to result in a sample of L2 ability sufficient for study, the bias in instructed SLA research to date has been toward *overly* constraining outcome measures, such that their construct validity is severely compromised. On Chaudron's continuum of available data-collection measures ranging from naturalistic

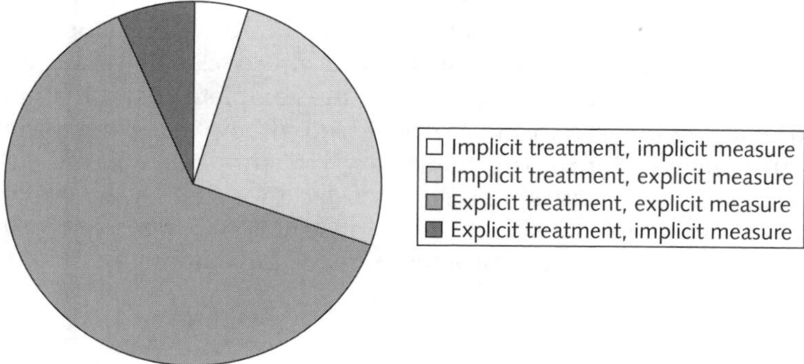

Figure 10.4 Match of treatments and measures (n = 182)

to decontextualized (this volume, p. 764), the vast majority used in type-of-instruction studies to date would be placed at the most decontextualized end, and many of them test metalinguistic rather than usable L2 knowledge.

These types of measures, termed "constrained, constructed responses" by Norris and Ortega, typically involve giving subjects much of a linguistic construction, together with some directions as to how to complete it (e.g., filling in blanks, being given the verb in its infinitive and told to use the direct object). Moreover, the tests look very much like the dominant approach to instruction, that is to say, explicit focus on forms. Such decontextualized focus-on-forms instruction and metalinguistic assessment measures draw neither upon L2 competence nor upon L2 performance during either the instruction or assessment phases of the studies. Rather, they merely teach and require knowledge of language as object. Furthermore, it should be noted that, even when L2 targets were taught by implicit pedagogical procedures, they still tended to be measured in this discrete, decontextualized fashion. Thus, compounding the problem of outcomes measures being overwhelmingly explicit in nature and number, measures are often mismatched with instructional type, as shown in figure 10.4. At the very least, both types of measures, implicit and explicit, should be employed. Having said all this, it remains to be noted that the research requirement to target (in order to be able to measure improvement in) a particular aspect of the L2 may, in part, be responsible for the over-representation of explicit instructional procedures.

The validity of instructed SLA outcome measures is compromised not only by decontextualization and the tapping primarily of metalinguistic knowledge, but also in terms of the analytic framework typically used to measure language change. Measures of interlanguage development have tended to be inappropriate, in the sense that they are overly target-language oriented. Child language researchers have long been employing analyses which enable the precise tracking of L1 development unencumbered by comparisons with the adult target. Adult SLA, being likewise systematic and non-linear in its progress, and, furthermore, seldom reaching the accuracy levels of the target language, must be studied in an interlanguage-sensitive fashion. For example, Doughty and Varela (1998) have shown that L2 instructional effects can be traced by looking at four types of evidence: (i) decreases in the complete absence of an L2 feature (zero marking or base form); (ii) increased attempts at expressing the L2 feature (in whatever form); (iii) temporary oversuppliance of the L2 features; and, eventually, (iv) increasing accuracy. Measures that set the target language as the only criterion for success of an instructional treatment will often fail to capture relevant evidence of interlanguage development.

3.4 *Summary*

In this overview of the empirical research on instructed SLA, we have seen that considerable understanding has been gained of instructional effects in the domains of rate, route, and ultimate attainment. In contrast, to date little is known concerning SLA processes in instructed settings. With respect to research on type of instruction, taking together biases revealed in approach to, and duration of, L2 instruction, and the demonstrated biases in measurement, we have more properly interpreted the apparent advantage for explicit instruction as an artifact of cumulative bias. More specifically, when the outcome of very short-term, explicitly focused instruction is measured on artificial, discrete-point tests, it has proven effective.[7] Put more simply, the case for explicit instruction has been overstated. This is because, although the primary aim is to understand SLA processes under instructed conditions, the design of L2 instruction and its assessment have tended to be based upon knowledge of language as object. That is to say, while ostensibly focusing on the psycholinguistic processes that operate in establishing form–meaning connections, once again researchers have used the wrong level of analysis. Furthermore, for the same reasons, the construct validity of L2 instructional treatments and measures is seriously in doubt.

In the remaining sections of this chapter, we will argue that a completely different approach is now needed in instructed SLA research. Rather than starting from a composite construct such as "method," or from static linguistic descriptions as bases for pedagogical procedures and measures, researchers must conceptualize instruction in terms of dynamic L2 processing. Accordingly, the remaining sections of this chapter examine processing-oriented research, much of which, heretofore, has been carried out in untutored settings, to shed light on how to investigate processing during instructed SLA.

4 Constraints on Adult SLA

Determination of the potential for L2 instruction, in terms of either absolute or relative effectiveness, hinges in part upon whether SLA processes are essentially the same as or different from those involved in child first language acquisition and, if different, how so. As noted at the outset of this chapter, the normal observation with regard to level of ultimate attainment in SLA is tremendous inter-learner variation, and frequently a poor, non-nativelike level of ultimate attainment. Given these vast differences in outcomes, a logical inference is that child language acquisition and adult SLA involve different types of processing for language learning. At least three positions in the literature make the claim that SLA is indeed radically different from child language acquisition. The Fundamental Difference Hypothesis (Bley-Vroman, 1990) proposes that whereas child language learning is implicit, automatic, and domain-specific (a UG first language acquisition view), adult SLA is best characterized by more explicit, general problem-solving strategies. DeKeyser (this volume) likewise argues that adult SLA is mainly explicit, and that adults rely on analytical thinking to acquire their second language. Similarly, the Competition Hypothesis (Felix and Hahn, 1985) claims that whereas implicit UG and explicit problem-solving processes initially compete in adult SLA, the latter eventually win out.

The explanation in common for these child–adult differences is that there are maturational constraints on language acquisition. Keeping to the very general outline of this account (see Hyltenstam and Abrahamsson, this volume, for details), such constraints are defined in terms of the onset and offset of special language-learning mechanisms that only operate when biologically scheduled to do so (i.e., during critical or sensitive periods). If exposure to input does not occur during the requisite time, the end result is an imperfectly learned language. As noted earlier, crucial in the critical period debate are the aforementioned considerable differences in ultimate attainment of learners whose ages of first exposure differ. In sum, what these three fundamental difference views have in common is the notion that processing for language learning shifts utterly from a child mode, involving automatic acquisition from exposure by a language-specific mechanism, to a non-domain-specific, adult mode involving explicit analytical thinking during the processing of L2 input.

In contrast to this drastic and complete, shift-of-processing type of explanation, a second possibility is that maturationally constrained changes in language processing result from and, in turn, subsequently influence the learner's experience with language input. More specifically, early in child language development, at a low, input-driven level of processing, there is a pronounced developmental sharpening of initially general and robust input-processing mechanisms for learning ambient language(s) (Nazzi, Jusczyk, and Johnson, 2000). The function of developmental sharpening of input processing is twofold: to enable the child initially to break into the language system of the surrounding environment, and, subsequently with greater ability, to facilitate everyday processing of rapid and continuous natural speech by use of perceptual cues to make predictions about the input. At a higher level of cognition, the onset of analytical thinking in later childhood changes the way information is processed overall. This enables the individual to advance in all areas of cognition. What is at issue in adult SLA is the extent to which the already developmentally sharpened low-level input processing mechanisms are useful (or detrimental) in breaking into a new language system, and whether the dominant adult mode of cognition (i.e., analytical thinking or explicit learning), which is designed to process non-linguistic information, can process language input in ways relevant to SLA.

The following is a necessarily brief consideration of the nature of language processing changes during primary language acquisition, all of which at once facilitate child cognitive and linguistic development, but conspire to make adult SLA more difficult. In section 5, the discussion turns to how instruction can potentially enhance L2 processing.

4.1 *Developmental sharpening*

Input processing in very early child language acquisition chiefly involves bootstrapping utterance structure from the speech signal (Jusczyk, 1997, 1999a, 2001). This is by no means an easy task. Although input to infants is certainly modified (slower, with exaggerated pitch, etc.), Van de Weijer (1999) has shown that 91 percent of the language addressed to an infant during all of her or his waking hours from age 6 months to 9 months was continuous speech, and, hence, that only 9 percent of the input consisted of isolated words. Thus, since fluent, adult language, even when directed at children, remains highly complex at the acoustic level (i.e., rapid, coarticulated, and variable within and across speakers), it does not enable one-to-one mapping of acoustic percepts to meaning. Nonetheless, despite the seemingly overwhelming complexity of the input, children do perceive, segment, encode, and remember the organization of linguistic information in the speech signal, enabling them subsequently to map acoustic forms onto meaning and, eventually, to figure out phrase and clause structure.

In order to explain how children accomplish this prosodic bootstrapping, L1 researchers posit that, from birth or perhaps even prenatally, infants have specialized, but ever adaptive, language-processing abilities that ultimately are constrained by both linguistic and cognitive factors (Jusczyk, 2001). Generally speaking, during the first year or so of life, children shift from processing primarily on the basis of acoustic features of the input (e.g., phonemes) to using their newly acquired knowledge as a foundation for processing other information (e.g., rhythm or distribution) salient in the input and relevant to the next developmental stage (e.g., determining word, phrase, and utterance boundaries). In the following sections we examine the evidence for, and consequences of, developmental sharpening in both child language acquisition and adult SLA. Table 10.7 provides a set of examples of the specialized language processing mechanisms.

The most dramatic example of developmental sharpening is the case of phonemic discrimination leading to categorization of the native language phoneme inventory. Whereas the capacity to process acoustic features is not determined initially by the child's native language (i.e., infants can process *any*

Table 10.7 Input processing mechanisms in L1A and SLA
A LA mechanisms that undergo developmental sharpening

	Mechanism				
Type of processing	*Initial*	*Developmental sharpening*	*Consequent processing change*	*Child L1A advantage*	*Adult SLA "disability"*
Segment sounds from speech (phonemic discrimination)	Categorical perception of all language contrasts	Tuning of phonetic segment perception to the adult language input 6–9 months	Decline in sensitivity to non-native contrasts	Early tuning of phonetic segment perception	L2 accent
Segment whole words from rapid, coarticulated speech (detect word boundaries) (metrical segmentation strategy)	No preference among syllables, morae, or stress patterns	Sensitivity to predominant rhythm pattern of the NL 6–9 months	Reliance upon only one segmentation strategy	Ignore "irrelevant" details to get major boundaries, thus narrowing the processing space	Mismatch of major segmentation strategy to input cues
Detect remaining word boundaries using less salient cues (phonotactics, distribution tallies, and allophonic variation)	Overly general rhythm-based segmentation strategy	Preference for NL over NNL and for frequent NL over infrequent NL phonotactic sequences; ability to track syllable following stress 6–9 months Preference for most frequent among allophonic variants 10.5 months	Decline in ability to process according to ALL features in the input (tuning to NL "details")	Pay attention to details within a narrowed processing space	Mismatch of details segmentation strategy to input cues

Table 10.7 *(Cont'd)*

Type of processing	*Mechanism*		*Consequent processing change*	*Child L1A advantage*	*Adult SLA "disability"*
	Initial	*Developmental sharpening*			
Detect phrase and clause boundaries	Sensitivity to prosodic cues (pause, pitch, final lengthening) in NL, NNL, and music input	Preference for native prosodic cues 4.5 months		Ignore "irrelevant" details to get major boundaries, thus narrowing the processing space	Mismatch of major segmentation strategy to input cues
Discover phrase and clause structure	Preference for real over nonsense function words	Ability to track position of function words 16 months		Pay attention to details within a narrowed processing space	Mismatch of details segmentation strategy to input cues

B Other constraining mechanisms

Type of processing	*Mechanism*		*Child L1A advantage*	*Adult SLA "disability"*
Encode and remember word	Segmentation	Store forms in the absence of meaning 9 months →	Enables fast mapping	Mismatch of segmentation strategy to input
Map word forms onto meaning (whole object, taxonomic, and mutual exclusivity constraints)	Fast mapping	Assume that labels refer to whole objects, entire classes, and are unique 12 months →	Narrows the hypothesis space for forms–meaning mapping	Unknown
Lexical	Joint attention	Ostensive → nouns Impending → verbs 6–21 months	Temporary facilitation of forms–meaning mapping	Unknown

language), between 6 and 9 months of age, this general processing receptivity declines, or more precisely stated, becomes attuned to the native language. In other words, although infants appear to be endowed with universal segmentation abilities – for instance, phoneme perception abilities that are sufficiently receptive to enable discrimination among any and all of the universal set of sounds (Eimas, Siqueland, Jusczyk, and Vigorito, 1971) – after six to nine months of experience with adult input, the influence of the native language begins to take hold, for instance such that the infant's sensitivity to non-native contrasts declines, and phonemic categories begin to organize along the lines of the adult language (Best, Lafleur, and McRoberts, 1995; Werker and Tees, 1984). The evidence for phoneme discrimination is found in high amplitude sucking rate and preferential head-turning experiments. The results of these studies clearly indicate a fine attunement of input processing to the native language, one which may already be complete by as early as 6 months of age.

Sensitivity to prosodic cues that indicate word boundaries, or "prosodic packaging," is another early and general processing capacity which gives way to more native-language-specific processing. During this same early time period (0–6 months), sensitivity to the predominant rhythm of the native language develops (Jusczyk, Cutler, and Redanz, 1993). Although very young infants learning any language exhibit no preference among rhythm types (e.g., stress-based, syllabic, or mora-based), studies have shown that American children at age 9 months prefer to listen to lists of English words with the dominant English stress pattern (strong/weak, as in *longer* rather than weak/strong as in *along*) (Jusczyk et al., 1993). The claim is that children use their preference for the dominant native language stress pattern as a first attempt to segment whole word forms from rapid, fluent input (Jusczyk, 1999a). Further evidence for this initial word segmentation approach is that, when just the strong initial syllables are trained and represented in a word, the listening preferences disappear, such that infants familiarized with strong/weak words do not prefer the passages containing monosyllabic words derived from the strong syllables (Jusczyk, 1998a). Thus, infants appear to be segmenting whole words using the complete rhythmic pattern of the native language, in this case, stress in English. (See Otake, Hatano, Cutler and Mehler, 1993, for a study showing a mora-based strategy for word segmentation in Japanese.) Cutler (Cutler, 1990, 1994; Cutler and Butterfield, 1992) has termed this the *metrical segmentation strategy*.

Of course, the dominant rhythmic pattern of a language is often incomplete as far as indicating the boundaries of all words is concerned. Nonetheless, infants appear to use the overly general approach – for example, the English word-initial segmentation stress cue – and this seems to be in order to derive smaller chunks of input which may then facilitate the discovery of other, initially less salient cues to word boundaries, such as distributional cues and allophonic variation (Jusczyk, Hohne, and Baumann, 1999). Once generalized phonetic and prosodic processing have been underway for six or more months, children demonstrate increasing sensitivity to the distribution of various types of information in the native language input, all of which are tied to features that are frequent in the language that surrounds them. For example, between 6 and 9 months of age, infants develop a preference for native over non-native phonotactic sequences, and for frequent native over infrequent native phonotactic sequences (Jusczyk et al., 1993). This is demonstrated by much longer listening times by 9-month-olds to lists of words in their native language than to lists in a non-native language (or longer listening times to frequent native word lists than to infrequent native word lists). Six-month-olds, on the other hand, listen to all types of lists for the same amount of time. Furthermore, additional experiments with 9-month-olds have shown that when all the phonotactic information is filtered from the lists, leaving only prosodic cues, infants no longer listen differentially, suggesting that, indeed, it is the phonotactic sequence information to which they are now paying attention in the input (Jusczyk et al., 1993).

Distributional cues help infants learning English to discover the problematic weak/strong pattern, where the strong stress now indicates a word-*final* boundary. To determine the difference between word-initial and word-final boundaries, children learning English appear to pay attention to the frequency of the next syllable (Jusczyk, Goodman, and Baumann, 1999). That is to say, they notice that initial strong stress is always followed by the same weak syllable (i.e., this is an entire word), and that final strong stress is always followed by a different weak syllable (i.e., this is the end of a word, followed by a new word). Evidence for this comes from studies showing that when children are fooled by regularizing the syllable following the weak/strong stress pattern, they no longer reveal a listening preference for the strong/weak word initial stress pattern (Newsome and Jusczyk, 1995; and see Jusczyk, 2001, for an overview). These findings are obtained with real and artificial language input (see Saffran, Newport, and Aslin, 1996, for artificial language studies). Furthermore, in studies of allophonic variation in which infants are familiarized with a pair of words like *nitrate* vs. *night rate*, where the differences between word-initial and word-medial segments are +/− aspiration of [t] and +/− voicing of [r], 9-month-olds listen equally long, regardless of word familiarized with, but by 10.5 months of age, they listen longer to, and hence are said to segment, the familiarized word (Hohne and Jusczyk, 1994; Jusczyk and Hohne, 1997).

The initial developmental milestones of prosodic bootstrapping for word learning can be summarized as follows: at age 7.5 months, word segmentation from fluent speech only approximates adult ability, but by 10.5 months, sensitivity to additional cues has developed. In other words, using a major cue, which is but part of the eventual adult parsing strategy, infants segment the input into developmentally relevant chunks, in effect limiting the search space, and thus enabling subsequent strategies to seek regularities in organization within the chunks (Nazzi, Bertoncini, and Mehler, 1998; Nazzi, Nelson, Jusczyk, and Jusczyk, 2000). As we have seen, infants then begin keeping track of phonotactic, distributional, and allophonic cues to infer other word boundaries.

By 10.5 months, English-learning infants seem to have developed segmentation abilities that are similar to those displayed by English-speaking adults. Infants need to use all of these cues for word segmentation because no one cue alone is sufficient for segmenting all words from highly complex continuous speech. Starting with one major and generally successful segmentation strategy enables the infant to pay attention to other, initially less noticeable, but relevant cues to word extraction.

Once the ability to segment words from the input has developed, the next task for children is to encode the words in memorial representation. The mechanism responsible for this is fast-mapping, which itself develops in two phases. Children appear first to encode and remember the segmented word forms; only later do they fast-map meanings onto the word forms. To demonstrate word-form encoding in the absence of meaning, researchers have used a modification of the head-turn-preference procedure, which is based on the principle of priming (Jusczyk and Aslin, 1995). In such experiments, very young infants are familiarized with particular targets (either in isolation or in fluent speech), and then researchers measure how long they listen to passages with the stimulus and with a relevant comparison. Results show that the recognition of familiarized word forms is a very precise ability, since if the familiarized words are changed by just one phoneme, infants no longer prefer the passage. Furthermore, they can recognize familiarized word forms in the presence of a distracting voice and generalize across speakers (this ability develops, too: at 7.5 months, only from one female to another, not female to male; at 10.5 months, to both) (Houston, Jusczyk, and Tager, 1998; Jusczyk, 2001). While, at this stage, infants are encoding word forms in the absence of processing for meaning, the resulting memorial representations lay the foundation for the later process, fast-mapping the lexicon (of forms to meanings), which they are then able to do at great speed.

In the second year, infants begin to link sound patterns to meaning. Mapping appears to be a constrained process, as well. For instance, research on children's word learning has suggested that children never consider the full range of hypotheses about what a given word could mean. Instead, they narrow the range of possible meanings for a word on the basis of innate constraints that force them to consider only certain relevant cues, for instance when trying to map a new word onto an object. Markman (1989, 1994) proposes three constraints on word meaning: the *whole-object constraint*, the *taxonomic constraint*, and the *mutual-exclusivity constraint*. When children see an adult point to an object and name it, they almost never assume the word refers to some part of the object; instead, they assume the person is naming the *whole* object, thus obeying the whole-object constraint. Similarly, the taxonomic constraint narrows children's guesses about word meaning by helping them to figure out the level of generality for which an object name is intended. In other words, the taxonomic constraint points children to the fact that, typically, a new word refers to a known *class* of things: *dog* refers to all members of the class of dogs, and not to this particular dog. Finally, when a child encounters two objects, one for which they already know a word, he or she will generally assume that the novel word applies to the object for which they do not already know a name – in other words, names for things are *mutually exclusive.*

Whereas these three constraints are considered necessary for lexical acquisition, another mechanism, joint attention, appears at least to be facilitative (Baldwin, 1993; Tomasello, 1995). Joint attention can be focused on objects (for noun learning) or actions (for verb learning). In naturalistic studies, children with the largest vocabularies are those whose mothers label the child's impending actions or their own completed actions (Tomasello and Kruger, 1992). In experimental studies, joint attention established during ostensive context is shown to lead to noun learning (Tomasello and Barton, 1994), and an impending context ("Now I'm going to roll the ball") is the most conducive to learning verbs (Tomasello and Kruger, 1992). Investigations of the capacity of infants to respond to the joint attention bids of others (e.g., gaze shift, pointing, and vocalizing) indicate that responding to joint attention at 6, 8, 10, 12, and 18 months is positively related to individual differences in vocabulary development (Morales et al., forthcoming). However, by 21 months of age, this correlation between response to joint attention bids and vocabulary growth no longer holds. Overall, joint attention with equal participation by the child in the activity appears to be the most effective for novel word learning (Tomasello and Todd, 1983).

Thus far, we have seen a number of examples of the approach taken by children to the enormously difficult problem of breaking into the native language in the face of complex input in the form of continuous speech. At first, guided by innate constraints, and ignoring "irrelevant" details, they adopt an overly general, but reasonably successful strategy to segmenting out the words. While it is certainly beyond the scope of this chapter to describe all of first language acquisition, it is important to point out that the same general-to-specific strategy, with increasing attention to distributional cues, has been demonstrated for the learning of phrase structure and syntax (for a collection of relevant studies, see Weissenborn and Höhle, 2001). For example, very early on, children (4.5 months old) demonstrate that they are sensitive to, and thus detect, prosodic cues to major phrase and clause boundaries (e.g., pitch, final lengthening, and pausing) in all of the following types of input: their native language, non-native languages, and music (Jusczyk, 1998a, 2001; Jusczyk and Krumhansl, 1993). The evidence for this is preference for listening to passages in which pauses coincide with boundaries rather than to passages with pauses inserted in mid-clause.

It is argued that, once the input has been divided into these smaller chunks, or "prosodic phrase packets," children may then be able to discover cues to syntactic organization within what is now a smaller processing space (Jusczyk, 1999b, 2001). Such cues include knowledge of the typical position of function words with respect to content words (Shady, 1996) and sensitivity to local dependencies like person–number agreement and between auxiliaries and verbs (Santelmann and Jusczyk, 1998). Interestingly, given a long-distance dependency, as when there is considerable intervening material between an auxiliary and a verb ("Grandma is almost always singing"), children no longer track dependencies (Santelmann and Jusczyk, 1997, p. 508). However, the longer the distance between the dependent elements, the less likely they are to appear in the same prosodic unit. As Jusczyk (2001, p. 22) has noted, "fortunately for language learners long adverbial phrases between adverbials and verb endings are apt to be very rare in the input." Apparently the everyday packaging of utterances in prosodic chunks is sufficiently effective for incrementally discovering the structure of language.

With respect to understanding the nature of input-processing mechanisms and developmental sharpening, it is worth noting that the metrical segmentation strategy and the preferences for salient or frequent cues in the native language input develop at just the same time as universal discrimination of non-native phonemic contrasts declines (Jusczyk, 1998a). Furthermore, for each language-learning problem (e.g., extracting word forms, mapping forms to meaning, determining phrase and clause boundaries, and discovering phrase and clause structure), the overly general strategy constrains the problem space such that children can then pay attention to less salient, previously ignored, but nonetheless now relevant cues in the input. Likewise, while detailed discussion of general cognitive development is well beyond the scope of the current chapter, a significant observation is that analytical thinking appears to develop in somewhat the same constrained fashion as do language input-processing mechanisms. That is to say, in very early life, children are generally perseverative in their approach to problem-solving tasks (Deák, 2000b), settling upon one successful solution (usually discovered in determinate tasks) and persisting in using it, even when encountering a new, indeterminate task, or in the face of explicit directions to adopt a new strategy. For example, while 3-year-olds can easily sort a group of objects according to their shape, the children cannot shift their sorting behavior when asked to sort according to function. At about age 4, children begin to use a more flexible style of induction, one that is based upon the original solution, but now takes into account more details of the problem. Four-year-olds can also follow instructions to change to a new sorting strategy. Deák (2000a) has termed this "adaptive-problem solving."

4.2 *Non-native speech processing*

We have seen that the preponderance of evidence in the studies of pre-lexical L1 processing, and of the subsequent association of forms with meaning, indicates that segmentation and mapping strategies used during child native language acquisition are constrained such that, while initially receptive to any type of salient cue, input processing rapidly becomes attuned to the ambient language during the first year of life. That is to say, segmentation and mapping procedures are refocused and readied to attend to previously unnoticed cues in the complex speech signal and in the agents, entities, and actions of the events in which the child participates, that is, those cues which now are most relevant to the next phase of language acquisition (see Jusczyk, 1993, 1997, 1998b, 2001). The consequence of this is that input processing during native language acquisition is highly efficient and relevant to the language-learning task at hand (e.g., extracting word forms, mapping forms to meaning, figuring out phrase structure, etc.). In child language acquisition, developmental sharpening is beneficial, since the attunement proceeds stepwise in concert with input and interaction. But what of adult SLA? An unfortunate drawback to the extreme efficiency of L1 processing, in particular to the developmental sharpening that it entails, is that adults are rendered "disabled second-language learners later in life" (Cutler, 2001). This is because speech-processing abilities are altered, through experience with the native language, so that adults acquiring their L2 typically process input with mechanisms already attuned to their L1.

To illustrate this, let us revisit the pre-lexical segmentation strategy that exploits the dominant rhythm pattern of the native language in order to extract word forms from continuous speech. When listening to their L2, adults face the same complexity in the input as do children, if not more.[8] Cutler and her colleagues have investigated the nature of speech segmentation by adults during native and non-native listening, adopting a cross-linguistic approach.[9] In a series of sound-segment monitoring experiments that were originally designed to test whether the syllable is the universal speech segmentation unit (as had been claimed by Mehler, Dommergues, Frauenfelder, and Segui, 1981), it was discovered that adult English speakers do not use a syllabification strategy when listening to their native language (Cutler, Mehler, Norris, and Segui, 1986). Since French is much more easily described in terms of syllables than English, the researchers wondered whether English speakers listening to French, a foreign language, but one which is much easier to syllabify, would be able to apply the syllabification strategy. Results showed clearly that, even when listening to French, English speakers do not use the strategy of syllabification. Native speakers of French, on the other hand, *always* use syllabification in speech segmentation, regardless of whether they are listening to familiar, easy-to-syllabify French or to foreign, hard-to-syllabify English (Cutler et al., 1986). In separate investigations, it was demonstrated that, rather than exploiting cues found in syllables, L1 English adults use a stress-based segmentation strategy when listening to their native language (Cutler and Butterfield, 1992; Cutler and Norris, 1988), and, crucially, that they use the same stress-based strategy when listening to a foreign language with a different rhythmic structure (in this case, Japanese, which is mora-based) (Otake, Hatano, and Yoneyama, 1996). Note that this is the very strategy which we discussed above in describing prosodic bootstrapping by infants learning English.

Likewise, Cutler and Otake (1994) have shown that Japanese adults do not use the syllabic strategy, but rather they segment their native Japanese by exploiting its mora-based rhythm. When English speakers listened to the same Japanese materials, they used neither the syllabic nor the mora-based strategy, and when French speakers listened to the Japanese materials, they clearly used their native syllabification rather than the Japanese-like mora-based segmentation strategy. In a second task involving phoneme detection, Japanese speakers were once again shown to use the native-language, mora-based strategy during non-native listening (to English), whereas English native speakers listening to the same materials were not influenced by the mora (Cutler and Otake, 1994). Thus, Japanese are sensitive to moraic structure even in L2 English, and even though native English speakers are not. Results such as these have been replicated with several combinations of rhythmically different native and non-native languages (see Cutler, 2001, for an overview). Taken together, the findings of the cross-linguistic speech segmentation studies suggest strongly that segmentation strategies are language-specific, not universal, processing routines (Cutler et al., 1986).[10] More specifically, Cutler et al. (1986, p. 397) claim that "[d]uring language acquisition, speakers adapt their perceptual routines so as to exploit with maximal efficiency the phonological properties of their native language."

Most important for the discussion at hand is another logical conclusion emanating from the findings of cross-linguistic speech segmentation comparisons: "Language-specific segmentation is in the listener, not in the speech signal" (Cutler, 2001, p. 11). That is to say, although it is indeed the salient features of the speech signal that initially attract the infant's processing attention very early on in native language acquisition, experience with the ambient input results in developmental sharpening such that one, and, as we shall now see, only one, dominant segmentation strategy is applied from that point onward, regardless of the features of the input encountered (including non-native languages). Evidence for this comes from studies of proficient bilinguals raised by native-speaking parents, one each of English and French (Cutler, Mehler, Norris, and Segui, 1989, 1992). Upon first analysis, the findings of the bilingual studies were perplexingly variable and not at all like the findings of the monolingual studies. It was then discovered that the group of bilingual subjects was not homogeneous in all regards. The difference among subjects was found not to be based on country of residence, or on the language of either parent. Rather, it was based on the subjects' stated language preference, that is, when asked, in case of brain injury, which language they would rather keep. When subjects were grouped according to their preferred language, the findings revealed that they commanded only the native strategy of the preferred language. Thus, subjects who said that they would keep French in the event of brain injury used the syllabic strategy, and those who preferred English exhibited stress-based segmentation. Further studies reveal that English–Dutch bilinguals use stress when processing both languages (both languages have stress-based rhythm), and that French-dominant French–Dutch bilinguals do not use stress-based segmentation in Dutch (van Zon, 1997, reported in Cutler, 2001). No studies have found simultaneous command of two processing strategies.

Interestingly, Cutler et al. (1992) note that, since the French–English bilinguals in their study were so high-functioning in both languages, listening clearly does not *depend* on the use of the strategy. Rather, the purpose of a dominant strategy is to facilitate the acquisition of the lexicon during native language acquisition. Whether or not the highly proficient bilinguals *ever* used more than one processing strategy during the simultaneous acquisition of their two languages is not known, as no such studies of early bilingual segmentation, in particular of infants exposed to rhythmically different languages from birth, have yet been carried out (Cutler, 2001). What does seem to be the case, however, is that the developmental change involved does not necessarily constitute a complete loss of "perceptual acuity" (Cutler, 2001). For instance, it has been shown that discrimination ability remains in adulthood for phonemes which are not present in the native language, but, crucially, which also are not pre-empted by any native language contrast: English speakers can, for example, discriminate Zulu clicks (Best, McRoberts, and Sithole, 1988). Cutler and Otake (1994) argue that such findings indicate that infants identify the acoustic distinctions that are important to pay attention to in order to learn the words of the native language, and, more importantly, that irrelevant variation, for instance between pronunciations within and across speakers, can be ignored.

For L2 purposes, this raises the crucial question of whether or not adults can be trained to use processing strategies other than their dominant native language ones. Cutler (2002, p. 3) offers an overall diagnosis: non-native listening skills are less flexible. In their native language, people cope effortlessly with unfamiliar voices and intra- and inter-speaker variations in pronunciation, and have little difficulty processing speech in the presence of noise or distraction. All of these factors cause great difficulty in non-native listening. Thus far it appears that, without training, listeners command a repertoire of procedures relevant to the efficient processing of their native language, and that they do not use new procedures more appropriate to L2 input. What is problematic is that they use their native language strategies even when mismatched to the input. This is clearly not efficient. Could second language instruction make a difference?

With regard to the discrimination of phonemes, the prognosis is not good. Intensive and laborious training in non-native discrimination results in only a small improvement (Lively et al., 1994). Once native phonemic categorization has taken place, it cannot be altered. Only phonemes that are not found in the native language inventory can be discriminated (Best et al., 1995). However, some evidence suggests that other segmentation strategies may not be so severely limited. Proficient German–English bilinguals have been shown to be sensitive to *both* their native German phonotactic sequence restrictions and non-native English constraints (Weber, 2000). In a word-spotting study, in which listeners had to detect the English word *luck* within nonsense words like *moysluck*, *moyshluck* or *moyfluck*, English speakers were fastest at detecting *luck* in *moyshluck*, presumably since *shl-* is not a possible onset in English, thus rendering the segmentation boundary more salient than *fl-* and *sl-*, which are both possible English onsets. Both *fl-* and *shl-* are possible onsets in German. Although the German–English proficient bilinguals found *luck* easiest to detect in *moysluck* (as would be predicted on the basis of the German phonotactic constraints), their detection responses were faster for *moyshluck* than for *moyfluck*. Weber interprets this to mean that, while the German listeners maintained sensitivity to their native sequencing constraints, they had also acquired some sensitivity to English phonotactics. With regard to segmentation on the basis of rhythm, recall the experiments with French–English bilinguals which revealed a language preference that was linked to its matching native language segmentation strategy (Cutler et al., 1992). Cutler (2001) discusses a very revealing finding in this study: the proficient bilinguals *never* misapplied their segmentation strategy in listening to their other language. That is to say, subjects who stated that they preferred French used the syllabic strategy in French listening but not in English listening. Exactly the same was true for the subjects who stated a preference for English. They exhibited the stress-based strategy in processing English, but not in French. Cutler (2001, p. 16) concludes the following: "Inappropriate language-specific segmentation is avoidable."

If, as evidence has shown, untutored bilinguals have developed an incipient sensitivity to phonotactic constraints in their less-preferred language, as well as the ability to inhibit a segmentation strategy that is mismatched to the rhythm of the language being processed, this suggests that adults retain something of the perceptual acuity they once called upon as child language learners. Furthermore, unlike the case of phonemic categorization, which appears to be immutable once completed, this constitutes tantalizing evidence that other patterns of language structure have not been unalterably fixed in memorial representation. Bilinguals still appear to be able to pay attention to the cues *located in the input*, as they did when they were infants first breaking their native language code.

A clear research priority in instructed SLA has thus presented itself: can L2 learners overcome the developmental sharpening effects of adopting procedures efficient for the processing of their L1, the outcome of which is a highly native-language-specific approach to input? More specifically, can they return to a mode of processing similar to that used during native language acquisition in which, *at least at first*, they pay attention to the cues in the input that are most useful in signaling the relevant lexical, phrasal, and syntactic boundaries of the L2, and use that information to narrow the processing problem space such that other cues may be perceived?

5 Enhancing Adult SLA

Ways in which to alter, with a view to enhancing, input processing by adults acquiring their second language have just begun to be investigated in SLA. Two recent lines of research – processing instruction studies and focus-on-form studies – both address the fundamental question of how L2 learner attention can most efficiently be directed to cues in the input which "disabled" adult learners fail to perceive when left to their own devices. Such work is motivated by the Noticing Hypothesis, which, stated in general terms, is as follows: "SLA is largely driven by what learners pay attention to and notice in target language input and what they understand the significance of noticed input to be" (Schmidt, 2001, pp. 3–4; and see also Robinson, this volume; Schmidt, 1990, 1992, 1993, 1995, 1998). On the face of it, this would appear to be the same type of process as drives primary language acquisition. However, given developmental sharpening, *what* is noticed differs, and presumably is less efficient, for adults acquiring their second language.

5.1 Processing instruction

Processing instruction studies address the issue of non-native input processing at the utterance level. As was the case with pre-lexical segmentation strategies discussed above, it has been shown that, when listening to their L2, adults rely upon L1 strategies for assigning grammatical roles in an utterance. For example, L1 English speakers consistently apply a word-order strategy which is highly reliable for identifying the subject of an utterance (i.e., since English sentences are nearly always SVO, the first noun encountered is going to be the subject of the utterance). They do so when processing their L1, and when processing their L2. Thus, L1 English speakers learning Spanish as a second language have difficulty with utterances like *Lo sigue la madre* ("His mother is following him"). Given the task of matching one of two pictures to an utterance which they hear, learners will assume, even though *lo* is an object pronoun, that "he" is the subject of the utterance, since it is a noun-like entity encountered sentence intially. Other cross-linguistic bilingual processing studies, most conducted within the competition model paradigm (Ellis, this volume; MacWhinney, 2001), have replicated this finding of reliance on L1 cues (for instance, to determine the grammatical subject, L1 Spanish speakers rely most on agreement cues found in morphology, and L1 Japanese speakers depend upon animacy cues). To overcome the mismatch between the L1 strategy and the L2 input, processing instruction informs learners that the L1 cues are not reliable, and alerts them to cues in the L2 to which they should pay attention instead. Learners are then given numerous opportunities (called structured processing) to interpret the L2 in the appropriate way (see VanPatten, 2002, for an overview).

While promising, there have been two problems with PI instruction studies to date. First, there is usually some component of explicitly presented, metalinguistic instruction that precedes (and, hence, is isolated from) the structured processing phase. Researchers working within the PI paradigm themselves have shown this component to be unnecessary in both classroom (VanPatten and Oikkenon, 1996) and computer-based (Sanz and Morgan-Short, 2002) environments. More specifically, in both of these studies, it was shown that explicit instruction had no effect beyond that of the structured processing component. A second difficulty with PI studies to date is that not all researchers adhere to the PI guidelines for designing L2 instruction. Processing instruction is supposed to address a *processing problem*, for example, the well-known first-noun strategy used by English speakers processing L2 Spanish input. More often than not, however, when the research has investigated something other than the first-noun strategy, it has been based on a linguistic description of an observed learner error. If the error was not a consequence of a processing problem, then PI would not be expected to be effective. Rather, the overall purpose of PI is to help learners process what is actually in the input, that is to say, to circumvent what their L1 systems expect.

5.2 *Focus on form*

Focus-on-form instruction is another approach to redirecting learner attention during input processing both within and across utterances. In accordance with the Noticing Hypothesis, the essential idea is that aspects of the L2 input learners need to notice, but do not (for whatever reason), will require some kind of pedagogical intervention. Well-known examples of recalcitrant L2 learning problems are found in research on the language competence of Canadian English–French bilinguals who have been immersed in their L2 at school for most of their academic careers. Arguably, this is the best possible context for L2 instruction, given the amount of time spent functioning in the second language. However, despite this opportunity, findings show that, after up to 12 years of immersion, while the listening, reading, and cognitive abilities of bilinguals are on a par with or superior to those of their monolingual counterparts in the two languages, their productive abilities (speaking and writing) are clearly non-native (Allen, Swain, Harley, and Cummins, 1990). Typical problems include grammatical gender agreement errors, absence of tense marking, and lack of politeness markers (Swain and Lapkin, 1982). Learners may not be able to notice these aspects of the L2 because they are not communicatively problematic, not conceptually similar to the L1, or perhaps not acoustically salient (perhaps because they are processed through the developmentally sharpened L1 mechanisms). Focus-on-form interventions draw learners' attention to these persistent problems when they arise incidentally during language use in the classroom that is otherwise meaning oriented (Doughty and Williams, 1998c; Long, 1988, 1991; Long and Robinson, 1998).

Examples of FonF pedagogical procedures include visual input enhancement and auditory recasting. (See table 10.4 for many others.) Studies of the former have tended to indicate that enhancements involving font manipulations or color coding are not salient enough for learners to notice (Jourdenais, 1998, 2001). In contrast, auditory recasts, although still among the more implicit of FonF pedagogical procedures, have been effective, with findings of both experimental (Long, Inagaki, and Ortega, 1998) and quasi-experimental, classroom (Doughty and Varela, 1998) research converging on the interpretation that the implicit negative evidence provided to learners by recasts contingent upon their interlanguage utterances is noticed and used in SLA (see Long, forthcoming, for an overview). The mechanism evoked in this explanation is cognitive comparison (Doughty, 2001). While precisely what the range of elements is that can effectively be brought into attentional focus during input processing is yet to be determined, how *many* should be attended to at once is clear. Learners benefit most from concentrated simple recasts (of one or two elements) of aspects of language for which they are developmentally ready to benefit from instruction.

Thus, the preliminary indication is that attention-oriented instruction is effective. However, it must be reiterated that most effects-of-instruction studies, even many that have ostensibly been operationalized in terms of attention to form, have been plagued by research bias, as discussed at length above (see section 3.3). In particular, pedagogical procedures, as well as the measures used to assess the L2 ability of subjects after instruction, have tended to be overly explicit, and in many cases excessively metalinguistic and decontextualized in nature (i.e., focus on forms, declarative knowledge). This has resulted in a false impression that explicit instruction is the most effective for SLA. In reality, what the evidence has shown is that explicit instruction involving decontextualized, declarative knowledge leads to an accumulation of metalinguistic knowledge. That FonF instruction has also been demonstrated to have a relatively large effect, even in the face of extreme research bias, suggests the robustness of attentional focus within implicit learning. However, since this type of instruction has, in practice, rarely, been properly investigated, modes of L2 processing that enable focus on form must now be prioritized in the research agenda.

5.3 *The "what" and "how" of the Noticing Hypothesis*

What must adults pay attention to in the L2 input, if not the kind of declarative knowledge offered up by explicit instruction? We have already seen that, during primary language acquisition, in a highly efficient manner, children initially notice regular and prosodically salient boundaries, and then, within this delimited processing space, begin to notice less salient details that provide cues to linguistic organization. Furthermore, we reviewed evidence that adults are somewhat, if not entirely, disabled by this tuning of their input processing mechanisms, such that they no longer notice cues in the input *per se*, but through the filter of the linguistic organization of their first language. To understand what adult learners need to notice to be successful in SLA, we now must address two issues that have largely been ignored by instructed SLA researchers: (i) the adequacy of conceptualizations of what learners pay attention to, and (ii) the nature of the default L2 processing mode and how it might be enhanced by instruction to promote noticing.

In specifying the Noticing Hypothesis beyond its general formulation, Schmidt has claimed that learners *must* pay attention to what he terms "surface elements" in order to acquire them. More specifically, he states that: "the objects of attention and noticing are elements of the surface structure of utterances in the input – instances of language, rather than any abstract rules or principles of which such instances may be exemplars" (Schmidt, 2001, p. 5). Noticing structural regularities, forming hypotheses, and making comparisons is a level beyond. Precisely what these "surface" elements of language input are is, as yet, little understood. However, Schmidt is clear about how these elements should *not* be construed: "Noticing is therefore used here in a restricted sense, as a technical term roughly equivalent to 'apperception' (Gass, 1988), to Tomlin and Villa's (1994) 'detection within selective attention' . . . My intention is to separate 'noticing' from metalinguistic awareness as clearly as possible" (Schmidt, 2001, p. 5).

The key point is that metalinguistic awareness and noticing are to be considered separate mental processes. The second crucial issue is *how* learners should be assisted through pedagogical procedures in noticing the "surface elements." Whereas explicit instruction (of the kind typical in studies to date) carves up the L2 for the learner, noticing enables learners to segment the input for themselves and, as such, is a mental process akin to segmentation in primary language acquisition. In the case of the former, metalinguistic approach, it is not at all clear how such declarative knowledge should be divided up for presentation to learners, or how the learner could reassemble the component parts of the L2. Although proceduralization of declarative knowledge through practice is sometimes invoked as a viable learning mechanism, it will become clear in the next section that exactly the opposite is closer to an accurate characterization of how complex knowledge is acquired. We shall see that implicit knowledge leading directly to procedural ability is first internalized, and, if the conditions require it (e.g., practice), declarative knowledge develops afterwards. If this is true, then instructional procedures that begin with declarative knowledge are putting the cart before the horse. Moreover, if complex L2 knowledge is primarily acquired implicitly, but through the filter of developmentally sharpened input-processing mechanisms, then all the more critical are precise conceptualizations of elements to which L2 learners must attend, particularly if instructional enhancements are to, in a sense, *reorganize* the processing space so that learners may overcome the effects of primary language acquisition.

5.4 *Modes of L2 processing*

Basic processing research thus far suggests that, to be successful, SLA must involve two modes of processing, a default implicit mode, and an available (and perhaps necessarily explicit) mode to be engaged only when implicit processing is insufficient. Modes of L2 processing are properly considered in the context of a debate that has been controversial in cognitive psychology for three decades. At issue is the question of how complex knowledge is learned from the available input – that is to say, whether implicitly or explicitly – and how such knowledge is represented in memory and accessed for use, typically in tests involving discrimination or generation and verbalizations of knowledge. Central to the discussion is how to characterize the memorial representations that arise immediately (during processing) and long-term (storage) in the learning of complex systems; whether such learning proceeds with or without awareness and with or without intention; and whether there is any interaction of the two types of knowledge. A version of this debate is embodied in Krashen's learning/acquisition distinction and non-interface position, and their counter-positions, as discussed earlier in the consideration of the case against L2 instruction (see section 2).

The view that the learning of complex knowledge is fundamentally explicit in nature underpins the three complete-shift-of-processing explanations of child–adult differences in language acquisition discussed in section 4. The underlying premise of such positions is that, since studies have failed to show a purely implicit learning mode for the processing complex input, the default mode must, therefore, be explicit. For instance, DeKeyser (this volume, p. 321), concludes that "a thorough reading of the literature on implicit learning . . . must leave one very skeptical about the possibility of implicit learning of abstract structure, at least by adults."

In contrast, following a growing consensus among implicit learning researchers (Stadler and Frensch, 1998), the view taken in the present chapter is that, indeed, the default processing mode in SLA, as in other types of complex learning, *is* implicit (Cleeremans and Jimenez, 1998). However, this need not and certainly does not rule out the occasional switch to explicit processing, which, in adult SLA – particularly instructed SLA – appears to be necessary to overcome the disabling influence of primary language learning. As a matter of fact, implicit learning studies have consistently shown evidence of concurrent explicit learning, such that researchers have all but abandoned the notion of a "pure" implicit learning processing mode (and, hence, the requirement that one be demonstrated).[11] In this light, the discussion will now turn to the evidence for implicit learning of complex systems, and to a consideration of the role of explicit processing therein.

5.4.1 Methodological entanglements and a solution

In general terms, the implicit view in cognitive psychology holds that learning of complex knowledge proceeds, in the main, without extensive understanding of the underlying system, either at the moment of learning or afterward (in the sense that the newly learned knowledge cannot be verbalized). Put more simply, people learn about the structure of a complex system without necessarily intending to do so, and in such a way that the resulting knowledge is difficult to express. Although the default implicit view is generally accepted by many cognitive psychologists (Berry, 1997; Berry and Dienes, 1993; Stadler and Frensch, 1998), a number of researchers have argued forcibly against it (e.g., Dulany, Carlson, and Dewey, 1984; Perruchet and Amorim, 1992; Perruchet and Pacteau, 1990; Shanks and St John, 1994). Typical points of contention have included what is noticed in the input at the time of learning, and how that noticed information is encoded into short-term and, ultimately, long-term memory representations. A related question is a methodological one: to what extent do the tests used in implicit learning studies themselves involve learning opportunities? Moreover, if such test effects operate, then is the newly acquired knowledge rendered different from that which resulted only from implicit learning? As we have seen, all of these are crucial considerations for the methodology of future instructed SLA studies as well, in terms of both the design of psycholinguistically appropriate instruction, and valid measurement.

Much of the controversy concerning implicit learning originally stemmed from these methodological entanglements, from the ensuing difficulty of interpreting findings of implicit–explicit learning experiments, and from the expectation that learning of complex systems proceeds *either* implicitly *or* explicitly, that is, the classic dissociation paradigm (Jacoby, 1991). After a fruitless period of research that sought to establish unequivocally that implicit learning occurs and is independent of explicit processing, recent assessments by cognitive psychologists have produced a consensus that (i) implicit and explicit learning occur simultaneously (Stadler and Frensch, 1998);[12] and, consequently, that (ii) implicit and explicit learning can never be disentangled empirically where the evidence for learning gathered is behavioral.[13] Accordingly, it appears reasonable that, in addition to being in the main implicit, SLA necessarily involves more than one mode of processing; that is to say, at times, explicit learning takes place alongside default implicit learning. What is important to determine is when and for what reason explicit learning mechanisms do, or perhaps should be encouraged to, override the default, somewhat disabled implicit processing mode in SLA. Such an understanding ultimately can inform the design of effective enhancements in instructed SLA.

5.4.2 Evidence for implicit learning of complex systems

Since a case for explicit learning has already been made by SLA researchers holding the complete-shift-of-processing view of child–adult differences in SLA (see section 4 and DeKeyser, this volume), we will now evaluate the evidence for the alternative view that instructed SLA processing should be in the main implicit, and only at times explicit. Assuming that implicit learning occurs, and that the nature of encoding at the time of learning is important, it is of great interest to cognitive psychologists to determine how complex learning differs qualitatively in aware (explicit) and unaware (implicit) conditions. To this end, the learning of at least four types of complex information has been investigated: artificial (finite-state) grammars (AGL); repeating patterns, either visual (e.g., lights) or auditory (e.g., tones, music sequences); complex systems (e.g., metropolitan traffic control); and invariant characteristics (e.g., analog and digital clock faces).

Studies of the first two types have often been criticized on the grounds that what is actually learned is not anything complex, but rather a set of bigram or trigram relations that enable successful discrimination at time of testing. Moreover, it is suggested that subjects often can (explicitly) verbalize these relations, even if they cannot state the entirety of the rules underlying the system (Perruchet and Pacteau, 1990; Shanks and St John, 1994). These criticisms are only valid in arguing against the pure implicit learning view of complex knowledge acquisition. More to the point when drawing implications for SLA, AGL experiments have also rightly been criticized as not representative of language systems because they are devoid of meaning (Mathews et al., 1989). To remedy this, Mathews and colleagues (Mathews et al., 2000) have embedded the AG learning task into a game that involves identifying food labels (some of which encode meaning about location and delivery routes of the items), as well as a form of feedback based on parental recasting. Subjects were assigned to either of two conditions: (i) an explicit "spy" condition, where they were told about a plot to poison the public, which they were to uncover via the code labels the spies used to keep themselves informed about the movement of food cans, or (ii) a second implicit condition in which they were instructed to memorize the known poison labels simply in order to identify them whenever they appeared. Findings from a series of experiments indicated overall that the contextualized, complex AG knowledge was acquired better implicitly from exposure to instances than by trying explicitly to induce rules.

When the underlying system involves complex rules, it may be that the time needed for learning (in both implicit and explicit modes) is lengthy, and learners may require some guidance. Decontextualized AGL experiments have also been criticized for not providing ample time, sufficient explicit information (in explicit conditions), or tools to assist in processing the input. In the third of their contextualized AGL experiments, Mathews et al. (2000) gave one group explicit instructions on what types of rules to look for, gave them plenty of time to do so, and allowed them to use pencil and paper ("model builders"). The memory group were given the same ample time and pencil and paper ("memorizers"). Practice on tasks was interspersed with practice-identify or practice-generate tests such that, when subjects reached the criterion on the practice tests, they did the final tests. What is critical to note is that these were optimal conditions for explicit model building.

Findings were analyzed in terms of how well subjects could classify as grammatical or could generate strings. Furthermore, since they were allowed to generate as many strings as they wished, "hit-rate," a sort of efficiency measure (i.e., the percentage of strings generated that were accurate), was calculated.[14] This replicated the standard implicit learning finding: the implicit mode led both to substantial knowledge of the set of grammatical strings and to more efficient generation of good strings. The researchers interpret the findings to mean that explicit model builders, much as they liked the explicit activities (and memorizers did not), relied on implicitly learned instances during tests. Thus, where complex knowledge is learned in context, implicit learning is more successful.

Much recent consideration has been given to what to make of verbalizable (i.e., declarative) knowledge of complex systems. The consistent empirical finding is that verbalizable knowledge of rules underlying complex systems is incomplete or absent. However, the absence of verbalized knowledge cannot be taken as evidence of the absence of explicit learning, and conscious accessibility of fragmentary knowledge does not necessarily constitute evidence *only* of explicit learning (Mathews and Roussel, 1997). This state of affairs prompts the following questions: what comes first, procedural or declarative knowledge? And how are the two related?

Stanley, Matthews, Buss, and Kotler-Cope (1989) investigated the relationship of verbalizations to the entirety of the knowledge that subjects have by examining whether verbalizations given to yoked subjects are sufficient for succeeding at complex tasks. If so, then it could be said that the subjects were able to verbalize the knowledge they had acquired. However, findings show that the hallmark of implicit learning is fragmentary knowledge. Subjects have explicit knowledge of fragments from the input, but, although they have the ability to recombine these fragments in accurate task performance, they cannot verbalize the rules underlying the recombination. After much practice, however, they then can verbalize this information such that others can follow it, indicating that, ultimately, it is possible for subjects to verbalize complex knowledge. These findings point to the conclusion that declarative knowledge is a by-product of practice during implicit learning.

In fact, in a series of studies described in more detail below, Berry and Broadbent (1984) and Stanley et al. (1989) have shown that improvements in performance *always* appear before participants are able to verbalize to any degree of completeness. Also, the declarative knowledge revealed does not appear at the moment of insight (where the performance improves), but much later in the set of trials. Evidence comes from studies of control tasks in which subjects receive input and target levels for variables, and then must interact in or observe a task. Performance improvements are measured, and then subjects are asked to verbalize in different ways. The types of knowledge tapped in these studies are (i) objective knowledge, measured in terms of performance, such as in accuracy of judgment (exemplar vs. string completion vs. patterns), reaction time, prediction, or generation; (ii) accessibility of knowledge in free recall or forced-choice recall (the latter intended to lessen the burden of articulating knowledge or to increase the sensitivity of the measure); and (iii) subjective knowledge operationalized as metaknowledge.

In all the studies, practice has the effect of performance improvement, but not improvement in articulating the basis for making decisions. Moreover, advance verbal instructions about how to do the task have no effect on performance (but do improve ability to answer questions). Finally, only when subjects practice a task in order to explain to someone else how to control it do findings show that extended practice increases verbalizable knowledge. That notwithstanding, performance always improves before subjects can tell someone how to control the task. And, consistently, individual learning curves show sudden improvements not accompanied by increased verbalizable knowledge, that is, insight. Taken together, the findings of control task studies suggest a very limited role, if any, for declarative knowledge in complex learning.

An important recent claim is that information which is processed in the unaware or implicit mode is more sophisticated than that which is processed explicitly (the so-called "smart unconscious") (Bornstein and Masling, 1998). In other words, implicit processing is more powerful than explicit thinking for learning complex systems involving many task variables (Mathews et al., 1989). This, of course, might explain why implicitly learned knowledge is so difficult to articulate. To cite an interesting example, in the case of neurological disorders such as prosopagnosia ("face blindness"), more information is processed in the unaware mode than explicitly. Whereas prosopagnosics can perceive faces and describe their component parts, they claim not to recognize who the people are. However, as shown by the fact that their galvanic skin responses are normal in the unaware mode (i.e., increased for familiar faces), they are able to do both.

To understand in some qualitative sense the nature of the elements in the input to which learners might be attending as they acquire the ability to control variables in complex systems, let us consider an example – city traffic management, that is, controlling the number of passengers using buses and the number of empty car parking spaces available by varying the parking fees and the time interval between buses. The underlying system algorithm is as follows: bus load increases linearly with time interval between buses, and number of parking spaces increases linearly with parking fee. There is also crosstalk between variables such that bus load increases linearly with parking fee, and parking space availability decreases linearly with time interval between buses. Subjects are given starting inputs and told to reach targets for the two variables. Scores on performance increase with practice, but ability to answer questions does not. In fact, verbalization of crosstalk decreases, even though to improve in performance one has to take that information into account (Broadbent, Fitzgerald, and Broadbent, 1986). The only clear interpretation of these findings is that subjects track and learn the relationships among variables implicitly.

With respect to concurrent explicit processing during the acquisition of control of variables in complex systems, Berry and Broadbent (1984) have examined experience, verbal instruction, and concurrent verbalization during sugar production and person interaction tasks (these two tasks involving the same underlying algorithms). In these complex systems, sugar output depended upon number of workers, and the computer–person interaction responses depended upon input of the subjects. As with the traffic control task, practice improved performance but not ability to verbalize, and detailed verbal instructions improved ability to verbalize, but not performance. Practice only helped performance when combined with a requirement to give a reason for each input *during* the task. Likewise, in the city transport system task described above, when a practice session on the individual relationships (e.g., time interval on bus load) was introduced, there was improvement in performance and in verbalization (Broadbent et al., 1986).

Stanley et al. (1989) also asked subjects to practice a complex task, and then explain it to someone else. Subjects in this study could choose their own words, quality of verbal instructions having been criticized in earlier studies. This time, their instructions were somewhat useful for yoked subjects, but still their own performance was better and improved before they were able to develop the explanation. Individual learning curves again showed sudden bursts of improvement that were not accompanied by similar increases in verbalizable knowledge. Finally, in a control task study using a talk-back method, subjects were told to verbalize for someone else, but then those instructions were actually used to develop a computer model (McGeorge and Burton, 1989). The more practice the subjects had, the better the verbalizations succeeded in the modeling.

Thus far, it is evident that, since increases in verbalization ability always appear after performance increases, explicit knowledge develops as a *result* of task experience. Moreover, providing explicit knowledge in advance of task practice is not helpful (even if generated by yoked subjects doing the tasks rather than by researchers), although providing actual task practice with relevant variables is. Thus, it is important to note that learning on the basis of declarative knowledge concerning the intricate relationships among complex system variables is much less efficient than implicit learning during actual task performance.

To explore the latter notion of practice with task variables further, researchers have asked whether making the underlying relationships more salient causes performance and variable knowledge to become associated (Berry and Broadbent, 1988). In a follow-up to the computer–person interaction study, the salient condition revealed the output to subjects immediately, while in the non-salient case, the computer person's output appeared after the next input (recall that output is contingent upon subjects' input). Results were in line with earlier practice studies. Berry and Broadbent then added an explicit instruction to the subjects: "The computer person's responses are determined by your inputs, and it helps to figure out how." Findings suggest that this information helps in the salient condition, but actually is detrimental in the non-salient condition.

To interpret these findings, Berry and Broadbent postulate two modes of processing: an implicit and unselective mode (i.e., store all contingencies), and a selective, explicit one (i.e., when relevant variables are obvious, selectively attend to these). The latter is only efficient if there are a few clear-cut variables, that is to say, if the variables selected are the right ones to which to attend. Otherwise, the non-selective mode is more effective, presumably since cases with many or unrelated variables might lead to attending to the wrong variable (but task experience ameliorates this). Next, because salience was confounded with task difficulty in the earlier studies, another was carried out combining the two modes into one task with salient and non-salient relationships (i.e., a sugar factory control task involving interaction with a union representative). The findings were the same as those of the independent studies (Berry and Broadbent, 1987). Finally, a further experimental modification revealed that watching someone do the salient person interaction task helps, but watching someone do the non-salient one does not (Berry, 1991).

Taken together, the findings on modes of processing during control of complex systems show five things: (i) without extensive or targeted practice, subjects learn to control the variables in the systems successfully, but they cannot articulate the bases for their decisions; (ii) with time and practice, they gain the ability to describe their mental models; (iii) improvement in performance always *precedes* the ability to explain how to control the complex system; (iv) explicit, declarative information is only helpful in improving performance in cases where complex tasks involve few and obvious variables; and (v) implicit practice at the relationships underlying the algorithms is beneficial. In sum, the findings of a pervasive implicit mode of learning, and the limited role of explicit learning in improving performance in complex control tasks, point to a default mode for SLA that is fundamentally implicit, and to the need to avoid declarative knowledge when designing L2 pedagogical procedures.

6 Conclusion

The difficulty for children in primary language acquisition is that they seemingly start from nothing, that is, they must bootstrap their way into language structure. Nonetheless, they are somehow able to rely upon the language which they hear for cues to segmentation. Their processing mechanisms appear to be constrained such that the approach they take is incremental and, consequently, efficient. In contrast, the difficulty for adults is that their special bootstrapping abilities have been altered by this experience. Left to their own devices, adults rely not upon signals in the language in the input, but on their native-language-processing strategies. That this happens is inevitable because developmental sharpening is a prerequisite to native listening ability. That is to say, what they have acquired is the ability to predict, on the basis of a few processible cues in rapid articulation, and in the face of a tremendous variation in the everyday speech of human beings, what the utterance is going to be. Moreover, research has generally shown that developmentally sharpened processing mechanisms are no longer tuned to the details of the input, that is, those "elements of surface structure" that are so critical to language acquisition. However, it is not clear that adult L2 learners are doomed to this fate, since something of their perceptual acuity remains.

What I have argued in this chapter is that the goal of L2 instruction should be to organize the processing space to enable adults to notice the cues *located in the input*, as they did when they were infants first breaking their native language code. A challenge for SLA researchers is to determine how the organization of L2 processing space might be implemented in pedagogical procedures. A guiding principle in this regard is to engage perceptual processes during implicit learning, rather than to promote metalinguistic awareness. Accordingly, "elements of surface structure" should be construed as prosodic packages, at least in the first few passes by the incrementally ordered mechanisms. Another suggestion is that, whereas processing-oriented instructional types, such as those in PI and FonF studies, have tended to target recalcitrant learning problems, organizing the input processing space early on in instructed SLA may help learners to revert sooner from their predictive adult comprehension mode to a more efficient acquisition mode.

A second challenge for researchers is to develop psycholinguistically relevant measures of SLA processing. For instance, if adults are to be guided to process efficiently and incrementally, then it becomes important to be able to measure the attainment of implicationally ordered processing preferences. For example, it appears to be important to develop a prerequisite sensitivity to salient, reliable prosodic cues to word boundaries in lexical acquisition, and to prefer pauses at phrasal and clausal boundaries. Only once these sensitivities have emerged should the processing space be organized such that learners focus attention on difficult-to-decipher input. Within this narrower processing space, learners can utilize less reliable, but nonetheless informative, cues to structure, such as distribution of syllables following weak stress or the position of function words with respect to content words in phrases. This is another instance of the phenomenon of developmental readiness, already discovered in the domain of SLA routes, now uncovered in the SLA processing domain.

Every day, adults, like children, must pay attention to cues in the language they hear. Operating in their L1, they are accustomed to using their acquired knowledge to predict utterance structure during comprehension. Acquiring a second language, however, requires a return to a discovery mode of processing, that is, perceiving clues to L2 structure found in the input. Thus, L2 learners must focus on elements of language. However, since L2 declarative knowledge can never be matched to the exacting needs of processing mechanisms, learners must so focus *themselves*. Nonetheless, L2 instruction, if conceived in SLA processing terms, can assist learners by organizing the processing space, hence perhaps re-enabling mechanisms that depend upon perceptual acuity.

APPENDIX: SPECIFIC MEASURES OF L2 ABILITY TYPICALLY EMPLOYED IN INSTRUCTED SLA

Constructed by the present author consulting (nearly all) the studies cited by Norris and Ortega (2000) and included in their final cohort.

Constrained, constructed responses (CCR)

Written "production":

- Cartoon task: unscramble words to make a sentence about a cartoon
- Cloze tests: missing verbs with infinitives provided below blanks
- Correct sentences

- Correction task: read a question, determine accuracy, reorder
- Fill in blank, given full translation
- Fill in blanks, given the English translation for blank filler and list of verb infinitives and translations
- Fill in blanks, given verb in its infinitive and told to use direct object pronoun
- Fill in the blank, given infinitive and the English translation
- Given a sentence and then expected to produce the dative alternate, if one is possible
- Given a situation, and told what to say in English, enter into a computer an L2 version
- Picture-based fill-in-blank sentence completion
- Picture-based sentence production, with patient given in prompt
- Rewrite sentences from active to passive
- See a picture and type in a sentence about it
- See a picture and type in or complete a sentence of two to three words, six to nine morphemes (reaction times and error rate)
- Sentence completion, verb infinitive provided
- Sentence combination, given two sentences; fill in the blank of new sentence combining two sentences
- Sentence completion, given the base form of a verb to use in the blank and its English translation
- Sentence completion: view pictures and using the second one, complete S, first part of which is the first picture

Oral "production":

- Structured interview with questions providing contexts for contrasting tense/aspect
- Oral picture description task, cued by cards with adverb to be used in sentence
- Shown a slide, and then asked to perform five named speech acts to that person
- Recall of isolated sentences
- Translation

Metalinguistic judgment responses (MJR)

- Judge sentences as correct or incorrect, untimed (accuracy)
- Judge correctness of sentences, timed (accuracy and RTs)
- Judge a sentence as correct or incorrect, giving a reason and circling errors (accuracy)
- Judge sentences as correct or not, timed (RTs) then later untimed with correction

Selected responses (SR)

"Comprehension":

- See four pictures and choose the one that matches the sentence (reaction time and error rate)
- Read or hear a sentence in L2; circle all possible referents from a list of English pronouns

- Read a dialog and select among four choices (by circling) for clitic pronouns
- Interpretation: hear a sentence and choose one of two pictures that matches meaning
- Interpretation: listen to a sentence and circle "past," "present," or "don't know"
- Look at a picture; hear a sentence and circle T/F to indicate match of picture to sentence
- Interpretation: choose one of four, given context, a dialog, and a question concerning implicature

"Production":

- Choose from a list the word to complete a sentence (past, present participials, and bare verbs)
- Circle "a," "an," "the," "0" for each blank in a list of unrelated sentences; same for a cloze paragraph
- Circle "a," "an," "the," "0" for each blank in a cloze paragraph
- Cloze test with missing verbs: circle one of two alternate forms provided under each blank
- Complete S by choosing among verbs and put in preterit, given infinitive and English translation
- Given a context, choose among three utterances which would be the appropriate one

Other:

- Recognize word: yes, no? (RTs)
- Semantic priming: see two words and decide whether the second one is a word (RTs)
- Translation: English–L2 pairs – same or different (RTs and accuracy)
- Word recognition: pairs of words: same or different (RTs)
- Read two sentences; decide whether one, the other, or both are correct (accuracy)

Free responses (FR)

Comprehension:

- Translate an L2 narrative into English

Production:

- Composition about a cartoon strip with prompt "Era diciembre del ano pasado . . ."
- Composition with prompt "Si j'etais . . ."
- Identify 10 differences between a set of pictures
- Interview: free conversation (R interviews S), role play (S interviews R) with prompt to be (more) polite
- Look at four pictures and ask questions until one of the four can be matched to an unseen picture
- Narration: describe video clip which has not been seen by the person who will read the description
- Production: picture description

- See pictures of four people; answer "who is number 1?"; see park scene and answer "Who is number X?"
- Write a narrative on a given topic
- Write a note from Mom to you about not cleaning room vs. note from you to landlord on having a dog

NOTES

1 While a discussion of the technique of meta-analysis is beyond the scope of this chapter, it is important to note that such an approach not only takes into account reported group differences, but also assesses effect size, thus enabling a more trustworthy level of scrutiny.

2 This excellent piece of research, carried out while the authors were doctoral students in the Ph.D. program in SLA at the University of Hawai'i, has won two awards: ACTFL's Pimsleur Award and the TESOL research prize.

3 A number of factors contribute to this bias: (i) that only published studies were included, excluding the so-called fugitive literature (e.g., unpublished doctoral research); (ii) that among the published studies, there were virtually none that reported null findings (suggesting that such manuscripts may not have been accepted for publication); (iii) only English-language journals were consulted, resulting in a research pool of studies of adult, university-level, mostly L2 English acquisition.

4 It is important to make two observations at the outset of the discussion of Norris and Ortega's findings: (i) the meta-analysis is a data-driven procedure, and so any problems with conceptualization of L2 instruction are due, at least in part, to the body of research being examined itself; (ii) their report of the meta-analysis includes far more than can be considered in this synopsis, so readers are urged to consult the original publication.

5 Another term sometimes appears in the effects-of-instruction literature: *form-focused*. Spada (1997), for instance, uses this term to encompass both focus on forms and focus on form. The difficulty with this notion – that is, that all types of attention to form be grouped – is that the psycholinguistically relevant distinction made clear here by Doughty and Williams is lost.

6 This order should not be interpreted as involving statistically significant differences between contiguous combinations. The only real difference was between all explicit and all implicit instructional types.

7 Like any other type of memorized knowledge, L2 knowledge learned in this way would be expected quickly to be forgotten. While not enough studies included delayed post-tests, a few studies have shown that explicitly learned knowledge, indeed, is forgotten, unless the feature is subsequently encountered in the input for a period of time (Lightbown, Spada, and White, 1993; Spada and Lightbown, 1993).

8 For example, L2 learners throughout the world are faced with an enormous amount of non-native input.

9 This impressive body of research includes a wide range of cross-linguistic comparisions. For the sake of simplicity, I will limit the discussion to studies of English, French, and Japanese.

10 A number of other language-specific processing strategies have been identified. English speakers have more difficulty discriminating word-medial vowels than word-medial consonants, even when listening to non-native languages with small inventories of clear vowels. The explanation for this is one of an effect of acquisition: since vowels are unreliable cues in English, the ability to detect them is not developed (Cutler and Otake, 1994). Similar findings for other language-specific strategies include vowel co-occurrence restrictions in Finnish and phonotactic constraints in Dutch, German, and Cantonese (see Cutler, 2001, for details).

11 This view is now held by the pioneer in implicit learning research, Arthur Reber.

12 In addition to the disentanglement offered by starting from the assumptions that implicit learning exists and coexists with explicit learning, a further advance is made by separating implicit learning from implicit memory. Frensch (1998, p. 49) argues persuasively that the following definition of implicit learning – one that is restricted to learning (as opposed to learning and retrieval) – is the scientifically most valid: "The non-intentional, automatic acquisition of knowledge about structural relations between objects or events" (see also Segalowitz, this volume).

13 Advances in cognitive neuroscience may enable separate observation of the two types of learning.

14 Results were as follows: for the explicit model builders with discrimination practice: 83 percent on classification, 45 percent generation, hit rate = 43 percent; and for those model builders with generate practice: 85 percent on classification, 45 percent generation, hit rate = 50 percent. For the memorizers with discrimination practice: 74 percent on classification, 38 percent generation, hit rate = 59 percent; and for those memorizers with generate practice: 90 percent on classification, 64 percent generation, hit rate = 71 percent.

REFERENCES

Allen, P., Swain, M., Harley, B., and Cummins, J. 1990: Aspects of classroom treatment: toward a more comprehensive view of second language education. In B. Harley, P. Allen, J. Cummins, and M. Swain (eds), *The Development of Second Language Proficiency*. New York: Cambridge University Press, 7–25.

Baldwin, D. 1993: Infants' ability to consult the speaker for clues to word reference. *Journal of Child Language*, 202, 395–418.

Berry, D. 1991: The role of attention in explicit learning. *Quarterly Journal of Experimental Psychology*, 43, 881–906.

Berry, D. 1997: *How Implicit is Implicit Learning?* New York: Oxford University Press.

Berry, D. and Broadbent, D. 1984: On the relationship between task performance and associated verbalizable knowledge. *Quarterly Journal of Experimental Psychology*, 36, 209–31.

Berry, D. and Broadbent, D. 1987: The combination of explicit and implicit learning processes. *Psychological Research*, 49, 7–15.

Berry, D. and Broadbent, D. 1988: Interactive tasks and the implicit–explicit distinction. *British Journal of Psychology*, 79, 251–72.

Berry, D. and Dienes, Z. (eds) 1993: *Implicit Learning: Theoretical and Empirical Issues*. Hove: Lawrence Erlbaum Associates.

Best, C. T., Lafleur, R., and McRoberts, G. W. 1995: Divergent developmental patterns for infants' perception of two non-native contrasts. *Infant Behavior and Development*, 18, 339–50.

Best, C. T., McRoberts, G. W., and Sithole, N. M. 1988: Examination of perceptual reorganization for non-native speech contrasts: Zulu click discrimination by English-speaking adults and infants. *Journal of Experimental Psychology: Human Perception and Performance*, 14, 345–60.

Bley-Vroman, R. 1990: The logical problem of foreign language learning. *Linguistic Analysis*, 201–2, 3–49.

Bornstein, R. and Masling, J. 1998: *Empirical Perspectives on the Psychoanalytic Unconscious*. Washington, DC: APA Books.

Broadbent, D., Fitzgerald, P., and Broadbent, M. 1986: Implicit and explicit knowledge in the control of complex systems. *British Journal of Psychology*, 77, 33–50.

Clark, R. (1985). Confounding in educational computing research. *Journal of Educational Computing Research*, 1, 137–48.

Cleeremans, A. and Jimenez, L. 1998: Implicit sequence learning: the truth *is* in the details. In M. Stadler and P. Frensch (eds), *Handbook of Implicit Learning*. Thousand Oaks, CA: Sage, 323–64.

Cutler, A. 1990: Exploiting prosodic probabilities in speech segmentation. In G. Altmann (ed.), *Cognitive Models of Speech Processing: Psycholinguistic and Computational Perspectives*. Cambridge, MA: MIT Press, 105–21.

Cutler, A. 2001: Listening to a second language through the ears of a first. *Interpreting*, 5, 1–18.

Cutler, A. 2002: Native listeners. *European Review*, 10, 27–41.

Cutler, A. and Butterfield, S. 1992: Rhythmic cues to speech segmentation: evidence from juncture misperception. *Journal of Memory and Language*, 31, 218–36.

Cutler, A. and Norris, D. G. 1988: The role of strong syllables in segmentation for lexical access. *Journal of Experimental Psychology: Human Perception and Performance*, 14, 113–21.

Cutler, A. and Otake, T. 1994: Mora or phoneme? Further evidence for language-specific listening. *Journal of Memory and Language*, 33, 824–44.

Cutler, A., Mehler, J., Norris, D. G., and Segui, J. 1986: The syllable's differing role in the segmentation of French and English. *Journal of Memory and Language*, 25, 385–400.

Cutler, A., Mehler, J., Norris, D., and Segui, J. 1989: Limits on bilingualism. *Nature*, 340, 229–30.

Cutler, A., Mehler, J., Norris, D., and Segui, J. 1992: The monolingual nature of speech segmentation by bilinguals. *Cognitive Psychology*, 24, 381–410.

Deák, G. 2000a: The growth of flexible problem-solving: preschool children use changing verbal cues to infer multiple word meaning. *Journal of Cognition and Development*, 1, 157–91.

Deák, G. 2000b: Hunting the fox of word learning: why constraints fail to capture it. *Developmental Review*, 20, 29–79.

DeKeyser, R. 1995: Learning second language grammar rules: an experiment with a miniature linguistic system. *Studies in Second Language Acquisition*, 17, 379–410.

Doughty, C. 1988: Effects of instruction on the acquisition of relativization in English as a Second Language. Ph.D. dissertation. University of Pennsylvania.

Doughty, C. 1991: Second language acquisition does make a difference: evidence from an empirical study of SL relativization. *Studies in Second Language Acquisition*, 13, 431–69.

Doughty, C. 1998: Acquiring competence in a second language: form and function. In H. Byrnes (ed.), *Learning Foreign and Second Languages*. New York: Modern Language Association, 128–56.

Doughty, C. 2001: Cognitive underpinnings of focus on form. In P. Robinson (ed.), *Cognition and Second Language Instruction*. Cambridge: Cambridge University Press, 206–57.

Doughty, C. and Varela, E. 1998: Communicative focus on form. In C. Doughty and J. Williams, (eds), *Focus on Form in Classroom Second Language Acquisition*. Cambridge: Cambridge University Press, 114–38.

Doughty, C. and Williams, J. (eds) 1998a: *Focus on Form in Classroom Second Language Acquisition*. Cambridge: Cambridge University Press.

Doughty, C. and Williams, J. 1998b: Issues and terminology. In C. Doughty and J. Williams (eds), *Focus on Form in Classroom Second Language Acquisition*. Cambridge: Cambridge University Press, 1–11.

Doughty, C. and Williams, J. 1998c: Pedagogical choices in focus on form. In C. Doughty and J. Williams (eds), *Focus on Form in Classroom Second Language Acquisition*. Cambridge: Cambridge University Press, 197–261.

Dulany, D. E., Carlson, R. A., and Dewey, G. I. 1984: A case of syntactical learning and judgment: how conscious and how abstract. *Journal of Experimental Psychology: General*, 113, 541–55.

Eckman, F., Bell, L., and Nelson, D. 1988: On the generalization of relative clause instruction in the acquisition of English as a Second Language. *Applied Linguistics*, 9, 10–20.

Eimas, P. D., Siqueland, E. R., Jusczyk, P. W., and Vigorito, J. 1971: Speech perception in infants. *Science*, 171, 303–6.

Felix, S. 1981: The effect of formal instruction on second language acquisition. *Language Learning*, 311, 87–112.

Felix, S. and Hahn, A. 1985: Natural processes in classroom second-language learning. *Applied Linguistics*, 63, 223–38.

Frensch, P. 1998: One concept, multiple meanings: on how to define the concept of implicit learning. In M. Stadler and P. Frensch (eds), *Handbook of Implicit Learning*. Thousand Oaks, CA: Sage, 47–104.

Gass, S. 1982: From theory to practice. In M. Hines and W. Rutherford (eds), *On TESOL '81*. Washington, DC: TESOL, 120–39.

Gass, S. 1988: Integrating research ideas: a framework for second language studies. *Applied Linguistics*, 9, 198–217.

Hohne, E. A. and Jusczyk, P. W. 1994: Two-month-old infants' sensitivity to allophonic differences. *Perception and Psycholinguistics*, 56, 613–23.

Houston, D., Jusczyk, P. W., and Tager, J. 1998: Talker-specificity and persistence of infants' word representations. In A. Greenhill, M. Hughes, H. Littlefield, and H. Walsh (eds), *Proceedings of the 22nd Annual Boston University Conference on Language Development. Vol. 1*. Brookline, MA: Cascadilla Press, 385–96.

Hulstijn, J. H. 1997: Second language acquisition research in the laboratory: possibilities and limitations. *Studies in*

Second Language Acquisition, 192, 131–43.

Hulstijn, J. 2002: Towards a unified account of the representation, acquisition, and automaticization of second-language knowledge. *Second Language Research*, 18, 193–223.

Jacoby, L. L. 1991: A process dissociation framework: separating automatic from intentional uses of memory. *Journal of Memory and Language*, 30, 513–41.

Jourdenais, R. 1998: The effects of textual enhancement on the acquisition of Spanish preterit and imperfect. Ph.D. dissertation. Georgetown University.

Jourdenais, R. 2001: Cognition, instruction, and protocol analysis. In P. Robinson (ed.), *Cognition and Second Language Instruction*. Cambridge: Cambridge University Press, 354–75.

Jusczyk, P. W. 1993: Pitch and rhythmic patterns affecting infants' sensitivity to musical phrase structure. *Journal of Experimental Psychology*, 193, 627–40.

Jusczyk, P. W. 1997: Finding and remembering words. *Current Directions in Psychological Science*, 6, 170–4.

Jusczyk, P. W. 1998a: Constraining the search for structure in the input. *Lingua*, 106, 197–218.

Jusczyk, P. W. 1998b: Dividing and conquering linguistic input. In M. C. Gruber, D. Higgins, K. S. Olson, and T. Wysocki (eds), *CLS 34. Vol. II: The Panels*. Chicago: University of Chicago, 293–310.

Jusczyk, P. W. 1999a: How infants begin to extract words from speech. *Trends in Cognitive Science*, 3, 323–8.

Jusczyk, P. W. 1999b: Narrowing the distance to language: one step at a time. *Journal of Communication Disorders*, 32, 207–22.

Jusczyk, P. W. 2001: Bootstrapping from the signal: some further directions. In J. Weissenborn and B. Hoehle (eds), *Approaches to Bootstrapping: Phonological, Lexical, Syntactic and Neurophysiological Aspects of Early Language Acquisition*. Amsterdam: John Benjamins, 3–23.

Jusczyk, P. W. and Aslin, R. N. 1995: Infants' detection of sound patterns of words in fluent speech. *Cognitive Psychology*, 291, 1–23.

Jusczyk, P. W. and Hohne, E. A. 1997: Infants' memory for spoken words. *Science*, 277, 1984–6.

Jusczyk, P. W. and Krumhansl, C. L. 1993: Pitch and rhythm patterns affecting infants' sensitivity to musical phrase structure. *Journal of Experimental Psychology: Human Perception and Performance*, 19, 627–40.

Jusczyk, P. W., Cutler, A., and Redanz, N. 1993: Preference for the predominant stress pattern of English words. *Child Development*, 64, 675–87.

Jusczyk, P. W., Goodman, M. B., and Baumann, A. 1999: 9-month-olds' attention to sound similarities in syllables. *Journal of Memory and Language*, 40, 62–82.

Jusczyk, P. W., Hohne, E. A., and Baumann, A. 1999: Infants' sensitivity to allophonic cues for word segmentation. *Perception and Psychophysics*, 61, 1465–76.

Krashen, S. 1982: *Principles and Practice in Second Language Acquisition*. Oxford: Pergamon.

Krashen, S. 1985: *The Input Hypothesis: Issues and Implications*. London: Longman.

Krashen, S. and Scarcella, R. 1978: On routines and patterns in language acquisition performance. *Language Learning*, 28 (2), 283–300.

Lightbown, P. 1983: Exploring relationships between developmental and instructional sequences in L2 acquisition. In H. Seliger and M. Long (eds), *Classroom-Oriented Research in Second Language Acquisition*. Rowley, MA: Newbury House, 217–43.

Lightbown, P. 2000: Classroom SLA research and second language teaching. *Applied Linguistics*, 21 (4), 431–62.

Lightbown, P. M., Spada, N., and White, L. (eds) 1993: The role of instruction in second language acquisition. *Studies in Second Language Acquisition*, 15 (2). Thematic issue.

Lively, S. E., Pisoni, D. B., Yamada, R. A., Tohkura, Y., and Yamada, T. 1994: Greater variety also improves phonetic category learning in foreign speakers. *Journal of the Acoustical Society of America*, 96, 2076–87.

Long, M. H. 1980: Inside the "black box": methodological issues in classroom research on language learning. *Language Learning*, 1, 1–42.

Long, M. H. 1983: Does instruction make a difference? *TESOL Quarterly*, 17, 359–82.

Long, M. H. 1988: Instructed interlanguage development. In L. Beebe (ed.), *Issues in Second Language Acquisition: Multiple Perspectives*. Rowley, MA: Newbury House, 115–41.

Long, M. H. 1991: The design and psycholinguistic motivation of research on foreign language learning. In B. F. Freed (ed.), *Foreign Language Acquisition Research and the Classroom*. Lexington, MA: Heath, 309–20.

Long, M. H. 1993: Second language acquisition as a function of age: research findings and methodological issues. In K. Hyltenstam and Å. Viberg (eds), *Progression and Regression in Language*. Cambridge: Cambridge University Press, 196–221.

Long, M. H. 2000: Focus on form in task-based language teaching. In R. L. Lambert and E. Shohamy (eds), *Language Policy and Pedagogy*. Amsterdam and Philadelphia: John Benjamins, 179–92.

Long, M. H. forthcoming: Recasts: the story thus far. In M. H. Long (ed.), *Problems in SLA*. Mahwah, NJ: Lawrence Erlbaum Associates.

Long, M. H., Inagaki, S., and Ortega, L. 1998: The role of implicit negative feedback in SLA: models and recasts in Japanese and Spanish. *Modern Language Journal*, 82, 357–71.

Long, M. H. and Robinson, P. 1998: Focus on form: theory, research, and practice. In C. Doughty and J. Williams (eds) *Focus on Form in Classroom Second Language Acquisition*. Cambridge: Cambridge University Press, 15–41.

MacWhinney, B. 2001: The Competition Model: the input, the context, and the brain. In P. Robinson (ed.), *Cognition and Second Language Instruction*. Cambridge: Cambridge University Press, 69–90.

Markman, E. M. 1989: *Categorization and Naming in Children: Problems of Induction*. Cambridge, MA: MIT Press.

Markman, E. M. 1994: Constraints on word meaning in early language acquisition. In L. Gleitman and B. Landau (eds), *The Acquisition of the Lexicon*. Cambridge, MA: MIT Press, 199–227.

Mathews, R. C. and Roussel, L. G. 1997: Abstractness of implicit knowledge: a cognitive evolutionary perspective. In D. Berry (ed.), *How Implicit is Implicit Learning?* Oxford: Oxford University Press, 13–47.

Mathews, R. C., Roussel, L. G., Cochran, B. P., Cook, A. E., and Dunaway, D. L. 2000: The role of implicit learning in the acquisition of generative knowledge. *Cognitive Systems Research*, 1, 161–174.

Mathews, R. C., Buss, R. R., Stanley, W. B., Blanchard-Fields, F., Cho, J. R., and Druhan, B. 1989: The role of implicit and explicit processes in learning from examples: a synergistic effect. *Journal of Experimental Psychology: Learning, Memory, and Cognition*, 15, 1083–100.

McGeorge, P. and Burton, M. 1989: The effects of concurrent verbalization on performance in a dynamic systems task. *British Journal of Psychology*, 80, 455–65.

Mehler, J., Dommergues, J. Y., Frauenfelder, U., and Segui, J. 1981: The syllable's role in speech segmentation. *Journal of Verbal Learning and Verbal Behavior*, 20, 298–305.

Morales, M., Mundy, P., Fullmer, C., Yale, M., Messinger, D., Neal, R., and Schwartz, H. forthcoming: Responding to joint attention across the 6- to 24-month age period and early language acquisition. *Journal of Applied Developmental Psychology*, 21 (3), 283–98.

Nazzi, T., Bertoncini, J., and Mehler, J. 1998: Language discrimination by newborns: towards an understanding of the role of rhythm. *Journal of Experimental Psychology: Human Perception and Performance*, 25, 755–66.

Nazzi, T., Jusczyk, P. W., and Johnson, E. K. 2000: Language discrimination by English-learning 5-month-olds: effects of rhythm and familiarity. *Journal of Memory and Language*, 43, 1–19.

Nazzi, T., Kemler Nelson, D. G., Jusczyk, P. W., and Jusczyk, A. M. 2000: Six-month-olds' detection of clauses embedded in continuous speech: effects of prosodic well-formedness. *Infancy*, 1, 123–47.

Newsome, M. and Jusczyk, P. W. 1995: Do infants use stress as a cue for segmenting fluent speech? In D. MacLaughlin and S. MacEwen (eds), *Proceedings of the 19th Annual Boston University Conference on Language Development. Vol. 2*. Somerville, MA: Cascadilla Press, 415–26.

Norris, J. and Ortega, L. 2000: Effectiveness of L2 instruction: a research synthesis and quantitative meta-analysis. *Language Learning*, 50 (3), 417–528.

Otake, T., Hatano, G., and Yoneyama, K. 1996: Speech segmentation by Japanese listeners. In T. Otake and A. Cutler (eds), *Phonological Structure and Language Processing: Cross-Linguistic Studies*. Berlin: Mouton de Gruyter, 183–201.

Otake, T., Hatano, G., Cutler, A., and Mehler, J. 1993: Mora or syllable? Speech segmentation in Japanese. *Journal of Memory and Language*, 32, 258–78.

Pavesi, M. 1986: Markedness, discoursal modes, and relative clause formation in a formal and an informal context. *Studies in Second Language Acquisition*, 81, 38–55.

Perruchet, P. and Amorim, M. A. 1992: Conscious knowledge and changes in performance in sequence learning: evidence against dissociation. *Journal of Experimental Psychology: Learning, Memory, and Cognition*, 18, 785–800.

Perruchet, P. and Pacteau, C. 1990: Synthetic grammar learning: implicit rule abstraction or explicit fragmentary knowledge. *Journal of Experimental Psychology: General*, 19, 264–75.

Pica, T. 1983: Adult acquisition of English as a second language under different conditions of exposure. *Language Learning*, 33, 465–97.

Pienemann, M. 1989: Is language teachable? Psycholinguistic experiments and hypotheses. *Applied Linguistics*, 10, 52–79.

Richards, J. and Rodgers, T. 1986: *Approaches and Methods in Language Teaching*. Cambridge: Cambridge University Press.

Robinson, P. (ed.) 2002: *Individual Differences and Instructed Language Learning*. Amsterdam: John Benjamins.

Saffran, J. R., Newport, E. L., and Aslin, R. N. 1996: Word segmentation: the role of distributional cues. *Journal of Memory and Language*, 35, 606–21.

Santelmann, L. and Jusczyk, P. 1997: What discontinuous dependencies reveal about the size of the learner's processing window. In E. Hughes,

M. Hughes, and A. Greenhill (eds), *Proceedings of the 21st Annual Boston University Conference on Language Development*. Somerville, MA: Cascadilla Press, 506–14.

Santelmann, L. and Jusczyk, P. 1998: 18-month-olds' sensitivity to relationships between morphemes. In E. Hughes, M. Hughes, and A. Greenhill (eds), *Proceedings of the 22nd Annual Boston University Conference on Language Development*. Somerville, MA: Cascadilla Press, 663–74.

Sanz, C. and Morgan-Short, K. 2002: Effects of different amounts of explicit instruction before and during input-based practice: a computer-based study. Paper presented at the Form–Meaning Connections in SLA conference. Chicago, February 23rd.

Schwartz, B. 1993: On explicit and negative data effecting and affecting competence and linguistic behavior. *Studies in Second Language Acquisition*, 15, 147–64.

Schwartz, B. and Sprouse, R. 1996: L2 cognitives states and the Full Transfer/Full Access Model. *Second Language Research*, 121, 40–72.

Schmidt, R. 1990: The role of consciousness in second language learning. *Applied Linguistics*, 112, 17–46.

Schmidt, R. 1992: Psychological mechanisms underlying second language fluency. *Studies in Second Language Acquisition*, 14, 357–85.

Schmidt, R. 1993: Awareness and second language acquisition. *Annual Review of Applied Linguistics*, 13, 206–26.

Schmidt, R. 1995: Consciousness and foreign language learning: a tutorial on the role of attention and awareness in learning. In R. Schmidt (ed.), *Attention and Awareness in Foreign Language Learning*. Honolulu: University of Hawai'i Press, 1–63.

Schmidt, R. W. 1998: The centrality of attention in SLA. *University of Hawai'i Working Papers in ESL*, 16 (2), 1–34.

Schmidt, R. W. 2001: Attention. In P. Robinson (ed.), *Cognition and Second Language Instruction*. Cambridge: Cambridge University Press, 3–32.

Shady, M. 1996: Infants' sensitivity to function morphemes. Ph.D. dissertation. SUNY, Buffalo.

Shanks, D. R. and St John, M. F. 1994: Characteristics of dissociable human learning systems. *Behavioral and Brain Sciences*, 17, 367–447.

Smith, P. 1970: *A Comparison of the Audio-Lingual and Cognitive Approaches to Foreign Language Instruction: The Pennsylvania Foreign Language Project*. Philadelphia: Center for Curriculum Development.

Spada, N. 1997: Form-focussed instruction and second language acquisition: a review of classroom and laboratory research. State of the Art article. *Language Teaching*, 30, 73–87.

Spada, N. and Lightbown, P. M. 1993: Instruction and the development of questions in L2 classrooms. *Studies in Second Language Acquisition*, 15, 205–24.

Stadler, M. and Frensch, P. (eds) 1998: *Handbook of Implicit Learning*. Thousand Oaks, CA: Sage.

Stanley, W., Matthews, R., Buss, R., and Kotler-Cope, S. 1989: Insight without awareness: on the interaction of verbalization, instruction, and practice in a process control task. *Quarterly Journal of Experimental Psychology*, 41, 553–77.

Swain, M. and Lapkin, S. 1982: *Evaluating Bilingual Education: A Canadian Case Study*. Clevedon: Multilingual Matters.

Tomasello, M. 1995: Theory or data? A response to Deuchar. *First Language*, 14, 110–30.

Tomasello, M. and Barton, M. 1994: Learning words in nonostensive contexts. *Developmental Psychology*, 30 (5), 305–14.

Tomasello, M. and Kruger, A. 1992: Joint attention on action verbs: acquiring verbs in ostensive and non-ostensive contexts. *Journal of Child Language*, 19, 311–33.

Tomasello, M. and Todd, J. 1983: Joint attention and lexical acquisition style. *First Language*, 4, 197–212.

Tomlin, R. and Villa, V. 1994: Attention in cognitive science and second language acquisition. *Studies in Second Language Acquisition*, 16, 183–203.

VanPatten, B. 1996: *Input Processing and Grammar Instruction*. Norwood, NJ: Ablex.

VanPatten, B. 2002: Processing instruction: an update. *Language Learning*, 52, 755–803.

VanPatten, B. and Oikkenon, S. 1996: Explanation versus structured input in processing instruction. *Studies in Second Language Acquisition*, 18, 495–510.

Van de Weijer, J. 1999: Language input for word discovery. Ph.D. thesis. University of Nijmegen.

van Zon, M. D. C. M. 1997: Speech processing in Dutch: a cross-linguistic approach. Ph.D. thesis. Tilburg University.

Weber, A. 2000: The role of phonotactics in the segmentation of native and non-native continuous speech. In A. Cutler and J. M. McQueen (eds), *Proceedings of the Workshop on Spoken Word Access Processes*. Nijmegen: MPI, 143–6.

Weissenborn, J. and Höhle, B. (eds) 2001: *Approaches to Bootstrapping: Phonological, Lexical, Syntactic and Neurophysiological Aspects of Early Language Acquisition*. Amsterdam: John Benjamins.

Werker, J. F. and Tees, R. C. 1984: Cross-language speech perception: evidence for perceptual reorganization during the first year of life. *Infant Behavior and Development*, 7, 49–63.

White, L. 1987: Against comprehensible input: the Input Hypothesis and the development of second-language competence. *Applied Linguistics*, 82, 95–110.

White, L. 1991: Adverb placement in second language acquisition: some effects of positive and negative evidence. *Second Language Research*, 7 (2), 133–61.

White, L., Spada, N., Lightbown, P. M., and Ranta, L. 1991: Input enhancement and L2 question formation. *Applied Linguistics*, 124, 416–32.

Zobl, H. 1982: A direction for contrastive analysis: the comparative study of developmental sequences. *TESOL Quarterly*, 16, 169–83.

IV Processes in SLA

11 Implicit and Explicit Learning

ROBERT DEKEYSER

1 Introduction

From both a practical and a theoretical point of view it is important to understand the difference between implicit and explicit learning mechanisms and the role they play in second language learning. One of the most frequently asked questions in language teaching circles is whether grammar should be taught explicitly, and one of the central issues in the psycholinguistics of second language acquisition is whether adults can learn a language fully through the same implicit learning mechanisms used by the child in learning a first language. The implicit/explicit dichotomy, however, is hard to define, and has often been confused with various other dichotomies. Therefore, this chapter will devote substantial attention to how implicit and explicit learning have been defined and studied in cognitive psychology, and to what the second language field can learn from this discipline, before reviewing the SLA literature on implicit and explicit learning itself, and discussing the differential role of the two learning mechanisms for different aspects of grammar and for learners of different ages.

2 The Cognitive Psychology of Implicit and Explicit Learning

2.1 *Definitions*

The definition of implicit learning has something in common with the well-known problem of defining intelligence. Just as intelligence researchers first developed a number of predictive tests, and only later started worrying about the psychological mechanisms that determine performance on such tests, the literature on implicit learning reflects an early focus on certain tasks, and subsequent attempts at analyzing the learning, storage, and retrieval mechanisms that explain this performance, and at defining their fundamental nature.

For Arthur Reber, the pioneer of implicit learning research, the central issue was lack of consciousness of the structure being learned. He defined implicit learning as "a primitive process of apprehending structure by attending to frequency cues" as opposed to "a more explicit process whereby various mnemonics, heuristics, and strategies are engaged to induce a representational system" (1976, p. 93). Hayes and Broadbent are slightly more precise in stating that implicit learning is "the unselective and passive aggregation of information about the co-occurrence of environmental events and features" (1988, p. 251).

Because of the difficulty of defining consciousness or awareness (see section 2.5), however, a number of alternative suggestions have been made, mainly involving intentionality and automaticity (for an overview, see Frensch, 1998). In my view, however, both of these concepts are clearly distinct from what is involved in implicit learning. Subjects in experiments on implicit learning usually have the intention of learning something, even though they may learn something different from what they intended to learn (something more abstract than the surface structure of the stimuli they try to memorize). Automaticity is really the result of a learning process, not a characteristic of the learning process itself, and is hard to define. (For recent overviews of automaticity, see Anderson and Lebiere, 1998; DeKeyser, 2001; Segalowitz, this volume. For more discussion of incidental learning, see Hulstijn, this volume.) Given that replacing awareness by intentionality or automaticity does not resolve the conceptual problems, and given that awareness is the defining feature used in the second language literature on implicit and explicit learning, implicit learning will be defined here as learning without awareness of what is being learned.

It is important, furthermore, to distinguish implicit learning from two concepts it is often confused with in the second language literature: inductive learning and implicit memory. Inductive learning (going from the particular to the general, from examples to rules) and implicit learning (learning without awareness) are two orthogonal concepts (see figure 11.1). Via traditional rule teaching, learning is both deductive and explicit. When students are encouraged to find rules for themselves by studying examples in a text, learning is inductive and explicit. When children acquire linguistic competence of their native language without thinking about its structure, their learning is inductive and implicit. The combination of deductive and implicit is less obvious, but the concept of parameter setting in Universal Grammar could be seen as

	Deductive	Inductive
Explicit	Traditional teaching	Rule discovery
Implicit	Using parameters	Learning L1 from input

Figure 11.1 The inductive/deductive and implicit/explicit dimensions

an example; supposedly learners derive a number of characteristics of the language being learned from the setting of the parameter, and this clearly happens without awareness.

In the same vein, implicit memory and implicit learning are in principle independent concepts. Even though implicitly acquired knowledge tends to remain implicit, and explicitly acquired knowledge tends to remain explicit, explicitly learned knowledge can become implicit in the sense that learners can lose awareness of its structure over time, and learners can become aware of the structure of implicit knowledge when attempting to access it, for example for applying it to a new context or for conveying it verbally to somebody else. In Reber's own experiments with artificial grammars, instructions encourage explicit retrieval, which may lead to making knowledge itself more explicit (cf. Buchner and Wippich, 1998).

2.2 *Basic findings*

Empirical research on implicit learning falls largely into three categories: artificial grammars, sequence learning, and control of complex systems. In each of these areas a considerable number of studies have shown that subjects can learn to use complex knowledge to perform on a variety of tasks without being aware of the exact nature of that knowledge (for a concise and readable overview, see, e.g., Cleeremans, Destrebecqz, and Boyer, 1998).

The oldest paradigm, and the one that continues to generate the most research to this day, is artificial grammar learning (AGL). The first such experiment by Reber (1967) did not draw much attention, but subsequent experiments (e.g., Reber 1976; Reber, Kassin, Lewis, and Cantor, 1980) and the controversy they generated (see, e.g., Dulany, Carlson, and Dewey, 1984; Reber, Allen, and Regan, 1985) led to a small industry of artificial grammar studies of ever increasing complexity and sophistication (e.g., Altmann, Dienes, and Goode, 1995; Buchner, 1994; Dienes, Broadbent, and Berry, 1991; Gomez, 1997; Gomez and Schvaneveldt, 1994; Knowlton and Squire, 1994, 1996; Meulemans and Van der Linden, 1997; Pothos and Bailey, 2000; Redington and Chater, 1996; Servan-Schreiber and Anderson, 1990; Shanks, Johnstone, and Staggs, 1997). Experiments in this paradigm expose learners to a set of letter strings (or equivalent series of symbols) generated by a set of rules in the form of a Markovian finite-state grammar. Subjects never get to see the rules, and are generally not aware of the rules after being exposed to a set of exemplar strings; yet they perform above chance when they are unexpectedly asked to classify new strings into those that conform to the structure of the exemplars and those that do not.

The sequence learning paradigm has also been quite productive. Since the early studies by Nissen and Bullemer (1987) and Lewicki, Czyzewska, and Hoffman (1987), a number of other experiments have confirmed that subjects exposed to a sequence of light flashes appearing in various locations or to long symbol strings with recurrent patterns become sufficiently sensitive to these patterns to be able to predict future sequences, again without being aware of the underlying patterns (e.g., Cleeremans and Jiménez, 1998; Cleeremans and McClelland, 1991; Cohen, Ivry, and Keele, 1990; Curran and Keele, 1993; Jiménez and Méndez, 1999).

In the third paradigm, control of complex systems, subjects learn to interact with a computer to control an output variable by manipulating input variables (e.g., Berry and Broadbent, 1984; Dienes and Fahey, 1995). For instance, they learn to keep production of a simulated sugar factory within bounds by manipulating variables such as amount of raw material processed. Again, they manage to do this without being aware of the complex formula the computer uses to relate input variables to output.

In all of these experimental paradigms, subjects learn to use complex knowledge without being aware of its underlying structure. Central to the ongoing debate about the nature of implicit learning, however, is Reber's (1976, 1989, 1993) claim that subjects learn abstract knowledge implicitly. Some researchers have claimed that the learning in such experiments is both explicit and concrete (e.g., Dulany et al., 1984; St John and Shanks, 1997); others have denied only the abstractness of the knowledge (e.g., Pothos and Bailey, 2000; Redington and Chater, 1996), the implicitness of the learning (e.g., Shanks and St John, 1994; Jiménez and Méndez, 1999), or the possibility of having both at the same time (e.g., Gomez, 1997; Perruchet and Pacteau, 1990, 1991). Let us now turn to a more detailed discussion of these issues.

2.3 *The implicitness issue*

Among the first to challenge Reber's claims of implicit learning of abstract rules were Dulany et al. (1984). These researchers actually quoted Reber and Allen (1978) to show that subjects in AGL experiments were aware of some knowledge: during retrospection these subjects mentioned "first and last letters, bigrams, the occasional trigram, and recursions" (1978, p. 202) as important in their decision-making. What allows subjects to make grammaticality judgments, Dulany et al. argued, was "conscious rules within informal grammars rather than . . . unconscious representations of a formal grammar" (1984, p. 541). In other words, subjects had not induced the finite-state grammar underlying the strings in Reber's experiments, but had explicitly remembered fragments of strings, which gave them enough information to perform reasonably well on the grammaticality judgment test. More importantly, these authors showed with data from their own experiment that subjects' judgments could be accounted for by their reported rules without significant residual. Several other studies have presented similar results (e.g., Perruchet and Pacteau, 1990, 1991; St John and Shanks, 1997).

An important piece of evidence in favor of the implicit interpretation of AGL comes from work with amnesic patients (e.g., Knowlton and Squire, 1994, 1996). As these patients' explicit memory is severely impaired, and as they still manage to perform as well as normals, implicit memory must be involved. This does not mean, however, that the learning itself was implicit; implicit memory does not necessarily imply implicit knowledge. Moreover, as several researchers have argued (e.g., Gomez, 1997; Redington and Chater, 1996), the fact that there were no control subjects in these studies leaves open the possibility that some learning takes place during the test. Finally, even amnesic patients may be able to remember explicitly some of the most salient features of the learning strings, such as initial trigrams (Gomez, 1997).

A different experimental approach was taken by Cleeremans and Jiménez (1998) and Jiménez and Méndez (1999). These researchers used a dual-task condition to show how diminished attention affects sequence learning. Cleeremans and Jiménez (1998) found the dual-task condition to be harmful for deterministic sequences only, not probabilistic ones. Jiménez and Méndez (1999) focused further on probabilistic sequences and found that, while division of attention barely affected learning, selective attention to the predictive dimensions was necessary to learn about the relation between these dimensions and the predicted one. Neither of these two studies, however, has anything precise to say about awareness.

We must conclude then, that there is very little hard evidence of learning without awareness, and agree with Carlson that "many if not most of the empirical demonstrations of supposedly unconscious phenomena are methodologically or theoretically flawed. Few stand up to serious attempts to replicate or to more carefully assess the contents of subjects' awareness and their relation to observed performance" (1997, p. 290).

2.4 *The abstractness issue*

Just as several studies have attempted to provide evidence to counter Dulany et al.'s (1984) claim that conscious knowledge can account completely for subjects' performance in AGL experiments, several researchers have tried to present evidence against their claim that subjects only learn concrete fragments and not abstract rules. This evidence is mainly of two kinds: separate manipulation and analysis of grammaticality and similarity, and transfer of learning to changed letter sets.

Beginning with Vokey and Brooks (1992), a number of studies have attempted to disentangle the effects of grammaticality (sensitivity to underlying structure) and mere surface similarity to training strings. Meulemans and Van der Linden (1997), for example, claimed to show that when subjects have seen few example strings, they are more sensitive to similarity. When they have seen most of the grammatical strings possible, the only effect observed is that of grammaticality. In principle grammaticality and similarity can be operationalized independently, because strings that are superficially similar can violate a structural rule, whereas strings that are very different from the ones seen previously can still follow that rule. It is very hard to avoid confounding the two variables, however. Johnstone and Shanks (1999) showed that information about grammatical rules and chunk locations was confounded in Meulemans and Van der Linden's (1997) study, and that all of their data could be explained by knowledge about the positional constraints on specific chunks. Finally, in one of the most sophisticated studies to date, drawing on Nosofsky's (1989) generalized context model (a similarity-based model of categorization), Pothos and Bailey (2000) did not find grammaticality to be an important predictor of string categorization in comparison with chunk strength and especially similarity. It appears doubtful, then, that grammaticality judgments in AGL experiments really reflect sensitivity to grammaticality instead of mere familiarity with surface characteristics.

The issue of transfer to changed letter sets has been called "the Granada of unconscious rule learning . . . the last remaining argument that implicit grammar learning produces abstract, rule-like knowledge that cannot be reported" (St John and Shanks, 1997, p. 189). If subjects can do well on grammaticality judgment tests for strings that use different letters but have the same underlying grammatical structure as the learning strings, then, the standard reasoning goes, they must have learned that underlying abstract structure rather than memorized concrete string fragments. A number of studies have indeed reported such findings (e.g., Brooks and Vokey, 1991; Gomez and Schvaneveldt, 1994; Knowlton and Squire, 1996; Mathews et al., 1989; Whittlesea and Dorken, 1993); some have even reported transfer across visual/auditory modalities (Altmann, Dienes, and Goode, 1995; Manza and Reber, 1997).

It is doubtful, however, that such transfer necessarily implies abstract learning. Redington and Chater (1996) argued strongly that such transfer phenomena are compatible with the hypothesis that subjects learn fragments (bigrams and/or trigrams) during the training phase of the experiment, and only abstract across the fragments at test time. They showed that a variety of models that include only fragment knowledge can equal or even exceed the performance by human subjects found in a variety of transfer experiments reported in the literature. Furthermore, they argued, control subjects without training have been observed to perform at the same above-chance levels as experimental subjects, which suggests that the performance of the latter too can be explained entirely by learning at test, and is not necessarily due to anything learned during training, let alone abstract knowledge.

Yet another problem for the abstractness account is the lack of a complexity effect under implicit learning conditions, as documented in various experiments described in Reed and Johnson (1998). They define complexity as the number of discrete elements that need to be taken into account in sequence learning experiments or other target location prediction tasks, and show that rules of different complexity show dramatically different learning rates under explicit but not implicit learning conditions. This absence of a complexity effect in the implicit condition, they argue, can be interpreted as showing that implicit learning results in less abstract representations, so that complexity is not an issue.

Finally, a question related to the abstractness issue is that of contiguity. Cleeremans and McClelland (1991), in an experiment on sequence learning, and Mathews et al. (1989) as well as St John and Shanks (1997), in AGL tasks, showed that implicit learning is severely hampered when the learning task requires establishing a relationship between elements that are at some distance, separated by several other elements.

In conclusion, then, it seems that implicit learning is at its best when only concrete and contiguous elements are involved. Neither the experimental disentangling of similarity and grammaticality nor the transfer phenomena documented in the AGL literature have provided convincing evidence that anything abstract is learned implicitly.

2.5 *Methodological problems*

The empirical studies listed in the previous sections already illustrate some of the methodological issues in the field of implicit learning. The crux of the issue is finding measures of implicit and explicit learning that are both pure and sensitive, so that they show exactly how much is learned through either process, nothing more and nothing less. This issue is all the more important as the amount of learning taking place in most experiments, even though statistically significant, is not very large. Typically subjects score 55–70 percent, where 50 percent reflects mere chance, given that most tests take the form of a simple yes/no grammaticality judgment. With such small amounts of learning, the slightest imperfection in the measures of what has been learned can have a big impact on the results. It is important then, that tests of implicit and explicit learning be equally sensitive, and that they probe the kind of knowledge that underlies performance. Shanks and St John (1994) refer to these two requirements as the sensitivity criterion and the information criterion, and they argue that tests of implicit learning tend to be more sensitive than tests of explicit learning (which often rely on verbalization).

As it is virtually impossible to design tests of implicit and explicit learning that are exactly equally sensitive, especially to find tests that measure explicit knowledge exhaustively, Reingold and Merikle (1988) have proposed a different solution to the measurement problem. If the explicit measure is at least as sensitive to conscious knowledge as the implicit measure, and the implicit measure shows more knowledge than the explicit measure, then this implies the existence of processing without awareness. There have been few attempts, though, to use this logic to demonstrate implicit learning (cf. Stadler and Roediger, 1998). The process-dissociation procedure proposed by Jacoby (1991) has been more influential (cf. Buchner and Wippich, 1998). It is a tool to estimate the separate contributions of the two types of processes to a single task, but has been questioned because of problems with differential response bias in explicit and implicit memory tests (Buchner, Erdfelder, and Vaterrodt-Plünnecke, 1995).

Furthermore, testing needs to be conducted at the right time; otherwise, if knowledge seems to be implicit, it can be claimed that learning was explicit but that explicit knowledge was lost in the meantime. Unfortunately, however, no clear criterion exists for deciding on an appropriate testing time (cf. Reed and Johnson, 1998).

Finally, while speeded tests undoubtedly are more problematic for the retrieval of explicit than implicit knowledge (e.g., Turner and Fischler, 1993), time pressure does not guarantee a pure measure of implicit knowledge. Conversely, any experiment of short duration is inherently biased against implicit learning, as the accumulation of instances in memory takes much more time than the short cut provided by explicit insight.

In conclusion, then, no perfect tests or procedures exist for distinguishing the results of implicit and explicit learning. At this point researchers have to content themselves with eliciting knowledge under conditions that are more or less conducive to the retrieval of implicit and explicit knowledge, and then infer to what extent the learning itself may have been implicit or explicit. Therefore, it seems prudent to follow Stadler and Roediger's advice to "focus on the differential effects of implicit and explicit orientations on learning, rather than on attempts to demonstrate that learning is implicit in some absolute sense" (1998, p. 107).

2.6 *Conclusion: implicit induction of abstract structure?*

How much can be learned implicitly? AGL experiments typically show a very limited amount of learning: 55–70 percent correct judgments on a grammaticality judgment post-test, where chance performance would be 50 percent. It is doubtful, however, that even this amount of knowledge is completely implicit (lack of verbalization is not a sufficient argument), let alone that it was acquired completely implicitly (as noted above, explicit memory resulting from explicit learning can be lost between learning and testing – especially in the case of amnesics).

Even if one believes that some knowledge is acquired, stored, and used implicitly, it is doubtful that this knowledge is ever really abstract in nature (even experiments with transfer to different symbols or modalities do not constitute conclusive proof). Perruchet and Pacteau (1990) argued that knowledge could be abstract or could be learned implicitly, but not both. Similarly, Gomez (1997) showed that "simple" knowledge (of first-order dependencies) could be learned implicitly, but not more complex knowledge (involved in learning second-order dependencies or in transfer to stimuli with the same underlying syntax but new surface features); and Shanks, Johnstone, and Staggs (1997) claimed to show implicit learning in some of their experiments and abstract learning in others, but admitted they had not done both in the same experiment. Their experiments 1 and 2 used the flawed transfer argument to show abstraction; their experiment 3 did not disentangle grammaticality from similarity (as they acknowledge); and most importantly, their experiment 4 showed that, when the rules (of a biconditional grammar) precluded learning by similarity, the implicit learners not only learned less than the explicit learners, but actually scored at the chance level.

A thorough reading of the literature on implicit learning, then, must leave one very skeptical about the possibility of implicit learning of abstract structure, at least by adults.

3 Implicit and Explicit Second Language Learning

Several recent literature reviews provide an overview concerning the role of a number of related concepts such as consciousness, awareness, attention, noticing, and focus on form in second language learning (see especially Doughty and Williams, 1998; Long and Robinson, 1998; Norris and Ortega, 2000; Spada, 1997). As these literature reviews show, a considerable amount of work suggests there is a positive role for some kind of attention to form, that is, either through the explicit teaching of grammar and explicit error correction, or at least through more indirect means such as input enhancement. These literature reviews also make it clear, however, that relatively few studies have consisted of a direct comparison of implicit and explicit learning, everything else being the same. The appendix to Norris and Ortega (2000), for example, lists 14 direct comparisons of implicit and explicit instruction or error correction (out of 77 studies reviewed). This classification was based on the definition of DeKeyser (1995) that an instructional treatment is explicit if rule explanation forms part of the instruction (deduction) or if learners are asked to attend to particular forms and try to find the rules themselves (induction). "Conversely, when neither rule presentation nor directions to attend to particular forms were part of a treatment, that treatment was considered implicit" (Norris and Ortega, 2000, p. 437).

Sections 3.1 and 3.2 will be limited to the SLA literature on implicit/explicit learning in this narrow sense of direct controlled comparisons between the two (comparisons with a no-treatment group are excluded). For broader issues concerning the role of attention or focus on form, see the aforementioned references as well as Robinson (this volume). First laboratory studies will be reviewed, and then classroom studies will be discussed. The following two sections will provide different kinds of evidence. Section 3.3 deals with the use of implicit and explicit knowledge after a substantial amount of learning has taken place, and section 3.4 examines connectionist models of SLA.

3.1 Laboratory studies

A small number of studies have compared implicit and explicit learning of new L2 material in a laboratory context (studies of error correction are not reviewed here). Some of these studies dealt with learners who simply volunteered for an experiment involving a language they had no contact with otherwise (Alanen, 1995; de Graaff, 1997; DeKeyser, 1995; N. Ellis, 1993); others dealt with learners who were studying the language in question in the classroom, but who were given a special experimental treatment on some point they had not covered before (Doughty, 1991; Leow, 1998; Robinson, 1996, 1997).

One of the earliest focused laboratory studies is N. Ellis (1993), an experiment involving the "soft mutation" of initial consonants in Welsh. Ellis compared three groups of learners. The random group received exposure to numerous examples of consonant alternations in random order. The grammar group received explicit explanation of the rules in question, followed by the same randomized examples. The structured group received explicit rule explanation, followed by two examples after each rule, and then the same random presentation of examples as the other two groups. While the random group was found to be the fastest in learning to judge the well-formedness of sentences seen before, it was also the slowest in generalizing its knowledge to judge new sentences. The grammar group showed solid explicit knowledge of the rules, but little ability to apply them to well-formedness judgments. Only the structured group did well on both tests of explicit rule knowledge and grammaticality judgments. Clearly the most explicit treatment, the only one that made learners aware of how rules apply to examples, outperformed the other two. Similar results were found by Michas and Berry (1994), in an experiment involving the pronunciation of Greek words by native speakers of English. One experiment showed the advantage of explicit rule presentation over word/pronunciation pairings; a second experiment showed that explicit presentation of the rules was useful only if followed by practice.[1]

Alanen (1995) used locative suffixes and a rule of "consonant gradation" in semi-artificial Finnish as the learning target. Four groups were involved in the experiment: mere exposure, input enhancement, rule presentation, and both rule presentation and input enhancement. The groups with rules did better than the other two on subsequent production tests, but the input enhancement group did not outperform the control (mere exposure) group. There was a qualitative difference between the latter two, however: the control group omitted more suffixes, while the input enhancement groups supplied more erroneous ones. It should be noted that rule presentation included examples in this study, so that both the rule presentation and rule presentation with input enhancement groups are comparable to Ellis's structured condition. The results then, are very comparable: in both studies the groups with the most explicit treatments (rules + examples) did best.

DeKeyser (1995) looked at the interaction between two treatment conditions (implicit, defined as mere exposure to numerous sentence/picture pairs, and explicit, defined as similar exposure along with explicit explanation of the relevant rules) and two types of rules (categorical rules, i.e., straightforward morphological form/function mappings, and prototypical rules, i.e., probabilistically applying rules of allomorphy) in a computerized experiment with an artificial language called Implexan. While there appeared to be a slight advantage for the implicit group with regard to the prototypicality patterns, the explicit group strongly outperformed the implicit group on the categorical rules. In fact, even after exposure to thousands of relevant examples, the performance of the implicit group was essentially random.

Advantages for explicit learning were also found in another computerized experiment involving an artificial language called eXperanto and resembling Spanish (de Graaff, 1997). One group (implicit) participated in a variety of structural as well as meaning-focused activities; the other group (explicit) received rule explanation in addition to these activities. De Graaff found a clear main effect for explicit instruction on several kinds of post-tests, but did not find the hypothesized interactions with rule complexity and the syntax/morphology distinction. Explicit instruction was simply better overall.

Both Doughty (1991) and Robinson (1996, 1997) worked with learners of ESL, Doughty in a computerized experiment, Robinson in a traditional format. Doughty (1991) targeted relative clauses, and compared three groups: rule-oriented learners (who were given explicit rules), meaning-oriented learners (who received enhanced and elaborated input), and learners who were simply exposed to many examples of the relative clause structures in question. Both instructed groups scored higher than the mere exposure group on production tests. The meaning-oriented group did better than the rule-oriented group in comprehension, possibly because this group received extra elaboration about meaning. It appears that both instructed groups had their awareness of the relevant aspects of relativization raised (the rule group through animation of moving sentences plus very simple metalinguistic rules; the meaning group through enhanced and elaborated input), and that, therefore, both did better than the mere exposure group in acquiring relativization.

Robinson (1996) compared four groups: incidental (focus entirely on meaning), implicit (subjects were told to remember sentences), rule-search (subjects were urged to find the rules), and instructed (the rules were presented to the subjects). The first two treatments can be called implicit in a broader sense, and the latter two explicit, respectively inductive and deductive. For both easy and hard rules (respectively about pseudoclefts of location and about subject–verb inversion after adverbials), the explicit-deductive group performed best, and the explicit-inductive group worst or nearly so on a grammaticality judgment post-test. This experiment agrees with the other ones mentioned in the sense that the groups with rule awareness do best. It provides the additional information that subjects may not be very good at becoming sufficiently aware of the rules through their own efforts: Robinson shows that the rule-search, incidental, and implicit groups respectively provided 11, 9, and 6 correct rule statements, compared to 22 for the instructed group (1996, p. 46, table 4).

A similar comparison between four groups was later made by Robinson (1997), but with a visual enhancement group instead of a rule-search group. This time the learning target was a rule of dative alternation applied to nonsense verbs embedded in English sentences. Here again the most explicit group, that is, the instructed group, was found to perform best on a grammaticality judgment post-test (except for sentences that were seen during the learning phase, where all conditions performed equally well).

Finally, two experiments with learners of Spanish as a second language also showed the advantage of learners with rule awareness over other groups. Leow (1998) compared four groups in an ingeniously designed experiment involving crossword puzzles: the four combinations of +/− orientation to, and +/− detection of, morphological irregularities in the morphology of the preterit. The two groups that were led to become aware of the irregularities because of the layout of the crossword puzzle ("+ detection") clearly outperformed the two other groups on a variety of post-tests, regardless of whether the instructions had drawn their attention to the irregularities or not ("+/− orientation").[2]

Rosa and O'Neill (1999) likewise found that awareness crucially determined the level of intake of a Spanish structure, in this case past counterfactual conditional sentences. They distinguished four treatments (+/− explicit rule instruction × +/− rule search during a problem-solving task) and a control group, and made a three-way distinction regarding awareness as assessed through a think-aloud protocol (at the level of understanding, at the level of noticing, and no awareness; cf. Schmidt, 1990, 1994, 1995, 2001). Their results showed significant effects of treatment on awareness, of awareness on intake (as measured by a multiple-choice post-test), and, not surprisingly then, of treatment on intake. Both explicit instruction and rule-search made a significant difference for awareness, but only awareness at the level of understanding made a significant difference for intake, and only the group with neither explicit instruction nor rule-search showed significantly less awareness than the other treatment groups.

In conclusion, all laboratory studies that involve a direct comparison of implicit and explicit learning conditions show an advantage for explicit learning, except perhaps where that learning is inductive (Robinson's, 1996, rule-search condition). Explicit induction worked better in Rosa and O'Neill's − instruction, + rule search group than in Robinson's rule-search condition, probably because of a more advantageous ratio between rule difficulty and learner sophistication (see section 4). The evidence from laboratory experiments, then, is overwhelmingly in favor of explicit learning. It should be taken into account, however, that nearly all these studies are of rather short duration; DeKeyser's (1995) study provided the longest treatment (about 12 weeks). Therefore, it could be argued that this body of literature based on laboratory experiments is biased against implicit learning.

3.2 Classroom studies

Very few studies have compared otherwise identical implicit and explicit treatments in a real classroom setting. In fact, Norris and Ortega (2000) identify only three, to which one older study can be added.

Scott (1989, 1990) conducted two very similar experiments with college students of French as a foreign language. In both studies, an explicit group was presented with rules about relative pronouns and the subjunctive, without any practice, while an implicit group read a text flooded with relevant forms (in the 1990 study this group was told about the presence of the forms in the text). Both studies showed a significant advantage for the explicit group on written post-tests; the 1989 study also included an oral post-test, which consisted of only five items, and did not yield any significant differences. Neither treatment condition appears very realistic, as the explicit condition subjects never received any practice, and the treatment was too short for implicit learning to work.

VanPatten and Oikkenon (1996) appears to be another study comparing implicit and explicit treatments, but does not really make that comparison upon closer inspection. Three groups were compared: explicit information only, structured input only (including comprehension exercises and feedback), and "regular processing instruction," the latter being a combination of explicit explanation, systematic practice, and explicit feedback referring back to the rules. Object pronouns in Spanish as a foreign language were the target of instruction. On the production post-test, the results were as follows: the most explicit group (regular processing instruction) did best, followed by the structured input group and the explicit information only group. (The post-test difference is largely due to pre-test differences, though; gain scores for the three groups were not significantly different.) On the comprehension post-tests, the results were similar, except that the first two groups virtually coincide, leaving the third far behind. VanPatten and Oikkenon conclude from these results that it was structured input and not explicit information that was helpful to the learners, but it is clear from their description of the treatments that the structured input group must also have engaged in explicit learning. Even though learners in this group were never given the rules, they were constantly given yes/no feedback, which must have led them to figure out the system (it boils down to a simple morphological alternation). Rather than an implicit group, then, this is an explicit inductive group. On the other hand, the explicit information group was never given any relevant practice; its poor results, then, are comparable to those of the "grammar group" in N. Ellis (1993). In other words, instead of an explicit and an implicit treatment, there was a good explicit-inductive and a poor explicit-deductive treatment. The order of performance of the three groups, then, is as one would expect: good explicit-deductive ("processing"), good explicit-inductive ("structured input"), and poor explicit-deductive ("explicit information only").[3]

One older study should be mentioned in this context. The Swedish GUME project is often quoted as evidence that global methods do not make a difference. Initial results, reported in Levin (1969), indeed showed no difference between implicit and explicit treatments for teaching three different ESL structures to 14-year-old Swedish students. Follow-up studies, however, yielded different results: "The Explicit method was almost uniformly superior at all age, proficiency, and aptitude levels, i.e. the difference in learning effect between the methods was the same irrespective of type of learner" (von Elek and Oskarsson, 1973, p. 39; cf. also Oskarsson, 1973).

Just as for the laboratory studies, then, we can conclude that the classroom studies that have focused narrowly on the implicit/explicit distinction have shown an advantage in explicit learning (Scott, 1989, 1990; von Elek and Oskarsson, 1973), or not really made an implicit/explicit comparison (VanPatten and Oikkenon, 1996). The evidence is very scant, however; surprisingly few studies have made this narrowly focused but essential comparison in a classroom context.

Both for the laboratory studies and the classroom studies, it should be pointed out that the dependent variable has always been a test that allows for some degree of monitoring of explicit knowledge. Even though there was some time pressure in various studies (de Graaff, 1997; DeKeyser, 1995; N. Ellis, 1993; Robinson, 1996, 1997), this probably merely made the use of explicit knowledge more difficult, and not impossible. The development of explicit declarative knowledge into fully implicit, automatized procedural knowledge takes more time than any of these studies allowed for. DeKeyser (1997), however, is a fine-grained analysis of how explicit knowledge of second language grammar rules can be gradually automatized through prolonged systematic practice.

3.3 *The use of implicit and explicit L2 knowledge*

Several studies since the early 1980s or so have investigated in some detail the role that implicit and explicit knowledge play in language use. An early example is Bialystok (1979). This often-quoted study involving 317 students of French as a second language showed that L2 learners at various levels of proficiency were equally good at making grammaticality judgments under time pressure (maximum three seconds allowed) and under more relaxed conditions. Only when they had to make more detailed judgments about what part of the sentence was problematic or what rule was violated did time pressure make a difference. Bialystok inferred from these data that learners make their grammaticality judgments on the basis of implicit knowledge, and only switch to the use of explicit knowledge when more fine-grained decisions are required. As mentioned in sections 2.5 and 3.2, however, time pressure makes the use of explicit knowledge harder, but does not exclude it completely. This is especially important as the learners in this study were relatively advanced, and as the mistakes in the incorrect sentences were rather elementary. It remains to be seen to what extent the results would generalize to more challenging grammaticality judgments or to situations with more extreme time pressure.

Also well known is Green and Hecht's (1992) large-scale study of the role that rules played in grammaticality judgments and sentence corrections made by 300 German students of English as a second language at various stages of learning, and in various school systems. The researchers found a rather low correlation between rule knowledge and ability to correct (and the degree of causality was probably even lower). Some of their figures, however, are open to reinterpretation. For instance, they show that in 43 percent of cases students could make a correction without knowing the relevant rules, but the researchers do not point out that students could often guess corrections (elements to be corrected were underlined, and many rules were dichotomous). On the other hand, at least some of their figures *do* suggest a rather strong correlation between rule knowledge and ability to correct. Where students knew the correct rules, they could correct the sentence 97 percent of the time; where they knew an "incorrect" (potentially just incomplete or very clumsily formulated) rule, they could correct 70 percent of the time; and where they knew no rule, they corrected 55 percent of the time. Most importantly, however, this study may be an instance of differential sensitivity of the testing to implicit and explicit knowledge (see section 2.5). Implicit knowledge is overestimated because guessing corrections is very easy for many items, while explicit knowledge is underestimated, because learners find it hard or impossible to formulate, even when it does help them in deciding between competing forms.

Han and Ellis (1998) used a very different methodology to get at the same question. They factor-analyzed a series of tests (oral production, grammaticality judgment, metalinguistic knowledge, TOEFL, SLEP), and found two factors that could be interpreted as implicit and explicit. Their results are hard to interpret too, however, because, as they make clear themselves, none of their tests is a pure measure of either implicit or explicit knowledge. Moreover, the results are of doubtful generalizability, because only one structure was at issue (verb complements), and this happens to be a case where it is very hard to formulate a rule, which puts explicit knowledge at a clear disadvantage.

More positive evidence for the role of explicit knowledge comes from Hulstijn and Hulstijn (1984), who found that learners of Dutch as a second language performed significantly better on word order rules in a story retelling task when they had explicit knowledge of these rules than when they did not. These results obtained for all the combinations of the experimental variables (+/− focus on grammar × +/− time pressure).

These four studies have all dealt with grammaticality judgments or other focused tests. It is, of course, well known that, in more spontaneous performance, the gap between explicit knowledge and use may be even bigger. An interesting recent illustration, for instance, is found in Macrory and Stone (2000). After four or five years of French in a British secondary school, students were found to have a fairly good grasp of the morphology of the French present perfect tense in the sense of being able to provide explicit rule statements or scoring highly on a discrete-point gap-filling test, but to omit the auxiliary most of the time in spontaneous discourse, except in largely formulaic utterances (cf. also Myles, Hooper, and Mitchell, 1998, on chunk learning of French verb forms in British secondary schools).

The literature reflects two diametrically opposite perspectives about how the second language teaching profession should deal with this gap between explicit knowledge and use. One point of view is often associated with Krashen (e.g., 1982, 1985, 1994, 1999), who posits that the results of (explicit) "learning" can never lead to implicit ("acquired") knowledge, and that the role of L2 instruction should really be to provide large quantities of comprehensible input for implicit learning ("acquisition"), not to provide explicit rules and systematic practice of these rules. In other words, in this view the gap cannot be bridged, or "learned competence does not become acquired competence" (Krashen, 1985, pp. 42–3). This view is often referred to as the non-interface position.

The other point of view is represented by, among others, DeKeyser (1997, 1998), Hulstijn (1995, 1999), McLaughlin (1978, 1990; McLaughlin and Heredia, 1996), Schmidt (e.g., 1990, 1994, 1995; Schmidt and Frota, 1986), and Swain (1985; Swain and Lapkin, 1995), who see explicit learning and practice as useful for at least some rules. In this view it is the role of practice to gradually bridge the gap between explicit knowledge and use. An intermediate point of view is that of proponents of focus on form, not focus on forms (cf., e.g., Doughty and Williams, 1998; Long and Robinson, 1998): learners are made to notice a feature of the input, in other words they become explicitly aware of a structure, but the focus-on-form techniques themselves (such as input enhancement) are not necessarily explicit. Another intermediate point of view is taken by R. Ellis (e.g., 1997, ch. 7), who argues that the role of explicit learning is really to help learners notice the gap between input and their own production, while the goal of systematic practice is limited to item learning and the improvement of fluency.

Unfortunately, very little empirical evidence exists that systematically documents the change of L2 knowledge as a result of practice over a long period of time. Studies on the role of different kinds of practice, such as Allen (2000), DeKeyser and Sokalski (1996), Robinson (1997), Salaberry (1997), VanPatten and Cadierno (1993), and VanPatten and Oikkenon (1996) all deal with short-term practice. DeKeyser (1997), however, traced students' performance on systematic comprehension and production exercises over a two-month period, and found the same learning curves in terms of error rate and reaction time that have been documented for a variety of cognitive domains outside of language learning. He also found the practice effect to be largely skill-specific (comprehension or production). DeKeyser concludes from these findings that "the ability to comprehend or produce sentences is not necessarily acquired through the implicit mechanisms of a separate mental module" (1997, pp. 211–13).

Krashen argues that DeKeyser's (1997) findings "only confirm that in his study we are dealing with learning, not acquisition" (1999, p. 253), that is, explicit not implicit learning. The point, however, is not whether students' (initial) learning was explicit; it clearly was, as DeKeyser (1997) makes clear. The point is whether the declarative knowledge that results from explicit learning processes can be turned into a form of procedural knowledge that is accessible in the same way as implicitly acquired knowledge. How one looks upon this issue depends in part on one's definition of "acquired" knowledge. If one takes lack of awareness to be as crucial for "acquired" knowledge as for implicit learning, then the end product of the learning process documented in

DeKeyser cannot be called implicit, as students are still aware of the rules. If, however, the criterion for "acquired" knowledge is that it be available with the same degree of automaticity as implicitly acquired knowledge, then it is not clear why the end product of automatization processes as documented in DeKeyser (1997) could not be considered "acquired." Moreover, it is quite possible that, after large amounts of communicative use and complete automatization of the rules, learners eventually lose their awareness of the rules. At that point they not only have procedural knowledge that is functionally equivalent to implicitly acquired knowledge, but even implicit knowledge in the narrow sense of knowledge without awareness.

This perspective is completely consistent with the general literature on cognitive skill acquisition (see, e.g., Anderson and Lebiere, 1998; DeKeyser, 2001) and implicit knowledge (see, e.g., Buchner and Wippich, 1998; Reed and Johnson, 1998). Moreover, there is no evidence in the second language acquisition literature that explicit learning and practice cannot lead to automatized procedural knowledge, only a dearth of evidence that it can – and the latter is not surprising as very little research has even tried to document automatization processes in L2. (Relative) absence of evidence is not evidence of absence.

3.4 Connectionist models of SLA

An overview of the empirical literature on implicit and explicit L2 learning and knowledge would not be complete without mentioning the small but growing body of work on connectionist modeling (see also Ellis, this volume). Connectionists claim that the linguistic knowledge usually represented by rules can be represented equally well or better by low-level associations between concrete forms, and that this is how humans actually represent such knowledge. This view, of course, makes the debate over implicit/explicit learning of rules moot; there are no rules in the connectionist concept of knowledge, only statistical associations between input and output patterns, and all knowledge is acquired and represented completely implicitly.[4] In the L1 literature, much of the debate for and against connectionism has focused on the past tense of English verbs (see, e.g., Rumelhart and McClelland, 1986, and Elman et al., 1996, for the connectionist viewpoint; Pinker, 1999, and Pinker and Prince, 1988, for the critique; and Jaeger et al., 1996, for an attempt at providing neurological evidence). The connectionist literature on L2, however, has largely been limited to gender assignment in French.

Sokolik and Smith (1992) showed how a system trained on a set of noun/gender pairings could generalize to new words with 75 percent accuracy after just five cycles through the learning set; apparently the system had become sensitive to the cues to gender present in the word endings. The Sokolik and Smith (1992) experiment has been criticized on a number of grounds. S. E. Carroll (1995), for example, pointed out that, unlike a human being, the model does not have to learn that French has gender, that only nouns have gender, and there are only two gender classes. Matthews (1999) carried out a series of experiments that strongly suggest that what happens in his (and by extension Sokolik and Smith's) model is mere memorization of the gender of specific nouns rather than the learning of phonological cues. More importantly, however, from the point of view of an SLA researcher, it is hard to take the Sokolik and Smith model as representative of the differences between L1 and L2 acquisition. The researchers formalized the difference between L1 and adult L2 by (i) zero initial weights for input/output connections for L1 and random initial weights for L2, and (ii) a slower learning rate for L2 than for L1. Neither of those formalizations seems realistic: (i) even if L1 influence could possibly be modeled as a set of pre-existing weights, it could hardly be argued that the pattern would be random, and (ii) slower learning is not characteristic of adult L2. On the contrary, adults learn faster initially, but are limited in ultimate attainment (see, e.g., Slavoff and Johnson, 1995).

For the time being then, researchers interested in how cues to French gender and similar fuzzy patterns can be learned in L2 will probably benefit more from studies with human learners. Tucker, Lambert, and Rigault (1977) show how native speakers are sensitive to phonological cues in the stem and use this knowledge to assign gender to new words; they also show, however, that native speakers are not explicitly aware of these cues. Holmes and Dejean de la Bâtie (1999) even provide experimental data which suggest that word endings are not the primary basis for gender attribution by native speakers, who seem to rely more on lexical associations. The data for L2 learners, however, suggest that the latter are more sensitive to word endings. S. E. Carroll (1999), on the other hand, conducted an experiment which "lends no support to the hypothesis that beginning anglophone learners of French are sensitive to or encode phonological patterns in stimuli that they then map onto gender classes" (p. 72). It should be pointed out, however, that the short duration of the experiment would bias in favor of the (explicit) learning of the semantic and morphological cues and against the (implicit) learning of the less salient phonological cues.

In conclusion, while L1 speakers can largely ignore phonological cues for existing words because they have memorized the gender of all but the rarest individual words, L2 learners have more of a need for such cues (Holmes and Dejean de la Bâtie, 1999). As they do not seem to pick these cues up very easily (S. E. Carroll, 1999), it may be useful to teach (at least the most common and reliable) cues explicitly, as Tucker, Lambert, and Rigault (1968) have already suggested on the basis of an experiment with college students of L2 French. (For further discussion of the learning of protypicality patterns, see section 4.)

Beyond the issue of the possible representation of French gender or other prototypicality patterns in advanced learners, it is not clear what connectionist models can contribute to a theory of second language learning at this point. While it appears to be true that the changes that take place in more advanced stages of L2 learning can often be modeled as a gradual change in sensitivity to different cues (see, e.g., MacWhinney, 1997), this does not mean that later stages of learning *have* to proceed this way, and certainly not that *initial* learning should also be a matter of implicit acquisition of sensitivity to these cues.

It is perfectly possible that, for many learners and many rules, the explicit learning of declarative rules and systematic practice to proceduralize them is a very convenient short cut to the point where connectionist-type fine-tuning of procedural knowledge can begin.

4 Which Learning for Which Elements of Language?

As indicated in sections 3.1 and 3.2, a modest number of studies have made comparisons between implicit and explicit learning for very specific structures (e.g., English dative alternation in Robinson, 1997; French relative pronouns and subjunctive forms in Scott, 1989; Welsh consonant mutation in N. Ellis, 1993). To some extent these studies give an idea of the range of structures that might be better learned explicitly than implicitly. Few empirical second language acquisition studies, however, have directly addressed the issue of differential effectiveness of implicit and explicit learning as a function of the nature of the element of grammar to be learned.

Both Reber (e.g., 1976, 1993; Reber et al., 1980) in cognitive psychology and Krashen (e.g., 1982, 1994) in applied linguistics have repeatedly argued that implicit learning is particularly advantageous for complex structures. As such structures are hard to grasp explicitly for most people – and can be impossible to grasp for many, especially without instruction – it is not surprising that implicit learning, however fragile it may be (see above, especially section 2.6), will show a relative advantage for such structures. Robinson (1996) did indeed find that implicit induction was second best out of four conditions and explicit induction worst out of four for hard rules, while the implicit condition was the worst out of four for easy rules. Hard rules involved pseudo-clefts of location and easy rules the optional subject–verb inversion after adverbials in English.

Drawing on what we know about the various roles of instruction in general for L2 acquisition (cf. especially Long, 1983, 1988; Long and Robinson, 1998), on Schmidt's (1990, 1994, 1995, 2001) hypothesis that noticing, but not necessarily understanding, is important for L2 acquisition, and on recent evidence that instruction is important to enhance subsequent noticing (Peckham, 2000), one can hypothesize different degrees of usefulness of explicit teaching for different levels of difficulty, as shown in table 11.1. It is important to note, however, that rule difficulty is an individual issue that can be described as the ratio of the rule's inherent linguistic complexity to the student's ability to handle such a rule. What is a rule of moderate difficulty for one student may be easy for a student with more language learning aptitude or language learning experience, and therefore the role of instruction for that element of grammar may vary from bringing about the learning of a structure that otherwise would not be learned to merely speeding up the learning process. Conversely, for a weaker student, the goal may not be to get the student to learn the rule at

Table 11.1 The role of instruction for rules of various levels of difficulty

Rule difficulty	*Role of instruction*
Very easy	Not useful (not necessary)
Easy	Speeding up explicit learning process
Moderate	Stretching ultimate attainment
Difficult	Enhancing later implicit acquisition by increasing chances of noticing
Very difficult	Not useful (not effective)

issue, but to draw enough attention to the forms involved so that the student will notice them more at some level and at least implicitly acquire some concrete uses of these forms through subsequent exposure rather than acquire the more abstract rule during instruction. Thus, for one and the same rule, the goal as well as the degree of effectiveness of explicit instruction will vary depending on the *subjective difficulty* of the rule.

A further complication, besides individual differences, is the fact that the *objective difficulty* of the rule itself is more than simply a matter of complexity. Novelty and abstractness of semantic categories also play a big role (e.g., in learning aspect, articles, or classifiers), as well as salience. DeKeyser (2000), for instance, argued that subject–verb inversion in yes-no questions is easily learned explicitly because of its salience, in contrast with subject–verb inversion in *wh*-questions. Bardovi-Harlig (1987) found that preposition stranding was learned before pied piping in L2 English, in spite of it being more marked, because it is more salient.

Hulstijn (1995; Hulstijn and de Graaff, 1994) hypothesizes an even wider variety of factors in determining when explicit rule learning is effective, among others complexity, UG status, subset–superset relationships, scope and reliability of the rule, semantic redundancy, and the possibility of item learning. De Graaff (1997) tested (the implications of) two of these hypotheses in his experiment with Dutch learners of a semi-artificial language ("eXperanto"). While the hypothesized interaction of implicit vs. explicit condition with complexity was partially confirmed (i.e., for syntax only and not for morphology), the hypothesis that there would be an interaction between implicit vs. explicit learning and morphology vs. syntax was not. The latter hypothesis was formulated because morphology was assumed to be more amenable to item learning than syntax.

DeKeyser (1995) made a distinction *within* morphology, which *did* interact with implicit vs. explicit learning. In an experiment with four morphological rules in an artificial language, he found that clear-cut categorical rules were learned much better in an explicit condition (which included traditional rule presentation along with picture/sentence pairs), whereas fuzzy prototypical rules, similar to the ones documented for English past tenses by Bybee and

Slobin (1982; see also Bybee and Moder, 1983), were learned slightly better in an implicit condition (involving exposure to picture/sentence pairs but no grammar explanation).

Williams (1999) also found an interaction between implicit/explicit learning and a distinction within morphology. In a series of experiments with native speakers of English learning pseudo-Italian, he found that the learning of (semantically redundant) agreement rules correlated strongly with various measures of memory, whereas the semantically non-redundant rules for marking plural on the noun or person on the verb usually did not correlate with these memory measures. Williams interpreted correlations between learning and memory as evidence of rather passive, implicit, "data-driven processes."

In comparing the findings from DeKeyser (1995) and Williams (1999) it is important to point out that the agreement rules in Williams's experiments all came down to euphony. What is being learned implicitly then, besides segmentation into morphemes, is concrete sound–sound correspondences, for instance the association of various occurrences of *–i* throughout the noun phrase (when article, noun, and adjective all mark the masculine plural). What was learned relatively well in the implicit condition in DeKeyser (1995) was also a concrete association between certain stems and certain allomorphs that go with those stems. Likewise, both the categorical rules in DeKeyser (1995) and the form–function mappings in Williams (1999) involve the learning of a more abstract pattern: associating certain morphemes with the semantic function not otherwise visible in the same phrase, and taking a different concrete form in the other (noun vs. verb) phrase. The two studies may have more in common, then, than would seem at first sight. Even though DeKeyser elicited implicit vs. explicit learning experimentally, while Williams inferred the learning processes from the results (correlations with memory), and even though Williams makes a distinction between form–function mapping and agreement, while DeKeyser distinguishes categorical rules and prototypical patterns, both studies show that implicit and explicit learning processes are differentially effective for the learning of abstract and concrete elements.

This finding is reminiscent, of course, of the position that a number of cognitive psychologists have taken, viz. that implicit learning is necessarily rather concrete, and that really abstract learning is necessarily explicit (see especially Gomez, 1997; Perruchet and Pacteau, 1990, 1991; Reed and Johnson, 1998). It also fits in with the finding of Saffran et al. (1997) that word boundaries in an artificial language were learned completely implicitly and incidentally by children as well as adults (through exposure to a tape-recording playing in the background while the subjects were engaged in a drawing task). As word boundaries can be learned merely on the basis of transitional probabilities between syllables, they are another example of implicit learning at its best: through association of concrete elements in close proximity.

This conclusion that implicit learning is best for the association of concrete elements in close proximity is not contradicted by the finding in N. Ellis and Schmidt (1997) that distant agreement in an artificial language was more correlated with memory than local agreement. The elements to be associated were still very concrete invariant morphemes, and the distance intervening between the words to be associated was one or two words. Clearly, as the burden on memory goes up with longer distances, the correlation with memory measures will go up till eventually the link between two morphemes becomes too difficult for associative memory to establish, and at that point the correlation between learning and memory measures will disappear. (See the findings from Cleeremans and McClelland, 1991, Mathews et al., 1989, and St John and Shanks, 1997, reported earlier, which show the limitations of implicit learning in this respect.)

In conclusion, abstractness and distance play a major role in the differential effectiveness of implicit and explicit learning, along with rule scope, rule reliability, and salience. The harder it is to learn something through simple association, because it is too abstract, too distant, too rare, too unreliable, or too hard to notice, the more important explicit learning processes become.

5 Age and Context Differences

It has often been hypothesized that children and adults use very different mechanisms for (second) language learning. The most elaborate formulation of this idea is to be found in Robert Bley-Vroman's (1988) Fundamental Difference Hypothesis. In order to explain a variety of observed differences in strategy and success between children and adults, Bley-Vroman posits that children use Universal Grammar and domain-specific learning procedures, while adults draw on native language knowledge and general problem-solving systems. Even though Bley-Vroman does not use the terms implicit and explicit, his distinction largely coincides with this dichotomy. Children's use of Universal Grammar and language-specific learning mechanisms happens outside of awareness, while adults can use their analytical abilities to think at least to some extent about the structure of the L2 (and its differences with L1).

Adults vary widely in their (verbal) analytical abilities, of course, and many studies have shown a strong correlation between such abilities, either in the broader sense of verbal intelligence or in the narrower sense of language learning aptitude (cf., e.g., J. B. Carroll, 1981, 1990; Sasaki, 1993; Skehan, 1989, 1998; Wesche, Edwards, and Wells, 1982; for recent overviews see Sawyer and Ranta, 2001, and Skehan, 1998). For children much lower correlations between aptitude and L2 learning have been found. Harley and Hart (1997), for instance, showed that analytic ability was not a significant predictor of second language proficiency for students who entered an immersion program in grade 1, while it was the only significant predictor of the same second language proficiency measures for students who started in grade 7. Harley and Hart (1997) left open the possibility that this may have been due to the degree of attention to form in the latter program, but other research (DeKeyser, 2000; Harley and Hart, 2002; Reves, 1982, quoted in Skehan, 1998) has shown that aptitude is a significant predictor of proficiency in naturalistic learning contexts too. DeKeyser (2000) focused on the interaction between age and aptitude in a study with Hungarian immigrants to the United States, showing that age was a significant predictor of proficiency for lower- but not for higher-aptitude learners, and that aptitude was a significant predictor for older, but not for younger learners. Such age differences in predictive validity of aptitude certainly fit with the hypothesis that adults learn largely explicitly, while children learn implicitly. DeKeyser (2000) argues that this is how the critical period hypothesis ought to be understood: somewhere between early childhood and puberty children gradually lose the ability to learn a language successfully through implicit mechanisms only. Skehan (1998, p. 234) also sees the close of the critical period as the end point of the separation between linguistic processing and general cognition.

The shift during childhood from implicit to explicit processes explains the two main findings about age differences in second language learning: children learn better and adults learn faster (for recent overviews, see Birdsong, 1999; Harley and Wang, 1997; Marinova-Todd, Marshall, and Snow, 2000). Children do better in terms of ultimate attainment because many elements of language are hard to learn explicitly (especially, of course, for those adults who have limited verbal ability); adults learn faster because their capacities for explicit learning let them take short cuts. As a result, given ample time in an unstructured environment, children come out on top. In a traditional school context, however, where time is limited and learning is highly structured, adults and older children learn more in the same amount of time. Muñoz (2001), for instance, recently demonstrated how, after the same number of EFL classroom hours in Barcelona, older learners (starting at age 11) performed better on a variety of tests than younger learners (starting at age 8). Particularly interesting in this context is also the finding from the GUME Project (von Elek and Oskarsson, 1973) that with an implicit method, children learned more than adults, while with an explicit method, adults learned more than children.

Such age differences have important practical implications that are often misunderstood. Rather than suggesting the importance of starting early, they indicate that the instructional approach should be different depending on age: full-scale immersion is necessary for children to capitalize on their implicit learning skills, and formal rule teaching is necessary for adolescents and adults to draw on their explicit learning skills.

6 Conclusions and Future Directions

In spite of a large body of sophisticated research, cognitive psychologists have not been able to provide convincing evidence that people can learn abstract patterns without being aware of them. The learning that takes place in artificial grammar and sequence learning tasks is not only quantitatively limited in the sense that subjects perform barely above chance; it also seems qualitatively limited to rather concrete patterns of contiguous elements, or accompanied by some kind of awareness, or both.

SLA researchers have similarly failed to show any significant learning of abstract patterns without awareness. At least one experiment has shown specifically that no abstract patterns were learned implicitly in spite of thousands of exposures to relevant examples of simple rules (DeKeyser, 1995). Several others have shown not only that explicit learning, especially deductive, is significantly more effective than implicit learning, but also that any learning that takes place in the "implicit condition" is often due to failure of the learners to stick to the instructions for implicit learning; thus their (partial) learning is the result of (partial) awareness (e.g., Robinson, 1996). Furthermore, L2 studies that have dealt with broader variables such as focus on form have provided evidence for the advantage of such focus compared to mere exposure or focus on meaning; the most likely interpretation of such research is that focus on form is necessary to make learners consciously notice the abstract patterns that are not easily learned implicitly.

It is only fair to say, however, that the amount of L2 research narrowly focused on the implicit–explicit distinction is, first, quite limited, not only in number of studies, but also in duration and in scope of the learning target. Second, most of this research has been conducted in laboratory studies of limited ecological validity rather than in classrooms, and no studies exist that trace the role of implicit and explicit learning longitudinally in untutored second language acquisition.[5] Third, the criterion measures invariably tend to be very constrained, involving grammaticality judgments or fill-in-the-blank tests rather than freely constructed discourse. Finally, while the criterion measures appear constrained and artificial from the point of view of the applied linguist or language teacher, they are far from being constrained enough to meet the methodological requirements identified in the psychological literature for guaranteeing pure implicit/explicit learning or for yielding a pure measure of implicit/explicit knowledge (see section 2.5). Nor has the issue of abstractness of knowledge been given much attention, except in one or two studies. How then can the field of SLA make progress toward a better understanding of a question of such fundamental importance both to theories of acquisition and to language teaching practice?

Clearly we cannot just extrapolate findings about AGL to SLA. A number of researchers have discussed the strong limits on the generalizability of AGL research (e.g., DeKeyser, 1994, 1995; Schmidt, 1994, 1995; VanPatten, 1994). We need to conduct research on actual second language learning, but what kind? The usual trade-off between internal and external validity is felt particularly strongly when the (operational) definition of what constitutes a treatment is as contentious as in the field of implicit learning. If hard-core experimental psychology cannot provide sufficient rigor to guarantee "pure" learning conditions, then how are we to attain such standards in more realistic contexts, where the whole grammar of a real second language is learned rather than a finite-state grammar that can be fully described on a square inch of paper, and where learners have a myriad of uncontrollable experiences in and out of the classroom before, during, and after the treatment?

Three different options exist. One is to conduct very narrow experiments, under strictly controlled conditions (probably by a computer), with very small fragments of a (real or made-up) second language. This can satisfy the cognitive psychologist, and maybe the SLA researcher, but probably not the applied linguist interested in classroom applications (see DeKeyser, 1997; N. Ellis and Schmidt, 1997; and especially Hulstijn, 1997; Yang and Givón, 1997, for further discussion of laboratory research on SLA). A second option is to conduct more realistic experiments, in actual classrooms, with much larger fragments of a language that the students are not just learning for the sake of the experiment, but making an effort to control the treatments more than is usually the case in classroom research. This may satisfy educational psychologists and applied linguists, and maybe classroom-oriented SLA researchers, but not cognitive psychologists. A third approach is to try to compromise even more than the previous two options already do, and to try to provide longer, broader, more varied, and therefore more realistic treatments than previous laboratory experiments, but to conduct the research in a more strictly controlled environment than a real classroom, either through an entirely computerized mini-curriculum or with specially designed materials, carefully trained teachers, and hand-picked students. I personally favor the third option, but certainly feel that the other two options are valuable to provide different pieces of the mosaic and to convince people with different disciplinary backgrounds.

Regardless of which option future researchers choose, however, they will have to come to grips with the issues discussed in section 4. We cannot keep generalizing about the psychology of SLA on the basis of a few structures in a few languages, but instead have to make a concerted effort to vary learning targets systematically along psycholinguistically relevant dimensions. Studies such as de Graaff (1997), DeKeyser (1995), Robinson (1996), and Williams (1999) already show the value of this approach, but much work remains to be done to define and operationalize concepts such as abstractness, complexity, contiguity, and difficulty in a way that will maximize the likelihood of detecting interactions between implicit/explicit learning processes and structural characteristics of learning targets.

Furthermore, we cannot ignore the interaction of both learning conditions and linguistic features with learners' aptitudes. Not only is the study of aptitude–treatment interactions of great potential value for educational practice (see, e.g., for educational practice in general, Corno and Snow, 1986; Cronbach and Snow, 1977; Jonassen and Grabowski, 1993; and for second language teaching, McLaughlin, 1980; Sawyer and Ranta, 2001; Skehan, 1989, 1998), but the study of the three-way interaction between aptitudes, treatments, and psycholinguistic features of the learning targets can provide much more insight into all three of these factors than the study of any one of them in isolation can hope to accomplish. Again, studies such as Robinson (1996) and Williams (1999) hold great promise in this regard (see box 11.1).

Box 11.1 Robinson (1996) and Williams (1999)

Robinson (1996)

Main research questions: Will implicit and incidental treatments yield similar results? Will rule search and instructed conditions similarly pattern together? Will complex structures be learned better by the implicit and incidental groups?

Subjects: One hundred and four intermediate ESL students (95 Japanese, 5 Chinese, 5 Korean).

Independent variables: Between subjects: four conditions (implicit, incidental, rule-search, instructed). Within subjects: simple vs. complex rules.

Dependent variables: Speed and accuracy of response in grammaticality judgment test for pseudoclefts of location (hard rule) and subject–verb inversion after adverbials (easy rule).

Results: Implicit/incidental learners do not outperform other learners on complex rules, but instructed learners outperform all others for simple rules.

Williams (1999)

Main research questions: What is the relationship between memory for input and inductive learning of morphological rules?

Subjects: Fifty-eight British university students (divided over three experiments).

Independent variables: Real vs. pseudo-Italian (the latter with random suffixes), typographical enhancement vs. control, memory performance during training.

Dependent variables: Agreement and form–function mapping on translation post-test.

Results: The findings are complex, but the correlations between memory during training and performance on the translation post-test suggest that agreement rules are largely the result of data-driven (implicit) learning, while form–function mappings result from conceptually driven (explicit) learning. (See section 4 for further discussion, as well as box 19.1 in this volume for more information on other aspects of this study.)

Comments

Robinson (1996) is particularly interesting because of its comparison of multiple treatments for different kinds of structures, which in this case showed an unexpected grouping of treatments, and an interaction between treatments and rule types. Far too often overly general conclusions are drawn from overly broad operationalizations of treatments and overly narrow operationalizations of learning targets.

Williams (1999) is very interesting because of the contrasting methodology. Instead of trying to control different learning processes experimentally through instructions and stimuli, Williams inferred them from the post-test correlations with different aptitude measures.

Both Robinson (1996) and Williams (1999), then, provide a more complete picture than many other studies by looking at the interaction between different learning processes, aptitudes, and L2 structures, but they do this in very different ways.

A disadvantage that both studies share with practically all other research that compares implicit and explicit L2 learning is the short duration of the treatment and the lack of ecological validity from the point of view of regular classroom teaching. Combining experimental rigor with ecological validity is an elusive goal in educational research. We agree with Kasper and Dahl (1991) that ecological validity should not be a sacred cow, but treatments of longer duration are desirable because shorter treatments are biased in favor of explicit learning.

Finally, the time may have come for SLA researchers to be more ambitious in their attempts to contribute to cognitive science. Prominent cognitive psychologists say that they "know of no comprehensive treatment of the role of consciousness at various stages of learning" (Carlson, 1997, p. 63), and advise researchers to "focus on the differential effects of implicit and explicit orientations on learning, rather than on attempts to demonstrate that learning is implicit in some absolute sense" (Stadler and Roediger, 1998, p. 107). We should not be too reluctant, then, to try to document the role of such different orientations in various aspects of the L2 learning process. This would provide cognitive science with a context that is not only more realistic than AGL or sequence learning experiments, but if we are lucky, may turn out to yield results that are easier to interpret too.

NOTES

1 For an excellent study on the interaction of rules and examples outside of the language domain, see Anderson, Fincham, and Douglass (1997).
2 It should be pointed out, however, that the learners in the + orientation/ – detection condition (crossword puzzle two) were implicitly given the wrong information about the irregular verb forms, which makes for a strange comparison.
3 VanPatten and Oikkenon (1996, p. 507) explicitly reject the role feedback could have played for the structured input group, because it was not explicit (metalinguistic). Clearly, given our definition of "explicit" as involving awareness, this lack of metalinguistic explicitness in the feedback does not matter, as long as the feedback brings about awareness by leading the learners to figure out the system inductively.
4 Rumelhart and McClelland (1986, p. 217) even reserve the term "implicit" for connectionist knowledge representation, and call Chomskyan-type rules "explicit inaccessible," in the sense that they are represented in the mind as rules, but without speakers being aware of them as such.
5 Claims have been made that the Tukano tribes in the Vaupes region of Amazonia routinely learn an L2 well

as adults (they can only marry a speaker of a different language). Studies of language among the Tukano (e.g., Sorensen, 1972; Jackson, 1983), however, invariably deal with language as an element of the marriage system and cultural identity, and have never documented learning processes in detail (or exact levels of ultimate attainment, for that matter).

REFERENCES

Alanen, R. 1995: Input enhancement and rule presentation in second language acquisition. In R. W. Schmidt (ed.), *Attention and Awareness in Foreign Language Learning*. Honolulu: University of Hawai'i Press, 259–302.

Allen, L. Q. 2000: Form–meaning connections and the French causative: an experiment in processing instruction. *Studies in Second Language Acquisition*, 22, 69–84.

Altmann, G. T. M., Dienes, Z., and Goode, A. 1995: Modality independence of implicitly learned grammatical knowledge. *Journal of Experimental Psychology: Learning, Memory, and Cognition*, 21, 899–912.

Anderson, J. R. and Lebiere, C. 1998: *The Atomic Components of Thought*. Mahwah, NJ: Lawrence Erlbaum Associates.

Anderson, J. R., Fincham, J. M., and Douglass, S. 1997: The role of examples and rules in the acquisition of a cognitive skill. *Journal of Experimental Psychology: Learning, Memory and Cognition*, 23, 932–45.

Bardovi-Harlig, K. 1987: Markedness and salience in second-language acquisition. *Language Learning*, 37, 385–407.

Berry, D. and Broadbent, D. 1984: On the relationship between task performance and associated verbalizable knowledge. *Quarterly Journal of Experimental Psychology*, 36, 209–31.

Bialystok, E. 1979: Explicit and implicit judgements of L2 grammaticality. *Language Learning*, 29, 81–103.

Birdsong, D. 1999: Introduction: whys and why nots of the critical period hypothesis for second language acquisition. In D. Birdsong (ed.), *Second Language Acquisition and the Critical Period Hypothesis*. Mahwah, NJ: Lawrence Erlbaum Associates, 1–22.

Bley-Vroman, R. 1988: The fundamental character of foreign language learning. In W. Rutherford and M. Sharwood Smith (eds), *Grammar and Second Language Teaching: A Book of Readings*. New York: Newbury House, 19–30.

Brooks, L. R. and Vokey, J. R. 1991: Abstract analogies and abstracted grammars: Comments on Reber 1989 and Mathews et al. 1989. *Journal of Experimental Psychology: General*, 120, 316–23.

Buchner, A. 1994: Indirect effects of synthetic grammar learning in an identification task. *Journal of Experimental Psychology: Learning, Memory, and Cognition*, 20, 550–66.

Buchner, A. and Wippich, W. 1998: Differences and commonalities between implicit learning and memory. In M. A. Stadler and P. A. Frensch (eds), *Handbook of Implicit Learning*. Thousand Oaks, CA: Sage, 3–46.

Buchner, A., Erdfelder, E., and Vaterrodt-Plünnecke, B. 1995: Toward unbiased measurement of conscious and unconscious memory processes within the process dissociation framework. *Journal of Experimental Psychology: General*, 124, 137–60.

Bybee, J. and Moder, C. 1983: Morphological classes as natural categories. *Language*, 59, 251–70.

Bybee, J. and Slobin, D. 1982: Rules and schemas in the development and use of the English past tense. *Language*, 58, 265–89.

Carlson, R. A. 1997: *Experienced Cognition*. Mahwah, NJ: Lawrence Erlbaum Associates.

Carroll, J. B. 1981: Twenty-five years of research on foreign language aptitude. In K. C. Diller (ed.), *Individual Differences and Universals in Language Learning Aptitude*. Rowley, MA: Newbury House, 83–118.

Carroll, J. B. 1990: Cognitive abilities in foreign language aptitude: then and now. In T. S. Parry and C. W. Stansfield (eds), *Language Aptitude Reconsidered*. Washington, DC: Center for Applied Linguistics, 11–29.

Carroll, S. E. 1995: The hidden dangers of computer modelling: remarks on Sokolik and Smith's connectionist learning model of French gender. *Second Language Research*, 11, 193–205.

Carroll, S. E. 1999: Input and SLA: adults' sensitivity to different sorts of cues to French gender. *Language Learning*, 49, 37–92.

Cleeremans, A. and Jiménez, L. 1998: Implicit sequence learning: the truth is in the details. In M. A. Stadler and P. A. Frensch (eds), *Handbook of Implicit Learning*. Thousand Oaks, CA: Sage, 323–64.

Cleeremans, A. and McClelland, J. L. 1991: Learning the structure of event sequences. *Journal of Experimental Psychology: General*, 120, 235–53.

Cleeremans, A., Destrebecqz, A., and Boyer, M. 1998: Implicit learning: news from the front. *Trends in Cognitive Sciences*, 21, 406–16.

Cohen, A., Ivry, R. I., and Keele, S. W. 1990: Attention and structure in sequence learning. *Journal of Experimental Psychology: Learning, Memory, and Cognition*, 16(1), 17–30.

Corno, L. and Snow, R. E. 1986: Adapting teaching to individual differences among learners. In M. C. Wittrock (ed.), *Handbook of Research on Teaching*. New York: Macmillan, 605–29.

Cronbach, L. J. and Snow, R. E. 1977: *Aptitudes and Instructional Methods: A Handbook for Research on Interactions*. New York: Irvington.

Curran, T. and Keele, S. W. 1993: Attentional and nonattentional forms of sequence learning. *Journal of Experimental Psychology: Learning, Memory, and Cognition*, 19 (1), 189–202.

de Graaff, R. 1997: The eXperanto experiment: effects of explicit instruction on second language acquisition. *Studies in Second Language Acquisition*, 19, 249–76.

DeKeyser, R. 1994: How implicit can adult second language learning be? *AILA Review*, 11, 83–96.

DeKeyser, R. M. 1995: Learning second language grammar rules: an experiment with a miniature linguistic system. *Studies in Second Language Acquisition*, 17, 379–410.

DeKeyser, R. M. 1997: Beyond explicit rule learning: automatizing second language morphosyntax. *Studies in Second Language Acquisition*, 19, 195–221.

DeKeyser, R. M. 1998: Beyond focus on form: cognitive perspectives on learning and practicing second language grammar. In C. Doughty and J. Williams (eds), *Focus on Form in Classroom Second Language Acquisition*. New York: Cambridge University Press, 42–63.

DeKeyser, R. M. 2000: The robustness of critical period effects in second language acquisition. *Studies in Second Language Acquisition*, 22, 499–533.

DeKeyser, R. M. 2001: Automaticity and automatization. In P. Robinson (ed.),

Cognition and Second Language Instruction. New York: Cambridge University Press, 125–51.

DeKeyser, R. M. and Sokalski, K. J. 1996: The differential role of comprehension and production practice. *Language Learning*, 46, 613–42.

Dienes, Z. and Fahey, R. 1995: The role of specific instances in controlling a dynamic system. *Journal of Experimental Psychology: Learning, Memory, and Cognition*, 21, 848–62.

Dienes, Z., Broadbent, D., and Berry, D. 1991: Implicit and explicit knowledge bases in artificial grammar learning. *Journal of Experimental Psychology: Learning, Memory, and Cognition*, 17, 875–87.

Doughty, C. 1991: Second language instruction does make a difference: evidence from an empirical study of SL relativization. *Studies in Second Language Acquisition*, 13, 431–69.

Doughty, C. and Williams, J. 1998: Pedagogical choices in focus on form. In C. Doughty and J. Williams (eds), *Focus on Form in Classroom Second Language Acquisition*. New York: Cambridge University Press, 197–261.

Dulany, D., Carlson, R., and Dewey, G. 1984: A case of syntactical learning and judgment: how conscious and how abstract? *Journal of Experimental Psychology: General*, 113, 541–55.

Ellis, N. 1993: Rules and instances in foreign language learning: interactions of explicit and implicit knowledge. *European Journal of Cognitive Psychology*, 5, 289–318.

Ellis, N. C. and Schmidt, R. 1997: Morphology and longer distance dependencies: laboratory research illuminating the A in SLA. *Studies in Second Language Acquisition*, 19, 145–71.

Ellis, R. 1997: *SLA Research and Language Teaching*. Oxford: Oxford University Press.

Elman, J. L., Bates, E. A., Johnson, M. H., Karmiloff-Smith, A., Parisi, D., and Plunkett, K. 1996: *Rethinking Innateness: A Connectionist Perspective on Development*. Cambridge, MA: MIT Press.

Frensch, P. A. 1998: One concept, multiple meanings: on how to define the concept of implicit learning. In M. Stadler and P. Frensch (eds), *Handbook of Implicit Learning*. Thousand Oaks, CA: Sage, 47–104.

Gomez, R. L. 1997: Transfer and complexity in artificial grammar learning. *Cognitive Psychology*, 33, 154–207.

Gomez, R. L. and Schvaneveldt, R. W. 1994: What is learned from artificial grammars? Transfer tests of simple association. *Journal of Experimental Psychology: Learning, Memory, and Cognition*, 20, 396–410.

Green, P. and Hecht, K. 1992: Implicit and explicit grammar: an empirical study. *Applied Linguistics*, 13, 168–84.

Han, Y. and Ellis, R. 1998: Implicit knowledge, explicit knowledge and general language proficiency. *Language Teaching Research*, 21, 1–23.

Harley, B. and Hart, D. 1997: Language aptitude and second language proficiency in classroom learners of different starting ages. *Studies in Second Language Acquisition*, 19, 379–400.

Harley, B. and Hart, D. 2002: Age, aptitude, and second language learning on a bilingual exchange. In P. Robinson and P. Skehan (eds), *Individual Differences and Second Language Instruction*. Philadelphia: John Benjamins, 301–30.

Harley, B. and Wang, W. 1997: The critical period hypothesis: where are we now? In A. M. B. De Groot and J. F. Kroll (eds), *Tutorials in Bilingualism: Psycholinguistic Perspectives*. Mahwah, NJ: Lawrence Erlbaum Associates, 19–51.

Hayes, N. A. and Broadbent, D. E. 1988: Two modes of learning for interactive tasks. *Cognition*, 28, 249–76.

Holmes, V. M. and Dejean de la Bâtie, B. 1999: Assignment of grammatical gender by native speakers and foreign learners of French. *Applied Psycholinguistics*, 20, 479–506.

Hulstijn, J. 1995: Not all grammar rules are equal: giving grammar instruction its proper place in foreign language teaching. In R. Schmidt (ed.), *Attention and Awareness in Foreign Language Learning*. Honolulu: University of Hawai'i at Manoa, 359–86.

Hulstijn, J. H. 1997: Second language acquisition research in the laboratory: possibilities and limitations. *Studies in Second Language Acquisition*, 19, 131–43.

Hulstijn, J. H. 1999: Vaardigheid zonder kennis? De rol van grammaticakennis en automatisering in de verwerving van een tweede taal. Inaugural lecture, November 5. Amsterdam: Vossiuspers AUP.

Hulstijn, J. H. and de Graaff, R. 1994: Under what conditions does explicit knowledge of a second language facilitate the acquisition of implicit knowledge? A research proposal. *AILA Review*, 11, 97–112.

Hulstijn, J. and Hulstijn, W. 1984: Grammatical errors as a function of processing constraints and explicit knowledge. *Language Learning*, 34, 23–43.

Jackson, J. E. 1983: *The Fish People: Linguistic Exogamy and Tukanoan Identity in Northwest Amazonia*. New York: Cambridge University Press.

Jacoby, L. L. 1991: A process dissociation framework: separating automatic from intentional uses of memory. *Journal of Memory and Language*, 30, 513–41.

Jaeger, J. J., Lockwood, A. H., Kemmerer, D. L., Van Valin, R. D., Murphy, B. W., and Khalak, H. G. 1996: A positron emission tomographic study of regular and irregular verb morphology in English. *Language*, 72, 451–97.

Jiménez, L. and Méndez, C. 1999: Which attention is needed for implicit sequence learning? *Journal of Experimental Psychology: Learning, Memory and Cognition*, 25, 236–59.

Johnstone, T. and Shanks, D. R. 1999: Two mechanisms in artificial grammar learning? Comment on Meulemans and Van der Linden 1997. *Journal of Experimental Psychology: Learning, Memory, and Cognition*, 25, 524–31.

Jonassen, D. H. and Grabowski, B. L. 1993: *Handbook of Individual Differences, Learning, and Instruction*. Hillsdale, NJ: Lawrence Erlbaum Associates.

Kasper, G. and Dahl, M. 1991: Research methods in interlanguage pragmatics. *Studies in Second Language Acquisition*, 13, 215–47.

Knowlton, B. J. and Squire, L. R. 1994: The information acquired during artificial grammar learning. *Journal of Experimental Psychology: Learning, Memory and Cognition*, 20, 79–91.

Knowlton, B. J. and Squire, L. R. 1996: Artificial grammar learning depends on implicit acquisition of both abstract and exemplar-specific information. *Journal of Experimental Psychology: Learning, Memory, and Cognition*, 22, 169–81.

Krashen, S. D. 1982: *Principles and Practice in Second Language Acquisition*. Englewood Cliffs, NJ: Prentice-Hall.

Krashen, S. D. 1985: *The Input Hypothesis*. London and New York: Longman.

Krashen, S. D. 1994: The input hypothesis and its rivals. In N. Ellis (ed.), *Implicit and Explicit Learning of Languages*. London: Academic Press, 45–77.

Krashen, S. D. 1999: Seeking a role for grammar: a review of some recent studies. *Foreign Language Annals*, 32, 245–57.

Leow, R. P. 1998: Toward operationalizing the process of attention in SLA: evidence for Tomlin and Villa's (1994) fine-grained analysis of attention. *Applied Psycholinguistics*, 19, 133–59.

Levin, L. 1969: *Implicit and Explicit: A Synopsis of Three Parallel Experiments in Applied Psycholinguistics. Assessing Different Methods of Teaching Grammatical Structures in English as a Foreign Language*. University of Gothenburg.

Lewicki, P., Czyzewska, M., and Hoffman, H. 1987: Unconscious acquisition of complex procedural knowledge. *Journal of Experimental Psychology: Learning, Memory and Cognition*, 13, 523–30.

Long, M. H. 1983: Does second language instruction make a difference? *TESOL Quarterly*, 17, 359–82.

Long, M. H. 1988: Instructed interlanguage development. In L. Beebe (ed.), *Issues in Second Language Acquisition: Multiple Perspectives*. New York: Harper and Row, 115–41.

Long, M. H. and Robinson, P. 1998: Focus on form: theory, research, and practice. In C. Doughty and J. Williams (eds), *Focus on Form in Classroom Second Language Acquisition*. New York: Cambridge University Press, 15–41.

Macrory, G. and Stone, V. 2000: Pupil progress in the acquisition of the perfect tense in French: the relationship between knowledge and use. *Language Teaching Research*, 4, 55–82.

MacWhinney, B. 1997: Second language acquisition and the competition model. In A. M. B. De Groot and J. F. Kroll (eds), *Tutorials in Bilingualism: Psycholinguistic Perspectives*. Mahwah, NJ: Lawrence Erlbaum Associates, 113–42.

Manza, L. and Reber, A. S. 1997: Representing artificial grammars: transfer across stimulus forms and modalities. In D. C. Berry (ed.), *How Implicit is Implicit Learning?* Oxford: Oxford University Press, 73–106.

Marinova-Todd, S. H., Marshall, D. B., and Snow, C. E. 2000: Three misconceptions about age and L2 learning. *TESOL Quarterly*, 34, 9–34.

Mathews, R., Buss, R., Stanley, W., Blanchard-Fields, F., Cho, J. R., and Druhan, B. 1989: Role of implicit and explicit processes in learning from examples: a synergistic effect. *Journal of Experimental Psychology: Learning, Memory, and Cognition*, 15, 1083–100.

Matthews, C. A. 1999: Connectionism and French gender attribution: Sokolik and Smith re-visited. *Second Language Research*, 15, 412–27.

McLaughlin, B. 1978: The Monitor model: some methodological considerations. *Language Learning*, 28, 309–32.

McLaughlin, B. 1980: Theory and research in second-language learning: an emerging paradigm. *Language Learning*, 30, 331–50.

McLaughlin, B. 1990: "Conscious" versus "unconscious" learning. *TESOL Quarterly*, 24, 617–34.

McLaughlin, B. and Heredia, R. 1996: Information-processing approaches to research on second language acquisition and use. In W. C. Ritchie and T. K. Bhatia (eds), *Handbook of Second Language Acquisition*. New York: Academic Press, 213–28.

Meulemans, T. and Van der Linden, M. 1997: Associative chunk strength in artificial grammar learning. *Journal of Experimental Psychology: Learning, Memory, and Cognition*, 23, 1007–28.

Michas, I. C. and Berry, D. C. 1994: Implicit and explicit processes in a second-language learning task. *European Journal of Cognitive Psychology*, 6, 357–81.

Muñoz, C. 2001: Factores escolares e individuales en el aprendizaje formal de un idioma extranjero. In S. Pastor Costeros and V. Salazar García (eds), *Estudios de Linguística*. Alicante: Universidad de Alicante, 249–70.

Myles, F., Hooper, J., and Mitchell, R. 1998: Rote or rule? Exploring the role of formulaic language in classroom foreign language learning. *Language Learning*, 48, 323–63.

Nissen, M. J. and Bullemer, P. 1987: Attentional requirements of learning: evidence from performance measures. *Cognitive Psychology*, 19, 1–32.

Norris, J. M. and Ortega, L. 2000: Effectiveness of L2 instruction: a research synthesis and quantitative meta-analysis. *Language Learning*, 50, 417–528.

Nosofsky, R. M. 1989: Further tests of an exemplar-similarity approach to relating identification and categorization. *Journal of Experimental Psychology: Perception and Psychophysics*, 45, 279–90.

Oskarsson, M. 1973: Assessing the relative effectiveness of two methods of teaching English to adults: a replication experiment. *IRAL*, 11, 251–62.

Peckham, D. W. 2000: Attention and consciousness in second language acquisition: an investigation into the effects of instruction on noticing. Ph.D. University of Pittsburgh.

Perruchet, P. and Pacteau, C. 1990: Synthetic grammar learning: implicit rule abstraction or explicit fragmentary knowledge? *Journal of Experimental Psychology: General*, 119, 264–75.

Perruchet, P. and Pacteau, C. 1991: Implicit acquisition of abstract knowledge about artificial grammar: some methodological and conceptual issues. *Journal of Experimental Psychology: General*, 120, 112–16.

Pinker, S. 1999: *Words and Rules: The Ingredients of Language*. New York: Basic Books.

Pinker, S. and Prince, A. 1988: On language and connectionism: analysis of a parallel distributed processing model of language acquisition. In S. Pinker and J. Mehler (eds), *Connections and Symbols*. Cambridge, MA: MIT Press, 73–193.

Pothos, E. M. and Bailey, T. M. 2000: The role of similarity in artificial grammar learning. *Journal of Experimental Psychology: Learning, Memory, and Cognition*, 26, 847–62.

Reber, A. S. 1967: Implicit learning of artificial grammars. *Journal of Verbal Learning and Verbal Behavior*, 6, 855–63.

Reber, A. 1976: Implicit learning of synthetic languages: the role of instructional set. *Journal of Experimental Psychology: Human Learning and Memory*, 2, 88–94.

Reber, A. S. 1989: Implicit learning and tacit knowledge. *Journal of Experimental Psychology: General*, 118, 219–35.

Reber, A. S. 1993: *Implicit Learning and Tacit Knowledge: An Essay on the Cognitive Unconscious*. Oxford: Oxford University Press.

Reber, A. S. and Allen, R. 1978: Analogy and abstraction strategies in synthetic grammar learning: a functionalist interpretation. *Cognition*, 6, 189–221.

Reber, A., Allen, R., and Regan, S. 1985: Syntactical learning and judgment, still unconscious and still abstract: comment on Dulany, Carlson and Dewey. *Journal of Experimental Psychology: General*, 114, 17–24.

Reber, A., Kassin, S., Lewis, S., and Cantor, G. 1980: On the relationship between implicit and explicit modes in the learning of a complex rule structure. *Journal of Experimental Psychology: Human Learning and Memory*, 6, 492–502.

Redington, M. and Chater, N. 1996: Transfer in artificial grammar learning: a reevaluation. *Journal of Experimental Psychology: General*, 125, 123–38.

Reed, J. M. and Johnson, P. J. 1998: Implicit learning: methodological issues and evidence of unique characteristics. In M. A. Stadler and P. A. Frensch (eds), *Handbook of Implicit Learning*. Thousand Oaks, CA: Sage, 261–94.

Reingold, E. M. and Merikle, P. M. 1988: Using direct and indirect measures to study perception without awareness. *Perception and Psychophysics*, 44, 563–75.

Reves, T. 1982: What makes a good language learner? Ph. D. Hebrew University of Jerusalem.

Robinson, P. 1996: Learning simple and complex second language rules under implicit, incidental, rule-search, and instructed conditions. *Studies in Second Language Acquisition*, 18, 27–67.

Robinson, P. 1997: Generalizability and automaticity of second language learning under implicit, incidental, enhanced, and instructed conditions. *Studies in Second Language Acquisition*, 19, 223–47.

Rosa, E. and O'Neill, M. D. 1999: Explicitness, intake, and the issue of awareness: another piece to the puzzle. *Studies in Second Language Acquisition*, 21, 511–56.

Rumelhart, D. and McClelland, J. 1986: On learning the past tenses of English verbs. In J. McClelland, D. Rumelhart, and PR Group (eds), *Parallel Distributed Processing*. Cambridge, MA: MIT Press, 217–71.

Saffran, J. R., Newport, E. L., Aslin, R. N., Tunick, R. A., and Barrueco, S. 1997: Incidental language learning: listening (and learning) out of the corner of your ear. *Psychological Science*, 8, 101–5.

Salaberry, M. R. 1997: The role of input and output practice in second language acquisition. *Canadian Modern Language Review*, 53, 422–51.

Sasaki, M. 1993: Relationships among second language proficiency, foreign language aptitude, and intelligence: a structural equation modeling approach. *Language Learning*, 43, 313–44.

Sawyer, M. and Ranta, L. 2001: Aptitude, individual differences, and instructional design. In P. Robinson (ed.), *Cognition and Second Language Instruction*. New York: Cambridge University Press, 319–53.

Schmidt, R. W. 1990: The role of consciousness in second language learning. *Applied Linguistics*, 11, 129–58.

Schmidt, R. W. 1994: Deconstructing consciousness in search of useful definitions for applied linguistics. *AILA Review*, 11, 11–26.

Schmidt, R. 1995: Consciousness and foreign language learning: a tutorial on the role of attention and awareness in learning. In R. Schmidt (ed.), *Attention and Awareness in Foreign Language Learning*. Honolulu: University of Hawai'i Press, 1–63.

Schmidt, R. W. 2001: Attention. In P. Robinson (ed.), *Cognition and Second Language Instruction*. New York: Cambridge University Press, 1–32.

Schmidt, R. W. and Frota, S. N. 1986: Developing basic conversational ability in a second language: a case study of an adult learner of Portuguese. In R. R. Day (ed.), *Talking to Learn: Conversation in Second Language Acquisition*. Rowley, MA: Newbury House, 237–326.

Scott, V. M. 1989: An empirical study of explicit and implicit teaching strategies in French. *Modern Language Journal*, 73, 14–22.

Scott, V. M. 1990: Explicit and implicit grammar teaching strategies: new empirical data. *French Review*, 63, 779–89.

Servan-Schreiber, E. and Anderson, J. R. 1990: Learning artificial grammars with competitive chunking. *Journal of Experimental Psychology: Learning, Memory, and Cognition*, 16, 592–608.

Shanks, D. R. and St John, M. F. 1994: Characteristics of dissociable human learning systems. *Behavioral and Brain Sciences*, 17, 367–95.

Shanks, D. R., Johnstone, T., and Staggs, L. 1997: Abstraction processes in artificial grammar learning.

Quarterly Journal of Experimental Psychology, 50, 216–52.

Skehan, P. 1989: *Individual Differences in Second Language Learning*. London: Edward Arnold.

Skehan, P. 1998: *A Cognitive Approach to Language Learning*. Oxford: Oxford University Press.

Slavoff, G. R. and Johnson, J. S. 1995: The effects of age on the rate of learning a second language. *Studies in Second Language Acquisition*, 17, 1–16.

Sokolik, M. and Smith, M. 1992: Assignment of gender to French nouns in primary and secondary language: a connectionist model. *Second Language Research*, 8, 39–58.

Sorensen, A. P. J. 1972: Multilingualism in the Northwest Amazon. In J. B. Pride and J. Holmes (eds), *Sociolinguistics*. Harmondsworth: Penguin, 78–93.

Spada, N. 1997: Form-focussed instruction and second language acquisition: a review of classroom and laboratory research. *Language Teaching*, 30, 73–87.

St John, M. F. and Shanks, D. R. 1997: Implicit learning from an information processing standpoint. In D. C. Berry (ed.), *How Implicit is Implicit Learning?* Oxford: Oxford University Press, 162–94.

Stadler, M. A. and Roediger, H. L. I. 1998: The question of awareness in research on implicit learning. In M. A. Stadler and P. A. Frensch (eds), *Handbook of Implicit Learning*. Thousand Oaks, CA: Sage, 105–32.

Swain, M. 1985: Communicative competence: some roles of comprehensible input and comprehensible output in its development. In S. M. Gass and C. G. Madden (eds), *Input in Second Language Acquisition*. Rowley, MA: Newbury House, 235–53.

Swain, M. and Lapkin, S. 1995: Problems in output and the cognitive processes they generate: a step towards second language learning. *Applied Linguistics*, 16, 371–91.

Tucker, G. R., Lambert, W., and Rigault, A. 1968: Students' acquisition of French gender distinctions: a pilot investigation. *International Review of Applied Linguistics*, 51–5.

Tucker, G. R., Lambert, W., and Rigault, A. 1977: *The French Speaker's Skill with Grammatical Gender: An Example of Rule-Governed Behavior*. The Hague: Mouton.

Turner, C. W. and Fischler, I. S. 1993: Speeded tests of implicit knowledge. *Journal of Experimental Psychology: Learning, Memory, and Cognition*, 19, 1165–77.

VanPatten, B. 1994: Evaluating the role of consciousness in second language acquisition: terms, linguistic features and research methodology. *AILA Review*, 11, 27–36.

VanPatten, B. and Cadierno, T. 1993: Explicit instruction and input processing. *Studies in Second Language Acquisition*, 15, 225–43.

VanPatten, B. and Oikkenon, S. 1996: Explanation versus structured input in processing instruction. *Studies in Second Language Acquisition*, 18, 495–510.

Vokey, J. R. and Brooks, L. R. 1992: Salience of item knowledge in learning artificial grammars. *Journal of Experimental Psychology: Learning, Memory, and Cognition*, 18, 328–44.

von Elek, T. and Oskarsson, M. 1973: *A Replication Study in Teaching Foreign Language Grammar to Adults*. Research Bulletin no. 16. Gothenburg School of Education.

Wesche, M., Edwards, H., and Wells, W. 1982: Foreign language aptitude and intelligence. *Applied Psycholinguistics*, 3, 127–40.

Whittlesea, B. W. A. and Dorken, M. D. 1993: Incidentally, things in general are particularly determined: an episodic-processing account of implicit learning. *Journal of Experimental Psychology: General*, 122, 227–48.

Williams, J. N. 1999: Memory, attention, and inductive learning. *Studies in Second Language Acquisition*, 21, 1–48.

Yang, L. R. and Givón, T. 1997: Benefits and drawbacks of controlled laboratory studies of second language acquisition: the Keck second language learning project. *Studies in Second Language Acquisition*, 19, 173–93.

12 Incidental and Intentional Learning

JAN H. HULSTIJN

1 Introduction

There are two popular views on what it means to learn a second language. One view holds that it means months and even years of "intentional" study, involving the deliberate committing to memory of thousands of words (their meaning, sound, and spelling) and dozens of grammar rules. The other, complementary, view holds that much of the burden of intentional learning can be taken off the shoulders of the language learner by processes of "incidental" learning, involving the "picking up" of words and structures, simply by engaging in a variety of communicative activities, in particular reading and listening activities, during which the learner's attention is focused on the meaning rather than on the form of language. These popular views on intentional and incidental learning reflect, at best, only partially the ways in which these terms have been and are being used in the academic literature. Some empirical researchers attribute to them only a specific methodological meaning, in the context of laboratory-type learning experiments. Apart from this methodological sense, incidental and intentional learning have been given various interpretations, sometimes indistinguishable from two more widely used terms, namely implicit and explicit learning, respectively. There are virtually no experimental L2 grammar learning studies which are explicitly presented as "intentional" learning studies, and only a handful which are explicitly presented as studies on "incidental" learning. There is a vast literature, however, of empirical studies in incidental and intentional vocabulary learning. These empirical studies reflect a wide variety of theoretical and educational/pedagogic research questions; they, therefore, do not constitute a coherent research domain, as will become apparent in this chapter.

The first aim of this chapter is to present the various ways in which the terms "incidental learning" and "intentional learning" are used in the psychological literature (section 2) and in the literature on L2 learning (section 3). The second aim is to give an overview of the empirical literature, in particular of the L2 vocabulary literature (section 4), as there are hardly any empirical studies on incidental and none on intentional L2 grammar learning (section 3.2). As the empirical literature on L2 vocabulary learning is so vast, and as the research questions differ so widely, section 4 confines itself to a number of illustrative examples. In section 5 follows a discussion of two pertinent methodological issues concerning the use of pre-tests and post-tests in incidental and intentional vocabulary learning studies. The chapter is concluded with some remarks concerning the diversity of issues addressed in it and the prospects of the labels "incidental learning" and "intentional learning" being used in the SLA field (section 6).

Readers interested in the various meanings of incidental and intentional learning are advised to turn to section 3; readers interested in vocabulary learning may find section 4 most worthy of their attention, while methodologically oriented readers may be most interested in sections 2.2, 2.4, and 5. Boxes 12.1 and 12.2 give two examples of empirical research. The first study (Horst, Cobb, and Meara, 1998) illustrates how incidental vocabulary acquisition through reading can be investigated; the second study (Griffin and Harley, 1996) illustrates how an intentional design was used in a controlled study to investigate the role of various factors in learning a list of L2 words.[1] These markedly contrasting studies are summarized in the boxes, and features not relevant in the present context have been omitted.

2 Incidental and Intentional Learning in the Psychological Literature

In this section, the notions of incidental and intentional learning are traced back to their roots in psychology. First the rise of incidental and intentional learning is described in the era of stimulus-response psychology. This is followed by a methodological subsection, characterizing so-called Type I and Type II designs in experiments involving incidental and intentional learning. Then the fall and subsequent resurrection of incidental and intentional learning are described in the era of cognitive psychology. In the last subsection, the notion of transfer-appropriate processing, important for a proper understanding of learning experiments, is highlighted.

2.1 *The origin of the notions of incidental and intentional learning in stimulus-response psychology*

According to early twentieth-century American psychologists such as James, Dewey, Watson, and Thorndike, learning is the forming of associations between sense impressions (stimuli – S) and impulses to action (responses – R). S-R psychologists distinguished various types of associative learning, ranging from

Box 12.1 Incidental learning (Horst et al., 1998)

Main research questions:

i Does reading a simplified novel lead to increased word knowledge?
ii Are words that occur more frequently in the text more likely to be learned?
iii Are words that occur more frequently in the language at large more likely to be learned?
iv Do learners with larger vocabulary sizes learn more words?

Methodology: This was a one-group pre-test–treatment–post-test study of incidental L2 vocabulary learning.

Subjects: 34 low-intermediate ESL learners in Oman (two intact classes), taking a reading course in preparation for the Cambridge Preliminary English Test.

Task: The teachers read aloud a simplified version of Thomas Hardy's *The Mayor of Casterbridge* (109 pages; 21,232 words), while learners followed along in their books. This required six sessions, over a ten-day period. With the reading-aloud and reading-along procedure all subjects were exposed to the entire text, while creating "the circumstances for incidental acquisition by precluding opportunities for intentional learning" (p. 211). Students "appeared to be absorbed by the story of secret love, dissolution and remorse, and tears were shed for the mayor when he met his lonely death at the end" (p. 211). Students were pre-tested (about a week before the reading session commenced) and post-tested on their knowledge of 45 words of low and middle frequency levels, occurring between 2 and 17 times in the text. It was assumed that the one-week time lapse "would allow the items to be forgotten to the extent that they would not be immediately recognized as testing points when they were encountered in the story. This seems to have been effective; in a discussion held after the post-test, students were surprised to learn that the tested words had occurred repeatedly in *The Mayor of Casterbridge*. Their response also suggests that any word learning that occurred was implicit and incidental" (p. 213).

Results: Mean vocabulary scores were 21.6 and 26.3 (out of 45) in pre- and post-test respectively ($t\ [33] = 5.81$; $p < 0.05$).

Conclusions: Concerning the first research question, the authors conclude that these findings "offer conclusive evidence that small but substantial amounts of incidental vocabulary learning can occur as a result of reading a simplified novel" (p. 214), but also that "the power of incidental L2 vocabulary learning may have been overestimated" (p. 220). Concerning the three remaining research questions, sizable word gains are reported (i) when words occurred eight times in the text, (ii) when words (nouns) referred to concrete concepts, and (iii) when readers' vocabulary size was at the (intermediate) 2000 level.

elementary to complex (Gagné, 1965), but all involving the four basic concepts of stimulus, response, feedback, and conditioning. The most elementary form of learning is *signal learning*, requiring the making of a general, diffuse response to a stimulus (e.g., producing tears at the sight of onions). The next form in the learning hierarchy is *stimulus-response learning* (proper), requiring

Box 12.2 Intentional learning (Griffin and Harley, 1996)

Research question: Is it more effective to learn word pairs in L1–L2 order or vice versa?

This practical general question was broken down into the following sub-questions:

i Given a word pair A–B, is the association between the two components of the word pair bi-directional?

ii If it is bi-directional, is the forward association, A–B, stronger than the backward association, B–A? Is A more likely to lead to the recall of B than vice versa? (Use of forward association means being tested in the same direction as learning. Use of backward association means being tested in the opposite direction.)

iii Given that one component is familiar and the other is unfamiliar, is it more effective to learn the familiar–unfamiliar association (L1–L2) or the unfamiliar–familiar association (L2–L1)?

iv Is production or comprehension the easier task? (Production and comprehension in this context mean, respectively, giving an L2 item in response to an L1 item cue and giving an L1 item in response to an L2 item cue, irrespective of the direction of learning.)

v Does the direction of learning have an effect on remembering over time? One possibility considered was that, although the French–English bond might appear to be easier to establish, the English–French bond might be stronger over time, due to the initial difficulty of learning and its lack of list dependence.

Methodology:

Subjects: 47 and 63 students from two high schools in Britain, between 11 and 13 years of age, after six months of learning French.

Task: Students were given 20 word pairs to learn, printed on a single sheet of paper. The instructions avoided the word "list" since the test would have the words in a different order from the original.

Students were told that they would have eight minutes to learn the word pairs, that they would then hand back their papers and receive a written test. The test forms contained 20 words (either the English or French members of the learned word pairs); students had to write down the other member of each pair (cued recall). No instruction was given on either the learning technique or the mode of testing. In each school, four groups were formed. The arrangement of experimental groups is shown in table 12.1.

Table 12.1 Arrangement of groups

Group	*Direction of learning*	*Use of forward or backward association at testing*	*Test condition*
1	English–French	Forward	Production
2	French–English	Forward	Comprehension
3	English–French	Backward	Comprehension
4	French–English	Backward	Production

The experiment adopted a 2 × 2 × 4 design, with two between-subject factors and one within-subjects factor. The between-subject factors were (i) use of forward or backward association at testing, and (ii) direction of learning (English–French or French–English). The within-subjects factor was time; students were tested four times: immediately after the learning session (day 1), as well as 3, 7, and 28 days later. No pre-test was administered. None of the French items had been encountered by students in their studies prior to the experiment, and students were not exposed to these words during the following 28 days. In order to answer the five research questions, performance of students in the following groups was compared:

Research questions i and ii: comparison between groups 1 and 2 and groups 3 and 4.
Research question iii: comparison between groups 1 and 3 and groups 2 and 4.
Research question iv: comparison between groups 1 and 4 and groups 2 and 3.
Research question v: a possible interaction between direction of learning and ability to recall over time.

Results: The four groups of school B performed consistently lower than the groups of school A (grand means of 29 percent and 47 percent respectively of words correctly recalled). For simplicity's sake, only performance of school A groups will be reported here. For details, see the original study:

Question i: The association was bi-directional: *contra* behaviorist claims, learning in one direction did not preclude performance in the opposite direction (37 percent in group 3 against 30 percent in group 4).
Question ii: Forward association was stronger than backward association (60 percent mean scores in groups 1 and 2 against 34 percent in groups 3 and 4).
Question iii: Direction of learning did not have a significant effect (45 percent mean scores for English–French learners in groups 1 and 3 and 48 percent for French–English learners in groups 2 and 4). Thus, there is nothing inherently more difficult about learning in the L1–L2 than in the L2–L1 direction.
Question iv: Comprehension scores (52 percent in groups 2 and 3) were significantly higher than production scores (41 percent in groups 1 and 4).
Question v: Performance on day 1 (53 percent) was significantly better than performance on day 3 (45 percent), day 7 (46 percent), and day 28 (43 percent). However, there was no significant interaction between language order at learning and day of testing. The English–French bond and the French–English bond decayed at much the same rate.

Conclusion: The L1–L2 learning condition is, on balance, "the more versatile direction for learning when both production and comprehension are required" (p. 453).

the making of a precise response to a discriminated stimulus. Learning L1–L2 word pairs is an example of stimulus-response learning. Sometimes, however, new words are learned through a series of S-R connections (so-called *chains*; more particularly, verbal chains, called *verbal associations*), as, for instance, when an English learner of French learns the L2 response *allumette* to the L1 stimulus *match* through the mediation of the English word *illuminate* and the word part *lum*, establishing the verbal chain *match–illuminate–lum–allumette*.[2] According to psychologists at the time, an important determinant of the formation of associations (in human learning) is the apparent preparedness or state of readiness on the part of the learner, commonly referred to as *set*, *intent*, or *motivation* (Gibson, 1941; Postman and Senders, 1946; Underwood and Schulz, 1960). For many years, approximately from 1940 to 1965, psychologists tried to develop a theory of learning set, intent, or motivation.[3] However, because of the difficulty of finding a satisfactory operationalization, researchers began to approach the concept merely in terms of the presence or absence of an explicit instruction to learn. The critical feature in this operationalization is whether or not (in incidental and intentional learning, respectively) participants are told in advance that they will be tested.

2.2 Experimental operationalization of incidental and intentional learning: Type I and Type II designs

In the heyday of S-R psychology, many studies were conducted to investigate the effect of a variety of manipulations of the stimulus materials, as well as of some learner variables such as age.[4] Two experimental methods were employed. The between-group Type I design is characteristic of the earlier studies. Participants in the incidental condition perform an orienting task on the stimulus materials, but they are given no instructions to learn and they are unexpectedly given a retention test afterwards. Participants in the intentional conditions are told in advance that they will later be tested. Early research aimed at demonstrating (i) that incidental learning did indeed exist and (ii) that intentional learning was superior to incidental learning. In the within-group Type II design, which was adopted in most later studies, all participants are instructed to learn some of the stimuli presented to them; but additional stimuli, which participants are not told to learn, are presented at the same time. Retention of the additional stimuli is unexpectedly tested afterwards. Thus, in the Type II design participants are their own controls, serving under both intentional and incidental conditions of learning, being exposed to two categories of stimuli, while expecting to be tested on only one of these. The additional stimuli in the Type II design may be either intrinsic or extrinsic, as illustrated with the following two hypothetical examples:

> *Example 1, illustrating the use of intrinsic additional stimuli:* The stimulus materials contain target words, which are printed either in bold face or in italics and in either red or blue (yielding a 2 × 2 design of stimulus form). The orienting task focuses participants' attention on color (instruction: "Try to remember which words appeared in red and which ones in blue"). Afterwards, participants are tested on their recall of red and blue words (intentional learning). But, unexpectedly, they are also requested to tell which

words originally appeared in bold face and in italics (incidental learning). In this experimental design, the additional stimuli (typefaces) are said to be intrinsic because they belong to the same entities to which the attended stimuli (colors) belong.

Example 2, illustrating the use of extrinsic additional stimuli: The stimulus materials consist of a list of words some of which are printed in capitals and some in lower case. The orienting task focuses participants' attention on the words in capitals (instruction: "Try to remember the capitalized words"). Afterwards, participants are tested on their recall of both capitalized (intentional) and lower-case words (incidental). The lower-case stimuli are said to be extrinsic to the experimenter-defined learning task, as they do not embody features of the attended stimuli.

2.3 *Incidental and intentional learning in cognitive psychology*

With the decline of S-R psychology and the advent of cognitive psychology in the 1960s and 1970s, marking a fundamental paradigm shift, psychologists lost interest in the concept of set or intention as a central construct in the explanation of human learning and memory performance. This would have meant the demise of the constructs of incidental and intentional learning had not the work of some cognitive psychologists in the 1970s saved them from oblivion, not for theoretical but mainly for methodological reasons. Researchers of *information processing* and *memory* (the labels that replaced *learning*, which was felt to be associated too much with S-R psychology) in the 1970s, unearthed the Type II incidental learning design because it appeared to serve as an excellent tool in the investigation of the effect of various types of information processing on long-term information retention. For instance, in a seminal paper, Hyde and Jenkins (1973) presented groups of participants with a number of words and asked each group to perform a different *orienting task*. Participants were not told in advance that they would be later tested on their recall of the words. Jenkins and Hyde demonstrated that retention on the unexpected test fluctuated with orienting task. For instance, retention scores of participants who had rated the words as to their pleasantness or unpleasantness on a five-point scale (a semantic orienting task) were much higher than those of participants who had to record the part of speech of the words (a non-semantic orienting task).[5] This and similar studies led Craik and Lockhart (1972) to propose their levels-of-processing theory, which engendered a lively theoretical debate and a great number of empirical investigations using incidental and (to a much lesser extent) intentional learning designs for many years to come (for a review, see Baddeley, 1997, ch. 7). It is through these studies that the notions of incidental and intentional learning have survived to the present day. For contemporary psychologists, their value is based on their record as research tools, rather than on their theoretical substance.

In conclusion, incidental and intentional learning refer, strictly speaking, only to the absence or presence of an announcement to participants in a psychological experiment as to whether they will be tested after the experimental task. Thus, in the incidental case, the experiment may not even be explicitly presented as a "learning experiment," because the word "learning" itself may already lead to testing expectancies among participants and hence to subject-generated information-processing strategies unwanted by the experimenter. In other words, incidental learning has acquired the status of a tool in the cognitive psychologist's experimental research kit to investigate some way or ways of information processing as intended by the investigator, not contaminated by ways of information processing not intended by the investigator. The presence or absence of an intention to learn does not figure as a theoretical construct in any current theory of human cognition.

2.4 *Transfer-appropriate learning and the crucial role of the orienting task*

Retention or criterial tasks to be performed after a learning phase may be compatible, incompatible, or neutral to the processing mode of the previous learning task. In connection with this phenomenon of (in)compatibility between learning and retention task, Bransford, Franks, Morris, and Stein (1979) introduced the notion of *transfer appropriateness*. Bransford and his associates (Morris, Bransford, and Franks, 1977) found an interaction between encoding processes (semantic and non-semantic learning tasks) and the product of retrieval processes (semantic and non-semantic retention tasks). Participants who had been administered compatible learning and retention tasks (semantic–semantic, or non-semantic–non-semantic) achieved higher retention scores than participants who were given incompatible learning and retention tasks (semantic–non-semantic, or non-semantic–semantic). The lesson to be learned here is that an accurate assessment of intentional and incidental learning experiments requires a joint consideration of learning and retention task (Eysenck, 1982, p. 225).[6] This can be illustrated with the study in box 12.2 (Griffin and Harley, 1996). In this intentional learning experiment, participants had to learn and memorize L2 words, which were paired to their L1 equivalents in either the L1–L2 productive order or in the L2–L1 receptive order. At test, the order was either the same as (productive–productive or receptive–receptive) or different from (productive–receptive or receptive–productive) the order during learning. It was found that retention scores on a same-order test were substantially higher than retention scores on a different-order test.

The notion of transfer appropriateness may help to illustrate the difference between incidental and intentional learning. For example, as participants in an intentional vocabulary learning task are told in advance that they will be tested after the learning phase, they will try to store the word information that is to be learned in a form perceived as transferable to the test situation;

and processing instructions during the learning phase in an incidental learning setting may or may not be conducive to successful transfer to the test situation. For instance, participants in an incidental learning vocabulary learning experiment who are instructed to pay attention to the meaning of some new words which appear in a reading text are likely to perform much better on an unexpected receptive post-test than on an unexpected productive post-test. The notion of transfer appropriateness also underscores the crucial importance of the orienting task given in a (Type I) learning study, because the orienting task is the instrument with which the researcher can control or manipulate participants' attention to the information to be learned, and attention is a necessary condition for noticing and learning (Robinson, this volume; Schmidt, 2001).[7]

3 Incidental and Intentional Learning in the L2 Learning Literature

This section will address the question of how incidental and intentional learning figure in the literature on L2 learning. As the field of L2 learning is fragmented into rather isolated sub-domains with little cross-talk, it comes as no surprise that the notions of incidental and intentional learning appear prominently in one domain but not at all in another. Incidental and intentional learning mainly figure in the area of vocabulary (including spelling). They do not appear at all in the areas of phonetics and phonology, however, and only exceptionally in the area of grammar (morphology and syntax).[8] The reason why the term "intentional learning" does figure in the vocabulary learning literature but hardly in the literature on grammar learning, whereas "incidental" figures in both literatures, is that "incidental," in principle, can apply to abstract as well as to factual declarative knowledge, whereas "intentional" appears to be applicable to factual knowledge only, as will be explained below in section 3.5.[9]

3.1 *Weak theoretical interpretations of incidental learning*

Incidental learning has often been rather loosely interpreted in common terms, not firmly rooted in a particular theory. It could therefore be said to have several theoretical meanings, in the weak sense. From Schmidt (1994a) three definitions can be derived:

i The most general meaning is couched in negative terms as learning without the intent to learn (p. 16).
ii Another interpretation is that it refers to the learning of one stimulus aspect while paying attention to another stimulus aspect. As Schmidt (1994a, p. 16) puts it, incidental learning is "learning of one thing (. . .) when the

learner's primary objective is to do something else (. . .)." This meaning of incidental clearly shows its descent from the methodological meaning, mentioned in section 2.1.

iii A slightly more specific interpretation of incidental learning is that it refers to the learning of formal features through a focus of attention on semantic features. Again, in the words of Schmidt (1994a, p. 16), but now with the previously omitted parenthetical phrases included: incidental learning is "learning of one thing (e.g., grammar) when the learner's primary objective is to do something else (e.g., communicate)."

Recently, Gass (1999) suggested a new, extended meaning for incidental learning as the learning of grammatical structures without exposure to instances of these structures. She refers to two studies on the acquisition of relative clauses (Eckman, Bell, and Nelson, 1988; Gass, 1982) in which learners were exposed to some but not all types of relative clauses and appeared to have learned not only the structures presented to them but also, "incidentally," the structures not presented in the input but implied by the ones that were presented. Thus, in addition to the distinction made in section 2.2 between intrinsic and extrinsic additional stimuli, and somewhat stretching the traditional notion of *stimulus*, one could even postulate a third category of implied, but not presented, and therefore not attended-to, stimuli.

Most L2 learning researchers use incidental learning in connection with the learning of vocabulary through reading.[10] As section 4.1 will show, it is widely believed that most people in literate societies enlarge their vocabularies through reading, focusing on the meaning of words and texts, rather than through the conscious, intentional memorization of lists of word forms and their meanings. A typical and well-known proponent of this view is Krashen (1989), who, in the context of his Input Hypothesis, argues that we acquire vocabulary and spelling through exposure to comprehensible input.

3.2 Empirical studies on incidental L2 grammar learning

In many empirical L2 grammar-learning studies, participants are exposed to L2 data under various experimentally manipulated conditions, without being told that these data represent instances of some feature (principle or rule) of the L2 grammar and that the investigator's aim is to assess the extent to which participants are able to acquire this feature under the experimental conditions. It could be argued that, methodologically speaking, these studies are concerned with incidental learning. For example, in a well-known experiment, Doughty (1991) studied the acquisition of different kinds of English relative clauses by adult ESL learners. The study adopted a between-subjects design that included two experimental groups (and a control group, not relevant in the present context). Participants in one experimental group received meaning-oriented instruction; participants in the other experimental group received rule-oriented instruction. Neither experimental group was told in advance that they would be tested afterwards on their acquisition of various types of relative clauses. Thus, from a methodological perspective, both experimental groups can be called incidental groups. However, as the use of the term "incidental learning" would not have had a theoretically relevant meaning in this study, Doughty, understandably, found no reason to use this term.[11]

Only three experimental L2 grammar-learning studies appear to have explicitly used the term "incidental," but none of them pitted incidental against intentional learning. The first study (Hulstijn, 1989) involved three experimental groups (Form, Meaning, and Form and Meaning). Theoretically, the study is presented as one of implicit learning, meaning that learners were not consciously aware of the grammatical target features under investigation. Methodologically, the study is presented as an incidental learning study: "Ss were not informed about the research questions until after the completion of the last test, and, while carrying out a current task, did not know whether a subsequent test would follow" (p. 54). The second and third studies (reported, respectively, in Robinson 1996a, 1996b, 1997) involved four experimental conditions: Implicit, Incidental, Explicit Rule Search, and Explicit Instruction (in the 1996 study), and Implicit, Incidental, Enhanced, and Instructed (in the 1997 study). The implicit and incidental conditions were alike "in not requiring a conscious focus on the grammatical form of the stimuli presented during training. In the implicit condition the task instruction is to memorize sentences, whereas in the incidental condition the task instruction is to read the sentences and understand their meaning" (Robinson, 1996b, p. 35). Robinson, who motivates his use of the term "incidental" by a reference to Paradis (1994, p. 394), whose definition will be quoted in section 3.4, appears to use "incidental" to refer to learning of L2 forms through a focus of attention on meaning, as in the third definition mentioned in section 3.1.

In summary, although some definitions of incidental L2 grammar learning have been proposed in the literature (in particular, Gass, 1999; Schmidt, 1994a), no reports of empirical L2 grammar learning studies have so far been published which explicitly base themselves on the Schmidt or Gass definitions. This is quite understandable, as the notion of implicit learning has had a greater appeal among SLA researchers than the notion of incidental learning (see section 3.4; DeKeyser, this volume; Doughty, this volume).[12]

3.3 *The meaning of "intentional" in the vocabulary-learning literature*

In the literature on vocabulary learning, when used at all, "intentional learning" is commonly given a cognitive interpretation, as the rehearsal and memorizing techniques invoked by learners when they have the explicit intention of learning and retaining lexical information (Schmitt, 1997).

3.4 *The differences between incidental and implicit and between intentional and explicit types of learning*

For many authors, incidental and intentional learning overlap with, or even become indistinguishable from, implicit and explicit learning respectively. There are several interpretations of the terms "implicit" and "explicit" learning (see DeKeyser, this volume). The most characteristic feature, however, distinguishing implicit from explicit learning is the absence or presence of "conscious operations" (N. Ellis, 1994, p. 1), a notion also referred to as the absence or presence of "awareness at the point of learning" (Schmidt, 1994a, p. 20). Note that none of the definitions of incidental and intentional listed in section 3.1 is synonymous with the definitions of implicit and explicit learning given by Ellis and Schmidt. In line with Schmidt (1994a), it is recommended here that the distinctions between incidental and implicit and between intentional and explicit should be maintained. Paradis (1994, p. 394), for instance, distinguishes incidental from implicit in the following definition of implicit competence, which "is acquired incidentally (i.e., by not focusing attention on what is being internalized, as in acquiring the form while focusing on the meaning), stored implicitly (i.e., not available to conscious awareness), and used automatically (i.e., without conscious control)." Thus, incidental learning, in all the definitions listed in section 3.1, is always implicated in implicit learning; implicit learning thus entails more than what is meant by incidental learning.

In a similar vein, it is recommended here that a distinction be maintained between intentional and explicit learning. Whereas explicit learning involves awareness at the point of learning (e.g., by trying to understand what the function of a certain language form is), intentional learning involves a deliberate attempt to commit new information to memory (e.g., by applying rehearsal and/or mnemonic techniques).

3.5 *Confusions concerning the interaction of the* **what** *and* **how** *of incidental and intentional learning*

The nagging problem in discussions concerning incidental and intentional (as well as implicit and explicit) learning is that, although the definitions of these terms appear to refer to the *how* of learning (learning mechanisms), their interpretations depend on authors' views on the *what* of learning (the representation of knowledge in the mind/brain).[13] For instance, it is relatively easy to imagine the intentional learning of a list of L2 words, as these form–meaning connections are readily conceived of as instances of declarative, factual knowledge. However, as soon as we define the *what* of learning as abstract knowledge of properties of L2 grammar (e.g., knowledge of the L2 setting of the pro-drop parameter), it is almost impossible to conceive of the acquisition of this abstract grammatical feature taking place through intentional learning.

It is much easier, it seems, to conceive of the acquisition of this feature taking place through implicit, and hence through incidental learning (see section 3.4). This and similar interactions between the *what* and *how* of L2 learning have caused, and continue to cause, confusions in the L2 learning literature.[14] It comes as no surprise, therefore, that the area in which "incidental" and "intentional" are used most frequently is that of vocabulary learning. Vocabulary knowledge can easily be conceived of as a type of declarative knowledge, and it is declarative knowledge which can be learned intentionally (e.g., with various memory aids) as well as incidentally (e.g., through reading and listening). It can be concluded that incidental and intentional learning are differentially important for different classes of target language features: whereas incidental is used in connection with the learning of both abstract and factual knowledge, the use of intentional is restricted to the learning of factual knowledge. When used in connection with factual knowledge, incidental and intentional learning in the realm of language (e.g., learning vocabulary items, writing systems, spelling rules, conventions for addressing people in oral or written discourse according to their age, sex, and status) does not appear to differ from incidental and intentional learning in other walks of life (e.g., learning geographical names, historical events).

3.6 *The issue of two poles on a continuum as opposed to two distinct categories*

Should incidental and intentional learning be thought of as two distinct learning processes or as poles on a continuum? There is no simple answer to this question. As Schmidt (1994a, 1994b) has argued, there is no learning without attention and noticing. This is true not only for implicit but also for incidental learning. Incidental and intentional share the involvement of attention and noticing (see the quotation from Paradis, 1994, p. 394, in section 3.4). Thus, in the dimension of attention and noticing, incidental and intentional do not form two distinct categories. However, this still leaves open possibilities of distinct processes in other dimensions. As was mentioned and illustrated in section 3.2, incidental and intentional are not juxtaposed to each other in the L2 grammar-learning literature. The polarity issue, therefore, does not seem to play a role in the domain of grammar learning. In the L2 vocabulary-learning literature, however, incidental and intentional learning are seen as distinct categories, in that intentional learning does, and incidental does not, imply the use of deliberate retention techniques.

In conclusion, on the one hand, both incidental and intentional learning require some attention and noticing. On the other hand, however, attention is deliberately directed to committing new information to memory in the case of intentional learning, whereas the involvement of attention is not deliberately geared toward an articulated learning goal in the case of incidental learning.

4 Empirical Studies on Incidental and Intentional L2 Vocabulary Learning

This section deals with the empirical research on incidental and intentional L2 vocabulary learning. Recent reviews of (parts of) the extensive literature can be found in Nation (2001), Singleton (1999), and collections edited by Coady and Huckin (1997), Schmitt and McCarthy (1997), and Wesche and Paribakht (1999).

4.1 *Incidental vocabulary learning through extensive reading*

This section addresses the popular view that people learn most of their L1 and L2 vocabularies through incidental learning (mostly, but not exclusively, reading) rather than through intentional learning. The issue itself is examined first (in section 4.1.1); the empirical evidence is reviewed next (in section 4.1.2).

4.1.1 The default argument

As stated in section 3.5, it is widely believed in the applied field of language pedagogy that most vocabulary, in L1 as well as in L2, is acquired in an incidental fashion, as the by-product of reading and listening activities not explicitly geared to vocabulary learning. Furthermore, it is widely held that little vocabulary is acquired in an intentional fashion, through activities aimed at deliberately committing lexical information to memory and keeping that information readily accessible. Influential in this respect have been publications by Nagy and Anderson (1984), Nagy and Herman (1987), and Nagy, Herman, and Anderson (1985). These researchers showed that American high school students know between 25,000 and 50,000 words, and argued that students cannot have learned such a large number of words solely by means of explicit vocabulary instruction. Rather, students must have learned most words in an incremental way through repeated encounters during extensive reading. A meta-analysis of 20 experiments examining incidental L1 word learning during normal reading, conducted by Swanborn and De Glopper (1999), showed that students learn around 15 percent of the unknown words they encounter. The learning of an unknown word while reading is affected by several factors, such as pre-test sensitization, students' grade levels, students' level of reading ability, the sensitivity of assessment methods to partial word knowledge, and the amount of text surrounding the target words.

The vocabulary-acquisition-through-reading argument is a default argument: because relatively few words are explicitly taught, most words must have been acquired from reading.[15] It has led, however, to various pedagogical interpretations (Coady, 1997). Some educationalists claim that students will learn all the vocabulary they need from context by reading extensively (Krashen, 1989). Others, however, while acknowledging the usefulness, even necessity, of extensive reading, have emphasized the importance of making L2 learners aware of their vocabulary learning task and of teaching explicit strategies for vocabulary learning (see Sökmen, 1997, for a review).[16]

4.1.2 Empirical L2 evidence

Studies of incidental vocabulary learning through extensive reading by L2 learners have been conducted by Cho and Krashen (1994) and Dupuy and Krashen (1993). These studies claim substantial vocabulary gains through reading. Wode (1999) conducted a pilot study of incidental learning of productive vocabulary over a seven-month period in a grade-7 immersion program in a German high school (English L2, German L1). One immersion class was compared with two control groups. The immersion class had, in addition to regular English-as-a-subject lessons, one subject (history) taught in English (by a German, non-native speaker). The two control classes, one from the same school as the immersion class, and one from another school which did not offer immersion, had only regular English-as-a-subject. Wode reports that, in an oral production post-test, the immersion group "used a considerably larger vocabulary than the two control groups in terms of both types and tokens" (p. 249).

Three studies have been conducted of the reading of a novel (in English) containing unknown words. These studies are, in chronological order: Saragi, Nation, and Meister (1978); Pitts, White, and Krashen (1989); and Horst et al. (1998). In the Saragi et al. study, 20 native speakers of English read Anthony Burgess's novel *A Clockwork Orange*, containing 241 unfamiliar words, mainly of Russian origin, that are used as a kind of slang called *nadsat*. Frequency of occurrence of these nadsat words ranged from 88 to 1, with a mean of 15. Participants did not know that the nadsat vocabulary would be tested afterwards; instead, they were told that they would be given a comprehension and literary criticism test. It was found that "repetition affects learning, but that the relationship is considerably complicated by other factors like meaningfulness of the context and similarity to words in the mother-tongue" (p. 76). In the Pitts et al. study, two groups of ESL learners read two chapters of *A Clockwork Orange* and were subsequently tested for their understanding of the nadsat words. Small vocabulary gains were recorded relative to control groups who had not read the text. The researchers claim this shows that L2 learners can acquire vocabulary by reading. The Horst et al. study is reported in box 12.1. The authors of this study conclude that the power of incidental L2 vocabulary learning may have previously been overestimated. (See section 4.3, for typical retention rates in more controlled experimental studies.)

4.2 Other incidental vocabulary studies under experimentally manipulated reading conditions

Many studies of incidental L2 vocabulary learning through reading or listening have been conducted to investigate the influence of a variety of factors pertaining to characteristics of target words, input modality (reading vs. listening;

reading vs. writing), frequency of exposure, characteristics of the verbal and non-verbal context, and presence or absence of cues as to the meaning of the target words (e.g., marginal glosses, opportunity to consult a dictionary). As almost all of these studies have been conducted since the behaviorist–cognitivist paradigm shift in psychology, most of them situate their research question, implicitly or explicitly, within an information-processing framework, sharing the assumption that "memory performance is determined far more by the nature of the processing activities engaged in by the learner than it is by the intention to learn per se" (Eysenck, 1982, p. 203). Most studies refer, in this respect, to the classical notions of *depth of processing* (Craik and Lockhart, 1972) and *elaboration* (Craik and Tulving, 1975). Recently, Laufer and Hulstijn (2001) tentatively proposed the notion of *involvement*, consisting of (i) a motivational component, comprising the *need* to determine a new word's meaning, and (ii) a cognitive component, comprising *search* (e.g., dictionary look-up) and *evaluation* (e.g., evaluating whether the information obtained from the dictionary applies to the verbal and non-verbal context). Each of these three factors can be absent or present during the processing of a new word in a natural or artificially designed task. The authors hypothesize that retention of hitherto unfamiliar words is conditional, in general, upon the degree of involvement in processing these words. The concept of involvement can be operationalized and submitted to empirical investigation by devising incidental-learning tasks with various degrees of need, search, and evaluation.

The following factors have been studied for their potential effects on incidental L2 vocabulary learning: new word density (Holley, 1973), new word frequency (Hulstijn, Hollander, and Greidanus, 1996; Rott, 1999), oral input (Loschky, 1994; R. Ellis, 1995; R. Ellis and Heimbach, 1997; and R. Ellis, Tanaka, and Yamazaki, 1994), oral vs. written input in watching subtitled cartoon films (d'Ydewalle and Pavakanun, 1995; Van de Poel and d'Ydewalle, 2001), reading vs. writing (Hulstijn and Trompetter, 1998), glossing and/or inferencing (Cobb, 1997; Cobb and Horst, 2001; Hulstijn, 1992; Hulstijn et al., 1996; Kost, Foss, and Lenzini, 1999; Watanabe, 1997), and dictionary use (Fischer, 1994; Hulstijn et al., 1996; Knight, 1994; Laufer and Hill, 2000). The results show a differentiated pattern, consistent with the view that it is elaboration of (Craik and Tulving, 1975) or involvement in (Laufer and Hulstijn, 2001) the lexical information being processed rather than any of these factors per se that determines retention. For L2 educators it is important to note that deep information processing normally requires more time than superficial information processing. Thus, for each device, the benefits must be assessed against the costs. For example, glossing gives a high return in terms of comprehension but a low return in terms of retention, when glossed words appear only once in a text. Retention of glossed words, however, increases substantially when they reoccur several times. On the other hand, retention of words whose meaning has to be inferred may be relatively high, but this benefit comes at the price of time and with the danger of incorrect inferencing (and consequently of learning incorrect word meanings) if no corrective feedback is given.

4.3 Differences in learning rates between incidental and intentional learning conditions

In general, retention rates under genuine incidental learning conditions are extremely low (Swanborn and De Glopper, 1999), depending, of course, on the factors mentioned above (frequency of occurrence, presence or absence of a cue, relevance of the target word, etc.). Retention rates under intentional learning conditions are, again on average, much higher than under incidental conditions. For example, in experiment 4 of a study conducted by Hulstijn (1992) native speakers of Dutch read an expository text of 907 words, containing 12 unfamiliar pseudo-words. Each pseudo-word occurred only once and was supplied with an L2 marginal cue as to its meaning. Half of the participants (N = 24) performed the reading task under incidental learning conditions. They were instructed to read the text carefully and prepare for answering some reading comprehension questions, which were to be given after reading, without the text being available. The other half of the participants (N = 28) performed the same task but under intentional conditions, that is, they were informed in advance that there would be a vocabulary-retention task after completion of their reading task. The average retention ratios of participants in incidental and intentional groups were 4 percent and 53 percent respectively on the immediate post-test in which all 12 target words were tested in isolation, and 43 percent and 73 percent on a subsequent post-test in which target words were tested in their original context. In a similar study, Mondria and Wit-de Boer (1991) asked Dutch high school students to learn eight French content words, which were presented in sentence contexts of varying strength along with their L1 translation. Study time was 10 minutes. The mean retention score under this form of intentional learning was 5.2 (65 percent).

In boxes 12.1 and 12.2, one incidental and one intentional vocabulary learning study are summarized (respectively Horst et al., 1998, and Griffin and Harley, 1996). Retention scores in these two studies differed substantially: an increase of 10 percent between pre- (48 percent) and post-test (58 percent) in the incidental study, and average retention scores of 29 percent and 47 percent in the two groups involved in the intentional study. These differences, in hindsight, may not be surprising, given the marked differences between the two studies in design and method. In order to avoid premature educational conclusions concerning the alleged superiority or inferiority of intentional over incidental learning, two points must be borne in mind.

The first is that it is almost impossible to control for "time on task" in comparisons conducted under educationally valid circumstances. For instance, in the study by Hulstijn (1992), mentioned above, students in both the incidental and intentional conditions did much more than processing unfamiliar lexical items. They were instructed to read the text and prepare for answering comprehension questions. Thus, the experimenter did not have control over how participants used the allotted time. Students in the intentional group may have spent more time on rehearsing the 12 unknown words and less on preparing for the upcoming comprehension questions than the incidental group, although performance on comprehension questions did not differ between the two groups. Studies which try to exert maximal control over information processing during exposure have little relevance for L2 pedagogy. A good example is a classic experiment conducted by Hyde and Jenkins (1973), typical of the sort of experiments conducted by psychologists at the time. Participants in this study were native English undergraduate psychology students. There were 20 experimental groups and two control groups. Participants listened to one of two lists of 24 English words, recorded at 3-second intervals. The lists consisted of 12 pairs of either unrelated (List 1) or associated words (List 2). While listening, students in the experimental groups had to perform one of five orienting tasks: (i) rating the words on a five-point rating scale of (un)pleasantness; (ii) estimating the frequency with which the words are used in the English language; (iii) making a check on whether the letters E and G occurred in the words; (iv) recording whether the words were nouns, verbs, or adjectives; and (v) indicating whether the words could or could not fit in two sentence frames ("It is —" and "It is a —"). Hyde and Jenkins classify the first two tasks as semantic and the remaining three as non-semantic.[17] Ten of the 20 experimental groups were told in advance that their recall of the 24 words would later be assessed (intentional condition); the other ten were not given this advance information (incidental condition). Students in the two control groups were not given orienting tasks but were simply instructed to remember the words and informed of an upcoming recall task (intentional condition). One control group was exposed to List 1 and the other to List 2. The design can be described as a 2 (List) × 5 (Orienting Task) × 2 (Intentionality) design, plus two control groups.

The following findings deserve to be mentioned in the present context. Semantically associated List 2 words were better recalled than unrelated List 1 words, regardless of other factors. Among the 20 experimental groups, groups in the two semantic orienting tasks (i and ii) outperformed groups in the three non-semantic orienting tasks (iii, iv, and v). Groups under intentional learning conditions obtained significantly and substantially higher recall scores than those under incidental conditions only when given the two semantic orienting tasks, whereas the two control groups (intentional condition – no orienting task) did *not* outperform the intentional groups in the semantic orienting tasks (i and ii). These results illustrate that retention is determined more by the nature of the processing activities than by learning intention (knowing or not knowing that retention will be assessed after exposure), as observed by Eysenck (1982, p. 203; see the quotation in section 4.2) and Postman (1964, p. 190). Thus, whereas most incidental L2 vocabulary-learning studies could not exert optimal control on information processing, the Hyde and Jenkins study was designed as a highly controlled study.[18] That study, however, has hardly any relevance for L2 pedagogy, as participants did not learn new words (form–meaning connections) and were exposed to each target item only once during a session which lasted only 72 seconds in total!

The second point is that most of the incidental L2 vocabulary-learning studies mentioned in section 4.2 were designed to assess the effect of information processing during the execution of a task in which new words were encountered for the first time. Their results are valid, and educationally relevant, only as far as this initial encounter is concerned.[19] What is far more relevant for educational practice is that long-term retention of new vocabulary normally requires frequent exposures or rehearsal, regardless of the conditions under which new words have initially been encountered.[20]

4.4 Studies of intentional L2 vocabulary learning

Researchers have used intentional learning designs to investigate a wide variety of research questions (cf. the classic experiments conducted by Crothers and Suppes, 1967). This subsection will confine itself to some illustrative examples of studies based on psycholinguistic and educational-pedagogical research questions (in sections 4.4.1 and 4.4.2 respectively).

4.4.1 Psycholinguistic studies

Most of the paired-associate research in the behaviorist era dealt with the pairing of two known words and has therefore not been considered relevant to the needs of L2 learners. Yet the method of paired-associate learning, involving L1–L2 word pairs, under intentional learning conditions, has occasionally been applied by cognitive psychologists in the post-behaviorist era, as the study by Griffin and Harley (1996) illustrates (see box 12.2). The experiments on the important role of the phonological loop in short-term memory for both L1 and L2 vocabulary learning, conducted by Baddeley and his co-workers, are famous. Papagno, Valentine, and Baddeley (1991) demonstrated that articulatory suppression of L2 items with high semantic association value did not impair learning, but that articulatory suppression of L2 items with low semantic value did, suggesting that articulatory rehearsal plays a role in L2 vocabulary learning, particularly when the words to be learned cannot be easily associated semantically with L1 words. Service and Craik (1993) manipulated the phonological similarity between English L1 words and the words to be learned (Finnish vs. pseudo-words) and the associative value of the L1 cue words (high vs. low imaginability) and found that both younger (age range between 20 and 40 years) and older adults (60 years and older) profited from phonological similarity and associative value.[21] Atkins and Baddeley (1998) demonstrated that individual differences in verbal, but not in non-verbal, working memory affect intentional L2 vocabulary learning substantially.

The intentional learning paradigm, in which participants are instructed to learn verbal information in association with other verbal or non-verbal (e.g., pictorial) information, offers an ideal testing ground for theories of the organization of the mental lexicon, monolingual as well as bilingual. Research in this vast area, mainly conducted in the laboratories of psychology departments and published in psychological journals, is reviewed by, for instance, Kroll and De Groot (1997). Recently, Lotto and De Groot (1998) examined the roles of learning method (translation vs. picture), word frequency, and cognate status. During the learning phase of the experiment, 80 L2 words were presented in three rounds, with either their L1 translation or a picture. During the test, which measured productive L2 vocabulary knowledge, either the pictures or the L1 translations constituted the cues for recall of the L2 words. The results showed that the translation learning condition resulted in better recall performance than the picture condition, and cognates and high-frequency words were easier to learn than non-cognates and low-frequency words (see also N. Ellis and Beaton, 1993).

Kroll, Michael, and Sankaranarayanan (1998) investigated L2 vocabulary learning under conditions differing in the allowance of L1 word mediation and concept mediation. The results show that, even when semantic (pictorial) information is salient, learners are likely to rely on mediation via L1. In contrast, the presence of novel perceptual information (pictures were presented in a non-canonical, upside-down, format) appears to benefit vocabulary learning. On the basis of their results, the authors hypothesize that "adding a unique cue in memory during L2 learning later facilitates the ability to think conceptually in the second language, as long as the cue can be associated to an already familiar concept" (p. 390).

The third and final example to be mentioned here is the study by Yang (1997), who conducted a longitudinal investigation of computer-aided learning of (artificial) vocabulary (word translation, word recognition, and semantic priming) over an instruction period of five weeks. Participants in this study were 29 American undergraduate students. In this unique study, which was partly based on earlier work by Kroll and her associates, Yang found that semantic priming – indicative of connectivity in the semantic network – was intact very early. This was reflected in the early accurate (but slow) performance in the translation and semantic priming tasks. However, speed of performance in the word recognition task increased slowly and continued to benefit from instruction. It is important to note that, as in so many psycholinguistic studies, vocabulary learning in many of these psycholinguistic L2 studies was measured in terms not only of response correctness but also of response latency (as an indication of degree of automatization).

4.4.2 *Practice-based, educational studies*

Intentional vocabulary learning can take place in a wide variety of instructional settings. A continuing debate among teachers and learners concerns the questions of (i) whether it is better to learn words in monolingual (new L2 item explained with familiar L2 item) or bilingual (new L2 item explained with L1 translation) lists, and (ii) whether it is better to present new words in context or in isolation (word list format). A classic study addressing the former issue is that by Oskarsson (1975), who presented adult Swedish learners of English with texts containing unfamiliar target words glossed either in English (monolingual glosses) or in Swedish (bilingual glosses). Students knew in advance that they would later be tested on their word knowledge. Retention over all groups and texts consistently favored the bilingual condition (with an average retention score of 18.6, over an average of 14.7 in the monolingual condition, out of a maximum of 35). Studies addressing the latter issue, context or no context (Grace, 1998; Lawson and Hogben, 1996; Mondria and Wit-de Boer, 1991; Prince, 1996; Qian, 1996; Seibert, 1930), have obtained mixed results, probably due to the fact that, as Nation (1982) and Nagy (1997) have pointed out, context is a multifaceted construct. Tinkham (1993), Waring (1998), and Schneider, Healy, and Bourne (1998) investigated whether it is good practice, as dictated by most L2 teaching materials, to have learners study lists of semantically related items (such as words for clothes) or whether it is better to have students learn lists of unrelated words. In all three studies it was found that presenting words in semantic clusters interferes with learning (see also Royer, 1973).

It appears that a number of researchers have investigated various presentation and rehearsal regimes (with and without feedback) in computer-aided instruction, but such studies are almost never published in international journals. These studies continue the tradition of the paired-associate learning experiments with "learning machines" that were so common in the behaviorist era. This line of research is of great practical interest, but it appears that, unfortunately, too little research money and interest are invested in it.

The last body of empirical research using intentional learning designs to be mentioned in this subsection concerns the study of mnemo-techniques. The technique most studied is the so-called *keyword method*, involving the use of memory-facilitating mediator words aimed at helping the learner make a link between the form and meaning of an L2 word that is to be learned. The mediating word should ideally be associated in sound with the form of the word to be learned, while simultaneously being available to a visual representation in which the meaning of the word to be learned can somehow be incorporated (preferably yielding a bizarre, and therefore highly memorable, picture). For example, an English person learning the German word *Raupe* (meaning *caterpillar*) could use the English word *rope* (similar in sound to *Raupe*) as a keyword, while constructing a mental image of a caterpillar stretched out to more than its fullest length (exaggeration helps) on a rope. Research in this area has been reviewed by Cohen (1987), N. Ellis and Beaton (1993), Hulstijn (1997a), and Rodríguez and Sadoski (2000). Cohen (1987) concludes his review with the claim that memory techniques have been shown to produce high retention rates but are not intended to replace other, more natural, approaches to vocabulary learning. Similarly, Hulstijn (1997a) advises that the keyword technique should only be used for words that, for whatever reason, have not been successfully acquired along normal routes.

5 Methodological Issues in Incidental and Intentional Vocabulary-Learning Studies

Boxes 12.1 and 12.2 contain examples of incidental and intentional vocabulary learning experiments (Horst et al., 1998, and Griffin and Harley, 1996, respectively). Both investigations were conducted with participants who already had some knowledge of the L2. This raises the problem of how to control for prior vocabulary knowledge in such investigations. Furthermore, in both studies participants' knowledge of the words to which they had been exposed in the treatment phase was tested only in a single post-test; no subsequent, delayed post-tests were administered to assess long-term retention. This absence of the measurement of long-term retention is often disapproved of. This section offers a methodological discussion of both these issues: (i) the possibility that learning targets (words to be learned) are already familiar to some of the subjects prior to the experiment (section 5.1), and (ii) the question of whether it is sufficient to use immediate post-tests only, or whether delayed post-tests are required (section 5.2).

5.1 *Pre-testing*

One of the problems in designing vocabulary-learning experiments is controlling for pre-knowledge of the target words. When participants already have some L2 knowledge, it is hard to rule out the possibility that they have (partial) knowledge of the target words used in the experiment. This was clearly the case with the study summarized in box 12.1 (Horst et al., 1998). The researchers of the study summarized in box 12.2 (Griffin and Harley, 1996) confined themselves to consulting the teachers concerned, according to whom none of the 20 selected target words had been encountered by students in their classes until then; but Griffin and Harley did not include a pre-test in their design in order to verify whether students were indeed unfamiliar with the target words.

One way of dealing with the pre-knowledge problem is to ask participants after the experiment proper to indicate whether they already knew the words before the experiment, and then to exclude the data on pre-known words from analysis. This method, adopted, for instance, by Hulstijn et al. (1996), has two disadvantages: (i) participants' responses will vary in reliability, and (ii) removal of data on some target words for some participants will limit the power and validity of statistical analyses.

To tackle the issue of reliability at least to some extent, the following method could be adopted.[22] Approximately one week prior to the experiment, participants are pre-tested. They are given a list of words (or rather letter sequences) and instructed to indicate which they do and do not know. Participants are told that the list contains some pseudo-words and that yes-responses to pseudo-words will be subtracted from their yes-responses to real words. These measures aim at limiting participants' tendencies to overestimate their word knowledge.

The list should be composed of (i) experimental target words, (ii) non-target words, and (iii) pseudo-words, in random order. To correct for guessing, the following formula could be used: the proportion of hits on words minus the proportion of false alarms on pseudo-words, divided by one minus the proportion of false alarms on pseudo-words (see Shu et al., 1995, p. 82).

After the experiment, participants must be tested again on both the target and non-target words in order to determine what proportion of any increase in knowledge of target words, between pre- and post-test, must be ascribed to learning and what proportion must be ascribed to the effect of retesting (to be calculated with the scores on the non-target words). Obviously, however, this method still does not rule out the possibility that some target words are already known before the experiment. To minimize this possibility the researcher could either use extremely rare or obsolete words, or words only used in professions to which participants do not belong; to rule out the possibility altogether, the researcher must use pseudo-words as target words.

In a series of five experiments of incidental word learning through text reading, Hulstijn (1992) adopted a so-called *twin approach*: the same Dutch reading text was used in all experiments; the target words were pseudo-words in two experiments, using native speakers of Dutch as participants; the target words were real (low-frequency) words in the three remaining experiments, using Dutch L2 learners as participants. The rationale for this twin approach, as discussed in Hulstijn (1997b, p. 136), is that an experiment with (partly) artificial input, such as pseudo-words, ranks relatively high on reliability (control of participants' prior knowledge) but possibly low on (ecological) validity. This is offset, however, by the accompanying experiment with natural language input ("real" L2 learners, learning a "real" L2, containing "real" and "useful" words), ranking relatively high on ecological validity but possibly low on reliability. The researcher then hopes that the results of the twin experiments dovetail nicely, allowing for interpretations that can be credited with both reliability and validity.

5.2 *Long-term retention and the use of immediate post-tests in incidental and intentional learning studies*

The results of vocabulary-learning experiments whose design includes immediate but no delayed post-tests often meet with skepticism from teachers as well as researchers. They question the validity and relevance for L2 instruction of studies showing that, after a single incidental or intentional learning session, method A yields higher retention rates than method B. They tend to dismiss results of such studies unless delayed post-tests, administered after days, weeks, or even months, reveal that method A remains superior to B. On first sight, this skepticism may seem justified. On closer inspection, however, this argument fails, as will be demonstrated in this subsection.

Research on this issue was conducted by Wang, Thomas, and Ouellette (1992) and Wang and Thomas (1995). Participants in the first investigation studied new words either by the keyword method or in rote rehearsal; participants in the second investigation studied new words either by the keyword method or using a non-mnemonic (i.e., semantic-context) strategy. In both studies, retention interval (immediate vs. delay) was treated as a between-subjects factor. The findings consistently indicated that whereas the keyword method yielded higher retention scores than the other two methods when participants were tested immediately after the learning session, the reverse pattern was obtained when participants were not tested immediately afterwards but only after some delay.[23] The authors conclude from these findings that keyword-based memories are especially fragile over time and will benefit from repeated testing and rehearsal.

The results of these studies and the conclusions of their authors, however, provide no evidence for claims that the results of vocabulary learning experiments using only immediate post-tests lack (theoretical or educational) relevance. In evaluations of learning experiments one must bear in mind two considerations: (i) with an immediate post-test, the researcher is able to measure the effect of cognitive processes during the learning session – nothing more, nothing less; and (ii) long-term retention of factual knowledge (such as lexical form–meaning pairs) will almost always require frequent exposure or frequent rehearsal. Research on vocabulary learning, whether under incidental or intentional learning conditions, aimed at addressing questions concerning the effect of cognitive processing during a learning session in which words are presented for the first time, requires only an immediate post-test. Inclusion of delayed post-tests in such research would make no sense, because it would not be possible to differentiate the extent to which performance on delayed post-tests is affected by processes during the experimental learning session or by processes (if any) after that session. In principle, these two types of processes could stand in coalition or in competition with one another. However, in vocabulary learning research aimed at addressing questions concerning maintenance or rehearsal of word knowledge, that is, after new words have initially been presented and processed in different learning modes, and in research on ease of relearning (Schneider et al., 1998), participants in all initial learning modes should be given time to reach the same level of (initial) learning so that the chances of maintaining or forgetting word knowledge is equal for them all. In conclusion, experiments comparing different methods of cognitive processing of new lexical material need only immediate post-tests; their educational significance should be evaluated independently from the issues of maintenance, rehearsal, and forgetting.

6 Conclusions

The issues raised and discussed in this chapter exhibit a wide diversity. The chapter deals with theories of language learning, methods of empirical research, grammar vs. vocabulary learning, and psycholinguistic vs. educational issues. The reason for the chapter's diversity resides in the fact that the labels "incidental" and "intentional" learning have been used to refer to widely differing constructs over a period of more than five decades. They have been used differently (i) across disciplines (e.g., psychology vs. first and second language acquisition vs. education and language pedagogy), (ii) over time within disciplines (e.g., behaviorist vs. early vs. late cognitive psychology; acquisition of grammar vs. acquisition of vocabulary), and (ii) between dimensions of academic inquiry (theory construction vs. development of research methods).

Having served so many different purposes during so many years, is there still a viable role for the labels "incidental" and "intentional" learning to play in the SLA field? Yes, there is. First, "incidental" and "intentional" learning will continue to be useful as technical terms in the experimental literature. As long as researchers continue to conduct L2 learning experiments with a pre-test–treatment–post-test design, it will be mandatory to consider whether participants at the beginning of the treatment (in the SLA literature often called "task" or "input exposure") will or will not be told that they will be tested afterwards, and if so, what sort of post-test to expect (section 2.2). In line with tradition, learning sessions with and without such a pre-warning can be conveniently referred to as "incidental" and "intentional" respectively. This is their *methodological* use. As far as SLA *theory* is concerned, it is not likely that either term will soon receive (or regain) a strong theoretical meaning (section 3). In the areas of second language education and pedagogy, however, the term "incidental learning" can still be fruitfully used as a convenient, informal, non-theoretical term referring to the more or less "unintentional," "incidental" acquisition (or "picking up") of language (grammar, vocabulary, orthography, pronunciation, etc.) during the performance of communicative tasks requiring an attentional focus on the meaning and function of language rather than on its form.

NOTES

1 In this chapter, no distinction is made between second and foreign language learning ("L2" is used throughout), or between acquisition and learning ("learning" is used throughout).
2 For an illustration of Gagné's learning types with examples taken from L2 learning, see Ingram (1975).
3 Eysenck (1982) gives a critical discussion of the most pertinent issues in the debate.
4 For an overview of the extensive literature, see McLaughlin (1965) and Postman (1964).
5 More information on this classic study is given in section 4.3.
6 Tulving (1979) therefore advocates the inclusion of at least two different

retention tasks in all learning experiments.

7 The notion of transfer-appropriate processing is also used in the context of the attainment of automaticity in fluent L2 performance (Segalowitz, 2000).

8 Standard textbooks on L2 learning, such as Cook (1993), R. Ellis (1994), Gass and Selinker (1994), Larsen-Freeman and Long (1991), Lightbown and Spada (1993), Mitchell and Myles (1998), Sharwood Smith (1994), Spolsky (1989), Towell and Hawkins (1994), and Van Els et al. (1984) include neither "incidental" nor "intentional" in their indexes. They are included, however, in the index of the volume edited by Ritchie and Bhatia (1996), referring to the chapter there by McLaughlin and Heredia (1996), quoted in n. 12 of this chapter, who use "incidental" and "intentional" in their methodological senses.

9 Schmidt (1994b, p. 173) acknowledges the importance that many L2 learners themselves attribute to the incidental learning of grammar rules, but dismisses incidental learning as a viable construct in the explanation of grammar acquisition.

10 A vocabulary item is commonly conceived of as the connection between one or more meanings and a phonological and orthographic form. Of course, a vocabulary item is much more than that. It bears, for instance, grammatical information which may be involved in highly abstract principles of grammar. It is now common to say that grammar acquisition takes place through the lexicon (Bates and Goodman, 1997; Gass, 1999).

11 The main finding of this study was that while "both instructional treatments were equally successful in facilitating the acquisition of relativization and both were more successful than the control treatment, the meaning-oriented treatment was shown to better facilitate comprehension than was the case in either the rule-oriented or control conditions" (Doughty, 1991, p. 463). The researcher attributed this difference to "the apparently successful combination of a focus on meaning and the bringing to prominence of the linguistic properties of relativization in the meaning-oriented group" (p. 463).

12 McLaughlin published, in 1965, a review on incidental and intentional learning and devoted much of his later work to L2 learning – his 1987 book was a classic for a decade or so. Interestingly, it is McLaughlin who dismisses the notions of incidental and intentional as outdated in a recent publication (McLaughlin and Heredia, 1996, pp. 221–2): "Years ago, a . . . discussion took place over the question of whether it was legitimate to distinguish two types of learning – intentional and incidental. . . . Data from research show quantitative differences between the instructions and no-instructions groups, but all that can be concluded on the basis of such data is that learning is more difficult under disadvantageous (no-instructions) conditions. . . . there is no justification for the implication that two qualitatively distinct types of learning are involved (McLaughlin, 1965)."

13 For an attempt to give a unified account of both the *what* and *how* of L2 learning, see Hulstijn (2002).

14 Connectionists and symbolists have different views on the *what* of language learning. According to

connectionists, language learners learn associations between units (in very complex configurations); according to symbolists, language learners internalize abstract principles and rules of grammar (apart from relatively simple constellations of declarative knowledge, such as vocabulary items and spelling rules). For connectionists, there is no reason to make a principled distinction between the *what* and *how* of processing, and hence between the *what* and *how* of learning. Connectionists speak of rule-like rather than of rule-governed behavior (see Ellis, this volume). Symbolists, however, see language use as the (automatic, unconscious) application of rules. Within the symbolic camp, however, there are different conceptions of the mechanisms through which symbolic knowledge representations come into existence. It is because of these underlying differences between connectionists and symbolists as well as among symbolists that interpretations of implicit and incidental learning differ widely (see Hulstijn, 2002).

15 In principle, it is possible for an L2 learner to follow up on L2 reading activities by activities of intentional learning, for example by rehearsing words encountered in a text, looked up in a dictionary, and written down in a notebook.

16 A detailed discussion of these pedagogical issues is beyond the scope of the present chapter, which is devoted to incidental and intentional learning rather than to the merits of various vocabulary-learning techniques. A more detailed account of the debate on the educational pros and cons of incidental and intentional vocabulary learning is given in Hulstijn (2001).

17 Thirty years later, one would find this classification rather questionable. But a criticism of the classification is irrelevant in the present context.

18 A nice illustration of how difficult it is to control participants' information processing can be found in the study by Eagle (1967). Two groups of participants in a vocabulary-learning experiment were instructed to use two different learning strategies, rehearsal and associative organization. After the administration of the retention test, participants were asked to report what learning strategies they had used. Neutral judges classified the reports into the categories of rote rehearsal, associate organization, or both. It was found that participants in the rehearsal group had actually learned more than half of the words with an associative strategy and that participants in the associative group had learned almost half of the words with a rote rehearsal strategy.

19 Section 5.2 makes some methodological points on studies limited to short-term retention.

20 For a discussion of educational implications see Hulstijn (2001).

21 A study by Feldman and Healy (1998) also suggests that L2 learners avoid learning L2 words with unfamiliar sounds or sound patterns. This study, however, was not designed as an incidental or intentional learning experiment.

22 This method is derived from, but not identical to, the one applied by Shu, Anderson, and Zhang (1995).

23 Avila and Sadoski (1996), however, obtained superior results for the keyword method even with delayed post-testing.

REFERENCES

Atkins, P. W. B. and Baddeley, A. D. 1998: Working memory and distributed vocabulary learning. *Applied Psycholinguistics*, 19, 537–52.

Avila, E. and Sadoski, M. 1996: Exploring new applications of the keyword method to acquire English vocabulary. *Language Learning*, 46, 379–95.

Baddeley, A. 1997: *Human Memory: Theory and Practice*. Revised edition. Hove: Psychology Press.

Bates, E. and Goodman, J. C. 1997: On the inseparability of grammar and the lexicon: evidence from acquisition, aphasia and real-time processing. *Language and Cognitive Processes*, 12, 507–84.

Bransford, J. D., Franks, J. J., Morris, C. D., and Stein, B. S. 1979: Some general constraints on learning and memory research. In L. S. Cermak and F. I. M. Craik (eds), *Levels of Processing in Human Memory*. Hillsdale, NJ: Lawrence Erlbaum Associates, 331–54.

Cho, K.-S. and Krashen, S. D. 1994: Acquisition of vocabulary from the Sweet Valley Kids Series: adult ESL acquisition. *Journal of Reading*, 37, 662–7.

Coady, J. 1997: L2 vocabulary acquisition: a synthesis of the research. In J. Coady and T. Huckin (eds), *Second Language Vocabulary Acquisition*. Cambridge: Cambridge University Press, 273–90.

Coady, J. and Huckin, T. (eds) 1997: *Second Language Vocabulary Acquisition*. Cambridge: Cambridge University Press.

Cobb, T. 1997: Is there any measurable learning from hands-on concordancing? *System*, 25, 301–15.

Cobb, T. and Horst, M. 2001: Reading academic English: carrying learners across the lexical threshold. In J. Flowerdew and M. Peacock (eds), *The English for Academic Purposes Curriculum*. Cambridge: Cambridge University Press, 315–29.

Cook, V. 1993: *Linguistics and Second Language Acquisition*. London: Macmillan.

Cohen, A. D. 1987: The use of verbal and imagery mnemonics in second-language vocabulary learning. *Studies in Second Language Learning*, 9, 43–61.

Craik, F. I. M. and Lockhart, R. S. 1972: Levels of processing: a framework for memory research. *Journal of Verbal Learning and Verbal Behavior*, 11, 671–84.

Craik, F. I. M. and Tulving, E. 1975: Depth of processing and the retention of words in episodic memory. *Journal of Experimental Psychology: General*, 104, 268–94.

Crothers, E. and Suppes, P. 1967: *Experiments in Second-Language Learning*. New York: Academic Press.

Doughty, C. 1991: Second language acquisition does make a difference: evidence from an empirical study of SL relativization. *Studies in Second Language Acquisition*, 13, 431–69.

Dupuy, B. and Krashen, S. D. 1993: Incidental vocabulary acquisition in French as a foreign language. *Applied Language Learning*, 4, 55–63.

d'Ydewalle, G. and Pavakanun, U. 1995: Acquisition of a second/foreign language by viewing a television program. In P. Winterhoff-Spurk (ed.), *Psychology of Media in Europe: The State of the Art – Perspectives for the Future*. Opladen: Westdeutscher Verlag, 51–64.

Eagle, M. 1967: The effect of learning strategies upon free recall. *American Journal of Psychology*, 80, 421–5.

Eckman, F., Bell, L., and Nelson, D. 1988: On the generalization of relative clause instruction in the acquisition of

English as a second language. *Applied Linguistics*, 9, 1–20.

Ellis, N. 1994: Implicit and explicit language learning – an overview. In N. Ellis (ed.), *Implicit and Explicit Learning of Languages*. London: Academic Press, 1–31.

Ellis, N. and Beaton, A. 1993: Psycholinguistic determinants of foreign language vocabulary learning. *Language Learning*, 43, 559–617.

Ellis, R. 1994: *The Study of Second Language Acquisition*. Oxford: Oxford University Press.

Ellis, R. 1995: Modified oral input and the acquisition of word meanings. *Applied Linguistics*, 16, 409–41.

Ellis, R. and Heimbach, R. 1997: Bugs and birds: children's acquisition of second language vocabulary through interaction. *System*, 25, 247–59.

Ellis, R., Tanaka, Y., and Yamazaki, A. 1994: Classroom interaction, comprehension, and the acquisition of L2 word meanings. *Language Learning*, 44, 449–91.

Eysenck, M. W. 1982: Incidental learning and orienting tasks. In C. R. Puff (ed.), *Handbook of Research Methods in Human Memory and Cognition*. New York: Academic Press, 197–228.

Feldman, A. and Healy, A. F. 1998: Effect of first language phonological configuration on lexical acquisition in a second language. In A. F. Healy and L. E. Bourne, Jr. (eds), *Foreign Language Learning: Psycholinguistic Studies on Training and Retention*. Mahwah, NJ: Lawrence Erlbaum Associates, 57–76.

Fischer, U. 1994: Using words from context and dictionaries: an experimental comparison. *Applied Psycholinguistics*, 15, 551–74.

Gagné, R. M. 1965: *The Conditions of Learning*. New York: Holt, Rinehart and Winston.

Gass, S. 1982: From theory to practice. In M. Hines and W. Rutherford (eds), *On TESOL '81*. Washington, DC: Teachers of English to Speakers of Other Languages, 129–39.

Gass, S. 1999: Discussion: incidental vocabulary learning. *Studies in Second Language Acquisition*, 21, 319–33.

Gass, S. M. and Selinker, L. 1994: *Second Language Acquisition: An Introductory Course*. Hillsdale, NJ: Lawrence Erlbaum Associates.

Gibson, J. J. 1941: A critical review of the concept of set in contemporary experimental psychology. *Psychological Bulletin*, 38, 781–817.

Grace, C. A. 1998: Retention of word meanings inferred from context and sentence-level translations: implications for the design of beginning-level CALL software. *Modern Language Journal*, 82, 533–44.

Griffin, G. and Harley, T. A. 1996: List learning of second language vocabulary. *Applied Psycholinguistics*, 17, 443–60.

Holley, F. M. 1973: A study of vocabulary learning in context: the effect of new-word density in German reading materials. *Foreign Language Annals*, 6, 339–47.

Horst, M., Cobb, T., and Meara, P. 1998: Beyond *A Clockwork Orange*: acquiring second language vocabulary through reading. *Reading in a Foreign Language*, 11, 207–23.

Hulstijn, J. 1989: Implicit and incidental second language learning: experiments in the processing of natural and partly artificial input. In H. W. Dechert (ed.), *Interlingual Processes*. Tübingen: Narr, 49–73.

Hulstijn, J. H. 1992: Retention of inferred and given word meanings: experiments in incidental vocabulary learning. In P. J. Arnaud and H. Béjoint (eds), *Vocabulary and Applied Linguistics*. London: Macmillan, 113–25.

Hulstijn, J. H. 1997a: Mnemonic methods in foreign-language vocabulary learning: theoretical considerations and pedagogical implications. In J. Coady and T. Huckin (eds), *Second Language Vocabulary Acquisition: A Rationale for Pedagogy*. Cambridge: Cambridge University Press, 203–24.

Hulstijn, J. H. 1997b: Second-language acquisition research in the laboratory: possibilities and limitations. *Studies in Second Language Acquisition*, 19, 131–43.

Hulstijn, J. H. 2001: Intentional and incidental second-language vocabulary learning: a reappraisal of elaboration, rehearsal and automaticity. In P. Robinson (ed.), *Cognition and Second Language Instruction*. Cambridge: Cambridge University Press, 258–86.

Hulstijn, J. H. 2002: Towards a unified account of the representation, processing and acquisition of second language knowledge. *Second Language Research*, 18, 193–223.

Hulstijn, J. H. and Trompetter, P. 1998: Incidental learning of second language vocabulary in computer-assisted reading and writing tasks. In D. Albrechtsen, B. Henriksen, I. M. Mees, and E. Poulsen (eds), *Perspectives on Foreign and Second Language Pedagogy*. Odense: Odense University Press, 191–200.

Hulstijn, J. H., Hollander, M., and Greidanus, T. 1996: Incidental vocabulary learning by advanced foreign language students: the influence of marginal glosses, dictionary use, and reoccurrence of unknown words. *Modern Language Journal*, 80, 327–39.

Hyde, T. S. and Jenkins, J. J. 1973: Recall for words as a function of semantic, graphic, and syntactic orienting tasks. *Journal of Verbal Learning and Verbal Behavior*, 12, 471–80.

Ingram, E. 1975: Psychology and language learning. In J. P. B. Allen and S. P. Corder (eds), *Papers in Applied Linguistics: The Edinburgh Course in Applied Linguistics. Vol.* 2. London: Oxford University Press, 218–90.

Knight, S. 1994: Dictionary: the tool of last resort in foreign language reading? A new perspective. *Modern Language Journal*, 78, 285–99.

Kost, C. R., Foss, P., and Lenzini, J. L., Jr. 1999: Textual and pictorial glosses: effectiveness on incidental vocabulary growth when reading in a foreign language. *Foreign Language Annals*, 32, 89–113.

Krashen, S. 1989: We acquire vocabulary and spelling by reading: additional evidence for the input hypothesis. *Modern Language Journal*, 73, 440–64.

Kroll, J. F. and De Groot, A. M. B. 1997: Lexical and conceptual memory in the bilingual: mapping form to meaning in two languages. In A. M. B. De Groot and J. F. Kroll (eds), *Tutorials in Bilingualism*. Mahwah, NJ: Lawrence Erlbaum Associates, 169–99.

Kroll, J. F., Michael, E., and Sankaranarayanan, A. 1998: A model of bilingual representation and its implications for second language acquisition. In A. F. Healy and L. E. Bourne, Jr (eds), *Foreign Language Learning: Psycholinguistic Studies on Training and Retention*. Mahwah, NJ: Lawrence Erlbaum Associates, 365–95.

Larsen-Freeman, D. and Long, M. H. 1991: *An Introduction to Second Language Acquisition Research*. Harlow: Longman.

Laufer, B. and Hill, M. 2000: What lexical information do L2 learners select in a CALL dictionary and how does it affect word retention? *Language Learning and Technology*, 3, 58–76.

Laufer, B. and Hulstijn, J. 2001: Incidental vocabulary acquisition in a second language: the construct of Task-Induced Involvement. *Applied Linguistics*, 22, 1–26.

Lawson, M. J. and Hogben, D. 1996: The vocabulary-learning strategies of foreign-language students. *Language Learning*, 46, 101–35.

Lightbown, P. and Spada, N. 1993: *How Languages are Learned*. Oxford: Oxford University Press.

Loschky, L. 1994: Comprehensible input and second language acquisition. *Studies in Second Language Acquisition*, 16, 303–23.

Lotto, L. and De Groot, A. M. B. 1998: Effects of learning method and word type on acquiring vocabulary in an unfamiliar language. *Language Learning*, 48, 31–69.

McLaughlin, B. 1965: "Intentional" and "incidental" learning in human subjects: the role of instructions to learn and motivation. *Psychological Bulletin*, 63, 359–76.

McLaughlin, B. 1987: *Theories of Second-Language Learning*. London: Arnold.

McLaughlin, B. and Heredia, R. 1996: Information-processing approaches to research on second language acquisition and use. In W. C. Ritchie and T. K. Bhatia (eds), *Handbook of Second Language Acquisition*. San Diego: Academic Press, 213–28.

Mitchell, R. and Myles, F. 1998: *Second Language Learning Theories*. London: Arnold.

Mondria, J.-A. and Wit-de Boer, M. 1991: The effects of contextual richness on the guessability and the retention of words in a foreign language. *Applied Linguistics*, 12, 249–67.

Morris, C. D., Bransford, J. D., and Franks, J. J. 1977: Levels of processing versus transfer appropriate processing. *Journal of Verbal Learning and Verbal Behavior*, 16, 519–33.

Nagy, W. 1997: On the role of context in first- and second-language vocabulary learning. In N. Schmitt and M. McCarthy (eds), *Vocabulary: Description, Acquisition and Pedagogy*. Cambridge: Cambridge University Press, 64–83.

Nagy, W. E. and Anderson, R. C. 1984: How many words are there in printed school English? *Reading Research Quarterly*, 19, 304–30.

Nagy, W. E. and Herman, P. A. 1987: Breadth and depth of vocabulary knowledge: Implications for acquisition and instruction. In M. G. McKeown and M. Curtis (eds), *The Nature of Vocabulary Acquisition*. Hillsdale, NJ: Lawrence Erlbaum Associates, 19–35.

Nagy, W. E., Herman, P. A., and Anderson, R. A. 1985: Learning words from context. *Reading Research Quarterly*, 20, 233–53.

Nation, I. S. P. 1982: Beginning to learn foreign vocabulary: a review of the research. *RELC Journal*, 13, 14–36.

Nation, P. 2001: *Learning Vocabulary in Another Language*. Cambridge: Cambridge University Press.

Oskarsson, M. 1975: On the role of the mother tongue in learning FL vocabulary: an empirical investigation. *ITL*, 27, 19–32.

Papagno, C., Valentine, T., and Baddeley, A. 1991: Phonological short-term memory and foreign-language vocabulary learning. *Journal of Memory and Language*, 30, 331–47.

Paradis, M. 1994: Neurolinguistic aspects of implicit and explicit memory: implications for bilingualism and SLA. In N. Ellis (ed.), *Implicit and Explicit Learning of Languages*. London: Academic Press, 393–419.

Pitts, M., White, H., and Krashen, S. 1989: Acquiring second language vocabulary through reading: a replication of the *Clockwork Orange* study using second language acquirers. *Reading in a Second Language*, 5, 271–5.

Postman, L. 1964: Short-term memory and incidental learning. In A. W. Melton (ed.), *Categories of Human Learning*. New York: Academic Press, 145–201.

Postman, L. and Senders, V. L. 1946: Incidental learning and generality of set. *Journal of Experimental Psychology*, 36, 153–65.

Pouwels, J. B. 1992: The effectiveness of vocabulary visual aids for auditory and visual foreign language students. *Foreign Language Annals*, 25, 391–401.

Prince, P. 1996: Second language vocabulary learning: the role of context versus translations as a function of proficiency. *Modern Language Journal*, 80, 478–93.

Qian, D. D. 1996: ESL vocabulary acquisition: contextualization and decontextualization. *Canadian Modern Language Review*, 53, 120–42.

Ritchie, W. C. and Bhatia, T. K. (eds) 1996: *Handbook of Second Language Acquisition*. San Diego: Academic Press.

Robinson, P. 1996a: *Consciousness, Rules, and Instructed Second Language Acquisition*. New York: Peter Lang.

Robinson, P. 1996b: Learning simple and complex second language rules under implicit, incidental, rule-search, and instructed conditions. *Studies in Second Language Acquisition*, 18, 27–67.

Robinson, P. 1997: Generalizability and automaticity of second language learning under implicit, incidental, enhanced, and instructed conditions. *Studies in Second Language Acquisition*, 19, 223–47.

Rodríguez, M. and Sadoski, M. 2000: Effects of rote, context, keyword, and context/keyword methods of retention of vocabulary in EFL classrooms. *Language Learning*, 50, 385–412.

Rott, S. 1999: The effect of exposure frequency on intermediate language learners' incidental vocabulary acquisition and retention through reading. *Studies in Second Language Acquisition*, 21, 589–619.

Royer, J. M. 1973: Memory effects for test-like events during acquisition of foreign language vocabulary. *Psychological Reports*, 32, 195–8.

Saragi, T., Nation, I. S. P., and Meister, G. F. 1978: Vocabulary learning and reading. *System*, 6, 72–8.

Schmidt, R. 1994a: Deconstructing consciousness in search of useful definitions for applied linguistics. *AILA Review*, 11, 11–26.

Schmidt, R. 1994b: Implicit learning and the cognitive unconscious: of artificial grammars and SLA. In N. Ellis (ed.), *Implicit and Explicit Learning of Languages*. London: Academic Press, 165–209.

Schmidt, R. W. 2001: Attention. In P. Robinson (ed.), *Cognition and Second Language Instruction*. Cambridge: Cambridge University Press, 3–32.

Schmitt, N. 1997: Vocabulary learning strategies. In N. Schmitt and M. McCarthy (eds), *Vocabulary: Description, Acquisition and Pedagogy*. Cambridge: Cambridge University Press, 199–227.

Schmitt, N. and McCarthy, M. (eds) 1997: *Vocabulary: Description, Acquisition and Pedagogy*. Cambridge: Cambridge University Press, 199–227.

Schneider, V. I., Healy, A. F., and Bourne, L. F., Jr 1998: Contextual interference effects in foreign language vocabulary acquisition and retention. In A. F. Healy and L. E. Bourne, Jr (eds), *Foreign Language Learning: Psycholinguistic Studies on Training and Retention*. Mahwah, NJ: Lawrence Erlbaum Associates, 77–90.

Segalowitz, N. 2000: Automaticity and attentional skill in fluent performance. In H. Riggenbach (ed.), *Perspectives on Fluency*. Ann Arbor: University of Michigan Press, 200–19.

Seibert, L. C. 1930: An experiment on the relative efficiency of studying French vocabulary in associated pairs versus studying French vocabulary in context. *Journal of Educational Psychology*, 21, 297–314.

Service, E. and Craik, F. 1993: Differences between young and older adults in learning a foreign vocabulary. *Journal of Memory and Language*, 32, 608–23.

Sharwood Smith, M. 1994: *Second Language Learning: Theoretical Foundations*. Harlow: Longman.

Shu, H., Anderson, R. C., and Zhang, H. 1995: Incidental learning of word meanings while reading: a Chinese and American cross-cultural study. *Reading Research Quarterly*, 30, 76–95.

Singleton, D. 1999: *Exploring the Second Language Lexicon*. Cambridge: Cambridge University Press.

Sökmen, A. J. 1997: Current trends in teaching second language vocabulary. In N. Schmitt and M. McCarthy (eds), *Vocabulary: Description, Acquisition and Pedagogy*. Cambridge: Cambridge University Press, 237–57.

Spolsky, S. 1989: *Conditions for Second Language Learning*. Oxford: Oxford University Press.

Swanborn, M. S. L. and De Glopper, K. 1999: Incidental word learning while reading: a meta-analysis. *Review of Educational Research*, 69, 261–85.

Tinkham, T. 1993: The effect of semantic clustering on the learning of second language vocabulary. *System*, 21, 371–80.

Towell, R. and Hawkins, R. 1994: *Approaches to Second Language Acquisition*. Clevedon: Multilingual Matters.

Tulving, E. 1979: Relation between encoding specificity and levels of processing. In L. S. Cermak and F. I. M. Craik (eds), *Levels of Processing in Human Memory*. Hillsdale, NJ: Lawrence Erlbaum Associates, 405–28.

Underwood, B. J. and Schulz, R. W. 1960: *Meaningfulness and Verbal Learning*. Philadelphia: Lippincott.

Van de Poel, M. and d'Ydewalle, G. 2001: Incidental foreign-language acquisition by children watching subtitled television programs. In Y. Gambier and H. Gottlieb (eds), *(Multi)media Translation: Concepts, Practices, and Research*. Amsterdam: John Benjamins, 259–73.

Van Els, T., Bongaerts, T., Extra, G., Van Os, C., and Janssen-van Dieten, A.-M. 1984: *Applied Linguistics and the Learning and Teaching of Foreign Languages*. London: Arnold.

Wang, A. Y. and Thomas, M. H. 1995: Effect of keywords on long-term retention: help or hindrance? *Journal of Educational Psychology*, 87, 468–75.

Wang, A. Y., Thomas, M. H., and Ouellette, J. A. 1992: Keyword mnemonic and retention of second-language vocabulary words. *Journal of Educational Psychology*, 84, 520–8.

Waring, R. 1998: The negative effects of learning words in semantic sets: a replication. *System*, 25, 261–74.

Watanabe, Y. 1997: Input, intake, and retention: effects of increased processing on incidental learning of foreign language vocabulary. *Studies in Second Language Acquisition*, 19, 287–307.

Wesche, M. and Paribakht, T. S. (eds) 1999: Incidental L2 vocabulary acquisition: theory, current research, and instructional implications. Thematic issue of *Studies in Second Language Acquisition*, 21 (2).

Wode, H. 1999: Incidental vocabulary acquisition in the foreign language classroom. *Studies in Second Language Acquisition*, 21, 243–58.

Yang, L. 1997: Tracking the acquisition of L2 vocabulary: the Keki language experiment. In J. Coady and T. Huckin (eds), *Second Language Vocabulary Acquisition*. Cambridge: Cambridge University Press, 125–56.

13 Automaticity and Second Languages

NORMAN SEGALOWITZ

1 Introduction

There are a number of different ways to understand second language acquisition (SLA), and each has its own strengths and limitations. One currently popular approach to SLA sees it as a special case of complex skill acquisition. From this point of view, one can ask whether SLA shares elements in common with other forms of complex skill acquisition such as learning to play the piano, developing mathematical abilities, or acquiring expertise in making medical diagnosis. In attempting to identify elements that might be common to all forms of complex skill acquisition, cognitive psychologists have focused on a number of issues, including the role of motivation and commitment (Ericsson, Krampe, and Tesch Roemer, 1993; Howe, 1990), the contribution of innate predispositions to mastery in the skill domain (e.g., a talent for language or music; Howe, Davidson, and Sloboda, 1998; Simonton, 1999), the role of practice (Ericsson and Charness, 1994), the operation of memory and attention (Gopher, 1992), and the question of why there exist individual differences in attainment (Ackerman, 1989; Obler, 1989; Obler and Fein, 1988; N. Segalowitz, 1997), among others. One aspect of skill acquisition that has long attracted considerable attention is the development and the role of "automaticity" in performance. This will be the focus of the present chapter.

Questions about automaticity are really part of a larger set of questions about the role played by attention and effort in skill acquisition. The interconnection between automaticity, attention, and skill can be appreciated by considering the following observation, which nearly everyone can attest to. As one's skill level in a domain increases, the amount of attention and effort required to perform generally appears to decrease. For example, when we begin learning to drive a car, we invest considerable effort in order to perform well, paying close attention to our every action and decision. We are usually aware that our performance can be easily disrupted by relatively trivial distractions, such as someone talking to us. After some amount of practice, however, our skill level improves and, along with this, we no longer experience performing as being as effortful as before. We are now able to pay attention to concurrent events that previously would have disrupted us. Indeed, we often interpret such an escape from the need to concentrate as evidence that skill level has improved. Why, then, does performance become less effortful and more resistant to interference? According to many authors, what has happened is that a number of the underlying components of the performance have become automatic, and it is this change that reduces the need for attention and effort.

As will become clear in a moment, the term *automatic* has a number of different technical meanings. Nevertheless, psychologists generally use the term in a sense similar to what is meant in ordinary language when we say, for example, that an automatic shift car changes gears without deliberate intervention by the driver, in contrast to a standard shift car which requires the driver to perform a manual operation. Thus, when we perform aspects of a task *automatically*, we perform them without experiencing the need to invest additional effort and attention (or at least with significantly less effort and attention). When the activity does become automatic in this sense, we often also find that performance has become relatively immune to disruption by potentially interfering events, such as external sights, sounds, concurrently performed tasks, intruding thoughts, or the like. Also, performance appears to be more efficient; it is faster, more accurate, and more stable. Such a transition from non-automatic to automatic performance seems to be a part of nearly all skill acquisition. In language learning, increased performance efficiency can be seen as contributing to fluency, that is, the ability to use language rapidly, smoothly, and accurately. For this reason, understanding what automatic processing is and how it comes about is important for understanding SLA and how to enhance language learning experiences.

This chapter contains five further sections. Section 2 considers how automaticity has been operationally defined by experimental psychologists. This section deals with what is perhaps the most important issue of all: what automaticity refers to. Section 3 reviews the concept of automaticity as it is found in theories of skill development, including SLA theory. Section 4 discusses some illustrative ways automaticity issues have figured into SLA research. Section 5 discusses the pedagogical implications for SLA that are raised by research on automaticity. Finally, the chapter concludes with a speculative discussion about future directions for research on automaticity in SLA.

2 Operational Definitions of Automaticity

To investigate how mechanisms become automatic during the course of skill acquisition, we need precise descriptions and operational definitions of the terms "automatic" and "non-automatic." Such definitions abound (e.g., Neely, 1977; Newell, 1990; Pashler, 1998; Posner and Snyder, 1975; Schneider and Shiffrin, 1977; Shiffrin and Schneider, 1977). Newell (1990, p. 136), for example, describes automatic processing in the context of searching for a target (say, a particular letter) in a display (of several letters). He characterizes an *automatic* process as follows: it is fast; it is unstoppable (ballistic); it is independent of the amount of information being processed; it involves exhaustive or complete search of all elements in the display; it involves no awareness of processing; and it involves "pop-out" of the target item from the display. In contrast, non-automatic processing, also called *controlled* processing, is characterized as follows: it is slow; it is capable of being inhibited; it depends on information load; it involves self-terminating search of the display; it involves awareness; and it does not involve target "pop-out." Other authors have similarly cited clusters of properties to characterize automaticity.

There are two points to be made about such characterizations. One is that they are contrastive. That is, any given characteristic of an automatic process can really only be understood in terms of a corresponding non-automatic, contrasting characteristic. For example, processing can only be considered to be fast in relation to some slower example of processing that serves as a reference point. To demonstrate that some aspect of processing is unstoppable, we need to compare it with a situation in which we observe an ability to interrupt processing. This contrastive aspect of definitions of automaticity is important, as we shall see, because in focusing on the place of automaticity in skill acquisition it is usually necessary to also focus on closely related *non*-automatic aspects.

The second point is that this way of characterizing automaticity gives rise to a set of important questions. For example, should the automatic/non-automatic distinction be viewed as strictly dichotomous (that is, a given process must always be either automatic or not) or as end points of a continuum stretching from very non-automatic to very automatic? Second, should automaticity be viewed as a unitary construct? That is, do automatic processes always have the same characteristics (e.g., are always fast, ballistic, immune to interference, etc.)? Or does automaticity refer to a number of possibly related but nevertheless logically independent phenomena? This latter view carries the implication that there exist different types of automaticity. Finally, one can ask whether becoming automatic should be viewed as a central goal of skill attainment or, instead, should be regarded as only one part of the larger picture of what skill acquisition entails.

With respect to SLA, interest in automaticity is nearly always connected to concerns about fluency. Is fluency – which we can define here as an ability in the second language to produce or comprehend utterances smoothly, rapidly, and accurately – accompanied by automaticity? Is fluency "merely" highly automatized performance? Do the conditions that promote automaticity necessarily also promote fluency? These and related questions are addressed later in this chapter.

We turn now to consider some of the different ways automaticity has been discussed and operationalized in the research literature. It is important that we do this for two reasons. One is that, as we shall see, the term "automaticity" has been used to refer to many logically distinct possibilities in the way psychological mechanisms may operate; it is an empirical question whether automaticity in any one of these senses entails automaticity in some or all of the other senses. The second reason is that one often sees reference in the literature to processes becoming or failing to become automatic without further specification of which sense of automaticity is intended. While it may be convenient to use "automaticity" as a shorthand term, the imprecision this entails can potentially create problems for the conduct and interpretation of research on the role of automaticity in skill.

2.1 *Fast processing*

The characteristic most frequently associated with automaticity is speed of processing. It is natural to think that once a mechanism has become automatic it will operate faster than it did earlier. For example, we normally expect (and find) word recognition in fluent first language readers to be faster than word recognition in most second language readers, and such differences have sometimes been attributed to the greater automaticity underlying first language reading. Speed of operation has thus become one of the hallmark characteristics of an automatic process in virtually all theories of automaticity (see, e.g., the review by DeKeyser, 2001).

There are, however, theoretical and practical difficulties in using speed as a defining characteristic of automaticity. While automatic processing may entail fast processing, it does not follow that all fast processing is necessarily automatic. This is because "fast" is nearly always understood in a relative rather than absolute sense. It is, for example, logically possible for a given individual to exhibit faster *non*-automatic processing on one occasion than on another, or for two individuals to differ in the speed of executing *non*-automatic aspects of task performance. Hence, merely observing that performance was fast does not necessarily indicate it was automatic. Of course, our intuitions may tell us that if processing has been accomplished within some very short duration – say, word recognition within less than 200 milliseconds – then the processing most likely was automatic in some useful sense of that word. However, in this case fast processing is only being taken as symptomatic of automaticity. All one can really say is that, as a consequence of the underlying brain mechanism being automatic (in some sense other than being fast, in order to avoid circularity), processing has become very fast. This contrasts with all the other operational definitions of automaticity discussed below. There, each operational criterion is considered, without circularity, part of the definition of what is meant by automaticity, and not merely a consequence of automaticity.

Some authors have tended to rely strongly on speed as an indication of automatic processing (e.g., Lambert, 1955). For example, Magiste (1986) studied the loss of mother-tongue fluency by immigrant German speakers living in Sweden. She found that the longer immigrants had resided in Sweden, the slower reaction time (RT) was in tests of word processing in German, their first language. She attributed this loss of processing speed to a loss of automaticity. While one may agree with the ultimate conclusion that first language loss involves the loss of some automaticity, by the criteria available today these conclusions cannot really be said to have been fully supported by the evidence. Additional evidence, beyond that provided by speed, is required to justify conclusions about automaticity (see, e.g., N. Segalowitz, 1991; N. Segalowitz and Segalowitz, 1993).

Recently, N. Segalowitz and Segalowitz (1993; S. J. Segalowitz, Segalowitz, and Wood, 1998) have suggested how it might be possible to use RTs to make inferences about automaticity without simply equating *fast* with *automatic*. Suppose that after some amount of practice RTs have become significantly faster than before. Has there been an increase in automaticity? Segalowitz and Segalowitz suggest that here the appropriate null hypothesis to reject is that the change simply reflects generalized speed-up, that is, due simply to the underlying processes operating faster, and nothing more. They proposed a way to use an individual's RTs and the associated coefficient of variability (the standard deviation of the individual's RTs divided by his or her mean RT) to reject this null hypothesis. With their method of data analysis it becomes possible to test whether a given set of RTs is significantly faster than what would have been expected from simple speed-up effects alone. According to Segalowitz and Segalowitz, such an outcome would indicate that there has been a *qualitative* change in performance, consistent with the idea of increased automaticity.

This brings us to the question of whether *automaticity* really refers to a qualitative or quantitative change in performance. Many authors do use the term to refer to a qualitative change, resulting perhaps from restructuring of the underlying mechanisms involved in carrying out the performance (Cheng, 1985; Neely, 1977; N. Segalowitz and Segalowitz, 1993; Schneider and Shiffrin, 1977; Shiffrin and Schneider, 1977). The contrasting view, of course, is that automaticity entails just better, more efficient processing of the same kind as occurs when performance is not automatic.

This debate about the quantitative/qualitative nature of automaticity may, in the end, turn out to be a non-issue. The brain mechanisms underlying second language performance (as in all complex skilled activity) are numerous and diverse, and their activities are no doubt executed in a complex pattern involving serial, parallel, and cascading organization (Carr and Curran, 1994). Different component mechanisms will have different lower limits for speed of operation; some can eventually be made to operate extremely quickly (e.g., some basic perceptual mechanisms) while others will always require significantly more time (perhaps certain decision mechanisms). As various component mental activities become practiced, their time of operation will speed up, and less of the total time of performance will be devoted to those particular mental operations. Mechanisms that were formerly rate-determining because they were quite slow may, after training, no longer be so because they operate so quickly that other, slower mechanisms become the rate-determining components by default. The now fast mechanisms may operate so rapidly that the remaining slower processes may not be able to interfere with their operation. The products of these now fast mental operations may no longer be available for verbal report and hence not experienced as being consciously executed, etc. In this sense, they have become automatic. In contrast, there will remain other mental activities with speed-up limits that are too high (too slow) to ever achieve the effects just described for the fast mechanisms. Because there are differences in speed-up limits among the diverse mechanisms underlying the skill in question, the overall order in which information is output and passed from one mechanism to another may change, with the consequence that the overall organization of processing may change. Thus, out of quantitative changes in speed come qualitative differences in the way information is processed. Just such a situation has been demonstrated in the connectionist literature regarding Piagetian stage-like behavior in the learning of the balance beam problem (by McLelland and Jenkins, as described in Elman et al., 1996, ch. 3). Incremental changes in connection weights ultimately resulted, in a learning simulation, in the emergence of what observers would recognize as a qualitatively higher stage of processing. It may well turn out to be a similar story for automaticity. The explanation of automatization may in the end reduce to a question of speed-up. But if *automaticity* is to be useful it should be more than a synonym for "fast processing." It should be used for situations where the change is of significant consequence, such as a restructuring of underlying processes (N. Segalowitz and Gatbonton, 1995), even if the ultimate explanation for this restructuring is selective speed-up of mechanisms.

It is worth mentioning that some qualitative changes resulting from selective speed-up of underlying mental activities might not actually enhance overall performance. For example, errors might be made due to premature processing of certain information or failure to inhibit or redirect other processing that has now occurred too quickly. Perhaps this leads to fossilization, that is, "fluent," robust habits of incorrect speech. On the other hand, many of the qualitative changes resulting from selective speed-up might indeed enhance overall processing by, for example, leaving relatively more time available for slower, centrally controlled processing to make important decisions. An example of this would be faster reading in L2 that results from very fast word recognition. Here, not only could reading be faster because the individual words are recognized faster, but the integration of the text into a coherent schema might be more efficient overall because a greater proportion of processing time can be devoted to that activity.

2.2 *Ballistic processing*

According to another definition, a process is considered automatic when its operation is shown to be ballistic or unstoppable. This corresponds to one ordinary language use of *automaticity*, as, for example, when we say that a computer automatically booted up when the power was turned on. One of the most famous demonstrations of such ballistic processing is the Stroop color word task (Stroop, 1935). It takes longer to name the colors in which words are written when the words themselves are incongruent color names (e.g., to say the color name "green" when the word RED is written in green ink) than to name the colours of patches or strings of Xs.

Neely (1977) constructed a clever experiment demonstrating that recognition of a word's meaning by skilled first language readers of English can be automatic in this ballistic sense (see box 13.1 for more details). In his study, subjects showed that within the first few hundred milliseconds of seeing a word they could not stop themselves from thinking about its usual meaning, even though a second or more later they could override that interpretation and think about the word differently. This demonstrated word recognition to be ballistic (automatic) in the early moments of each trial.

What was clever about this experiment was that it demonstrated the subjects' inability to avoid processing a word's meaning *despite* their conscious attempt to do so. In this study, non-automatic or controlled processing was pitted against automatic processing; the results demonstrated that when processing time was limited, the output of that part of the process that was fast off the mark and unstoppable – the part Neely called automatic – prevailed. In contrast, when longer processing time was available, controlled processing overtook automatic processing and its output prevailed. Other authors have also used ballisticity or the involuntary nature of a mechanism's operation as a criterion for automatic processing (Favreau and Segalowitz, 1983; Pashler, 1998; Tzelgov, Henik, and Leiser, 1990).

2.3 *Load independent processing*

Shiffrin and Schneider have conducted a set of seminal studies examining the conditions under which practice leads to automatic performance (Schneider

Box 13.1 Neely's (1977) demonstration of ballistic (automatic) word recognition

Neely (1997) presented an experiment that neatly and convincingly demonstrated the ballistic or unstoppable, involuntary nature of meaning access upon seeing a familiar word. The design used a method of opposition in which automatic and controlled processes were set to operate in opposite directions within a trial. While the reported original study was rather complex, involving numerous conditions, the basic design of the study is elegant, and it is the general logic of that design for demonstrating automaticity that is presented here.

Methodology: Neely's subjects were instructed to make a lexical decision (word/non-word) judgment about a target stimulus appearing on the screen. Prior to the appearance of the target subjects saw a priming stimulus, either XXX, BIRD, BODY, or BUILDING. When the priming word was BIRD, on two-thirds of word trials the target was a bird name, on one sixth ("surprise" trials) it was a body part name, and on one sixth a building-related word. When the priming word was BODY, on two-thirds of word trials the target was a building-related word, on one sixth it was a bird name, and on one sixth a body part name. Finally, when the priming word was BUILDING, on two-thirds of word trials the target named a body part, on one sixth it named a bird, and on one sixth it was a building-related word. Thus, on BIRD priming trials, the expectation was that if a real word followed, that word would be semantically related to the prime. In contrast, on BODY priming trials, the expectation was that if a word followed, that word would be semantically unrelated to the prime. Word trials with XXX as prime were followed equally often with words from the *bird*, *body*, and *building* categories. Of course, on half of all trials the target following the prime was a non-word.

The time interval between the onset of the prime and the onset of the target (stimulus onset asynchrony: SOA) was varied between 250 and 2000 milliseconds.

This design provided for the following four basic test conditions on word trials: long SOA, expect a related word; long SOA, expect an unrelated word; short SOA, expect a related word; short SOA, expect an unrelated word.

Reaction times (RTs) on word trials with XXX as prime provided baseline data (neutral prime). The primes BIRD, BODY, and BUILDING could have the effect of facilitating RTs to the target word (faster responding), inhibiting RTs (slower responding), or neither in comparison to the baseline RT data.

Results: The most interesting results came from trials where a prime is followed by a word that was *un*expected. In the long SOA condition, when the target was unexpected (e.g., BIRD–door; BODY–heart; BUILDING–door) there was inhibition. When the target was expected, there was facilitation. This demonstrated the influence of non-automatic or controlled, strategic processes based on expectations triggered by the priming stimulus. Note that facilitation occurred if the target was expected and inhibition occurred if it was unexpected regardless of whether the word was actually semantically related to the prime or not.

On the short SOA trials the story was different. When the target was related there was facilitation with respect to XXX trials even when this was a "surprise" trial, that is, the target word was not expected (e.g., BODY–heart, where the target was semantically related but a building-related word was expected). When the target was unrelated (e.g., BIRD–door; BODY–robin) there was neither facilitation or inhibition. The crucial finding here is that there was facilitation for related words, *even when those related words were not expected.*

Conclusion: This study demonstrated the influence of automatic, unstoppable processes triggered by the priming stimulus. Subjects could not prevent themselves from accessing the normal meaning of the prime word even though in the long SOA condition they exhibited inhibition with this same prime due to the mismatch with their expectations. Thus, the study demonstrated how automaticity can be operationally defined as ballistic processing, and it demonstrated that access to the meaning of words in fluent readers of English was (in the present case) automatic.

and Shiffrin, 1977; Shiffrin and Schneider, 1977). In this case, automatic processing was operationally defined as load-independent processing. A process was said to be automatic if it operated without regard to how much information had to be processed. The paradigm these authors developed involved searching a small display of items (letters, digits) for a remembered target. The researchers reasoned that if the response time to locate a target was slower the larger the display, then processing was load dependent, and by definition, not automatic. If the response time was the same to large and small displays, the items in that display could be said to have been processed in parallel – that is, all items were processed at the same time; the target just "popped" out – and processing was load independent (or automatic). They found that processing started out as non-automatic or load dependent but under certain conditions could become automatic or load independent. This qualitative shift resulted only when the stimuli were mapped onto responses in what the authors called a consistent mapping relation. This means that any item, say the letter R, that appeared as a target on a given trial always appeared only as a target during the experiment; it never appeared as a non-target element on some trial. In contrast, in some experimental conditions, stimuli were sometimes mapped onto responses in a variable mapping relation, that is, a target item on one trial might appear later on another trial as a non-target. Shiffrin and Schneider found that with variable mapping, load-independent processing was not achieved, even after thousands of trials, and even though processing became faster. This result, that automatic (load-independent) processing resulted from stimulus-response experiences involving consistent mapping, has important pedagogical implications (see below). (See, however, Nakayama and Joseph, 1998, for a different analysis of "pop-out" effects, and Pashler, 1998, for a different interpretation of Shiffrin and Schneider's results.)

2.4 *Effortless processing*

Posner and Boies (1971) reported a study that demonstrated letter processing to be automatic in the sense of not requiring attention or effort. "Effort" refers here to the expenditure of a limited attentional resource (Kahneman, 1973). The logic of Posner and Boies's study was the following. They argued that performing a primary task that is effortful (non-automatic) should interfere with simultaneously performing a secondary effortful task. They indexed such interference by the extent to which performance on the secondary task was slowed down. On the other hand, they argued that if the primary task is largely automatic and therefore does not draw attention capacity or effort away from performance of the secondary task, then there should be no slowing down on the secondary task.

In their study, subjects performed a primary task involving the following sequence of events. Subjects viewed a fixation point on a screen followed after a fixed interval by a single letter. After a short fixed interval another letter appeared in the same location as the first. Subjects had to indicate by pressing one of two buttons on a reaction time panel with their right hand whether the two letters had the same name or not (e.g., "A, a" versus "A, b"). Subjects concurrently performed a secondary task in which they pressed a different reaction time panel with their left hand whenever they heard a burst of white noise in their left ear. There was only one noise burst on any given trial and it could occur at any one of eight time positions after the fixation point appeared, up to the period after a response was made. The attention or effort required by the primary task (letter matching) was operationalized as the amount of slowing down of reaction time on the secondary task.

Posner and Boies found that when the noise burst occurred any time after the onset of the fixation point but before the onset of the first letter, reaction time to the noise burst remained relatively fast, indicating that general preparation for the upcoming first letter did not consume attentional resources. However, as the time of the noise burst occurred closer and closer to the onset of the second letter, reaction time on the secondary task slowed down considerably, indicating that mental preparation for comparing the second letter with the first did involve effort (possibly, for example, to rehearse the first letter in memory; to generate an image of what the second letter might look like given the first letter, etc.). Most interesting, however, was the finding that when the noise burst occurred within a few hundred milliseconds *after* the onset of the first letter but well before the onset of the second letter – that is, during the time when recognition of the first letter took place – there was no slowing down of the secondary task reaction time. This was interpreted as indicating that simple letter recognition itself (a highly practiced skill) did not require redirecting attention or effort away from the secondary task, whereas letter matching did (a far less well-practiced skill). In this sense, letter recognition was said to be automatic.

2.5 *Unconscious processing*

Jacoby has addressed the role of automaticity in recognition memory by showing how one can separate the contributions of unconscious, automatic processes from those of consciously controlled processes (Jacoby, 1991; Jacoby, McElree, and Trainham, 1999). Jacoby makes the distinction as follows. Consider the case where a person recollects information or a previously learned response that was encountered earlier during a study or training period. On the one hand, memory access for that information will be increased by the degree to which the individual is able, through deliberate effort, to consciously reconstruct or retrieve the target information. On the other hand, memory access may also be increased by virtue of the operation of automatic encoding processes which at the time of learning promote perceptual fluency with the information that is to be remembered. In other words, the encoding processes during the study/ training phase will have primed representations of that information. Thus, we may remember something because we can actually recall having encountered it earlier by a process of conscious recollection. Or we may recall it because it has a "ring" of familiarity about it due to earlier automatic priming, even though we may not really be sure about having encountered it before. Usually, of course, these two sources of remembering are confounded.

Jacoby (1991) devised a process dissociation procedure to tease these two factors apart as follows. Let us refer to the two components as A (automatic) and C (conscious recollection). Jacoby designed experiments with two types of conditions, one labeled "inclusion," in which the A and C factors are set to work in the same direction to facilitate memory, and the other labeled "exclusion," in which the A and C factors are set to work in opposite directions.

For example, subjects may be given two lists of words, one presented visually, one aurally. They are subsequently given a recognition test consisting of old (previously encountered) and new items (not previously encountered). In the inclusion condition, subjects are told to say that they recognize as old all items regardless of whether they had been seen or heard in the previous lists. Here, items could be remembered either because they were consciously recollected, or because they achieved some level of familiarity from exposure during the presentation of the visual and aural lists and are now processed with greater perceptual fluency than are new items. The probability that an item will be correctly recognized in this inclusion condition will be jointly determined by the probability of conscious recollection (C) plus the probability of relying on automatic processes (A) when recollection fails $(1 - C)$, that is, $A(1 - C)$. Thus the probability of a previously seen item being correctly accepted in this inclusion condition is given by $C + A(1 - C) = C + A - AC$.

In the exclusion condition, subjects are asked to recognize as old only items that were heard, and to reject previously seen items (to treat them as new). They are told that if they see an item which they recognize as one having been seen earlier, they may conclude that they did not hear it and so should reject it. Thus, any previously seen item that is incorrectly accepted must have seemed familiar because of automatic processing and was not consciously recollected (if it had been consciously recollected, it would have been rejected). Thus the probability of incorrectly accepting an item that is to be excluded is $A(1 - C) = A - AC$. One can compare performance on inclusion and exclusion conditions. That is, one can look at actual probabilities for correctly accepting previously encountered items in the inclusion condition and incorrectly accepting items in the exclusion condition. By doing simple algebra with the above equations, one can obtain separate estimates of the contribution of automatic and conscious processes in recognition memory. Jacoby and his colleagues have conducted a number of experiments to estimate the separate contribution of automatic and conscious processes in memory (see, e.g., Jacoby et al., 1999, for a review). In principle, by using this technique it should be possible to compare the degree to which encoding of L2 versus L1 information is automatic as a function of individual differences, level of L2 mastery, type of L2 learning or exposure, etc.

2.6 *Shift to instance processing*

Logan (1988) has investigated the improvements in performance that derive from practice using "alphabet arithmetic" tasks. An alphabet arithmetic task involves dealing with expressions such as "B + 3 = E," which states that E is three letters down the alphabet after B. Logan noticed that initially reaction times to make judgments about such expressions were quite slow. After some practice they soon speeded up, but the rate of speed-up was negatively accelerated and could be described by a power function of the form $RT = a + bN - c$, where RT is the time to respond, N is the number of practice trials, and a, b, and c are constants. This relation of RT to the number of practice trials has been observed frequently in the literature (Newell and Rosenbloom, 1981) and has been proposed by Logan as a hallmark of automaticity (Logan, 1988).

Logan explains this effect as follows. Initially, the subject computes the alphabet arithmetic result by rule; the response is based on the use of an algorithm by which the expression is evaluated. The result ("B + 3 = E") is placed in memory every time it is computed. After many trials, memory becomes populated with many tokens of this information. On each trial there is a race to find the solution, a race between computing the solution by algorithm versus finding a token or instance of the solution stored in memory. Eventually, when many tokens are represented in memory, the instance-based solution is encountered sooner than the algorithm-based solution. This shift from algorithm to instance is automatization, according to Logan.

Interestingly, DeKeyser (2001) makes a convincing argument that this approach to automaticity may not be appropriate for many issues in SLA. In Logan's model, an encountered stimulus must be identical to the one encoded in memory for the instance retrieval to take place. But as DeKeyser points out, this is often not true in language comprehension. We are likely to encounter stimuli that are only similar, not identical, to those encountered before. Palmeri (1997), on the other hand, provides an exemplar-based theory in which retrieval is based on the similarity of items. This may provide a step toward making an exemplar-based approach more useful for SLA theory (but see DeKeyser, 2001, for general comments on the limitations of such approaches).

2.7 *Brain activity measures*

Finally, it is interesting to note that recent developments in brain imaging have made it possible to obtain brain-based, as opposed to behavior-based, information related to automaticity issues. The literature in this field is growing very rapidly and it is beyond the scope of this chapter to review it here (see, e.g., Fischler, 1998). One interesting finding, however, merits consideration. It is that, as an individual becomes more skilled and thus presumably more automatic in at least some of the senses described above, the size of the region of the brain devoted to carrying out the task appears, on current evidence, to become smaller (Fischler, 1998; Haier et al., 1992). This is interesting because one might have supposed that, with increased skill and increased performing experience, additional regions of the brain would be recruited to provide a richer basis for executing the task at hand. Instead, what may be happening is that processing becomes more efficient – less noisy in the sense that less brain tissue is recruited for carrying out the same task. Raichle et al. (1994) conducted a positron emission tomography (PET) study in which they compared the performance of practiced and unpracticed subjects in a task requiring participants to generate verbs in response to pictured objects. Practiced subjects responded faster, which the authors took as an indication of learning and increased automaticity. The areas of the brain that were the most active during unpracticed performance included the anterior cingulate, the left prefrontal and left posterior temporal cortices, and the right cerebellar hemisphere. These areas became markedly *less* active after 15 minutes of practiced performance. In contrast, there was increased bilateral activity in the sylvian insular cortices. The authors concluded that these areas represented two neural circuits that become differentially involved depending on whether or not a task is well learned and performed with some degree of automaticity. It should be noted that their study did not provide an independent behavioral measure of automaticity; they simply assumed that the skilled group was more automatic by virtue of being faster. Their conclusion is probably correct, although the case would have been stronger with evidence that something other than simple speed-up was involved (see earlier discussion). In general, however, it is clear that brain-based measures open an exciting range of possibilities of studying the role of automatic processes in skill development.

3 Automaticity in Skill Development and SLA

Automaticity figures as an important issue in nearly all theories of cognitive skill acquisition, including treatments of first language performance (e.g., Levelt, 1993; Perfetti, 1985) and in many discussions of second language acquisition (e.g., DeKeyser, 2001; Ellis and Laporte, 1997; Hulstijn, 2001; Johnson, 1996; Koda, 1996; MacWhinney, 1997; McLaughlin and Heredia, 1996; Pienemann, 1998; Robinson, 1997; Schmidt, 2001; Skehan, 1998; Tomlin and Villa, 1994). In general, the question of how to define automaticity (as fast, ballistic, effortless, and/or unconscious, etc., processing) is not the focus of these theories. It is usually assumed, often implicitly, that automatic processing will have one or some of the above characteristics. Rather, such theories focus on what it is that is automatized, under what conditions the process of becoming automatized occurs, and what role automatizing plays in the larger picture of skill acquisition.

3.1 Anderson's ACT theory

Perhaps the best-known general theory of skill acquisition is Anderson's adaptive control of thought (ACT) (Anderson, 1983; Anderson and Lebriere, 1998).

This theory has undergone an evolution since 1983 to the present, the most recent version appearing in a volume entitled *The Atomic Components of Thought* (Anderson and Lebriere, 1998). The theory can be implemented on computer and thus allows one to test predictions derived from it. ACT theory assumes that skill acquisition involves a transition from a stage characterized by declarative knowledge to one characterized by procedural knowledge. Declarative knowledge (knowledge "that") refers to consciously held, skill-relevant knowledge that is describable. An example might be the explicit knowledge one may have about how to form a particular grammatical construction in one's L2. Procedural knowledge (knowledge "how") is knowledge evident in a person's behavior but which the person is not consciously aware of and hence cannot describe in words. An example might be the knowledge most native speakers have about forming correct grammatical constructions in their L1. Initially, the execution of a cognitive skill involves retrieving and using declarative knowledge to solve the problem at hand, a process involving the application of production rules upon the declarative knowledge. These rules function like "procedural atoms" or units of skill acquisition (Anderson and Lebriere, 1998, p. 26). The transition from declarative knowledge to procedural knowledge through the application of production rules occurs via a process called proceduralization. This involves passing from a cognitive stage where rules are explicit, through an associative phase where rules are applied repeatedly in a consistent manner, to an autonomous stage where the rules are no longer explicit and are executed automatically, implicitly in a fast, coordinated fashion. The process is sometimes referred to as compilation, analogous to the compiling of computer routines written in a higher-level language into a lower-level language. Automaticity, then, describes an end point in the acquisition of skill in this model.

Other well-known general purpose theories of cognitive skill development include Newell's SOAR theory (Lehman, Laird, and Rosenbloom, 1998; Newell, 1990) and Meyer and Kieras's EPIC model (Meyer and Kieras, 1997, 1999). ACT, SOAR, and EPIC differ in terms of the scope of issues they address and of course, in the cognitive architecture they propose (see Meyer and Kieras, 1999, for a brief comparison of the models). For purposes of the present discussion, they are similar insofar as they accord an important place to the acquisition of automatic processing in the overall scheme of skill development.

As regards SLA, it appears that no author has yet attempted to model SLA broadly within any of the frameworks of ACT, SOAR, EPIC , or other universal theories of cognition. Nevertheless, a number of SLA theorists have made reference to such theories, especially ACT, in the course of developing their own approach to second language development. Two in particular deserve mention.

Johnson (1996, pp. 91–101) makes the point that proceduralization should result in encodings that are inflexible and non-generative because the knowledge contained in the encoding is in the production rule itself, not in the larger knowledge base. This knowledge is therefore not available for other encodings. He suggests that this might be one way to account for fossilization in learners. He goes on to point out how it is important for successful SLA that the declarative knowledge which has become proceduralized nevertheless continue to be available so that learning does not become inflexible. Johnson discusses ways to extend Anderson's model by providing for forms of declarative knowledge that come after the emergence of procedural knowledge.

DeKeyser (2001) also discusses Anderson's model in considerable detail. He draws attention to a directional asymmetry that characterizes skill acquisition, as discussed by Anderson (Anderson and Fincham, 1994; Anderson, Fincham, and Douglass, 1997). This refers to the idea that procedural knowledge, once formed, cannot generalize to other uses even if those other uses are based on the same declarative knowledge. In other words, procedural knowledge is committed to a specific operation. In contrast, declarative knowledge used in one situation may facilitate its use in another; it is generalizable. This asymmetry increases with learning. DeKeyser (1997) reports evidence for such directional asymmetry in a study of grammar acquisition with a miniature linguistic system (see below for more on this).

In Anderson's (1983) theory, the shift to using rules (the proceduralization of declarative knowledge) is a primary characteristic of automatic performance. This can be seen to contrast with Logan's (1988) instance-theory approach to automaticity, described earlier, where automaticity reflects a shift from the use of rules in guiding performance to the retrieval of specifically stored solutions (instances). This raises the question about which approach better addresses what happens when a skill is automatized, a question that is far from being resolved at the present time. Some intermediate positions are emerging in the literature (e.g., Anderson et al., 1997; Palmeri, 1997; Rickard, 1997) and are leading to revisions of earlier theories. Of special interest here is work on the learning of dynamically complex tasks, such as computerized fighter-pilot simulation games (Gopher, 1992), where one can observe the evolution of controlled and automatic processing components. For example, Shebilske, Goettl, and Regian (1999), in reviewing this area, stress how this research points to different conclusions from earlier studies that used tasks that were very much simpler. These studies of complex task learning indicate that automatic processing plays a role both early and late in training. They also indicate that executive control processes increase in importance as skill develops and that there is an interactive relationship between controlled and automatic processes.

Second language performance is itself undoubtedly complex in ways similar to task performance in the simulation games described in Gopher (1992) and Shebilske et al. (1999). For example, second language learners have to attend to many unpredictable, changing features of a dynamically complex communicative environment. The input to the L2 user can be a critical factor in shaping the way the individual engages in the "negotiation of meaning" (Long, 1996). Second language communication requires one to draw on linguistic knowledge and various cognitive strategies in order to meet immediate communicative needs, just as in the case of complex simulation games.

In recent years the study of attention has added to our understanding of the role of automaticity in the performance of cognitive skills. One interesting development is the following. Allport and Wylie (1999) report studies involving tasks where subjects have to switch task goals from one trial to the next. This generally slows performance compared to situations where no switching is involved (the full story about the effects of task switching is quite complicated and is currently the subject of much research; Allport and Wylie, 1999; Rogers and Monsell, 1995). Allport and Wylie report what they refer to as "a new form of *priming*, at the level of competing condition-action rules in procedural working memory" (p. 277). They go on to suggest that, as regards the automatic/controlled processing distinction, "task-set, the prototypical constituent of 'control', is itself subject to 'automatic' priming effects" (p. 277). This can be seen as one example of how automatic and controlled processes may interact. For an example of attention switching related to SLA see N. Segalowitz, O'Brien, and Poulsen (1998).

Another example of the interplay of automatic and controlled processes is seen in the work of Wegner (1994) on mental control. Wegner has studied why people say or do the very thing they had been trying so hard to avoid (let slip out a confidence, for example), or why it is hard sometimes to stop thinking a certain thought. He calls such "slips" the result of "ironic" processes, which he explains as follows. When we try to direct ourselves away from a target thought or utterance, we employ controlled, effortful processes to do so. However, at the same time, we must activate an automatic monitoring process in order to detect the onset of any internally generated or external stimulus that might trigger the behavior we are trying to avoid. Normally, when our monitor detects such a stimulus, the controlled process is sent into action to suppress the unwanted thought. However, if our attentional capacity is depleted for any reason (stress, information overload, etc.) then the control process will fail, leaving our automatic monitoring system free to determine our behavior. Thus, when we are tired or under stress we are more likely to make the very errors we normally try so hard to avoid. Wegner's explanation of ironic processes may be relevant to understanding the role automatic processes can play in so-called backsliding or "U-shaped" behavior (Lightbown, 1985; McLaughlin and Heredia, 1996), as when a student reverts to using incorrect forms of language that recently had been under control. The hypothesis here is that the control processes normally responsible for the student selecting correct forms are not functioning; the student may be tired, the communicative situation may be too demanding, etc. It may even be possible that new learning can lead to restructuring of existing linguistic knowledge so that some controlled process is no longer operative. When this happens, background automatic processes that normally coordinate with controlled processes by detecting error-potential situations now determine behavior alone, and the student makes the very error that she or he had so recently appeared to have learned to overcome. There does not appear to be any research addressing this hypothesis, but it seems to be one worth investigating.

4 Automaticity in SLA

It is only in recent years that SLA researchers have begun to realize the importance of understanding automaticity. Work in this area has restricted itself mainly to certain areas of performance – visual word recognition, acquisition of grammatical rules, and acquisition of orthographic knowledge. It is to be expected, however, that as techniques for measuring automaticity improve, researchers will cast a wider net. Illustrative examples from the SLA literature involving automaticity in word recogntion and grammar acquisition follow below.

4.1 Word recognition in reading

One of the basic skills that underlies fluency is single word recognition. Several authors have investigated this in the case of visual word recognition in second language reading. For a general review and discussion of issues, see Haynes and Carr (1990) and Koda (1994). The role of automaticity in visual word recognition was directly investigated in Favreau and Segalowitz (1983). They extended Neely's (1977; see box 13.1) paradigm by comparing performance in first and second language conditions, and by comparing bilinguals who were either very fluent readers of L2 (they read L1 and L2 at the same speed) or quite fluent but nonetheless slower readers in L2. As an index of automaticity, Favreau and Segalowitz used Neely's measure of ballistic processing, namely the facilitation effect in the short SOA condition for words related to the prime but nevertheless unexpected (see box 13.1 for explanation). They found that the highly fluent bilinguals showed significant facilitation in both L1 and L2, indicating automaticity in both languages, while the less fluent bilinguals showed it in L1 only. This result supported the conclusion that automaticity of single word recognition underlies fluency (see also the discussions in N. Segalowitz, Poulsen, and Komoda, 1991; N. Segalowitz, 2000). Similar studies of auditory word recognition and word production have yet to be undertaken in the same vein.

In the research just cited, automaticity was understood to imply that some kind of restructuring of processing has taken place. DeKeyser (2001, pp. 144–5) makes a useful distinction between fine-grained changes in performance and more holistic changes. For example, he points out that McLeod and McLaughlin (1986) did not find evidence for restructuring, whereas N. Segalowitz and Segalowitz (1993) and S. J. Segalowitz et al. (1998) did. DeKeyser argues that one needs to recognize the important difference between restructuring of mechanisms within word recognition (fine-grained structuring) and higher-level restructuring involved in utterance comprehension; restructuring may occur at one level but not the other.

This line of research has interesting implications for vocabulary development in L2 (as well as, of course, in L1). Many theorists argue that new vocabulary is generally acquired through learning in context (Nagy, Anderson, and Herman, 1987; Sternberg, 1987). Nation (1993) points out that a very high threshold of vocabulary comprehension is required if one is to be able to learn new vocabulary from reading a text. That is, one must have a basic vocabulary that enables one to understand on the order of 90 percent of the words of a given text if new words are to be learned effectively. Moreover, Nation (1993; also Meara, 1993) points out that the learner must have *fluency of access* to this basic vocabulary to be useful. This idea has never been directly tested, and it would seem that the techniques for studying automaticity described here could be used to investigate it. The idea that there is a threshold of automaticity in accessing basic vocabulary that must be crossed before additional vocabulary learning can take place is reminiscent of the idea (Alderson, 1984) that transfer of reading strategies from L1 to L2 cannot proceed until there is some threshold level of mastery of L2. Such transfer may also involve a threshold level of automatic processing in L2, in addition to some threshold level of knowledge of L2. Again, current techniques for assessing automaticity could be used in such a study.

4.2 *Grammar*

A number of authors in recent years have investigated the role of automatic processes in the acquisition of grammatical knowledge or grammar-like structure (Leow, 1998; Schmidt, 1994; Tomlin and Villa, 1994; Whittlesea and Dorken, 1993; see also contributions in Stadler and Frensch, 1998).

DeKeyser (1997) conducted a study in which learners were exposed to a miniature language system consisting of a number of artificial nouns and verbs; morphemic inflections to indicate gender, number, and grammatical case; and picture stimuli to illustrate the meanings of sentences expressed in this language. Subjects were trained and tested over a period of 8 weeks, during which they learned to comprehend (match a sentence to the appropriate picture) and produce (generate a sentence or fill in morpheme slots to describe a picture). DeKeyser was interested principally in whether the evidence of increased skill in this language-learning situation would resemble learning of other cognitive skills. His conclusions were that this generally was the case. Subjects' reaction times decreased gradually in a manner that was well fitted by a power curve of the type others have found in skill-learning situations (Logan, 1988, 1990). DeKeyser interpreted the observed decreasing speed of performance as a sign of increasing automaticity. In further discussing this research elsewhere, however, DeKeyser (2001, pp. 141–2) pointed out results from this study could be seen as evidence against Logan's instance-retrieval interpretation of automaticity. At the end of the study, the subjects had to use rules that were learned during either comprehension or production sessions in new comprehension or production tasks. One group used the rules in the same type of task (comprehension or production). A second group reversed the tasks (having now to apply a production rule to a comprehension task, etc.). DeKeyser found large reaction time and error differences between the two groups, favoring the same-task application of the rules. He argued that instance theory cannot explain this asymmetry of rule application, since once the solution instances are registered in memory they should be available equally for either type of task. He suggests that instance theory probably applies exclusively in situations where only memory is required for performance. Where production rule learning is the important requirement, as in SLA, the theory may not apply.

Robinson (1997) reported a study in which he compared the effects of focusing the attention of Japanese learners of English on grammatical form while they learned a rule governing a structure in English. The study was designed to test predictions derived from Logan's (1988) instance theory of automatization. In Robinson's study, the learners were placed in conditions that varied the kind of instruction they received (instructed, enhanced, incidental, and implicit) and the number of practice examples given before knowledge of the rule was tested. He found facilitation effects (faster responding) for old grammatical sentences in the transfer test (consistent with Logan's theory), but no effect of faster responding to examples that had been seen more frequently (not consistent with Logan's theory). In reviewing his findings, Robinson concluded that "two knowledge bases are contributing to transfer task performance" (p. 241), one that fits the description of controlled processes ("slow, effortful hypothesis testing"), the other automatic processes ("fast, efficient memorization of instances and fragments").

To summarize, the research on automaticity in grammar acquisition does not provide a tidy picture whereby learning grammatical structure proceeds simply from knowledge of examples to automatized (proceduralized) rules (ACT theory). Nor does it seem that grammar acquisition proceeds simply from the effortful application of rules to the retrieval of memorized instances. Some kind of integration of rule-based and exemplar-based processes may ultimately be called for, as DeKeyser (2001) has suggested.

5 Pedagogical Implications of Automaticity

The concept of automaticity obviously has implications for second language pedagogy (DeKeyser, 2001; Hulstijn, 2001; Johnson, 1996; Robinson, 2001; Skehan, 1998). In this section we consider two practical issues: (i) should teachers promote automaticity in SLA, and if so, why; and (ii) how should this be done?

There are several possible reasons to expect learning to benefit from automaticity. The most commonly cited one is that because automatic processing consumes fewer attentional resources than does controlled processing, the more automatic performance becomes the more attentional resources there are left over for other purposes. Thus, for example, if one can handle the phonology and syntax of a second language automatically, then more attention can be paid to processing semantic, pragmatic, and sociolinguistic levels of communication.

A second reason to favor automaticity is that once a mechanism becomes automatic it will process information very quickly and accurately, being immune to interference from other sources of information. This in itself improves the quality of performance. It has even been suggested that this consideration may be more important than the freeing up of resources (Stanovich, 1991), although there does not appear to be any research to directly test this.

Third, there are strong reasons for associating automaticity with important (but, of course, not all) aspects of fluency (N. Segalowitz, 2000; Skehan, 1998). To the extent that fluency represents the ability to speak or read quickly, accurately, and without undue hesitation, then automatic execution of certain aspects of L2 performance such as pronunciation, grammatical processing, and word recognition would, by definition, promote fluency. Fluency is, of course, a worthwhile goal in itself, insofar as it facilitates communication. In addition, however, increasing learners' fluency may increase their motivation to use the language, which in turn assists them in seeking out and profiting from increased L2 contact.

A number of authors have emphasized the importance of automaticity as one pedagogical goal in SLA. For example, Hulstijn (2001) discusses what he sees as a regrettable lack of appreciation in curriculum development for automatic skills in listening and reading word recognition, and he makes some practical suggestions regarding how this situation might be corrected. Robinson (2001) proposes ways in which learning tasks might be sequenced according to various criteria of complexity in order to facilitate automatization, among other things. Johnson (1996) develops in some detail a proposal to promote automaticity through management of the "required attention" for the task at hand.

All automaticity proposals for enhancing SLA are based, in one way or another, on the idea that extended practice, under particular conditions and circumstances, will increase fluency by developing automaticity. Where theorists differ is in terms of how explicit they are about the boundary conditions under which this will happen. We might start with a very basic question: what is the evidence that practice will enhance fluency? The literature, actually, is not so very clear on this question. A useful discussion of the issues can be found in Ellis and Laporte (1997), who review both field and laboratory studies dealing with various types of practice and their impact on SLA.

Ericsson et al. (1993) and Ericsson and Charness (1994) discuss the role of practice in other fields of expertise. They conclude that massive practice, on the order of 10,000 hours, is required to achieve expert levels in many areas of skill. In the case of L1 development, a simple calculation will show that by age 4 or 5, or even earlier, a child will have logged in hours of communicative activity on this order of magnitude. Unfortunately, this amount of time is rarely available to more mature second language learners unless they are fully immersed in a second language milieu. It is generally assumed, nevertheless, that even over shorter periods, say weeks or months, properly organized practice can lead to great improvements in second language skill. This is especially true in vocabulary learning and in the learning of chunks of language – phrases, collocations, formulaic utterances – that some have suggested is critical to the learning of syntactic patterns (Ellis, 1997). As Ellis suggests, the more automatic the learner's access to frequent language sequences stored in long-term memory, "the more fluent is the resultant language use, concomitantly freeing attentional resources for analysis of the meaning of the message, either for comprehension or for production planning . . . [I]t is this long-term knowledge base of word sequences which serves as the database for the acquisition of language grammar" (p. 139).

How, then, to best promote automaticity? Here, the challenge is the potential conflict that may exist between methods used specifically to promote automaticity and the larger methodological framework used to promote second language learning in the classroom. DeKeyser (2001) identified this problem explicitly: "It is the task of applied linguists, then, to determine how consistent practice, distributed practice, and quality feedback can be incorporated into the curriculum and reconciled with other desiderata for classroom activities, such as communicativeness and variety, not to mention how activities designed to automatize grammar can be integrated with the automatization of vocabulary" (pp. 145–6). Now, promoting automaticity is generally believed to require massive repetition experiences and consistent practice, most likely in the sense defined by Shiffrin and Schneider (1977). Traditionally, however, opportunities for massive repetition have been created in the language class through drills and practice exercises. These activities tend to operate in a way that may undermine the goals of communicative orientations to language teaching. Drill and practice are usually boring, reduce motivation, and tend to involve highly artificial, non-communicative uses of language. It has been suggested (Gatbonton and Segalowitz, 1988) that the very success of communicative language methods derives from the fact that they capitalize on an important principle of learning and memory, namely the principle of transfer-appropriate processing (Roediger and Guynn, 1996) or procedural reinstatement (Healy and Bourne, 1998). The challenge then is to incorporate activities that promote automaticity into the language learning situation in a manner that respects transfer-appropriate processing and other positive features of communicative practices (for concrete examples see Gatbonton, 1994; Gatbonton and Segalowitz, 1988; N. Segalowitz and Gatbonton, 1995). It was mentioned earlier that Shebilske et al. (1999) and others have shown that in complex skill-learning situations the transfer of automatized skills depends on the psychological similarity of the learning and transfer contexts. This consideration will be important too in designing L2 curricula. Future research will have to determine which dimensions of psychological similarity (e.g., whether the learners' intentions, feelings, etc., are important, or whether only linguistic contexts are important) are relevant to the establishment of automaticity that is transferable to new situations.

6 Summary and Conclusion

By way of summary, several points can be made. First, automaticity has been operationally defined in various ways. It is important, therefore, for researchers to be clear about which sense of automaticity they have in mind when attributing some aspect of performance to automaticity. Automaticity should not be used merely as a synonym for fast processing. Rather, automaticity refers to a significant change in the way processing is carried out (some form of restructuring). Research techniques exist for distinguishing fast automatic from fast non-automatic processes. Second, automaticity appears to be implicated in similar ways in all skill development. Third, research into the development of complex skills in dynamically changing environments points to the importance of developing automaticity in coordination with the development of attention management skills. While automaticity certainly appears to be important in the development of second language fluency, fluency also requires skilled use of controlled processes. It is important, therefore, that more research be done on the co-development of automatic processing and attention management in the acquisition of language fluency.

Where should researchers focus future work on automaticity in second language acquisition? First, in the area of measurement, it would be useful to develop practical measures of automaticity that can be easily administered in learning settings, and that do not require complex research designs involving only laboratory-based testing. In particular, it would be helpful to have measures that could be used in single case studies so that the role of automaticity in a learner's language-skill development could be traced over time. Second, more research needs to be done on how considerations of automaticity interact with the development of attention management skills. For example, it has been suggested that it is important early on for learners to have automatic access to prefabricated chunks of language stored in memory. This stored language may serve as a database from which the learner abstracts recurrent patterns, leading to the mastery of grammatical regularities. Researchers need to fill in the specific details about how this actually comes about, showing the interplay between the development of automatic access and the abstracting of regularities for the construction of rule-based knowledge or rule-like behaviors. Third, more research needs to be done on the conditions of automatization that allow skills to be transferred to new contexts, and the conditions that limit such transfer. It was suggested that the principle of transfer-appropriate processing may be crucial here; more research needs to be done on this in the context of second language development. Finally, if we are to see pedagogical benefits from research on automaticity, it is important that curriculum developers and researchers agree on how automaticity and attention are to be operationally defined, so that meaningful connections can be made between work done in the laboratory and in the field.

ACKNOWLEDGMENT

The author gratefully acknowledges the comments of Elizabeth Gatbonton, Catherine Poulsen, and Vivien Watson on earlier versions of this chapter. This work was supported by grants to the author from the Natural Sciences and Engineering Research Council of Canada and from the Quebec Ministry of Education (FCAR).

REFERENCES

Ackerman, P. L. 1989: Individual differences and skill acquisition. In P. L. Ackerman, R. J. Sternberg, and R. Glaser (eds), *Learning and Individual Differences: Advances in Theory and Research*. New York: W. H. Freeman, 165–217.

Alderson, J. C. 1984: Reading: a reading problem or a language problem? In J. C. Alderson and A. H. Urquhart (eds), *Reading in a Foreign Language*. Harlow: Longman, 1–24.

Allport, A. and Wylie, G. 1999: Task-switching: positive and negative priming of task set. In G. W. Humphreys, J. Duncan, and A. Treisman (eds), *Attention, Space and Action: Studies in Cognitive Neuroscience*. Oxford: Oxford University Press, 273–96.

Anderson, J. R. 1983: *The Architecture of Cognition*. Cambridge, MA: Harvard University Press.

Anderson, J. R. and Fincham, J. M. 1994: Acquisition of procedural skills from examples. *Journal of Experimental Psychology: Learning, Memory and Cognition*, 20, 1322–40.

Anderson, J. R. and Lebriere, C. 1998: *The Atomic Components of Thought*. Mahwah, NJ: Lawrence Erlbaum Associates.

Anderson, J. R., Fincham, J. M., and Douglass, S. 1997: The role of examples and rules in the acquisition of a cognitive skill. *Journal of Experimental Psychology: Learning, Memory, and Cognition*, 23, 932–45.

Carr, T. H. and Curran, T. 1994: Cognitive factors in learning about structured sequences: applications to syntax. *Studies in Second Language Acquisition*, 16, 205–30.

Cheng, P. 1985: Restructuring versus automaticity: alternative accounts of skill acquisition. *Psychological Review*, 92, 414–23.

DeKeyser, R. 1997: Beyond explicit rule learning: automatizing second language morphosyntax. *Studies in Second Language Acquisition*, 19, 195–222.

DeKeyser, R. M. 2001: Automaticity and automatization. In P. Robinson (ed.), *Cognition and Second Language Instruction*. New York: Cambridge University Press, 125–51.

Ellis, N. C. 1997: Vocabulary acquisition: word structure, collocation, word-class, and meaning. In N. Schmitt and M. McCarthy (eds), *Vocabulary: Description, Acquisition and Pedagogy*. Cambridge: Cambridge University Press, 122–39.

Ellis, N. C. and Laporte, N. 1997: Contexts of acquisition: effects of formal instruction and naturalistic exposure on second language acquisition. In A. M. B. de Groot and J. F. Kroll (eds), *Tutorials in*

Bilingualism: Psycholinguistic Perspectives. Mahwah, NJ: Lawrence Erlbaum Associates, 53–83.

Elman, J. L., Bates, E. A., Johnson, M. H., Karmiloff-Smith, A., Parisi, D., and Plunkett, K. 1996: *Rethinking Innateness: A Connectionist Perspective on Development.* Cambridge, MA: MIT Press.

Ericsson, K. A. and Charness, N. 1994: Expert performance: its structure and acquisition. *American Psychologist*, 49, 725–47.

Ericsson, K. A., Krampe, R. T., and Tesch Roemer, C. 1993: The role of deliberate practice in the acquisition of expert performance. *Psychological Review*, 100, 363–406.

Favreau, M. and Segalowitz, N. S. 1983: Automatic and controlled processes in the first- and second-language reading of fluent bilinguals. *Memory and Cognition*, 11, 56–74.

Fischler, I. 1998: Attention and language. In R. Parasuraman (ed.), *The Attentive Brain.* Cambridge, MA: MIT Press, 381–99.

Gatbonton, E. 1994: *Bridge to Fluency: Speaking.* Scarborough, Ontario: Prentice-Hall Canada.

Gatbonton, E. and Segalowitz, N. 1988: Creative automatization: principles for promoting fluency within a communicative framework. *TESOL Quarterly*, 22, 473–92.

Gopher, D. 1992: The skill of attention control: acquisition and execution of attention strategies. In D. Meyer and S. Kornblum (eds), *Attention and Performance XIV: Synergies in Experimental Psychology, Artificial Intelligence, and Cognitive Neuroscience.* Cambridge, MA: MIT Press, 299–322.

Haier, R. J., Siegel, B. V., MacLachlan, A., Soderling, E., et al. 1992: Regional glucose metabolic changes after learning a complex visuospatial/motor task: a positron emission tomographic study. *Brain Research*, 570, 134–43.

Haynes, M. and Carr, T. H. 1990: Writing system background and second language reading: a component skills analysis of English reading by native speaker-readers of Chinese. In T. H. Carr and B. A. Levy (eds), *Reading and its Development: Component Skills Approaches.* San Diego: Academic Press, 375–421.

Healy, A. F. and Bourne, J. L. 1998: *Foreign Language Learning.* Mahwah, NJ: Lawrence Erlbaum Associates.

Howe, M. J. A. (ed.) 1990: *Encouraging the Development of Exceptional Skills and Talents.* Leicester: British Psychological Society.

Howe, M. J. A., Davidson, J. W., and Sloboda, J. A. 1998: Innate talents: reality or myth? *Behavioral and Brain Sciences*, 21, 399–442.

Hulstijn, J. 2001: Intentional and incidental second language vocabulary learning: a reappraisal of elaboration, rehearsal and automaticity. In P. Robinson (ed.), *Cognition and Second Language Instruction.* New York: Cambridge University Press, 258–86.

Jacoby, L. L. 1991: A process dissociation framework: separating automatic from intentional uses of memory. *Journal of Memory and Language*, 22, 485–508.

Jacoby, L. L., McElree, B., and Trainham, T. 1999: Automatic influences as accessibility bias in memory and Stroop tasks: toward a formal model. In D. Gopher and A. Koriat (eds), *Attention and Performance XVII.* Cambridge, MA: MIT Press, 461–86.

Johnson, K. 1996: *Language Teaching and Skill Learning.* Oxford: Blackwell.

Kahneman, D. 1973: *Attention and Effort.* Englewood Cliffs, NJ: Prentice-Hall.

Koda, K. 1994: Second language reading research: problems and possibilities. *Applied Psycholinguistics*, 15, 1–28.

Koda, K. 1996: Second language word recognition research: a critical review. *Modern Language Journal*, 80, 450–60.

Lambert, W. E. 1955: Measurement of the linguistic dominance of bilinguals. *Journal of Abnormal and Social Psychology*, 50, 197–200.

Lehman, J. F., Laird, J., and Rosenbloom, P. 1998: A gentle introduction to Soar: an architecture for human cognition. In D. Scarborough and S. Sternberg (eds), *An Invitation to Cognitive Science. Vol. 4: Methods, Models, and Conceptual Issues*. Cambridge, MA: MIT Press, 211–53.

Leow, R. P. 1998: Toward operationalizing the process of attention in SLA: evidence for Tomlin and Villa's (1994) fine-grained analysis of attention. *Applied Psycholinguistics*, 19, 133–59.

Levelt, W. J. M. 1993: *Speaking: From Intention to Articulation*. Cambridge, MA: MIT Press.

Lightbown, P. M. 1985: Great expectations: second language acquisition research and classroom teaching. *Applied Linguistics*, 6, 173–89.

Logan, G. D. 1988: Toward an instance theory of automatization. *Psychological Review*, 95, 492–527.

Logan, G. D. 1990: Repetition priming and automaticity: common underlying mechanisms? *Cognitive Psychology*, 22, 1–35.

Long, M. 1996: The role of the linguistic environment in second language acquisition. In W. C. Ritchie and T. K. Bhatia (eds), *Handbook of Second Language Acquisition*. New York: Academic Press, 413–68.

MacWhinney, B. 1997: Second language acquisition and the Competition Model. In A. M. B. de Groot and J. F. Kroll (eds), *Tutorial in Bilingualism: Psycholinguistic Perspectives*. Mahwah, NJ: Lawrence Erlbaum Associates, 113–42.

Magiste, E. 1986: Selected issues in second and third language learning. In J. Vaid (ed.), *Language Processing in Bilinguals: Psycholinguistic and Neuropsychological Perspectives*. Hillsdale, NJ: Lawrence Erlbaum Associates, 97–122.

McLaughlin, B. and Heredia, R. 1996: Information-processing approaches to research on second language acquisition and use. In W. C. Ritchie and T. K. Bhatia (eds), *Handbook of Second Language Acquisition*. New York: Academic Press, 213–28.

McLeod, B. and McLaughlin, B. 1986: Restructuring or automaticity? Reading in a second language. *Language Learning: A Journal of Applied Linguistics*, 36, 109–23.

Meara, P. 1993: The bilingual lexicon and the teaching of vocabulary. In R. Schreuder and B. Weltens (eds), *The Bilingual Lexicon*. Amsterdam: John Benjamins, 279–97.

Meyer, D. E. and Kieras, D. E. 1997: A computational theory of executive cognitive processes and multiple-task performance. Part 1: Basic mechanisms. *Psychological Review*, 104, 3–65.

Meyer, D. E. and Kieras, D. E. 1999: Précis to a practical unified theory of cognition and action: some lessons from EPIC computational models of human multiple-task performance. In D. Gopher and A. Koriat (eds), *Attention and Performance XVII*. Cambridge, MA: MIT Press, 17–88.

Nagy, W. E., Anderson, R. C., and Herman, P. A. 1987: Learning word meanings from context during normal reading. *American Educational Research Journal*, 24, 237–70.

Nakayama, K. and Joseph, J. S. 1998: Attention, pattern recognition, and pop-out in visual search. In R. Parasuraman (ed.), *The Attentive Brain*. Cambridge, MA: MIT Press, 279–98.

Nation, P. 1993: Using dictionaries to estimate vocabulary size: essential, but rarely followed, procedures. *Language Testing*, 10, 27–40.

Neely, J. H. 1977: Semantic priming and retrieval from lexical memory: roles of inhibitionless spreading activation and limited-capacity attention. *Journal of Experimental Psychology: General*, 106, 226–54.

Newell, A. 1990: *Unified Theories of Cognition*. Cambridge, MA: Harvard University Press.

Newell, A. and Rosenbloom, P. S. 1981: Mechanisms of skill acquisition and the law of practice. In J. R. Anderson (ed.), *Cognitive Skills and their Acquisition*. Hillsdale, NJ: Lawrence Erlbaum Associates, 1–55.

Obler, L. K. 1989: Exceptional second language learners. In S. Gass, C. Madden, D. Preston, and L. Selinker (eds), *Variation in Second Language Acquisition. I: Discourse and Pragmatics. II: Psycholinguistic Issues*. Clevedon: Multilingual Matters, 141–59.

Obler, L. K. and Fein, D. 1988: *The Exceptional Brain*. New York: Guilford Press.

Palmeri, T. 1997: Exemplar similarity and the development of automaticity. *Journal of Experimental Psychology: Learning, Memory and Cognition*, 23, 324–54.

Pashler, H. E. 1998: *The Psychology of Attention*. Cambridge, MA: MIT Press.

Perfetti, C. 1985: *Reading Ability*. New York: Oxford University Press.

Pienemann, M. 1998: Developmental dynamics in L1 and L2 acquisition: Processability Theory and generative entrenchment. *Bilingualism: Language and Cognition*, 1, 1–20.

Posner, M. I. and Boies, S. J. 1971: Components of attention. *Psychological Review*, 78, 391–408.

Posner, M. and Snyder, C. 1975: Attention and cognitive control. In R. C. Solso (ed.), *Information Processing and Cognition: The Loyola Symposium*. Hillsdale, NJ: Lawrence Erlbaum Associates, 55–85.

Raichle, M. E., Fiez, J. A., Videen, T. O., MacLeod, A. K., Pardo, J. V., Fox, P. T., and Petersen, S. E. 1994: Practice-related changes in human brain functional anatomy during nonmotor learning. *Cerebral Cortex*, 4, 8–26.

Rickard, T. 1997: Bending the power law: a CMPL theory of strategy shifts and the automatization of cognitive skills. *Journal of Experimental Psychology: General*, 126, 288–311.

Robinson, P. 1997: Generalizability and automaticity of second language learning under implicit, incidental, enhanced, and instructed conditions. *Studies in Second Language Acquisition*, 19, 223–48.

Robinson, P. 2001: Task complexity, cognitive resoures, and syllabus design: a triadic framework for examining task influences on SLA. In P. Robinson (ed.), *Cognition and Second Language Instruction*. New York: Cambridge University Press, 287–318.

Roediger, I. H. L. and Guynn, M. J. 1996: Retrieval processes. In E. L. Bjork and R. A. Bjork (eds), *Memory*. New York: Academic Press, 197–236.

Rogers, R. D. and Monsell, S. 1995: The cost of a predictable switch between simple cognitive tasks. *Journal of Experimental Psychology: General*, 124, 207–31.

Schmidt, R. 1994: Implicit learning and the cognitive unconscious: of artificial grammars and SLA. In N. C. Ellis (ed.), *Implicit and Explicit Learning of Languages*. New York: Academic Press, 165–209.

Schmidt, R. 2001: Attention. In P. Robinson (ed.), *Cognition and Second Language Instruction*. New York: Cambridge University Press, 1–32.

Schneider, W. and Shiffrin, R. M. 1977: Controlled and automatic human information processing. 1: Detection, search and attention. *Psychological Review*, 84, 1–66.

Segalowitz, N. 1991: Does advanced skill in a second language reduce automaticity in the first language?

Language Learning: A Journal of Applied Linguistics, 41, 59–83.

Segalowitz, N. 1997: Individual differences in second language acquisition. In A. de Groot and J. Kroll (eds), *Tutorials in Bilingualism*. Hillsdale, NJ: Lawrence Erlbaum Associates, 85–112.

Segalowitz, N. 2000: Automaticity and attentional skill in fluent performance. In H. Riggenbach (ed.), *Perspectives on Fluency*. Ann Arbor: University of Michigan Press, 200–19.

Segalowitz, N. and Gatbonton, E. 1995: Automaticity and lexical skills in second language fluency: implications for computer assisted language learning. *Computer Assisted Language Learning*, 8, 129–49.

Segalowitz, N. and Segalowitz, S. J. 1993: Skilled performance, practice, and the differentiation of speed-up from automatization effects: evidence from second language word recognition. *Applied Psycholinguistics*, 14, 369–85.

Segalowitz, N., O'Brien, I., and Poulsen, C. 1998: Evidence for a domain-specific component of attentional control in skilled performance. *Brain and Cognition*, 37, 129–32.

Segalowitz, N., Poulsen, C., and Komoda, M. 1991: Lower level components of reading skill in higher level bilinguals: implications for reading instruction. *AILA Review*, 8, 15–30.

Segalowitz, S. J., Segalowitz, N. S., and Wood, A. G. 1998: Assessing the development of automaticity in second language word recognition. *Applied Psycholinguistics*, 19, 53–67.

Shebilske, W., Goettl, B., and Regian, J. W. 1999: Executive control and automatic processes as complex skills develop in laboratory and applied settings. In D. Gopher and A. Koriat (eds), *Attention and Performance XVII. Cognitive Regulation of Performance: Interaction of Theory and Application*. Cambridge, MA: MIT Press, 401–32.

Shiffrin, R. M. and Schneider, W. 1977: Controlled and automatic human information processing. 2: Perceptual learning, automatic learning and a general theory. *Psychological Review*, 84, 127–90.

Simonton, D. 1999: Talent and its development: an emergenic and epigenetic model. *Psychological Review*, 106, 435–57.

Skehan, P. 1998: *A Cognitive Approach to Language Learning*. Oxford: Oxford University Press.

Stadler, M. A. and Frensch, P. A. 1998: *Handbook of Implicit Learning*. Thousand Oaks, CA: Sage.

Stanovich, K. E. 1991: Word recognition: changing perspectives. In R. Barr & M. L. Kamil (eds), *Handbook of Reading Research. Vol. 2*. Mahwah, NJ: Lawrence Erlbaum Associates, 418–52.

Sternberg, R. J. 1987: Most vocabulary is learned from context. In M. McKeown and M. Curtis (eds), *The Nature of Vocabulary Acquisition*. Hillsdale, NJ: Lawrence Erlbaum Associates, 89–106.

Stroop, J. R. 1935: Studies of interference in serial and verbal reactions. *Journal of Experimental Psychology*, 18, 643–62.

Tomlin, R. S. and Villa, V. 1994: Attention in cognitive science and second language acquisition. *Studies in Second Language Acquisition*, 16, 183–203.

Tzelgov, J., Henik, A., and Leiser, D. 1990: Controlling Stroop interference: evidence from a bilingual task. *Journal of Experimental Psychology: Learning, Memory, and Cognition*, 16, 760–71.

Wegner, D. M. 1994: Ironic processes of mental control. *Psychological Review*, 101, 34–52.

Whittlesea, B. W. and Dorken, M. D. 1993: Incidentally, things in general are particularly determined: an episodic-processing account of implicit learning. *Journal of Experimental Psychology: General*, 122, 227–48.

14 Variation

SUZANNE ROMAINE

1 Introduction

The process of second language acquisition (SLA) is highly variable. Indeed, Young (1988, p. 281) identifies variation as "one of the abiding problems of second language acquisition." Variation is immediately obvious in the fact that Japanese learners of English, for instance, sometimes pronounce English /r/ as /l/, or that Chinese and Vietnamese learners of English do not always mark noun plurals, etc. Many such differences between learners' performance and that of native speakers were traditionally attributed to interference or transfer from the learner's first language (L1), (see Odlin, this volume, on cross-linguistic influence).

Contrastive analysis of the learner's language with the target language (TL) was used to pinpoint areas of difference and hence predict learner errors. Thus, within this framework the failure of Japanese learners to produce English /r/ consistently was explained by the fact that Japanese does not distinguish phonologically between /l/ and /r/. Likewise, the variability in plural marking among Chinese and Vietnamese learners of English can be attributed to the fact that Chinese and Vietnamese do not regularly mark plurals.

On closer examination, however, variability clearly has sources and causes other than cross-linguistic influence. Czech learners of English, for instance, also mark noun plurals variably, and Czech does mark plurality in a way similar to English by means of inflectional morphology. Furthermore, variability is not totally random or idiosyncratic. Low-proficiency Chinese learners, for example, more often mark plurals on nouns ending in stops, such as *dog*. Grammatical accuracy also varies depending on the demands of the task, with more target-like performance typically more frequent on formal tests than in casual conversation.

Until the 1970s such phenomena were not generally discussed in variationist terms or indeed within the larger context of linguistic theory, because the learner's language was not considered as a system in its own right. Since then, however, researchers have turned their attention away from contrastive analysis and analysis of individual errors defined in terms of the mature TL system, in order to concentrate instead on the notion of SLA as a dynamic process characterized in terms of a variable and changing system over time. The introduction in particular of the notion of *interlanguage*, the variable learner systems of increasing complexity that develop during the process of acquiring a second language, marked an important paradigm shift in the field of SLA. The observation that learners from different L1 backgrounds acquiring the same TL appeared to go through the same stages of development, whether they were receiving formal classroom instruction or learning the language informally, led to claims that SLA was influenced by internally driven mechanisms independent of the learner's L1 and the TL (see, e.g., the papers in Rutherford, 1984).

With the shift in emphasis toward accounting for variability and explaining its sources and causes, there was initially much cross-fertilization between the fields of sociolinguistics and SLA, as well as between the study of pidgin and creole languages and SLA, because scholars in both those fields were also engaged in analyzing variation. During the 1970s and 1980s there were a number of attempts to develop taxonomies of variation within sociolinguistics as well as within SLA (see Adamson, 1988; Preston, 1989). Klein and Dittmar (1979), for example, pioneered the systematic study of learner varieties with their work on the natural or untutored (i.e., outside the classroom) acquisition of German by foreign workers. Recognition of the central concern of students of SLA to describe and account for the variability in interlanguage systems led in some cases to the adoption of sociolinguistic procedures for collecting and analyzing data, in particular recognition of the need to collect data in different contexts which might affect the occurrence of individual linguistic features. Correspondingly, there has been a growing interest in the influence of external variables of the kind investigated by sociolinguists, such as setting (see, especially, the chapters by Siegel and by Watson-Gegeo and Nielsen, this volume), attitudes and motivation, peer group influence, amount of planning time, topic, and interlocutor.

2 Sources of Variation in SLA

2.1 *Systematic and unsystematic variation*

The most basic (though not uncontroversial) distinction is that between systematic (i.e., rule-governed) and non-systematic (or free) variation not conditioned by any observable factors or governed by rule. As an example of non-systematic variation, consider the case of an 11-year-old Portuguese learner of English who used pre-verbal negation (e.g., *No look my card*) and *don't* + V (e.g., *Don't look my card*) in apparently random fashion (Ellis, 1992). The development of negation actually began with the generalized use of pre-verbal negation. Then *don't* entered the boy's repertoire and for a time was in free variation with *no* until other forms were added, such as *can't* and *won't*. The stage of free variation rapidly gave way to systematic variation and target-like invariance once he mastered the system. It is still an open question, however, whether cases of seemingly free variation are instead the result of inadequate research methods and lack of sufficient data for analysis. Other researchers looking at the same or similar data in more detail have not agreed with Ellis's claims about free variation and its role in the learner's interlanguage (see further in Ellis, 1999; Towell, Hawkins, and Bazergui, 1993; and section 5 below).

As an example of systematic variation, we can take the case of another learner mentioned by Ellis who marked third person singular present tense verbs with the suffix *-s* when the clause subject was a pronoun, but tended not to do so when the subject was a noun. Compare *he eats turkey* with *John eat turkey*. Here, variation is systematic because constraints can be observed and used to predict the appearance of the variants.

2.2 Internal and external variation

Quantitative sociolinguistic research of the type established by Labov (1966) identified both internal and external factors which had systematic effects in constraining the occurrence of phonological variables; for example the pronunciation of post-vocalic /r/ in words such as *farm, car,* final -t/d in *missed/grabbed, mist/hand,* or grammatical variables such as the third person singular present tense suffix *-s*, etc.

Internal variation is conditioned by linguistic factors, such as the phonetic environment in which a sound occurs. Over two decades of research on these and other variables in a number of different varieties of English and English-based creoles has revealed that variation previously reported and described as unsystematic or free was in fact conditioned by linguistic factors, such as environment. In the case of -t/d deletion, for example, it matters whether a word beginning with a vowel or a consonant follows (e.g., *missed train* v. *missed Alice*) or whether the final member of the cluster is the past tense morpheme (e.g., *missed* v. *mist*).

In addition, there are regular external or social factors affecting the realization of -t/d, including social class of the speaker, with higher-status speakers deleting less often than lower-status ones; style, with more deletion in less formal styles than in formal ones; and age, with younger speakers differing from older speakers with respect to the treatment of verbs such as *keep*, where past tense is marked by both the final /t/ and vowel change of the type found in strong verbs such as *come* (see Guy and Boyd, 1990). There are also differences relating to ethnicity and region, with African-Americans, for instance, deleting more frequently than whites.

2.3 Constraint hierarchies

An important finding of quantitative sociolinguistic research is that variable constraints can be ordered in a hierarchy according to how great an influence they exert on deletion. In this example, the linguistic constraints follow the hierarchy:

i Monomorphemic > Bimorphemic
ii C > V

This means that the phonetic environment promotes deletion more than the grammatical constraint: monomorphemic forms such as *mist* are more likely to show deletion than bimorphemic forms such as *missed*, where there is a morpheme boundary between *miss* and the final *-ed* signaling the past tense. Where a word beginning with a consonant follows word final -t/d, as in *missed train*, deletion is most likely.

One of the first SLA studies to adopt this kind of explicitly variationist perspective in both methodology and analysis was Dickerson's (1975) study of the variable phonology of ten Japanese learners of English. Dickerson incorporated the sociolinguistic concept of variable rule, an analytical construct which attempts to capture the observation that variation is sensitive to various constraints in the internal and external environment. Figure 14.1 shows the variable performance of learners in the pronunciation of /z/ in four linguistic contexts: before a following vowel (e.g., *jazzy*); before a following consonant other than interdental fricatives, affricates, and alveolar stops (e.g., *jasmine*); before a following silence; and before interdental fricatives, affricates, and alveolar stops (e.g., *buzzed*).

There are a number of theoretical and practical implications of Dickerson's findings. The first is that learners' pronunciation is most target-like before

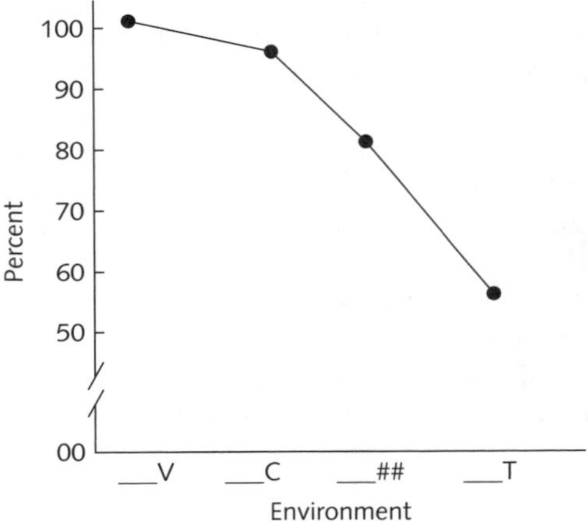

Figure 14.1 Accuracy of Japanese learners' pronunciation of English /z/ in four linguistic contexts
Source: Dickerson (1975, p. 403)

vowels, and least target-like before interdental fricatives, affricates, and alveolar stops. Thus, variation is sensitive to internal linguistic conditioning factors of the same type identified by sociolinguists in their study of native speakers. Another is that new sounds of a foreign language are easier to acquire in some contexts than others, a fact which is pedagogically useful for designing teaching materials. Learners can be taught to master difficult sounds in the easiest environments first before moving onto more difficult ones. Quantitative analysis can reveal the ordering of environments according to difficulty of acquisition. In later work, Adamson and Regan (1991) characterized the learning of constraints as "horizontal variation" (by comparison to "vertical variation," which is of a developmental nature). The problem posed by horizonal variation is that learners must learn the external and internal constraint rankings on variation.

3 Explanations for Internal Variability

3.1 Markedness

Explanations for internal linguistic variability in both native and non-native performance have appealed to a variety of factors, such as markedness and universals. A number of sociolinguists, for instance, have treated -t/d deletion as a slightly more specific version of a more general articulatory reduction rule. The loss of final consonants is a universal phonetic tendency operative in a wide range of languages. Thus, speakers tend to simplify consonant clusters, presumably because sequences of consonants are more marked than a sequence of consonant followed by vowel. This constraint operates to maintain the preferred universal canonical syllable structure, CVC. In fact, deletion of -t/d in consonant clusters is normal in casual, non-standard speech throughout native-speaker varieties of English.

Likewise, it has been assumed that a one-to-one relationship between form and meaning is the most natural one. Kiparsky's (1972) Distinctiveness Condition, for example, states that there is a tendency for semantically relevant information to be retained in surface structure. Therefore, the final /t/ of *mist* is more likely to be deleted than the final /t/ of *missed*, which carries meaning. A meaningful feature is more marked if it has no phonetic realization. Grammars tend to block rules which would wipe out surface morphological distinctions. We can then predict that a phonological rule of deletion would tend not to operate across morpheme boundaries. Thus, in general terms, we could say that the grammatical constraint reflects a functional principle because deletion in this environment would result in syncretism between the present (except for 3rd person singular forms) and past tense forms.

Kiparsky (1972, p. 645) claims that processes such as -t/d deletion are better treated as the result of general functional conditions impinging on speech performance than as specific rules in individual grammars. Phonological change

Table 14.1 Markedness metric for t/d/ deletion

	Constraints	
Environments	*[morpheme boundary]*	*[syllabic]*
i mist #C	u	u
ii mist #V	u	m
iii miss+ed #C	m	u
iv miss+ed #V	m	m

works against the demands of ideal morphology, with optimal encoding being expressed by uniform encoding of one form/one function.

Using these insights, we can generate a markedness metric for the environments in which -t/d deletion occurs, as shown in table 14.1. The constraint of a following consonant outranks that of a preceding morpheme boundary, so environment (i) is the most favorable to deletion because the unmarked values for both features [morpheme boundary] and [syllabic] co-occur; and environment (iv) is most resistant because here both features are marked.

Morphological and syntactic studies also show that variability reflects universal principles of markedness rather than simply the influence of L1 and L2. Typological work on relative clause formation strategies led to a variety of predictions that were tested by SLA researchers. Gass and Ard (1984), for example, found that acquisition of English relative clauses by learners of various L1 backgrounds proceeded from left to right in the noun phrase accessibility hierarchy postulated by Keenan and Comrie (1977): Subject > Direct object > Indirect object > Oblique > Genitive > Object of comparison. The hierarchy predicts universal constraints on relativization by means of an implicational ordering of noun phrases according to their degree of accessibility to relativization. The hierarchy predicts that subject position will be the most frequently relativized (e.g., *the woman who works with me rides a bike to the office*). If a language has a relative clause formation strategy that works on two possible NP positions, then it must work on all intermediate positions. This means that we would not expect to find a language with relative clause formation strategies that apply only to subject and oblique position.

Gass and Ard also found that the lower the position in the hierarchy, the more likely resumptive pronouns were used, for example, *the woman that I gave the book to her*. Here the relative clause is in oblique position (i.e., object of a preposition) and *her* is a resumptive pronoun occupying that slot. The frequency of occurrence of resumptive pronouns also occurred in inverse proportion to proficiency.

Similarly, Hyltenstam (1984) showed that learners of Swedish as a second language from a variety of L1 backgrounds used resumptive pronouns with greater frequency further down the hierarchy. Some of the learners' languages allowed resumptive pronouns. Swedish, however, like English, does not permit resumptive relative pronouns.

3.2 *The relationship between variation and change*

One of the tenets of sociolinguistic theory is that synchronic variation represents a stage in long-term change. We can also use this constraint hierarchy to predict the development through time of varieties, on the assumption that linguistic change proceeds in step-wise increments, with rules generalizing as they spread through time and space, as suggested, for instance, in Bailey's (1973) wave model. Initially, a rule may have a probability of application of zero in all environments, and then the probability of application increases environment by environment. This is shown in table 14.2, where the onset of change is in variety A at time i in environment a. Using the kind of calculus applied by Bailey (1973), we can generate the continuum of varieties in table 14.2, in which the environments a, b, c, and d are temporally successive.

In assigning the heavier weight to the following consonant and the lighter one to the morpheme boundary, the model predicts that more deletions will occur in monomorphemic than bimorphemic clusters. The assumption here is that, all other things being equal, "normal" linguistic change proceeds from heavier to lighter environments. Bailey also predicts, however, that rules operate faster in heavier than lighter environments. Thus, the oldest environment is the earliest and fastest. It becomes categorical earliest, before the last environment begins to be variably operative. In other words, what is heavier has a greater effect on the application of the rule. What is quantitatively less is slower and later. In variety E, deletion is categorical in the heaviest environment,

Table 14.2 Temporal development of varieties for the rule of -t/d deletion

		Environment			
		a	*b*	*c*	*d*
Time	*Variety*	*mist #C*	*mist #V*	*miss+ed #C*	*miss+ed #V*
i	A	mis(t)	mist	missed	missed
ii	B	mis(t)	mis(t)	missed	missed
iii	C	mis(t)	mis(t)	miss(ed)	missed
iv	D	mis(t)	mis(t)	miss(ed)	miss(ed)
v	E	mis	mis(t)	miss(ed)	miss(ed)
vi	F	mis	mis	miss(ed)	miss(ed)
vii	G	mis	mis	miss	miss(ed)
viii	H	mis	mis	miss	miss

while the others are variable. Variety H, which is furthest in time and space from the point of origin, displays categorical deletion, while variety A is the least advanced. Here the rule applies variably only in the most favorable environment. Environments are implicationally ordered so that a variety which shows categorical deletion in environment c, for example, must also show categorical deletion in the lighter environments to the left, a and b. This is shown in variety E.

Rules, of course, can become stagnant, die out, or be aborted at any point in their temporal development. They may also be stable over long periods of time, as is the case for -t/d deletion, for instance. There is no reason to believe that one day all final instances of -t/d will disappear, because literacy acts as a brake on change. Constraints on rules may also be reweighted as they develop in a particular direction or variety. Rules can also compete for the same territory, and the same linguistic environment can host more than one change at the same time.

Dickerson (1975) also showed that it is possible to model SLA as continuous change over time, comprised of a series of transitions from one variety to the next, with each stage and transition characterized by systematicity. She monitored the learners' performance by recording them on three separate occasions over a nine-month period and found that development involved an increase in the proportion of target and target-like variants over time.

A number of SLA researchers have employed the same kinds of statistical procedures used by sociolinguists, such as VARBRUL analysis, a statistical program to calculate the probabilities for each factor (see, e.g., the studies in Bayley and Preston, 1996, and the appendix by Young and Bayley, 1996), as well as the kind of implicational model of change embodied in Bailey's dynamic paradigm, frequently employed by creolists in the analysis of variable data.

Gatbonton (1978) was one of the first to apply the dynamic model of language change to the acquisition of English interdental fricatives by French Canadian learners, who tend to substitute the equivalent stops. Her results for the voiced interdental fricative [d], shown in table 14.3, illustrate that new pronunciations move through learner interlanguage systems in a similar way to forms undergoing change in native-speaker varieties (or lects, as Bailey called them).

Like Dickerson, Gatbonton found that the correct TL pronunciation was mastered in some environments more readily than others. Variety 1, for instance, shows the system used by three learners who do not use the correct TL pronunciation at all. Variety 11 shows complete mastery of the TL pronunciation, a stage none of the learners in this study has reached. In fact, only two of the learners have progressed to the stage illustrated in varieties 8 and 9, where the use of the correct TL variant is categorical in the heaviest three environments, but still variable in the lightest two environments.

Note that Gatbonton's findings do not match exactly the predictions made by Bailey's wave theory, where only one variant appears in one environment

Table 14.3 Acquisition of English interdental fricatives by French Canadian learners

Linguistic environments[a]						
Heaviest					*Lightest*	
Lect	*V___*	*VCT___*	*VS___*	*VLCT___*	*VLS___*	*Number of subjects*
1	1	1	1	1	1	3
2	1,2	1	1	1	1	7
3	1,2	1,2	1	1	1	3
4	1,2	1,2	1,2	1	1	0
5	1,2	1,2	1,2	1,2	1	2
6	1,2	1,2	1,2	1,2	1,2	2
7	1,2	1,2	1,2	1,2	1,2	3
8	2	2	1,2	1,2	1,2	1
9	2	2	2	1,2	1,2	1
10	2	2	2	2	1,2	0
11	2	2	2	2	2	0

[a] V, preceding vowel; VCT, preceding voiced continuant; VS, preceding voiced stop; VLCT, preceding voiceless continuant; VLS, preceding voiceless stop. 1 = categorical presence of non-native substitute for English; 2 = categorical presence of native or nativelike English; 1,2 = variation of 1 and 2.

Source: Adapted from Gatbonton (1978), in Preston (1996, p. 244)

at a time. Once the learners in Gatbonton's study introduce a new form into an environment, it does not completely replace the old one. There is a stage where the old and new form alternate in apparent free variation. Otherwise, there is a good match between the model and the data. Only 6 of the 28 learners in the study did not fit into one of the predicted lect patterns. For Ellis (1992), such "free" variation is the clue to development because it is restructuring of competing rule systems which leads to change (see section 5).

3.3 *Implications of variation in developing systems*

The possibility that there may be universal constraints, such as markedness, driving the progression of linguistic systems from more simple to more complex also prompted a good deal of fruitful interaction between creolists and SLA researchers, as scholars sought to identify the similarities across both first and second language acquisition and language change, particularly contact-induced change of the type resulting in pidgins and creoles (see Andersen, 1983; Romaine, 1988, ch. 6, for an examination of the relevance of SLA to the study of pidgins and creoles). If there is a tendency to use less complex, more universal, and less marked forms in all these settings, then the sorts of systems that emerge ought to be similar.

Such ideas launched a series of studies aimed at detailing the similarities and differences among these developing variable systems. With respect to grammatical morphemes in first language acquisition, for instance, Brown (1973, p. 257) noted some time ago that performance does not pass from total absence to reliable presence: "There is always a considerable period, varying in length with the particular morpheme, in which production-where-required is probabilistic." Bickerton's (1977, pp. 54–5) characterization of pidginization as second language acquisition with limited input, and creolization as first language acquisition with restricted input, sparked a number of studies showing how the early stages of SLA shared features with pidgins. Schumann's (1978) longitudinal study of negation strategies used by Spanish speakers, in particular by Alberto, a 33-year-old Costa Rican Spanish speaker who acquired a rather limited proficiency in English, emphasized Alberto's continued use of pre-verbal negation, the preferred strategy of negation in English-based pidgins. Stauble (1978) suggested that developmental stages of the interlanguage continuum could be called basilang, mesolang, and acrolang, by analogy with the portions of the creole continuum referred to as basilect (i.e., that furthest away from the target), mesolect, and acrolect.

A strict universalist interpretation would lead to the prediction that there is a single series of changes or sequence of developments in any continuum linking the basilect/basilang to the acrolect/acrolang, between particular pairings of source and target languages. This encouraged consideration of cross-linguistic data from learners with different L1 backgrounds acquiring the same TL, which contrasted along major parameters of variation. The European Science Foundation project on adult second language acquisition among immigrants employed this methodology. Six teams of researchers based in different countries of Europe undertook paired comparisons of the learning of one TL by speakers of different source languages (SL) and the learning of different TLs by speakers of the same SL. This systematic comparison allowed a distinction to be drawn between features of the learning process specific to one linguistic pairing and features which were recurrent.

Overall, there appeared to be little TL influence in the acquisition of major semantic domains, such as temporality (see Dietrich, Klein, and Noyau, 1995). In the early stages, it seems that learners create a system of communication rather than acquire specific TL features. Learners begin by using lexical means before proceeding to grammaticalized ones. Systematic morphological distinctions emerge rather late, if at all. In the case of French, for instance, Noyau, Houdaïfa, Vasseur, and Véronique (1995, p. 205) found that although French has a grammaticalized aspectual distinction in the past, even advanced learners did not acquire it. This suggests that acquisition is dictated not by the TL, but by the constraints of the developing interlanguage system over time.

3.4 Transfer

An approach based on markedness and universals does not, however, explain everything, partly because there is no single definition of markedness. As Janda (1995, p. 207) has remarked, the notion has "survived decades of imprecise definitions and . . . developed into a cluster of (dis)similar concepts." Nor does markedness eliminate the need to invoke a role for transfer (see Odlin, this volume). As work becomes more sophisticated, researchers have resisted the temptation to look for single causes and accepted that interlanguage variability may have more than one source.

Gilbert (1983), for instance, examined the acquisition of the definite article in German by foreign workers of different language backgrounds. Four of the six source languages included in this study possess definite articles (i.e., Spanish, Greek, Italian, and Portuguese) in syntactic environments corresponding to those of German. A simple interpretation of transfer theory would predict that speakers of these languages should find it easier to learn a category in a second language equivalent to one already existing in their own. In addition, if such learners omit definite articles, this has to be attributed to pidginization rather than transfer. Absence of the definite article is a significant indicator of pidginization, because the definite article is nearly universal in all Germanic- and Romance-based pidgins and creoles. Moreover, the only instance in which the definite article is omitted in native-speaker German is in foreigner talk. Conversely, Turks and Yugoslavs, whose languages have no matching category, would face a more difficult task because they would have to create a whole new category.

Table 14.4 shows that speakers of languages with definite articles do make more use of definite articles, as would be predicted by transfer theory. However, they do not use articles categorically, which argues against the "bulk transfer hypothesis." The differences among Portuguese, Spanish, Italian, and Greek speakers is partly due to period of residence. Those with longer

Table 14.4 Frequency of occurrence of the definite article in the German of learners of different language backgrounds

Nationality	*% of occurrence of definite article*
Turkish	15
Yugoslav	19
Portuguese	35
Italian	69
Greek	75
Spanish	87

Source: Adapted from Gilbert (1983, p. 173)

residence produced more definite articles. The lower rate of use of definite articles among learners with shorter periods of residence is evidence of pidginization operative in the early stages of SLA.

Another effect of pidginization is in evidence in the forms of the definite article actually used. German has six distinct forms inflected for case, number, and gender. Italian and Greek are the languages most similar to German in this respect, and according to transfer theory, we would expect these two groups to produce a greater variety of marked forms (even if incorrectly distributed) than Spanish, Italian, and Portuguese speakers, whose definite articles differ in terms only of gender and number. This is not the case, however. In fact, Italian speakers used *die* categorically, just as speakers of Rabaul Creole German used *de* categorically. The form *die* is actually the most frequently occurring form in native-speaker German, occurring over 50 percent of the time. In fact, all groups tended to overgeneralize the use of *die*, regardless of period of residence. Overall, this study supports the idea that there are universal principles of pidginization, as well as positive and negative transfer effects. These manifest themselves in variable frequencies of occurrence of different features in L2. The study also suggests that learners with the same L1 make up learner communities.

The acquisition of the definite article in English is one of the major difficulties faced by second language learners, particularly those who speak languages with no definite articles. Similar effects may be found to those of the German acquisition study, namely that learners with articles in their first languages perform better than those who do not (Oller and Redding, 1971). Zobl (1982) shows how Spanish and Italian learners of English move directly from zero representation of the definite article to the target form. Chinese speakers, whose L1 does not have a definite article, follow a different evolutionary route in which a demonstrative pronoun is used as a first approximation to mark definiteness. Likewise, Zobl's (1984) study of the acquisition of nominal possessives in German by Turkish and Romance speakers shows that each group follows a distinct route which relates directly to typological differences between Romance languages and Turkish.

Another approach drawing on markedness, universals, and typological variation has followed the principles and parameters model account of the language faculty (Chomsky, 1981) to explain both order of acquisition and the effects of transfer in SLA. Within this perspective the grammar contains a core of fixed principles and certain open parameters which are set in accordance with experience. An associated theory of markedness dictates that in the absence of evidence to the contrary, the child will select the unmarked options. If we assume, not uncontroversially, that second language learners still have access to universal grammar, the problem is how to reconcile possible differences in parameter setting between the first language and the TL.

Some have argued that all parameters are initialized at the unmarked setting, and thus the second language learner will first adopt the unmarked form, irrespective of first language parameter settings. Meisel (1983, p. 202), for example, argued that deletion of pronouns can be found across a range of second language learners with different first language backgrounds in accordance with the fact that pro-drop constitutes the unmarked case (see also Hyams, 1986, for first language acquisition). However, there is also evidence that where the same parameter is marked in both languages, learners do not reset to the unmarked value. This, in effect, predicts that transfer will have no effect, and is too strong a claim. White (1986), for example, discusses evidence to show that speakers sometimes transfer a marked parameter setting from their first to a second language, in which the parameter is unmarked. There are also other cases where the learner's first language does not have a particular parameter at all, but nevertheless, the learner acquires the marked setting found in the second language rather than going through a stage of treating the parameter as if it had the unmarked setting.

There will also be ambiguous cases where it is impossible to distinguish transfer from the application of the default parameter setting. For example, some Spanish speakers apply pro-drop to English, but since English has the marked setting for this parameter and Spanish does not, the use of the unmarked parameter setting in English could be due to transfer or to more general markedness principles, or both. Other indeterminate cases arise from the fact that markedness theory does not dictate any particular setting as marked or unmarked. Thus, core grammar allows a number of different unmarked word orders. There is also some disagreement on the markedness values assigned to different parameter settings, which will affect how the evidence is interpreted. White (1986, p. 319), for instance, argues that pro-drop is the marked setting, and suggests that it might be harder for native speakers of Spanish learning English to abandon pro-drop than it is for native speakers of English learning Spanish to acquire it. In effect, this means that it should be harder to go from marked to unmarked than from unmarked to marked, if pro-drop is the marked setting. Phinney (1987, p. 235) provides evidence to support White's claim that English speakers are more easily able to acquire the pro-drop system of Spanish than Spanish speakers are able to acquire the non-pro-drop system of English, but she assumes that pro-drop constitutes the unmarked case.

More interesting perhaps, however, are cases where the languages in contact are typologically very different with respect to more than one parameter or with respect to a parameter which has far-reaching structural consequences, such as the head-final/head-initial parameter, which dictates basic principles of word order in a language (see, e.g., Flynn, 1989, on the acquisition of English relative clauses by Japanese and Spanish learners). More carefully controlled contrastive studies of a number of different language combinations must be conducted before these differing findings can be properly evaluated and understood, or indeed before it is clear whether a developmental interpretation of parameter setting is coherent (see Saleemi, 1992).

4 External Factors in Variation

External variables, such as social class, network, age, sex, ethnicity, or style, may come into play in both native and non-native performance. Although social class distinctions have been of paramount interest in accounting for sociolinguistic variation, they are of limited use within SLA. Interlanguage variants seldom have social significance for learners, although they may convey such distinctions to native speakers (see section 5).

4.1 *Style/task-based variation*

Stylistic variation, understood in terms of amount of attention paid to speech in different situations or while performing different tasks, however, is pertinent to both native and non-native speakers (see also Siegel, this volume, on context more generally). Dickerson (1975) found that Japanese learners of English produced more target-like variants in situations where they were able to monitor their speech, such as reading word lists, and fewer target-like forms in situations where they were less able to monitor their speech, such as free speech. This, too, has a direct parallel in sociolinguistic studies of native speaker varieties, where prestige forms are usually produced more frequently in carefully monitored styles.

Figure 14.2 shows Tarone's interlanguage continuum, which attempts to account for variation in learner speech by hypothesizing the existence of a number of varieties arranged along a continuum, which also represents the progression from zero to ultimate attainment. The learner moves up or down according to amount of attention paid to speech.

There are problems, however, with respect to both the measurement of amount of attention and the equation between attention and formality (see Sato, 1985; Traugott and Romaine, 1985). Different tasks make different demands

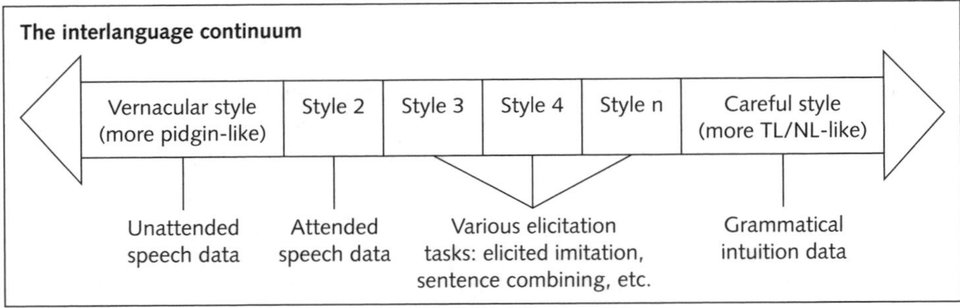

Figure 14.2 The interlanguage continuum
Source: Tarone (1985, p. 152)

on native speakers as well as learners. Where spelling suggests a more standard pronunciation, as, for instance, it does in forms ending in -t/d, native speakers may produce the more standard variants in reading style for reasons that have nothing to do with formality per se. In other cases, spelling may bias speakers to produce a non-standard variant, such as in the case of speakers of some non-standard varieties of British English who pronounce the final ending of words such as *singing* as [ng] rather than with a velar nasal [n]. In other varieties of English, this feature is also variable, but the main variants are an alveolar nasal [n] and a velar nasal [n]. Here we have an example of the same process leading to two completely different outcomes.

In his study of -t/d deletion, Bayley (1996) found that although both native English speakers and Chinese learners of English were affected in the same way by style, with more deletion occurring in more informal styles, the learners were more likely to omit -t/d from past tense forms. The magnitude of the effect varied according to the social circumstances of the learner. Learners who regularly interacted with native speakers in informal contexts behaved more like native speakers, omitting -t/d from past tense clusters more frequently than those whose use of English was restricted to the classroom. It is tempting to suggest that socialization patterns are the cause of the variation, which would parallel explanations based on network theory within sociolinguistics, where scholars such as Milroy (1980) proposed that the kind of social network speakers are involved in has significant effects on language patterns. However, learners rarely form cohesive communities and networks of the type sociolinguists typically investigate, with the possible exception of indigenized varieties, such as Singapore English, which have been heavily shaped by substratum influence (see Ho and Platt, 1993). Hence, we would not expect the same types of sociolinguistic explanations based on the identity functions served by the maintenance of non-standard norms of speech to apply to second language learners.

In any case, Bayley offers a different explanation for the behavior of the Chinese learners, who he says have not learned to delete final -t/d, but simply have failed to acquire target-like patterns fully. Similarly, Romaine (1984) has argued that it makes no sense to talk of deletion in earlier stages of the history of English before we have a system containing bimorphemic clusters. It was not until fairly late in the history of English that the verb system contained the relevant environments for deletion. The same could be said for most pidgin and creole varieties of English, where it makes more sense to speak of addition of -t/d as a late rule. Even in the most favorable environments, presence of past tense marking is rare. Once these clusters emerge regularly, they are picked up, so to speak, by the phonetic rule which was already operating more generally on final consonant clusters. The fact that this environment is relatively late would explain why it is quantitatively less. There is no need to invoke a distinctiveness condition (a notion which has been criticized on other grounds by both sociolinguists and SLA researchers; see, e.g., Labov, 1994, pp. 553–5; Young, 1993). Thus, early absences of -t/d do not represent cases of true deletion but, rather, sporadic failures to insert. Here we have a case where different processes or rules may lead to the same outcome. It is not always possible to tell if surface zero results from deletion or failure to insert. Divergent grammars may be concealed by surface similarity.

Sociolinguists have also observed some regular interactions between change and external factors. The effect of style, for instance, is such that more formal styles tend to be more conservative, while more casual speech tends to be more innovative. Tarone (1985) suggests that new forms may be produced first in unmonitored styles and spread later to more carefully monitored styles, or conversely, they may appear first in monitored speech and spread to casual speech. Ellis (1992), however, predicts that free variability will occur first in more carefully monitored styles and spread from there. Preston (1989) speculates that more marked forms develop more quickly in monitored styles of interlanguage production and that unmarked ones are acquired earlier in less monitored styles (see also Major, 1999). This is an attempt to draw a specific parallel between interlanguage development and variationist notions of change from above (i.e., conscious change which originates in more formal styles and in the upper end of the social hierarchy) and change from below (i.e., below the level of conscious awareness and in the lower end of the social hierarchy).

More carefully monitored styles may also be open to aberrant, marked, and SL forms. Beebe (1980), for instance, found that Thai learners of English showed less accuracy in pronouncing English initial /r/ in elicitation environments which promoted greater attention to form (word lists) because a non-target-like trilled /r/ in Thai in initial position has high prestige. A more English-like /r/ is actually more frequent in initial position in casual styles. Thus, transfer itself may be responsive to social constraints, such as prestige. Prestige, in turn, may operate differently for men and women. If women are more sensitive to prestige norms, as suggested by a variety of sociolinguistic studies, this might lead to greater transfer among women in certain contexts. Schmidt (1987) found more evidence of transfer in more formal styles.

The clear effects of style and task on phonological variability are not always evident in morphology. Tarone's (1985) study of variable morphology by Japanese and Arabic learners of English, for instance, showed that some features, such as the third person singular indicative marker /s/, were also more frequently present in more formal elicitation contexts, such as on grammar tests, and less frequently present in less formal contexts, such as narratives. Overall, Japanese learners produced more target-like forms than Arabic learners. Other features, however, such as noun plurals, showed no sensitivity to elicitation environment or to language background.

Pienemann (1998), however, explains the task-based variation observed by Tarone (1988) and others in terms of the different components of the language production system utilized by different tasks, rather than in terms of differences in underlying knowledge (see box 14.1). Some tasks are more successful than others in eliciting particular structures. When a learner does not produce a particular structure in a given task, but uses it in another, we have to ask

Box 14.1 Task variation and the steadiness hypothesis (Pienemann, 1998, 6.5)

Research question: what is the variability of learners' interlanguage in response to task?

Hypothesis: Pienemann proposes a Steadiness Hypothesis, which predicts that the basic nature of the grammatical system of a learner's interlanguage does not change in different communicative tasks as long as those tasks are based on the same skill type in language production. Learners, thus, do not use grammatical rules which are beyond their current level of processability.

Methodology: Two groups (one consisting of learners of English, the other of English native speakers) with six subjects each, similar in age range (19–25 years) and gender composition (four females, two males), were asked to carry out six time-controlled tasks in sequence. The study also aimed to test the effectiveness of tasks in eliciting morphosyntactic structures. The tasks produced 12 hours of recorded speech.

Tasks:

Task 1: Habitual actions
Structure: 3 sg. *-s*
Participants: Subject + researcher

This task involved a set of photographs depicting a day in the life of someone such as a police officer or a librarian. Subjects were asked questions such as "What does a librarian do every day?"

Task 2: Story completion
Structure: *Wh*-questions
Participants: Subject + researcher

Subjects were shown a set of pictures in order, then instructed to find a story behind the pictures. They were encouraged to ask for information.

Task 3: Informal interview
Structure: General
Participants: Subject + researcher

Subjects were interviewed informally by researcher.

Task 4: Picture sequencing
Structure: Questions
Participants: Subject + subject

Subjects were each given part of a sequence of pictures, which together made up a story. Questions had to be asked to enable the subjects to sequence the pictures.

Task 5: Picture differences
Structure: Negatives/questions
Participants: Subject + subject

Subjects were given one picture each of the "Spot the difference" variety. They had to ask questions to determine the differences.

Table 14.5 Third person singular -s and plural -s marking by learner 1 in six different tasks

Structure	*1 Habitual actions*	*2 Story completion*	*3 Informal interview*	*4 Picture sequencing*	*5 Picture differences*	*6 Meet partner*
3 sg. -*s*	26	21	17	15	0	25
Plural -*s*	88	50	57	29	100	33

Source: adapted from Pienemann, 1998, p. 304, table 6.5–18.

Task 6: Meet partner
Structure: Questions
Participants: Subject + subject

Subjects in dyads asked each other questions to find out information and then were asked to introduce each other to the researcher.

Conclusion: Fluctuations in correctness levels across tasks do not reflect different levels of acquisition, but are brought about by the specific lexical needs of the individual tasks and the status of morphological marking in different entries to the learner's lexicon.

Discussion of selected results: Results showed the expected fluctuation in rule application associated with task. Table 14.1 illustrates variability in the rate of plural -*s* insertion and for third person singular -*s* for one subject who displayed some of the greatest amounts of variation in each of the tasks. The numbers are percentages reflecting the rate of application of the rule. The plural rule, for example, has a rate of application varying between 29 percent (picture sequencing task) and 100 percent (picture differences task), whereas the third person singular varies between 0 percent (picture differences task) and 26 percent (habitual actions task).

The differential effects of task are evident. The fact that the habitual actions task prompted the highest use of third person singular -*s* is a logical response to the expressive needs of the task, which requires a singular third person referent and reference to present and non-continuous action. This task produced 23 contexts for the third person singular. The story completion task only makes reference to different time relations, with some of the action placed in the past, and so produces fewer contexts for the occurrence of the third person singular -*s*. Likewise, the picture differences task shows the highest rate of plural marking because it had the highest number of plural referents. Moreover, accuracy rates are affected by lexical choice, which in turn is determined by the task. A highly frequent use of correctly marked items increases the accuracy rate.

This conclusion is reinforced by the fact that native speakers responded in a similar way to the tasks, as shown in table 14.2, which details the results for third person singular -*s* in three tasks. Here we see the number of environments produced by natives and non-natives for the three tasks, along with the number of T-units (minimal terminal units) for each group, and a measure of the rate of occurrence of

Table 14.6 Frequency of the production of the environment for subject–verb agreement in three different tasks by native speakers and non-native speakers of English

Structure	*1 Habitual actions*	*2 Story completion*	*3 Informal interview*
Natives:			
3rd sg. -*s*	113	88	40
T-units	398	551	722
3rd sg./T-unit	0.28	0.16	0.06
Non-natives:			
3rd sg. -*s*	146	101	34
T-units	291	423	450
3rd sg./T-unit	0.50	0.24	0.08

Source: adapted from Pienemann, 1998, p. 302, table 6.5–17.

the third person singular -*s* per T-unit (i.e., what Pienemann calls "data density"). The main difference is that non-native speakers produce a greater number of environments for the feature, which may reflect the fact that learners produce a greater number of T-units to accomplish the same task.

The study underlines the importance of controlling for task variation in data collection. If speech samples are collected in the context of tasks which produce few contexts for the feature under study, then the researcher may draw incorrect conclusions about the state of the learner's grammar.

The study also casts some doubt on the use of quantitative acquisition criteria as accurate measures of development. This notion occurred in response to the question of when we can consider a learner to have acquired a particular structure. Some researchers have suggested that an item is acquired when a learner produces it 80–90 percent of the time. Non-application of a rule could, however, reflect the fact that no contexts for its application occurred in the environment in which the data were collected. If we adopted an arbitrary 80 percent criterion in the case of learner 1 in this study, for instance, the plural -*s* has been acquired in only two tasks (i.e., picture differences and habitual actions), while the third person singular -*s* has not been acquired at all.

Note that steadiness does not refer to consistency across individuals but to developmental consistency. Pienemann found that none of the subjects underperformed in any task, that is, failed to produce structures at or above the developmental level displayed in other samples.

whether each task produces enough relevant contexts for the rule to appear. Pienemann demonstrated that native and non-native speakers behaved very similarly in terms of the extent to which they produced particular structures, such as the third person singular present tense, in response to different tasks. This means that the nature of the communicative task itself produces the variable effect on the production of subject–verb agreement.

4.2 *Gender-based variation*

Few studies have focused on gender differentiation as a source of explanation for SLA variability, although gender has been of increasing concern within sociolinguistics (see, e.g., Romaine, 1999). When taken into account in the usual way by correlating linguistic variables with sex, results have generally not produced much of interest. Selinker (1969), for instance, found no difference in interlanguage word order for men and women. However, other studies taking a broader approach to the issue of gender as a social and cultural variable have found some significant effects.

Gass and Varonis (1986), for instance, studied sex differences in conversational interactions among Japanese learners of English. They found that mixed-sex dyads showed a greater number of negotiations than single-sex dyads, and that females were responsible for twice as many such negotiations as males. Males led in the number of conversational turns taken in mixed-sex dyads, and tended to lead the conversation in a picture-description task even when women were assigned the role of describing the picture to the male who could not see it. Men more often than women also gained the floor after interruptions. Single-sex dyads showed a more equitable distribution of talk.

Not surprisingly, these findings replicate patterns well known to gender scholars, such as Holmes (1994) and others, who have looked at the distribution of talk in various settings and found that men often dominate in public settings and in mixed-sex interaction. Many researchers have noted that from the very outset of schooling through to university level, male students talk more than females, and receive more class time than females. Studies have shown how this gender bias results in lower levels of achievement and self-esteem for girls. Since talk is crucial to learning, and input crucial to acquisition, males and females should have equal time. Informal reports suggest that the same kind of gender bias may also apply to second language classrooms. Lillian (1996) offered personal testament to her own unsuccessful efforts to give equal time to male and female students in her eighth-grade French-as-a-second-language class. On a "good" day, if she "used every scrap of energy and determination," she might manage to give the girls the floor 40 percent of the time, but on such days, the class was "absolute pandemonium," with the boys calling out, banging their feet and desks, and even verbally abusing her. In order not to have bedlam, she estimated she could allow the girls no more than about 25–30 percent of the talk time. In spite of what she perceived as her own failure to give equal time to the girls, she was regularly accused of favoring the girls and giving them all of her attention. One father even came to her classroom to complain that she was a "man-hater," just like his ex-wife!

Another way in which women learners may not receive equal time is suggested by Polanyi (1995), who offered an explanation for the findings of Brecht, Davidson, and Ginsberg (1995) that listening and speaking skills of American women learning Russian in a study-abroad program did not improve as much as the scores of the male learners, otherwise matched for ability, aptitude, and other factors. She found that the linguistic growth of the women had been compromised by routine incidents of sexual harassment from Russian males, which made their communicative encounters unpleasant and awkward, and thus placed limits on their language learning opportunities.

The extent to which gender differentiation is encoded in the TL may also be an inhibiting factor for women. Japanese, for instance, is well known for its linguistic encoding of information relating to social status, politeness, and gender differences. The complexity of this system poses a special difficulty for foreign learners, in terms of not only the range of expressions available, but also the level of social and cultural competence required to use them appropriately. Even after a year abroad, students still have difficulty.

Although norms are changing (in many cases faster than textbooks appear to allow), Japanese women tend to use more polite and honorific forms than men. Western women who come from more egalitarian societies may feel they must project too subservient and alien a persona in order to speak Japanese properly as females. Japanese language teachers in the US report that female students reject the images of women's language projected in the textbooks and say they would not speak Japanese if they had to speak in such a fashion. One woman commented (Siegal and Okamoto, 1996, p. 675): "I don't think I've found my Japanese persona yet, who I am when I am speaking Japanese – I was listening to this lady speaking on the telephone in a little squeaky voice <imitates voice> it's like no, I don't think I can do that, it's not for me – um – I don't know." Gender, then, in the larger sense may be an important factor affecting the outcome of the SLA process.

5 Variability in Outcome

Although there are strong similarities in the structure of the acquisition process for all learners acquiring a given TL, there is considerable variation in its final point, as well as in its speed. In contrast to first language acquisition, which produces fluent speakers, there are wide differences in the outcome of the SLA process. The systems of many second language learners maintain a degree of variability in areas where native speakers show none (i.e., they maintain non-target variants such as *I no like it*). At the same time, learners do not display some of the more complex kinds of sociostylistic variation found in native varieties. Coppieters (1987) found that even highly fluent, near-native speakers of French had different intuitions about grammaticality and different semantic interpretations of a range of French constructions from native speakers (see Sorace, this volume).

These facts have led some researchers to claim there is evidence of variability in competence as well as performance between native and non-native speakers. This issue of whether learners' underlying competence is also variable (see Gregg, 1989; Pienemann, 1998, pp. 237–9) parallels a debate which had its heyday in sociolinguistics in the 1970s and 1980s (see, e.g., Cedergren and Sankoff, 1974; Romaine, 1985), but does not seem to have influenced the field of SLA. As Preston (1986, p. 246) points out, Ellis has misunderstood the notion of free variation as well as the concept of variable rule.

Other explanations can often be found for instances in which Ellis (1992), for instance, has argued for variable competence. The fact that Zambian learners of English mark the third person singular present tense of verbs in main but not subordinate clauses falls out more generally from the processability theory argued for by Pienemann (1998). Although the theory does not define the set of conditions which determines the individual form of variation, it does attempt to delineate the scope within which interlanguage variability can occur. Processability Theory contains a hierarchy of processing procedures and routines ordered according to their activation. Pienemann predicts that in the acquisition of language processing procedures, the assembly of the component parts will follow an implicational sequence. Subordinate clause procedures are the last ones to be implemented. Within this theory, then, variability is explained in terms of the constraints imposed on the learning process by the architecture of the language processor. The task of language acquisition is seen as the acquisition of processing skills. Learners cannot acquire what they cannot process (see further in Pienemann, this volume).

Likewise, another of Ellis's examples of free variation between pre-verbal negation and *don't* + V (see section 2.1) has been challenged by Berdan's (1996) detailed analysis of negation in Schumann's (1978) study, which also claimed variation was not rule-governed. Berdan showed how the use of *don't* + V in Alberto's speech changed from being the least likely variant to the more likely variant over time, and identified a number of constraints governing choice of variants. Schachter (1986), too, concluded after an examination of variation in the development of negation among learners of English as a second language that the variation between pre-verbal negation and *don't*, which Ellis believed to be unsystematic, was in fact conditioned by function; pre-verbal negation was used to express denial or non-existence. Findings such as these call for more careful attention to methodology to ensure that studies are designed to control for as many conditioning factors as possible.

It is, however, still puzzling that learners should progress beyond a very basic level if they have control over a system which enables them to communicate reasonably well. Dietrich and Perdue (1995, p. 6), for instance, point out that learners are perfectly able to express temporal reference and relations despite the complete absence of verb morphology, and even of verbs, in a large proportion of their utterances. This means that there is no way of marking temporality by grammatical means.

Moreover, a high degree of proficiency is needed for second language learners to master nativelike sociolinguistic variation. Native-speaking English children between the ages of 5 and 8, for example, have already acquired the constraints on -t/d deletion and other variable features routinely exploited by native speakers as part of sociolinguistic competence. As Lavandera (1978) points out, failure to exploit the sociostylistic dimensions of such variables, where the choices among variants are not referentially distinctive but socially diagnostic, carries the connotation of foreignness, no matter how proficient a speaker is otherwise, and limits the ability of the speaker to express sociostylistic meaning.

As an example, consider how the first element of the French negator *ne . . . pas* is variably deleted and is a highly sensitive marker of status, style, power and solidarity, and even political orientation (see, e.g., Sankoff and Vincent's 1980 study of Montreal French). Regan (1995) found that although advanced learners of French increased their deletion of *ne* dramatically after spending a period of study abroad, thus improving their sociolinguistic competence, they still tended to overgeneralize it. The deletion rule strengthened in nearly all environments and the ordering of constraints was generally the same as for native French speakers, and became even more nativelike over time.

The appearance of socially sensitive variable behavior is most likely to be found in learners with a high degree of proficiency. Among groups with lower levels of proficiency, the most importance influence is that of linguistic environment. Some learners may make no overt progress in the pronunciation of unfamiliar sounds due to peer pressure, and thus fossilize for social reasons. Accommodation theory thus has a role to play in explaining learner variability. A high degree of motivation and identification with the group whose language is being learned are more likely to result in a greater degree of convergence and, thus, greater L2-like accuracy, as the earlier example of Japanese honorific language illustrates.

6 Conclusion

The study of SLA requires an understanding of variation and the nature of the constraints on variable systems over time. Variation is usually conditioned by multiple causes, which means that researchers will be concerned with identifying multiple factors and assessing the relative contribution of each. There is still much to learn about the intersection of grammatical and phonological variation. Likewise, although task-based variability is well established, it is still not well understood. The conspiring influence of transfer and universals makes careful cross-linguistic work essential.

The study of SLA offers potential for greater understanding of language change. A broad developmental perspective of the type outlined in section 3.3

allows us to view both first and second language acquisition, as well as pidginization and creolization, within a larger framework of variation and change. Such insights are captured in ongoing work on grammaticalization theory and cognitive linguistics, which attempts to map routes between source and target categories (see Romaine, 1992).

The application of quantitative techniques of analysis from sociolinguistics to second language learners' performance can be used to solve both practical and theoretical problems. Unfortunately, Preston (1996, p. 246) observes that sociolinguistics and SLA have not had much in common recently, due to greater interest on the part of SLA researchers in the generative paradigm (particularly, the principles and parameters approach) and the reluctance or inability of sociolinguists to propose convincing psycholinguistic explanations of variability.

REFERENCES

Adamson, H. D. 1988: *Variation Theory and Second Language Acquisition.* Washington, DC: Georgetown University Press.

Adamson, H. D. and Regan, V. 1991: The acquisition of community speech norms by Asian immigrants learning English as a second language. *Studies in Second Language Acquisition*, 13, 1–22.

Andersen, R. W. (ed.) 1983: *Pidginization and Creolization as Language Acquisition.* Rowley, MA: Newbury House.

Bailey, C.-J. N. 1973: *Variation and Linguistic Theory.* Washington, DC: Center for Applied Linguistics.

Bayley, R. 1996: Competing constraints on variation in the speech of adult Chinese learners of English. In R. Bayley and D. Preston (eds), *Second Language Acquisition and Linguistic Variation.* Amsterdam: John Benjamins, 96–120.

Bayley, R. and Preston, D. (eds) 1996: *Second Language Acquisition and Linguistic Variation.* Amsterdam: John Benjamins.

Beebe, L. 1980: Sociolinguistic variation and style shifting in second language acquisition. *Language Learning*, 2, 433–48.

Berdan, R. 1996: Disentangling language acquisition from language variation. In R. Bayley and D. Preston (eds), *Second Language Acquisition and Linguistic Variation.* Amsterdam: John Benjamins, 203–45.

Bickerton, D. 1977: Pidginization and creolization: language acquisition and language universals. In A. Valdman (ed.), *Pidgin and Creole Linguistics.* Bloomington: Indiana University Press, 49–69.

Brecht, R. D., Davidson, D. E., and Ginsberg, R. B. 1995: Predictors of foreign language gain during study abroad. In B. F. Freed (ed.), *Second Language Acquisition in a Study Abroad Context.* Amsterdam: John Benjamins, 37–67.

Brown, R. 1973: *A First Language.* Cambridge, MA: Harvard University Press.

Cedergren, H. and Sankoff, D. 1974: Performance as a statistical reflection of competence. *Language*, 50, 333–55.

Chomsky, N. 1981: Principles and parameters in syntactic theory. In

N. Hornstein and D. Lightfoot (eds), *Explanation in Linguistics: The Logical Problem of Language Acquisition*. London: Longman, 32–76.

Coppieters, R. 1987: Competence differences between native and fluent non-native speakers. *Language*, 63, 544–73.

Dickerson, L. J. 1975: The learner's interlanguage as a system of variable rules. *TESOL Quarterly*, 9, 401–7.

Dietrich, R. and Perdue, C. 1995: Introduction. In R. Dietrich, W. Klein, and C. Noyau (eds), *The Acquisition of Temporality in a Second Language*. Amsterdam: John Benjamins, 1–17.

Dietrich, R., Klein, W., and Noyau, C. (eds) 1995: *The Acquisition of Temporality in a Second Language*. Amsterdam: John Benjamins.

Ellis, R. 1992: *Second Language Acquisition and Language Pedagogy*. Clevedon: Multilingual Matters.

Ellis, R. 1999: Item versus system learning: explaining free variation. *Applied Linguistics*, 20 (4), 460–80.

Flynn, S. 1989: Spanish, Japanese and Chinese speakers' acquisition of English relative clauses: new evidence for the head direction parameter. In K. Hyltenstam and L. Obler (eds), *Bilingualism Across the Lifespan: Aspects of Acquisition, Maturity, and Loss*. Cambridge: Cambridge University Press, 116–31.

Gass, S. M. and Ard, J. 1984: Second language acquisition and the ontology of language universals. In W. E. Rutherford (ed.), *Language Universals and Second Language Acquisition*. Amsterdam: John Benjamins, 33–67.

Gass, S. M. and Varonis, E. M. 1986: Sex differences in non-native speaker/ non-native speaker interaction. In R. R. Day (ed.), *Talking to Learn: Conversation in Second Language Acquisition*. Rowley, MA: Newbury House, 327–51.

Gatbonton, E. 1978: Patterned phonetic variability in second language speech: a gradual diffusion model. *Canadian Modern Language Review/La Revue Canadienne des Langues Vivantes*, 34, 335–47.

Gilbert, G. 1983: Transfer in second language acquisition. In R. W. Andersen (ed.), *Pidginization and Creolization as Language Acquisition*. Rowley, MA: Newbury House, 168–81.

Gregg, K. R. 1989: The variable competence model and why it isn't. *Applied Linguistics*, 11, 364–83.

Guy, G. R. and Boyd, S. 1990: The development of a morphological class. *Language Variation and Change*, 2, 1–18.

Ho, M.-L. and Platt, J. T. 1993: *Dynamics of a Contact Continuum: Singaporean English*. Oxford: Oxford University Press.

Holmes, J. 1994: *Women, Men and Politeness*. London: Longman.

Hyams, N. 1986: *Language Acquisition and the Theory of Parameters*. Dordrecht: Reidel.

Hyltenstam, K. 1984: The use of typological markedness conditions as predictors of second language acquisition. In R. Andersen (ed.), *Second Languages: A Cross-Linguistic Perspective*. Rowley, MA: Newbury House, 39–58.

Janda, L. 1995: Unpacking markedness. In E. Casad (ed.), *Cognitive Linguistics in the Redwoods: The Expansion of a New Paradigm in Linguistics*. Berlin: Mouton de Gruyter, 207–33.

Keenan, E. L. and Comrie, B. 1977: Noun phrase accessibility and universal grammar. *Linguistic Inquiry*, 8, 63–99.

Kiparsky, P. 1972: Explanation in phonology. In S. Peters (ed.), *Goals of Linguistic Theory*. Englewood Cliffs, NJ: Prentice-Hall, 189–227.

Klein, W. and Dittmar, N. 1979: *Developing Grammars: The Acquisition of German Syntax by Foreign Workers*. Berlin: Springer.

Labov, W. 1966: *The Social Stratification of English in New York City*.

Arlington, VA: Center for Applied Linguistics.

Labov, W. 1994: *Principles of Linguistic Change: Internal Factors*. Oxford: Blackwell.

Lavandera, B. R. 1978: The variable component in bilingual performance. In J. E. Alatis (ed.), *International Dimensions of Bilingual Education*. Washington, DC: Georgetown University Press, 391–409.

Lillian, D. 1996: Posting to Fling internet discussion list. December 14. fling@listserv.oit.unc.edu.

Major, R. 1999: Chronological and stylistic aspects of second language acquisition of consonant clusters. *Language Learning*, 49 (Supplement 1: *Phonological Issues in Language Learning*), 123–49.

Meisel, J. 1983: A linguistic encounter of the third kind or, will the non-real interfere with what the learner does? Reply to discussants. In R. W. Andersen (ed.), *Pidginization and Creolization as Language Acquisition*. Rowley, MA: Newbury House, 196–209.

Milroy, L. 1980: *Language and Social Network*. Oxford: Blackwell.

Noyau, C., Houdaïfa, E.-H., Vasseur, M.-T., and Véronique, D. 1995: The acquisition of French. In R. Dietrich, W. Klein, and C. Noyau (eds), *The Acquisition of Temporality in a Second Language*. Amsterdam: John Benjamins, 145–209.

Oller, J. W. and Redding, E. Z. 1971: Article usage and other language skills. *Language Learning*, 21, 85–95.

Phinney, M. 1987: The pro-drop parameter in second language acquisition. In T. Roeper and E. Williams (eds), *Parameter Setting*. Dordrecht: Reidel, 221–39.

Pienemann, M. 1998: *Language Processing and Second Language Development*. Amsterdam: John Benjamins.

Polanyi, L. 1995: Language learning and living abroad: stories from the field. In B. F. Freed (ed.), *Second Language Acquisition in a Study Abroad Context*. Amsterdam: John Benjamins, 271–93.

Preston, D. R. 1989: *Sociolinguistics and Second Language Acquisition*. Oxford: Blackwell.

Preston, D. R. 1996: Variationist linguistics and second language acquisition. In W. C. Ritchie and T. K. Bhatia (eds), *Handbook of Second Language Acquisition*. New York: Academic Press, 229–65.

Regan, V. 1995: The acquisition of sociolinguistic native speech norms: effects of a year abroad on second language learners of French. In B. F. Freed (ed.), *Second Language Acquisition in a Study Abroad Context*. Amsterdam: John Benjamins, 245–67.

Romaine, S. 1984: The sociolinguistic history of t/d deletion. *Folia Linguistica Historica*, V/2, 221–55.

Romaine, S. 1985: Variable rules, O.K.? Or can there be sociolinguistic grammars? *Language and Communication*, 5, 53–67.

Romaine, S. 1988: *Pidgin and Creole Languages*. London: Longman.

Romaine, S. 1992: The evolution of complexity in a creole language: the acquisition of relative clauses in Tok Pisin. *Studies in Language*, 16, 139–82.

Romaine, S. 1999: *Communicating Gender*. Mahwah, NJ: Lawrence Erlbaum Associates.

Rutherford, W. E. (ed.) 1984: *Language Universals and Second Language Acquisition*. Amsterdam: John Benjamins.

Saleemi, A. P. 1992: *Universal Grammar and Language Learnability*. Cambridge: Cambridge University Press.

Sankoff, G. and Vincent, D. 1980: The productive use of *ne* in spoken Montreal French. In G. Sankoff (ed.), *The Social Life of Language*.

Philadelphia: University of Pennsylvania Press, 295–310.

Sato, C. J. 1985: Task variation in interlanguage phonology. In S. M. Gass and C. Madden (eds), *Input in Second Language Acquisition*. Rowley, MA: Newbury House, 181–96.

Schachter, J. 1986: Three approaches to the study of input. *Language Learning*, 36(2), 211–25.

Schmidt, R. W. 1987: Sociolinguistic variation and transfer. In G. Ioup and S. Weinberge (eds), *Interlanguage Phonology: The Acquisition of a Second Language Sound System*. Cambridge, MA: Newbury House, 365–77.

Schumann, J. 1978: *The Pidginization Process*. Rowley, MA: Newbury House.

Selinker, L. 1969: Language transfer. *General Linguistics*, 9, 67–92.

Siegal, M. and Okamoto, S. 1996: Imagined worlds: language, gender and sociocultural "norms" in Japanese language textbooks. In N. Warner, J. Ahlers, M. Oliver, S. Wertheim, and M. Chen (eds), *Gender and Belief Systems*. Proceedings of the Fourth Berkeley Women and Language Conference. Berkeley: Berkeley Women and Language Group. University of California at Berkeley, 667–79

Stauble, A.-M. 1978: Decreolization as a model for second language development. *Language Learning*, 28, 29–54.

Tarone, E. 1985: Variability in interlanguage use: a study of style shifting in morphology and syntax. *Language Learning*, 35, 373–403.

Tarone, E. 1988: *Variation in Interlanguage*. London: Edward Arnold.

Towell, R., Hawkins, R., and Bazergui, N. 1993: Systematic and non-systematic variability in advanced language learning. *Studies in Second Language Learning*, 15, 439–60.

Traugott, E. C. and Romaine, S. 1985: Some questions for the definition of "style" in socio-historical linguistics. In S. Romaine and E. C. Traugott (eds), *Papers from the Workshop on Socio-historical Linguistics. Folia Linguistica Historica*, VI, 7–39.

White, L. 1986: Markedness and parameter setting: Some implications for a theory of adult second language acquisition. In F. R. Eckman, E. Moravcsik, and J. R. Wirth (eds), *Markedness*. New York: Plenum Press, 309–26.

Young, R. 1988: Variation and the interlanguage hypothesis. *Studies in Second Language Acquisition*, 10, 281–302.

Young, R. 1993: Functional constraints on variation in interlanguage morphology. *Applied Linguistics*, 14, 76–97.

Young, R. 1996: Form-function relations in articles in English interlanguage. In R. Bayley and D. Preston (eds), *Second Language Acquisition and Linguistic Variation*. Amsterdam: John Benjamins, 135–75.

Young, R. and Bayley, R. 1996: VARBRUL analysis for second language acquisition research. In R. Bayley and D. Preston (eds), *Second Language Acquisition and Linguistic Variation*. Amsterdam: John Benjamins, 253–306.

Zobl, H. 1982: A direction for contrastive analysis: the comparative study of developmental sequences. *TESOL Quarterly*, 16, 169–83.

Zobl, H. 1984: Uniformity and source-language variation across developmental continua. In W. E. Rutherford (ed.), *Language universals and Second Language Acquisition*. Amsterdam: John Benjamins, 185–218.

15 Cross-Linguistic Influence

TERENCE ODLIN

1 Introduction

Researchers interested in cross-linguistic influence have several phrases to choose from in referring to the phenomenon, including the following: *language transfer, linguistic interference, the role of the mother tongue, native language influence,* and *language mixing*. In this chapter, *language transfer* and *cross-linguistic influence* will be used interchangeably, as they are the most commonly employed in contemporary second language research. No single term is entirely satisfactory, however, and linguists have often noted various problems. Cook (2000), for example, observes that *transfer* and *cross-linguistic influence* spuriously suggest some kind of movement. In this chapter, moreover, the drawbacks of the term *interference* will be discussed.

Whatever term is employed, there remains the problem of definition. One characterization is as follows: "Transfer is the influence resulting from the similarities and differences between the target language and any other language that has been previously (and perhaps imperfectly) acquired" (Odlin, 1989, p. 27). Such a definition suffices to restrict the area under study, but it says little about just what constitutes "influence." Selinker (1992, p. 208) considers transfer to be a cover term for a number of behaviors which intersect with input from the target language and with universal properties of human language (cf. Dechert and Raupach, 1989; Gass and Selinker, 1993). Much of what is meant by transfer involves "retentions" of one kind or another, as Jarvis and Odlin (2000) observe, yet the notion of retention does not take into account other relevant phenomena such as avoidance and hypercorrection, as well as some of the behaviors associated with the notion of "simplification" (even though that concept is sometimes viewed as diametrically opposed to transfer).

This chapter uses a few terminological conventions that may seem to sacrifice precision, but doing so will avoid some cumbersome phrasing. The term *second language* will usually be employed, though one section specifically addresses the problem of cross-linguistic influence in cases where the target is not the second but rather the third language – and in some cases even a fourth or fifth language. Most of the discussion will consider transfer in relation to adult language learners, though again one section will look at younger as well as older learners. Since most research deals with either second language speech or second language writing, the emphasis will be on production as opposed to comprehension, but at a number of points the significance of transfer for listening and reading comprehension will also be discussed.

Several books, collections of articles, and state-of-the-art papers in the last fifteen years or so show that interest in cross-linguistic influence remains strong (e.g., Dechert and Raupach, 1989; Gass, 1996; Gass and Selinker, 1993; Kellerman, 1984, 1995; Kellerman and Sharwood-Smith, 1986; Odlin, 1989; Ringbom, 1987; Selinker, 1992). Moreover, cross-linguistic influence attracts considerable attention from researchers in fields where transfer is not the primary object of study but where it constitutes an important topic: language contact (e.g., Siegel, 1999), second language phonetics and phonology (e.g., Leather and James, 1996), language universals and linguistic typology (e.g., Eckman, 1996; White, 2000), and second language writing (e.g., Connor, 1996). The very plenitude of sources on cross-linguistic influence creates something of a problem. Because so much research is available, anyone seeking to understand transfer itself in all its manifestations needs to try to become familiar with a wide range of linguistic research; neglecting to do so can result in making claims that do not square with the available evidence (as has happened fairly often). The highly diverse evidence for transfer has impeded attempts to develop truly comprehensive theories of cross-linguistic influence. In the more credible attempts at theory-building, researchers have focused on what is admittedly only part of an overall model, as in the characterization of second language speech production by De Bot (1992).

Language transfer affects all linguistic subsystems including pragmatics and rhetoric, semantics, syntax, morphology, phonology, phonetics, and orthography. (As will be seen, some have been skeptical about transfer in syntax and morphology, but such skepticism is unwarranted.) It is beyond the scope of this chapter to deal thoroughly with cross-linguistic influence in each subsystem, though one book attempts to provide such coverage (Odlin, 1989). Instead of looking in detail at each subsystem, this chapter will consider several topics that have remained important over the years, including the methods for determining transfer, the concept of transferability, the age factor in relation to transfer, the notion of typology and universals, and the influence of a second language on the acquisition of a third. There will also be a discussion of a topic less often considered but clearly important for cross-linguistic influence: linguistic relativity. To begin, however, it will help to consider language transfer in historical terms.

2 Weinreich and the Notion of Interference

Some fifty years have elapsed since the publication of Uriel Weinreich's *Languages in Contact* (1953), a work that looked at cross-linguistic influence far more closely than any previous investigation had. Even though Weinreich's scope was not confined to the question of transfer in second language acquisition, his monograph will serve as a useful benchmark for assessing change and continuity in research on transfer. Many historical treatments of the research take Robert Lado's *Linguistics Across Cultures* (1957) as their starting point, but Weinreich's work reviewed many more actual studies of language mixing, and Lado himself invoked *Languages in Contact* as empirical support for the importance of transfer. However, transfer in second language acquisition is only one of the phenomena associated with language mixing, two others being the influence of a second language on one's native language and the influences arising in the coexisting knowledge systems of bilinguals who have (more or less) equal facility with two languages (Odlin, 1989; Thomason and Kaufman, 1988).

Some second language researchers (e.g., Dulay and Burt, 1974) have claimed that *Languages in Contact* does not consider the role that one's native language can play in the acquisition of another language, but more careful readings (e.g., Selinker, 1992) show that claim to be mistaken. Indeed, even while Weinreich expressed a disinterest in applied linguistics, he saw second language research as relevant to his focus on language mixing. With its strong historical orientation, *Languages in Contact* emphasizes patterns of negative transfer, or (to use the term usually found in the book) "interference." This interest in hybridization and interference has probably affected views of transfer in second language acquisition, with many studies focusing on the ways in which a learner's knowledge of a second language may diverge from the target language. In fact, the widely used term *interlanguage* (Selinker, 1972) presupposes some difference between a learner's knowledge and that of native speakers; moreover, research by Nemser (1971), which Selinker has seen as conceptually close to his own, invoked the notion of interference. Researchers have debated whether or not the interlanguage concept is applicable in all instances of second language acquisition, though it is clear that the notion does apply in the vast majority of cases (cf. Selinker, 1992; Sridhar and Sridhar, 1986).

With his emphasis on interference, Weinreich tacitly assumed that negative transfer is inherently more interesting than positive transfer, which can be defined as the facilitating influences that may arise from cross-linguistic similarities. While some second language researchers seem to share Weinreich's assumption, others, most notably Ringbom (1987, 1992), have argued that positive transfer will affect acquisition much more than will negative transfer. The teaching of English in Finland is not very different for speakers of Finnish or speakers of Swedish, yet the latter group of learners generally has a much easier time with English. As Swedish and English are Indo-European (and Germanic) languages, and Finnish is non-Indo-European, the greater success of the "Swedes" (the term used by Ringbom) seems mainly due to positive transfer, and Ringbom's research as well as other studies provides many details to support that inference. Given the importance of facilitating effects, it is clear that transfer should not be equated with interference.

Although Weinreich's emphasis on negative transfer had some unfortunate consequences, his analysis of cross-linguistic influence shows clearly that neither he nor many of the researchers whose work he cites held behaviorist views. This point is important since one of the most common misrepresentations of the intellectual history of transfer claims that the idea of cross-linguistic influence was spawned from behaviorist theories by proponents of contrastive analysis (i.e., systematic comparisons of languages). It is true that some proponents of contrastive analysis assumed that learning a new language largely consisted of acquiring new "habits," as Charles Fries argued in the preface to Lado's book. Such assumptions naturally led to a strong reaction when generative grammarians and cognitive psychologists challenged the validity of behaviorist thinking about language (Odlin, 1989). Even so, Weinreich showed considerable skepticism about any psychological models proposed to account for bilingualism and interference, noting that "they vary from one school of psychology to another" (p. 71). While he recognized the importance of ultimately achieving a workable psychological account, the linguistic evidence was what convinced him about the importance of cross-linguistic influence.

3 Transfer in Relation to Linguistic Subsystems

Few if any researchers have ever denied that cross-linguistic influence plays some role in second language acquisition, but skeptics have maintained that transfer matters much more for some subsystems than for others, with phonetics and phonology usually the systems where widespread transfer is conceded, in contrast to morphology and syntax (e.g., Dulay, Burt, and Krashen, 1982). Such claims are sometimes taken to imply that language universals or target language influence matter more in syntax and morphology than in phonetics and phonology, despite considerable evidence for the importance of other factors in addition to transfer in second language pronunciation (Leather and James, 1996; Odlin, 1989). Moreover, such claims presuppose that there exists a reliable way to measure the relative contributions of the native language to the ease or difficulty learners have with each subsystem and, by implication, the total contribution of transfer to the process of second language acquisition. Weinreich's assessment a half century ago of efforts to quantify subsystem contributions to transfer is worth recalling: "All the cited opinions on the relative amount of borrowing are rather superficial and premature, if they are meaningful at all" (p. 67). Despite considerable progress in the study of cross-linguistic influence, Weinreich's estimation still holds true. The discussion in this section will focus on certain problems in attempting to gauge subsystem contributions and on related issues such as the importance of transfer for comprehension and production.

A quarter of a century ago, Schachter (1974) noted one of the biggest obstacles to comparing the relative contribution of phonological and syntactic transfer: frequencies of occurrence. Many syntactic structures important to a grammatical system may nevertheless be rare in comparison with the phonemes of a language. Cleft sentences, for example, serve a variety of discourse functions including contrastive focus, as in *It's tomorrow that she arrives – not today*. In a large corpus of spoken English as used by individuals from southern England, Filppula (1986) found less than one cleft sentence used for every thousand words (0.7, to be exact). The infrequency of clefts arises from many factors, one of them being that the syntactic structure is optional in many discourse contexts: in the preceding example, one could also choose to say *She arrives tomorrow – not today*. Such options are rare in phonology; if one has settled on using a particular word – *rabbit*, for example – all the phonemes are obligatory, and the sequence of them is invariant (/rabit/), with the only options being at the sub-phonemic level (where, e.g., one could choose a tap, retroflex, or some other variant of /r/). In the speech of many learners of English and of some bilinguals, it is easy to spot cases of cross-linguistic influence involving /r/ because of its general frequency and the unavoidability of the phoneme in many contexts. On the other hand, the obvious influences related to /r/ should not imply that a less frequent structure such as clefting is never implicated in transfer; in fact, work on language contact in the British Isles suggests that transfer has affected the use of clefting in some regions (Filppula, 1999; Odlin, 1997a). Even so, comparing the importance of transfer related to /r/ and to clefting would be a classic example of comparing the incomparable.

In instances such as /r/ and clefts, meaningful quantitative comparisons seem dubious, and the prospect seems even worse in cases where learners fail to use a structure and where failure arises from a cross-linguistic contrast. Transfer and simplification are often thought of as distinct phenomena, but it is becoming increasingly clear that the absence of, for example, obligatory prepositions in a learner's interlanguage can often have something to do with the learner's native language. Jarvis and Odlin (2000) found frequent cases of zero prepositions in the written narratives of speakers of Finnish who watched a silent film, as in the sentence *C[harlie] C[haplin] and the woman go to sit the grass*. The absence of *on* or *in* before the phrase *the grass* might be viewed as simply the lapses of non-native speakers of any language (or even of native speakers) were it not for the fact that a comparable group of students whose native language was Swedish never omitted the preposition. The difference in performance here is directly related to the difference between Swedish and Finnish, with the former language employing prepositions much the same way as English does and with the latter language using a much larger set of options to indicate spatial reference, most importantly, inflectional morphemes.

With regard to prepositions, then, their absence can have a great deal to do with the native language, but quantifying this factor in relation to other transfer phenomena seems nigh impossible.

The similarity of the prepositional system of Swedish gives native speakers of that language a tremendous advantage in learning English, as does the much greater amount of cognate vocabulary. For speakers of non-Indo-European languages (including Finnish), countless hours must be spent in trying to remember English words having little or no similarity to those of their native languages. By the same token, learners whose native language is English will find virtually all non-Indo-European languages to be much harder than Germanic and Romance languages such as Swedish or French. This point may seem obvious, but one implication is well worth stressing. The advantage that cognate vocabulary confers can allow learners to take advantage of positive transfer to increase their comprehension of the target language with far greater ease, thereby freeing many cognitive resources for other language learning tasks (cf. Ringbom, 1992).

It is difficult to quantify the advantage that easier listening and reading comprehension can give to speakers of similar languages, and thus the difficulty increases further still for anyone wishing to measure the relative contributions of, for example, phonology and syntax. Should such measurement be taken with more emphasis on speaking than on listening – or vice versa? Should advantages that accrue to new readers and writers of a target language similar to their native language count for more or for less than advantages in oral skills? Such questions remain quite difficult to answer.

4 Predicting Cross-Linguistic Influence

Whether transfer is positive or negative, the similarities and differences between languages have naturally led teachers and researchers to make predictions. Both in Weinreich's *Languages in Contact* and in Lado's *Linguistics Across Cultures*, similarities are judged to help language learners and differences to hinder them. The challenge of making sound predictions has become increasingly evident, however, and critics of contrastive analysis have emphasized cases where cross-linguistic comparisons fail to predict actual difficulties and where difficulties predicted do not always materialize (cf. Gass, 1996; Odlin, 1989). A detailed study of perception and production by Nemser (1971) showed how complex the issues can be even at the phonetic level. The Hungarian learners he tested usually perceived the English voiceless interdental fricative /θ/ as a voiceless labiodental (/f/), but the same individuals produced a voiceless apical stop (/t/). A different sort of predictive difficulty is evident in a study by Giacobbe (1992), who observes that a Spanish-speaking learner of French named Berta did not quickly use motion verbs that are cognate in Spanish and French (e.g., *va*, "goes"), but she did latch on to prepositions that were cognate (e.g., *a* and *de*) to express ideas involving motion. Even though contrastive analysts might not necessarily see it, Berta clearly saw, however unconsciously, a chance to draw on spatial prepositions in her native language to express motion concepts in an interlanguage that diverges significantly from the native as well as the target language.

Another problem in making sound contrastive predictions is that different individuals may pursue different options, as is evident in the study of spatial reference by Jarvis and Odlin (2000) mentioned above. In writing a summary of part of the film *Modern Times*, some Finnish speakers chose to write *sit to the grass* while others used *sit on the grass* and still others *sit in the grass*. Finnish can be seen as an influence on all three choices (as well as on the omissions of prepositions discussed above) since there are different case inflections that correspond to each preposition even while only the latter two choices are target-like. In contrast to the Finnish speakers, comparable groups of Swedish speakers never chose *sit to the grass* (and there is no corresponding Swedish collocation). Accordingly, any sound contrastive prediction must take into account the reality of individual variation in interlingual identifications, that is, in what any particular learner may view as similar between the native and target language.

As many examples in this chapter will show, cross-linguistic influence can surface in a wide variety of ways. Accordingly, generalizations about the importance of transfer with regard to a particular structure or, even more, an entire subsystem seem risky at best. In effect such generalizations constitute predictions about when transfer will or will *not* occur (the latter type of prediction often termed a *constraint*), and without a thorough look at all the possible ways that transfer might manifest itself, prognostications about occurrence or non-occurrence can often go wrong. The domain of bound morphology can illustrate vividly the myriad ways that one language can influence another. Jarvis and Odlin (2000) note that cross-linguistic influence might involve actual phonological forms or simply the semantic structures represented by the form; it might involve either production or comprehension, or both; it might involve inflectional as well as derivational morphology or simply one or the other; and it could involve either positive or negative transfer. To make highly accurate predictions about bound morphology, then, will depend on understanding how transfer can work in a wide range of ways (e.g., positive or negative transfer involving comprehension vs. positive or negative transfer involving production). In light of the complexity of the issues, it seems unlikely that researchers will achieve such a detailed understanding any time soon.

5 Interlingual Identifications and Learner Perceptions

As the complexity of second language research has become ever clearer, there might seem little that has remained constant in the study of cross-linguistic influence. However, Weinreich, Lado, and other structuralists recognized the importance of language distance, a concept that has enduring importance for the study of transfer. Which will take longer for an English speaker to learn to do: read this morning's news in a newspaper written in French or in one in Chinese? To most educated people, the answer is obvious, and the response will not likely change significantly if some other task is alluded to in the question (e.g., understanding the morning news in a television report or carrying on a conversation about the news with a friend). Some might argue that it is mainly a common cultural heritage that will make French an easier language for English speakers. However, even while cultural distance obviously matters, language distance matters even more, as is evident in Ringbom's comparison of Finnish-speaking and Swedish-speaking students in Finland. Ringbom (1987) stresses the great cultural similarity of these two groups of learners yet also the very different degrees of success in learning English.

Although Weinreich used the notion of the interlingual identification to focus on negative transfer, the notion also works well for understanding positive transfer in cases such as Finland: Swedish learners generally have the advantage of being able to look for cross-linguistic similarities that their native language affords them. Having such opportunities, however, does not guarantee that any particular learner will do the necessary looking or come to the right conclusion about just how congruent a cross-linguistic correspondence is. Weinreich repeatedly stressed that any language contact is mediated in a bilingual's mind, thus recognizing the difference between the abstract comparison of languages and the behavior of actual people.

Much of what is called cross-linguistic influence depends on the individual judgments of language learners and bilinguals that there exist certain cross-linguistic similarities. In cases where the judgments are accurate, the transfer is positive, but regardless of their accuracy, the judgments are by definition subjective. One of the most important insights about transfer research in the last half century has been the observation by Kellerman (1977, 1978) and others that learners can sometimes be highly skeptical that they should take advantage of what is in fact a bona fide similarity between the native and target language, as will be discussed below. Kellerman's results show the importance of subjectivity in any assessment of cross-linguistic similarity, and, not surprisingly, such subjectivity is related to background factors such as age, motivation, literacy, and social class (Odlin, 1989). These factors and others combine in myriad ways that make the learning situations of virtually all individuals unique – and also make contrastive predictions even more subject to qualification. As will be seen, this subjectivity has crucial implications for a number of issues related to transfer, such as the role that a second language may play in the acquisition of a third.

Although learners sometimes do not take advantage of similarities that would lead to positive transfer, the successes documented by Ringbom show that they often do – to the point where, he notes, the Swedes sometimes get complacent about the relatively small distance between Swedish and English. The ease of making interlingual identifications (including incorrect ones) no doubt arises from similar psycholinguistic routines available to native speakers as they attempt to cope with variation in their own language, be it involving dialect or register differences. The likelihood that such routines are similar or even the same in bilingual settings supports Schachter's contention (1993) that there is nothing unique in second language acquisition about language transfer. Many linguists have observed that the difference between a language and a dialect often arises on sociohistorical grounds instead of on structural ones (e.g., Chambers and Trudgil, 1980; Ferguson, 1959; Haugen, 1966; Joergensen and Kristensen, 1995), and the competence needed to deal with variation in any context makes the routines inherent in the interlingual identification available in monolingual as well as bilingual settings.

So far, the discussion has referred to cases where learners recognize at least the possibility of making an interlingual identification, whether or not they actually choose to do so. In cases where learners fail to notice a cross-linguistic parallel, the consequence will often be something other than cross-linguistic influence, according to Gass (1996). She points to evidence indicating that universal meaning-based strategies will be invoked when no grammatical parallels seem to exist. This explanation could account for much of the similarity seen in early interlanguage development in cases of naturalistic second language acquisition (e.g., Klein and Perdue, 1997). Even so, it would be mistaken to view all cases of simplification as unrelated to the native language of a learner; the zero prepositions discussed earlier in this chapter suggest that the difference between Finnish and English sometimes impedes learners in forming accurate hypotheses about the target language.

Moreover, two other behaviors will sometimes indicate cross-linguistic influence: avoidance and hypercorrection. Schachter (1974) attributed the underproduction of English relative clauses by speakers of Chinese and Japanese to the very great differences between the target and the native languages in relativization. In contrast to those learners, speakers of Arabic and Persian, languages more like English in their patterns of relativization, did not avoid using relative clauses even though these speakers produced more errors than did the Chinese and Japanese speakers. Schachter interpreted the infrequent use of relative clauses as evidence that learners were avoiding the English structure, though this interpretation has been disputed by Kamimoto, Shimura, and Kellerman (1992). While the results in the Schachter study do indicate a significant difference in patterns of production between the Chinese and Japanese speakers, on the one hand, and Arabic and Persian speakers on the other, more than one explanation might work, including some notion of simplification like that mentioned for zero prepositions. Whether or not the students in Schachter's study deliberately tried to avoid using relative clauses, there are unambiguous cases of avoidance involving taboo forms (Haas, 1951), and they will be discussed later in this chapter. Along with avoidance, hypercorrection can sometimes be attributed to cross-linguistic influence even when no overt form in the native language is directly responsible, as seen in an example involving spelling hypercorrections (Odlin, 1989, p. 38).

A final caveat concerning interlingual identification is that even when learners discover and try to use a real similarity between the native and target language, they may be unwilling or unable to assess just how sound their judgment is. Such an inability would presumably explain the relative clause errors made by Arabic and Persian speakers in the Schachter study. The difficulty of noticing cross-linguistic differences may be especially acute in the area of pronunciation. Flege (1999) and others have repeatedly stressed the difficulty that learners confront when they hear a sound phonetically similar – but not identical – to one in their native language (cf. Leather and James, 1996). Evidence by Bongaerts (1999) discussed below suggests that overt training can help learners to overcome such perceptual difficulties, but it seems that interlingual identifications will often sacrifice details that matter for anyone interested in a nativelike pronunciation of the target language.

6 Methods and Sources

Second language researchers have made considerable progress in the last thirty years or so in establishing methods to determine whether cross-linguistic influence has played a role in some particular acquisition situation. Two methods have proven to be especially important. One relies on comparisons of the use of a particular structure in the native language, the target language, and the interlanguage, with this approach having been successfully used by Selinker (1969). The second approach relies on a comparison of how learners with two (or more) native languages do with regard to a target language structure present in one NL but absent in the other; this method is well exemplified by Mesthrie and Dunne (1990) and Master (1987). After a closer look at the two methods, there will be a discussion of the approach taken by Jarvis (2000), who argues for the need to employ both methods along with additional refinements.

The logic of the approach taken by Selinker is evident in his investigation of word order in the English interlanguage of native speakers of Hebrew. In interviews with school children he found a frequent placement of adverbs in structures that correspond more closely to Hebrew than to English, as in the case of *I like very much movies*, as opposed to *I like movies very much*. Having also interviewed native speakers in Hebrew and native speakers in English, Selinker was able to make statistically significant associations in a number of structures where the interlanguage data resembled the word order of Hebrew more than the word order of the target language. It is also noteworthy that Selinker went to great lengths to ensure that the discourse contexts of the interlanguage speakers and of the native speakers of Hebrew and English would be highly comparable.

In cases where researchers have access to interlanguage data from two or more groups of learners who are similar except in terms of their native language, the opportunity arises for comparing how distinct structural patterns in the native languages may lead to different outcomes reflecting language transfer. One striking example of differing interlanguage structures comes from a study rarely cited in second language research (Mesthrie and Dunne, 1990). The individuals studied were speakers of South African Indian English and had either an Indic or Dravidian language as the mother tongue. Mesthrie and Dunne focused on relativization patterns partly because the native languages show very different ways of forming relative clauses. Indic languages use correlative constructions whereas Dravidian languages rely on clauses that premodify a head noun. The authors provide the following examples from Gujarati, an Indic language, and Tamil, a Dravidian:

(1) Gujarati:
Je veparii marii sathe avyo, te veparii
CORRELATIVE businessman me with came that businessman
Harilal ka bhaaii che
Harilal of brother is
The businessman who came with me is Harilal's brother.
(Literally, "Which businessman came with me, that businessman is Harilal's brother.")

(2) Tamil:
Taccaan aṯicca vaṉṉaan ceṉṉeki
carpenter.nom beat.past.rel part washerman.nom Madras.
poonaan
dat go.past.3sg.masc
The washerman whom the carpenter beat went to Madras.
(Literally, "The carpenter-beat(en) washerman went to Madras.")

The correlatives *je . . . te* in the Gujarati example function somewhat like forms such as *either . . . or* and *neither . . . nor* in English (which does not, however, use such forms to make relative clauses). In the Tamil example, the closest parallel in English is the occasional clause that can occur before the noun modified as in *a-never-to-be-forgotten-experience*. In South African Indian English, two structurally different interlanguage patterns of relativization appear in the speech of less proficient individuals (the square brackets are inserted to allow for easy identification in the Dravidian example):

(3) Indic:
But now, which-one principal came here, she's just cheeky like the other one.
"The principal who arrived recently is just as stern as the previous one."

(4) Dravidian:
People [who got working-here-for-them] sons, like, for them nice they can stay

"It is nice for people who have sons [who are] working for the company, since they are allowed to stay on in the barracks."

The structural contrast between the Indic and Dravidian native languages emerges rather clearly in such examples, with the contrast thus suggesting a strong likelihood of cross-linguistic influence. Mesthrie and Dunne find that other sources besides transfer account better for certain other relativization patterns seen, but their evidence indicates that Indic and Dravidian influence frequently affects the clauses of speakers not especially proficient in English.

It might be possible to argue that such clear cases as the Dravidian example make comparisons with Indic patterns unnecessary; using Selinker's approach, one could conceivably compare the frequency of such patterns in Tamil with those in South African Indian English and in turn with those seen in a native-speaker variety of English. Even so, the comparison of the interlanguage with the native and target language has certain limitations, especially with regard to positive transfer. If the NL and TL show little or no difference in some structure common to both, any pattern of positive transfer should not differ much, and any actual difference in interlanguage patterns in such cases will not automatically say much about transfer (though it might well prove interesting for understanding other factors in second language acquisition). One case illustrating the methodological problem is in the use of definite and indefinite articles. Speakers of languages using these structures might or might not have an advantage in using articles in a new language (e.g., a Spanish speaker learning English). Certainly, researchers sympathetic to contrastive analysis might take any success to indicate positive transfer, but skeptics might argue that any success results simply from acquisition strategies common to first and second language acquisition. Clearly, the way to resolve such an impasse is to compare learners whose languages have articles with learners whose languages do not. One detailed look at speakers of different languages in this regard is work by Master (1987), and the results indicate a very clear advantage for the learners whose languages have articles. Other research to be mentioned later in this survey corroborates Master's findings.

Apart from articles, several other structural points have shown a difference in success depending on the presence or absence of a structure in the native language. In addition to the Mesthrie and Dunne study, there are other convincing investigations of relativization (e.g., Gass 1979; Hyltenstam, 1984; Singler, 1988), word order (Bickerton and Givón, 1976; Jansen, Lalleman, and Muysken, 1981), nominal case prefixation (Orr, 1987), spatial expressions (Ijaz, 1986; Jarvis and Odlin, 2000; Schumann, 1986), phrasal verbs (Sjöholm, 1995), causative constructions (Helms-Park, 2001), use of overt subject pronouns (White, 1985), existential constructions (Schachter and Rutherford, 1979), and lexical tones (Gandour and Harshman, 1986). Moreover, at least two studies show that speakers of Romance and Germanic languages show greater understanding of English vocabulary than do speakers of non-Indo-European languages (Ard and Homburg, 1993; Ringbom, 1987). Still other areas showing differences between native language groups are the pragmatics of apologies (Olshtain, 1983), the ability to recall kanji forms in written Japanese (Mori, 1998), and the metalinguistic recognition of a learner's native language in writing errors (Odlin, 1996). The differences between native language groups is also evident at the global level. As noted earlier, Ringbom (1987) finds that Swedish speakers generally have an easier time with English than do Finnish speakers, and Elo (1993) comes to the same conclusion in a study of the acquisition of French by Swedish and Finnish speakers: once again, the former were more successful.

The two different methods discussed so far have different strengths. The approach employed by Selinker requires a quantitative analysis of the native language and the target language as well as of the interlanguage variety under study, in contrast to other studies (e.g., Master, 1987) which identify a source-language pattern relevant to transfer but which do not always focus on how the patterns actually work in the native language. On the other hand, the approach used by Selinker could not work to demonstrate positive transfer beyond a reasonable doubt. Clearly, there are methodological advantages to be gained by employing both approaches in the same investigation. Jarvis (1998, 2000) argues that the most convincing evidence for transfer will demonstrate three characteristics: intra-group homogeneity, inter-group heterogeneity, and similarities between native language and interlanguage performance. The second of these criteria is more or less the same as seen in the method used by Mesthrie and Dunne and by Master comparing learners with different native languages. Likewise, the third criterion characterizes the method employed by Selinker comparing native language and interlanguage patterns. In addition to combining the two methods, Jarvis stresses the importance of intra-group homogeneity. One expectation implicit in this criterion is that there will be internal consistencies in what learners do in their native language and in their interlanguage. Although Jarvis's approach constitutes a major methodological advance, there remains some uncertainty as to whether it is as feasible for studies of comprehension as it is for ones focusing on production. In any case, how Jarvis applies these criteria in his own research is evident in box 15.1.

The methods exemplified in the studies of Selinker, Jarvis, Master, and Mesthrie and Dunne (as well as many others) have shown that it is possible to subject claims about cross-linguistic influence to rigorous tests. Such testing has often indicated language transfer to be at work, and the reality of the phenomenon is undeniable even though much remains to be understood. Nevertheless, many discussions of transfer do not rely on such methods but instead use data based simply on comparisons of an interlanguage structure with something in the native language. In such cases, claims that transfer has – or has not – taken place may be indeterminate, as when, for example, Spanish learners of English use double negators: for example, *I didn't see nothing*. Since the native language translation equivalent has two negators (***No** vi **nada***), a claim about cross-linguistic influence is plausible. However, there remains the possibility that *I didn't see nothing* reflects the influence of a non-standard

Box 15.1 Jarvis (1998, 2000)

Research question: What is the effect of the native language on learners' lexical choices?

Jarvis (1998, 2000) investigated using methods employed by previous researchers but also adding refinements that make his conclusions all the more credible. His procedures follow straightforwardly from the three criteria for identifying transfer discussed in this chapter: intra-group homogeneity, inter-group heterogeneity, and similarities between native language and interlanguage performance. Other strengths of the study include: (i) a large sample size from a very appropriate population to study, (ii) a use of the same materials employed by other second language researchers, and (iii) a clear account of the methods he used, which will enable future researchers to conduct either replications or parallel studies with other groups.

Methodology: Focusing on the acquisition of English in Finland, Jarvis was able to compare two groups of learners not very different culturally, but quite different in terms of language, Finnish being non-Indo-European and Swedish being Germanic as well as Indo-European (and thus historically rather close to English).

Subjects: Jarvis recruited 537 students in Finland, their ages ranging from 11 to 16, and also 98 native speakers of American English of about the same ages. Through random sampling, he distinguished four groups, each of 35 learners, whose native language was Finnish (the "Finns") and two groups of 35 whose native language was Swedish (the "Swedes"). In addition he had three groups of native speakers of Finnish writing in that language, as well as two groups of native speakers of Swedish writing in their mother tongue, each group having 22 individuals. The native speaker sample was likewise pared down to three groups, with 22 pupils in each.

Task: One complicating factor in studying the acquisition of English in Finland is that Finns usually study Swedish and Swedes Finnish, and the design Jarvis used considered that, as well as the number of years of English that learners had had. He also wished to compare the effects of the native language in production and in comprehension, so there were three different tasks: a written description of part of the Charlie Chaplin film *Modern Times*, a vocabulary listing test (to measure productive vocabulary), and a vocabulary recognition test. The written task required everyone to provide a narrative of the film, with about a quarter of an hour allowed.

Results: The results of this investigation of transfer indicate all of the following: intra-group homogeneity, inter-group heterogeneity, and similarities between native language and interlanguage performance. One problem Jarvis encountered was that the lexical choices of pupils writing in their native languages were not always very different. Thus, for example, both groups often referred to a bakery truck by the same kind of denotation, *auto* ('auto') in the case of the Finnish writers and *bil* ('car') in the case of the Swedish writers. Accordingly, such convergences make the performance of the Finns and Swedes sometimes hard to distinguish. When, for example, a Finn wrote *a woman stoles bread from a car*, the use of *car* probably reflects the use of *auto* in Finnish, but Swedes used the same lexical item as in *She stoled bread into a car*. On the other hand, distinct lexical forms sometimes surfaced. One event in the film involves a collision in the street between Charlie Chaplin and Paulette Goddard, and students writing in Swedish often referred to the event with one of two different verbs, *krocka* ('crash') and *springa på* ('run on'), whereas those writing in Finnish overwhelmingly chose *törmätä* ('crash') and almost never *juosta* ('run'). In the English of the Swedes, several learners are apparently influenced by *springa på*, as in *She run on Charlie Chaplin*. As this verb–particle construction was never used by the Finns, its frequent appearance in the English of the Swedes strongly argues for cross-linguistic influence.

Conclusion: The theoretical framework that Jarvis adopted was prototype research, and he argues that his findings on inter-group differences support a relativist notion of conceptual transfer. Both relativism and prototypes will be discussed elsewhere in this chapter, but here it will suffice to note that Jarvis and Odlin (2000) have employed similar methods with the same database of Finns and Swedes to examine issues related to morphological type, spatial reference, and transfer, and Jarvis (2002) has used a similar approach in a study of the acquisition of articles.

variety of the target language, and it may also be that natural principles of language acquisition are at work (Odlin, 1989). In such a case it would clearly help to look at what kind of target language input learners hear and also to compare how often speakers of another language use double negation. Without those methodological improvements, claims that Spanish is or is not involved remain inconclusive.

Although the Spanish example shows the risk of making inferences based simply on cross-linguistic similarity, not all comparisons lead to such indeterminacy. An uncontroversial case of cross-linguistic influence is seen in the so-called *after* perfect still common in Ireland and some parts of Scotland, as in the following example from Sabban (1982, p. 155), *I'm after forgetting all that lot now*, which is equivalent to *I have forgotten all that now*. The individual whom Sabban recorded was an elderly native speaker of Scottish Gaelic, which uses a very similar perfect construction signaled in part either by *an déidh* or *air* ('after'), with equivalent forms used in Ireland, *tar éis* and *i ndiaidh*. For virtually all researchers, the *after* perfect is the result of intensive language contact in centuries past when many speakers of Irish and Scottish Gaelic were learning English as a second language (Filppula, 1999). What makes this case different from the Spanish example is, first, the fact that no dialects of English outside of the Celtic regions use the construction, and second, the fact that *after* perfects are not all common in the interlanguage verb phrases of speakers of other languages as they acquire English. Since neither target language influence nor universal principles (which would presumably lead to widespread use of the structure) can explain the *after* perfect, the cross-linguistic similarity here constitutes strong evidence for transfer.

The methods used by Selinker and the other researchers cited in this section rely on statistical comparisons, but cases such as the *after* perfect show that powerful evidence can come simply from the presence of a structure in the speech or writing of a distinct population of learners and, very crucially, its absence in groups whose native languages have nothing analogous. The *after* perfect is compatible with Selinker's assertion that there should be a close resemblance between the native language and the interlanguage, and the occurrence of the *after* perfect in a distinct population allows for an implicit comparison with the transfer patterns of speakers of other languages where the structure is absent (Odlin, 1989). When such implicit comparisons are possible, then, they provide strong evidence of transfer. This point is an especially important one because a great deal of language contact research does not – and sometimes cannot – use statistics.

Evidence from language contact research requires careful interpretation for any real contribution to the study of transfer (cf. Odlin, 1992). As noted above, much of the evidence discussed by Weinreich deals with issues other than second language acquisition. Moreover, historical linguists have often suggested alternative explanations besides cross-linguistic influence for the ontogeny of particular characteristics in a language. Even so, the vast number of encounters between speakers of highly different languages and the countless cases of naturalistic acquisition at many points in history make it unwise to ignore the insights about transfer to be found in language contact research. Many studies of pidgins and creoles have identified likely cases of substrate influence (i.e., influence from the native language or some other previously learned language), and some creolists have found much in common in the findings of research in their field and in second language acquisition (e.g., Mufwene, 1990; Siegel, 1999). Indeed, Mufwene (1998) has argued that pidginization and creolization, which creolists usually view as highly distinct phenomena, often amount to cases of second language acquisition. Whether or not pidgins and creoles always qualify as second language varieties, much of the creolist research strongly suggests the transferability of structures which are not so often discussed in the mainline journals for the field called second language acquisition, such as the inclusive/exclusive distinction in pronoun categories (Keesing, 1988) and serial verb constructions (Migge, 1998). Apart from the issue of transferability, creolist research can obviously contribute to understanding the topic in the next section, the importance of social factors in transfer research.

The evidence for cross-linguistic influence takes many forms not only because of the wide range of geographic and social settings but also because of the different kinds of data collection that researchers have engaged in, resulting in a highly diverse array of clues about how transfer can operate. The studies run a gamut from recordings of speech in naturalistic settings to highly controlled experimental procedures, and no single data collection procedure will necessarily provide better evidence about transfer. Speech samples might seem to offer the best data in many cases, but inferences about positive transfer based only on speech will likely underestimate the facilitating effects arising from large numbers of shared words in languages such as English and French. Moreover, some syntactic structures are comparatively rare, as noted above, yet they may still be highly significant for understanding transfer. Such infrequency, however, can lead to interpretive problems. If the only way to get evidence about transferability comes from the analysis of linguistic intuitions, there can be room for doubt as to whether the intuitions obtained have any relation to actual positive or negative transfer in production or comprehension. When possible, the most convincing evidence will come from multiple sources: spoken and written performances as well as responses to measures of perception, comprehension, or intuition.

7 Language Transfer and Social Setting

All language acquisition takes place in a social matrix, and so it will be useful to consider some of the social factors relevant to transfer. Not all conceivable background factors will play a role in cross-linguistic influence, but some clearly do make a difference. For instance, in research focusing on semantic influences from the target as well as the native, Pavlenko (1999) found that the use of words related to the notion of privacy by Russian–English bilinguals varied according to whether they were living in Russia or in the United States. Looking at differences correlated with social class, Schmidt (1987) found that variation in Arabic consonants affected the consonants used by learners of English. In a study of transfer in West Africa, Chumbow (1981) found there to be more influence from African languages among learners who did not live in cities. The homogeneity of bilingual interlocutors also appears to be a powerful factor in confirming learners' hypotheses about what the target language is like, and cross-linguistic influence can often arise, as Singler (1988) found in comparing the relativization patterns of two groups of speakers, one fairly homogeneous in terms of the native languages that they spoke, and the other not. Somewhat similarly, Mesthrie (1992) saw the social isolation caused by apartheid as a contributing factor to the patterns of syntactic transfer seen in South African Indian English.

Social factors can also account for certain discrepancies seen in transfer research, as is evident in the case of idioms. Kellerman (1977) found Dutch learners to be skeptical about the possibility of using Dutch idioms in English even though there are sometimes word-for-word correspondences, as in the case of *to have victory in the bag*. However, Sridhar and Sridhar (1986) criticized Kellerman's claims about the non-transferability of idioms, arguing that in countries such as India and Nigeria, speakers often create idioms in English based on ones in their native language. On the other hand, results similar to those of Kellerman have also been evident in studies conducted in schools in Syria and Finland (Abdullah and Jackson, 1998; Sjöholm, 1983). Odlin (1991, 1989) has suggested the discrepancy in such results has to do primarily with social context. The historical language contact situation in Ireland resembled that of India and Nigeria, since English was once a language spoken by only a small but dominant group. In Holland, Finland, and Syria, English has never played a role comparable to what it has in Nigeria or India or to what it had in Ireland (before becoming the native language of virtually the entire population). The Irish case also differs from those in Holland, Finland, and Syria in that many Irish learners acquired English in a naturalistic setting (Odlin, 1997b).

It thus appears that formal language instruction often makes students wary about cross-linguistic correspondences. By the same token, schooling and literacy conventions can affect the stance that learners take in writing in a second language, as seen in work in contrastive rhetoric (e.g., Connor, 1996). Although researchers and teachers have sometimes taken too literally the impressionistic observations of Kaplan (1966/84) about discourse patterns across cultures, there are in fact numerous differences in the conventions of written language (usually considered the domain of contrastive rhetoric) as well as in spoken language (usually considered the domain of pragmatics). There will later be attention given to implications of pragmatic differences, but the focus now will be on written conventions as reflections of differing patterns of socialization.

Differences in literacy conventions can be hard to characterize accurately; societies such as China with long traditions of literacy have varied at different times on, for example, the desirability of questioning a past authority (Bloch and Chi, 1995). Nevertheless, only some strands of the tradition may affect individual learners – and the variations in instruction may account for differing views of the importance of contrastive rhetoric (e.g., Connor, 1996; Mohan and Lo, 1985). While there is a need in this field for comparative research of the kind outlined by Jarvis (2000), the evidence already available points to yet another area where learners' social background matters a great deal. Just as the diary studies by linguists have yielded useful insights about transfer (and some will be discussed below), certain accounts of becoming literate in a new language indicate the great difficulty occasioned by different conventions of written discourse in the native and target languages. Shen (1989, p. 465) describes how he finally succeeded in learning to write in a new language – and only after he had learned to distance himself from the conventions that he had been taught:

> The change is profound: through my understanding of new meanings of words like "individualism," "idealism," and "I," I began to accept the underlying concepts and values of American writing, and by learning to use "topic sentences" I began to accept a new logic. Thus, when I write papers in English, I am able to obey all the rules of English composition. In doing this, I feel that I am writing through, with, and because of a new identity . . . I am not saying that I have lost my Chinese identity . . . Any time I write in Chinese, I resume my old identity and obey the rules of Chinese composition such as "make the 'I' modest" and "Beat around the bush before attacking the central topic."

Not all writers in a second language may have such a strong sense of changing identities. However, Shen's experience indicates that native language literacy practices can indeed affect the hypotheses that learners may have of discourse in the target language, and that those practices have the potential to interact with cross-linguistic influence involving rhetoric, pragmatics, and other linguistic subsystems.

8 Constraints on Transfer

Discussions of language transfer have often invoked the notion of constraints, but not in identical ways. The most global notion is Schachter's (1993) characterization of transfer itself as a constraint on the hypotheses that learners will formulate about the target language. More often, however, there have appeared claims about localized constraints on cross-linguistic influence, as in the above-noted claims about the non-transferability of idioms. Moreover, researchers have sometimes believed that other structural characteristics are not transferable, most notably basic word order (Rutherford, 1983; Zobl, 1986), bound morphology (Eubank, 1993/4; Krashen, 1983), and what are known in Universal Grammar as "functional projections" (Vainikka and Young-Scholten, 1998). Such claims have not proven true in all acquisition settings, however. There are cases of basic word-order transfer (Odlin, 1990), and likewise bound morphology is not always immune to cross-linguistic influence (Dušková, 1984; Jarvis and Odlin, 2000; Orr, 1987; Sulkala, 1996). The problem with the recent claim about functional heads will be discussed in the section on language universals.

Any highly generalizable claim about constraints must hold true for all social settings (and there is, of course, the difficulty of determining the full range of such settings). On the other hand, there is also a problem in claiming, as Thomason and Kaufman (1988) do, that there are no constraints at all, their assertion a reaction to unsuccessful attempts to formulate constraints. In fact, Thomason and Kaufman consider markedness a constraining factor, although they do not say much about just how markedness functions in that capacity (cf. Eckman, 1996).

Regardless of how many or how few constraints there may be, it will help to consider the notion of constraint itself. As noted above, much of what is considered cross-linguistic influence depends on interlingual identifications, that is, the judgments that something in the native language and something in the target language are similar. Accordingly, a constraint could be anything that prevents a learner either from noticing a similarity in the first place or from deciding that the similarity is a real and helpful one. Furthermore, constraints might involve general cognitive capacities including perception and memory, or they might involve principles of language either totally or partially independent of other human capacities. Although the existence of some kinds of constraints seems probable, there remains much uncertainly about how many kinds of constraints there are or what their exact nature is.

Two of the most interesting attempts to elucidate constraints have looked at interactions between linguistic and general cognitive capacities. The Transfer to Somewhere Principle (Andersen, 1983) focuses on the conditions that will induce learners to make interlingual identifications, while the Transfer to Nowhere Principle (Kellerman, 1995) considers how cross-linguistic influence can occur even when there might seem to be no basis for an interlingual identification. The Transfer to Somewhere Principle draws on earlier thinking on cross-linguistic influence and is compatible with notions of "congruence" as expounded by Weinreich (1953) and others. Andersen articulates the principle in the following very general form: "Transfer can only function in conjunction with the operating principles that guide language learners and users in their choice of linguistic forms to express the intended meaning" (1983, p. 180). While this statement intentionally has few specifics, Andersen elaborates on the principle through a close look at several operating principles, that is, heuristics, identified by Slobin (1973) as crucial for children acquiring their native language, including these: (i) "pay attention to the end of words"; (ii) "pay attention to the order of words and morphemes"; (iii) "avoid interruption or rearrangement of linguistic units"; and (iv) "underlying semantic relations should be marked overtly and clearly." These and other principles (which Slobin has added to over the years) seem to provide children with a way to look for cues in the input. Although the heuristics focus on linguistic structures, Slobin sees them as closely related to a more general cognitive system that matures and enables children's thinking and perception to tune into language.

Andersen accordingly examines Slobin's operating principles for evidence of their importance in second language acquisition. In a look at a number of case studies he finds that both positive and negative transfer can occur when learners perceive (however unconsciously) some cross-linguistic similarity consonant with the operating principles. For instance, he compares a 5-year-old Spanish-speaking girl named Marta with a Japanese-speaking girl of the same age named Uguisu for their success with each of the following English structures: articles, copulas, auxiliaries, plural morphemes, the prepositions *in* and *on*, and the possessive inflection in words such as *brother's*. Marta showed earlier success than Uguisu on all of the structures except for *on* (and Uguisu showed no greater success with that preposition) and the possessive inflection. All of the structures that Marta found easy meet the following criteria established by Andersen: they are frequent, they are more or less transparent in meaning, and they are congruent between English and Spanish. Other factors (e.g., phonetic similarity) help with some but not all, and no factor seems to give Uguisu any advantage except with the possessive inflection, which is congruent with a possessive morpheme in Japanese. In effect, then, Marta is able to take advantage of cross-linguistic similarities that conform to cognitive principles involving ease of perception and interpretation. Drawing as it does on notions of cross-linguistic congruence as a condition for transfer, the Transfer to Somewhere Principle has a commonsense appeal. On the other hand, there are problems. For one thing, the exact conditions for congruence in any given acquisition setting may not always be clear, especially since the very number of principles deemed important by Slobin is large yet perhaps incomplete. Moreover, individuals may vary in terms of which principle has priority in any given context.

Kellerman doubts the applicability of the Transfer to Somewhere Principle in all cases, and he proposes a complementary Transfer to Nowhere Principle, which states that "there can be transfer which is not licensed by similarity to the L2, and where the way the L2 works may very largely go unheeded" (1995, p. 137). Kellerman cites two types of cross-linguistic contrasts to illustrate where his principle may apply. In the first instance, he summarizes a discussion by Slobin (1993) of work on Panjabi learners of English sponsored by the European Science Foundation. These learners appear to equate progressive verb forms of English with forms in Panjabi marking imperfective aspect. In contrast, Italian speakers in a related ESF project were accurate in marking English verbs for tense and made relatively little use of progressive forms. Slobin and Kellerman attribute the Panjabi speakers' choices to the influence of their native language, in which tense is considered to play a less important systemic role than aspect. The second example cited by Kellerman involves contrasts between verbs in Dutch and English indicating space and motion (e.g., the cognate pair *brengen* and *bring*). Semantic differences between such verbs lead to learning difficulties for English-speaking learners of Dutch and Dutch-speaking learners of English. Along with Slobin, Kellerman espouses a mildly relativistic view to account for difficulties in both the Panjabi and Dutch cases: "learners may not be able to capitalize on cross-linguistic correspondences because some types of 'thinking for speaking' [a term used by Slobin] may be beyond individual awareness" (1995, p. 143).

Although Kellerman intends Transfer to Nowhere to complement Transfer to Somewhere, it seems possible to consider the examples he offers as instances where the latter principle does in fact apply. In the first example, the equivalence made between progressive forms in English and imperfective forms in Panjabi seems explainable through an analysis of progressive aspect as a subcategory of an imperfective category that may underlie the aspectual systems of all human languages (Comrie, 1976). Thus, Panjabi speakers might well consider the English progressive a "somewhere": in fact, other research indicates that learners frequently make interlingual identifications between categories of tense, aspect, or modality in their native language and categories showing only a partial semantic overlap in the target language (e.g., Ho and Platt, 1993; Klee and Ocampo, 1995; Wenzell, 1989). In the case of the Dutch–English cognates, there is an even clearer cross-linguistic correspondence, and so it would be surprising if learners did not make interlingual identifications. If Kellerman's principle really can cover cases not understandable as Transfer to Somewhere, it will be necessary to offer other examples of "unlicensed" cross-linguistic influence.

The Transfer to Nowhere Principle may prove to be superfluous, but the issues raised by Andersen, Kellerman, and Slobin will no doubt reappear in one form or another. There most probably are "natural acquisition principles," but their exact character remains incompletely understood. On the other hand, language-specific characteristics may interact with cognition in ways that make it more difficult for learners to notice differences between the native language and target languages.

9 Transfer, Fossilization, and Multiple Effects

Schachter (1988) has argued that two characteristics of second language acquisition make it substantively different from the acquisition of a first language: transfer and fossilization. The latter term can be defined informally as the cessation of learning, although just how researchers can demonstrate either partial or total cessation is problematic, as is the psychological or social reality of the phenomenon for highly proficient individuals (cf. Long, this volume; Selinker, 1972, 1992; Selinker and Lamendella, 1981; Sridhar and Sridhar, 1986). Whatever the difficulties related to the concept, there is little question that learners often do not become proficient in the target language and that several factors contribute to learner difficulties, one of them being transfer. The apparent permanence of foreign accents is perhaps the most salient – but not the only – indicator that cross-linguistic influence contributes to fossilization.

Like transfer, fossilization is probably best understood as a cover term for a variety of factors which in this case result in the cessation of learning. Selinker (who earlier coined the term *fossilization* itself) has recently considered how various factors interact and has posited a "multiple effects principle": "It is a general law in SLA that when two processes work in tandem, there is a greater chance for stabilization of forms leading to possible fossilization" (1992, p. 262). He also advances the following corollary: "In every instance of the multiple effects principle, language transfer will be involved" (1992, p. 263). In a closer look at this corollary, Selinker and Lakshmanan (1993) discuss strong and weak versions, the latter formulated, accordingly: "language transfer is a *privileged* co-factor in setting multiple effects" (1993, p. 198, emphasis in the original). The strong version posits transfer as a necessary co-factor, but later in the article Selinker and Lakshmanan suggest that only the weak version is tenable.

Their discussion of transfer includes diverse examples that indeed suggest the interaction of cross-linguistic influence with other factors. Citing instances from Dušková (1984), they note that Czech learners of Russian use bound morphology from their native language as in the interlanguage form *rabotnice* ("workwomen"), with the suffix (*-nice*) differing from the target language suffix (*-nicy*) in the Russian *rabotnicy*. Even while the stem of the equivalent Czech word, *pracovnice*, is different, the suffixes of the native language and interlanguage forms are identical. Selinker and Lakshmanan see three factors at work in producing such forms: (i) transfer; (ii) the existence of numerous cognates in Czech and Russian; and (iii) learners' perceptions that the two languages are more similar than Czech and English are (Dušková did not find learners using suffixes such as *-nice* in their English). Another example given by Selinker and Lakshmanan comes from the investigation of interlanguage word order of Hebrew speakers discussed earlier. Learners frequently placed adverbs that normally do not directly follow the verb, as in an example discussed above: *I like very much movies*. Similar factors are also seen to be at work in this instance, including transfer (post-verbal adverbs being common in Hebrew) but also the fact that English allows many adverbs to occur in initial, medial, and final parts of clauses.

These and other instances considered by Selinker and Lakshmanan are certainly intriguing, but they also raise a number of questions. In the Czech example, the second and third of the multiple effects are arguably just preconditions for language transfer, although in the Hebrew example, the target language itself may contribute to learners' difficulty. One question, then, that these examples bring to mind is just what factors may interact under the Multiple Effects Principle. This question does not necessarily argue against the significance of the Multiple Effects Principle, but it does suggest that second language researchers are not yet in a position to specify the exact conditions under which fossilization occurs or just how transfer interacts with it (see Long, this volume).

10 Universals, Typology, and Transfer

As much of this chapter has already shown, the study of transfer intersects with many other concerns in linguistics, and work on what is termed *Universal Grammar* has given considerable attention to certain areas where cross-linguistic influence may operate. Most UG researchers do not make transfer their primary concern, but many recognize its importance; moreover, their abiding interest in trying to understand, within a Chomskian framework (e.g., Chomsky, 1995), just how much (or how little) first and second language acquisition will overlap has led to numerous studies that seek, among other goals, to determine if transfer has affected particular patterns of acquisition.

Second language research within the UG framework has normally focused on the question of whether or not learners have access to Universal Grammar. In the last two decades, universalist research in the Chomskian tradition has attempted to identify universal principles and language-specific parameters (which are often typologically relevant to many languages) that constrain the hypotheses learners will formulate about what the target language could be like. If universal principles (or related technical constructs such as features and projections) are available to learners, there will be at least some overlap between first and second language acquisition, with certain innate principles putatively available to all learners. On the other hand, if there is little or no access to the principles (because of maturational or other factors), specific parameters (e.g., word order or the use or non-use of pronouns) may steer second language acquisition in ways not seen in the language learning of children. If parametric variation does play a major role, it could interact with universal principles or it could operate largely independently of them, but either way, language transfer has been a real concern of UG researchers.

In the large and growing body of research on these issues, highly diverse positions have emerged. White (2000; see, also, White, this volume) identifies five approaches, four of which envision some role for cross-linguistic influence: (i) full transfer/partial access; (ii) no transfer/partial access; (iii) full transfer/full access; (iv) partial transfer/full access; and (v) partial transfer/partial access. As she acknowledges, even this range does not adequately capture the diversity of positions on the issues. For one thing, there exists another position one might take, "no transfer/no access" – and in fact, some work goes in that direction (e.g., Meisel, 1997). All of the five positions contrasted above, however, do envision some role for UG, and all but the second envision some role for transfer.

The expanding range of positions on the access question departs from earlier tendencies in the literature to characterize transfer and access in absolute terms. Apart from the "no transfer/no access" position, the most opposed stances are the first and second, and variants of them have long been part of the UG literature. The "full transfer/partial access" position maintains that UG is available to learners but only as instantiated in whatever ways the learner's native language may reflect UG principles (e.g., Bley-Vroman, 1989). Conversely, "no transfer/partial access" has held that the principles of UG that a learner has access to are not mediated by the native language at all but instead are accessible directly through acquisition just as these principles presumably are in the acquisition of the first language (e.g., Flynn and Martohardjono, 1994). Research for some two decades has led to many conflicting results; not surprisingly, then, many researchers are now unwilling to espouse all-or-nothing positions. As White (2000) suggests, it is certainly conceivable that some but not all UG properties would be accessible. Moreover, research both in and outside the UG tradition suggests that there are some kinds of constraints on cross-linguistic influence, even though specifying the nature of the constraints has proven very difficult.

Research in the UG framework covers a fairly wide range of structures and raises a host of issues, some more relevant to the study of transfer than others. Accordingly, it seems best in a survey such as this not to address any one specific approach (e.g., "full transfer/full access"), but rather to consider some issues that will be of lasting importance regardless of whether any one approach continues to shape much of the research landscape in the future. Even if any particular UG approach is misguided (or, indeed, the overall Chomskian framework is so), problems that arise in interpreting the research will no doubt continue to be problems for transfer researchers for a long time. Two especially important concerns – and interrelated ones – are the nature of parameters and the scope of Universal Grammar.

The notion of "parameter" can be defined fairly succinctly, as in the following gloss in an introductory textbook: "*Parameter* A universal dimension along which languages may vary" (O'Grady, Dobrovolsky, and Aronoff, 1993, p. 589). It is easy enough to give examples of parameters, and often the illustrations involve cross-linguistic contrasts, as in the case of a word-order property where English and French differ:

(5) Louise mange toujours du pain.
Louise eats always bread
*Louise toujours mange du pain.

As Haegeman and Guéron (1999) note, English adverbs normally precede a verb in cases where they would immediately follow the verb in French (though, of course, many adverbs in both languages can also appear in clause-initial or clause-final position). As a contrastive description, the one given here is no better or worse than many outside the UG tradition. However, most if not all parameters are generalizations that necessarily ignore exceptions, and these exceptions may matter for the study of transfer. The following sentences all come from users of the Internet (emphases added):

(6) I remember *vaguely* some of the threads on the Forum, and that they . . .

(7) Read *carefully* everything received from the Office of Admissions . . .

(8) . . . you must understand *thoroughly* the major ideas and concepts . . .

The position of each adverb in relation to the verb constitutes an exception to the generalization of the parameter described by Haegeman and Guéron. No doubt various explanations can be given to account for such exceptions, and they do not invalidate the cross-linguistic contrast. However, if an English-speaking learner of French says *Lisez soigneusement* ("read carefully"), the word order might reflect cross-linguistic influence even though the pattern departs from the native language parameter. Such a case could alternatively result from simply a correct apprehension of the target language pattern, and to demonstrate positive transfer it would be necessary to use a method such as described above, that is, to contrast learners' performances with those of a group of learners whose native language never allowed an adverb to appear right after a verb. The example here does not invalidate UG research on adverb placement, but it does show that language-specific influences may not always be synchronized with native language parameters even in areas focused on in Universal Grammar.

Some parameters such as word order have long gotten attention in the literature (in some cases, long enough to generate controversy over just how to define the parameter). Exactly how many parameters there are in any language remains an open question, and it is likewise not certain just what the scope of a parameter is in any adequate description of a language or in an account of how the parameter is (or is not) acquired. The parameter of aspect illustrates the boundary problem of the relation of Universal Grammar to other areas of linguistics. Slabakova (1999) discusses this parameter in relation to syntactic properties such as double objects and verb–particle constructions. Whatever the merits of her specific analysis, it would be mistaken to conclude that the cluster of properties studied is all that is relevant to aspect. Whether or not the notion of parametric variation applies well in this case, aspect has semantic and pragmatic dimensions that matter a great deal in second language acquisition (Andersen and Shirai, 1996; Bardovi-Harlig, 1992). Moreover, there is good evidence for aspectual transfer in a number of studies outside the UG framework (e.g., Ho and Platt, 1993; Sabban, 1982; Wenzell, 1989).

Most UG researchers acknowledge that there are domains relevant to language acquisition beyond Universal Grammar, and it is not unusual to find statements such as the following: "UG is not a comprehensive theory of the acquisition process; many other factors enter into the language-specific instantiation of principles and parameters" (Flynn and Martohardjono, 1994, p. 319). Even so, this world beyond sometimes impinges on the claims of UG researchers, as in one made by Vainikka and Young-Scholten (1998) about functional projections, an important concept in recent UG research: "there is evidence that in L2 development these projections are not available for transfer. Thus the development of functional projections in L2 acquisition is very similar to what has been observed in L1 development" (p. 29).

The terminology in this claim may obscure its sweeping nature. If it were true, a number of function-word categories such as the article would be acquired with no significant influence from the native language. There is, however, abundant evidence that learners whose languages have articles often do avail themselves of real cross-linguistic correspondences, thus leading to a great deal of positive transfer (e.g., Andersen, 1983; Dulay and Burt, 1974; Jarvis, 2002; Kempf, 1975; Master, 1987; Myers, 1992, Oller and Redding, 1971; Ringbom, 1987; Shannon, 1995). It should go without saying that to ignore research outside the UG framework is to run the risk of making empirically unsound claims.

In all probability, researchers will not decide soon on the exact relation between the concerns of Universal Grammar and concerns in other areas of second language acquisition. However, two points made elsewhere (Odlin, forthcoming) are relevant here: (i) the significance of transfer for SLA does not stand or fall on the access issue; and (ii) research on Universal Grammar deals with only a subset of possible language universals, and accordingly there remains a need for universalist research looking beyond the issues raised by UG theorists. With regard to the first point, it is worth mentioning four areas largely outside of UG that clearly matter to many transfer researchers as well as to language learners and teachers: phonetics, cognate vocabulary, pragmatics, and literacy. Fortunately, there is a considerable work in all of these areas (e.g., Connor, 1996; Kasper, 1992; Leather and James, 1996; Schweers, 1993).

With regard to the second point, some transfer research has considered language universals and linguistic typology but not in the UG framework (e.g., Eckman, 1996; Wolfe-Quintero, 1996). The study of typology has had a life of its own outside the Chomskian tradition (e.g., Givón, 1984; Tomlin, 1994), as has the notion of linguistic innateness. A great deal of typologically oriented research assumes that communicative needs play a key role in shaping the grammatical options that characterize any language. Not surprisingly, such assumptions have often been challenged by generative theorists (e.g., Gregg, 1989). In any case, typological research outside the UG framework has also led to interesting insights about transfer. For example, work by Clark (1978) on existential and possessive constructions provided the basis for a study of transfer patterns in the English of a native speaker of Cambodian (Duff, 1993). Many languages of the world do not make the kind of distinction that English does between verbs of possession (as in *have*) and verbs predicating existence (as in the construction *There is*). Such is the case with Cambodian, and Duff provides a longitudinal analysis of the changes in one speaker's interlanguage from a stage where *has* serves as both an existential and possessive marker to one where it marks possession, but not existence (the form *has* being much more frequent in the data than *have*).

Duff notes another change evident in the development of separate ways of expressing existence and possession: the use of overt syntactic subjects becomes more and more common. Like Chinese, Cambodian does not have a category closely comparable to that of subject in English where syntactic phenomena such as agreement often depend on what the subject of the clause is. Accordingly, languages such as Cambodian and Chinese are sometimes designated "topic-prominent" languages in contrast to "subject-prominent" languages such as English (e.g., Rutherford, 1983). A study by Jin (1994) indicates an interesting case of bi-directional symmetry. Just as speakers of Cambodian find it difficult to acquire an overtly marked subject category, speakers of English learning Chinese have difficulties at first in suppressing overt subjects in their interlanguage. The studies of Duff and Jin suggest that the interlingual identifications made by learners can draw on either communicative categories such as topic (as in the Duff study) or formal categories not closely tied to a particular communicative principle (as in the Jin study). Whatever learners can notice in their native language, whether formal or discourse-functional, seems to motivate interlingual identifications in such cases.

Although discourse-functional studies and UG research aim at understanding different parts of the human language capacity, both have drawn on facts in other fields, not only from linguistic typology but also from what is sometimes termed prototype research. In the last fifty years or so, thinkers in several fields have questioned whether linguistic and general cognitive knowledge can be adequately represented in the classical notions of categorization that assume that every category has a set of necessary and sufficient conditions (e.g., Lakoff, 1987; Rosch, 1973). In contrast to such characterizations in which every member of a category has the same status, characterizations by prototype distinguish core from peripheral members of a set (as where, for instance, a robin is considered a more typical kind of bird than is a penguin). One of the earliest examples of the application of prototype analysis to second language research comes from work by Kellerman (1978) looking at the intuitions of native speakers about the transferability of sentences such as *Hij brak zijn been* ("He broke his leg") and *Zijn val werd door een boom gebroken* ("His fall was broken by a tree"). The judges generally considered sentences such as the former to be more transferable, the use of *break* in such cases being closer to a core meaning of the Dutch–English cognate *breken/break*, as Kellerman determined through a test of native speaker intuitions about the senses of the Dutch verb *breken*. What makes these intuitions especially interesting is the fact that even though both of the above sentences are acceptable in Dutch and English, notions of centrality appear to affect what learners regard as transferable. Kellerman's results, then, show how important it is to take into account the judgments of actual learners and not rely simply on a contrastive analysis.

The cognates *breken/break* constitute a case where there exists an extremely close correspondence (even though learners often do not see it that way). However, the value of prototype research for transfer is also evident in studies involving languages less similar than Dutch and English. Since most cross-linguistic correspondences are rougher than the case of *breken/break*, it is necessary to determine whether learners speaking different languages will agree on what the core meanings of a target language word are. Evidence that they sometimes agree comes from a study by Ijaz (1986) of the use of English spatial terms by native speakers of Urdu and German. Both groups responded similarly to cloze test items, such as *Two watches are____the table*, to which both non-native groups, as well as a group of native speakers, nearly always supplied the preposition *on*. In this instance, using *on* conforms to the prototypical sense characteristics of static contact from a vertical direction. In contrast, the test item *The keys are hanging____the hooks* elicited very different responses. Native speakers of English, Urdu, and German all chose *on* in many cases (especially the first group), but other responses were common in this context, which involves a more peripheral sense of *on* (contact from a horizontal direction). Along with *on*, another acceptable response that some individuals in all three groups chose was *from*, but non-native speakers sometimes chose spatial terms influenced by their native languages. In the case of the Urdu speakers, *with* was often selected, whereas some German speakers chose *at*. Non-central instances thus elicited considerable negative transfer.

The notion of core and periphery has also been used to study the acquisition of grammatical structures, as in the case of tense and aspect (Andersen and Shirai, 1996). Similarly, the notion of markedness often overlaps with notions of prototypes, with less marked structures being closer to the core and more marked ones closer to the periphery (cf. Eckman, 1996). In the most ambitious characterizations, linguists sometimes posit a core and periphery in language itself (e.g., Cook, 1994). Along the same lines, some second language researchers have argued that there exists a Basic Variety (more or less a core interlanguage) in all cases of naturalistic acquisition (Klein and Perdue, 1997). Needless to say, the wider the scope of the claim, the more details there are that require explanation, and in the broadest claims, it is far from clear what role language transfer should have. Universalist research, including work on the so-called Basic Variety, looks for commonalities in acquisition patterns, but there is plenty of evidence for the influence of the native language in naturalistic as well as scholastic settings, and as Schwartz (1997) suggests, such influence can reduce the uniformity of acquisition patterns.

11 Conceptual Transfer and Linguistic Relativity

As described in the preceding section, Ijaz (1986) found differences between the prepositional choices of speakers of Urdu and German in identical discourse contexts, and this evidence supports her contention that "Concepts underlying words in the L1 are transferred to the L2 and mapped onto new linguistic labels, regardless of differences in the semantic boundaries of corresponding words" (p. 405). Other researchers have adopted a similar approach, looking at influences from the semantics and pragmatics of the native language as "conceptual transfer" (e.g., Jarvis, 1998; Pavlenko, 1999). Not surprisingly, then, discussions of transfer have addressed once again the issue of linguistic relativity.

The notion that language can affect thinking has a long intellectual history, and at least from the nineteenth century some have considered thought patterns in the native language to be a possible source of difficulty in learning a new language (Odlin, forthcoming). In the twentieth century, Lado (1957) discussed the arguments of Benjamin Lee Whorf, and Kaplan (1966/84) likewise invoked relativistic thinking in relation to contrastive rhetoric. Nevertheless, linguists of the later part of the century more often than not took a dim view of linguistic relativism (e.g., Pinker, 1994), and even in contrastive rhetoric some researchers have remained skeptical about the value of relativistic analyses (e.g., Connor, 1996). Despite such skepticism, recent empirical work indicates some clear effects of language-specific structures on cognition (e.g., Lucy, 1992; Pederson et al., 1998). It seems likely, then, that such work will stimulate further interest in the relation between relativism and cross-linguistic influence.

Pavlenko (1999) focuses on cognitive changes that may come with the transition from monolingualism to bilingualism, especially in cases where cross-linguistic correspondences are tenuous at best. Observing that the English word *privacy* has no close translation equivalent in Russian, she compares the ways that four groups discussed scenes in a film showing an example of an "invasion of privacy," to use an expression common in the native English-speaking group. A group of Russian immigrants in the United States likewise invoked the notion of privacy in their retellings of the events in the film, although they sometimes used constructions influenced by Russian phrasing, as in "she had some personal emotions, and she felt she was intruded upon, her personal space was intruded." Pavlenko notes that this construction constitutes a hybrid of English *personal space* and a Russian collocation *vmeshivatsia v chuzhiye chuvstva* ("invading/interfering with someone's feelings"). Comparable influences of English on the Russian of the immigrants were also evident, and such hybridization was conspicuously absent in the retellings of monolingual Russian speakers and Russian learners of English living in St Petersburg. The difference between the immigrants and the English speakers living in Russia supports Pavlenko's view that bilingual memory representations are not static: using English as a second language in a native speaker environment can lead to the development of new concepts such as privacy which one's native language may not encode in any straightforward way. The results also suggest how much a social variable such as place of residence can correlate with or decrease the likelihood of cross-linguistic influence.

Since Pavlenko's Russian informants often spoke of emotions in relation to the incidents in the film, a question arises as to whether there exists any language-specific coding of affect, which in turn intersects with the question of whether the same repertory of emotions exists in all cultures. Many psychologists and anthropologists have debated the latter question (cf. Lazarus, 1991; Lutz and White, 1986), and both univeralists and relativists can cite considerable evidence to support either position (Odlin, forthcoming). In Pavlenko's analysis, emotion has culture-specific and language-specific dimensions that can influence acquisition. Indeed, other evidence indicates that avoidance behaviors sometimes arise from taboos in the native language. Haas (1951), for example, cites the reluctance of speakers of Nootka to use the word *such* since the English form is phonetically similar to a Nootka word for the vagina, and similar instances of avoidance by Thai speakers are cited in the same article. As an alternative to avoidance, native language euphemisms and related speech acts may sometimes be translated in order to get around taboos (Odlin, 1998).

If there exist language-specific affective codings and if they can influence how learners acquire the target language, the problem of personal identity raised in the earlier quotation from Shen (1989) intersects in crucial ways with the problem of language transfer. The most obvious area where affect can matter is no doubt pragmatic transfer. Adults speaking their native language have a repertoire enabling them to choose how polite and how expressive to be, even if they do not always choose the best options for a given occasion. Learning to speak a second language normally requires learning a repertoire at least somewhat different in how affect is coded, and difficulties may arise either from "being at a loss for words" or from using a pragmatic routine acceptable in the native language but not in the target language. Olshtain (1983) contrasts the perceived need for apologies felt by native speakers of Russian, English, and Hebrew. For speakers of English, she found, there can be a problem of sounding too apologetic when speaking Hebrew, whereas for Hebrew speakers of English, the danger may come from not sounding apologetic enough. Adopting new pragmatic routines seems to entail the issue of identity raised by Shen with regard to written discourse. If so, the native language may not simply be a cognitive filter constraining hypotheses about the target language: it may also be an affective filter.

Although relativistic approaches will probably inform many future investigations of transfer, there will be a need to clarify just what conceptual transfer entails. It would be mistaken to equate a verbal concept in Ijaz's sense of the term with a cognitive concept. Otherwise, there are the pitfalls of a kind of relativism one might read into de Saussure's observation that words do not stand for pre-existing concepts. To illustrate this point, de Saussure provided a contrastive analysis of French *louer* and German *mieten,* where the former can designate either paying for or receiving payment for something, while the German verb cannot indicate the second meaning (de Saussure, 1915/59, p. 116). De Saussure's example naturally leads to a prediction that French learners of German will have difficulties with *mieten,* including the fact that they will have to learn a second German verb, *vermieten,* to speak accurately about cases of receiving payment. Likewise, German learners of French may have some difficulty in using *louer* to designate actions that in their native language are lexically distinct. The difference between French and German does not suggest any breathtaking conceptual gulf between the two languages, however. The notion of payment in either language inevitably implies both giving and receiving, and the different patterns of lexicalization in the two languages do not alter that fact. De Saussure apparently did not argue either for or against the existence of concepts independent of language, though he does suggest that such a concern belongs to psychology, not linguistics. Whether or not a linguist employs two different terms such as *concept* and *notion* (as was done in this paragraph), precision seems to require an assumption about different levels of cognition.

While Ijaz, Pavlenko, and others have demonstrated cross-linguistic influence involving concepts coded through language, it remains unclear how many conceptual levels are relevant and how "deep" transfer may run through those levels. Lucy (1992) stresses the difference between cases where non-verbal interpretations are affected by language-specific structures and cases where they are not. Whether particular structures in the native language might influence non-verbal memory or categorization in a learner's use of an interlanguage remains an empirical issue. It is worth considering, then, some structures and methods that future researchers might employ to address the issue. Lucy's own research focused on the mass–count distinction in Yucatec and in English, and to study differences in monolinguals' cognitive patterns, he employed verbal and non-verbal tasks involving pictures as well as sorting tasks, all of which helped to show differences in non-verbal categorization and memory. Similar contrasts in mass–count noun systems could certainly be explored in transfer research (and a natural starting point for such research would be, of course, to look at interlanguage Spanish noun phrases used by those Yucatec speakers who have only an intermediate proficiency in Spanish). Writing about the noun classifier system of Yucatec, Lucy notes the following intriguing parallel: "the classifiers resemble the category of aspect in the verb phrase which gives the logical or temporal perspective being applied to or presupposed of the predicate. Numeral classifiers give the logical or spatial perspective being applied to or presupposed of the noun phrase complement" (p. 74). It is also worth noting that the study by Pederson et al. (1998) of spatial constructs used methods also employed in second language research (e.g., Bongaerts, Kellerman, and Bentlage, 1987).

Spatial and temporal constructs thus seem promising sites for future research exploring the connection between transfer and relativism. Indeed, the analyses of Kellerman (1995) and Slobin (1993) regarding constraints on transfer point in the same direction, even though their stance on relativism is somewhat more qualified than the research discussed in this section. In the case of aspect, there are frequent overlaps with other categories including tense and mood. The latter category also seems a promising one for future research. Klee and Ocampo (1995) found Quechua influence on Spanish involving evidentiality, a verb category important in Quechua as well as many other languages since it concerns speakers' evaluation of evidence (Givón, 1984), and thus there might be non-verbal cognitive effects related to linguistic coding.

If, as seems likely, future transfer research focuses sharply on the question of relativism, there will still be a need for universalist approaches. Indeed, Lucy and other researchers recognize typology as the natural link between universalist and relativist approaches. Categories such as aspect have universal as well as language-specific dimensions, and none should be neglected (cf. Chung and Timberlake, 1985; Comrie, 1976; Slobin, 1993). At the same time, much of what is interesting about cross-linguistic influence involves the variations in outlook that language learners show, and relativist investigations may say a great deal about such variations.

12 The Age Factor and Language Transfer

For people who do not read second language research it may often seem self-evident that children learn a second language more easily than adults do. In fact, many of those who believe whole-heartedly that "younger is better" can give interesting anecdotal evidence to support their belief. On the other hand, the growing specialist literature on the subject shows the complexity of the issues related to age and acquisition (e.g., Birdsong, 1999; Long, 1990; see also Hyltenstam and Abrahamsson, this volume). Not surprisingly, cross-linguistic influence figures prominently in the problems investigated (e.g., Singleton, 1989). If it is true that younger is better, perhaps adults show different patterns of transfer. Alternatively, if age differences matter less than is commonly supposed, perhaps the native language plays more or less the same role for both adult and child bilinguals. Whatever the correct account of transfer and the age factor turns out be (and that account still seems very far in the future), it clearly has major implications for other concerns in second language research, including the role of universals and the problem of fossilization.

One name often used as a cover term for age issues in second language research is the Critical Period Hypothesis. As Birdsong (1999) notes, there is really more than one hypothesis which researchers have formulated, but a common question they address is whether or not there exists some cut-off point in a person's life beyond which it becomes impossible to achieve nativelike proficiency in another language. In his survey of varying approaches to the Critical Period Hypothesis, Birdsong lists several explanations including the following: a loss of neural plasticity in the learner's brain, a loss of access to Universal Grammar (or even a loss of UG itself), and a "maladaptive gain" in processing resources as a learner matures. The third of these accounts focuses on the overall relation between language and cognition. The problem-solving approaches that adults use in other aspects of life can also be used in second language acquisition – but perhaps at a cost. For example, the deductive reasoning used in many kinds of problem solving can also help in analyzing unfamiliar grammatical patterns in the new language. Even so, the strain on neural processing resources to perform such analyses may make it harder to adopt simpler but ultimately more successful learning strategies, ones presumably used by young children. In the section after this, a developmental argument made by Krashen (1983) with regard to cross-linguistic influence will be discussed.

The above explanations all have some supporting evidence, but each also fails in some respects, as do other accounts. In fact, considerable counter-evidence suggests that there may not actually be a critical period in the first place. If there really is no cut-off point, there might still exist significant age-related effects, but in that case some of the proposed explanations become less likely (e.g., total loss of access to Universal Grammar). Pronunciation might seem to be one area in which to find strong support for a critical period: after all, children often seem to have an easier time with the sound system of a new language. Beyond anecdotal evidence, some researchers have looked closely at the fossilized pronunciation of many adult bilinguals and inferred the existence of a critical period, though there has not been complete agreement about just how early on the period may end – whether early adolescence or somewhere around age 6, for example, is the cut-off point, or perhaps somewhat later (cf. Long, 1990; Scovel, 1988). However, there have been other studies suggesting that adults can achieve nativelike pronunciation, some of the most recent work coming from Bongaerts (1999) and his colleagues. The researchers taped several adult native speakers of Dutch whose English pronunciation proved to be indistinguishable from that of speakers of British English when the samples were played for listeners in England. Moreover, a comparable group of speakers of French as a second language proved to be impossible to distinguish from native speakers of French. One inherent problem in these and other studies is the uncertainty of whether the non-native speakers taped could, to use Long's phrase, "fool all of the raters all of the time" (1990, p. 267). Yet despite such inevitable sampling problems, it is clear that negative transfer and other inhibiting factors play a minimal role if any in the pronunciation of such highly proficient learners.

Bongaerts concedes that such individuals are few and far between, but no matter how few, they do challenge the notion of a critical period for acquiring nativelike second language pronunciation. Further difficulty for such a notion is evident in work by Flege (1999) and others on pronunciation. Flege, Murray, and MacKay (1995) found that immigrants to Canada from Italy showed age differences in their pronunciation of English, but not ones that accord well with the notion of a critical period. For one thing, some individuals who had arrived in Canada well before age 6 had accents detectable to native speakers of English. More seriously still, there was a strong relation between the age of arrival and the degree of accentedness judged by each rater. While such a correlation does support the notion of age-related differences in pronunciation, it also suggests that neither age 6 nor any subsequent stage marks a drastic cut-off point. Although other factors can also contribute to a foreign accent, cross-linguistic influence often plays a major role, and the Canadian studies indirectly suggest that age of arrival interacts with transfer.

There have also been claims that a cut-off point exists for the acquisition of nativelike morphology and syntax (e.g., Patkowski, 1980), but once again some evidence calls into question the credibility of any version of the Critical Period Hypothesis. A study by Coppetiers (1987) has often been cited to argue for a critical period, as this investigation focused on individuals extremely proficient in French as a second language. Coppetiers found substantial differences between his sample of near-native speakers and a group of native speakers of French in their intuitions of certain syntactic structures. Nevertheless, a counter-study by Birdsong (1992) of a different sample of near-native speakers identified several individuals whose intuitions of French syntax were not substantially different from those of native speakers. As with the Bongaerts studies, one can always wonder whether the near-natives in Birdsong's investigation would invariably perform as they did in the study; it is possible, for example, that these individuals might produce non-native grammatical forms under certain conditions (e.g., great fatigue). Even so, the work of Bongaerts, Birdsong, and others suggests that the gap between native and near-native proficiency is at the very least much smaller than has often been supposed.

The results of such work on second language pronunciation and grammar accordingly call into question whether there is a cut-off in second language acquisition. Unless researchers can succeed in showing that there is a critical period that has subtle but real effects on the acquisition process, explanations of any age-related differences will have to take another form, quite possibly invoking multiple causes. Birdsong (1999) deems it conceivable "that the attested straight-line age function in L2A over the lifespan is the product of different causal mechanisms along the way, that is, the result of developmental factors up to the end of maturation, and of nondevelopmental factors thereafter" (p. 12) If the notion of a critical period is ultimately salvageable, the native language might prove to be the underlying difficulty in all cases. On the other hand, if Birdsong's speculation is correct, the role of transfer in age-related effects will probably be one contributing factor – but only one among several others.

Whatever the outcome of the critical period debate, the relation between cross-linguistic influence and age-related factors appears likely to be complex.

Even so, one supposition about transfer seems possible to rule out now: namely, that transfer is inevitable in child bilingualism. Children who start acquiring two languages in early childhood have sometimes shown little or no mixing of their languages, though some kinds of mixing (including what might be called transfer) do arise, as seen in studies described by Odlin (1989). In fact, the simultaneous acquisition of two languages may have more in common with first than with second language acquisition. Writing about a child learning Dutch and English simultaneously, de Houwer (1990) states, "it seems that Katie can, so to speak, be seen as two monolingual children in one" (p. 339). Very few other studies have identified bilingual children quite like Katie, yet however rare such cases are, they imply that cross-linguistic influence may be inevitable only when a second language begins to develop and only after the processes of primary language acquisition are well underway.

Up to this point, the comparison of first and second language acquisition has proceeded with the tacit assumption that the differences in social context have little bearing on the issues. However, some observations of one child language researcher show the risk inherent in discounting social factors. Slobin (1993) lists a number of advantages that child languages learners normally enjoy: "They are young . . . Their communication is not vital to their survival . . . Their communicative intentions do not seriously outstrip their communicative capacities . . . They are learning the social functions of language along with the language itself" (p. 240). Slobin's observations suggest some difficulties in comparing the successes of adults and children. For example, adults who learn English in order to practice medicine in, say, Britain or the United States will require a specialist vocabulary that neither adults nor children in the target language community usually know. Even in primary language settings, social variation affects acquisition in a variety of ways (e.g., Heath, 1983), but the kinds of target language competence that adults need will generally vary even more. In the case of medical terminology, positive transfer may prove especially important for speakers of languages sharing many of the Latin and Greek words used by English-speaking doctors. Accordingly, there are real problems in trying to compare the importance of positive transfer for some adults and for bilingual children. The comparability problem is not restricted to lexis, either. Highly literate adults will likely prove more adept at writing in genres shared in the discourse traditions of historically connected languages, as in the case of writing summaries (Hatzitheodorou, 1994). Once again, comparing adults and children in terms of the possible effects of positive transfer seems difficult if not impossible.

The social differences seen in the acquisition of literacy show the danger of simplistic conclusions about the relation between age and language transfer. Even assuming a highly parallel development of pronunciation and grammar is open to question. Flege, Yeni-Komshian, and Liu (1999) studied a large sample of Korean speakers who had come to the United States at varying ages, and as in other studies, those who had arrived at younger ages tended to have more nativelike pronunciation. The authors attribute the success of the younger learners to a different pattern of interaction between Korean and English. Age-related differences were also evident in the grammaticality intuitions of the child and adult bilinguals, but Flege et al. find that educational differences and other social factors play a much greater role in such variation in comparison with what was seen in pronunciation. Accordingly, the interaction of age, social variation, and language transfer seems likely to differ from one linguistic subsystem to the next.

13 Transfer in Trilingual and Multilingual Settings

The study by Dušková cited earlier indicates that the much greater similarity of Czech to Russian than of Czech to English affects learners' judgments about what may be transferable. Some work has been done explicitly on the distances that learners perceive (e.g., Schweers, 1993), but the implications for transfer have been studied in the greatest detail in research in which the target language is a third, not a second, language.

Studies conducted on both sides of the border between Nigeria and Cameroon have been among the most interesting investigations of trilingualism, since there has been a great deal of contact involving the languages of two former colonial powers as well as several indigenous languages. In studies of the acquisition of French and English, Chumbow (1981) found their relative similarity leading to more frequent cross-linguistic influence than did Ngemba and Yoruba. Thus, for example, in his examination of sources of pronunciation errors in French as a third language, Chumbow found over twice as many English-inspired types as of types due to Ngemba influence. Although the cross-linguistic similarity (or lack thereof) is a powerful factor, Chumbow notes others including one mentioned earlier: the influence of African languages varied according to how proficient individuals were, city-dwellers using them less often than rural people. Chumbow's results are in general consonant with those of a study of learner intuitions in Cameroon by Ahukana, Lund, and Gentile (1981), as described by Odlin (1989). Other similar studies are discussed by Ringbom (1987).

Ringbom's own work on native speakers of Finnish and Swedish in Finland (whom he terms "Finns" and "Swedes" respectively) offers especially clear evidence of the importance of language distance. Looking at hundreds of writing samples in English from both groups, he found that the two languages were involved in many lexical errors but in different ways. The Finns produced many transfer errors based on both Finnish and Swedish, whereas the errors of the Swedes almost always reflected Swedish influence (and this despite years of study of Finnish by the Swedes in school). Moreover, the two groups also differed in the extent to which they employed forms cognate between Swedish and English. Swedes occasionally used low-frequency forms such as *marmor* ('marble') as in *A new house made of marmor* (Ringbom, 1987,

p. 146). However, the Finns proved far more willing to assume that any Swedish form was cognate with an English one, even in the case of frequent words such as *lösa* ('solve'), with the result often being false friends as in *This couldn't lose the problem* (p. 157). For the Finns, forms from their native language only rarely seemed to be possible cognates, as in *Our perils will see what we have had and will understand us better* (p. 162), where Finnish *perillinen* means 'descendant.' On the other hand, the Finns often drew on both Finnish and Swedish in what Ringbom calls "loan translations," as in *Weather moves quickly from the other kind to the other kind* (p. 125), which reflects the Finnish repetition of the same word (*toinen*, 'other'), which is semantically equivalent to *one . . . another* (*toinen . . . toinen*). Swedes likewise produced many loan translations, although these were nearly always based on their native language and only rarely on Finnish.

The fact that the Finns drew rather freely from both of their previously acquired languages indicates that their estimation of the language distances between English, Swedish, and Finnish is somewhat different from the cross-linguistic perceptions of the Swedes. Even though Swedish was used by both groups, the Finns showed a greater willingness to believe that there were many formal similarities between the two Germanic languages. At the same time, these learners also were influenced by Finnish even while the Swedes were not. Accordingly, the following generalization seems viable: a very different language can influence the acquisition of another, but mainly in cases where it is a learner's native language. If this generalization is correct, one implication naturally follows: it is not just cross-linguistic distance that matters in transfer, but also the specific acquisition history of every learner.

The importance of individual learner histories for transfer is also evident in a recent study of trilingualism in Belgium (Dewaele, 1998) in which the target language was French and the native language Dutch. For some of the learners, French was the third language they had studied (English being the second), whereas for a different group French was the second language (with English being the third). The transfer errors for the two groups differed primarily in frequency: the L2 French group produced errors influenced by English but their native language was the primary source of cross-linguistic influence, whereas the L3 French group showed fewer Dutch-based innovations and far more based on their second language (i.e., English). Another result in Dewaele's study also points to the importance of learner histories in that the L2 French group produced a higher proportion of intralingual errors, where French characteristics, not English or Dutch ones, influenced learners, as in:

> Aors euh dans la Wallonie on a le concurrence entre Filmnet, Tévéclub, et Canal Plus pour euh *pouver* [puve] entrer dans le cable. (TL form: *pouvoir*)
>
> "And then ugh in French-speaking Belgium you have competition between Filmnet, Tévéclub, and Canal Plus to ugh to be able to get into the cable (network)." (p. 478)

The L3 French group also produced intralingual errors (though not as many), yet in both groups interlingual (i.e., transfer) errors were more numerous. Even so, cases such as *pouver* are valuable reminders of the importance of the target language as a source for interlanguage constructions (cf. Laufer-Dvorkin, 1991).

One limiting factor in Dewaele's study is the close cross-linguistic distances involved. Dutch and English share much basic vocabulary, and French and English overlap a great deal in the overall extent of the lexicon. The Belgian research certainly indicates the importance of learner histories, but it remains unclear whether language distance would matter more if one of the two previously acquired languages in such a study were structurally more distant from the target language.

In cases involving more than two previously learned languages, the possible interactions between the languages may be even more complex, and the methodological complications of studying such cases are certainly greater, as seen in a study by Singleton (1987) of the spoken French of a learner named Philip. A native speaker of English, Philip had also learned some Latin and Irish in school, although it appears that his proficiency in these languages was marginal. On the other hand, he had acquired considerably more spoken (and written) Spanish, and Singleton deems this language to be the chief source of influence on Philip's French, although transfer from English figures in his speech, as well. There may also be influence from Latin and Irish, although these are more problematic; even so, Philip's self-reports indicate that he would sometimes "Frenchify" a Latin word. In the appendix to the study, examples of influence solely from English and solely from Spanish are listed, but also cases showing various combinations of possible influences: English/Irish, English/Spanish, Spanish/Latin, English/Irish/Spanish, English/Irish/Latin, English/Spanish/Latin, and English/Irish/Spanish/Latin. The idea that more than one source language can contribute to an interlanguage construction is certainly plausible, and in fact some researchers have also seen this as likely in trilingual settings (Ho and Platt, 1993; Leung, 1998). Nevertheless, as the combination of possibly contributing languages grows, so does the methodological difficulty of deciding whether an error is due to, for example, a combination of English/Irish/Spanish or of English/Irish/Latin.

Singleton deliberately excluded cases where Philip made no attempt to Frenchify words from other languages, but such intrusions also characterize interlanguage and perhaps play an especially large role in the behavior of multilingual learners. Especially illuminating are the introspective studies of three second language researchers, Richard Schmidt, Larry Selinker, and the late Sarah Williams, of their own transfer patterns (Schmidt and Frota, 1986; Selinker and Baumgartner-Cohen, 1995; Williams and Hammarberg, 1998). Although any kind of self-report data will present interpretive problems, the reflections of individuals with unusually high metalinguistic awareness can shed light on some of the complexities of cross-linguistic influence. Schmidt's detailed diary of his experiences does not focus on transfer, but it provides striking examples of cross-linguistic influence from English and Arabic, the former his native language and the latter a second language he had spoken for many years. Not surprisingly, there were cases where he placed adjectives in front of nouns, the normal order in English, whereas Portuguese adjectives normally follow nouns. On the other hand, he notes with puzzlement some influences from Arabic, a language much less similar to Portuguese than is English: "This morning in class I said Arabic *yimkin* [Arabic "perhaps"] without realizing it wasn't Portuguese until L [his teacher] looked at me and smiled in noncomprehension" (p. 255). He also notes an article error that no doubt has its source in Arabic syntax.

The Selinker study is also based on a diary record of a native speaker of English, but in this case the target language is German, which the author had studied before, but with a lapse of three years before using it again during the time of the diary-keeping. Other languages studied that he mentions are Hebrew and French, with both being influences on his German, as in the following examples (p. 117), with underlines added to indicate the intrusions:

- *Sie haben quellen <u>là-bas</u>.* (Intended meaning: *'They have springs there.'*)
- *<u>Tu as</u> mein Fax bekommen?* (Intended meaning: *'Did you get my fax?'*)
- <u>eyze</u> Denkmal . . . ? For *welche Denkmal . . .* ? (Intended meaning: *'which monument . . . ?'*)

The first two examples show French intrusions but differ in that the second may owe something to a phonetic similarity between French *tu* and German *du* (cognate forms of the familiar second person pronoun). In the third case, the intrusion comes from Hebrew and there is no phonetic similarity. Selinker and Baumgartner-Cohen list several possible factors that may be at work in such cases, including the semantic plausibility of the intrusion, the phonetic similarity of the intrusion to a target language form, a common functional class, transfer of training, and reinforcing influences from the native language. In discussing these and other possible factors, the authors speculate that the native language has a status rather different from other languages as a source of influence, and that much of the impetus for the intrusions comes from a "talk foreign" cognitive mode.

Support for something like the "talk foreign" mode is evident in the Williams and Hammarberg study, which in fact offers a more detailed explanation for the difference between influences from the native language and other languages known to the learner. Williams was, once again, a native speaker of English, and had some proficiency in a number of other languages including German, French, and Italian. The target language focused on in this study was Swedish, with English and German being the chief influences. Looking at over 800 instances of "language switches" in Williams's speech, the authors conclude that English has what they call an instrumental role, whereas German has a supplier role. The cases of English switches consisted mainly of instances of self-repair and similar functions, or metalinguistic comments on what Williams had said in Swedish or to get assistance. On the other hand, it was "almost always German that supplied material for L3 lexical construction (other than Swedish itself)" (p. 318). The supplier role arises from varied factors, four of which Williams and Hammarberg consider especially important: the learner's relative proficiency in each of the languages, the cross-linguistic distance of the languages (which they refer to as "typology"), the recency of each of the languages in the learner's active repertory, and whether or not the learner has a native speaker's competence in the language. The authors acknowledge that understanding the exact interplay of these four and other factors will require much more investigation.

The three diary studies described here raise difficult issues not only for transfer but also for second language research generally. In the Schmidt and Selinker studies, there are cases of intrusions from languages very dissimilar to both the target and native languages, which clearly complicates any contrastive predictions in trilingual settings. On the other hand, the nature of the influence of German and English in the Williams study suggests that the processing roles associated with each previously learned language can be quite distinct, and such differences suggest that performance as well as competence can greatly affect the language mixing seen in trilingual data. At present there seems to be no theory or methodology capable of showing the extent to which performance as opposed to competence is at work.

14 Transfer and Cognitive Models

As stated in the introduction, the problems related to cross-linguistic influence are so varied and so complex that there does not exist any really detailed theory of language transfer. On the other hand, a good deal of second language research addresses more general questions on language and cognition, including what role transfer plays. This section looks at the following questions: (i) how transfer works in speech production; (ii) whether transfer is involved in "knowing" vs. "knowing about" language; and (iii) how much the learning involved in transfer resembles patterns of learning beyond second language acquisition.

14.1 Transfer and speech production

As noted earlier, there has never been good reason to associate cross-linguistic influence with behaviorist theories of language, and for over twenty years some second language researchers have attempted to specify the overall working of transfer in a cognitivist framework (Sajavaara, 1981; Sharwood-Smith, 1979, 1986). Sharwood-Smith emphasized the creative construction that underlies much cross-linguistic influence, his models being among the first to conceive of such influence in terms of information processing. In his attempt to make more explicit the notion of "strategy," his characterization of transfer makes a point similar to one raised in the preceding section: namely, that the relation between performance and competence is a complex one. In contrast to Sharwood-Smith's focus on models of cross-linguistic influence, recent proposals by De Bot (1992) attempt to build on a highly elaborated model of the human speech capacity (Levelt, 1989) with special reference to bilinguals. Although De Bot's model does not address transfer exclusively, it recognizes the importance of cross-linguistic influence, and it, too, reflects some problems discussed in this chapter. A completely adequate model (which De Bot does not claim to have achieved) must take language distance into account. He argues that when the languages involved are highly similar, there is no need to posit separate knowledge stores, in contrast to what is necessary in the case of highly different languages. As De Bot notes, however, much remains unclear about the implications of having separately stored knowledge systems – a problem that seems especially difficult in the case of historically related languages that are nevertheless quite different (e.g., English and Russian). Also problematic is how such a model will treat differences in concepts, such as the three-way distance contrast seen in many languages, as in Spanish *aquí* ('here'), *ahí* ('there'), and *allá* ('yonder'), as opposed to the two-way contrast in Dutch *hier/daar* ('here'/'there'). Further work on conceptual transfer will certainly have to address such problems.

14.2 Declarative and procedural knowledge

The difficulties that older children and adults normally experience with a new language contrast strikingly with the apparently effortless facility that they often show in using even highly complex structures in their native language. While automaticity coupled with accuracy seems beyond the reach of adult language learners, the role of transfer in this regard remains unclear. Krashen (1983) distinguishes "acquisition" from "learning," with the former notion more or less equivalent to what other researchers have called "implicit" or "procedural" knowledge, and the latter notion more or less equivalent to "explicit" or "declarative" knowledge. For Krashen, cross-linguistic influence cannot play much of a role in "acquisition," which proceeds much as it does for monolingual children. The native language can and does play a role, he acknowledges, but primarily as one of the phenomena associated with "learning." Möhle and Raupach (1989), however, take a diametrically opposed stance, arguing that very little transfer involves declarative knowledge (i.e., "learning") at least in cases of instructed second language acquisition. Because procedural knowledge develops only gradually, they argue, the classroom environment can foster declarative knowledge that eventually becomes procedural (something Krashen has denied); furthermore, the native language can facilitate procedural knowledge when it is similar to the target language. Möhle and Raupach concede that some procedural knowledge will constitute negative transfer when the cross-linguistic correspondences are less than exact; even so, they clearly ascribe a more central role to transfer than Krashen does.

14.3 Language transfer and lateral transfer

As noted above, Sharwood-Smith (1979) outlined a cognitive model for cross-linguistic influence, and in doing so he drew on work on general learning theory (e.g., Ausubel, 1968). As an alternative to the stimulus-response approaches of behaviorism, cognitive models emphasize the importance of characteristics such as clarity and stability in the knowledge base that people draw upon to solve new learning problems, and Ausubel terms the operation of such previous knowledge "transfer." Thus it is natural to wonder about the relation between language transfer and transfer of learning in other contexts.

Singley and Anderson (1989) discuss learning in terms of two types of transfer: vertical and lateral. The former requires a hierarchical plan of action to use skills already learned in order to build new ones showing greater complexity. One example the authors provide is a proposed hierarchy involved in solving mathematical equations. In contrast to vertical transfer, lateral transfer involves reapplying skills at the same level of complexity, and one example they cite is second language acquisition where French and English would be either the native or target language. Unfortunately, they do not cite any actual second language research, and they primarily discuss a series of experiments where individuals learned to adjust to new editing programs. Comparing positive and negative transfer in the transitions from one text editor to the next, Singley and Anderson conclude that the former had a much greater effect in their experiments. Although the evidence draws on a very different domain, it is compatible with the claims of Ringbom (1992, 1987) that positive transfer has a greater potential to affect acquisition. It is tempting to identify vertical transfer with the kind of developmental pattern seen in first and second language acquisition, such as has been observed in the development of syntactic negation (Odlin, 1989). Likewise, the parallels between the positive transfer seen in text editing and that seen in learning foreign language vocabulary make it natural to wonder how much the notion of lateral transfer may be applicable in both cases. Even so, there are good reasons to be cautious, one of them being Singley and Anderson's assumption (p. 198) that the learning of grammatical rules in a foreign language constitutes one kind of declarative knowledge. As the discussion above indicates, however, the relation between transfer and procedural and declarative knowledge remains an open question in second language acquisition.

The three problems related to cognitive modeling discussed in this section are by no means the only ones relevant to transfer, and relevant research takes even more diverse forms, as seen in research on neural networks that has attempted to develop computer modeling of interlingual identifications (Gasser, 1990). It may be wondered just how applicable such modeling is to cases of acquisition involving actual people, especially with regard to questions such as affect and linguistic relativity, discussed earlier. Even so, such research may help develop more plausible models relevant to human cognition and transfer.

15 Conclusion

This chapter has considered a wide range of phenomena associated with cross-linguistic influence, although space does not permit much of a look at some related topics that are also important (e.g., effects of the native language on spelling the target language). From the complexity of the issues addressed, however, it should come as no surprise that there does not yet exist any comprehensive theory of language transfer – and the appearance of one any time soon seems unlikely. Even so, the last fifty years or so have seen considerable progress on several empirical issues that are prerequisites for any viable theory. Equally important has been the growing clarity about methodology: several researchers have formulated falsifiable claims about cross-linguistic influence and have subjected the claims to rigorous tests. Transfer is evident in all linguistic subsystems, and when a highly similar language is the target, the native language can greatly facilitate acquisition. These empirical findings are reasonably clear, but understanding whatever underlies the very real effects of transfer remains elusive, as Dewaele (1998) and others have observed.

The complexity of cross-linguistic influence partially explains the controversy that has sometimes surrounded the topic. When second language researchers started looking more closely at the differences between certain contrastive predictions and actual learner difficulties, the promise of contrastive analysis seemed to some to be illusory (Odlin, 1989). Even so, study after study has shown real effects of the native language, and researchers increasingly realize that good predictions require close study of what learners understand and produce. Looking at the effects of explicit instruction on question making in a second language, Spada and Lightbown (1999) argue that making learners aware of cross-linguistic differences will help with certain difficulties in the target language. Support for that claim is evident in a study of pronunciation already discussed (Bongaerts, 1999), and also in an investigation of the effects of contrastive instruction in certain areas of syntax (Kupferberg and Olshtain, 1996). It seems likely that further research will lead to similar results.

REFERENCES

Abdullah, K. and Jackson, H. 1998: Idioms and the language learner: contrasting English and Syrian Arabic. *Languages in Contrast*, 1, 83–107.

Ahukana, J., Lund, N., and Gentile, R. 1981: Inter- and intra-lingual interference effects in learning a third language. *Modern Language Journal*, 65, 281–7.

Andersen, R. 1983: Transfer to somewhere. In S. Gass and L. Selinker (eds), *Language Transfer in Language Learning*. Rowley, MA: Newbury House, 177–201.

Andersen, R. and Shirai, Y. 1996: The primacy of aspect in first and second language acquisition: the pidgin–creole connection. In W. Ritchie (ed.),

Handbook of Second Language Acquisition. New York: Academic Press, 527–70.

Ard, J. and Homburg, T. 1993: Verification of language transfer. In S. Gass and L. Selinker (eds), *Language Transfer in Language Learning*. Amsterdam: John Benjamins, 47–70.

Ausubel, D. 1968: *Educational Psychology: A Cognitive View*. New York: Holt, Rinehart, and Winston.

Bardovi-Harlig, K. 1992: The relationship between form and meaning: a cross-sectional study of tense and aspect in the interlanguage of learners of English as a second language. *Applied Psycholinguistics*, 13, 253–78.

Bickerton, D. and Givón, T. 1976: Pidginization and syntactic change: from SXV and VSX to SVX. In C. W. Stanford Stever and S. Mufwene (eds), *Papers from the Parasession on Diachronic Syntax*. Chicago: Chicago Linguistic Society, 9–39.

Birdsong, D. 1992: Ultimate attainment in second language acquisition. *Language*, 68, 706–55.

Birdsong, D. 1999: Introduction: whys and why nots for the Critical Period Hypothesis in second language acquisition. In D. Birdsong (ed.), *Second Language Acquisition and the Critical Period Hypothesis*. Mahwah, NJ: Lawrence Erlbaum Associates, 1–22.

Bley-Vroman, R. 1989: What is the logical problem of foreign language learning? In S. Gass and J. Schachter (eds), *Linguistic Perspectives on Second Language Acquisition*. Cambridge: Cambridge University Press, 41–68.

Bloch, J. and Chi, L. 1995: A comparison of the use of citations in Chinese and English academic discourse. In D. Belcher and G. Braine (eds), *Academic Writing in a Second Language: Essays on Research and Pedagogy*. Norwood, NJ: Ablex, 231–74.

Bongaerts, T. 1999: Ultimate attainment in L2 pronunciation: the case of very advanced late L2 learners. In D. Birdsong (ed.), *Second Language Acquisition and the Critical Period Hypothesis*. Mahwah, NJ: Lawrence Erlbaum Associates, 133–59.

Bongaerts, T., Kellerman, E., and Bentlage, A. 1987: Perspective and proficiency in L2 referential communication. *Studies in Second Language Acquisition*, 9, 171–200.

Chambers, J. K. and Trudgill, P. 1980: *Dialectology*. Cambridge: Cambridge University Press.

Chomsky, N. 1995: *The Minimalist Program*. Cambridge, MA: MIT Press.

Chumbow, B. 1981: The mother tongue hypothesis in a multilingual setting. In J.-G. Savard and L. Laforge (eds), *Proceedings of the 5th Congress of the International Association of Applied Linguistics*. Quebec: Laval University Press.

Chung, S. and Timberlake, A. 1985: Tense, aspect, and mood. In T. Shopen (ed.), *Syntactic Description and Linguistic Typology. Vol. III*. Cambridge: Cambridge University Press, 202–58.

Clark, E. 1978: Locationals: existential, locative, and possessive constructions. In J. Greenberg (ed.), *Universals of Human Language*. Stanford, CA: Stanford University Press, 85–126.

Comrie, B. 1976: *Aspect*. Cambridge: Cambridge University Press.

Connor, U. 1996: *Contrastive Rhetoric*. Cambridge: Cambridge University Press.

Cook, V. 1994: Universal Grammar and the learning and teaching of second languages. In T. Odlin (ed.), *Perspectives on Pedagogical Grammar*. Cambridge: Cambridge University Press, 25–48.

Cook, V. 2000: Is *transfer* the right word? Paper presented at International Pragmatics Association, Budapest, July 11.

Coppetiers, R. 1987: Competence differences between native and non-native speakers. *Language*, 63, 544–73.

De Bot, K. 1992: A bilingual production model: Levelt's "Speaking" model adapted. *Applied Linguistics*, 13, 1–24.

Dechert, H. and Raupach, M. (eds) 1989: *Transfer in Language Production*. Norwood, NJ: Ablex.

de Houwer, A. 1990: *The Acquisition of Two Languages from Birth: A Case Study*. Cambridge: Cambridge University Press.

de Saussure, F. 1915/59: *Course in General Linguistics*. New York: McGraw-Hill.

Dewaele, J.-M. 1998: Lexical inventions: French interlanguage as L2 versus L3. *Applied Linguistics*, 19, 471–90.

Duff, P. 1993: Syntax, semantics, and SLA: the convergence of possessive and existential constructions. *Studies in Second Language Acquisition*, 15, 1–34.

Dulay, H. and Burt, M. 1974: Natural sequences in child second language acquisition. *Language Learning*, 24, 37–53.

Dulay, H., Burt, M., and Krashen, S. 1982: *Language Two*. New York: Oxford University Press.

Dušková, L. 1984: Similarity – an aid or hindrance in foreign language learning? *Folia Linguistica*, 18, 103–15.

Eckman, F. 1996: A functional-typological approach to second language acquisition theory. In W. Ritchie and T. K. Bhatia (eds), *Handbook of Second Language Acquisition*. San Diego: Academic Press, 195–211.

Elo, A. 1993: Le Francais parlé par les étudiants finnophones et suedophones. Ph.D. dissertation. University of Turku.

Eubank, L. 1993/4: On the transfer of parametric values in L2 development. *Language Acquisition*, 3, 183–208.

Ferguson, C. 1959: Diglossia. *Word*, 15, 325–40.

Filppula, M. 1986: *Some Aspects of Hiberno-English in a Functional Sentence Perspective*. Joensuu: Joensuu Publications in the Humanities.

Filppula, M. 1999: *The Grammar of Irish English*. London: Routledge.

Flege, J. 1999: Age of learning and second language speech. In D. Birdsong (ed.), *Second Language Acquisition and the Critical Period Hypothesis*. Mahwah, NJ: Lawrence Erlbaum Associates, 101–31.

Flege, J., Murray, M., and MacKay, I. 1995: Factors affecting strength of perceived foreign accent in a second language. *Journal of the Acoustical Society of America*, 97, 3125–34.

Flege, J., Yeni-Komshian, G., and Liu, S. 1999: Age constraints on second language acquisition. *Journal of Memory and Language*, 41, 78–104.

Flynn, S. and Martohardjono, G. 1994: Mapping from the initial state to the final state: the separation of universal principles and language-specific principles. In B. Lust, M. Suner, and J. Whitman (eds), *Syntactic Theory and First Language Acquisition: Cross-Linguistic Perspectives. Vol. 1: Heads, Projections, and Learnability*. Hillsdale, NJ: Lawrence Erlbaum Associates, 319–35.

Gandour, J. and Harshman, R. 1978: Crosslanguage differences in tone perception: a multidimensional scaling investigation. *Language and Speech*, 21, 1–33.

Gass, S. 1979: Language transfer and universal grammatical relations. *Language Learning*, 29, 327–44.

Gass, S. 1996: Second language acquisition and linguistic theory: the role of language transfer. In W. Ritchie and T. K. Bhatia (eds), *Handbook of Second Language Acquisition*. San Diego: Academic Press, 317–45.

Gass, S. and Selinker, L. (eds) 1993: *Language Transfer in Language Learning*. Amsterdam: John Benjamins.

Gasser, M. 1990: Connectionism and universals in second language acquisition. *Studies in Second Language Acquisition*, 12, 179–99.

Giacobbe, J. 1992: A cognitive view of the role of L1 in the L2 acquisition process. *Second Language Research*, 8, 232–50.

Givón, T. 1984: *Syntax. Vol. I.* Amsterdam: John Benjamins.

Gregg, K. 1989: Second language acquisition theory: a generativist perspective. In S. Gass and J. Schachter (eds), *Linguistic Perspectives on Second Language Acquisition*. Cambridge: Cambridge University Press, 15–40.

Haas, M. 1951: Interlingual word taboos. *American Anthropologist*, 53, 338–44.

Haegeman, L. and Guéron, J. 1999: *English Grammar: A Generative Perspective*. Oxford: Blackwell.

Harris, J. 1984: Syntactic variation and dialect divergence. *Journal of Linguistics*, 20, 303–27.

Hatzitheodorou, A.-M. 1994: An analysis of summary writing by students of English as a second language. M.A. thesis. Ohio State University.

Haugen, E. 1966: Dialect, language, nation. *American Anthropologist*, 68, 922–35.

Heath, S. 1983: *Ways with Words*. Cambridge: Cambridge University Press.

Helms-Park, R. 2001: Evidence of lexical transfer in learner syntax: the acquisition of English causatives by speakers of Hindi-Urdu and Vietnamese. *Studies in Second Language Acquisition*, 23, 71–102.

Ho, M.-L. and Platt, J. 1993: *Dynamics of a Contact Continuum: Singaporean English*. Oxford: Oxford University Press.

Hyltenstam, K. 1984: The use of typological markedness conditions as predictors in second language acquisition. In R. Andersen (ed.), *Second Languages: A Cross-Linguistic Perspective*. Rowley, MA: Newbury House, 39–58.

Ijaz, I. H. 1986: Linguistic and cognitive determinants of lexical acquisition in a second language. *Language Learning*, 36, 401–51.

Jansen, B., Lalleman, J., and Muysken, P. 1981: The alternation hypothesis: acquisition of Dutch word order by Turkish and Moroccan foreign workers. *Language Learning*, 31, 315–36.

Jarvis, S. 1998: *Conceptual Transfer in the Interlanguage Lexicon*. Bloomington: Indiana University Linguistics Club.

Jarvis, S. 2000: Methodological rigor in the study of transfer: identifying L1 influence in the interlanguage lexicon. *Language Learning*, 50, 245–309.

Jarvis, S. 2002: Topic continuity in L2 English article use. *Studies in Second Language Acquisition*, 24, 387–418.

Jarvis, S. and Odlin, T. 2000: Morphological type, spatial reference, and language transfer. *Studies in Second Language Acquisition*, 22, 535–56.

Jin, H. G. 1994: Topic prominence and subject prominence in L2 acquisition. *Language Learning*, 44, 101–22.

Joergensen, J. N. and Kristensen, K. 1995: On boundaries in linguistic continua. *Language Variation and Change*, 7, 153–68.

Kamimoto, T., Shimura, A., and Kellerman, E. 1992: A second language classic reconsidered – the case of Schachter's avoidance. *Second Language Research*, 8, 251–77.

Kaplan, R. 1966/84: Cultural thought patterns and inter-cultural education. In S. Mackay (ed.), *Composing in a Second Language*. Rowley, MA: Newbury House, 43–62.

Kasper, G. 1992: Pragmatic transfer. *Second Language Research*, 8, 203–31.

Keesing, R. 1988: *Melanesian Pidgin and the Oceanic Substrate*. Stanford, CA: Stanford University Press.

Kellerman, E. 1977: Towards a characterization of the strategy of transfer in second language learning. *Interlanguage Studies Bulletin*, 21, 58–145.

Kellerman, E. 1978: Giving learners a break: native language intuitions about transferability. *Working Papers in Bilingualism*, 15, 59–92.

Kellerman, E. 1984: The empirical evidence for the influence of L1 on interlanguage. In A. Davies, C. Criper, and A. P. R. Howatt (eds), *Interlanguage*. Edinburgh: Edinburgh University Press, 98–122.

Kellerman, E. 1995: Crosslinguistic influence: transfer to nowhere? *Annual Review of Applied Linguistics*, 15, 125–50.

Kellerman, E. and Sharwood-Smith, M. 1986: *Cross-Linguistic Influence in Second Language Acquisition*. New York: Pergamon Press.

Kempf, M. 1975: A study of English proficiency level and the composition errors of incoming foreign students at the University of Cincinnati, 1969–1974. Ph.D. dissertation. Ohio State University.

Klee, C. and Ocampo, A. 1995: The expression of past reference in Spanish narratives of Spanish–English bilingual speakers. In C. Silva-Corvalán (ed.), *Spanish in Four Continents*. Washington, DC: Georgetown University Press, 52–70.

Klein, W. and Perdue, C. 1997: The Basic Variety (or: couldn't natural languages be much simpler?) *Second Language Research*, 13, 301–47.

Krashen, S. 1983: Newmark's "Ignorance Hypothesis" and current second language acquisition and theory. In S. Gass and L. Selinker (eds), *Language Transfer in Language Learning*. Rowley, MA: Newbury House, 135–53.

Kupferberg, I. and Olshtain, E. 1996: Explicit L2 instruction facilitates the acquisition of difficult L2 forms. *Language Awareness*, 5, 149–65.

Lado, R. 1957: *Linguistics Across Cultures*. Ann Arbor: University of Michigan Press.

Lakoff, G. 1987: *Women, Fire, and Dangerous Things: What Categories Reveal about the Mind*. Berkeley: University of California Press.

Laufer-Dvorkin, B. 1991: *Similar Lexical Forms in Interlanguage*. Tübingen: Gunter Narr.

Lazarus, R. 1991: Progress on a cognitive-motivational-relational theory of emotion. *American Psychologist*, 46, 819–34.

Leather, J. and James, A. 1996: Second language speech. In W. Ritchie and T. K. Bhatia (eds), *Handbook of Second Language Acquisition*. San Diego: Academic Press, 269–326.

Leung, I. Y.-K. 1998: Transfer between interlanguages. In A. Greenhill, M. Hughes, H. Littlefield, and H. Walsh (eds), *Proceedings of the 22nd Annual Boston University Conference on Language Development*, 2, 478–87.

Levelt, W. 1989: *Speaking: From Intention to Articulation*. Cambridge, MA: MIT Press.

Long, M. 1990: Maturational constraints on language development. *Studies in Second Language Acquisition*, 12, 251–85.

Lucy, J. 1992: *Grammatical Categories and Cognition*. Cambridge: Cambridge University Press.

Lutz, C. and White, G. 1986: The anthropology of emotions. *Annual Review of Anthropology*, 15, 405–36.

Master, P. 1987: A cross-linguistic interlanguage analysis of the acquisition of the English article system. Ph.D. dissertation. University of California at Los Angeles.

Meisel, J. M. 1997: The L2 Basic Variety as an I-language. *Second Language Research*, 13, 374–85.

Mesthrie, R. 1992: *English in Language Shift*. Cambridge: Cambridge University Press.

Mesthrie, R. and Dunne, T. 1990: Syntactic variation in language shift: the relative clause in South African Indian English. *Language Variation and Change*, 2, 31–56.

Migge, B. 1998: Substrate influence in the formation of the Surinamese Plantation Creole: a consideration of sociohistorical data and linguistic data from Ndyuka and Gbe. Ph.D. dissertation. Ohio State University.

Mohan, B. and Lo, W. A.-Y. 1985: Academic writing and Chinese students: transfer and developmental factors. *TESOL Quarterly*, 19, 515–34.

Möhle, D. and Raupach, M. 1989: Language transfer of procedural knowledge. In H. Dechert and M. Raupach (eds), *Transfer in Language Production*. Norwood, NJ: Ablex, 195–216.

Mori, Y. 1998: Effects of first language and phonological accessibility on kanji recognition. *Modern Language Journal*, 82, 69–82.

Mufwene, S. 1990: Transfer and the substrate hypothesis in creolistics. *Studies in Second Language Acquisition*, 12, 1–23.

Mufwene, S. 1998: What research on creole genesis can contribute to historical linguistics. In W. Schmid, J. Austin, and D. Stein (eds), *Historical Linguistics 1997*. Amsterdam: John Benjamins, 315–38.

Myers, S. 1992: In search of the genuine article: a cross-linguistic investigation of the development of the English article system in written compositions of adult ESL students. Ph.D. dissertation. Florida State University.

Nemser, W. 1971: *An Experimental Study of Phonological Interference in the English of Hungarians*. Bloomington: Indiana University Linguistics Club.

Odlin, T. 1989: *Language Transfer*. Cambridge: Cambridge University Press.

Odlin, T. 1990: Word order, metalinguistic awareness, and constraints on foreign language learning. In B. VanPatten and J. F. Lee. (eds), *Second Language Acquisition/Foreign Language Learning*. Clevedon: Multilingual Matters, 95–117.

Odlin, T. 1991: Irish English idioms and language transfer. *English World-Wide*, 12, 175–93.

Odlin, T. 1992: Transferability and linguistic substrates. *Second Language Research*, 8, 171–202.

Odlin, T. 1996: On the recognition of transfer errors. *Language Awareness*, 5, 166–78.

Odlin, T. 1997a: Bilingualism and substrate influence: a look at clefts and reflexives. In J. Kallen (ed.), *Focus on Ireland*. Amsterdam: John Benjamins, 35–50.

Odlin, T. 1997b: Hiberno-English: pidgin, creole, or neither? *CLCS Occasional Paper No. 49*. Centre for Language and Communication Studies, Trinity College Dublin.

Odlin, T. 1998: On the affective and cognitive bases for language transfer. In R. Cooper. (ed.), *Compare or Contrast?* Tampere: University of Tampere, 81–106.

Odlin, T. forthcoming: Language transfer and cross-linguistic studies: relativism, universalism, and the native language. In R. Kaplan (ed.), *The Oxford Handbook of Applied Linguistics*. New York: Oxford University Press.

O'Grady, W., Dobrovolsky, M., and Aronoff, M. 1993: *Contemporary Linguistics: An Introduction*. New York: St Martin's Press.

Oller, J. and Redding, E. 1971: Article usage and other language skills. *Language Learning*, 20, 183–9.

Olshtain, E. 1983: Sociocultural competence and language transfer: the case of apology. In S. Gass and L. Selinker (eds), *Language Transfer in*

Language Learning. Rowley, MA: Newbury House, 232–49.

Orr, G. 1987: Aspects of the second language acquisition of Chichewa noun class morphology. Ph.D. dissertation. University of California, Los Angeles.

Patkowski, M. 1980: The sensitive period for the acquisition of syntax in a second language. *Language Learning*, 30, 449–72.

Pavlenko, A. 1999: New approaches to concepts in bilingual memory. *Bilingualism, Language and Cognition*, 2, 209–30.

Pederson, E., Danziger, E., Wilkins, D., Levinson, S., Kita, S., and Senft, G. 1998: Semantic typology and spatial conceptualization. *Language*, 74, 557–89.

Pinker, S. 1994: *The Language Instinct: How the Mind Creates Language*. New York: Morrow.

Ringbom, H. 1987: *The Role of the First Language in Foreign Language Learning*. Clevedon: Multilingual Matters.

Ringbom, H. 1992: On L1 transfer in L2 comprehension and production. *Language Learning*, 42, 85–112.

Rosch, E. 1973: On the internal structure of perceptual and semantic categories. In T. Moore (ed.), *Cognitive Development and the Acquisition of Language*. New York: Academic Press, 95–121.

Rutherford, W. 1983: Language typology and language transfer. In S. Gass and L. Selinker (eds), *Language Transfer in Language Learning*. Rowley, MA: Newbury House, 358–70.

Sabban, A. 1982: *Gälisch–Englischer Sprachkontakt*. Heidelberg: Julius Groos.

Sajavaara, K. 1981: Psycholinguistic models, second-language acquisition, and contrastive analysis. In J. Fisiak (ed.), *Contrastive Linguistics and the Language Teacher*. Oxford: Pergamon Press, 87–120.

Schachter, J. 1974: An error in error analysis. *Language Learning*, 24, 205–14.

Schachter, J. 1988: Second language acquisition and its relation to universal grammar. *Applied Linguistics*, 9, 215–35.

Schachter, J. 1993: A new account of language transfer. In S. Gass and L. Selinker (eds), *Language Transfer in Language Learning*. Amsterdam: John Benjamins, 32–46.

Schachter, J. and Rutherford, W. 1979: Discourse function and language transfer. *Working Papers in Bilingualism*, 19, 1–12.

Schmidt, R. W. 1987: Sociolinguistic variation and language transfer in phonology. In G. Ioup and S. Weinberger (eds), *Interlanguage Phonology*. Rowley, MA: Newbury House, 365–77.

Schmidt, R. W. and Frota, S. 1986: Developing basic conversational ability in a second language: a case study of an adult learner. In R. R. Day (ed.), *Talking to Learn: Conversation in Second Language Acquisition*. Rowley, MA: Newbury House, 237–326.

Schumann, J. 1986: Locative and directional expressions in basilang speech. *Language Learning*, 36, 277–94.

Schwartz, B. 1997: On the basis of the Basic Variety. *Second Language Research*, 13, 386–402.

Schweers, C. W. 1993: Variation in cross-linguistic influence on interlanguage lexicon as a function of perceived first-language distance. Ph.D. dissertation. New York University.

Scovel, T. 1988: *A Time to Speak: A Psycholinguistic Inquiry into the Critical Period for Human Speech*. Rowley, MA: Newbury House.

Selinker, L. 1969: Language transfer. *General Linguistics*, 9, 67–92.

Selinker, L. 1972: Interlanguage. *International Review of Applied Linguistics*, 10, 209–31.

Selinker, L. 1992: *Rediscovering Interlanguage*. London: Longman.

Selinker, L. and Baumgartner-Cohen, B. 1995: Multiple language acquisition: "Damn it, why can't I keep these two languages apart?" *Language, Culture, and Curriculum*, 8, 115–21.

Selinker, L. and Lakshmanan, U. 1993: Language transfer and fossilization: the Multiple Effects Principle. In S. Gass and L. Selinker (eds), *Language Transfer in Language Learning*. Amsterdam: John Benjamins, 197–216.

Selinker, L. and Lamendella, J. 1981: Updating the inter-language hypothesis. *Studies in Second Language Acquisition*, 3, 201–20.

Shannon, J. 1995: Variability and the interlanguage production of the English definite article. Ph.D. dissertation. Ohio State University.

Sharwood Smith, M. 1979: Strategies, language transfer and the simulation of second language learners' mental operations. *Language Learning*, 29, 345–61.

Sharwood Smith, M. 1986: The Competence/Control Model, cross-linguistic influence and the creation of new grammars. In E. Kellerman and M. Sharwood Smith (eds), *Crosslinguistic Influence and Second Language Acquisition*. New York: Pergamon Press, 10–20.

Shen, F. 1989: The classroom and the wider culture: identity as a key to learning English composition. *College Composition and Communication*, 40, 459–66.

Siegel, J. 1999: Transfer constraints and substrate influence in Melanesian Pidgin. *Journal of Pidgin and Creole Languages*, 14, 1–44.

Singler, J. 1988: The homogeneity of the substrate as a factor in pidgin/creole genesis. *Language*, 64, 27–51.

Singleton, D. 1987: Mother and other tongue influence on learner French. *Studies in Second Language Acquisition*, 9, 327–45.

Singleton, D. 1989: *Language Acquisition: The Age Factor*. Clevedon: Multilingual Matters.

Singley, M. and Anderson, J. 1989: *The Transfer of Cognitive Skill*. Cambridge, MA: Harvard University Press.

Sjöholm, K. 1983: Problems in "measuring" L2 learning strategies. In H. Ringbom (ed.), *Psycholinguistics and Foreign Language Learning*. Turku: Publications of the Research Institute of the Abo Akademi Foundation.

Sjöholm, K. 1995: *The Influence of Crosslinguistic, Semantic, and Input Factors on the Acquisition of English Phrasal Verbs*. Turku: Abo Akademi University Press.

Slabakova, R. 1999: The parameter of aspect in second language acquisition. *Second Language Research*, 15, 283–317.

Slobin, D. 1973: Cognitive prerequisites for the development of grammar. In C. Ferguson and D. Slobin (eds), *Studies in Child Language Development*. New York: Holt, Rinehart, and Winston, 175–208.

Slobin, D. 1993: Adult language acquisition: a view from child language study. In C. Perdue (ed.), *Adult Language Acquisition: Cross-Linguistic Perspectives. Vol. II: The Results*. Cambridge: Cambridge University Press, 239–52.

Spada, N. and Lightbown, P. 1999: Instruction, first language influence, and developmental readiness in second language acquisition. *Modern Language Journal*, 83, 1–22.

Sridhar, K. and Sridhar, S. N. 1986: Bridging the paradigm gap: second language acquisition theory and indigenized varieties of English. *World Englishes*, 5, 3–14.

Sulkala, H. 1996: Finnish as a second language for speakers of related languages. In M. Martin and P. Muikko-Werner (eds), *Finnish and Estonian: New Target Languages*. Jyväskylä: Center for Applied

Language Studies, University of Jyväskylä.

Thomason, S. and Kaufman, T. 1988: *Language Contact, Creolization, and Genetic Linguistics*. Berkeley: University of California Press.

Tomlin, R. 1994: Functional grammars, pedagogical grammars, and communicative language teaching. In T. Odlin (ed.), *Perspectives on Pedagogical Grammar*. Cambridge: Cambridge University Press, 140–78.

Vainikka, A. and Young-Scholten, M. 1998: The initial state in the L2 acquisition of phrase structure. In S. Flynn, G. Martohardjono, and W. O'Neil (eds), *The Generative Study of Second Language Acquisition*. Mahwah, NJ: Lawrence Erlbaum Associates, 17–34.

Weinreich, U. 1953/68: *Languages in Contact*. The Hague: Mouton.

Wenzell, V. 1989: Transfer of aspect in the English oral narratives of native Russian speakers. In H. Dechert and M. Raupach (eds), *Transfer in Language Production*. Norwood, NJ: Ablex, 71–97.

White, L. 1985: The "pro-drop" parameter in adult second language acquisition. *Language Learning*, 35, 47–62.

White, L. 2000: Second language acquisition: from initial to final state. In J. Archibald (ed.), *Second Language Acquisition and Linguistic Theory*. Oxford: Blackwell, 130–55.

Williams, S. and Hammarberg, B. 1998: Language switches in L3 production: implications for a polyglot speaking model. *Applied Linguistics*, 19, 295–333.

Wolfe-Quintero, K. 1996: Nativism does not equal Universal Grammar. *Second Language Research*, 12, 335–73.

Zobl, H. 1986: Word order typology, lexical government, and the prediction of multiple, graded effects on L2 word order. *Language Learning*, 36, 159–83.

16 Stabilization and Fossilization in Interlanguage Development

MICHAEL H. LONG

1 Introduction

A construct first introduced into the field of SLA by Selinker in 1972, fossilization has become widely accepted as a psychologically real phenomenon of considerable theoretical and practical importance. The literature reveals several problems, however. Fossilization is alternately explanandum and explanans. Its definition and alleged scope vary markedly across writers and studies. So do the research designs, subjects, data, and measurement criteria considered relevant. So do the explanations offered for it when fossilization is treated as product, not process. And while it is often said that fossilization is pervasive, especially in adult SLA, the evidence to date has been largely impressionistic.

After tracing the history and evolution of the idea, a review of empirical studies on fossilization, including some recent longitudinal work, will show almost all to have suffered from one or more of four problems: assuming, not demonstrating, fossilization; selecting inappropriate learners for study; basing findings on insufficient data; and using inadequate analyses. For a variety of reasons, most explanations for fossilization are equally unsatisfactory. It will be concluded, therefore, that fossilization of IL grammars may occur, but that until research shows convincingly that it does, researchers would do better to focus on describing and explaining the well-attested phenomenon of stabilization, a strategy with several advantages from a theory-construction perspective.

2 The Theory

"Fossilization" is a construct first introduced into the SLA literature by Selinker (1972), who appears to have seen it as a way of both characterizing and explaining the product of the SLA process in terms of what many observers consider one of its single most salient qualities (compared to L1A), that is, relative failure. The end-state was viewed as a grammar which differed from that of the target-language variety, among other ways, in its permanent retention of deviant rules and forms, despite adequate opportunity for improvement – forms which persistently reappeared in L2 performance long after they were thought to have been supplanted, a phenomenon referred to by Selinker as "backsliding." The permanent non-nativelike state was termed "fossilization" (as product), while "fossilization" (as process), constrained by L1 transfer, was viewed as part of the individual learner's underlying psychological structure, a putative cognitive mechanism which could explain the failure. Fossilization was:

> a mechanism which is assumed also to exist in the latent psychological structure . . . Fossilizable linguistic phenomena are linguistic items, rules, and subsystems which speakers of a particular NL will tend to keep in their IL relative to a particular TL, no matter what the age of the learner or the amount of explanation and instruction he [*sic*] receives in the TL . . . A crucial fact which any adequate theory of second language learning will have to explain is this regular reappearance or re-emergence in IL productive performance of linguistic structures which were thought to be eradicated. This behavioral reappearance is what has led me to postulate the reality of fossilization and ILs. (Selinker, 1972, p. 215)[1]

Recognition of how widespread acceptance of the notion quickly became can be seen in its qualifying as an entry in a non-field-specific dictionary just five years later, a feat apparently accomplished by no other SLA term before or since:

> *fossilize* 5. *Ling*. (of a linguistic form, feature, rule, etc.) to become permanently established in the interlanguage of a second-language learner in a form that is deviant from the target-language norm and that continues to appear in performance regardless of further exposure to the target language. (*The Random House Dictionary of the English Language*, 1987, p. 755)

And just five years after that, while admitting that definitions of fossilization varied widely, Selinker reported the existence of "literally hundreds of studies in the literature which claim to have shown a fossilized phenomenon, or speculate on a fossilizable phenomenon, or assume fossilization and speculate on its possible cause in the case under study" (Selinker, 1992, p. 250).

While permanence and deviance despite favorable conditions for change, and L1 transfer as a causal factor (see below), have been retained by Selinker as defining criteria over the years, other emphases have shifted somewhat, from a predominant focus on performance to one on underlying competence, and from fossilization as a global IL phenomenon to a more differentiated approach. Paradoxically, the changes have made the construct more restricted, yet less verifiable. Thus, Selinker and Lamandella wrote: "Fossilization is the permanent cessation of IL learning [*sic*][2] before the learner has attained target language norms at all levels of linguistic structure and *in all discourse domains* in spite of the learner's positive ability, opportunity or motivation to learn or acculturate into target society" (Selinker and Lamendella, 1978, p. 187, emphasis added). While increasing the power of the theory (a negative), implying that fossilization may occur in individual "domains" appears to make identification easier for the researcher than verifying that change has ceased everywhere in a grammar, yet really makes it harder, since, as detailed below, "discourse domain" remains a nebulous construct to this day. A year later, Selinker suggested that fossilization was not only domain-dependent, but context-dependent, and so could be evidenced by variability ("fluctuation") across contexts, not just by uniformity in performance across all contexts, and was meaningfully sought under conditions of natural exposure, that is, in second, as opposed to foreign, language settings. Again, "context" was undefined, and in practice difficult to operationalize. Selinker also attempted to deal with the obvious problem of what would constitute "permanence," and more to the point, what the lower bounds might be for an empirical test. Fossilization was now:

> a situation in which the learner might produce a target language form correctly in one context but not in another, thereby evidencing a fluctuation in interlanguage performance. In order to qualify as fossilization, this fluctuation would have to have persisted in the learner's speech for an extended period of time (perhaps two to five years at the very least) – in spite of copious interaction with native speakers in an environment where the learner's L2 is spoken as a first language. (Selinker, 1989, p.c., cited in Bean and Gergen, 1990, p. 206)

Again, unless it is possible to specify where one "context" (and/or "discourse domain") ends and another begins, testing a claim that all or part of a grammar has fossilized becomes impossible. And if persistence of unvarying IL phenomena for from at least two to five years is required to qualify as evidence of fossilization, it should be noted right away that only three studies of putative fossilization in nearly 30 years (Han, 1998, 2000a; Lardiere, 1998a, 1998b; Long, 1997) have lasted that long.[3]

Finally, if, as seems uncontroversial, and as has been recognized by Selinker (Selinker and Han, 1996; Selinker and Lakshmanan, 1992), stabilization is the first sign of (putative) fossilization, and if the only difference between stabilization and fossilization is permanence (see, e.g., Bley-Vroman, 1989),[4] then including persistent "fluctuation" as a legitimate index of fossilization creates another problem. The dictionary already quoted defines stabilization thus:

> *stabilize* 2. to maintain at a given or *unfluctuating* level or quantity. (*The Random House Dictionary of the English Language*, 1987, p. 1852, emphasis added)

Fluctuation is not part of stabilization, yet stabilization is the precursor to fossilization, which can supposedly include fluctuation.

The various definitions of fossilization as process and product raise several methodological difficulties concerning, among other matters, testability, scope, learner age, unit of analysis, and deviance. First, where *testability* is concerned, a claim that something in a person's make-up is "permanent" is unfalsifiable during her or his lifetime, yet permanence is the only quality distinguishing fossilization from stabilization. Either an inevitably somewhat arbitrary minimum period must be specified as acceptably long for permanence to be inferred, therefore, or a claim of fossilization remains untestable. However, given that both U-shaped behavior and renewed language development after periods of plateau-like stability, some lasting for several years, are widely attested characteristics of normal child first and second language acquisition (see, e.g., Bowerman, 1982; Harley and Swain, 1984, respectively), understanding the causes of *stabilization* (and destabilization) would seem to promise as much for SLA theory as work on fossilization, and do so without fossilization's attendant theoretical and empirical baggage. Selinker recognizes the empirical problem, but not the potential implication: "at any point in time it is nonetheless very difficult, if not impossible, to tell, at a particular point in time, if a learner's *stabilized* IL is in fact fossilized. Thus it is common in SLA discussion to distinguish theoretically 'permanent fossilization' from 'temporary stabilization' of the IL" (Selinker, 1993, p. 16). The question, however, is not whether such a distinction can be made "theoretically," but whether it is useful for SLA theory construction to do so, and with what theoretical and empirical consequences.[5] Also, the two processes might share the same surface characteristics, but differ in their underlying causes.[6]

Second, as noted above, the *scope* of putative fossilization remains unspecified. Learners do not fossilize, and neither do whole ILs or whole IL systems (syntax, phonology, etc.); rather, IL development within certain contexts and "discourse domains" – roughly, topics mediated by personal life history – supposedly does. Thus, according to Selinker and Douglas (1985, 1989), a structure can be fossilized in one discourse domain, while still developing in another. But contexts are often vague, defined by a host of sometimes rather nebulous sociolinguistic and social-psychological parameters (see Douglas, 2000, pp. 41–74), and discourse domains turn out to be even more elusive. Douglas writes:

> Douglas and Selinker (1985) use the term *discourse domain* to refer to the [learner's] internal interpretation of context . . . Douglas and Selinker define discourse domain as a cognitive construct created by a language learner as a context for interlanguage development and use. Discourse domains are engaged when strategic competence, in assessing the communicative situation, recognizes cues in the environment that allow the language user to identify the situation and his or her role in it. If there are insufficient cues, if they are unrecognized by the language user, or if they are contradictory or ambiguous, the result will be uncertainty and stumbling around. (Douglas, 2000, p. 46)

Identification of discourse domains, that is to say, involves considerable ambiguity and risk of misinterpretation by both learner and researcher. Discourse domains, moreover, are idiosyncratic (Selinker and Douglas, 1985), only identifiable for each learner empirically, a posteriori. This means not only that testing a fossilization claim is laborious, involving identification of discourse domains for that learner first, but that generalization and prediction are impossible.[7]

Third, Selinker repeatedly asserts that fossilization, resulting in non-target-like ultimate attainment, operates in learners regardless of *age*; for example, as quoted above, "no matter what the age of the learner" (1972, p. 215). While its appearance in *child*, as well as adult, SLA is necessary if fossilization is to qualify as a phenomenon characterizing *second*, as opposed to *adult*, language acquisition, or just *adult second* language acquisition (an issue to which we return), the fact is that no studies have shown fossilization in child L2 acquirers,[8] and it is doubtful whether this would ever happen with children learning an L2 any more than with child L1A. On the contrary, given adequate opportunity, children appear to attain nativelike levels in a second language, just as they do in their first. A more likely scenario, albeit still a controversial one in some quarters (see, e.g., Birdsong, 1999), is that the ability to acquire either a first or a second language to nativelike levels is maturationally constrained: learners first exposed before the offset of one or more sensitive periods for language development can reach nativelike levels; those first exposed later cannot (for a comprehensive review of the literature on maturational constraints, see Hyltenstam and Abrahamsson, this volume).

Fourth, at what level does fossilization supposedly occur? What is the appropriate *unit of analysis*: the whole IL, the module, the linguistic rule, particular forms, words, meanings, collocations, form–function relationships, ranges of variation, all of these, or something else? Does fossilization halt IL development at the level of type or token? For instance, is it necessary to show that (target-like or non-target-like) plural *-s* marking remains the same on all noun phrases to support a fossilization claim, or just on particular NPs, perhaps always supplied accurately on some, but always omitted on others? Would a claim that fossilization has occurred be supported by proof of stability (within discourse domain X, context Y, and over time period Z) in a learner's failure to use the regular past tense morpheme *-ed* in English appropriately on any verbs, that is, at the level of type, or on particular verbs, that is, at the level of token? What if, for example, a learner's average target-like use (TLU) for regular past remained constant at around 50 percent (or varied only within a narrow range) over time, but the marking of individual verbs changed during that period? And even if conducting an analysis at the level of token (particular plural NPs, or particular verbs marked, or not, for past time), does the researcher further need to take precise linguistic contexts, collocations, and intended meanings into account when comparing multiple uses of the same tokens? Suppose, for example, that a learner invariably uses singular and plural forms of some "measure words" (*days*, *years*, etc.) and a few other lexical items (e.g., *ladies*) correctly, but marks plurality variably or not at all on some other NPs. Is one to conclude that plural *-s* (either the rule or the form) has fossilized altogether, has fossilized in the case of some NPs but not others, some uses but not others, or that it has not fossilized at all?[9] And if structures, such as English relative clauses (Schachter, 1974) or passives (Seliger, 1989), are produced with increasing accuracy over time (a matter of the system), but are persistently and consistently undersupplied, or "avoided," by speakers of a particular L1 (a matter of norms), can it be said that while the structures are still developing, the uses have fossilized?

Fifth, is fossilization a matter of *deviance* only, or, as might reasonably be supposed, of correct, nativelike rules and forms, too?[10] A cognitive mechanism that could differentiate nativelike from non-nativelike elements and apply only to the latter requires some imagination. Yet, given that many target-like, as well as non-target-like, rules and forms are acquired early, even by ultimately unsuccessful learners, and remain unchanged "permanently," belief in such an uncannily sophisticated device is what acceptance of the construct entails. Conversely, positing that target-like forms fossilize, too, increases plausibility, but creates another problem, for what kind of cognitive mechanism could simultaneously apply and not apply to different structures, "freezing" grammatical ones while allowing ungrammatical ones to continue to develop, or as noted above, simultaneously apply and not apply to the same structure in different discourse domains?

3 The Evidence

In light of the widespread acceptance of fossilization as a force in SLA,[11] or at least the pervasive casual use of the term in the SLA literature,[12] the scarcity – until recently, the complete absence – of even potentially supporting evidence is surprising, to say the least. Numerous studies over the past 30 years or so have purported to demonstrate and/or explain fossilization, but each finding may be questioned, often on multiple grounds.[13] Common problems include, but are not limited to: (i) assuming, not demonstrating, fossilization (or stabilization); (ii) selecting inappropriate learners for study; (iii) basing findings on insufficient data; and (iv) using inadequate analyses.

3.1 *Assuming, not demonstrating, fossilization*

A number of researchers start by asserting that various structures or whole ILs – and sometimes even learners, or whole groups of learners – have fossilized, a claim usually accompanied by speculations about the reasons why (see, e.g., Lin, 1995; Washburn, 1992). The most common justifications offered for such a priori classifications are that certain errors are frequent[14] or that the informants have resided in a society in which the target language is widely spoken for what the researcher considers long enough for them to have learned more than they have in fact learned. Other factors occasionally invoked include length and type of prior language-learning experience. Thus, in an interesting study of self-correction and incorporation of other-correction by eight Mandarin-speaking Taiwanese learners of Spanish, Lin (1995) compared two groups of four informants, one group supposedly fossilized, the other not. The allegedly fossilized group consisted of three men and one woman, all of low proficiency in Spanish, three of them restaurant workers, one a manager, who ranged in age from 36 to 53, and who, to qualify for the study, had to have lived in Spain for at least 10 years, have acquired Spanish naturalistically for the most part (starting Spanish after their arrival in Spain, with an average of about eight months of instruction), (for reasons not clear to me) not be married to a Spaniard, and have had continual contact with native speakers throughout their period of residence. The comparison group consisted of four women, two graduate students and two professionals, ranging in age from 26 to 33, all of whom had majored in Spanish at university in Taiwan, had received from three to four additional years of instruction in Spanish in Spain, had lived in Spain for from three to five years, and had attained considerably higher levels of proficiency in the L2 than members of the supposedly fossilized group. After studying transcripts of single conversations, lasting between 23 and 45 minutes, between each of the informants and one of four native speakers of Spanish (and in one case, two such conversations), Lin reported a clear difference between the two groups in their sensitivity to, and use, of self- and other-repair. The non-fossilized group incorporated 69 percent of other-corrections, compared with the allegedly fossilized group's 7 percent, and self-corrected seven times as often as the longer-term residents.

Lin expresses a belief in multiple causes of fossilization, and in different ones affecting different learners. Those he lists include time available for, and interest in, L2 study, basic educational level, and aptitude (Lin, 1995, p. 140), psychological and social distance, and felt communicative need (1995, p. 149). He also recognizes (1995, p. 143) that the (on numerous grounds, non-equivalent control group) design of his study precludes any assignment of causality. Lin nevertheless suggests that an important factor might also be a learner's metalinguistic ability, as evidenced by the two groups' differential rates of self-correction and sensitivity to negative feedback (Lin, 1995; Lin and Hedgcock, 1996). Lin may well be right, but his findings do not support such a conclusion for several reasons, most obviously the fact that one brief conversational sample from each informant precludes any assessment of the persistence of elements in that person's IL over time, and hence, any judgment as to whether that informant has stabilized, much less fossilized. Asserting that some informants were fossilized (or stabilized), and others not, on the basis of differing personal histories, language-learning profiles, and L2 proficiency is no substitute for longitudinal data. The findings on self-correction and negative feedback, valuable though they are, might be due to one or more of several differences between the two groups, including those mentioned by Lin, and might have nothing to do with fossilization, if such a thing exists.

3.2 Selecting inappropriate learners for study

A pervasive problem in fossilization studies involves selection of inappropriate informants. Given that even under optimal conditions, it takes several years to learn a second language, it is clearly essential to base findings, as Selinker has always rightly stressed, on learners who have had adequate ability, motivation, and opportunity to learn. It would be absurd to show that the ILs of classroom foreign language learners or of low-proficiency learners recently arrived in an L2 environment were still developing, and to claim, therefore, that learners do not fossilize (quite apart from the impossibility of proving a negative). But it is equally absurd to base a fossilization claim on such learners, for example, those in foreign language settings, who, motivated or not, could not have had adequate time or opportunity to acquire the target language, and when the researcher could not have studied the learner long enough to show lack of change persistent enough even to meet Selinker's lowest suggested minimum of at least two to five years. Even learners who have resided in a target-language community for periods of ten years or more may be unsuitable for study, at least before data are collected on their ability, motivation, and opportunity to learn during that time. Many such individuals spend considerable proportions of their lives in L1 linguistic ghettos. Others, while enjoying plenty of L2 exposure, have little need for, or interest in, acquiring the new language, perhaps due to use of the L1 at home and/or at work, their own social status, the relative sociolinguistic status of the L1 and L2 involved, or low intended (as opposed to actual) length of residence. Yet a number of fossilization claims have been based on studies of learners of these types (see, e.g., Agnello, 1977; Bean and Gergen, 1990; Bruzzese, 1977; Mukattash, 1986; Sola, 1989; Thep-Ackrapong, 1990; Washburn, 1992).

Washburn (1992, 1994), for example, divided 18 undergraduate students enrolled in the same level of a writing course at a US university into two groups of nine, which she designated "fossilized" and "non-fossilized" on the basis of length of residence (LOR) and whether or not the student had ever failed an ESL course (thereby also making this another case of a study where fossilization was assumed, not demonstrated). Washburn writes: "Since there is no operationalized definition of fossilized speakers based on linguistic behavior, a working definition was employed" (1994, p. 72). LOR ranged from six months to four-and-a-half years for the "non-fossilized" group, and from five to seven years for the "fossilized" group. No students in the "non-fossilized" group had failed a previous ESL course; all students in the "fossilized" group had failed at least one. Students participated in three sessions for the research during the semester, each lasting about 45 minutes: an interview designed to elicit certain structures known to be problematic; a session where students completed a cloze test and a combined grammaticality judgment and imitation task (the latter based on deviant utterances from the particular informant's earlier interview); and finally, a short-term learning task in which each student received intensive corrective feedback on structures on which he or she had continued to make errors in the grammaticality judgment and imitation task. The feedback took the form, in sequence, of correct models, repetition of the correct models with emphasis, breaking the utterance into smaller units, backwards build-up, and overt correction. The "treatments" during the second and third sessions were innovative and especially interesting because instead of focusing on arbitrarily chosen structures, they targeted items for each student which were more likely to be "learnable" in a processing sense (Pienemann, 1984), as suggested by that student's attempts at production during previous sessions.[15]

As Washburn predicted, the "non-fossilized" group improved in accuracy more quickly (measured in numbers of turns required) than the allegedly fossilized learners following the intensive corrective feedback. Interestingly – that is, when potential explanations of fossilization are considered – Washburn's allegedly fossilized learners, like those in several other studies (e.g., Lennon, 1991a, 1991b; Lin, 1995; Lin and Hedgcock, 1996; Mukkatash, 1986; Thep-Ackrapong, 1990), seemed less sensitive to negative feedback. Students in the two groups were not distinguishable by the errors they made, many of these being the same, although the quantity of errors was higher in the "fossilized" group. Rather, it was in two patterns of errors across tasks that (again, quantitative) differences emerged. First, students in the "fossilized" group exhibited statistically significantly less stability in their production of correct forms during the feedback sessions, providing them one moment, and then what Washburn calls "regressing" the next. Second, their TLU across the interview and elicitation tasks was consistent for only 36.5 percent of the target structures, accuracy being lower during the interview, compared with 52 percent consistency for the "non-fossilized" group (a clear, if statistically non-significant, trend). How these two indications of greater *in*stability among the allegedly "fossilized" group are to be reconciled with fossilization is unclear. It could presumably be argued that "regression" was suggestive of Selinker's "backsliding," and so an indication of fossilization, and that the instability across tasks was due to their constituting different contexts or discourse domains. However, one would then want to know why the supposedly "non-fossilized" learners exhibited the same patterns, if less markedly. An alternative, simpler interpretation of Washburn's results is that students in the supposedly "fossilized" group performed less accurately and more unstably because they were of lower proficiency, as suggested by their cloze test scores, which Washburn reports (1994, p. 73) were considerably (and statistically significantly) lower, and that neither group was fossilized, as shown by the ability of both to benefit from corrective feedback. A period of from six months to seven years is insufficient for most adults to acquire a new language. However intriguing Washburn's findings, this means that the initial classification of informants as "fossilized" or "non-fossilized" chiefly on the basis of LOR (with no data on L2 exposure and use during that period), as in several other studies, was arbitrary and by assertion. In all probability, none of the students was an appropriate choice for a fossilization study.

3.3 *Basing findings on insufficient data*

A surprising number of studies have purported to investigate fossilization using cross-sectional designs. Some, for example, Lin (1995), based their findings on a single sample of learner speech or writing. Some, for instance Bean and Gergen (1990), gathered data from the same learner(s) on two or more tasks, but at one time. Some collected two or more (sometimes many more) samples, but over too short a period for fossilization to be ascertained, especially if a five-year-minimum period of observation is required; for example two samples in six weeks (Mukkatash, 1986), three samples during a semester (Washburn, 1994), 16 samples in six months (Lennon, 1991a, 1991b), multiple samples in nine months (Han and Selinker, 1997), and three samples in 18 months (Thep-Ackrapong, 1990). Such studies can provide useful insights on stabilization, and often have, but arguably not on fossilization. This is so even if they are otherwise methodologically sound, unless Selinker's suggested two-to-five-year criterion and what is already known about the normal irregular pace of SLA are disregarded, in which case a distinction between stabilization and fossilization would no longer be sustainable. As Selinker and Mascia put it:

> only with longitudinal interlanguage data in the context of positive evidence to the learner where there exists the motivational criterion are we able to show instances of fossilization. Otherwise, we just do not believe fossilization can be demonstrated. That is, cross-sectional studies by definition just do not capture what is happening to individual learners, the necessary locus of fossilization. (Selinker and Mascia, 1999, p. 257)

Possibly emulating Schumann's (unsuccessful) attempt to teach Alberto negation at the end of a study of common simplification processes underlying early naturalistic SLA and pidginization (Schumann, 1978), another popular approach to buttressing fossilization claims is to show that learners persist with errors despite attempts to "correct" them through instruction and/or negative feedback of one or more kinds.[16] Mukkatash (1986), for example, argued that 80 Jordanian fourth-year college English majors with an average of 11 years of prior classroom EFL instruction had fossilized when explicit grammatical explanations and error correction failed to improve their written production of various constructions, including *be*-deletion, confusion of simple present and simple past forms, and retention of pronominal copies in relative clauses (allowed in Arabic), as evidenced by two written assignments over a six-week period. Similarly, Thep-Ackrapong (1990) collected a speech sample from Lin, a Chinese speaker, tutored her for four months, collected a second sample, and then collected a third one year later. Errors with infinitival complements and related structures were frequent and persisted in all three samples, leading Thep-Ackrapong to claim Lin had fossilized. Obvious potential problems with this approach include the inadequate time allowed for improvement, failure to ascertain whether some or all of the targeted structures are "teachable" and "learnable" for the students concerned,[17] use of non-comparable data over time, analysis at the level of type, not token, a variety of well-known methodological difficulties in measuring the effects of any kind of instructional intervention (Mellow, Reeder, and Forster, 1996), and the possibility that the instruction or error-correction is inadequate.

More reasonably, some, such as Kellerman (1989) and Schouten (1996), have employed pseudo-longitudinal, panel designs, buttressed by evidence from typological studies and diachronic language change. The reasoning is that if single samples obtained at one point in time from groups of progressively more advanced learners with the same L1 show widespread persistence of the same errors (e.g., use of 'would' in the protasis of hypothetical conditionals, as in **If he would be taller, he would be a better player*, by most Dutch learners of English), especially when all the groups are highly proficient, then it is safe to assume that such structures are at the very least vulnerable to fossilization. This may well be true, but it is not the same (and Kellerman or Schouten do not claim it is) as showing that the structure concerned is stabilized or fossilized in any individual's IL (where it may still be improving, even though still not target-like), and it is the individual IL that is the appropriate unit of analysis when advancing a claim of fossilization in IL development, meaning that longitudinal studies of one or more individuals are required. The well-documented tendency of speakers of various L1s to retain common errors in their L2 is good prima facie evidence of transfer, but not, alone, sufficient evidence of fossilization, since some speakers of those L1s do *not* persist with those particular errors. Thus, while many Spanish-speaking learners of English operate with pre-verbal negation for long periods (see, e.g., Schumann, 1978; Stauble, 1984), many Spanish speakers can be found who control a fully analyzed English negation system – and the same appears to be true for any well-attested common error, allegedly L1-influenced or not. Like their pure cross-sectional counterparts, pseudo-longitudinal studies can be useful sources of hypotheses about fossilization, but a claim to have demonstrated fossilization must be supported (among other things) by evidence of lack of change in an individual IL over time. Again, true longitudinal studies are needed.

Data are also sometimes inadequate not only because of the single time at which they were collected, and/or the short period over which they were collected, and/or the type of informants from whom they were collected, but due to the kind collected. Preference will usually be accorded spontaneous speech (supplemented by elicited spoken data and data on comprehension as needed). Speech data will be closer to the vernacular, and hence, more likely to offer a window on whatever is systematic in the IL concerned – and systematicity, as opposed to variability, is potentially a key indication of stabilization. Conversely, test scores, especially if grouped across linguistic features and/or informants, and written data of any kind (as in Mukkatash, 1986), especially if from formal genres, such as academic papers (see, e.g., Han, 1998), are more vulnerable to various well-known sources of variability, such as transfer and monitoring. That is, they are more permeable, and so likely to be less useful (although still potentially useful in some cases if such sources of systematic variation are taken into account during the analysis). In addition, when (minimally) two sets of data are available on the same (appropriate) informants, and gathered over an adequate time period, they need to be comparable – not, say, supplied-in-obligatory-context (SOC) morpheme test scores at time 1 and SOC morpheme scores from free speech at time 2, or target-like-use (TLU) scores for past time reference in informal conversation at time 1 and in a picture-strip narration at time 2. All the usual sociolinguistic parameters of speech or writing need to be considered, given their well-documented roles as potential sources of variation (see, e.g., Tarone, 1988), and hence, in concealing stabilization or fossilization, especially in light of Selinker's caveats concerning fossilization's possible sensitivity to context and discourse domain.

In sum, rather than one factor alone determining the worth of a fossilization claim, it is a combination of appropriate informant(s) and adequate data that is required. A five-year longitudinal study, using (in various senses) adequate data, of a learner who had already lived in the target-language community for 20 years when the study began, with good motivation and opportunity to acquire, could be more valuable than a 10-year study of a learner in a foreign language setting or of a learner who had only recently arrived in the target-language setting and started SLA when the study began. Conversely, the shorter study could be more useful if it involved multiple samples of comparable free speech, while the longer study relied exclusively on test scores or translation. All other things being equal, a study involving advanced learners is more likely to be successful in identifying persistent errors, simply because errors remaining in the ILs of advanced learners are more likely to be potentially permanent problems than errors found in the ILs of less proficient learners, which will include a greater variety and number, but many that will disappear with increasing proficiency. Similarly, errors known to be common in highly proficient speakers of a particular L1 background are more likely to include persistent ones, or they would not be more common with advanced learners from a particular L1 background. A constellation of methodological factors needs to be evaluated, in other words. The problem is that very few studies indeed have managed to avoid all of the pitfalls described, and some almost none of them, meaning that in addition to its theoretical problems, fossilization suffers from a paucity of credible supporting evidence. Moreover, data to be presented below (section 3.4.) suggest that the level at which many, possibly all, analyses are conducted needs to include not just type, but token, something found in no published study of fossilization to date.

3.4 *Using inadequate analyses*

Given the present state of ignorance about fossilization – not least, uncertainty as to whether such a thing exists – it is difficult to be sure how to analyze data appropriately. It is possible to be sure that many methods are *in*appropriate, however, and the analyses employed in virtually every study of fossilization have arguably been flawed in one or more ways. Common problems have included (i) use of group means (e.g., for a whole class of children) instead of individual scores, meaning that changes in some informants' ILs risk canceling out changes in others, giving the false appearance of overall "fossilization" at the level of the group; (ii) use of pooled data (e.g., mean SOC percentages for 10 morphemes) within an individual, meaning that changes in some morphemes risk canceling out changes in others, again giving the false appearance of overall "fossilization" at the level of morphology; (iii) use of accuracy or accuracy ranges (e.g., SOC or TLU measures) instead of stability/change measures, regardless of whether or not the rules or elements studied are target-like; and (iv) conducting analyses at the level of types, not tokens. All such analyses are also likely to miss changes in form–function relationships over time, zig-zag developmental curves, and U-shaped behavior.

By way of illustration, Bean and Gergen (1990) sought to determine whether the ILs of fossilized speakers (*sic*) varied across tasks in the L2, and whether fossilized ILs (*sic*) varied among individuals with the same L1 when they performed similar tasks in the L2. The subjects were two young women, Jean and May. Jean was an ethnic Chinese Malaysian, aged 33, with a LOR of about 10 years and a bachelor's degree in business from a US university, working at a bank in Los Angeles at the time of the study. May was from Hong Kong, aged 21, with a LOR of three years, in her last year of a business degree at a university in Los Angeles, working in a related area, and intending to stay in the US. Both women had been raised in upper-middle-class families, with Cantonese L1 spoken in the home. Both had been exposed to English from the age of 5 at school in their countries of origin, but reported having had minimal opportunity or need to speak the language in or out of school until coming to the US (see Bean and Gergen, 1990, p. 216n.3). There were several obvious problems, in other words, with the initial choice of informants for such a study.

Data consisted of speech production on three tasks – an informal interview, a picture story narration, and an oral morphology test (the Solomonick-Williams Morpheme Test, which uses pictures and sentence completion) – gathered at one point in time. There was really no possibility of determining whether the informants had stabilized, in other words, much less fossilized, regardless of what the analysis revealed.[18] For each informant, Bean and Gergen calculated percentage accurate SOC across the three tasks for 11 morphemes: progressive *-ing*, regular noun plural, copula (*is*, *am*, *are*, *was*, and *were*), auxiliary *be*, modal auxiliaries, two regular auxiliaries (*have* and *do*), articles (*a*, *an*, and *the*), regular past, third person singular *-s*, and possessive *s*. Drawing an innovative but unmotivated distinction between "what appears to be fossilized and what may actually be acquired . . . and thus not eligible for analysis as fossilized morphemes" (1990, p. 211), they then assigned morphemes to one of three categories for each informant:

Table 16.1 SOC percentages for "fossilized" morphemes

Jean				*May*			
Morpheme	*I*	*N*	*T*	*Morpheme*	*I*	*N*	*T*
Copula	66	96	100	*-ing*	100	100	60
Article	83	100	65	Plural	81	67	100
Regular past	16	18	30	Auxiliary *be*	100	50	60
				Regular past	26	50	80
				3rd person sing. *-s*	20	5	70

Source: based on Bean and Gergen (1990)

> (1) those that appear to be acquired (that is, 80 percent or more accurate on all three tasks), (2) those that are candidates for the designation "fossilized" (that is, those showing *wide variation in accuracy within or across tasks*), and (3) those which occur too infrequently for analysis (that is, fewer than 10 occurrences in two of the three tasks). (Bean and Gergen, 1990, p. 211, emphasis added)

Table 16.1 shows the morphemes Bean and Gergen classified as fossilized, together with the percentage accuracy scores across the three tasks: interview (I), story narration (N), and test (T).

Aside from the impossibility of ascertaining whether IL development has ceased on the basis of data from a cross-sectional study, this analysis raises a number of questions. Not least, if (i) acquired items are considered irrelevant (despite the potential support that their relative stability both within and across tasks might be thought to lend a fossilization claim) – that is, if fossilization is assumed to be able to affect some items *within* a task, discourse domain, or context, while leaving others untouched, as well as the same items across tasks, domains, or contexts – and if (ii) "wide variation in accuracy within or across tasks" is considered evidence of fossilization, what is left that could constitute counter-evidence? Bean and Gergen concluded, "This study's findings demonstrate that fossilization entails idiosyncratic, task-based variation in interlanguage morphological production" (1990, p. 215). But if considerable variation is evidence of fossilization, what would constitute evidence of development? Moreover, how can a researcher tell that, say, Jean's 66 percent accuracy with copula in her interview, compared with her near-perfect (96 percent accurate) and perfect (100 percent) suppliance during the story narration and on the test, respectively, or May's perfect accuracy with *-ing* during the interview and story narration, but 60 percent score on the test, are indications of fossilization and not simply of acquisition of copula and *-ing* being incomplete, but still in progress (especially given the relatively short period over which either woman had actually spoken English – about three years in May's case)? In any case, how could the same linguistic item simultaneously be acquired perfectly and not acquired, depending on task? And if acquired items, that is, those supplied with 80 percent accuracy or better across all three tasks, are not to be considered fossilized, how can items like May's *-ing*, supplied with 100 percent accuracy on two tasks and 60 percent on the third, be considered fossilized, not acquired?[19]

In addition to these problems, accuracy percentage for morphemes in spontaneous spoken or written data (even if longitudinal) is potentially a highly unreliable measure of whether development of an item has ceased, since the analysis is conducted at the level of type, such as third person singular *-s* or regular past, not token. To illustrate (using round numbers for ease of exposition), a learner on task 1 or at time 1 might produce 20 tokens of third person singular verbs, of which 10 were marked accurately with word-final *-s*, and 10 not, yielding an average accuracy score of 50 percent. Ten of 20 tokens on task 2 or at time 2 might also be accurately marked, again giving an overall accuracy score of 50 percent. Yet this result could just as well indicate development as stabilization (or fossilization), depending on which verbs were accurately and inaccurately marked in each case. Leaving aside additional problems, such as the fact that error rates can rise with increased development (see, e.g., Meisel, Clahsen, and Pienemann, 1981), meaning that similar SOC percentages over time may not indicate stability over time, or the way intended meanings of the same form sometimes change from one use to the next, or the way new functions are sometimes attempted with a given form, of 10 verbs common to both samples, seven might be unmarked for past time on the first occasion, and marked accurately on the second. Meanwhile, of a second group of 10 different verbs, each appearing in one sample only, seven might be accurately supplied in the first, whereas only three were accurately supplied in the second. That might justifiably be taken as evidence of development, and certainly of change, not stability. Similarly, outcomes and interpretations might easily be influenced by the presence of several instances (tokens) of the same verb (type), marked correctly or incorrectly, in one sample, but not another, say as a result of particular topics discussed. These and other problems (for additional examples, see Long and Sato, 1984) are threats to the validity not just of SOC analysis of morphemes, but of any analysis conducted at the level of type, not token.

In sum, while widely taken to be a proven universal feature of IL development, the empirical evidence for fossilization in the 30 or so years since the construct's first appearance in the SLA literature has been vanishingly small. Studies offered in support of fossilization claims turn out simply to have assumed, not demonstrated, fossilization; to have used inappropriate subjects, insufficient data, and inadequate analyses; or in many cases to have been marred by two or more of these flaws. Partly in response to this state of affairs, three ongoing longitudinal studies have been undertaken, finally offering to determine whether fossilization is myth or reality.

4 Three Longitudinal Studies

The need for longitudinal empirical studies of IL stabilization and putative fossilization is clear (for discussion, see Selinker and Han, 2001), and the first work of this kind is under way. A study by Han (1998, 2000) just meets the lower bound of Selinker's minimum requirement of from two to five years to substantiate a fossilization claim, and studies by Lardiere (1998a, 1998b, 2000a, 2000b) and Long (1997) comfortably exceed the upper bound.

While recognizing (1998, p. 89, and elsewhere) that not all stabilization is a precursor to, or an indication of, fossilization, Han (1998) views stabilization and fossilization as two parts of a continuum. She conceptualizes fossilization as a cognitive process, properly inferable only from long-term stabilization, demonstrable only by longitudinal studies, occurring at the level of IL subsystems rather than the entire system, and manifesting itself in three ways: invariant appearance of IL forms over time, backsliding over time, and stabilized variations over time (Han, 1998, p. 87).

Two Chinese speakers, F and G, aged 32 and 36, served as informants for Han's research. Both had studied English in the People's Republic of China, and both had lived in an English-speaking country for two years when the study began. A LOR of only two years made them questionable subjects for a fossilization study, but this was offset somewhat by their high level of prior L2 attainment, each having achieved TOEFL scores of over 600 ten years earlier, and by Han's focusing on a typical IL construction for Chinese-speaking learners of English. F was first a post-doctoral civil engineer at a British university, and subsequently an engineer in a computer software company in Australia; G was a researcher in astrophysics at a US university. Both needed to research and publish as part of their work, and both were motivated to improve their English. Data consisted primarily of drafts of academic papers, and formal and informal letters, supplemented by results from translation, grammaticality judgment and correction tasks, and a cloze test. In a detailed analysis that involved both type and token, Han focused on three related constructions: (i) pseudo-passives, such as "The letter about graphics file has not received," a common error in Chinese–English IL – due, among other reasons, she claims, to its matching the topic-comment structure of Chinese; (ii) a subset of target-like passives; and (iii) cases of "over-passivization," that is, passivized unaccusatives, such as "This problem is originated from some numerical error" (1998, p. 168).

There were three main findings. First, in their writing, the informants produced pseudo-passive sentences, such as "Fanta's software can use to model processing procedure" and "The reference keeps at the central surface" (1998, pp. 101–2), throughout the period of observation, even though the pseudo-passives occasionally featured in backsliding. Such errors, that is, novel unaccusatives, were more common in informal letters (perhaps because the writer's attention was focused proportionately more on message than form in that genre), were rare in the research papers, and did not occur in data from the experimental tasks. In addition, the pseudo-passives involved only a small set of verbs, which usually appeared or reappeared when the context favored function-to-form transfer, that is, when the pseudo-passive was used to express what would have been a null-subject topic-comment structure in Chinese; for example, "I also received a card that my health check-up has already sent to the office" (p. 136) and "The letter about graphics file has not received" (p. 139). It is those persistent, L1-influenced, "non-developmental" novel unaccusatives that Han considers vulnerable to fossilization, as opposed to the transitional, "developmental" novel unaccusatives like those found in child language acquisition, such as "The stupid Nintendo unplugged" and "The table knocked over" (p. 126), which result mostly from incorrect lexical entries.

Second, a subset of target-like passives, such as "Your email message was received" and "My reply will be sent to you following this mail," which Han took to be a monitored form of the pseudo-passive, appeared invariably, again in informal writing. Han noted that these target-like passives were essentially driven by the same type of L1 topic-comment influence that induced the pseudo-passives; pragmatically, they differ from true English passives but are identical to the IL pseudo-passives.

Third, passivised unaccusatives, such as "The reflection 'hump' could be disappeared" and "Cough is almost disappeared" (1998, p. 149), appeared in variation with non-passivized ones, such as "We notice that the 'hump' disappear from the composite spectrum" and "My teeth pain almost disappeared" (1998, p. 149) throughout the observation, that is, they manifested stabilized variation. Han suggested that in this case, it was the dual factors of input and learnability, not L1 influence as in the case of pseudo-passives, that will be implicated in fossilization. Thus, all three characteristics of fossilization posited by Han and Selinker (1999) were observed: backsliding over time, invariant appearance of IL forms over time, and stabilized variation over time.

Lardiere (1998a, 1998b, 2000a, 2000b) reports findings from a thus far nearly 10-year study of grammatical knowledge in what appears to be the end-state in the acquisition of English by Patty, a native speaker of Chinese who arrived in the USA at the age of 22. The study began when Patty had already lived in the target-language environment for 10 years. She was immersed in English throughout the observation period – for nearly 20 years by the time of the later recordings – so had had plenty of opportunity to acquire the target language. The data consist of three relatively short conversations between Patty and the researcher,[20] supplemented by two grammaticality judgment tasks administered 18 months apart. Lardiere's focus is not fossilization per se, but a claim by some UG theorists that a contingent relationship exists between the acquisition of verbal morphological inflection and underlying syntactic knowledge – a claim which Lardiere rejects, arguing instead for a dissociation between morphology and syntax even in end-state grammars – and the broader question of whether the underlying abstract syntactic knowledge posited to be involved in child language acquisition is available to the adult L2 acquirer.

Patty does indeed seem to provide evidence of a dissociation between morphology and syntax, and of continued adult access to innate syntactic knowledge. This can be seen in the supposed relationship between the abstract syntactic property of finiteness and pronoun morphology. Patty's past tense marking on verbs has remained low and very stable, at close to 34 percent SOC, over the entire period of the study. Nominative case marking on pronominal subjects, conversely, has been perfect (100 percent SOC) throughout the same period, and clearly a function of finiteness, since only subjects in finite contexts receive subject case, at the same time as subjects in non-finite contexts are also always correctly marked (100 percent SOC) for object case. Patty's grammatical knowledge, that is, includes the functional category T(ense), specified for [+/– finiteness], even though her tense marking on verbs is relatively poor. Patty's grammar is described in detail in an ongoing series of papers summarized by Lardiere for this volume (see box 16.1).

Despite its somewhat different principal focus, Lardiere's research is of great interest for the light it throws on fossilization. Patty's LOR and history of plentiful L2 exposure make her an appropriate informant. The duration of the study (nearly 10 years to date) and the use of comparable samples collected over that period mean that the data constitute a legitimate basis for a potential fossilization claim. The study's motivation by a detailed linguistic theory helps guide data collection and analysis and means that the researcher has a coherent explanation for her findings. In addition to the stability in past tense marking mentioned above, Lardiere has reported that Patty's production of third person singular *-s* on thematic (lexical) verbs has remained stable throughout

Box 16.1 Lardiere (1998a, 1998b, 2000a, 2000b)

Research question: Does a morphological deficiency in production data reflect a corresponding deficit in the abstract representation of functional features and phrase structure in the syntax?

This ongoing study focuses on the nature of grammatical knowledge in the "fossilized" end-state of adult SLA. The results so far indicate a dissociation between morphology and syntax; in other words, the contingent relation often argued in the literature to hold between the acquisition of verbal morphological inflection and underlying syntactic knowledge is not supported. The long-term goal of the study is to revisit the question of access to UG in adult SLA by considering how and/or whether the scope of UG extends to the often highly complex procedures for mapping from abstract grammatical features in the syntax to language-specific morphophonological forms. (For the situating of this study in its larger theoretical context, see Lardiere 2000a.)

Methodology: The findings are based on a detailed longitudinal case study comprising naturalistic L2 production data collected in three audiotaped recordings spanning nearly nine years and, more recently, on elicited task-based data from Patty, a native

Chinese speaker who arrived in the US at the age of 22. Data collection began after Patty had already been living continuously in the US for about 10 years. From the beginning of data collection, Patty was immersed totally and virtually exclusively in the target language environment, English, spoken by native speakers. Fossilization cannot, therefore, be due to any relative paucity of input in quantity or quality, or to lack of assimilation into the target culture.

Results: Although Patty's morphological marking on verbs has apparently fossilized at a production rate well below the usual criteria typically assumed throughout the literature for "acquisition," we can nonetheless find alternative types of evidence suggesting knowledge of the functional categories and features associated with verbal inflection. Three kinds of evidence have been investigated to date: (i) pronominal case on subjects (indicating abstract knowledge of finiteness); (ii) the position of verbs with respect to negation and adverbs (indicating knowledge of feature strength and/or UG general economy principles prohibiting overt verb raising in English); and (iii) the extensive presence in the data of *wh*-questions and embedded clauses, many with overt complementizers (indicating the representation of a CP functional category and therefore, presumably, all lower functional projections as well). Taking a brief look at each of these in turn:

i In English (as in many languages), there is a relation between finiteness – an abstract feature of the grammar – and the form of subject pronouns. Within both Minimalist and pre-Minimalist approaches to generative grammar, if the functional category I(nfl) or T(ense) is specified as [+ finite], the pronominal subject will require nominative or subject case; otherwise it will receive the default case marking for English, object case. Lardiere (1998a) examined the suppliance of past tense marking on verbs in Patty's data and found it to be stable and low over the entire period of data collection, at only about 34 percent suppliance in obligatory contexts. Nonetheless, the distribution of subject case marking on Patty's pronominal subjects in the same contexts was absolutely perfect, at 100 percent suppliance over the entire period of data collection. Moreover, pronominal case marking on subjects was clearly a function of finiteness: only subjects in finite contexts received subject case, whereas all subjects in non-finite contexts (such as infinitive, ECM, and small clauses) were correctly produced in the object case form. A few first person examples of the latter follow:

(1) he make *me*, uh, spending money
(2) that doesn't have anything to do with *me* leaving home
(3) it's, uh, best for *me* to stay in Shanghai
(4) she didn't tell me to . . . like let *me* know that there's nothing going on in China

These findings indicate that Patty's grammatical representation of English includes the functional category T(ense), specified for [± finiteness], despite the relative impoverishment of tense marking on verbs.

ii This study again departs from recent claims in the theoretical and acquisition literature that posit a contingent relation between (the acquisition of) the verbal morphological paradigm for agreement (in English, 3sg *-s*) and the parameterized possibility of verb raising in the target language. The relevant abstract feature in English is "weak," thereby prohibiting thematic verb raising past adverbs and negation, and necessitating *do*-support in the case of negation. Thus, the following are ungrammatical in English:

(5) *they drink not beer
(6) *they drink frequently beer

Knowledge of the "weak" specification of English should result in evidence that the learner knows thematic verbs do not raise in English and will reject sentences such as those above as ungrammatical. The data from Patty, including both naturalistic production data and elicited grammaticality judgments, unequivocally show this, despite the fact that Patty produces 3sg *-s* agreement marking on thematic verbs in only about 4 percent of obligatory contexts. Lardiere (1998b) examined all possible contexts for verb raising over negation and/or adverbs in the production data and found that verb raising does not occur and does not appear to be an option. Additionally, Lardiere (2000b) reported the results of two grammaticality judgment tasks administered 18 months apart assessing the acceptability of verb raising over adverbs (the second test included 25 native speaker controls). Both yielded identical results: Patty correctly rejected all ungrammatical sentences involving verb raising past adverbs, a finding completely convergent with the production data. Again, the data suggest a total dissociation between morphological inflection and abstract featural knowledge; that is, even though Patty has *never* acquired verbal agreement affixation, she was still able to determine the status of verb raising in the target L2.

iii Finally, the presence of a CP, the highest functional projection in the clause, is claimed within nearly all models of language acquisition to implicate the presence of the lower functional categories as well. These include the categories of IP, such as Tense and Agreement which are typically associated with verbal inflectional morphology. Lardiere (1998a, 2000a) observes that, despite the very low suppliance rates for tense and agreement marking on verbs, Patty's grammatical representation of English nonetheless clearly includes a CP projection, indicating the presence of fully extended clausal phrase structure. The data provide abundant evidence for a CP projection in the form of embedded clauses with various complementizers, relative and free relative clauses, and *wh-* and yes-no questions involving subject–aux inversion. A few examples follow:

(7) why do you want me to go?
(8) he have the inspiration to say what he want to say
(9) something that have to show the unbeliever that you are in spirit
(10) can I have onion?

In sum, Patty's representation of English phrase structure appears to be complete, and clearly not contingent on the acquisition of verbal inflectional morphology.

Conclusion: Taken together, the results support the modularity of grammatical domains, and suggest that some domains are more susceptible to fossilization than others. In Patty's case, the mapping from morphosyntactic features to morphophonological spell-out appears to be particularly vulnerable; in contrast, her knowledge of finiteness and feature strength and the development of extended phrase structure in English all seem quite nativelike.

the period of observation, and very low, at around just 4 percent SOC. Related abstract syntactic knowledge – parameterized knowledge of verb raising, shown by correct placement of verbs with adverbs and in negation – however, is again intact. Lardiere suggests that such findings in grammatical subsystems in Patty's IL support the notion that adult L2 acquirers have continued access to innate knowledge of abstract syntactic features, but not to the complex procedures for mapping from those features to language-specific morpho-phonological forms, procedures which may lie outside the scope of UG. She concludes:

> In sum, Patty's representation of English phrase structure appears to be complete, and clearly not contingent on the acquisition of verbal inflectional morphology . . . Taken together, the results support the modularity of grammatical domains, and suggest that some domains are more susceptible to fossilization than others. (Lardiere, box 16.1, p. 506)

In a very recent, ongoing study conducted within the same linguistic framework, White (2002) reports on what may also turn out to be the end-state grammar of SD, a 50-year-old adult Turkish woman whose family emigrated to Montreal when she was 40. SD speaks Turkish at home, but has otherwise been exposed to a considerable amount of English over the past decade through a college course in interior design and subsequent work in English-speaking environments. She is a fluent, "advanced" speaker, as judged by her score of 93 percent on a University ELI placement test, but makes some errors, particularly with articles, of which she is well aware. Data were obtained from four interviews conducted over a two-month period, as well as a series of communication tasks targeting various morphological items, and several written tasks. Since there appeared to be few or no changes over the four interviews, the data were collapsed for the initial analysis.[21]

Production of several morphological inflections in obligatory contexts was found to be variably accurate, 60 percent or better on definite article, indefinite article, plural *-s*, third person singular *-s*, all persons aux + cop, lexical past verbs, and past aux + cop. In the realm of syntax, however, SD had moved from her subject and object pro-drop L1 to the English system virtually perfectly, and made no case errors at all: her choice of nominative and accusative pronoun forms was always appropriate, with subject pronouns nominative even when the verb was uninflected. White notes that these findings reveal SD's unconscious knowledge of certain syntactic requirements in English; for example, that subjects must be overt, and subject pronouns must be marked nominative. Similarly, SD's accuracy with pronouns and with definite and indefinite articles on an elicitation task suggest that the +/– definite feature is intact, and the lack of verb raising also argues against "inert" feature strength (cf. Eubank, 1995). White concludes that her results suggest missing surface inflection, and support Lardiere's findings of access problems, rather than representational deficits (cf. Hawkins, 2000).

Long (1997) has reported preliminary findings from a thus far 16-year study of "Ayako," a Japanese woman, born in 1926, now 75, who immigrated to Hawai'i in 1948, aged 22. A "war bride," Ayako came as the wife of a local third-generation Japanese-American man who had served as an interpreter in the US army of occupation in Japan. He was a blue-collar worker (now retired) and native speaker of Hawai'i Creole English (HCE). They have been happily married ever since. Ayako had already lived in the L2 environment for 37 years when the study began in 1985. She is very popular and has a wide circle of English-speaking and some Japanese-speaking friends in Honolulu. Except for the first three or four years after her arrival, English has been the main language at home, a fact made necessary, among other things, by the need to communicate with her three children, their friends, and neighbors, and later by her two jobs, the first working in a florist's for four years, the second as a salesperson at the local PX store for 16 years before retiring in 1988. While Ayako still uses both languages for a variety of purposes, she has used English more frequently for most of the past 52 years – she estimates about 75 percent of the time with her husband, for instance, and more than that outside the home. She is, and considers herself to be, highly acculturated, and often says she much prefers life in Hawai'i to what she would have experienced, especially as a woman, had she stayed in Japan.

Data collection began in 1985, when Ayako completed a battery of six oral production tasks designed to elicit a variety of narrative and expository discourse:

i a semi-structured interview, during which she spoke freely in response to eight intentionally broad, open-ended questions, such as "In as much detail as possible, would you please tell me about your childhood?" and "What differences do you think there are between Japan and America and between Japanese and Americans?";

ii a picture description of a detailed street scene showing a serious traffic jam, followed by her reply to the question, "What do you think caused the traffic jam in the first place?";

iii a 20-item repetition test, using pre-recorded stimulus sentences, each designed to reflect one of six differing degrees of processing complexity as (then) specified in work by Meisel et al. (1981, and elsewhere);

iv a second picture description, this time of a six-frame cartoon strip story about a young boy, John, being knocked off his bicycle by a careless motorist, the narrative started by the researcher with the prompt "One day last year . . . ," and recounted by Ayako without the pictures after a two-minute period of silent study and planning with the pictures present;

v a second, 60-item repetition test, using a pre-recorded stimulus tape, designed to probe a wide range of grammatical features;

vi a brief, open-ended discussion of Ayako's reflections on her experience completing tasks (i)–(v).

Cue cards with written Japanese translations of the eight questions and of the instructions for each task were available when needed. The whole session lasted approximately one hour.

In the interest of comparability, exactly the same procedure was repeated 10 years later, in 1995, and except for the two repetition tests, which proved too difficult for Ayako, repeated again in 1996, 1998, and 2000. The 1995 and subsequent sessions usually lasted two hours or longer, despite removal of the two repetition tasks from 1996 on, due to Ayako's volunteering more information and the researcher's improved use of follow-up prompts. One question in the informal conversation each year asks, "How important is English in your life?" In addition to eliciting speech data, this, plus follow-up questions, serves to help keep track of any changes in Ayako's language attitudes and use, and her perceptions thereof. The two highly controlled picture-description tasks are intended to provide sub-samples over time that are not only exactly comparable in terms of content and procedure, but in which almost everything Ayako intends to say is unambiguous. That is often not the case in spontaneous speech with lower-proficiency learners, sometimes making analyses difficult.[22] Data from these sessions have been supplemented by a few audio-recordings at informal family gatherings over the years, by occasional notes on interesting spontaneous utterances written down verbatim when they occurred, and in 2000 by a written version of the bicycle story, completed after the usual spoken version.[23]

Ayako has had both motivation and opportunity to learn English for the past 52 years, and at first sight appears to have been quite successful. She speaks and understands HCE fluently in face-to-face conversation with familiar topics and people in partly routinized informal situations, such as at mealtimes, when discussing family matters, out shopping, or during social visits with friends. However, communication on most such occasions is made easier not only by the routinization factor, but by the fact that frequent interlocutors are tuned into her English, and she to theirs. Ayako and many of her family members and friends use a variety of strategies to pre-empt and repair trouble. She can have difficulty in less familiar situations, especially when they involve more impersonal expository discourse dealing with displaced time and space. Transcripts of her speech show numerous lexical gaps, little complex syntax, and many persistent morphological errors.[24] For example, plural *s*-marking, which varies across tasks and time, was supplied correctly only 71 percent of the time in obligatory contexts in free conversation in 1985, and 48 percent of the time in free conversation in 1995, while reference to past time, which also varies greatly, was marked accurately in fewer than 50 percent of obligatory contexts in the bicycle story narrative in both 1985 and 1995.

What is most noticeable about Ayako's speech is that while performing far short of nativelike levels, with pervasive and persistent errors despite ample opportunity to acquire the target language, and so constituting an apparently perfect candidate for a fossilization claim, her interlanguage exhibits extensive amounts of variation, both synchronic and diachronic. Some of this variability may turn out to be systematic, but much of it appears not to be. Therefore, unless considerable and unpredictable synchronic and diachronic IL change are acceptable indices of fossilization, which would surely be to bleed the construct of any remaining meaning,[25] some subsystems in Ayako's IL, at least, are not, in fact, stabilized, much less fossilized.

To illustrate, consider Ayako's plural marking during her responses to questions 1 (about her childhood) and 2 (about Japanese–American differences) in the informal interview in 1985 and 1995, shown in table 16.2. Within just a few lines, she supplies and fails to supply plural *-s* in identical linguistic contexts, with identical referents and identical intended meanings. This kind of variability is seen both synchronically, within and across "tasks," or what Selinker would probably call "discourse domains" (here, responses to the two questions), as in *ten month/s old, sister/s*, and *(girl)friend/s* in 1985, and *sister/s* and *friend/s* in 1995, and diachronically, within the same task or discourse domain (here, responses to the two questions) over time, as in *month/s, sister/s*, and *friend/s*. This variability is seen with these and other tokens throughout the transcripts, and with a variety of features, not just plural *-s*. Thus, while recounting the bicycle story in 1985, and due to a procedural error, twice in

Table 16.2 Ayako's plural *-s* marking across tasks and time

Question	*1985*	*1995*
1	Ten months old (85, 1, 3)	Ten months old (× 3)
	Ten month_ old (85, 1, 5)	
	Five sisters	Da older sisters (95, 8, 22)
	My sisters	Older sister_ (95, 9, 28)
	Three sister_	My older sister_ (95, 9, 30)
		My sisters all (95, 9, 38)
	Seven years old	Six years old
	A couple of years	Four years
		Olden days time
2	Those things (× 2)	
	Stories	
	Book_	Her friends
	My friend_ (85, 2, 4)	My friend_ (× 3)
	My girlfriends (85, 2, 5)	We become close friend_
		Retirees
		Sometime_
		Trip_
		News

1995 (once with the strip-story pictures present, and then a day later, without the pictures), past time marking shows similar variability, again sometimes with the same verbs, within identical linguistic contexts, and with identical referents and intended meanings; for example *fix/fixed his bike, he _/was riding, he see/saw a car, he's trying to/was try to/try to fix the car*. Elsewhere in the data, Ayako shows that plurality and past time reference, and the forms used to mark each morphologically in English, are both known to her and are used correctly on some noun phrases and verbs fairly consistently, while consistently being omitted on others. Pairs like *lady/ladies, child/children, day/days,* and *year/ years,* for instance, and *have/had, go/went, doesn't/didn't, cannot/couldn't,* are almost invariably used correctly and productively, whereas some other noun phrases, such as *horn, noun, textbook,* and *sentence* (generally, but not only, those involving lower-frequency items for Ayako), are rarely or never marked for plural, and some verbs, such as *look, pass, stop, try,* and *want,* are rarely, if ever, marked for past.[26]

This combination of (i) relatively stable suppliance of appropriate marking on certain nouns and verbs, (ii) relatively stable omission of the same marking on others, and (iii) highly variable, unpredictable performance, that is, free variation, on still others, seems different in kind from the "free" variation often reported in the SLA literature, and is here termed *volatility*. *Free variation* is commonly defined as cases where two or more forms or variants of a form occur interchangeably with the same meaning or function in the same linguistic, discoursal, and situational context, and with no evidence of difference in the degree of attention to form during their production (see Ellis, 1999, and elsewhere).[27] Ellis claims that free variation is the result of items having been learned, but *not yet integrated* into an IL system for lack either of internal linguistic or external communicative pressure for the integration to occur. This would cover cases under (iii), above, where Ayako's suppliance is seemingly random, were it not for the fact that cases under (i) show that she *has* learned and integrated the forms in question for some nouns and verbs, if not others. Accordingly, I have tentatively defined *volatility* as cases where:

> a target-like or non-target-like form has been learned and integrated into the grammar with a target-like or non-target-like form–function relationship, yet where that form still also occurs interchangeably with one or more other forms or variants with different lexical types in the same linguistic, discoursal and situational context to express the same meaning or function, with no evidence of different degrees of attention during its production. (Long, 1997, p. 4)

What makes volatility of particular methodological relevance in a study of stabilization or fossilization is that a case where a learner seems to have integrated productive (in this case, also target-like) rules into his or her underlying grammar, but only applies them with certain subsets of the classes of items to which they should apply, will only be discernible through an analysis conducted at the level of token, not type. This means that claims of stabilization or fossilization in IL framed in terms of SOC or TLU accuracy percentages, or of other measures at the level of type, may obscure considerable synchronic or diachronic change, and so be unfounded. Despite the volatility described above, for example, Ayako's SOC percentages for past time reference in the two comparable 1995 and 1996 renditions of the bicycle story (without the pictures present) were 48 percent and 45 percent, respectively, giving the illusion of stabilization.[28]

In sum, two of the three longitudinal studies briefly summarized here, those by Han and Lardiere, appear to provide the strongest evidence to date for fossilization as *product*, and each comes accompanied by (very different) interesting putative explanations for the findings. In addition, Patty's (and SD's) data suggest that if fossilization occurs, it operates locally, not globally throughout an IL. Fossilization would not simply be the same thing as general non-nativelike L2 attainment by adult starters, in other words. In this context, it is important to note, however, that to substantiate such a claim and show that fossilization affects specific modules or structures, or consistent access to them, it is necessary to provide evidence that the items concerned have ceased to develop while other IL subsystems continue to make progress. Failing that, it is unjustified to argue for fossilization of particular items as distinct from maturational constraints on the whole system – a separate issue. No study to date has sought, much less provided, such evidence.

It is too early to say, on the other hand, whether parts of Ayako's IL have fossilized. The evidence so far suggests that they have not, and that the two small grammatical domains reported on above, at least, may not even have stabilized, in spite of the fact that Ayako's speech is far from nativelike after plenty of motivation and opportunity to have advanced further. Should this be the eventual finding, it will not show that fossilization does not exist (it is impossible to prove a negative, of course), but it may serve as a note of caution for those purporting to show fossilization in learners with less optimal profiles than Ayako, using cross-sectional designs, less complete data, and more superficial analyses.

5 Explanations for Stabilization and/or Fossilization

Whether or not fossilization is a psychological reality is a question of how the construct is defined, and whether or not cases of fossilization have been documented depends not only on the definition, but very much on one's evaluation of the methodology employed in the search. Already assuming fossilization to be a proven reality, however, researchers have advanced a variety of explanations, some as well founded as many of the fossilization claims themselves, some more serious. Surprisingly, no one seems to have considered the possibility that if fossilization is, as Selinker (1972) claimed, a cognitive mechanism producing the non-target-like end-state also called "fossilization," there is no need for other explanations, or conversely, that if L1 transfer, learnability, markedness, etc., or some combination of linguistic and psycholinguistic factors is responsible, there is no need for "fossilization" as an explanation.

There seem to be two problems. First, for many, "fossilization" has simply become a general, non-technical name for non-target-like ultimate attainment, that is, a performance descriptor, a broad-brush method of characterizing what a learner did not do, not a competence issue, a matter of what he or she could not do, which is what made the original claim interesting. In Selinker's original formulation, fossilization (as product) was supposedly a technical term for a special state of permanent non-target-like ultimate attainment that was due to a change in an individual's underlying capacity for SLA, also known as "fossilization" – a process which, it has since been suggested, appears to affect particular structures, modules, domains, etc., rather than whole ILs. The second problem is that, even in Selinker's original definition, reference was made to the process manifesting itself in "linguistic phenomena . . . which speakers of a particular NL will tend to keep in their IL relative to a particular TL" (Selinker, 1972, p. 215). In other words, Selinker himself was positing the existence of a cognitive mechanism, fossilization, responsible for fossilization as product, but simultaneously suggesting that the mechanism was in turn controlled or constrained by other factors, such as L1 transfer. On that view, fossilization (as process) is not itself an explanation, but really a cover term for one or more causal variables in SLA, such as transfer, that is, a process itself in need of explanation. Selinker has continued to elaborate on his belief in a central role for transfer ever since (see, e.g., Selinker, 1992; Selinker and Lakshmanan, 1992), and others have joined him in the search for an explanation for the explanation.

Factors proposed as causes of fossilization[29] include (but are not limited to) the following: lack of negative feedback on error, both external, and internal in the form of self-monitoring, and/or provision of positive feedback on successful communication despite error (Higgs and Clifford, 1982; Vigil and Oller, 1976; Yorio, 1994), especially when the latter co-occurs with unavailability of negative evidence in natural L2 input (White, 1987); insensitivity to negative feedback (Lin, 1995); age-related loss of sensitivity to language data, caused by learners reaching the steady state in the L1 (Schnitzer, 1993); maturational constraints (Seliger, 1978); lack of access to various components of UG, either computational resources, with mapping problems between the lexicon and syntax (Lardiere, 1998b; White, 2002; and others), representational resources (Beck, 1998; Eubank, 1995; and others), or representational resources not instantiated in the L1 (Hawkins, 2000; and others); loss of access to UG altogether (Bley-Vroman, 1989; Clahsen, 1988; Meisel, 1991, 1997); L1 transfer (Selinker, 1972; and others); idiosyncratic transfer of L1 elements which particular learners (as opposed to all learners from that L1 background) perceive as equivalent to elements in the L2, so as to avoid duplicating them in the new language (Nakuma, 1998); a combination of L1 transfer and one or more other factors, such as perceived typological markedness or a desire for symmetry, converging on the same error (Kellerman, 1989; and others), as expressed in the weak form of the Multiple Effects Principle (MEP), in which L1 transfer is a privileged factor (Selinker and Lakshmanan, 1992); the strong form of the MEP, in which L1 transfer is a necessary factor, in combination with one or more other factors (Selinker and Lakshmanan, 1992); processing constraints (as distinct from lack of grammatical knowledge) producing fossilized random variation, especially of semantically light morphology (Schachter, 1996); failure to acculturate (Schumann, 1978); a variety of social-psychological variables (Preston, 1989);[30] premature communicative pressure (Higgs and Clifford, 1982); automatization of incorrect forms and rules, with resulting errors more likely to appear in casual than careful style due to less attention to form being exercised there (Hulstijn, 1989); satisfaction of communicative needs (Corder, 1967; and others); the ease of using what learners may know is a simplified system, but one that handles their basic communicative needs (Klein, 1986); communication breakdown, leading to avoidance of contact with native speakers, and hence to early fossilization (Perdue, 1993); inability to notice input–output discrepancies, that is, the Matching Problem Hypothesis (Klein, 1986); unwillingness to risk restructuring (Klein and Perdue, 1993); and ungrammatical input from native speakers (Gass and Lakshmanan, 1991) or non-native speakers (Harley and Swain, 1978). What almost all explanations on offer have in common is that they do not work – at least, not for fossilization, even when they may for stabilization, and not for some learners or for some supposedly fossilized features of L2 performance.

As in any area of SLA theory construction, one way of evaluating proposals to account for stabilization and/or fossilization is to subject them to empirical test. Short of other problems, any that can survive such testing are candidate explanations. Any that cannot are probably not. What is sought of an explanation is predictive power,[31] not an ability after the fact to describe cases where the proposed causal factors (supposedly) did work, while ignoring those where they did not. That would be to return to the pseudo-explanations of the Error Analysis period.[32] Does the explanation potentially apply to all learners and all supposedly fossilized structures? It loses credibility if it can be shown that it only applies to some learners, and/or only to some structures alleged to have fossilized, and not to others, or predicts stabilization or fossilization which does not occur.[33] Is there counter-evidence, in other words?

To illustrate, a claim that stabilization is caused by transfer operating in tandem with one or more additional factors, such as typological markedness, perceptual saliency, or general cognitive constraints underlying developmental sequences, has plenty of empirical support (Andersen, 1983; Harley and Swain, 1984; Jain, 1974; Wode, 1981; Zobl, 1982). Zobl (1982), for example, reviews evidence from a number of studies showing, among other things, that learners tend to persist longer with an interlingual structure, such as *No V* negation in ESL, when it is the same as, or similar to, one with the same function in their L1. Thus, Spanish speakers stay with pre-verbal negation longer than Japanese speakers, whose L1 has post-verbal negation. A claim that fossilization is caused by transfer operating in tandem with one or more additional variables is equally obviously unfounded, however. While many Spanish speakers, and some Japanese speakers, as shown by Stauble (1984), never progress beyond the *No V* stage, many do. The claim cannot survive the universality test, in other words – it simply does not work for all learners; indeed, it fails for a large proportion of them.

One need look no further than the same findings to show that the MEP, too, cannot be correct, in either its strong or weak form. The four-stage development of negation in ESL is probably the single best-documented developmental sequence in SLA to date, and has been shown to occur in the ILs of speakers from every L1 background yet studied (for review, see, e.g., Schumann, 1979), including those like Japanese, Swedish, and Turkish (Hyltenstam, 1977), whose post-verbal L1 systems mean that the two initial stages (*No V* and *Don't V*) cannot be the result of L1 influence (probably not even in the cases of speakers of L1s which do have pre-verbal negation), and so must be due to other factors. Here, then, is a clear case where L1 and one or more other factors combine, but where the fact that many learners progress beyond *No V* negation shows that the L1 + X combination cannot predict fossilization. The MEP, too, fails the universality test. It is potentially a more accurate predictor of learning *difficulty* than transfer alone, but not of fossilization.

Quite apart from the poor empirical track record of transfer and several other factors in the above list of putative explanations for fossilization, very few of the many suggested even have the *potential* to predict fossilization, due to the simple, but crucial, fact that they concern either universal human characteristics or pervasive qualities of the linguistic environment, whereas fossilization, according to Selinker, is supposedly a process constrained by L1 properties, but manifesting itself idiosyncratically at the level of the individual. Factors which are immutable and the same for everyone could only work as explanations for the entire population of L2 learners and for all structures if they worked at all. They involve: (i) unchanging facts about L1–L2 relationships (e.g., the MEP); (ii) cognitive abilities and processes which are presumably universal, or at least vary only in degree, not kind (e.g., processing constraints, automatization of incorrect forms or rules, ease of using simpler IL systems); (iii) changes in language-learning ability (e.g., loss of sensitivity to language data, complete or partial loss of access to UG, and other effects of putative maturational constraints), which are supposedly part of the human biological inheritance, and so universal; or (iv) pervasive characteristics of language use (e.g., the absence of negative feedback and/or presence of positive feedback on error in non-instructional talk, the ungrammaticality of natural speech, communication breakdown, and unwillingness to risk restructuring), which, again, are presumably roughly the same for everyone (if extremely hard, or even impossible, to measure in some cases). A few supposed universals or constants are serious candidates (some far more plausible, and with much stronger empirical credentials) for explaining putatively universal non-nativelike ultimate attainment in general, but arguably should not be considered as explanations for fossilization at the level of the individual. They can explain neither differences among individuals – why one IL stabilizes or fossilizes, but not another, given learners with basically the same genetic endowment, the same cognitive abilities, similar input, and so on – nor differences within individuals – why some structures but not others are affected.

Conversely, because they themselves can and do vary from one individual to another, a second set of factors in the above list might appear to have the *potential* to account for fossilization (but less so universal non-nativelike ultimate attainment, if that is indeed the end-state for all adult starters, as many researchers maintain). They include satisfaction of communicative needs, social-psychological variables, (in)sensitivity to feedback (including internal self-monitoring), and (in)ability to notice mismatches between input and output. In practice, however, the first two fail empirically. First, it is well known that language development continues to progress in many individuals long after they are capable of satisfying their communicative needs (just as it does in children doing L1A). Second, despite unsupported assertions to the contrary (see Schumann, 1993), various arrays of social and psychological factors have repeatedly failed to account for age-related success and failure in SLA at the level of individuals (see, e.g., Schmidt, 1983) and groups (see, e.g., Schumann, 1986), and have no obvious potential, either, for explaining differential success within the same individual at the level of linguistic domain or grammatical structure.

This leaves only (in)sensitivity to feedback (including internal self-monitoring), and (in)ability to notice mismatches between input and output, which are clearly very similar proposals. If it were only deviant structures that stabilized or (supposedly) fossilized, one might propose sensitivity to (negative) feedback as an explanation. For reasons discussed earlier, however, correct rules and structures stabilize, and must be subject to the same mental processes as incorrect ones. It is highly unlikely, moreover, that the same individual would be differentially (in)sensitive to positive and negative input, as opposed to input in general. Accordingly, while several factors predict stabilization, including L1–L2 and typological markedness relationships, and various combinations of social-psychological factors, just one factor, *sensitivity to input*, is the most likely explanation for fossilization (as product, in the sense of a frozen end-state grammar), if fossilization itself turns out to be a reality. It would, of course, also be a predictor of stabilization, which certainly is a reality.

Common input characteristics, such as occasional ungrammaticality, typically vary very little from one setting to another, and with the exception of comprehensibility, such variance as has been studied appears to affect first or second language acquisition very little, either.[34] Individual learners' sensitivity to input, conversely, can vary a great deal, and beyond the importance for acquisition in general of "noticing," in the sense of registering the existence of items in the input (see Schmidt, 1995), there are several hints in the literature as to the possible importance of individual differences in this ability. One well-known example is the discussion of possible reasons for Wes's poor rate of development (Schmidt, 1983). Another, perhaps less obvious, case may be the solid empirical track record of language aptitude as a predictor of success in SLA (for review, see Skehan and Dörnyei, this volume). Sensitivity to input is arguably a key component of aptitude, tapped, for instance, in both the spelling clues and words in sentences subtests of the Modern Language Aptitude Test (Carroll and Sapon, 1959). In fact, three of the four components which Carroll proposed made up language aptitude could be viewed as involving input sensitivity: phonetic coding ability, grammatical sensitivity, and inductive language learning ability. Grammatical sensitivity, for instance, supposedly concerns the ability to recognize the grammatical functions of words or other linguistic elements in sentence structures. As noted earlier (with due caveats about methodological aspects of the studies concerned), there are reports (e.g., Lin, 1995; Lin and Hedgcock, 1996) within the fossilization literature itself that learners whom the researchers considered fossilized showed relatively low sensitivity to feedback. Indeed, as also reported earlier, several researchers have (unjustifiably) treated the apparent failure of learners to destabilize following corrective feedback of various kinds as a key indicator that they had fossilized. A thorough test of the current hypothesis would require a validated measure of sensitivity to input, with scores predicted to be lower for learners whose ILs revealed longer periods of stabilization.

An obvious problem for input sensitivity as an explanation for stabilization or fossilization is the question of why, if it is a general characteristic of an individual's language learning ability (or aptitude), only some structures are affected, and not others.[35] Hence, an adequate account of stabilization or fossilization will also need to recognize the importance of various characteristics of target structures in the input, especially perceptual saliency, which is in turn often related to frequency, communicative value, semantic weight, and so forth. In sum, the interaction of *input sensitivity* (a constant within the individual, but varying across individuals) with *perceptual saliency* (which varies across structures) has the potential to account for stabilization or fossilization of some structures, but not others, observed in some individuals, but not others.[36]

If this proposal is correct, it should predict accurately which classes of linguistic elements are more likely to stabilize (or fossilize) than others. In a valuable contribution on this issue (see also Kellerman, 1989), Todeva (1992, pp. 232–9) suggested that three high-risk categories (HRCs) of linguistic features are especially prone to fossilization: (i) categories lacking a straightforward form–function relationship, such as articles; (ii) semi-productive rules, whose exceptions (unlike, say, irregular English past tense forms) do not constitute clearly defined sets, such as English negative prefixation, dative alternation, and stress shift in verb-to-adjective formations (e.g., analyze/analyzable, present/presentable, but admire/admirable); and (iii) units of a highly arbitrary nature, such as prepositions, collocations, and gender assignment. A similar search for classes of linguistic features potentially vulnerable to maturational constraints on language acquisition (Long, 1993b) involved a survey of findings from studies of a range of situations in which language is developed, lost, or impaired late in life or under other abnormal circumstances, including pidginization, aphasia, and first and second language acquisition by older children and adults. Morphology was found to be more vulnerable than syntax, inflections more at risk than free morphemes, and exceptional cases within a language-specific paradigm especially problematic. Counter-examples to every generalization were not hard to find, however. Given that language development, not language, is the object of study, a better strategy, it was suggested, should be to combine linguistic classifications with psycholinguistically relevant qualities, such as frequency, regularity, semantic transparency, communicative redundancy, and perceptual saliency. In other words, a processing dimension is needed, one which combines cognitive factors with input characteristics. It is not the case that all inflectional morphology is vulnerable to maturational constraints – or, in the present context, likely to stabilize, or if such a thing exists, fossilize – but perhaps non-salient, irregular inflections, for example, or ambiguous, optional pragmatic rules, are the items that even good learners are most likely to miss and which are especially problematic for learners with low input sensitivity. This is obviously an area where some painstaking research is needed. Meanwhile, it is possible to assess the findings to date on fossilization as process and product, along with implications for the role of the construct in SLA theory.

6 The Status of Fossilization in SLA Theory

Fossilization has been beset with definitional and methodological ambiguities from the outset, not least as to whether it is (i) a term used to *describe* the permanent end-state of IL development (in some subsystems and/or discourse domains, for some learners), (ii) a term used to *explain* permanent cessation of learning short of the target, despite ample opportunity, motivation, and ability to acquire the target language, or (iii) *both*. In other words, fossilization has sometimes been explanandum, the phenomenon to be explained, sometimes explanans, the putative explanation, and sometimes explanandum *and* explanans.

Even its use simply as a descriptor of the product of learning has become vaguer over time, with an increasing tendency in the SLA literature (and outside it) to equate fossilization and general non-nativelike attainment (not necessarily with permanent connotations).[37] This is a mistake. The original, narrower use of the term involves a potentially interesting claim that the current level of development is the permanent end-state because a learner *cannot* progress any further (in one or more IL subsystems), a claim about a *loss of capacity to acquire*. The latter is simply an observation about the level of one or more individuals' L2 proficiency – a statement about what they have not (perhaps, simply, have not yet) accomplished.

A similar dilution of the construct has begun to occur at the process level, as well, with fossilization sometimes being offered as an explanation for general age-related differences in the capacity for language learning. The link became clear in Selinker's work in 1996:

> fossilization is the process whereby the learner creates a cessation of interlanguage learning [*sic*], thus stopping the interlanguage from developing, it is hypothesized, in a permanent way . . . The argument is that no adult can hope to ever speak a second language in such a way that s/he is indistinguishable from native speakers of that language. (Selinker, 1996, cited in Han, 2000b, p. 5)

Again, conflating fossilization in SLA and general maturational constraints on (all) language acquisition is a mistake. Few dispute that ultimate attainment in child L1A and adult L2A – native in the former, non-native (nearly always markedly so) in the latter – is one of the most salient differences between the two processes, although disagreement persists as to the principal underlying cause(s), commonly, but not universally, held to be age of onset and/or a constellation of linguistic factors dealt with under the general rubric of "L1 transfer." If fossilization is to have value as a construct in SLA theory, it must refer to something other than this general age-related decline in the capacity to acquire any language, first or additional, that is, to a loss of ability to acquire a *second* (including foreign) language. Put another way, the important questions both for SLA theory and for a variety of practical matters are (i) whether typically poor adult L2 attainment is due to circumstantial environmental and personal factors (inadequate opportunity to acquire, lack of motivation, etc.), that is, simple *failure to acquire*, or to a qualitative or quantitative *loss of ability to acquire* even when conditions are optimal; and (ii) whether the factor(s) underlying failure are peculiar to L2A, as opposed to language acquisition, in general.

Two broad bodies of research findings speak to the first issue: that on putative universal maturational constraints on the human capacity to learn languages, including work on so-called "sensitive periods" (for review, see Hyltenstam and Abrahamsson, this volume), and that, reviewed above, on fossilization, an allegedly localized loss of capacity supposedly affecting individual second language acquirers differently (although all learners eventually, on some accounts), not necessarily age-related and not necessarily system-wide in its effects. General maturational constraints, on the one hand, and fossilization (as cognitive mechanism), on the other, are supposedly very different in pervasiveness, scope, timing, and more, in other words, and the two should not be equated. As Hyltenstam (1988, p. 69) points out, young second language learners provide the test case on the second issue. If fossilization only occurs (if it occurs at all) in adult starters, it should be seen as an age-related learning phenomenon. If it is found in the ILs of child starters, as well, it will be seen as constituting a pure second language, as opposed to first language, phenomenon.[38]

As product, unless fossilization and mere non-nativelike proficiency are clearly distinguished, and as process, unless fossilization remains a claim about what is possible in adult language learning separate from a general belief in maturational constraints, the construct can be expected to disappear from SLA theory (if not from colloquial pedagogic parlance) for being redundant in each case. With the more restricted and thus potentially theoretically interesting meanings, therefore, how does fossilization fare as description and/or explanation?

To assess its *descriptive* value, the relevant question is whether there is evidence of the phenomenon to be thus described, that is, evidence of permanently immobilized IL grammars, or parts thereof, which cannot undergo further development. In light of the research findings to date, there would appear to be little compelling evidence that IL grammars fossilize. Only two studies, those by Lardiere and Han, have obtained results potentially interpretable as evidence of fossilization, and their findings on this issue (as opposed to others they speak to) may be questioned methodologically: in Han's research, on the basis of the kind of (primarily planned, written) data employed, and the study's limited duration, and in both cases due to the lack of evidence that one or more other aspects of the informants' ILs were still developing, and the level (type, not token) at which analyses were conducted. All other studies to date have suffered from one or more serious problems invalidating their findings as far as the fossilization issue is concerned (although, as noted earlier, many remain interesting and very valuable for other reasons): to reiterate, assuming, not demonstrating, fossilization, selecting inappropriate learners for study, basing findings on insufficient data, and using inadequate analyses. In other words, while fossilization may yet turn out to exist, as the studies by Lardiere (1988a, and elsewhere) and White (2002), in particular, suggest, there is little evidence that it does thus far, and hence, currently little or nothing to explain.

It would certainly be premature to dismiss fossilization as an empty construct at this stage, however, just as it is quite unwarranted to assume its reality. Fossilization may very well occur in some ILs. The fact is that the very problems that have beset almost all the empirical work to date mean that the notion remains largely unexplored. Several methodological improvements needed in future research were outlined above. To recapitulate, to have any potential for substantiating a claim of fossilization (as product), the subject(s) chosen for study need to have had the ability, motivation, and opportunity to acquire the L2 for many years (perhaps 10 or more) before the study begins. Then, accompanied by evidence of continuing ability, motivation, and opportunity, repeated comparable observations are required over time (perhaps five years or more), ideally involving ample samples of the spoken vernacular, supplemented where appropriate by elicited data of various kinds. Analyses should be carried out at the level of token, as well as type, with a rational account provided of the analyst's treatment of the inevitable synchronic and diachronic variation.[39] If a resulting fossilization claim is specified to apply to certain IL subsystems, data should be provided to show that one or more other subsystems continue to develop. If a claim is specified to apply within a certain discourse domain, context, task, or other unit, the unit(s) concerned need to be defined operationally before the analysis begins, and data need to be provided to show that the linguistic elements covered by the fossilization claim continue to progress in one or more other discourse domains, etc. These are stringent requirements, but requirements needing to be met if a case of fossilization is to be distinguished from the more general one of an IL grammar affected by general maturational constraints, or even from an IL grammar that is still developing uninhibited by either.

Whatever the current or future verdict on its validity as a description of the end-product of at least some cases of SLA, as an *explanation* fossilization clearly fails. Left to stand on its own, it is a "black box," no more revealing than saying that learners cannot progress any further because of "Force X." Alternatively, if itself to be explained by other factors, as seems to be the consensus even among true believers, it is redundant: if the MEP, input sensitivity, or whatever, is the reason for linguistic rigor mortis having set in, then that is the reason, not Force X. In fact, however, in the absence to date, at least, of convincing evidence of fossilization as product, the more relevant object of study for researchers becomes *stabilization*, not fossilization, and explanations for that. From a theory-construction perspective, too, such a shift in focus has several advantages: (i) the existence of stabilization is not in doubt; (ii) it avoids the methodologically problematic "permanence" issue; (iii) it makes an additional subset of claims empirically testable; and (iv) unless and until solid evidence appears of the psychological reality of fossilization, it lightens the burden of SLA theory and theories by one variably operationalized and as yet empirically unsubstantiated construct.

ACKNOWLEDGMENT

My initial realization of the urgent need to re-examine the whole notion of fossilization was triggered by a superb presentation on the subject by Malcolm Johnston at the Australian Association for Applied Linguistics conference in Adelaide in 1986. For their contributions to the sections of the present chapter describing their studies, I thank ZhaoHong Han and Donna Lardiere. For constructive feedback on the whole manuscript, I am grateful to Georgette Ioup, Malcolm Johnston, and Larry Selinker. None is responsible for the errors of fact or interpretation which no doubt remain.

NOTES

1 Selinker regards fossilization as having been foundational for SLA: "It could be argued that the field of second language acquisition was spurred into existence by the phenomenon usually labeled 'fossilization.' That is, the idea that no matter what the learner does, the learner will always 'be stuck' in the second language at some distance from the expected target. The phenomenon of 'being stuck' in the L2 seems to occur to most if not all learners even at the most advanced stages. This phenomenon seemed to force early SLA researchers, who believed they were working in a contrastive analysis framework (e.g., Briere, 1966; Nemser, 1971; and Selinker, 1966) into positing intermediate linguistic systems that in some serious sense did not seem to change. These systems were thought to be 'intermediate' between and, importantly, different from, the native language and from the target language, an 'approximative system' in Nemser's terms. What is interesting is that until the late 1960s none of these researchers knew about the others' work and each discovered the phenomenon independently." (Selinker, p.c., September 27, 2000)

2 "Interlanguage learning" is an unfortunate term. Each interlanguage is an idiosyncratic variety of the target language created by a particular learner. Each interlanguage is unique, the incomplete product of the L2 learning process, not an existing variety available to be learned (except, probably, in the rare case where another non-native speaker might be a learner's sole model).

3 More recently, Selinker appears to favor the higher figure:

> we often get asked how much time is enough to show fossilization? At the end of the day, we believe the number will be arbitrary. What we mean by a "substantial period" of time in any case must veer towards the years side of the continuum, perhaps a minimum of five years. (Selinker and Mascia, 1999, p. 258)

A five-year-minimum requirement would rule out Han's study, it should be noted, leaving just two potential cases, Patty and Ayako (discussed below), in the entire literature.

4

> It has long been noted that foreign language learners reach a certain stage of learning – a stage short of success – and that learners then permanently stabilize at this stage. Development ceases, and even serious conscious efforts to change are often fruitless. Brief changes are sometimes observed, but they do not "take." The learner backslides to the stable state. (Bley-Vroman, 1989, pp. 46–7)

5 A variety of unfortunate terms and unwarranted prescriptions surrounding fossilization have appeared in the SLA and (especially) pedagogical literatures over the years (see, e.g., Calve, 1992; Johnson, 1993; Valette, 1991). If fossilization is, by definition, permanent, "permanent

fossilization" is tautologous, "temporary fossilization" an oxymoron, and "defossilization" impossible. Yet Selinker himself urges research to answer the question: "Is it possible for a person to 'de-fossilize' at some point and, if so, under what conditions, internal/external to the learner?" (Selinker, 1993, p. 18). Despite assertions to the contrary (see, e.g., Graham, 1981; Johnson, 1993; Linn and Sucher, 1995; Wales, 1993), the answer *must* be negative, or fossilization is an empty construct. By contrast, "de-stabilization of previously considered fossilized forms" (Selinker and Mascia, 1999, p. 258) is conceptually coherent.

6 In this light, some clarification of statements like the following would be useful: "in terms of the logic of fossilization, if we can demonstrate at any one time that highly [?] stabilized forms are cognitively present, then the case is closed and the forms are permanently stabilized and we can call them 'fossilized'" (Selinker and Mascia, 1999, p. 258).

7 Differential performance across discourse domains also raises the specter of variable rules, an unfortunate import from group-level variationist sociolinguistics to theorizing at the level of the individual in SLA – an example of the ecological fallacy. Todeva (1992, p. 220) suggests that differential performance across discourse domains is a question of control, not knowledge.

8 Early reports of fossilized errors in the speech of sequential child bilinguals (Naiman, 1974; Selinker, Swain, and Dumas, 1975) were based on insufficient data and inadequate analyses (see sections 3.3. and 3.4). Plann (1976, 1977) discussed apparent three-year plateaus in the Spanish of anglophone children in the Culver City immersion program in terms of fossilization and the emergence of a classroom L2 dialect, but her claims were supported by a lack of evidence of significant progress across grade levels in the average morpheme accuracy scores in pooled data on different groups of children, as opposed to data on the same individuals over (sufficient) time. Also, Plann suggested that whatever lack of progress she had documented might have been due to the relatively low status of Spanish in California and to the fact that the immersion children lacked native-speaking Spanish peers with whom to bond. If that is true, the children were not a test case for fossilization, given Selinker's stipulation of lack of progress in the face of adequate ability, *motivation*, and *opportunity* to learn. Similarly, and again using cross-sectional data on groups of school-age children, Harley and Swain (1984) reported plateaus as long as four years, from grades 1 to 4, in the L2 development of French by anglophone youngsters in two immersion programs in Canada, but noted that this was followed by renewed, often substantial, progress by grade 10. Harley and Swain recognized that there was "to date no evidence of fossilization in any particular L2 domain at any particular level" (1984, pp. 301–2). A third study involving young learners, this time six children in a Canadian French immersion program (Pellerin and Hammerly, 1986), concluded that various errors had indeed fossilized, this despite the authors' data showing considerable improvement from time 1 to time 2 in three of five

grammatical domains examined. The study was flawed in several other respects, as well, including its inadequate duration for a fossilization claim, and the use of mean accuracy scores at the level of type (prepositions, verb forms, gender, pronouns, and reflexive pronouns), not token. All five categories, most obviously "verb forms," potentially concealed development among a miscellany of forms and structures falling under those headings (for useful discussion, see VanPatten, 1988, pp. 248–9, 256n.3). In fact, evidence of the need for caution in such grade-level comparisons of French immersion data had already been provided by Harley (1979) with respect to the development of gender marking from grades 2 to 5.

9 These and other cases will be returned to below in the discussion of data on Ayako.

10 Todeva (1992, p. 221) argues that it is easy to demonstrate fossilization of correct structures, as well, by showing that very advanced speakers consistently overuse correct structures in contexts where native speakers of the target language use different ones, that is, by identifying persistent deviations from the norms (for use), as opposed to deviations from the system. One well-attested example she cites is Bulgarian and Russian speakers' use of correctly formed relative clauses in place of attributive infinitives at ratios of 17:1 and 23:1, respectively.

11 In an encyclopedia entry on interlanguage, for instance, the reader is informed, "A central characteristic of any interlanguage is that it fossilizes – that is, it ceases to develop at some point short of full identity with the target language" (Tarone, 1994, p. 1715). Tarone provides no evidence for her assertion, but if she is right, and fossilization not only exists, but is inevitable in all cases of SLA, equally unsubstantiated pedagogic recipes for preventing it (see, e.g., Valette, 1991) must be doomed to failure.

12 Casual use of the term is something I have been guilty of myself; for instance "Japanese acquirers (with post-verbal L1 negation) also pass through a *No V* stage in English . . . some Japanese–English ILs appearing to fossilize at that stage" (Larsen-Freeman and Long, 1991, p. 260).

13 Few of the more than 40 investigations of fossilization to date of which I am aware will be cited here – and then only the better ones – as there is no value, or advantage to the field, in dwelling upon flawed studies by named researchers. Rather, the aim should be to identify what is and is not known about fossilization, what sort of data and analysis permit what kind of claim, and, in general, to improve future research in the area. It should also be noted that some of the studies cited critically in what follows are useful in other ways, and that the present focus is exclusively on what they show, or do not show, about fossilization, and how the researchers went about it. It should also be pointed out that Selinker is not responsible for methodologically inadequate work on fossilization conducted by third parties.

14 To illustrate:

> The criterion used to determine whether some specific error types could be considered fossilized was their frequency across subjects and speech modes. If that error was made frequently by all

> the subjects of the study in both free-elicited speech and writing, then the error in question may be attributed to the fact that the rules controlling its production have fossilized. (Sola, 1989, p. 63)

An obvious problem with this approach is that many successfully mastered aspects of a L2 (or L1) were once prone to frequent errors.

15 A related, but vaguer, construct utilized by sociocultural theorists is Vygotsky's "Zone of Proximal Development." Malcolm Johnston (p.c.) considers the uncertain validity of most measures utilized in fossilization studies to be one of their greatest, largely unrecognized, weaknesses.

16 This reasoning also appears to underlie the "pedagogic corollary" to the Multiple Effects Principle (see below) advanced by Selinker and Lakshmanan (1992): apparently fossilized structures will not become open to destabilization through consciousness-raising strategies when multiple effects apply.

17 For example, errors with some relative clause constructions and with nominal and pronominal copies have been found to persist in the Italian–English ILs of both instructed and naturalistic acquirers, even though Italian licenses neither type of copy (Pavesi, 1986).

18 Bean and Gergen write: "While the present study relies on a cross-sectional analysis of fossilized interlanguage, the benefits of longitudinal data are not to be overlooked [*sic*]. Ideally, a more comprehensive study of fossilization would involve a longitudinal, comparative analysis of many speakers of the same L1 who have fossilized in the same L2" (1990, p. 215n.1). Later, however, they defend a different aspect of their methodology, the use of only two informants in cross-sectional research, with the comment, "However, the design of the study has been most efficacious" (1990, p. 209).

19 Bean and Gergen write: "Future studies of fossilization will need to contend with the issue of what counts as 'fossilized.' For the sake of space and time, we have chosen not to engage in this debate here" (1990, p. 216).

20 The first conversation lasted 34 minutes, the second, eight years later, lasted 75 minutes, and the third, two months after that, 31 minutes.

21 White (p.c.) reports that a second set of data, gathered 18 months after those reported on in her paper, will soon be analyzed, thereby helping to determine whether SD's grammar has really reached end-state.

22 For discussion of strengths and weaknesses of a range of elicitation tasks used with adult second language learners, see Doughty and Long (2000) and Chaudron (this volume).

23 It is hoped that this and other written samples, possibly later supplemented by grammaticality judgment data, will help determine which of certain persistent problems are due to production constraints (for example, on word-final consonants and consonant clusters) interfering with overt marking of some grammatical relations, including plurality and past time reference, as distinct from lack of knowledge. Writing in English is hard for Ayako, however, and something she rarely does, save for the occasional greeting card message, and grammaticality

judgments are often problematic for learners of this kind, too (for discussion of this problem, see Long, 1993a).

24 Care has to be taken when analyzing Ayako's speech to distinguish what would be errors in "standard" spoken English in Hawai'i from what are perfectly grammatical constructions in HCE. Whether or not a given form is deviant is relatively unimportant in a fossilization study compared to whether or not it is supplied consistently. However, determining consistency is sometimes made difficult by the fact that, like most native speakers of the local variety, Ayako's command of HCE is not limited to one level, but allows her to shift up and down within a certain range on a creole continuum according to such factors as topic and, especially, interlocutor. In some contexts, for example, variation in Ayako's suppliance or omission of copula, morphological markers of past time reference, and other forms can be due to a shift toward or away from "standard" spoken English in Hawai'i rather than to variation in her suppliance of the item within a variety. Ambiguous cases are eliminated from the analysis, as, of course, are all instances where suppliance of a targeted item is unclear acoustically, such as past time /t/ or /d/ preceding an initial consonant on the following word.

25 If considerable and unpredictable synchronic and diachronic IL change were acceptable indices of fossilization, what would constitute counter-evidence for a fossilization claim? See the earlier discussion of Bean and Gergen (1990).

26 This is probably for phonological reasons in some cases. Japanese has CV syllable structure and disallows all word-final consonants except /n/, and all consonant clusters – a constraint known to affect adversely production of English past tense marking by speakers of Vietnamese (Sato, 1984, 1985, 1990). Ayako does, however, produce word-final consonants in many words, including /d/ and /t/, for example, *child, died, that, not, childhood, polite,* and *eight*, and even some word-final consonant clusters, for example, *it's, that's, raised,* and *passed*. Written data and grammaticality judgment data collected from Ayako will help clarify this matter.

27 IL variation initially pronounced to be "free" has sometimes turned out to be systematic when more carefully analyzed, as shown, for instance, by Berdan (1996), and that may yet turn out to be the case with Ayako's data.

28 Malcolm Johnston (p.c.) notes that if a totally systematic fossilized IL is at least a hypothetical possibility, but something always obscured in practice by the kinds of variation inevitable in samples of performance, a proper definition of fossilization would have to rule such a case out, thereby making the construct even more circumscribed than it already is or need be. He writes:

> My feeling is that, if fossilization were to exist, it would have to be something like the case of Ayako, where in a general context of cessation, there is still a kind of "head-banging" variation, i.e., the learner has been stopped by a "wall," but still continues to move back and forth laterally, oscillating as he or she "tries" to breach the

obstacle at different places. So variation would be fundamental to any postulated definition of fossilization.

29 Some of the factors that follow in the main body of the chapter – specifically, diminished access to UG, failure to reset parameters, and maturational constraints – were originally discussed by some of the authors concerned (but not others) as potential explanations of (allegedly universal) failure to acquire an L2 to nativelike levels in general, rather than of fossilization of particular subsystems within individual IL grammars. Others, such as failure to acculturate and automatization, were discussed in both contexts.

30 Preston (1989) claims that fossilization in Selinker's sense, which Preston terms "social fossilization," is caused by "the social and psychological make-up of the learners, their relationship to other learners, especially shared L1, and their feelings toward their reception in the L2 community" (1989, p. 254). He suggests (p. 255) that a second, symbolic kind of fossilization, which he terms "socio-linguistic fossilization," can occur when learners deliberately retain variability in their ILs as a marker of their identity in the speech community. While an interesting claim in its own right, it is doubtful whether it meets Selinker's criteria for fossilization, given that this variability is supposedly under the learner's control.

31 The requirement of predictive power rules out proposals like Nakuma's. On that account, fossilized structures are the result of entirely idiosyncratic perceptions of interlingual identification of L1–L2 equivalents, with consequent avoidance of L2 forms. Even if testable, this proposal could never predict the future course of development (or arrested development) even for the learner under study, much less for any other learner.

32 For discussion and illustrations of the hollowness of such accounts, see Long and Sato (1984, pp. 255–8). Selinker (1972, p. 24) recognizes the danger when he rejects overgeneralization as a potential explanation for fossilization on the grounds that some learners recover from overgeneralizations, whereas others do not, and that some learners recover from some overgeneralizations but not others. He endorses the search for an explanation with predictive power, not descriptive power. Unfortunately, however, as explained below, lack of predictive power is a problem for several candidate explanations, including the MEP.

33 Some might claim that while very few, if any, variables can successfully predict stabilization or fossilization, a variety, like those listed earlier, can genuinely account for individual cases after the fact. Put another way, stabilization and/or fossilization might be caused by different factors in different individuals and/or grammatical subsystems and/or discourse domains. Quite apart from the unwelcome enormous increase in the power of the theory such a stance allows (in this as in any other domain of SLA), with data potentially being "explicable" after the fact by any variables the theorist likes – anything goes, and no claim is falsifiable – to take this stance is to forget that fossilization is supposedly a cognitive mechanism

affecting all L2 learners, albeit manifesting itself in a variety of linguistic domains in different learners.

34 Variation in the interactional structure of conversation, on the other hand, does appear to affect both comprehension and acquisition (for review, see Gass, this volume; Long, 1996).

35 Klein (1986) implicitly recognizes this problem in his brief discussion of the relevance of "rule criticalness," "confirmation index," "target heterogeneity," and "reflection," in learners' failure to notice input–output mismatches.

36 The fact that there is nothing perceptually non-salient about structures like those marking the four stages of ESL negation means that at least some stabilization, for example at the *No V* stage, must simply reflect failure to develop, not loss of capacity to do so. That is, it must reflect factors associated with general success and failure in SLA, like impoverished input, rather than a change in underlying competence, such as that envisaged when fossilization sets in.

37 The extent of the problem can be seen in the opening paragraph of a recent encyclopedia entry on fossilization:

> Fossilization is the term used to describe incomplete language learning. This is identified by certain features of the learner's language being different from the speech of the target population, marking the point when progress in that aspect of the target language stops and the learner's language becomes fixed at an intermediate state. This is considered to occur because the learner's internalised rule system differs from that of the target system. Fossilization can take a number of forms, such as fossilized accent or syntax, in which case it might approximate to pidginization. Fossilization would normally be judged in relation to native speaker skills and would be seen as a permanent feature of the learner's language, although some authorities (Brown, 1980) describe it as "relatively permanent." (Daniels, 2000, p. 218)

38 Hyltenstam (1988) found that, while near-native in most respects, the speech and writing of 24 17- and 18-year-old Swedish high school students, native speakers of Spanish or Finnish who had begun acquiring Swedish between the ages of 4 and 12, still exhibited a number of lexical errors that might indicate fossilization in child SLA. Hyltenstam (1988, pp. 82–3) was careful to note, however, that the cross-sectional nature of his data precluded a definitive answer. The phenomena in question might have reflected permanent problems of the kind associated with fossilization; alternatively, they might simply turn out to have concerned late-acquired items, errors that disappeared at an extremely low rate, that is, incompleteness (see Schachter, 1988) and/or processing capacity restrictions in bilinguals. For further insightful discussion of the difficulty in distinguishing problems of competence or control in such data, see Hawkins (2000), Hyltenstam (1992), and White (2001).

39 The status of variation, in particular, clearly remains a major unresolved

issue. Can rules or structures which exhibit wide within-task or cross-task (context, discourse domain, etc.) variation be said to have stabilized, let alone fossilized? If so, is this not to immunize the claim against falsification? How much variation is permissible? Where does one task, context, discourse domain (and what other units?) end and the next begin? Why should variation (especially, but not only, within-task variation) be taken as evidence for, or consistent with, a claim of fossilization, as opposed to an *un*stable IL or, indeed, of the very opposite, that is, IL *development*? Free variation, after all, is claimed to play a catalytic role in some theories of SLA (see, e.g., Ellis, 1985, 1999).

REFERENCES

Agnello, F. 1977: Exploring the pidginization hypothesis: a study of three fossilized negation systems. In C. Henning (ed.), *Proceedings of the Los Angeles Second Language Research Forum 1977*. Los Angeles: TESL Section, Department of English, University of California, 246–61.

Andersen, R. W. 1983: Transfer to somewhere. In S. M. Gass and L. Selinker (eds), *Language Transfer in Language Learning*, Rowley, MA: Newbury House, 177–201.

Bean, M. and Gergen, C. 1990: Individual variation in fossilized interlanguage performance. In H. Burmeister and P. Rounds (eds), *Variability in Second Language Acquisition. Proceedings of the Tenth Second Language Research Forum. Vol. 1*. Eugene, OR: Department of Linguistics, University of Oregon, 205–19.

Beck, M.-L. 1998: L2 acquisition and obligatory head movement: English-speaking learners of German and the local impairment hypothesis. *Studies in Second Language Acquisition*, 20 (4), 311–48.

Berdan, R. 1996: Disentangling language acquisition from language variation. In R. Bayley and D. Preston (eds), *Second Language Acquisition and Linguistic Variation*. Amsterdam: John Benjamins, 203–44.

Birdsong, D. 1999: Introduction: whys and why nots of the critical period hypothesis for second language acquisition. In D. Birdsong (ed.), *Second Language Acquisition and the Critical Period Hypothesis*. Mahwah, NJ: Lawrence Erlbaum Associates, 1–22.

Bley-Vroman, R. 1989: The logical problem of second language learning. In S. M. Gass and J. Schachter (eds), *Linguistic Perspectives on Second Language Acquisition*. Cambridge: Cambridge University Press, 41–68.

Bowerman, M. 1982: Starting to talk worse: clues to language acquisition from children's late speech errors. In S. Strauss and R. Stavy (eds), *U-Shaped Behavioral Growth*. New York: Academic Press, 101–45.

Briere, E. 1966: An investigation of phonological interference. *Language*, 42, 768–96.

Brown, H. D. 1980: *Principles of Language Learning and Teaching*. Englewood Cliffs, NJ: Prentice-Hall.

Bruzzese, G. 1977: English/Italian secondary hybridization: a case study of the pidginization of a second language learner's speech. In C. Henning (ed.), *Proceedings of the Los Angeles Second Language Research Forum 1977*. Los Angeles: TESL Section, Department of English, University of California, Los Angeles, 235–45.

Calve, P. 1992: Corriger ou ne pas courriger, ça n'est pas la question. *Canadian Modern Language Review*, 48, 458–71.

Carroll, J. B. and Sapon, S. 1959: *The Modern Languages Aptitude Test*. San Antonio, TX: Psychological Corporation.

Clahsen, H. 1988: Parameterized grammatical theory and language acquisition: a study of the acquisition of verb placement and inflection by children and adults. In S. Flyn and W. O'Neil (eds), *Linguistic Theory in Second Language Acquisition*. Dordrecht: Kluwer, 47–75.

Corder, S. P. 1967: The significance of learners' errors. *IRAL*, 5, 161–9.

Daniels, J. 2000: Fossilization. In M. Byram (ed.), *Routledge Encyclopedia of Language Teaching and Learning*. London: Routledge, 218–20.

Doughty, C. J. and Long, M. H. 2000: Eliciting second language speech data. In L. Menn and N. Bernstein Ratner (eds), *Methods for Studying Language Production*. Mahwah, NJ: Lawrence Erlbaum Associates, 149–77.

Douglas, D. 2000: *Assessing Languages for Specific Purposes*. Cambridge: Cambridge University Press.

Douglas, D. and Selinker, L. 1985: Principles for language tests within the "discourse domain" theory of interlanguage: research, test construction and interpretation. *Language Testing*, 2, 205–26.

Ellis, R. 1985: Sources of variability in interlanguage. *Applied Linguistics*, 6, 118–31.

Ellis, R. 1999: Item versus system learning: explaining free variation. *Applied Linguistics*, 20 (4), 461–80.

Eubank, L. 1995: Generative research on second language acquisition. *Annual Review of Applied Linguistics*, 15, 93–107.

Gass, S. M. and Lakshmanan, U. 1991: Accounting for interlanguage subject pronouns. *Second Language Research*, 7, 181–203.

Graham, J. 1981: Overcoming fossilized English. ERIC Document No. ED 209 924.

Han, Z.-H. 1998: Fossilization: an investigation into advanced L2 learning of a typologically distant language. Doctoral dissertation. Birkbeck College, University of London, Department of Applied Linguistics.

Han, Z.-H. 2000a: Persistence of the implicit influence of NL: the case of the pseudo-passive. *Applied Linguistics*, 21 (1), 55–82.

Han, Z.-H. 2000b: Fossilization: the state of the art. Ms. Teachers College, New York.

Han, Z.-H. and Selinker, L. 1997: Multiple effects and error persistence: a longitudinal case study. Ms. Birkbeck College.

Han, Z.-H. and Selinker, L. 1999: Error resistance: towards an empirical pedagogy. *Language Teaching Research*, 3 (3), 248–75.

Harley, B. 1979: French gender "rules" in the speech of English-dominant, French-dominant and monolingual French-speaking children. *Working Papers on Bilingualism*, 19, 129–56.

Harley, B. and Swain, M. 1978: An analysis of the verb system by young learners of French. *Interlanguage Studies Bulletin*, 3, 35–79.

Harley, B. and Swain, M. 1984: The interlanguage of immersion students and its implications for second language teaching. In A. Davies, C. Criper, and A. P. R. Howatt (eds), *Interlanguage*. Edinburgh: Edinburgh University Press, 291–311.

Hawkins, R. 2000: Persistent selective fossilization in second language acquisition and the optimal design of the language faculty. *Essex Research Reports in Linguistics*, 34, 75–90.

Higgs, T. and Clifford, R. 1982: The push toward communication. In T. Higgs (ed.), *Curriculum, Competence and the Foreign Language Teacher*, Skokie, IL: National Textbook Company, 57–79.

Hulstijn, J. H. 1989: A cognitive view on interlanguage variability. In M. Eisenstein (ed.), *The Dynamic Interlanguage: Empirical Studies in Second Language Variation*. New York: Plenum Press, 17–31.

Hyltenstam, K. 1977: Implicational patterns in interlanguage syntax variation. *Language Learning*, 27, 383–411.

Hyltenstam, K. 1988: Lexical characteristics of near-native second-language learners of Swedish. *Journal of Multilingual and Multicultural Development*, 9 (1 and 2), 67–84.

Hyltenstam, K. 1992: Non-native features of near-native speakers: on the ultimate attainment of childhood L2 learners. In R. J. Harris (ed.), *Cognitive Processing in Bilinguals*. Amsterdam: Elsevier Science, 351–68.

Jain, M. P. 1974: Error analysis: source, cause and significance. In J. C. Richards (ed.), *Error Analysis*. London: Longman, 189–215.

Johnson, H. 1993: Defossilizing. In J. Oller and L. Richards d'Amato (eds), *Methods that Work: Ideas for Literacy and Language Teachers*. Second edition. Boston, MA: Heinle and Heinle, 281–8.

Kellerman, E. 1989: The imperfect conditional. In K. Hyltenstam and L. K. Obler (eds), *Bilingualism Across the Lifespan*. Cambridge: Cambridge University Press, 87–115.

Klein, W. 1986: *Second Language Acquisition*. Cambridge: Cambridge University Press.

Klein, W. and Perdue, C. 1997: The Basic Variety (or: couldn't natural languages be much simpler?). *Second Language Research*, 13 (4), 301–47.

Lardiere, D. 1998a: Case and tense in the "fossilized" steady-state. *Second Language Research*, 14, 1–26.

Lardiere, D. 1998b: Dissociating syntax from morphology in a divergent L2 end-state grammar. *Second Language Research*, 14, 359–75.

Lardiere, D. 2000a: Mapping features to forms in second language acquisition. In J. Archibald (ed.), *Second Language Acquisition and Linguistic Theory*. Malden, MA: Blackwell, 102–29.

Lardiere, D. 2000b: On optionality and grammaticality in L2 knowledge. Paper presented at the 4th Meeting on Generative Approaches to Second Language Acquisition (GASLA). MIT, April 1.

Larsen-Freeman, D. and Long, M. H. 1991: *An Introduction to Second Language Acquisition Research*. London: Longman.

Lennon, P. 1991a: Error and the very advanced learner. *IRAL*, 19 (1), 31–44.

Lennon, P. 1991b: Error elimination and error fossilization: a study of an advanced learner in the L2 community. *ITL*, 93–4, 129–51.

Lin, Y.-H. 1995: Un analysis empirico de la estabilizacion/fosilizacion: la incorporacion y la autocorreccion en unos sujetos chinos. Doctoral thesis. Departamento de Didactica de la Lengua y la Literatura, Universidad de Barcelona.

Lin, Y.-H. and Hedgcock, J. 1996: Negative feedback incorporation among high-proficiency and low-proficiency Chinese-speaking learners of Spanish. *Language Learning*, 46 (4), 567–611.

Linn, C. A. and Sucher, K. 1995: De-fossilization through memorization of the perfect paragraph. Paper presented at the International TESOL Convention. Long Beach, CA, March.

Long, M. H. 1993a: Second language acquisition as a function of age:

substantive findings and methodological issues. In K. Hyltenstam and A. Viberg (eds), *Progression and Regression in Language*. Cambridge: Cambridge University Press, 196–221.

Long, M. H. 1993b: Sensitive periods in second language acquisition. Paper presented at the invitational seminar "SLA and the Philosophy of Science." Washington, DC, National Institutes of Mental Health.

Long, M. H. 1996: The role of the linguistic environment in second language acquisition. In W. C. Ritchie and T. K. Bahtia (eds), *Handbook of Second Language Acquisition*. New York: Academic Press, 413–68.

Long, M. H. 1997: Fossilization: Rigor mortis in living linguistic systems? Plenary address to the EUROSLA 97 conference. Universitat Pompeu Fabra, Barcelona, May 22–4.

Long, M. H. and Sato, C. J. 1984: Methodological issues in interlanguage studies: an interactionist perspective. In A. Davies, C. Criper, and A. P. R. Howatt (eds), *Interlanguage*. Edinburgh: Edinburgh University Press, 253–79.

Meisel, J. M. 1991: Principles of Universal Grammar and strategies of language learning: some similarities and differences between first and second language acquisition. In L. Eubank (ed.), *Point Counterpoint: Universal Grammar in the Second Language*. Amsterdam: John Benjamins, 231–76.

Meisel, J. M. 1997: The acquisition of the syntax of negation in French and German: contrasting first and second language acquisition. *Second Language Research*, 13, 227–63.

Meisel, J. M., Clahsen, H., and Pienemann, M. 1981: On determining developmental stages in natural second language acquisition. *Studies in Second Language Acquisition*, 3 (2), 109–35.

Mellow, D., Reeder, K., and Forster, E. 1996: Using time-series research designs to investigate the effects of instruction. *Studies in Second Language Acquisition*, 18 (3), 325–50.

Mukkatash, L. 1986: Persistence in fossilization. *IRAL*, 24 (2), 187–203.

Naiman, N. 1974: Imitation, comprehension, and production of certain syntactic forms by young children acquiring a second language. Doctoral dissertation. University of Toronto.

Nakuma, C. 1998: A new theoretical account of "fossilization": implications for L2 attrition research. *IRAL*, 36 (3), 247–56.

Nemser, W. 1971: Approximative systems of foreign language learners. *IRAL*, 9 (2), 115–24.

Pavesi, M. 1986: Markedness, discoursal modes, and relative clause formation in a formal and an informal context. *Studies in Second Language Acquisition*, 8 (1), 38–55.

Pellerin, M. and Hammerly, H. 1986: L'expression orale apres treize ans d'imersion francaise. *Canadian Modern Language Review*, 42, 592–606.

Perdue, C. 1993: *Adult Language Acquisition: Cross-Linguistic Perspectives. Vol. 1: Field Methods*. Cambridge: Cambridge University Press.

Pienemann, M. 1984: Psychological constraints on the teachability of languages. *Studies in Second Language Acquisition*, 6, 186–214.

Plann, S. 1976: The Spanish immersion program: towards nativelike proficiency or a classroom dialect? MA in TESL thesis. University of California, Los Angeles.

Plann, S. 1977: Acquiring a second language in an immersion situation. In H. D. Brown, C. Yorio, and R. Crymes (eds), *On TESOL '77*. Washington, DC: TESOL, 213–23.

Preston, D. 1989: *Sociolinguistics and Second Language Acquisition*. Oxford: Blackwell.

The Random House Dictionary of the English Language 1987: Second edition, unabridged. New York: Random House.

Sato, C. J. 1984: Phonological processes in second language acquisition: another look at interlanguage syllable structure. *Language Learning*, 34 (4), 43–57. Also in G. Ioup and S. Weinberger (eds), *Interlanguage Phonology*. Cambridge, MA: Newbury House, 248–60.

Sato, C. J. 1985: Task variation in interlanguage phonology. In S. M. Gass and C. Madden (eds), *Input in Second Language Acquisition*. Rowley, MA: Newbury House, 181–96.

Sato, C. J. 1990: *The Syntax of Conversation in Interlanguage Development*. Tubingen: Gunter Narr.

Schachter, J. 1974: An error in error analysis. *Language Learning*, 27, 205–14.

Schachter, J. 1988: The notion of completeness in second language acquisition. Paper presented at the Boston University Conference on Language Development.

Schachter, J. 1996: Maturation and the issue of Universal Grammar in second language acquisition. In W. R. Ritchie and T. J. Bhatia (eds), *Handbook of Second Language Acquisition*. San Diego: Academic Press, 159–93.

Schmidt, R. W. 1983: Interaction, acculturation, and the acquisition of communicative competence: a case study of an adult. In N. Wolfson and E. Judd (eds), *Sociolinguistics and Second Language Acquisition*. Rowley, MA: Newbury House, 137–74.

Schmidt, R. W. 1995: Consciousness and foreign language learning: a tutorial on the role of attention and awareness in learning. In R. W. Schmidt (ed.), *Attention and Awareness in Foreign Language Learning*. Honolulu: University of Hawai'i Press, 1–63.

Schnitzer, M. L. 1993: Steady as a rock: does the steady state represent cognitive fossilization? *Journal of Psycholinguistic Research*, 22 (1), 1–20.

Schouten, E. 1996: Crosslinguistic influence and the expression of hypothetical meaning. In E. B. Kellerman, B. Weltens, and T. Bongaerts (eds), *EUROSLA 6: A Selection of Papers. Toegepaste Taalwetenschap in Artikelen* [*Applied Linguistics in Article Form*], 55, 161–74.

Schumann, J. H. 1978: *The Pidginization Process: A Model for Second Language Acquisition*. Rowley, MA: Newbury House.

Schumann, J. H. 1979: The acquisition of English negation by speakers of Spanish: a review of the literature. In R. W. Andersen (ed.), *The Acquisition and Use of Spanish and English as First and Second Languages*. Washington, DC: TESOL, 3–32.

Schumann, J. H. 1986: Research on the acculturation model for second language acquisition. *Journal of Multilingual and Multicultural Development*, 7, 379–92.

Schumann, J. H. 1993: Some problems with falsification: an illustration from SLA research. *Applied Linguistics*, 14, 295–306.

Seliger, H. W. 1978: Implications of a multiple critical periods hypothesis for second language learning. In W. Ritchie (ed.), *Second Language Acquisition Research*. New York: Academic Press, 11–19.

Seliger, H. W. 1989: Semantic transfer constraints on the production of English passive by Hebrew–English bilinguals. In H. Dechert and M. Raupach (eds), *Transfer in Language Production*. Norwood, NJ: Ablex, 21–34.

Selinker, L. 1966: A psycholinguistic study of language transfer. Ph.D. dissertation. Department of Linguistics, Georgetown University.

Selinker, L. 1972: Interlanguage. *IRAL*, 10 (3), 209–31.

Selinker, L. 1992: *Rediscovering Interlanguage*, New York: Longman.

Selinker, L. 1993: Fossilization as simplification? In M. L. Tickoo (ed.), *Simplification: Theory and Application*. Singapore: Regional Language Centre, 14–28.

Selinker, L. 1996: Research proposal for grant application submitted to the British Library. Ms.

Selinker, L. and Douglas, D. 1985: Wrestling with "context" in interlanguage theory. *Applied Linguistics*, 6, 190–204.

Selinker, L. and Douglas, D. 1989: Research methodology in contextually based second language research. *Second Language Research*, 5 (1), 1–34.

Selinker, L. and Han, Z.-H. 1996: Fossilization: what we think we know. Paper presented at EUROSLA 96. Nijmegen, May 30.

Selinker, L. and Han, Z.-H. 2001: Fossilization: moving the concept into empirical longitudinal study. In C. Elder, A. Brown, E. Grove, K. Hill, N. Iwashita, T. Lumley, T. McNamara, and K. O'Loughlin (eds), *Studies in Language Testing*: *Experimenting with Uncertainty*. Cambridge: Cambridge University Press, 276–91.

Selinker, L. and Lakshmanan, U. 1992: Language transfer and fossilization: the multiple effects principle. In S. M. Gass and L. Selinker (eds), *Language Transfer in Language Learning*. Amsterdam: John Benjamins, 176–217.

Selinker, L. and Lamendella, J. T. 1978: Two perspectives on fossilization in interlanguage learning. *Interlanguage Studies Bulletin*, 3 (2), 143–91.

Selinker, L. and Mascia, R. 1999: Fossilization: trying to get the logic right. In P. Robinson (ed.), *Representation and process*: *Proceedings of the 3rd Pacific Second Language Research Forum. Vol. 1*. Tokyo: Pacific Second Language Research Forum, 257–65.

Selinker, L., Swain, M., and Dumas, G. 1975: The interlanguage hypothesis extended to children. *Language Learning*, 25 (1), 139–52.

Sola, D. 1989: Fossilized errors and the effect of formal instruction on highly proficient Hispanic learners of English. M.A. thesis. University of South Carolina, Linguistics Program.

Stauble, A.-M. 1984: A comparison of the Spanish–English and Japanese–English interlanguage continuum. In R. W. Andersen (ed.), *Second language: A Cross-Linguistic Perspective*. Rowley, MA: Newbury House, 323–53.

Tarone, E. 1988: *Variation in Interlanguage*. London: Edward Arnold.

Tarone, E. 1994: Interlanguage. In R. E. Asher (ed.), *The Encyclopedia of Language and Linguistics*. Oxford: Pergamon Press, 1715–19.

Thep-Ackrapong, T. 1990: Fossilization: a case study of practical and theoretical parameters. Doctoral dissertation. Illinois State University. DAI-A 51/09.

Todeva, E. 1992: On fossilization in (S)LA theory. In D. Staub and C. Delk (eds), *Proceedings of the Twelfth Second Language Research Forum*. East Lansing: Center for International Programs, Michigan State University, 216–54.

Valette, R. 1991: Proficiency and the prevention of fossilization – an editorial. *Modern Language Journal*, 75 (3), 325–8.

VanPatten, B. 1988: How juries get hung: problems with the evidence for a focus on form in teaching. *Language Learning*, 38 (2), 243–60.

Vigil, N. A. and J. W. Oller, Jr 1976: Rule fossilization: a tentative model. *Language Learning*, 26 (2), 281–95.

Wales, L. 1993: The benefits of literacy development for fossilized ESL learners. *ELT Journal*, 47 (2), 144–56.

Washburn, G. 1992: Fossilization in second language acquisition: a Vygotskian analysis. Ph.D. dissertation. University of Pennsylvania.

Washburn, G. 1994: Working in the ZPD: fossilized and nonfossilized nonnative speakers. In J. P. Lantolf and G. Appel (eds), *Vygotskian Approaches to Second Language Research*. Norwood, NJ: Ablex, 69–81.

White, L. 1987: Against comprehensible input: the input hypothesis and the development of second language competence. *Applied Linguistics*, 8 (1), 95–110.

White, L. 2002: Morphological variability in endstate L2 grammars: the question of L1 influence. In B. Skarabela, S. Fish, and A.H.-J. Do (eds), *Proceedings of the 26th Annual Boston University Conference on Language Development*. Somerville, MA: Cascadilla Press, 758–68.

Wode, H. 1981: *Learning a Second Language*. Tubingen: Gunter Narr.

Yorio, C. 1994: The case for learning. In R. M. Barasch and C. Vaughn James (eds), *Beyond the Monitor Model*. Boston, MA: Heinle and Heinle, 125–37.

Zobl, H. 1982: A direction for contrastive analysis: the comparative study of developmental sequences. *TESOL Quarterly*, 16 (2), 169–83.

V Biological and Psychological Constraints

17 Maturational Constraints in SLA

KENNETH HYLTENSTAM AND NICLAS ABRAHAMSSON

1 Introduction

Adult second language acquisition sometimes results in the extraordinary achievement of ultimate levels of proficiency comparable to those of native speakers. When this happens, it is the object of much admiration and even astonishment. For child learners, however, everything short of nativelike levels is seen as failure. This difference in judgments is of course due to different implicit standards for adults and children: both the entirely successful adult learner and the slightly unsuccessful child deviate from the unspoken norm.

That children are more efficient second language learners than adults was given its first scientific formulation by Penfield and Roberts (1959) in an account where the biological and neurological basis for children's advantages in language learning was specified. These neuroscientists contended that "the child's brain has a specialized capacity for learning language" (p. 240) and that "[t]here is a biological clock of the brain" (p. 237). They further suggested an age limit of approximately 9 years on cerebral flexibility allowing "direct learning" from the input, and explained the poorer attainment levels resulting from later ages of onset (AOs) with reference to the fact that children become "more analytical" and learn "indirectly" via their first language after that age. Working from studies of recovery from aphasia, Lenneberg (1967) suggested that the loss of this biological predisposition for language acquisition could be explained by the completion of hemispheric lateralization, which in his view coincided with puberty, and labeled the time span between age 2 and puberty a *critical period* for language acquisition (cf. p. 175f).

Since the late 1960s, the existence of a critical period for language acquisition has been one of the most widely debated issues in second language acquisition research. While few researchers today would deny long-term advantages for child starters – especially after reviews have found no counter-evidence to this contention (Krashen, Long, and Scarcella, 1979; Long, 1990; cf. also Singleton,

1989, 2001) – views differ as to whether these observations should be explained by biological scheduling, that is, by constraints imposed on the learner along with maturation, or by social/psychological factors. Thus, the controversy about the existence of a critical period remains as intense as ever (see contributions in Birdsong, 1999a; Hyltenstam and Abrahamsson, 2001; Marinova-Todd, Marshall, and Snow, 2000; Scovel, 2000; Singleton, 2001); indeed, few empirical results in the field remain uncontroversial.

It would seem that many of the disagreements are related to, or can be seen in the light of, Lenneberg's original formulation of the *Critical Period Hypothesis* (CPH). Lenneberg claimed that:

> automatic acquisition from mere exposure to a given language seems to disappear [after puberty], and foreign languages have to be taught and learned through a conscious and labored effort. Foreign accents cannot be overcome easily after puberty. However, a person *can* learn to communicate at the age of forty. This does not trouble our basic hypothesis. (1967, p. 176)

Thus, what was central to the original formulation of the CPH was the "possibility to acquire a language, be it L1 or L2, to normal nativelike levels" (Birdsong, 1999b, p. 1). More recently, several authors have underscored just that: the CPH, or maturational constraints in general, concern the ability to reach nativelike attainment (e.g., Birdsong, 1999b; Eubank and Gregg, 1999; Long, 1993). As with other types of maturationally constrained behavior, what is of interest is not just the development of *any* behavior in the area studied, but rather the exact species-specific behavior. A parallel example often mentioned is the familiar case of song-birds, where the young bird must experience singing from adult birds in order for its species-specific singing to develop. Claiming for an individual bird that "it sings" is clearly not relevant – it must sing *exactly* in the way that other birds of that specific species sing. If it does not, it would be considered not to have received the appropriate triggering from the environment at the right time in development.

As we will see in the literature review below, research on maturational constraints, or on the CPH specifically, has developed research questions based either on factors that were actually mentioned by Lenneberg, or on factors that could be derived from his formulation; other questions have – intentionally or unintentionally – disregarded one or more of the central aspects of his hypothesis. At least three different conceptualizations on which research questions have been based can be discerned.

The first conceptualization is fully congruent with Lenneberg's formulation and focuses on the attainability of *nativelike* ultimate proficiency *from mere exposure* to a given language. Here, the CPH would be falsified if nativelike proficiency were found in learners who started acquiring a language outside a certain age limit (i.e., puberty in Lenneberg's specific formulation) *and* who have acquired the language naturalistically without tutoring. However, most studies of nativelike second language proficiency have not addressed the restrictions that follow from the hypothesis's qualification, "from mere exposure." That is, the CPH is frequently considered falsified if nativelike proficiency is found in learners who start acquiring a language outside a certain age limit regardless of how they have acquired it.

Being somewhat less restricted, the second conceptualization concerns the relationship between age and *ultimate attainment*, and suggests that younger learners outperform older learners with respect to eventual outcome. However, as with the younger-is-better version below, it disregards the constraint of *nativelike* outcomes, and is falsified, therefore, if older learners reach comparatively higher ultimate attainment levels than younger learners, given equal learning conditions.

The third conceptualization is that the *younger* learner *is better* at language learning than the older learner. This version is unrestricted, and so in research based on it, younger and older learners have been compared in one respect or another. The hypothesis is falsified if older learners are "better" than younger learners on a certain measure of success given the same learning conditions (e.g., Snow and Hoefnagel-Höhle, 1978). Research based on this conceptualization, amazingly enough, completely disregards both the condition of ultimate attainment and the condition of nativelike proficiency.

The fact that different researchers have implicitly based their research on conceptually different interpretations of the CPH is, of course, one source of confusion in the field. Additional sources for disagreement about maturational constraints comprise the many ways in which the notion of "language" has been defined and operationalized. This question will be dealt with below. Suffice it to say at this point that, in our view, the domain for maturational constraints in general is the human capacity for language both at the level of knowledge and at the level of processing. On such an assumption, the critical period relates to a comprehensively defined notion of language proficiency, including but not restricted to "grammatical competence."

It is obvious that several of the questions that have been investigated over the years remain unanswered. One of the most basic ones is: if it is at all possible to attain full nativelike proficiency in a second language, is there an AO limit for such attainment? Or is it possible to reach nativelike proficiency starting at any age? Several related issues, not dealing specifically with the attainability of nativelike proficiency, are also central within this area. For example, as certain age-related factors are obviously involved in determining ultimate proficiency levels even during later phases of the life span (Bialystok and Hakuta, 1999; Birdsong, 1999b), language proficiencies resulting from AOs beyond a possible critical period also need to be dealt with in order to fully understand the implications of maturational constraints and their interaction with other determining factors. It is also reasonable to ask what levels of *near-native* and *non-native* proficiency are attained at which age ranges. Another question is what effects an increasingly constrained language learning mechanism would have across sub-components of language and across different phenomena within sub-components.[1]

This chapter does not intend to suggest final answers to these questions, but will rather be specifically concerned with discussing how such questions have been approached. We will propose that the empirical data discussed in this research area are not sufficiently rich to constitute a basis for the falsification of hypotheses, primarily because the notion of "nativelike proficiency" is highly elusive. In our view, however, the most reasonable interpretation of the limited data that exist does support a maturational constraints hypothesis, although this hypothesis is not necessarily identical to the original or any other prevalent formulation of the CPH. We will conclude by attempting to provide an integrated perspective, where maturational constraints in interaction with other factors play a definite role for second language acquisition. Some methodological requirements for future research will also be discussed.

2 Maturational Constraints as the Default Hypothesis

The theoretically unmarked position is to postulate one comprehensive account for different manifestations of human language learning rather than having to deal with each type on its own terms. Therefore, if language acquisition is maturationally constrained, the theoretical constructs employed to define the workings of such constraints should have identifiable implications for language acquisition under all conditions, that is, in first, second, atypical, etc., language acquisition (cf. Harley and Wang, 1997; Long, 1990). Long (1990) argues that "positing maturational constraints . . . is the *un*marked hypothesis" (p. 253); we should expect there to be such constraints "because they are so well attested in the development of other animal species, in other types of human learning, and in other human neurological abilities" (ibid.).

In Gleitman and Newport (1995), a wealth of facts from first language acquisition, language deprivation, and delayed first language acquisition are discussed under such assumptions. The observations discussed can be given a consistent explanation if maturational constraints exist, but these observations would require different and at times arbitrary explanations if one assumes the *non*-existence of such constraints. We will briefly review these facts in order to position data from second language acquisition within this wider context.

Gleitman and Newport (1995, p. 21) argue that "biologically given dispositions" are reflected in all types of language acquisition. Given normal environmental exposure to any language, the child acquires it relatively rapidly in a universally uniform development. The development is marked by a strict set of milestones (cf. Singleton, 1989, pp. 8ff), including early phonological distinctions and a one-word stage at about 1 year, a sudden growth of vocabulary and a two-word stage during the second year, then, by the age of 3, an increase of syntactic complexity and development of function morphemes until, finally, a principally complete system has developed by the age of 5. Such regular sequencing is typically seen in other areas where an inborn biological timetable for development must be postulated, such as in motor and cognitive development. Indeed, "[t]he learning of the mother tongue is normally an *inevitable* process" (Penfield and Roberts, 1959, p. 240; our italics), except in cases of deprivation from input caused by either severe abuse or inherent physiological or mental disabilities. This uniform development occurs irrespective of a wide range of individual, social, and cultural variation in input qualities and quantities that children receive under normal conditions. An obvious interpretation is that the range of input that is sufficient for language acquisition to take place is a wide one: "virtually any exposure conditions short of total isolation and vicious mistreatment will suffice to bring [language] forth in every child" (Gleitman and Newport, 1995, p. 21).

There are data, admittedly sparse and difficult to interpret, suggesting that AOs delayed beyond 6 or 7 – due to deprivation or isolation – result in a less than complete ultimate attainment in first language acquisition. Gleitman and Newport's (1995, pp. 10ff) comparison of the well-known case of "Genie" (Curtiss, e.g., 1977, 1988) with the cases of "Chelsea" (Curtiss, 1988, 1989) and "Isabelle" (Davis, 1947) illustrates the effects of being severely deprived of linguistic input. Genie was isolated and deprived of linguistic input from the time she was 1½ years old until she was discovered at the age of 13. Chelsea was born with a hearing deficit, but was erroneously diagnosed as mentally retarded or emotionally disturbed. It was not until she had reached the age of 31 that a neurologist rightly diagnosed her as hard of hearing, and when tested with hearing aids she reached near-normal hearing levels. Isabelle had been hidden away in an attic and given only minimal attention until she was discovered at the age of 6. While Isabelle reached "native-level fluency" (p. 11) after only one year of exposure, Genie stopped at a level similar to that of 2-year-olds, and Chelsea did not develop "even the rudimentary aspects of grammatical structure" (p. 12) that were characteristic of Genie's speech. To the extent that cases of abuse, as with Genie, can be taken as evidence, the differences between the two cases of Isabelle and Genie support the view that a pronounced decrease in potential to acquire nativelike proficiency in a first language occurs between the age of 7 (Isabelle) and puberty (Genie).

However, there are empirical results that suggest even lower age limits for nativelike ultimate attainment. Data from deaf children who started to acquire their first language, American Sign Language (ASL), between the ages of 4 and 6 showed slight differences from native proficiency levels even after 30 years or more of using the language; in addition, and as expected, a group of learners who started their first language acquisition from puberty onwards, as expected, showed clear signs of non-native proficiency (Newport, 1990). Similar results were obtained in studies by Mayberry and her colleagues (see summary in Morford and Mayberry, 2000, and below). Likewise, in studies reported by Ruben (1997),[2] hearing children who, due to otitis media, suffered from continuing hearing impairment during their first 12 months of life, and then recovered, scored significantly lower than controls for verbal memory and phonetic perception when tested at age 9. On the basis of these results, Ruben suggests that a critical period for phonology might already terminate by age 1, and he further speculates that "[i]nsufficient early phonological input results in flawed semantic and syntactic capacities" (p. 117).

Therefore, although the general belief until now has been that full nativelike proficiency in a first language is attainable given AOs up to the age of approximately 6 or 7, data showing effects of deprivation during very early phases actually call this contention into question. As a matter of fact, the only empirical evidence that directly supports the age limit of 6–7 is the case of Isabelle. However, the statement that she achieved full nativelike fluency after one year may not be totally reliable as it is not substantiated by detailed linguistic analysis. Neither is the absolute absence of input during her first six years wholly clear.

Gleitman and Newport (1995) contend that the atypical cases mentioned above aptly illustrate what takes place in *all* individual children: "Every learner is an isolate"; that is, individual learners have to identify for themselves the regularities of the target language. According to the position that Newport and Gleitman represent, these regularities or generalizations cannot be arrived at from experience alone, that is, from the examples of the target language; learners have to rely on an innate mechanism that allows them to acquire any language they encounter in their environment, "just because in some sense they know, from their biological predispositions, the essence of language" (p. 17). What facts like these underscore is the child's ability to reach perfection even on the basis of reduced input. The uniformity of the child's creativity and inventiveness across the various conditions can be understood only if we assume that "significant aspects of language development are dictated by our biology" (p. 10).

If it is the case that the human brain is particularly adapted for language acquisition during an early period of life, but less so later in life, there should be manifestations of this adaptation in a second language context that are parallel to the manifestations in first language contexts. Even if this does seem to be the case at some level of comparison, in second language acquisition the effects of exposure later than the early childhood years are not nearly as dramatic as in the L1 cases just mentioned. What we see, rather, when we compare L2 starters at the age ranges of Genie or Chelsea, is "neither nativelike mastery of the L2 . . . nor the near-total incompetence in the L2 that Genie and Chelsea manifested in their first" (Eubank and Gregg, 1999, p. 79). As we will see from the review of studies in the following section, much of the research appears to support the view that nativelike proficiency can also be reached in a second language given early AOs (Hyltenstam, 1992; Johnson and Newport, 1989; Oyama, 1978; Patkowski, 1990). Furthermore, it is also almost certainly the case that most learners who start acquisition after early childhood can reach nativelike attainment in certain sub-components of language, as demonstrated in studies on nativelike behavior on, for example, intuitive judgment tasks (Birdsong, 1992; White and Genesee, 1996) and pronunciation (Bongaerts, 1999;

Bongaerts, Mennen, and van der Slik, 2000; Moyer, 1999) among adult second language starters. An important apparent difference from the first language context is that nativelike proficiency in a second language is not *inevitable*, even with AOs in early childhood. Several studies note enduring non-native features in the ultimate attainment even of some very young starters (Bialystok and Miller, 1999; Butler, 2000; DeKeyser, 2000; Ekberg, 1998; Flege, 1999; Hene, 1993; Hyltenstam, 1992; McDonald, 2000; see also summary in Harley and Wang, 1997, p. 38). One factor that these studies single out is the effect a bilingual speaker's languages may have on each other at any age. It also seems that the nature of input (amount, quality, etc.) is much more decisive in the second language context – or in the case of bilingualism generally – than in first language contexts. It has been suggested that early childhood bilingualism is typically unbalanced, with one of the languages weaker than the other (Pulvermüller and Schumann, 1994; Schlyter, 1993; Wong Fillmore, 1991). This weaker language, be it L1 or L2, or one of two simultaneously acquired L1s, characteristically exhibits non-native features; in fact, as Harley and Wang (1997) conclude, "[m]onolingual-like attainment in each of a bilingual's two languages is probably a myth (at any age)" (p. 44). The long-term effects of "weak" language development have not been studied, however, and they therefore remain unclear.

3 The Empirical Evidence

Literature reviews on age-related differences in L2 acquisition usually either start or conclude by iterating the now well-known generalizations by Krashen et al. (1979) that "(1) adults proceed through early stages of morphological and syntactic development faster than children (where time and exposure are held constant): (2) older children acquire faster than younger children (again in early stages of morphology and syntax, where time and exposure are held constant: and (3) child starters outperform adult starters in the long run" (Krashen, Scarcella, and Long, 1979, p. 573). What motivated the pioneering review by Krashen et al. (1979) was that the then existing empirical results concerning age-related differences in L2 acquisition seemed to be inconsistent and conflicting, insofar as some studies demonstrated an advantage for younger learners, while others seemed to show that older children and adults are "better" language learners than young children. These apparent inconsistencies dominated the theoretical debate during the 1970s, and raised questions about whether children have a greater L2 learning ability than adults, and, consequently, whether there are biologically determined constraints on language acquisition. Krashen et al. (1979) resolved this problem by dividing the empirical studies into two types, "initial rate" and "eventual attainment." The generalizations given above simply state that older learners acquire (certain aspects of) a second language at a faster rate than younger learners in the beginning of the acquisition process, but that younger learners, especially small children, catch up and eventually surpass older children and adults. Even though the last generalization is neutral about the final state of L2 proficiency (Long, 1990, p. 260), research has demonstrated that young starters seem to end up as nativelike speakers of the L2, which is rarely, if ever, the case for adult or adolescent starters.

3.1 *Age effects on initial learning efficiency: who is faster in the short run?*

Studies addressing the issue of acquisition rate have been both naturalistic and experimental in nature. In naturalistic rate studies, the subjects have been exposed to the target language in an L2 environment, while in experimental laboratory studies, there has been no such natural exposure, but rather the subjects have first been taught limited aspects of a language previously unknown to them, and shortly thereafter tested for their acquired L2 "proficiency." The vast majority of rate studies have been short-term studies with "acquisition" periods ranging from a few minutes to a number of weeks or months.

Despite Krashen et al.'s (1979) efforts in bringing some order to age studies, some conflicting results still remain for the rate studies. While some have indeed pointed to greater success for older learners (e.g., Asher and Price, 1967; Loewenthal and Bull, 1984; Olson and Samuels, 1973; Snow and Hoefnagel-Höhle, 1977, 1978), others have indicated that younger learners have advantages over older learners (e.g., Cochrane, 1980; Cochrane and Sachs, 1979; Tahta, Wood, and Loewenthal, 1981a, 1981b; Yamada, Takatsuka, Kotake, and Kurusu, 1980), and still others have indicated no significant rate differences between younger and older learners (e.g., Slavoff and Johnson, 1995).

The crucial question is, however, what studies of initial rate of L2 acquisition, in fact, are able to tell us about the existence of a critical period/maturational constraints. First of all, do laboratory studies, in which "[c]hildren and adults [are] brought into the lab, taught some property of a second language, and then immediately tested on what they [have] learned" (Slavoff and Johnson, 1995, p. 3), represent a reasonable procedure for investigating the ability to acquire a second language? Do such studies measure L2 proficiency at all, or are the frequently reported advantages for older learners just an artifact of the experimental nature of the studies? Long (1990) believes the latter to be the case, and argues that such studies "probably favor older learners because of their "teach and test" or laboratory interview formats and their occasional use of tasks where superior cognitive skills and/or test-wiseness can obviously play a role" (p. 260). Similarly, Loewenthal and Bull (1984) speculate whether older–faster results could be due to the social psychology of the testing situation, rather than to older learners being "better" at L2 acquisition.

Moreover, even though many naturalistic rate studies (e.g., Snow and Hoefnagel-Höhle, 1978) probably reflect language acquisition more accurately than laboratory studies do, there are still reasons to doubt their relevance to the issue of maturational constraints. Learning *rate*, in contrast to *attainment*, is, as indicated above, of little relevance to the existence or non-existence of a critical period, as is *initial*, in contrast to *ultimate*, proficiency. Long (1990) argues that initial rate advantages for older over younger learners in early morphosyntax "should be interpreted as just that – a short-lived rate advantage" (p. 274). For him, older–faster results constitute no evidence that older children and adults are better learners. Patkowski (1990) basically holds the same position when stating that "the issue of initial learning rates is a separate one, and one which does not bear directly upon the validity of the CPH" (p. 75). According to Patkowski, the only evidence with any validity for the CPH is that of eventual proficiency of differently aged learners.[3]

3.2 *Age effects on eventual learning outcomes: who is better in the long run?*

As a consequence of the doubts concerning their applicability to the question of a critical period or maturational constraints in L2 acquisition, rate studies more or less fell out of fashion in the 1980s, and the focus moved instead to long-term AO effects. The consistent pattern observed in a number of ultimate attainment studies – for example, Asher and García (1969), Oyama (1976, 1978), and Patkowski (1980) – is a significant correlation between AO and ultimate L2 outcomes, while other factors, such as length of residence (LOR) and degree of motivation, cannot account for the variation in ultimate attainment.

The most frequently cited study of this type is that of Johnson and Newport (1989),[4] who showed that when factors other than starting age are controlled for, such as LOR, motivation, or amount of formal instruction, AO turns out to be the only relevant predictor for eventual proficiency in a second language. Using a 276-item grammaticality judgment test, Johnson and Newport (1989) investigated the grammatical intuitions of 46 adult Chinese and Korean L2 learners of English who had arrived in the United States between the ages of 3 and 39. Results showed that the youngest AO group (3–7) performed within the range of native controls; for subjects with AOs above 7, there was a linear decline in performance up through puberty; from the age of 17 and upwards, the linear decline in performance with increasing age vanished. Except for the overall poorer performance than that of the younger arrivals, the adult learners thus demonstrated a high degree of inter-learner variability, something that was absent among younger arrivals. Johnson and Newport (1989) concluded that their results support a maturational account, since "the age effect is present during a time of ongoing biological and cognitive maturation and absent after maturation is complete (i.e., after puberty)" (p. 90).

The Johnson and Newport (1989) study has a central position within the field, and it has been given a great deal of attention in the literature – by both proponents and opponents of maturationally based explanations for age-difference effects. Proponents have described it as the best-designed and most important ultimate attainment study, providing the CPH debate with "[the] least ambiguous evidence to date of maturational constraints operating in the morpho-syntactic domain" (Long, 1990, p. 271); Birdsong (1999b) states that in SLA research on ultimate attainment, "no single study has contributed more to the case for critical period effects" (p. 10); DeKeyser (2000, p. 517) refers to it as a "landmark study." The critics, on the other hand, have expressed reservations about the methods and materials used (for example, that a minimum of five years was probably not enough for some learners to have reached their ultimate proficiency levels, and that the length of the test may have resulted in concentration difficulties; see, e.g., Bialystok and Hakuta, 1994; Juffs and Harrington, 1995; Kellerman, 1995), as well as about various aspects of the statistical analyses adopted (see, e.g., Bialystok, 1997; Bialystok and Hakuta, 1994).

In a recent replication of the Johnson and Newport (1989) study, DeKeyser (2000) managed to avoid most of these methodological weaknesses. A modified version of the grammaticality judgment test used by Johnson and Newport was distributed to 57 Hungarian L2 learners of English with 10 years of residence or more in the United States and with AOs between 1 and 40 years. Instead of 276 test items, DeKeyser's test included only 200 sentences; a few of the original sentences were also deleted or changed, and some structures were included that were predicted to be particularly difficult for Hungarian learners. In addition to the grammaticality test, a language learning aptitude test was distributed to the subjects.[5] The main purpose of the study was to test the *fundamental difference hypothesis* (Bley-Vroman, 1989; see further below), which states that while children learn language through implicit, domain-specific mechanisms, adults have lost most of their ability to learn languages implicitly, and must instead use their explicit, problem-solving capacities in L2 acquisition.

As with the Johnson and Newport (1989) data, DeKeyser's results exhibited no significant correlations between test scores and variables such as LOR, years of schooling, or age at time of the test; only the predicted negative overall correlation between AO and grammaticality judgment scores was found. All child arrivals (AO < 16) scored above 180 out of 200 (except for one who reached 170), while most adult arrivals (AO > 16) scored below this 180 limit. However, a certain overlap between the two groups was found: six of the late starters produced relatively high test scores (over 175), and three of these scored within the range of child arrivals (i.e., above 180). DeKeyser explains this result with the significant correlation between grammaticality judgment scores and aptitude scores among these successful adult starters; in the AO < 16 group, there was no correlation between grammatical competence and aptitude. In other words, and as was predicted, those late starters who performed near or within the range of early starters also had high verbal aptitude, which would have allowed them to learn the L2 through explicit reflection on grammatical rules (cf. also Harley and Hart, 1997, for similar results from the immersion setting). Moreover, DeKeyser's study showed that some structures are less sensitive to age effects than others (see further below), something that is explained by their differing perceptual saliency.

Even though DeKeyser's (2000) study must in many ways be viewed as an improvement and development of Johnson and Newport (1989), it still suffers from some weaknesses. First, one might question the accuracy of the aptitude scores obtained by most of the learners. DeKeyser concludes, on the basis of data in Ottó (1996), that the average score for monolingual Hungarian speakers is 10 rather than 4.72, as was obtained by the bilingual subjects in this study. The fact that verbal aptitude was assessed with a test in Hungarian, even though 20 of the 57 learners reported that they felt more comfortable in English, may have blurred the results in unpredictable ways. Second, the argument that only those adult starters who have high verbal analytical abilities will score within the range of child starters is weakened by the fact that one of the three most successful adult starters did not, in fact, have a high score on the aptitude test. The criterion for high aptitude was set at "6 or higher on the aptitude test" (p. 24), but this individual (the second best adult, with a grammaticality judgment score of 186/200) had an aptitude score of only 3.[6] Third, since no native English controls were included in the study, it is difficult to relate the scores to nativelike proficiency.

As White and Genesee (1996) note, studies that have used randomly selected learners with different AOs only indicate that children typically achieve higher ultimate levels than adults – by now a fully established fact – but "leave unanswered the question of whether late L2 learners can ever attain linguistic competence that is indistinguishable from monolingual native speakers" (p. 235). In other words, although the youngest arrivals in both Johnson and Newport (1989) and DeKeyser (2000) scored very high (in the range of native controls in the Johnson and Newport study), a fact that significantly separated them from the rest of the subjects, the question remains whether there actually are nativelike adult L2 learners who, because of their infrequency, were not captured by these studies or by any of the other ultimate attainment studies mentioned above. White and Genesee (1996) argue that, in order to investigate the absolute potentials of late learners, only subjects who seem to have reached nativelike L2 proficiency levels should be selected, because "[if] such subjects give the appearance of having attained nativelike use of the L2, one can then ask whether they have in fact attained nativelike competence" (p. 234). If so, such individuals would constitute evidence against the claim that late starters cannot obtain nativelike proficiency – and, thus, against the existence of maturational constraints.

3.3 *Age effects on ultimate learning potentials: who can become nativelike in a second language?*

Bearing most directly on the issue of maturational effects is the research that has consciously attempted to locate second or foreign language learners who – after initial screening for nativelikeness/near-nativeness – have undergone careful testing or assessment of their *actual* L2 proficiency. Ever since rate studies disappeared in the 1980s, leaving the opponents of the CPH with no empirical data to support their critique of maturational effects in L2 acquisition, the crucial empirical task for researchers has been to demonstrate that adult L2 starters – under advantageous learning circumstances – are in fact able to perform within the range of native speakers, that is, to reach native levels of L2 proficiency. If such individuals are to be found, then there is some justification for the belief that factors other than maturation are responsible for late starters' typical failure in achieving nativelike proficiency (Patkowski, 1990). In this section, we will discuss those ultimate attainment studies that have challenged the CPH and/or maturational constraints by claiming to have found late L2 starters who have reached native levels of proficiency.

The first study to adopt this approach was that of Coppieters (1987). He distributed a syntactic/semantic judgment task to 21 highly successful and highly educated adult foreign language learners of French, and also engaged them in follow-up interviews. These learners were selected because of the absence of any salient foreign accent in several of the subjects. However, even though the learners were initially judged as nativelike and even though they managed to respond to judgment items correctly, their overall performance was still distinctly below that of native controls; the recorded interviews revealed errors in structures that were mastered in the judgment task. However, in a replication of Coppieters (1987), although using stricter criteria for subject screening, Birdsong (1992) found that 15 of his 20 late foreign language learners of French performed within the same range as native speakers on a difficult grammaticality judgment task.

In the area of phonology, Bongaerts (1999; see also Bongaerts, Planken, and Schils, 1995; Bongaerts, van Summeren, Planken, and Schils, 1997) reports on the nativelike pronunciation of some highly proficient post-puberty Dutch foreign language students of English and French in the Netherlands. These subjects were chosen for the study because EFL and FFL[7] experts had designated them as exceptionally successful and advanced learners. A read-aloud task was used, where subjects were to read sentences and phrases which contained sounds that were predicted to be particularly difficult for Dutch learners. Results showed that significant proportions of these subjects passed as native speakers according to panels of native judges; in fact, they performed in the *upper* range of native controls. In a similar fashion, Bongaerts et al. (2000) investigated the pronunciation of very successful, immersed/naturalistic learners of Dutch as L2. By asking experts of Dutch as a second language, and through a personal networking procedure, they managed to select 30 highly educated L2 speakers, with a variety of L1 backgrounds, who had settled in the Netherlands between the ages of 11 and 34. Ten native controls also participated in the study. The subjects read aloud 10 sentences three times, and the second attempt was used for the rating procedure (except when this attempt included reading errors or slips). Pronunciation was then rated on a five-point scale (from "very strong accent; definitely non-native" to "no foreign accent at all; definitely native") by 21 Dutch judges, some with linguistic training, some without. Details aside, the results showed that two participants in particular (with AOs 21 and 14; Bongaerts, p.c.) stood out from the general pattern, and received ratings in the lower range of native controls; in other words, they passed as native speakers.

In another recent ultimate attainment study of phonology, Moyer (1999) investigated the pronunciation of 24 late, though very advanced and highly motivated, American learners of German as a foreign language. They were all graduate students and employed as teachers in a German program at an American university. In addition, their exposure included up to several years of immersion in Germany. Four native German controls also participated. Three read-aloud tasks were used (word list, sentences, and paragraph) in addition to one free oral production task. The speech samples were then rated independently by four native German judges, using a six-point scale (from "definitely native" to "definitely non-native"). Results clearly showed that the native judges were able to differentiate the L2 subjects from the native subjects; in other words, the L2 speakers performed distinctly below native pronunciation. However, there was one subject who performed within the range of native controls across all four pronunciation tasks. Moyer describes this individual as an exceptional learner, who was largely self-taught and who had "a strong desire to sound German (a goal very few of the other subjects had)" (p. 98).[8]

One interesting aspect of Moyer's (1999) results is that there was a trend toward more native accent ratings for more isolated task items: word list reading resulted in the lowest accent ratings, followed by the reading aloud of sentences, and, next, the reading of paragraphs; free production resulted in the highest foreign accent ratings. In light of these findings, one might argue that, despite the fact that some learners reported in Bongaerts (1999) and Bongaerts et al. (2000) appear to have reached nativelike L2 pronunciation, there is a risk that these studies highlight skills other than "real" pronunciation skills. It is not surprising that some very advanced learners perform very well, even within the same range as native speakers, when they read relatively few, short sentences. But in the absence of evidence to the contrary, we find it reasonable, at this point, to question whether Bongaerts's learners would perform as well on tasks involving longer units of spontaneous speech (say, five minutes) such as story-retelling or free conversation, or on reading tasks involving paragraphs or longer texts. Although their pronunciation most certainly would get exceptionally high ratings on such tasks, there are reasons to doubt that they would still be able to pass as native speakers for any native judge.[9] However, as Moyer (1999) points out, "the inclusion of tasks beyond word recitation naturally involves suprasegmental features as well as lexical, syntactic, and pragmatic fluency" (p. 86); therefore, "a clean measure of phonological fluency alone is not possible for extended, naturalistic speech," since raters are "indeed influenced by structures beyond L2 phonological production in their assessments of performance" (ibid.).

Ioup, Boustagui, El Tigi, and Moselle (1994; see also Ioup, 1995), in a case study, report on Julie, a talented L2 speaker of Egyptian Arabic who had immigrated to Cairo from Britain at the age of 21. Her acquisition of Arabic was naturalistic, in that she had received no formal L2 instruction, and she was not literate in Arabic. Her LOR in Egypt was 26 years at the time of the study. She was married to an Egyptian man, had two children, and worked as an EFL teacher at an Egyptian school. In addition to Julie, this study reported on a second subject: Laura, also an exceptionally talented, yet tutored, L2 speaker of several varieties of Arabic. Her L1 was American English, she had taken Arabic at different universities and in different countries (France, Morocco, etc.), and was at the time of the study living in Cairo with her Egyptian husband. Her LOR was 10 years, and she worked as a university professor of Standard Arabic.

What makes the Ioup et al. study methodologically interesting for the assessment of nativelikeness is the employment of a large set of elicitation instruments that included some particularly demanding tasks. Julie and Laura were assessed for production, dialect differentiation abilities (two tests), and grammatical competence (translation, grammaticality judgment, and interpretation of anaphora). Results showed that both Julie and Laura performed as well as (and even better than) some native controls on the dialect differentiation test, and Julie performed somewhat better than Laura. Where production was concerned, a majority of 13 judges (all native speakers of Egyptian Arabic and teachers of Arabic as a foreign language) rated both Julie and Laura as native speakers; judges who gave non-native ratings commented on some element of pronunciation. Finally, both subjects also scored high on tests of grammatical intuition, although slightly below native controls. In other words, there were small differences between the two subjects and native controls and small differences between Julie and Laura.[10] Ioup et al. (1994) conclude that, if there are exceptions to the critical period, the assumed neurocognitive change does not happen in the usual way, although it remains uncertain whether the ordinary acquisition system continues to function or whether an alternative learning system takes over.

White and Genesee (1996) point out that individuals who *appear* to have achieved nativelike proficiency nevertheless frequently differ from native speakers "in subtle ways" (p. 234). Therefore, prior to investigating the accessibility of the Universal Grammar (UG) features *Subjacency* and the *Empty Category Principle* (*ECP*) in adult L2 acquisition, they adopted a strict and extensive criteria-based screening procedure in order to separate "truly" near-native L2 speakers from non-native ones.[11] Randomly selected portions of tape-recorded language samples from 89 differently aged advanced learners of L2 English (AOs: 0–7 [*n* = 28], 8–11 [*n* = 12], 12–15 [*n* = 18], 16+ [*n* = 31]) were independently evaluated by two native English judges for pronunciation, morphology, syntax, vocabulary, fluency, and overall impression of nativeness. Samples from native English control subjects were also included. The screening resulted in one group of 45 near-native subjects (i.e., L2 learners who passed as native speakers) and one group of 44 non-native subjects (i.e., those learners who, despite being highly advanced L2 learners, did *not* pass as native speakers). As frequently observed, there was a biased distribution in terms of learners' AOs in these two groups: the majority of the near-native learners (29 out of 45) had started their acquisition of English before age 12, while the majority of the non-native learners (33 out of 44) had started after that age. After this initial screening process, the "real" testing procedure took place. A grammaticality judgment test (a computerized task that, besides recording yes-no answers, also measured reaction times) and a question formation test (an untimed pen-and-paper task) – both of which included sentences relevant to Subjacency and the ECP – were administered to the subjects individually. The results exhibited significant differences between the non-native group and the native group, although no significant differences were found between the near-native group and the native control group on either of the measures, even for reaction times. In addition, there were no effects for age within groups, that is, late starters performed as well as young starters. These findings led White and Genesee (1996) to conclude that access to UG is unaffected by starting age, and thus that nativelike proficiency levels in a second language are indeed attainable even by adult L2 starters, at least in the domain they chose to investigate (p. 261).

Despite the careful screening procedure, ironically, perhaps the most serious objection that one might have to the White and Genesee study concerns another aspect of subject selection. Most of the L2 learners were L1 speakers of French, a language in which Subjacency and ECP work largely as they do in English. From this one might expect these learners to experience little or no difficulty with sentences involving these aspects of UG. Eubank and Gregg (1999) speculate that the White and Genesee data perhaps reflect continued access to L1 principles – in combination with high metalinguistic awareness – rather than continued access to UG principles.

In order to put the above results on late learners' potentials into perspective it is crucial to consider as well the few studies that have paid attention to the ultimate attainment of very young starters. Hyltenstam (1992; see also Hyltenstam, 1988) investigated the grammatical and lexical performance of 24 near-native 17–18-year-old Spanish and Finnish L2 learners of Swedish. Among these, 16 subjects had AOs at 6 years or earlier, and 8 had AOs at 7 years or later. These highly proficient learners were selected by their teachers because they were "not . . . immediately identifiable as non-native speakers in their manifestation of phonology, grammar and/or lexicon" (p. 355).[12] The subjects were active bilinguals, in that they used both their L1 and L2 on a regular basis. A group of 12 native Swedish speakers served as controls. Free speech was elicited through oral retellings of four prepared texts (two presented on tape, two in written format) and one untimed written composition about a section of Charlie Chaplin's silent film *Modern Times*. Each group produced approximately 12,000 words. Although an error analysis revealed an extremely low error frequency in all groups, the native controls made 1–10 errors, the AO < 6 subjects 1–23 errors, and the AO > 7 group 13–26 errors; in other words, the older learner group did not overlap with the native group, whereas the younger learner group overlapped with both the other groups. Hyltenstam concluded that "[the] age 6 or 7 does seem to be an important period in distinguishing between near-native and nativelike ultimate attainment" (p. 364). However, as not all of the early learners performed within the range of native controls, it was further suggested that "an early AO may be a necessary although not sufficient requirement for nativelike ultimate attainment" (ibid.).

Other studies of very early L2 starters suggest that frequency differences may exist between native and near-native speakers of a language, for example, in the use of specific structures, or in the size and quality of vocabulary. These characteristics of near-native language proficiency are not directly detectable, as errors are, but observable only in the results of linguistic analyses. Ekberg (1998) investigated the use of certain discourse and grammatical structures among 13 bilingual adolescents who had grown up in Sweden, spoke Swedish at school and in out-of-home contexts, but spoke a language other than Swedish at home. The study included a control group comprising 14 Swedish monolingual children. Ekberg found significant differences between the two groups in frequencies of the following: sentence connectors, presentation, pseudo-coordinations expressing progressive aspect, and complex predicates. Hene (1993) studied several aspects of the vocabulary of 24 10–12-year-old children who had been adopted from other countries by Swedish families when the children were between the ages of 3 months and 6 years. The children were compared to 24 native speakers of Swedish of the same ages. The results showed differences between the two groups in several respects. The largest differences were found in the comprehension of some quite frequent words and phrases that appear in school materials for their age groups (e.g., *anse* 'be of the opinion'; *avskaffa* 'abolish'; *början av* 'the beginning of') in tasks that involved prepositions of place, and in giving lexical explanations using synonyms or paraphrases (p. 204). Unfortunately, however, the results are not presented in a way that makes it possible to distinguish L2 children with different AOs.

In a further investigation along the same lines but with a more elaborate design, Hyltenstam and Abrahamsson (forthcoming) studied 20 highly educated adult L2 speakers of Swedish who had been carefully screened for nativelikeness in an informal conversational setting. The subjects were distributed evenly across four AO groups (4–5, 8–10, 12–15, and 19–23), had a LOR of 10 years or more, and used both their L1 and L2 on a regular basis. They were compared to two control groups matched for age and educational background, one of which comprised first language speakers of Swedish (n = 5) and the other advanced but clearly non-nativelike speakers (n = 5, AOs between 4 and 25). Three different instruments were used: a test of perception in white noise, a cloze test, and a grammaticality judgment test.[13] Results consistently revealed significant differences between first language speakers on the one hand and second language speakers of *all* AO groups on the other – that is, even the very early starters differed significantly from native controls. However, differences between the different AO groups were small and in most cases non-significant. Furthermore, within-group variation among the second language speakers was salient, but minimal among first language speakers.[14]

Similar results were demonstrated by Butler (2000) for adult Chinese L2 speakers of English. Three AO groups and one native control group ($n = 8$ per group) were compared with regard to their performance on three different grammaticality judgment tests. Early arrivals (AO 3–5 years) performed significantly below native controls, but above mid arrivals (AO 5–10 years), who, in turn, scored better than late arrivals (AO 10–15 years). Thus, as in the Hyltenstam and Abrahamsson (forthcoming) study, not even the very young starters exhibited completely nativelike proficiency. Similarly, Bialystok and Miller (1999) and McDonald (2000) report on some very early starters with less than nativelike ultimate attainment.

Thus, results such as those obtained by Butler (2000), Ekberg (1998), Hene (1993), Hyltenstam (1992), and Hyltenstam and Abrahamsson (forthcoming) for second language learners with very low AO are consistent with those reported by Ruben (1997) and Morford and Mayberry (2000) in the first language acquisition context: they all seem to indicate that even a very short delay in onset has effects on the ultimate level of language proficiency.

Likewise, studies that have examined late, advanced L2 learners have failed to localize completely nativelike individuals. While some studies were simply not able to demonstrate full proficiency in the L2 for their advanced learners (Coppieters, 1987; Hyltenstam and Abrahamsson, forthcoming; Ioup et al., 1994; Moyer, 1999),[15] others indicated that their subjects were non-nativelike in areas of the L2 *outside* the areas investigated. For example, referring to his 1992 replication of Coppieters (1987), Birdsong (1999b) claims that several of the 15 participants who had passed as native speakers "deviated very little from native norms" (p. 9), thereby indicating that these learners had *not* attained full nativelike L2 proficiency. Similarly, Bongaerts (p.c.) observed from pilot studies that non-native features beyond pronunciation (e.g., deviant frequency distributions or avoidance of certain lexical/grammatical items) occurred in some of his advanced learners during free oral production. Similarly, although maintaining that late L2 starters can indeed achieve nativelike proficiency, at least in the domain of (certain) UG principles, White and Genesee (1996) see it as a challenging further question "whether this is true of all domains and, if not, in which areas nativelike success is not attainable and why not" (p. 262).

However, research has convincingly demonstrated that, although not entirely nativelike in every aspect of the L2, there is a small population of late L2 learners who, under exceptionally advantageous circumstances, have a potential of reaching high overall levels, perhaps even nativelike proficiency in one or several areas of the L2. In fact, in normal verbal interaction, it may be difficult, even impossible, for native listeners to distinguish such individuals from native speakers. Furthermore, these learners have frequently been characterized as either being highly motivated (Moyer, 1999), or having a high degree of aptitude for language learning (DeKeyser, 2000; Harley and Hart, 1997; Ioup et al., 1994), or having received intensive and focused L2 instruction (Bongaerts, 1999; Moyer, 1999).

Having presented portions of the relevant empirical research, we will now review some of the theoretical discourse which has framed studies in this area.

4 Theoretical Foundations

4.1 Formulations of maturational constraints

In the most general sense, the notion of maturational constraints suggests that there is a causal relationship between biologically scheduled changes in the developing human brain, on the one hand, and language acquisition potential, on the other. The formulation of maturational constraints most often referred to is Lenneberg's original *Critical Period Hypothesis* (CPH). A second, fairly common formulation has been labeled the *Sensitive Period Hypothesis* (SPH). While the SPH formulation shares with the CPH the view of a heightened sensitivity for natural language input in an early phase of life, the two versions entail different interpretations of the workings of maturational constraints.

The concept of *critical period* is typically associated with those types of behavioral developments that have sudden onsets and offsets, result in all-or-nothing events, depend on instinct, are unlearned and irreversible, and for which environmental influences such as motivation do not play any role (see summaries in Harley and Wang, 1997; Long, 1990). Most importantly, in the *critical period* formulation, maturation is thought to take place and come to an end within an early phase of the life span, abruptly set off from the rest at a specific age (puberty or earlier). However, it is not always the case that periods of special adaptability in any area of temporally scheduled development are sharply set off from what comes before or follows them. This type of pattern has often been referred to as a *sensitive period* (Harley and Wang, 1997, p. 20; Long, 1990, p. 252; Oyama, 1978). As in the critical period formulation, the special adaptation is thought to occur during an early phase, but in this weaker formulation, the sensitivity does not disappear at a fixed point; instead it is thought to fade away over a longer period of time, perhaps covering later childhood, puberty and adolescence. The concept of a critical period, in other words, would represent "a comparatively well-defined *window of opportunity*" (Eubank and Gregg, 1999, p. 68), while a sensitive period would represent "a progressive inefficiency of the organism, or a gradually declining effectiveness of the peripheral input" after a certain time (ibid.). In spite of the fact that this distinction between sensitive and critical periods has been generally acknowledged, and although some people, therefore, prefer the notion of sensitive to critical and see the SPH as a revised form of the CPH (see Obler and Hannigan, 1996, p. 510), in practice, the two terms are often used interchangeably. This may be due in part to the extreme difficulty of drawing a clear distinction between the two phenomena, which led researchers such as Eubank and Gregg (1999, p. 72) "to use [critical period] in its more widely accepted sense, while ignoring the term *sensitive period* as unhelpful."[16]

4.2 Exercise and maturational state versions of the CPH

Another dimension of maturational constraints and how they are formulated concerns the relevance of maturation in L2 acquisition as compared to L1 acquisition. Johnson and Newport (1989) suggested two possible versions of the CPH, "one which does not include second language acquisition in its effects and one that does" (p. 64). They call these the *exercise* version and the *maturational state* version, respectively. The exercise hypothesis predicts that if the language learning capacity is not exercised in early childhood, through the learning of an L1 (cf. Genie and Chelsea), it will disappear with maturation. If this capacity is exercised during this time, however, it will remain intact. The exercise version of the CPH thus predicts that late first language learners will inevitably arrive at levels lower than native proficiency, while late second language learners will not necessarily do so, but may well reach fully nativelike levels of the L2. On the other hand, the maturational state hypothesis, which is the most common version of the CPH, states that maturation has an effect on the acquisition of *any* language; that is, if nativelike levels are to be achieved, the acquisition of a first or second (or third, etc.) language must begin early in life, since the human capacity for learning languages declines with maturation, whether exercised in early life or not. This version of the CPH thus predicts non-native proficiency levels for anyone first exposed to the L2 after a critical period.

However, even though a maturational state version of the CPH emphasizes the negative effects of maturation, it does not necessarily ignore the positive effects of exercise. As was pointed out above, adult L2 acquisition results neither in the rudimentary levels reached by Genie or Chelsea, nor the proficiency levels of native speakers, but in outcomes somewhere between those extremes. A study by Mayberry (1993) confirmed just this. In a comparison of late first and second language learners of ASL (AOs 9–15) who had all used ASL for an average of 50 years, the second language users clearly outperformed the first language users. For facts such as these, Eubank and Gregg (1999) offer the explanation that in adult L2 acquisition, "the neural architecture is already developed" (p. 78) as a result of normal and successful acquisition of an L1 during the critical period, whereas in the case of Chelsea's late acquisition of her mother tongue, "the relevant neural architecture is presumably unorganized and unspecific" (p. 77) because "a [critical period] has been missed outright" (ibid.). Thus, as Harley and Wang (1997) point out, "the exercise and maturational state versions of the critical period hypothesis are not mutually exclusive" (p. 27).

4.3 Characteristics of a critical period

Being the formulation of maturational constraints referred to most frequently, the CPH has been characterized in greater detail than other formulations. In a recent summary of earlier discussions of what constitutes a critical period in any area of behavioral development, Harley and Wang (1997) mention the following six characteristics: (i) an onset, (ii) a terminus, (iii) an intrinsic component, (iv) an extrinsic component, (v) an affected system, and (vi) ultimate causes. It is the offset, or terminus, characteristics that actually distinguish the formulations of maturational constraints discussed above; the other characteristics are neutral with regard to these differences and can be said to be valid for maturational constraints in general. We will briefly comment on the characteristics in (i)–(v) here; (vi) will be discussed in a separate section.

There are definitely few elaborated suggestions as to the age at which the *onset* of a critical period for language acquisition occurs. Lenneberg's (1967) proposal of an onset at the age of 2, among other things coinciding with the development of increased syntactic complexity, contrasts with suggestions that such a period begins at 6 months, when the child is clearly sensitive to phonetic categories, or even at birth, when sensitivity to segmental and prosodic distinctions, as well as turn-taking, has been reported (see discussion in Singleton, 1989, p. 78). The question of a critical period's onset is obscured by the fact that some authors equate the onset of the period with the onset of primary language acquisition in general, while others seem to refer to an onset where there is a characteristic acceleration in linguistic development. In his review, Singleton (1989) presents a detailed discussion of onsets in the domains of phonology, grammar, lexicon, and discourse, paying attention to documented "milestones" of language development. Indeed, such milestones are reflections of the fact that different aspects of language have their different onsets. According to what Schachter (1996) refers to as the Windows of Opportunity hypothesis, "principles or properties of [competence] mature, like other biological properties, and become available to the learner at particular points in their linguistic development" (p. 183). The notion of *multiple critical periods* (cf. Seliger, 1978) captures this observation that there are different onsets (and offsets) for different sub-components of language, for example phonology and morphosyntax, or for different (sets of) features within or cutting across these sub-components. In short, with few exceptions (notably Bialystok, 1997, pp. 120, 134), authors prefer to talk about "different [critical periods] with different time courses" (Eubank and Gregg, 1999; see also Long, 1990, among many others).

A critical period should have an identifiable *offset* (or *terminus* in the terminology that Harley and Wang use). The offset issue, in fact, is the most debated question in the field. As we saw above, Penfield and Roberts (1959) suggested that the critical period ends at the age of 9, on the basis of their observation that at this age the child no longer learns language directly but via the units of the first language, due to a reduced cerebral flexibility. Lenneberg (1967) pointed to puberty as the end of the critical period, and suggested that it coincides with the completion of lateralization. His view on the lateralization process has later been challenged; the process is believed to be completed well before puberty, possibly at the age of 5 or earlier (Krashen, 1973). However, Lenneberg's suggestion of puberty is congruent with observations often made by lay people and with the interpretations in some empirical studies (e.g., Patkowski, 1980; cf. also Scovel, 1988). Since the appearance of empirical work in the late 1970s and in the 1980s, where different AOs are correlated with ultimate level of attainment, an upper limit has been suggested for the acquisition of phonology at age 6 "in many individuals" and at the age of 12 for the rest (Long, 1990, p. 280). For morphology and syntax, Long (1990) concludes on the basis of his review that the age of 15 seems to be the upper limit for nativelike abilities. However, there are indications that the age of 6 or 7 may also be relevant for morphosyntax (Johnson and Newport, 1989) or morphosyntax and lexicon (Hyltenstam, 1992). On the basis of such research, Long (1993, p. 204) suggests that the placement of the upper limit at puberty may be "due to studies having used insufficiently sensitive measures and/or inadequate corpora to detect L2 [phenomena]."

According to the third general characteristic of maturational constraints, there should be some genetically determined mechanism that accounts for the route that language acquisition takes. This *intrinsic component* covers the idea of such an inborn predisposition for language acquisition, that is, some form of linguistic nativism. There have been few expansions on how an intrinsic component specifically would constrain second language acquisition, except within the UG framework. Although, as Wolfe-Quintero (1996, p. 340) notes, "the theory of UG has been the most widely researched variant of linguistic nativism in the field of language acquisition," all current theories of language development are nativist (p. 336) and could therefore be researched specifically for their claims on maturational constraints.

The *extrinsic component* deals with the issue of how environmental factors influence language development. Harley and Wang (1997, p. 24) point out that the effect of environmental factors is "underplayed in critical period studies." From studies of young starters, for example, it is obvious, as we have pointed out above, that a low AO does not necessarily lead to a nativelike ultimate attainment. Among other factors, frequency and quality of input as well as identity issues seem to play an important role and interact with maturational constraints for the outcome even at a low age (Hyltenstam, 1992, p. 364).

The *affected system* – in our context, language proper – is often described as simply as that, especially in early discussions of the CPH. Obviously, more detailed specification is needed in order to support empirical statements, and caution should be exercised in generalizing from empirical results in a specific domain to "language." However, although one must agree with Eubank and Gregg's (1999, p. 66f) contention that "discussions of the [critical period] conducted at the level of Language [i.e., a folk-psychological notion of language] are inherently unfruitful" and that it is necessary to define which components or elements are discussed, it seems premature to exclude factors other than "linguistic competence" from the agenda of maturational constraints, as they do. Instead, one should recognize the relevance and validity of "the human capacity to utter sounds, to learn words, to construct narratives, to participate in conversations, to produce and understand metaphor, to accommodate to another's speech, to persuade . . . , and, in general, to engage in social discourse" (Schumann, 1995, p. 60). In short, a framework for the understanding of the notion of "language" would be the "human cognitive capacity for language learning (language knowledge, learning, and processing)" (Wolfe-Quintero, 1996, p. 335).

Because, as we have tried to underscore in this chapter, maturational constraints make predictions about the ability to become nativelike in a second language, an important goal for second language acquisition theory is to specify what aspects of language are maturationally affected. As the human capacity for second language acquisition allows learners at any age to acquire large portions of the target language, specifications should concern features that not everyone seems to be able to acquire. Therefore, it is just those features which distinguish near-native and native speakers of a language that are of particular interest. Schachter's (1996, p. 160) discussion of differences between "the child L1 and the adult L2 cases" captures some of this. Schachter points to four differences, two of which distinguish the ultimate attainment even of very successful L2 learners from that of L1 learners: (i) incompleteness with regard to the grammar of the L2; and (ii) fossilized variation, that is, "errors and non-errors in the same linguistic environments." (The other two differences concern transfer and lack of equipotentiality for all languages due to L1 characteristics.) The issue of completeness concerns linguistic competence, while fossilized variation most likely should be considered primarily a processing phenomenon at this level (p. 161). With regard to completeness of competence, there is at present little clear evidence for specific phenomena being maturationally constrained. Among those researchers arguing for the existence of maturational constraints from a UG perspective, Schachter (1996, p. 188) notes that "evidence . . . is just beginning to emerge," and suggests on the basis of various investigations that there is support for the view that the Subjacency Principle is maturationally constrained. Likewise, empirical results by Lee (1992; cited in Schachter, 1996) are taken as support for the Governing Category Principle being sensitive to maturational constraints. Eubank and Gregg (1999, p. 89) draw a different conclusion with reference to a study by Beck (1997), where a theoretical framework relying on the idea of lexical parameters is used, when they suggest that "adult L2 learners, however proficient they may be in other areas of language, share an inability to represent parametric values drawn from the lexicon."

DeKeyser's (2000) data, covering both UG and non-UG features, suggest a distinction between morphosyntactic aspects that are sensitive to maturational effects (the use of articles, the use and position of auxiliaries, the position of adverbs, certain elements of verb sub-categorization, and some uses of the plural morpheme) and aspects that, due to their saliency, are not (basic word order and pronoun gender).

Evidence from studies outside the UG framework seem to be more reliable for the simple reason that they have more frequently investigated the type of subjects which are crucial for the issue of maturational constraints, namely seemingly nativelike (or near-native) second language learners. As we have seen above, studies that have identified second language learners who perform within the range of native speakers have in most cases concluded that there are still some minor differences between the two groups (e.g., Coppieters, 1987; Ekberg, 1998; Hene, 1993; Hyltenstam, 1992; Hyltenstam and Abrahamsson, forthcoming; Ioup et al., 1994; Moyer, 1999; cf. also Sorace's, 1993, distinction between "divergent" and "incomplete" L2 competence).

4.4 *Ultimate causes: proposed explanations for age effects*

4.4.1 Biological explanations

Ever since the early suggestions by Penfield and Roberts (1959) and Lenneberg (1967), biological explanations have addressed the brain's steady loss of flexibility or plasticity. Even though little is known about the exact cerebral mechanisms that are responsible for differential outcomes of language learning at different phases of life, there is enough independent knowledge of changes in the brain taking place during the time when language acquisition outcomes differ systematically to be suggestive of hypothesized relations between the two.

A broad characterization of the notion of *cerebral plasticity* is "the ability of neurons to make new connections, and varied connections depending on the stimulus" (Eubank and Gregg, 1999, p. 69). Furthermore, the "[s]trengthening of connections between neurons probably represents the neurobiological basis for learning," including language acquisition (Pulvermüller and Schumann, 1994, p. 691). The question, then, is what physiological cerebral correlates might have implications for the ability of neurons to make new connections.

This issue has often been discussed with reference to the process of *myelination*. The myelination of cortical neurons is a physical-chemical process in the brain in which glial cells wrap the axons of the neurons with myelin. (Myelin is a substance contained in the glial cells that consists of lipids and proteins.) The function of this wrapping of the axons with myelin is to provide the neurons with nutrition and to increase their ability to conduct electrical signals more rapidly. This promotes the ability for the transfer of information at larger cerebral distances. At the same time, it increasingly makes connections between neighboring neurons more difficult. The process of myelination starts at the fetus stage and continues for at least several decades; there is, however, evidence that a high number of neurons in the adult brain remain unmyelinated. Since the beginning of the twentieth century, it has been known that different cortical areas myelinate at different times (see references in Pulvermüller and Schumann, 1994, p. 711). By the age of 12 months, the primary sensory and motor areas along the Rolandic fissure are myelinated. Higher-order association areas of the cortex, such as the angular gyrus, are myelinated much later, and it is in these regions that some neurons remain unmyelinated in adults. The language areas around the Sylvian fissure myelinate after the primary sensory and motor areas, but before the higher-order association areas: "Around puberty, all cortical areas, except perhaps the higher-order association cortices, have reached their full level of myelination" (Pulvermüller and Schumann, 1994, p. 713). The "maturation of the brain" is indeed often equated with the process of myelination.

These aspects of myelination are coupled with another well-established fact about cortical network organization in an interpretation that Pulvermüller and Schumann (1994) present of the relationship between brain correlates on the one hand and language acquisition potential on the other. They refer to the existence of two systems of cortical connections between neurons, one using what are called apical dendrites and axons that reach far from the cell body and connect different cortical areas, and another system using basal dendrites which are close to the cell body and local branches of the axons, which are called axon collaterals (these two systems are labeled the A-system and the B-system, respectively, by Braitenberg, 1978). Before myelination of a certain area has severed connections between neighboring neurons, a strengthening of connections naturally takes place locally through the B-system. This provides an explanation for why the learning of "how to sequence phonemes, syllables, and words" (Pulvermüller and Schumann, 1994, p. 713) – in other words, the acquisition of the phonological and syntactic system – is easy early in life but becomes increasingly difficult with age. Thus, it is assumed that the acquisition of these aspects of language relies on connections within a limited cortical area. Pulvermüller and Schumann account for the fact that maturation (i.e., myelination) has less of an effect on semantics, pragmatics, and vocabulary with the explanation that these aspects of language rely on connections handled by the A-system, which typically has the ability to connect different cortical areas, not least to involve the higher association areas. With myelination, the electrical signals can be conducted more efficiently between the language areas and other relevant cortex areas through the apical axons, while, at the same time, local connections are enhanced within these areas because myelination is absent.

Of course, a number of facts remain unexplained or ignored in Pulvermüller and Schumann's proposal. It would, for example, be interesting to speculate on how the coupling of prosodic and segmental features should be accounted for in such a framework, or what explains the sudden growth of vocabulary in the 2–3-year-old child. However, it is not unreasonable also to see explanations for such phenomena in terms of myelination.

Interestingly, the model can to some extent be said to find corroboration in recent ERP (Event-Related Brain Potentials) work by Weber-Fox and Neville (see 1999, pp. 27ff, for a summary of studies). For example, in a study of ERP responses for content and function (or grammatical) words, it was demonstrated that in native speakers and early second language learners (AO < 7 years), these two word classes led to different responses, while in groups of second language learners with AOs above that age, there was no obvious difference. Weber-Fox and Neville conclude that "grammatical and syntactic aspects of language processing appear to be more vulnerable to alterations in the timing of language experience compared to more semantic or lexical processing" (1999, p. 34).

Other proposals of cerebral correlates for differences in second language acquisition outcomes include metabolic differences in pre-puberty and post-puberty brains (see references in Pulvermüller and Schumann, 1994, p. 710), thickening of the corpus callosum (Seliger, 1978), and, of course, lateralization (Lenneberg, 1967; see discussion in Long, 1990, p. 278).

4.4.2 *Social/psychological explanations*

As has already been made clear, there is certainly no consensus on a biological interpretation of differences in outcome of child and adult second language learning. Alternative explanations, with no basis in biology, refer to *social/psychological factors* that are thought to co-vary with age, including motivational, affective/attitudinal, and input factors. That is, it is sometimes claimed that children are inherently more motivated than adults to acquire nativelike levels of the L2, that younger learners develop positive attitudes toward the L2, its culture, and its speakers more easily than older learners do, or that children receive more and simpler input than adults (e.g., Bialystok and Hakuta, 1999). As Long (1990) points out, however, there are some major problems with accounts that use these factors as explanations for child–adult differences. For example, there is no direct evidence that children would be inherently more motivated to learn the L2, or that they receive more input than adults; on the contrary, children may vary in their desire to acquire the L2 and in the input they receive, but invariantly end up with much higher ultimate attainment than most adults. In addition, several empirical studies (e.g., Johnson and Newport, 1989; Oyama, 1978) have shown that motivational factors cannot account for the decrease in ultimate attainment with increasing AOs. Moreover, as was mentioned initially, even though children may generally receive simpler L2 input than adults, research on caretaker talk (or motherese) indicates that course, speed, and success in *first* language acquisition are relatively insensitive to qualitative and quantitative variation in input and interaction. This is true both within and across cultures, and there is no obvious reason to doubt that children can reach very high, if not nativelike, L2 standards from quite poor and sparse input/interaction (see, further, Gleitman and Newport, 1995; see also Ellis, 1994, pp. 267–9).[17]

As there is no convincing counter-evidence to the default assumption that biology constrains L2 acquisition, we must maintain that maturation does have a significant impact on decreasing learning potentials with higher AOs. As maturation clearly plays a major role in L1 acquisition, it would be surprising if L2 acquisition were not strongly influenced by learners' maturational states as well. However, it would be equally surprising if social/psychological factors were shown to have no effect at all on L2 outcomes. There is most certainly an interplay between maturational and non-maturational factors, where the latter sometimes combine into advantageous learning circumstances that may "compensate for the biological disadvantages of a late start" (Bongaerts et al., 1995, p. 45).

In cases of late L2 learning, the advantageous learning circumstances embrace not only motivational, affective/attitudinal, and input factors, but also social/psychological factors relating to amount and type of instruction, verbal analytical ability, metalinguistic awareness, and a general talent for acquiring languages. While maturation would seem to be responsible for the inevitable overall age-related decline in learning potential (for delayed L1 learners and "normal" L2 learners, as well as for exceptionally successful late L2 learners), the variability between exceptionally successful and other L2 learners *of the same starting age* may be seen as a result of (a certain combination of) these non-maturational factors. The study by Moyer (1999) mentioned earlier showed that, in addition to degree of motivation, the amount and type of instruction that post-puberty L2 learners receive strongly correlate with success, whereas varying starting ages after the completion of maturation do not correlate with levels of proficiency (i.e., ultimate outcomes become statistically unpredictable from AOs after puberty; cf. Johnson and Newport, 1989). Similarly, Bongaerts and his colleagues have suggested that the intensive training in the perception and production of L2 sounds that their foreign language students had received, in combination with high motivation and continued access to ample L2 input, may have been decisive for their attainment of a nativelike pronunciation (Bongaerts, 1999, pp. 154–5). Furthermore, all but one of the late L2 starters in DeKeyser's (2000) study who had achieved scores within the range of child starters on a grammaticality judgment test also scored high on a test of verbal analytical ability. This result led DeKeyser to conclude that only adults with such special abilities can reach near-native L2 competence. Similarly, Ioup et al. (1994; see also Ioup, 1995) stressed the importance for adult learners of focusing on form. Julie reported that from the very beginning of her acquisition of spoken Egyptian Arabic she "consciously manipulated the grammatical structure of the language" (p. 92), that she noticed redundant morphological structure, and that her "attitude toward grammar was that it needed to be mastered correctly" (ibid.). However, another factor is given even more prominence by Ioup et al. (1994), namely an innate talent for learning languages. This trait has been hypothesized (and to some extent observed) to correlate with characteristics "such as left-handedness, twinning, and allergies, among others"[18] (p. 92), and it is also manifest in the speed of L1 acquisition, all of which seemed to fit Julie's profile well.[19] Talent for language learning is also hypothesized by Ioup et al. to originate in "unusual brain organization where a greater proportion of cortex is devoted to language" (ibid.), which leads them to suggest that "any apparent exceptions to the CPH will manifest some aspects of the neuropsychological profile that characterize language learning talent" (p. 93), although just "how the talented brain acquires language in comparison with the normal brain" (ibid.) remains unclear.

4.4.3 Cognitive explanations

Finally, a general consensus exists around the position that "cognitive factors must be implicated in sensitive period effects at some level" (Long, 1990, p. 277), although this consensus does not extend to views on exactly how cognition comes into play; in fact, these views are not at all consentient. Cognitive explanations for children's superiority at second language acquisition are often based on different versions of the idea that general problem-solving mechanisms are involved in the older learner's processing of second language data. Penfield and Robert's (1959) view of the development of analytical thinking in children by the age of 9 is an early predecessor of explanations built upon Piagetian theorizing about the development of the formal operations stage. Conscious reflections on the structure of the target language are supposed to counteract the normal "direct" processing of target language input. Similar reasoning lies behind later cognitive explanations linked to UG assumptions on language competence. According to the *fundamental difference hypothesis* (Bley-Vroman, 1989), adult learners differ from child learners in that they no longer have access to the inborn language acquisition device specified in UG and instead have to rely on general problem-solving procedures. In contrast, the *competition hypothesis* (Felix, 1985) assumes continued access to UG and suggests that the language acquisition device competes with general problem-solving mechanisms, which eventually win out over the language acquisition device. According to the *less is more hypothesis* (Newport, 1990), limitations on cognitive capacity allow the child to focus on and store component pieces of the input, while adults unsuccessfully try to analyze complex chunks of input simultaneously.[20]

A different perspective on the role of cognition in explaining age-related differences is that of Bialystok and Hakuta (1999). On the basis of categorical, self-reported census data from 63,690 Spanish- and Chinese-speaking immigrants to the United States, with AOs between zero and 70+ and with 10 years of exposure or more, these researchers claim to demonstrate a perfectly linear relationship between AO and ultimate proficiency in L2 English. According to Bialystok and Hakuta, "there appears to be nothing special about the age range before puberty," and rather "[the] decline in proficiency remains constant across ages" (p. 175).[21] They interpret this linear pattern as evidence against a critical period, and propose an explanation based on certain cognitive mechanisms.[22] More specifically, "studies of lifespan cognition" provide evidence that in learning experiments, older subjects are more sensitive to timing factors in the presentation of materials and need longer recall time. There is also a general decline in the recall of details and a tendency for older learners to remember "only the gist." Moreover, the cognitive decline is gradual and constant, just as the levels of language proficiency become gradually poorer with increasing AOs. As all of these deteriorating cognitive abilities are involved in the learning and use of a new language, "age-related changes in ultimate language proficiency are to be attributable to these cognitive changes and not to a specific language module that is constrained by a maturational schedule" (ibid., p. 172). Similarly, although expressing a preference for a maturational interpretation, Johnson and Newport (1989) admit that their results are also congruent with this kind of cognitive account, adding that "future research will [hopefully] provide more detailed results which may differentiate these views from one another" (p. 97). However, Long (1990, p. 277) discusses problems associated with particular cognitive explanations and with cognitive explanations in general. The strongest argument against general problem-solving and metalinguistic abilities as explanations for age-related differences in outcome is the fact that there is no co-variation between language proficiency and these specific types of cognitive ability. Furthermore, cognitive explanations would predict fundamentally different learning processes for children and adults (in terms of order and sequence of acquisition etc.), which does not seem to be the case.

5 Toward an Understanding of the Role of Maturation

The preceding sections have demonstrated some of the complexities that characterize research on maturational constraints. As mentioned, few empirical results remain uncontroversial, and authors and researchers have taken a wide range of theoretical stances on the basis of quite different – and, at times, similar – empirical data. The aim of this section is to arrive at an understanding of the reasons for these conflicting positions and to suggest a unitary interpretation of existing data.

5.1 *Age of onset and ultimate attainment: a unitary interpretation of conflicting observations*

From the review of empirical results and theoretical arguments above, we find that different authors claim to have made one of two main kinds of empirical observations of the relationship between AO and nativelike ultimate attainment in a second language:

i Nativelike L2 proficiency is observed in early starters only.
ii Nativelike L2 proficiency is observed in early starters, and also in individual late starters.

That is, while some studies suggest that only child learners can reach nativelike levels, others indicate that nativelike proficiency can be reached regardless of starting age. However, our review has also shown that there are results, especially in more recent research, that give us reason to reinterpret these observations and suggest a third possibility:

iii Nativelike L2 proficiency is observed in neither early nor late starters.

In other words, some studies indicate less than nativelike ultimate attainment even in very early learners; in fact, some studies suggest that ultimate attainment already begins to correlate negatively with AO from birth.

The observations in points (i)–(iii) are displayed graphically in figures 17.1–17.3 respectively.

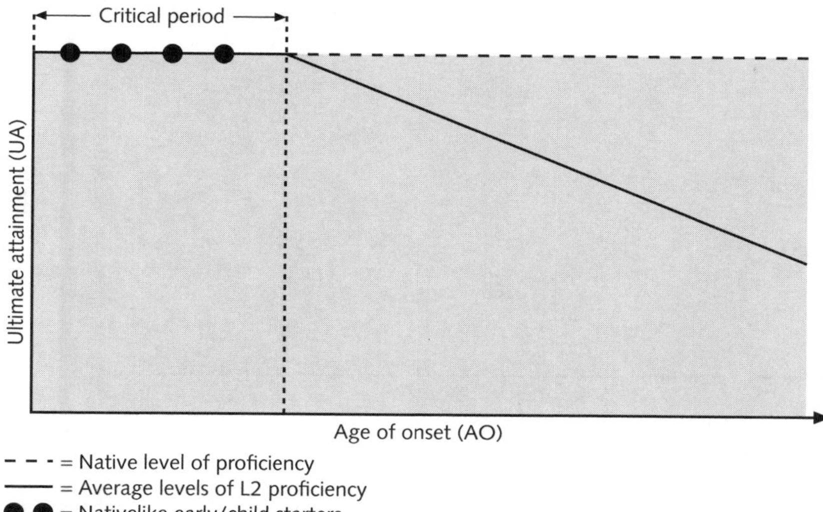

Figure 17.1 Observations of nativelike ultimate attainment in early starters only
Notes: This is based on studies showing that the average UA seems to be uniformly nativelike in early starters, and that UA begins to correlate negatively with higher AO after a certain age (e.g., Johnson and Newport, 1989; Patkowski, 1980, 1990). The typical interpretation attributes this to biological critical period effects (e.g., DeKeyser, 2000; Johnson and Newport, 1989; Patkowski, 1980, 1990). An alternative interpretation attributes it to other, non-biological changes at a certain age, such as identity, motivation, cognition, input, formal training, and other social conditions (e.g., Bialystok and Hakuta, 1999; Bialystok and Miller, 1999).

As can be seen in figure 17.1, which displays the observations formulated in point (i) above, all AOs below a certain age are associated with nativelike ultimate proficiency; AOs after a specific age limit are generally associated with successively lower ultimate attainment. In addition, although not indicated in the figure, inter-learner variability in achieved ultimate proficiency becomes increasingly greater, as has been mentioned earlier.

The pattern in figure 17.1 has typically been interpreted as support for the existence of a biologically defined critical or sensitive period, and thus the existence of maturational constraints, with the implication that the language learning mechanism is less effective after the completion of maturation. However, this has not been the only interpretation. Non-biologically based positions postulate systematically higher degrees of motivation or more supportive input for learners below a certain age than for learners beyond that age limit.

Figure 17.2 illustrates the situation in which we find nativelike L2 proficiency in early starters generally, but also in individual late starters, as stated in point (ii) above. The typical interpretation of this pattern is that there are no maturational constraints on L2 acquisition. It is not an inherent biological restriction on language acquisition that causes the uneven distribution of nativelike

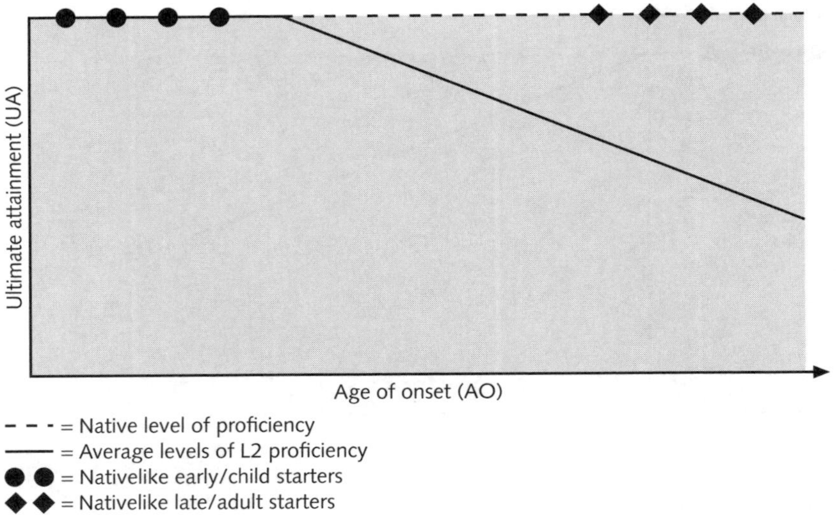

Figure 17.2 Observations of nativelike ultimate attainment in early starters and individual late starters

Notes: This is based on studies demonstrating that late L2 starters who have become highly successful do exist, some of whom even seem to have reached nativelike proficiency (e.g., Birdsong, 1992; Bongaerts, 1999; Bongaerts et al., 2000; Moyer, 1999; White and Genesee, 1996). The typical interpretation is that there is no biological critical period, and learners at any age can, in principle, reach nativelike UA (e.g., Birdsong, 1992; White and Genesee, 1996). An alternative interpretation is that even though a biological critical period exists (see figure 17.1), a few late starters are able to "beat the predictions of the CPH" through compensatory factors, such as high aptitute (e.g., DeKeyser, 2000; Ioup et al., 1994), high motivation (Bongaerts, 1999; Bongaerts et al., 2000; Moyer, 1999), formal training and input (Bongaerts, 1999), etc.

ultimate proficiency among learners with different AOs, but rather differences in their learning circumstances. Within this interpretive framework, a frequently made claim is that motivation and input factors are more favorable for children than for adults. Cognitive factors have also been mentioned as a source of the variability. In particular, it has been claimed that the deterioration of certain cognitive abilities across the life span correlates with the more limited achievement we see in the average learner (Bialystok and Hakuta, 1999).

A biologically based interpretation of the pattern observed in figure 17.2 is related directly to the uneven AO distribution of nativelike ultimate proficiencies. While most younger learners have a special predisposition for acquiring language from mere exposure, this ability is lost with maturation. However, we find exceptional adult learners who have either a different psychological setup in terms of verbal memory and ability to focus on form (Novoa, Fein, and Obler, 1988), or a willingness to adopt a new cultural identity (Schneiderman and Desmarais, 1988), or a high verbal analytical ability (DeKeyser, 2000), or some other more unspecified talent for language generally (Ioup et al., 1994).

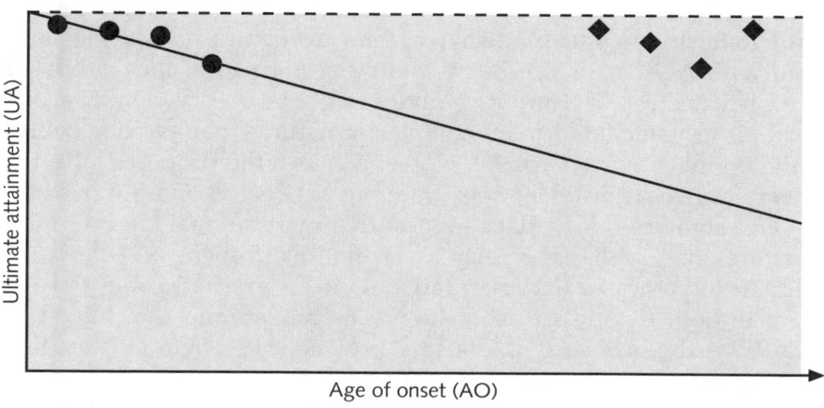

- - - = Native level of proficiency
—— = Average levels of L2 proficiency
● ● = Near-native (rather than nativelike) early/child starters
◆ ◆ = Near-native (rather than nativelike) late/adult starters

Figure 17.3 A reassessment of the nativelikeness of both early and late starters
Notes: This is based on:

i evidence suggesting that even very early L2 starters reach slightly non-nativelike UA (Ekberg, 1998; Hene, 1993; Hyltenstam, 1992; Hyltenstam and Abrahamsson, forthcoming; McDonald, 2000);
ii evidence or indications that the UA reported for the highly successful late starters in figure 17.2 is actually not completely nativelike, at least not in all relevant aspects of the L2 (e.g., Coppieters, 1987; Ioup et al., 1994; Moyer, 1999; White and Genesee, 1996);
iii suggestions that UA declines linearly with increasing AO, rather than abruptly at a certain AO (e.g., Bialystok and Hakuta, 1999; Birdsong, 1999; Butler, 2000; Flege, 1999; Guion et al., 2000).

Interpretation 1: Biological/maturational effects from birth with no abrupt cut-off point at a certain AO (e.g., Hyltenstam and Abrahamsson, forthcoming; cf. also Birdsong, 1999, pp. 11–12).
Interpretation 2: Lowered language learning ability as a function of a linear decline of cognitive abilities generally (e.g., Bialystok and Hakuta, 1999), or of different amounts of L1 and L2 use for learners with different AOs (e.g., Flege, 1999).

Both the "critical" and "sensitive" formulations suggest that there is a certain period during which the language acquisition ability is not maturationally constrained. This period has a more (in the CPH) or less (in the SPH) abrupt offset. Figure 17.3 shows observations according to which second language ultimate attainment decreases from birth. This pattern is based on studies of non-nativelike early starters as well as on recent research suggesting a linear relationship between AO and ultimate attainment instead of a non-linear one, as implied by the CPH. Here, the curve that describes language acquisition potentials at different AOs thus has no level phase before falling off, but rather describes a continuous decrease from birth over the life span.

However, this idea is not entirely new. Johnson and Newport (1989) speculated whether a critical period for L2 acquisition might terminate much earlier than age 7, which was the age limit for nativelike attainment suggested by their L2 data. Referring to data on delayed L1 acquisition of ASL which show that children with AOs 4–6 score below native performance, they proposed that such an early decrease in learning abilities might be observed in L2 acquisition, as well, if tests included more complex structures that avoided ceiling effects for the younger starters (p. 96). However, since the proposed offset of a CP has been located at different ages (ranging between 6 and 15) over the years, and since some recent L1 data suggest that maturational effects can be detected much earlier, perhaps as early as 12 months (Ruben, 1997), it is not unreasonable to hypothesize that maturational effects are noticeable as early as from birth in both L1 and L2 acquisition. The few studies that have performed detailed analyses of early L2 starters' proficiency seem to indicate this.

Consequently, we would like to suggest that those studies that claim nativelike ultimate attainment in young learners generally do so on the basis of underanalyzed data. Similarly, it is clear from our review above that claims of nativelikeness for late L2 starters are also based on underanalyzed data. Therefore, the hypothesis that language learning must start "from the beginning" in order to result in full nativelike ultimate proficiency (see point (iii) above) seems to be in agreement with recent suggestions of a linear decline with increasing AOs rather than an abrupt cut-off point at a certain age (see Birdsong, 1999b, p. 11).

The maturational interpretation of observations of this type would be that biological factors play a prominent role in the ultimate attainment of young learners who do reach near-native levels, but that social/psychological and cross-linguistic factors also come into play even at an early age. With increasing AOs, maturational factors play a successively diminished role, whereas other factors become more influential, which is reflected in the greater inter-learner variability among learners with higher AOs (DeKeyser, 2000; cf. also Birdsong, 1999b, p. 12). A formulation along these lines might be considered a less spectacular view of maturational constraints, according to which it is true that biology constrains language acquisition, but not necessarily in terms of a critical period.

The maturational interpretation is not, however, a view that is unanimously embraced. Bialystok and Hakuta (1999), for example, seem to interpret a linear decline in ultimate attainment as evidence not only against a critical period, which it undoubtedly is – "discontinuity [i.e., a salient offset] is the minimal essential evidence needed to reject the null hypothesis of no critical period" (ibid., p. 173) – but against maturational constraints in general, that is, as an absence of biological causes for age-related differences. In such an interpretation, the observed distribution of ultimate attainment levels would again be accounted for by different learning conditions. According to Bialystok and Hakuta (1999), "social factors conspire to ease the effort for young children by providing a nurturing environment, simplified input, educational opportunities, cooperative peers, and other supporting aspects of a social context that facilitate the acquisition of any language" (p. 178). As mentioned earlier, they also suggest that the deterioration of general cognitive mechanisms over the life span affects the ability to learn a new language. However, in our view, a perfectly linear, negative correlation between ultimate attainment and AO seriously weakens – perhaps even disqualifies – any kind of social/psychological explanation. A linear decline hypothesis predicts average differences in ultimate attainment even between learners with a minimal difference in AO, and at any point on the AO continuum. To our knowledge, no theory can specify the social/psychological (i.e., affective, motivational, educational, input-related, etc.) factors that enable the average 8-month-old starter to reach a slightly higher ultimate attainment than the average 12-month-old starter. Similarly difficult to specify is what cognitive changes during this early period of life would leave more negative traces in the ultimate attainment of the 12-month-old. Such differences in ultimate learning potential are better explained with reference to biological factors. In fact, we see these recent research findings of a linear decline in ultimate attainment as even stronger evidence for the role of maturation than the typical, non-linear pattern.

5.2 *The observations revisited: bringing the patterns together*

We would like to present figure 17.4 as a device for unifying and reinterpreting the quite diverse patterns presented in figures 17.1–17.3.

Earlier in this chapter, we mentioned the fact that it is inherently difficult, perhaps even impossible, to distinguish native from near-native speakers. The slight differences that exist between them may well be unnoticeable. Much of the data discussed in the literature on maturational constraints, and specifically on the CPH, has not been analyzed in sufficient detail to make possible any claims about whether the subjects are nativelike in all respects. On the contrary, it is only in exceptional cases that these very advanced L2 speakers have been the subject of in-depth studies over a range of phenomena that would reflect various aspects of their proficiency.

We can, therefore, readily imagine that many of the L2 learners identified in studies to be "within the range of native controls" should in actual fact be characterized as near-native rather than nativelike speakers. This would actually allow us to merge all types of observations presented in figures 17.1–17.3, and thereby envisage a situation where no L2 learners, irrespective of AO, can become nativelike. The observation in figure 17.1, that is, that only children eventually reach nativelike proficiency, is explained by the fact that most learners with AOs before a certain age limit (say puberty) and practically speaking all before an earlier age limit (say 6) reach proficiency levels above *the limit of perceivable non-nativeness*, thus making them *appear* to be nativelike. This, incidentally, gives an *apparent* cut-off point at a certain AO and consequently an "apparent" critical period prior to that AO. The same explanation may be used for the observation in figure 17.2 (i.e., that of nativelike late starters): because they have reached proficiency levels above this limit of perceivable

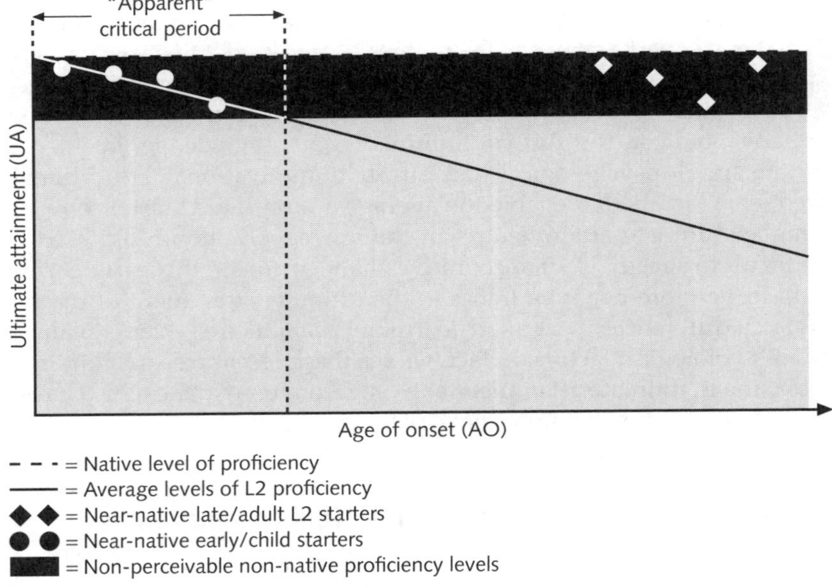

Figure 17.4 A reinterpretation of (i) nativelikeness as non-perceivable non-nativeness, and (ii) the critical period as an "illusion" based on data from underanalyzed early starters

Notes: This is based on all observations behind the patterns in figures 17.1–17.3. Our conclusions are that:

i underanalyzed subjects (both very early and late starters) have near-native (rather than nativelike) L2 proficiency levels that are extremely difficult to distinguish from native levels;

ii what seems to be a critical period is actually the time span prior to the AO point where average L2 learners' UA levels begin to be perceivable as non-nativelike.

non-nativeness, they are seemingly nativelike. In addition, this account helps to explain why the pattern in figure 17.3 has as yet only been hinted at as a possibility, perhaps due to the fact that it does not appear to correspond to observations in everyday life. Thus, the seemingly conflicting data can be given a unitary interpretation, provided that a dimension of "non-perceivable non-nativeness" is included.

In the next section, an attempt is made at integrating the various observations and perspectives into a composite picture that incorporates the interactional effects of the factors that seem to be decisive for the ultimate outcomes of second language acquisition.

5.3 *The composite picture*

Figure 17.5 presents a "consensus model" of what we believe constitutes our present knowledge. It is intended to exhibit and consolidate the existing

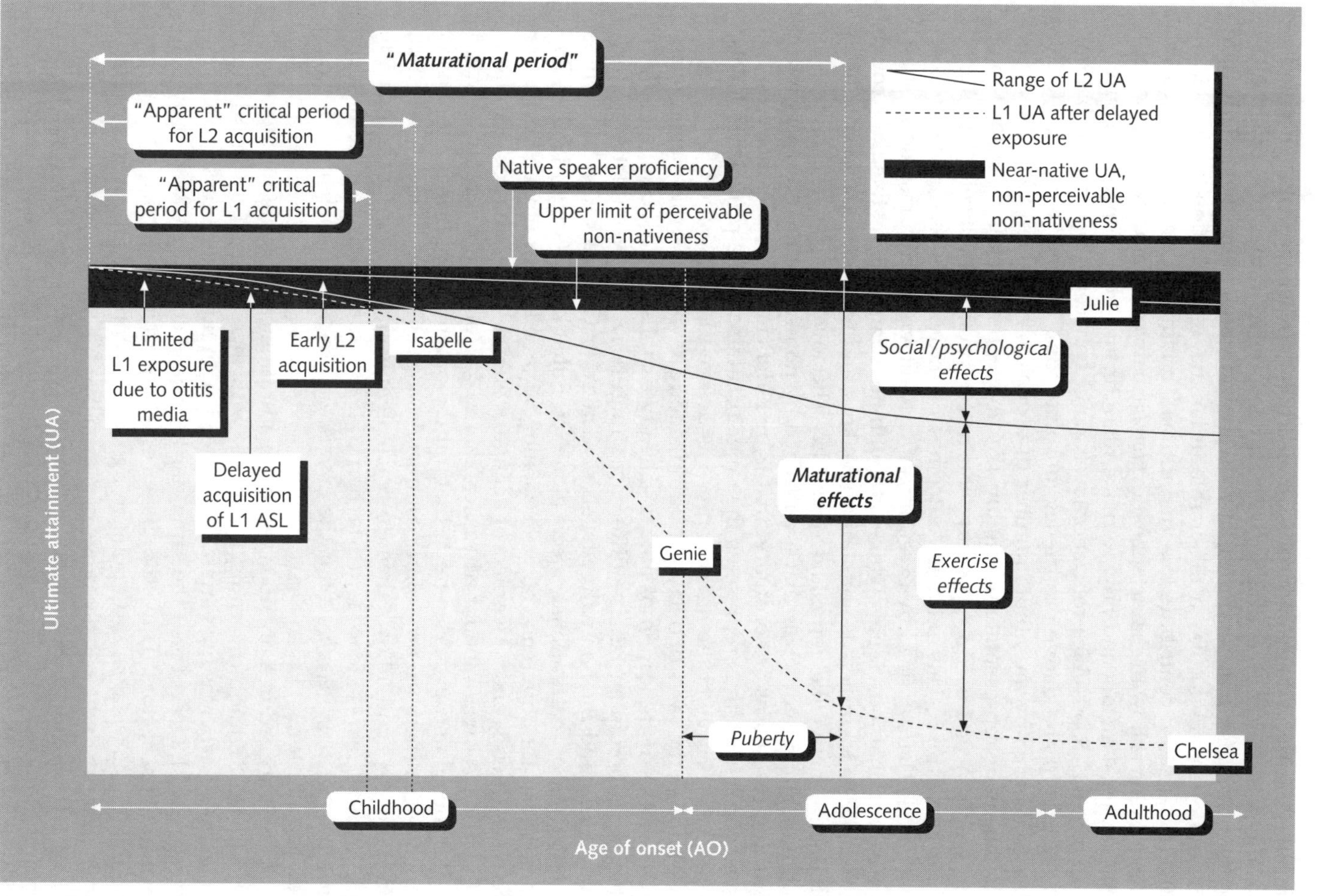

Figure 17.5 A model of the interplay between maturation, exercise, and social/psychological factors

empirical facts and the relationships among them. We believe that such a model has the potential of providing us with an interpretive framework for simultaneously appraising the empirical and theoretical status of our field. Although maturation seems to play a major role in language acquisition, as we see it, other factors also contribute to actual ultimate attainment in individual cases. The question is how to characterize the *interplay* between maturation and social/psychological factors and how to make them fit into the composite picture.

In figure 17.5, possible proficiency levels range between zero (absolute bottom of the graph) and native proficiency (absolute top). In other words, logically, one could identify an infinite number of proficiency levels in between. As in the schematic representation in figure 17.4 above, the black layer at the top of the graph in figure 17.5 represents *near*-native proficiency levels. The upper solid curve represents ultimate outcomes of individuals (e.g., Julie) whose learning is characterized by exceptionally advantageous circumstances. These are exceptional individuals who – although not completely nativelike – could not easily be identified as non-native speakers, and who instead *appear* to have attained a nativelike command of the L2. The lower solid curve represents ultimate attainment levels that are reached by non-exceptional learners when learning conditions are ordinary, that is, non-deficient. The area between the two solid curves thus represents the range of attainable L2 proficiency levels. The dashed curve in the figure represents delayed L1 acquisition.

Although the cases of delayed L1 acquisition are very rare, they nevertheless give us a clear indication of how an already established L1 positively affects the acquisition of an L2. The difference in figure 17.5 between native proficiency levels and the non-native levels of Genie's or Chelsea's L1 attainment is a reflection of maturational effects alone (cf. Eubank and Gregg, 1999, p. 78). In contrast, the difference between Genie and any 13-year-old L2 learner, or between Chelsea and L2 learners of her age, would be due to the positive effects of *exercise*. As was mentioned earlier, there is an obvious interplay between maturational and exercise effects that, on the one hand, prevents late second language learners from reaching completely nativelike proficiency levels, but, on the other hand, allows them to reach significantly higher levels than late L1 learners (as evidenced in Mayberry, 1993); something that neither the *maturational state hypothesis* nor the *exercise hypothesis* – in their pure forms – can account for.

As was argued in a previous section, maturation can account for the overall and linear decline in learning potentials with increasing AOs (for all kinds of learners), whereas the variability between exceptionally successful and non-exceptional L2 learners of the same starting age is accounted for best by non-maturational factors. Thus, the distance between native proficiency and *any* non-native curve at *any* AO point in figure 17.5 represents the negative effect of maturation, whereas the range of non-native L2 levels represents the effect of social/psychological factors. In other words, social/psychological factors may explain why one 25-year-old starter reaches higher levels of proficiency than another 25-year-old starter, but cannot explain why 4-year-old starters generally perform better than 25-year-old starters – only maturational factors can. The empirical data on delayed *first* language acquisition are very sparse, and therefore we are not able to tell whether social/psychological factors would result in the same kind of inter-learner variability in the first language context.

It seems, however, that the role of social/psychological factors becomes increasingly important with age. At least up to AOs 6 or 7, all learners will automatically reach levels that allow them to pass as native speakers – provided that there is sufficient input and that the learning circumstances are not deficient. The relatively early phase of the maturation process thus allows for learning to result in seemingly nativelike proficiency from mere L2 exposure. With increasing AOs after this age, however, certain social/psychological factors must be increasingly advantageous in order to compensate for the successively negative effects of maturation. That is, 8-year-old starters must have a certain (albeit small) degree of extraordinary motivation (and/or positive affect, input, instruction, aptitude, etc.) in order to reach the same levels that are automatically reached by their 6-year-old friends; the 25-year-old starter will have to encounter a variety of such advantageous circumstances, and to a much greater degree, in order to compensate for maturational effects. In contrast, non-maturational factors seem to play only a marginal role in early childhood: talented and highly motivated 4-year-olds do not have any significant advantage over their less talented/motivated peers of the same age (cf. DeKeyser, 2000). This is not only because the absolute difference between their levels of L2 proficiency will be very small, but also because they will all end up in the near-native layer anyway, thus attaining levels of proficiency at which non-nativeness cannot be detected easily by native listeners.

As in figure 17.4 above, there are no ultimate attainment curves in figure 17.5 that ever touch the ceiling; perfect proficiency in a first or second language is displayed here as never being attained when acquisition is delayed in the least. However, given our present state of knowledge, this aspect of figure 17.5 remains a conjecture that requires extensive empirical corroboration. Nevertheless, given the fact that there are no published accounts of a single adult starter who has reached nativelike overall L2 proficiency, and given the frequent observation of non-native features even in very early starters, we would suggest the *possibility* that absolute nativelike command of an L2 may in fact never be possible for any learner. According to such a view, the language learning mechanism would be designed in such a way that it requires immediate triggering from the environment in order for it to develop and work appropriately; that is, the learning mechanism inevitably and quickly deteriorates from birth if not continuously stimulated.

Finally, the general notion "maturational period," which is depicted here as occurring between birth and (approximately) age 15, has been included instead of specific notions such as "critical/sensitive/optimal period(s)." The continued decline of all curves after age 15 is meant to be interpreted as dependent on non-maturational factors. Note that a "maturational period" concept implies only that maturation *is going on*; that is, it predicts that acquisition will be increasingly difficult during this period, but remains neutral as to the exact levels of ultimate attainment (since the degree of motivation, talent, instruction, and other compensatory potentials of individual learners is unpredictable from AO). This contrasts with the notion "critical period," which predicts nativelike levels if acquisition begins at any AO within this period. However, as was shown in figure 17.4 above, there are certain time spans that may be interpreted as critical periods. The bottom of the black layer (i.e., the upper limit of perceivable non-nativeness) in figure 17.5 is eventually broken, first by the L1 curve, then by the lower L2 curve. If the bottom line of the near-native layer has been interpreted earlier as (absolute) nativelike proficiency, then there are *apparent* critical periods, within which proficiency levels that are perceived as nativelike by native listeners are attainable. Exactly where (or if) the upper L2 curve crosses the limit of perceivable non-nativeness is still an open question.

In the scenario given here, some of the established research results connected with the topic of the CPH would be seen as an illusion. Many aspects of the CPH would be seriously questioned, although at the same time there would be strong support for the role of maturation in both first and second language acquisition.

6 Future Research: Basic Methodological Requirements

We believe that the most fruitful way to research maturational constraints is to focus explicitly on ultimate L2 learning *potentials* – in late as well as in early starters. Because ultimate attainment studies using randomly selected learners of different ages manage only to demonstrate that early starters generally reach higher levels of L2 proficiency than late starters, future research must continue in the direction developed during the 1990s, namely to focus specifically on the question of whether late/adult starters can ever attain nativelike L2 proficiency. This should be done by continuing the intensive examination of exceptionally successful late starters who appear to have reached nativelike levels of L2 proficiency. However, as has been clear from our previous discussion, the careful investigation of the ultimate L2 proficiency of very young starters is equally important. In other words, learners of all ages who we, as native speakers, cannot immediately identify as non-native speakers should be selected as subjects. Long (1993) points out that screening procedures prior to investigation are important, as "there is no value in studying obviously non-nativelike individuals intensively in order to declare them non-nativelike" (p. 204).

A problem with ultimate attainment studies in general has to do with a tendency among researchers to equate "language" with "grammatical competence." As was mentioned in the introductory section, the domain for maturational constraints should, in our view, be the human capacity for language both at the level of knowledge and at the level of processing. Therefore, the notion of "language" needs to be defined in terms of "language proficiency," *including* "grammatical competence" (as defined, for example, within the UG framework). Learners' L2 proficiencies should thus be evaluated on the basis not only of their grammatical competence, but also of their ability to utilize such competence, in oral or written production/comprehension, as well as in grammaticality judgment and other formal tasks. Furthermore, it is important to investigate the extent to which advanced L2 speakers can pass as nativelike speakers under a variety of conditions, such as in stressful versus relaxed situations of language production/comprehension.

With the exception of a few studies using test batteries, and thereby covering various aspects of the L2 (e.g., Ioup et al., 1994), most studies have drawn far-reaching conclusions about maturational constraints from learners' performance on a limited set of structures within, perhaps, one sub-component of one linguistic level of the L2, without evaluating the full range of learners' L2 proficiency. In order to avoid such unwarranted generalizations, and be able instead to arrive at a global understanding of this proficiency, researchers should either employ large sets of elicitation techniques for varied aspects of language proficiency, or explicitly relate the specific area investigated to empirical results in the field in general.

Furthermore, the tasks and tests should be highly demanding, in order to distinguish, where possible, between non-native and native subjects (that is, to avoid ceiling effects; cf. Johnson and Newport, 1989, p. 96). It is, therefore, important to include not only core features (such as UG principles or parameters) but also language-specific, peripheral features (such as metaphors, idiomatic expressions, and "unusual" structures), since these are usually predicted as being difficult, if not impossible, to master (Ekberg, 1998; Yorio, 1989). Long (1993) points out that different kinds of forced production, such as elicited imitation, are useful tools for probing low-frequency items that are easily avoided; since such items might never occur in free oral or written production, "it would be unwarranted to assume either (a) lack of knowledge on the basis of non-use, or (b) that error-free performance on what the learner did say or write can be interpreted as nativelike competence in all unobserved domains, as well" (p. 209). Moreover, non-nativelike L2 proficiency may also be manifest through very infrequent and subtle phonological deviance (cf. Julie and Laura in Ioup et al., 1994), through the slightly deviant or unusual (although not directly erroneous) use or representation of certain lexical items or grammatical structures (cf. Hyltenstam, 1992; Sorace, 1993), through deviance in frequency of certain words or grammatical constructions (Ekberg, 1998; Hene, 1993), through slightly slower speaking rate (cf. Guion, Flege, Liu, and Yeni-Komshian, 2000), or through small but significant comprehension and perception difficulties that do not occur in native speakers (Hyltenstam and Abrahamsson, forthcoming; McAllister, 2000). In other words, there may well be minor non-native features that are difficult to detect in everyday conversation or with crude testing techniques. Since these kinds of subtle non-native features are most likely present, and since our focus when researching adult learners' potentials should be on what they *cannot* do (Long, 1993, p. 208), refined analyses/measurements of learner behavior are necessary.

Finally, we see it as an important task for future research to systematically identify and describe the social/psychological characteristics that can be associated with the near-native adult learner. Exactly what psychological traits and social circumstances distinguish such learners from average early starters and other, less successful, late starters? Indeed, as we have mentioned above, several researchers have already begun to investigate such factors: Moyer (1999) singled out high motivation as the determining factor for the exceptional learner in her study of L2 pronunciation; Bongaerts (1999) suggested both high motivation and intensive instruction in pronunciation as crucial factors for reaching advanced levels of foreign language proficiency; Ioup et al. (1994) discussed the psychological profile of Julie, and pointed to both focus on form and a general talent for learning languages as important features; DeKeyser (2000) suggests that high verbal analytical abilities may be a prerequisite for reaching high levels of L2 proficiency in adulthood.

In conclusion, as has become evident from our review of empirical work, no single study meets all of the methodological requirements mentioned above. On the other hand, some studies have successfully met one or two of the requirements (see boxes 17.1–17.3). Ioup et al. (1994) included a relatively large test-battery, embracing various elicitation techniques for different subcomponents of language. White and Genesee (1996) employed rigorous initial screening of near-native and non-native speakers. DeKeyser (2000) attempted to describe a potentially important characteristic of the high-scoring adult learner, verbal aptitude, thereby providing an explanation for the relative success in some late learners. Jointly, these aspects of research design cover many of the requirements outlined above, and the three studies mentioned here illustrate how each of these methodological features can be incorporated in the design of future work.

7 A Final Remark

We started this chapter by stating that both adults, in rare cases, and children, in most cases, seem to reach nativelike proficiency in a second language. We have ended up with a qualified guess that "seem to" is a central part of that formulation. Thus, it may appear that we began with a quite optimistic remark but finished with a pessimistic one. Such an interpretation of our discussion is, however, unwarranted.

Given that maturation has the strong influence on second language outcomes that our review has indicated, it should come as no surprise that nativelike proficiency in a second language is unattainable. More surprising, we would like to claim, are the miraculous levels of proficiency that second language learners (at all ages) in fact *can* reach, despite the constraints that are imposed by our biological scheduling. That maturational effects, to a very

Box 17.1 Assessment of L2 proficiency: the design of a demanding and rigorous test-battery (Ioup et al., 1994)

Speech production:
Audiotaped spontaneous speech (detailed narration of favorite recipe).

Accent identification:
Recorded speech samples of various Arabic dialects, viz. Libyan, Syrian, Palestinian, Kuwaiti, and Sudanese, as well as whether an Egyptian accent was the Cairene variety or not.

Grammatical intuitions:

- *translation:* of constructions reflecting language-specific rules relating to relative clauses, yes-no questions, *wh*-questions, and conjoined NPs;
- *grammaticality judgment*: 37 Egyptian Arabic sentences either pertaining to constraints in UG or following from language-particular rules;
- *interpretation of anaphora*: conjoined sentences, backward pronominalization, and relative clauses, all in conditions of both adjacent and remote reference.

Box 17.2 Selection of subjects: identification and initial screening of near-native speakers (White and Genesee, 1996)

Identification of near-native L2 speakers:
Solicitation through notices posted at the university and in local newspapers; 89 advanced L2 speakers were identified; 19 native English controls were also included.

Initial selection of language samples for evaluation of nativelikeness:
Individual, face-to-face interviews (using selected pictures from the Thematic Apperception Test; Murray, 1971) recorded on tape.

Evaluation for nativelikeness prior to the actual testing:

- A randomly selected portion of the samples were evaluated independently by two native English-speaking judges. Judges were informed that the samples came from non-native and native speakers of English.
- Samples were evaluated for: pronunciation, morphology, syntax, choice of vocabulary, fluency, and overall impression of nativeness. Each of these aspects was independently evaluated on a "non-native"–"native" continuum.
- Only those L2 speakers who were rated within the range of native speakers qualified as near-natives (n = 45); those with ratings below that range were labelled non-natives (n = 44).

Box 17.3 Exceptional learners: identifying learner traits and learning conditions (DeKeyser, 2000)

Research aim: To test the *fundamental difference hypothesis* (Bley-Vroman, 1989).
Methodology: A grammaticality judgment test and a language learning aptitude test were administered to 57 Hungarian learners of English with AOs ranging between 1 and 40.

Results: The grammaticality judgment test results showed a strong, negative correlation with AO, with a small overlap between early (AO<16) and late starters (AO>16). Aptitude scores did not correlate with AOs. Correlations between grammaticality judgment scores and aptitude scores were: non-significant for the group as a whole; non-significant for the group of early starters; significant for the group of late starters. Those late starters (except for one) who scored within or close to the range of early starters all had above average aptitude scores.

Conclusion: Aptitude plays no role in ultimate attainment by child starters, but is a necessary condition for near-native proficiency in adult learners.

large extent, can be compensated for is indeed encouraging. The subtle differences that we have assumed to exist between near-native and native proficiency are probably highly insignificant in all aspects of the second language speaker's life and endeavors, although *very* significant for a theory of human capacity for language learning. The highly successful L2 speakers that we have characterized as having reached "only" near-native proficiency *are*, in fact, nativelike in all contexts except, perhaps, in the laboratory of the linguist with specific interest in second language learning mechanisms.

ACKNOWLEDGMENTS

We are indebted to the editors and an anonymous reviewer for valuable comments on an earlier draft of this chapter. We would also like to gratefully acknowledge Thomas Lavelle's indispensable work in removing most of the non-native features from our English.

NOTES

1 Although acknowledging the numerous complexities associated with the definition, assessment, and social implications of "nativelike proficiency" (and related notions, such as "nativeness" and "native speaker"; see, e.g., Cook, 1999; Davies, 1991), we have chosen to

disregard these complexities, in order to attain a reasonable level of generality in our discussion.

2 See Moody et al. (1996); Wallace et al. (1988).

3 For comprehensive and detailed overviews of rate studies, see, for example, Harley (1986, pp. 25–33); Long (1990, pp. 260–5); Singleton (1989, pp. 94–107).

4 See also Johnson and Newport (1991) and Johnson (1992).

5 The Hungarian Language Aptitude Test, Words in Sentences (Ottó, 1996), which is an adaptation of the Modern Language Aptitude Test, Words in Sentences (Carroll and Sapon, 1959).

6 It is, of course, possible to interpret this learner's high score as an effect of other beneficial factors.

7 EFL = English as a foreign language; FFL = French as a foreign language.

8 The aim of Moyer's study was to investigate the relationship between AO, motivation, instruction, and foreign accent. We will return to her study later in this chapter when we discuss alternative explanations to age-related differences in ultimate L2 outcomes, and the possible interaction between social/psychological factors (motivation, talent, etc.) and maturational constraints.

9 Ringbom (1993) notes that "we have all met or heard people, especially actors and singers, with a singular excellence in producing nativelike speech in fixed situations, even though their actual knowledge of the language may be minimal, even practically non-existent" (p. 7) (for individual adults' phonetic imitation abilities, see, e.g., the studies by Neufeld, 1977, 1978; cf. also Markham, 1997). Moreover, after a sufficient amount of rehearsal, it seems that the odds of sounding nativelike when *singing* in a (highly familiar) foreign language are much greater than when spontaneously *speaking* it. In fact, we would venture the claim that even Agnetha and Frida might, at times, have been mistaken for native singers of English, although, *surely*, no native English speaker would ever make such a judgment on the basis of an Abba interview.

10 Similarly, in an unpublished paper, Zhang (1992) reports on two native speakers of English with seemingly nativelike L2 proficiency in Chinese. Although they passed as native speakers for the majority of a group of native judges, a detailed linguistic analysis revealed subtle cases of divergence from native controls on various linguistic aspects. For example, although they did not violate syntactic rules in their use of pauses and fillers, both subjects exhibited a relatively high frequency of such elements sentence-internally, a feature that distinguished them from the native controls.

11 This screening procedure was very much in accordance with the criteria for subject selection originally proposed by Long (1993, pp. 204–13).

12 For details about these subjects' literacy skills, see Stroud (1989).

13 In addition to these tests, several other instruments were used in this study, including an oral interview, a self-assessment, the retelling of written and oral texts, a reading-aloud task, and a written composition; the results from these tasks will be reported elsewhere.

14 In addition, preliminary analyses of lexical and grammatical errors not discussed in Hyltenstam and Abrahamsson (forthcoming) show the same tendency.

15 Except for one outlier in Moyer (1999) who was rated as a native speaker.

16 An alternative terminology is *optimal period* for language acquisition (Patkowski, 1980). Patkowski uses this term interchangeably with *critical* and *sensitive period*. However, Bialystok (1997, p. 116f) suggests that these terms should not be used as synonyms. As she points out, the use of the terms *critical* and *sensitive periods* entails assumptions about the paradigm from which they are taken, that is, biologically defined bases for second language acquisition outcomes, while an optimal period of acquisition could be used without making claims about a biological cause. She believes that it is reasonable to talk about an optimal time for language acquisition as "such factors as social, experiential or educational aspects of second language learning . . . tend to favor younger learners" (p. 117).

17 For further criticism of non-maturational explanations for age-related differences, see Long (1990, pp. 275–6).

18 That is, characteristics belonging to what is usually referred to as the "Geschwind cluster" (see, e.g., Obler, 1989).

19 Julie's mother reported her to have been precocious in L1 acquisition, and that "she spoke in full sentences at 18 months" (Ioup et al., 1994, p. 93).

20 See Harley and Wang (1997, pp. 40ff) for a more detailed discussion of cognitive explanations.

21 See Bialystok and Miller (1999) and Butler (2000) for similarly linear relations between starting age and ultimate attainment.

22 However, such a linear pattern over the life span does not necessarily need to be interpreted in non-biological terms, as will be evident from the following sections in this chapter.

REFERENCES

Asher, J. and García, G. 1969: The optimal age to learn a foreign language. *Modern Language Journal*, 38, 334–41.

Asher, J. and Price, B. 1967: The learning strategy of total physical response: some age differences. *Child Development*, 38, 1219–27.

Beck, M.-L. 1997: Regular verbs, past tense and frequency: tracking down a potential source of NS/NNS speaker competence differences. *Second Language Research*, 13, 95–115.

Bialystok, E. 1997: The structure of age: in search of barriers to second language acquisition. *Second Language Research*, 13, 116–37.

Bialystok, E. and Hakuta, K. 1994: *In Other Words: The Science and Psychology of Second-Language Acquisition*. New York: Basic Books.

Bialystok, E. and Hakuta, K. 1999: Confounded age: linguistic and cognitive factors in age differences for second language acquisition. In D. Birdsong (ed.), *Second Language Acquisition and the Critical Period Hypothesis*. Mahwah, NJ: Lawrence Erlbaum Associates, 161–81.

Bialystok, E. and Miller, B. 1999: The problem of age in second-language acquisition: influences from language, structure, and task. *Bilingualism: Language and Cognition*, 2, 127–45.

Birdsong, D. 1992: Ultimate attainment in second language acquisition. *Language*, 68, 706–55.

Birdsong, D. (ed.) 1999a: *Second Language Acquisition and the Critical Period Hypothesis*. Mahwah, NJ: Lawrence Erlbaum Associates.

Birdsong, D. 1999b: Introduction: whys and why nots of the critical period hypothesis for second language acquisition. In D. Birdsong (ed.), *Second Language Acquisition and the Critical Period Hypothesis*. Mahwah, NJ: Lawrence Erlbaum Associates, 1–22.

Bley-Vroman, R. 1989: What is the logical problem of foreign language learning? In S. Gass and J. Schachter (eds), *Linguistic Perspectives on Second Language Acquisition*. Cambridge: Cambridge University Press, 41–68.

Bongaerts, T. 1999: Ultimate attainment in L2 pronunciation: the case of very advanced late L2 learners. In D. Birdsong (ed.), *Second Language Acquisition and the Critical Period Hypothesis*. Mahwah, NJ: Lawrence Erlbaum Associates, 133–59.

Bongaerts, T., Mennen, S., and van der Slik, S. 2000: Authenticity of pronunciation in naturalistic second language acquisition: the case of very advanced late learners of Dutch as a Second Language. *Studia Linguistica*, 54, 298–308.

Bongaerts, T., Planken, B., and Schils, E. 1995: Can late learners attain a native accent in a foreign language? A test of the critical period hypothesis. In D. Singleton and Z. Lengyel (eds), *The Age Factor in Second Language Acquisition*. Clevedon: Multilingual Matters, 30–50.

Bongaerts, T., van Summeren, C., Planken, B., and Schils, E. 1997: Age and ultimate attainment in the pronunciation of a foreign language. *Studies in Second Language Acquisition*, 19, 447–65.

Braitenberg, 1978: Cortical architectonics: General and areal. In M. A. B. Vrazier and H. Petsche (eds), *Architectonics of the Cerebral Cortex*. New York: Raven Press, 443–65.

Butler, Y. G. 2000: The age effect in second language acquisition: Is it too late to acquire native-level competence in a second language after the age of seven?. In Y. Oshima-Takane, Y. Shirai, and H. Sirai (eds), *Studies in Language Sciences 1*. Tokyo: Japanese Society for Language Sciences, 159–69.

Carroll, J. B. and Sapon, S. 1959: *Modern Language Aptitude Test. Form A*. New York: Psychological Corporation.

Cochrane, R. 1980: The acquisition of /r/ and /l/ by Japanese children and adults learning English as a second language. *Journal of Multilingual and Multicultural Development*, 1, 331–60.

Cochrane, R. and Sachs, J. 1979: Phonological learning by children and adults in a laboratory setting. *Language and Speech*, 22, 145–9.

Cook, V. 1999: Going beyond the native speaker in language teaching. *TESOL Quarterly*, 33, 185–209.

Coppieters, R. 1987: Competence differences between natives and near-native speakers. *Language*, 63, 544–73.

Curtiss, S. 1977: *Genie: A Psycholinguistic Study of a Modern-day "Wild Child"*. New York: Academic Press.

Curtiss, S. 1988: Abnormal language acquisition and the modularity of language. In F. J. Newmeyer (ed.), *Linguistics: The Cambridge Survey. Vol. II*. Cambridge: Cambridge University Press, 99–116.

Curtiss, S. 1989: The case of Chelsea: a new test case of the critical period for language acquisition. Ms. University of California, Los Angeles.

Davies, A. 1991: *The Native Speaker in Applied Linguistics*. Edinburgh: Edinburgh University Press.

Davis, K. 1947: Final note on a case of extreme social isolation. *American Journal of Sociology*, 52, 432–7.

DeKeyser, R. M. 2000: The robustness of critical period effects in second language acquisition. *Studies in Second Language Acquisition*, 22 (4), 493–533.

Ekberg, L. 1998: Regeltillämpning kontra lexikonkunskap i svenskan hos invandrarbarn i Malmö. In J. Møller, P. Quist, A. Holmen, and J. N. Jørgensen (eds), *Nordiske sprog som andetsprog*. København: Institut for humanistiske fag, Danmarks Lærerhøjskole, 99–116.

Ellis, R. 1994: *The Study of Second Language Acquisition*. Oxford: Oxford University Press.

Eubank, L. and Gregg, K. R. 1999: Critical periods and (second) language acquisition: divide et impera. In D. Birdsong (ed.), *Second Language Acquisition and the Critical Period Hypothesis*. Mahwah, NJ: Lawrence Erlbaum Associates, 65–99.

Felix, S. 1985: More evidence on competing cognitive systems. *Second Language Research*, 1, 47–72.

Flege, J. E. 1999: Age of learning and second language speech. In D. Birdsong (ed.), *Second Language Acquisition and the Critical Period Hypothesis*. Mahwah, NJ: Lawrence Erlbaum Associates, 101–31.

Gleitman, L. and Newport, E. 1995: The invention of language by children: environmental and biological influences on the acquisition of language. In L. Gleitman and M. Liberman (eds), *Language: An Invitation to Cognitive Science. Vol. 1*. Second Edition. Cambridge, MA: MIT Press, 1–24.

Guion, S. G., Flege, J. E., Liu, S. H., and Yeni-Komshian, G. H. 2000: Age of learning effects on the duration of sentences produced in a second language. *Applied Psycholinguistics*, 21, 205–28.

Harley, B. 1986: *Age in Second Language Acquisition*. Clevedon: Multilingual Matters.

Harley, B. and Hart, D. 1997: Language aptitude and second language proficiency in classroom learners of different starting ages. *Studies in Second Language Acquisition*, 19, 379–400.

Harley, B. and Wang, W. 1997: The critical period hypothesis: where are we now? In A. M. B. De Groot and J. F. Kroll (eds), *Tutorials in Bilingualism: Psycholinguistic Perspectives*. London: Lawrence Erlbaum Associates.

Hene, B. 1993: *Utlandsadopterade barns och svenska barns ordförståelse: en jämförelse mellan barn i åldern 10–12 år*. Göteborg: Göteborgs universitet.

Humes-Bartlo, M. 1989: Variation in children's ability to learn second languages. In K. Hyltenstam and L. K. Obler (eds), *Bilingualism Across the Lifespan. Aspects of Acquisition, Maturity, and Loss*. Cambridge: Cambridge University Press, 41–54.

Hyltenstam, K. 1988: Lexical characteristics of near-native second-language learners of Swedish. *Journal of Multilingual and Multicultural Development*, 9, 67–84.

Hyltenstam, K. 1992: Non-native features of near-native speakers: on the ultimate attainment of childhood L2 learners. In R. J. Harris (ed.), *Cognitive Processing in Bilinguals*. Amsterdam: Elsevier Science, 351–68.

Hyltenstam, K. and Abrahamsson, N. 2001: Age and L2 learning: the hazards of matching practical "implications" with theoretical "facts." (Comments on Stefka H. Marinova-Todd, D. Bradford Marshall, and Catherine E. Snow's "Three misconceptions about age and L2 learning"). *TESOL Quarterly*, 35, 151–70.

Hyltenstam, K. and Abrahamsson, N. forthcoming: Age of onset and ultimate attainment in near-native speakers of Swedish. In K. Fraurud and K. Hyltenstam (eds), *Multilingualism in Global and Local Perspectives: Papers from the 8th Nordic Conference on*

Bilingualism, November 1–3, 2001, Stockholm-Rinkeby. Stockholm: Rinkeby Institute of Multilingual Research.

Ioup, G. 1989: Immigrant children who have failed to acquire native English. In S. Gass, C. Madden, D. Preston, and L. Selinker (eds), *Variation in Second Language Acquisition. Vol. 2: Psycholinguistic Issues*. Clevedon: Multilingual Matters, 160–75.

Ioup, G. 1995: Evaluating the need for input enhancement in post-critical period language acquisition. In D. Singleton and Z. Lengyel (eds), *The Age Factor in Second Language Acquisition*. Clevedon: Multilingual Matters, 95–123.

Ioup, G., Boustagui, E., El Tigi, M., and Moselle, M. 1994: Reexamining the critical period hypothesis: a case study in a naturalistic environment. *Studies in Second Language Acquisition*, 16, 73–98.

Johnson, J. S. 1992: Critical period effects in second language acquisition: the effects of written versus auditory materials on the assessment of grammatical competence. *Language Learning*, 42, 217–48.

Johnson, J. S. and Newport, E. L. 1989: Critical period effects in second language learning: the influence of maturational state on the acquisition of English as a second language. *Cognitive Psychology*, 21, 60–99.

Johnson, J. S. and Newport, E. L. 1991: Critical period effects on universal properties of language: the status of subjacency in the acquisition of second languages. *Cognition*, 30, 215–58.

Juffs, A. and Harrington, M. 1995: Parsing effects in second language sentence processing: subject and object asymmetries in *wh*-extraction. *Studies in Second Language Acquisition*, 17, 483–516.

Kellerman, E. 1995: Age before beauty: Johnson and Newport revisited. In L. Eubank, L. Selinker, and M. Sharwood Smith (eds), *The Current State of Interlanguage*. Amsterdam: John Benjamins, 219–31.

Krashen, S. 1973: Lateralization, language learning, and the critical period: some new evidence. *Language Learning*, 23, 63–74.

Krashen, S., Long, M., and Scarcella, R. 1979: Age, rate, and eventual attainment in second language acquisition. *TESOL Quarterly*, 13, 573–582.

Lee, D. 1992: Universal Grammar, learnability, and the acquisition of English reflexive binding by L1 Korean speakers. Ph.D. dissertation. University of Southern California, Los Angeles.

Lenneberg, E. 1967: *Biological Foundations of Language*. New York: John Wiley.

Long, M. H. 1990: Maturational constraints on language development. *Studies in Second Language Acquisition*, 12, 251–85.

Long, M. H. 1993: Second language acquisition as a function of age: research findings and methodological issues. In K. Hyltenstam and Å. Viberg (eds), *Progression and Regression in Language*. Cambridge: Cambridge University Press, 196–221.

Loewenthal, K. and Bull, D. 1984: Imitation of foreign sounds: what is the effect of age? *Language and Speech*, 27, 95–7.

Marinova-Todd, S. H., Marshall, D. B., and Snow, C. E. 2000: Three misconceptions about age and L2 learning. *TESOL Quarterly*, 34, 9–34.

Markham, D. 1997: *Phonetic Imitation, Accent, and the Learner*. Lund: Lund University Press.

Mayberry, R. I. 1993: First-language acquisition after childhood differs from second-language acquisition: the case of American Sign Language. *Journal of Speech and Hearing Research*, 36, 1258–70.

McAllister, R. 2000: Perceptual foreign accent and its relevance for simultaneous interpreting. In B. Englund Dimitrova and K. Hyltenstam (eds), *Language Processing and Simultaneous Interpreting.* Amsterdam: John Benjamins, 45–63.

McDonald, J. L. 2000: Grammaticality judgments in a second language: Influences of age of acquisition and native language. *Applied Psycholinguistics*, 21, 395–423.

Moody, M., Schwartz, R. G., Gravel, J. S., Wallace, I. F., Ellis, M. A., and Lee, W. W. 1996: Speech perception and verbal memory in children with otitis media. In M. L. Casselbrant, D. Lim, and C. D. Bluestone (eds), *Recent Advances in Otitis Media: Proceedings of the 6th International Symposium.* Toronto: B. C. Decker, 339–42.

Morford, J. P. and Mayberry, R. I. 2000: A reexamination of "early exposure" and its implications for language acquisition by eye. In C. Chamberlain, J. P. Morford, and R. I. Mayberry (eds), *Language Acquisition by Eye.* Mahwah, NJ: Lawrence Erlbaum Associates, 111–27.

Moyer, A. 1999: Ultimate attainment in L2 phonology: the critical factors of age, motivation, and instruction. *Studies in Second Language Acquisition*, 21, 81–108.

Murray, H. A. 1971: *Thematic Apperception Test*. Cambridge, MA: Harvard University Press.

Neufeld, G. 1977: Language learning ability in adults: A study on the acquisition of prosodic and articulatory features. *Working Papers on Bilingualism, University of Ontario*, 12, 45–60.

Neufeld, G. 1978: On the acquisition of prosodic and articulatory features in adult language learning. *Canadian Modern Language Review*, 34, 163–94.

Newport, E. L. 1990: Maturational constraints on language learning. *Cognitive Science*, 14, 11–28.

Novoa, L., Fein, D., and Obler, L. K. 1988: Talent in foreign languages: a case study. In L. K. Obler and D. Fein (eds), *The Exceptional Brain: Neuropsychology of Talent and Special Abilities.* New York: Guilford Press, 294–302.

Obler, L. K. 1989: Exceptional second language learners. In S. Gass, C. Madden, D. Preston, and L. Selinker (eds), *Variation in Second Language Acquisition. Vol. II: Psycholinguistic Issues.* Clevedon: Multilingual Matters, 141–59.

Obler, L. K. and Hannigan, S. 1996: Neurolinguistics of second language acquisition and use. In W. C. Ritchie and T. K. Bhatia (eds), *Handbook of Second Language Acquisition.* San Diego: Academic Press, 509–23.

Olson, L. and Samuels, S. J. 1973: The relationship between age and accuracy of foreign language pronunciation. *Journal of Educational Research*, 66, 263–7.

Ottó, I. 1996: *Hungarian Language Aptitude Test. Words in Sentences*. Budapest: Department of English Applied Linguistics, Eötvös Loránd University.

Oyama, S. 1976: A sensitive period for the acquisition of a nonnative phonological system. *Psycholinguistic Research*, 5, 261–85.

Oyama, S. 1978: The sensitive period and comprehension of speech. *Working Papers on Bilingualism*, 16, 1–17.

Patkowski, M. S. 1980: The sensitive period for the acquisition of syntax in a second language. *Language Learning*, 30, 449–72.

Patkowski, M. S. 1990: Age and accent in a second language: a reply to James Emil Flege. *Applied Linguistics*, 11, 73–89.

Penfield, W. and Roberts, L. 1959: *Speech and Brain Mechanisms.* New York: Athenaeum.

Pulvermüller, F. and Schumann, J. H. 1994: Neurobiological mechanisms of language acquisition. *Language Learning*, 44, 681–734.

Ringbom, H. 1993: Introduction: on near-native proficiency. In H. Ringbom (ed.), *Near-Native Proficiency in English*. Åbo: Åbo Akademi University, 5–8.

Ruben, R. J. 1997: A time frame of critical/sensitive periods of language development. *Acta Otolaryngologica*, 117, 202–5.

Schachter, J. 1996: Maturation and the issue of universal grammar in second language acquisition. In W. C. Ritchie and T. K. Bhatia (eds), *Handbook of Second Language Acquisition*. San Diego: Academic Press, 159–93.

Schlyter, S. 1993: The weaker language in bilingual Swedish–French children. In K. Hyltenstam and Å. Viberg (eds), *Progression and Regression in Language*. Cambridge: Cambridge University Press, 289–308.

Schneiderman, E. I. and Desmarais, C. 1988: A neuropsychological substrate for talent in second-language acquisition. In L. K. Obler and D. Fein (eds), *The Exceptional Brain: Neuropsychology of Talent and Special Abilities*. New York: Guilford Press, 103–26.

Schumann, J. H. 1995: Ad minorem theorae gloriam: a response to Eubank and Gregg. *Studies in Second Language Acquisition*, 17, 59–63.

Scovel, T. 1988: *A Time to Speak: A Psycholinguistic Inquiry into the Critical Period for Human Speech*. New York: Newbury House.

Scovel, T. 2000: A critical review of the critical period research. *Annual Review of Applied Linguistics*, 20, 213–23.

Seliger, H. W. 1978: Implications of a multiple critical periods hypothesis for second language learning. In W. Ritchie (ed.), *Second Language Acquisition Research*. New York: Academic Press, 11–19.

Singleton, D. 1989: *Language Acquisition. The Age Factor*. Clevedon: Multilingual Matters.

Singleton, D. 2001: Age and second language acquisition. *Annual Review of Applied Linguistics*, 21, 77–89.

Slavoff, G. R. and Johnson, J. S. 1995: The effects of age on the rate of learning a second language. *Studies in Second Language Acquisition*, 17, 1–16.

Snow, C. and Hoefnagel-Höhle, M. 1977: Age differences in the pronunciation of foreign sounds. *Language and Speech*, 20, 357–65.

Snow, C. and Hoefnagel-Höhle, M. 1978: The critical period for language acquisition: evidence from second language learning. *Child Development*, 49, 1114–28.

Sorace, A. 1993: Incomplete vs. divergent representations of unaccusativity in non-native grammars of Italian. *Second Language Research*, 9, 22–47.

Stroud, C. 1989: Literacy in a second language: a study of text-construction in near-native speakers of Swedish. In A. Holmen (ed.), *Bilingualism and the Individual*. London: Multilingual Matters, 235–51.

Tahta, S., Wood, M., and Loewenthal, K. 1981a: Age changes in the ability to replicate foreign pronunciation and intonation. *Language and Speech*, 24, 363–72.

Tahta, S., Wood, M., and Loewenthal, K. 1981b: Foreign accents: factors relating to transfer of accent from the first language to a second language. *Language and Speech*, 24, 265–72.

Wallace, I. F., Gravel, J. S., McCarton, C., Stapells, D. R., Bernstein, R. S., and Ruben, R. J. 1988: Otitis media and language development at 1 year of age. *Journal of Speech and Hearing Disorders*, 53, 245–51.

Weber-Fox, C. M. and Neville, H. J. 1999: Functional neural subsystems are differentially affected by delays in second language immersion: ERP and behavioral evidence in bilinguals. In D. Birdsong (ed.), *Second Language Acquisition and the Critical Period Hypothesis*. Mahwah, NJ: Lawrence Erlbaum Associates, 23–38.

White, L. and Genesee, F. 1996: How native is near-native? The issue of ultimate attainment in adult second language acquisition. *Second Language Research*, 12, 233–65.

Wolfe-Quintero, K. 1996: Nativism does not equal Universal Grammar. *Second Language Research*, 12, 335–73.

Wong Fillmore, L. 1991: When learning a second language means losing the first. *Early Childhood Research Quarterly*, 6, 323–46.

Yamada, J., Takatsuka, S., Kotake, N., and Kurusu, J. 1980: On the optimum age for teaching foreign vocabulary to children. *International Review of Applied Linguistics in Language Teaching*, 18, 245–7.

Yeni-Komshian, G. H., Flege, J. E., and Liu, S. 2000: Pronunciation proficiency in the first and second languages of Korean–English bilinguals. *Bilingualism: Language and Cognition*, 3, 131–49.

Yorio, C. A. 1989: Idiomaticity as an indicator of second language proficiency. In K. Hyltenstam and L. K. Obler (eds), *Bilingualism Across the Lifespan. Aspects of Acquisition, Maturity, and Loss.* Cambridge: Cambridge University Press, 55–72.

Zhang, Y. 1992: The ultimate attainment of Chinese as a second language: a case study. Term paper. Department of English as a Second Language, University of Hawai'i at Manoa.

18 Individual Differences in Second Language Learning

ZOLTÁN DÖRNYEI AND
PETER SKEHAN

1 Introduction

An appropriate starting point for a discussion of individual differences in second language learning is what might be termed "the correlational challenge." This is that individual differences in second language learning, principally foreign language aptitude and motivation, have generated the most consistent predictors of second language learning success. Correlations of aptitude or motivation with language achievement range (mostly) between 0.20 and 0.60, with a median value a little above 0.40. Since aptitude and motivation do not show particularly high correlations with one another, they combine to yield multiple correlations which are frequently above 0.50.

Aside from age of onset, no other potential predictors of second language learning success consistently achieve such levels. Yet it is fair to say that learner differences, such as aptitude, style, and strategies, as a sub-area of second language acquisition, and applied linguistics more generally, have not been integrated into other areas of investigation, and have not excited much theoretical or practical interest in recent years. Other sub-areas, principally those associated with universal processes, have generated a much higher level of empirical research, for example, route of second language development, or features of input or interaction hypothesized to promote second language development. Other SLA areas have also been more central to theoretical developments, for example, processability theory. And finally, more universal areas have enjoyed clearer perceptions of practical, classroom-oriented relevance, for instance, task-based instruction.

This is a curious state of affairs. It is difficult, after all, to ignore such impressive correlations. We are left to conclude that the study of most areas of individual differences in language learning is simply not fashionable, and has been avoided because other areas have appeared to have greater promise. It will be the aim of this chapter to try to redress this imbalance. We will survey work in several areas of individual differences, and will conclude that there are now signs that the study of areas such as aptitude and motivation is ready for reintegration into mainstream SLA, as well as being closer to generating active intervention in the language classroom. For reasons of space and duplication, some individual differences will not be covered in this chapter. The age factor is addressed by Hyltenstam and Abrahamsson (this volume). The broad sub-domain of personality is not explored here, partly because it is so extensive, and also because progress in this area has been slow, in terms of both methodology and systematic patterns of results. A recent review of the area can be found in Dewaele and Furnham (1999).

The chapter is organized into four main parts. We review research and theorizing in the areas of foreign language aptitude (sections 2–5), learning style (section 6), learner strategies (section 7), and motivation (section 8), in turn. It will be seen that research into aptitude has languished somewhat, but is now gathering pace again. A significant influence upon this is that aptitude researchers are now exploring relevant constructs against the sort of progress in SLA reported in other chapters in this volume. Learning style and cognitive style are still elusive concepts, and, not for the first time, are assessed as containing more promise than attested relevance. Learner strategies research, which was extremely active a few years ago, seems to be losing vitality somewhat. Finally, the study of language learning motivation, which has generated by far the most research in this area, will be seen to have changed character in significant ways in the last 10 years. A concluding section offers generalizations which indicate links between the various areas of individual difference research.

2 Foreign Language Aptitude

2.1 *Preliminaries*

The central claim in foreign language aptitude research is very simple. It is that there is a specific talent for learning foreign languages which exhibits considerable variation between learners. Expressed in these terms, it would be unremarkable in nature, and comparable to the myriad other domains where there is variation between human beings. The complexities with aptitude derive from a number of related questions:

i Is such a talent innate?
ii Is it relatively fixed?
iii If it is not fixed, is it amenable to training?
iv Is foreign language aptitude a distinct ability, or does it relate to more general abilities, such as intelligence, effectively functioning as a subset of a more general view of human variation?

v Could such a talent be used as the basis for prediction of language learning success? If so, how effective might it be for such prediction, and how would predictions based on it compare with predictions made from other sources?
vi Could such a talent be used as the basis for adaptation of instruction?
vii Does such a talent always apply in a similar manner, without influence of:
  a learning context (e.g., FL vs. SL);
  b learning methodology;
  c L1 to L2 combination?
viii Is such a talent undifferentiated, or does it have sub-components?
ix What is the theoretical basis for any such talent or sub-talents?

Finally, and in a sense, more importantly, and most mundanely:

x Can such a talent be measured effectively?

This section will address these questions, providing answers to some, and at least surveying what is known about the others. It will be seen that the concept of aptitude, long regarded as out of date, has much to offer, but needs new conceptualizations to link it to insights and findings from SLA research. It also merits an active research program.

2.2 *Carroll's initial work*

It is appropriate to start the discussion of aptitude with a review of the work of the American psychologist J. B. Carroll. Rarely has a sub-area been so dominated by one person. Carroll researched foreign language aptitude (as well as an enormous range of other phenomena) and established the parameters within which the sub-field still operates. It is instructive to explore his ideas about aptitude, as well as his methods of inquiry.

Carroll conducted the relevant research during the 1950s. Together with co-researcher Stanley Sapon, he devised a practical (and commercially available) aptitude test battery (Carroll and Sapon, 1959). In the fullest account of the way this was done, Carroll (1965) reported how he and Sapon started by devising a large number of potential predictor tests of foreign language learning. They then administered these potential tests (over 40 of them) to learners, and gathered data on the achievement scores of the learners at the end of the course of instruction. Armed with those data, Carroll and Sapon then examined:

i which potential aptitude sub-tests correlated with one another highly;
ii which sub-tests actually correlated highly with end-of-course performance on achievement tests.

As a result of this work, those sub-tests which did not correlate with end-of-course performance were eliminated, along with those which correlated with

Table 18.1 Carroll's four-component model of aptitude

Component name	*Nature and function*
Phonemic coding ability	Capacity to code unfamiliar sound so that it can be retained over more than a few seconds and subsequently retrieved or recognized
Grammatical sensitivity	Capacity to identify the grammatical functions that words fulfill in sentences
Inductive language learning ability	Capacity to extract syntactic and morphological patterns from a given corpus of language material and to extrapolate from such patterns to create new sentences
Associative memory	Capacity to form associative bonds in memory between L1 and L2 vocabulary items

one another, whatever their correlations with achievement, since they were clearly duplicating one another. In other words, only the best of such "clusters" were retained. In this way, a small group of sub-tests was selected, each of which made sufficiently separate contributions to the prediction of end-of-course performance.

This entirely pragmatic aim of predicting language learning success went hand in hand with a parallel, and much more interesting and enduring, aim of understanding the components of foreign language aptitude. On the basis of an analysis of skills required in the groups of tests which survived the "statistical winnowing" in the research project, Carroll (1965) proposed the components shown in table 18.1.

Clearly, these four components have an intriguing relationship to one another, a relationship which has been clarified in a series of papers by Carroll (1973, 1979, 1981, 1991). Phonemic coding ability represents an interesting perspective on the auditory component of foreign language learning. Earlier approaches had focused on simple sound-discrimination tasks, based, essentially on minimal pairs. Carroll, in contrast, realized that perceiving sound discriminations was not enough. It was more relevant to focus on *stretches* of sound, and then on the coding (analysis) procedures which operated upon this sound, that is, the processes which made encoding and retrieval of material more likely. Thus, there was a memory link-up, even to the auditory component of aptitude. The second and third components are both concerned with the processing of language material. Grammatical sensitivity focuses on the capacity to analyze language material, and consequently has a rather passive quality. Inductive language learning is more active, in that it requires learners to go beyond the information given and to generalize, so that new language can be produced. Finally, associative memory concerns the linkages that are formed in memory. Clearly, this component was strongly influenced by associationist accounts of memory prevailing in psychology when Carroll's research program was operating. The emphasis is simply on memory as bonds. As we shall see, this is a limited conception.

Surprisingly, in reading Carroll's work, one has the impression that the separation into components was a tactical affair, accomplished because the identification of related but distinct components had the most effective outcome in terms of prediction equations derived from regression analyses. The actual test battery which resulted from the research (Carroll and Sapon, 1959) consisted of five sub-tests, *but those sub-tests were mainly hybrid mixtures of the different underlying components*. In other words, understanding and construct validity were sacrificed in favor of predictive validity. This decision has occurred at other times with aptitude research (Petersen and Al-Haik, 1976), and while it has enabled more predictive tests to result, it has had a disastrous impact upon the place of aptitude within applied linguistics over the years. It has led to the lack of appreciation of the explanatory contribution that foreign language aptitude can make to the field of SLA.

2.3 *Post-Carroll research*

Since Carroll's influential work, the story of aptitude has not changed very much. In fact, it is only in very recent years that interesting and challenging reconceptualizations of aptitude have emerged. We will return to these below. First, however, it is worth briefly surveying how the fields of applied linguistics and of language teaching have positioned themselves with respect to aptitude, and what research has actually been completed within the framework established by Carroll.

Two major influences have caused the study of aptitude to become a marginal activity over the last 30–40 years. First, aptitude has been poorly regarded within language teaching. One reason for this has been that aptitude is perceived as anti-egalitarian, in that if a fixed, immutable interpretation of aptitude is taken, it is seen as potentially disadvantaging many learners, with no hope offered of overcoming the handicap of low aptitude. It may not be a logical reaction, but many researchers have turned away from the study of aptitude as a result of drawing essentially this conclusion. Another negative response within the language teaching profession derives from the place of learner differences more generally. Even though virtually all teachers would quickly agree that learners differ from one another (with the acceptable face of these differences often being referred to as "mixed ability teaching"), the bulk of language teaching materials have assumed that all learners are the same. Certainly a major feature of the language teaching profession over the last 20 years or so has been the rise and rise of the main coursebook series. These series, now produced with immense care and resourcing, necessarily assume that all learners are essentially the same (thereby maximizing sales potential), and so downplay how the individual learner may be catered for. As a result, there has been something of a mismatch between the actual learner variation in real classrooms, and the homogeneity implied by most coursebooks (a mismatch which it has been the teacher's lot to cope with, as best she or he can).

The second marginalizing influence concerns the putative link between aptitude and learning context. Many within the language teaching profession have associated foreign language aptitude with the methodologies that prevailed at the time of Carroll's research, methodologies which do not, any longer, survive scrutiny from SLA researchers. Krashen (1981), in particular, linked foreign language aptitude to *learning*, and to the sorts of activities which are teacher-led and occur exclusively in classrooms, that is, explicit rule-focus, non-communicative practice activities, and awareness of language items on the learner's part. Krashen proposed that aptitude was not relevant for *acquisition* and the subconscious induction and internalization of language rules that he advocated. For many years, this seemed the kiss of death for aptitude, since it associated the aptitude construct very strongly with the sorts of activities that were anathema to communicative classrooms. (In passing, it is worth noting that the claim was made without any evidence: simply guilt by association.) We return to this issue below.

Despite discouraging attitudes such as these, there has been a steady flow of aptitude research, albeit firmly within the framework established by Carroll. It is useful to review the studies which have appeared briefly. First, it is important to mention that there has been large-scale work aimed at the production of aptitude test batteries other than the MLAT produced by Carroll and Sapon. Working during the 1960s, Pimsleur produced the only alternative, commercially available battery, the PLAB (Pimsleur, 1966), targeted at high school students. This set of sub-tests is broadly similar to Carroll's MLAT, but places greater emphasis on auditory factors, and less on memory. It is also noteworthy that Pimsleur's interest in aptitude was connected with his belief that many language students in US high schools underachieve because of auditory difficulties. This accounts for the auditory emphasis built into the PLAB, and connects with Pimsleur's proposals that use of the PLAB could enable early diagnosis of remediable learning difficulties in high-school foreign language programs.[1] Such early diagnosis could then trigger remedial work, so that the purpose of the aptitude testing would be to facilitate instructional adaptation.[2]

Other attempts to produce complete aptitude batteries have had a more restricted quality. The Defense Language Aptitude Battery (Petersen and Al-Haik, 1976) was produced for the US military because it was felt that the MLAT did not discriminate sufficiently well at the higher end of the language aptitude range. The DLAB was intended to be more searching for high-aptitude learners. It emphasized Carroll's inductive language learning ability, and also phonemic coding ability and memory. Sub-tests, though, were not "pure" measures of particular aptitude sub-components, but rather effective predictive amalgams: pragmatically effective for the contexts in which they were used, but unenlightening otherwise. The battery did not really produce more effective predictions than the MLAT, and the "closed" nature of the research (i.e., restricted to military applications) has meant that the battery has not proved to be particularly influential. The same is true for subsequent developments with aptitude batteries produced in association with military contexts, such as VORD (Parry and Child, 1990). It will be interesting to see what happens with the latest of these ventures, the production of the CANAL-F battery (Grigorenko, 2002; Grigorenko, Sternberg, and Ehrman, 2000; Sternberg, forthcoming), a battery grounded in Sternberg's theory of human intelligence, which focuses on recall and inferencing with linguistic material under immediate and delayed conditions.

Most researchers have tended not to explore how new aptitude batteries can be produced, but instead to focus on particular aspects of the aptitude construct, or on particular contexts in which aptitude might operate. Regarding contexts, Reves (1983) demonstrated that aptitude functions as an effective predictor in second (acquisition-rich, with exposure to naturalistic language use) as well as foreign (acquisition-poor, with exposure only or mainly to classroom language) contexts. Reves administered aptitude tests to a group of Arabic L1 learners of Hebrew (SL context) and English (FL context). The aptitude tests generated the best prediction of language learning success in *both* contexts, and there was little difference in levels of prediction for each of the languages. This contrasts with Krashen's (1981) claims that aptitude is only relevant for instructed (learning-oriented) contexts. Reves's findings are consistent with Skehan's (1989) proposal that aptitude should be equally relevant in second language contexts precisely because learners have to confront situations in which there is not the pedagogic selection of materials which attempts to structure the sequences in which learning takes place. Naturalistic second language contexts do not offer the learner any protection, by way of sequencing or selection, with the result that the problem of extracting structure from data is more, rather than less, difficult, and learner differences may have more of an impact upon development. DeKeyser (2000), whose work is discussed more extensively below, has also reported that aptitude scores are an important predictor of achievement in acquisition-rich contexts.

Wesche (1981) studied how instruction can be adapted to take account of aptitude differences. Working in the context of a Canadian government language training program for civil servants, she categorized learners as analytic- or memory-oriented on the basis of the profiles of aptitude sub-test scores. She then explored the consequences of such learners being matched or mismatched with teaching methodologies, one of which was analytic in nature, and the other of which was audiolingual, and so regarded as memory-oriented. She reports that analytic learners matched with an analytic methodology did better than such learners matched with the audiolingual methodology, and also that they evidenced greater satisfaction with these conditions. Memory-oriented learners also did better with a memory-oriented methodology. These results, showing an interaction between learner characteristics and instructional conditions, are important, since they bring out the potential of aptitude information to go beyond global scores and to provide potentially vital diagnostic information. Skehan (1986) also reported results suggesting that the same two learner types, analytic and memory-oriented, emerge from learner score profiles on aptitude test batteries, and that either sort of learner can be successful.

Other researchers have explored the relationship between foreign language aptitude and other variables, such as age and intelligence. Harley and Hart (1997) have shown that the predictive qualities of different aptitude components change with age. They researched grade 7 and grade 11 immersion children, and investigated which components of aptitude were most significantly implicated at these different ages. With younger children, the stronger correlations were with the memory components of aptitude. In contrast, with older learners, it was the language analysis sub-tests which had the higher correlations. Sasaki (1996) also took a more differentiated view of aptitude, and examined the relationship between foreign language aptitude and intelligence. At a first-order level of factor analysis (i.e., an analysis based on the matrix of correlations between the different measures), she showed that aptitude and intelligence were distinct. A second-order analysis (i.e., an analysis based on the factor loadings of the first-order analysis), however, did show connections between the two constructs. Interestingly, Sasaki demonstrated that this second-order relationship was strongest for what Skehan (1998) has termed the "central" component of aptitude, language analytic ability, but that more peripheral components (phonemic processing and memory) were more weakly related to intelligence.

3 Foreign Language Aptitude and SLA

The discussion so far has attempted to capture the way that aptitude has been perceived as a self-contained area, largely unrelated to broader issues in SLA. This has recently begun to change. For example, Skehan (1998) proposed that different components of aptitude could be related to stages of information processing. Phonemic coding ability can be related to input processing; language analytic ability (grammatical sensitivity, inductive language learning) can be related to central processing; and memory-as-retrieval can be related to output and fluency. Such a set of linkages shows how aptitude, at a fairly general level, is consistent with a cognitive view of SLA.

But this analysis can be extended, as table 18.2 shows, to incorporate putative SLA processes at a more detailed level. In the table, existing foreign language aptitude constructs are shown in normal text, while *potential* aptitude constructs are shown in italics. These are discussed further below.

The left-hand column in this table attempts to portray a range of processing stages consistent with an information-processing account of SLA. Most of these have been the focus for active investigation over the last 20 or so years. The list is not intended to be controversial – merely to reflect things that have preoccupied researchers. More important here is the right-hand column. If we assume the relevance of the processing stage implied in the left-hand column, the operative questions are as follows:

Table 18.2 SLA stages and aptitude constructs

SLA stage	*Corresponding aptitude constructs*
Input processing strategies, such as segmentation	*Attentional control* *Working memory*
Noticing	Phonemic coding ability *Working memory*
Pattern identification	Phonemic coding ability *Working memory* Grammatical sensitivity Inductive language learning ability
Pattern restructuring and manipulation	Grammatical sensitivity Inductive language learning ability
Pattern control	*Automatization* *Integrative memory*
Pattern integration	*Chunking* *Retrieval memory*

i Is there relevant variation between learners?
ii Is it justifiable to postulate an aptitude component in this area?
iii Does an existing aptitude component apply, or do we need to explore the nature and measurement of additional aptitude constructs?

We can take noticing as an example. Schmidt (1990, 1994, 2001; Schmidt and Frota, 1986) has argued convincingly that noticing is a necessary precursor to development, a point of view which complements nicely current discussions of the need for a focus on form in foreign language instruction (Doughty, 2001; Doughty and Williams, 1998). Discussion in this area has generally implied that noticing is a universal process and that its effects will vary from individual to individual only as a function of factors such as salience and frequency in input, together with variations in task conditions, etc. (Schmidt, 1990). But it is possible that there are individual differences between learners in noticing abilities: other things being equal, some learners may be more likely to notice relevant qualities of input than others (Sawyer and Ranta, 2001). We could postulate a range of reasons why this might be so. Some learners might be able to segment the input stream better than others (VanPatten, 1996); some might have better working memory (Miyake and Friedman, 1999; Sawyer and Ranta, 2001; Walter, 2000); some might be more field-independent (Chapelle and Green, 1992). The point is that there may be relevant individual differences which bear upon the likelihood of noticing.

There is also a component of aptitude, phonemic coding ability, which might be relevant in this case. The component has been defined (see above) as the capacity to code input material so that it can be retained over more than a few seconds. The questions we can now ask are these:

i Does such an ability (assuming its existence) cover the same areas as the above SLA processes?
ii Are there individual differences (IDs) in noticing which go beyond what is measured by phonemic coding ability?
iii Can operationalizations of such IDs be produced which are reliable and valid and which go beyond simply the measurement of phonemic coding ability?

If the answers to these questions are positive (and it is central to this discussion that the questions are *empirical* and susceptible to experimental investigation), then it is clear that there is scope for relating the mainstream SLA construct of noticing to an individual differences construct which would then make a major contribution to explaining language development.

Noticing is taken here only as an example: all the other SLA stages shown in table 18.2 can be interpreted in similar fashion. Prior to the stage of noticing, we have the need to segment the input stream effectively, and to control attentional and perceptual processes so that the stream of noise which is encountered is handled in such a way that it can be subsequently analyzed. This links clearly with the construct of phonemic coding ability. Phonemic coding ability, it will be recalled, is the ability to code unfamiliar sound in such a way that it can be retained for more than a few seconds. This seems very close to the imposition of structure on the incoming speech stream that input processing strategies themselves are concerned with. Perhaps this needs to be supplemented with additional constructs from contemporary psychology, such as the phonological loop component of working memory (Baddeley and Logie, 1999; Baddeley, Gathercole, and Papagno, 1998; Gathercole and Baddeley, 1993). If this is the case, then the research motivation originating from SLA for the stages of information processing will have provided interesting input to clarify which aptitudinal constructs can fit in to this sequence, *and which additional aptitudinal constructs are needed.* Sawyer and Ranta (2001), for example, argue forcefully that working memory, as measured by a reading span test, should be represented in language aptitude test batteries.

Clearly, as we move through the first four stages outlined in table 18.2, there is a shift in emphasis from the processing of input, on the one hand, to what is done with material which has been extracted in this way. So the third stage, pattern identification, goes beyond the focus on "simple" noticing, and has more emphasis on wider-ranging patterns, where the learner is likely to wrestle with more complex language structures, with elements containing some degree of internal relationship. While there may still be some role for phonemic coding ability and working memory here, the emphasis shifts toward grammatical sensitivity and inductive language learning ability as relevant aptitudinal constructs. In other words, the presumption is that, given exactly the same input/intake data, there will be differences in pattern-extraction capacities, that is, some people are able to analyze material and make generalizations based upon it better than others. Such learners will also then benefit from the greater degree of structuring of the input material into the form of rules (correct or not), and retain material more effectively.

In some ways, the fourth stage, pattern restructuring and manipulation, appears hardly any different from pattern extraction. The crucial difference, however, is that this stage concerns a *change* in existing rules in the interlanguage system. In other words, the acquisition problem consists not simply of the extraction of a rule from input data, but of the overhaul of an existing rule whose incorrectness or incompleteness has been (belatedly) apprehended. To look at this from another perspective, it is the "anti-fossilization" stage of development, in which the prospect of a previous and limited pattern persisting unhelpfully has been overcome.

We finally reach two stages which concern how control over an emerging interlanguage system is achieved. In the earlier of these, pattern control, the focus is on accuracy and automatization. The extracted pattern or generalization from earlier stages is, as a result, produced with less effort, and with avoidance of error. The focus is on production, in other words, and the way that perceived patterns can be the basis for effective speech or writing. The final stage, pattern integration, is even more production-oriented. Here, the existence of a rule, pattern, or generalization is presupposed, as is the capacity to use such a pattern largely without error and without undue effort. What is at issue in the final stage is that a different level of routinization may be achieved, in which a pattern may be used not simply as quickly produced, rule-based language, but as a lexicalized chunk, in that it can be accessed as a whole or "gestalt," perhaps based on a formulaic piece of language (Pawley and Syder, 1983; Skehan, 1998). In this case, processing costs are significantly reduced, since internal computation is no longer necessary.

Clearly, this reinterpretation of aptitude and its linkage with SLA processing stages, goes beyond the models of aptitude which currently exist. The right-hand column in table 18.2 shows that some of the existing aptitude constructs may be serviceable starting points for this reconceptualization of aptitude, but may well need some operational updating. There are a number of other areas which are simply unrepresented at present, however, and which will need to be addressed at an operational level if SLA and aptitude are to come into a more satisfactory relationship. Table 18.2, in other words, implies a significant research program.

4 SLA-Informed Aptitude Research

There is already interesting work consistent with this framework which tries to link SLA at the process level with aptitudinal constructs. DeGraaf (1997) reports a study into the effects of rule explanation (and non-explanation) on the performance of learners of eXperanto (an artificial language) and Spanish, with each of these represented by simple and complex versions of morphological and syntactic rules. In this regard, the study resembles many SLA studies where the focus is on the contrast between implicit and explicit learning. In addition, however, DeGraaf (1997) gave subjects in his study an aptitude test. This test correlated significantly with performance in both eXperanto and Spanish, and for the explicit *and* implicit conditions. Indeed, there was no difference in strength of relationship with aptitude between these two conditions.

Consistently with this, Robinson (1995) examined the level of correlation between aptitude measures (grammatical sensitivity and memory) and performance, for both an easy and a hard rule, for four conditions: instructed (where learners were given explicit instruction); rule-search (where they were provided with material and told to search for a rule); implicit (where learners were simply provided with material which was consistent with the rule in question, but where their attention was not drawn to this); and incidental (where learners were given a meaning-related task, but with the same rules built in to the material). There were significant correlations with the aptitude measures for all conditions except the incidental one, with correlations in all the significant conditions being above 0.50, for both easy and hard rules.

These two sets of results are intriguing. They suggest that aptitude is relevant not simply for conventional, explicit, rule-focused teaching contexts, but also when the learning is implicit, an interpretation consistent with the analysis of SLA stages presented in table 18.2. In fact, the one non-significant correlation in Robinson's (1995) study (for the incidental condition) is equally intriguing. This suggests that aptitude may not be so relevant when the focus is on meaning. As DeGraaf (1997, pp. 158–9) puts it, this suggests that "the evidence cannot be generalized to non-instructed learning without any focus on form." Aptitude, it would seem, presupposes a requirement that there is a focus on form, precisely the same claim made currently by a range of SLA researchers (Doughty and Williams, 1998).

This interpretation is also consistent with the findings of some aptitude research in naturalistic settings. Reves (1983, and see above) reports that L1 Arabic learners of L2 Hebrew (in naturalistic conditions) and L2 English (in instructed conditions) evidenced significantly and equally elevated correlations in each of the conditions. In fact, out of a range of predictors of language learning success, aptitude was the most effective in each condition. More recently, DeKeyser (2000), following Johnson and Newport's (1989, 1991) study of critical period effects (see Hyltenstam and Abrahamsson, this volume, for coverage of this area), has examined the effects of age on second language acquisition. Researching Hungarian learners in the Pittsburgh area, he has replicated Johnson and Newport's (1989) findings that:

i there is a strong negative correlation between age on arrival, and level of attained proficiency, up till the age of around 17;

ii there is no correlation between age on arrival and attained proficiency beyond that point.

In addition to gathering data directly comparable to that of Johnson and Newport (although with a few research design improvements), DeKeyser also administered an aptitude test to these learners. Very interestingly, he shows that:

iii there is no correlation between aptitude scores and attained proficiency up till the age of 17;
iv there is a correlation (0.60) between aptitude and attained proficiency after this age;
v the few subjects who arrived in the US after the age of 17 but who have reached nativelike levels of English are all high aptitude scorers.

This research, too, is consistent with the interpretation that the concept of aptitude is complementary to general SLA research, and that its relevance is not confined to traditional instructed settings.

5 Aptitude: Conclusion

This seems a propitious moment to be discussing aptitude research. For many years, aptitude has been isolated from the wider area of foreign language learning and acquisition. It has been perceived as moderately effective as a predictor, but undemocratic with respect to learners, out of date conceptually, and of little explanatory value. The research over the last six years or so has indicated that this judgment is unwarranted. Aptitude may well be a central construct when there is a focus on form in SLA, precisely the condition many SLA researchers now call for. If we accept that there is a critical period for second language learning (see Hyltenstam and Abrahamsson, this volume), and that totally meaning-based acquisition is a hazardous undertaking, then aptitude may well represent a constellation of individual differences which bear upon the effectiveness with which learners are able to focus on form when the conditions for doing so are operative.

6 Cognitive and Learning Style

The study of cognitive and learning styles within SLA has long been an interesting puzzle. Studies of style represent a clear case of the importation of a concept from a neighboring discipline, psychology in this case, in a manner which has proved simultaneously attractive and unsatisfactory. Various factors combine to account for the attractiveness of style concepts to SLA researchers. First of all, in some contrast to aptitude, a predisposition to deal with learning situations or to process information implies that each of the different choices or styles may have strengths and weaknesses. As a result, *different* styles may be equally valid and advantageous. This leads to a second attraction: that it is possible to envision all styles as making contributions, even if in different domains. From this viewpoint, it seems less appropriate, therefore, to think of someone as low in style (as one may well think of someone low in aptitude) than as having a characteristic style, with its strengths and weaknesses. Finally, there is also the attraction that style may concern attributes which do not have such a fixed status as aptitudes. A predisposition may be deep-seated, but it does imply some capacity for flexibility, and scope for adaptation of particular styles to meet the demands of particular circumstances.

Keefe and Perrell define style as: "A complexus of related characteristics in which the whole is greater than its parts. Learning style is a gestalt combining internal and external operations derived from the individual's neurobiology, personality and development, and reflected in learner behavior" (Keefe and Ferrell, 1990, p. 16). This definition can be developed slightly to bring out a contrast between cognitive and learning styles, a distinction sometimes left unclear in the literature. The former can be defined as a predisposition to process information in a characteristic manner while the latter can be defined as a typical preference for approaching learning in general. The former, in other words, is more restricted to information-processing preferences, while the latter embraces all aspects of learning.

The review which follows starts by focusing on cognitive style, and then moves to consider issues of learning style more broadly. The major interpretation of cognitive style has been through studies of the constructs of field independence and field dependence. Drawing on the original proposals of Witkin (1962), this view of style has contrasted an analytic predisposition to the processing of information with a preference for a more holistic approach. Field independents are seen as more likely to analyze information into its component parts, and to distinguish the essential from the inessential. Field dependents, in contrast, are more likely to deal with information structures as wholes, or "gestalts." At a personal level, field independents are portrayed as aloof, preferring to find solutions to problems for themselves. Field dependents, in contrast, are sociable and work well in groups. Each of these putative preferences could have advantages in language learning: the former should link with a capacity to analyze linguistic material, and perhaps learn systematically; the latter to engage in communicative language use, and to "talk to learn." The FI/D concept, in its original form, also includes, besides such an analytic predisposition, related contrasts between internal and external frames of reference, and between different interpersonal competencies (Chapelle and Green, 1992).

A range of studies motivated by the FI/D contrast has been conducted in the second language domain (see reviews in Chapelle and Green, 1992; Ehrman, 1996; Griffiths and Sheen, 1992; Reid, 1995; Skehan, 1989, 1998). Generalizing from the empirical results:

i Coefficients obtained have usually indicated a low correlation between FI/D and language learning achievement, with a value of around 0.30 being typical.

ii Despite the claims that each different style has its advantages, the significant positive correlations are always in favor of the FI style.
iii Not all studies report significant correlations.
iv The correlations are lowered when intelligence scores are partialed out, leading to the allegation that the FI/D interpretation of cognitive style is simply a disguised measure of intelligence.

Two general difficulties, with the construct of field independence itself and with operationalizations thereof, have bedeviled work in this area, and understanding these difficulties may point to ways forward. With respect to the underlying construct of field independence, the case against has been forcefully put by Griffiths and Sheen (1992). They have argued that:

i field independence is now outdated within psychology, its origin;
ii it does not translate well to the language domain;
iii it is indeed a surrogate measure of intelligence;
iv it has generated no results that are impressive.

It is a powerful case that they make.

Chapelle and Green (1992; Chapelle, 1992) have offered a spirited defense of the construct. While acknowledging problems of measurement (see below), they follow Witkin and Goodenough (1981) in analyzing it into the three components: (whether people rely on internal (self-reliant) referents, or external (other-oriented) referents); cognitive restructuring, (i.e., ease with analysis and capacity to manipulate and organize cognitive structures); and interpersonal competencies (i.e., capacity to work effectively with other people). The first of these, frame of reference, is seen as fundamental, and "remains the value-neutral cognitive style, denoting that individuals differ in how they perceive rather than how accurately they perceive" (Chapelle and Green, 1992, p. 50). The remaining two components are then associated with the two poles of the underlying construct. Restructuring links directly with the field-independent end of the continuum, and has connections with constructs of ability. Interpersonal competencies then connect with the field-independent end of the continuum, and link with interactional style. This implies that, while the restructuring component of field independence may be linked to intelligence, the frame of reference and interpersonal components do still have separate research promise. It appears, therefore, that if the measurement problem can be solved, a style-linked predisposition to deal with problem solving in different functional ways may be established, a predisposition which in turn is derived from style.

Skehan (1998), in slight contrast, critiques the bipolar status of field independence, that is, the fact that the "classic" interpretation of FI/D is in terms of a contrast between analytic and holistic processing, implying that one of these has to be at the expense of the other. He proposes instead that the contrast should be between an analytic orientation and a memory orientation (see section 2.3). This would imply capacities in each of these areas, *as well as* predispositions to process information in one way or the other. This, he argues, is more consistent with the literature on individual differences in the second language field. One could therefore envision learners who have strong analytic abilities and strong memory, or learners who are weak in either case, or learners who are mixed, with stronger ability in one domain than the other. While there may be a tendency for people to prefer a style which complements their own strengths and weaknesses, it does not follow automatically that they will take this approach. Hence it may be that someone with strong analytic abilities will prefer a memory orientation. To recapitulate, this approach has two parts. First, there is the distinction between ability and style. Second, each of the two dimensions of ability/style is a continuum in its own right: in other words, it is possible to do well in analysis, and also in memory. In this way, memory/holistic processing is not at the expense of analysis: it is simply another option.

The second major difficulty with FI/D constructs is measurement. The most widely used (but clearly unsatisfactory) measure is the Group Embedded Figures Test (GEFT), a convenient but flawed method of assessing cognitive style. Although very easy to use, the measure lacks validity (see Cronbach, 1970, for review), relying as it does on an excessively visual interpretation of style. There are also questions to be asked about cultural bias in the GEFT. More valid, but probably less practical, is a computer-based measuring instrument developed by Riding (1991; Riding and Cheema, 1991). This approach distinguishes between an analytic–holistic dimension of style, and a verbalizer–imager dimension Crucially, it is possible to score highly *on each pole of each dimension*, so that, unlike with the GEFT, a holistic style is not simply the absence of an analytic style. This implies that it is also possible to have low scores on each dimension, suggesting that someone can be "low" in style options. The computer-based administration system also enables latency of response to be recorded, allowing more sophisticated scoring systems to be developed which base style decisions on processing preferences.

Any balanced assessment of cognitive style would have to conclude that it is not a construct which has generated robust and impressive findings. But the concept does have its attractions, and our understanding of the construct itself, and the pitfalls in its measurement, have improved considerably. There is a still a case to be proved, but it would seem that because of the current promise of the reconceptualizations and new measurement tools, there may be scope for additional research where, just a few years ago, the area looked very unpromising.

So far, we have restricted the discussion to *cognitive* style. But the concept of style also applies to other domains, and to other applications than processing information. In terms of domain, Reid (1995), for example, goes beyond the cognitive domain to include such areas as sensory preference and personality. Regarding the sensory domain, she proposes auditory, visual, kinesthetic and tactile preferences.

Oxford and Anderson (1995) take an even broader perspective. They state that individual learners have a composite of at least 20 style dimensions, of which eight seem to be particularly important for L2 learning:

i global vs. analytic;
ii field dependent vs. field independent;
iii feeling vs. thinking;
iv impulsive vs. reflective;
v intuitive-random vs. concrete-sequential;
vi closure-oriented vs. open;
vii extroverted vs. introverted;
viii visual vs. auditory vs. hands-on (or tactile/kinesthetic).

More generally, they argue that learning styles have six interrelated aspects: *cognitive* (concerning the preferred or habitual patterns of mental functioning), *executive* (concerning the degree to which the person seeks order, organization, and closure, and manages his or her own learning process), *affective* (concerning values, beliefs, and attitudes that influence what an individual pays attention to in a learning situation), *social* (concerning the preferred extent of involvement with other people while learning), *physiological* (concerning at least partly the person's anatomically based sensory and perceptual tendencies), and *behavioral* (concerning the extent to which someone actively seeks to satisfy his or her learning preferences).

But if we broaden the concept of style to embrace learning, rather than simply cognition, the interpretation that seems to enjoy the most current attention is that of Kolb (1984), especially as this relates to the place of the individual learner and the development of learner autonomy, two issues of some significance to SLA. Kolb (1984) proposes that there is an ideal learning cycle, which starts from concrete experience (CE), moves to observation and reflection upon that experience (RO), then conceptualizes the experience at a more abstract level, as a result of the reflection (AC). The learner then uses the results of the conceptualization to achieve a deeper level of understanding. This conceptualization is used to transform the underlying experience in such a way that the learner acts and "experiments" to change the nature of experience (AE). After this, the entire cycle is repeated, with (the newly arrived at) concrete experience setting the whole process in motion again.

This cycle can be applied to learning in a number of domains, from higher education, and the learning of, for example, geography (Healey, 1999), to management and the business domain, and to teacher education (Barduhn, 1998). There are several potential applications to acquisition. One could consider the CE stage to represent exposure to input, which would be followed by observation and reflection (RO). If we were dealing with the past tense form in English, this could be the *noticing* of the existence of a wide range of past tense forms indicated by the morphological "-ed" ending. This observation and tentative generalization might lead to the conceptualization that the past tense in English is invariably formed in this way (AC). Then, the conceptualization, reflecting its tentative status, might provoke the learner to choose to use this form for the past tense while observing the reactions of others (AE). In other words, the learner would come back to concrete experience having transformed this experience in some way, with the result that the experience itself would be different. In this case, highly idealized as it is, the learner might overuse the regular past, and then, at a later RO stage, reflect on the consistently raised eyebrows that its application to verbs such as "go" or "give" had provoked. This, in turn, might lead to a new conceptualization of past tense formation, and so on.

Two opposing dimensions supposedly underlie the Kolb cycle. The first concerns the way we perceive, grasp, and represent experiences, and contrasts the CE and AC stages of the cycle. The second takes the remaining two stages, RO and AE, and concerns how we process and transform experience. This leads to the central insight of Kolb's work in terms of learning style. In the present discussion, movement through the four stages of the cycle has been idealized. But in reality the different stages do not take equivalent amounts of time: some learning problems may require longer periods of RO, for example. In fact, Kolb proposes that different learners may *characteristically* linger at particular points of the learning cycle, with the result that whatever point of the four-stage sequence they prioritize will overly influence how they learn. In an ideal situation, it is important to pass through all stages of the cycle in a reasonably complete way, because learning is an iterative process. Consistently focusing on one stage is therefore likely to be disadvantageous and inefficient, because the necessary contributions of the other stages are not being sufficiently exploited. This can again be illustrated through the past tense example. Not to reflect at all will seriously retard progress. But to spend too much time simply observing and reflecting and never to get around to theorizing (or, in SLA terms, focusing on form) would also slow progress. Equally, to experiment remorselessly without taking stock often enough would generate considerable "busy" work, but would not produce sufficient cumulative progress.

The emphasis in the Kolb model is on learning in general, not acquisition specifically. Indeed the applications of the model are not at all confined to the language learning domain, as the earlier examples made clear. Even within language learning, the focus need not be on acquisition, since areas such as teacher education, learner autonomy, and many others would be equally appropriate for application. The attractions of the model are that, unlike the concept of cognitive style, the research foundations in this case do give some basis for encouragement, even though it is necessary to go outside the language domain for such findings (see Robotham, 1999, for review). Interesting results have been published, for example, relating to the effects of matching and mismatching students with instructional programs (Hayes and Allinson, 1996). Indeed, there is a significant literature on how educational programs can be adapted to cater for differences in learning style, and overcome learning style difficulties. There is a significant additional advantage: the Kolb cycle does seem to be accompanied by measuring instruments which are valid and reliable as well as fairly stable in the results they deliver at the individual level. Kolb (1976, 1984) himself published the *Learning Styles Inventory*. In addition, there seem to be widely accepted derivative measures, such as Honey and Mumford's *Using Your Learning Styles* (1986; see also Honey and Mumford, 1992). This instrument, which is easy to administer, provides useful norming data, and may be a practical method of obtaining learning style information.

The different approaches to "learning style" demonstrate that the term has been used very broadly in the literature to cover a wide range of learning patterns or orientations at various psychological and behavioral levels. In this respect, learning styles are very similar to learning strategies, sharing their basic theoretical shortcoming of a lack of precise definition, which results in a somewhat openended and eclectic list of potential components (see below). Indeed, Schmeck (1988) argues that learning styles and learning strategies are closely related, as a learning style refers to a habitual, cross-situational use of a class of learning strategies. This being the case, however, it is difficult to decide whether learning styles are independent individual difference factors or if the term is merely a convenient way of referring to certain patterns of information-processing and learning behaviors whose antecedents lie in a wide range of diverse factors, such as varying degrees of acquired abilities and skills, idiosyncratic personality traits, and different exposures to past learning experiences.

As concluded by others (Skehan, 1989; Griffiths and Sheen, 1992), it appears from a review of findings on style that such concepts may not deserve high research priority, but they have not been eliminated as potentially relevant second language linked measures. What is now needed is more evidence of educationally linked applications of such concepts. If such evidence is forthcoming, style concepts may become more central in SLA once again.

7 Language Learning Strategies

Three books published at the beginning of the 1990s, by O'Malley and Chamot (1990), Oxford (1990), and Wenden (1991), indicated that the concept of "language learning strategy" – reflecting the learner's active contribution to enhancing the effectiveness of his or her own learning – had reached mainstream recognition in the L2 field. Indeed, right from its introduction in L2 research in the late 1970s, the notion of "learning strategy" was intuitively very appealing to researchers and was also embraced with enthusiasm by language teachers. The initial phase of strategy research focused primarily on what could be learned from the "good language learner," that is, what characteristics made some learners more successful than others in learning a second language (Naiman, Fröhlich, Stern, and Todesco, 1978; Rubin, 1975; Stern, 1975; Wong Fillmore, 1979). The results indicated in a fairly consistent manner that it was not merely a high degree of language aptitude and motivation that caused some learners to excel, but also the students' own active and creative participation in the learning process through the application of individualized learning techniques. Following this early research, the study of language learning strategies was taken up by a number of scholars in the 1980s. By 1987, Wenden and Rubin were able to compile a rich collection of research studies on "learner strategies," which underlined the important role they played in the acquisition of an L2. The publication of the three summary books mentioned above further added to the general momentum, so that in an article describing a social psychological model of strategy use published in the mid-1990s, MacIntyre (1994) started his discussion by stating that "One of the most fertile areas of research in language learning in recent years is the topic of language learning strategies" (p. 185).

Looking back, it may seem peculiar that virtually nobody has examined the theoretical soundness of the concept of "learning strategy" critically, particularly in view of the fact that the definitions and conceptualizations offered in the L2 literature were rather inconsistent and elusive. Oxford (1989) provided a seemingly straightforward functional definition for language learning strategies – "behaviours or actions which learners use to make language learning more successful, self-directed, and enjoyable" (p. 235) – but when she described the scope of these strategies in her well-known taxonomy (Oxford, 1990), she also included cognitive and affective strategies that involved *mental processes* rather than "behaviours or actions." In order to eliminate this inconsistency, the 1990 volume simply replaced the phrase "behaviours and actions used by the learner" with the more general "steps taken by the learner," which could accommodate both behavioral and mental steps. Oxford's strategy taxonomy was made up of six strategy classes: cognitive, memory, metacognitive, compensation, affective, and social strategies. This division raises further questions inasmuch as (i) "compensation" (i.e., communication) strategies are primarily related to language *use* rather than language *learning* (and were included on the basis that language use leads to language acquisition), and (ii) cognitive and memory strategies are treated as separate categories of equal status, even though the latter is obviously a sub-class of the former.

An alternative definition of language learning strategies was offered by O'Malley and Chamot (1990), according to which these strategies involve "special thoughts or behaviours that individuals use to help them comprehend, learn, or retain new information" (p. 1). This conceptualization differed from Oxford's functional definition in that it highlighted the *cognitive* aspects of strategy use. Even though the cautious wording of the definition did actually allow learning strategies to be "behaviours," the addition of "thoughts" was an important alteration, as was the restriction of the purpose of strategy use to comprehending, learning, and retaining new information. All these reflected the fact that O'Malley and Chamot attempted to ground learning strategy research in Anderson's (1983, 1985) general cognitive psychological theory. However, when the authors listed concrete examples of learning strategies, we find an inventory that is not at all dissimilar to Oxford's (1990). O'Malley and

Chamot distinguish three main classes of strategy: *cognitive*, which correspond to Oxford's "cognitive" and "memory" categories; *metacognitive*, which have a direct equivalent in Oxford's system; and *social/affective*, which correspond roughly to Oxford's "social," "affective," and "communication" categories. The odd one out in O'Malley and Chamot's taxonomy is clearly the last group, "social/affective strategies," which includes diverse behaviors, such as "cooperation," "questioning and clarification," and "self-talk." These strategies are not related to the cognitive theoretical basis outlined by the authors, and they admittedly represent a "broad grouping" (p. 45), a miscellaneous category that appears to have been introduced simply to accommodate all the strategies that did not fit into the first two types but which could not be left out either. Also, it is interesting to see that in order to eliminate the problematic issue of the relationship between "behaviours" and "thoughts" in their definition, O'Malley and Chamot (1994) followed a strategy similar to Oxford's (1990) by replacing these words with the more general formula of "methods and techniques that individuals use."

In spite of the different emphases and concerns in the approaches by Oxford and O'Malley and Chamot, their strategy systems are highly compatible. If we make three justifiable changes to the two taxonomies – (i) exclude communication strategies from the scope of learning strategies (for a justification, see Cohen, 1998; Tarone, 1981), (ii) combine Oxford's (1990) memory and cognitive strategies, and (iii) separate O'Malley and Chamot's (1990) social/affective strategies – we end up with two matching typologies, each comprising four main classes of learning strategy:

i *cognitive strategies*, involving the manipulation or transformation of the learning materials/input (e.g., repetition, summarizing, using images);
ii *metacognitive strategies*, involving higher-order strategies aimed at analyzing, monitoring, evaluating, planning, and organizing one's own learning process;
iii *social strategies*, involving interpersonal behaviours aimed at increasing the amount of L2 communication and practice the learner undertakes (e.g., initiating interaction with native speakers, cooperating with peers);
iv *affective strategies*, involving taking control of the emotional (affective) conditions and experiences that shape one's subjective involvement in learning.

Although the theoretical inconsistencies of the learning strategy literature in general were quite obvious, leading Ellis (1994) to conclude that "(D)efinitions of learning strategies have tended to be *ad hoc* and atheoretical" (p. 533), it was not at all unreasonable that the L2 field showed remarkable tolerance of these shortcomings. After all, learning strategies represented one of the hottest topics in the broader field of educational psychology in the 1980s and – what was just as important – research studies that included language learning strategies as either dependent or independent variables produced very interesting results. There was an increasing body of research evidence that learning strategies contributed to the effectiveness of L2 attainment, and the practical significance of this claim was further augmented by the emerging view that learning strategies could be specifically trained/taught to language learners (cf. Cohen, 1998; Nyikos, 1996; for a critical exchange on the teachability of learning strategies, see Chamot and Rubin, 1994; Rees-Miller, 1993, 1994). Strategy research also contributed to the growing awareness of cross-cultural differences in SLA, as attested by a collection of papers edited by Oxford (1996) that examined the varying importance of certain strategies across diverse sociocultural contexts.

L2 strategy research appeared to constitute such an important advance in our understanding of how the actual process of "learning" took place that it was easy to put aside any doubts by saying that significant developments are often accompanied by a theoretical muddle that will eventually be cleared away by the subsequent restructuring of our existing knowledge. Skehan's (1989) summary of the learning strategy research illustrates the research climate well:

> If, now, we review the whole of the learner-strategies research, we have to say that the area is at an embryonic stage. Conflicting results and methodologies proliferate. There are few hard findings. Even the causal role and intervention potential of strategies could be disputed . . . Yet the area of research has considerable attractions. A lot of useful and suggestive research has now been reported. There are the beginnings of systematicity in the categorisation schemes for strategies, so that new investigators need not gather information blindly . . . This suggests that we are ready for the first attempts at theorising within the learner-strategies field. (p. 98)

Regrettably, the "clearing away" process never happened and the conceptual ambiguity about learning strategies prevailed. This resulted – in the educational psychology literature – in the abandonment of the term "learning strategy" in favor of the more versatile concept of "self-regulation." Researchers in the L2 field have not made this transition yet, and "learning strategy" is still a frequently used phrase. Because of its shaky theoretical foundation, a significant change in L2 strategy research paradigms appears inevitable.

7.1 *Learning strategies in the psychological literature*

In one of the more recent theoretical overviews of learning strategies in mainstream educational psychology, Weinstein and Meyer (1994) state that learning strategies include "thoughts, emotions, and behaviours that facilitate the acquisition of knowledge and skills, or the reorganisation of one's knowledge base" (p. 3335). This is a precise summary that clearly reveals the weaknesses of the concept: how can something be either cognition or affect or behavior? How can it contribute to the acquisition of both knowledge and skills, and even to the reorganization of existing knowledge? To satisfy all these criteria, either learning strategies must be some sort of superordinate magic tools, or the term has been used in far too broad a sense, including a number of different things that do not necessarily belong together.

In a theoretical discussion of the concept, Schmeck (1988) indicates that "strategy" was originally a military term, referring to procedures for implementing the plan of a large-scale military operation, and in non-military usage has come to refer to the implementation of a set of procedures (tactics) for accomplishing something. Thus, a *learning strategy* in a more general sense is a "sequence of procedures for accomplishing learning" (p. 5). Kirby (1988) took Schmeck's reasoning further by trying to specify the relationship between "strategies," "skills," and "abilities." As he argues,

> *skills* are existing cognitive routines for performing specified tasks, and *strategies* are the means of selecting, combining, or redesigning those cognitive routines. Skills range from *knowledge skills*, the accessing by stimulus patterns of stored representations and associations (e.g., knowing that "7" says "seven") to *action skills*, the transforming of input information to obtain desired results . . . Skills are fundamentally related to *abilities*, to the extent that the latter sets some sort of upper limit to the development of the former. (p. 230)

Thus, broadly speaking, skills are the things we can do (constrained by our ability), whereas strategies and tactics involve the conscious decisions to implement these skills. Although this appears to be an adequate clarification, it leaves the exact level of analysis of strategies and skills open. At which conceptual level are the processes governed by strategies and skills best conceived? Are we talking about neurological, cognitive, or behavioral processes? And how do knowledge systems, emotional states/processes, cognitive operations, and motor skills interplay in leading to action? To answer these questions – and therefore to be able to use the term "learning strategy" in a scientifically rigorous sense – we would need to produce a coherent neurobiological account of behavior, which is a formidable task yet to be achieved.

In order to extricate themselves from this deadlock, educational psychologists in the 1990s took an alternate route. They simply dropped the term "strategy" (which seemed to cause most of the confusion) and focused instead on what was seen as the essence of strategic learning: the learner's conscious and proactive contribution to the enhancement of her or his own learning process. The new term introduced to cover this learner-specific perspective was *self-regulation*.

7.2 *Self-regulatory learning*

Self-regulation refers to the degree to which individuals are active participants in their own learning; it is a more dynamic concept than "learning strategy," highlighting the learners' own "strategic efforts to manage their own achievement through specific beliefs and processes" (Zimmerman and Risemberg, 1997, p. 105). The notion of *self-regulation of academic learning* could also be perceived as a multidimensional construct, including cognitive, metacognitive, motivational, behavioral, and environmental processes that learners can use to enhance academic achievement. Thus, self-regulation is clearly distinct from measures of mental ability, and the self-regulated learner can be portrayed as "calling on a library of information and applying a suite of varied skills during studying activities in which achievements are forged" (Winne, 1995, p. 173). By switching to this new concept, researchers had not, by any means, solved the theoretical problems undermining the term "learning strategy," but they had successfully shifted the emphasis from the product to the process, thereby creating more leeway for themselves. This is well demonstrated by the fact that in the lead article of a special issue of the journal *Educational Psychologist* entirely devoted to the topic of self-regulation, Winne (1995) set out to define the concept by providing a description of the self-regulating *learner* rather than of *self-regulatory mechanisms*. This is indeed an appropriate validation of the term, because the existence of "self-regulating learners" is well documented in educational psychology. As Winne summarizes:

> When they begin to study, self-regulating learners set goals for extending knowledge and sustaining motivation. They are aware of what they know, what they believe, and what the differences between these kinds of information imply for approaching tasks. They have a grasp of their motivation, are aware of their affect, and plan how to manage the interplay between these as they engage with a task. They also deliberate about small-grain tactics and overall strategies, selecting some instead of others based on predictions about how each is able to support progress towards chosen goals. (p. 173)

It is almost as if the magic term "learning strategy" had been replaced by the superhuman person of the "self-regulating learner."

Self-regulation is a very active field of research in educational psychology (for a recent summary, see Boeakaerts, Pintrich, and Zeidner, 2000). Using the new paradigm, researchers attempt to synthesize learner-initiated cognitive, metacognitive, and motivational processes and strategies. These are strongly linked to the subject of the final section of our review, which focuses on language learning motivation. Indeed, from a self-regulatory point of view, learners can enhance the effectiveness of their learning not only by means of applying creative cognitive operations that suit their particular learning styles, but also by generating motivation to learn and finding ways of maintaining their commitment when persistence appears to be flagging. In a more general sense, therefore, self-regulation and motivation are inextricably bound together, as they both concern the antecedents of increased learner achievement.

8 Motivation

The concept of "motivation" is just as surrounded with theoretical controversies as is the concept of learning strategy, yet motivation research during the past 10 years or so has shown a very different pattern of development: rather than gradually going into decline, the study of L2 motivation reached an unprecedented boom in the 1990s, with over 100 journal articles published on the topic and a wide array of alternative theoretical constructs proposed (for reviews, see Clément and Gardner, 2001; Dörnyei, 1998, 2001). This difference in development is, to a large extent, due to the differing historical backgrounds of the two fields. In contrast to the study of language learning strategies, which goes back to exploratory observations of the "good language learner," L2 motivation research was characterized by a well-articulated and theoretically explicit position right from the start, as represented by the influential work of Wallace Lambert, Robert Gardner, Richard Clément, and their associates in Canada (e.g., Clément, 1980; Clément and Gardner, 2001; Gardner, 1985; Gardner and Lambert, 1972; Gardner and MacIntyre, 1993). This position was firmly grounded in social psychology, which allowed the researchers to adopt a range of well-researched terms and metaphors to describe L2 motivation, and to adapt the elaborate quantitative research repertoire of social psychological measurement to the needs of L2 motivation testing. As a result, L2 motivation research soon developed a special data-based research tradition in which the various theoretical propositions were explicitly operationalized and empirically tested.

8.1 The Canadian social psychological approach

A key tenet of the Canadian social psychological approach is that *attitudes* related to an L2 community exert a strong influence on one's L2 learning. This makes sense, since few learners are likely to be successful in learning the language of a low-status community. Gardner (1985) also assumed that language learners' goals fall into two broad categories: (i) an *integrative orientation*, which reflects a positive disposition toward the L2 group and the desire to interact with and even become similar to valued members of that community; and (ii) an *instrumental orientation*, whereby language learning is primarily associated with the potential pragmatic gains of L2 proficiency, such as getting a better job or a higher salary. Although these two orientations have become widely known in the L2 field, the most elaborate and researched aspect of Gardner's theory is not the integrative/instrumental duality but the broader concept of the *integrative motive*. This is a complex construct made up of three main components: (i) *integrativeness*, subsuming integrative orientation, interest in foreign languages, and attitudes toward the L2 community; (ii) *attitudes toward the learning situation*, comprising attitudes toward the teacher and the course; and (iii) *motivation*, which according to Gardner is made up of motivational intensity, desire to learn the language, and attitudes toward learning the language. In an important addition to Gardner's motivation model, Clément (1980; Clément, Dörnyei, and Noels, 1994) has introduced the concept of *linguistic self-confidence* as a significant motivational subsystem, which is very much in line with the increasing importance attached to self-efficacy in mainstream psychological research (see below).

The Canadian social psychological approach dominated the field of L2 motivation research for over two decades, and, interestingly, the real challenge to it did not originally come from L2 researchers but from the field of mainstream psychology. The 1980s brought about a cognitive "revolution" resulting in a range of exciting new motivation theories, and the emerging new paradigms found a particularly fertile ground within educational psychology. The study of student motivation became a topical issue, with virtually all the leading motivational psychologists taking an active interest in it. Therefore, L2 motivation researchers who followed the mainstream psychological literature could not help noticing the range of interesting developments. This growing recognition was accompanied by the fact that by the 1990s, the initial research inspiration and standard-setting empirical and theoretical work coming from Canada had borne fruit by educating a new generation of L2 motivation researchers, who were ready to test their muscles by experimenting with novel paradigms and applying their acquired expertise in diverse contexts and in creative ways. As a consequence, within a few years, a series of position papers, new theoretical constructs, and alternative theoretical approaches was published, resulting in an unexpectedly colorful and confusing scene (e.g., Brown, 1994; Crookes and Schmidt, 1991; Dörnyei, 1994; Julkunen, 1993; Oxford and Shearin, 1994; Schmidt, Boraie, and Kassagby, 1996; Skehan, 1991; Tremblay and Gardner, 1995; Ushioda, 1994; Williams, 1994).

It is a reflection of the strong theoretical basis of Gardner's work that virtually nobody in the "reform movement" wanted to discard the established findings of the social psychological approach. Rather, most researchers tried to extend the existing paradigms. Naturally, such a supplementation process is not at all simple, since it requires an overall restructuring of the existing knowledge. Therefore, an increasing number of researchers decided that in order to be able to make progress, one first needed to go back to the basics of motivation research. (See box 18.1)

8.2 *What is motivation?*

In the most general sense, motivation research addresses the basic question of why humans think and behave as they do; that is, motivation concerns the direction and magnitude of human behavior, or, more specifically (i) the choice of a particular action, (ii) the persistence with it, and (iii) the effort expended on it. In broad terms, motivation is responsible for *why* people decide to do something, *how long* they are willing to sustain the activity, and *how hard* they are going to pursue it.

The range of potential influences on human behavior, that is, the range of possible motives, is very broad, so motivation psychology has traditionally expended a great deal of effort on producing "underlying constructs." These are models of motivation in which the multitude of potential determinants of human behavior is reduced by identifying a relatively small number of key variables that are assumed to subsume or mediate other motivational

Box 18.1 Gardner et al. (1997)

Research question: What is the interrelationship of a large number of learner characteristics (including various attitudinal measures) and language achievement in a unified framework?

Methodology:
Subjects: 102 Canadian university students enrolled in introductory French (although 86 percent of them had at least nine years of prior French training).

Task: Three self-report questionnaires were issued, focusing on a total of 34 variables within the domains of attitudes, motivation, achievement, perceived French competence, anxiety, learning strategies, aptitude, field dependence/independence, and language history. Participants were offered $15 for volunteering to take part in two data-collection sessions (90 minutes each), and their French grades were also obtained.

Results: Both factor analysis and structural equation modeling were carried out (the former will not be reported here), the latter by means of the Amos 3.51 program. The modification indices of the Amos program suggested one added link to the initially proposed model, and having taken this into account, a causal model with reasonable goodness of fit indices was obtained.
main results are as follows:

- "Language attitudes" were seen to cause "motivation" (the latter referring to a combination of "attitudes toward learning French," "motivational intensity," and "desire to learn French."
- "Motivation" caused both "self-confidence" and "language learning strategies."
- "Motivation," "language aptitude," and "language learning strategies" were all seen as antecedents of "language achievement."
- "Field independence" correlated significantly with "language aptitude."
- "Language achievement" caused "self-confidence."
- An unexpected result is the negative path between "language learning strategies" and "Language Achievement," suggesting that strategy use, as measured by the "SILL" (Oxford, 1990), is associated with low levels of achievement. The authors argued that this was due to the psychometric shortcomings of the self-report measurement of learning strategies.

components, and so are able to explain a significant proportion of the variance in people's actions. Thus, the main difference between the various competing theories in motivational psychology lies in the selection of the principal factors on which to anchor the underlying theory. Let us briefly summarize the dominant contemporary approaches.

Expectancy-value theories assume that motivation to perform various tasks is the product of two key factors: the individual's expectancy of success in a given task and the value the individual attaches to success in that task (for reviews, see Brophy, 1999; Wigfield, 1994). Within this framework, we can identify a variety of sub-theories that attempt to explain the cognitive processes that shape the individual's expectancy of success: *attribution theory* (Weiner, 1992) places the emphasis on how one processes past achievement experiences (successes or failures); *self-efficacy theory* (Bandura, 1993) refers to people's judgment of their capabilities to carry out certain specific tasks; and *self-worth theory* (Covington, 1998) claims that the highest human priority is the need for self-acceptance and to maintain a positive face.

Goal theories (Ames, 1992; Locke and Latham, 1990) propose that human action is triggered by a sense of purpose, and for action to take place, goals have to be set and pursued by choice. Accordingly, the key variables in goal theories concern goal properties. The underlying principle of a third main direction in current motivation research, *self-determination theory* (Deci and Ryan, 1985; Vallerand, 1997), and the accompanying intrinsic vs. extrinsic motivational paradigm, is that the desire to be self-initiating and self-regulating is a prerequisite for any human behavior to be intrinsically rewarding, and, therefore, the essence of motivated action is a sense of autonomy. Finally, the key tenet in *social psychological theories of action* (Ajzen, 1988; Eagly and Chaiken, 1993) is the assumption that it is attitudes that exert a directive influence on people's behavior, since people's attitude toward a target influences the overall pattern of their responses to the target.

None of the available theories in motivational psychology offers a comprehensive overview of all the critical motivational factors, in the sense that their absence can cancel or significantly weaken any other existing motives, whereas their active presence can boost learning behavior. Furthermore, there are some basic challenges that most motivation theories have failed to address adequately, such as accounting for unconscious motives (since the emphasis has traditionally been on conscious, rational ones); integrating emotional influences into the primarily cognitive paradigms; addressing the interplay of multiple parallel influences on human behavior (rather than treating one type of action and the underlying motives in isolation); explaining the complex interrelationship of the individual organism, the individual's immediate environment, and the broader sociocultural context; and accounting for the diachronic nature of motivation, that is, portraying motivational processes as they happen in time (for a detailed discussion, see Dörnyei, 2001).

8.3 Motivation in education

Along with a number of researchers (e.g., Graham, 1994; Stipek, 1996; Weiner, 1984), Dörnyei (2001) argues that in order to account for the intricate motivational life of classrooms, comprehensive rather than reductionist models that cover a wide range of academic and social motives are needed. Only such multifaceted, and most probably eclectic, constructs can explain the relationship between (i) general motives concerning L2-related values, beliefs and attitudes; (ii) learner-specific motives, such as self-confidence and self-esteem; (iii) motives rooted in the social micro-context of the language classroom, such as the informal class norms designated by the peer group; (iv) the teacher's motivational influence; (v) the motivational characteristics of the curriculum and the teaching materials; (vi) the distracting effects of alternative actions; and (vii) the learner's self-regulatory activity to control his or her own motivational state. Although this list is incomplete, it shows that the complex of student motivation subsumes a number of facets.

Besides the multifaceted nature of student motivation, motivation to learn in educational settings has another significant aspect, namely the important role played by "time" in it. During the lengthy process of mastering certain subject matters, motivation does not remain constant, but is associated with a dynamically changing and evolving mental process, characterized by constant (re)appraisal and balancing of the various internal and external influences that the individual is exposed to. Indeed, even within the duration of a single course of instruction, most learners experience a fluctuation of their enthusiasm/commitment, sometimes on a day-to-day basis. In Ushioda's (1996) words, "within the context of institutionalised learning especially, the common experience would seem to be motivational flux rather than stability" (p. 240). In order to account for the daily "ebb and flow" of motivation (i.e., the level of effort invested in the pursuit of a particular goal oscillating between ups and downs), an adequate model of student motivation needs to have a distinct temporal dimension that can accommodate systematic patterns of transformation and evolution in time (Dörnyei, 2000).

One influential theoretical approach in motivational psychology, proposed by the German psychologists Heinz Heckhausen, Julius Kuhl, and their associates (for reviews, see Heckhausen, 1991; Kuhl and Beckmann, 1994), offers a framework with a prominent time component. A central feature of Heckhausen and Kuhl's theory, often referred to as "Action Control Theory" (see Robinson, this volume), is the separation of the *predecisional phase* of motivation, referring to the pre-actional stage of deliberation associated with planning, goal setting, and intention formation, and the *post-decisional phase* associated with influences that come into force when action has started and therefore concern motivational maintenance and control, perseverance, and overcoming various internal obstacles to action. Heckhausen (1991) argued that these two phases are energized and directed by largely different motives: "Why one wants to do something and that one wants to do it is one thing, but its actual implementation and successful completion is another" (p. 163).

8.4 A synthesis of L2 motivation research: a dynamic perspective

In an attempt to address the challenge of time in theories of student motivation, Dörnyei and Ottó (1998; Dörnyei, 2000, 2001) proposed a process-oriented conceptualization of motivation. They define it as the dynamically changing cumulative arousal in a person that initiates, directs, coordinates, amplifies, terminates, and evaluates the cognitive and motor processes whereby initial wishes and desires are selected, prioritized, operationalized, and (successfully or unsuccessfully) acted out. They argued that such a dynamic perspective is a potentially fruitful method of interpreting and integrating the manifold motivational factors that affect the student's language learning behavior in classroom settings. Using *time* as an organizing principle offers a "natural" way of ordering the relevant motivational influences into various distinct stages of the motivational sequence along a temporal axis. In fact, because the different sub-phases of the motivation process may be associated with different motives, ignoring "time" in motivation models can (and often does) result in a situation where two theories are equally valid and yet contradict one another – simply because they refer to different *phases* of the motivation process. In fact, Dörnyei (2001) maintains that the differences between the traditional, social psychological conceptions of L2 motivation and many of the subsequent "reform" conceptualizations are largely rooted in the different perceptions of the temporal reality of motivation, and that by adopting a dynamic model, the various approaches can be successfully synthesized.

Figure 18.1 shows the schematic representation of a motivation construct offered by Dörnyei (forthcoming) that is based on process-oriented principles. Following Heckhausen and Kuhl's approach, the construct separates three phases of motivation: *choice motivation*, associated with the pre-actional phase; *executive motivation*, associated with the actional phase; and *motivational retrospection*, which involves the learner's final analysis of the actional process once it has been completed or terminated. The figure summarizes the main motivational functions and influences, broken down into the three phases.

How does such a process-oriented construct relate to Gardner's (1985) established social psychological conception of L2 motivation? The Canadian approach has traditionally targeted the more general and stable aspects of motivation, such as language attitudes, beliefs, and values. From a process-oriented perspective, these motivational aspects are primarily associated with the pre-actional stage of motivation and are, therefore, particularly useful in predicting issues such as *language choice* or the initial intention to *enrol in a language course*. They are less adequate for predicting actual L2 learning behaviors demonstrated in the classroom (e.g., rate of attendance, level of attention paid, degree of task engagement), because learner behaviors during the actional stage tend to be energized by executive motives. These are largely rooted in the situation-specific characteristics of the learning context and show few overlaps with motives fueling the pre-actional stage. This was demonstrated in a study focusing on the motivational background of student engagement in communicative L2 tasks by Dörnyei (2000), who also found that even within situation-specific motives, two clusters can be distinguished: (i) course-specific motives (associated with the appraisal of the L2 course), and (ii) task-specific motives (i.e., attitudes toward a particular task).

Although Gardner and his colleagues have included certain aspects of the learning situation in their paradigm – namely the appraisal of the L2 teacher and course – these were fairly general measures that were selected to provide a broad index usable across various contexts (Gardner and MacIntyre, 1993).

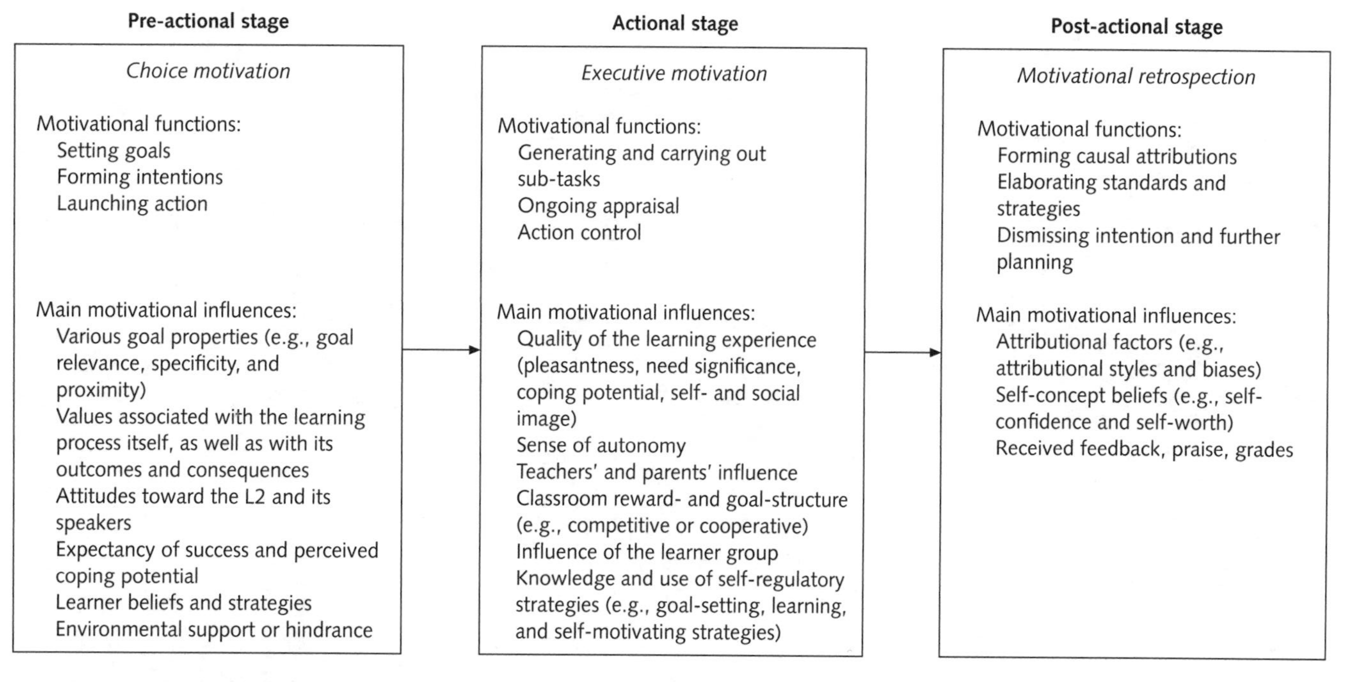

Figure 18.1 A process model of learning motivation in the L2 classroom
Source: Dörnyei (2001)

More specific executive motives were the target of a great deal of research in the 1990s, resulting in what can be seen as an "educational shift" (e.g., Crookes and Schmidt, 1991; Dörnyei, 1994; Oxford and Shearin, 1994; Skehan, 1991). Some perceived the initial articles promoting this more situated approach as attacks on Gardner's theory, whereas from a temporal perspective they can be seen as playing a merely complementary role by focusing on the actional phase of motivation, which had not been the main focus of previous research. This line of investigation, which is aimed at examining the situation-specific motivational underpinnings of language learning as an ongoing social activity, is likely to be further pursued in future motivation research, particularly because it can accommodate a wide range of novel emerging themes and approaches. The following lines of research are representative.

Schumann's (1997) neurobiological research: This was one of the first attempts in the L2 field to incorporate the findings of neuroscience and to link the study of language to this particularly dynamically developing discipline within cognitive science. The key constituent of Schumann's theory is *stimulus appraisal*, which occurs in the brain along five dimensions: *novelty* (degree of unexpectedness/familiarity); *pleasantness* (attractiveness); *goal/need significance* (whether the stimulus is instrumental in satisfying needs or achieving goals); *coping potential* (whether the individual expects to be able to cope with the event); and *self- and social image* (whether the event is compatible with social norms and the individual's self-concept). Thus, stimulus appraisal can be seen as a key process underlying executive motivation. Recently Schumann (2001) has broadened his theory by outlining a conception of learning as a form of *mental foraging* (i.e., foraging for knowledge), which engages the same neural systems as the ones used by organisms when foraging to feed or mate, and which is generated by an incentive motive and potentiated by the stimulus appraisal system.

Self-determination theory in L2 motivation: Because learning an L2 almost always involves a combination of external and internal regulatory factors, Kim Noels and her colleagues (Noels, 2001; Noels, Clément, and Pelletier, 1999; Noels, Pelletier, Clément, and Vallerand, 2000) set out to explore how the orientations proposed by self-determination theory (see above) relate to various orientations that have traditionally been identified in the L2 field, such as instrumental and integrative. Noels argues convincingly that applying the intrinsic/extrinsic continuum can be helpful in organizing language learning goals systematically, and that the paradigm is particularly useful for analyzing classroom climate in terms of how controlling or autonomy-supporting it is.

Willingness to communicate (WTC): A recent extension of motivation research that has both theoretical and practical potential involves the study of L2 speakers' *willingness* to engage in the act of L2 communication. Originally inspired by research in L1 communication studies (e.g., McCroskey and Richmond, 1991), Peter MacIntyre and colleagues (e.g., MacIntyre, Babin, and Clément, 1999; MacIntyre, Clément, Dörnyei, and Noels, 1998) have conceptualized *willingness to communicate* (WTC) in the L2, attempting to explain an individual's "readiness to enter into discourse at a particular time with a specific person or persons, using a L2" (MacIntyre et al., 1998, p. 547). The L2 WTC construct thus conceived is made up of several layers and subsumes a range of linguistic and psychological variables, including linguistic self-confidence (both state and trait); the desire to affiliate with a person; interpersonal motivation; intergroup attitudes, motivation, and climate; parameters of the social situation; communicative competence and experience; and various personality traits. Thus, the model attempts to draw together a host of learner variables that have been well established as influences on second language acquisition and use, resulting in a construct in which psychological and linguistic factors are integrated in an organic manner.

Motivational self-regulation: This is an intriguing new area within motivational psychology, exploring ways by which learners can be endowed with appropriate knowledge and skills to motivate themselves. Motivational self-regulation involves self-management skills that help to overcome environmental distractions and competing/distracting emotional or physical needs or states. Ushioda (1994, 2001) has conducted some pioneering analyses of the positive motivational thinking patterns that help someone to keep going even in adverse learning conditions, and on the basis of Kuhl's (1987) and Corno and Kanfer's (1993) typologies, Dörnyei (forthcoming) has proposed a taxonomy of self-motivating strategies made up of five main classes: commitment control strategies, metacognitive control strategies, satiation control strategies, emotion control strategies, and environmental control strategies. Some of the actual techniques listed under these categories are very similar to the "affective learning strategies" conceptualized by Oxford (1990) and O'Malley and Chamot (1990).

In sum, the study of L2 motivation reached an exciting turning point in the 1990s, with a variety of new models and approaches put forward in the literature, resulting in what Gardner and Tremblay (1994) have called a "motivational renaissance." The pioneers of the field have been joined by a new generation of international scholars, and the scope of motivation research has been extended to cover a variety of related issues. As a result, there is now a colorful mix of approaches to the understanding of L2 motivation, comparable on a smaller scale to the multifaceted motivational arena in psychology. The renewed interest in L2 motivation is at the same time indicative of a more general trend in applied linguistics, whereby an increasing number of scholars combine psychological/psycholinguistic and linguistic approaches in order better to understand the complex mental processes involved in SLA.

9 Individual Differences: Conclusions

An assessment of individual difference research has to portray a mixed picture. First of all, it is difficult to avoid the conclusion that the study of learning and cognitive style is a problematic area. That is not to say that it is without interest, but simply that the promise that the concepts contain has not been fulfilled. There is a need for more than a seductive account of how people differ; it is also important to ground claims in research, and better still, to show how the ideas which may be relevant to educational settings generate reliable and robust findings in such settings. Similarly, the current formulations of learning strategies, while containing pedagogic promise, seem to lack a clear theoretical basis. The classification schemes which have been proposed have pragmatic utility, but do not stand up to serious scrutiny. It appears that the sub-field needs to renew itself by returning to its original roots within psychology and then exploring how self-regulated learning can be facilitated in the context of second and foreign language learning.

The two individual difference areas which show signs of immediate promise and the capacity to generate research programs are aptitude and motivation. The interest with aptitude is that it may now reintegrate itself within mainstream SLA, a move which could be to the benefit of both areas. The crucial development here is that aptitude constructs are being related to acquisitional processes. A theory of aptitude can lead to the exploration of the extent to which putative SLA processes can be linked to differences between learners, for example, in areas such as noticing, or with different types of learning. If such linkages can be established, aptitude will function significantly in a wider range of accounts of SLA success, across a wider range of contexts. This would allow a different perspective on pedagogic application, since it would be feasible to undertake analyses at a more micro-level of research. It is also striking here that this new approach to aptitude is grounded in a more cognitive view of SLA, with connection through constructs such as working memory to mainstream psychology.

The new orientation to the study of motivation shares some of these qualities. This renewal, too, has been partly stimulated by developments in mainstream psychology, which have been more able to capture the fluidity of the operation of motivation. There is also the common factor that a concern for classrooms, as the arena within which such fluidity operates, is central to the revised perspective: action control theory, while incorporating "orientational" approaches to motivation, also treats rather distinctly what is happening inside the classroom. The result may well be that more direct routes to offering practical advice will become available, as effective means of managing motivation and sustaining learning duration and intensity are understood and exploited.

There are also some interesting connections among the individual differences variables covered in this chapter. It is clear that foreign language aptitude and cognitive style have some degree of relationship (see, e.g., Gardner, Tremblay, and Masgoret, 1997). It has been argued (Chapelle and Green, 1992) that this connection is accounted for by the way each draws upon the common underlying factor of intelligence. In slight contrast, Skehan (1998) argues that the connection arises because within aptitude, one can propose an analytic learner type and a memory-oriented learner type. This is related to, but not identical with, the analytic–holistic contrast in the style literature. As indicated above,

Skehan argues that if cognitive style is interpreted as not one continuum but two, this, combined with a style vs. predisposition interpretation, can accommodate, separately, both aptitudinal and style concepts. We also saw above that Schmeck (1988) argues that learning style is connected to learning strategies, in that style relates to consistency of strategy use across contexts.

More interesting, perhaps, is the potential connection between motivation and learning strategies. If one accepts the distinction between pre- and post-decisional stages in the operation of motivational variables, then it may be the case that the operation of learning strategies is, in effect, a subset of action control strategies. In other words, the effective use of learning strategies may be precisely the sort of behavior that causes motivational levels to be sustained within the learning situation (Dörnyei, 2001). Their use may give encouragement to the learner, provide benchmarks for evaluation and progress, and enable motivational goal setting to be accomplished. If strategies are viewed in this way, they may re-emerge within a more elaborated theoretical framework.

NOTES

1 A distinguished applied linguist once said to one of the authors at a conference: "I like your interest in aptitude. But I always feel: aptitude is there, but what can you do with it?" Pimsleur's work is an interesting early approach which begins to answer this question.

2 In many language testing textbooks, it is traditional to consider that there are four test types: aptitude, achievement, proficiency, and diagnostic. The viewpoint taken here is that diagnostic tests are not a separate category, but rather a use that any sort of test may be put to. Pimsleur, in other words, was using aptitude tests diagnostically. The information derived from them, in other words, would be obtained prior to a language course, and therefore could be a design factor for such a course. Aptitude, that is, would give information for pre-emptive course design decisions which would predict learning difficulties to come, *and do something about them.*

REFERENCES

Ajzen, I. 1988: *Attitudes, Personality and Behavior*. Chicago: Dorsey Press.

Ames, C. 1992: Classrooms, goals, structures and student motivation. *Journal of Educational Psychology*, 84, 267–71.

Anderson, J. R. 1983: *The Architecture of Cognition*. Cambridge: Cambridge University Press.

Anderson, J. R. 1985: *Cognitive Psychology and its Implications*. Second edition. New York: Freeman.

Baddeley, A. D. and Logie, R. H. 1999: Working memory: the multiple component model. In A. Miyake and P. Shah (eds), *Models of Working Memory: Mechanisms of Active Maintenance and Executive Control*. Cambridge: Cambridge University Press, 28–62.

Baddeley, A. D., Gathercole, S., and Papagno, C. 1998: The phonological loop as a language learning device. *Psychological Review*, 105, 158–73.

Bandura, A. 1993: Perceived self-efficacy in cognitive development and functioning. *Educational Psychologist*, 28, 117–48.

Barduhn, S. 1998: Factors influencing success on the CELTA initial teacher training course. Ph.D. dissertation. Thames Valley University.

Boekaerts, M., Pintrich, P. R., and Zeidner, M. (eds) 2000: *Handbook on Self-Regulation*. San Diego: Academic Press.

Brophy, J. E. 1999: Toward a model of the value aspects of motivation in education: developing appreciation for particular learning domains and activities. *Educational Psychologist*, 34, 75–85.

Brown, H. D. 1994: *Teaching by Principles*. Englewood Cliffs, NJ: Prentice-Hall.

Carroll, J. B. 1965: The prediction of success in intensive foreign language training. In R. Glaser (ed.), *Training, Research, and Education*. Pittsburgh, PA: University of Pittsburgh Press.

Carroll, J. B. 1973: Implications of aptitude test research and psycholinguistic theory for foreign language teaching. *International Journal of Psycholinguistics*, 2, 5–14.

Carroll, J. B. 1979: Psychometric approaches to the study of language abilities. In C. J. Fillmore, D. Kempler, and W.-S. Y. Wang (eds), *Individual Differences in Language Ability and Language Behavior*. New York: Academic Press, 13–32.

Carroll, J. B. 1981: Twenty-five years of research in foreign language aptitude. In K. C. Diller (ed.), *Individual Differences and Universals in Language Learning Aptitude*. Rowley, MA: Newbury House, 83–118.

Carroll, J. B. 1991: Cognitive abilities in foreign language aptitude: then and now. In T. Parry and C. Stansfield (eds), *Language Aptitude Reconsidered*. Englewood Cliffs, NJ: Prentice-Hall, 11–29.

Carroll, J. B. and Sapon, S. 1959: *The Modern Languages Aptitude Test*. San Antonio, TX: Psychological Corporation.

Chamot, A. U. and Rubin, J. 1994: Comments on Janie Rees-Miller's "A critical appraisal of learner training: theoretical bases and teaching implications." *TESOL Quarterly*, 28, 771–6.

Chapelle, C. 1992: Disembedding "Disembedded figures in the landscape . . .": an appraisal of Griffiths and Sheen's "Reappraisal of L2 research on field dependence/independence." *Applied Linguistics*, 13, 375–84.

Chapelle, C. and Green, P. 1992: Field independence/dependence in second language acquisition research. *Language Learning*, 42, 47–83.

Clément, R. 1980: Ethnicity, contact and communicative competence in a second language. In H. Giles, W. P. Robinson, and P. M. Smith (eds), *Language: Social Psychological Perspectives*. Oxford: Pergamon Press, 147–54.

Clément, R. and Gardner, R. C. 2001: Second language mastery. In W. P. Robinson and H. Giles (eds), *The New Handbook of Language and Social Psychology*. Second edition. New York: John Wiley, 489–504.

Clément, R., Dörnyei, Z., and Noels, K. A. 1994: Motivation, self-confidence and group cohesion in the foreign language classroom. *Language Learning*, 44, 417–48.

Cohen, A. D. 1998: *Strategies in Learning and Using a Second Language*. Harlow: Longman.

Corno, L. and Kanfer, R. 1993: The role of volition in learning and performance. *Review of Research in Education*, 19, 301–41.

Covington, M. 1998: *The Will to Learn*. Cambridge: Cambridge University Press.

Cronbach, L. 1970: *Essentials of Psychological Testing*. Third edition. New York: Harper and Row.

Crookes, G. and Schmidt, R. W. 1991: Motivation: reopening the research agenda. *Language Learning*, 41, 469–512.

Deci, E. L. and Ryan, R. M. 1985: *Intrinsic Motivation and Self-Determination in Human Behavior*. New York: Plenum.

DeGraaf, R. 1997: *Differential Effects of Explicit Instruction on Second Language Acquisition*. The Hague: Holland Institute of Generative Linguistics.

DeKeyser, R. 2000: The robustness of critical period effects in second language acquisition. *Studies in Second Language Acquisition*, 22 (4), 493–533.

Dewaele, J.-M. and Furnham, A. 1999: Extraversion: the unloved variable in applied linguistic research. *Language Learning*, 43 (3), 509–44.

Dörnyei, Z. 1994: Motivation and motivating in the foreign language classroom. *Modern Language Journal*, 78, 273–84.

Dörnyei, Z. 1998: Motivation in second and foreign language learning. *Language Teaching*, 31, 117–35.

Dörnyei, Z. 2000: Motivation in action: towards a process-oriented conceptualisation of student motivation. *British Journal of Educational Psychology*, 70, 519–38.

Dörnyei, Z. 2001: *Teaching and Researching Motivation*. Harlow: Longman.

Dörnyei, Z. forthcoming: *Motivational Strategies: Creating and Maintaining Student Motivation in the Foreign Language Classroom*. Cambridge: Cambridge University Press.

Dörnyei, Z. and Kormos, J. forthcoming: The role of individual and social variables in oral task performance. *Language Teaching Research*.

Dörnyei, Z. and Ottó, I. 1998: Motivation in action: a process model of L2 motivation. *Working Papers in Applied Linguistics (Thames Valley University, London)*, 4, 43–69.

Doughty, C. 2001: Cognitive underpinnings of focus on form. In P. Robinson (ed.), *Cognition and Second Language Instruction*. New York: Cambridge University Press, 206–57.

Doughty, C. and Williams, J. 1998: *Focus on Form in Classroom Second Language Acquisition*. New York: Cambridge University Press.

Eagly, A. H. and Chaiken, S. 1993: *The Psychology of Attitudes*. New York: Harcourt Brace.

Ehrman, M. E. 1996: *Understanding Second Language Difficulties*. Thousand Oaks, CA: Sage.

Ellis, R. 1994: *The Study of Second Language Acquisition*. Oxford: Oxford University Press.

Gardner, R. C. 1985: *Social Psychology and Second Language Learning: The Role of Attitudes and Motivation*. London: Edward Arnold.

Gardner, R. C. and Lambert, W. E. 1972: *Attitudes and Motivation in Second Language Learning*. Rowley, MA: Newbury House.

Gardner, R. C. and MacIntyre, P. D. 1993: A student's contributions to second-language learning. Part II: Affective variables. *Language Teaching*, 26, 1–11.

Gardner, R. C. and Tremblay, P. F. 1994: On motivation, research agendas, and theoretical frameworks. *Modern Language Journal*, 78, 359–68.

Gardner, R. C., Tremblay, P. F., and Masgoret, A.-M. 1997: Towards a full model of second language learning: an empirical investigation. *Modern Language Journal*, 81, 344–62.

Gathercole, S. and Baddeley, A. 1993: *Working Memory and Language*. Hillsdale, NJ: Lawrence Erlbaum Associates.

Graham, S. 1994: Classroom motivation from an attributional perspective. In H. F. O'Neil, Jr, and M. Drillings (eds), *Motivation: Theory and Research*. Hillsdale, NJ: Lawrence Erlbaum Associates, 31–48.

Griffiths, R. and Sheen, R. 1992: Disembedded figures in the landscape: a reappraisal of L2 research on field dependence/independence. *Applied Linguistics*, 13, 133–48.

Grigorenko, E. L. 2002: Language-based learning disabilities. In P. Robinson (ed.), *Individual Differences and Instructed Language Learning*. Amsterdam and Philadelphia: John Benjamins, 95–113.

Grigorenko, E., Sternberg, R. J., and Ehrman, M. 2000: A theory based approach to the measurement of foreign language learning ability: the Canal-F theory and test. *Modern Language Journal*, 84 (3), 390–405.

Harley, B. and Hart, D. 1997: Language aptitude and second language proficiency in classroom learners of different starting ages. *Studies in Second Language Acquisition*, 19 (3), 379–400.

Hayes, J. and Allinson, C. W. 1996: The implications of learning styles for training and development: a discussion of the matching hypothesis. *British Journal of Management*, 7, 63–73.

Healey, M. 1999: Learning cycles and learning styles: Kolb's experiential learning theory and its application in geography in higher education. Available from /www.chelt.ac.uk/

Heckhausen, H. 1991: *Motivation and Action*. New York: Springer.

Honey, P. and Mumford, A. 1986: *Using your Learning Styles*. Maidenhead: Peter Honey.

Honey, P. and Mumford, A. 1992: *The Manual of Learning Styles*. Maidenhead: Peter Honey.

Johnson, J. S. and Newport, E. 1989: Critical period effects in second language learning: the influence of maturational state on the acquisition of English as a second language. *Cognitive Psychology*, 21, 60–99.

Johnson, J. S. and Newport, E. 1991: Critical period effects on universal properties of language: the status of subjacency in the acquisition of a second language. *Cognition*, 39, 215–58.

Julkunen, K. 1993: On foreign language learning motivation in the classroom. In S. Tella (ed.), *Kielestä mieltä – Mielekästä kieltä*. Helsinki: University of Helsinki, Teacher Education Department, 70–8.

Keefe, J. W. and Ferrell, B. G. 1990: Developing a defensible learning style paradigm. *Educational Leadership*, 48 (2), 57–61.

Kirby, J. R. 1988: Style, strategy, and skill in reading. In R. R. Schmeck (ed.), *Learning Strategies and Learning Styles*. New York: Plenum, 3–19.

Kolb, D. A. 1984. *Learning Style Inventory*. Revised edition. Boston, MA: McBer.

Krashen, S. 1981: Aptitude and attitude in relation to second language acquisition and learning. In K. C. Diller (ed.), *Individual Differences and Universals in Language Learning Aptitude*. Rowley, MA: Newbury House, 155–75.

Kuhl, J. 1987: Action control: the maintenance of motivational states. In F. Halish and J. Kuhl (eds), *Motivation,*

Intention and Volition. Berlin: Springer, 279–91.

Kuhl, J. and Beckmann, J. (eds) 1994: *Volition and Personality: Action versus State Orientation*. Seattle, WA: Hogrefe and Huber.

Locke, E. A. and Latham, G. P. 1990: *A Theory of Goal Setting and Task Performance*. Englewood Cliffs, NJ: Prentice-Hall.

MacIntyre, P. D. 1994: Toward a social psychological model of strategy use. *Foreign Language Annals*, 27, 185–95.

MacIntyre, P. D. and Noels, K. A. 1996: Using social-psychological variables to predict the use of language learning strategies. *Foreign Language Annals*, 29, 373–86.

MacIntyre, P. D., Babin, P. A., and Clément, R. 1999: Willingness to communicate: antecedents and consequences. *Communication Quarterly*, 47, 215–29.

MacIntyre, P. D., Clément, R., Dörnyei, Z., and Noels, K. A. 1998: Conceptualizing willingness to communicate in a L2: a situated model of confidence and affiliation. *Modern Language Journal*, 82, 545–62.

McCroskey, J. C. and Richmond, V. P. 1991: Willingness to communicate: a cognitive view. In M. Booth-Butterfield (ed.), *Communication, Cognition and Anxiety*. Newbury Park, CA: Sage, 19–37.

Miyake, A. and Friedman, D. 1998: Individual differences in second language proficiency: working memory as language aptitude. In A. Healy and L. Bourne (eds), *Foreign Language Learning: Psycholinguistic Studies on Training and Retention*. Mahwah, NJ: Lawrence Erlbaum Associates.

Naiman, N., Fröhlich, M., Stern, H., and Todesco, A. 1978: *The Good Language Learner*. Toronto: Ontario Institute for Studies in Education.

Noels, K. A. 2001: New orientations in language learning motivation: toward a contextual model of intrinsic, extrinsic, and integrative orientations and motivation. In Z. Dörnyei and R. Schmidt (eds), *Motivation and Second Language Acquisition*. Honolulu: University of Hawai'i, Second Language Teaching and Curriculum Center, 43–68.

Noels, K. A., Clément, R., and Pelletier, L. G. 1999: Perceptions of teachers' communicative style and students' intrinsic and extrinsic motivation. *Modern Language Journal*, 83, 23–34.

Noels, K. A., Pelletier, L. G., Clément, R., and Vallerand, R. J. 2000: Why are you learning a second language? Motivational orientations and self-determination theory. *Language Learning*, 50, 57–85.

Nyikos, M. 1996: The conceptual shift to learner-centred classrooms: increasing teacher and student strategic awareness. In R. L. Oxford (ed.), *Language Learning Strategies around the World: Cross-Cultural Perspectives*. Honolulu: University of Hawai'i Press, 109–17.

O'Malley, J. M. and Chamot, A. U. 1990: *Learning Strategies in Second Language Acquisition*. New York: Cambridge University Press.

O'Malley, J. M. and Chamot, A. U. 1994: Learning strategies in second language learning. In *The International Encyclopedia of Education. Vol. 6*. Oxford: Pergamon Press, 3329–35.

Oxford, R. L. 1989: Use of language learning strategies: a synthesis of studies with implications for strategy training. *System*, 17, 235–47.

Oxford, R. L. 1990: *Language Learning Strategies: What Every Teacher Should Know*. Boston, MA: Heinle and Heinle.

Oxford, R. L. (ed.) 1996: *Language Learning Motivation: Pathways to the New Century*. Honolulu: University of Hawai'i Press.

Oxford, R. L. and Anderson, N. J. 1995: A crosscultural view of learning styles. *Language Teaching*, 28, 201–15.

Oxford, R. L. and Shearin, J. 1994: Language learning motivation: expanding the theoretical framework. *Modern Language Journal*, 78, 12–28.

Parry, T. S. and Child, J. R. 1990: Preliminary investigation of the relationship between VORD, MLAT, and language proficiency. In T. S. Parry and C. W. Stansfield (eds), *Language Aptitude Reconsidered*. Washington, DC: Center for Applied Linguistics, 30–66.

Pawley, A. and Syder, F. 1983: Two puzzles for linguistic theory: nativelike selection and nativelike fluency. In J. C. Richards and R. Schmidt (eds), *Language and Communication*. London: Longman, 191–227.

Petersen, C. and Al-Haik, A. 1976: The development of the Defense Language Aptitude Battery. *Educational and Psychological Measurement*, 36, 369–80.

Pimsleur, P. 1966: *The Pimsleur Language Aptitude Battery*. New York: Harcourt, Brace, Jovanovic.

Rees-Miller, J. 1993: A critical appraisal of learner training: theoretical bases and teaching implications. *TESOL Quarterly*, 27, 679–89.

Rees-Miller, J. 1994: The author responds . . . *TESOL Quarterly*, 28, 776–81.

Reid, J. M. (ed.) 1995: *Learning Styles in the ESL/EFL Classroom*. Boston, MA: Heinle and Heinle.

Reves, T. 1983: What makes a good language learner? Ph.D. dissertation. Hebrew University.

Riding, R. 1991: *Cognitive Styles Analysis*. Birmingham: Learning and Training Technology.

Riding, R. and Cheema, I. 1991: Cognitive styles – an overview and integration. *Educational Psychology*, 11, 193–215.

Robinson, P. 1995: Learning simple and complex rules under implicit, incidental, rule-search, and instructed conditions. *Studies in Second Language Acquisition*, 18, 27–67.

Robotham, D. 1999: The application of learning style theory in higher education teaching. Available at /www.chelt.ac.uk/

Rubin, J. 1975: What the "Good Language Learner" can teach us. *TESOL Quarterly*, 9, 41–51.

Sasaki, M. 1996: *Second Language Proficiency, Foreign Language Aptitude, and Intelligence*. New York: Peter Lang.

Sawyer, M. and Ranta, L. 2001: Aptitude, individual differences, and instructional design. In P. Robinson (ed.), *Cognition and Second Language Acquisition*. New York: Cambridge University Press, 319–53.

Schmeck, R. R. 1988: An introduction to strategies and styles of learning. In R. R. Schmeck (ed.), *Learning Strategies and Learning Styles*. New York: Plenum, 3–19.

Schmidt, R. 1990: The role of consciousness in second language learning. *Applied Linguistics*, 11, 129–58.

Schmidt, R. 1994: Deconstructing consciousness: in search of useful definitions for applied linguistics. *AILA Review*, 11, 11–26.

Schmidt, R. 2001: Attention. In P. Robinson (ed.), *Cognition and Second Language Acquisition*. New York: Cambridge University Press, 3–32.

Schmidt, R. and Frota, S. 1986: Developing basic conversational ability in a second language: a case study of an adult learner of Portuguese. In R. Day (ed.), *Talking to Learn*. Rowley, MA: Newbury House, 237–326.

Schmidt, R., Boraie, D., and Kassagby, O. 1996: Foreign language motivation: internal structure and external connections. In R. Oxford (ed.), *Language Learning Motivation: Pathways to the New Century*. Honolulu: University of Hawai'i Press, 9–70.

Schumann, J. H. 1997: *The Neurobiology of Affect in Language*. Blackwell, Oxford.

Schumann, J. H. 2001: Learning as foraging. In Z. Dörnyei and R. Schmidt (eds), *Motivation and Second Language Acquisition*. Honolulu: University of Hawai'i, Second Language Teaching and Curriculum Center, 21–8.

Skehan, P. 1986: Cluster analysis and the identification of learner types. In V. Cook (ed.), *Experimental Approaches to Second Language Acquisition*. Oxford: Pergamon Press, 81–94.

Skehan, P. 1989: *Individual Differences in Second Language Learning*. London: Edward Arnold.

Skehan, P. 1991: Individual differences in second language learning. *Studies in Second Language Acquisition*, 13, 275–98.

Skehan, P. 1998: *A Cognitive Approach to Language Learning*. Oxford: Oxford University Press.

Stern, H. H. 1975: What can we learn from the good language learner? *Canadian Modern Language Review*, 31, 304–18.

Sternberg, R. forthcoming: The theory of successful intelligence and its implications for language aptitude testing. *Journal of Contemporary Psychology*.

Stipek, D. J. 1996: Motivation and instruction. In D. C. Berliner and R. C. Calfee (eds), *Handbook of Educational Psychology*. New York: Macmillan, 85–113.

Tarone, E. 1981: Some thoughts on the notion of "communication strategy." *TESOL Quarterly*, 15, 285–95.

Tremblay, P. F. and Gardner, R. C. 1995: Expanding the motivation construct in language learning. *Modern Language Journal*, 79, 505–20.

Ushioda, E. 1994: L2 motivation as a qualitative construct. *Teanga*, 14, 76–84.

Ushioda, E. 1996: Developing a dynamic concept of motivation. In T. Hickey and J. Williams (eds), *Language, Education and Society in a Changing World*. Clevedon: Multilingual Matters, 239–45.

Ushioda, E. 2001: Language learning at university: exploring the role of motivational thinking. In Z. Dörnyei and R. Schmidt (eds), *Motivation and Second Language Acquisition*. Honolulu: University of Hawai'i, Second Language Teaching and Curriculum Center, 91–124.

Vallerand, R. J. 1997: Toward a hierarchical model of intrinsic and extrinsic motivation. *Advances in Experimental Social Psychology*, 29, 271–360.

VanPatten, B. 1996: *Input Processing and Grammar Instruction*. New York: Ablex.

Walter, C. 2000: The involvement of working memory in reading in a foreign language. Ph.D. dissertation. University of Cambridge.

Weiner, B. 1984: Principles for a theory of student motivation and their application within an attributional framework. In R. Ames and C. Ames (eds), *Research on Motivation in Education: Student Motivation. Vol. 1*. San Diego: Academic Press, 15–38.

Weiner, B. 1992: *Human Motivation: Metaphors, Theories and Research*. Newbury Park, CA: Sage.

Weinstein, C. E. and Meyer, D. K. 1994: Learning strategies: teaching and testing for. In T. Husén and T. N. Postlethwaite (eds), *The International Encyclopedia of Education*. Oxford: Pergamon Press, 3335–40.

Wenden, A. 1991: *Learner Strategies for Learner Autonomy*. Hemel Hempstead: Prentice-Hall.

Wenden, A. and Rubin, J. 1987: *Learner Strategies in Language Learning*. Hemel Hempstead: Prentice-Hall.

Wesche, M. 1981: Language aptitude measures in streaming, matching students with methods, and diagnosis of learning problems. In K. C. Diller (ed.), *Individual Differences and Universals in Language Learning Aptitude*. Rowley, MA: Newbury House, 119–54.

Wigfield, A. 1994: Expectancy-value theory of achievement motivation: a developmental perspective. *Educational Psychology Review*, 6, 49–78.

Williams, M. 1994: Motivation in foreign and second language learning: an interactive perspective. *Educational and Child Psychology*, 11, 77–84.

Winne, P. H. 1995: Inherent details in self-regulated learning. *Educational Psychologist*, 30, 173–87.

Witkin, H. 1962: *Psychological Differentiation*. New York: John Wiley.

Witkin, H. and Goodenough, D. 1981: *Cognitive Styles: Essence and Origin*. Psychological Issues Monograph 51. New York: International Universities Press.

Wong Fillmore, L. 1979: Individual differences in second language acquisition. In C. J. Fillmore, W.-S. Y. Wang and D. Kempler (eds), *Individual Differences in Language Ability and Language Behavior*. New York: Academic Press, 203–28.

Zimmerman, B. J. and Risemberg, R. 1997: Self-regulatory dimensions of academic learning and motivation. In G. D. Phye (ed.), *Handbook of Academic Learning*. San Diego: Academic Press, 105–25.

19 Attention and Memory during SLA

PETER ROBINSON

1 Introduction and Overview

Attention to and subsequent memory for attended language input are both essential for SLA, and are intricately related. Attention is the process that encodes language input, keeps it active in working and short-term memory, and retrieves it from long-term memory. Attention and memory structures can be viewed hierarchically. The focus of attention is a subset of short-term memory, and short-term memory is that part of long-term memory in a currently heightened state of activation. Long-term memory is where instances of encoded input are stored and assume (or confirm, in some innatist theories of SLA) the representational shape that recognition processes match to new instances of input in working memory during parsing and comprehension. These representations also form the basis of speech production "plans," which guide retrieval processes during grammatical and phonological encoding, and articulation of a message. Attention, then, can be viewed as a process for which memory provides structure and constraint.

Research into attention and memory during SLA has begun to accumulate in the last decade or so, addressing such issues as the following: what levels of attention and awareness are necessary for encoding L2 input in short-term working memory? What is the nature of the encoding, rehearsal, and retrieval processes that operate on attended input? How do L2 task demands affect the allocation of memory and attention? And is memory simply functionally differentiated, or also neurophysiologically differentiated, reflecting the operation of distinct learning and memory systems? Many of these issues also dominate recent debate in cognitive psychology concerned with distinctions between implicit, incidental, explicit, and intentional learning – issues that are discussed elsewhere in this volume, but not in any detail here (see Ellis, DeKeyser, and Hulstijn, this volume). Research into attention and memory during SLA is relevant to a transition theory (see Gregg, 2001, this volume) of the cognitive mechanisms that move L2 knowledge from point A to point B, and so has largely been concerned with specifying the universal cognitive architecture of attention and memory during learning. A transition theory predicates a property theory (how knowledge at points A and B is represented) and specifies mechanisms which can be activated by attentional processes and memory structures (spreading activation, parameter resetting, cue strengthening, etc.) that give knowledge at point B representational shape (see Ellis, O'Grady, and White, this volume, for substantive discussion of options in SLA property theories).

Arising, in part, out of interest in the architecture of attention and memory during SLA is resurgent interest in the implications of individual differences in attentional and memory resources. Issues this research addresses include the following: do individual differences in L2 working memory capacity affect skill development? Can the influence of age differences on SLA be explained by developmentally regulated changes in attentional and memory resources? Do individual differences in resource availability affect explicit but not implicit learning? And how are differences in attentional and memory resources related to language learning aptitude?

Attention and memory can be studied and measured at various levels, including ecological/adaptive (Reed, 1996), cognitive/information-processing (Sanders, 1998), and neurophysiological/biochemical (Carter, 1998; Posner and Petersen, 1990). This chapter presents a cognitive-level characterization of attention and memory that describes the information-processing operations and stages mediating stimulus input and response selection. This raises issues of both learning – the attentional and memory processes responsible for the acquisition of new and the restructuring of existing representations – and performance – the skilled deployment of existing knowledge to achieve task goals. Comprehensive accounts of human cognition view a theory of learning as embedded within, and commensurate with, a theory of action (Allport, 1987; Clark, 1997; Hazelhurst and Hutchins, 1998; Korteling, 1994; Shallice, 1978; Thelen and Smith, 1994), which describes how attentional and memory resources are drawn on in task and context analysis, and during adaptive responses to both. Consequently, I will describe the role of attention and memory in selection and maintenance of new information in memory (see also Schmidt, 1995, 2001; Tomlin and Villa, 1994, for reviews of this area), as well as in control of action, and sustained attention to the goals of action – areas where there has been less theoretical discussion of the role of cognitive factors in SLA research.

In what follows I focus on the interrelated areas of attention and memory separately, describing current theoretical issues and models of each, then summarizing research that has examined the influence of these cognitive factors on SLA, using a variety of methodologies.

2 Attention

2.1 *Overview*

Three general stages of information processing at which attention operates are captured in figure 19.1. The stages correspond broadly to three current themes in attentional research and theory (Sanders, 1998; Sanders and Neumann, 1996; Sergeant, 1996); (i) auditory and visual information intake and processing; (ii) central control and decision-making functions, such as allocation of attention to competing task demands, and automatization; and (iii) response execution and monitoring via sustained attention. These three themes and stages also correspond to three uses of the concept of attention; to describe selection of information (we pay attention to things as a way of selecting them for further processing); to describe the capacity of attentional resources (sometimes we are able to pay a lot of attention to a task, while at other times we are not); and to describe the effort involved in sustaining attention to task goals (we can maintain the level of attention we pay to a task, or attention and performance can decline over time). These are distinct but related uses of the concept of attention; each one related to separate functions, which, however, often operate in conjunction with each other.

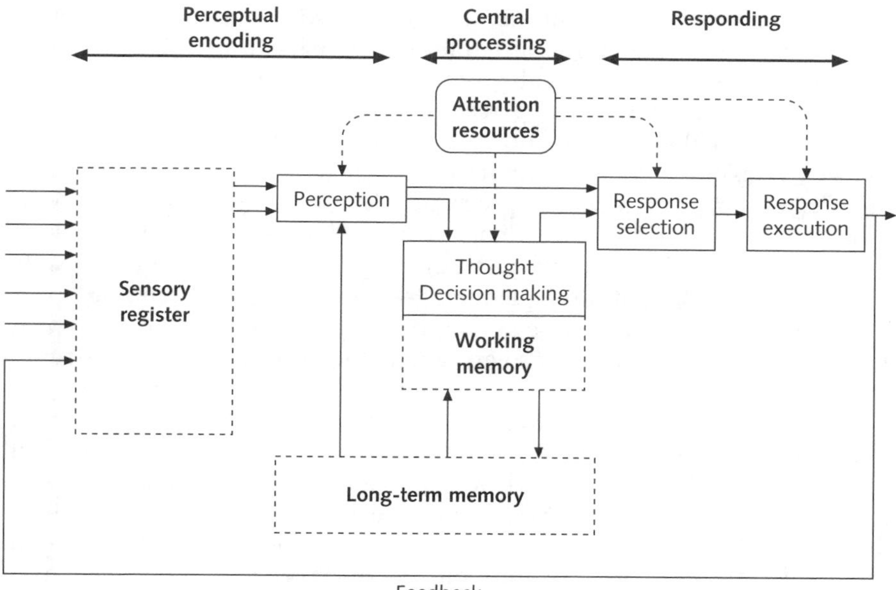

Figure 19.1 A generic model of human information processing with three memory systems

Source: Wickens, Gordon, and Liu (1997, p. 147)

2.2 Attention as selection

Learning and performance both involve selection and subsequent encoding of information available in the environment. A traditional distinction in SLA theory is between linguistic "input" to the learner and "intake" or mental registration of the input (Corder, 1967). Recent SLA research and theory have examined the role of attention in mediating this process by studying, for example, the level of attention needed for selecting input for processing (S. Carroll, 1999; Chaudron, 1985; Gass, 1988, 1997; Leow, 1993; Tomlin and Villa, 1994); whether pedagogic intervention can facilitate switches of attention from meaning to aspects of the (syntactic, morphological phonological, semantic, and pragmatic) form of input which otherwise may lack saliency for learners and so remain unattended to during communication (Doughty, 2001; Doughty and Williams, 1998; Long, 1996); and what, if any, level of awareness must accompany or follow the selection process if intake is to be permanently registered in memory (Philp, 1998; Schmidt, 1990, 1995, 2001; Sharwood-Smith, 1981, 1991). Three important theoretical issues are: (i) when and how does selection of information happen; (ii) why is information selectively attended for further processing; and (iii) what mechanisms guide the selection process?

2.2.1 *When and how does selection happen?*

As figure 19.1 shows, during the first stage of information processing preattentively processed sensory information is detected and held temporarily in the sensory register, where it is selected for perceptual encoding by attentional mechanisms. Auditory and visual processing dominated early research into the role of selective attention in perception, and two issues largely divided early theories; whether the attention allocated to information selection from the sensory register is limited or unlimited in capacity, and whether information is selected early or late during processing. These issues concern the "why" and the "when" of selection. Broadbent (1958, 1971) assumed that attentional capacity is limited and that therefore auditory and visual information must be channeled and specific stimuli sequentially selected early, via a filtering operation, for further processing. These assumptions appeared necessary to explain findings such as the following: answering two different questions that overlap temporally interferes with performance, but prior knowledge that one question will be irrelevant enables it to be screened out, or inhibited, thereby facilitating performance on the relevant question, which receives subsequent full semantic analysis. Selection, that is, was viewed as a functional consequence of limited attentional capacity (Neumann, 1996, p. 395) and was thought to be made early on the basis of a partial analysis of specific features of the input. Once widely accepted, these assumptions were challenged by evidence from both letter discrimination tasks (Sperling, 1960) and dichotic listening tasks, in which different messages are presented simultaneously in each ear (Treisman, 1971), which showed that multiple sources of information can be processed in parallel (messages presented in either ear, all letters presented briefly in a visual display), and that selection of any one may be late, and based on full semantic, not partial feature analysis. Late selection theories, consequently, argue selection takes place in working memory after stimuli have been fully analyzed (Allport, 1987).

2.2.2 *Why does selection happen?*

If many inputs can be processed in parallel, and the attention available to the sensory register and the central processor is potentially unlimited, then Broadbent's main reason for proposing the "when" (early) and "how" (a filter) of selection disappears. Why then is information selected if it is not a functional response to capacity limitations? It is as well to separate answers to this question that are principally concerned with the broader issue of general information processing, efficiency, and performance from those that are principally concerned with information specific to language learning, representational change, and competence. The performance argument made variously by Allport (1987, 1989), Korteling (1994), Neumann (1987, 1996), and van der Heijden (1992) is that selection serves as a means of action control rather than as a response to capacity limitations. Actions are responses to task demands, and allocation of attention to input with the goal of meeting these demands is the result of control processes, operationalized in short-term/working memory. Selection of input relevant to the dominant action also serves the important function of inhibiting and suppressing perception of the many other stimuli which are detected and held in the sensory register, and which may be called for by alternative, contradictory speech and action plans (Faust and Gernsbacher, 1996; Neely, 1977; Shallice, 1972, 1978; Tipper, 1992). Thus, the requirement for coherent speech and action, and continued adherence to a plan, not scarcity of resources, forces selective perception and thought.

2.2.3 *What guides selection of L2 input?*

Carroll has recently argued that in SLA theory "the idea of attention as a selection function cannot be maintained" (S. Carroll, 1999, p. 343). Clearly it cannot be maintained as an *autonomous function*. Input is detected (via peripheral attention) and stored in the sensory register, then selected (via focal attention) from the stimulus array. But selection is at the same time a response to *control processes* such as attention allocation policy, scheduling and switching between concurrent task demands, and strategy monitoring. Selection of linguistic input is therefore just one aspect of action control, guided by the supervisory attentional system, and executive control mechanisms. There are a number of accounts of these control mechanisms in cognitive psychology, which can be broadly grouped into three categories: those involved in task analysis, in selection and control of the cognitive and metacognitive strategies for performing the task, and in monitoring the effectiveness of strategies (see Baddeley, 1986; Butterfield and Albertson, 1995; Case, 1992; Eslinger, 1996; Sternberg, 1985).

SLA theories diverge, as S. Carroll (1999) points out, on the role of control processes in guiding selection of input for language learning, and the mechanisms and parsing procedures available to them (see Harrington, 2001). In some views, selection is guided by innate representations of abstract phonetic and grammatical knowledge, which enable auditory cues in the input to be detected, analyzed, categorized, and parsed. Compatible with these views are models of L1 and L2 speech perception and word recognition that propose a categorical process of phoneme identification, drawing on knowledge of universal phonological "features" (Liberman and Mattingly, 1989) upon which L1 phonetic categories are based, and which may interfere with L2 speech perception (Flege and Munro, 1994). Such non-semantic representations may be modularly encapsulated (Fodor, 1983; Schwartz, 1999), distinct from (but interfaced with) the conceptual system (Jackendoff, 1997; White, this volume) or not (O'Grady, this volume), and activated early, automatically, and involuntarily. But automatic activation still requires attention (Boronat and Logan, 1997; Holender, 1986; Hsiao and Reber, 1998; Logan, 1990; Mulligan, 1997).

Alternatively, constructivist accounts of SLA argue no modular, encapsulated knowledge is available to guide language development, and recognition and selection of input. Compatible with these views are models of speech perception that propose a non-categorical, continuous process of pattern recognition, which is non-specialized (Massaro, 1987). Some argue that knowledge of language emerges out of an automatic distributional analysis of co-occurring features of the input (Broeder and Plunket, 1994; N. Ellis and Schmidt, 1997; Elman, 1990; Gasser, 1990; Gasser and Smith, 1998), contributing to chunk strength and knowledge of sequencing constraints (N. Ellis, 2001, this volume), represented as a pattern of associations over neurons, and that this occurs late during full semantic processing. In MacWhinney's Competition Model (1987, 2001) this distributional analysis is guided by selective attention to cues in the input (e.g., word order, case marking) which enable form–function relations to be mapped during L2 message comprehension. While they disagree on issues of whether speech perception is a specialized/categorical or general/continuous process of pattern recognition, and whether representations of language properties are modular and encapsulated or not, and innate rather than emergent, all agree that selection of detected auditory input happens (whether early or late), and that attention is required for it to happen, but that it need not (but very often does) implicate awareness (N. Ellis, 2001; Hsiao and Reber, 1998; Schmidt, 1990, 1995, 2001; Tomlin and Villa, 1994). Issues of the relation between detection, selection, and awareness during L2 learning are taken up again below in reporting findings from SLA research.

2.3 SLA research into attention as selection

2.3.1 Input, intake, and awareness

The role of attention, and awareness, in selecting input as intake for L2 learning has been a controversial issue in SLA theory for some time. Krashen (1985,

1994) has argued that adult learners have access back to the "unconscious" processes and innate mechanisms that guide L1 "acquisition," and that conscious "learning" is minimally influential on the ability to learn and use an L2 in communication. However, Schmidt (1990) argues that the critical notion of "unconscious" is inadequately described in Krashen's work, and can be used to describe three different things: learning without intention (unconscious learning is possible in this sense, since we can learn without intending to); learning without explicit metalinguistic knowledge (unconscious learning is possible in this sense, since nobody has metalinguistic knowledge of all the rules of their L2); and learning without awareness. It is in this last sense that learning must be conscious, Schmidt argues, since we must pay attention to input and also have the momentary subjective experience of "noticing" it, if we are to subsequently learn. Schmidt argues that a higher level of awareness than noticing, rule understanding, is not necessary for learning, but can be facilitative. Schmidt's "noticing" hypothesis has been the focus of recent debate. Two broad theoretical objections have been raised to it. It has been claimed that attention without awareness can lead to learning (Tomlin and Villa, 1994), and also that the noticing hypothesis is pre-theoretic, since it does not specify what properties of input are available for noticing and learning (S. Carroll, 1999). A third objection is methodological (Truscott, 1998): it has been argued the noticing hypothesis is unfalsifiable given the difficulties of precisely measuring awareness.

First, Tomlin and Villa (1994) argue "detection," not selection accompanied by noticing, is the attentional level at which SLA must operate, since detected information can be registered in memory, and dissociated from awareness. Experiments by Marcel (1983) appear to show this. In these experiments rapidly presented words which subjects cannot report awareness of, such as "doctor," prime and so speed the time taken for reading subsequent words, such as "nurse," to which they are semantically related, but do not prime others, such as "balloon," which consequently are read more slowly. As Schmidt (1995) has pointed out, however, these findings do not address the issue of "learning," or new memory for input, since subjects already know the priming and primed words. Such studies are evidence only of automatic, unaware, activation of existing knowledge that Schmidt does not deny could occur. In fact it must occur, as I make clear below.

While detection is clearly necessary for further processing of novel stimuli, Schmidt argues only that the subset of detected information that is selected via focal attention can be "noticed," and that this is the attentional level at which input becomes "intake" for learning. I have argued (Robinson, 1995b) that memory processes, such as maintenance and elaborative rehearsal, which allocation of focal attention activates, are coresponsible for noticing and the durability and extent of awareness that noticing is accompanied by. These relationships are illustrated in figure 19.4 below and are discussed more fully in the following section on memory in SLA. Importantly, however, as described previously, while focal attention and noticing are selective of input, they are also *inhibitory* of the much larger set of detected information, and suppress perception of it in the interests of maintaining continuity of action and preventing interference. Thus detection is necessary as a stage prior to intake, but cannot be coextensive with it. Yet on occasions, *involuntary* switches of focal attention do occur (Naatanan, 1992; Posner, 1980) when automatic activation of existing knowledge calls for them (e.g., when you pause in conversation because you notice a burning smell coming from the kitchen), or when an assumed regularity in the input (based on an internal model of, e.g., word order, pronunciation, or morphological affixation) is seemingly randomly violated (Prinz, 1986). Speech and other plans are important to maintain, but must be interruptible. These issues are important to understanding the role of attention during incidental learning and the rationale for "focus on form" described below, which aims to facilitate switches of attention from meaning to form during communication.

A second objection, made by S. Carroll (1999) and Truscott (1998), is that the noticing hypothesis is representationally empty, or pre-theoretic regarding properties of the input signal that "trigger" noticing. While a property theory is essential to a theory of SLA, these are not valid objections to the noticing hypothesis per se, which is not a comprehensive theory, and was not proposed as one. Schmidt describes what must be noticed as "elements of the surface structure of utterances in the input, instances of language, rather than any abstract rules or principles of which such instances may be exemplars" (2001, p. 5). Comments that "we do not notice and are not consciously aware of the properties or categories of our own mental representations of the signal . . . we do not notice and have no awareness of the internal organization of aspects of logical form or scope" (S. Carroll, 1999, pp. 354, 356) are thus irrelevant to the noticing hypothesis as stated. These two objections are linked, of course. If innate representational knowledge of the shape of possible grammars is accessible in adulthood, then positive evidence of the L2, detected outside of awareness, could prime and automatically activate it, as in Marcel's experiments described above, triggering learning mechanisms such as parameter resetting. Schmidt's noticing hypothesis stands as a simple challenge to these "Minimalist" accounts of the role of attention and awareness in SLA.

The third objection to the noticing hypothesis – the difficulty of measuring awareness precisely – cuts both ways: any counter-claim that learning is possible without the momentary subjective experience of awareness must also demonstrate its absence. Schmidt (1990) operationally defined "noticing" as the availability for verbal report. Admittedly, this raises complicated methodological and interpretive issues, since the contents of awareness are sensitive to, but not always coextensive with, what can be reported, given that awareness may be momentary and fleeting, that subjects differ in their propensity and ability to verbalize, and that some things that are noticed are easier to put into words than others (Faerch and Kasper, 1987; Jourdenais, 2001; Kasper, 1999; Schmidt, 1995, 2001; Shanks and St John, 1994). For this reason, recognition measures of awareness, such as those adopted in implicit memory studies (e.g., preference rating, word fragment completion tests; for discussion see Richardson-Klavehn and Bjork, 1988; Robinson, 1995b, 1996a) may be more sensitive measures than those requiring on- or off-line production and verbalization of the contents of awareness. Given this caveat, however, results of a number of recent studies using verbal reports as data appear to support Schmidt's hypothesis.

2.3.2 *Operationalizing "noticing"*

Methodologies for studying the role of awareness and noticing in learning (in a variety of linguistic domains, across a variety of L2s) have included both *off-line* verbal report measures, such as diary entries, questionnaire responses, and immediate and delayed retrospection, and *on-line* measures such as protocols. Schmidt (Schmidt and Frota, 1986) found that diary entries describing aspects of L2 input (Portuguese) that he noticed in the input corresponded strongly with the subsequent appearance of these features in his production during interaction with a native speaker in planned, monthly conversations.

Robinson (1996a, 1997a) found that written questionnaire responses asking participants exposed to L2 input in an immediately prior experiment if they had searched for rules, and could say what the rules were, correlated positively and significantly with learning in an implicit (memorize examples) learning condition, and that ability to verbalize rules correlated positively and significantly with learning in a condition where participants were instructed to try and find rules during exposure to the input. In both conditions, positive correlations of language learning aptitude and awareness suggest that this is an ability variable that can trigger awareness at the levels of noticing, rule search, and verbalization.

Kim (1995) used immediate off-line retrospective verbal reports to examine the relationship between phonological awareness and L2 listening comprehension (measured as the ability to correctly match a picture to one of 30 aurally delivered texts). Finding slow speech rate resulted in greater comprehension than normal speech rate, Kim established a tentative implicational hierarchy of phonological awareness based on verbal reports of those clues in the speech stream learners attended to in arriving at answers to the comprehension questions: perception of key words > of phrases > of clauses > and of conjoined clauses. Coding learners based on this hierarchy, however, failed to distinguish level of awareness of learners exposed to slow vs. normal speech, though there was a trend to higher levels of phonological awareness for those exposed to slowed speech, who also demonstrated significantly greater comprehension.

Philp (1998) also used an immediate off-line simulated recall technique, in this case to assess whether learners had noticed the relevant properties of orally delivered recasts. Immediately following provision of a recast during dyadic NS–NNS interaction, the NS prompted recall via a signal (a knock on the table). Correct recall and repetition of the recast form was assumed to demonstrate noticing. Philp found that, in general, and particularly for higher-level learners, those who demonstrated greater noticing during the simulated recalls also demonstrated greater gain and development of question forms from pre- to immediate and delayed post-tests.

Other studies have used on-line measures of awareness, such as protocols (Alanen, 1995; Jourdenais et al., 1995; Leow, 1997, 2000; Rosa and O'Neill, 1999) to examine uptake and learning of information during treatments designed to draw learners' attention to forms while processing for meaning (these involved italicizing and underlining words in a text; completing a crossword puzzle; and completing a multiple choice textual jigsaw puzzle). Alanen (1995), Jourdenais et al. (1995), Leow (1997, 2000), and Rosa and O'Neill (1999) all reported that those subjects demonstrating greater noticing and awareness during the on-line protocols also demonstrated greater intake and gain, at least on some aspects of the targeted forms in each study (aspects of Finnish grammar in Alanen, 1995, and of Spanish grammar in Jourdenais et al., 1995; Leow, 1997, 2000, and Rosa and O'Neill, 1999) than those whose protocols demonstrated less noticing and awareness of the targeted forms.

While of theoretical interest, zero-point issues of whether learning is possible without attention or without "noticing" are of much less practical interest to SL pedagogy than the findings summarized above. Few would argue the zero-point issue with regard to attention. Gass (1997), however, claims that evidence of the generalizability of relative clause instruction on more marked (and complex) objects-of-preposition relative clauses to less marked subject and object relative clauses is evidence of non-attentional learning. Yet in both Gass (1982) and Eckman, Bell, and Nelson (1988), who found similar effects, there was pre-testing, and attended exposure to all forms of relative clause, before the instructional treatment, and there is additionally no guarantee that in their prior learning experience learners in these studies had not attended to the three forms of relative clause in question. In experimental studies, where such control is guaranteed, there are few advocates of the zero-point option for attention and learning. For example, most explanations of "implicit" learning of artificial grammars, or rules governing repeating sequences of letters or lights (Hsiao and Reber, 1998; Nissen and Bullemer, 1987; Stadler, 1992), clearly state that attention is required for processing the learned stimuli. As Hsiao and Reber observe, in implicit sequence learning experiments, increasing the structural constraints on and therefore the complexity of rules describing the repeating sequences also increases the probability of event sequences/letter strings occurring after other event sequences. The probability learning that is facilitated by and results from exposure to such sequences is merely *less* demanding of attention, not independent of it: "The fewer the constraints, the more attentional resources will be required to learn that sequence" (Hsiao and Reber, 1998, p. 475).

In summary, the necessity of noticing and awareness is more controversial than the necessity of attention for SLA (Schmidt, 1995, 2001) and is difficult to prove conclusively, given that no measurement instrument or technique can be assumed to be entirely coextensive with, and sensitive to, the contents of awareness and noticing. Nonetheless, cumulative findings from the studies reported above are predominantly in line with Schmidt's noticing hypothesis, and are certainly not contrary to it. Furthermore, many have argued that, even if it is not necessary, noticing certainly contributes to learning and retention, and that consequently consciousness raising (Rutherford, 1987), input enhancement (Sharwood-Smith, 1991), processing instruction (VanPatten, 1996), or focus on form (Long, 1991; Long and Robinson, 1998), which aim to induce it, are likely to be beneficial to learners.

2.3.3 *Focus on form*

The noticing hypothesis offers a partial explanation of why a focus on meaning alone, with plentiful opportunities for exposure and processing of input, as in Canadian immersion classrooms, often results in levels of high comprehension ability and fluency, but poor accuracy in production (Harley, 1993; Harley and Swain, 1984). Learners did not selectively attend to and notice communicatively redundant, perceptually non-salient, or infrequent and rare forms in the input. In these and other cases, Long (1991) has argued *focus on form*, in the context of meaningful use of language, may be necessary to promote and guide selective attention to aspects of input which otherwise may go unnoticed, unprocessed and unlearned:

> Focus on form refers to how focal attentional resources are allocated . . . during an otherwise meaning-focussed classroom lesson, focus on form often consists of an occasional shift of attention to linguistic code features – by the teacher and/or one or more students – triggered by perceived problems in communication. (Long and Robinson, 1998, p. 23)

Undoubtedly, while processing oral L2 input for meaning, as in naturalistic or immersion environments and during L2 reading, learners do unintentionally attend to, notice, and learn many vocabulary or grammatical and pragmatic features of the L2 (incidental learning) (Gass, 1999; Huckin and Coady, 1999; Hulstijn, this volume; Rott, 1999; Schmidt, 1990, 1995). However, in those areas where unguided incidental learning is slow and inefficient (Long, 1996), or just not possible for learnability reasons (L. White, 1991), guided focus on form is widely accepted to be a necessary pedagogic intervention. More controversial is the nature of the pedagogic technique that intervention should adopt in order to be optimally effective, while being minimally intrusive on the communicative activity (Doughty and Williams, 1998). For example, is it more effective to proactively instruct learners in targeted features prior to communicative activities, via a brief rule explanation or metalinguistic summary (instructed learning)? Or is it better to adopt less communicatively intrusive techniques for focusing attention on form, by giving learners instructions to process for meaning (e.g., to read a news article in preparation for a debate) while drawing their attention, through underlining or highlighting, to targeted forms in the text (enhanced learning)? Alternatively, reactive techniques for focus on form, such as oral recasts of problematic learner utterances, involve no a priori decision about which forms to target.

Recent experimental laboratory research has investigated these issues by comparing differences in learning under incidental, instructed, and enhanced conditions across a variety of linguistic domains (see Hulstijn, 1997, for review). This research has often also been concerned to match the difficulty or complexity of the targeted instructional form to the best learning condition. While conceptualizations and/or operationalizations of rule complexity differ across studies (see Doughty, 1998; Hulstijn and DeGraaff, 1994; Robinson, 1996b, for discussion), a general summary of the laboratory research findings is that proactive rule instruction can lead to short-term rate advantages over incidental and enhanced learning in simple grammatical domains (DeGraaff, 1997a, 1997b; DeKeyser, 1995; N. Ellis, 1993; Robinson, 1996a, 1997a), but the positive effects of rule instruction are much less obvious for complex grammatical domains.

There is also evidence from experimental laboratory research (Robinson, 1997b; Williams, 1999) and classroom studies (Alanen, 1995; S. Carroll and Swain, 1993; Doughty, 1991; Doughty and Varela, 1998; Fotos, 1993; Iwashita, 1999; Jourdenais et al., 1995; Leeman, Arteagoitea, Fridman, and Doughty, 1995; Leow, 1997, 2000; Muranoi, 1996, 2000; Spada and Lightbown, 1993; J. White, 1998; L. White, Spada, Lightbown, and Ranta, 1991) that enhanced learning conditions, adopting (i) techniques for off-line, proactive, textual input enhancement of targeted forms and (ii) reactive, on-line, aural/interactive, or gestural enhancement of problematic aspects of production during communicative tasks (which are both assumed to induce selective attention and noticing) can positively affect learning, relative to unstructured and unenhanced exposure alone. However, relying, as they may, to a much greater extent on individual differences in cognitive ability variables such as aptitude (Robinson, 1997a, 2001b) or working memory capacity (Mackey et al., 2002; Philp, 1999; Robinson, 2001b, 2002; Robinson and Yamaguchi, 1999; Robinson, Strong, Whittle, and Nobe, 2001; Williams, 1999), group effects for input and output enhancement have been less robust than those for explicit rule instruction. Nevertheless, given the short-term nature of most of the experimental laboratory studies of the effects of rule instruction, it may be that the positive effects of input and output enhancement obtained in classroom studies – which are typically studied over much longer, and more ecologically valid, periods of exposure – while showing less immediate short-term gain, are more durable and permanent (see Doughty and Williams, 1998; N. Ellis and LaPorte, 1997; Long and Robinson, 1998; Norris and Ortega, 2000; and Spada, 1997, for extended reviews and interpretations of these findings).

2.4 *Attention as capacity*

2.4.1 Overview

Tasks differ in the demands they make on our attention. Elsewhere in this volume this issue is dealt with in terms of important distinctions between controlled and automatic L2 processing (DeKeyser, 1997, 2001; Segalowitz, this volume), the former being traditionally viewed as more attention demanding than the latter; and between explicit and implicit L2 learning (DeKeyser, this volume; N. Ellis, 1994), the former also being traditionally viewed as more attention demanding than the latter. Some argue that speed-up of control processes and withdrawal of attention (McLaughlin, 1990; Shiffrin and Schneider, 1977) and unconscious abstract rule induction (Reber, 1993) in a separate implicit memory store (Paradis, 1994; Schacter, 1996) can explain these differentials in attentional demands. Others have argued (Logan, 1988, 1990; Shanks and St John, 1994) that automatic decision making (Robinson, 1995b; Robinson and Ha, 1993) and implicit L2 learning (Robinson, 1995b, 1996a, 1996b, 1997b) are memory-based processes involving storage and retrieval of attended instances in memory.

Differentials in the attentional demands of L2 tasks, and of dual versus single-task performance have also been proposed as one cause of within-learner interlanguage variation. Complex tasks are more attention demanding than simpler tasks, and performing two tasks simultaneously is more attention demanding than performing one alone (Gopher, 1992; Heuer, 1996), and varying these attentional demands may systematically affect the accuracy, fluency, and complexity of learner speech (Crookes, 1988, 1989; Hulstijn, 1989; Robinson, 1995a, 2000, 2001a, 2002, forthcoming; Robinson and Niwa, 2001; Robinson, Ting, and Urwin, 1995; Skehan, 1998; Skehan and Foster, 2001; Tarone, 1985). The specific issue addressed here, then, is the relationship of task demands to attention used in the sense of *capacity*, since capacity limits are often invoked to explain the greater "mental load" and therefore difficulty of controlled processing, explicit learning, and L2 processing during complex and dual-task performance. Three positions on the structure and significance of capacity limits can be identified.

2.4.2 Single capacity and multiple resources

Kahneman (1973) proposed that a single finite volume of attention is available for allocation to competing task demands. Attention is allocated in working memory, and is selective of actions, not incoming messages. Capacity limits are not fixed and unchanging, but vary with the level of arousal. Task difficulty is defined in terms of capacity consumption, as reflected in physical indices of "effort" such as pupilliary dilation. More complex and less automatized tasks consume more attentional capacity, and require greater effort. Multiple-resource models (Wickens, 1984, 1989, 1992) go beyond simple single-capacity models by proposing distinctions between separate resource pools from which attention is allocated to different task dimensions, such as processing mechanisms required by the task (perceptual vs. response), codes of processing (spatial vs. verbal), and modality (auditory vs. visual; see figure 19.2). This modification to Kahneman's model is necessary since structural alterations in a secondary task, while keeping its difficulty constant, are known to affect performance. For example, when simultaneously performed tasks both require manual responses (steering and written recall of digits), there is more interference/worse

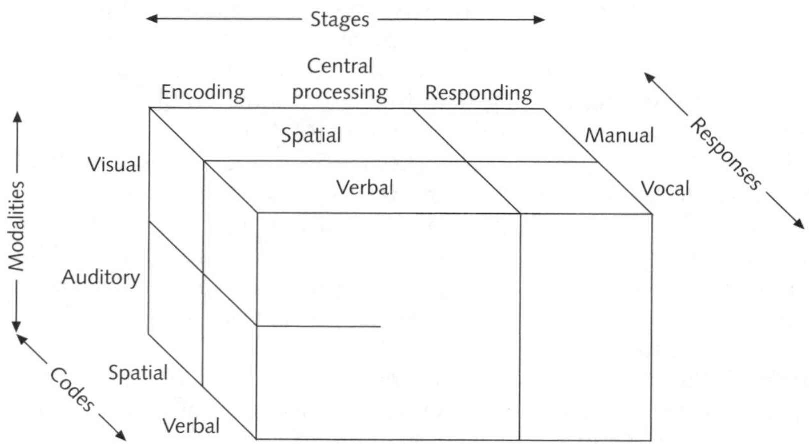

Figure 19.2 The proposed structure of processing resources
Source: Wickens (1992, p. 375)

performance than when one requires a manual and the other a verbal response (steering and verbal recall of digits). Thus, resource competition was argued to exist within, but not between, separate attentional pools.

While multiple-resource theory has influenced some L2 research concerned with awareness and intake (Rosa and O'Neill, 1999), and the effects of task dimensions on input processing and production (see figure 19.3 below), and proven a productive framework for the study of human workload and workplace design (Wickens, 1992), it has a number of problems, one of which concerns its key theoretical assumption, that is, that attention is limited in capacity. First, performance limits are simply *ascribed* to capacity limits; it is not specified *how* or *why* capacity is limited – a key theoretical objection (Neumann, 1987). Second, interference between competing tasks is often more specific than is predicted on the basis of the resource pools identified (Navon, 1989). For example, performing arithmetic tasks simultaneously causes more interference than performing a spelling and arithmetic task simultaneously (Hirst and Kalmar, 1987), despite the fact that they are both classified, in Wicken's model, as drawing on the same resource pools. Third, inventing new classifications of resource pools to account for examples of successful and unsuccessful time-sharing is unsatisfactorily post hoc, and unconstrained. These issues of explaining interference beyond those predicted by classifications of resource pools have led to the development of an alternative account of the relation between attention and task demands.

2.4.3 Interference and/or capacity?

Interference models argue that increasing the number of stimuli and response alternatives or the similarity between them will sometimes lead to confusion, reducing performance efficiency. This can be caused by competition for the same types of codes during information flow, or by "cross-talk" between similar codes. For example, while typing auditorily presented words, at the same time as shadowing (repeating) visually presented words (the same code), visually presented words are sometimes mistakenly typed (Shaffer, 1975). Interference is therefore caused by involuntary attention shifts, not by resource limitations, and is a breakdown in action control (Navon, 1989; Neumann, 1987). Within this approach:

> considerations of resource scarcity or the performer's ability to allocate sufficient processing efforts are irrelevant. The limits on task performance are not conceived in these terms. Attention control is constrained to a decision to engage, disengage and shift attention between tasks and the pursuit of intentions. In interference models the only limited resource is time and its derived scheduling constraints. (Gopher, 1992, pp. 279–80)

While there are clearly structural constraints on human information-processing ability, and limits on the information that can be stored in short-term working memory, these accounts nonetheless question the utility of the notion of "capacity limits" on attention in explanations of degraded task performance (Logan, 1992). Connectionist models of representation, processing, and attention (e.g., Phaf, van der Heijden, and Hudson, 1990; Schneider and Detweiler, 1988) complement these non-limited attention capacity accounts. Such models consist of "mutually activating and inhibiting units among and within various levels of processing. From this perspective, processing limits are due to interference, confusion and cross-talk among elements of a neural net and not to capacity constraints" (Sanders, 1998, p. 15).

2.4.4 Task demands, capacity, and interference

Two points are worth making with regard to these three theoretical views of central processing, task demands, and attention. First, single-resource, limited-capacity models cannot explain many of the effects of structural alterations in task demands on task performance, whereas multiple-resource theory can. Second, multiple-resource theory may be able to accommodate interference models: interference models are lower-level (implementational) approaches to describing the causes of attention switching and task competition during control of information flow. This may mean that multiple-resource theory maintains the distinction between resource pools, but abandons the notion of capacity limitations (which interference models do not assume) within those pools.

Much SLA research within an information-processing framework assumes attentional capacity is limited, and, as a result, that accuracy, fluency, and complexity may compete for resource allocation during L2 task production (Skehan, 1998) or that "form" and "function" compete for scarce attentional resources during input processing (VanPatten, 1996). Tomlin and Villa (1994) have argued that these assumptions, and the single-resource, limited-capacity model of attention they are based on, are too "coarse-grained." Whether or not the notion of capacity limits during single- and multiple-task performance is retained in theories of attention, it seems clear that invoking limits on *undifferentiated* attention capacity as an explanation of various SLA processes (e.g., the inefficiency of input processing, transfer at a variety of levels, lapses in fluency and accuracy during task production) is unsatisfactory. As described above, current theories of attentional allocation to input are "rapidly moving away from the limited capacity processor" (Sanders, 1998, p. 356), and do not see this as a major constraint on why and when selection of input, or of action, takes place. Consequently, these trade-off effects (form vs. function, accuracy vs. fluency) may be better explained not in terms of a priori capacity limits on a single pool of attention but in terms of control functions during central processing (allocation policy, time constraints on scheduling attention allocation), and interference occurring during resource allocation to those specific *task demands* which central processing responds to. From the perspective of interference theory, explanations linking relative ease or difficulty of L2 comprehension, or different characteristics of L2 production, to task demands may be more legitimately framed in terms of confusion and cross-talk between codes (of L1, interlanguage, and L2 syntax, morphology, semantics, and phonology/orthography) within specific resource pools during task performance, rather than in terms of global capacity limitations.

Abandoning invocation of undifferentiated attention capacity limits to explain the effects of task demands on comprehension and production will require more precise specifications of constraints affecting attention allocation during language processing. Codes would have to be representationally specified, as would resource pools. The competition model (MacWhinney, 1987, 2001) offers one framework (there are others) for describing codes and their peaceful coexistence, or the competition and interference between them caused by task demands on comprehension and production – that is, the extent to which L1 and L2 differ in their cues to form–function relations. For example, pre-verbal positioning is a highly reliable and available cue to assigning agency in English, but less reliable in Spanish, and simply not available in verb-initial languages like Samoan (Samoan uses an ergative marker *e* to mark the subject of transitive verbs). Interference and misinterpretation (confusion) occur where the same cue is available but differs in reliability across languages (as with pre-verbal positioning in English and Spanish) (see MacWhinney, 2001). The search for a cue not available in the L2 (English) which is available in the L1 (Samoan), such as an ergative marker, can also lead to interference (cross-talk).

Investigating the structure of attentional resource pools drawn on in L2 processing is a recent area of SLA research, and some models have been proposed to guide research (Robinson, 2001a, 2001c). Task design features can *disperse* attention between pools (e.g., by requiring two task components to be performed concurrently), or *direct* attention to specific needed areas of the L2 within a pool (e.g., by requiring continual reference to events happening now, and so to use of the present tense), and it is possible that dispersal may lead to a higher probability of trade-offs and interference of the kind described above (Robinson, 2001c). These issues are further taken up in discussion of SLA findings below.

2.5 SLA research into attention as capacity

2.5.1 Resources, task demands, and language production

Recent SLA research has begun to examine the extent to which design features of L2 tasks make differential demands on attention, and here the notion of attention as capacity is most important to understanding the effects of these demands on perception and selection of input, as well as on production. Allocation of attentional capacity to task demands is a control process, and as task components and demands proliferate, so does the difficulty of managing allocation policy, with consequent lapses in perception and production. In studies of L1 and general intellectual development the relation between tasks, attentional capacity, and learning has most often been studied by contrasting performance on simple (less capacity-demanding) and complex (most capacity-demanding) versions of tasks at different ages, or stages of linguistic and cognitive development (see Case, 1985, 1992; Halford, 1993; Karmiloff-Smith, 1992; Nelson, 1996; Thelen and Smith, 1998). The same simple–complex task paradigm, along with studies of single vs. dual and multiple-task performance, has also been adopted in studies of the effects of task demands on attentional capacity in the acquisition of complex skills in adulthood (see Fleishman and Quaintance, 1984; Holding, 1989; Sanders, 1998; Wickens, 1992). Drawing to varying degrees on this research into L1 linguistic, cognitive, and skill development, as well as on previous classifications of the interactive demands of L2 tasks (Crookes, 1986; Duff, 1986; Long, 1989; Pica, Kanagy, and Falodun, 1993) and SLA research into the effects of attention to speech on L2 accuracy (Hulstijn, 1989; Tarone, 1985; Tarone and Parrish, 1988), SLA researchers have begun to theorize and operationalize the attentional demands of L2 tasks and to study their effects on production, comprehension, and learning (see Norris, Brown, Hudson, and Yoshioka, 1998; Robinson, 1996c, 2001a, 2001c; Skehan, 1996, 1998, for theoretical discussion and reviews of findings).

2.5.2 Attentional demands and task output

Figure 19.3 illustrates a number of dimensions of task demands that have been argued to affect attentional allocation and consequently the quality of L2 production and comprehension. Tasks where planning time and prior knowledge are available, and which involve only a single activity, are simpler and less attention demanding than dual tasks requiring simultaneous activities, and where no prior knowledge or planning time is available. Increasing complexity along these dimensions alone has the effect of depleting the attention available to perform the task, and dispersing it over many, non-specific linguistic aspects of production and comprehension. On the other hand, tasks which

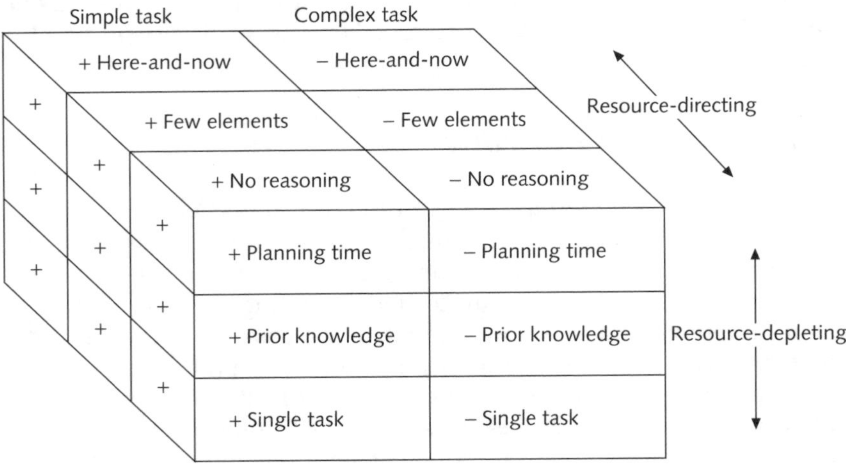

Figure 19.3 Resource-directing and resource-depleting dimensions of task complexity

require reasoning and reference to many elements, and which are displaced in time and space, are more complex and attention demanding than their simpler counterparts, but these dimensions have the potential to direct learner attentional resources to needed aspects of language code, such as conjunctive coordinators to establish causality, past tense morphology and temporal expressions, and complex nominalizations to distinguish numerous similar elements. Increasing task complexity and attentional demands simultaneously along both these types of dimension have the effect of approximating the performance constraints of real-world task activity. For example, a simple task might involve giving directions to a partner after a period of planning using a simplified small map (few elements) of a known area (prior knowledge available) where the route from A to B was already marked on (making it a single task, as opposed to thinking up the route and describing it simultaneously). A complex, real-world version of this task would involve giving directions from an authentic map of a large area, which is unfamiliar to the information giver and receiver, without a route marked on, and with no planning time, as when a passenger gives directions to a driver from a road map as they travel quickly through an unfamiliar town.

A great deal of previous research has focused on the dimension of planning time (Crookes, 1989; R. Ellis, 1987; Foster and Skehan, 1996; Mehnert, 1998; Ortega, 1999; Skehan and Foster, 1997, 2001; Ting, 1996), finding, in general, that planned tasks result in greater fluency and complexity of production, with some studies also showing gains in accuracy on planned tasks. What has yet to be shown, but which might be expected, is the effect of planning time on the accuracy and complexity of production during tasks made complex along different resource-directing dimensions – such as tasks requiring reasoning vs.

tasks requiring reference to many similar elements. Planning time for the former could be expected to optimize time available for producing complex syntax to express logical causality (if-then), belief justification (X because Y), and conditionality (if it/I were, it/I would), for example: planning time for the latter to encourage planning of complex nominal predicates, use of relative clauses, and article and determiner use. These considerations point to the potential dangers of predicting global effects on accuracy and complexity of production on one resource-depleting dimension of complexity and attentional demands, such as the availability of planning time, regardless of its interaction with other dimensions that have the potential to differentially direct attentional resources to task-relevant aspects of language code.

Nonetheless, the tendency in this descriptive data-gathering period of research has been to examine the effects of differences in attentional demands along one dimension independently of others. Effects have been found for greater fluency but lower accuracy on narratives performed in the here-and-now (stories performed in the present tense, while looking at picture sequences illustrating the story) than in the more complex there-and-then (stories performed in the past tense while remembering the picture sequences; Rahimpour, 1997, 1999; Robinson, 1995a). Increasing the reasoning demands and number of elements that need to be referred to and described has also been shown to negatively affect fluency (Niwa, 1999; Robinson, 2001a, 2001c; Robinson and Niwa, 2001) while having positive effects on some aspects of lexical range and linguistic complexity (Brown, 1996; Brown, Anderson, Shillcock, and Yule, 1984; Niwa, 1999; Robinson, 2001a; Robinson and Niwa, forthcoming). Similarly, dual tasks have been shown to result in less fluent production than single tasks (Robinson and Lim, 1993; Robinson et al., 1995), as do tasks performed where no prior knowledge is available (Chang, 1999; Robinson, 2001a, 2001c). Lack of prior knowledge has also been shown to negatively affect comprehension during reading and listening tasks (Barry and Lazarte, 1998; Carrell, 1987; Clapham, 1996; Dunkel, 1991; Urwin, 1999), with prior knowledge of related content facilitating listening comprehension measured by inferencing questions, and prior knowledge of formal organizational schemas facilitating comprehension measured by recall questions (Urwin, 1999).

2.5.3 Attentional demands and task intake

One pedagogic motivation for examining the attentional demands of tasks and the effects of these on production has been a concern to design pedagogic tasks for learners which optimize production practice in the three areas of fluency, accuracy, and complexity of output (Bygate, 1996, 1999; Skehan, 1996, 1998; Skehan and Foster, 1997, 2001). A second motivation stems from proposals for "analytic" approaches to pedagogy, such as Long's proposals for Task Based Language Teaching (see Long, 1998, forthcoming; Long and Norris, 2000), which reject linguistic units of analysis (either grammatical rules, lexical items, or notions and functions, etc.) and associated criteria for grading sequencing units of instruction, in favor of a syllabus made up of a series of pedagogic tasks. One proposal for operationalizing such syllabuses is to base task sequencing on empirical evidence of differences in the cognitive demands of tasks, so that pedagogic tasks progressively approximate the full information-processing complexity of real-world target task demands over a course of instruction (Long, 1998; Long and Crookes, 1992; Robinson, 1996c, 2001a, 2001c).

A third and fundamentally important motive for studying the attentional demands of tasks lies in the effect these have on learning. Schmidt (1990) argued that along with input factors, such as perceptual saliency and frequency of forms, task demands are also powerful determinants of what is noticed and selected via focal attention for further processing. Unfortunately, to date there has been almost *no* research into the effect of task complexity and dual-task performance on selection and intake of new, previously unknown, task-relevant linguistic information. Two theoretical positions have been put forward, however, which promise to stimulate future research. One position is that increasing the complexity of tasks and their multiple components reduces a pool of generally available attention capacity (Kahneman, 1973), thus negatively affecting detection, selection, and subsequent memory for new linguistic forms in the input. This is compatible with VanPatten (1996) and Skehan's assumption of a single-resource, limited-capacity model of attention (Skehan, 1996, 1998; Skehan and Foster, 2001), which predicts that as learners' attentional limits are reached, learners prioritize processing for meaning over processing form. The researchers argue that this leads learners to adopt a strategy of paying attention to content words at the expense of grammatical morphology during message comprehension, and to an increasingly lexicalized, ungrammatical mode of speech production.

Alternatively, if different components of task demands draw on attention allocated from within separate resource pools (Wickens, 1984, 1989), then increasing the cognitive demands of tasks could, in a number of cases, be argued to increase the attention learners pay to input and output, and to process it more deeply and elaborately, without necessarily being constrained by capacity limits or competition for attentional resources. In this view, increasing task complexity along compatible, separately resourced, dimensions may increase the likelihood of detecting and selecting seeded aspects of the input (Robinson, 1995b, 2001a, 2001c), made salient through such techniques as flooding, visual enhancement (in the case of written text), or recasting (in the case of oral interaction).

To illustrate how tasks can be made complex along compatible, separately resourced dimensions, take the example referred to earlier, that of a simple direction-giving task (requiring reference to few elements where prior knowledge is available) vs. a complex direction-giving task (requiring reference to many elements, with no prior knowledge). I would argue the resource-directing dimensions of complexity identified in figure 19.3, such as *reference to few vs. many elements*, draw on the resource pools Wickens identified for *verbal encoding and vocal responding* (see figure 19.2), whereas this is not necessarily so of the resource-depleting dimensions. *Lack of prior knowledge* of an area described by a map, that is, would affect only visual encoding of the many elements (roads, buildings, other landmarks, etc.) the map contains and would draw on the *visual spatial encoding* resource pool in figure 19.2. Multiple-resource theory predicts little interference between the attentional demands of tasks which increase in complexity – as in this case – along two separately resourced dimensions, which can be time-shared successfully (i.e., no prior knowledge of an area illustrated by a map/visual-spatial-encoding resource pool; reference to many elements/vocal-responding resource pool).

Increasing task complexity may also lead to greater retention of noticed input. For example, Schneider, Healy, and Bourne (1998) showed that increasing the "intra task interference," and hence processing demands, of vocabulary word-list learning tasks (presenting words randomly vs. grouped into simplifying conceptual categories) led learners to process the randomly ordered group more elaborately (see Craik and Lockhart, 1972, and discussion in section 3.3 below), resulting in more retention for these words than for those grouped into categories. Further, since increasingly complex interactive tasks result in greater amounts of negotiation (see Robinson, 2001a) they also increase learner opportunities for, and maybe therefore the likelihood of, making cognitive comparisons between input and output, leading to noticing "gaps" or holes in production (see Doughty, 2001, this volume; Muranoi, 2000; Swain, 1995).

In summary, Skehan assumes attentional capacity is generally available and limited, and that increases in task complexity drain attentional resources and are therefore likely to have the effect of degrading the fluency, accuracy, and complexity of output, as well as perception of input and intake (see Skehan, 1998, p. 174). In cases where complex tasks make demands that exceed the learners' available attentional resources, Skehan argues additional task structure is necessary to attract learner attention to relevant aspects of form, which would otherwise not be processed. A similar rationale underlies VanPatten's (1996) proposals for processing instruction. The alternative position I have described lays less emphasis on capacity limits, and makes the prediction that where dimensions of task complexity are separately resourced, and can be time-shared, then increases in task complexity along multiple dimensions will not degrade output, perception of input, and intake, and may lead to qualitative increases in all three relative to performing simpler tasks. These issues are speculative, unresolved, testable, of great practical relevance to SL pedagogy and syllabus design, and in much need of further SLA research.

2.6 Attention as effort

Sustained attention to an activity over time is a third, separable use of the term "attention" and is a central notion in studies of vigilance, energetic states, and the causes of decline in performance on a task. Attention in this sense is a "state" concept referring to energy or activity in the processing system, not to structural processes such as selecting, allocating resources, and rehearsing information in memory. To maintain performance on a task, the attentional energy devoted to it must remain at a constant state. Three energetic pools have been proposed (Sanders, 1986), which correspond to the three information-processing stages in figure 19.1; the *arousal* pool (concerned with encoding and affected by variables such as cue salience, intensity, and novelty); the *activation* pool (concerned with central processing and affected by such variables as task preparedness and alertness); and the *effort* pool (concerned with responding, monitoring output, and the feedback it elicits, and affected by such variables as task complexity, time spent on task, and type of feedback provided). Since issues of attention in encoding and central processing are discussed above, I briefly focus here on sustained attention at the third stage of information processing in figure 19.1.

Failure to sustain attention to a task and maintain the level of *effort* expended results in a decline in performance over time. Failure to sustain attentional effort is caused not only by prolonged time on task, but also by the complexity of the task as determined by the number and compatibility of task components and sources of input (Koelega, 1996; Wickens, 1992). This is manifest in a decline in vigilance – failure to detect a target signal (in studies of visual search) and failure to correctly identify and interpret auditory input (in studies of comprehension), as well as failures in grammatical encoding and production leading to mistakes and speech errors (in studies of speech production). In psycholinguistic theories of speech production applied to SLA, failure to sustain attention to a communicative task can be identified as one cause of declines in self-repair and monitoring of output (Crookes, 1988; De Bot, 1996; Kormos, 1999; Levelt, 1989). Swain's notion of "pushed" output (Izumi, Bigelow, Fujiwara, and Fearnow, 1999; Swain, 1985, 1995; Swain and Lapkin, 1995) also appears to implicate the sense of attention as effort; pushed L2 production is more effortful than the normal production level of a learner. Coordinating joint attention to language through the provision and uptake of feedback during L1 child–caregiver (Tomasello and Farrar, 1986) or L2 interaction (Doughty, 2001, this volume; Gass, 1997, this volume; Iwashita, 1999; Lyster, 1998; Lyster and Ranta, 1997; Mackey, Gass, and McDonough, 2000; Muranoi, 2000; Oliver, 1995; Philp, 1998; Pica, 1988, 1992) also requires sustained, effortful attention, and this may increase as the number of participants in the interaction increases (Tomasello, Manle, and Kruger, 1989).

2.7 SLA research into attention as effort

The relationship of attention as effort to attention as capacity is currently controversial. Kahneman's (1973) model of attention, implicitly adopted by Skehan (1996, 1998) and VanPatten (1996), assumed that sustaining attention to tasks which were high in their capacity demands was more effortful than sustaining attention to tasks which were low in their capacity demands. Kahneman argued that greater effort in sustaining attention was indexed by physiological measures, such as increased heart rate and pupilliary dilation, and by greater declines in vigilance and less freedom from distraction over time, compared to less effortful and capacity-consuming tasks. The alternative view I have described above, that is, that there are plentiful attentional resources within separate pools, suggests effortful tasks are those requiring coordinated attention to, and executive time-sharing between, task components drawing concurrently on the same resource pools. Where task components draw on separately resourced pools, sustained attention to a task will be less effortful, and performance will show less decline in vigilance (more effective monitoring and uptake and incorporation of feedback) over time than when there is competition for resources within the same pools. In this view, then, the effort involved in sustaining attention to L2 output and input results from the interaction of time constraints and coordination of attentional resources, not from their scarcity (Logan, 1992; Navon, 1989; Neumann, 1996).

Arousal and the effort pool are also related. Increases in stress lead to greater arousal and also to temporary increases in effort to perform the task, though there are limits to this equation, as described by the Yerkes-Dodson law. Levels of stress, arousal, and performance increase to a point beyond which performance declines, and this point is reached earlier on complex tasks than simpler ones. Attention as effort is therefore related to affective influences on SLA, such as motivation (Dörnyei, 1998, 2002), and the distinction between facilitating and debilitating anxiety (Holthouse, 1995; Horwitz, Horwitz, and Cope, 1986; Jacob, 1996), issues that are dealt with in more detail elsewhere in this volume (see the chapter by Dörnyei and Skehan).

3 Memory

3.1 Overview

As the review above illustrates, research into the necessity of attention and awareness in selection of intake for learning has dominated recent SLA research. There is growing interest too in the issue of capacity constraints on attentional allocation. The role of memory has been less controversial, and so, perhaps, less studied. Recently, however, three issues have attracted theoretical interest: the relationship of selective attention and awareness to memory during noticing; the role of memory in implicit and incidental L2 learning; and the effect of individual differences in short-term, working memory capacity on SLA. A fourth issue – the organization and accessibility of information in long-term memory – has been addressed in a number of studies of listening and reading comprehension processes, as well as in studies of bilingual processing (Bialystok, 1991), lexical acquisition (Crutcher, 1998; Hulstijn , 2001), and lexical access and retrieval during SL production (Doughty, 2001), though full review of these areas is beyond the scope of this chapter.

3.2 Attention and memory

It is uncontroversial that memory processes are functionally differentiated, and that the modal view of memory proposed by Atkinson and Shiffrin (1968), distinguishing between perceptual/sensory memory, short-term/working memory, and long-term/episodic and semantic memory, captures some of these functional distinctions (Pashler and Carrier, 1997). Short-term, working memory is capacity limited, whereas long-term memory is not. Information in short-term memory decays rapidly; information in long-term memory does not. Evolutionary explanations (e.g., Reber, 1993) argue capacity limitations on short-term, working memory are necessary – and so have evolved – if fast decisions (based on limited information), which are often necessary to survival, are to be guaranteed. In short, these accounts argue that capacity limits on short-term memory are the result of a decision-making trade-off in evolutionary development between speed (more necessary) and accuracy (less necessary).

More controversial in memory research is whether these functional distinctions correspond to neurophysiologically separate systems, or whether passive short-term and active working memory are distinct stores (Baddeley, 1986; Cowan, 1993, 1995; Nairne, 1996; Schachter, 1996; Shiffrin, 1993; Squire, 1992). However, most memory researchers do hold the view that short-term, working memory is that part of long-term memory in a currently heightened state of activation, and further, that awareness and working memory are isomorphic, and correspond to the contents of short-term memory which are within the focus of attention (Cowan, 1988, 1993, 1995; Nairne, 1996).

3.3 *Memory, rehearsal, and awareness*

Consistently with the position described above, figure 19.4 illustrates the following set of relationships between memory and attention. Detected information can briefly enter short-term memory and automatically access previously encoded information in long-term memory outside of awareness (as illustrated by subliminal exposure, priming experiments, such as those of Marcel, 1983, referred to earlier). Automatic, unaware activation of long-term memory representations is the result of categorization mechanisms which compute the similarity distance of the detected input to prior instances encoded in memory (see Estes, 1992; Nosofsky, 1992; Nosofsky, Krushke, and McKinley, 1992; Smith and Sloman, 1994). This is evidence, however, only of unaware recognition, not of learning, since the categories which are activated pre-exist the input. For newly detected information to be encoded in long-term memory, which is "uncalled for" by similarity computing mechanisms, and which needs, therefore, to be learned, the information must enter focal attention and so short-term working memory, where rehearsal processes operate prior to encoding in long-term memory. Rehearsal processes can be of two kinds; *maintenance rehearsal*, requiring data-driven, instance-based processing, and *elaborative rehearsal*, requiring conceptually driven, schema-based processing (Craik and Lockhart, 1972; Hulstijn, 2001).

Schmidt (1990, 1995) has argued that noticing and focal attention are essentially isomorphic. This position is illustrated in figure 19.4. However, unvariegated focal attention alone cannot explain the differential learning consequences

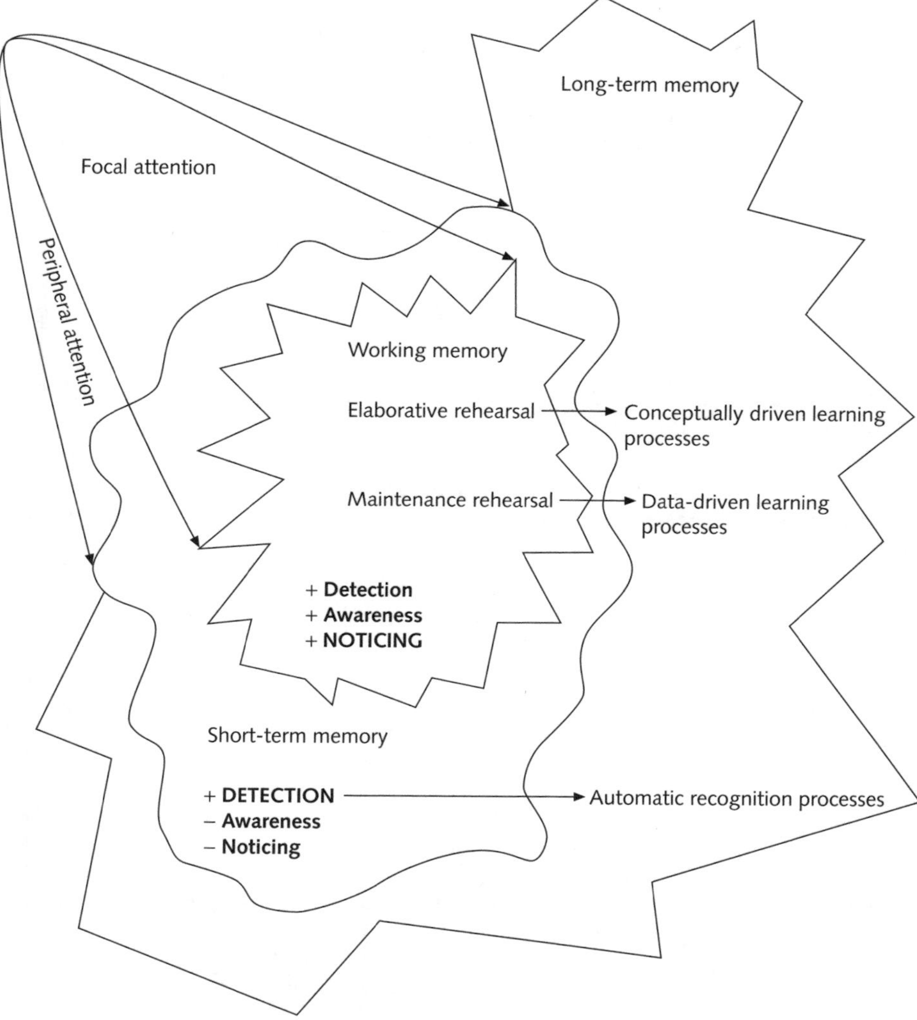

Figure 19.4 "Noticing" as selective focal attention and rehearsal in working memory: "detection" as recognition outside of awareness in passive short-term memory

of noticing under different conditions of exposure, as revealed in laboratory studies of learning under implicit, incidental, and explicit conditions (see Hulstijn, 1997, for review; DeKeyser, this volume; box 19.1 below). In addition, one must invoke memory processes. I would argue that "noticing" involves that subset of detected information that receives focal attention, enters short-term working memory, and is rehearsed. Noticing and higher levels of awareness, that is, are the result of rehearsal mechanisms (maintenance or elaborative rehearsal) which send (however temporarily) information in short-term memory to long-term memory. It is these rehearsal processes that give rise to awareness, place limits on the extent of awareness, and constrain what can be verbalized during verbal reports. In this regard I have argued (Robinson, 1995b, 1996a, 1997b) that data-driven, instance-based processing and conceptually driven, schema-based processing correspond to those implicit and explicit learning processes that some, in contrast, (Krashen, 1985; Paradis, 1994; Reber, 1989; Schachter, 1987, 1996; Squire, 1992) argue result from neurophysiologically distinct implicit/explicit learning and memory systems.

3.4 SLA research into memory, rehearsal, and elaboration

Williams (1999) addressed the issue of whether inductive SLA could be characterized as a data-driven learning process, requiring maintenance rehearsal of instances and "chunks" in unanalyzed form in working memory, as opposed to a conceptually driven learning process, requiring activation of schemas in long-term memory which are drawn on in elaboratively rehearsing and analyzing the input (see box 19.1 for further details). In a series of three (between-groups) computerized, experimental studies, Williams presented 40 sentences in a previously unknown language (Italian) in a display which illustrated the meaning of the sentences semi-graphically. Subjects both read and heard the sentences. The ability to recall each sentence verbatim following each presentation during training was used as a measure of memory, and was assumed to require predominantly maintenance rehearsal and data-driven

Box 19.1 Williams (1999)

Research question: What is the relationship between verbatim memory for input and inductive learning of aspects of grammar?

The relationship between memory for language input (without awareness of, or intention to search for, grammatical rules) and subsequent induction of grammar has been a central issue in cognitive psychology, and in experimental SLA research throughout the 1990s. In a series of three laboratory experiments, Williams investigated the relationship between verbatim memory for input and inductive learning of aspects of grammar. The target grammar was Italian, a language none of the participants was familiar with. Williams explained the task as an exercise in memorizing sentences.

Methodology:

The verbatim memory task – presentation phase: Williams presented a semi-graphical display on a computer screen. Participants were asked to say aloud the sentence depicted by the display in English. After this they saw the correct English sentence on the screen. They then heard, and saw on the computer screen, an Italian sentence describing the graphical display. Following this participants heard segments of the Italian sentences, accompanied by highlighted portions of the relevant aspects of the graphic. They were asked to repeat each segment aloud after they heard it. Finally, they heard and viewed (for 3 seconds) the whole sentence once more and were asked to repeat it.

Williams thus ensured that the meaning of each Italian sentence (a total of 40) had been understood, and had a taped record of the accuracy of recall of segments and the whole sentence.

The verbatim memory task – recall phase: After every two sentences presented and memorized following the above procedure, Williams presented the graphical representation of each sentence again with instructions to recall the Italian sentence aloud. Following this, to prompt further accuracy in recall, participants were allowed to view some letters of the Italian *content* words that appeared on the graphical display, and say the sentence aloud again if they wished to change their initial response. No aspects of Italian grammar, such as verb or article noun agreement inflections, were presented on the display during the recall phase.

Testing learning: Williams tested the learning that had occurred following the memorization task via a computerized translation test. This involved the presentation of a series of semi-graphical displays. Participants had to click the correct verb form, and noun and article forms, to construct the corresponding Italian sentence.

Results: Williams found considerable variance in accuracy of recall at the begining of training (individual differences in memory), for the first eight Italian sentences viewed and heard (block 1) but rather less variance at the end of training, on the last eight sentences viewed and heard (block 5). Williams also found the translation task revealed accurate learning of *some* of the aspects of grammar, such as verb inflections, but not of others, such as article–noun agreement.

Importantly, Williams found that accuracy of recall early during training (on block 1) correlated significantly and positively with accuracy during the translation post-test. In fact, accuracy of early recall correlated much *more* strongly than accuracy of later, block 5 recall. Williams concludes: "It would appear from this result that there is at least some sense in which knowledge of grammatical rules emerges out of memory for input and that individual differences in memory ability that are apparent even in the earliest stages of exposure have consequences for ultimate levels of learning. The results suggest that the learning occurring in this experiment can be characterized as data driven" (p. 22).

Conclusion: Three brief comments are worth making, considering the issues raised in this chapter. First, Williams's findings contradict the claims of Krashen (1985) and Reber (1993), reported in section 3.6, that incidental and implicit learning are insensitive to measures of individual differences. Second, the finding that verb inflections were learned more easily than article noun agreement rules is in line with the findings of DeKeyser (1995) and DeGraaff (1997a) that implicit and incidental learning processes interact with the complexity of the learning domain. Finally, Williams found (though not reported in my summary) that techniques for making salient aspects of the targeted structures also interacted with the complexity of the linguistic domain, and led to greater learning of some forms, supporting the claims reported in section 2.3.3 for the value of focus on form.

processing (since learners had no prior conceptual knowledge of the language to draw on in processing the input). Individual differences in the memory-recall task were then examined to see if they related to performance on a transfer translation task which was used as a measure of learning. The transfer translation task also presented a semi-graphical representation of a sentence, and subjects had to select words to make the matching Italian sentences, by clicking on an array of possible words presented on the computer screen.

Williams found strong significant correlations between accurate recall early in training, and performance on the transfer translation task. There were lower positive correlations with recall performance later in training (when learners, particularly those with greater grammatical sensitivity, might have been expected to switch to conceptually driven processing and hypothesis testing), suggesting that the inductive learning that had occurred did draw predominantly on data-driven processing and maintenance rehearsal. In a second experiment Williams introduced a technique to enhance, or make visually salient, aspects of form during presentation of the sentences. There were still significant positive correlations of memory, as measured by early training task recall ability, and learning, as evidenced by accurate performance on the transfer translation task. However, enhancement had the effect of dramatically increasing learning on some aspects of grammar (e.g., knowledge of morphemes for marking article–noun agreement) which had been imperfectly recalled during training. These results suggest that enhancement techniques, for selectively inducing learner attention to form during processing for meaning, are effective for *some* forms, in the short term, but that the learning processes they activate result from a more conceptually driven mode of processing and elaborative rehearsal, in contrast to the data-driven maintenance rehearsal reflected in accurate verbatim recall of sentences presented early in training. Inducing selective attention via enhancement, that is, induces noticing and elaborative rehearsal, resulting in a different pattern of learning outcomes than that which results from noticing and maintenance rehearsal (see box 19.1 for further discussion). However, in a third experiment Williams found that providing feedback on accuracy of recall attempts during training (a more explicit form-focusing technique than visual enhancement, which might be expected to facilitate greater conceptually driven processing, hypothesis testing, and more elaborative rehearsal) did not significantly alter the extent of learning, and led to worse learning on some forms than did the second experiment.

In short, Williams found evidence for a complex interplay of data-driven and conceptually driven processing during inductive second language learning, in which individual differences in working memory for written and aural input largely (and positively) predicted the extent of subsequent learning in all experiments. Compared to the unstructured, memorize-only training condition in the first experiment, inducing selective attention to form via visual enhancement in the second experiment facilitated greater learning of some forms, though explicit feedback about accuracy of recall during training (which might be expected to induce rule search) in the third experiment led to decreases in learning of some forms. These findings are consistent with those for more successful learning under enhanced conditions of exposure than in unenhanced, memorize-only conditions (Robinson, 1997b), and for the negative effects of explicit rule search where forms to be acquired are complex (Robinson, 1997a). Studies such as Williams (1999), motivated by attentional, learning, *and* memory theory, are therefore to be encouraged for the additional insight they provide into the cognitive processes activated by the focus-on-form techniques described earlier in this review.

3.5 Short-term and working memory

Passive measures of short-term storage, such as backward digit span, in which subjects hear and repeat, in reverse order, a list of numbers, are distinguished from active measures of short-term storage, such as reading span tests. In reading span tests (Daneman and Carpenter, 1983; Osaka and Osaka, 1992), subjects read sets of sentences aloud from written cue cards in which selected words are underlined; subjects are then instructed to recall the underlined words. These tests measure the extent to which information is actively maintained and periodically refreshed in short-term memory while other processing operations (reading, speaking) take place. While the relationship between them is controversial, both types of test are argued to reflect important memory processes. Baddeley (1986) has proposed a model of working memory to account for the effects of active measures of short-term memory, in which information is maintained via rehearsal in two slave-systems of working memory, the *phonological loop* and the *visuospatial sketchpad*, which are jointly coordinated by a *central executive*. However, figure 19.4 represents working memory as *within* short-term memory (Nairne, 1996), since priming and subliminal exposure experiments such as those of Marcel (1983) show automatic access to long-term memory, and may exhibit primacy and recency effects, but these cannot be attributed to working memory and the focus of attention (see Baddeley, 1986; Cowan, 1993, 1995; N. Ellis, 2001; Gathercole and Baddeley, 1993; Shiffrin, 1993, for discussion).

3.6 SLA research into the role of short-term and working memory

A number of studies have examined the relationship between individual differences in short-term, working memory and SLA. Cook (1977) found a closer relationship between performance on passive measures of short-term storage in the L1 and the L2 than on measures of long-term memory, and suggested short-term L1 memory capacity was more transferable to L2 learning and use than long-term L1 memory capacity. Harrington and Sawyer (1992) found active measures of L2 working memory, measured by reading span tests, predicted superior L2 reading skill more than did passive, digit span measures of short-term storage. Similarly, Geva and Ryan (1993) found a closer relationship between L2 proficiency and measures of L2 working memory than between L2 proficiency and passive measures of short-term storage. Miyake, Friedman, and Osaka (1998) also found a close positive relationship between working memory and L2 linguistic knowledge and L2 listening comprehension. Working within the framework of MacWhinney's (1987) competition model (see discussion and examples given in section 2.2 above), they found that Japanese learners of English with high working memory capacity, measured by a listening span version of Daneman and Carpenter's (1983) reading span test, demonstrated more accurate cue assignment strategies (correctly assigning agency to nouns in English sentences on the basis of word order) than did learners with low working memory capacity, who preferred the L1 (Japanese) based strategy of assigning agency on the basis of animacy. High working memory learners also demonstrated greater comprehension of complex sentences read at natural speed.

As might be expected, then, following Schmidt's "noticing" hypothesis, measures of working memory capacity, which affects the extent and efficiency of focal attention allocation, are closely and positively related to second language proficiency and skill development. Miyake and Friedman (1998) argue that for this reason, working memory measures should be included in tests of language learning aptitude. Surprisingly, this is not currently the case, since traditional measures of language learning aptitude, such as the Modern Language Aptitude Test (J. B. Carroll and Sapon, 1959) and tests based on it (Sasaki, 1996), use only rote, passive measures of short-term memory ability (see Robinson, 2001b; Dörnyei and Skehan, this volume). In addition to the *inferential* evidence provided by the correlational studies of working memory capacity and existing levels of L2 proficiency and L2 reading and listening skill reported above, recent experimental studies of second language learning lend more *direct* support to the claim that working memory is an important contributor to second language learning ability, under *some* conditions of exposure. This issue is taken up in the following section.

3.7 Implicit and explicit memory: individual differences and child and adult L2 learning

Direct tests of memory (in which subjects are instructed to attend to material presented in a study phase in order to complete a later recall test) are assumed to access explicit memory, whereas indirect tests (in which material is simply presented in a study phase with no instructions to remember the information for a later recall test) are assumed to access implicit memory (see Kelley and Lindsay, 1997; Merickle and Reingold, 1991; Robinson, 1993, 1995b). Separate systems accounts argue that attention and awareness regulate access to (recognition and retrieval from) explicit but not implicit memory, and that explicit and implicit learning encode new information differentially into each. However, this neat equation is problematic. One problem is the fact that implicit memory measures (Marcel's priming experiments are just one example) generally show strong task and modality effects, such that information presented during a study phase on one task, in one modality (written words), may often not be recognized or recalled when tested later in another task, in another modality (aurally presented words). However, when implicit memory study/test tasks are similar and modality is the same, recognition and recall are much higher (Buchner and Wippich, 1998). In contrast, implicit learning experiments (see Reber, 1989, 1993) have been argued to show robust *generalizability* of learned information across different study/test tasks, and across modalities (though many disagree; see DeKeyser, this volume; Shanks and St John, 1994).

These issues have interesting implications for Universal Grammar (UG) explanations of SLA (S. Carroll, 1999; Cook, 1994; Gregg, this volume; Krashen, 1985; Schwartz, 1999; Truscott, 1998; White, this volume). Some UG explanations argue innate representations of the shape of possible languages persist into adulthood and so pre-exist adult exposure to L2 input, and that "full access" (Schwartz, 1999) to these representations can be triggered by exposure to positive evidence of the L2 alone, during processing for meaning, with no conscious attention to form. In this case, adult access to UG *may* be interpreted as implicit memory for existing knowledge or unconscious "acquisition" (Krashen, 1985), and dissociable from the learning that draws on consciously accessed explicit memory (Paradis, 1994). If so, the available evidence suggests modal specificity, so that positive evidence presented in one modality (reading) will have limited transfer to another (listening). This, of course, would be consistent with *child* L1 or L2 language development (before the age of 6 and the onset of maturational constraints; see Long, 1990), which is aural/oral modality dependent. However, it poses problems for UG accounts of *adult* L2 development (Krashen, 1985, 1994; Schwartz, 1999) that claim positive evidence obtained via *reading*, with no conscious attention to or noticing of form, can trigger access (via implicit memory) to representations which subsequently promote grammatical development in other modalities, such as *speaking*. The interesting possibility raised by studies of implicit memory, then, is that if separate systems are proposed in a transition theory, "full access" to UG during adulthood may be modality specific.

Some non-UG explanations of SLA assume that access to innate representations and cognitive mechanisms available in childhood is attenuated or not possible for adults, and that child and adult L2 learning are fundamentally different (see Bley-Vroman, 1988; Long, 1990; Skehan, 1998). Compatible with this assumption, effects for adult implicit learning are likely attributable not to separate systems, but to a preponderance of data-driven processing, maintenance rehearsal, and instance learning of noticed information (accounting for the difficulty of verbalizing the contents of awareness during implicit learning), whereas adult explicit learning likely results from a preponderance of conceptually driven processing, and elaborative rehearsal of noticed information (see Doughty, this volume, for another view). The preponderance of one or the other is largely a consequence of the way the study tasks force the material to be processed. Evidence for implicit memory and learning reflects study/test overlaps in data-driven processing, and evidence for explicit memory and learning reflects study/test overlaps in conceptually driven processing – different systems are not involved (cf. Healy et al., 1992; Jacoby and Dallas, 1981; Roediger, Weldon, and Challis, 1989; Shanks and St John, 1994, for similar proposals). To this extent, implicit and explicit learning in adulthood are fundamentally similar, requiring focal attention and rehearsal of input in memory, and are both sensitive to individual differences in relevant cognitive capacities. Differences in consciously attended task demands, together with individual differences in relevant cognitive variables, such as working memory capacity or speed (N. Ellis, 1996, 2001; N. Ellis, Lee, and Reber, forthcoming; Gathercole and Thorn, 1998; Harrington and Sawyer, 1992; Miyake and Friedman, 1998; Robinson, 2002), or language learning aptitude (Robinson, 1997a, 2001b; Sasaki, 1996; Sawyer and Ranta, 2001; Skehan, 1998), cause differences in learning outcomes. However, those who adopt separate-systems explanations of implicit/explicit learning argue implicit learning will be unaffected by individual differences, and be much more homogeneous across populations of learners than explicit learning, where individual differences in cognitive abilities *are* predicted to play a significant role in determining the extent of learning (Krashen, 1985; Reber, 1993; Reber, Walkenfield, and Hernstadt, 1991; Zobl, 1992, 1995). These and related issues have begun to be addressed in recent SLA research.

3.8 SLA research into the role of memory and individual differences

Reber (1989; Reber et al., 1991) and Krashen (1985; cf. similar proposals by Zobl, 1992, 1995) have argued that individual differences in cognitive abilities will affect consciously regulated explicit learning, but not unconscious implicit or incidental learning. In support of this claim, Reber et al. showed nonsignificant correlations of intelligence (using the Wechsler adult intelligence scale) with implicit learning of an artificial grammar, but significant positive correlations of intelligence and explicit learning during a forced choice series-solution task. Similarly, Robinson (1996a, 1997a) found that learning in an incidental, process-for-meaning condition alone was unrelated to measures of aptitude (the MLAT measures of rote memory for paired associates and grammatical sensitivity), in contrast to learning under explicit instructed and rule-search conditions. This finding appears to support Krashen's claims for the aptitude independence of supposedly unconscious acquisition processes activated by incidental learning conditions, and is in line with Reber et al's. findings that unaware, implicit learning is insensitive to measures of individual differences. Robinson (2002), however, argued that this may have been because the measure of paired-associates rote memory used in the earlier study did not reflect the active nature of the processing demands of the incidental learning task – processing sentences for meaning while incidentally noticing grammatical information.

In contrast to the earlier finding, in an extended replication of Reber et al. (1991), Robinson showed that incidental learning of a previously unknown L2 (Samoan) by Japanese learners (exposed during training to 450 sentence strings, which were processed in order to answer comprehension questions over a period of three hours; training took place on two separate days, one to three days apart) did correlate positively and significantly with measures of L1 working memory capacity (Osaka and Osaka's, 1992, reading span test). This was so for one-week and six-month delayed (not immediate) post-tests using grammaticality judgment measures of responses to novel Samoan sentences not encountered during training, as well as post-test measures of production of sentences (a word ordering test of sentence construction). However, in contrast to the findings of Reber et al. (1991), in a repeated-measures design using the same implicit and explicit training conditions operationalized in Reber et al., there were significant *negative* correlations of intelligence and implicit artificial grammar learning, as well as significant positive correlations of intelligence and explicit learning of the series-solution task. Learning during the implicit and explicit tasks, however, unlike incidental L2 learning, did not correlate positively and significantly with working memory. Once again, as in Robinson (1996a, 1997a), language learning aptitude, as measured by Sasaki's (1996) Language Aptitude Battery for the Japanese (based on J. B. Carroll and Sapon's, 1959, MLAT), did not correlate significantly with learning in the incidental L2 learning condition on the immediate post-test, and even correlated significantly and negatively with learning of some of the complex rules present in the training sentences. However, aptitude did positively predict six-month delayed post-test performance, but only as measured by the ability to produce sentences on the word-ordering task.

This study suggests, then, that incidental L2 learning, contrary to arguments put forward by Krashen (1985) and also by Zobl (1992, 1995), *is* sensitive to measures of individual differences in cognitive abilities, but that the measures used must correspond with, and be sensitive to, the processing demands of the particular training condition under which exposure takes place, and, importantly, that individual differences will be most likely to show delayed (not immediate) effects on incidental learning. To this extent, current L2 aptitude measures, as Miyake and Friedman (1998) suggest, and as this study shows, may appear to lack treatment validity, if perfomance on immediate post-tests is the measure of learning. The results of delayed post-tests, however, show aptitude to be a predictor of learning, but only when the measure is a productive one. Further, while the results of the implicit and explicit learning experiments partially replicate the findings of Reber et al. (showing intelligence to be positively related to explicit learning), the study demonstrates (what has often been asserted though not directly shown) that claims based on evidence of implicit learning of artificial grammars cannot be validly generalized to incidental L2 learning. Incidental L2 learning shows a different pattern of correlations with individual difference measures than learning in the other two conditions.

4 Conclusion

If this chapter has been relatively long, and inconclusive, in part it is because discussion of the role of cognitive variables in transition theories of SLA is often short and conclusive – learning is "triggered" (somehow) by input; implicit learning (or "acquisition") happens automatically, outside of awareness, and is insensitive to individual differences in cognitive capacities. What, then, could there be to discuss in a chapter on the role of attention and memory in SLA, except their irrelevance?

I have argued, however, that current views of attentional resources, and the contribution of individual differences in memory processes and capacities, are underrepresented, little explored, and sometimes misconceptualized in SLA research that has referred to them. Much recent attentional theory questions the oft-invoked SLA notion of "capacity" constraints. Why are there capacity constraints on attention? If these are general and undifferentiated across task demands, why then have multiple-resource theories been able to predict successful and unsuccessful competition for, and time-sharing between, attentional resources as a function of different task demands? Clearly memory "structures" are capacity limited, and impose constraints on attentional processes, but what learning processes do these structures and constraints give rise to: implicit/explicit learning, or different kinds of attentionally regulated rehearsal during processing, which appear to correspond to different learning systems? These and other questions raised (but not answered) in this review will hopefully prompt further research into cognitive processes and the role of cognitive variables during SLA, adding to, and refining, the findings which have begun to accumulate in the field, and resonating with research findings that have accumulated in other related fields of psychological inquiry and learning theory.

ACKNOWLEDGMENT

Preparation of this chapter was made possible by support provided by the Aoyama Gakuin Soken Research Institute.

REFERENCES

Alanen, R. 1995: Input enhancement and rule presentation in second language acquisition. In R. Schmidt (ed.), *Attention and Awareness in Foreign Language Learning and Teaching*. Second Language Teaching and Curriculum Center Technical Report No. 9. Honolulu: University of Hawai'i Press, 259–302.

Allport, D. A. 1987: Selection for action: some behavioral and neurophysiological consequences of attention and action. In H. Heuer and A. Sanders (eds), *Perspectives on Perception and Action*. Hillsdale, NJ: Lawrence Erlbaum Associates, 395–419.

Allport, D. A. 1989: Visual attention. In M. Posner (ed.), *Foundations of Cognitive Science*. Cambridge, MA: MIT Press.

Atkinson, R. and Shiffrin, R. 1968: Human memory: a proposed system and its control processes. In K. Spence (ed.), *Psychology of Learning and Motivation: Advances in Research and Theory. Vol. 2*. New York: Academic Press, 89–195.

Baddeley, A. 1986: *Working Memory*. Oxford: Oxford University Press.

Barry, S. and Lazarte, A. A. 1998: Evidence for mental models: how do prior knowledge, syntactic complexity, and reading topic affect inference generation in a recall task for nonnative readers of Spanish? *Modern Language Journal*, 82, 176–93.

Bialystok, E. (ed.) 1991: *Language Processing in Bilingual Children*. Cambridge: Cambridge University Press.

Bley-Vroman, R. 1988: The fundamental character of foreign language learning. In W. Rutherford and W. Sharwood-Smith (eds), *Grammar and Second Language Teaching*. New York: Newbury House, 19–30.

Boronat, C. and Logan, G. 1997: The role of attention in automatization: does attention operate at encoding or retrieval or both? *Memory and Cognition*, 25, 36–46.

Broadbent, D. 1958: *Perception and Communication*. London: Pergamon Press.

Broadbent, D. 1971: *Decision and Stress*. New York: Academic Press.

Broeder, P. and Plunkett, K. 1994: Connectionism and second language acquisition. In N. Ellis (ed.), *Implicit and Explicit Learning of Languages*. London: Academic Press, 421–54.

Brown, G. 1995: *Speakers, Listeners and Communication*. Cambridge: Cambridge University Press.

Brown, G., Anderson, A., Shillcock, R., and Yule, G. 1984: *Teaching Talk: Strategies for Production and Assessment*. Cambridge: Cambridge University Press.

Buchner, A. and Wippich, W. 1998: Differences and commonalities between implicit learning and implicit memory. In M. Stadler and P. Frensch (eds), *Handbook of Implicit Learning*. Thousand Oaks, CA: Sage, 3–46.

Butterfield, E. and Albertson, L. 1995: On making cognitive theory more general and developmentally pertinent. In F. Weinert and W. Schneider (eds), *Research on Memory Development*. Hillsdale, NJ: Lawrence Erlbaum Associates, 73–99.

Bygate, M. 1996: Effects of task repetition: appraising the developing language of learners. In J. Willis and M. Willis (eds), *Challenge and Change in Language Teaching*. Oxford: Heinemann, 136–46.

Bygate, M. 1999: Task as a context for the framing, reframing and unframing of language. *System*, 27, 33–48.

Carrell, P. 1987: Content and formal schemata in ESL pedagogy. *TESOL Quarterly*, 21, 461–81.

Carroll, J. B. and Sapon, S. 1959: *The Modern Language Aptitude Test*. San Antonio, TX: Psychological Corporation.

Carroll, S. 1999: Putting "input" in its proper place. *Second Language Research*, 15, 337–88.

Carroll, S. and Swain, M. 1993: Explicit and implicit negative feedback. *Studies in Second Language Acquisition*, 15, 357–86.

Carter, R. 1998: *Mapping the Mind.* London: Weidenfeld and Nicolson.

Case, R. 1985: *Intellectual Development: Birth to Adulthood.* Norwood, NJ: Ablex.

Case, R. 1992: *The Mind's Staircase: Exploring the Conceptual Underpinnings of Children's Thought and Knowledge.* Hillsdale, NJ: Lawrence Erlbaum Associates.

Chang, Y. F. 1999: Discourse topics and interlanguage variation. In P. Robinson (ed.), *Representation and Process: Proceedings of the 3rd Pacific Second Language Research Forum. Vol. 1.* Tokyo: PacSLRF, 235–41.

Clapham, C. 1996: *The Development of IELTS: A Study of the Effect of Background Knowledge on Reading Comprehension.* Cambridge: Cambridge University Press.

Clark, A. 1997: *Being There: Putting Brain, Body, and World Together Again.* Cambridge, MA: MIT Press.

Cook, V. 1977: Cognitive processes in second language learning. *International Review of Applied Linguistics*, 15, 1–20.

Cook, V. 1994: The metaphor of access to Universal Grammar in L2 acquisition. In N. Ellis (ed.), *Implicit and Explicit Learning of Languages.* New York: Academic Press, 477–502.

Corder, S. P. 1967: The significance of learners' errors. *IRAL*, 5, 161–70.

Cowan, N. 1988: Evolving conceptions of memory storage, selective attention, and their mutual constraints within the human information processing system. *Psychological Bulletin*, 104, 163–91.

Cowan, N. 1993: Activation, attention and short-term memory. *Memory and Cognition*, 21, 162–7.

Cowan, N. 1995: *Attention and Memory: An Integrated Framework.* Oxford: Oxford University Press.

Craik, F. and Lockhart, R. 1972: Levels of processing: a framework for memory research. *Journal of Verbal Learning and Verbal Behavior*, 11, 671–84.

Crookes, G. 1986: *Task Classification: A Cross-Disciplinary Review.* Technical Report No. 4, Center for Second Language Research, Social Science Research Institute, University of Hawai'i at Manoa.

Crookes, G. 1988: *Planning, Monitoring and Second Language Development.* Technical Report No. 6, Center for Second Language Research, Social Science Research Institute, University of Hawai'i at Manoa.

Crookes, G. 1989: Planning and interlanguage variation. *Studies in Second Language Acquisition*, 11, 183–99.

Crutcher, R. 1998: The role of prior knowledge in mediating foreign language vocabulary acquisition and retention: a process analytic approach. In A. Healy and L. Bourne Jr (eds), *Foreign Language Learning: Psycholinguistic Studies on Training and Retention.* Mahwah, NJ: Lawrence Erlbaum Associates, 91–112.

Daneman, M. and Carpenter, P. 1983: Individual differences in integrating information within and between sentences. *Journal of Experimental Psychology: Learning, Memory and Cognition*, 9, 561–83.

De Bot, K. 1996: The psycholinguistics of the output hypothesis. *Language Learning*, 46, 529–55.

DeGraaff, R. 1997a: The eXperanto experiment: effects of explicit instruction on second language acquisition. *Studies in Second Language Acquisition*, 19, 249–97.

DeGraaff, R. 1997b: *Differential Effects of Explicit Instruction on Second Language Acquisition.* HIL Dissertations No. 35. The Hague: Holland Institute of Generative Linguistics.

DeKeyser, R. 1995: Learning second language grammar rules: an experiment with a miniature linguistic system. *Studies in Second Language Acquisition*, 17, 379–410.

DeKeyser, R. 1997: Beyond explicit rule learning: automatizing second language morphosyntax. *Studies in Second Language Acquisition*, 19, 195–224.

DeKeyser, R. 2001: Automaticity and automatization. In P. Robinson (ed.), *Cognition and Second Language Instruction*. New York: Cambridge University Press, 125–51.

Dörnyei, Z. 1998: Motivation in foreign and second language learning. *Language Teaching*, 31, 117–35.

Dörnyei, Z. 2002: The motivational basis of language learning tasks. In P. Robinson (ed.), *Individual Differences and Instructed Language Learning*. Amsterdam: John Benjamins, 137–58.

Doughty, C. 1991: Second language instruction does make a difference: evidence from an empirical study of relativization. *Studies in Second Language Acquisition*, 13, 431–69.

Doughty, C. 1998: Acquiring competence in a second language: form and function. In H. Byrnes (ed.), *Learning Foreign and Second Languages*. New York: MLA, 128–56.

Doughty, C. 2001: Cognitive underpinnings of focus on form. In P. Robinson (ed.), *Cognition and Second Language Instruction*. New York: Cambridge University Press, 206–57.

Doughty, C. and Varela, E. 1998: Communicative focus on form. In C. Doughty and J. Williams (eds), *Focus on Form in Classroom Second Language Acquisition*. New York: Cambridge University Press, 114–38.

Doughty, C. and Williams, J. 1998: Pedagogical choices in focus on form. In C. Doughty and J. Williams (eds), *Focus on Form in Classroom Second Language Acquisition*. New York: Cambridge University Press, 197–262.

Duff, P. 1986: Another look at interlanguage talk: taking task to task. In R. Day (ed.), *Talking to Learn: Conversation in Second Language Development*. Rowley, MA: Newbury House, 147–81.

Dunkel, P. 1991: Listening in the native and second/foreign language: towards an integration of research and practice. *TESOL Quarterly*, 25, 431–57.

Eckman, F., Bell, L., and Nelson, D. 1988: On the generalization of relative clause instruction in the acquisition of English as a second language. *Applied Linguistics*, 9, 1–20.

Ellis, N. 1993: Rules and instances in foreign language learning: interactions of explicit and implicit knowledge. *European Journal of Cognitive Psychology*, 5, 289–318.

Ellis, N. 1994: Implicit and explicit learning: an overview. In N. Ellis (ed.), *Implicit and Explicit Learning of Languages*. London: Academic Press, 1–16.

Ellis, N. 1996: Sequencing and SLA: phonological memory, chunking and points of order. *Studies in Second Language Acquisition*, 18, 91–126.

Ellis, N. 2001: Memory for language. In P. Robinson (ed.), *Cognition and Second Language Instruction*. New York: Cambridge University Press, 33–68.

Ellis, N. and LaPorte, N. 1997: Contexts of acquisition: effects of formal instruction and naturalistic exposure on second language acquisition. In A. De Groot and J. Kroll (eds), *Tutorials in Bilingualism: Psycholinguistic Perspectives*. Hillsdale, NJ: Lawrence Erlbaum Associates, 53–83.

Ellis, N. and Schmidt, R. 1997: Morphology and longer distance dependencies: laboratory research illuminating the A in SLA. *Studies in Second Language Acquisition*, 19, 145–71.

Ellis, N., Lee, M., and Reber, A. forthcoming: Phonological working memory in artificial language acquisition. MS.

Ellis, R. 1987: Interlanguage variability in narrative discourse: style shifting and use of the past tense. *Studies in Second Language Acquisition*, 9, 1–20.

Elman, J. 1990: Finding structure in time. *Cognitive Science*, 14, 179–212.

Eslinger, P. 1996: Conceptualizing, describing and measuring components of executive function. In G. Reid Lyon and N. A. Krasnegor (eds), *Attention and Executive Function*. Baltimore, MD: Paul H. Brookes, 395–421.

Estes, W. 1992: Mental psychophysics of categorization and decision making. In H. Geissler, S. Link, and J. Townsend (eds), *Cognition, Information Processing and Psychophysics: Basic Issues*. Hillsdale, NJ: Lawrence Erlbaum Associates, 123–41.

Faerch, C. and Kasper, G. 1987: From product to process – introspective methods in second language research. In C. Faerch and G. Kasper (eds), *Introspection in Second Language Research*. Clevedon: Multilingual Matters, 5–24.

Faust, M. and Gernsbacher, M. 1996: Cerebral mechanisms for suppression of inappropriate information during sentence comprehension. *Brain and Language*, 53, 234–59.

Flege, J. and Munro, M. 1994: The word as a unit in second language speech perception and production. *Studies in Second Language Acquisition*, 16, 381–411.

Fleishman, E. and Quaintance, M. 1984: *Taxonomies of Human Performance: The Description of Human Tasks*. New York: Academic Press.

Fodor, J. 1983: *The Modularity of Mind*. Cambridge, MA: MIT Press.

Foster, P. and Skehan, P. 1996: The influence of planning and task type on second language performance. *Studies in Second Language Acquisition*, 18, 299–324.

Fotos, S. 1993: Consciousness raising and noticing through focus on form: grammar task performance versus formal instruction. *Applied Linguistics*, 14, 385–407.

Gass, S. 1982: From theory to practice. In M. Hines and W. Rutherford (eds), *On TESOL '81*. Washington, DC: TESOL, 129–39.

Gass, S. 1988: Integrating research areas: a framework for second language studies. *Applied Linguistics*, 9, 198–217.

Gass, S. 1997: *Input, Interaction, and the Second Language Learner*. Mahwah, NJ: Lawrence Erlbaum Associates.

Gass, S. 1999: Incidental learning: a commentary. *Studies in Second Language Acquisition*, 21, 319–34.

Gasser, M. 1990: Connectionism and universals of second language acquisition. *Studies in Second Language Acquisition*, 12, 179–99.

Gasser, M. and Smith, L. 1998: Learning nouns and adjectives: a connectionist account. In K. Plunkett (ed.), *Language Acquisition and Connectionism*. Hove: Psychology Press, 269–306.

Gathercole, S. and Baddeley, A. 1993: *Working Memory and Language*. Hillsdale, NJ: Lawrence Erlbaum Associates.

Gathercole, S. and Thorn, A. 1998: Phonological short-term memory and foreign language learning. In A. Healy and L. Bourne Jr (eds), *Foreign Language Learning: Psycholinguistic Studies on Training and Retention*. Mahwah, NJ: Lawrence Erlbaum Associates, 141–60.

Geva, E. and Ryan, E. 1993: Linguistic and cognitive correlates of academic skills in first and second languages. *Language Learning*, 43, 5–42.

Gopher, D. 1992: Analysis and measurement of mental workload. In G. d'Ydewalle, P. Eelen, and P. Bertelson (eds), *International Perspectives on Psychological Science. Vol. 2. State of the Art*. Hillsdale, NJ: Lawrence Erlbaum Associates, 265–91.

Gregg, K. 2001: Learnability and second language acquisition theory. In P. Robinson (ed.), *Cognition and Second Language Instruction*. New York: Cambridge University Press, 152–82.

Halford, G. 1993: *Children's Understanding: The Development of Mental Models*. Hillsdale, NJ: Lawrence Erlbaum Associates.

Harley, B. 1993: Instructional strategies and SLA in early French immersion. *Studies in Second Language Acquisition*, 15, 245–60.

Harley, B. and Swain, M. 1984: The interlanguage of immersion students and its implications for second language teaching. In A. Davies, C. Criper, and A. Howatt (eds), *Interlanguage: Studies in Honor of S. Pit Corder*. Edinburgh: Edinburgh University Press, 219–311.

Harrington, M. 2001: Sentence processing. In P. Robinson (ed.), *Cognition and Second Language Instruction*. New York: Cambridge University Press, 91–124.

Harrington, M. and Sawyer, M. 1992: L2 working memory capacity and L2 reading skill. *Studies in Second Language Acquisition*, 14, 25–38.

Hazelhurst, B. and Hutchins, E. 1998: The emergence of propositions from the coordination of talk and action in a shared world. In K. Plunkett (ed.), *Language Acquisition and Connectionism*. Hove: Psychology Press, 373–424.

Healy, A., Fendrich, D., Crutcher, R., Wittman, W., Gesi, A., Ericsson, K., and Bourne, L. Jr 1992: The long term retention of skills. In A. Healy, S. Kosslyn, and R. Shiffrin (eds), *From Learning Processes to Cognitive Processes: Essays in Honor of William Estes. Vol. 2*. Thousand Oaks, CA: Sage, 1–29.

Heuer, H. 1996: Dual-task performance. In O. Neumann and A. Sanders (eds), *Handbook of Perception and Action. Vol. 3: Attention*. New York: Academic Press, 113–48.

Hirst, W. and Kalmar, D. 1987: Characterizing attentional resources. *Journal of Experimental Psychology: General*, 116, 68–81.

Holding, D. (ed.) 1989: *Human Skills*. New York: John Wiley.

Holender, D. 1986: Semantic activation without conscious identification in dichotic listening tasks, parafoveal vision and visual masking: a survey and appraisal. *Behavioral and Brain Sciences*, 9, 1–66.

Holthouse, J. 1995: Anxiety and second language learning task type. M.A. dissertation. University of Queensland.

Horwitz, E. K., Horwitz, M. B., and Cope, J. 1986: Foreign language classroom anxiety. *Modern Language Journal*, 70, 125–32.

Huckin, T. and Coady, J. 1999: Incidental vocabulary acquisition in a second language. *Studies in Second Language Acquisition*, 21, 181–94.

Hulstijn, J. 1989: A cognitive view on interlanguage variability. In M. Eisenstein (ed.), *The Dynamic Interlanguage*. New York: Plenum, 17–32.

Hulstijn, J. 1997: Second language acquisition research in the laboratory: possibilities and limitations. *Studies in Second Language Acquisition*, 19, 131–44.

Hulstijn, J. 2001: Intentional and incidental second language learning: a reappraisal of elaboration, rehearsal and automaticity. In P. Robinson (ed.), *Cognition and Second Language Instruction*. New York: Cambridge University Press, 258–86.

Hulstijn, J. and DeGraaff, R. 1994: Under what conditions does explicit knowledge facilitate the acquisition of implicit knowledge? A research proposal. *AILA Review*, 11, 97–112.

Iwashita, N. 1999: The role of task-based conversation in the acquisition of Japanese grammar and vocabulary. Ph.D. dissertation. University of Melbourne.

Izumi, S., Bigelow, M., Fujiwara, M., and Fearnow, S. 1999: Testing the output hypothesis: effects of output on noticing and second language acquisition. *Studies in Second Language Acquisition*, 21, 421–52.

Jackendoff, R. 1997: *The Architecture of the Language Faculty*. Cambridge, MA: MIT Press.

Jacob, A. 1996: Anxiety and motivation during second language task performance in Singaporean schools. M.A. dissertation. National University of Singapore/RELC.

Jacoby, L. and Dallas, M. 1981: On the relationship between autobiographical memory and perceptual learning. *Journal of Experimental Psychology: General*, 3, 306–40.

Jourdenais, R. 2001: Cognition, instruction, and protocol analysis. In P. Robinson (ed.), *Cognition and Second Language Instruction*. New York: Cambridge University Press, 354–75.

Kahneman, D. 1973: *Attention and Effort*. Englewood Cliffs, NJ: Prentice-Hall.

Karmilloff-Smith, A. 1992: *Beyond Modularity*. Cambridge, MA: MIT Press.

Kasper, G. 1999: Self report data in pragmatics research. In N. O. Jungheim and P. Robinson (eds), *Pragmatics and Pedagogy: Proceedings of the 3rd Pacific Second Language Research Forum. Vol. 2*. Tokyo: PacSLRF, 1–15.

Kelley, C. and Lindsay, D. S. 1997: Conscious and unconscious forms of memory. In E. L. Bjork and R. Bjork (eds), *Memory*. San Diego: Academic Press, 31–63.

Kim, H. 1995: Intake from the speech stream: speech elements that learners attend to. In R. Schmidt (ed.), *Attention and Awareness in Foreign Language Learning and Teaching*. Second Language Teaching and Curriculum Center Technical Report No. 9. Honolulu: University of Hawai'i Press, 65–84.

Koelega, H. 1996: Sustained attention. In O. Neumann and A. Sanders (eds), *Handbook of Perception and Action. Vol. 3: Attention*. San Diego: Academic Press, 277–322.

Kormos, J. 1999: Monitoring and self repair in L2. *Language Learning*, 49, 303–42.

Korteling, J. 1994: *Multiple Task Performance and Aging*. Groningen: Bariet, Ruinen.

Krashen, S. 1985: *The Input Hypothesis: Issues and Implications*. Oxford: Pergamon Press.

Krashen, S. 1994: The input hypothesis and its rivals. In N. Ellis (ed.), *Implicit and Explicit Learning of Languages*. London: Academic Press, 45–78.

Leeman, J., Arteagoitia, I., Fridman, B., and Doughty, C. 1995: Integrating attention to form with meaning: focus on form in content-based Spanish instruction. In R. Schmidt (ed.), *Attention and Awareness in Foreign Language Learning and Teaching*. Second Language Teaching and Curriculum Center Technical Report No. 9. Honolulu: University of Hawai'i Press, 217–58.

Leow, R. 1993: To simplify or not to simplify: a look at intake. *Studies in Second Language Acquisition*, 15, 333–55.

Leow, R. 1997: Attention, awareness and foreign language behavior. *Language Learning*, 47, 467–505.

Leow, R. 2000: A study of the role of awareness in foreign language behavior: aware vs. unaware learners. *Studies in Second Language Acquisition*, 22, 557–84.

Levelt, W. J. M. 1989: *Speaking: From Intention to Articulation*. Cambridge, MA: MIT Press.

Liberman, A. and Mattingly, I. 1989: A specialization for speech perception. *Science*, 243, 489–94.

Logan, G. D. 1988: Toward an instance theory of automatization. *Psychological Review*, 95, 492–527.

Logan, G. D. 1990: Repetition priming and automaticity: common underlying mechanisms? *Cognitive Psychology*, 22, 1–35.

Logan, G. D. 1992: Attention and memory. In L. Squire (ed.), *Encyclopedia of Learning and Memory*. New York: Macmillan, 63–7.

Long, M. H. 1989: Task, group, and task–group interactions. *University of Hawai'i Working Papers in ESL*, 8, 1–25.

Long, M. H. 1990: Maturational constraints on language development. *Studies in Second Language Acquisition*, 12, 251–85.

Long, M. H. 1996: The role of the linguistic environment in second language acquisition. In W. Ritchie and T. Bhatia (eds), *Handbook of Research on Second Language Acquisition*. New York: Academic Press, 413–68.

Long, M. H. 1998: Focus on form in task-based language teaching. *University of Hawai'i Working Papers in ESL*, 161, 49–61.

Long, M. H. forthcoming: *Task Based Language Teaching*. Oxford: Blackwell.

Long, M. H. and Crookes, G. 1992: Three approaches to task-based syllabus design. *TESOL Quarterly*, 26, 55–98.

Long, M. H. and Norris, J. 2000: Task based language teaching. In M. Byram (ed.), *Encyclopedia of Language Education*. London: Routledge, 597–603.

Long, M. H. and Robinson, P. 1998: Focus on form: theory, research, practice. In C. Doughty and J. Williams (eds), *Focus on Form in Classroom Second Language Acquisition*. New York: Cambridge University Press, 15–41.

Lyster, R. 1998: Recasts, repetition and ambiguity in L2 classroom discourse. *Studies in Second Language Acquisition*, 20, 51–81.

Lyster, R. and Ranta, L. 1997: Corrective feedback and learner uptake: negotiation of form in communicative classrooms. *Studies in Second Language Acquisition*, 19, 37–66.

Mackey, A., Gass, S. M., and McDonough, K. 2000: Do learners recognize implicit negative feedback as feedback? *Studies in Second Language Acquisition*, 22, 471–97.

Mackey, A., Philp, J., Eri, T., Fuji, A., and Takaguchi, T. 2002: The outcomes of implicit feedback in conversational interaction: an exploration of the role of aptitude in phonological short-term memory. In P. Robinson (ed.), *Individual Differences and Instructed Language Learning*. Amsterdam: John Benjamins, 181–210.

MacWhinney, B. 1987: The competition model. In B. MacWhinney (ed.), *Mechanisms of Language Acquisition*. Hillsdale, NJ: Lawrence Erlbaum Associates, 249–308.

MacWhinney, B. 2001: The competition model: the input, the context and the brain. In P. Robinson (ed.), *Cognition and Second Language Instruction*. New York: Cambridge University Press, 69–90.

Marcel, A. 1983: Conscious and unconscious perception: experiments on visual masking and word recognition. *Cognitive Psychology*, 15, 197–237.

Massaro, D. 1987: *Speech Perception by Ear and by Eye: A Paradigm for Psychological Inquiry*. Hillsdale, NJ: Lawrence Erlbaum Associates.

McLaughlin, B. 1990: Restructuring. *Applied Linguistics*, 11, 113–28.

Mehnert, U. 1998: The effects of different lengths of time for planning on second language performance. *Studies in Second Language Acquisition*, 20, 83–108.

Merickle, P. and Reingold, E. 1991: Comparing direct (explicit) and indirect (implicit) measures to study unconscious memory. *Journal of Experimental Psychology: Learning, Memory and Cognition*, 17, 224–33.

Miyake, A. and Friedman, N. 1998: Individual differences in second language proficiency: working memory as language aptitude. In A. Healy and L. Bourne Jr (eds), *Foreign Language Learning: Psycholinguistic Studies on Training and Retention*. Mahwah, NJ: Lawrence Erlbaum Associates, 339–64.

Miyake, A., Friedman, N., and Osaka, M. 1998: Cue acquisition and syntactic comprehension in second language learning. Findings reported in A. Miyake and N. Friedman 1998: Individual differences in second language proficiency: working memory as language aptitude. In A. Healy and L. Bourne Jr (eds), *Foreign Language Learning: Psycholinguistic Studies on Training and Retention*. Mahwah, NJ: Lawrence Erlbaum Associates, 339–64.

Mulligan, N. 1997: Attention and implicit memory tests: the effects of varying attentional load on conceptual priming. *Memory & Cognition*, 25, 11–17.

Muranoi, H. 1996: Effects of interaction enhancement on restructuring of interlanguage grammar: a cognitive approach to foreign language instruction. Ph.D. dissertation. Georgetown University, Department of Linguistics.

Muranoi, H. 2000: Focus on form through interaction enhancement: integrating formal instruction into a communicative task in EFL classrooms. *Language Learning*, 50, 617–73.

Naatanen, R. 1992: *Attention and Brain Function*. Hillsdale, NJ: Lawrence Erlbaum Associates.

Nairne, J. 1996: Short-term/working memory. In E. L. Bjork and R. Bjork (eds), *Memory*. San Diego: Academic Press, 102–30.

Navon, D. 1989: The importance of being visible: on the role of attention in a mind viewed as an anarchic intelligence system. *European Journal of Cognitive Psychology*, 1, 191–238.

Neely, J. 1977: Semantic priming and retrieval from lexical memory: roles of inhibitionless spreading activation and limited capacity attention. *Journal of Experimental Psychology: General*, 106, 226–54.

Nelson, K. 1996: *Language in Cognitive Development: The Emergence of the Mediated Mind*. New York: Cambridge University Press.

Neumann, O. 1987: Beyond capacity: a functional view of attention. In H. Heuer and A. Sanders (eds), *Perspectives on Perception and Action*. Berlin: Springer, 361–94.

Neumann, O. 1996: Theories of attention. In O. Neumann and A. Sanders (eds), *Handbook of Perception and Action. Vol. 3: Attention*. San Diego: Academic Press, 389–446.

Nissen, M. and Bullemer, P. 1987: Attentional requirements of learning: evidence from performance systems. *Cognitive Psychology*, 19, 1–32.

Niwa, Y. 1999: Reasoning demands of L2 tasks and L2 narrative production: effects of individual differences in working memory, intelligence, and aptitude. M.A. dissertation. Aoyama Gakuin University, Department of English.

Norris, J. and Ortega, L. 2000: Effectiveness of L2 instruction: a research synthesis and meta-analysis. *Language Learning*, 50, 417–528.

Norris, J., Brown, J. D., Hudson, T., and Yoshioka, J. 1998: *Developing Second Language Performance Tests*. University of Hawai'i Second Language Teaching and Curriculum Center Technical Report No. 19. Honolulu: University of Hawai'i Press.

Nosofsky, R. 1992: Exemplar-based approach to relating categorization, identification and recognition. In F. G. Ashby (ed.), *Multidimensional Models of*

Perception and Categorization. Hillsdale, NJ: Lawrence Erlbaum Associates, 363–95.

Nosofsky, R., Kruschke, J., and McKinley, S. 1992: Combining exemplar-based category representations and connectionist learning rules. *Journal of Experimental Psychology: Learning Memory and Cognition*, 15, 282–304.

Oliver, R. 1995: Negative feedback in child NS/NNS conversation. *Studies in Second Language Acquisition*, 17, 459–83.

Ortega, L. 1999: Planning and focus on form in L2 oral performance. *Studies in Second Language Acquisition*, 21, 109–48.

Osaka, M. and Osaka, N. 1992: Language-independent working memory as measured by Japanese and English reading span tests. *Bulletin of the Psychonomic Society*, 30, 287–9.

Paradis, M. 1994: Neurolinguistic aspects of implicit and explicit memory: implications for bilingualism. In N. Ellis (ed.), *Implicit and Explicit Learning of Languages*. New York: Academic Press, 393–419.

Pashler, H. and Carrier, M. 1997: Structures, processes, and the flow of information. In E. L. Bjork and R. Bjork (eds), *Memory*. San Diego: Academic Press, 3–29.

Phaf, R., van der Heijden, A., and Hudson, P. 1990: SLAM: a connectionist model for attention in visual selection tasks. *Cognitive Psychology*, 22, 273–341.

Pica, T. 1988: Interlanguage adjustments as an outcome of NS–NNS negotiated interaction. *Language Learning*, 38, 45–73.

Pica, T. 1992: The textual outcomes of NS–NNS negotiation: what do they reveal about learning? In C. Kramsch and S. McConnel-Ginet (eds), *Text and Context*. Cambridge, MA: Heath, 198–237.

Pica, T., Kanagy, R., and Falodun, J. 1993: Choosing and using communication tasks for second language teaching and research. In G. Crookes and S. Gass (eds), *Tasks in Language Learning: Integrating Theory and Practice*. Clevedon: Multilingual Matters, 1–42.

Posner, M. 1980: Orienting of attention. *Quarterly Journal of Experimental Psychology*, 32, 3–25.

Posner, M. and Petersen, S. 1990: The attention system of the human brain. *Annual Review of Neuroscience*, 13, 25–42.

Prinz, W. 1986: Continuous selection. *Psychological Research*, 48, 231–8.

Rahimpour, M. 1997: Task condition, task complexity and variation in oral L2 discourse. Ph.D. dissertation. University of Queensland.

Rahimpour, M. 1999: Task complexity and variation in interlanguage. In N. Jungheim and P. Robinson (eds), *Pragmatics and Pedagogy: Proceedings of the 3rd Pacific Second Language Research Forum. Vol. 2*. Tokyo: PacSLRF, 115–34.

Reber, A. 1989: Implicit learning and tacit knowledge. *Journal of Experimental Psychology: General*, 118, 219–35.

Reber, A. 1993: *Implicit Learning and Tacit Knowledge: An Essay on the Cognitive Unconscious*. Oxford: Oxford University Press.

Reber, A., Walkenfield, F., and Hernstadt, R. 1991: Implicit and explicit learning: individual differences and IQ. *Journal of Experimental Psychology: Learning, Memory and Cognition*, 17, 888–96.

Reed, E. 1996: *Encountering the World: Toward an Ecological Psychology*. New York: Oxford University Press.

Richardson-Klavehn, A. and Bjork, R. 1988: Measures of memory. *Annual Review of Psychology*, 39, 475–543.

Robinson, P. 1993: Problems of knowledge and the implicit/explicit distinction in SLA theory. *University of*

Hawai'i Working Papers in ESL, 12, 99–146.

Robinson, P. 1995a: Task complexity and second language narrative discourse. *Language Learning*, 45, 99–140.

Robinson, P. 1995b: Attention, memory and the "noticing" hypothesis. *Language Learning*, 45, 283–331.

Robinson, P. 1996a: Learning simple and complex second language rules under implicit, incidental, rule search and instructed conditions. *Studies in Second Language Acquisition*, 18, 27–67.

Robinson, P. 1996b: *Consciousness, Rules and Instructed Second Language Acquisition*. New York: Lang.

Robinson, P. 1996c: Connecting tasks, cognition and syllabus design. In P. Robinson (ed.), *Task Complexity and Second Language Syllabus Design: Data-Based Studies and Speculations. University of Queensland Working Papers in Applied Linguistics*, 1, 1–16.

Robinson, P. 1997a: Individual differences and the fundamental similarity of implicit and explicit adult second language learning. *Language Learning*, 47, 45–99.

Robinson, P. 1997b: Generalizability and automaticity of second language learning under implicit, incidental, enhanced and instructed conditions. *Studies in Second Language Acquisition*, 19, 223–47.

Robinson, P. 2000: The cognition hypothesis of task-based language development and its implications. In *Proceedings of the 3rd Acquisition of Japanese as a Second Language Conference, Ochanomizu University, Tokyo, December*, 10–15.

Robinson, P. 2001a: Task complexity, task difficulty, and task production: exploring interactions in a componential framework. *Applied Linguistics*, 22, 27–57.

Robinson, P. 2001b: Individual differences, cognitive abilities, aptitude complexes and learning conditions: an aptitude complex/ability differentiation framework for SLA research. In Larry Selinker and Usha Lakshmanan (eds), *Second Language Research*, 17, 368–92: Special Issue on Explanation and Scientific Method in SLA Research: Festschrift for Paul van Buren.

Robinson, P. 2001c: Task complexity, cognitive resources, and syllabus design: a triadic framework for investigating task influences on SLA. In P. Robinson (ed.), *Cognition and Second Language Instruction*. New York: Cambridge University Press, 287–318.

Robinson, P. 2002: Effects of individual differences in working memory, intelligence and aptitude on incidental second language learning: a replication and extension of Reber, Walkenfield and Hernstadt 1991. In P. Robinson (ed.), *Individual Differences and Instructed Language Learning*. Amsterdam: John Benjamins, 211–66.

Robinson, P. forthcoming: *Task Complexity, Second Language Development and Syllabus Design*. Cambridge: Cambridge University Press.

Robinson, P. and Ha, M. 1993: Instance theory and second language rule learning under explicit conditions. *Studies in Second Language Acquisition*, 13, 413–38.

Robinson, P. and Lim, J. J. 1993: Cognitive load and the Route-Marked/Not-Marked Map Task. Unpublished data. University of Hawai'i at Manoa, Department of ESL.

Robinson, P. and Niwa, Y. 2001: Task complexity and reasoning demands of second language narratives: effects on production and perceptions of task difficulty. Ms.

Robinson, P. and Yamaguchi, Y. 1999: Communication, corrective feedback and aptitude: interactions of classroom, task and learner factors. Paper presented at the 13th AILA

World Congress of Applied Linguistics, Waseda University, Tokyo, August.

Robinson, P., Strong, G., Whittle, J., and Nobe, S. 2001: The development of academic discussion ability. In J. Flowerdew and M. Peacock (eds), *Research Perspectives on English for Academic Purposes*. Cambridge: Cambridge University Press, 347–59.

Robinson, P., Ting, S., and Urwin, J. 1995: Investigating second language task complexity. *RELC Journal*, 25, 62–79.

Roediger, H., Weldon, M., and Challis, B. 1989: Explaining dissociations between implicit and explicit measures of memory: a processing account. In H. Roediger and F. Craik (eds), *Varieties of Memory and Consciousness*. Hillsdale, NJ: Lawrence Erlbaum Associates, 3–41.

Rosa, E. and O'Neill, M. 1999: Explicitness, intake and the issue of awareness: another piece to the puzzle. *Studies in Second Language Acquisition*, 21, 511–56.

Rott, S. 1999: The effect of exposure frequency on intermediate language learners' incidental vocabulary acquisition and retention through reading. *Studies in Second Language Acquisition*, 21, 589–620.

Rutherford, W. 1987: *Second Language Grammar: Learning and Teaching*. London: Longman.

Sanders, A. 1986: Energetical states underlying task performance. In G. R. Hockey, A. W. Gaillard, and M. G. Coles (eds), *Energetics and Human Information Processing*. Dordrecht: Martinus Nijhoff, 139–54.

Sanders, A. 1998: *Elements of Human Performance*. Mahwah, NJ: Lawrence Erlbaum Associates.

Sanders, A. and Neumann, O. 1996: Introduction. In O. Neumann and A. Sanders (eds), *Handbook of Perception and Action. Vol. 3: Attention*. San Diego: Academic Press, 1–5.

Sasaki, M. 1996: *Second Language Proficiency, Foreign Language Aptitude and Intelligence*. New York: Lang.

Sawyer, M. and Ranta, L. 2001: Aptitude, individual differences and program design. In P. Robinson (ed.), *Cognition and Second Language Instruction*. New York: Cambridge University Press, 319–53.

Schachter, D. 1987: Implicit memory: history and current status. *Journal of Experimental Psychology: Learning, Memory and Cognition*, 13, 501–18.

Schachter, D. 1996: *Searching for Memory: The Brain, the Mind, and the Past*. New York: Basic Books.

Schmidt, R. 1990: The role of consciousness in second language learning. *Applied Linguistics*, 11, 129–58.

Schmidt, R. 1995: Consciousness and foreign language learning: a tutorialon the role of attention and awareness in learning. In R. Schmidt (ed.), *Attention and Awareness in Foreign Language Learning and Teaching*. Second Language Teaching and Curriculum Center Technical Report No. 9. Honolulu: University of Hawai'i Press, 1–64.

Schmidt, R. 2001: Attention. In P. Robinson (ed.), *Cognition and Second Language Instruction*. New York: Cambridge University Press, 3–32.

Schmidt, R. and Frota, S. 1986: Developing basic conversational ability in a second language: a case study of an adult learner of Portuguese. In R. Day (ed.), *Talking to Learn: Conversation in Second Language Acquisition*. Rowley, MA: Newbury House, 237–322.

Schneider, W. and Detweiler, M. 1988: The role of practice in dual-task performance: toward workload modeling in a connectionist-control architecture. *Human Factors*, 30, 539–66.

Schneider, W., Healy, A., and Bourne, L. Jr 1998: Contextual interference effects in foreign language vocabulary acquisition and retention. In A. Healy and L. Bourne Jr (eds), *Foreign Language Learning: Psycholinguistic Studies on Training and Retention*. Mahwah, NJ: Lawrence Erlbaum Associates, 77–90.

Schwartz, B. 1999: Let's make up your mind: "special nativist" perspectives on language, modularity of mind, and nonnative language acquisition. *Studies in Second Language Acquisition*, 21, 635–56.

Sergeant, J. 1996: A theory of attention: an information processing perspective. In G. Reid Lyon and N. A. Krasnegor (eds), *Attention and Executive Function*. Baltimore, MD: Paul H. Brookes, 57–69.

Shaffer, L. 1975: Multiple attention in continuous verbal tasks. In P. Rabbitt and S. Dornic (eds), *Attention and Performance. Vol. 4*. New York: Academic Press, 157–67.

Shallice, T. 1972: Dual functions of consciousness. *Psychological Review*, 79, 383–93.

Shallice, T. 1978: The dominant action system: an information processing approach to consciousness. In K. Pape and J. Singer (eds), *The Stream of Consciousness*. New York: Plenum Press, 117–57.

Shanks, D. and St John, M. 1994: Characteristics of dissociable human systems. *Behavioral and Brain Sciences*, 17, 367–447.

Sharwood-Smith, M. 1981: Consciousness-raising and the second language learner. *Applied Linguistics*, 2, 159–68.

Sharwood-Smith, M. 1991: Speaking to many minds: on the relevance of different types of language information for the L2 learner. *Second Language Research*, 7, 118–32.

Shiffrin, R. 1993: Short-term memory: a brief commentary. *Memory & Cognition*, 21, 193–7.

Shiffrin, R. and Schneider, W. 1977: Controlled and automatic human information processing II: perceptual learning, automatic attending and a general theory. *Psychological Review*, 84, 127–90.

Skehan, P. 1996: A framework for the implementation of task-based instruction. *Applied Linguistics*, 17, 38–62.

Skehan, P. 1998: *A Cognitive Approach to Language Learning*. Oxford: Oxford University Press.

Skehan, P. and Foster, P. 1997: Task type and task processing conditions as influences on foreign language performance. *Language Teaching Research*, 1, 185–212.

Skehan, P. and Foster, P. 2001: Cognition and tasks. In P. Robinson (ed.), *Cognition and Second Language Instruction*. New York: Cambridge University Press, 183–205.

Smith, E. E. and Sloman, S. 1994: Similarity-versus rule-based categorization. *Memory & Cognition*, 22, 377–86.

Spada, N. 1997: Form-focussed instruction and second language acquisition: a review of classroom and laboratory research. *Language Teaching*, 29, 1–15.

Spada, N. and Lightbown, P. 1993: Instruction and the development of questions in the L2 classroom. *Studies in Second Language Acquisition*, 1 (15), 205–21.

Sperling, G. 1960: The information available in brief visual presentations. *Psychological Monographs*, 74 (11) (no. 498).

Squire, L. 1992: Declarative and nondeclarative memory: multiple brain systems supporting learning and memory. *Journal of Cognitive Neuroscience*, 4, 232–43.

Stadler, M. 1992: Statistical structure and implicit serial learning. *Journal of Experimental Psychology: Learning, Memory and Cognition*, 18, 318–27.

Sternberg, R. 1985: *Beyond IQ: A Triarchic Theory of Human Intelligence*. Cambridge: Cambridge University Press.

Swain, M. 1985: Communicative competence: some roles of comprehensible input and comprehensible output in its development. In S. Gass and C. Madden (eds), *Input in Second Language Acquisition*. Rowley, MA: Newbury House, 235–53.

Swain, M. 1995: Three functions of output in second language learning. In G. Cook and B. Seidlhoffer (eds), *Principle and Practice in Applied Linguistics: Studies in Honor of H. G. Widdowson*. Oxford: Oxford University Press, 125–44.

Swain, M. and Lapkin, S. 1995: Problems in output and the cognitive processes they generate. *Applied Linguistics*, 16, 370–91.

Tarone, E. 1985: Variability in interlanguage use: a study of style-shifting in morphology and syntax. *Language Learning*, 35, 373–403.

Tarone, E. and Parrish, B. 1988: Task-based variation in interlanguage: the case of articles. *Language Learning*, 38, 21–44.

Thelen, E. and Smith, L. 1998: *A Dynamic Systems Approach to the Development of Cognition and Action*. Cambridge, MA: MIT Press.

Ting, S. C.-C. 1996: Tasks and planning time in the acquisition of Chinese as a second language. In P. Robinson (ed.), *Task Complexity and Second Language Syllabus Design: Data-Based Studies and Speculations*. Brisbane: University of Queensland Working Papers in Applied Linguistics, 30–63.

Tipper, S. 1992: Selection for action: the role of inhibitory mechanisms. *Current Directions in Psychological Science*, 1, 105–9.

Tomasello, M. and Farrar, M. 1986: Joint attention and early language. *Child Development*, 57, 1454–63.

Tomasello, M., Manle, S., and Kruger, A. 1989: Linguistic environment of 1- to 2-year-old twins. *Developmental Psychology*, 22, 169–76.

Tomlin, R. and Villa, V. 1994: Attention in cognitive science and SLA. *Studies in Second Language Acquisition*, 16, 185–204.

Treisman, A. 1971: Shifting attention between the ears. *Quarterly Journal of Experimental Psychology*, 23, 157–67.

Truscott, J. 1998: Noticing in second language acquisition: a critical review. *Second Language Research*, 14, 103–35.

Urwin, J. 1999: Second language listening task complexity. Ph.D. dissertation. Monash University.

van der Heijden, T. 1992: *Selective Attention in Vision*. London: Routledge.

VanPatten, B. 1996: *Input Processing and Grammar Instruction: Theory and Research*. Norwood, NJ: Ablex.

White, J. 1998: Getting the learner's attention: a typographical input enhancement study. In C. Doughty and J. Williams (eds), *Focus on Form in Classroom Second Language Acquisition*. New York: Cambridge University Press, 85–113.

White, L. 1991: Adverb placement in second language acquisition: some effects of positive and negative evidence in the classroom. *Second Language Research*, 7, 122–61.

White, L., Spada, N., Lightbown, P., and Ranta, L. 1991: Input enhancement and L2 question formation. *Applied Linguistics*, 12, 416–32.

Wickens, C. 1984: Processing resources in attention. In R. Parasuraman and D. Davies (eds), *Varieties of Attention*. New York: Academic Press, 63–102.

Wickens, C. 1989: Attention and skilled performance. In D. Holding (ed.), *Human Skills*. New York: John Wiley, 71–105.

Wickens, C. 1992: *Engineering Psychology and Human Performance*. Second edition. New York: HarperCollins.

Wickens, C., Gordon, S. E., and Liu, Y. 1997: *An Introduction to Human Factors Engineering*. New York: Longman.

Williams, J. 1999: Memory, attention and inductive learning. *Studies in Second Language Acquisition*, 21, 1–48.

Zobl, H. 1992: Sources of linguistic knowledge and uniformity of nonnative performance. *Studies in Second Language Acquisition*, 14, 387–403.

Zobl, H. 1995: Converging evidence for the acquisition/learning distinction. *Applied Linguistics*, 16, 35–57.

20 Language Processing Capacity

MANFRED PIENEMANN

1 Introduction

In this chapter I will focus on the development of L2 processing capacity. In section 2, an overview will be provided of different approaches to SLA that entail a processing perspective. The bulk of the chapter is devoted to one specific approach, processability theory (PT), because it affords an explicit account of L2 processing capacity. Within this framework, I will show that research on L2 processing skills contributes to an explanation of linguistic development by defining which linguistic forms are processable at different points in development. I will further show that the concept of "processability" makes testable predictions for developmental routes across typologically different languages, that it applies to L2 as well as to L1 acquisition, and that it delineates the scope of interlanguage variation as well as L1 transfer.

2 Processing Approaches to SLA

The notion of limited processing capacity is a standard assumption in work on human cognition. For instance, short-term memory is thought to be limited in capacity and duration (e.g., Baddely, 1990). The assumption that the processing capacity of L2 learners is limited forms the basis of several approaches to SLA. The limited-capacity view of L2 processing constitutes a basic assumption in work on L2 input processing (e.g., Krashen, 1982; VanPatten, 1996), in research on L2 skill acquisition (e.g., McLaughlin, 1987), in work on operating principles (e.g., Andersen, 1984), in the "competition model" (e.g., Bates and MacWhinney, 1981), and in Clahsen's (1984) L2 processing strategies, as well as in my own work on processability.

In this section I will briefly review the above approaches in an attempt to assess how explicitly the L2 processor is specified, because in my view only an explication of L2 processing procedures permits one to integrate a theoretical model of L2 processing with a module of L2 knowledge, and only procedural explicitness allows the processing module to be falsified. One needs to bear in mind, however, that the above approaches were not solely designed to model L2 processing. Instead they also touch upon issues dealt with in other chapters of this volume, such as automatization, memory, and attention. Nevertheless, it should be noted that this chapter will focus as far as possible on the architecture of the language processor and its impact on second language development. Other issues will therefore be mentioned only in passing.

2.1 *Input processing*

One early approach to SLA that incorporates, amongst other things, a processing perspective is Krashen's (1985) monitor model. This work received a great amount of attention in the 1980s and has been subjected to extensive critiques (e.g., Gregg, 1984; Long, 1985; McLaughlin, 1978, 1987).

In his Input Hypothesis, Krashen claims that: "humans acquire language in only one way – by understanding messages, or by receiving 'comprehensible input' . . . We move from *i*, our current level, to *i+1*, the next level along the natural order, by understanding input containing *i+1*" (Krashen, 1985, p. 2). As this quotation illustrates, the Input Hypothesis is aimed at explaining two things, namely (i) the inferential mechanisms that drive the acquisition process, and (ii) the assumed universal order of acquisition. It has been pointed out in the above-mentioned critiques that the Input Hypothesis cannot be operationalized for any of its components. As a result, it cannot be tested empirically. How are *i* and *i+1* defined? What is the exact process by which the learner incorporates *i+1* into his or her interlanguage system? And what is the relationship between linguistic input and the representation of L2 knowledge? In other words, Krashen's model evades the issue of specifying the architecture of the L2 processor and the inferential mechanisms involved. As research of the past two decades has shown, these turned out to be monumental tasks.

VanPatten's (1996) work is an example of later mainstream research on input processing. VanPatten follows the main idea of the Input Hypothesis and stipulates two sets of input-processing strategies in an attempt to spell out aspects of the architecture of the L2 processor. The first set consists of five cognitive strategies that are supposed to regulate which aspects of the linguistic input are attended to and processed first (VanPatten, 1996, p. 14f). The second set consists of three Bever-style (Bever, 1970) strategies for the assignment of grammatical and semantic roles to nouns (VanPatten, 1996, p. 32). VanPatten follows Corder (1967) in distinguishing between "input" and "intake" and stipulates attention as the necessary condition for input to be transformed into intake. In his model the first set of strategies is intended to operationalize "attention," and the second, aspects of "sentence processing." However, these processing strategies are limited to one narrow domain of language processing and are subject to the same conceptual limitations as Clahsen's (1984) strategies approach, which will be summarized at the end of this section.

Carroll (1999, 2000) reviews the literature on L2 input processing and concludes that the standard assumption, based on Corder's (1967) input–intake distinction, according to which "perception is regulated only by attention, which in turn is regulated by intention" (Carroll, 1999, p. 343), is not supported by any explicit theory of attention. Her own view on the matter contrasts sharply with the attention-filter assumption. Carroll seeks to demonstrate that signal detection is regulated by human knowledge systems independently of intention and concludes that: "[i]nput is . . . determined by our grammars" (Carroll, 1999, p. 343). Carroll (1999, 2000) proposes the Autonomous Induction Theory, which is an explicit theoretical framework for the induction of linguistic representation from linguistic input. In this induction process, Carroll distinguishes between the input to speech processing and the input to language-learning mechanisms. This position is compatible with a modular view of processing and a UG-position on cognition, and is thus juxtaposed to the functionalist orientation of the standard view on the attention filter in processing. Irrespective of one's theoretical inclination, this work highlights the enormity of the task of specifying the inferential mechanisms that explain how input becomes intake. In other words, Carroll's work focuses on the inferential mechanisms and is not designed as a contribution to specifying the architecture of the L2 processor.

This brief summary of trends in theory on L2 input processing also illustrates that work in this area involves a large number of factors in addition to language-processing capacity, which is the focus of this chapter.

2.2 *Procedural skills*

Reference to language-processing capacity is also made in research on the acquisition of L2 procedural skills. From their cognitive perspective, McLaughlin and his associates (McLaughlin, 1987; McLaughlin, Rossman, and McLeod, 1983) assume that "[t]o learn a second language is to learn a *skill*" (McLaughlin, 1987, p. 133) and that L2 learning "requires the automatization of component sub-skills" (McLaughlin, 1987, p. 133). Similarly, other authors have also expressed the view that language acquisition entails the acquisition of procedural skills (e.g., Hulstijn, 1990; Levelt, 1978; Schmidt, 1992). In line with his cognitive perspective, McLaughlin views humans as limited-capacity processors for controlled processes. He assumes that L2 processing skills become more efficient through automatization, which allows them to be processed automatically and thus without the limitation of controlled processes. He concludes that "[t]he notion of a capacity-free (automatic) process provides an explanation for improvement in performance" (McLaughlin, 1987, p. 136).

McLaughlin's work is not directly concerned with language-processing procedures. Instead it focuses on two key notions: *automaticity* and *restructuring*. Automaticity makes recourse to the dichotomy of *controlled* and *automatic processing* (Posner and Snyder, 1975; Schneider and Shiffrin, 1977; Shiffrin and Schneider, 1977). Restructuring refers to the replacement of existing procedures by more efficient ones. McLaughlin believes that "once the procedures at any phase become automatized . . . learners step up to a 'metaprocedural' level, which generates representational change and restructuring" (McLaughlin, 1987, p. 138). In other words, McLaughlin's approach is aimed at the skills that underlie L2 processing, as well as at the acquisition of these skills. And automatization is seen as the process by which the overall L2 processing capacity can be increased. As far as the explicitness of his approach and of cognitive theory generally is concerned, McLaughlin makes the following cautious statement: "Cognitive theory does not represent a highly articulated theoretical position. There have been relatively few attempts to spell out with any degree of precision what the predictions of such a theory would be for second language learning" (McLaughlin, 1987, p. 150).

2.3 *Operating principles*

Andersen (1984, 1988) based his approach to SLA on a different set of assumptions. Following the basic design of Slobin's (1973, 1985) approach to L1 acquisition, he proposed a set of "operating principles" for SLA which concern two aspects of the acquisition process: the processing of language and the discovery of its formal and functional properties. In other words, Andersen's approach goes beyond language processing and incorporates learning mechanisms. An example is the "one-to-one principle," which states that "[a]n interlanguage system should be constructed in such a way that an intended underlying meaning is expressed with one clear invariant surface form" (Andersen, 1984, p. 79).

Andersen's and Slobin's approaches have been criticized for being difficult to test, because the operating principles are not clearly separated from each other (e.g., Larsen-Freeman, 1975); instead, they compete with one another. This leads to typical post-factual explanations. If an IL phenomenon cannot be attributed to principle A, then it can be attributed to a competing principle B. Bowerman (1985) points out that operating principles are not falsifiable, because evidence against existing principles can be countered by the introduction of ever new principles. The reason why operating principles are not testable is because they do not contain procedural information to implement the micro-structure of language processing. For instance, to make Slobin's (1973) operating principle "Be semantically expressive" productive for the speaker, one needs to specify the exact procedures required to generate the surface structures which best express the semantic structures intended by the speaker. In sum, operating principles lack linguistic or procedural explicitness.

2.4 *The competition model*

The competition model (Bates and MacWhinney, 1981, 1982, 1987) is a further approach to language acquisition that assumes limited processing resources in L2 learners. It is a functionalist approach that is based on the assumption that linguistic behavior is constrained, among other things, by general cognition (and not by a language-specific cognitive module) and communicative needs. Following the functionalist tradition, Bates and MacWhinney assume that "the surface conventions of natural languages are created, governed, constrained, acquired, and used in the service of communicative functions" (Bates and MacWhinney, 1981, p. 192).

As the above quotation indicates, the competition model is claimed to be applicable to child language, language processing in general, and second language acquisition. According to this model, it is the task of the language learner to discover the specific relationship between the linguistic forms of a given language and their communicative functions. The linguistic forms used to mark grammatical and semantic roles differ from language to language. For instance, agreement marking, word order, and animacy play a different role in the marking of subject-hood and agency in different languages. Linguistic forms are seen as "cues" for semantic interpretation in on-line comprehension and production, and different cues may compete, as in the above case of the marking of subject-hood. Hence, the name: competition model.

In the competition model, the process of learning linguistic forms is driven by the frequency and complexity of form–function relationships in the input. In this context, the majority of L2 learning problems is modeled in connectionist terms. MacWhinney (1987) exemplifies this with the pre-verbal positioning of a linguistic form as a (processing) cue for the semantic actor-role. He states that the strength of this cue "can be viewed as the weight on the connection between the preverbal positioning node (an input node) and the actor role (an output node). If the preverbal positioning node is activated, it then sends activation to the actor node in proportion to the weight on the connection" (MacWhinney, 1987, p. 320).

The competition model has formed the conceptual basis of experiments on bilingual sentence processing (e.g., Gass, 1987; Harrington, 1987; Kilborn and Ito, 1989; McDonald and Heilenman, 1991; Sasaki, 1991). In these studies, bilingual speakers of different languages have to identify the function of different "cues" in L1 and L2. Input material is designed to reflect the coordination and competition of cues. For instance, Harrington (1987) studies the (competing) effect of word order, animacy, and stress on the comprehension of Japanese and English sentences by native speakers and non-native speakers of the two languages who are all speakers of both languages. Obviously, the three cues have different weights in the two target languages concerned. The results show that L2 learners transfer their L1 processing strategies (i.e., weighting of cues) when interpreting L2 sentences. This overall result is predicted by the competition model, since within this framework, processing cues are not initially separated by languages and their weighting can therefore be predicted to be transferred. However, the above studies also produced a host of effects that are not predicted by the model or that cannot even be captured by it. Aside from the limitations of the connectionist framework (cf. Pinker and Prince, 1987), which MacWhinney (1987) recognizes, the competition model can presently offer only fragments of the architecture of the language processor.

2.5 Processing strategies

The use of processing strategies in Clahsen's (1984) approach yielded a considerable number of testable hypotheses. It therefore warrants a somewhat more explicit summary and critique. Clahsen's (1984) "strategies" approach was designed to explain the stages in the acquisition of German L2 word order found in the ZISA study (Clahsen, Meisel, and Pienemann, 1983):

x	Canonical order	SVO
x + 1	Adverb preposing (ADV)	adv SVO
x + 2	Verb separation (SEP)	X SVOV
x + 3	Inversion (INV)	X VSY
x + 4	Verb final (V-END)	comp SOV

Clahsen (1984) assumed a set of speech-processing strategies which constrain the otherwise overly powerful grammar of the learner. These strategies are stated below:

i *Canonical Order Strategy (COS)*: "In underlying sequences [x1 + x2 . . . Xn] Cx [ ] Cx + 1 [ ] Cx + m, in which each of the subconstituents contributes information to the internal structure of the constituent Cx, no subconstituent is moved out of Cx, and no material from the subsequent constituents Cx + 1, Cx + 2, Cx + n is moved into Cx."

ii *Initialization-Finalization Strategy (IFS)*: "In underlying sequences, [X Y Z]s permutations are blocked which move X between Y and Z or Z between X and Y."

iii *Subordinate Clause Strategy (SCS)*: "In subordinate clauses permutations are avoided." (Clahsen, 1984, pp. 219–42)

This work was originally carried out in the late 1970s (Clahsen, 1979). Clahsen based these strategies on research into speech processing and language acquisition. COS was based on Bever's (1970) experiments on comprehension. IFS was based on findings from memory research, and SCS on the finding that subordinate clauses are processed in a different mode than main clauses. Table 20.1 shows schematically how the above strategies account for the observed order of acquisition.

In principle, the above strategies are understood as heuristic principles which allow the learner to short cut the comprehension-production process. For instance, the COS, which is based on Bever's (1970) postulation of an NVN strategy, permits direct mapping of semantic structure onto syntactic forms. In the psycholinguistic discussion of the 1970s, Bever-style strategies were conceptualized as "performance short cuts" of the derivational process. This view

Table 20.1 Processing stages and acquisition order

Stage	*Rule*	*Strategies*		
x	Canonical order		+COS	+SCS
x + 1	Adverb prep[illegible]	+IFS	+COS	+SCS
x + 2	Verb s[illegible]	+IFS	−COS	+SCS
x + 3	[illegible]	−IFS	−COS	+SCS
x + 4	[illegible]	−IFS	−COS	−SCS

[illegible] namely (i) the validity of the
[illegible] theory, and (ii) its lack of
[illegible] ese strategies to the concept
[illegible] ntence comprehension, he
[illegible] ture is dependent on the
[illegible] erial involved in the pro-
[illegible] ms. From this perspect-
iv[illegible] nstraint shedding.[1]
C[illegible] uistic concepts which
wer[illegible] erspective is at odds
with [illegible] d out the shortcomings o[illegible] ade:

- The [illegible] lear (e.g., Towell
and [illegible] grammars are
underc[illegible] learner at any given
stage o[illegible] arner does not have sufficient
informat[illegible] ction of interlanguage speech on the
basis of s[illegible] egies can only operate as complements to a
grammar, [illegible] nar substitutes.
- Processing [illegible] egies are based on comprehension-related phenomena and formulated through the interpretation of empirical findings on comprehension, although it is clear that comprehension and production are not mirror images of one another (White, 1989, 1991). The NVN strategy (Bever, 1970), in particular, accounts for observational facts in speech comprehension.
- Strategies are stated in such a way that they are constraints on movement transformations as conceptualized in TG. This has a rather important side effect: the strategies approach is set up to prevent the movement of "materialized" sub-constituents across the boundaries of major constituents. This view automatically limits the strategies approach to the domain of word order.
- A final problem with the strategies approach is its relation to learnability and extendibility (e.g., Pinker, 1984). I pointed out above that the strategies

> in Clahsen's framework are not sufficient prerequisites for the learnability of the structures in question. At the same time, they serve to predict the order of complexity once the structures are described with recourse to an additional paradigm, namely, aspects of a grammatical formalism. Only in this latter sense is the processing approach predictive.

In the final analysis, the strategies approach proves to lack the degree of procedural explicitness required to integrate it into a theory of SLA, even though the approach does produce falsifiable hypotheses and withstood a fair number of empirical tests.

To sum up, the processing-oriented approaches reviewed above (with the exception of Clahsen's) are not focused solely on L2 processing and its effect on L2 development. Instead, L2 processing is studied as one of several interacting factors that contribute to L2 acquisition. In other words, those approaches are aimed at explaining more than developmental trajectories. For instance, most of them also include the inferential process as an explanandum. And more than one explanatory component is used to account for the explananda. The wide scope of these approaches comes at the cost of explicitness. Since I view procedural explicitness as a necessary prerequisite for the operationalizibility of an approach to L2 processing capacity, the remainder of this chapter will focus on a modular processing approach to SLA that aims at procedural explicitness, namely processability theory (Pienemann, 1998a).

3 Processability Theory

3.1 *Step 1: A hierarchy of processing procedures*

The logic underlying processability theory (PT) is the following: at any stage of development, the learner can produce and comprehend only those L2 linguistic forms which the current state of the language processor can manage. It is, therefore, crucial to understand the architecture of the language processor and the way in which it handles a second language. This enables one to predict the course of development of L2 linguistic forms in language production and comprehension across languages.

The architecture of the language processor (e.g., Levelt's, 1989, model) accounts for language processing in real time and within human psychological constraints, such as word access and human memory. The incorporation of the language processor into the study of second language acquisition, therefore, brings to bear a set of human psychological constraints that are crucial for the processing of languages. PT (Pienemann, 1998a), which is based on Levelt's (1989) skill-based approach to language production and Bresnan's (1982) lexical-functional grammar, was designed to overcome the limitations of the strategies approach by which it was originally inspired:

- *The role of grammar*: Rather than assuming a set of strategies which operate on grammar, processes which create complexity are identified and implemented into a theory of grammar that is closely related to a psychologically plausible performance grammar.
- *Restriction to movement*: This limitation of the strategies approach was due to the choice of grammatical theory, namely transformational grammar. In PT, processing factors are integrated into lexical-functional grammar, a grammatical theory which is based on the systematic utilization of a psychologically plausible operation: feature unification. This process has implications for syntax and morphology.
- *Comprehension and production*: Processing strategies were conceptualized as short cuts within a full derivational process of TG. The features of language processing utilized in PT are far more general in nature. They are related to the linearity of speech production and the exchange of grammatical information.

PT is based on a universal hierarchy of processing procedures, which is derived from the general architecture of the language processor. This hierarchy is related to the requirements of the specific procedural skills needed for the TL. In this way, predictions can be made for language development which can be tested empirically.

The view of language production followed in PT is largely that described by Levelt (1989), which overlaps to some extent with the computational model of Kempen and Hoenkamp (1987), which in turn emulates much of Merrill Garrett's work (e.g., Garrett, 1976, 1980, 1982), on which the corresponding section of Levelt's model is based. The basic premises of that view are the following.

i Processing components, such as procedures to build NPs, are relatively autonomous specialists which operate largely automatically. Levelt (1989) describes such grammatical procedures as "stupid," because their capacity is strictly limited to the very narrow but highly efficient handling of extremely specific processing tasks (e.g., NP-procedures, VP-procedures, etc.). The automaticity of these procedures implies that their execution is not normally subject to conscious control.

ii Processing is incremental. This means that surface lexicogrammatical form is gradually constructed while conceptualization is still on-going. A key implication of incremental language processing is the need for grammatical memory. For the next processor to be able to work on still-incomplete output of the current processor and for all of this to result in coherent surface forms, some of the incomplete intermediate output has to be held in memory.

iii The output of the processor is linear, even though it may not be mapped onto the underlying meaning in a linear way. This is known as the "linearization problem" (Levelt, 1981), which applies to the mapping of conceptual structure onto linguistic form, as well as to the generation of morphosyntactic structures. One example is subject–verb agreement, as illustrated in the sentence *"She gives him a book."* The affixation of the agreement marker to the verb depends, amongst other things, on the storage of information about the grammatical subject (namely number and person), which is created before the verb is retrieved from the lexicon.

iv Grammatical processing has access to a grammatical memory store. The need for a grammatical memory store derives from the linearization problem and the automatic and incremental nature of language generation. Levelt (1989) assumes that grammatical information is held temporarily in a grammatical memory store which is highly task-specific and in which specialized grammatical processors can deposit information of a specific nature (e.g., the value of diacritic features). In Kempen and Hoenkamp's (1987) Incremental Procedural Grammar, the locus of the grammatical buffer is the specialized procedures which process NPs, VPs, etc. Pienemann (1998a) presents evidence from on-line experiments and aphasia research in support of these assumptions (e.g., Cooper and Zurif, 1983; Engelkamp, 1974; Paradis, 1994; Zurif, Swinney, Prater, and Love, 1994).

The process of incremental language generation as envisaged by Levelt (1989) and Kempen and Hoenkamp (1987) is exemplified in figure 20.1, which illustrates some of the key processes involved in the generation of the example sentence *"A child gives a cat to the mother."* The concepts underlying this sentence are produced in the Conceptualizer.

The conceptual material produced first activates the lemma CHILD in the lexicon. The lemma contains the category information N, which calls the categorial procedure NP. This procedure can build the phrasal category in which N is head, that is, NP. The categorial procedure inspects the conceptual material of the current iteration (the material currently being processed) for possible complements and specifiers and provides values for diacritic features. Given certain conceptual specifications, the lemma "A" is activated and the NP-procedure attaches the branch Det to NP. During this process the diacritic parameters of Det and N are checked against each other. This implies that the grammatical information "singular" is extracted from each of the two lemmas at the time of their activation and is then stored in NP until the head of the phrase is produced. This process of exchange of grammatical information is a key feature of language production. Below, we will see that in LFG it can be modeled by feature unification.

The production process has now proceeded to the point where the structure of a phrase has been created and the associated lemmata are activated. What is still needed to make this the beginning of a continuous and fluent utterance is the establishment of a relation between the phrase and the rest of the intended message. This is accomplished by assigning a grammatical function to the newly created phrase. The outcome of all of this is depicted by a tree structure in figure 20.1. And while this structure was produced and the associated lemmata were activated, the next conceptual fragment would have been processed in parallel and the output of the Formulator would have been delivered

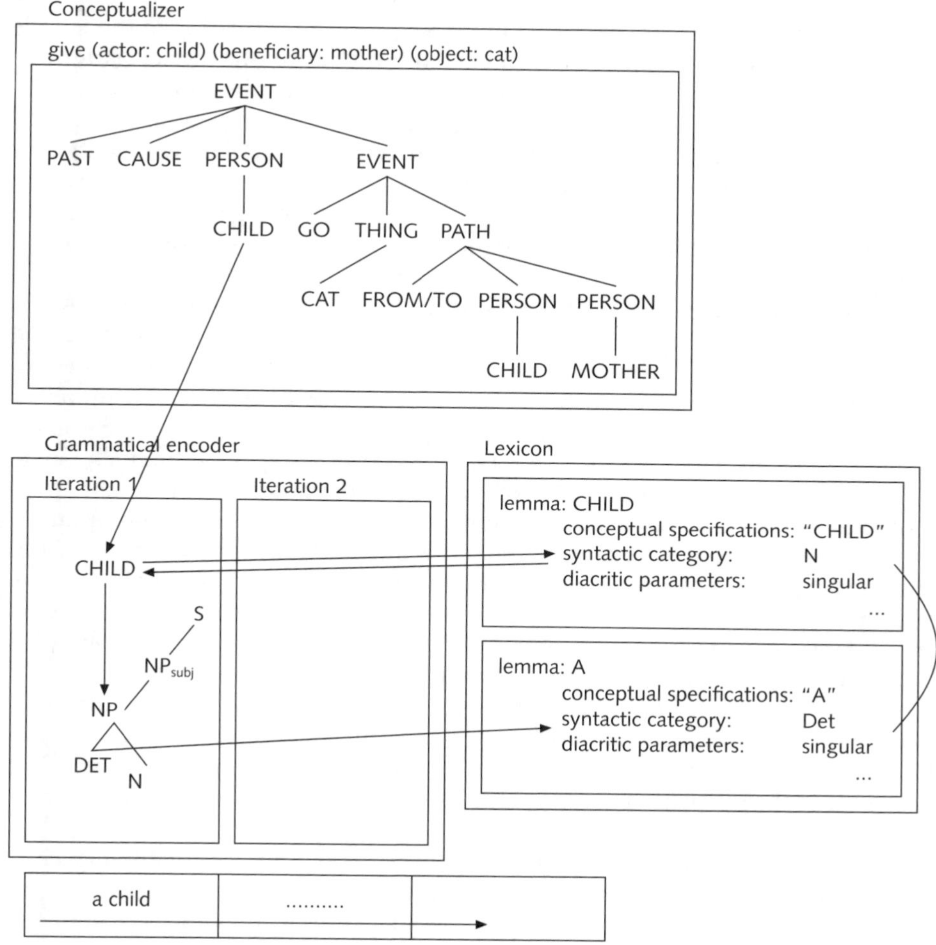

Figure 20.1 Incremental language generation

to the Articulator. This means that new conceptualization occurs while the conceptual structure of the previous iteration is being produced. The whole process then moves on from iteration to iteration.

In the process of incremental language generation the following processing procedures and routines are activated in the sequence indicated:

i lemma access;
ii the category procedure;
iii the phrasal procedure;
iv the S-procedure;
v the subordinate clause procedure, if applicable.

Pienemann (1998a) hypothesizes that this set of key grammatical encoding procedures is arranged according to the items' sequence of activation in the language generation process, and this sequence follows an implicational pattern in which each procedure is a necessary prerequisite for the following procedures. The basic thesis of PT is that in the acquisition of language-processing procedures, the assembly of the component parts will follow the above-mentioned implicational sequence. The key to predicting processable grammars is which pieces of grammatical information can be exchanged between which constituents, given the availability of the different procedures and their storage capacity.

It is important to note that the above processing procedures are operational only in mature users of a language, not in language learners. While even beginning second language learners can make recourse to the same *general* cognitive resources as mature native language users, they have to create language-specific processing routines. In this context, it is important to ensure that Levelt's model (and Kempen and Hoenkamp's specific section of it) can, in principle, account for language processing in bilinguals, since second language acquisition will lead to a bilingual language processor.

De Bot (1992) adapted Levelt's model to language production in bilinguals. On the basis of work by Paradis (1987), he shows that information about the specific language to be used is present in each part of the pre-verbal message, and this subsequently informs the selection of language-specific lexical items and of language-specific routines in the Formulator. The key assumption of De Bot's work for L2 processing is that in all cases where the L2 is not closely related to the L1, different (language-specific) procedures have to be assumed. Therefore, most of the above processing procedures have to be acquired by the L2 learner. The differences in the lexical prerequisites for language processing are obvious in diacritic features, such as "tense," "number," "gender," and "case," which vary between languages.

What happens when an element is missing in this implicational hierarchy? Pienemann (1998a) hypothesizes that the hierarchy will be cut off in the learner grammar at the point of the missing processing procedure, and the rest of the hierarchy will be replaced by a direct mapping of conceptual structures onto surface form, as long as there are lemmata that match the conceptually instigated searches of the lexicon. In other words, it is hypothesized that processing procedures and the capacity for the exchange of grammatical information will be acquired in their implicational sequence, as depicted in table 20.2.

If the hierarchy in table 20.2 is to be universally applicable to language acquisition, it needs to be interpretable in relation to grammatical structures of individual languages. This is achieved by interpreting the processability hierarchy through a theory of grammar which is typologically and psychologically plausible. The theory of grammar used for this purpose in PT is LFG. The reason for that choice is that every level of the hierarchy of processing procedures can be captured through feature unification in LFG, which also shares three key features with Kempen and Hoenkamp's procedural account of language generation, namely (i) the assumption that grammars are lexically driven, (ii)

Table 20.2 Hypothetical hierarchy of processing procedures

Procedure	*t1*	*t2*	*t3*	*t4*	*t5*
S′ (embedded S)	–	–	–	–	+
S	–	Simplified	Simplified	Inter-phrasal information	Inter-phrasal information
Phrasal	–	–	Phrasal information	Phrasal information	Phrasal information
Category	–	Lexical morphemes	Lexical morphemes	Lexical morphemes	Lexical morphemes
Word/lemma	+	+	+	+	+

the functional annotations of phrases (e.g., "subject of"), and (iii) reliance on lexical feature unification as a key process in sentence generation. In other words, an LFG description of the structure to be learned affords an analysis of the psycholinguistic process of grammatical information exchange, and the latter is the key component of the processability hierarchy.

3.1.1 A brief sketch of LFG

Before I demonstrate how the processability hierarchy is implemented into an LFG-based description of a target language (and the developing interlanguage), I will give a brief outline of lexical-functional grammar. LFG is a unification grammar, the most prominent characteristic of which is the unification of features. Put simply, the process of feature unification ensures that the different parts that constitute a sentence do actually fit together.

LFG consists of three parts: (i) a constituent structure (c-structure) component that generates "surface structure" constituents and c-structure relationships; (ii) a lexicon, whose entries contain syntactic and other information relevant to the generation of sentences; and (iii) a functional component which compiles for every sentence all the grammatical information needed to interpret the sentence semantically.

All c-structures are generated directly by phrase structure rules without any intervening transformations. Hence the mapping of predicate–argument structures onto surface forms is achieved without any intervening levels of representation. Grammatical functions assume the role of grammatical primitives, and major constituents are annotated for their grammatical function. The c-structure of the sentence "Peter owns a dog," for instance is shown in figure 20.2, which can be generated by the annotated phrase structure rules shown in figure 20.3. A simplified account of the lexical entries relating to figure 20.2 is given in table 20.3.

As is obvious from these simplified examples, lexical entries specify a number of syntactic and other properties of lexical items by assigning values to features (e.g., NUM = SG). In most cases, such equations *define* the value of

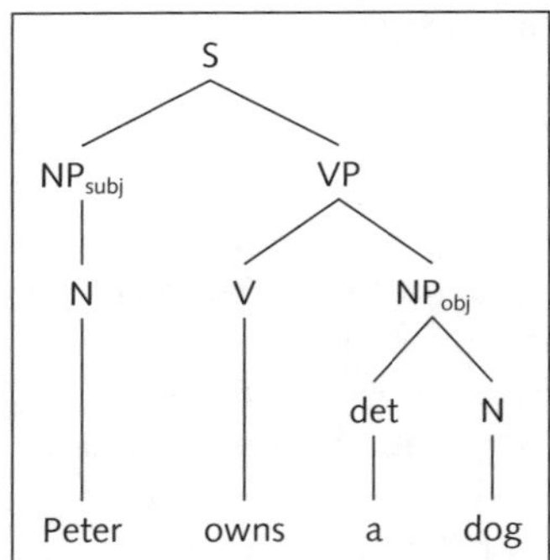

Figure 20.2 Example of a constituent structure

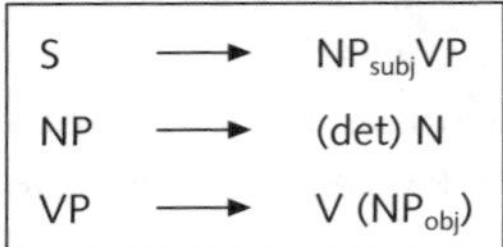

Figure 20.3 C-structure rules

Table 20.3 Lexical entries

Peter:	N,	PRED	=	"Peter"
owns:	V,	PRED	=	"own" (SUBJ, OBJ)
		TENSE	=	present
		SUBJ PERSON	=	3
		SUBJ NUM	=	SG
a:	DET,	SPEC	=	"a"
		NUM	=	SG
dog:	N,	PRED	=	"dog"
		NUM	=	SG

features. In some cases they may also "demand" certain values elsewhere in the functional description of a sentence. One example for such a constraining equation would be:

$$WH =_c +$$

This equation stipulates that the phrase to which it is attached must be a *wh*-word.

The functional structure or "f-structure" of a sentence is a list of those pieces of grammatical information needed to semantically interpret the sentence. It

Table 20.4 Functional structure

PRED	"own" (SUBJ, OBJ)	
TENSE	present	
SUBJ	PRED	"Peter"
OBJ	SPEC	"a"
	NUM	SG
	PRED	"dog"

is generated by the interaction between c-structure and the lexicon. The f-structure of the sentence in figure 20.2 is given in table 20.4.

The predicate entry [PRED "own" (SUBJ, OBJ)] is taken from the lexical entry of the verb. Listing the stem of the verb in quotation marks ("own") is simply a shorthand convention for a semantic representation of the word. The slots to the right of the verb, which are filled by SUBJ and OBJ in table 20.4, list the arguments of the predicate: first the *owner*, then the *item owned*. The PRED entry of the f-structure, therefore, makes it possible to relate the different constituents to the "players" described by the sentence (actor, patient, etc.). This forms the link between the syntactic form and its underlying predicate–argument relations.

3.2 *Step 2: Implementing a processing hierarchy into LFG*

The implementation of the processability hierarchy into an LFG-based description of a given language affords us a prediction of the stages in which the language can develop in L2 learners. The main point of the implementation is to demonstrate the flow of grammatical information in the production of linguistic structures. I will demonstrate this with the example of three English morphological rules.

In LFG, the morphological component operates on the basis of a functional description of the sentence. The following sentence may illustrate this:

A man owns many dogs.

Note that lexical entries contain schemas which are relevant here. These are listed in table 20.5.

The well-formedness of sentences is guaranteed, amongst other things, by ensuring that functional descriptions of the sentence and lexical entries match; for example, the phrase "a man" is functionally well-formed because, amongst other things, the value for NUM is "SG" in the subsidiary function NUM = SG under SUBJ, as well as in the lexical entry for "man." In the same way, "many dogs" is well-formed because of a match of the feature "NUM."

The actual structure of the morphological component is not crucial to the present line of argument. The central point here is that morphological processes

Table 20.5 Lexical entries for 'A man owns many dogs'

a:	DET,	SPEC	=	"A"
		NUM	=	SG
man:	N,	PRED	=	"MAN"
		NUM	=	SG
		PERS	=	3
owns:	V,	PRED	=	"OWN" (SUBJ) (OBJ)
		SUBJ NUM	=	SG
		SUBJ PERS	=	3
		TENSE	=	PRESENT
many:	DET,	SPEC	=	"MANY"
		NUM	=	PL
dogs:	N,	PRED	=	"DOG"
		NUM	=	PL

are informed by feature unification. One can now see that the unification of the NUM value in noun phrases is an operation which is restricted entirely to the NP. In PT this type of affixation is called *phrasal* because it occurs inside phrase boundaries (cf. Pienemann, 1998a). An example of a *lexical* morpheme is regular English tense marking (V+ "-ed"), the information for which can be read off the lexical entry of the verb, as can be seen in figure 20.1 above.

Subject–verb agreement, in contrast, involves the matching of features in two distinct constituents, namely NP_{subj} and VP. The insertion of the -s affix for subject-verb agreement marking requires the following syntactic information:

S-V affix	TENSE	=	present
	SUBJ NUMBER	=	sg
	SUBJ PERSON	=	3

While the value of the first two equations is read off the functional description of sentences as illustrated above, the values for NUMBER and PERSON must be identical in the f-structure of SUBJ and the lexical entry of V. Hence, this information has to be matched across constituent boundaries from inside both constituents. One may informally describe this process as follows:

[A man]$_{NP_{subj}}$			[{holds} . . .]$_{VP}$ (Present, imperfective)		
PERSON	=	3	PERSON	=	3
NUM	=	sg	NUM	=	sg

From a processing point of view, the two morphological processes, plural agreement in NP_{subj} and SV-agreement, have a different status. While the first occurs exclusively inside one major constituent, the second requires that

Table 20.6 Processing procedures applied to English

Processing procedure	*L2 process*	*Morphology*	*Syntax*
5 Subordinate clause procedure	Main and subordinate clause		Cancel INV
4 S-procedure	Interphrasal information	*SV agreement* (= 3sg-s)	Do2nd, INVERSION
3 Phrasal procedure	Phrasal information	*NP agreement*	ADV, Do-Front, Topi Neg+V
2 Category procedure	Lexical morpheme	*plural, past -ed,* possessive pronoun	Canonical order
1 Word/lemma	"Words"	Invariant forms	Single constituent

grammatical information be exchanged across constituent boundaries. This type of morphological process is referred to as *interphrasal affixation*.

We are now in a position to locate three English morphological phenomena within the hierarchy of processability. These structures have been highlighted in table 20.6. The table also lists a range of further structures and their position within the hierarchy. However, due to limited space, a full exposition of ESL development within PT will not be possible here.

The predicted ESL sequence is supported by Johnston's (1985) cross-sectional study of 16 Polish and Vietnamese learners of English, which includes 12 of the grammatical rules contained in the ESL table. Johnston's data result in an implicational table with 100 percent scalability. Additional evidence is provided by a cross-sectional study of 13 child ESL learners (Pienemann and Mackey, 1993), which includes 14 of the structures from the ESL table and also results in an implicational table with 100 percent scalability. The ESL scale also contains several items that relate to interrogatives. The developmental sequence of interrogatives implicit in the ESL scale is fully supported by a longitudinal study by Cazden, Cancino, Rosansky, and Schumann (1975) of six Spanish ESL learners (cf. also Ravem, 1974) and by a longitudinal study of child ESL by Felix (1982).

4 Cross-Linguistic Predictions for Development

If the processing factors employed in the approach described above are to be generic for human languages (as L2s), then they have to apply cross-linguistically. In addition, an empirical test of factors determining the acquisition process will have a higher degree of validity if it is performed not in terms of general trends (e.g., "more of X co-occurs with more of Y"), but specifically at the level of identifiable linguistic forms ("prerequisite A can process structures X, Y, and Z, but not structures U or V"). This ensures that the theory to be tested is conceptually refined to the point where such specific predictions can be made.

PT has been tested against an array of data at this precise level of detail, with English, Swedish, German, and Japanese as target languages. The first step in such a test is to relate a set of target-language linguistic structures to the general hierarchy of processability and, more specifically, to the exchange of grammatical information involved in producing those structures. The outcome of the process is a language-specific prediction for the sequence in which these structures will be acquired. In a second step, the hypothesized sequence is compared with empirical data from the acquisition of the given language. It may be useful to illustrate these two steps with examples from Japanese, the language of the group of four tested with the greatest typological distance from German and English, and for which PT was originally conceptualized. For reasons of space, I will restrict this exercise to the identification of phrasal and lexical morphemes in Japanese.

Japanese is a morphologically rich, agglutinative language. According to Shibatani (1990, p. 306f), verbal affixes usually occur in the following order:

Vstem – causative – passive – aspect – desiderative – negation – tense.

This is exemplified by several morphological forms of *kak-u* ('write') in (1) to (4):[2]

(1) kak-areru (passive)
stem-(passive)

(2) kak-aseru (causative)
stem-(causative)

(3) kak-aser-areru (causative-passive)
stem-(causative)-(passive)

(4) kak-aser-are-tai (causative-passive-desiderative)
stem-(causative)-(passive)-(desiderative)

In other words, one morpheme usually expresses one function. However, because of a large set of morphological classes and morphophonological variation (compare examples (3) and (4) for the form of the passive morpheme), complex form–function relationships create learning problems of a different kind.

Most or all of the verbal morphemes listed above (expressing causative, passive, aspect, desiderative, negation, and tense) can be derived directly from conceptual structure. In other words, the only processing requirement for the insertion of these morphemes is that the formal lexical class "verb" is so marked in the lexicon. These morphemes are therefore lexical. However, information distribution is crucial in the verbal system when more than one verb occurs. In this case, Japanese is no different from European languages, in that only one of the verbs can be finite. One can see this in examples (5) and (6), where the penultimate verb is marked with the -te morpheme, which is a marker of non-finiteness and seriality: *shi-te mi-ta* [do-(serial) try (-past)] in (5) and *tabe-te iru* [eat (serial) (progressive)] in (6). The verb marked *'-te'* appears in penultimate position and cannot be marked for any of the features causative, passive, aspect, desiderative, negation, or tense. To achieve this, the two verbs have to exchange the information INF = + in the encoding process. The entry for the verb 'shi-te' in (5) contains, amongst other things, the following information:

shi-te: V, PRED = 'shi-te (SUBJ) (OBJ)'
INF = +

The entry for the verb 'mi-tä' contains the following information:

mi-tä: V, PRED = 'mitä, V-COMP (SUBJ)'
V-COMP INF $=_c$ +

Because the information INF = + has to be exchanged between the two verbs, -te is a phrasal morpheme:

(5) *Tomoko ga* *Kimiko ni* *denwa* *o* *shi-te*
(name) (subj-part.) (name) (indir.obj part.) telephone (obj-part.) do-(serial)
mi-ta
try (-past)
"Tomoko tried to give Kimiko a ring."

(6) *Tomoko ga* *gohan o* *tabe-te* *iru.*
(name) (subj-part.) rice (obj part.) eat (serial) (progressive)
"Tomoko is eating rice."

In this very brief discussion, two types of morphemes have been identified in Japanese according to the exchange of grammatical information required for their production. This is summarized in table 20.7.

This predicted sequence was confirmed in two empirical studies (Huter, 1998; Kawaguchi, 1996), the key findings of which are shown in tables 20.8 and 20.9.

Given that English, German, and Swedish are all Germanic languages, it is much easier to transfer the analysis of morphosyntax within the processability framework from one of these languages to the others. For instance, all three

Table 20.7 Japanese as L2

Processing procedure	*L2 process*	*Morphology*
3 Phrasal procedure	Phrasal information	V-te V
2 Category procedure	Lexical morpheme	V_{aff}
1 Word/lemma	"Words"	Invariant forms

Table 20.8 Kawaguchi's (1996) study

Affix	*Meg*	*Kat*	*Sim*	*Iri*	*Sam*	*Nat*	*Hel*
No affix	/	/	/	/	/	/	/
Lexical affix	+	+	+	+	+	+	+
Phrasal affix	–	–	–	+	+	+	+

Table 20.9 Huter's (1998) study

Affix	*M1*	*K1*	*K2*	*K3*	*M2*	*M3*	*M4*	*K4*	*K5*	*J1*	*J2*	*J3*	*J4*	*J5*
No affix	/	/	/	/	/	/	/	/	/	/	/	/	/	/
Lexical affix	+	+	+	+	+	+	+	+	+	+	+	+	+	+
Phrasal affix	–	–	–	–	–	–	–	–	–	–	–	–	+	+

languages display some form of subject–verb inversion. INVERSION is indeed positioned at the same level of processability for each of these languages, and the exchange of grammatical information involved in the production of inversion structures is in fact very similar to the above account for the English language. Also, all three languages differentiate syntactically between main and subordinate clauses. One way in which this manifests itself is that INVERSION is blocked in subordinate clauses. Again, this syntactic feature is positioned at the same level of processability across the three languages.

A number of examples of English lexical, phrasal, and interphrasal morphemes was given above. Tables 20.10 and 20.11 list further examples for Swedish and German. In each case, the identification of the level of processing depends on the type of exchange of grammatical information. It is worth noting that despite some structural similarities between German, Swedish, and English syntax, most morphological regularities do not overlap. Pienemann (1998a) analyzed the exchange of grammatical information involved in each of the morphological and syntactic structures of English, German, and Swedish shown in tables 20.6, 20.10, and 20.11 and identified the corresponding level of processability in this way.

Table 20.10 German as L2

Processing procedures	*L2 process*	*Syntax*	*Morphology*
6 Subordinate clause procedure	Main and subordinate clause	V-End	
5 S-procedure	Interphrasal information	INV	SV-agreement
4 VP-procedure	Phrasal information VP	SEP	
3 Phrasal procedure	Phrasal information NP	ADV	Plural agreement
2 None	Lexical morphemes	Canonical order	Past-te, etc.
1 Word/lemma	"Words"	Single constituent	Invariant forms

Table 20.11 Swedish as L2

Processing procedures	*L2 structure*	*Morphology*	*Syntax*	*Negation*
5 Subordinate clause procedure	Main and subordinate clause		Cancel INV	neg V_f
4 S-procedure	Interphrasal information	Predicate agreement	INV	X V_f NP_s neg
3 Phrasal procedure	Phrasal information	NP agr VPagr	ADV WH fronting	V_f neg
2 Category procedure	Lexical morpheme	pl, def	Canonical order	(Aux) V neg (Aux) neg V neg V
1 Word/lemma	"Words"	Invariant forms	Single const.	neg+X

The empirical support for each of these hierarchies is very strong. A series of longitudinal and cross-sectional studies by Boss (1996), Clahsen (1980), Clahsen et al. (1983), Jansen (1991), Meisel et al. (1981), and Pienemann (1980, 1981, 1987) all demonstrate that German L2 morphosyntactic forms emerge in the sequence predicted by PT.

Vainikka and Young-Scholten (1994) analyzed cross-sectional data from the acquisition of German by 11 Turkish and 6 Korean adults. Their study also supports the processability hierarchy. However, an evaluation of this study in relation to the processability hierarchy will be easier to contextualize after an analysis of German L1 acquisition within this framework. I will therefore return to this study at the end of section 6.

The case of Swedish as a second language was examined in detail by Pienemann and Håkansson (1999), who surveyed 14 major studies of Swedish as L2 to test the predicted processability hierarchy for Swedish morphology, syntax, and negation. These studies are based on over 1000 informants. Some of the studies are longitudinal, others are cross-sectional. This survey did not reveal one single piece of counter-evidence to the predicted hierarchy.

5 Variation and Processing Constraints

Perhaps the strongest doubts about the universality of grammatical development have been expressed by scholars who study L2 variation, and by language testers. For instance, Bachman (1988) voices the following concern about acquisition-based profiling procedures: ". . . to what extent is the procedure sensitive to individual variations that may result from different elicitation contexts, and to what extent will this affect the determination of the developmental stage?" (p. 204). Similarly, Douglas (1986) is concerned about ". . . the problem of characterizing a learner's competence when it would appear that 'competence' varies with task" (p. 158).

There is indeed ample evidence that the shape of an interlanguage varies within one and the same learner on one and the same day depending on which linguistic task the learner performs in which context (e.g., Crookes, 1989; Crookes and Gass, 1993; Selinker and Douglas, 1985; Tarone, 1983). For instance, Tarone (1989) observed that the frequency of producing /r/ may vary between 50 percent and almost 100 percent where the latter occurs in the reading of word lists and the first in "free speech." However, the issue at stake is not whether interlanguage performance is constant across tasks, but whether the developmental stage is constant across tasks. Obviously, if the stage can change from situation to situation, the concept of universal routes of development becomes vacuous.

The question of the stability of stages is one that can be answered empirically. Pienemann (1998a) put forward the "steadiness hypothesis," which predicts that the basic nature of the grammatical system of an IL does not change in different communicative tasks, as long as these are based on the same skill type in language production (such as "free conversation"). Pienemann (1998a) tested the steadiness hypothesis in a sample containing six ESL learners, each of whom carried out six different communicative tasks. The IL profiles of all learners were found to be *perfectly consistent* across all tasks in the area of syntax according to the emergence criterion. For the area of morphology, a total of three out of 324 possible cases of "underproduction," and not a single case of "overproduction," were found. This amounts to a 99.1 percent fit of the data in this area. In other words, these data constitute strong support for the steadiness hypothesis.

Pienemann (1998a) further demonstrated that fluctuations in correctness levels across tasks do not reflect different levels of acquisition and that they are instead brought about by the specific lexical needs of individual tasks and the status of morphological marking in different entries to the learner's lexicon. In all these analyses, it is essential to compare learner behavior with measures that are well defined, theoretically motivated, and applied consistently across different corpora. For all measurements of learner behavior, Pienemann (1998a) provided quantified distributional analyses for each individual speaker. He further used the emergence criterion because of its suitability as a measure of the in-principle acquisition of processing skills. In addition, implicational scaling was used to determine developmental stages.

It should be added that within PT, interlanguage variation is not merely defined as fluctuations in correctness levels. Instead it is defined a priori by the learner's current level of processing. In other words, it is defined as a specific range of structural options that are available to the learner. This range of structural options results from the fact that the learner's limited processing resources constrain the way in which he or she can avoid structures which have not yet been acquired. An example is the acquisition of English inversion. As noted above, this rule is acquired at stage 4 in the ESL hierarchy. The rule describes the observational fact that auxiliaries are placed in second position in English *wh*-questions, as in the following example:

(7) Where is he going?

Variability occurs in *wh*-questions before this rule is acquired. At the prior stage, some learners leave out one or more constituents:

(8) Where he going?

(9) Where is going?

Other learners produce *wh*-questions using canonical word order:

(10) Where he is going?

The range of possible solutions to the formation of *wh*-questions simply derives from the state of the learner's grammar before stage 4. The ESL processability hierarchy specifies the following for stage 4:

$$S'' \rightarrow (XP) \qquad S' \\ \left\{ \begin{array}{l} \text{wh} =_c + \\ \text{adv} =_c \text{“seldom, rarely ...”} \\ \text{SENT MOOD = INV} \end{array} \right\}$$

$$S' \rightarrow (V) \qquad\qquad S$$
$$\left\{ \begin{array}{l} \text{aux} =_c + \\ \text{ROOT} =_c + \\ \text{SENT MOOD} =_c \text{INV} \end{array} \right\}$$

In other words, the information "SENT MOOD = INV" has to be exchanged between XP and V to achieve the desired position of the auxiliary in second position. However, before stage 4, the interlanguage processor cannot carry out this operation because the S-node is not available yet as the information store for this process (cf. Pienemann, 1998a, pp. 175f, 239f). Quite logically, the learner has only a limited number of options for resolving this problem: (i) leaving out one of the constituents involved in the exchange of grammatical information, which ensures that the impossible information exchange becomes obsolete; or (ii) applying a canonical sentence schema to the sentence (S → wh NP_{subj} V X), which makes the crucial exchange of information obsolete; or (iii) avoiding the context for this structure (i.e., no *wh*-questions), which again avoids the impossible operation. However, these are all the options that are available. There is no alternative way to exchange the crucial grammatical information and thus to produce inversion (except in rote-memorized chunks). In other words, the full range of solutions to the developmental problem is dictated by the current state of the learner's production grammar.

This brief summary of the treatment of variation within the processability approach highlights a key feature of that approach, namely the fact that it provides a coherent formal framework for the treatment of the dynamics of second language development. On the one hand, it makes testable predictions about stages of development across languages by defining those classes of grammars that are processable at each stage. On the other hand, processability leaves a certain amount of leeway, which allows the learner to develop a range of solutions to developmental problems. However, this range is strictly constrained.

Mentioning testable predictions triggers the question as to how PT can be falsified. The simple answer is: "when it makes incorrect predictions." To be more specific, predictions on processability involve implicational hierarchies, such as A before B before C. If such a prediction is made and it can be demonstrated in a corpus with sufficient data on A, B, and C that C is acquired before, say B, then the prediction is falsified.

6 L1–L2 Differences and the Processability Hierarchy

I will show in this section that the same dynamics as are present in IL variation also apply to the comparison of L1 and L2 development.

There is overwhelming evidence for fundamental differences between L1 and L2 acquisition in ultimate attainment (cf. Long, 1990). Remarkable differences between L1 and L2 acquisition also exist in the developmental schedule. Clahsen (1982, 1990, 1992) found a developmental pattern in the acquisition of German as a first language that is shown below. This pattern differs markedly from the one observed in the acquisition of German as a second language:

L1 sequence:	*L2 sequence:*
(1) Variable word order	(1) SVO
(2) SOV	(2) ADV
(3) V-2nd and SV-agreement marking	(3) SEP
(4) Subordinate clauses (without any errors in the positioning of the verb)	(4) INVERSION, SV-agreement sometimes
	(5) V-Final in subordinate clauses (with errors in the positioning of the verb)

The differences between L1 and L2 go beyond that of the developmental path. Clahsen observed that as soon as the child uses complementizers, the position of verbal elements in subordinate clauses is completely in line with the structure of the adult language. He also found that in German child language development, SV-agreement is acquired at exactly the same point in time as V–2nd position. This is not the case in the acquisition of German as L2.

Despite these differences in the course of development, it can be shown that the L1 schedule is constrained by the processability hierarchy. Similarly to SVO structures in L2 acquisition, the initial word order hypothesis in L1 acquisition (i.e., SOV) can be accounted for simply by a c-structure rule along the lines of (R-a). Since grammatical functions can be read off c-structure and no exchange of grammatical information is required, SOV order is positioned at the lowest level in the processability hierarchy.

This simple analysis of initial word order in L1 acquisition also highlights an important difference between Clahsen's strategies and the processability approach. As Vainikka and Young-Scholten (1994) and Towell and Hawkins (1994) point out, Clahsen's strategies would predict that the initial hypothesis in L2 acquisition is formed on the perceptual array "actor, action, acted-upon," thus producing universal SVO patterns for all L2s. No such assumption is made in PT. The only stipulation that exists at this level is that no grammatical information be exchanged within the sentence. This constrains the language processor to produce only structures that can be processed without such information exchange. SVO and SOV both satisfy this condition.

The Verb-2nd phenomenon found in the L1 sequence can be produced by (R-b) and (R-c) in a way similar to German and English INVERSION. For the V-2nd position to be produced, the grammatical information SENT MOOD has to be exchanged between two constituents (XP and V). This places V-2nd at the same level in the processability hierarchy as INVERSION and SV-agreement. In other words, SOV and V-2nd do indeed fall within the constraints of the processability hierarchy and their sequence of acquisition is predicted correctly.

Note that the rule SEP is absent from the L1 sequence. To explain why this is the case, one has to consider the effect of the rules R–a-c: on the basis of an SOV c-structure, these three rules have the same effect as the combined application of SEP and INVERSION on the basis of an SVO c-structure. Since in R-a, the verb is in final position, and R-b jointly with R-c permit the finite verb to appear in second position, the "split verb" position is also permitted.

The sentence-final position of the verb in subordinate clauses is predicted to occur at level 6 of the processability hierarchy. The final stage of the L1 sequence is therefore also in line with PT:

(R-a) $S \rightarrow NP_{subj}\ VP$
$VP \rightarrow (NP_{obj1})(NP_{obj2})\ V\ (V)$

(R-b) $\bar{S} \rightarrow (XP)\ \ S$
$$\left\{\begin{array}{l} wh =_c + \\ adv =_c + \\ N =_c + \\ \text{SENT MOOD} = \text{INV} \end{array}\right\}$$

(R-c) $\bar{S} \rightarrow (V)\ \ S$
$$\left\{\begin{array}{l} \text{ROOT} =_c + \\ \text{SENT MOOD} =_c \text{INV} \end{array}\right\}$$

Table 20.12 provides an overview of this comparison of grammatical development in the acquisition of German as a second and as a first language; it shows at a glance that both developmental paths fall within the confines of the processability hierarchy. In other words, there are no differences in the temporal order in which processing procedures are activated. All grammars are processable at the time they develop, and each grammar builds upon the processing procedures acquired at the previous stages in a cumulative fashion. However, the L1 learner achieves this in two key "moves," SOV and V-2nd (with SV agreement), while the L2 learner takes five "moves," most of which introduce ungrammatical structures that have to be modified in later moves.

Two questions remain after this comparison. (i) Why are there different routes of development? And (ii) Where do the initial structural hypotheses come from? Both questions are outside the intended scope of the processability approach, which focuses on the explanation of sequences and variation in development. Pienemann (1998a) developed an additional explanatory module that interacts with PT, and according to which the route of development is caused largely by the initial hypothesis. The structural properties contained in the initial hypothesis propagate throughout development by a dynamic process known as "generative entrenchment" that is mathematically well described.

The above summary of my position concerning processing similarities in the L1 and the L2 has been described in more detail in a "keynote article"

Table 20.12 Development in German L1 and L2 from a processability perspective

Stage	*Exchange of information*	*Resources*	*German L2*	*German L1*
6	Within subordinate clause	+/– ROOT	V-End	V-End (no errors)
5	Interphrasal	WO rules S-Procedure	INV +/–agr	V-2nd +agr
4	Phrasal	WO rules VP-Procedure	PART	–
3	None	Lexical categories Saliency	ADV	–
2	None	Lexical categories	SVO	SOV Variable word order
1	None	Lexical entres	Words	Words

(Pienemann, 1998b) which was published together with eight partly critical peer commentaries. For instance, De Bot (1998) queries the relationship between the Formulator and LFG, Bialystok (1998) wonders how LFG can capture language processing, and Schachter (1998) discusses the neurophysiological plausibility of the proposed processing similarity between L1 and L2.

It is now time to return briefly to the study by Vainikka and Young-Scholten (1994), which adds an interesting twist to the comparison of developmental schedules. As mentioned above, the researchers studied 11 Turkish and 6 Korean adult learners of German. It is important to bear in mind that both source languages follow an SOV pattern. These authors claim to have found that "the development of phrase structure in . . . [their L2 corpus, MP] follows a pattern noted in first language acquisition" (Vainikka and Young-Scholten, 1994, p. 295). Specifically, their learners are reported to produce SOV structures before verb-second. In other words, these authors claim that the Turkish and Korean learners of German start out with a different initial hypothesis on word order from that of Italian and Spanish learners of German, and that the hypothesis of the first group of L2 learners is identical to that of L1 learners.

From the above observations, Vainikka and Young-Scholten (1994) infer that L2 learners will transfer certain basic constituent structure features, but not the basic prerequisites for morphological processes, such as SV-agreement marking. As the above L1–L2 comparison demonstrated, such a variable initial hypothesis would be within the confines of the hypothesis space defined by

PT. However, Vainikka and Young-Scholten's hypothesis is merely a generalization of their observations and does not withstand the test of cross-linguistic validity, since it is inconsistent with the observation that English learners of Japanese do not transfer the basic SVO pattern to Japanese (cf. Huter, 1998; Kawaguchi, p.c.).

7 Developmental Constraints on L1 Transfer

A further key aspect of PT is its capacity to spell out developmental constraints on L1 transfer. The assumption that L1 transfer may be developmentally constrained is not new. For instance, Wode (1976, 1978) demonstrated that for the acquisition of ESL negation and interrogatives, certain L1 forms appear in the interlanguage only after learners gradually develop the structural prerequisites for them in the L2. Similar observations were made by Zobl (1980) and Kellerman (1983).

PT provides a formal framework within which such developmental constraints on L2 transfer can be formally delineated. The logic behind this is quite straightforward. If L1 structures were able to be transferred "in bulk," as assumed in the "full transfer" hypothesis by Schwartz and Sprouse (1996), one would have to assume that the learner can generally utilize L1 procedures for the L2. In Pienemann (1998a), I demonstrated that this assumption is implausible, given the lexically driven nature of human language processors.

Using L1 procedures for the L2 would lead to internal problems in the processor because all of the processing procedures described above need to be orchestrated in a language-specific way. If any of them is missing or incompatible with the rest, the Formulator is inoperable. If, for instance, the lexical category information is missing, category and phrasal procedures cannot be called. If diacritic features are missing or have no values or values which are incompatible with those listed in agreeing phrases, or if they are incompatible with the Functorization rules, then the processor will be inoperable. This does not mean that the learner will never attempt to form diacritic features and Functorization rules that reflect L1 regularities. However, a "bulk transfer" of the L1 Formulator would lead to very unwieldy hypotheses (Pienemann, 1998a, pp. 80ff).

The case of constraints on the transfer of morphological and lexical regularities is obvious. As the above LFG treatment of subject–verb inversion shows, similar constraints also apply to word order. The key point of the argument is that the positioning of verbs is controlled by the unification of a lexical feature that is specific to the verb. In other words, word-order phenomena may also depend on the correct annotation of lexical entries. Therefore, word order is as much dependent on the delicate mechanics of the developing language processor as morphological and lexical patterns. This is demonstrated particularly strongly in a study by Håkansson, Pienemann, and Sayehli (2002), which shows that Swedish learners of German do not transfer the verb-second pattern from the L1 to the L2, even though this pattern is part of both languages. Instead, the informants produce a structure (XSVO) which is ungrammatical in both languages. The authors argue with reference to PT that this is the case because the L2 processor cannot initially handle verb-second due to a lack of the necessary L2 processing procedures (see box 20.1).

8 Linguistic Knowledge, Language Use, and Performance Grammars

In the discussion of processing approaches to SLA, the relationship between competence and performance has been critically examined. As I showed in the early part of this chapter, most of the key criticisms of processing strategies such as Clahsen's (1984) have been addressed in later work on L2 processing. One key point of interest in current discussion of language processing and SLA is the relationship between the processor and linguistic knowledge. White (1991) equates research on acquisition with research on linguistic knowledge only, and she relegates everything else to the domain of language use. Kaplan and Bresnan (1982) have a different view. In the context of language acquisition, they put research on language processing on an equal footing with research on linguistic knowledge, as the following quotation illustrates: "[Children] acquire knowledge and skills that enable them to produce and comprehend an infinite number of novel utterances . . . The major goal of psycholinguistic research is to devise an explanatory account of the mental operations that underlie these linguistic abilities" (Kaplan and Bresnan, 1982, p. 177).

PT is positioned in this tradition. It therefore does not fit White's dichotomy. As Kaplan and Bresnan (1982) point out, the various components of a theory of language acquisition can be studied separately as long as they ultimately fit together in a coherent model. And it is for reasons of overall coherence that LFG was chosen as the grammatical framework for PT, because it provides a basis for relating linguistic knowledge to the processor. However, the issue of this relationship is not the focus of PT. In other words, PT is constructed in a modular fashion, and the study of the relationship between the processor and grammatical knowledge is one that can be pursued within the processability framework, since the language processor is seen as the computational routines that operate on, but are separate from, linguistic knowledge (cf. Kaplan and Bresnan, 1982).

Such an integrative line of research could prove highly productive. For instance, White (1991) is concerned that production data may not reveal a learner's linguistic knowledge because the learner may fail to produce certain structures for reasons to be found in the production routines rather than in his or her linguistic knowledge. In fact, White's concern highlights the fact that the interface between the processor and linguistic knowledge is of particular relevance to those SLA researchers who focus on the study of linguistic knowledge. As Chomsky (1978, p. 10) pointed out, we do not know a priori which aspects of

Box 20.1 Håkansson et al. (2002)

Research question: One of the key issues in SLA research has been the question of L1 transfer. Håkansson et al. (2002) provide strong empirical evidence to demonstrate that L1 transfer is developmentally moderated as predicted by PT.

The study focuses on the acquisition of German by Swedish school children. The L1 and the L2 share the following word order regularities in affirmative main clauses: SVO; adverb fronting (ADV); and subject–verb inversion (INV) after ADV.

Results: The results of this study are summarized in table 20.13, which treats all learner samples as parts of a cross-sectional study. Therefore, table 20.13 represents an implicational analysis of the data which demonstrates that the learners follow the sequence (i) SVO, (ii) ADV, and (iii) INV. In other words, ADV and INV are not transferred from the L1 at the initial state even though these rules are contained in the L1 and the L2. This implies that for a period of time the learners produce the constituent order:

* adverb+ S + V + O,

which is ungrammatical in the L1 as well as in the L2.

Conclusion: Håkansson et al. (2002) argue on the basis of Processability Theory (Pienemann, 1998a) that the L2 system can utilize L1 production mechanisms only when the L2 system has developed the necessary prerequisites to process L1 forms, and that, therefore, the procedures required for INV in the L1 cannot be utilized before the full S-procedure has developed in the L2.

Table 20.13 Implicational scale based on all learners in the study by Håkansson et al. (2002)

Name	*SVO*	*ADV*	*INV*
Gelika (year 1)	+	–	–
Emily (year 1)	+	–	–
Robin (year 1)	+	–	–
Kennet (year 1)	+	–	–
Mats (year 2)	+	–	–
Camilla (year 2)	+	–	–
Johann (year 1)	+	+	–
Cecilia (year 1)	+	+	–
Eduard (year 1)	+	+	–
Anna (year 1)	+	+	–
Sandra (year 1)	+	+	–
Erika (year 1)	+	+	–
Mateus (year 2)	+	+	–
Karolin (year 2)	+	+	–
Ceci (year 2)	+	+	–
Peter (year 2)	+	+	–
Johan (year 2)	+	+	+
Zandra (year 2)	+	+	+
Zofie (year 2)	+	+	+
Caro (year 2)	+	+	+

linguistic data are attributable to grammatical competence and which to innumerable other factors. Language acquisition studies that focus on linguistic competence, therefore, ought to place special emphasis on the interface between the processor and grammatical knowledge, since the latter is accessible only through the first, especially in SLA, where it cannot be taken for granted that individual utterances are representative of the structure of the underlying linguistic system. Utilizing an explicit production grammar and a compatible theory of linguistic representation would allow one to explore this issue in detail. Such a study could potentially shed light on the relationship between production routines and linguistic representation. Naturally, it assumes that the researcher accepts that the study of both the language processor and linguistic knowledge is a valid contribution to a theory of second language acquisition.

NOTES

1 It may be worthwhile at this point to clarify that the strategies approach to SLA is a separate proposition from the Multidimensional Model of SLA (cf. Meisel, Clahsen, and Pienemann, 1981). These two approaches tend to be conflated in reference works, for instance in Ellis (1994). The first approach is designed to explain sequences of acquisition, while the latter is a framework for the description of dynamic acquisition processes.

2 I want to thank Satomi Kawaguchi for allowing me to use these examples. They are taken from her M.A. thesis on simplified registers in Japanese (Kawaguchi, 1996).

REFERENCES

Andersen, R. 1984: The one-to-one principle of interlanguage construction. *Language Learning*, 34, 77–95.

Andersen, R. 1988: Models, processes, principles, and strategies: second language acquisition in and out of the classroom. *IDEAL*, 3, 77–95.

Bachman, L. F. 1988: Language testing–SLA interfaces. *Annual Review of Applied Linguistics*, 9, 193–209.

Baddeley, A. 1990: *Human Memory: Theory and Practice*. Hillsdale: Lawrence Erlbaum Associates.

Bates, E. and MacWhinney, B. 1981: Second-language acquisition from a functionalist perspective: pragmatic, semantic, and perceptual strategies. In Winity H. (ed.), *Native Language and Foreign Language Acquisition*. New York: Annals of the New York Academy of Sciences, 379, 190–214.

Bates, E. and MacWhinney, B. 1982: Functionalist approaches to grammar. In E. Wanner and L. R. Gleitman (eds), *Language Acquisition: The State of the Art*. Cambridge: Cambridge University Press, 173–218.

Bates, E. and MacWhinney, B. 1987: Competition, variation and language learning. In B. MacWhinney (ed.),

Mechanisms of Language Acquisition. Hillsdale, NJ: Lawrence Erlbaum Associates, 157–93.

Bever, T. G. 1970: The cognitive basis for linguistic structures. In J. Hayes (ed.), *Cognition and the Development of Language.* New York: John Wiley, 279–362.

Bialystok, E. 1998: What's in a process? Explaining development in language acquisition. *Bilingualism: Language and Cognition,* 1 (1), 21–2.

Boss, B. 1996: German grammar for beginners – the Teachability Hypothesis and its relevance to the classroom. In C. Arbonés Solá, J. Rolin-Ianziti, and R. Sussex (eds), *Who's Afraid of Teaching Grammar? Papers in Language and Linguistics.* Queensland: University of Queensland, 93–103.

Bowerman, M. 1985: What shapes children's grammars? In D. Slobin (ed.), *The Cross-Linguistic Study of Language Acquisition. Vol. 2.* Hillsdale, NJ: Lawrence Erlbaum Associates, 1257–1320.

Bresnan, J. (ed.) 1982: *The Mental Representation of Grammatical Relations.* Cambridge, MA: MIT Press.

Carroll, S. E. 1999: Putting "input" in its proper place. *Second Language Research,* 15 (4), 337–88.

Carroll, S. E. 2000: *Input and Evidence: The Raw Material of Second Language Acquisition.* Amsterdam: John Benjamins.

Cazden, C. E., Cancino, H., Rosansky, E., and Schumann, J. 1975: *Second Language Acquisition in Children, Adolescents and Adults: Final Report.* Washington, DC: National Institute of Education.

Chomsky, N. 1978: A theory of core grammar. *GLOT,* 1, 7–26.

Clahsen, H. 1979: Syntax oder Produktionsstrategien. Zum natürlichen Zweitspracherwerb der "Gastarbeiter." In R. Kloepfer (ed.), *Bildung und Ausbildung in der Romania.* Munich: W. Fink, 343–54.

Clahsen, H. 1980: Psycholinguistic aspects of L2 acquisition. In S. Felix (ed.), *Second Language Development.* Tübingen: Narr, 57–79.

Clahsen, H. 1982: *Spracherwerb in der Kindheit. Eine Untersuchung zur Entwickung der Syntax bei Kleinkindern.* Tübingen: Narr.

Clahsen, H. 1984: The acquisition of German word order: a test case for cognitive approaches to second language acquisition. In R. Andersen (ed.), *Second Languages.* Rowley, MA: Newbury House, 219–42.

Clahsen, H. 1990: The comparative study of first and second language development. *Studies in Second Language Acquisition,* 12, 135–53.

Clahsen, H. 1992: Learnability theory and the problem of development in language acquisition. In J. Weissenborn, H. Goodluck, and T. Roeper (eds), *Theoretical Issues in Language Acquisition: Continuity and Change.* Hillsdale, NJ: Lawrence Erlbaum Associates, 53–76.

Clahsen, H. and Muysken, P. 1989: The UG paradox in L2 acquisition. *Second Language Research,* 2, 1–29.

Clahsen, H., Meisel, J. and Pienemann, M. 1983: *Deutsch als Zweitsprache: Der Spracherwerb ausländischer Arbeiter.* Tübingen: Narr.

Cooper, W. E. and Zurif, E. B. 1983: Aphasia: information-processing in language production and reception. In B. Butterworth (ed.), *Language Production. Vol. 2.* London: Academic Press, 225–56.

Corder, S. P. 1967: The significance of learners' errors. *International Review of Applied Linguistics,* 5, 161–70.

Crookes, G. 1989: Planning and interlanguage variation. *Studies in Second Language Acquisition,* 11 (4), 367–83.

Crookes, G. and Gass, S. (eds) 1993: *Tasks and Language Learning: Integrating Theory and Practice.* Clevedon: Multilingual Matters.

De Bot, K. 1992: A bilingual production model: Levelt's "speaking" model adapted. *Applied Linguistics*, 13 (1), 1–24.

De Bot, K. 1998: Does the formulator know its LFG? *Bilingualism: Language and Cognition*, 1(1), 25–6.

Douglas, D. 1986: Communicative competence and the tests of oral skills. In C. W. Stansfield (ed.), *TEFOL Research Reports, 21: Toward Communicative Competence Testing. Proceedings of the Second TEFOL Invitational Conference*. Princeton, NJ: Educational Testing Service, 157–75.

Ellis, R. 1994: *The Study of Second Language Acquisition*. Oxford: Oxford University Press.

Engelkamp, J. 1974: *Psycholinguistik*. Munich: Ullstein.

Felix, S. W. 1982: *Psycholinguistische Aspekte des Zweitsprachenerwerbs*. Tübingen: Narr.

Garrett, M. F. 1976: Syntactic processes in sentence production. In R. Wales and E. Walker (eds), *New Approaches to Language Mechanisms*. Amsterdam: North-Holland, 231–56.

Garrett, M. F. 1980: Levels of processing in language production. In B. Butterworth (ed.), *Language Production. Vol. 1: Speech and Talk*. London: Academic Press, 170–220.

Garrett, M. F. 1982: Production of speech: observations from normal and pathological language use. In A. W. Ellis (ed.), *Normality and Pathology in Cognitive Functions*. London: Academic Press, 19–76.

Gass, S. M. 1987: The resolution of conflicts among competing systems: a bidirectional perspective. *Applied Psycholinguistics*, 8, 329–50.

Gregg, K. 1984: Krashen's Monitor and Occam's Razor. *Applied Linguistics*, 5, 79–100.

Håkansson, G., Pienemann, M., and Sayehli, S. 2002: Transfer and typological proximity in the context of L2 processing. *Second Language Research*, 18(3), 250–73.

Harrington, M. 1987: Processing transfer: language-specific processing strategies as a source of interlanguage variation. *Applied Psycholinguistics*, 8, 351–77.

Hulstijn, J. 1990: A comparison between information-processing and the analysis/control approaches to language learning. *Applied Linguistics*, 11, 30–45.

Huter, K. 1998: The acquisition of Japanese as a second language. Ph.D. dissertation. Australian National University.

Jansen, L. 1991: The development of word order in natural and formal German second language acquisition. *Australian Working Papers in Language Development*, 5, 1–42.

Johnston, M. 1985: *Syntactic and Morphological Progressions in Learner English*. Canberra: Commonwealth Dept of Immigration and Ethnic Affairs.

Kaplan, R. and Bresnan, J. 1982: Lexical-functional grammar: a formal system for grammatical representation. In J. Bresnan (ed.), *The Mental Representation of Grammatical Relations*. Cambridge, MA: MIT Press, 173–281.

Kawaguchi, S. 1996: Referential choice by native speakers and learners of Japanese. M.A. thesis. Australian National University.

Kellerman, E. 1983: Now you see it, now you don't. In S. Gass and L. Selinker (eds), *Language Transfer in Language Learning*. Rowley, MA: Newbury House, 37–57.

Kempen, G. and Hoenkamp, E. 1987: An incremental procedural grammar for sentence formulation. *Cognitive Science*, 11, 201–58.

Kilborn, K. and Ito, T. 1989: Sentence processing in a second language: the timing of transfer. *Language and Speech*, 32 (1), 1–23.

Krashen, S. 1982: *Principles and Practice in Second Language Acquisition*. Oxford: Pergamon Press.

Krashen, S. 1985: *The Input Hypothesis: Issues and Implications*. London: Longman.

Larsen-Freeman, D. 1975: The acquisition of grammatical morphemes by adult ESL students. *TESOL Quarterly*, 9, 409–30.

Levelt, W. J. M. 1978: Skill theory and language teaching. *Studies in Second Language Acquisition*, 1, 53–70.

Levelt, W. J. M. 1981: The speaker's linearization problem. *Philosophical Transactions*, Royal Society, London, B295, 305–15.

Levelt, W. J. M. 1989: *Speaking: From Intention to Articulation*. Cambridge, MA: MIT Press.

Long, M. H. 1985: A role for instruction in second language acquisition: task-based language training. In K. Hyltenstam and M. Pienemann (eds), *Modelling and Assessing Second Language Acquisition*. Clevedon: Multilingual Matters, 77–100.

Long, M. H. 1990: Maturational constraints on language development. *Studies in Second Language Acquisition*, 12 (3), 251–85.

McDonald, J. L. and Heilenman, L. K. 1991: Determinants of cue strength in adult first and second language speakers of French. *Applied Psycholinguistics*, 12, 313–48.

McLaughlin, B. 1978: The Monitor Model: some methodological considerations. *Language Learning*, 28 (2), 309–32.

McLaughlin, B. 1987: *Theories of Second Language Learning*. London: Edward Arnold.

McLaughlin, B., Rossman, T., and McLeod, B. 1983: Second language learning: an information-processing perspective. *Language Learning*, 33 (1), 135–57.

Meisel, J. M., Clahsen, H., and Pienemann, M. 1981: On determining developmental stages in natural second language acquisition. *Studies in Second Language Acquisition*, 3, 109–35.

Paradis, M. 1987: *The Assessment of Bilingual Aphasia*. Hillsdale: Lawrence Erlbaum Associates.

Paradis, M. 1994: Neurolinguistic aspects of implicit and explicit memory: implications for bilingualism and SLA. In N. Ellis (ed.), *Implicit and Explicit Learning of Languages*. San Diego: Academic Press, 393–419.

Pienemann, M. 1980: The second language acquisition of immigrant children. In S. W. Felix (ed.), *Second Language Development: Trends and Issues*. Tübingen: Narr, 41–56.

Pienemann, M. 1981: *Der Zweitspracherwerb ausländischer Arbeiterkinder*. Bonn: Bouvier.

Pienemann, M. 1987: Determining the influence of instruction on L2 speech processing. *Australian Review of Applied Linguistics*, 9, 92–122.

Pienemann, M. 1998a: *Language Processing and Second Language Development: Processability Theory*. Amsterdam: John Benjamins.

Pienemann, M. 1998b: Developmental dynamics in L1 and L2 acquisition: Processability Theory and generative entrenchment. *Bilingualism: Language and Cognition*, 1 (1), 1–20.

Pienemann, M. and Håkansson, G. 1999: A unified approach towards the development of Swedish as L2: a processability account. *Studies in Second Language Acquisition*, 21, 383–420.

Pienemann, M. and Mackey, A. 1993: An empirical study of children's ESL development and Rapid Profile. In P. McKay (ed.), *ESL Development: Language and Literacy in Schools. Vol. 2*. Canberra: Commonwealth of Australia and National Languages and Literacy Institute of Australia, 115–259.

Pinker, S. 1984: *Language Learnability and Language Development.* Cambridge, MA: Harvard University Press.

Pinker, S. and Prince, A. 1987: On language and connectionism: analysis of a parallel distributed processing model of language acquisition. Occasional Paper No. 33. Center for Cognitive Science, MIT.

Posner, M. I. and Snyder, C. R. R. 1975: Attention and cognitive control. In R. L. Solso (ed.), *Information Processing and Cognition: The Loyola Symposium.* Hillsdale, NJ: Lawrence Erlbaum Associates, 55–85.

Ravem, R. 1974: The development of *wh*-questions in first and second language learners. In J. Richards (ed.), *Error Analysis.* London: Longman, 134–55.

Sasaki, Y. 1991: English and Japanese interlanguage comprehension strategies: an analysis based on the competition model. *Applied Psycholinguistics,* 12, 47–73.

Schachter, J. 1998: The need for converging evidence. *Bilingualism: Language and Cognition,* 1 (1), 32–3.

Schmidt, R. 1992: Psychological mechanisms underlying second language fluency. *Studies in Second Language Acquisition,* 1, 357–85.

Schneider, N. and Shiffrin, R. M. 1977: Controlled and automatic processing. I: Detection, search and attention. *Psychological Review,* 84, 1–64.

Schwartz, B. D. and Sprouse, R. A. 1996: L2 cognitive states and the Full Transfer/Full Access model. *Second Language Research,* 12 (1), 40–72.

Selinker, L. and Douglas, D. 1985: Wrestling with "context" in interlanguage theory. *Applied Linguistics,* 6, 190–204.

Shibatani, M. 1990: *The Languages of Japan.* Cambridge: Cambridge University Press.

Shiffrin, R. M. and Schneider, W. 1977: Controlled and automatic human information processing. II: Perceptual learning, automatic, attending, and a general theory. *Psychological Review,* 84, 127–90.

Slobin, D. I. 1973: Cognitive prerequisites for the development of grammar. In C. A. Ferguson and D. I. Slobin (eds), *Studies of Child Language Development.* New York: Holt, Rinehart, and Winston, 175–208.

Slobin, D. I. 1985: Cross-linguistic evidence for the language-making capacity. In D. Slobin (ed.), *The Cross-Linguistic Study of Language Acquisition. Vol. 2.* Hillsdale, NJ: Lawrence Erlbaum Associates, 1157–1256.

Tarone, E. 1983: On the variability of interlanguage systems. *Applied Linguistics,* 4, 142–63.

Tarone, E. 1989: On the variability of interlanguage systems. In F. Eckman, L. H. Bell, and D. Nelson (eds), *Universals in Second Language Acquisition.* Rowley, MA: Newbury House, 9–23.

Towell, R. and Hawkins, R. 1994: *Approaches to Second Language Acquisition.* Clevedon: Multilingual Matters.

Vainikka, A. and Young-Scholten, M. 1994: Direct access to X′-theory: evidence from Korean and Turkish adults learning German. In T. Hoekstra and B. D. Schwartz (eds), *Language Acquisition Studies in Generative Grammar: Papers in Honour of Kenneth Wexler from the 1991 GLOW Workshops.* Philadelphia, PA: John Benjamins, 7–39.

VanPatten, B. 1996: *Input Processing and Grammar Instruction in Second Language.* Norwood, NJ: Ablex.

White, L. 1989: *Universal Grammar and Second Language Acquisition.* Amsterdam: John Benjamins.

White, L. 1991: Second language competence versus second language performance: UG or processing strategies? In L. Eubank (ed.),

Point–Counterpoint: Universal Grammar in the Second Language. Amsterdam and Philadelphia: John Benjamins, 67–189.

Wode, H. 1976: Developmental sequences in naturalistic L2 acquisition. *Working Papers on Bilingualism*, 11, 1–31.

Wode, H. 1978: Developmental sequences in naturalistic L2 acquisition. In E. Hatch (ed.), *Second Language Acquisition*. Rowley, MA: Newbury House, 101–17.

Zobl, H. 1980: The formal and developmental selectivity of L1 influence on L2 acquisition. *Language Learning*, 30 (1), 43–57.

Zurif, E., Swinney, D., Prather, P., and Love, T. 1994: Functional localization in the brain with respect to syntactic processing. *Journal of Psycholinguistic Research*, 23 (6), 487–97.

VI Research Methods

21 Defining and Measuring SLA

JOHN NORRIS AND
LOURDES ORTEGA

1 Introduction: A Framework for Understanding Measurement in SLA Research

Research within the social and cognitive sciences frequently calls upon measurement to provide a systematic means for gathering evidence about human behaviors, such that they may be interpreted in theoretically meaningful ways. The scientific value of resulting interpretations, which explain what is observed in light of what is known, depends in large part on the extent to which measurement practice within a given research domain adheres to standards for the development, use, and evaluation of measurement instruments and procedures (e.g., AERA, APA, NCME, 1999). Where such standards are not in place, or where they are not rigorously followed, measurement practice will produce research "findings" which lack interpretability and generalizability, which do not contribute to the accumulation of knowledge, and which therefore, as Wright (1999) has observed, provide little more than "a transient description of never-to-be-reencountered situations, easy to doubt with almost any replication" (p. 71).

Measurement is used within second language acquisition (SLA) research to elicit, observe, and record the language (and language-related) behaviors of L2 learners, and to enable the interpretation of resulting evidence in light of explanatory theories of the language acquisition process. Although by no means in a state of theoretical accord, the field of SLA is, on the whole, interested in describing and understanding the dynamic processes of language learning (learning used here in its broadest sense) under conditions other than natural, first language acquisition (Beretta, 1991; Bley-Vroman, 1989; Crookes, 1992; Ferguson and Huebner, 1991; Gregg, 1993; Lambert, 1991; Long, 1990, 1993; McLaughlin, 1987). Accordingly, measurement in SLA research generally provides evidence for interpretations about: (i) a learner's linguistic system (i.e., the underlying mental representations of the L2); (ii) development or change (or the lack thereof) in a learner's linguistic system; and (iii) factors which may contribute to or hinder a learner's developmental approximations of the target L2.

Despite similarities, theoretical accounts of SLA differ widely according to the ways in which acquisition is defined and the types of evidence that are brought to bear in associated research; so, too, do measurement practices differ systematically according to the varying theoretical premises. Although a number of these measurement practices have enjoyed rather lengthy traditions of use within particular SLA research communities, doubts continue to be voiced regarding the extent to which: (i) theoretical constructs are being defined in measurable ways (e.g., Bachman, 1989; Bachman and Cohen, 1998); (ii) measurement instruments and procedures are being systematically developed and implemented (e.g., Polio, 1997); (iii) measurement practices are being subjected to adequate validity evaluation (e.g., Chapelle, 1998); and (iv) the reporting of measurement-based research is adequate for enabling scientific replication and knowledge accumulation (e.g., Norris and Ortega, 2000; Polio and Gass, 1997; Whittington, 1998). Furthermore, it is likely that advances in measurement theory are not afforded consistent attention within measurement-based SLA research (see, e.g., discussions in Bachman and Cohen, 1998; Grotjahn, 1986; Hudson, 1993; Paolillo, 2000; Saito, 1999; Shohamy, 2000), as has been noted with respect to other social science research domains (see, e.g., Embretson, 1999; Thompson, 1998).

The purpose of the current chapter is to address these concerns and to discuss how SLA researchers might organize their thinking about measurement in order better to serve the research endeavor. In the remainder of this first section, we present a framework which defines the scope and process of measurement and which we use throughout the chapter to analyze measurement practices in SLA. We then present an overview of the primary epistemological approaches to be found in the field. This overview establishes the link between the nature of SLA theories, the ways in which acquisition has been defined, and the types of evidence brought to bear in interpretations about "acquisition." We then examine measurement practices and problems associated with SLA research, and we offer recommendations for resolving problems and generally improving measurement practice. Where applicable throughout the chapter, we also indicate recent advances in measurement theory which seem pertinent to the measurement of L2 acquisition. Finally, we end with a discussion of several implications for the future of measurement-based SLA research.

1.1 Constructs, data, and the measurement process

Measurement is at once a data- and theory-driven undertaking (Messick, 1989). This implies, on the one hand, that the kinds of theoretical interpretations to be made have been defined, and on the other, that the kinds of data to be accepted as relevant evidence for such interpretations have been specified. The first of these assumptions is treated traditionally under the notion of *construct definition*, and the second concerns the nature of *measurement data*.

Historically, constructs were considered unobservable explanatory entities residing within theory and only inferred via the interactions between sets of observable variables. More recently, however, the notion of construct has evolved to acknowledge the interplay between a theoretical explanation of a phenomenon and the data that may be gathered about the phenomenon (see Angoff, 1988; Cronbach, 1988; Cronbach and Meehl, 1955; Loevinger, 1957; Messick, 1975, 1989). This current view is reflected by Chapelle (1998), who maintains: "[a] construct is a meaningful interpretation of observed behavior" (p. 33). Construct definitions, then, provide an explicit delineation of the interpretations that are intended to be made on the basis of a measure. As such, they dictate the theoretical meanings which may be attached to measurement data; without construct definitions, measurement data are meaningless.

Measurement *data* are composed of repeated observations of particular patterns in behaviors (Chapelle, 1998; Cronbach, 1980), and these observations are condensed into scores of some kind, which can be defined as "any coding or summarization of observed consistencies on a test, questionnaire, observation procedure, or other assessment device" (Messick, 1989, p. 14). The types of data which constitute acceptable evidence about a construct are typically drawn from an empirical knowledge base. For example, accumulated findings from a series of longitudinal descriptive studies of the given phenomenon may lead to an association between particular observable behaviors and a theoretical explanation for those behaviors. Given such an empirical association and an explicit definition of the construct, the kinds of data which may serve as evidence for interpretations can be specified.

Measurement, then, involves the collection of data, the transformation of those data into evidence, and the use of that evidence for making a theory-based interpretation. In practice, measurement proceeds according to several interrelated but distinguishable stages (see discussions in Bennett, 1999; Messick, 1989, 1994; Mislevy, 1994, 1995; Mislevy et al., forthcoming), which are outlined in figure 21.1. Note that the measurement process there begins and ends with interpretation; thus, intended interpretations are the starting point for developing appropriate measures, and actual interpretations are the culmination of using measures. Note also that the arrows in figure 21.1 proceed only in one direction, with each stage feeding into the next. This unidirectionality shows the chronological progression of stages in measurement development and use. At the same time, the graduated shading in the model and its cyclical composition indicate that the process is not static; while individual stages are primarily conceptual or primarily procedural, decisions and discoveries at each stage of the process may influence developments at all other stages. Finally, the ultimate outcomes of the measurement process obviously feed back into revised theoretical interpretations.

Each of the stages in figure 21.1 implies particular actions on the part of researchers. The first three stages require that researchers *conceptualize* the

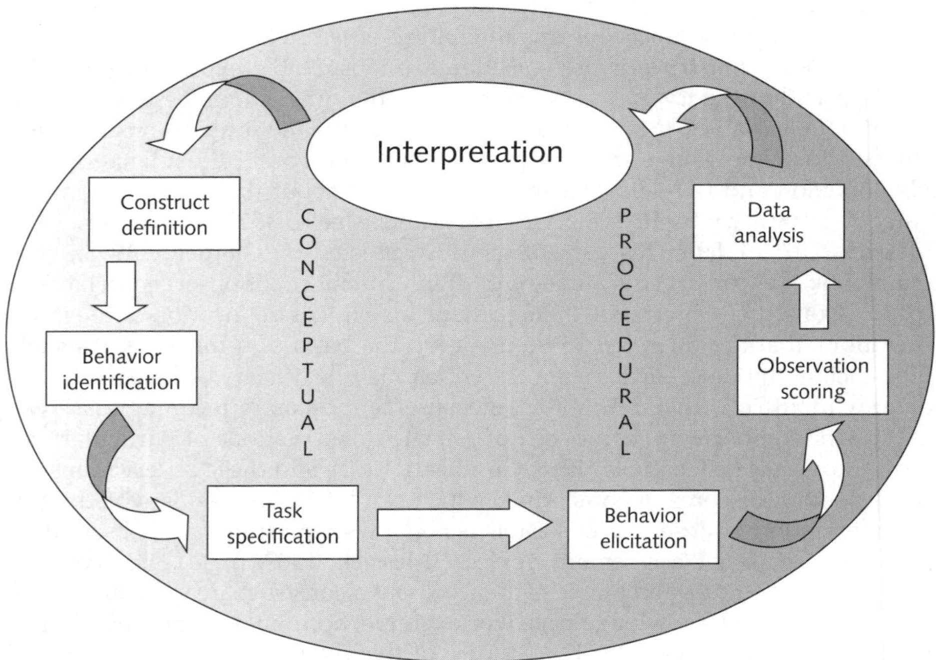

Figure 21.1 The measurement process

evidence to be provided with a given measure, by defining intended construct interpretations and linking them with observable behaviors:

1 *Construct definition*: For a given measure, researchers explicate exactly what it is that they want to know based on what kinds of interpretations are going to be made. Constructs should be defined in specific terms, such that observable behaviors may be obviously linked with them, and they should provide a clear indication of the theoretical assumptions that they represent.
2 *Behavior identification*: Researchers decide what particular behavior or constellation of behaviors needs to be observed, as well as what qualities or variations in those behaviors are important, in order to provide sufficient evidence for a given construct interpretation. The link between target behaviors and constructs emerges from an empirical knowledge base; that is, researchers draw on accumulated knowledge about the construct in order to identify evidentiary requirements in the form of behaviors.
3 *Task specification*: The researcher specifies a particular set of tasks or situations for the elicitation/observation of targeted behaviors. Tasks/situations should also be linked to behaviors via an empirical knowledge base.

In practice, this implies the careful analysis of tasks/situations in order to determine whether they can provide the behavioral evidence required of them (see Bachman and Palmer, 1996; Mislevy, Steinberg, and Almond, 1999; Norris, Brown, Hudson, and Yoshioka, 1998; Skehan, 1998). Tasks/situations should be defined in terms explicit enough to enable exact replication.

In the next three stages, researchers *proceduralize* the outcomes of the conceptual stages, implementing mechanisms for the elicitation, scoring, and analysis of behavioral data in order to provide evidence for interpretations:

4 *Behavior elicitation*: Data on targeted behaviors are elicited, observed, and recorded via the administration of tasks or the observation of situations, while the potential influence of other variables is carefully controlled or accounted for (this incorporates the whole of instrument operationalization and administration; see practical guides in AERA, APA, NCME, 1999; Bachman and Palmer, 1996; J. D. Brown, 1996, forthcoming; Linn, 1989; Popham, 1981; Seliger and Shohamy, 1989).
5 *Observation scoring*: Data are attributed initial construct-relevant meaning by researchers classifying variations in observed behaviors according to the range of previously identified criterial values; the score should summarize observations in a way that may be clearly linked to intended interpretations. In practice, scoring is based on the use of numeric scales which reflect meaningful values, including categorical, ordinal, interval, and ratio types (see Angoff, 1984; Bachman and Palmer, 1996; Brindley, 1998; J. D. Brown, 1996; Wright, 1999). The reliability of scoring is also evaluated, in order to establish the extent to which score summaries represent systematic versus unknown or unintended sources of variability, by estimating classical and other sorts of reliability (see Feldt and Brennan, 1989; Hambleton, Swaminathan, and Rogers, 1991; Orwin, 1994; Shavelson and Webb, 1991; Traub, 1994).
6 *Data analysis*: Individual scores and patterns of scores are compared and summarized in light of various categorical and probabilistic properties. Behavioral predictions from the construct definition stage (e.g., in the form of hypotheses) are evaluated using various techniques (statistical description and inference, implicational scalar analysis, etc.; see J. D. Brown, 1988, 1996; Hatch and Lazaraton, 1991; Tabachnick and Fidell, 1996; Woods, Fletcher, and Hughes, 1986).

In a final stage, which forms the culmination of the cyclical measurement process outlined in figure 21.1, measurement outcomes are incorporated as evidence for construct interpretations. At this point, researchers (and the research community) discuss the outcomes from their measures in light of theoretical predictions, and they integrate the new evidence into an existing research knowledge base.

1.2 Construct validation

The objective of proceeding through each of the measurement stages above, carefully building on the foundations of the previous stage, is to produce a *warranted* interpretation about the construct of interest. An interpretation is warranted when researchers can demonstrate that a measure has provided trustworthy evidence about the construct it was intended to measure. Of course, the intended construct interpretation, as originally defined from the point of view of theory, is susceptible to becoming *un*warranted at any and all of the stages in measurement on *each* occasion of measurement use. As such, it is incumbent on individual researchers as well as the research community to investigate the construct validity of measurement, asking to what extent their practices in developing and using a measure result in an interpretation or set of interpretations that may be warranted (see AERA, APA, NCME, 1999; Messick, 1989). Comprehensive validation in educational measurement generally involves an evaluation of the entire process of test use, including the social consequences and values implications of applied test use and the relevance/utility of particular test scores for decisions and other actions (see, e.g., Kane, 1992; Linn, 1997; Messick, 1989; Moss, 1992; Shepard, 1993, 1997). However, when measures are employed as research tools, validation may be usefully constrained to a focus on the measurement stages outlined above and on the resulting construct interpretations (indeed, it is these interpretations which generally define the extent to which research measures are intended to be used).

The major threats to construct validity in measurement are of two types. *Construct underrepresentation* indicates the "degree to which a test fails to capture important aspects of the construct," whereas *construct-irrelevant variance* is the "degree to which test scores are affected by processes that are extraneous to its [*sic*] intended construct" (AERA, APA, NCME, 1999, p. 10). Problems of construct underrepresentation typically occur during the conceptualization of a measure (stages 1–3 above), when researchers fail adequately to consider (and demonstrate) a relationship between intended interpretations and the observable behaviors which will provide evidence about them. Construct-irrelevant variance is usually introduced during the proceduralization of a measure (stages 4–6 above), when researchers fail to control or account for the potential influence of the act of measuring itself (including scoring and analysis, as well as elicitation) on construct interpretations.

In order to engage in sound measurement practice in SLA research, and to better understand the extent to which their interpretations may be threatened by construct underrepresentation or construct-irrelevant variance, researchers will need to understand the relationship between SLA theories and the ways in which each of the stages in the measurement process is pursued. Therefore, we now turn to an examination of the link between SLA theories and their definitions for acquisition, the types of evidence brought to bear upon acquisition constructs, and the measurement practices employed within acquisition research.

2 What Counts as L2 Acquisition? Conceptual Bases for Measurement in SLA

Since the inception of SLA as a field (see discussion in Huebner, 1991; Larsen-Freeman, 2000), theories of acquisition have multiplied, reflecting both a broadening scope of inquiry and interdisciplinary excursions by researchers. Diverging epistemologies have also led, undoubtedly, to "conflicting views about the 'best' way to gather data and/or the 'correct' questions to be asked" (Gass, 1988, p. 199). As a consequence, what counts as L2 acquisition – including what constructs are of interest, how they are defined, and what kinds of observable data are accepted as evidence – has become increasingly complex, varied, and at times disputed.

A persistent concern of many SLA researchers has been the relevance of linguistic theory for explaining L2 acquisition, and vice versa (for example, see articles in Huebner and Ferguson, 1991). As Huebner (1991) pointed out, "to the extent that linguistic theories are concerned with diachronic change, language development, language universals, or the nature and acquisition of grammatical and communicative competence, the phenomena involved in SLA must be of central concern to linguistic theory" (p. 4). Since the 1970s, the predominant linguistic theory, at least in the US, has been of a Chomskian generativist bent. However, as Lightbown and White (1987) observed, it was not until the mid-1980s that some SLA researchers paid more than lip service to generative linguistics, in vague references to a universal grammar, and started developing a research agenda for a formal linguistic theory of learnability in SLA (see, e.g., Eubank, 1991; Gass and Schachter, 1989; Rutherford, 1984). Thus, generative SLA researchers have begun to investigate the extent to which purportedly innate Universal Grammar (UG) principles and parameters are accessible in L2 acquisition (see White, 1996, 2000, this volume, for an overview of the various positions). Another line of research has concentrated on investigating the fundamental similarity or difference (Bley-Vroman, 1989) not only between L1 and L2 acquisition, but also between child L2 and adult L2 acquisition (e.g., Schwartz, 1992). Finally, an area of research receiving increased attention in generative SLA concerns the hypothesis of a critical period and associated maturational constraints on the attainment of nativelike, UG-constrained competence by non-native speakers (e.g., Birdsong, 1999; Hyltenstam and Abrahamsson, this volume; Sorace, 1993; White and Genesee, 1996).

For other researchers, linguistic theory alone has not been epistemologically sufficient. The need for SLA to explain differential success and, often, failure among second (particularly adult) language learners fostered a two-fold focus on linguistic and non-linguistic (social, affective, and cognitive) variables that influence the L2 acquisition process. From such research concerns stemmed a second theoretical strand that has gained prominence since the early 1980s: that of interactionist SLA (or interactionalist SLA; see Chapelle, 1998). Interactionist approaches to SLA focus on the relationship between learner-internal and external processes in L2 acquisition. Input, interaction, and output were the essential external variables identified within initial social interactionist research agendas (see Krashen's, 1981, input hypothesis; Long's, 1980, interaction hypothesis; and Swain's, 1985, 1995, output hypothesis). More sociolinguistically oriented research has investigated the influence of social context on acquisition, as in IL variation theories (R. Ellis, 1985; Tarone, 1988), and the interaction of learner variables with social context, as in Gardner's (1979) social psychological model and Schumann's (1978) acculturation model. Interest in the role of learner-internal variables, influenced by theories of learning within an information-processing approach to cognitive psychology, has spurred the development of cognitive interactionist theories of SLA, such as a skill theory of L2 acquisition (Bialystok, 1991; McLaughlin, 1987), a psycholinguistic theory of universal operating principles for L2 acquisition (Andersen, 1984), and a processing constraint theory of L2 acquisition (Pienemann, 1984, 1998).

Until recently, these two distinct theoretical perspectives, generativist and interactionist, comprised the SLA research mainstream. The 1990s brought two new types of theories into the field, along with unique epistemologies: emergentism and sociocultural theory. Sociocultural theories maintain that learning of any kind (including language learning) is an essentially social process rather than one generated within the individual. Second language, like first language and thought itself, develops in the social, inter-mental plane, and only subsequently is it appropriated by the individual into the intramental plane (Lantolf, 1994; Vygotsky, 1986). Because research driven by sociocultural theories of L2 acquisition does not, in general, employ measurement of the sort discussed in this chapter, we make no further reference to such work (although sociocultural approaches are by no means exempt from the concerns raised in this chapter, wherever measurement is employed). Emergentist theories view L2 learning, like all human learning, as the outcome of a neurobiological tendency of the brain to attune itself to primary sensory experience through the strengthening and weakening of connections among the billions of neurons that it typically develops. Linguistic knowledge (or the phenomenological experience thereof) emerges as a by-product of the establishment of networked connections upon exposure to probabilistic patterns underlying the (L1 or L2) linguistic input (e.g., N. Ellis, 1998, 1999). In fact, emergentism is radically different from both generativist and interactionist epistemologies. On the one hand, it is incompatible with generative SLA because it denies symbolism, modularity, and innatism, and it removes linguistics from the center of the research domain, replacing it with cognitive architecture. On the other hand, in spite of the shared interest in functionalist explanations and cognitive constructs, emergentist theory resonates little with interactionist SLA. The highly specialized neurobiological treatment of cognitive processes, the lack of a traditional dichotomy between representation and access, and the absence of interest in non-cognitive variables (social, affective, educational, etc.) all differentiate emergentist from interactionist perspectives.

Although fundamental differences in the theories outlined above often lead to sharp divisions among SLA researchers according to what may or may not count as acquisition, it is not our intention here to address theory construction or evaluation (see Beretta, 1991; Crookes, 1992; Gregg, 1993; Long, 1990, 1993). Instead, we maintain that whatever theoretical questions are posed and however data are gathered, where measurement is used, careful construct definition and adherence to measurement standards will provide a rational guide for enabling and improving the research process. Therefore, we turn now to an examination of the first three conceptual stages of the measurement process outlined in figure 21.1, asking of SLA research:

i How are constructs defined via the interpretations made about acquisition from different theoretical perspectives?
ii Have criterial behaviors and behavioral qualities been identified which can provide sufficient evidence for making such construct interpretations?
iii Are measurement tasks/situations designed to elicit adequate and accurate behavioral data?

2.1 *Construct definition: interpretations about L2 acquisition*

In order to define acquisition as a construct for measurement purposes, the particular interpretations to be made about L2 acquisition must first be sought within existing SLA theories. Table 21.1 summarizes some of the essential features (interpretive as well as evidentiary) for three main theoretical approaches to SLA.

Generative SLA views language as a symbolic system, autonomous from cognition, and too complex to be acquired by training or through inductive or deductive learning from the input. Since it adheres to the tenets of first language nativism, generative SLA research aims at elucidating empirically whether learners can have indirect, partial, full, or no access to the principles of Universal Grammar in the process of acquiring an L2, and it prioritizes interpretations about linguistic competence, not language performance (Gregg, 1990; Schwartz, 1993; White, 1991). Further, this epistemological approach to L2 acquisition focuses on constructs which describe and explain the origins of linguistic mental representations (the "competence problem" central in a property theory) and does not concern itself so much with interpreting how such representations unfold or become available to the learner in a predictable route (the "developmental problem" central in a transition theory) (see Gregg, 1996). Therefore, generative SLA research confines itself to formal descriptions of interim learner grammars (i.e., syntax) as reflected in a learner's tacit ability to judge ungrammaticality in the L2, because it assumes that the goal of SLA as a theory is to explain how learners can acquire a full mental representation of many of the complexities of the L2, and why they cannot acquire all aspects of an L2 syntax (and precisely which aspects learners may fail to acquire).

Table 21.1 What counts as L2 acquisition for three types of SLA theories

Stage	*Generative SLA*	*Interactionist SLA*	*Emergentist SLA*
Epistemology and construct interpretations	Language as symbolic representation which is autonomous from cognition Learning mediated by UG and L1 Grammatical competence Property theory: initial state and end state in L2 acquisition	Language as symbolic representation which is constrained by cognition Learning mediated by social, affective, and cognitive variables Communicative competence Transition theory: developmental course of L2 acquisition (For information-processing theories) automatization of declarative knowledge	Language as complex rule-like behavior, epiphenomenal result of functional needs Learning as interaction of the organism with the environment Neural networks Transition theory: specification of input frequency and regularity plus learning mechanisms
Target behaviors	Tacit intuiting of what is ungrammatical in the L2	Appropriate and fluent performance when using the L2 communicatively (and in controlled tasks)	Accurate and fluent performance in laboratory tasks Output that matches attested learning curves and eventually matches characteristics of fed input
Elicitation tasks/situations	Grammaticality judgment tasks of various kinds	Spoken and written discourse production Tests of implicit and explicit knowledge: verbalization of understanding of rules; controlled performance on comprehension and production tasks; grammaticality judgment tasks	Implicit memory tasks and forced-choice reaction-times tasks with human learners in laboratory Computer simulations of neural networks

Generative linguistic studies of SLA are likely to rely almost exclusively on the outcomes of grammaticality judgment tasks of various kinds, where *acquired* means nativelike levels of rejection of illegal exemplars of the target grammar.

Interactionist SLA, on the other hand, is based on functionalist views of language as a symbolic system that develops from communicative needs (Tomlin, 1990; Tomasello, 1998a). Language is believed to be a complex faculty that is acquired by the learner through engagement with the environment, through inductive and/or deductive learning from input, and in a constructive process (in the Piagetian sense) constrained by general cognition (see Long, 1996; Richards and Gallaway, 1994). Hence, language acquisition is thought of as a gradual process of active form/function mapping, and the traditional dichotomy between competence and performance is not maintained; instead, language learning is inextricably related to language use in that performance is viewed as driving competence (Hymes, 1972; see papers in G. Brown, Malmkjaer, and Williams, 1996; and discussion in McNamara, 1996, ch. 3). Interactionist epistemologies, drawing on functionalist linguistic theories, such as variationist sociolinguistics (Preston, 1989), functional grammar (Givón, 1979), and discourse analysis (Sinclair and Coulthard, 1975), focus not so much on the origin and description of linguistic representation as on the "developmental problem" (e.g., Pienemann, 1998). Not only, therefore, do interactionist SLA theories need to describe and explain learner transitional grammars, but their interpretations must also invoke non-linguistic (i.e., cognitive and environmental) constructs thought to be crucial in accounting for how learning of an L2 takes place on a predictable route and with differential ultimate success. Interactionist SLA researchers maintain that acquisition of L2 forms cannot be demonstrated until such forms are productively used in a variety of contexts in spontaneous performance; a multiplicity of performance data is therefore required to produce a complete picture of language development. In addition, this type of theory argues that incremental, non-linear *changes* (not necessarily target-oriented improvements) in patterns of language use can be taken as indications that gradual learning is taking place (e.g., Mellow, Reeder, and Forster, 1996). Consequently, interactionist studies (at least logically ought to) draw on measures of implicit and explicit memory for L2 forms (i.e., recognition tasks where *acquired* means detected or noticed), measures of explicit knowledge of rules (i.e., metalinguistic verbalization tasks, where *acquired* means understood with awareness), and measures of the use of L2 forms in spontaneous, meaning-driven discourse (i.e., comprehension and production tasks involving sentence-level and, preferably, text-level performance, where ability for use is demonstrated). In sum, under interactionist approaches to SLA, *acquired* may mean a number of gradual and non-linear changes in the linguistic (and, in some theories, metalinguistic) behavior that characterize the developmental course of L2 acquisition, based on construct interpretations such as: (i) a form has "emerged," has been "detected," "noticed," "attempted," or "restructured"; (ii) a learner is "aware" of a form or a form-related pattern; and/or (iii) a learner is "able to use a form appropriately and fluently."[1]

Finally, emergentism provides a combined functional and neurobiological approach to language acquisition that views grammar as a complex, rule-like, but not rule-governed system arising from the interaction of very simple learning mechanisms in the organism (the architecture of the human brain) with the environment (massive exposure to input). Emergentist theories of L2 acquisition seek to explain the frequency and regularity of linguistic input to which the learner must be exposed in order for the processing system (i.e., the brain) to develop a functional set of weights (i.e., degree of interconnectivity among nodes) that will match patterns underlying that input (Sokolik, 1990). Speeded, accurate production of output that matches the input provides evidence that such functional sets of weights in the neural networks have been established on the basis of simple learning algorithms and exposure to positive input alone (N. Ellis, 1998). Consequently, emergentist-connectionist studies typically employ computer modeling experiments and trials with human subjects under laboratory conditions, with interpretations based on reaction-time decision tasks involving carefully controlled input (e.g., N. Ellis and Schmidt, 1997). *Acquired,* for emergentists, means fast, accurate, and effortless performance attained along attested learning curves that reflect non-linear, exemplar-driven learning.

Obviously, each of the preceding theoretical approaches to SLA defines acquisition in unique ways and calls for particular construct interpretations to be made on the basis of measurement data. Indeed, what counts as acquisition is so dependent on the theoretical premises of the research domain that the same measurement data may be interpreted as evidence of acquisition or the lack thereof, depending on the theoretical approach adopted. A good illustration of this point can be found in a well-known study by Trahey and White (1993). Measurement outcomes from this study showed that young francophone learners in intensive ESL programs in Quebec, after a two-week regime of exposure to English input flooded with adverbs, accepted more cases of Subject-Adverb-Verb-Object sentences (ungrammatical in the L1 but grammatical in English) than they had accepted before. However, positive evidence alone (i.e., exposure to only correct SAVO exemplars in the flooded input) did not cause these learners to reject Subject-Verb-Adverb-Object sentences (grammatical in the L1 and ungrammatical in English). From the generativist perspective of the authors, these measurement observations were interpreted to show that acquisition had not occurred, because there was no evidence of parameter resetting, which would require simultaneous acceptance of SAVO and rejection of *SVAO. However, arguments from interactionist SLA, including developmental accounts of L2 learning (e.g., Meisel, Clahsen, and Pienemann, 1981; Mellow et al., 1996) and claims about the role of attention and awareness in L2 learning (e.g., Schmidt, 1993, 1994; Tomlin and Villa, 1994), would call for an alternative interpretation of the same data as evidence for incipient acquisition of adverb placement in L2 English. In fact, in studies of implicit and incidental instructional conditions (i.e., external interventions that do not orient learners to learning with intention; see Schmidt, 1993) researchers have repeatedly found evidence for acquisition in small post-instructional increases in recognition of or preference for the targeted form (a behavior typically observed in input flood treatments, as in Trahey and White, 1993) and/or in increased, albeit initially unsuccessful, attempts to produce the targeted form (a behavior typically observed in typographical input treatments; see Alanen, 1995; Jourdenais et al., 1995).

To summarize, what counts as acquisition (theoretically defined), as well as the utility of viewing L2 acquisition in particular ways, may be disputed by researchers from differing paradigms. However, such disagreements themselves bear witness to the fact that construct definitions are available. Given theoretical construct definitions, additional conceptual bases for measurement may be evaluated. Therefore, we turn now to an examination of the evidence required for making interpretations about acquisition and the measurement tasks used to provide such evidence.

2.2 *Behaviors and tasks: evidence for acquisition*

As indicated in section 1.2, the major threat to validity during the conceptualization of measurement involves construct underrepresentation. Construct underrepresentation occurs when the complex *link* between a theoretical interpretation and required behavioral evidence is inadequately understood and/or conveyed into practice. In order to avoid underrepresentation of a construct, researchers must carefully define the evidentiary requirements (in the form of behaviors) for their intended interpretations, then link these requirements to empirically, or at least logically, related elicitation tasks or situations, which are themselves understood in terms of the behavior(s) that they elicit. Given the range of measurement tasks actually employed by SLA researchers, from discrete-point recognition items to full-blown spontaneous communicative performance, as well as the range of construct interpretations that are based on them, the possible sources for construct underrepresentation are many. In this section, we address four of the most serious (and most common) conceptual problems: providing evidence for both causal and outcomes interpretations (section 2.2.1); understanding and matching complex interpretations with complex behaviors (section 2.2.2); specifying the variable qualities of behaviors in meaningful units that are sensitive to the levels of interpretation to be made (section 2.2.3); and avoiding the "valid test" fallacy (section 2.2.4).[2]

2.2.1 *Evidence for causes and outcomes*

Where interpretations are to be made about the relationship between causal or moderating processes (noticing, comprehension, cognitive resources of memory and attention, attentional focus, language aptitude, etc.) and L2 acquisition products, behavioral evidence for such constructs will also need to be specified and associated measurement tasks selected. SLA research frequently employs dependent variable measures which only provide evidence bearing on the linguistic "products" of acquisition (vocabulary recognition items, grammaticality judgment tasks, elicited imitation, communicative performance, etc.). Such measures do little to inform interpretations about the independent variables to which acquisition-related behavioral patterns are ascribed; the actual construct interpretations (i.e., about the relationship between certain causes and linguistic outcomes in acquisition) will thus be underrepresented within measurement practice.

Two recent cognitive interactionist proposals for task-based second language learning, advanced by Robinson (2001b) and Skehan (1998), provide a good illustration of theories which call on measurement simultaneously to inform both causal and outcomes interpretations. These two theoretical models invoke distinct explanatory processes while predicting very similar changes in L2 behavior. In both theories, the more cognitively complex a task (a meaning-oriented communicative activity), the more likely it will yield increasingly more complex but less fluent language output by learners. Both models posit this relationship on the assumption that cognitive complexity of tasks is positively related to L2 learning. However, Robinson (2001b) argues that the linguistic processing demanded by cognitively more complex tasks entails a mobilization of attentional pools dedicated to language production, and thus pushes the internal system in several ways (i.e., by fostering deeper linguistic processing that promotes rehearsal in short-term memory and eventual reorganization of form/function connections; see also Robinson, 1995). This is essentially an emergentist or functionalist rationale (see N. Ellis, 1998; MacWhinney, 1998; Tomasello, 1998b) that rests on a multiple-resource model of attention and memory (Wickens, 1989). By contrast, Skehan (1998) claims that unmitigated/uncensored cognitive complexity can have the undesirable effect of overloading a learner's limited attentional resources and fostering an easy way out through lexical (as opposed to syntactic) processing of L2 input and output. Therefore, according to Skehan, during competence-expanding L2 performance, it is necessary to orchestrate learner-external interventions to ensure that learners consciously attend to the linguistic code and prioritize accuracy goals during performance. This is in essence an information-processing and skills-acquisition rationale that assumes limited attentional capacity (see Anderson, 1993; McLaughlin, 1987).

Since both Robinson (2001b) and Skehan (1998) predict, as a result of task-based learning, very similar outcomes in terms of L2 performance (with regard to productive complexity and fluency; accuracy is much-debated terrain – see Ortega, 1999), the only way to inform the full range of interpretations that need to (and will) be made in related research is by gathering evidence bearing on the explanatory constructs invoked in each theory in addition to language performance data. For Robinson's predictions to be measurable, this will mean eliciting behaviors that reflect psycholinguistic operations (e.g., deeper processing and rehearsal in short-term memory), which reside beyond conscious control. For Skehan's theory, behaviors must be elicited which reflect metalinguistic operations (e.g., strategic attention to the code and a prioritization of accuracy), which are subject to conscious learner control. Each type of interpretation calls for distinct, indirect techniques to provide empirical evidence for either psycholinguistic or metalinguistic operations. For instance, introspective methodologies (see Ericsson and Simon, 1993; Sugrue, 1995) seem the best available options for accessing metalinguistic operations, whereas implicit memory tasks (priming tasks, implicit recognition tasks, etc.) may be the most appropriate choices for attempting to tap psycholinguistic, automatic operations (see Bjork and Bjork, 1996; Stadler and Frensch, 1998). Finally, measurement in the service of both theories will also need to provide evidence for interpretations about the so-called cognitive "complexity" of L2 performance tasks (see discussion in Norris, Brown, Hudson, and Yoshioka, 1998; Robinson, 2001a; Skehan, 1998). Of course, establishing a link between the full sets of interrelated constructs (cognitive complexity, linguistic complexity, strategic accuracy-orienting operations, deeper processing operations, complexity/fluency/accuracy in performance) and long-term L2 learning, rather than immediate L2 performance, raises additional questions regarding the timing and frequency of measurement that will be necessary to provide adequate evidence for such complex interpretations.

This example underscores the necessity of defining the evidentiary requirements for *all* construct interpretations to be based on measurement, such that an adequate range of corresponding behaviors may be elicited. Other explanations for SLA which are based on the contribution of causal processes run a similar risk of construct underrepresentation, including: the role of noticing and awareness (e.g., Leow, 1997) and attentional focus (e.g., Williams, 1999); the potential contribution of uptake (e.g., Lyster, 1998; Mackey and Philp, 1998); the moderating influence of aptitude (e.g., Sawyer and Ranta, 2001; Grigorenko, Sternberg, and Ehrman, 2000); and the relationship between interactional modifications and actual L2 learning, via either facilitated comprehension (e.g., Loschky, 1994) or provision of negative feedback (e.g., Iwashita, 1999; Mackey, 1999). For these and other approaches to acquisition research which make reference to cognitive processes, advances in measurement within the cognitive sciences should prove instructive, where, as a rule, a multiplicity of behavioral observations is gathered to inform and triangulate interpretations (see Pellegrino, 1988; Siegler, 1989; Snow and Lohman, 1989; Sugrue, 1995). For example, Royer, Cisero, and Carlo (1993) point out that "cognitive assessment procedures should be able to provide indices of change in knowledge organization and structure and indices of the accuracy, speed, and resource load of the activities being performed" (p. 202). Bennett (1999) also shows how developing technologies will enable researchers simultaneously to capture and measure a much wider array of behavioral evidence bearing on cognitive constructs.

2.2.2 *Matching complex interpretations with complex behaviors*

Whereas the previous section addressed problems in construct underrepresentation which occur when researchers fail to employ multiple measures for multiple interpretations, this section addresses problems arising from the multidimensional or complex nature of both the evidence required by particular constructs and the evidence provided by particular behaviors. In the context of correlational and experimental research on child language acquisition, Richards (1994) calls the problem of ignoring or underestimating the complexity of variables at play the *holistic fallacy*. This fallacy arises when the relationship between behaviors and constructs is conceptualized as being "more widely applicable or more uniform than may be the case" (p. 100). The holistic fallacy can take several forms in SLA research. On the one hand, researchers may fail to recognize the complex nature of the behavioral evidence that is required by a given construct interpretation; in such cases, resulting measurement data tend to be overinterpreted because the behaviors selected to be observed do not, in fact, provide sufficient evidence for the full construct interpretation. On the other hand, researchers may fail to recognize the complexity of the behavioral evidence that will be provided by measurement tasks/situations, when the actual sources of variability within the selected behaviors are not understood; in these cases, measurement data tend to be underinterpreted because the observed variations in behavior may really be attributable to factors beyond those found in the construct interpretation.

Nichols and Sugrue (1999) have observed that many educational tests and test items fail adequately to reflect intended constructs because of a mismatch between "the simple cognitive assumptions often embedded in conventional test development practices and the cognitively complex nature of the constructs to be measured" (p. 18). Several measurement examples in SLA research underscore similar problems. In a meta-analytic review of experimental and quasi-experimental studies of L2 instruction, Norris and Ortega (2000) compared the observed magnitude of effects when instructional outcomes were measured using metalinguistic judgments (various kinds of grammaticality judgment tasks), free constructed responses (discourse-level communicative L2 performance), and constrained responses (selecting or producing word- or clause-level linguistic responses). They found that the observed effects associated with constrained response types ranged from half again up to as much as three times the effects associated with metalinguistic judgments and free constructed response types. Obviously, in light of the consistent differences in observed effects, researchers would come to very different conclusions about acquisition if they chose to elicit constrained response behaviors instead of the other evidence types. Indeed, there is good reason to believe that the constrained response type of measure does not adequately reflect the complexity of interpretations being made about L2 acquisition in such studies. Constrained response tests reduce language behavior to the single instance of "ticking the right box" or producing a form out of extended discursive context. Given the disjuncture between such isolated language-like behaviors and either communicative language use or a learner's underlying mental representation of the L2 grammar, the link with complex interpretations about changes in ability for use or grammatical competence is at best tenuous. While not without their own problems, it can be argued that the behaviors elicited in metalinguistic judgments and free constructed response measures better reflect constructs like "grammatical competence" and "ability for use." Metalinguistic judgments directly ask learners to indicate which aspects of the grammar they find acceptable and which they do not, behaviors which, if carefully planned and elicited (e.g., Sorace, 1996), may provide a much more complete depiction of the learner's internal L2 grammar than the suppliance of "correct" responses to isolated grammar questions. Likewise, free constructed response behaviors offer insights into how a learner actually deploys acquired L2 forms in real-time, meaning-focused communication, as opposed to how a learner responds to selected language forms presented out of context.

A number of other complex construct interpretations in SLA research call for complex behaviors to be elicited. For example, as Sorace (1996) has pointed out, interpretations about grammatical competence which attempt to incorporate inherently variable phenomena (i.e., as opposed to ignoring variable phenomena which "are not representative of a learner's linguistic knowledge," Gass, 1994, p. 308), such as grammatical indeterminacy, optionality, and hierarchies of grammatical acceptability, will be poorly served by grammaticality measures which simply ask learners to judge sentences categorically as either acceptable or not. In order to inform such interpretations, measurement will need to enable a greater range in elicited response behaviors which may better reflect the range of actual interpretations (e.g., magnitude estimation techniques in Bard, Robertson, and Sorace, 1996; Sorace, 1996; Sorace and Robertson, forthcoming; Yuan, 1997). Where interpretations are to be made about dynamic constructs, such as grammatical development along attested routes of acquisition, multiple instances of behaviors will need to be elicited over time, in order to determine what rules or forms may already be present or not within the learner's interlanguage system, and what a change in behavior with a rule or form may indicate (emergence of a rule, U-shaped or omega-shaped developmental behavior, etc.). Where only static behaviors are elicited, as is often the case in cross-sectional research or pre-test/post-test design studies (see Willett, 1988), unidentified baseline trends in behavior may go undetected at a single point of measurement because the dynamic nature of the construct is not reflected (see Mellow et al., 1996; Pienemann, 1998). Finally, because of the accidental statistical structure of an impoverished language corpus, interpretations about the existence or absence of a given rule/form in the IL system may be unwarranted (Bley-Vroman, 1983). For example, where interpretations are to be made about the emergence of linguistic phenomena which exhibit both variational and developmental characteristics (such as emergence of word order rules in L2 German acquisition; Meisel et al., 1981), measurement will need to elicit behaviors across numerous linguistic and communicative contexts in order to show that interpretations are not based on a lack of evidence, as opposed to evidence for the lack of emergence (see discussion in Hudson, 1993; Pienemann, 1998; and potential solutions in Pienemann, 1998; Pienemann, Johnston, and Brindley, 1988).

Although measurement data may often be overinterpreted as SLA researchers attempt to provide evidence for complex constructs, it is likely that measurement data are more frequently underinterpreted when researchers do not adequately conceptualize the complexities of measurement behaviors that they intend to elicit. Thus, while elicited behaviors may reflect intended constructs in part, no elicitation procedure, regardless of how much control is exercised by the researcher, is immune to variability introduced by the interaction of the human subject with the measurement task or situation. In this regard, an issue raised some time ago by Grotjahn (1986) rings particularly true for measurement in SLA research: "in order to really understand what a (language) test measures [. . .], we first have to understand the individual task-specific cognitive processes on which the observed performance depends" (p. 162). Making warranted interpretations on the basis of elicited performance will depend, then, on understanding to what extent observed behaviors are influenced by the interaction of learner variables with task/situation variables (see Bachman and Cohen, 1998; J. D. Brown, Hudson, Norris, and Bonk, forthcoming; Norris, 2000).

Observed performances on L2 measurement tasks may be influenced by a number of learner variables which may or may not be reflected in intended construct interpretations. For example, undocumented differences in learners' prior L2 knowledge (in terms of overall proficiency; see discussions in Hulstijn, 1997; Thomas, 1994) and/or current interlanguage status (e.g., in terms of developmental readiness to acquire a particular structure; see Pienemann, 1998) will prove problematic for developmental as well as causal interpretations in SLA research. Unless learners have been characterized according to language ability or psycholinguistic readiness vis-à-vis the acquisition construct in focus (Chaudron, 1985), elicited behaviors, especially if they are summarized at the group level, may lead to misinterpretations about L2 development or the lack thereof, the relative effectiveness of a given instructional treatment, etc. Likewise, differences in how learners respond to a measurement task at motivational, cognitive, and metacognitive levels will determine in part the performance behaviors that may be observed (Royer et al., 1993; Sugrue, 1995). For example, Leow (2000) found that learners who became aware of targeted forms during experimental exposure, as opposed to those who remained unaware of them, increased in their ability to recognize and produce the same forms immediately after the experiment (cf. similar findings in Alanen, 1995). In such cases, construct interpretations would need to tease out the learner's state of awareness in terms of the structures being measured in order comprehensively to understand elicited language performance behaviors. A number of additional individual learner differences may also influence the language behaviors elicited during measurement, including language aptitude, memory capabilities, learning backgrounds, first language, linguistic training, and mental state (see Bardovi-Harlig, 1994a; de Graaff, 1997; DeKeyser, 1995; Robinson, 1997; Sorace, 1996; Zobl, 1995).

Observed performances may also be influenced by characteristics of the measurement tasks/situations themselves, which again may or may not be reflected in intended construct interpretations. For example, the linguistic contexts elicited in measurement may vary according to communicative activity type. Tarone and Parrish (1988) found that a narrative activity was inherently less demanding on learners' abilities to apply English article rules than was an interview activity. Whereas the narrative primarily elicited linguistic contexts for the least difficult type of reference (i.e., reference to an entity already introduced in the narration), the oral interview elicited a balanced mixture of contexts for all three types of reference involving article use (see Huebner, 1983). Obviously, interpretations about learners' abilities with this particular grammatical subsystem would depend largely on an understanding of the particular elicitation tasks selected. Similarly, language performance behaviors may depend in part on the formatting and presentation of measurement tasks. For example, Bley-Vroman and Chaudron (1994) demonstrated that learners' performances on elicited imitation tasks were systematically influenced by stimulus length and serial order effects (see also Chaudron and Russell, 1990). Thus, depending on both the length of the sentence to be repeated and the placement within the sentence of targeted structures, learners would either correctly or incorrectly repeat the structure to be measured. Numerous other characteristics of measurement tasks may introduce systematic variability into the performances elicited from learners, including characteristics of the measurement setting, the communicative or linguistic context, and task instructions and formatting (see extensive treatment in Bachman and Palmer, 1996; R. Ellis, 1994; Loschky and Bley-Vroman, 1993; Norris et al., 1998; Tarone, 1998; Wolfram, 1985; Yule, 1997).

In sum, SLA researchers will need to conceptualize carefully the link between intended construct interpretations and the behaviors selected to provide evidence about them. Recent empirical and theoretical approaches to cognitive task analysis should prove helpful in conceptualizing the cognitive demands made by characteristics of measurement tasks and the ways in which learners deal with such demands during task performance (e.g., Baxter and Glaser, 1998; Mislevy et al., 1999; Nichols and Sugrue, 1999; Royer et al., 1993; Sugrue, 1995). More fundamentally, measurement for SLA research purposes would be well served by adopting an *evidence-centered* approach to the design of instruments and procedures. Bennett (1999) summarizes evidence-centered design as the process of "identifying the evidence needed for decision making in terms of some complex of student characteristics, the behaviors or performances required to reveal those constructs, and the tasks needed to elicit those behaviors" (p. 5). Recent work on the application of evidence-centered design principles to educational and occupational assessment problems offers detailed and useful examples of this process (e.g., Mislevy et al., 1999, forthcoming).

2.2.3 *Specifying meaningful qualities of behavior*

Even if behaviors to be elicited in measurement are carefully selected in order to provide adequate evidence for intended construct interpretations, construct underrepresentation remains a threat unless the variable qualities of behaviors are specified in units of analysis which are sensitive to the intended interpretations. Chaudron (1988) has pointed out, "when we test hypotheses with a quantitative method, we have derived them from qualitative, conceptual considerations. Before we count, we have to decide what categories to count" (p. 16). In SLA research, meaningful categories may include, among others: (i) frequency or amount of behaviors; (ii) duration of behaviors; (iii) sequences of behaviors; (iv) combinations of behaviors; and (v) comparisons of one sort of behavior with others. Each of these approaches to synthesizing behavioral observations requires a corresponding scale with units that match the scope of intended interpretations (e.g., counting milliseconds, seconds, or minutes will obviously affect the level at which chronometric research findings may be discussed; see related problems in Siegler, 1989). In addition, it may frequently be the case that a single set of scales/units will prove insufficient for capturing the complexity of construct interpretations. For example, while "error" counts may offer evidence for interpretations about the extent of a learner's knowledge, they will do little in the way of informing interpretations about the cognitive resource demands or expertise in performing a task using that knowledge, especially when "improvements in skilled performance continue long after errorless performance is achieved" (Royer et al., 1993, p. 210). Therefore, conceptualizing the variable qualities of elicited behaviors in construct-meaningful ways will prove critical for maintaining construct validity during the scoring and analysis of measurement outcomes.

Interlanguage analysis techniques, typically carried out within interactionist approaches to SLA, offer a useful example of problems which researchers encounter when criterial qualities of behavior do not match the scope of intended interpretations. For example, Pica (1983) found that the application of different levels of analysis to the same interlanguage performance data "resulted in two different interpretations regarding the role of L2 exposure conditions in second language acquisition" (p. 73). Pica compared accuracy results from the measurement of suppliance in obligatory contexts (SOC; see R. Brown, 1973) with results from the measurement of target-like use (TLU), a technique developed to account for oversuppliance errors. She found that the results of TLU analyses, but not of SOC, revealed a marked tendency among instruction-only learners to oversupply certain morphemes, a tendency which was absent in the L2 performance of naturalistic learners. Further TLU analyses based on types (where only different word types were counted for accurate use), but not based on tokens of the same data (where each word token was entered into the accuracy count), revealed that naturalistic learners and instruction-only learners had a smaller expressive vocabulary and used the English plural morpheme with fewer word types than instruction-plus-exposure learners. Had the data been subjected solely to SOC and token-based TLU analyses, these two patterns would have gone undetected. Another illustration of how increased sensitivity of analytical units and procedures may contribute to a better understanding of the behaviors of interest within a given theory is found in Oliver (1995). In her study of the provision of negative feedback during task-based interactions, Oliver observed that only 10 percent of recasts produced by English native-speaking children during interactional exchanges were incorporated by their ESL interlocutor peers. However, when she introduced a finer level of analysis for NNS third turns in recast episodes, by adding to her coding scheme the category "no opportunity to incorporate" (due to discursive-pragmatic constraints on turn-taking), she found that over one-third of all recasts were incorporated.

A particularly thorny issue in interlanguage research is adjudication of the extent to which accuracy in production of L2 forms should be taken as reflective of IL development. An early caution against accuracy as a viable criterion for L2 acquisition (as traditionally established in L1 acquisition studies by R. Brown, 1973) was advanced by Meisel et al. (1981; see also Pienemann, 1998). These authors argued that emergence, defined as the first documented occasion of productive (i.e., non-formulaic) use of a given form, is the most IL-sensitive approximation for measuring development. Likewise, measures of grammatical accuracy have difficulty accounting for attested IL developmental phenomena, such as threshold and stage-related effects (Meisel et al., 1981), flooding (Huebner, 1983), and U-shaped behavior (Kellerman, 1985), all of which can obscure interpretations. Additional qualities of interlanguage development have been proposed which may further constrain interpretations based on grammatical accuracy. For instance, Wolfe-Quintero, Inagaki, and Kim (1998, pp. 73–4) have suggested a phenomenon that they call omega-shaped behavior, referring to a temporary increase in the frequency of (possibly less-than-accurate) suppliance of a recently emerged form, followed by a normalization in rate of suppliance, once the new form has been worked out by the learner. Another underexplored quality of learner L2 production is the gradual extension of suppliance of a form from a few simple contexts to a wider range of (possibly more complex) contexts (see Richards, 1990, on L1 acquisition; and Pishwa, 1994, on L2 acquisition).

What the existence of such interlanguage processes and phenomena suggests is that curvilinear rather than linear relationships can be expected between accuracy in producing a given L2 form and IL development of that form. These curvilinear relationships need to be taken into account when conceptualizing criteria for behavioral qualities and when planning analyses of L2 performance, as they will certainly affect the interpretations that follow. An IL analytical approach that combines emergence and accuracy (of the same form or of related forms) may prove more informative and useful than an exclusive focus on emergence or, no doubt, on accuracy. For example, by combining analyses of emergence and accuracy in a longitudinal corpus, Bardovi-Harlig (1994b) was able to establish that the emergence of initial instances of past perfect marking in L2 English was dependent upon learners reaching a reasonable level of stability (i.e., productive accuracy of around 85 percent SOC) in the marking of past tense morphology. In the end, the most desirable approach, particularly with longitudinal data, may be to adopt a three-step coding process which gauges: (i) first suppliance (or emergence), (ii) non-target-like but more sustained suppliance (frequency of functional contexts attempted), and (iii) target-like suppliance at optimal ultimate levels of attainment (accuracy).

This multifaceted approach to characterizing qualities of behavior might most precisely reflect the gradual processes in IL development that many SLA researchers are interested in mapping (see Stromswold, 1996, for similar methodological suggestions in L1 acquisition research).

These examples of interpretive problems arising in interlanguage analysis underscore what should be a fundamental concern for SLA researchers who utilize measurement data. That is, for all measures, researchers should be able to demonstrate how a particular type and level of behavioral analysis enable construct-relevant interpretations to be made. What does it mean for a learner to score 60 percent correct on a post-test as compared with 50 percent correct on the pre-test? What does an observed difference in "amount of interaction" have to do with differences in acquisition? How can similar reaction times in sentence-matching tasks from advanced and novice learners be explained? What does an "incorrect" answer on a grammatical acceptability item tell us about the learner's internal grammar? How does frequency of "errors" in a written narrative offer insights into a learner's developing interlanguage? Where basic questions like these about the qualities of observed behaviors cannot be answered, researchers will remain "unenlightened" about the meanings attributable to measurement outcomes (Chaudron, 1988; Schachter, 1998), and construct interpretations will remain unwarranted. It should also be obvious from the examples above that the only source for answers to such questions, and the basis for establishing meaningful qualities of measurement behaviors, resides in empirical knowledge that has been accumulated about the acquisition-related behaviors of interest. In this regard, as has been recommended for measurement in other domains of inquiry (e.g., the measurement of automatization in cognitive processing; Royer et al., 1993), there is an obvious increased role to be played in SLA research by descriptive longitudinal studies which establish norms of performance for particular processes and phenomena in L2 acquisition (e.g., Ortega, 2000). Indeed, attempting to "measure" acquisition without a sound descriptive basis for meaningful differences in particular acquisition-related behaviors would be akin to timing a runner's performance over a mile without knowing how many times around the track a mile happens to be.

2.2.4 The "valid test" fallacy

From time to time, SLA researchers adopt measures employed in previous studies, or in other non-research contexts, for the purposes of their own investigations. In itself, repeated use of identical measurement instruments/procedures for measuring the *same construct(s)* is a fundamentally worthwhile endeavor. As Norris and Ortega (2000) have pointed out for studies of L2 instructional effectiveness, it is only through such exact replication (e.g., by measuring the same dependent variable) across research settings that trustworthy findings about a given variable may begin to accumulate (see also Bangert-Drowns, 1986; Cohen, 1997; Light and Pillemer, 1984; Rosenthal, 1979). However, when SLA researchers adopt pre-existing measures wholesale, simply because they seemed valid in other studies or measurement contexts, the researchers are guilty of the "valid test" fallacy.

In such cases, researchers or other measurement users mistakenly assume that validity is a property of test instruments and procedures, rather than the uses that are made of them. As the *Standards for Educational and Psychological Testing* (AERA, APA, NCME, 1999) make clear, validation is a process of gathering evidence and theoretical arguments supporting the *use* of test scores for particular interpretations and related purposes. As such, the *Standards* emphasize, "When test scores are used or interpreted in more than one way, each intended interpretation must be validated" (p. 9). If SLA researchers assume that a given measure is a "valid" indicator of acquisition (or learning or proficiency or knowledge or aptitude, etc.), then apply that measure to their own situated purposes, without taking the time to establish the link between behavioral evidence provided by the measure and their own intended constructs, the validity of resulting interpretations will be threatened (see related discussion in Messick, 1989; Thompson, 1998).

For example, Shohamy (1994) observed that tests intended for educational decision making, such as the Test of English as a Foreign Language (TOEFL), are frequently utilized by SLA researchers as measures of learning or acquisition, even though such tests were designed as indicators of global academic language abilities. Likewise, holistic proficiency measures, such as the ACTFL (1986) *Guidelines* and related procedures, may be used as a basis for assigning learners to instructional research conditions, even though the scores on such measures may have nothing to do with the particular L2 forms or abilities being investigated (see discussion in Norris, 1996, 1997; Young, 1995b). The "valid test" fallacy applies equally to so-called "objective" measures, such as those used in analyzing spoken or written L2 performance (e.g., accuracy, complexity, and fluency measures; see Polio, 1997; Wolfe-Quintero et al., 1998), when researchers misguidedly assert or hope that such units of analysis will be "valid" for all reasons (Foster, Tonkyn, and Wigglesworth, 1998). We are not suggesting that for every research study new measures need to be developed; this would only serve to limit generalizability of findings and hinder the accumulation of knowledge. We are suggesting that SLA researchers need to conceptualize carefully their constructs and the evidence that will be brought to bear on them, and then match these conceptual bases with corresponding instruments and procedures, in order for each occasion of measurement use to inform warranted interpretations.

3 How Should Acquisition be Counted? Procedural Concerns for Measurement in SLA

Given adequate conceptualization of what counts as acquisition, the mechanics of measurement may take place, following several procedural stages (4–6 in section 1.1): (i) selected tasks/situations are employed to elicit behaviors;

(ii) meaningful qualities in observed behaviors are summarized in the form of scores; and (iii) scores are analyzed to produce evidence for intended interpretations about acquisition. As conceptual decisions are translated into practice, the particular actions that are taken by researchers may influence resulting interpretations. Such unintended or unsystematic sources of variance which issue from the act of measurement itself can be summarized under the heading of measurement error. The fundamental construct validity question for these procedural stages, then, asks to what extent patterns in the behavioral data which are actually elicited, scored, and analyzed can be attributed to the construct interpretations that researchers want to make, as opposed to construct-*irrelevant* variance due to measurement error.

There are numerous approaches to developing and using measures which may help to reduce the influence of measurement error. For practical guides, readers are referred to several sources directly related to applied linguistics (e.g., Bachman, 1990; J. D. Brown, 1996; Hatch and Lazaraton, 1991; Henning, 1987; Scholfield, 1995; Woods, Fletcher, and Hughes, 1986) as well as to the educational and psychological measurement literature (e.g., Anastasi and Urbina, 1997; Gronlund and Linn, 1990; Linn, 1989; Orwin, 1994; Pedhazur and Schmelkin, 1991; Popham, 1981; Traub, 1994). Our purpose in the current section is briefly to address a few of the most critical concerns associated with the proceduralization of measurement in SLA research, and to suggest directions in research practice which might help to reduce the threat of construct-irrelevant variance due to measurement error.

3.1 *Reliability in elicitation and scoring*

Reliability reflects the extent to which a measure leads to *consistent* interpretations about a particular construct on each measurement occasion. Such consistency is traditionally viewed (e.g., Traub, 1994) as the relationship between an observed score or any quantified outcome of measurement, the amount of that observed score which is attributable to the construct of interest, and the amount of observed score which is attributable to measurement error: observed score = true score + error. As behavioral data are elicited and scored, varying amounts of error may be introduced from a number of sources, including: (i) environmental factors associated with the data-collection or test-administration context; (ii) data-collection or test-administration procedures; (iii) characteristics of items or other components of the measurement instrument; (iv) data-coding or test-scoring procedures; and (v) idiosyncrasies of research participants, such as interest, attention, and motivation (see J. D. Brown, 1996; Traub, 1994). Obviously, the greater the influence of such error types, the less reliable measurement outcomes will be (i.e., the less an observed score on a measure will represent a learner's true score vis-à-vis the construct). In order for measurement-based SLA research to inform warranted interpretations, such sources of measurement error should be reduced where possible. It is also essential to observe, analyze, and report reliability and error for each use of a measure, as indicated by the American Psychological Association task force on statistical inferencing: "[A]uthors should provide reliability coefficients of the scores for the data being analyzed even when the focus of their research is not psychometric. Interpreting the size of observed effects requires an assessment of the reliability of the scores" (Wilkinson and the Task Force on Statistical Inference, 1999, p. 596). Furthermore, the *Standards for Educational and Psychological Testing* (AERA, APA, NCME, 1999) hold that reports of reliability should include discussion of: (i) the operationalization and administration of instruments and procedures; (ii) the development and use of scoring or coding schemes; (iii) the training of coders or raters; (iv) the performance of coders or raters; (v) the characteristics of participants or populations; and (vi) the characteristics of scores.

3.1.1 *Error in behavior elicitation*

The behavior elicitation and observation stage of measurement is particularly susceptible to the introduction of error, owing to the multitude of factors to be considered in order to maintain procedural consistency (see, e.g., the detailed list in J. D. Brown, 1996, p. 189). On the one hand, researchers must ensure that all critical aspects of tasks or situations are faithfully translated into measurement instruments and procedures as conceptualized, such that the scope of behaviors and behavioral qualities may be fully captured. For example, in research on developmental sequences in L2 syntax and morphology, the design of measurement tasks must reflect a number of considerations in order to elicit consistent behavioral patterns. Because initial emergence of particular syntactic and morphologic forms is posited to be implicationally related with the preceding or subsequent emergence of other forms, behavioral data must be gathered across a variety of linguistic contexts. Furthermore, given the fact that initial emergence of a form may occur in different communicative contexts for different learners, behavioral data must be gathered using a variety of communication tasks (or in a variety of situations). In light of such evidentiary requirements, it is only through the elicitation of extensive amounts and types of L2 behaviors that measurement can show that particular forms have emerged, that implicationally preceding forms have also emerged, and that subsequent forms have not emerged. If measurement tasks fail to provide the range of linguistic and communicative contexts necessary for patterns in emergence to be displayed, then interpretations about learners' developmental stages will remain inconclusive at best (see discussion in Clahsen, Meisel, and Pienemann, 1983; Hudson, 1993; Pienemann, 1998; Pienemann, Johnston, and Brindley, 1988; Pienemann and Mackey, 1993).

On the other hand, researchers must also be wary of potentially unpredictable sources of error that may be associated with features of the measurement context, measurement forms or instructions, individual learners, etc. For example, for SLA research which seeks to make interpretations based on learners' oral L2 discourse, characteristics of the interlocutor as well as particular actions undertaken by the interlocutor may unpredictably influence a learner's L2 performance. Research on oral interview types of language tests, wherein one or more examinees interact with one or more interlocutors, has demonstrated that such characteristics as gender and age of the interlocutor may substantially affect the amount and quality of language produced by the examinee (e.g., McNamara and Lumley, 1997; O'Sullivan, 2000). Likewise, the particular activities engaged in by interlocutors (especially interviewers), such as discourse accommodation, have been demonstrated to influence what an examinee says and how it is said (e.g., Lazaraton, 1992, 1996; Ross and Berwick, 1990; Young, 1995a; Young and He, 1998; Young and Milanovic, 1992).

In order to reduce the effect of these and many other problems that may emerge during the elicitation of behaviors for measurement purposes, there is much to be said for following systematic methods in the production of tests and other procedures, and especially for careful pilot-testing and revision of instruments, directions, and administration guidelines (see Bachman, 1990; Bachman and Palmer, 1996; J. D. Brown, 1996, forthcoming; Campbell and Reichardt, 1991; Lynch and Davidson, 1994; Popham, 1981). Recent developments in measurement theory and technology may also prove useful in this respect, for example, in the form of computerized item-generation capabilities (e.g., Irvine and Kyllonen, 2001).

3.1.2 Error in scoring

Even if they are consistently elicited and observed, measurement behaviors on their own are typically insufficient for enabling intended interpretations; hence, they are almost always summarized or scored in light of particular qualities which are relevant to the L2 acquisition constructs. Measurement error may also be introduced during this scoring process. First, the particular scoring procedures employed by researchers may serve as sources of error, if they are not consistently carried out. Second, important qualities of measurement behaviors may be distorted or obscured by characteristics of the scores that have been selected to represent them.

The coding of learners' spoken or written L2 production for patterns in interlanguage development offers a good example of the possible sources of error which may be introduced during measurement scoring. Such "interlanguage coding" involves the subjective application of particular criteria by raters or coders in order to identify various attested or predicted phenomena within learner performances, such as: (i) target-like grammatical accuracy of syntactic or morphologic forms; (ii) lexical range, density, and diversity; (iii) rate of speech, number and length of pauses, hesitations, and other features of fluency; (iv) range, length, and suppliance of various clausal types; and (v) length, amount, and frequency of various semantic and/or phonological units (see overviews in Crookes, 1990, 1991; Norris, 1996; Ortega, 1999, 2000; Polio, 1997; Richards and Malvern, 1997; Skehan, 1998; Wolfe-Quintero et al., 1998). Typically, in coding for these and related phenomena, individual coders work through recordings, transcripts, or written products, identifying and marking the phenomena in question as they go. A number of problems may occur during this coding process which introduce error into the resulting scores. Coders may be insufficiently knowledgeable of, or trained to recognize, the IL phenomenon in the first place, or the phenomenon may be defined so poorly within the research domain as to defy accurate coding of complex data (e.g., the coding of utterances or T-units for spoken discourse, as Crookes, 1990, and Foster et al., 1998, have pointed out). When working with a lengthy corpus, coders may become fatigued, frustrated, or bored. Over time, they may "drift" in their assessments of how a phenomenon is realized in the data. Finally, coders may be biased to identify or ignore the particular IL phenomena that they are investigating. Each of these problems can cause coders to miscode, or simply miss, characteristics of the behavioral data which have been elicited. In order to minimize the impact of such coding problems, a systematic series of error-reduction strategies (Orwin, 1994) can be employed, including the careful development and pilot-testing of coding protocols, the sufficient training of coders, the use of multiple codings of the same data, and the scheduling of coding rounds in a staged fashion to minimize coder drift (e.g., Ortega, 2000). In addition, the periodic and overall calculation of intercoder agreement coefficients will enable the identification and reduction of coder error, as well as provide evidence regarding the extent to which such error influences the final scores attributed to individual learners.

Once codings are completed, they are tallied and converted into numerical scores which represent the interlanguage phenomena in various ways (number of pauses, number of different clause types per total number of clauses, target-like forms supplied in obligatory contexts, etc.). Of course, simple miscounts of the codings or miscalculations of comparisons among them will distort the actual behaviors observed, although the mechanization of counting and calculating can greatly reduce such error (e.g., MacWhinney, 2000). At the same time, the index or scale selected for scoring may itself introduce error into eventual interpretations. For example, a host of reliability problems have been associated with discrepancies between scores, the overall size of a corpus and variable text length within a corpus, and intended interpretations (see discussions in Biber, 1990; Bley-Vroman, 1983; Richards, 1994). Simple raw frequency counts of a phenomenon (e.g., number of relative clauses) can prove problematic when scores are to be compared among different learners' texts, because lengthier texts increase the likelihood that a given phenomenon will be observed more frequently (Richards, 1994). Thus, general learner *productivity* may serve to confound interpretations about a learner's use or knowledge of a given L2 form. In addition, the exclusive reporting of raw frequencies makes it difficult to compare results across studies yielded by total corpora of differing lengths (Wolfe-Quintero et al., 1998).

One solution favored by many researchers is to convert frequency tallies into ratio scores (e.g., words per second, clauses per T-unit, unique lexemes per total lexemes, etc.). However, ratios are not impervious to reliability problems associated with the size of a corpus and the relative size of the texts (or samples) which comprise it. For example, the lexical type–token ratio (number of lexical types per total number of lexical tokens) has been shown repeatedly to have a non-linear, and often negative, relationship with corpus size and to be a very unstable score when text samples of varying lengths are compared (see Hess, Sefton, and Landry, 1986; Richards, 1987). This instability occurs because closed-class words as well as high-frequency words are likely to be repeated increasingly in extended production by a given learner, while new words are progressively less likely to be used (i.e., relative to the other words). Thus, shorter samples tend to display inflated type–token ratios relative to longer samples. As a solution to this productivity bias, it has been suggested that a minimum standardized length of 300 tokens (e.g., words, T-units, etc.) per sample may be necessary for lexical ratios to stabilize (see Hess et al., 1986). However, perhaps the most accurate, if somewhat more computationally demanding, approach to resolving such problems has been proposed by Richards and Malvern (1997), who have shown that a statistical model of lexical diversity better reflects lexical differences among learners. Such modeling of multiple sources of variance in observed behaviors may be the only means for accurately summarizing interlanguage codings in a way that is adequately consistent and relevant to intended construct interpretations.

These examples underscore the extent to which error may be introduced into measurement through the scoring process. Among other problems (e.g., violation of a cardinal assumption for statistical inferencing), resulting low reliability in measurement scores can cloud outcomes to the point that findings are not interpretable or actual relationships and effects are not detected. As such, it is essential that researchers seek to understand the error involved in each use of a measure. Along these lines, Thompson (1994) has emphasized:

> The failure to consider score reliability in substantive research may exact a toll on the interpretations within research studies. For example, we may conduct studies that could not possibly yield noteworthy effect sizes, given that score reliability inherently attenuates effect sizes. Or we may not accurately interpret the effect sizes in our studies if we do not consider the reliability of the scores we are actually analyzing. (p. 840)

There are several major theoretical approaches to, and numerous techniques for, estimating the amount and type of error in measurement scoring and scores. In addition to classical test theory approaches and techniques (e.g., J. D. Brown, 1996; Traub, 1994), developments in reliability theory over the past several decades have led to a much more sophisticated understanding of how and to what extent error may be influencing scores. Item response theory and associated computerized analyses (e.g., Linacre, 1998), which focus on the probabilities of various score patterns, not only enable the calculation of learner ability and task difficulty estimates according to a single true interval scale, but also allow for the estimation of error associated with each individual score point, as opposed to the traditional and much less informative single reliability estimate for an entire set of scores (see discussion in Embretson and

Hershberger, 1999; Hambleton, Swaminathan, and Rogers, 1991). An even more thorough understanding of the amount of error contributed to scores by each of any number of different sources (raters, tasks, forms, examinee populations, etc.) may be achieved through the use of generalizability theory and related techniques (e.g., Marcoulides, 1999; Shavelson and Webb, 1991). Of course, while more sophisticated approaches to reliability estimation will help researchers better understand the extent to which error is affecting their measurement scores, it is only through improvements in scoring practices that researchers will be able to reduce the influence of error on their eventual interpretations about acquisition (see discussion of innovations in test scoring methods in Thissen and Wainer, 2001).

3.1.3 Reporting reliability of measurement scores

A major concern which directly influences the interpretability of SLA research findings and the accumulation of trustworthy knowledge about acquisition constructs is the fact that reliability and error in measurement scoring are at best infrequently considered and only inconsistently reported. For example, Norris and Ortega (2000) found that only 16 percent of 77 studies on the effectiveness of L2 instruction, published between 1980 and 1998, reported any kind of reliability information for scores on dependent variable measures. Similarly, in a review of 39 studies of L2 writing research, published between 1974 and 1996, Wolfe-Quintero et al. (1998) observed that only 18 percent reported any information about the reliability of procedures used to measure accuracy, complexity, and fluency in written performance data. In smaller-scale reviews of more recent bodies of L2 research (e.g., 10 planning studies reviewed in Ortega, 1999; 16 writing studies reviewed in Polio, 1997; 10 recent SLA studies surveyed by Shohamy, 2000), findings show that at best only half of the studies addressed reliability, and that most researchers reported only global or averaged reliability estimates without specifying, let alone discussing, the indices employed or the particular sources for error (this is not a phenomenon unique to SLA or applied linguistics research; see Royer et al., 1993; Vacha-Hasse, Ness, Nilsson, and Reetz, 1999; Whittington, 1998).

The failure to estimate, report, and discuss reliability and error may generate several problems for SLA research. First, unless reliability or error estimates are reported, individual study findings will be uninterpretable, because it will remain unclear to what extent measurement outcomes reflect the construct of interest versus other unintended sources of variance. Second, as Hunter and Schmidt (1994) have pointed out, unless reliability estimates are reported in individual studies, the influence of measurement error on a range of findings accumulated from studies which investigate the same variable cannot be understood. As such, syntheses of an overall effect or relationship observed across studies will be less accurate, because correction for overall score attenuation due to error will be impossible. Third, without accurate reporting of the *sources* of error influencing score reliability, as well as the *amount* of error involved, systematic efforts at reducing measurement error in future studies will be hindered. Where reliability of measurement scores *is* consistently reported within a domain of inquiry, there may be unique possibilities for researching and better understanding the amounts and sources of error associated with particular measures, scoring procedures, learner populations, and features of measurement contexts. Vacha-Hasse et al. (1999) propose the notion of "reliability generalization," a meta-analytic method for combining the reliability results of the use of similar dependent variables across a range of studies in order to make interpretations about sources of measurement error associated with such measures and measurement contexts.

3.2 *Analyzing measurement scores*

SLA researchers employ a variety of analytic techniques (statistical inference, implicational scaling, correlational analyses, statistical modeling, etc.) to summarize, compare, and interpret scores in light of research questions, hypotheses, and predicted relationships among and between variables, thereby completing the transformation of measurement-based data into evidence. Because appropriate analyses are determined in part by the particular research questions and methods of a study, their selection falls within the scope of overall research design (see Chaudron, this volume) and is not a concern isolated to measurement per se. Nevertheless, it is often the case that measurement data are further manipulated within such analyses; thus, the link between behavioral evidence and intended interpretations is also susceptible to construct-irrelevant variance at this stage in the measurement process. In this section, we highlight a few examples of analytic problems in measurement-based SLA research.

A most basic problem involves the selection of analytic tools which may be inappropriate for the particular kinds of interpretations to be made. For example, Paolillo (2000) demonstrated how response patterns on grammaticality judgment tasks (GJTs) can lead to spurious findings (which then become reified within the research community), owing to the application of statistical analyses which are insufficiently sensitive to the actual range and sources of variance in elicited behavioral data. Paolillo (2000) first showed how a chi-test for independence, which has been recommended as the appropriate statistical approach to analyzing GJTs (Bley-Vroman, Felix, and Ioup, 1988), is incapable of disentangling whether GJT response patterns are due to: (i) a systematic (and UG-predicted) interaction between the correctness of learners' judgments and the grammaticality or ungrammaticality of items (an asymmetry effect); or (ii) simple indeterminacy in learners' responses. Paolillo then employed a multivariate analysis (logistic regression) to reveal a more complex relationship in response patterns than that which had been predicted; namely, in the particular data set he was studying, GJT behaviors were best modeled as an interaction between learner conservatism (i.e., a tendency to judge items as ungrammatical), the types of grammatical constructions being measured, and target grammaticality norms for these items, in addition to the UG-predicted asymmetry effect. Paolillo concluded by emphasizing that all such potential effects on GJT response patterns "need to be examined and factored into the explanation of the data in order to arrive at the intended UG-based interpretation" (2000, p. 223).

As Paolillo demonstrates, for certain approaches to SLA the application of multivariate statistics and related analyses can help to clarify exactly what measurement data may reveal about constructs. At the same time, in much of the research on L2 acquisition, there is a virtually default practice of utilizing inferential statistics for all analytic purposes. Unfortunately, the "quest" for statistical significance may actually obscure what measurement data have to say, especially when: (i) the use of inferential statistics leads to insufficient reporting of other forms of measurement data; (ii) the results of statistical analyses are inaccurately interpreted; and (iii) studies are not adequately planned to meet the basic assumptions for such techniques. For example, in their review of 77 studies on L2 instructional effectiveness, Norris and Ortega (2000) found that researchers were more likely to report the outcomes of inferential statistical analyses than basic descriptive statistics, such as means, standard deviations, and number of test items, even though the latter provide the only direct indication of the behavioral patterns that were actually observed on measures. Norris and Ortega also found that researchers frequently interpreted the results of statistical significance tests to be indicative of the *magnitude* of effects or relationships observed via measurement, as opposed to the probability levels associated with particular observations, and that research designs and measurement data types often violated the assumptions of the statistics being used. One consequence of these problems in the reporting and interpretation of inferential statistics is that meaningful patterns in measurement scores may be obscured to the point that accurate interpretations about intended constructs are no longer feasible (see related discussion in Carver, 1978; Cohen, 1988, 1990; Cooper, 1998; Cooper and Hedges, 1994; Harlow, Mulaik, and Steiger, 1997; Light and Pillemer, 1984; Rosenthal, Rosnow, and Rubin, 2000; Rosnow and Rosenthal, 1989; Wilkinson and the Task Force on Statistical Inference, 1999).

In order for researchers to understand what measurement data have to say about their research questions and hypotheses, they will need to know what analyses are available, what kinds of analyses are appropriate for what kinds of data, and how to interpret and report the outcomes of these analyses. In this regard, and in light of the propensity of SLA researchers to employ inferential statistics, any of the available treatments of standard univariate and multivariate statistical analyses would be a good place to start (e.g., Tabachnik and Fiddell, 1996; Woods et al., 1986). At the same time, the potential role to be played by alternative analytic tools should be further explored, as these may offer more direct and appropriate means for summarizing and understanding what measurement data have to say. For example, analytic approaches to research designs which have inherently small data sets (Hoyle, 1999), as well as analyses appropriate for longitudinal, multiwave studies (Willett, 1988), may prove particularly useful for many SLA research studies. Furthermore, the potential analytic role to be played by simple effect sizes, confidence intervals, and graphic displays should not be overlooked (e.g., Cooper, 1998; Light and Pillemer, 1984; Rosenthal et al., 2000). Finally, it will be critical for researchers to pay closer attention to the nature of measurement scores and the ways in which various score types may interact with particular analytic tools. For example, problems with the use of raw scores from tests and other measures in parametric statistical analyses have begun to be widely discussed, in light of the fact that raw scores never provide the true interval data, or equal reliabilities for all score points, that are assumed by such analyses (see related discussions in Embretson and Hershberger, 1999).

4 Making it Count: Accumulating Measurement-Based Knowledge

As a concluding stage in the measurement process, final construct interpretations are made on the basis of the evidence provided, and research findings are integrated by primary and secondary researchers into the cumulative knowledge of the domain of inquiry. The extent to which these construct interpretations will contribute warranted and relevant knowledge to theories of SLA will depend on how well researchers have countered threats to construct validity at each of the stages in measurement practice (see figure 21.1). In particular, we have raised several fundamental weaknesses in the conceptualization and proceduralization of measurement in SLA which will demand attention. First, SLA researchers must acknowledge that a single measure will not provide sufficient evidence for informing the range of interpretations typically sought in most SLA studies and that theories which posit cognitive constructs will need to incorporate means for observing the full range of these constructs, not simply the language performance outcomes attributed to them. Second, serious efforts will need to be made by SLA researchers in order to develop the empirical knowledge bases required for understanding what observed behaviors may tell us about acquisition in the first place; this implies much broader implementation of descriptive, longitudinal studies of various L2 acquisitional phenomena. Third, measurement error will continue to play an unknown role in most measurement-based SLA research until researchers begin to report appropriate reliability estimates and to consider the various sources for error in their measures. Fourth, SLA researchers need to recognize that inferential statistics do not provide the only, and in many cases do not provide the appropriate, analytic tools for understanding measurement scores and incorporating scores into research findings. Fifth, it will be crucial for SLA researchers who intend to utilize measurement as a primary research tool to be trained in the fundamentals of measurement, so that they may attend to advances within measurement theory and practice which are of direct relevance to their own methods. Finally, researchers and editors alike will need to recognize that much more explicit and thorough reporting of all phases of measurement practice will be necessary for the accumulation of scientifically worthwhile knowledge about SLA to be possible.

Within the language testing field, it has been suggested for some time now that a research priority should be the development of comprehensive programs of validation for the various intended uses of language ability tests (Bachman, 1989; Bachman and Clark, 1987; Bachman and Cohen, 1998). We would suggest that validity *generalization* of this sort (see also Wiley, 1991) should also be a priority for measurement used within SLA research and should constitute the site of true collaboration between language testers or measurement specialists and measurement-informed SLA researchers. It should not be incumbent on the individual researcher alone to pursue a comprehensive program of measurement development, use, and validation for each construct interpretation to be made (indeed, as Messick, 1989, has suggested, this would be virtually impossible). Rather, we believe that where entire SLA research communities engage in a comprehensive approach to all of the stages in the measurement process, the field will find itself much better able to make theoretically meaningful interpretations about its constructs and to pursue the accumulation of scientifically worthwhile knowledge.

NOTES

1 A particular cognitive theory within interactionist SLA must be singled out here because of some notable differences. Skills acquisition theories (e.g., DeKeyser, 1997) argue that fast, accurate, and effortless application of L2 knowledge to novel cases provides evidence of true learning. Further, interpretations about automatization are central to this type of theory, and automatization is thought to be typically reflected in "gradual drop-offs in reaction time and error rates, and diminished interference from and with simultaneous tasks" (DeKeyser, 1997, p. 196). Thus, skills acquisition studies are more likely than other interactionist studies to include measures of reaction times and nativelike accuracy over multiple trials in order to document changes in speed and accuracy of rule application to novel cases. From this theoretical perspective, *acquired* means fast, accurate, and effortless performance that reflects automatized production and/or comprehension resulting from sufficient practice guided by declarative knowledge (i.e., conceptually driven learning). It is important to note that, although the similarities with emergentist-connectionist theories are striking, the theoretical models of learning that are assumed in skills acquisition theory and in emergentism are radically different.

2 Readers will note that many of the measurement examples we employ throughout this chapter are typically associated with interactionist approaches to SLA research. This unbalanced treatment simply reflects

our own research backgrounds and training; we do not wish to suggest that measurement in interactionist SLA is either particularly problematic or particularly effective relative to other epistemologies and associated measures. Naturally, we hope that readers will be able to generalize from our examples to their own measurement applications and problems.

REFERENCES

Alanen, R. 1995: Input enhancement and rule presentation in second language acquisition. In R. Schmidt (ed.), *Attention and Awareness in Foreign Language Learning and Teaching*. Technical Report No. 9. Honolulu: University of Hawai'i, Second Language Teaching and Curriculum Center, 259–302.

ACTFL (American Council on the Teaching of Foreign Languages) 1986: *Proficiency Guidelines*. Yonkers, NY: ACTFL.

AERA, APA, NCME (American Educational Research Association, American Psychological Association, and National Council on Measurement in Education) 1999: *Standards for Educational and Psychological Testing*. Washington, DC: American Educational Research Association.

Anastasi, A. and Urbina, S. 1997: *Psychological Testing*. Upper Saddle River, NJ: Prentice-Hall.

Andersen, R. 1984: The one-to-one principle of interlanguage construction. *Language Learning*, 34, 77–95.

Anderson, R. J. 1993: *Rules of the Mind*. Hillsdale, NJ: Lawrence Erlbaum Associates.

Angoff, W. H. 1984: *Scales, Norms and Equivalent Scores*. Princeton, NJ: Educational Testing Service.

Angoff, W. H. 1988: Validity: an evolving concept. In H. Wainer and H. I. Braun (eds), *Test Validity*. Hillsdale, NJ: Lawrence Erlbaum Associates, 19–32.

Bachman, L. F. 1989: Language testing–SLA research interfaces. *Annual Review of Applied Linguistics*, 9, 193–209.

Bachman, L. F. 1990: *Fundamental Considerations in Language Testing*. Oxford: Oxford University Press.

Bachman, L. F. and Clark, J. L. D. 1987: The measurement of foreign/second language proficiency. *Annals of the American Academy of Political and Social Science*, 490, 20–33.

Bachman, L. F. and Cohen, A. D. 1998: Language testing–SLA interfaces: an update. In L. F. Bachman and A. D. Cohen (eds), *Interfaces between Second Language Acquisition and Language Testing Research*. Cambridge: Cambridge University Press, 1–31.

Bachman, L. F. and Palmer, A. S. 1996: *Language Testing in Practice: Designing and Developing Useful Language Tests*. Oxford: Oxford University Press.

Bangert-Drowns, R. L. 1986: Review of developments in meta-analytic method. *Psychological Bulletin*, 99, 388–99.

Bard, E. G., Robertson, D., and Sorace, A. 1996: Magnitude estimation of linguistic acceptability. *Language*, 72, 32–68.

Bardovi-Harlig, K. 1994a: Anecdote or evidence? Evaluating support for hypotheses concerning the development of tense and aspect. In

E. Tarone, S. Gass, and A. Cohen (eds), *Research Methodology in Second-Language Acquisition*. Hillsdale, NJ: Lawrence Erlbaum Associates, 41–60.

Bardovi-Harlig, K. 1994b: Reverse-order reports and the acquisition of tense: beyond the principle of chronological order. *Language Learning*, 44, 243–82.

Baxter, G. and Glaser, R. 1998: Investigating the cognitive complexity of science assessments. *Educational Measurement: Issues and Practice*, 17 (3), 37–45.

Bennett, R. E. 1999: Using new technology to improve assessment. *Educational Measurement: Issues and Practice*, 18 (3), 5–12.

Beretta, A. 1991: Theory construction in SLA: complementary and opposition. *Studies in Second Language Acquisition*, 13, 493–511.

Bialystok, E. 1991: Achieving proficiency in a second language: a processing description. In R. Philipson, E. Kellerman, L. Selinker, M. S. Smith, and M. Swain (eds), *Foreign/Second Language Pedagogy Research*. Clevedon: Multilingual Matters, 63–78.

Biber, D. 1990: Methodological issues regarding corpus-based analyses of linguistic variation. *Literary and Linguistic Computing*, 5, 257–69.

Birdsong, D. (ed.) 1999: *Second Language Acquisition and the Critical Period Hypothesis*. Mahwah, NJ: Lawrence Erlbaum Associates.

Bjork, E. and Bjork, R. (eds) 1996: *Memory: Handbook of Perception and Cognition*. 2nd edition. New York: Academic Press.

Bley-Vroman, R. 1983: The comparative fallacy in interlanguage studies: the case of systematicity. *Language Learning*, 33, 1–17.

Bley-Vroman, R. 1989: What is the logical problem of foreign language acquisition? In S. M. Gass and J. Schachter (eds), *Linguistic Perspectives on Second Language Acquisition*. Cambridge: Cambridge University Press, 41–68.

Bley-Vroman, R. and Chaudron, C. 1994: Elicited imitation as a measure of second-language competence. In E. Tarone, S. Gass, and A. Cohen (eds), *Research Methodology in Second-Language Acquisition*. Hillsdale, NJ: Lawrence Erlbaum Associates, 245–61.

Bley-Vroman, R., Felix, S., and Ioup, G. 1988: The accessibility of Universal Grammar in adult language learning. *Second Language Research*, 4, 1–32.

Brindley, G. 1998: Describing language development? Rating scales and SLA. In L. Bachman and A. Cohen (eds), *Interfaces between Second Language Acquisition and Language Testing Research*. Cambridge: Cambridge University Press, 112–40.

Brown, G., Malmkjaer, K., and Williams, J. (eds) 1996: *Performance and Competence in Second Language Acquisition*. Cambridge: Cambridge University Press.

Brown, J. D. 1988: *Understanding Research in Second Language Learning: A Teacher's Guide to Statistics and Research Design*. London: Heinemann.

Brown, J. D. 1996: *Testing in Language Programs*. Englewood Cliffs, NJ: Prentice-Hall.

Brown, J. D. forthcoming: *Using Surveys in Language Programs*. Englewood Cliffs, NJ: Prentice-Hall.

Brown, J. D., Hudson, T. D., Norris, J. M., and Bonk, W. forthcoming: *Investigating Task-Based Second Language Performance Assessment*. Honolulu: University of Hawai'i Press.

Brown, R. 1973: *A First Language: The Early Stages*. Cambridge, MA: Harvard University Press.

Campbell, D. T. and Reichardt, C. S. 1991: Problems in assuming the comparability of pretest and posttest in autoregressive and growth models. In C. E. Snow and D. E. Wiley (eds), *Improving Inquiry in Social Science*.

Hillsdale, NJ: Lawrence Erlbaum Associates, 201–19.

Carver, R. 1978: The case against statistical significance testing. *Harvard Educational Review*, 48, 389–99.

Chapelle, C. A. 1998: Construct definition and validity inquiry in SLA research. In L. F. Bachman and A. D. Cohen (eds), *Interfaces between Second Language Acquisition and Language Testing Research*. Cambridge: Cambridge University Press, 32–70.

Chaudron, C. 1985: Intake: on models and methods for discovering learners' processing of input. *Studies in Second Language Acquisition*, 7, 1–14.

Chaudron, C. 1998: *Second Language Classrooms: Research on Teaching and Learning*. Cambridge: Cambridge University Press.

Chaudron, C. and Russell, G. 1990: The validity of elicited imitation as a measure of second language competence. Ms. University of Hawai'i.

Clahsen, H., Meisel, J., and Pienemann, M. 1983: *Deutsch als Zweitsprache: Der Spracherwerb ausländischer Arbeiter*. Tübingen: Narr.

Cohen, J. 1988: *Statistical Power Analysis for the Behavioral Sciences*. 2nd edition. Hillsdale, NJ: Lawrence Erlbaum Associates.

Cohen, J. 1990: Things I have learned so far. *American Psychologist*, 45, 1304–12.

Cohen, J. 1997: The earth is round ($p < .05$) In L. Harlow, S. Mulaik, and J. Steiger (eds), *What If There Were No Significance Tests?* Mahwah, NJ: Lawrence Erlbaum Associates, 21–36.

Cooper, H. 1998: *Synthesizing Research: A Guide for Literature Reviews*. 3rd edition. Thousand Oaks, CA: Sage.

Cooper, H. and Hedges, L. V. (eds) 1994: *The Handbook of Research Synthesis*. New York: Russell Sage Foundation.

Cronbach, L. J. 1980: Validity on patrol: how can we go straight? In *New Directions for Testing and Measurement: Measuring Achievement, Progress Over a Decade, No. 5*. San Francisco: Jossey-Bass, 99–108.

Cronbach, L. J. 1988: Five perspectives on validity argument. In H. Wainer and H. I. Braun (eds), *Test Validity*. Hillsdale, NJ: Lawrence Erlbaum Associates, 3–45.

Cronbach, L. J. and Meehl, P. E. 1955: Construct validity in psychological tests. *Psychological Bulletin*, 52, 281–302.

Crookes, G. 1990: The utterance and other basic units for second language discourse. *Applied Linguistics*, 11, 183–99.

Crookes, G. 1991: Second language speech production research. *Studies in Second Language Acquisition*, 13, 113–32.

Crookes, G. 1992: Theory formation and SLA theory. *Studies in Second Language Acquisition*, 14, 425–99.

de Graaff, R. 1997: *Differential Effects of Explicit Instruction on Second Language Acquisition*. The Hague: Holland Institute of Generative Linguistics.

DeKeyser, R. 1995: Learning second language grammar rules: an experiment with a miniature linguistic system. *Studies in Second Language Acquisition*, 17, 379–410.

DeKeyser, R. 1997: Beyond explicit rule learning: automatizing second language morphosyntax. *Studies in Second Language Acquisition*, 19, 195–221.

Ellis, N. C. 1998: Emergentism, connectionism and language learning. *Language Learning*, 48, 631–64.

Ellis, N. C. 1999: Cognitive approaches to SLA. *Annual Review of Applied Linguistics*, 19, 22–42.

Ellis, N. C. and Schmidt, R. 1997: Morphology and longer-distance dependencies: laboratory research illuminating the A in SLA. *Studies in Second Language Acquisition*, 19, 145–71.

Ellis, R. 1985: A variable competence model of second language acquisition.

International Review of Applied Linguistics, 23, 47–59.

Ellis, R. 1994: *The Study of Second Language Acquisition*. Oxford: Oxford University Press.

Embretson, S. E. 1999: Issues in the measurement of cognitive abilities. In S. E. Embretson and S. L. Hershberger (eds), *The New Rules of Measurement: What Every Psychologist and Educator Should Know*. Mahwah, NJ: Lawrence Erlbaum Associates, 1–15.

Embretson, S. E. and Hershberger, S. L. (eds) 1999: *The New Rules of Measurement: What Every Psychologist and Educator Should Know*. Mahwah, NJ: Lawrence Erlbaum Associates.

Ericsson, K. A. and Simon, H. A. 1993: *Protocol Analysis: Verbal Reports as Data*. Revised edition. Cambridge, MA: MIT Press.

Eubank, L. (ed.) 1991: *Point Counterpoint: Universal Grammar in the Second Language*. Philadelphia: John Benjamins.

Feldt, L. S. and Brennan, R. L. 1989: Reliability. In R. L. Linn (ed.), *Educational Measurement*. 3rd edition. New York: Macmillan, 105–46.

Ferguson, C. A. and Huebner, T. 1991: Foreign language instruction and second language acquisition research in the United States. In K. De Bot, R. B. Ginsberg, and C. Kramsch (eds), *Foreign Language Research in Cross-Cultural Perspective*. Philadelphia: John Benjamins, 3–19.

Foster, P., Tonkyn, A., and Wigglesworth, G. 1998: Measuring spoken language: a unit for all reasons. *Applied Linguistics*, 21, 354–75.

Gardner, R. 1979: Social psychological aspects of second language acquisition. In H. Giles and R. S. Clair (eds), *Language and Social Psychology*. Oxford: Blackwell.

Gass, S. M. 1988: Integrating research areas: a framework for second language studies. *Applied Linguistics*, 9, 198–217.

Gass, S. M. 1994: The reliability of second-language grammaticality judgments. In E. Tarone, S. Gass, and A. Cohen (eds), *Research Methodology in Second-Language Acquisition*. Hillsdale, NJ: Lawrence Erlbaum Associates, 303–22.

Gass, S. M. and Schachter, J. (eds) 1989: *Linguistic Perspectives on Second Language Acquisition*. Cambridge: Cambridge University Press.

Givón, T. 1979: *On Understanding Grammar*. London: Academic Press.

Gregg, K. 1990: The variable competence model of second language acquisition, and why it isn't. *Applied Linguistics*, 11, 364–83.

Gregg, K. R. 1993: Taking explanation seriously: or, let a couple of flowers bloom. *Applied Linguistics*, 14, 276–94.

Gregg, K. R. 1996: The logical and developmental problems of second language acquisition. In W. Ritchie and T. Bhatia (eds), *Handbook of Second Language Acquisition*. New York: Academic Press, 49–81.

Grigorenko, E. L., Sternberg, R. J., and Ehrman, M. E. 2000: A theory-based approach to the measurement of foreign language learning ability: the CANAL-F theory and test. *Modern Language Journal*, 84, 390–405.

Gronlund, N. E. and Linn, R. L. 1990: *Measurement and Evaluation in Teaching*. 6th edition. New York: Macmillan.

Grotjahn, R. 1986: Test validation and cognitive psychology: some methodological considerations. *Language Testing*, 3, 159–85.

Hambleton, R. K., Swaminathan, H., and Rogers, H. J. 1991: *Fundamentals of Item Response Theory*. Newbury Park, CA: Sage.

Harlow, L. L., Mulaik, S. A., and Steiger, J. H. (eds) 1997: *What If There Were No Significance Tests?* Mahwah, NJ: Lawrence Erlbaum Associates.

Hatch, E. and Lazaraton, A. 1991: *The Research Manual: Design and Statistics for Applied Linguistics*. New York: HarperCollins and Newbury House.

Henning, G. 1987: *A Guide to Language Testing: Development, Evaluation, Research*. Cambridge, MA: Newbury House.

Hess, C. W., Sefton, K. M., and Landry, R. G. 1986: Sample size and type–token ratios for oral language of preschool children. *Journal of Speech and Hearing Research*, 29, 129–34.

Hoyle, R. H. (ed.) 1999: *Statistical Strategies for Small Sample Research*. Thousand Oaks, CA: Sage.

Hudson, T. 1993: Nothing does not equal zero: problems with applying developmental sequences findings to assessment and pedagogy. *Studies in Second Language Acquisition*, 15, 461–593.

Huebner, T. 1983: *A Longitudinal Analysis of the Acquisition of English*. Ann Arbor, MI: Karoma.

Huebner, T. 1991: Second language acquisition: litmus test for linguistic theory? In T. Huebner and C. A. Ferguson (eds), *Crosscurrents in Second Language Acquisition and Linguistic Theories*. Amsterdam and Philadelphia: John Benjamins, 3–22.

Huebner, T. and Ferguson, C. A. (eds) 1991: *Crosscurrents in Second Language Acquisition and Linguistic Theories*. Amsterdam and Philadelphia: John Benjamins.

Hulstijn, J. H. 1997: Second language acquisition research in the laboratory: possibilities and limitations. *Studies in Second Language Acquisition*, 19, 131–44.

Hunter, J. E. and Schmidt, F. L. 1994: Correcting for sources of artificial variation across studies. In H. Cooper and L. V. Hedges (eds), *The Handbook of Research Synthesis*. New York: Russell Sage Foundation, 323–36.

Hymes, D. H. 1972: On communicative competence. In J. B. Price and J. Holmes (eds), *Sociolinguistics*. Baltimore: Penguin, 269–93.

Irvine, S. and Kyllonen, P. (eds) 2001: *Item Generation for Test Development*. Mahwah, NJ: Lawrence Erlbaum Associates.

Iwashita, N. 1999: The role of task-based conversation in the acquisition of Japanese grammar and vocabulary. Doctoral dissertation. University of Melbourne.

Jourdenais, R., Ota, M., Stauffer, S., Boyson, B., and Doughty, C. (1995): Does textual enhancement promote noticing? A think-aloud protocol analysis. In R. Schmidt (ed.), *Attention and Awareness in Foreign Language Learning*. Technical Report No. 9. Honolulu: University of Hawai'i, Second Language Teaching and Curriculum Center, 183–216.

Kane, M. T. 1992: An argument-based approach to validity. *Psychological Bulletin*, 112, 527–35.

Kellerman, E. 1985: If at first you do succeed . . . In S. M. Gass and C. Madden (eds), *Input in Second Language Acquisition*. Rowley, MA: Newbury House, 345–53.

Krashen, S. 1981: *Second Language Acquisition and Second Language Learning*. Oxford: Pergamon Press.

Lambert, R. D. 1991: Pros, cons, and limits to quantitative approaches in foreign language acquisition research. In K. De Bot, R. B. Ginsberg, and C. Kramsch (eds), *Foreign Language Research in Cross-Cultural Perspective*. Philadelphia: John Benjamins.

Lantolf, J. (ed.) 1994: *Sociocultural Theory and Second Language Learning*. Special issue of *Modern Language Journal*, 78, 4.

Larsen-Freeman, D. 2000: Second language acquisition and applied linguistics. *Annual Review of Applied Linguistics*, 20, 165–81.

Lazaraton, A. 1992: The structural organisation of a language interview: a conversational analytic perspective. *System*, 20 (3), 373–86.

Lazaraton, A. 1996: Interlocutor support in Oral Proficiency Interviews: the case of CASE. *Language Testing*, 13 (2), 151–72.

Leow, R. P. 1997: Attention, awareness, and foreign language behavior. *Language Learning*, 47, 467–506.

Leow, R. P. 2000: A study of the role of awareness in foreign language behavior: aware vs. unaware learners. *Studies in Second Language Acquisition*, 22, 557–84.

Light, R. and Pillemer, D. 1984: *Summing Up: The Science of Reviewing Research*. Cambridge, MA: Harvard University Press.

Lightbown, P. and White, L. 1987: The influence of linguistic theories on language acquisition research: description and explanation. *Language Learning*, 37, 483–510.

Linacre, J. M. 1998: *Facets 3.17*. Computer program. Chicago: MESA Press.

Linn, R. L. (ed.) 1989: *Educational Measurement*. 3rd edition. New York: American Council on Education and Macmillan.

Linn, R. L. 1997: Evaluating the validity of assessments: the consequences of use. *Educational Measurement: Issues and Practice*, 16 (2), 14–16.

Loevinger, J. 1957: Objective tests as instruments of psychological theory. *Psychological Reports*, 3, 635–94.

Long, M. H. 1980: Input, interaction and second language acquisition. Doctoral dissertation. University of California at Los Angeles.

Long, M. H. 1990: The least a second language acquisition theory needs to explain. *TESOL Quarterly*, 24, 649–66.

Long, M. H. 1993: Assessment strategies for second language acquisition theories. *Applied Linguistics*, 14, 225–49.

Long, M. H. 1996: The role of the linguistic environment in second language acquisition. In W. C. Ritchie and T. K. Bahtia (eds), *Handbook of Second Language Acquisition*. New York: Academic Press, 413–68.

Loschky, L. 1994: Comprehensible input and second language acquisition: what is the relationship? *Studies in Second Language Acquisition*, 16, 303–23.

Loschky, L. and Bley-Vroman, R. 1993: Grammar and task-based methodology. In G. Crookes and S. Gass (eds), *Tasks and Language Learning: Integrating Theory and Practice*. Philadelphia: Multilingual Matters, 123–67.

Lynch, B. and Davidson, F. 1994: Criterion-referenced language test development: linking curricula, teachers, and tests. *TESOL Quarterly*, 28, 727–43.

Lyster, R. 1998: Negotiation of form, recasts, and explicit correction in relation to error types and learner repair in immersion classrooms. *Language Learning*, 48, 183–218.

Mackey, A. 1999: Input, interaction, and second language development: an empirical study of question formation in ESL. *Studies in Second Language Acquisition*, 21, 557–87.

Mackey, A. and Philp, J. 1998: Conversational interaction and second language development: recasts, responses, and red herrings? *Modern Language Journal*, 82, 338–56.

MacWhinney, B. (ed.) 1998: *The Emergence of Language*. Hillsdale, NJ: Lawrence Erlbaum Associates.

MacWhinney, B. 2000: *The CHILDES project: Tools for Analyzing Talk. Vol. I: Transcription Format and Programs*. 3rd edition. Mahwah, NJ: Lawrence Erlbaum Associates.

Marcoulides, G. A. 1999: Generalizability theory: picking up where the Rasch IRT model leaves off? In S. Embretson and S. Hershberger (eds), *The New*

Rules of Measurement: What Every Psychologist and Educator Should Know. Mahwah, NJ: Lawrence Erlbaum Associates, 129–52.

McLaughlin, B. 1987: *Theories of Second Language Learning*. London: Edward Arnold.

McLaughlin, B. 1990: Restructuring. *Applied Linguistics*, 11, 1–16.

McNamara, T. 1996: *Measuring Second Language Performance*. New York: Longman.

McNamara, T. F. and Lumley, T. 1997: The effect of interlocutor and assessment mode variables in overseas assessments of speaking skills in occupational settings. *Language Testing*, 14 (2), 140–56.

Meisel, J., Clahsen, H., and Pienemann, M. 1981: On determining developmental stages in natural second language acquisition. *Studies in Second Language Acquisition*, 3, 109–35.

Mellow, D., Reeder, K., and Forster, E. 1996: Using time-series research designs to investigate the effects of instruction on SLA. *Studies in Second Language Acquisition*, 18, 325–50.

Messick, S. 1975: The standard problem: meaning and values in measurement and evaluation. *American Psychologist*, 30, 955–66.

Messick, S. 1989: Validity. In R. L. Linn (ed.), *Educational Measurement*. 3rd edition. New York: American Council on Education and Macmillan, 13–103.

Messick, S. 1994: The interplay of evidence and consequences in the validation of performance assessments. *Educational Researcher*, 23 (2), 13–23.

Mislevy, R. J. 1994: Evidence and inference in educational assessment. Presidential address to the Psychometric Society. *Psychometrika*, 59, 439–83.

Mislevy, R. J. 1995: Test theory and language-learning assessment. *Language Testing*, 12, 341–69.

Mislevy, R. J., Steinberg, L. S., and Almond, R. G. 1999: *On the Roles of Task Model Variables in Assessment Design*. CSE Technical Report 500. Los Angeles, CA: Center for the Study of Evaluation, Graduate School of Education and Information Studies at the University of California, Los Angeles.

Mislevy, R. J., Steinberg, L. S., Almond, R. G., Haertel, G. D., and Penuel, W. R. forthcoming: Leverage points for improving educational assessment. In B. Means and G. D. Haertel (eds), *Designs for Evaluating the Effects of Technology in Education.*

Mislevy, R. J., Steinberg, L. S., Breyer, F. J., Almond, R. G., and Johnson, L. 1999: A cognitive task analysis, with implications for designing a simulation-based assessment system. *Computers and Human Behavior*, 15, 335–74.

Moss, P. A. 1992: Shifting conceptions of validity in educational measurement: implications for performance assessment. *Review of Educational Research*, 62 (3), 229–58.

Nichols, P. and Sugrue, B. 1999: The lack of fidelity between cognitively complex constructs and conventional test development practice. *Educational Measurement: Issues and Practice*, 18 (2), 18–29.

Norris, J. M. 1996: A validation study of the ACTFL guidelines and the German Speaking Test. Master's thesis. University of Hawai'i.

Norris, J. M. 1997: The German Speaking Test: utility and caveats. *Die Unterrichtspraxis*, 30 (2), 148–58.

Norris, J. M. 2000: *Tasks and Language Assessment*. Paper presented in the colloquium "Key issues in empirical research on task-based instruction" at the annual American Association for Applied Linguistics conference (AAAL). Vancouver, British Columbia, Canada, March 14.

Norris, J. M. and Ortega, L. 2000: Effectiveness of L2 instruction: a research synthesis and quantitative meta-analysis. *Language Learning*, 50, 417–528.

Norris, J. M., Brown, J. D., Hudson, T., and Yoshioka, J. 1998: *Designing Second Language Performance Assessments*. Technical Report No. 17. Honolulu: University of Hawai'i, Second Language Teaching and Curriculum Center.

Oliver, R. 1995: Negative feedback in child NS/NNS conversation. *Studies in Second Language Acquisition*, 17, 459–81.

Ortega, L. 1999: Planning and focus on form in L2 oral performance. *Studies in Second Language Acquisition*, 21, 109–48.

Ortega, L. 2000: Understanding syntactic complexity: the measurement of change in the syntax of instructed L2 Spanish learners. Doctoral dissertation. University of Hawai'i at Manoa.

Orwin, R. G. 1994: Evaluating coding decisions. In H. Cooper and L. V. Hedges (eds), *The Handbook of Research Synthesis*. New York: Russell Sage Foundation, 139–62.

O'Sullivan, B. 2000: Exploring gender and oral proficiency interview performance. *System*, 28 (3): 373–86.

Paolillo, J. C. 2000: Asymmetries in Universal Grammar: the role of methods and statistics. *Studies in Second Language Acquisition*, 22, 209–28.

Pedhazur, E. J. and Schmelkin, L. P. 1991: *Measurement, Design, and Analysis: An Integrated Approach*. Hillsdale, NJ: Lawrence Erlbaum Associates.

Pellegrino, J. W. 1988: Mental models and mental tests. In H. Wainer and H. Braun (eds), *Test Validity*. Hillsdale, NJ: Lawrence Erlbaum Associates, 49–60.

Pica, T. 1983: Methods of morpheme quantification: their effect on the interpretation of second language data. *Studies in Second Language Acquisition*, 6, 69–79.

Pienemann, M. 1984: Psychological constraints on the teachability of languages. *Studies in Second Language Acquisition*, 6, 186–214.

Pienemann, M. 1998: *Language Processing and Second Language Development: Processability Theory*. Philadelphia: John Benjamins.

Pienemann, M. and Mackey, A. 1993: An empirical study of children's ESL development and Rapid Profile. In P. McKay (ed.), *ESL Development: Language and Literacy in Schools, vol. 2*. Commonwealth of Australia and National Languages and Literacy Institute of Australia, 115–259.

Pienemann, M., Johnston, M., and Brindley, G. 1988: Constructing an acquisition-based procedure for second language assessment. *Studies in Second Language Acquisition*, 10, 217–43.

Pishwa, H. 1994: Abrupt restructuring versus gradual acquisition. In C. A. Blackshire-Belay (ed.), *Current Issues in Second Language Acquisition and Development*. New York: University Press of America, 143–66.

Polio, C. G. 1997: Measures of linguistic accuracy in second language writing research. *Language Learning*, 47, 101–43.

Polio, C. and Gass, S. 1997: Replication and reporting: a commentary. *Studies in Second Language Acquisition*, 19, 499–508.

Popham, W. J. 1981: *Modern Educational Measurement*. Englewood Cliffs, NJ: Prentice-Hall.

Preston, D. R. 1989: *Sociolinguistics and Second Language Acquisition*. New York: Blackwell.

Richards, B. 1987: Type/token ratios: what do they really tell us? *Journal of Child Language*, 14, 201–9.

Richards, B. J. 1990: *Language Development and Individual Differences:*

A Study of Auxiliary Verb Learning. New York: Cambridge University Press.

Richards, B. J. 1994: Child-directed speech and influences on language acquisition: methodology and interpretation. In C. Gallaway and B. J. Richards (eds), *Input and Interaction in Language Acquisition*. Cambridge: Cambridge University Press, 74–106.

Richards, B. J. and Gallaway, C. (eds) 1994: *Input and Interaction in Language Acquisition*. Cambridge: Cambridge University Press.

Richards, B. J. and Malvern, D. D. 1997: *Quantifying Lexical Diversity in the Study of Language Development*. Reading: University of Reading, New Bulmershe Papers.

Robinson, P. 1995: Attention, memory, and the "noticing" hypothesis. *Language Learning*, 45, 283–331.

Robinson, P. 1997: Individual differences and the fundamental similarity of implicit and explicit adult second language learning. *Language Learning*, 47, 45–99.

Robinson, P. 2001a: Task complexity, cognition and second language syllabus design: a triadic framework for examining task influences on SLA. In P. Robinson (ed.), *Cognition and Second Language Instruction*. New York: Cambridge University Press, 287–318.

Robinson, P. 2001b: Task complexity, task difficulty, and task production: exploring interactions in a componential framework. *Applied Linguistics*, 22, 27–57.

Rosenthal, R. 1979: Replications and their relative utility. *Replications in Social Psychology*, 1, 15–23.

Rosenthal, R., Rosnow, R. L., and Rubin, D. B. 2000: *Contrasts and Effect Sizes in Behavioral Research*. New York: Cambridge University Press.

Rosnow, R. L. and Rosenthal, R. 1989: Statistical procedures and the justification of knowledge in psychological science. *American Psychologist*, 44, 1276–84.

Ross, S. and Berwick, R. 1990: The discourse of accommodation in oral proficiency interviews. *Studies in Second Language Acquisition*, 14, 159–76.

Royer, J. M., Cisero, C. A., and Carlo, M. S. 1993: Techniques and procedures for assessing cognitive skills. *Review of Educational Research*, 63 (2), 201–43.

Rutherford, W. 1984: Description and explanation in interlanguage syntax: the state of the art. *Language Learning*, 34, 127–55.

Saito, H. 1999: Dependence and interaction in frequency data analysis in SLA research. *Studies in Second Language Acquisition*, 21, 453–75.

Sawyer, M. and Ranta, L. 2001: Aptitude, individual differences, and instructional design. In P. Robinson (ed.), *Cognition and Second Language Instruction*. New York: Cambridge University Press, 424–69.

Schachter, J. 1998: Recent research in language learning studies: promises and problems. *Language Learning*, 48, 557–83.

Schmidt, R. 1993: Awareness and second language acquisition. *Annual Review of Applied Linguistics*, 13, 206–26.

Schmidt, R. 1994: Deconstructing consciousness in search of useful definitions for applied linguistics. *AILA Review*, 11, 11–26.

Scholfield, P. 1995: *Quantifying Language: A Researcher's and Teacher's Guide to Gathering Language Data and Reducing it to Figures*. Bristol, PA: Multilingual Matters.

Schumann, J. 1978: The acculturation model for second-language acquisition. In R. C. Gringas (ed.), *Second Language Acquisition and Foreign Language Teaching*. Washington, DC: Center for Applied Linguistics, 27–50.

Schwartz, B. 1992: Testing between UG-based and problem-solving models of L2A: developmental sequence data. *Language Acquisition*, 2, 1–19.

Schwartz, B. D. 1993: On explicit and negative data effecting and affecting competence and linguistic behaviour. *Studies in Second Language Acquisition*, 15, 147–63.

Seliger, H. W. and Shohamy, E. 1989: *Second Language Research Methods*. Oxford: Oxford University Press.

Shavelson, R. J. and Webb, N. M. 1991: *Generalizability Theory: A Primer*. Newbury Park, CA: Sage.

Shepard, L. A. 1993: Evaluating test validity. *Review of Research in Education*, 19, 405–50.

Shepard, L. 1997: The centrality of test use and consequences for test validity. *Educational Measurement: Issues and Practice*, 16 (2), 5–13.

Shohamy, E. 1994: The role of language tests in the construction and validation of second-language acquisition theories. In E. Tarone, S. Gass, and A. Cohen (eds), *Research Methodology in Second-Language Acquisition*. Hillsdale, NJ: Lawrence Erlbaum Associates, 133–42.

Shohamy, E. 2000: The relationship between language testing and second language acquisition, revisited. *System*, 28, 541–53.

Siegler, R. S. 1989: Strategy diversity and cognitive assessment. *Educational Researcher*, 18 (9), 15–20.

Sinclair, J. M. and Coulthard, R. M. 1975: *Towards an Analysis of Discourse: The English Used by Teachers and Pupils*. London: Oxford University Press.

Skehan, P. 1998: *A Cognitive Approach to Language Learning*. Oxford: Oxford University Press.

Snow, R. and Lohman, D. 1989: Implications of cognitive psychology for educational measurement. In R. L. Linn (ed.), *Educational Measurement*. 3rd edition. Washington, DC: American Council on Education and National Council on Measurement in Education, 263–332.

Sokolik, M. E. 1990: Learning without rules: PDP and a resolution of the adult language learning paradox. *TESOL Quarterly*, 24, 685–96.

Sorace, A. 1993: Incomplete vs. divergent representations of unaccusativity in near-native grammars of Italian. *Second Language Research*, 9, 22–48.

Sorace, A. 1996: The use of acceptability judgments in L2 acquisition research. In W. Ritchie and T. Bhatia (eds), *Handbook of Second Language Acquisition*. New York: Academic Press, 375–409.

Sorace, A. and Robertson, D. 2001: Measuring development and ultimate attainment in non-native grammars. In C. Elder, A. Brown, N. Iwashita, E. Grove, K. Hill, and T. Lumley (eds), *Experimenting with Uncertainty: Essays in Honour of Alan Davies*. Cambridge: Cambridge University Press, 264–74.

Stadler, M. A. and Frensch, P. A. (eds) 1998: *Implicit Learning Handbook*. Thousand Oaks, CA: Sage.

Stromswold, K. 1996: Analyzing children's spontaneous speech. In D. McDaniel, C. McKee, and H. S. Cairns (eds), *Methods for Assessing Children's Syntax*. Cambridge, MA: MIT Press, 23–53.

Sugrue, B. 1995: A theory-based framework for assessing domain-specific problem-solving ability. *Educational Measurement: Issues and Practice*, 14 (3), 29–36.

Swain, M. 1985: Communicative competence: some roles of comprehensible input and comprehensible output in its development. In S. M. Gass and C. G. Madden (eds), *Input in Second Language Acquisition*. Rowley, MA: Newbury House, 235–53.

Swain, M. 1995: Three functions of output in second language learning. In G. Cook and B. Seidhofer (eds),

Principles and Practice in the Study of Language. Oxford: Oxford University Press, 125–44.

Tabachnick, B. G. and Fidell, L. S. 1996: *Using Multivariate Statistics.* 3rd edition. New York: HarperCollins.

Tarone, E. 1988: *Variation in Interlanguage.* London: Edward Arnold.

Tarone, E. 1998: Research on interlanguage variation: implications for language testing. In L. F. Bachman and A. D. Cohen (eds), *Interfaces Between Second Language Acquisition and Language Testing Research.* Cambridge: Cambridge University Press, 71–89.

Tarone, E. and Parrish, B. 1988: Task-related variation in interlanguage: the case of articles. *Language Learning*, 38, 21–44.

Thissen, D. and Wainer, H. (eds) 2001: *Test Scoring.* Mahwah, NJ: Lawrence Erlbaum Associates.

Thomas, M. 1994: Assessment of L2 proficiency in second language acquisition research. *Language Learning*, 44, 307–36.

Thompson, B. 1994: Guidelines for authors. *Educational and Psychological Measurement*, 54, 837–47.

Thompson, B. 1998: Five methodology errors in educational research: the pantheon of statistical significance and other faux pas. Presentation at the American Educational Research Association annual conference. San Diego, April 15. Available at: <http://acs.tamu.edu/~bbt6147/>

Tomasello, M. 1998a: Introduction: a cognitive-functional perspective on language structure. In M. Tomasello (ed.), *The New Psychology of Language: Cognitive and Functional Approaches to Language Structure.* Mahwah, NJ: Lawrence Erlbaum Associates, vii–xxiii.

Tomasello, M. (ed.) 1998b: *The New Psychology of Language: Cognitive and Functional Approaches to Language Structure.* Mahwah, NJ: Lawrence Erlbaum Associates.

Tomlin, R. 1990: Functionalism in second language acquisition. *Studies in Second Language Acquisition*, 12, 155–77.

Tomlin, R. S. and Villa, V. 1994: Attention in cognitive science and second language acquisition. *Studies in Second Language Acquisition*, 16, 183–203.

Trahey, M. and White, L. 1993: Positive evidence and preemption in the second language classroom. *Studies in Second Language Acquisition*, 15, 181–204.

Traub, R. E. 1994: *Reliability for the Social Sciences: Theory and Applications.* Thousand Oaks, CA: Sage.

Vacha-Haase, T., Ness, C., Nilsson, J., and Reetz, D. 1999: Practices regarding reporting of reliability coefficients: a review of three journals. *Journal of Experimental Education*, 67 (4), 335–41.

Vygotsky, L. 1986: *Thought and Language.* Translation newly rev. and ed. Alex Kozulin. Cambridge, MA: MIT Press.

White, L. 1991: Second language competence versus second language performance: UG or processing strategies. In L. Eubank (ed.), *Point Counterpoint: Universal Grammar in the Second Language.* Amsterdam: John Benjamins, 167–89.

White, L. 1996: Universal Grammar and second language acquisition: current trends and new directions. In W. C. Ritchie and T. K. Bhatia (eds), *Handbook of Second Language Acquisition.* San Diego: Academic Press, 85–120.

White, L. 2000: Second language acquisition: from initial to final state. In J. Archibald (ed.), *Second Language Acquisition and Linguistic Theory.* New York: Blackwell, 130–55.

White, L. and Genesee, F. 1996: How native is near-native? The issue of ultimate attainment in adult second language acquisition. *Second Language Research*, 12, 233–65.

Whittington, D. 1998: How well do researchers report their measures? An evaluation of measurement in published educational research. *Educational and Psychological Measurement*, 58, 21–37.

Wickens, C. D. 1989: Attention and skilled performance. In D. H. Holding (eds), *Human Skills*. Chichester: John Wiley, 71–104.

Wiley, D. E. 1991: Test validity and invalidity reconsidered. In R. E. Snow and D. E. Wiley (eds), *Improving Inquiry in Social Science*. Hillsdale, NJ: Lawrence Erlbaum Associates, 75–107.

Wilkinson, L. and the Task Force on Statistical Inference 1999: Statistical methods in psychology journals: guidelines and explanations. *American Psychologist*, 54 (8), 594–604.

Willett, J. B. 1988: Questions and answers in the measurement of change. *Review of Research in Education*, 15, 345–422.

Williams, J. N. 1999: Memory, attention, and inductive learning. *Studies in Second Language Acquisition*, 21, 1–48.

Wolfe-Quintero, K., Inagaki, S., and Kim, H.-Y. 1998: *Second Language Development in Writing: Measures of Fluency, Accuracy, and Complexity*. Technical Report No. 17. Honolulu: University of Hawai'i, Second Language Teaching and Curriculum Center.

Wolfram, W. 1985: Variability in tense marking: a case for the obvious. *Language Learning*, 35, 229–53.

Woods, A., Fletcher, P., and Hughes, A. 1986: *Statistics in Language Studies*. New York: Cambridge University Press.

Wright, B. D. 1999: Fundamental measurement for psychology. In S. E. Embretson and S. L. Hershberger (eds), *The New Rules of Measurement: What Every Psychologist and Educator Should Know*. Mahwah, NJ: Lawrence Erlbaum Associates, 65–104.

Young, R. 1995a: Conversational styles in language proficiency interviews. *Language Learning*, 54, 3–42.

Young, R. 1995b: Discontinuous interlanguage development and its implications for oral proficiency rating scales. *Applied Linguistics*, 6, 13–26.

Young, R. and He, A. W. 1998: *Talking and Testing: Discourse Approaches to the Assessment of Oral Proficiency*. Studies in Bilingualism, 14. Philadelphia: John Benjamins.

Young, R. and Milanovic, M. 1992: Discourse variation in oral proficiency interviews. *Studies in Second Language Acquisition*, 14, 403–24.

Yuan, B. 1997: Asymmetry of null subjects and null objects in Chinese speakers' L2 English. *Studies in Second Language Acquisition*, 19, 467–97.

Yule, G. 1997: *Referential Communication Tasks*. Mahwah, NJ: Lawrence Erlbaum Associates.

Zobl, H. 1995: Converging evidence for the "acquisition–learning" distinction. *Applied Linguistics*, 16, 35–56.

22 Data Collection in SLA Research

CRAIG CHAUDRON

1 Introduction

Although professionals working in second/foreign language pedagogy have always displayed interest in assessing learners' achievement, the approach to doing so has typically involved tests developed within an instructional/achievement/normative paradigm (see Chaudron, 2001, for a review of foreign language research), so that a record of individuals' or groups of learners' L2 development was not the principal focus of research. In contrast to this tradition, research on second language acquisition (SLA), deriving from studies of child language acquisition of the 1950s and 1960s, began in earnest in the late 1960s with the advent of the notion of interlanguage development (see Hatch, 1978b, for a review).

The application of research methods in second language acquisition since the early 1970s has intensified and become more refined in substantial ways, by adopting or expanding upon methodologies employed especially in psychology, sociology, anthropology, and linguistics, all of which were themselves fledgling fields with hybrid research approaches barely a century ago. *Research design*, as in experimental studies, case studies, and correlational studies, and many other approaches and techniques for *data analysis* are equally critical to successful, informative research (see overview texts such as Hatch and Lazaraton, 1991; D. Johnson, 1992; Nunan, 1992; see also, for example, the treatment of issues with respect to time-series designs in Mellow, Reeder, and Forster, 1996). However, because the principles underlying reliable and valid adoption and refinement of these approaches are largely common to research in the broader disciplines, and can, therefore, be reviewed and accessed through that literature, this chapter will adopt a narrower focus – on the core of research procedures in SLA, namely *data-collection procedures* as employed since the early 1980s in SLA research (see descriptions of instrumentation and procedures in Doughty and Long, 2000; Larsen-Freeman and Long, 1991, pp. 26–38; Seliger and Shohamy, 1989, pp. 158–80).[1] It has become clear in the development of the SLA research tradition that, regardless of the particular approach or design adopted by the researcher, a variety of data-collection procedures is feasible,[2] if not desired, in order for the researcher to obtain the best sample of learners' performance potential. The various approaches to the elicitation and collection of data on learner performance in second languages will therefore be outlined, with a concern for the appropriate methodologies that ensure valid SLA analysis.

This overview will focus on the following primary questions:

i What procedures have been applied in SLA research, and what are the conditions and characteristics of each?
ii How reliable and valid are the procedures and methods for collecting SLA data?
iii As a specific outcome of the question of validity, what are the limits to interpretation from data collected by each procedure as reflections of underlying SLA performance/competence?
iv As a matter of the generalizability of procedures, to what extent can procedures adopted for L1 research be applied in L2 research?
v What new or additional procedures or adaptations are possible or needed for L2 research?

A wide range of procedures and methods will be described, each illustrated by a number of exemplary studies, and overviews of SLA research using each procedure, when they exist, will be identified for further study.

1.1 General dimensions of data collection

First language data-collection methodologies have been characterized by Bennett-Kastor (1988) either as "naturally observed" or as elicited under "controlled observation" (p. 26). Of the naturally observed data sources, she includes three types: "indirect or anecdotal evidence; native speaker 'intuitions', especially as judgments of the acceptability of utterances; and 'raw' data actually manifested in conversational and other naturally occurring forms" (p. 26). Bennett-Kastor acknowledges, however, that data may also be experimentally elicited through controlled procedures, which are necessarily used to obtain judgment data, but which involve as well "manipulation of objects, pictures or even the child's postures . . . and the elicitation of descriptions by the child of object configurations," and even imitation or other verbal manipulation tasks (p. 29ff). This naturalistic/experimental dimension for classifying research methodologies (recapitulated by Nunan, 1996, with reference to research design and general methodology) has been applied under various guises by many L2 theorists, as in Cook's (1986) "authentic" vs. "non-authentic" distinction, van Lier's (1988) "± interventionist" dichotomy, Seliger and Shohamy's (1989, pp. 158ff) "low explicitness/heuristic" vs. "high explicitness/deductive," and Larsen-Freeman and Long's (1991, pp. 14–15) "qualitative/quantitative continuum." These characterizations, at times, include the entire perspective

Table 22.1 Data collection methods classified on the naturalistic to experimental continuum

Naturalistic (contextualized)	*Elicited production*	*Experimental (decontextualized)*
Learner speech production		
Recorded natural (spontaneous) speech	Role play	On-line processing measures (sentence matching/verification, signal detection, word recognition, decision)
Communication task	(meaning-focused)	
	Story (video) retelling	
Unstructured interviews	Structured interview	Utterance completion
		Elicited imitation
	Picture description/picture prompts	
	Instruction giving	
Classroom observation	Discourse completion	Word association
		Elicited translation
		Sentence manipulation
Communication task	(structure-focused)	
	Structured questionnaire	
	OPI	
	SOPI	
	Stimulated recall (verbal reports, etc.)	
Diary (self)	Integrated (e.g., cloze) tests	Discrete-point tests
		Metalinguistic tests (card sorting, grammaticality judgments, magnitude scaling, paired comparisons, sentence correction, rule expression)
Observational notes		
Reflection on production: perception/interpretation		

undertaken in the research (distinguished as in Grotjahn, 1987, on a continuum from "nomothetic" to "heuristic"), rather than the specific data-collection procedures, any one of which might be applicable to a diverse array of designs and research purposes. In this chapter, however, we will avoid entering into the question of general research orientations, restricting the overview to the description of the procedures and their specific characteristics and capacity for obtaining valid data.[3]

Given a dimension, as in Bennett-Kastor, from "naturalistic" to "experimental," where the degree of *contextualization for meaningful and purposeful language use* is a key criterion to be used to place a method on the continuum, the data-collection techniques to be reviewed here can be laid out as in table 22.1. Here, a vertical dimension has been added to suggest the *extent of direct vs. indirect elicitation* of L2 linguistic forms or competence, that is, the extent to which the subjects/learners are led to produce without further reflection, or to express their reflections and interpretations of the language they have produced or are presented with. In a related view, this dimension is referred to by Kasper and Dahl (1991, p. 217) as "modality of language use: perception/comprehension → production." (See also Chaudron, 1985b, for the input–intake relationship.)

To some extent, the naturalistic–experimental continuum may seem related, as well, to the "interlanguage continuum" distinction made by Tarone (1979, 1983; following Labov, 1969), with spontaneous free speech ("vernacular" is a term that is often used, but may be inappropriate for L2 speech) on one end and careful controlled speech on the other. SLA researchers are cautious about disentangling L2 production effects that are based on implicitly acquired knowledge from those that derive from explicit knowledge and its influence in monitored speech (see discussion in Doughty and Long, 2000, pp. 154–6). But this important factor of speech-style monitoring that can increase intra-subject variability is somewhat independent of the specific elicitation methodology chosen, and more contingent on certain contextual conditions that can be manipulated or altered in any given methodology, such as the amount of time allowed to the subject to plan or reflect on his or her performance; the degree of social demand for more polished performance, which occurs in interaction with larger groups or higher-status interlocutors; and the extent of feedback.

After an introductory note on reliability and validity (see also Norris and Ortega, this volume), a topic which will be reprised at the end of this review, the methods reviewed will be grouped according to three primary types, following the horizontal dimension on table 22.1 from left to right: *naturalistic*, *elicited production*, and *experimental*, or more decontextualized, performance stimuli.

1.2 Reliability and validity

A key concern of this review is whether the particular methods employed by researchers have proven to be reliable and valid, that is, whether they have consistently led to successful elicitation of learners' language performance and, possibly, competence, and whether the analysis of this performance matches other, independent measures of or expectations for the learners' production. It is frequently impossible to tell from a given collection of data whether the forms produced are simply an artifact of the method. This is why many researchers today employ multiple measures, in order to "triangulate" their findings, and to differentiate the possible effects of the method employed from the stable or developing traits of the learners' underlying language capacity. The use of multiple measures is exemplified in three procedures discussed by Doughty and Long (2000) in their review of data elicitation, all of which employ various tasks to elicit a range of language abilities: the *developmental linguistic profiling* procedures of Pienemann and his associates (Pienemann, 1998); the *descriptive linguistic profiling* employed by both the European Science Foundation (ESF) project (Dietrich, Klein, and Noyau, 1995; W. Klein and Perdue, 1992; Perdue, 1982) and the FLIRT research project at Georgetown University (see the web page at <http://cfdev.georgetown.edu/flirt/docs/advlearn.htm>); and the research of Pica and her colleagues (Pica, Kanagy, and Falodun, 1993) and Swain and her colleagues (Swain and Lapkin, 1998) on *production via interaction on tasks*, which involves performance on multiple or sequential communication tasks. At the end of the following review of procedures, we will attempt to determine which comparisons among distinct methods and tasks appear to confirm or to question the validity of particular data elicitation procedures.

2 Naturalistic Data Collection Procedures

Some of the earliest approaches to and sources of productive data on SLA involved *observation of children's language use in play and normal interaction* with parents and others (Leopold, 1939, 1948; Ravem, 1968, 1970). Well-known early SLA research of this sort also includes studies by Hakuta (1974, 1976) and Huang and Hatch (1978); see the collection of studies in Hatch (1978a). Procedures for observing and recording children's (or adults') speech in such naturalistic settings have gradually been elaborated and are outlined and critiqued in some detail regarding L1 research in Milroy (1987), Bennett-Kastor (1988, pp. 55–73), and Demuth (1996), where recommendations for the use of video- and audio-recording devices are made.

2.1 *Advantages and disadvantages*

Naturalistic observation must be systematic, and details of the physical and verbal context in which observations and recordings are made must be recorded, in order to retrieve sources of deictic reference, restrictive/non-restrictive relative clause contexts, and possible social-interactive events that would influence pragmatic meanings and interpretations, and, whenever possible, to supplement potentially unintelligible linguistic information in the recordings. Assuming a context for observation in a naturally occurring social event, the advantage of data collected in this way is that the learner's production will be a true sample of his or her L2 speech, possibly in open communication with familiar colleagues or friends, and uninfluenced by artifactual aspects of an elicitation method, as well as potentially less influenced by the learner's careful monitoring or application of learned rules of production. Also, extended research studies can collect very large amounts of learner production data in this manner, without substantially preparing new materials or altering any procedures for data collection. As will be clear in later sections, the preparation of quality materials for eliciting more controlled speech forms is a highly complicated, intensive process.

The disadvantages of naturalistic observation include a number of well-known limitations. Obviously, the quality of recordings made can be a significant factor in reducing or enhancing the validity of the data. Mechanical failures in recording equipment (or failure to plug it in or turn it on!) are frequent sources of difficulty for researchers (cf. Swain and Cumming, 1989), and the observer's written record may omit contextual features or distort speech production data if no independent recording is available. But more significant is the major concern of researchers that particular target structures or competences of the L2 may be avoided or underrepresented and thus not assessed: it is difficult to interpret the absence of structures in the learners' performance, and comprehension is typically not easily evaluated. Especially in records of younger children interacting, whether or not a particular form is productive in use cannot be determined. A further limitation is that naturalistic observation is highly labor-intensive, owing to the need for a trained observer at all data-collection moments and later during elaborate transcription of the data; as a consequence, only smaller numbers of subjects can be studied. This is why naturalistic observation is typically used in case studies of only a few children or a single classroom. In such research, the value of the data will depend more on the variability that arises through the natural interaction that might occur, or possible differences between the few subjects, or because the procedure is used in a longitudinal design to discover trends in acquisition.

2.2 *Observation of child and adult learning in context*

Among a number of studies using naturalistic observation are those displayed in table 22.2, which include recent examples of the use of naturalistic observation in studies of young bilingual children (ages from less than 2 to 4) engaged in free play with their parents or a TL-speaking research assistant (in most cases, each parent is a native speaker of a different language) over a period of from one to two years (Meisel, 1994a, 1994b; Nicolaidis and Genesee, 1996; Paradis and Genesee, 1996; Schlyter, 1993).

In such studies, the number of children observed or analyzed is small (from two to six – though Meisel's group, cf. Meisel, 1994b, has collected data from 13 children), but the large number of longitudinal data obtained can allow for a very wide range of analyses. Typically, the researchers will only sample from the large amount of data collected (from one-third to half of the data) for the

Table 22.2 Studies of natural language production in bilingual children

Study	*Languages*	*N*	*Ages*	*Context and period*	*Frequency*	*Focus*
Studies involving natural play with parents or interlocutors:						
Swain and Wesche (1973)	French English	1	3	$1\frac{1}{2}$-hour play with two TL researchers for 9 months	Every 2 weeks	Language mixing and switching elicited translation
Schlyter (1993)	French Swedish	6	2–4	$\frac{1}{2}$-hour play with each parent for 2 years	Every 4 months	Constraints on finiteness, negation, word order, pronouns in stronger/weaker language
Meisel (1994a)	French German	2 (out of larger n = 13)	1:3–3:0	1-hour play with TL speakers/ parents for 3+ years	Every 2 weeks	Mixing of L1/L2, acquisition of structural constraints on mixing/switching
Paradis and Genesee (1996)	French English	3	1:11–3:3	1-hour play with each parent and both for 1 year	Every 4 months	Development of finiteness, negation, pronominals

Nicolaidis and Genesee (1996)	French English	4	1:5–3:8	≈ 1-hour play with each parent for $1\frac{1}{2}$ years	Every 2 months	Language choice with parents, use of translation
Studies involving guided conversations, play or interviews:						
Pfaff (1992)	Turkish German	3 (out of larger n = 31)	1–5	$\frac{1}{2}$-hour play with researchers over 3 years	Twice a month (once each language)	Grammaticalization, pragmatic/syntactic categories
Tomiyama (2000)	Japanese English	1	8–11	1+-hour English conversation + elicited productions over almost 3 years	Every month, then every 2 months	Attrition of English morphology and lexis
Haznedar (2001)	Turkish English	1	4–5:6	40–90-minute play interaction in English	Three times per month	Development of copula, aux., tense agreement, subject pronouns
Bardovi-Harlig and Hartford (1996)	English Various	16	Adults	≈ 15–20-minute academic interviews	Twice an academic year	Pragmatic competence development

sake of transcription and detailed analysis. While Nicolaidis and Genesee focus on the developmental changes in the children's code switching and appropriateness of language choice with their parent interlocutors, the others – Meisel, Paradis and Genesee, and Schlyter – attempt to compare the children's patterns of structural constraints in the dual acquisition of French with German, English, and Swedish, respectively, to expectations for universal L1 patterns of acquisition in each (e.g., structural constraints on language mixing within utterances, acquisition of finite marking and pronominal subjects), or to assess transfer effects from the dominant into the weaker language and vice versa.

Researchers employing naturalistic observation and recording with older subjects are less likely to use this technique without some form of intervention or control, minimally an *interview* or *conversation* with the subject, whether unstructured or structured. (However, see research on code switching in adult bilinguals by, for example, Poplack and her colleagues – Poplack, Wheeler, and Westwood 1989 – which employs "standard social network techniques" to record and analyze free conversations. Also, Bardovi-Harlig and Hartford, 1993, 1996, used recordings of authentic academic interviews with non-native students in order to evaluate the development of their pragmatic competence.) Thus, even when studying a subject as young as 3 years of age, in her groundbreaking research on early childhood bilingualism, Swain (1972; Swain and Wesche, 1973) and her co-researcher interacted with their subject, each in a different language, in order to elicit the child's abilities, occasionally asking the child to translate for the other language speaker. Likewise, while researching the same topic as Paradis and Genesee, Haznedar (2001) chose to engage in play-like interaction with a 4-year-old Turkish child learning L2 English, primarily in order to elicit L2 use. And Tomiyama (2000) employed English conversation interviews for 33 months with an 8-year-old Japanese native child returning from a seven-year residence in the United States.

A number of European studies of L2 development in adults and children, such as the ESF project, obtained data from the natural "free conversation" of informants and occasionally observation of their speech with others. Generally, these studies have relied more on *participant observation* records, informant self-recorded *diaries*, and unstructured and structured *conversational interviews* (Perdue, 1982, pp. 56–61), along with more controlled and experimental procedures (see, e.g., studies by Perdue and Klein, Pfaff, Giacalone Ramat, and Skiba and Dittmar, all in Dittmar, 1992; chapters in Dietrich et al., 1995; and all articles in Perdue, 2000). In the US, Park (2000) reports an analysis of data collected on Korean children acquiring L2 English, as part of an early 1980s project of the National Center for Bilingual Research in Los Angeles. The data were collected with individualized tape-recorders both at home and in school, with some semi-structured and structured elicitation. Finally, an innovative approach to the use of "diaries" with adults is the study by Brown, Sagers, and LaPorte (1999), who examined oral and written *dialog journals* (interactions between EFL learners and their teachers) as a basis for the analysis of vocabulary acquisition.

It deserves mention that the use of *self-report diaries* maintained by researchers on their own language-learning experiences has not seen a significant continued use in the investigation of L2 production and development. Aside from reports of such studies, primarily in the 1980s, whose focus was on affective and cognitive effects of learning or teaching in uninstructed and classroom contexts (e.g., Bailey, 1983, 2001; F. Schumann, 1980; see Bailey and Nunan, 1996, for reports of classroom use of student and teacher diary-keeping), one diary study that gained notoriety for its analysis of linguistic features in the acquisition of Portuguese by Schmidt (Schmidt and Frota, 1986) remains a model for too few subsequent studies (see Jones, 1995, for a self-study of Hungarian vocabulary acquisition). Schmidt's detailed diaries were also compared with analyses of his Portuguese use in monthly recordings of unstructured conversations with his co-author. In this way, the researcher was especially able to compare the relationship between his sometimes unconscious production and use in interaction and his development in Portuguese grammar.

2.3 Classroom observation

As a special case of naturalistic observation, techniques for the *observation of learning in classrooms* have been developed since the mid-1960s (as reviewed in Allwright, 1988; Allwright and Bailey, 1991; Chaudron, 1988; van Lier, 1988; and many more). Such approaches have not typically been used to examine SLA development directly, as they usually involve global observation schedules or checklists, and focus on teacher behavior or classroom interaction processes. However, through analyses of additional measures of interaction and learning opportunities arising from classroom behaviors, researchers have pointed to contexts and processes that might influence SLA. (See, e.g., Markee, 1994, who analyzed vocabulary awareness from transcripts of lessons during which all participants recorded separately on their own lapel microphones; Lyster, 1998a, 1998b, and Lyster and Ranta, 1997, who evaluated student performance relative to teacher feedback treatments; and Williams, 1999, who evaluated the nature of student interaction during language form-related activities.) It deserves note, however, that a few such studies have made use of the analysis of classroom transcripts or direct observation of learner production in order to characterize L2 progress. An early such study was that of Adams (1978, originally conducted in 1971), who maintained a systematic record of Spanish-speaking ESL learners' production of a variety of morphemes and syntactic structures over a two-year period. These results were compared with elicited imitation and translation tasks involving similar structures. Likewise, Ellis (1992) studied learners' classroom performance, although his analysis was based on his hand-recorded notes on two learners' productions and interaction, with audio-recordings used only to confirm analyses. Both of these researchers lamented the high degree of background noise that often affects classroom recordings, which is an argument for individually assigned microphones and recorders. For the most part, however, classroom-based observations of learner development have made use of more controlled tasks that will be described in later sections.

3 Elicited Production Procedures

Although the data obtained from naturalistic observation are demonstrably extensive and informative, especially insofar as intra- and inter-subject longitudinal development can be analyzed, the disadvantages of such data, noted above, have been a concern for many researchers interested in more specific L2 learning targets. Therefore, a number of techniques have been developed that are designed to elicit learners' productive language performance in a more concentrated and focused fashion, by providing some initial verbal or physical context selected by the researcher. These include *structured interviews* intending to elicit particular target forms (e.g., past tense, hypotheticals, adjectives, and relative clauses) or topics (e.g., family relationships), a very wide range of *communication tasks* with greater or lesser attention to meaning vs. form (as suggested in table 22.1, the more attention is directed to form, the more reflective the task), *role plays, picture descriptions* and *instruction-giving, story-retelling, discourse completion, stimulated recall* and other *structured questionnaires,* and combinations of these as used in the *Oral Proficiency Interview* and *Simulated Oral Proficiency Interview.* For most of these procedures, first language researchers have created many more extensive uses, although owing to the lesser cognitive maturity of the subjects of such studies, a number of more meaningful communication tasks (such as role plays and debates) have not normally been used to elicit L1 linguistic performance per se. (For reviews of L1 methods, see chapters 5, 6, and 9–13 in Menn and Bernstein Ratner, 2000; see Crookes, 1991, for L2 research methodology.)

3.1 *Advantages and disadvantages*

The advantages in general of such elicitation tasks relative to naturalistic observation are that, first, they can be tailored to specific points of L2 learning that are the theoretical focus of the research, especially certain communication tasks or picture descriptions that can be designed to promote specific productions, known as "task essentialness" (cf. Loschky and Bley-Vroman, 1993). Second, they can be employed in a more mechanical fashion using recording instruments, so that the researcher and assistants can elicit more subjects' data with less concern for observational reliability. A third advantage is that they lend themselves to use with learners of virtually any level of L2 competence, because translations of instructions or materials can be provided. Finally, fourth, they tend to be more easily analyzed and scored, although transcription and coding of protocols do require reliability assessments.

Relative to more decontextualized or receptive experimental measures, these tasks also have the following advantage: depending on the volume of language elicited and the extent of naturalistic context provided (e.g., as in a role play), they can elicit an extensive range of potentially natural, unmonitored learner performance appropriate to a given genre of speech behavior or style. For the above reasons, most researchers have tended to elicit data using more than one such method, thereby allowing for better cross-task validation of their findings.

Among some possible disadvantages are ones similar to those for naturalistic observation. First, there remains sufficient lack of control over linguistic context that subjects may still avoid targeted structures or language use. Second, as with more decontextualized, experimental techniques, the social and psychological demands of the task, which can interact with norms of the L1 culture or personal anxieties, may lead to hesitance on the part of subjects to comply with the task demands. Finally, with very small children, some procedures require thoughtful adjustment to make the expectations for execution of the task clear and to stimulate the children to perform.

Several recent reviews of SLA have cited the use of many of these data-collection methods (and other more controlled, experimental ones that we will review in the following main section), frequently with several used concurrently, in the study of speech acts (Ellis, 1994, pp. 169–71), tense and aspect development (Bardovi-Harlig, 1999), Swedish L2 morphology and word order (Pienemann and Håkansson, 1999), and the effects of pre-task planning on L2 performance (Ortega, 1999). Regrettably, however, those reviews did not propose to evaluate the methods per se. But, as in the case of naturalistic observation, if findings from the use of different procedures lead to results that are consistent with specific theoretical interpretations, then this amounts to a cross-task validation of the procedures. Table 22.3 summarizes a number of representative studies that have employed multiple tasks; when comparable, or divergent, results are obtained with their procedures, we can thereby draw conclusions about their validity.

3.2 *(Un)structured interviews*

Many researchers use (un)structured interviews in order to obtain what is often referred to as "free conversation," even though the data do not constitute "overheard" speech, rather speech by the informant(s) following sequences of questions by the researcher or other interviewer. Surprisingly, in most of this literature, there is little description of exactly what sort of protocols, guidelines, questions, or procedures are employed (for some guidelines, see Seliger and Shohamy, 1989, pp. 166–8, or qualitative research manuals such as Glesne and Peshkin, 1992, especially ch. 4). The reason appears to be that SLA researchers use interview data, unlike more naturalistic research, as a context within which to elicit particular target structures. The target linguistic focus intended can be word order and negation (Bolander, 1989), past time reference and propositional encoding (Sato, 1990), lexical development (Viberg, 1993), subject/topic prominence and pro-drop (Hendriks, 2000; Jin, 1994; Liceras and Díaz, 1999), existentials (Duff, 1993), tense and aspect (Bayley, 1994; and Klein

Table 22.3 Example studies using multiple elicited production procedures and tasks

Study	*Languages*		N	Procedures used	Topic focus	Design
Study	*Target*	*L1*	*N*	*Procedures used*	*Topic focus*	*Design*
Bolander (1989)	Swedish Swedish Swedish	Finnish Polish Spanish	20 20 20	15-minute interview Picture description	Inversion Negation	4-month longitudinal pre-/post-test
Rintell and Mitchell (1989)	English (NS comparison group)	Various	34 37	Discourse completion: role play	Speech acts: requests, apologies	Comparative experiment
Sato (1985, 1990)	English	Vietnamese	2	Conversation with researcher Communication games Picture description, sequences Story translation Conversational translation Elicited imitation Oral reading, spelling	Past time reference Propositional encoding	Longitudinal sampling (every week for 10 months, less often over 2 more years)
Duff (1993)	English	Cambodian	1	Free conversation Personal narrative Picture description Story-telling	Possessive and existential	Longitudinal sampling (3 years)

Viberg (1993)	Swedish	13 languages	23	Free conversation Story-retelling (video) Play with flannel board	Lexical development: verb semantics	Cross-sectional and longitudinal development
Jin (1994)	Chinese	English	46	Oral interview Story-retelling Free composition	Subject- and topic-prominence in transfer	Lumped data from all tasks
Ioup, Boustagui, El Tigi, and Moselle (1994)	Arabic	English	2	Recipe description Accent identification Sentence translation Grammatical judgment Anaphora referent choice	NS-level accuracy in accent, syntax	NS judges, multi-task
W. Klein, Coenen, van Helvert, and Hendriks (1995)	Dutch	Turkish Moroccan	2 2	Conversation Personal narrative Story-retelling	Tense and aspect	Cross-sectional and longitudinal
Flanigan (1995)	English	8 language groups	23	Written answers to anaphora questions Story-telling L1 story-telling Sentence combining	Anaphora in relative clauses, reflexives	Correlations with proficiency measures
House (1996)	English	German	32	Interviews Pair interactions Role play Self-perception	Pragmatic gambits and competence	Instructional experiment over 1 term

Table 22.3 *(cont'd)*

	Languages					
Study	*Target*	*L1*	*N*	*Procedures used*	*Topic focus*	*Design*
Myles, Mitchell, and Hooper (1999)	French	English	16	Picture description Story retelling Information gap (one-way) Problem-solving (two-way) Role play (group) Vocabulary test	Formulaic phrases, interrogatives	6 samples over 2+ years
Mackey (1999)	English	9 languages	34	Picture sequencing Picture description Picture differences Story completion	Question formation	Experimental task orders Output pooled across tasks
Rosa and O'Neill (1999)	Spanish	English	67	Multiple-choice Think-aloud	Past conditional (subjunctive)	Between-group Pre-/post-test
Helms-Park (2001)	English	Hindi-Urdu Vietnamese	47 45	Picture description-written (1 sentence, w/verb prompt) Multiple-choice response to question Grammatical judgment task	Lexis Causative verbs Picture context	Cross-sectional comparison

et al., 1995, which is representative of many of the ESF studies, as also found in Dietrich et al., 1995, and Dittmar, 1992), and speech acts and pragmatics (House, 1996; other studies in Kasper, 1996). More often than not, additional more specific tasks are included in the course of the interviews, such as picture descriptions (Bolander, 1989; M. Carroll, Murcia-Serra, Watorek, and Bendiscioli, 2000; Holmen, 1993; Sato, 1990), experimental elicitation tasks (Sato, 1990), personal narratives (Duff, 1993; Klein et al., 1995), story-retelling (Jin, 1994; Klein et al., 1995; Sato, 1990; Viberg, 1993), instruction-giving (Ahrenholz, 2000), or focused interactions and self-reflections (House, 1996).

With such varied procedures being employed, the same data can be analyzed for many different features, as is evident in the second stage of analysis of the ESF data (Perdue, 2000), where the data that had been originally analyzed for basic morphology and phrase structure, as in Dittmar (1992) and Dietrich et al. (1995), was then analyzed for negation, interclausal relations, and discourse structure. In few of the studies just cited, however, have researchers made a clear comparison between the analyses of the data gathered from the basic interviews and of those elicited by means of more controlled production tasks. Many primarily report on the more spontaneous conversation portions, and Jin (1994) claims (without displaying their separate frequencies) that since no significant differences occurred in the results for different tasks, the data are collapsed across tasks. Typically, of course, the nature of the specific target analysis is such that the key data are derived from the more focused task. A notable exception to this lack of comparison is Sato's (1985, 1990) longitudinal study of two Vietnamese boys, whose speech was analyzed after conducting various tasks – conversation, reading aloud, elicited imitation, and prepared text recitation. Sato's (1985) analysis of one of the boys' target-like final consonants and final consonant clusters revealed considerable cross-task consistency on the former by the end of the 10-month period. However, on final consonant clusters, on which his performance was overall much worse (generally lower than 30 percent accuracy, compared to nearly 70 percent for single consonants), there was substantial cross-task differentiation. The imitation task resulted in most target-like production, while conversation was the lowest (with consequent greater variability) for all but the final sample. Oral reading and text recitation led to gradual lower accuracy in later elicitations, possibly due to the competing demands on the boy to attend to other linguistic features than phonology. It would appear to be important for researchers to make more such comparisons across tasks, in order to assess learners' underlying competence with respect to their performance in less structured conversation. That is to say, more controlled elicited production procedures like the ones following in this section need to be used to complement data from interviews and personal narratives.[4]

3.3 *Communication tasks*

Although a large number of communication tasks have been developed and employed for the purpose of direct L2 instruction since the mid-1960s, their use as a tool for eliciting L2 speech production in research has only gradually developed since the late 1970s. Much of the focus of early research making use of such tasks has been on the study of the effects of interaction on SLA (see the articles collected in Gass and Mackey, 1998; recent studies such as Shehadeh, 1999, using *picture dictation* and *opinion exchange*, and Van den Branden, 1997, using *picture description*; and previous reviews by Long, 1983; Pica, 1994). Yet such tasks have also been used to elicit learner production data for SLA analysis (some examples are given in table 22.3 above).

Communication tasks vary considerably, from map reading, real-world sales exchanges and *information-getting* tasks, and *problem-solving* discussions, to narrower searching for differences in pictures, *picture description*, or sorting out the order of unordered picture sequences (see Yule, 1997, for representative types; and Norris, Brown, Hudson, and Yoshioka, 1998, for sample tasks within a schematic approach to the development of task-based performance assessment). Despite their variety, Skehan's (1998, p. 95) itemization of characteristics typical of communication tasks is essentially adequate:

i meaning is primary;
ii there is some communication problem to solve;
iii there is some sort of relationship to comparable real-world activities;
iv task completion has some priority; and
v the assessment of the task is in terms of outcome.

There have furthermore been various proposals for describing and designing tasks, such as the following ones for the principal factors or dimensions of variation among tasks:

- *Nunan (1989)*: goals, input and materials, activity, teacher and learner roles, and context;
- *Pica et al. (1993)*: interactional activity (relationship and requirements) and communicative goal (orientation and outcome options);
- *Skehan (1998, p. 99)*: code complexity, cognitive complexity (familiarity and processing), and communicative stress;
- *Robinson (2001, p. 30)*: complexity (resource-directing and resource-depleting), conditions (participation and participant variables), and difficulty (affective and ability variables).

Choices from among the options for any given dimension can lead to differences in the complexity and linguistic demands on the subjects. Examples of the use of communicative tasks to elicit learners' speech for basic SLA analyses include Bolander (1989) and Ellis (1989) – picture descriptions for negation and/or word order; Ioup et al. (1994) – *description* of a favorite recipe in order to assess nativelikeness; Myles et al. (1999; see also Myles, Hooper, and Mitchell, 1998) – several one-way and two-way *information gap tasks* administered to French L2 secondary school children to elicit interrogatives; Wode (1999) – a complex *problem-solving* task to examine grade seven English FL learners' lexical development; and Robertson (2000) – *one-way information gap* task to elicit English article use by Chinese L1 speakers. Also, from the earliest period of SLA research on communication strategies (see especially the collection of reprinted studies in Færch and Kasper, 1983; and more recent research in Kasper and Kellerman, 1997; as well as discussion on methodology by Bialystok, 1990, pp. 50–1), picture descriptions and many information-exchange tasks have been widely used to elicit learners' use of communication strategies.

As noted before, however, and as Doughty and Long (2000) exemplify, communicative tasks have been employed in SLA research in order to explore the influence of instruction and interaction on learners' acquisition, in which only certain narrowly defined target and interlanguage forms have been analyzed – along with more global measures of fluency, complexity, and accuracy – with respect to their improvement following task performance. Thus for example, studies employing communication tasks for the evaluation of effects of task dimensions on learner speech have included those on the amount of *planning time* allowed before performance: Crookes (1989), using Lego construction and *map description* tasks; Mehnert (1998), using instructions in telephone messages; Foster and Skehan (1996) and Skehan and Foster (1997), using information exchange and *decision-making* tasks; and Ortega (1999), using *picture/story-retelling*. Despite the differences among task types, relatively consistent effects of planning on these measures have been found. These include the result that, while fluency and complexity improve, accuracy does not change in any dramatic direction, except for some measures for which planning enhances accuracy (e.g., target-like use of Spanish noun modification in Ortega's study). In addition, some results point to increased effects of planning on some of these measures when the tasks vary on a dimension such as *complexity* (as in Foster and Skehan, 1996). Further, using a two-way interactive map-direction task of varying complexity, Robinson (2001) demonstrates, for instance, that task complexity tends to exert a favorable effect on accuracy and lexical variety, while diminishing fluency.

3.4 Story-retelling

The use of a pre-selected story presented to a learner in either written, picture, or video mode has been a widely used technique in (narrative) language elicitation. As early as Perkins and Larsen-Freeman (1975), non-dialog films have been used to elicit L2 English production. Perkins and Larsen-Freeman had to alter their elicitation, however, by interspersing the viewing of the film with questions, because their subjects were avoiding the morphological features they were investigating. More recently, this procedure has been used to elicit L2 lexical development (Hyltenstam, 1988, 1992, who used segments of Charlie Chaplin's *Modern Times*), and anaphoric reference and evidence of topic- or subject-prominence by several researchers, for example, Flanigan (1995; see table 22.3), who used a wordless picture story to elicit children's L1 and

L2 story-retellings in order to assess anaphoric reference; Jin (1994; also in table 22.3), who used silent cartoon films retold in L2 Chinese; and Polio (1995), who used the *Pear Film* to elicit L2 Chinese reference (see considerable L1 research using the "Pear Stories," starting with Chafe, 1980). Also, recently Rose (2000), who had earlier questioned the validity of discourse completion tasks (see the next section) in eliciting speech acts cross-culturally (Rose, 1994; cf. Rose and Ono, 1995, for an L1 Japanese comparison), employed cartoon strips to elicit politeness speech acts, and Gass, Mackey, Alvarez-Torres, and Fernández-García (1999) used video story-retelling (in fact, on-line simultaneous description of events) in a complex design to investigate the degree of improvement in Spanish L2 production (measured in terms of holistically rated speech, morphosyntax – *ser/estar* distinction – and complexity of vocabulary), after repeated viewings of the same video or repeated performances on different videos.

Retelling has been used especially to elicit L2 tense and aspect features (as in the ESF studies – cf. Perdue, 1982, and others' use of *Modern Times*). An early L2 report of this sort analyzed in terms of foreground–background relationships in ESL was Tomlin (1984). And Bardovi-Harlig (2000, pp. 199–202) reviews this methodology especially with respect to the use of silent films and variations in the context and frequency with which they are presented, noting several advantages of this procedure: "[i] the sequence of events is known to the researcher . . . [ii] such narratives can be compared across learners . . . [iii] retell tasks may encourage some learners to produce longer samples than they would otherwise . . . [iv] the content of stories . . . may be manipulated" (pp. 199–200). To this one might add that, if a particular source for retelling is long, omissions of events are likely, unless the recipient of the retelling assists the subject. Among the disadvantages Bardovi-Harlig points to are: "there is still noteworthy variation in number of the tokens that learners produce . . . [and] certain types of predicates appear more frequently than others" (p. 201). The result of these disadvantages is that researchers have had to resort to narrower elicitation measures such as cloze passages in conjunction with retellings. A study that attempted to alleviate some of the disadvantages noted is that of Salaberry (1999) (who previously – 1998 – had used the *Pear Film* to elicit L2 French tense/aspect marking), as he presented segments of *Modern Times* individually in private to college students of Spanish L2. For purposes of motivation and authenticity, the students were then asked to relate the story to another student playing the role of a detective, who would, in turn, retell the events to a native or near-native listener.

3.5 *Role plays and discourse completion*

Some techniques have been developed primarily in order to elicit only certain domains of target structure. This is the case with *role plays* and *discourse-completion tests* (DCT), which have been used predominantly in L2 research to elicit data on pragmatic abilities in a variety of speech acts, with requests and apologies being the most commonly studied. An anthology of such research is presented in Blum-Kulka, House, and Kasper (1989), in which a particular DCT the editors developed is employed in various studies. Further, Hudson, Detmer, and Brown (1995) provide a model for the development of DCTs, and Kasper and Dahl (1991) and Kasper (1998) provide extensive reviews of research methodology in L2 pragmatics.

In an early effort to make cross-procedure comparisons, Rintell and Mitchell (1989) explicitly contrasted results from oral role plays and written discourse-completion responses by ESL learners and native controls, with respect to length, variety, and directness of apologies and requests. They found that, while oral interaction led to less direct and longer speech acts than written responses, there were mainly similarities in the range of strategies used. Aside from the added length that indirectness leads to, the writer's opportunity to reflect on appropriate forms in the written response resulted in more concise, less hesitant responses. A quite similar result was found in a within-subject comparison in a recent study by M. Sasaki (1998) on Japanese L1 EFL learners. These findings suggest that while DCTs may provide legitimate data, they may also elicit a narrower range of pragmatic performance than learners are actually capable of.

Kormos (1999) conducted a slightly different but consistent comparison between role-play results and typical language-testing "interview" procedures for EFL in Hungary. In intra-subject comparisons of 30 learners being tested via a conversational interview and guided role play with the same interviewer, Kormos found that the role plays allowed much more opportunity for the subjects to display their conversational competence, in topic management in particular. That study is but a more recent investigation into a long-standing issue, that is, the adequacy of a structured or unstructured oral proficiency interview to assess a learner's ability.

3.6 *(Simulated) oral proficiency interview*

Research has also been conducted on the use of (simulated) oral proficiency interviews to elicit overall learner proficiency or more specific L2 performance. Space does not permit a more extensive review of the history of the OPI (and ACTFL scales – see Clark and Clifford, 1988), or the British-based Cambridge Certificate Examination (UCLES, 1990), but, as these formats include a combination of the sorts of semi-structured tasks that we have been reviewing, it seems reasonable to consider combinations of such procedures as legitimate measures as well.

It is sufficient to note that such formal examinations, besides playing a major role in educational and occupational placement, have been used by researchers, as well, as a comparative standard in evaluating learners' development in second languages. Yet, criticism of their validity as specific measures of SLA has mounted over the years, with particularly strong arguments arising from SLA-oriented analyses of topic- and conversational management of the interaction during such interviews (as seen above in Kormos, 1999; see also articles in M. Johnson, 2000; S. Ross and Berwick, 1992; Valdman, 1988; Young, 1995; Young and He, 1998; and Young and Milanovic, 1992). The upshot of these critiques is that, as the OPI/UCLES procedures involve interaction between a status-dominant and guiding interviewer, the nature of the language performance that results is less than optimal, especially with respect to the elicitation of a full range of verbal and pragmatic competence on the part of the learner. Similarly, because a SOPI does not involve a real interlocutor, performance on it in comparison to an OPI results in different discourse and strategic use of the L2 (Koike, 1998).

3.7 Stimulated recall

The final general type of elicitation that falls within the group of more naturalistic, less decontextualized procedures is that of *stimulated recall*, which is a cover term for what are described in the literature as *think-aloud* (protocols), *introspective/retrospective interviews*, *verbal reports*, and *cued recall*, among other terms. These all have in common the elicitation from L2 subjects not of a direct linguistic performance, but of a more reflective, metalinguistic analysis or description of their language use, and internal representations or reconstructions of what they have said and how they arrived at their performance. These methods are reviewed most currently in Gass and Mackey (2000), but L2 researchers' interest in evaluating them dates back over 20 years to seminal L1 research, such as Ericsson and Simon (1980), and L2 surveys, such as Cohen and Hosenfeld (1981), and Færch and Kasper (1987a, 1987b). Cohen and Olshtain (1994, p. 148) suggest that verbal reports are vital to the validation and interpretation of learner behavior at each stage in the cycle of research on speech acts, that is, from (i) observation, to (ii) role play, to (iii) discourse completion, to (iv) learner acceptability checks.

Færch and Kasper's (1978a, p. 11) classification of the methodological framework that can be used to analyze most forms of stimulated recall is useful here (see table 22.4). Stimulated recall has been used to elicit learners' awareness and explanations of such phenomena as their tense and aspect use (Liskin-Gasparro, 1998); general grammar rule awareness and correction (P. Green and Hecht, 1992); vocabulary knowledge and decoding or translation processes (Dechert and Sandrock, 1986; Fraser, 1999 – who used both retrospection about processing and cued recall as a test; and Paribakht and Wesche, 1999 – who used both concurrent and retrospective introspection, along with training tasks and other measures of vocabulary comprehension; cf. also Wolter, 2001); and metalinguistic processes and awareness of noticing forms in input (e.g., Ellis, 1991, on learners' processing of grammaticality decisions; Leow, 1997; Rosa and O'Neill, 1999; and most of the research collected in Schmidt, 1995a; for example, Jourdenais et al., 1995, who provide a detailed description of their procedures and analytical coding), and reflections on planning processes (Ortega, 1999).

While introspective methods have gained a high degree of acceptability in L2 research, as most of the above studies have displayed findings that shed

Table 22.4 Abridged framework for classification of introspective methods

1 Object of introspection:
  linguistic, cognitive, affective, social
  declarative vs. procedural knowledge
  modality (spoken vs. written, receptive vs. productive, etc.)
  continuous process vs. specific aspect
2 Relation to concrete action:
  concrete/specific to non-specific/abstract
3 Temporal relation to action:
  simultaneous, immediately consecutive to delayed.
4 Participant training:
  ± instructions, ± training
5 Elicitation procedure:
  degree of structure
  ± media support
  self-initiated vs. other-initiated
  ± interaction between informant and experimenter
  ± integration with action
  ± interference with action
6 ± Combination of methods

Source: Færch and Kasper (1978a)

additional light on concurrent measures (such as vocabulary comprehension measures and other evidence of learner processing in uptake of input, for example), there remain concerns about the extent of application of these methods. Cohen (1991), an advocate of verbal reporting, following the work of Ericsson and Simon (1984), recognizes a number of criticisms of the method, which he summarizes (pp. 136–8): data from verbal reports (i) do not access unconscious skill learning; (ii) may simplify a particular process just by virtue of accessing it; (iii) may distort the original process by virtue of constructing a verbal report, and, therefore, become distant from the underlying events; (iv) may repress information (e.g., for social-affective reasons); (v) may intrude on the process investigated; and (vi) may also distort the reality of the process by using a different (target or native) language for the report. Jourdenais (1998, 2001) has documented in an SLA study influences of type (v).

4 Experimental Procedures and Tasks

The final principal group of data-collection procedures (as in the procedures in table 22.1 in the right-hand column) will be referred to here as "experimental" procedures and tasks, as they tend to be employed under more controlled conditions, with elicitation of L2 production or performance on perceptual-receptive tasks, with less communicatively driven and decontextualized constraints. Although some of these may also be considered broadly as "elicited production," as in the previous section, we are making the distinction here with respect to the more meaningful context and generally lengthier nature of the language production process or result that obtains in those procedures discussed previously, compared to the shorter, controlled productions typical of experimental procedures.

The current set of methods (see table 22.5, which lists representative studies for each grouping of them) includes, first, a variety of "on-line" (often computer-managed) target language processing tasks like those frequently used in L1 psycholinguistic research, such as *signal detection* tasks (of target phonemes, lexis – *word recognition*, or semantic content), *sentence-* (or other linguistic form) *matching, verification, reading* and *discrimination*, and certain *decision* (yes/no identification) tasks. For a review of several such tasks in L1 psycholinguistics, see Murdock (1982); Olson and Clark (1976); and more recent methods in McKee (1996); cf. L2 discussion by Simard and Wong (2001).

Second, many tasks that involve more cognitive processing of stimuli, and possibly learning, have been used in many SLA experiments, such as *utterance completion, elicited imitation, word association, word/list memorization, elicited translation, sentence manipulation* (*combining, transformation*), *recall* of linguistic elements following exposure to them, *rule learning, act-out* of presented structures (as a measure of comprehension) and a large variety of *discrete-point* and *cloze-type tests* measuring L2 productive knowledge of morphology, syntax, discourse, and lexis.

Finally, a very large range of methods that involve more extensive use of reflective capacities and access to higher levels of L2 knowledge have been used to elicit learners' *metalinguistic knowledge* (*grammaticality judgment tests – GJT*), *magnitude scaling* and other *judgments* (ratings), *paired comparisons, card sorting*, and ability to *express* (grammatical) *rules* or *lexical definitions* and apply them in *correction* or *editing* tasks. A number of chapters in McDaniel, McKee, and Cairns (1996) provide extensive discussions on some of these techniques as employed in child L1 studies, especially on elicited production (of the experimental sort), elicited imitation, picture selection, act-out, and judgments (including grammaticality).

It is helpful to bear several methodological issues in mind in this section. First, for the sake of distinguishing SLA linguistic performance/competence from many other topics dealt with in the L2 literature, in this review we are distinguishing the linguistic from the non-linguistic focused targets of the above procedures or methods. This is to say that many of the above procedures have been used to elicit data from subjects on such matters as their attitudes (as in many attitude surveys or scales and the use of the matched guise technique), anxiety, reflections on learning strategies, and general cognitive measures, such as aptitude or memory functioning (e.g., digit span, musical memory, analogical ability, cognitive styles). While much of this research has been vital to

Table 22.5 Example studies using experimental procedures and tasks

Study	Languages			Procedures used	Topic focus	Design analysis
	Target	L1	N			
On-line tasks:						
Juffs and Harrington (1995)	English	Chinese	26	Word-by-word reading Grammaticality judgments: (whole and paced sentences) ["Moving window"]	± grammaticality of *wh*-extraction	Cross-task comparisons Reaction time and accuracy measures
Juffs and Harrington (1996)	English	Chinese	(25?)	Same procedures as in Juffs and Harrington (1995)	± grammaticality of *wh*-extraction Garden Path sentences: ± infinitive, ± inside theta	Same as in Juffs and Harrington (1995)
Verification, decision, and reading tasks:						
Trahey and White (1993)	English	French	54	Sentence manipulation Correctness of sentence pairs Grammaticality judgment Cartoon and verbal stimulus: sentence production	Effects of instruction Verb-movement (adverb placement)	Between-group comparisons Accuracy and rate of adverb placement
Y. Sasaki (1994)	Japanese	English	30	Choice of first noun as subject/actor	Competition Model: animacy, case, word order	Mixed ANOVA on choice proportions

Table 22.5 *(cont'd)*

Study	*Languages*			*Procedures used*	*Topic focus*	*Design analysis*
	Target	*L1*	*N*			
Matsumura (1994)	English	Japanese	110	Choice of referent for reflexive	Reflexive binding Proficiency differences	Between-group comparisons Accuracy
VanPatten and Oikkenon (1996)	Spanish	English	59	Picture selection Picture description: prompted completion	Object word order Effects of instruction	2 experimental, 1 control group comparisons
DeKeyser and Sokalski (1996)	Spanish	English	82	Comprehension: object selection Production: sentence completion, translation, answering questions	Direct object clitics Conditional Effects of instruction	2 experimental groups, pre-test/post-test
Ying (1996)	English	Various	45	Preference selection of NP or VP	Ambiguous NP/VP attachment ± referential context, lexical context type, aural vs. reading input	Within-subject correlations Choice means
Beck (1998)	German	English	48	Sentence-matching Elicited oral translation	Verb-raising ± grammaticality ± inversion	Within-subject correlations Reaction time and grouping by translation performance

Salaberry and López-Ortega (1998)	Spanish	English	74	Cloze completion text Multiple choice completion Written narrative from picture stimulus	Cross-task performance ± communicative pressure Attention to form Articles, pro-drop, aspect	Between-groups comparisons Accuracy
Moyer (1999)	German	English	24	Reading: word lists, sentences, paragraph text Topical conversation	Motivation effects on high-level pronunciation	Rating of nativeness, confidence of judge
Bongaerts (1999) [3 studies]	English English French	Dutch Dutch Dutch	22 21 27	Reading aloud: sentences, words Personal narratives	Pronunciation: high- vs. low-proficiency learners, age of acquisition	Accent ratings Comparability with native speaker ratings
Ju (2000)	English	Chinese	31	Preference for active/passive setence	Active/passive Lexical (± transitive) Cognitive effects (± external) + Context	Error rate within-group
EI:						
Grigg (1986)	English	Various	18	EI ± stimulus repetition Dictation, grammar correction, rule statement	Plural -S, article Relative pronoun marker	Within-subject correlations Mean accuracy
Munnich et al. (1994)	English	Japanese	12	EI oral vs. taped GJT: oral vs. taped	Relative clause structure ± Grammatical	Within-subject correlations Accuracy, error analysis

Table 22.5 (*cont'd*)

	Languages					
Study	*Target*	*L1*	*N*	*Procedures used*	*Topic focus*	*Design analysis*
Yang and Givón (1997)	Keki (artificial)	English	29	Word recognition Lexical decision-priming Word translation EI ("recall") ± delay GJT, Picture description Narrative translation and comprehension	Simplified (pidgin) vs. grammatical input	Longitudinal accuracy Reaction time Lexical/grammar recall
Ortega (2000)	Spanish	English	16	EI, GJT Spanish simulated oral proficiency interview Compositions	Cross-task comparisons SLA measures Syntactic/lexical complexity	Longitudinal (pre-test/post-test) Accuracy, ratings
Metalinguistic tasks (GJT, magnitude estimation):						
White (1986)	English	Spanish/ Italian	34	Sentence transformation (questions from statements)	Pro-drop ± grammaticality: VS word order, subject pronoun omission *Wh*-extraction	Between-group comparisons Accuracy
		French	37	GJT		
Bley-Vroman, Felix, and Ioup (1988)	English	Korean	92	GJT	*Wh*-movement: ± grammaticality	Group % accuracy Consistency within-subject
Robinson (1994)	Samoan	English	29	GJT	Noun incorporation ± Grammaticality Empty category principle	Within-subject correlations Reaction time, Accuracy, certainty

Yuan (1995)	Chinese	English	102	GJT with magnitude estimation	Proficiency level Base-generated topics ± Gapped NPs	Between-group comparisons Accuracy
Yuan (1997)	English	Chinese	159	GJT with magnitude estimation Animacy	Proficiency level Null subjects and objects	Between-group comparisons Accuracy
Mandell (1999)	Spanish	English	91	GJT Sentence construction ("dehydrated" sentences)	Proficiency, S-V inversion ± *Wh*-questions Adverb placement	Between-group comparisons Accuracy
Complex tasks (paired comparisons, rule statement, editing):						
White (1989)	English French	French English	95 151	GJT (paced, scaled) GJT (multiple choice) Sentence comparisons (preference)	Proficiency/age levels Adjacency (adverb placement)	Between-group comparisons Accuracy Cross-task comparisons
Liceras (1989)	Spanish	French English	32 30	GJT Correction Translation	Proficiency Pro-drop parameter: inversion, that-trace, complementizer	Cross-sentence type Between-group comparisons
Alanen (1995)	Finnish	English	36	Sentence completion Comprehension test Word translation GJT with correction or explanation Rule statement Think-aloud	Input enhancement Rule presentation Locative suffixes Consonant alternation	Between-group comparisons Pre-test/post-test

Note: ANOVA = analysis of variance; EI = elicited imitation; GJT = grammaticality judgment task; L1 = first language; N = number of subjects; NP = noun phrase; S = subject; V = verb; VP = verb phrase.

understanding the psychological processes of language acquisition, these measures do not provide direct information about learners' L2 development. Second, we separate the procedures here from various *analytical measures of performance* that might be associated with them (see Norris and Ortega, this volume). Aside from more detailed linguistic analyses, many of these procedures are typically assessed with respect to normative *accuracy*, or speed of access and degree of neurological activity in responses (*reaction time*, as in Robinson and Ha, 1993, and *event-related potentials – ERP*), and, depending on the particular measure, different results may ensue, but how these measures are applied will not be our main concern here.[5]

Finally, as in any experimental design and methodology, there are many *conditions* for the elicitation, such as those described previously for communicative task dimensions (e.g., time constraints, such as planning time, repetition of stimuli, aural or visual context, nature of the instructions for the task, prior learning tasks, and structuring of input). Only insofar as there have been notable effects associated with a given measure or condition when used in a procedure will we call attention to it.

4.1 Advantages and disadvantages

As Cook (1986, p. 13) put it succinctly: "Controlled data has the advantage that it yields the information we are looking for. It has the disadvantage of artificiality. . . . [T]he behaviour that is studied must correspond with something outside the laboratory if it is to have any ultimate relevance. There is, then, a continual tension between 'internal validity' . . . and 'external validity.'" Following the outline of advantages and disadvantages already seen for the previous two principal groups of data-collection methods, it should be evident here that experimental tasks are very different from naturalistic methods, but they share some of the advantages of elicited production. With respect to the four advantages noted above for elicited production – more tailored targets, more mechanical administration, a wider range of access to subjects, and ease of scoring – these most controlled tasks tend to achieve even more or better outcomes. Moreover, because of the degree of control over target forms, they alleviate one of the disadvantages of elicited production: well designed and analyzed experimental techniques should be able to determine whether target forms were avoided or not. At the same time they elicit less contextualized and less extensive L2 production, thereby also exaggerating at least two of the disadvantages of elicited production: that subjects, especially young children, may find experimental techniques too alien or off-putting, and performance will be avoided.

4.2 On-line methods/word (etc.) recognition

In first language psycholinguistic research, the use of a large number of on-line language processing procedures is very common, yet such procedures have rarely been employed in SLA research. Technologically sophisticated methods in SLA have principally been incorporated in research on L2 phonetics and phonology perception and production (see Cebrian, 2000; Hardison, 1996; Leather, 1999; Major, 1998; Watson, 1991), and especially psycholinguistic research on bilinguals (see, e.g., the special issue on bilingualism in *Language and Cognition*, 4 (1), 2001; De Bot et al., 1995; De Groot and Kroll, 1997; Schreuder and Weltens, 1993; Weber-Fox and Neville, 1999). The greater availability of computer hardware and software for such research is now allowing more researchers to conduct experiments in speech processing and memory, but many of the L1 methods and procedures described in McKee (1996), such as on-line search and cross-modal priming, have not been widely adopted in the SLA literature.

An early example of *word recognition* (signal detection) in a Spanish L2 and English L1 lexical search task is Meara's (1986) study of learners' progress (determined by reaction time in recognition) over time in acquiring lexis during an instructional program. As an example of *morphological* recognition, Leow (1993) used a multiple choice (M/C) recognition question to assess whether learners in a ± simplified input contrast had recognized either the present perfect or present subjunctive L2 Spanish forms in a reading passage. Recently, Yang and Givón (1997) used word recognition and lexical decision priming to assess learners' acquisition of an artificial language taught via both simplified and normal input procedures.

Juffs and Harrington (1995, 1996) conducted an on-line processing study of *wh*-extraction and Garden Path sentences presented by computer, with both accuracy and reaction time as dependent measures. The target decision for Chinese learners of English was whether or not sentence strings were grammatical ("possible/impossible"), but Juffs and Harrington compared learners' decisions both after reading the sentences as whole sentences, and after being presented the sentences in a "moving window" mode (see Just and Carpenter, 1987; Rayner, 1983), a word-by-word presentation according to the subjects' own pace of reading. The researchers then assessed reading times through the key grammatical segments, as well as decision times on their judgments. (See also Hoover and Dwivedi's, 1998, study of advanced French learners' window-paced reading of causative sentences.)

4.3 Decision tasks: sentence matching, verification, discrimination

It is likely that the largest number of researchers in SLA experimental studies have employed some variant of *decision tasks*, in which subjects are instructed to make some decision among options (categories, pictures, sentences, multiple choices, preferences for appropriateness, referents, and so on). A basic on-line task, for example, is that of *sentence-matching* (proposed for L2 by Bley-Vroman and Masterson, 1989; see also Eubank, 1993), which involves a time-controlled presentation of two sentences (simultaneously or in sequence), with the subject having to decide whether the two are the same or different. Analyses are based on the reaction time to decide on matching ("same") sentences, so that eventual contrasts are made only for the grammaticality differences between whatever syntactic phenomena are studied. For example, Beck (1998) used such a procedure to test German L2 verb-raising. For this, however, because she predicted a developmental effect dependent on subjects' knowledge of German agreement and S-V inversion rules, she used scores on an *elicited translation* task to group subjects developmentally. Some SLA researchers have made use of a *preference choice* on pairs of sentences (a form of *discrimination* – and also *metalinguistic judgment* – see below) illustrating target features in order to elicit (receptive) comparative judgments of learners' developing sensitivity. This procedure avoids forcing learners to make absolute judgments (of, say, grammaticality), because in many cases, it is the relative contrast between items that is of interest, rather than a judgment of them one at a time on an absolute scale. Trahey and White (1993), White (1989), and White, Spada, Lightbown, and Ranta (1991), for instance, used this task to elicit French (and English FSL in White, 1989) learners' ratings of ESL target sentences involving adjacency conditions (in adverb placement), and question formation. Lakshmanan and Teranishi (1994) used the task to elicit judgments on reflexive binding in L2 English, and Duffield and White (1999) used it in combination with grammaticality judgments to assess L2 knowledge of Spanish clitic placement.

Probably the most common passive/receptive form of experimental decision task is the *M/C response selection* (among picture options, responses to questions, categorical choices, etc.). This is illustrated in many studies exploring the Competition Model of language learning/processing (cf. Gass, 1987; MacWhinney, 1987, 1997; cross-linguistic and L2 studies in *Applied Psycholinguistics*, 8 (3); and MacWhinney and Bates, 1989). In the most frequent application of this paradigm in L2 studies, where word order preferences (e.g., SVO vs. VSO), case markings, and animacy preferences differ across the typologically distinct languages, simple lexical combinations of grammatical cues and word orders are presented aurally to learners, who are to respond by selecting the actor or subject of the "sentences." Ungrammatical strings are also used to force learners to demonstrate their preferences for specific cues, and learner proficiency level is typically included as an independent variable. Examples of this procedure are Harrington (1987), with Japanese L1 learners of English; Kempe and MacWhinney (1998), with Russian and German L2; Rounds and Kanagy (1998), with child L2 immersion learners of Japanese; Y. Sasaki (1994), with adult English L1 learners of Japanese; and Su (2001), with both English and Chinese L1 learners of the other group's language. These studies lend themselves especially to comparisons between native speaker and learner performance in the source and target languages, as the contrasting high and low percentages of choice of "first noun" as agent/subject reveals the degree of interpretation based on processing strategies derived from the L1, L2, or the learner's interlanguage. Kempe and MacWhinney (1998) provide a very detailed accounting of the quantitative analysis that is possible with both the proportion of first noun choices and reaction time measures.

Other examples of (M/C) response selection (often by way of a picture choice) are choice of referent or definition for lexical items (Ellis and He, 1999; Rott, 1999); phrasal verbs (Laufer and Eliasson, 1993); anaphora (and reflexives – Eckman, 1994); reflexives (Matsumura, 1994; Thomas, 1992); object pronouns (DeKeyser and Sokalski, 1996; VanPatten and Oikkenon, 1996); phrasal prosody (Harley, Howard, and Hart, 1995); verb tense/aspect (Salaberry, 1998; Salaberry and López-Ortega, 1998); and NP/VP attachment (Ying, 1996). Some researchers present lengthier response alternatives, such as Tanaka and Kawade (1982) with politeness strategies, Ju (2000) with active/passive sentences, and Helms-Park (2001) with description of causative situations.

4.4 *Reading aloud, utterance completion, elicited productions*

A further wide range of tasks has been employed in SLA experiments that prompts learners to produce forms in a more active and sometimes extended fashion. These tasks include *reading aloud* tasks to assess all levels of speech production, but particularly phonological and lexical abilities; *utterance completion* to assess syntactic and lexical competences; and other *elicited production* (from picture stimuli, questions, or other prompts) with constrained options, but which allow for free access to the learners' knowledge base and more extended speech routines. Some of the earliest SLA research typically adopted such procedures from L1 research, as in the case of d'Anglejan and Tucker's (1975) use of Chomsky's (1969) research methods on questions about infinitive complements, with and without *picture choice,* and Fathman's (1975) use of Berko's (1958) type of materials for *picture prompts* for morphology and syntax. Recent examples of these are *text, sentence,* and/or *word list reading* for phonological/lexical evaluation (Bongaerts et al., 1997; Flege et al., 1998; Major and Faudree, 1996; Moyer, 1999; Riney and Flege, 1998) and syntactic speed of access to French L2 syntax (Hoover and Dwivedi, 1998); *sentence completion* or *blank filling (cloze)* prompting French aspect (Harley, 1989);[6] phrasal verbs (Laufer and Eliasson, 1993); Spanish conditionals and object pronouns (DeKeyser and Sokalski, 1996); instrument attachments to either NPs or VPs in ambiguous sentences (Ying, 1996); *picture cued descriptions* (with occasional verbal prompt) eliciting lexical items (Snodgrass, 1993); head NPs of relatives or *wh*-questions (Wolfe-Quintero, 1992); English *adverb placement* (Trahey and White, 1993); Spanish clitic objects (VanPatten and Cadierno, 1993; VanPatten and Oikkenon, 1996); causatives (Helms-Park, 2001); and past hypothetical conditionals (Izumi, et al., 1999).

4.5 *Elicited imitation*

Elicited imitation (EI) is a special sort of elicited production that has gained considerable research attention since its early use in the child language research of the 1960s (Fraser, Bellugi, and Brown, 1963; Slobin and Welsh, 1973; see

Bernstein Ratner, 2000, and Lust, Flynn, and Foley 1996, for reviews of L1 research; see J. Schumann, 1978, and Swain et al., 1974, for early L2 research; and see Bley-Vroman and Chaudron, 1994, for review of L2 research). The procedure involves preparing a stimulus string (usually a sentence, although lower- or higher-order texts have been used to control length and discourse context) that illustrates some grammatical feature (only occasionally has phonology been studied in this fashion), and subjects are instructed to repeat exactly what they hear. The assumption of the procedure is that success at exact imitation demonstrates the subject's possession of the grammatical (or lexical, etc.) feature in her or his knowledge store, unless the stimulus is too short and thereby allows for echoic repetition. Failure to repeat exactly, and any modifications or transformations of the stimulus, can be taken to represent the limits or other representations of the subject's grammatical competence. Thus, the procedure, being apparently relatively simple to prepare, can be used to elicit potentially a very wide range of target structures. Both grammatical and ungrammatical structures can also be tested with the method (e.g., Masterson, 1992), in order to detect greater subject difficulty or ability to reconstruct grammatical forms.

There have been numerous applications of this technique in L2 research: Grigg (1986) used a single and a repeated stimulus to elicit ESL morphology for comparisons with other measures; Flynn (1987) compared ESL imitation of various structures with L1 Spanish and Japanese adults; Verhoeven (1994) elicited L2 Dutch and L1 Turkish sentence imitations in bilingual children in order to establish their bilinguality; Munnich et al. (1994) compared different procedures to elicit repetitions with grammaticality judgments on relative clause structures; Scott (1994) compared Spanish L2 EI performance with other auditory and fluency measures in order to differentiate age differences among learners; Yang and Givón (1997) employed EI to test learning of their artificial Keki language; Roebuck, Martínez-Arbelaiz, and Pérez-Silva (1999) provide their elicitation stimuli in a study of English L2 complementizer phrase production ("filled CP") by Spanish and Chinese L1 speakers; and Ortega (2000) evaluated Spanish L2 EI as a pre- and post-instructional period measure of SLA change. Chaudron (forthcoming) reviews this L1 and L2 research in detail.

4.6 *Elicited translation*

An alternative manner in which to attempt to constrain the elicitation of specific target structures is to use *translation* sentences. An early use of translation was the study by Perkins and Larsen-Freeman (1975) for Spanish L1 to English L2 morpheme production. Among various measures for eliciting L2 production of Arabic from their near-native learner, Ioup et al. (1994) used an English-to-Arabic translation of selected syntactic structures. Other researchers include Snodgrass (1993), who used *word translation* in comparison with *picture naming*; de Graaff (1997), who used this technique among his measures of learning from instruction in the artificial language eXperanto; and similarly, Yang and

Givón (1997) employed an L2-to-L1 translation task for both words and an entire narrative (sentence by sentence). Beck (1998) used a translation task as a grouping (developmental stage) variable when analyzing her results for sentence-matching in L2 German, and Pérez-Leroux and Glass (1999) used *sentence translation* following picture stories to elicit L2 Spanish ± anaphora. See Malakoff and Hakuta (1991) for a discussion of the role of metalinguistic skill in translation, where they found that translation skills were distinct from source or target language proficiency in helping to predict translation accuracy for words and sentences.

4.7 Word (paired) association, and lexical assessment

A wide range of measures of vocabulary knowledge has been employed in SLA research, following the extensive research of this nature in the L1 psycholinguistic literature (see De Groot and Keijzer, 2000; Kroll and De Groot, 1997; P. Nation, 2001; Smith, 1997; and the special issue of *SSLA*, 21 (2), 1999, on vocabulary acquisition). Wolter (2001), for example, illustrates a number of approaches to assessing word knowledge in bilinguals via *word association* and depth of knowledge (cf. Wesche and Paribakht, 1996); Schmitt and Meara (1997) assess word knowledge via both receptive and productive measures of Japanese L1 learners' knowledge of English suffixation; and Scarcella and Zimmerman (1998) use a knowledge/familiarity rating to determine learners' knowledge of academic vocabulary.

4.8 Discrete-point tests

It is natural that many SLA researchers would employ tests with discrete-point assessment of knowledge of particular target forms, for these are easier to develop and standardize. This overview cannot, however, begin to examine the extensive number of tests and test batteries that have been developed and applied to such purposes, as such a review belongs broadly to the domain of language testing. Such tests do fortunately tend to be subjected to more rigorous analytical procedures than many of the measures described thus far, with respect to their reliability and validity.

4.9 Sentence manipulation (combining, transformation)

A number of researchers have employed *sentence manipulation (combining, transforming)* tasks, which frequently resemble the typical sort of classroom construction exercise used to guide learners in creating interclausal links, anaphora, and many other targets. Such tasks have been used to elicit learners' production of relative clauses, by providing two separate clauses which are to be combined into one (see Doughty, 1991; Eckman, Bell, and Nelson, 1988; Gass, 1980; Hamilton, 1994), and adverb placement, for example, has also been a target (Trahey and White, 1993). Doughty (1991) also elicited similar relative clauses with a more constrained *sentence completion* task in which a portion of the targeted structure was used as a prompt to elicit the embedded relative clause.

4.10 Act-out

One method that has been very widely employed in child L1 acquisition research but very rarely in SLA research is the *act-out* task (see Goodluck, 1996). This method for assessing comprehension has been used with children primarily because of their lower capacity in productive language relative to receptive abilities, but also because it can more accurately assess matters relative to anaphora, missing subject or object constructions, relative clauses, passives, or *that*-trace in *wh*-questions. SLA researchers, however, have not widely availed themselves of such a measure, with the exception of Flynn (1987), who conducted research on anaphora in comprehension, and recently Finney (1997), who assessed various factors that influence the interpretation of gaps and referents in purpose clauses ("[in order] to" clauses). Flynn (1987), for instance, used sentences with temporal relations and physical movements expressed via main and adverbial subordinate clauses, in order to determine which referents subjects were interpreting for pronouns occurring in either the main or subordinate clause. Learners' actions with objects named in the sentences demonstrated their choice, whereas EI productions of similar sentences could not provide any such indication of contextualized interpretation.

4.11 Metalinguistic knowledge tasks

A final major group of elicitation techniques can be treated together as involving the expression, application, or invoking of learners' "metalinguistic knowledge." That is, instead of direct elicitations of language produced or interpreted, learners are presented with linguistic stimuli, in reaction to which they must make other active decisions, ratings, comparisons, and revisions about the form or meaning of the stimuli. We have seen one variant of this method in the simple "preference" decision task, which does invoke a judgment of acceptability or "correctness." Others include: grammaticality judgments, ratings, paired comparisons and card sorting, rule expression and definitions, and editing and correcting. These procedures have been widely used in the SLA research, particularly because adult learners are thought to be more readily able to carry out the often more complex tasks and decisions involved. As proposed by Bialystok and Ryan (1985), several of these tasks might be viewed as falling on a continuum of increasing use of "analyzed knowledge," from grammaticality judgments to locating ungrammaticality, to correcting ungrammaticality, then explaining ungrammaticality, and stating a rule that is violated. Ellis (1991) employs this notion in a table (p. 163) which suggests the differential nature of the possible responses for each type of metalinguistic operation, mainly in terms of the extent of verbalization of judgment – from "discrimination" of well-formedness, to "location," then "correction," then "description" of errors. These features thus can be used to differentiate (i) intuitive from analytical responses, (ii) non-verbalizable from verbalizable knowledge, and (iii) recognition from production.

The most familiar and widely used form of metalinguistic knowledge elicitation is the *grammaticality judgment test (GJT)*, which was adopted by theoretical linguists in the 1960s and afterwards as a standard, albeit solitary and individualized, assessment of the acceptability of surface syntax (see studies in Greenbaum, 1977; J. Ross, 1979; a review by McDaniel and Cairns, 1996; and a complete review of this research, also L2-related, in Schütze, 1996). The second language acquisition literature was reviewed by Birdsong (1989), Chaudron (1983), Ellis (1991), and Sorace (1996); see also a mini-analysis of UG-based grammaticality studies by Zobl (1992). As in the analysis of communicative tasks (see the previous section), there are many features of GJT that can influence their effectiveness, of which Ellis (1991) mentions at least the following:

- *target items*: syntactic, lexical, phonological;
- *order of presentation*: ± randomized;
- *distractors*: ± other target structures;[7]
- *medium of presentation*: written/aural;
- *complexity*: controlled or not;
- *contextualized*: in discourse or not;
- *nature of response*: binary, multiple choice, preference, ranking;
- *immediacy of response;*
- *timed response;*
- *familiarization with task requirements.*

Under "familiarization," one would note factors such as training and task instructions, not to mention inter-subject differences in their interpretation of the notions "grammaticality," "acceptability," "correctness," and so on. See the discussion of the acceptable/grammatical contrast in Birdsong (1989), Chaudron (1983), Gass (1994), and Sorace (1996), as well as the very helpful provision of their complete instructions and test items in Bley-Vroman et al. (1998).

With respect especially to the nature of the response, the scale or options used have varied considerably across studies. As Gass (1994) demonstrates, the differences in response format can lead to differences in the interpretation of findings.[8] In order to enhance the sensitivity of grammaticality judgments, researchers have tended to avoid singular or dichotomous decisions. Nonetheless, researchers such as Munnich et al. (1994, p. 231) state that they only "recorded whether or not [the subject] believed the sentence to be grammatical," while most researchers elicit other actions or decisions: for example, Gass (1979, 1980) asked subjects to correct ungrammatical sentences; Lightbown,

Spada, and Wallace (1980) had them label sentences as "C[orrect]," or provide error *corrections* of them if they were judged not correct; and a similar correction-only procedure was used by Liceras (1985). These researchers favor at least three-point decisions to allow for a "not sure"/"I don't know" choice, which is sometimes: (i) counted categorically, occasionally with a correction procedure in order to verify the subjects' attention to and conception of the source of error[9] (Ellis, 1991; Mandell, 1999; Seliger, 1989; Towell, et al., 1993; White, 1986); (ii) considered as "incorrect" (Bley-Vroman et al., 1988); (iii) eliminated from analysis (Felix and Weigl, 1991; Shirai and Kurono, 1998, who had subjects judge each one from among four possible responses using Japanese L2 tense and aspect – a multiple-choice procedure also adopted by White, 1989); (iv) viewed as correct (Coppetiers, 1987); or (v) counted independently as a measure of certainty of response (Robinson, 1994). For the most part, indications of uncertainty in these studies have been limited to less than 3 percent of the responses (but as high as 29 percent in Robinson's study), so that researchers have been confident in ignoring such responses. Likert scale ratings of four or more, and up to even ten points (Gass, 1994; Inagaki, 1997; Papp, 2000; Schachter and Yip, 1990; Wang and Lee, 1999), have been used more in recent years, and White (1989) employed an unscaled line with ± correct polarity, on which subjects were to place a stroke wherever they preferred.

An alternative to a judgment on each sentence, that is, *preference comparisons* between pairs of sentences, was used in early studies, as already mentioned (e.g., studies by White and her colleagues). This procedure, which is a variation on the psychometric method of *paired comparisons* (Edwards, 1957; B. Green, 1954) has been used partly in order to avoid forcing absolute judgments, which researchers have suspected of being less reliable, as different subjects may use very different standards, but also because in many cases, the point of comparison is to determine subjects' *relative* sensitivity to variant structures of the same sort, and within-subject reliability can be increased thereby. These are among Sorace's (1996) arguments in favor of various mechanisms for rank ordering of L2 stimuli by learners. See Chaudron's (1985a) application of paired comparisons to ranking of the comprehensibility of a range of topic reinstatement devices, as well as Mohan (1977) and Walters (1979). This method can be expanded to include more than just pairs of items. The principle of ranking or rating a group of items with respect to some criterion was used, for instance, by Carrell and Konneker (1981) for judgments of politeness, White (1989) for a correctness decision/ranking of four adjacency condition sentences, and Cowan and Hatasa (1994) for sets of four similar grammatical Japanese relative clause sentences to be ranked with respect to their difficulty (targeting complexity of relatives).

Several other procedures have made use of learners' metalinguistic judgments. An interesting one, which has not been used (to my knowledge) since its early applications by Kellerman (1978) and Carrell and Konneker (1981), is *card sorting* (or "Q-sort"; see Miller, 1969), or a type of scaling/grouping according to judgments of same/different. In order to determine learners' perception of the literal or figurative meanings of English L2 "break," Kellerman had subjects place sentences using "break" in a number of its meanings into distinct groups or piles. Just as with paired comparisons, accumulation of the responses of a number of subjects allows for a pooled rank order of preferences and clusters in perceptions about meaning (in this case – see research on cluster analysis, such as Skehan, 1986). A second method is *magnitude scaling* or *estimation*, a technique derived from psychophysical research traditions, which allows subjects to set their own standard or scale for comparing judgments (see Bard, Robertson, and Sorace, 1996, on L1 acceptability judgments evaluated using magnitude scaling, as well as Sorace, 1990, 1996). Yuan (1995, 1997), for instance, used magnitude estimation in eliciting subjects' "acceptability" judgments on Chinese topic structure by English-speaking learners of Chinese L2, and on English (ungrammatical and grammatical) ± subject or object constructions by Chinese-speaking learners of L2 English. In this procedure, subjects are presented sentences, as in a GJT, but they are asked to create their own value for the degree of acceptability of the first sentence. Then, for each successive sentence, they provide a value relative to the first that represents their judgment. Subjects' scores must then be standardized in order to carry out further analysis, but this procedure is deemed to provide a more sensitive within-subject (and comparative) measure of learners' perceptions and intuitions. Recently, Gass et al. (1999) used magnitude estimation for Spanish native-speaker raters' evaluations of L2 Spanish learners' film-retelling narratives, and Dube (2000) provides the instructions for a magnitude estimation study of Zulu L2 acquisition by learners of a large range of proficiency levels, as measured by a (apparently general) cloze test.

A third method, and arguably the one that accesses the highest level of metalinguistic knowledge, consists of procedures that elicit learners' expression of grammatical or other rule knowledge, vocabulary definitions (e.g., Snow, Cancino, de Temple, and Schley, 1991), or other verbalized intuitions about (e.g., pragmatic) acceptability (see also Ellis's 1991 analysis of learners' think-aloud reports about the strategies and deliberations they went through when making grammaticality judgments). An early study that compared such rule expression with other tasks (elicited imitation, dictation, and grammar correction) was that of Grigg (1986), who asked ESL learners to write out the rules for the phonology of plural *-s*, articles, and relative pronouns ("who," "which," "that"). He evaluated the adequacy of their responses according to a fixed target description, using a 10-point scale. A larger-scale study by P. Green and Hecht (1992) had young German learners of English express the rules for certain grammatical errors of morphology and syntax, while correcting them, as well. The students evaluated the relationship between rule knowledge and ability, in comparison with native English-speaking school children. Green and Hecht provide a description of their scheme for counting various types of rule descriptions, but they do not discriminate among them in any scaled way, with only a binary "correct/incorrect" score calculated.

One of several dependent measures used by Alanen (1995) was rule descriptions for two types of rules in L2 Finnish, as she compared four experimental groups receiving various sorts of input to process. Two of her groups were also given the Finnish rules, so that she could immediately determine the extent of learning of the rules. Her simultaneous elicitation of grammaticality judgments with explanations and think-aloud protocols allowed her to triangulate subjects' extent of awareness of rules with their performance. A similar comparison of rule description and think-aloud protocol analysis allowed Rosa and O'Neill (1999) to assess the degree of noticing or awareness of L2 Spanish learners related to their learning achievement.

5 Reliability and Validity

5.1 *Reliability*

Although researchers should ultimately be concerned about the validity of their data and conclusions, the reliability of the data-collection procedure or instrument needs to be determined first. In most of the studies involving the measures discussed above, the researchers failed to establish one or more of the following: inter-rater reliability, "test–retest" reliability, or internal consistency reliability; or to apply other such measures traditionally used in the domain of psychometrics (for standard psychometric measures, see, e.g., Bachman, 1990, ch. 6; also see Chaudron, Crookes, and Long, 1988, regarding observational and linguistic coding judgments; and see Norris and Ortega, this volume). In the case of naturalistic observations, for example, most researchers state that their transcriptions were verified by at least one other researcher, but as is typical in linguistic analysis of this sort, quantitative (inter-rater) reliability measures have generally not been reported, and regrettably, there is little mention in these studies of concerns over the issue. Similarly, and somewhat surprisingly, data collected even in most of the more experimental studies have not frequently been assessed for internal consistency or other measures of reliability. Most researchers using forms of elicited production appear to take it as given that the linguistically focused analyses they conduct on the data elicited by their instruments are inherently reliable, and that the researcher, or a pair or team of researchers in consultation with one another, is or are competent to judge reliability without submitting their analyses to objective or independent comparison. It is true, in fact, that many of the results obtained using such instruments involve relatively low-inference structures. So concern for validity and reliability tends only to appear in L2 research using more experimental tasks, in particular procedures such as standardized tests. In contrast, as perusal of virtually any journal will demonstrate, researchers in child L1 acquisition, and especially in language impairment studies, adopt more rigorous measures of reliability and validity for many linguistically oriented analyses (e.g., Bucks, Singh, Cuerden, and Wilcock, 2000; Damico, Oller, and Tetnowski, 1999; Fenson et al., 2000).

5.2 *Validity*

Assuming reliable measurement, learner data elicited by any of the above procedures may be valid information on SLA, depending on the degree of conformity and consistency of such data with one or more of the following (see Norris and Ortega, this volume, for specific discussion of forms of validation in SLA research):

i Theoretical proposals (*prediction*): researchers investigate underlying linguistic and developmental phenomena in search of differences in performance among learners, so that outcomes that confirm their predictions tend to "validate" their theories, but at the same time confirm that the measures used are effective, and thus "valid." This occurs whether the predictions arise out of comparative linguistic analyses, or assumptions about differences among learners based on proficiency levels, learning experiments, or development over time via maturation. (See, however, the cautions expressed by Thomas, 1994, concerning the lack of use of proficiency measures in L2 research.)

ii Comparable data from other studies of a similar nature (*replication*, in the case of intentional retesting of a prior finding, or *convergence*, if two researchers happen to have carried out comparable studies): to the extent that outcomes on the same or related measures with respect to similar target features point consistently to the same fundamental conclusion, those measures may be judged valid.

iii Simultaneous measures within a study using other techniques (*triangulation*): only slight differences in outcomes on different tasks can frequently accentuate the consistency of predictions of learner production; on the other hand, if specific dimensions on which the techniques are expected to differ result in distinct outcomes, the limits of generalizability of the methods can be determined (a form of validation).

5.3 *Theoretical predictions*

As an example of comparability of data across naturalistic studies (not strictly *replication*, as the researchers have operated independently of one another), Meisel (1994a), Paradis and Genesee (1996), Schlyter (1993), and Swain and Wesche (1973) are all concerned with the appearance of comparable structural constraints on the acquisition of the children's two languages. On the whole, they arrive at similar findings with respect to a natural sequence of acquisition according to L1 norms of at least the stronger of the children's languages, but there is evidence of greater variability, non-L1 type errors, and failure to attain structural differentiation in the weaker of the children's languages, even when linguistic developmental level is controlled (mean length of utterance in Schlyter, 1993). Similarly, Meisel (1994a) and Swain and Wesche (1973) both find language mixing (especially of lexical items) occurring early in development, but code switching begins to be constrained by structural factors once functional categories such as agreement and tense appear. Also, apart from some degree of early use of one language's lexis within the other's syntax (as also in Swain and Wesche, 1973), Paradis and Genesee's (1996) data illustrate that neither of the two simultaneously acquired (and more equally balanced) languages has either a strong negative or a facilitating influence on the syntactic development of the other, as each one follows an L1 developmental sequence. Likewise, Polio (1995) and Jin (1994), independently investigating, among other targets, evidence for zero pronoun production by L2 Chinese learners doing story-retelling, found no evidence in speech by beginning learners, regardless of whether the L1 of the subjects was a subject- or a topic-prominent language (Polio's subjects were both Japanese and English speakers). Finally, as already noted in the section on elicited production, the feature of +planning, as an aspect of communicative task design, had proved to result in consistent findings using various tasks and measures across studies.

Many studies involve theoretical predictions of L2-influenced performance as shown by comparison with data from native speakers. For example, in their on-line sentence-reading task, Juffs and Harrington (1995, 1996) found L2 GJT error rates for *wh*-extraction (18–40 percent) higher than L1 rates (especially problematic were *wh*-extraction of subject from infinitives); however, error rates were lower and closer to NS performance on garden path sentences, by which NSs also were predicted to be misled. There was a corresponding variability in response time to judgments of grammaticality relative to NS performance. Also, in reading time per word on the garden path sentences, the NNSs were slower at comparable critical points, although in a more exaggerated pattern. Likewise, among the numerous measures employed by Ioup et al. (1994) in order to distinguish their advanced NNSs of Arabic from NSs, while most measures did not clearly discriminate between them, an anaphora-interpretation task involving discourse semantics clearly distinguished Julie, their advanced subject, from NSs. Of interest here was that this was one of the few tasks which showed a weaker performance for Julie than for another advanced L2 speaker who was an instructed learner of Arabic, and who may thus have benefited from instruction in learning the relevant structures.

Very frequently, researchers who investigate the effects of instruction on acquisition will predict that a particular instructional treatment will lead to changes in L2 performance (cf. Norris and Ortega's, 2000, review of the overall effects of instruction). Although design problems may lead to questionable results, and some instruction fails to achieve an effect, numerous tasks have been successful in detecting the effects of instruction. Many of the studies by White and her colleagues (e.g., Trahey and White, 1993; White, 1991; White, Spada, Lightbown, and Ranta, 1991), have measured the effects of theoretically motivated instruction with sentence-comparison preference tasks, picture descriptions or responses, judgment tasks, and others. In most of these, clear effects of instruction (on question formation and adverb order) have been revealed. For instance, Trahey and White (1993) showed subjects' sensitivity to training or input on the target form (adverb order in L2 English), with a differential effect between the training and control groups on most measures, according to predictions of the value of negative input for French L1 learners to unlearn incorrect SAV order. Of interest was their finding that the preference task was sensitive to the learning effects of explicit training on English adverb order, while it was not as sensitive in distinguishing between their control training groups (question formation and input flood). Trahey (1996) further shows that these results endure over a full year's time. Other training studies, such as Rosa and O'Neill's (1999) comparison of formal instruction and rule-search procedures in the acquisition of Spanish L2 past hypotheticals, and Alanen's (1995) study of explicit rule presentation and input enhancement with Finnish L2 locative morphology, found positive effects on a variety of measures: multiple-choice recognition selection of the correct verb form in the former, and rule statements and sentence completion in the latter.[10] And DeKeyser (1997) showed that comprehension and production training in an artificial language, as measured by multiple-choice and metalinguistic tests of the same modality format, resulted in linear improvement in reaction time, but that "students with comprehension practice only . . . improve more in comprehension skills than students with production practice only and vice versa, whereas students with an equal amount of practice in both skills . . . perform at an intermediate level in both skills" (p. 213).

Another type of prediction of effects on tasks is that they would be sensitive to basic differences in subjects' level of proficiency (as determined by external factors, such as amount of prior instruction or natural developmental growth – correlations between proficiency measures and tasks will be addressed in a later section). For example, Salaberry and López-Ortega (1998) compared two (placement) levels of L2 Spanish learners' abilities on several measures of article and subject pronoun use, and aspect: multiple-choice sentence completion, open-ended fill-in-the-blank, and a written narration based on a picture stimulus. They report all measures as being sensitive to the increased level of proficiency, with the fill-in-the-blank task, being the more difficult task, showing the greatest sensitivity. Similarly, among a number of elicited production and experimental tasks employed by Ortega (2000) to assess theoretically expected developmental changes in complexity and accuracy in the course of a semester of advanced L2 Spanish – student journal writing, academic paper writing, written and oral picture narratives, as well as GJT and elicited imitation – the oral narratives showed consistent change in complexity, while the GJT and EI showed significant improvement in accuracy.[11]

5.4 *Replication*

It will be recalled that there were convergent findings by both Rintell and Mitchell (1989) and M. Sasaki (1998) in which role plays were superior to DCTs in their elicitation of more complex speech act behavior, and a finding also by Kormos (1999) with respect to learners' greater conversational competence in a guided role play compared to an interviewer conducting a guided interview (a general finding against OPI-type procedures). Such findings justify other researchers' efforts to employ role plays as a more sensitive measure of speech acts. Another method that has been found to produce similar results across tasks is EI, or sentence repetition, in particular when the stimulus is repeated or there is a delay prior to the prompt to repeat. Among his several measures, Grigg (1986) employed two different versions of the EI task, one with the stimuli repeated twice. These intercorrelated highly ($r = .76$), and both correlated with a dictation task (.68), but while the EI task with one repetition of the stimulus showed little relation to his grammar rule knowledge task ($r = .19$), the EI task with a repetition, and thus more adequate time for responding, correlated significantly with the rule knowledge task ($r = .51$, $p < .05$). Just as in the L1 study by McDade, Simpson, and Lamb (1982), which assessed the effects of a delay before repeating, the implication is that, with time to process the stimuli, L2 subjects will best be able to call upon their rule-based competence in production. A different experimental adjustment with much the same conclusion was used by Yang and Givón (1997), who injected a distracter task for 15 seconds, so that subjects who were better able to process the grammatical and lexical information in the stimuli proved more successful in eventual repetition: the delay resulted in a better discrimination of ability between their training groups than the immediate repetition. The authors caution, however, that "these findings suggest that elicited sentence recall may not be a valid measure of grammatical competence for aspects of grammar that are subject to surface information loss" (p. 186), such as morphological or phonological information.

5.5 *Triangulation*

The final major means by which researchers can validate the findings of their elicitation measures is by confirming that their results are consistent across different intra-study and intra-subject tasks. Yang and Givón (1997), for instance, who used a large number of measures to attempt to discriminate between their full-instruction vs. simplified ("pidgin") input of an artificial language, found most measures discriminating consistently between the treatments, although vocabulary measures did so less, since the input in the two treatments was virtually the same. Likewise, almost all of Alanen's various measures tended to discriminate in favor of the rule-based over the non-rule-based treatments.

Among naturalistic examples of intra-subject, cross-task validation are Schmidt and Frota's (1986) comparison of data from Schmidt's self-observations with those elicited in their conversations, and Tomiyama's (2000) use of other elicitation measures for the purpose of triangulation. In the former, discrepancies between observations of his awareness and his productions led, in particular, to Schmidt's theorizing on the importance of conscious awareness and attention in learning (cf. Schmidt, 1995b). In Tomiyama's study, there was concurrence in the findings based on objective measures of differential rates of attrition in syntax and lexis and those based on the subject's spontaneous speech. In the same way, Rosa and O'Neill (1999) compared groups who explicitly mentioned rules for L2 Spanish contrary-to-fact conditionals, and were able to formulate them, with those who did not, and the rule formulators were significantly better in performance.

Very many comparisons between different tasks demonstrate that some may be more sensitive relative to other criterion performances, and these differences are important in order for future researchers to exploit particular differences in elicitation procedures. For example, Helms-Park (2001) used picture production and multiple-choice picture selection (comprehension) tasks to investigate English L2 causative acquisition by Vietnamese and Hindi-Urdu learners. She found the subjects to perform similarly on production, but they were distinguished according to L1 transfer predictions on the comprehension measure, with some effects revealed by level of proficiency. Similarly, Flanigan's (1995) study of relative clause structure showed weaker success on production than comprehension, and the more difficult production measure revealed a predicted order of OS-OO-SS-SO, while the easier comprehension task did not. Flanigan also noted a significant correlation between scores on the Bilingual Syntax Measure and her question-answering task.

5.6 *Grammaticality judgments and validity*

Perhaps the most widely used measure in SLA research has been the GJT, which we have already noted in comparison with other measures and predicted outcomes. Owing to its experimental and quantifiable nature, as well as the widespread application of GJT for diverse target structures, many researchers have shown concern for the absolute (i.e., theoretically distinct and predicted) and concurrent validity of this method, so we have saved a discussion of this method until the end of this section. That GJTs do exhibit concurrent (triangulated) validity has been demonstrated not only in several of the studies cited above, but, for example, in consistency between it and a (SOPI-like) Spanish Speaking Test ($r = .87$; Ortega, 2000), on-task performance in dative movement training (S. Carroll and Swain, 1993), introspective evidence (R. Nation and McLaughlin, 1986), a paragraph story-task (White et al., 1997), "Dehydrated Sentence" reconstruction of several Spanish L2 structures (Mandell, 1999), and sentence-matching examining L2 Spanish clitic placement (Duffield and White, 1999). Also, as a matter of "predicted" performance, comparing GJTs presented with audio and written input, D. J. Johnson (1992; see also Slavoff and Johnson, 1995) found that age of onset of L2 exposure, thus earlier initiation of target language literacy, tended to favor more accurate performance on the written version.

However, GJTs have not always resulted in findings consistent with other measures (such as the comparison of picture-cued description using English hypothetical past and GJTs on the same targets, in Izumi, Bigelow, Fujiwara, and Fearnow, 1999; see early comments on discrepant results in Ellis, 1991; Gass, 1983). It is clear from much discussion on this procedure that a number of factors must be considered in interpreting results from its use.[12]

In an early review of this procedure, Chaudron (1983) found generally that there was a correspondence between GJT findings and other measures. However, Gass (1983) conducted a study on a set of English L2 learners in order to determine their ability to correct their own and peers' productions. On the basis of high variability in performance, which included inconsistent and erroneous judgments, Gass argued that learners do not progress in a natural way to improve their judgments, but instead rely on an increasing degree of analytical knowledge in order to evaluate and correct errorful target structures. Thus, if task conditions do not promote access to such knowledge, the measure may not succeed in eliciting performance comparable to subjects' other productive capacities. The question of absolute validity arises, then, of what the relationship is between performance on a GJT and underlying competence. The problem of variability in learner performance, not only in general interlanguage (IL) production, but also in access to metalinguistic knowledge, is therefore an important one for the study of the GJT as a valid measure. Sorace (1996) refers to this as "indeterminacy":

> First, native judgments themselves can be indeterminate, particularly when the objects of investigation are highly marked or very subtle syntactic properties . . . At the most basic level, [target language] constructions are indeterminate because the learners do not have any knowledge of them . . . [IL indeterminacy due to ignorance] characterizes nonnative grammars throughout the acquisition process, although it is more conspicuous at the initial and intermediate stages of IL development. At more advanced stages, constructions may become indeterminate (after a period of relative stability) because of the increased amount and sophistication of the learner's knowledge. (pp. 385–6)

Sorace then suggests "that the UG-driven specification of [SLA] core properties is narrower in scope and strength than in native grammars . . . The result is a wider periphery and consequently more room for permeability and variation" (p. 387).[13] Sorace takes this point to the extreme end of comparison between NS judgments and those of near-natives (as in Birdsong, 1992; Coppetiers, 1987; Davies and Kaplan, 1998; Ioup et al., 1994), where she notes: "near-native grammars may also be indeterminate in the same sense as native grammars . . . [which] leads to inconsistent and variable judgments" (p. 390). She uses this observation eventually to argue in favor of various mechanisms for rank ordering of L2 stimuli.

At the same time, other researchers have noted that the basis for non-native judgments of grammaticality (or acceptability) lies not strictly in linguistic knowledge, but in varying degrees of application of other sources of intuitions and cognitive operations (Birdsong, 1989; Davies and Kaplan, 1998; Ellis, 1991; Gass, 1989; Goss, Zhang, and Lantolf, 1994; Schütze, 1996; and see debate between Birdsong, 1994; and Felix and Zobl, 1994). Cowan and Hatasa (1994), for example, comment on the concurrent validity of the GJT with a scalar judgment task on a criterion measure:

> Our results indicate that no matter how delicate the scale, native speaker and L2-learner judgment data will, at best, reflect sensitivity to only some structural characteristics that affect processing, and that they will always vary with on-line data, which are far more indicative of complexity . . . processing research must employ some on-line task that elicits reaction or reading time plus some measure that provides an indication of the extent to which the stimuli used in the on-line task were comprehended. (p. 297)

Gass (1994), however, who scrutinizes the variability in reliability of judgments by learners on the Noun Phrase Accessibility Hierarchy, is more cautious: "there is evidence to suggest that low reliability occurs in just those areas where greater indeterminacy is predicted . . . [I]t has been shown that judgment data can, when used properly and appropriately, be useful in second language acquisition research" (p. 320). Her evidence showed that NNS variability in automaticity of L2 perception and processing interferes with access to L2 knowledge representation. Many other studies have found similar results; for example, Ortega (2000) found that with familiarity with the target language, L2 Spanish learners' certainty in judgments and their eventual consistency increased; and in Juffs and Harrington (1996) those with longer reading times were more accurate,

6 Adaptability and Innovation of Research Methods between L1 and L2 Research

We are now left with the last two questions posed at the beginning of this chapter:

iv To what extent can procedures adopted for L1 research be applied to L2 research?
v What new or additional procedures or adaptations are possible or needed for L2 research?

To the first of which it now seems appropriate to add the reverse question:

vi What L2 procedures can be applied to L1 research?

As for the first question, it would seem as if, since most of the procedures employed in L2 research have indeed arisen in some form from prior L1 research, we have only to look to L1 research for guidance as to the next stages. To some extent this is true. Among technologically sophisticated techniques, L2 research has clearly recognized and taken advantage of computerized, on-line experiments and data collection (e.g., Beck, 1998; Hagen, 1994; Hulstijn and DeKeyser, 1997; Juffs, 1998; Juffs and Harrington, 1995, 1996; Robinson, 1997). These studies all used reading time or reaction time to judgments. Also, the use of event-related potentials and magnetic resonance imaging (Weber-Fox and Neville, 1999) is beginning to find a place in SLA research. What remains to be examined with such procedures, of course, is how much the data derived from them are subject to greater within- and between-subject error variability, owing to the higher degree of indeterminacy and alternative sources of knowledge in L2 learners' grammars, as was pointed out about GJTs. Hulstijn (1997) raises just such a cautious note. Yet Kempe and MacWhinney (1998) illustrate in some detail how decision latencies (reaction time) can be analyzed fruitfully to reveal predictable tendencies in acquisition (comparing case-marking processing between learners of L2 German and Russian in a competition-model word-order experiment). A wider application of such procedures is warranted.

Despite the evidence of greater overall variability in L2 than L1 learners' grammars and performance, it is difficult to imagine that there could not be an application for L1-associated research methodology and data-elicitation procedures of the most sophisticated sort, if only because L2 learners are human, as well, and they possess all the potential abilities of any native speaker. Certainly, all manner of direct naturalistic observation and standard elicited production measures is already well within the repertoire of SLA researchers. But a number of on-line procedures used in the psycholinguistic literature rely on full and highly automatized access by subjects to their mature grammars and perceptual processing, so that subjects with too high variability in reaction time and accuracy are more likely to be excluded from L1 research, whereas they are more of the natural population in SLA studies.[14] Thus, L2 learners may exhibit too much variability and uncertainty for some of these procedures to be applied. But beyond this not insurmountable problem, whatever limitations there may be lie more in the question of access to facilities and financial resources, and possibly the incidental problems of accessing and putting through the rigors of laboratory training L2 learners who may at times be more reluctant than the captive audience of first-year psychology students.

As for the final question, concerning which L2 procedures can be applied in L1 research, it is fair to say that it has been SLA research, rather than L1 research, which has developed most thoroughly a number of methods and measures of language performance and use. Examples of these include: (i) observational measures of classroom language use; (ii) description of pragmatic language abilities in social interaction; (iii) detailed methods for tapping into learners' introspective, metalinguistic knowledge; (iv) elicited production techniques and variables in design of picture sequences and tasks (as indicated in section 3.3); and (v) many other procedures for which the focus is the learners' manipulation of linguistic form versus meaning. Some reasons for this greater development in SLA research are that researchers have had the benefit of subjects with greater maturity than infants and young children, who could employ world knowledge in their operations with tasks. Also, the greater concern in SLA studies with developing grammars during later stages of cognitive maturation has motivated more elaborate designs, methodologies, and tests, in order to examine complex linguistic performance. Therefore, it will be incumbent on L1 researchers to have a closer look at SLA research in order to discover some of the implications and expansions of their own methods and interpretations in the realm of language acquisition and processing, which they ought to perceive as the natural testing ground for claims about the uniformity of human linguistic experience.

NOTES

1 For reasons of length, this review focuses on L2 oral production; the quite extensive research on L2 writing or reading, for example, cannot be included. See Wolfe-Quintero, Inagaki, and Kim (1998) for an extensive review of analytical procedures in the writing domain.

2 Throughout this review, in one effort to avoid stylistic boredom, the terms "procedure," "task," "method," and "technique" will be used interchangeably to refer to types of data collection, although at times each of these may refer to a more specific or distinct referent (as when we refer to "communicative" tasks as one type of technique).

3 See other chapters in this volume, especially Norris and Ortega, regarding approaches to SLA and measurement.

4 As space is limited, and as we are unaware of a primary source of research about personal narratives and their elicitation in second language research, we can only point to the vast literature on the elicitation and analysis of narrative in L1 research. See the extensive, partly annotated bibliography by Handorf, Watson-Gegeo, and Sato (1993).

5 Reaction time and ERP are among the psycholinguistic processing measures commonly employed in L1 research, but they have been used very little in L2 research, a point to be discussed in the concluding section of this review.

6 Cloze tests as employed in SLA research are highly varied, and can be constructed with many distinct targets. A basic distinction is between "random" deletion of cloze items for more global assessment and "rational" deletion for specific target form assessment. It is beyond the scope of this review to address these variations.

7 It is not uncommon for researchers to include as distracters other sets of items that are to be used for a different investigation, but the nature of which is unmentioned in the study. The issue of fatigue and other task-internal effects (e.g., perseverance errors) on the part of the subject in cases of large sets of items is rarely discussed.

8 See discussion in Schütze (1996, pp. 62–77) on L1 theorists' concerns about the dichotomous or scalar nature of grammaticality.

9 Correction is often used to confirm that subjects' grounds for rejection are justified. It has been used in the above studies, as well as E. Klein (1995), Salaberry (1998), Schachter

(1989), and Trahey and White (1993).

10 Surprisingly, Alanen found that on the GJT for locatives, the Rule group was best and the Rule+Enhance condition was the weakest. Her analysis suggested that the latter group were systematically rejecting one of the correct alternative forms.

11 Ortega also reports very high Cronbach's alpha reliability of the GJT and EI, at both the beginning and end of the semester – all but the GJT at the beginning, which was .86, were .95–6. The lack of a control group leaves open the possibility that improvement in these accuracy measures could be due to test–retest experience, although that is an unlikely explanation, given the 14 weeks that intervened.

12 Note that the sociolinguist Milroy (1987, ch. 7, p. 146 ff), discussing "elicitation techniques" for L1 data collection to supplement naturally occurring data, refers principally to acceptability ratings, but questions the reliability of linguistically naive informants' judgments.

13 This notion fits with Zobl's (1992) proposal of two main sources of metalinguistic (grammatical) knowledge – from "input-independent" (e.g., core UG) and "input-dependent" knowledge (language-particular parameters and elements outside core grammar) – which lead to more homogeneity for judgments based on core principles, but more heterogeneity for decisions about input-dependent, L1-specific structures.

14 Except perhaps in research literature on the language-impaired population, for which, see research by, for example, Gathercole and Baddeley (1993) for examples of L2-appropriate methods and research questions.

REFERENCES

Adams, M. 1978: Methodology for examining second language acquisition. In E. Hatch (ed.), *Second Language Acquisition: A Book of Readings*. Rowley, MA: Newbury House, 278–96.

Ahrenholz, B. 2000: Modality and referential movement in instructional discourse: comparing the production of Italian learners of German with native German and native Italian production. *Studies in Second Language Acquisition*, 22 (3), 337–68.

Alanen, R. 1995: Input enhancement and rule presentation in second language acquisition. In R. Schmidt (ed.), *Attention and Awareness in Foreign Language Learning*. Honolulu: University of Hawai'i Second Language Teaching and Curriculum Center, 259–302.

Allwright, D. 1988: *Observation in the Language Classroom*. London: Longman.

Allwright, D. and Bailey, K. M. 1991: *Focus on the Language Classroom: An Introduction to Classroom Research for Language Teachers*. New York: Cambridge University Press.

Bachman, L. F. 1990: *Fundamental Considerations in Language Testing*. Oxford: Oxford University Press.

Bailey, K. M. 1983: Competitiveness and anxiety in adult second language learning: looking *at* and *through* the diary studies. In H. W. Seliger and M. H. Long (eds), *Classroom Oriented*

Research in Second Language Acquisition. Rowley, MA: Newbury House, 67–103.

Bailey, K. M. 2001: Action research, teacher research, and classroom research in language teaching. In M. Celce-Murcia (ed.), *Teaching English as a Second or Foreign Language*. 3rd edition. Boston, MA: Heinle and Heinle, 489–98.

Bailey, K. M. and Nunan, D. (eds) 1996: *Voices from the Language Classroom*. New York: Cambridge University Press.

Bard, E. G., Robertson, D., and Sorace, A. 1996: Magnitude estimation of linguistic acceptability. *Language*, 72 (1), 32–68.

Bardovi-Harlig, K. 1999: From morpheme studies to temporal semantics: tense-aspect research in SLA. *Studies in Second Language Acquisition*, 21 (3), 241–82.

Bardovi-Harlig, K. 2000: Tense and aspect in second language acquisition: form, meaning, and use. *Language Learning 50: Supplement 1*. Ann Arbor: Blackwell.

Bardovi-Harlig, K. and Hartford, B. S. 1993: Learning the rules of academic talk: A longitudinal study of pragmatic change. *Studies in Second Language Acquisition*, 15 (3), 279–304.

Bardovi-Harlig, K. and Hartford, B. S. 1996: Input in an institutional setting. *Studies in Second Language Acquisition*, 18 (2), 171–88.

Bayley, R. 1994: Interlanguage variation and the quantitative paradigm: past tense marking in Chinese-English. In E. Tarone, S. M. Gass, and A. D. Cohen (eds), *Research Methodology in Second-Language Acquisition*. Hillsdale, NJ: Lawrence Erlbaum Associates, 157–81.

Beck, M.-L. 1998: L2 acquisition and obligatory head movement: English-speaking learners of German and the Local Impairment Hypothesis. *Studies in Second Language Acquisition*, 20 (3), 311–48.

Bennett-Kastor, T. 1988: *Analyzing Children's Language: Methods and Theories*. Oxford: Blackwell.

Berko, J. 1958: The child's learning of English morphology. *Word*, 14, 150–77.

Bernstein Ratner, N. 2000: Elicited imitation and other methods for the analysis of trade-offs between speech and language skills in children. In L. Menn and N. Bernstein Ratner (eds), *Methods for Studying Language Production*. Mahwah, NJ: Lawrence Erlbaum Associates, 291–311.

Bialystok, E. 1990: *Communication Strategies: A Psychological Analysis of Second-Language Use*. Oxford: Blackwell.

Bialystok, E. and Ryan, E. B. 1985: A metacognitive framework for the development of first and second language skills. In D. Forrest-Presley, G. E. MacKinnon, and T. G. Waller (eds), *Metacognition, Cognition, and Human Performance. Vol. 1: Theoretical Perspectives*. Orlando: Academic Press, 207–52.

Birdsong, D. 1989: *Metalinguistic Performance and Interlinguistic Competence*. Berlin: Springer-Verlag.

Birdsong, D. 1992: Ultimate attainment in second language acquisition. *Language*, 68, 706–55.

Birdsong, D. 1994: Asymmetrical knowledge of ungrammaticality in SLA theory. *Studies in Second Language Acquisition*, 16 (4), 463–73.

Bley-Vroman, R. and Chaudron, C. 1994: Elicited imitation as a measure of second-language competence. In E. Tarone, S. M. Gass, and A. D. Cohen (eds), *Research Methodology in Second-Language Acquisition*. Hillsdale, NJ: Lawrence Erlbaum Associates, 245–61.

Bley-Vroman, R. and Masterson, D. 1989: Reaction time as a supplement to grammaticality judgments in the investigation of second language learners' competence. *University of Hawai'i Working Papers in ESL*, 8 (2), 207–45.

Bley-Vroman, R., Felix, S., and Ioup, G. 1988: The accessibility of Universal Grammar in adult language learning. *Second Language Research*, 4, 1–32.

Blum-Kulka, S., House, J., and Kasper, G. (eds) 1989: *Cross-Cultural Pragmatics: Requests and Apologies*. Norwood, NJ: Ablex.

Bolander, M. 1989: Prefabs, patterns and rules in interaction? Formulaic speech in adult learners' L2 Swedish. In K. Hyltenstam and L. K. Obler (eds), *Bilingualism Across the Lifespan*. Cambridge: Cambridge University Press, 73–86.

Bongaerts, T. 1999: Ultimate attainment in L2 pronunciation: the case of very advanced late L2 learners. In D. Birdsong (ed.), *Second Language Acquisition and the Critical Period Hypothesis*. Mahwah, NJ: Lawrence Erlbaum Associates, 133–59.

Bongaerts, T., van Summeren, C., Planken, B., and Schils, E. 1997: Age and ultimate attainment in the pronunciation of a foreign language. *Studies in Second Language Acquisition*, 19 (4), 447–65.

De Bot, K., Cox, A., Ralston, S., Schaufeli, A., and Weltens, B. 1995: Lexical processing in bilinguals. *Second Language Research*, 11, 1–19.

Brown, C., Sagers, S. L., and LaPorte, C. 1999: Incidental vocabulary acquisition from oral and written dialogue journals. *Studies in Second Language Acquisition*, 21 (2), 259–83.

Bucks, R. S., Singh, S., Cuerden, J. M., and Wilcock, G. K. 2000: Analysis of spontaneous, conversational speech in dementia of Alzheimer type: evaluation of an objective technique for analysing lexical performance. *Aphasiology*, 14 (1), 71–91.

Carrell, P. L. and Konneker, B. H. 1981: Politeness: comparing native and nonnative judgments. *Language Learning*, 31 (1), 17–30.

Carroll, M., Murcia-Serra, J., Watorek, M., and Bendiscioli, A. 2000: The relevance of information organization to second language acquisition studies. *Studies in Second Language Acquisition*, 22 (3), 441–66.

Carroll, S. and Swain, M. 1993: Explicit and implicit negative feedback: an empirical study of the learning of linguistic generalizations. *Studies in Second Language Acquisition*, 15 (3), 357–86.

Cebrian, J. 2000: Transferability and productivity of L1 rules in Catalan–English interlanguage. *Studies in Second Language Acquisition*, 22 (1), 1–26.

Chafe, W. (ed.) 1980: *The Pear Stories: Cognitive, Cultural, and Linguistic Aspects of Narrative Production*. Norwood, NJ: Ablex.

Chaudron, C. 1983: Research on metalinguistic judgments: a review of theory, methods, and results. *Language Learning*, 33 (3), 343–77.

Chaudron, C. 1985a: The role of simplified input in classroom language. In G. Kasper (ed.), *Learning, Teaching and Communication in the Foreign Language Classroom*. Århus: Århus University Press, 99–110.

Chaudron, C. 1985b: Intake: on models and methods for discovering learners' processing of input. *Studies in Second Language Acquisition*, 7 (1), 1–14.

Chaudron, C. 1988: *Second Language Classrooms: Research on Teaching and Learning*. Cambridge: Cambridge University Press.

Chaudron, C. 2001: Progress in language classroom research: evidence from *The Modern Language Journal*, 1916–2000. *Modern Language Journal*, 85 (1), 57–76.

Chaudron, C. forthcoming: *Elicited Imitation: Second Language and First Language Applications*.

Chaudron, C., Crookes, G., and Long, M. H. 1988: *Reliability and Validity in Second Language Classroom Research.* Technical Report No. 8, Center for Second Language Research. Honolulu: University of Hawai'i.

Chomsky, C. 1969: *The Acquisition of Syntax in Children from 5 to 10.* Cambridge, MA: MIT Press.

Clark, J. L. D. and Clifford, R. T. 1988: The FSI/ILR/ACTFL proficiency scales and testing techniques: development, current status, and needed research. *Studies in Second Language Acquisition,* 10 (2), 121–47.

Cohen, A. D. 1991: Feedback on writing: the use of verbal report. *Studies in Second Language Acquisition,* 13 (2), 133–59.

Cohen, A. D. and Hosenfeld, C. 1981: Some uses of mentalistic data in second language research. *Language Learning,* 31 (2), 285–313.

Cohen, A. D. and Olshtain, E. 1994: Researching the production of second-language speech acts. In E. Tarone, S. M. Gass, and A. D. Cohen (eds), *Research Methodology in Second-Language Acquisition.* Hillsdale, NJ: Lawrence Erlbaum Associates,143–56.

Cook, V. 1986: The basis for an experimental approach to second language learning. In V. Cook (ed.), *Experimental Approaches to Second Language Learning.* Oxford: Pergamon Press, 3–21.

Coppetiers, R. 1987: Competence differences between native and near-native speakers. *Language,* 63 (3), 545–73.

Cowan, R. and Hatasa, Y. A. 1994: Investigating the validity and reliability of native speaker and second-language learner judgments about sentences. In E. Tarone, S. M. Gass, and A. D. Cohen (eds), *Research Methodology in Second-Language Acquisition.* Hillsdale, NJ: Lawrence Erlbaum Associates, 287–302.

Crookes, G. 1989: Planning and interlanguage variation. *Studies in Second Language Acquisition,* 11 (4), 367–83.

Crookes, G. 1991: Second language speech production research. *Studies in Second Language Acquisition,* 13 (2) 113–32.

Damico, J. S., Oller, J. W., Jr, and Tetnowski, J. A. 1999: Investigating the interobserver reliability of a direct observational language assessment technique. *Advances in Speech-Language Pathology,* 1 (2), 77–94.

d'Anglejan, A. and Tucker, G. R. 1975: The acquisition of complex English structures by adult learners. *Language Learning,* 25 (2), 281–96.

Davies, W. D. and Kaplan, T. I. 1998: Native speaker vs. L2 learner grammaticality judgements. *Applied Linguistics,* 19 (2), 183–203.

Dechert, H. W. and Sandrock, U. 1986: Thinking-aloud protocols: the decomposition of language processing. In V. Cook (ed.), *Experimental Approaches to Second Language Learning.* Oxford: Pergamon Press, 111–26.

DeKeyser, R. M. 1997: Beyond explicit rule learning: automatizing second language morphosyntax. *Studies in Second Language Acquisition,* 19 (2), 190–221.

DeKeyser, R. M. and Sokalski, K. J. 1996: The differential role of comprehension and production practice. *Language Learning,* 46 (4), 613–42.

Demuth, K. 1996: Collecting spontaneous production data. In D. McDaniel, C. McKee, and H. Smith Cairns (eds), *Methods for Assessing Children's Syntax.* Cambridge, MA: MIT Press, 3–22.

Dietrich, R., Klein, W., and Noyau, C. 1995: *The Acquisition of Temporality in a Second Language.* Philadelphia: John Benjamins.

Dittmar, N. (ed.) 1992: Grammaticalization in second language acquisition. Special issue.

Studies in Second Language Acquisition, 14 (3).

Doughty, C. 1991: Second language instruction does make a difference: evidence from an empirical study of SL relativization. *Studies in Second Language Acquisition*, 13 (4), 431–69.

Doughty, C. and Long, M. H. 2000: Eliciting second language speech data. In L. Menn and N. Bernstein Ratner (eds), *Methods for Studying Language Production*. Mahwah, NJ: Lawrence Erlbaum Associates, 149–77.

Dube, B. 2000: Where are the minimal trees? Evidence from early Zulu L2 subordination. *Second Language Research*, 16 (3), 233–65.

Duff, P. A. 1993: Syntax, semantics, and SLA: the convergence of possessive and existential constructions. *Studies in Second Language Acquisition*, 15 (1), 1–34.

Duffield, N. and White, L. 1999: Assessing L2 knowledge of Spanish clitic placement: converging methodologies. *Second Language Research*, 15 (2), 133–60.

Eckman, F. R. 1994: Local and long-distance anaphora in second-language acquisition. In E. Tarone, S. M. Gass, and A. D. Cohen (eds), *Research Methodology in Second-Language Acquisition*. Hillsdale, NJ: Lawrence Erlbaum Associates, 207–25.

Eckman, F. R., Bell, L. H., and Nelson, D. 1988: On the generalization of relative clause instruction in the acquisition of English as a second language. *Applied Linguistics*, 9 (1), 1–20.

Edwards, A. L. 1957: *Techniques of Attitude Scale Construction*. New York: Appleton-Century-Crofts.

Ellis, R. 1989: Are classroom and naturalistic acquisition the same? A study of the classroom acquisition of German word order rules. *Studies in Second Language Acquisition*, 11, 305–28.

Ellis, R. 1991: Grammaticality judgments and second language acquisition. *Studies in Second Language Acquisition*, 13 (2), 161–86.

Ellis, R. 1992: Learning to communicate in the classroom: a study of two language learners' requests. *Studies in Second Language Acquisition*, 14 (1), 1–23.

Ellis, R. 1994: *The Study of Second Language Acquisition*. Oxford: Oxford University Press.

Ellis, R. and He, X. 1999: The roles of modified input and output in the incidental acquisition of word meanings. *Studies in Second Language Acquisition*, 21 (2), 285–301.

Ericsson, K. A. and Simon, H. A. 1980: Verbal reports as data. *Psychological Review*, 87, 215–51.

Ericsson, K. A. and Simon, H. A. 1984: *Protocol Analysis*. Cambridge, MA: MIT Press.

Eubank, L. 1993: Sentence matching and processing in L2 development. *Second Language Research*, 9 (3), 253–80.

Færch, C. and Kasper, G. (eds) 1983: *Strategies in Interlanguage Communication*. London: Longman.

Færch, C. and Kasper, G. (eds) 1987a: *Introspection in Second Language Research*. Clevedon: Multilingual Matters.

Færch, C. and Kasper, G. 1987b: From product to process: introspective methods in second language research. In C. Færch and G. Kasper (eds), *Introspection in Second Language Research*. Clevedon: Multilingual Matters, 5–23.

Fathman, A. 1975: The relationship between age and second language productive ability. *Language Learning*, 25 (2), 245–53.

Felix, S. W. and Weigl, W. 1991: Universal Grammar in the classroom: the effects of formal instruction on second language acquisition. *Second Language Research*, 7 (2), 162–81.

Felix, S. and Zobl, H. 1994: Asymmetries in second language acquisition data.

Studies in Second Language Acquisition, 16 (4), 475–84.

Fenson, L., Bates, E., Dale, P., Goodman, J., Reznick, J. S., and Thal, D. 2000: Measuring variability in early child language: don't shoot the messenger. *Child Development*, 71 (2), 323–8.

Finney, M. A. 1997: Markedness, operator movement and discourse effects in the acquisition of purpose clause constructions in a second language. *Second Language Research*, 13 (1), 10–33.

Flanigan, B. O. 1995: Anaphora and relativization in child second language acquisition. *Studies in Second Language Acquisition*, 17 (3), 331–51.

Flege, J. E., Frieda, E. M., Walley, A. C., and Randazza, L. A. 1998: Lexical factors and segmental accuracy in second language speech production. *Studies in Second Language Acquisition*, 20 (3), 155–87.

Flynn, S. 1987: *A Parameter-Setting Model of L2 Acquisition: Experimental Studies in Anaphora*. Dordrecht: D. Reidel.

Foster, P. and Skehan, P. 1996: The influence of planning and task type on second language performance. *Studies in Second Language Acquisition*, 18 (3), 299–323.

Fraser, C. A. 1999: Lexical processing strategy use and vocabulary learning through reading. *Studies in Second Language Acquisition*, 21 (2), 225–41.

Fraser, C., Bellugi, U., and Brown, R. 1963: Control of grammar in imitation, comprehension, and production. *Journal of Verbal Learning and Verbal Behavior*, 2 (2), 121–35.

Gass, S. M. 1979: Language transfer and universal grammatical relations. *Language Learning*, 29 (2), 273–91.

Gass, S. M. 1980: An investigation of syntactic transfer in adult second language learners. In R. C. Scarcella and S. D. Krashen (eds), *Research in Second Language Acquisition*. Rowley, MA: Newbury House, 132–41.

Gass, S. M. 1983: The development of L2 intuitions. *TESOL Quarterly*, 17 (2), 273–91.

Gass, S. M. 1987: The resolution of conflicts among competing systems: a bidirectional perspective. *Applied Psycholinguistics*, 8 (3), 329–50.

Gass, S. M. 1989: How do learners resolve linguistic conflicts? In S. M. Gass and J. Schachter (eds), *Linguistic Perspectives on Second Language Acquisition*. Cambridge: Cambridge University Press, 183–99.

Gass, S. M. 1994: The reliability of second-language grammaticality judgments. In E. Tarone, S. M. Gass, and A. D. Cohen (eds), *Research Methodology in Second-Language Acquisition*. Hillsdale, NJ: Lawrence Erlbaum Associates, 303–22.

Gass, S. M. and Mackey, A. (eds) 1998: The role of input and interaction in second language acquisition. Special issue: *Modern Language Journal*, 82 (3).

Gass, S. M. and Mackey, A. 2000: *Stimulated Recall Methodology in Second Language Research*. Mahwah, NJ: Lawrence Erlbaum Associates.

Gass, S., Mackey, A., Alvarez-Torres, M. J., and Fernández-García, M. 1999: The effects of task repetition on linguistic output. *Language Learning*, 49 (4), 549–81.

Gathercole, S. E. and Baddeley, A. D. 1993: *Working Memory and Language*. Hillsdale, NJ: Lawrence Erlbaum Associates.

Giacalone Ramat, A. 1992: Grammaticalization processes in the area of temporal and modal relations. *Studies in Second Language Acquisition*, 14 (3), 297–322.

Glesne, C. and Peshkin, A. 1992: *Becoming Qualitative Researchers: An Introduction*. London: Longman.

Goodluck, H. 1996: The act-out task. In D. McDaniel, C. McKee, and H. Smith Cairns (eds), *Methods for Assessing Children's Syntax*. Cambridge, MA: MIT Press, 147–62.

Goss, N., Zhang, Y.-H., and Lantolf, J. P. 1994: Two heads may be better than one: mental activity in second-language grammaticality judgments. In E. Tarone, S. M. Gass, and A. D. Cohen (eds), *Research Methodology in Second-Language Acquisition*. Hillsdale, NJ: Lawrence Erlbaum Associates, 263–86.

de Graaff, R. 1997: The eXperanto experiment: effects of explicit instruction on second language acquisition. *Studies in Second Language Acquisition*, 19 (2), 249–76.

Green, B. 1954: Paired comparison scaling procedures. In G. Lindzey (ed.), *Handbook of Social Psychology. Vol. 1*. Reading, MA: Addison-Wesley, 344–7.

Green, P. S. and Hecht, K. 1992: Implicit and explicit grammar: an empirical study. *Applied Linguistics*, 13 (2), 168–84.

Greenbaum, S. (ed.) 1977: *Acceptability in Language*. The Hague: Mouton.

Grigg, T. J. 1986: The effects of task, time, and rule knowledge on grammar performance for three English structures. *University of Hawai'i Working Papers in ESL*, 5 (1), 37–60.

De Groot, A. M. B. and Keijzer, R. 2000: What is hard to learn is easy to forget: the roles of word concreteness, cognate status, and word frequency in foreign-language vocabulary learning and forgetting. *Language Learning*, 50 (1), 1–56.

De Groot, A. M. B. and Kroll, J. F. (eds) 1997: *Tutorials in Bilingualism: Psycholinguistic Perspectives*. Mahwah, NJ: Lawrence Erlbaum Associates.

Grotjahn, R. 1987: On the methodological basis of introspective methods. In C. Færch and G. Kasper (eds), *Introspection in Second Language Research*. Clevedon: Mulitilingual Matters, 54–81.

Hagen, L. K. 1994: Constructs and measurement in parameter models of second-language acquisition. In E. Tarone, S. M. Gass, and A. D. Cohen (eds), *Research Methodology in Second-Language Acquisition*. Hillsdale, NJ: Lawrence Erlbaum Associates, 61–87.

Hakuta, K. 1974: A preliminary report on the development of grammatical morphemes in a Japanese girl learning English as a second language. *Working Papers on Bilingualism*, 3, 18–43.

Hakuta, K. 1976: A case study of a Japanese child learning English as a second language. *Language Learning*, 26 (2), 321–51.

Hamilton, R. L. 1994: Is implicational generalization unidirectional and maximal? Evidence from relativization instruction in a second language. *Language Learning*, 44 (1), 123–57.

Handorf, S., Watson-Gegeo, K., and Sato, C. J. 1993: *Research on Narrative: A Bibliography and Selected Annotations*. Technical Report No. 10, Center for Second Language Research. Honolulu: University of Hawai'i.

Hardison, D. M. 1996: Bimodal speech perception by native and nonnative speakers of English: factors influencing the McGurk effect. *Language Learning*, 46 (1), 3–73.

Harley, B. 1989: Functional grammar in French immersion: a classroom experiment. *Applied Linguistics*, 19 (3), 331–59.

Harley, B., Howard, J., and Hart, D. 1995: Second language processing at different ages: do younger learners pay more attention to prosodic cues to sentence structure? *Language Learning*, 45 (1), 43–71.

Harrington, M. 1987: Processing transfer: language-specific processing strategies as a source of interlanguage variation. *Applied Psycholinguistics*, 8 (3), 351–77.

Hatch, E. (ed.) 1978a: *Second Language Acquisition: A Book of Readings*. Rowley, MA: Newbury House.

Hatch, E. 1978b: Introduction. In E. Hatch (ed.), *Second Language*

Acquisition: A Book of Readings. Rowley, MA: Newbury House, 1–18.

Hatch, E. and Lazaraton, A. 1991: *The Research Manual*. Rowley, MA: Newbury House.

Haznedar, B. 2001: The acquisition of the IP system in child L2 English. *Studies in Second Language Acquisition*, 23 (1), 1–39.

Helms-Park, R. 2001: Evidence of lexical transfer in learner syntax: the acquisition of English causatives by speakers of Hindi-Urdu and Vietnamese. *Studies in Second Language Acquisition*, 23 (1), 71–102.

Hendriks, H. 2000: The acquisition of topic marking in L1 Chinese and L1 and L2 French. *Studies in Second Language Acquisition*, 22 (3), 369–97.

Holmen, A. 1993: Syntactic development in Danish L2. In K. Hyltenstam and Å. Viberg (eds), *Progression and Regression in Language: Sociocultural, Neuropsychological, and Linguistic Perspectives*. Cambridge: Cambridge University Press, 267–88.

Hoover, M. L. and Dwivedi, V. D. 1998: Syntactic processing by skilled bilinguals. *Language Learning*, 48 (1), 1–29.

House, J. 1996: Developing pragmatic fluency in English as a foreign language: routines and metapragmatic awareness. *Studies in Second Language Acquisition*, 18 (2), 225–52.

Huang, J. and Hatch, E. 1978: A Chinese child's acquisition of English. In E. Hatch (ed.), *Second Language Acquisition: A Book of Readings*. Rowley, MA: Newbury House, 118–31.

Hudson, T., Detmer, E., and Brown, J. D. 1995: *Developing Prototypic Measures of Cross-Cultural Pragmatics*. Honolulu: University of Hawai'i Second Language Teaching and Curriculum Center.

Hulstijn, J. 1997: Second language acquisition research in the laboratory: possibilities and limitations. *Studies in Second Language Acquisition*, 21 (2), 131–43.

Hulstijn, J. and DeKeyser, R. (eds) 1997: Testing SLA theory in the research laboratory. Special issue. *Studies in Second Language Acquisition*, 19 (2).

Hyltenstam, K. 1988: Lexical characteristics of near-native second-language learners of Swedish. *Journal of Multilingual and Multicultural Development*, 9 (1 and 2), 67–84.

Hyltenstam, K. 1992: Non-native features of near-native speakers: on the ultimate attainment of childhood L2 learners. In R. J. Harris (ed.), *Cognitive Processing in Bilinguals*. Amsterdam: Elsevier Science, 351–68.

Inagaki, S. 1997: Japanese and Chinese learners' acquisition of the narrow-range rules for the dative alternation in English. *Language Learning*, 47 (4), 637–69.

Ioup, G., Boustagui, E., El Tigi, M., and Moselle, M. 1994: Reexamining the critical period hypothesis: a case study of successful adult SLA in a naturalistic environment. *Studies in Second Language Acquisition*, 16 (1), 73–98.

Izumi, S., Bigelow, M., Fujiwara, M., and Fearnow, S. 1999: Testing the output hypothesis: effects of output on noticing and second language acquisition. *Studies in Second Language Acquisition*, 21 (3), 421–52.

Jin, H. G. 1994: Topic-prominence and subject-prominence in L2 acquisition: Evidence of English-to-Chinese typological transfer. *Language Learning*, 44 (1), 101–22.

Johnson, D. M. 1992: *Approaches to Research in Second Language Learning*. New York: Longman.

Johnson, J. S. 1992: Critical period effects in second language acquisition: the effect of written versus auditory materials on the assessment of grammatical competence. *Language Learning*, 42 (2), 217–48.

Johnson, M. 2000: Interaction in the Oral Proficiency Interview: problems of validity. *Pragmatics*, 10 (2), 215–31.

Jones, F. R. 1995: Learning an alien lexicon: a teach-yourself case study. *Second Language Research*, 11 (2), 95–111.

Jourdenais, R. 1998: The effects of textual enhancement on the acquisition of Spanish preterit and imperfect. Ph.D. dissertation. Georgetown University.

Jourdenais, R. 2001: Cognition, instruction, and protocol analysis. In P. Robinson (ed.), *Cognition and Second Language Instruction*. Cambridge: Cambridge University Press, 354–75.

Jourdenais, R., Ota, M., Stauffer, S., Boyson, B., and Doughty, C. 1995: Does textual enhancement promote noticing? A think-aloud protocol analysis. In R. Schmidt (ed.), *Attention and Awareness in Foreign Language Learning*. Honolulu: University of Hawai'i Second Language Teaching and Curriculum Center, 183–216.

Ju, M. K. 2000: Overpassivization errors by second language learners: the effect of conceptualizable agents in discourse. *Studies in Second Language Acquisition*, 22 (1), 85–111.

Juffs, A. 1998: Main verb versus reduced relative clause ambiguity resolution in L2 sentence processing. *Language Learning*, 48 (1), 107–47.

Juffs, A. and Harrington, M. 1995: Parsing effects in second language sentence processing. *Studies in Second Language Acquisition*, 17 (4), 483–516.

Juffs, A. and Harrington, M. 1996: Garden Path sentences and error data in second language sentence processing. *Language Learning*, 46 (2), 283–326.

Just, M. A. and Carpenter, P. A. 1987: *The Psychology of Reading and Language Comprehension*. Boston: Allyn and Bacon.

Kasper, G. (ed.) 1996: The development of pragmatic competence. Special issue. *Studies in Second Language Acquisition*, 18 (2).

Kasper, G. 1998: Datenerhebungsverfahren in der Lernersprachenpragmatik. *Zeitschrift für Fremdsprachenforschung*, 9 (1), 85–118.

Kasper, G. and Dahl, M. 1991: Research methods in interlanguage pragmatics. *Studies in Second Language Acquisition*, 13 (2), 215–47.

Kasper, G. and Kellerman, E. (eds) 1997: *Communication Strategies: Psycholinguistic and Sociolinguistic Perspectives*. London: Longman.

Kellerman, E. 1978: Giving learners a break: native language intuitions as a source of predictions about transferability. *Working Papers on Bilingualism*, 15, 59–92.

Kempe, V. and MacWhinney, B. 1998: The acquisition of case marking by adult learners of Russian and German. *Studies in Second Language Acquisition*, 20 (4), 543–87.

Klein, E. C. 1995: Second versus third language acquisition: is there a difference? *Language Learning*, 45 (3), 419–65.

Klein, W. and Perdue, C. 1992: *Utterance Structure: Developing Grammars Again*. Philadelphia: John Benjamins.

Klein, W., Coenen, J., van Helvert, K., and Hendriks, H. 1995: The acquisition of Dutch. In R. Dietrich, W. Klein, and C. Noyau (eds), *The Acquisition of Temporality in a Second Language*. Philadelphia: John Benjamins, 117–43.

Koike, D. A. 1998: What happens when there's no one to talk to? Spanish foreign language discourse in simulated oral proficiency interviews. In R. Young and A. W. He (eds), *Taking and Testing: Discourse Approaches to the Assessment of Oral Proficiency*. Philadelphia: John Benjamins, 69–98.

Kormos, J. 1999: Simulating conversations in oral-proficiency assessment: a conversation analysis of role plays and non-scripted interview in language exams. *Language Testing*, 16 (2), 163–88.

Kroll, J. F. and De Groot, A. M. B. 1997: Lexical and conceptual memory in the bilingual: mapping form to meaning in two languages. In A. M. B. De Groot and J. F. Kroll (eds), *Tutorials in Bilingualism: Psycholinguistic Perspectives*. Mahwah, NJ: Lawrence Erlbaum Associates, 169–99.

Labov, W. 1969: The study of language in its social context. *Studium General*, 23, 30–87. Reprinted in 1972, *Sociolinguistic Patterns*. Philadelphia: University of Pennsylvania Press.

Lakshmanan, U. and Teranishi, K. 1994: Preferences versus grammaticality judgments: some methodological issues concerning the governing category parameter in second-language acquisition. In E. Tarone, S. M. Gass, and A. D. Cohen (eds), *Research Methodology in Second-Language Acquisition*. Hillsdale, NJ: Lawrence Erlbaum Associates, 185–206.

Larsen-Freeman, D. and Long, M. H. 1991: *An Introduction to Second Language Acquisition Research*. London: Longman.

Laufer, B. and Eliasson, S. 1993: What causes avoidance in L2 learning: L1–L2 difference, L1–L2 similarity, or L2 complexity? *Studies in Second Language Acquisition*, 15 (1), 35–48.

Leather, J. (ed.) 1999: *Phonological Issues in Language Learning: A Supplement to Language Learning*, 49, Supplement 1.

Leopold, W. 1939: *Speech Development of a Bilingual Child. Vol. I: Vocabulary Growth in the First Two Years*. Evanston, IL: Northwestern University Press.

Leopold, W. 1948: The study of child language and infant bilingualism. *Word*, 4, 1–17.

Leow, R. P. 1993: To simplify or not to simplify: a look at intake. *Studies in Second Language Acquisition*, 15 (3), 333–55.

Leow, R. P. 1997: Attention, awareness, and foreign language behavior. *Language Learning*, 47 (3), 467–505.

Liceras, J. M. 1985: The role of intake in the determination of learners' competence. In S. M. Gass and C. G. Madden (eds), *Input in Second Language Acquisition*. Rowley, MA: Newbury House, 354–73.

Liceras, J. M. 1989: On some properties of the "pro-drop" parameter: looking for missing subjects in non-native Spanish. In S. M. Gass and J. Schachter (eds), *Linguistic Perspectives on Second Language Acquisition*. Cambridge: Cambridge University Press, 109–33.

Liceras, J. M. and Díaz, L. 1999: Topic-drop versus pro-drop: null subjects and pronominal subjects in the Spanish L2 of Chinese, English, French, German and Japanese speakers. *Second Language Research*, 15 (1), 1–40.

Lightbown, P., Spada, N., and Wallace, R. 1980: Some effects of instruction on child and adolescent ESL learners. In R. Scarcella and S. D. Krashen (eds), *Research in Second Language Acquisition*, Rowley, MA: Newbury House, 162–72.

Liskin-Gasparro, J. 1998: Linguistic development in an immersion context: how advanced learners of Spanish perceive SLA. *Modern Language Journal*, 82, (2), 159–75.

Long, M. H. 1983: Native speaker/non-native speaker conversation and the negotiation of comprehensible input. *Applied Linguistics*, 4 (2), 126–41.

Loschky, L. and Bley-Vroman, R. 1993: Grammar and task-based methodology. In G. Crookes and S. Gass (eds), *Tasks and Language Learning: Integrating Theory and Practice*. Clevedon: Multilingual Matters, 123–67.

Lust, B., Flynn, S., and Foley, C. 1996: What children know about what they say: elicited imitation as a research method for assessing children's syntax. In D. McDaniel, C. McKee, and H. Smith Cairns (eds), *Methods for Assessing Children's Syntax*. Cambridge, MA: MIT Press, 55–76.

Lyster, R. 1998a: Recasts, repetition, and ambiguity in L2 classroom discourse. *Studies in Second Language Acquisition*, 20 (1), 51–81.

Lyster, R. 1998b: Negotiation of form, recasts, and explicit correction in relation to error types and learner repair in immersion classrooms. *Language Learning*, 48 (2), 183–218.

Lyster, R. and Ranta, L. 1997: Corrective feedback and learner uptake. *Studies in Second Language Acquisition*, 19 (1), 37–66.

Mackey, A. 1999: Input, interaction, and second language development: an empirical study of question formation in ESL. *Studies in Second Language Acquisition*, 21 (4), 557–587.

MacWhinney, B. 1987: The Competition Model. In B. MacWhinney (ed.), *Mechanisms of Language Acquisition*. Hillsdale, NJ: Lawrence Erlbaum Associates, 249–308.

MacWhinney, B. 1997: Second language acquisition and the Competition Model. In A. M. B. De Groot and J. F. Kroll (eds), *Tutorials in Bilingualism: Psycholinguistic Perspectives*. Mahwah, NJ: Lawrence Erlbaum Associates, 113–42.

MacWhinney, B. and Bates, E. (eds) 1989: *The Crosslinguistic Study of Sentence Processing*. Cambridge: Cambridge University Press.

Major, R. C. (ed.) 1998: Interlanguage phonetics and phonology. Special issue. *Studies in Second Language Acquisition*, 20 (2).

Major, R. C. and Faudree, M. C. 1996: Markedness universals and the acquisition of voicing contrasts by Korean speakers of English. *Studies in Second Language Acquisition*, 18 (1), 69–90.

Malakoff, M. and Hakuta, K. 1991: Translation skill and metalinguistic awareness in bilinguals. In E. Bialystok (ed.), *Communication Strategies: A Psychological Analysis of Second-Language Use*. Oxford: Blackwell, 141–66.

Mandell, P. B. 1999: On the reliability of grammaticality judgement tests in second language acquisition research. *Second Language Research*, 15 (1), 73–99.

Markee, N. P. 1994: Toward an ethnomethodological respecification of second-language acquisition studies. In E. Tarone, S. M. Gass, and A. D. Cohen (eds), *Research Methodology in Second-Language Acquisition*. Hillsdale, NJ: Lawrence Erlbaum Associates, 89–116.

Masterson, D. 1992: Instruments for measuring grammaticality and preference: the status of modified NPs in English and Korean. *University of Hawai'i Working Papers in ESL*, 11 (1), 125–56.

Matusmura, M. 1994: Japanese learners' acquisition of the locality requirement of English reflexives. *Studies in Second Language Acquisition*, 16 (1), 19–42.

McDade, H. L., Simpson, M. S., and Lamb, D. E. 1982: The use of elicited imitation as a measure of expressive grammar. *Journal of Speech and Hearing Disorders*, 47 (1), 19–24.

McDaniel, D. and Cairns, H. Smith. 1996: Eliciting judgments of grammaticality and reference. In D. McDaniel, C. McKee, and H. Smith Cairns (eds), *Methods for Assessing Children's Syntax*. Cambridge, MA: MIT Press, 233–54.

McDaniel, D., McKee, C., and Cairns, H. Smith (eds) 1996: *Methods for Assessing Children's Syntax*. Cambridge, MA: MIT Press.

McKee, C. 1996: On-line methods. In D. McDaniel, C. McKee, and H. Smith Cairns (eds), *Methods for Assessing Children's Syntax*. Cambridge, MA: MIT Press, 189–208.

Meara, P. 1986: The *Digame* project. In V. Cook (ed.), *Experimental Approaches to Second Language Learning*. Oxford: Pergamon Press, 101–10.

Mehnert, U. 1998: The effects of different lengths of time for planning on second language performance. *Studies in Second Language Acquisition*, 20 (1), 83–108.

Meisel, J. M. 1994a: Code-switching in young bilingual children. *Studies in Second Language Acquisition*, 16 (4), 413–39.

Meisel, J. M. (ed.) 1994b: *Bilingual First Language Acquisition: French and German Grammatical Development*. Philadelphia: John Benjamins.

Mellow, J. D., Reeder, K., and Forster, E. 1996: Using time-series research designs to investigate the effects of instruction on SLA. *Studies in Second Language Acquisition*, 18 (3), 325–50.

Menn, L. and Bernstein Ratner, N. (eds) 2000: *Methods for Studying Language Production*. Mahwah, NJ: Lawrence Erlbaum Associates.

Miller, G. A. 1969: A psychological method to investigate verbal concepts. *Journal of Mathematical Psychology*, 6, 169–91.

Milroy, L. 1987: *Observing and Analysing Natural Language*. Oxford: Blackwell.

Mohan, B. A. 1977: Acceptability testing and fuzzy grammar. In S. Greenbaum (ed.), *Acceptability in Language*. The Hague: Mouton, 133–48.

Moyer, A. 1999: Ultimate attainment in L2 phonology. *Studies in Second Language Acquisition*, 21 (1), 81–108.

Munnich, E., Flynn, S., and Martohardjono, G. 1994: Elicited imitation and grammaticality judgment tasks: what they measure and how they relate to each other. In E. Tarone, S. M. Gass, and A. D. Cohen (eds), *Research Methodology in Second-Language Acquisition*. Hillsdale, NJ: Lawrence Erlbaum Associates, 227–43.

Murdock, B. B., Jr 1982: Recognition memory. In C. R. Puff (ed.), *Handbook of Research Methods in Human Memory and Cognition*. New York: Academic Press, 1–26.

Myles, F., Hooper, J., and Mitchell, R. 1998: Rote or rule? Exploring the role of formulaic language in classroom foreign language learning. *Language Learning*, 48 (3), 323–63.

Myles, F., Mitchell, R., and Hooper, J. 1999: Interrogative chunks in French L2. *Studies in Second Language Acquisition*, 21 (1), 49–80.

Nation, P. 2001: *Learning Vocabulary in Another Language*. Cambridge: Cambridge University Press.

Nation, R. and McLaughlin, B. 1986: Language learning in multilingual subjects: an information-processing point of view. In V. Cook (ed.), *Experimental Approaches to Second Language Learning*. Oxford: Pergamon Press, 41–53.

Nicolaidis, E. and Genesee, F. 1996: A longitudinal study of pragmatic differentiation in young bilingual children. *Language Learning*, 46 (3), 439–64.

Norris, J. M. and Ortega, L. 2000: Effectiveness of L2 instruction: a research synthesis and quantitative meta-analysis. *Language Learning*, 50 (3), 417–528.

Norris, J. M., Brown, J. D., Hudson, T., and Yoshioka, J. 1998: *Designing Second Language Performance Assessments*. Honolulu: University of Hawai'i Second Language Teaching and Curriculum Center.

Nunan, D. 1989: *Designing Tasks for the Communicative Classroom*. Cambridge: Cambridge University Press.

Nunan, D. 1992: *Research Methods in Language Learning*. Cambridge: Cambridge University Press.

Nunan, D. 1996: Issues in second language acquisition research: examining substance and procedure.

In W. C. Ritchie and T. K. Bhatia (eds), *Handbook of Second Language Acquisition*. New York: Ritchie and Bhatia, 349–74.

Olson, G. M. and Clark, H. H. 1976: Research methods in psycholinguistics. In E. C. Carterette and M. P. Friedman, (eds), *Handbook of Perception. Vol. VII: Language and Speech*. New York: Academic Press, 25–74.

Ortega, L. 1999: Planning and focus on form in L2 oral performance. *Studies in Second Language Acquisition*, 21 (1), 109–48.

Ortega, L. 2000: Understanding syntactic complexity: the measurement of change in the syntax of instructed L2 Spanish learners. Ph.D. dissertation. University of Hawai'i.

Papp, S. 2000: Stable and developmental optionality in native and non-native Hungarian grammars. *Second Language Research*, 16 (2), 173–200.

Paradis, J. and Genesee, F. 1996: Syntactic acquisition in bilingual children: autonomous or interdependent? *Studies in Second Language Acquisition*, 18 (1), 1–25.

Paribakht, T. S. and Wesche, M. 1999: Reading and "incidental" L2 vocabulary acquisition: an introspective study of lexical inferencing. *Studies in Second Language Acquisition*, 21 (2), 195–224.

Park, H. 2000: *When*-questions in second language acquisition. *Second Language Research*, 16 (1), 44–76.

Perdue, C. (ed.) 1982: *Second Language Acquisition by Adult Immigrants: A Field Manual*. Strasbourg: European Science Foundation.

Perdue, C. (ed.) 2000: The Structure of Learner Varieties. Special issue. *Studies in Second Language Acquisition*, 22 (3).

Perdue, C. and Klein, W. 1992: Why does the production of some learners not grammaticalize? *Studies in Second Language Acquisition*, 14 (3), 259–72.

Pérez-Leroux, A. T. and Glass, W. 1999: Null anaphora in Spanish second language acquisition: probabilistic versus generative approaches. *Second Language Research*, 15 (2), 220–49.

Perkins, K. and Larsen-Freeman, D. 1975: The effect of formal language instruction on the order of morpheme acquisition. *Language Learning*, 25 (2), 237–43.

Pfaff, C. W. 1992: Grammaticalization processes in the area of temporal and modal relations. *Studies in Second Language Acquisition*, 14 (3), 273–96.

Pica, T. 1994: Research on negotiation: what does it reveal about second-language learning conditions, processes, and outcomes? *Language Learning*, 44 (3), 493–527.

Pica, T., Kanagy, R., and Falodun, J. 1993: Choosing and using communication tasks for second language instruction. In G. Crookes and S. Gass (eds), *Tasks and Language Learning: Integrating Theory and Practice*. Clevedon: Multilingual Matters, 9–34.

Pienemann, M. 1998: *Language Processing and Second Language Development: Processability Theory*. Philadelphia: John Benjamins.

Pienemann, M. and Håkansson, G. 1999: A unified approach toward the development of Swedish as L2: a processability account. *Studies in Second Language Acquisition*, 21 (3), 393–420.

Polio, C. 1995: Acquiring nothing? The use of zero pronouns by nonnative speakers of Chinese and the implications for the acquisition of nominal reference. *Studies in Second Language Acquisition*, 17, 353–77.

Poplack, S., Wheeler, S., and Westwood, A. 1989: Distinguishing language contact phenomena: evidence from Finnish–English bilingualism. In K. Hyltenstam and L. Obler (eds), *Bilingualism Across the Lifespan*.

Cambridge: Cambridge University Press, 132–54.

Ravem, R. 1968: Language acquisition in a second language environment. *International Review of Applied Linguistics*, 6, 165–85. Reprinted 1974 in J. Richards (ed.), *Error Analysis*. London: Longman, 124–33.

Ravem, R. 1970: The development of Wh-questions in first and second language learners. *Occasional Papers*, Language Centre, University of Essex. Reprinted 1974 in J. Richards (ed.), *Error Analysis*. London: Longman, 134–55.

Rayner, K. (ed.) 1983: *Eye Movements in Reading: Perceptual and Language Processes*. New York: Academic Press.

Riney, T. J. and Flege, J. E. 1998: Changes over time in global foreign accent and liquid identifiability and accuracy. *Studies in Second Language Acquisition*, 20 (3), 213–43.

Rintell, E. M. and Mitchell, C. J. 1989: Studying requests and apologies: an inquiry into method. In S. Blum-Kulka, J. House, and G. Kasper (eds), *Cross-Cultural Pragmatics: Requests and Apologies*. Norwood, NJ: Ablex, 248–72.

Robertson, D. 2000: Variability in the use of the English article system by Chinese learners of English. *Second Language Research*, 16 (2), 135–72.

Robinson, P. 1994: Universals of word formation processes: noun incorporation in the acquisition of Samoan as a second language. *Language Learning*, 44 (4), 569–615.

Robinson, P. 1997: Generalizability and automaticity of second language learning under implicit, incidental, enhanced, and instructed conditions. *Studies in Second Language Acquisition*, 19 (2), 223–47.

Robinson, P. J. 2001: Task complexity, task difficulty, and task production: exploring interactions in a componential framework. *Applied Linguistics*, 22 (1), 27–57.

Robinson, P. J. and Ha, M. A. 1993: Instance theory and second language rule learning under explicit conditions. *Studies in Second Language Acquisition*, 15 (4), 413–38.

Roebuck, R. F., Martínez-Arbelaiz, M. A., and Pérez-Silva, J. I. 1999: Null subjects, filled CPs and L2 acquisition. *Second Language Research*, 15 (3), 251–82.

Rosa, E. and O'Neill, M. D. 1999: Explicitness, intake, and the issue of awareness: another piece to the puzzle. *Studies in Second Language Acquisition*, 21 (4), 511–56.

Rose, K. R. 1994: On the validity of DCTs in non-western contexts. *Applied Linguistics*, 15 (1), 1–14.

Rose, K. R. 2000: An exploratory cross-sectional study of interlanguage pragmatic development. *Studies in Second Language Acquisition*, 22 (1), 27–67.

Rose, K. R. and Ono, R. 1995: Eliciting speech act data in Japanese: the effect of questionnaire type. *Language Learning*, 45 (2), 191–223.

Ross, J. R. 1979: Where's English? In C. J. Fillmore, D. Kemper, and W. S.-Y. Wang (eds), *Individual Differences in Language Ability and Language Behavior*. New York: Academic Press, 172–83.

Ross, S. and Berwick, R. 1992: The discourse of accommodation in oral proficiency interviews. *Studies in Second Language Acquisition*, 14 (2), 159–76.

Rott, S. 1999: The effect of exposure frequency on intermediate language learners' incidental vocabulary acquisition and retention through reading. *Studies in Second Language Acquisition*, 21 (4), 589–619.

Rounds, P. L. and Kanagy, R. 1998: Acquiring linguistic cues to identify AGENT: evidence from children learning Japanese as a second language. *Studies in Second Language Acquisition*, 20 (4), 509–42.

Salaberry, M. R. 1998: The development of aspectual distinctions in L2 French classroom learning. *Canadian Modern Language Review/La revue canadienne des langues vivantes*, 54 (4), 508–42.

Salaberry, M. R. 1999: Procedural vocabulary: lexical signalling of conceptual relations in the development of past tense verbal morphology in classroom L2 Spanish. *Applied Linguistics*, 20 (2), 151–78.

Salaberry, M. R. and López-Ortega, N. 1998: Accurate L2 production across language tasks: focus on form, focus on meaning, and communicative control. *Modern Language Journal*, 82 (4), 514–32.

Sasaki, M. 1998: Investigating EFL students' production of speech acts: a comparison of production questionnaires and role plays. *Journal of Pragmatics*, 30 (4), 457–84.

Sasaki, Y. 1994: Paths of processing strategy transfers in learning Japanese and English as foreign languages. *Studies in Second Language Acquisition*, 16 (1), 43–72.

Sato, C. J. 1985: Task variation in interlanguage phonology. In S. M. Gass and C. G. Madden (eds), *Input in Second Language Acquisition*. Rowley, MA: Newbury House, 181–96.

Sato, C. J. 1990: *The Syntax of Conversation in Interlanguage Development*. Tübingen: Gunter Narr.

Scarcella, R. and Zimmerman, C. 1998: Academic words and gender: ESL student performance on a test of academic lexicon. *Studies in Second Language Acquisition*, 20 (1), 27–49.

Schachter, J. 1989: Testing a proposed universal. In S. M. Gass and J. Schachter (eds), *Linguistic Perspectives on Second Language Acquisition*. Cambridge: Cambridge University Press, 73–88.

Schachter, J. and Yip, V. 1990: Why does anyone object to subject extraction? *Studies in Second Language Acquisition*, 12 (4), 379–92.

Schlyter, S. 1993: The weaker language in bilingual Swedish–French children. In K. Hyltenstam and Å. Viberg (eds), *Progression and Regression in Language: Sociocultural, Neuropsychological, and Linguistic Perspectives*. Cambridge: Cambridge University Press, 289–308.

Schmidt, R. (ed.) 1995a: *Attention and Awareness in Foreign Language Learning*. Honolulu: University of Hawai'i Second Language Teaching and Curriculum Center.

Schmidt, R. 1995b: Consciousness and foreign language learning: a tutorial on the role of attention and awareness in learning. In R. Schmidt (ed.), *Attention and Awareness in Foreign Language Learning*. Honolulu: University of Hawai'i Second Language Teaching and Curriculum Center, 1–63.

Schmidt, R. and Frota, S. 1986: Developing basic conversational ability in a second language: a case study of an adult learner of Portuguese. In R. Day (ed.), *Talking to Learn: Conversation in Second Language Acquisition*. Rowley, MA: Newbury House, 237–326.

Schmitt, N. and Meara, P. 1997: Researching vocabulary through a word knowledge framework. *Studies in Second Language Acquisition*, 19 (1), 17–36.

Schreuder, R. and Weltens, B. (eds) 1993: *The Bilingual Lexicon*. Philadelphia: John Benjamins.

Schumann, F. M. 1980: Diary of a language learner: a further analysis. In R. C. Scarcella and S. D. Krashen (eds), *Research in Second Language Acquisition*. Rowley, MA: Newbury House, 51–7.

Schumann, J. 1978: *The Pidginization Process: A Model for Second Language Acquisition*. Rowley, MA: Newbury House.

Schütze, C. T. 1996: *The Empirical Base of Linguistics: Grammaticality Judgments and Linguistic Methodology*. Chicago: University of Chicago Press.

Scott, M. L. 1994: Auditory memory and perception in younger and older adult second language learners. *Studies in Second Language Acquisition*, 16 (3), 263–281.

Seliger, H. 1989: Deterioration and creativity in childhood bilingualism. In K. Hyltenstam and L. Obler (eds), *Bilingualism Across the Lifespan*. Cambridge: Cambridge University Press, 173–84.

Seliger, H. W. and Shohamy, E. 1989: *Second Language Research Methods*. London: Oxford University Press.

Shehadeh, A. 1999: Non-native speakers' production of modified comprehensible output and second language learning. *Language Learning*, 49 (4), 627–75.

Shirai, Y. and Kurono, A. 1998: The acquisition of tense-aspect marking in Japanese as a second language. *Language Learning*, 48 (2), 245–79.

Simard, D. and Wong, W. 2001: Alertness, orientation, and detection: the conceptualization of attentional functions in SLA. *Studies in Second Language Acquisition*, 23 (1), 103–24.

Skehan, P. 1986: Cluster analysis and the identification of learner types. In V. Cook (ed.), *Experimental Approaches to Second Language Learning*. Oxford: Pergamon Press, 81–94.

Skehan, P. 1998: *A Cognitive Approach to Language Learning*. Oxford: Oxford University Press.

Skehan, P. and Foster, P. 1997: Task type and task processing conditions as influences on foreign language performance. *Language Teaching Research*, 1, 185–211.

Skiba, R. and Dittmar, N. 1992: Pragmatic, semantic, and syntactic constraints and grammaticalization. *Studies in Second Language Acquisition*, 14 (3), 323–49.

Slavoff, G. R. and Johnson, J. S. 1995: The effects of age on the rate of learning a second language. *Studies in Second Language Acquisition*, 17 (1), 1–16.

Slobin, D. I. and Welsh, C. A. 1973: Elicited imitation as a research tool in developmental psycholinguistics. In C. Ferguson and D. Slobin (eds), *Studies of Child Language Development*. New York: Holt, Rinehart, and Winston, 485–97. Reprint of D. I. Slobin and C. A. Welsh (1968) Elicited imitation as a research tool in developmental psycholinguistics. Working Paper 10. Language Behavior Research Laboratory, University of California, Berkeley.

Smith, M. C. 1997: How do bilinguals access lexical information? In A. M. B. De Groot and J. F. Kroll (eds), *Tutorials in Bilingualism: Psycholinguistic Perspectives*. Mahwah, NJ: Lawrence Erlbaum Associates, 145–68.

Snodgrass, J. G. 1993: Translating *versus* picture naming: similarities and differences. In R. Schreuder and B. Weltens (eds), *The Bilingual Lexicon*. Philadelphia: John Benjamins, 83–114.

Snow, C. E., Cancino, H., de Temple, J., and Schley, S. 1991: Giving formal definitions: a linguistic or metalinguistic skill? In E. Bialystok (ed.), *Communication Strategies: A Psychological Analysis of Second-Language Use*. Oxford: Blackwell, 90–112.

Sorace, A. 1990: Indeterminacy in first and second languages: theoretical and methodological issues. In J. de Jong and D. Stevenson (eds), *Individualizing the Assessment of Language Abilities*. Clevedon: Multilingual Matters, 127–53.

Sorace, A. 1996: The use of acceptability judgments in second language acquisition research. In W. C. Ritchie and T. K. Bhatia, (eds), *Handbook of Second Language Acquisition*. San Diego: Academic Press, 375–409.

Su, I.-R. 2001: Transfer of sentence processing strategies: a comparison of

L2 learners of Chinese and English. *Applied Psycholinguistics*, 22 (1), 83–112.

Swain, M. 1972: Bilingualism as a first language. Ph.D. dissertation. University of California at Irvine.

Swain, M. and Cumming, A. 1989: Beyond methodology: behind research. In J. H. Esling (ed.), *Multicultural Education and Policy: ESL in the 1990s*. Toronto: OISE Press, 88–106.

Swain, M. and Lapkin, S. 1998: Interaction and second language learning: two adolescent French immersion students working together. *Modern Language Journal*, 82 (3), 320–37.

Swain, M. and Wesche, M. 1973: Linguistic interaction: case study of a bilingual child. *Working Papers on Bilingualism*, 1, 10–34.

Swain, M., Dumas, G., and Naiman, N. 1974: Alternatives to spontaneous speech: elicited translation and imitation as indicators of second language competence. *Working Papers on Bilingualism*, 4, 68–79.

Tanaka, S. and Kawade, S. 1982: Politeness strategies and second language acquisition. *Studies in Second Language Acquisition*, 5 (1), 18–33.

Tarone, E. 1979: Interlanguage as chameleon. *Language Learning*, 29 (1), 181–91.

Tarone, E. 1983: On the variability of interlanguage systems. *Applied Linguistics*, 4, 143–63.

Thomas, M. 1992: What do elicited imitation data reveal about comprehension? In D. Staub and C. Delk (eds), *The Proceedings of the Twelfth Second Language Research Forum*. East Lansing, MI: Michigan State University, 187–99.

Thomas, M. 1994: Assessment of L2 proficiency in second language acquisition research. *Language Learning*, 44 (2), 307–36.

Thornton, R. 1996: Elicited production. In D. McDaniel, C. McKee, and H. Smith Cairns (eds), *Methods for Assessing Children's Syntax*. Cambridge, MA: MIT Press, 77–102.

Tomiyama, M. 2000: Child second language attrition: a longitudinal case study. *Applied Linguistics*, 21 (3), 304–32.

Tomlin, R. S. 1984: The treatment of foreground–background in the on-line descriptive discourse of second language learners. *Studies in Second Language Acquisition*, 6 (2), 115–42.

Towell, R., Hawkins, R., and Bazergui, N. 1993: Systematic and nonsystematic variability in advanced language learning. *Studies in Second Language Acquisition*, 15 (4), 439–60.

Trahey, M. 1996: Positive evidence in second language acquisition: some long-term effects. *Second Language Research*, 12 (2), 111–39.

Trahey, M., and White, L. 1993: Positive evidence and preemption in the second language classroom. *Studies in Second Language Acquisition*, 15 (2), 181–204.

UCLES (University of Cambridge Local Examinations Syndicate) 1990: *First Certificate in English/Certificate of Proficiency in English: Instructions to Oral Examiners*. Cambridge: UCLES.

Valdman, A. (ed.) 1988: The assessment of foreign language oral proficiency. Special issue. *Studies in Second Language Acquisition*, 10 (2).

Van den Branden, K. 1997: Effects of negotiation on language learners' output. *Language Learning*, 47 (4), 589–636.

van Lier, L. 1988: *The Classroom and the Language Learner*. London: Longman.

VanPatten, B. and Cadierno, T. 1993: Explicit instruction and input processing. *Studies in Second Language Acquisition*, 15 (2), 225–43.

VanPatten, B. and Oikkenon, S. 1996: Explanation versus structured input in processing instruction. *Studies in*

Second Language Acquisition, 18 (4), 495–510.

Verhoeven, L. T. 1994: Transfer in bilingual development: the linguistic interdependence hypothesis revisited. *Language Learning*, 44 (3), 381–415.

Viberg, Å. 1993: Crosslinguistic perspectives on lexical organization and lexical progression. In K. Hyltenstam and Å. Viberg (eds), *Progression and Regression in Language: Sociocultural, Neuropsychological, and Linguistic Perspectives*. Cambridge: Cambridge University Press, 340–85.

Walters, J. 1979: The perception of politeness in English and Spanish. In C. A. Yorio, K. Perkins, and J. Schachter (eds), *On TESOL '79: The Learner in Focus*. Washington, DC: TESOL, 288–96.

Wang, C. and Lee, T. H. 1999: L2 acquisition of conflation classes of prenominal adjectival participles. *Language Learning*, 49 (1), 1–36.

Watson, I. 1991: Phonological processing in two languages. In E. Bialystok (ed.), *Communication Strategies: A Psychological Analysis of Second-Language Use*. Oxford: Blackwell, 25–48.

Weber-Fox, C. and Neville, H. J. 1999: Functional neural subsystems are differentially affected by delays in second language immersion: ERP and behavioral evidence in bilinguals. In D. Birdsong (ed.), *Second Language Acquisition and the Critical Period Hypothesis*. Mahwah, NJ: Lawrence Erlbaum Associates, 23–38.

Wesche, M. and Paribakht, T. S. 1996: Assessing vocabulary knowledge: depth vs. breadth. *Canadian Modern Language Review*, 53 (1), 13–40.

White, L. 1986: Implications of parametric variation for adult second language acquisition: an investigation of the pro-drop parameter. In V. Cook (ed.), *Experimental Approaches to Second Language Learning*. Oxford: Pergamon Press, 55–72.

White, L. 1989: The adjacency condition on case assignment: do L2 learners observe the Subset Principle? In S. M. Gass and J. Schachter (eds), *Linguistic Perspectives on Second Language Acquisition*. Cambridge: Cambridge University Press, 134–58.

White, L. 1991: Adverb placement in second language acquisition: some effects of positive and negative evidence in the classroom. *Second Language Research*, 7 (2), 133–61.

White, L., Spada, N., Lightbown, P. M., and Ranta, L. 1991: Input enhancement and L2 question formation. *Applied Linguistics*, 12 (4), 416–32.

White, L., Bruhn-Garavito, J., Kawasaki, T., Pater, J., and Prévost, P. 1997: The researcher gave the subject a test about himself: problems of ambiguity and preference in the investigation of reflexive binding. *Language Learning*, 47 (1), 145–72.

Williams, J. 1999: Learner-generated attention to form. *Language Learning*, 49 (4), 583–625.

Wode, H. 1999: Incidental vocabulary acquisition in the foreign language classroom. *Studies in Second Language Acquisition*, 21 (2), 243–58.

Wolfe-Quintero, K. 1992: Learnability and the acquisition of extraction in relative clauses and *Wh*-questions. *Studies in Second Language Acquisition*, 14 (1), 39–70.

Wolfe-Quintero, K., Inagaki, S., and Kim, H. 1998: *Second Language Development in Writing: Measures of Fluency, Accuracy and Complexity*. Honolulu: University of Hawai'i Second Language Teaching and Curriculum Center.

Wolter, B. 2001: Comparing the L1 and L2 mental lexicon. *Studies in Second Language Acquisition*, 23 (1), 41–69.

Yang, L. R. and Givón, T. 1997: Benefits and drawbacks of controlled laboratory studies of second language acquisition. *Studies in Second Language Acquisition*, 19 (2), 173–93.

Ying, H. G. 1996: Multiple constraints on processing ambiguous sentences: evidence from adult L2 learners. *Language Learning*, 6 (4), 681–711.

Young, R. 1995: Conversational styles in language proficiency interviews. *Language Learning*, 45 (1), 3–42.

Young, R. and He, A. W. (eds) 1998: *Taking and Testing: Discourse Approaches to the Assessment of Oral Proficiency*. Philadelphia: John Benjamins.

Young, R. and Milanovic, M. 1992. Discourse variation in oral proficiency interviews. *Studies in Second Language Acquisition*, 14 (4), 403–24.

Yuan, B. 1995: Acquisition of base-generated topics by English-speaking learners of Chinese. *Language Learning*, 45 (4), 567–603.

Yuan, B. 1997: Asymmetry of null subjects and null objects in Chinese speakers' L2 English. *Studies in Second Language Acquisition*, 19 (4), 467–97.

Yule, G. 1997: *Referential Communication Tasks*. Mahwah, NJ: Lawrence Erlbaum Associates.

Zobl, H. 1992: Sources of linguistic knowledge and uniformity of nonnative performance. *Studies in Second Language Acquisition*, 14 (4), 387–402.

VII The State of SLA

23 SLA Theory: Construction and Assessment

KEVIN R. GREGG

1 Introduction

Anyone who has read the preceding chapters will agree that SLA is a terribly complex process, that understanding the process requires the contributions of numerous fields, from linguistic theory to anthropology to brain science, and that the process is not yet very well understood. In this chapter, we step back a bit from the trees, as it were, of the previous chapters, to look at the forest; to situate SLA within scientific inquiry in general, and within the field of cognitive science in particular.

I speak of SLA as a science here both without apology, despite the arguably quite meager empirical results so far obtained, and without invidious presuppositions about the relative intellectual merit of different objects and methods of study. The world is full of phenomena, only some of which lend themselves to scientific study. It may very well be that only a relatively small part of human nature falls within the area amenable to scientific study.[1] But language acquisition certainly seems to lie in that possibly constricted area, and to that extent I see nothing misleading or pretentious in talking about SLA as a scientific enterprise.[2]

But of course science is anything but monolithic. Scientists can differ not only in the objects of their research, but also in their epistemological stances toward those objects and their methodological stances toward the research, as well as in what they see as the important problems to be solved. In what follows we will look at some of the variation, possible and actual, in SLA theorizing.

2 Attitudes Toward Theories and Theoretical Entities

2.1 *Three epistemological stances*

To start with, SLA researchers, like other scientific researchers, can differ among themselves in the commitments they make as to what can in principle be known about the phenomena of interest and what the epistemological status is or can be of theories and the entities they posit. Very roughly, one can distinguish three positions: realism, empiricism, and relativism.

Realism is essentially the claim "that the characteristic product of successful scientific research is knowledge of largely theory-independent phenomena and that such knowledge is possible (indeed actual) even in those cases in which the relevant phenomena are not, in any non-question-begging sense, observable" (Boyd, 1989, p. 6). Empiricists would reject the term "knowledge," at least insofar as it is based on non-observable phenomena. "Knowledge" presupposes "truth," and empiricists claim that the most one can attribute to a theory is "empirical adequacy"; we are warranted in believing only what we can observe, although of course we are free to make use in our theories of constructs that go beyond the observable. An empiricist, in other words, can take an *instrumentalist* attitude toward theoretical constructs, using them to make predictions, for instance, but will withhold from them the status of real entities. A relativist denies the theory-independence of phenomena, and further denies, *contra* realists and empiricists alike, that knowledge or empirical adequacy is either actually or potentially of universal validity. Rather, theories are only true relative to some specific personal point of view, cultural or temporal context, Kuhnian paradigm, etc.

I don't propose to spend much time on relativist views of theory, SLA or otherwise, as there seems to be very little reason to take them seriously. For one thing, there are, to a first approximation, no scientists who take a relativist position. This is hardly surprising: it is inherently self-contradictory to conduct empirical research in order to reach conclusions that could be reached without all that bother, and which could not persuade, or even be comprehensible to, anyone outside the researcher's culture/paradigm/mindset. As Long put it, "it is not clear . . . why relativists would bother to do research at all" (Long, 1993, p. 230).

Of course, scientists themselves might be mistaken; they may be blind to the fact that they are not discovering facts but constructing them, as Latour and Woolgar (1986; Latour, 1987) argue (Latour and Woolgar themselves are evidently immune to this blindness; *they* have not constructed facts about how scientific research is done, but discovered them, on the basis of objective observation). Thus, more important than the fact that scientists, including SLA researchers, do not conduct research within a relativist framework is the fact that no one has provided any convincing reason to think that relativism is a defensible, or even a coherent, epistemology. As Brueckner says, "It is difficult to formulate an even remotely plausible view that deserves the title *conceptual relativism*" (1998, p. 295). (For detailed discussion of the problems of relativism, see Laudan, 1990, 1996.)[3] So, since no one has given us any reason to deny the claim, supported by realists and empiricists alike, that "there are some hypotheses and some logically and nomologically possible states of affairs such that we're absolutely warranted in believing the hypothesis if we find ourselves in the indicated state" (Kukla, 1998, p. 112), and since virtually all SLA research takes that claim for granted, we may safely give relativism short shrift, and concentrate on the differences between realist and empiricist takes on SLA.

2.2 *Theory and observation*

Perhaps the fundamental question dividing realists and empiricists is the theory/observation distinction. For the empiricist, remember, we are warranted in believing only observational statements (although we may, of course, agnostically employ theoretical ones as well). For this claim to go through, however, there must be a non-arbitrary way to distinguish observational statements from theoretical ones. But it has long been argued that any such distinction is inevitably arbitrary, that observation is, as they say, *theory-laden* (Hacking, 1983; Hanson, 1958; Kuhn, 1970; Maxwell, 1962), and these arguments do not seem to have been satisfactorily refuted (Sober, 1994a; see Kukla, 1998, for extensive discussion). Now, if empiricists cannot convincingly maintain the theory–observation distinction, then they have no principled ground on which to withhold belief in the existence of theoretical entities. This becomes particularly germane, perhaps, in the case of sciences like linguistics, which posit entities, such as Universal Grammar, that are on anyone's account unobservable in principle.[4]

If we accept the idea of the theory-ladenness of observation, we can run with it in a couple of very different directions. One direction leads to the relativist claim that theory-neutral observation is impossible: if even the most innocent-seeming observation is tainted with theoretical presupposition, so the reasoning runs, then two observers, starting with different presuppositions, will not be in a position to agree about what inferences from that observation are legitimate. If, as the relativist maintains, there is no theory-neutral observation, we cannot expect there to be observational statements whose veridicality could be accepted by all rational observers. Indeed, on a radical interpretation of theory-ladenness, observers who don't share the same presuppositions actually observe different things.

Fortunately, theory-ladenness simply does not, *pace* the relativists, entail the impossibility of theory-neutral observation. For one thing, as Kukla points out, there is simply no reason to think that our observations are affected by our beliefs in anything like the degree assumed by this relativist position: "To show the impossibility of theory-neutral observation, one would have to establish that *all* cognitive differences have an effect on perception – and this goes beyond what the New Look research program has established on even the most sanguine reading" (1998, p. 115; cf. J. A. Fodor, 1983).[5] And in fact there are countless observational statements about whose veridicality no rational observer disagrees.

For another thing, there is usually no reason to think that a given observation is "laden" with the particular theory being tested by that observation (Hacking, 1983; Nagel, 1997). Nor do we need to demand that *all* observations be neutral relative to *all* possible theories; it is enough (but it is essential) that the observations at issue be neutral with respect to the two or more theories that are being tested (Sober, 1999). Observation of cell mitosis, or of the surface of Mars, is "laden" with various theories from optics that explain how microscopes and telescopes work, for instance. But those theories don't affect the observations, although they may, of course, affect the interpretation of the observations, which is a different question: whether the lines we see are canals or not doesn't alter the fact that we – all of us – see lines. We may refuse to accept the results of a grammaticality judgment test because we think there's no reliable causal connection between the subjects' knowledge and their responses, or because we reject the grammar-theoretical categories being tested, or because we disagree with the judgments; but we will not disagree as to what was in fact observed, which was a set of marks on paper.

This leads to a final, important point about observation, theory-laden or other: as Bogen and Woodward (1988) argue, if "we use 'observe' to mean 'perceive' or 'detect by means of processes which can be usefully viewed as extensions of perception,' then scientific theories typically do not predict and explain facts about what we observe" (p. 305). What we actually observe in a grammaticality judgment test, for example, is the subject making marks on paper or punching keys on a computer keyboard; we do not observe grammaticality judgments. We infer (with a very high degree of confidence, of course) from the observed acts to the judgments, and (with a good deal lower degree of confidence) from the inferred judgments to the hypothesized grammatical knowledge. On the other hand, we want to predict (and explain) not the observable markings and punchings but the judgments, which we can't observe. It is these unobservable *phenomena*, not the observable *data*, that are the objects of inquiry; thus "it is a mistake to think of claims about phenomena as theory-laden observational claims" (p. 315; cf. Woodward, 1989; see Gregg, 1993, for SLA-related discussion).

In short, to say that observations are theory-laden is not by any means to say that objective comparison and assessment of theories are impossible. But there are other inferences one can make from the claim that there is no criterion or algorithm for distinguishing theoretical statements from observational statements. As we saw above, denying the theory–observation distinction opens up the possibility of rationally accepting the existence of "purely" theoretical – that is to say, unobservable – entities, which is precisely what the realist does.[6] But since (unlike relativists) realists do not believe that "anything goes," they must give us some sort of criteria for deciding when a given unobservable construct warrants our belief. Since the criterion of observability is obviously out, it follows that the realist is committed to appealing to, or at least allowing the appeal to, non-empirical virtues such as simplicity, explanatory power, or inference to the best explanation as criteria for preferring one theory over another. This raises a range of problems, as we will see below.

2.3 *Realism and empiricism in SLA*

SLA researchers are not given to publishing their epistemological allegiances or arguing about issues in the philosophy of science. (But see, e.g., Beretta, 1991;

Beretta and Crookes, 1993; Gregg, 1989, 1993; Long, 1990a, 1993; Tarone, 1994.) Even those SLA textbooks that devote some space to more general questions of theory (as opposed to simply presenting and comparing various theories), such as Larsen-Freeman and Long (1991) or McLaughlin (1987), are not that explicit.

One could perhaps characterize the majority of SLA researchers as holding to what Kukla (following Leplin, 1997) calls "minimal epistemic realism," the belief that "it's logically and nomologically possible to attain to a state that warrants belief in a theory" (Kukla, 1998, p. 11). Note that this position does not imply any strong realist commitment. It is indeed a minimalist position, little more than an articulation of the common ground shared by realists and empiricists (notably, the rejection of relativism and its works), leaving open most of the questions that divide those two camps.

Foremost among those questions is the role of non-observables. In SLA, as in all areas of psychology, opinion differs as to how far we should be willing to attribute causal powers to distinct, but of course unobservable, elements of the mind. Empiricist psychologists begrudge every such attribution, wishing to appeal wherever possible to the environment; hence, for instance, their peculiar insistence on operationalization.[7] Realists are perfectly at ease with a proliferation of mental elements, and willing to justify them on theoretical rather than operational grounds. We will see how this opposition plays itself out in SLA below, when we look at SLA property theories.

3 The Domain of an SLA Theory

SLA theorists can differ not only in their epistemological commitments, but in their view of the domain of SLA theory: what is an SLA theory a theory of?

On the face of it, this would seem to be a fairly simple and uncontroversial question: SLA theory is the theory of the acquisition of a second language. Since acquisition is at least something like learning, if not in fact the very same thing, it should follow that SLA falls within the scope of cognitive science, as opposed to social science. SLA research is thus first and foremost an *internalist* rather than an *externalist* discipline, to borrow terms from Chomsky (1995). That is to say that we are primarily concerned with learner-internal changes of state, not with the behavior of learner groups (or even of individual learners), and not with abstract "learner languages," or "E-languages," to apply Chomsky's (1986) term to SLA.

Of course, just because this may seem to go without saying (or at least *with* saying: e.g., Gregg, 1989, 1990) doesn't mean that it has been accepted without question. Firth and Wagner (1997), for instance, make the bizarre claim that current SLA research is too cognitive, although they fail to offer any reasons for changing the direction of research in the way they seem to favor (see commentary by Gass, 1998; Kasper, 1997; Long, 1997). No one, however, has presented a coherent argument against the position that second language acquisition involves individual mental states and their changes, so I think that we can accept that position as a working definition of the domain of SLA theory.

This does not, I stress, mean that externalist L2 research is inconsequential, uninteresting, misguided, or irrelevant. And it certainly does not mean that learner behavior can be ignored by researchers trying to explain SLA. The point is simply that we must distinguish between evidence for an SLA theory (learner behavior) and the object of that theory (learner mental states).

3.1 Natural kinds

One way of comparing internalist and externalist approaches to SLA theory is to consider whether they can identify natural kinds among the objects of study. Ideally, that is, a theory should be able to pick out a set of objects such that, however it is defined, one can make interesting generalizations that apply to all and only the members of that set. Biology distinguishes, say, between mammals and fish, but not between terrestrial and aquatic animals, because once you've identified something as a mammal you can predict all kinds of things about its physiology regardless of where it lives, whereas identifying something as an aquatic animal tells you little more of biological interest than that it's an animal and that it lives in the water. ("Interesting," of course, means scientifically interesting, not culturally. The distinction in Jewish law between clean and unclean animals is interesting, but not to the biologist. Chemistry recognizes a class of heavy metals, but not a class of precious metals, no matter how much more interesting you and I find the latter.)

The question, then, is whether an externalist or an internalist approach to SLA is more likely to be able to distinguish natural kinds. Non-native utterances, for instance, are often ungrammatical from the point of view of the target language, but then so are some native utterances, and many if not most non-native utterances (if it even makes sense to quantify them) are grammatical. So it's hard to see how the set of non-native utterances could be characterized so as to distinguish it from the set of native utterances, let alone how we could go beyond the definition of non-native utterances to make other claims than that they are utterances made by non-natives. Again, many L2 learners learn their L2 primarily in classrooms, and thus could fall within the domain of a pedagogical theory, for instance, or a sociological theory about power relations in schools; but then other students learn, and other subjects are taught, in classrooms on the one hand, and many L2 learners learn the L2 outside of classrooms on the other. Many L2 learners are immigrants learning the L2 on the job, and as immigrants in low-paying jobs are the victims of oppression and discrimination; but then many aren't immigrants, and there are many natives who suffer oppression and discrimination. In short, it appears that it will be hard to identify the class of L2 learners in a way that could define them as a natural class for an externalist SLA theory.

Of course, we are not by any means guaranteed that an internalist SLA theory will do better, but the possibilities at least seem a bit more promising.

We need to ask whether the set of L2 learners – or rather, the set of L2 learner grammars – regardless of L1 and regardless of target language, constitutes an interestingly distinct natural kind, different from the knowledge states of learners in general, and from the grammars of L1 learners in particular. And we need to ask whether adult language learners constitute an interestingly different kind from bilingual child language learners. These questions are all still open – albeit to varying degrees, perhaps – and the answers may turn out to be "No." Language acquisition, first or second, could turn out to be nothing other than learning, in which case the class of L2 learners would be of no more specific scientific interest than the class of mathematics learners. More plausibly, perhaps, adult SLA could turn out to be the same as child language acquisition, in which case L2 learners could be merely a source of dirtier than normal data. But at least the possibility seems to remain that there are interesting things to say about the mental states of adult L2 learners *qua* adult L2 learners that one cannot say about children or about learning in domains other than language.

3.2 *Idealization*

If we are working toward an internalist theory, it may be objected, a theory of mental states and changes of state, while at the same time tentatively assuming that the set of adult L2 learners forms a natural kind, are we not ignoring the seemingly gross variation that obtains across learners? Yes, that's exactly what we're doing. *Any* theory, as a matter of course, idealizes over its subject matter. The very idea of a natural kind presupposes certain attributes shared by all the members and by them only; the problem for the theorist is to identify those common attributes that specify the kind. But that means that, for the purposes of specifying the kind, we can and should ignore variation across members. Once we are in a position to identify what distinguishes the class of L2 learners from other learners, we are in a better position to characterize and explain the variation among L2 learners.

We are tentatively allowing for a couple of different possibilities, which need to be confirmed or rejected on empirical grounds:

i The possibility that nativelike competence can be attained. This view is consistent with, although it doesn't necessarily entail, the position that SLA is essentially the same process as child first language acquisition, and just as first language acquisition theory assumes an ideal learner who attains perfect competence, so would an SLA theory. The self-evident disjunction between this idealization and the reality of SLA variation would then need to be explained (or explained away) by secondary, extrinsic causes: quantitative or qualitative deficiencies in input, motivational, or other affective variation, degrees of acculturation, what have you.

ii The possibility that there are one or more (relevant) universal differences between the initial state of adult learners and that of child learners, hence universal (minimal) "deficits" in final L2 competence. Here again we would be postulating a uniform ideal final state, albeit one that differs from the final state attained by the L1 native speaker. (If we don't mind committing the "comparative fallacy" (Bley-Vroman, 1983), we could say that non-native learners "fail to acquire the target language completely," or have "imperfect L2 competence.") Thus, one could posit the effects of input and affect as in (i), while claiming that even if, in the ideal situation, these were all overcome, there would still be differences between the final state of the ideal native and that of the ideal non-native. One could argue, say, that the adult L2 learner has lost one or more specific learning mechanisms used by children (O'Grady, this volume; White, 1989); or that the adult L2 learner is not able to fix parameter values for the L2 (to "reset" parameters, as it is often put) (Eubank and Gregg, 1999; Hawkins and Chan, 1997; Schachter, 1996; Smith and Tsimpli, 1995; Strozer, 1994).

Note that on either view, (i) or (ii), we are idealizing away from the actual variation that one can observe across individual learners; note further that this is exactly what we should want to do. Take parameter-setting, for one example. One could consistently claim that all L2 learners are different from natives, and identical to each other, in one specific respect – inability to reset parameters – while allowing for, indeed predicting, wide variation across learners according to what specific L1–L2 parametric differences obtain. One might predict, for instance, different L2 English competences – and hence different behaviors – with respect to expletives and pronoun use depending on whether the L1 was a pro-drop language or not. At the same time, by positing a certain uniformity across learners – a uniformity that is, moreover, not observable – we have the possibility of making a principled, testable distinction between possible and impossible variation (or predictable and non-predictable) and thus have a potential means of explaining variation, rather than merely describing it. Indeed, failing to idealize in this way virtually guarantees the sort of theoretical sterility found in much of the SLA variationist literature (Gregg, 1990).

4 SLA Property Theories

Given an internalist perspective – given, that is, that we are hoping to explain the internal state of an individual learner with respect to an L2 – it may not be too question-begging to assume that an SLA theory will characterize the L2 *knowledge*, or *competence*, of an idealized learner. Those terms, of course, have been the object of a great deal of contention, but not from within the internalist perspective, where perhaps the only principled rejection of the terms would come from those who prefer to talk of dispositions to behave rather than of knowledge. The arguments against such a view are well known (see, e.g., Chomsky, 1959, 1980a, 1986), and there's no need to rehash them here. In short, an SLA theory needs to explain the knowledge state of the L2 learner vis-à-vis the L2. Indeed, it needs to explain at least two such states: the initial state, immediately preceding first exposure to L2 input, and the final state, after which input ceases to have any significant instructional effect.

A theory of this sort is sometimes referred to as a *property theory* (Cummins, 1983; for SLA, see Gregg, 1993, 1996a, 2001). A property theory answers the question, "In virtue of what does system S have property P?" (Cummins, 1983); it explains the instantiation of a property in a system. Thus, for example, theories of dispositions – acidity, solubility, heritability, etc. – are property theories. Linguistic theory is an excellent example of a property theory, answering the question of how linguistic knowledge is instantiated in a mind. Property theories do not account for sequential processes – these are the domain of a *transition theory*, which answers the question, "How does system S change from one state to the next?" But this is not to say that property theories are not causal. To claim, for example, that such-and-such a sentence is ungrammatical by virtue of the Empty Category Principle is to claim that there is a causal relation between the ECP and the ungrammaticality. To put it somewhat differently, a property theory that appeals to the ECP in this way is claiming that the ECP is real; not just "psychologically real," whatever that peculiar phrase is supposed to mean, but real: "To be real is to have causal efficacy; to be unreal is to be a mere artefact of some causal process" (Sober, 1994b, p. 220). This is what makes property theories explanations, not mere descriptions.

Property theories of SLA can vary on any number of parameters, but we will look at the following:

i *modularity* (section 4.1): is L2 knowledge in any interesting way modular?
ii *innateness* (section 4.2): is L2 knowledge in any interesting way attained or possessed independently of environmental influence?
iii *the nature of L2 representations* (section 4.3): specifically, does L2 knowledge consist in a hierarchically ordered, structured system of representations, or is it distributed across essentially unstructured representations?

4.1 Modularity

A module is a comparatively autonomous subsystem within a larger system, which acts more or less independently of other subsystems, and has structures and functions that are more or less recognizably different from those of other subsystems. Cognitive science recognizes a couple of different senses of modularity. One difference is in the level of analysis: modularity at the anatomical level vs. modularity at the functional level. A claim of *anatomical* modularity for L2 knowledge would be a claim that L2 knowledge is localized in a specific, well-defined area of the brain. Such a claim, though, stands or falls independently of a claim of *cognitive* modularity, the claim that L2 knowledge, however instantiated physiologically and wherever located, is a module within a larger system of knowledge. The mutual independence of these two modularity claims needs to be stressed, as it is often overlooked in the literature. If, for instance, we were to find that all L2 performance – silent reading, conversation, listening, etc. – activated one specific corner of the brain and no other, that would certainly be suggestive evidence for the cognitive modularity of L2 knowledge. And if that L2 corner were different from the L1 corner, it might suggest that L1 knowledge and L2 knowledge were cognitively different. But such a conclusion would not automatically follow, any more than the conclusion that the books on the third floor of the library stacks are categorically different from those on the first. And by the same token, just as books on the same subject may be shelved in two widely separate locations simply according to age or size or date of acquisition, so would the discovery of multiple "L2 areas" in the brain be consistent with L2 as a cognitive module.

The question of anatomical modularity ("localization of function") is of course an interesting one, but for SLA as a cognitive-scientific discipline, it is secondary to the question of cognitive modularity. As Coltheart and Langdon point out (1998, p. 151), "even if there is anatomical modularity, if the module in which one is interested itself has an internal modular structure, each of these submodules may well be instantiated in a different part of the brain." Coltheart and Langdon go on to draw an important conclusion, one that is often misunderstood in the SLA literature (e.g., Jacobs and Schumann, 1992): "That is why the development of an adequately fine-grained abstract theory of the structure of cognitive systems must precede any attempts to map the neural substrate of cognition."[8]

Putting aside anatomical modularity, we can perhaps distinguish between two different (but mutually compatible) understandings of cognitive modularity, what we might call Chomsky-modularity and Fodor-modularity (see Schwartz, 1998, 1999, for discussion). L2 knowledge would be Chomsky-modular if it is part of a hypothesized language module. The language faculty is modular in that, and to the extent that, it comprises structures and conforms to principles not found in other modules: binding principles, say, or c-command, or the Subset Principle. L2 knowledge would be Fodor-modular (J. A. Fodor, 1983; Schwartz, 1986) if it is (to a significant degree) *cognitively impenetrable* and *informationally encapsulated*: that is to say, if the processing of linguistic input is not significantly affected by or accessible to higher cognitive functions (beliefs, say) or by other input systems.

Some of the contributions to this volume reflect the various possible stances one can take on L2 modularity. UG/SLA positions, for instance, assume modularity for language as a whole and extend that assumption to L2. But one can with consistency claim that L1 knowledge is modular (in whatever sense) while L2 knowledge isn't (Bley-Vroman, 1990). (For that matter, it's logically possible to claim that L2 knowledge is modular while L1 knowledge isn't, although I can't imagine anyone making such a claim.) A "cognitive nativist" position such as O'Grady's (1996, 1999b, this volume) rejects at least the strong Chomsky-modularity claimed by UG theorists. Although allowing some language-specific principles and mechanisms (such as the Subset Principle), the thrust of cognitive nativism is away from Chomsky-modularity (as reflected (e.g., O'Grady, 1996) in O'Grady's earlier term for his position, "general nativism").

It is, of course, hard to say in principle when a cognitive system is or is not modular "to an interesting degree," but connectionism is certainly anti-modular, at least in practice. This anti-modularity, it is worth noting, is not a logically necessary one. One could have a language module in which linguistic knowledge is acquired by connectionist learning mechanisms, for instance. And, as Ramsey and Stich (1991, p. 308) say, "If the best connectionist models of language acquisition exploit a learning algorithm that is particularly adept at language learning and largely useless in other domains, then again rationalism and connectionism will turn out to be comfortably compatible." But in fact most connectionists would probably reject this possibility (Broeder and Plunkett, 1994) and deny that language has any interesting domain-specific components, such as the principles and parameters of linguistic theory. Just what it is that connectionists think linguistic knowledge *does* consist of, however, is another question, and one that is not at all easy to answer; we'll return to this problem below.

4.2 *Innateness*

"Innateness" is an infelicitous term, and indeed "many biologists consider the concept of innateness to verge on incoherence" (Sterelny and Griffiths, 1999, p. 6; cf. Ariew, 1996, 1999; Wimsatt, 1986, 1999). Since no one thinks the mind is truly a *tabula rasa*, and no one thinks there are genes for foreign languages, the question is to what extent acquisition of an L2 depends on knowledge that exists independently of environmental input, *and* that applies specifically to the domain of language. Everyone, that is, postulates *some* innate component to language acquisition; at issue is to what extent the innate component is domain-specific, and to what extent the domain-specific component is innate. A comparison may be helpful: knowledge of baseball includes domain-specific knowledge, such as knowledge of what a squeeze play is, of when to throw to first base rather than second, etc. This domain-specific knowledge is learned, not innate. On the other hand, there is an innate component to baseball; bipedal movement, for instance. But clearly, running in baseball is just running; an innate capacity, but not domain-specific. Here again, the point where this "innateness" becomes "interesting" cannot be determined in advance, but useful distinctions can nonetheless be made among SLA theories.

As with modularity, UG/SLA theories stand at one extreme. Although other innate knowledge enters into language acquisition and use – for instance, the "mindreading" capacities (Baron-Cohen, 1995) that enable us to interpret the intentions underlying the utterances of others – the foundation of language knowledge is UG; and UG is innate and domain-specific. Also domain-specific, but not innate, is the peripheral information that varies from one natural language to another – the knowledge that "automobile" is used to refer to automobiles, for instance, or the knowledge of honorifics. But the essence of linguistic knowledge – the principles or mental structures that characterize the language faculty and distinguish it from other mental faculties – is, for UG/SLA theorists, innate. Cognitive nativism would reduce, perhaps drastically, the amount of domain-specific innate knowledge in language; the key properties of the computational faculty, for instance, while innate, are shared, on this view, with mathematical knowledge. Domain-specific non-innate knowledge is of two kinds: the sort of specific learned lexical information for a given language, as in UG theories, but also derived, "module"-specific knowledge. (O'Grady's idea that grammar is a "new machine built out of old parts" (1997, p. 328; quoting Bates and MacWhinney, 1988, p. 147) is reminiscent of Karmiloff-Smith's, 1992, idea of, in effect, learned modularity.)

On the face of it, connectionism would seem to deny the domain-specificity of innate knowledge totally. What is innate, presumably, is merely the general learning capacity that inheres in the system of nodes and the susceptibility of their connections to strengthening and weakening. On this view, linguistic knowledge is almost entirely learned; there are no underlying rules or principles or structures that obtain only for language.

The problem, though, is where do the nodes come from? A connectionist simulation starts with elements of some sort on which to base the growth of a distributed system; say, lexical items and plural forms as in Ellis and Schmidt (1998), or gender markers as in Sokolik and Smith (1992). But what we don't know from the simulation is how those forms were themselves acquired. Does a learner have an inborn concept of plurality, say, or gender? Since gender, at least, is a purely formal (i.e., domain-specific) concept, connectionists would seem to be committed to denying its innateness; yet nothing is said about how the concept of gender (*mutatis mutandis*, plurality, tense, etc.) is learned. But the problem of language acquisition, as Fodor says, "is that of how a child acquires grammatical structure, not how he learns *correlates* of grammatical structure" (J. A. Fodor, 1998e, p. 150). In the absence of specific connectionist proposals about such structures, we seem to have nothing to replace nativist theories such as UG. After all, if they weren't acquired, they must be innate, which is hardly what a connectionist should want to claim. Hence, for instance, Carroll's criticism of Sokolik and Smith, namely that their results merely "show that if the learning device is given *a priori* means to solve a given linguistic learning problem, it does very well indeed. This is just the claim innatists make" (Carroll, 1995, p. 202).

4.3 *L2 representations*

The crucial distinction between SLA theories here is whether or not they assume that the mental representations of L2 knowledge are structured. Most theories at least tacitly assume some sort of so-called "classical" view of knowledge representation, such that knowledge (e.g., L2 knowledge) is organized in a highly structured system of representations (e.g., a syntax); UG theories, of course, make that structure fairly explicit. Connectionists, on the other hand, generally see L2 knowledge as instantiated in unstructured, distributed representations. (Cf. J. A. Fodor, 1998a, p. 11 fn. 6: "Connectionists are committed, willy-nilly, to *all* mental representations being primitive.")[9] To be more precise, this is the position taken by those connectionists – often referred to as "eliminativist connectionists" – who see connectionism as offering a rival account of mental representation to the "classical" account. Rey refers to this strong form of connectionism as RCON (radical connectionism) to distinguish it from LCON (liberal connectionism), the view of connectionist processes as merely implementing, rather than eliminating, a classical representational system. "The crucial feature that distinguishes RCON from LCON . . . is the claim that there is no causally efficacious constituent structure to the mental representations that play a role in the processing" (Rey, 1997, p. 227). It has often been pointed out (e.g., J. A. Fodor and Pylyshyn, 1988; Rey, 1997; Sterelny, 1990) that a connectionist learning process à la LCON is consistent with a structured, classical representational architecture; but, as Broeder and Plunkett (1994) suggest, most connectionists are not content with that role. Certainly SLA connectionists seem to lean toward RCON (e.g., Ellis and Schmidt, 1998), and in any case LCON is of no interest to us here as a property theory of L2 knowledge, since it doesn't provide an alternative to classical theories like UG/SLA. In what follows, then, I will use "connectionist" and "connectionism" to refer to RCON, or eliminativist connectionism.

What's at stake in the choice between structured and unstructured representations? The fundamental problem is the one raised by J. A. Fodor and Pylyshyn (1988): the problem of *systematicity*. Briefly, it is uncontroversial that in any natural language, if that language allows a sentence of the form, say, "John loves Mary," it will also allow "Mary loves John" (similarly, anyone who can think that John loves Mary – in effect, anyone – can think that Mary loves John). This sort of fact is easily enough explained if you allow syntactic categories and rules that control them: noun phrases are structures that can fill certain roles within a larger structure (a sentence), and if X is a noun phrase, then by virtue of its category membership it can play those roles, etc. Put somewhat differently, the undoubted systematicity of language can be explained if it is *nomologically necessary*: systematicity (syntacticity) is a necessary condition on being a natural language.

On a connectionist account, on the other hand, it would seem that this sort of systematicity is purely contingent: it just so happens that all humans have this capacity. In the absence of appropriate input, it should be perfectly possible for there to be a human who can say "John loves Mary" but cannot say "Mary loves John." This seems, to say the least, counterintuitive; as Fodor says, "I think we had better take it for granted, and as part of what is not negotiable, that systematicity and productivity are grounded in the 'architecture' of mental representation and not in the vagaries of experience. If a serious alternative proposal should surface, I guess I'm prepared to reconsider what's negotiable. But the prospect hasn't been losing me sleep" (J. A. Fodor, 1998a, p. 27).

The systematicity debate rages on, and at least some connectionists have recognized it as an important challenge to connectionism (e.g., Clark, 1993),[10] and have taken it seriously enough to try to overcome it (e.g., Smolensky, 1987, 1995; for responses see J. A. Fodor, 1998c; J. A. Fodor and McLaughlin, 1998), but the consensus so far seems to be that this challenge has yet to be met. Aizawa, indeed, goes so far as to say (1997, p. 126), "Independent discoveries by future science might one day vindicate Connectionism against Classicism, but what future science will not change is the fact that Connectionism cannot explain the systematicity of thought. At most, future science can show that Connectionism is true, *despite* its inability to explain the systematicity of thought" (but cf. Cummins, 1996). In any case, the systematicity problem seems to have been largely ignored in SLA theorizing, and it is hardly likely that it will be resolved there.

5 SLA Transition Theories

Where the SLA property theory will explain the nature of the cognitive states of an L2 learner, the SLA transition theory will explain the causal processes that effect changes in those states such that L2 knowledge becomes instantiated in the learner's cognitive system. As with the property theory, the transition theory should be an idealized one, abstracting away from a specific L1 and L2 or from a specific group of learners. To borrow terms from Sterelny and Griffiths (1999), a general SLA transition theory should aim for a *robust process explanation* rather than an *actual sequence explanation*:

> *Actual sequence explanations* seek to explain the nuances of the causal history of the world we find ourselves in. They explain the contrasts between our actual history and the histories of the nearby possible worlds. For such purposes, the more fine-grained the explanation, the better . . . *Robust process explanations* reveal the *insensitivity* of a particular outcome to some feature of its actual history. Thus an explanation of World War I that appeals to the political divisions of Europe is a robust process explanation, seeking to show that some World War I-like event was very probable. The detailed unraveling of diplomatic and military maneuverings is an actual sequence explanation, showing how we got our actual World War I. (p. 84)

As Sterelny and Griffiths go on to point out, the two types of explanation are not rivals, and each has its own legitimacy. However, in so far as we are trying to formulate a theory of L2 acquisition as such, and not simply an account of how certain learners acquired a certain L2, we need a robust process explanation. As with the case of the property theory and variation in final states, once we have something like a robust process explanation we should be in a better position to offer actual sequence explanations, to account for the various specific deviations from the ideal process that are actually attested.

On any account, the result of SLA is a set of representations of the L2, however different they may be from the native speaker's representations. Since those new representations are representations of the L2, and vary rather neatly according to what L2 input is provided – you need input of English to get representations of English – it seems a safe bet to assume that input is the major causal factor in SLA. (I am using "input" here in the atheoretical sense in which it's generally used in the SLA literature, viz. to refer to the *utterances* of speakers other than the learner, heard (or read) by that learner. The actual characterization of the input to the learning mechanism depends on the property theory being assumed. See Carroll, 1999, forthcoming, for detailed discussion.) This assumption is all the safer given that we are, tentatively at least, restricting ourselves to adult SLA, and hence can eliminate maturational processes as causal powers in the forming of an L2 representational system.

Finally, since our transition theory is an internalist one, we will need to posit some sort of mental mechanism – a learning mechanism – that can act on the input to create the representations. There will no doubt be other internal causal factors – motivation, for instance – but these will necessarily be secondary, for the simple reason that they cannot themselves process linguistic input. Motivation can directly affect the amount and frequency of input, for instance – by getting the learner to go to class and pay attention, say – but motivation alone cannot tell a noun from a verb, let alone parse a sentence or set a parameter value.

In a word, an SLA theory minimally must account for the role of input and must provide for a learning mechanism to create L2 representations based on that input.

5.1 *Learning mechanisms*

Learning has generally been taken to be an inductive process of trial and error. Hence the often-used term, "hypothesis-testing": on the basis of environmental stimuli, the learner (consciously or unconsciously) makes tentative hypotheses, which are then confirmed or disconfirmed by further stimuli. Certainly some forms of language learning are inductive on anyone's account. A child hears a few examples of verbs in the past and present forms, and finally induces a rule of past-tense formation, say. Of course the term "rule" is highly tendentious; a connectionist, no doubt, would prefer to say that the child develops an extremely strong tendency to associate what a linguist would describe as the past tense form with new verbs, in the absence of disconfirming evidence. The effect is the same, however stated; the learner inductively acquires the past tense marker and can use it expertly once a certain number of exemplars have been presented.

Of course, some learning could not be inductive, again on anyone's account: you can't induce the existence of D, E, and F on the basis of hearing A, B, and C, for instance, but rather must have the entire alphabet presented to you. This is sometimes referred to as brute force enumeration: simply all the exemplars of a given set are presented to the learner. In the same way, it might be possible to present the learner – at least an adult learner – not with a small sampling of the set of past-tense verbs to be learned, but rather with an explicit rule for producing those verbs. But it should be clear that the possibilities in language learning for brute force enumeration will be fairly limited, and I will say no more about it.

In any case, there seems to be a serious insufficiency with inductive learning as an explanation of the language acquisition process. Induction is notoriously *fallible*; the next raven we run into may be white, the next verb irregular. This is a problem, for first language acquisition theorists at least, because first language acquisition is standardly taken to be *in*fallible.[11] This simple but immense fact has, as we all know, led theorists to posit some sort of deductive learning mechanism, pre-eminently parameter-setting triggered by appropriate input. What sorts of input are appropriate, of course, is the big question (see, e.g., J. D. Fodor, 1998; Gibson and Wexler, 1994); but in any case it is assumed that the input feeds into a *parser*, which processes the information if it can, and revises the current grammar if it can't, in order to be able to handle the problematic input. Thus, for a theory that assumes some sort of rule-like, systematic representational system in its property-theory component, the transition theory will largely consist of a theory of grammatical parsing of input.

It will, of course, have occurred to the reader that "infallibility" is not the most apt term for characterizing SLA. And indeed, one might want to attribute the pretty much general failure, or seeming failure, to acquire nativelike L2 competence to the parser's inability to learn from its failures. The adult learner, it could be argued, has a representational system of the same general type as the native – not, *pace* Bley-Vroman (1990), a fundamentally different one – but a parser that can no longer make adjustments in the developing grammar to correct for parsing failures.

5.2 *The role of input*

An SLA transition theory will, of course, vary according to the property theory with which it is linked. Thus, depending on whether the property theory is a "classical" one of some sort – a UG/SLA theory, say, or a cognitive nativist theory – or a connectionist one, we will have different views of the role of input in acquisition.

5.2.1 Frequency

One question, simple enough on the face of it, is the relation between frequency of input and acquisition: how often does input of X need to be provided in order for X to be acquired? Actually, the question is badly put, since we don't receive input of X. What we want to know, rather, is this: in order to create representation R, how often does input that (in some sense that needs to be made clear by the property theory) "contains" R need to be presented to the learner?

On a connectionist view, it would seem that for any and every R, a good deal of relevant input would be necessary. A connectionist learning system learns by adjusting the weights of connections between nodes, and those adjustments, although not monotonic, are comparatively slow and gradual. For connectionists, as Ellis and Schmidt point out, one advantage of connectionist models is that they are "data-driven with prototypical representations emerging as a natural outcome of the learning process rather than being prespecified and innately given by the modellers as in more nativist cognitive accounts" (1998, p. 317). Put a bit differently, "What distinguishes between [connectionist and classical systems] is that, although both can learn, the former can't be programmed but have to be trained. As it turns out, that's a mixed blessing" (J. A. Fodor, 1998d, p. 85). Training takes time, and since the input is the trainer, that means a good deal of input is needed. Language learning seems to be a gradual process, so the gradual, input-based nature of connectionist models is often touted as a plus.

Of course, as Fodor says, this blessing is mixed. Learning a language certainly takes time, but that does not mean that learning any and every specific element of a language takes time. As Sterelny notes, "Lots of human learning is quick; there is a lot of one-shot learning from perception and language. Connectionist learning looks a good model for skill learning, but not for information gathering" (Sterelny, 1990, p. 193; cf. Schmidt, 1994). It is thus perhaps not surprising that, despite talk of representations, connectionists tend to speak in terms of skills.

Theories that, unlike connectionist theories, allow for the existence of rules nonetheless recognize the need for repeated input of R in some cases at least, but there is an important difference. In order to acquire, say, knowledge of plural formation in English, all theories agree that the learner needs to be presented with exemplars of regular nouns in the singular and the plural (putting aside for the moment the possibility of being presented with an explicit rule for plural formation; see "negative evidence" in section 5.2.2). The question is what happens next. A classical theory would see the input acting as the basis for inducing a rule, which would become the *de*ductive basis for determining the plural of nouns not yet presented in input. A connectionist theory, on the other hand, would see the relevant input as merely increasing the strength of association between input nouns and plural *-s*; an asymptotic increase, perhaps, but still only a statistical association, not a rule-based one.[12]

Where connectionist theories may be embarrassed by one-shot learning, UG/SLA theories have the opposite problem. Although UG theories can accept the need for perhaps fairly large doses of input in the formation of specific rules like English pluralization, the core of language learning presumably lies in parameter-setting. And where rule-formation is an inductive process, parameter-setting is supposed to be deductive. Hence the idea of triggering. Input for parameter-setting is not intended as evidence for a hypothesis, but rather as a stimulus that will reliably provoke the learning mechanism to fix one element of the grammar. Triggering is deductive not in the sense that the learner actually engages in anything like deductive reasoning, but rather in the sense that the chain from input to grammar-formation is infallible in the way that the chain from premises to conclusion is infallible in a deductive syllogism. Triggering is deductive in the way that imprinting is: the newly hatched duckling acts *as if* reasoning, "If it moves, it's Mom; that thing just moved; *ergo*, that thing is Mom."

This is all well and good if you're a duck, or if you're an ethologist studying ducks; there's a well-demonstrated relation between cause and effect that should be highly satisfactory to the both of you. The language acquisition theorist is not in such an enviable position; very little is even thought to be known about what specific stimuli in the input could act as the trigger for the setting of a specific parameter in a specific language. And in SLA, discussion of triggering, and of parsing in general, is close to non-existent. In any case, if there is triggering in SLA, one would expect – at least, in the absence of an extenuating explanation – fairly clear-cut results, in the form of a very steep learning curve following the triggering act. Indeed, one exemplar of whatever it is that is necessary to set a given parameter should suffice for that parameter to be correctly and permanently set.[13] We do not seem to have evidence showing such sudden effects in SLA, and indeed there is evidence (e.g., Kanno, 1999; O'Grady, 1999a) that L2 parameter setting may take years, even under seemingly ideal conditions.

5.2.2 *Negative evidence and modified input*

In first language acquisition, the child succeeds in acquiring native competence without benefit of negative evidence – explicit correction, or explicit metalinguistic information, such as about how to make the past tense. But of course it is widely believed that adults can benefit from negative evidence; so widely, indeed, that there is a multimillion-dollar publishing industry based on this belief. Still, that doesn't mean the belief is incorrect. If I tell you that in Japanese the past tense form of *asobu* is *asonda*, you may very well learn that fact, and even go on to infer that the past tense form of *yobu* is *yonda*. I rather doubt that anyone in SLA has ever believed that *no* negative evidence is *ever* usable, or that negative evidence can never accelerate the *speed* of acquisition. Nor do I imagine that anyone is claiming that negative evidence is always usable; no one, I trust, is arguing that learners will benefit from having ECP violations called to their attention. The real questions for an SLA theory are, is negative evidence ever *necessary* in SLA, and if so, when? One fairly concrete suggestion that has been made (White, 1987, 1989) is that when the L1 and L2 are in a superset/subset relation with respect to a given parameter, the learner will be unable to reset the parameter to the more restrictive subset value, in the absence of negative evidence (for some critical comments on the treatment of the Subset Principle in SLA, see Gregg, 1996a, 2001; White, 1989). In general, as always, the question is still open.

One's position on this question, and the fervor with which one defends it, will depend to some extent on the kind of property theory one supports. A UG/SLA theorist, for instance, should be perfectly comfortable with negative evidence being useful sometimes, so long as the evidence does not implicate UG. UG, after all, is posited as a solution to the problem of the poverty of the stimulus; but if the teacher or the textbook tells you all you need to know about forming the past tense of Japanese verbs, then the stimulus is not impoverished, and there's no puzzle about why you now know about Japanese past-tense formation. The point – or the claim, at least – about language competence is that it vastly transcends the kinds of knowledge that could conceivably be acquired through provision of this sort of evidence; not that 100 percent of language competence consists of such knowledge, only that it includes such knowledge to an important extent. Thus, while UG/SLA theorists can live with a role for negative evidence, that role must needs be a minor one at best.

Ironically, perhaps, a connectionist would seem to need to be more strongly committed to the non-efficacy of negative evidence than a UG/SLA theorist. Language acquisition, like all other learning, is for the connectionist a strengthening of associations, say between verb stems and past tense forms. The strengthening is accomplished by repeated input of the relevant forms, not by explicit metalinguistic reference to the forms. It's not clear (to me, anyway) how input of a sentence like, "The past tense is *-ed*," even repeated a hundred times a day, can be used by a "neural network" to strengthen the connection between verbs and their past tense forms. Thus in this sense it would seem that the connectionist SLA theorist must rely on positive evidence – everyday input – to an even greater extent than the UG/SLA theorist.[14]

A child L1 acquirer also seems to do just fine without any special modifications of the input; despite years of heroic effort, researchers have failed to show the necessity of "motherese," expansions, repetition, recasts, or other forms of input modification. But adult L2 learners *don't* do just fine in general, so perhaps modified input is necessary, or at least useful (Long, 1996). That is a theoretical possibility, of course, although the jury is still not in. But even if it turns out to be the case that input modification is essential for the acquisition of nativelike competence, this would not be much more of a contribution to the framing of a transition theory than would the discovery that motivation is essential, and for the same reason. Modifying the input is basically a way of making the input cleaner, more easily handled by the learning mechanism, whatever that is; in the extreme case, input modification makes the input input. By the same token, sitting attentively in the language classroom each day, rather than hanging out in the quad, makes the input in that classroom input, rather than noises off. But neither a theory of motivation nor a theory of input modification will tell us how the learning mechanism operates on the input, howbeit modified, to produce a bit of grammar.

6 Evaluating SLA Theories

It's not really clear that we yet have anything worth calling a theory of SLA, in which case it may seem premature to discuss evaluating them. Still, there are at least proposals on the table, if not perhaps very detailed proposals, and we can at least consider what sorts of problems these proposals, or future theories, may face.

6.1 Red herrings

First, though, we need to dismiss a couple of non-problems that get raised all too often in the literature.

6.1.1 Plausibility

Proposals are often evaluated – prematurely, I would say – in terms of their plausibility. Connectionists, for instance, are fond of pointing to the putative similarity of their somewhat tendentiously named "neural network" models to the way the brain really works.[15] More often, plausibility arguments take the form of an attack on a rival proposal for being *im*plausible on one ground or another. These attacks usually are simply examples of what Dawkins (1986) calls the Argument from Personal Incredulity; rather than providing empirical or theoretical evidence contradicting the proposal, one simply appeals to one's sense of what is and is not likely. In SLA, proposals based on theories of Universal Grammar have been especially subject to such attacks, especially perhaps from adherents of what Stoljar and Gold (1998, p. 111) call the "Biological Neuroscience Thesis," the thesis that mental science is *biological* neuroscience, "where 'biological neuroscience' is intended to include only those sciences traditionally regarded as part of neurobiology, roughly: neuroanatomy, neurophysiology, and neurochemistry." Thus Jacobs and Schumann (1992), for instance, along with numerous others, dismiss the constructs of generative linguistic theory as no better than metaphors. Similarly, Ellis tells us that "Innate specification of synaptic connectivity in the cortex is unlikely. On these grounds, linguistic representational nativism seems untenable" (Ellis, 1999, p. 25).

Arguments such as these simply have no force. Implausibility is one of the hallmarks of the natural world, from gravity and quarks to echolocation and metamorphosis, and the mind is one of the most implausible things around. Not, mind you, that we should adopt Tertullian's motto (*Credo quia absurdum est*, I believe because it is absurd), but the appeal to unlikeliness is simply no argument at all. Whether, say, UG exists or not is an open question, of course. But UG is posited not because it's plausible, but because it can explain certain phenomena – phenomena, moreover, about the existence of which there is little dispute. And in science, one normally rejects an explanation only when one has a superior explanation to replace it. At the moment, no adherent of the Biological Neuroscience Thesis has anything like an explanation to rival those offered by linguistic theories that posit something like UG.[16]

Now, scientists do, of course, reject certain theories out of hand, on grounds that may seem like the Argument from Personal Incredulity. No scientist accepts so-called "creation science," for instance, or time travel, or ESP. But these "theories" are not rejected because of their implausibility – a concept for which there is no useful standard against which to measure theories – but because they lack any empirical confirming evidence, while simultaneously contradicting well-confirmed theories that explain a great many phenomena. To accept these truly implausible theories would entail abandoning those well-confirmed theories and the explanations they provide, in exchange for nothing, a price no rational person should be willing to pay.

This is definitely *not* the case with UG, or more generally with cognitive theories that posit mental organization at a level higher than, and not directly reducible to, the neurological. Accepting a UG theory does, of course, require abandoning certain other possible theories of the mind. But unlike creationism or ESP, UG theory does not contradict any well-confirmed theory of the mind, and hence does not require us to abandon well-supported explanations of mental phenomena. The unhappy fact is that we don't *have* much in the way of well-supported explanations of mental phenomena; in fact, linguistics is about the most advanced of the cognitive sciences. At this point at least, McLaughlin and Warfield claim, "there is nothing known about the human brain that gives any reason whatsoever to doubt that it contains a classical cognitive architecture" (1994, p. 381; cf. Smolensky, 1999). This does not mean for a minute that UG theories are correct, of course; it merely means they are not to be rejected on such a flimsy ground as implausibility.[17]

6.1.2 Simplicity

Akin to plausibility is the red herring of simplicity. As we saw above, realists are willing to appeal to non-empirical factors, including simplicity, to adjudicate between rival theories, while empiricists are not. Putting aside the unsettled question whether such an appeal can ever be justified, it certainly is the case that it cannot *always* be justified. Occam's Razor, for instance (entities are not to be multiplied beyond necessity), can only be usefully invoked if it's clear whether a given theoretical construct is truly otiose, where one can compare a theory with the construct and the same theory without it. Thus, in perhaps the first explicit invocation of Occam's Razor in SLA, Gregg (1984) argued that the Affective Filter of Krashen (1981) was otiose in just this way. Such easy targets are rare, however, and it is normally quite difficult to decide, even intuitively, which of two theories is the simpler; all the more difficult when it's not even clear whether one has two theories to compare. As Chomsky said in relation to linguistic theory and first language acquisition, where far greater progress has been made than in SLA, "The issue of relative 'simplicity,' even if this notion can be given some content relevant to choice among theories, can hardly be sensibly raised in connection with theories so meager in confirming evidence and explanatory force as those that have been proposed to account for learning and behavior" (1980b, pp. 288–9).

Appeals to simplicity in SLA tend to be made, ironically enough, against realist positions such as UG/SLA theories. As with plausibility, the appeals are usually general metatheoretical claims, rather than specific comparisons between two theories, say one with binding principles and one without. Thus Ellis, for instance, notes that connectionists are fond of appealing to Morgan's Canon, the principle introduced by the evolutionary biologist Lloyd Morgan, which holds that "in no case may we interpret an action as the outcome of a higher psychical faculty if it can be interpreted as the outcome of one which stands lower in the psychological scale" (Ellis, 1999, p. 28). The canon here seems to be being used as a form of Occam's Razor (although that may not be the appropriate interpretation; cf. Sober, 1998), but in fact the argument doesn't go through. As Morgan himself noted, "the canon by no means excludes the interpretation of a particular activity in terms of the higher processes, if we already have independent evidence of the occurrence of these higher processes in the animal under observation" (Morgan, 1903, p. 59; cited in Sober, 1998, p. 240, fn. 1). But we have such independent evidence, and in abundance, for relevant higher processes in humans; the systematicity argument is based on just such evidence. Morgan's Canon will keep us from attributing beliefs to bacteria and syntax to snakes, but it's of no use in assessing claims about the nature of language and language acquisition.

6.2 Explanatory problems

We are still left with plenty of real problems for an SLA theory to overcome, a few of which I'll discuss briefly.

6.2.1 Replacing UG

If we exclude UG/SLA theories for the moment, probably the most fundamental problem facing SLA property theories is that they don't exist. For better or worse, SLA theories of L2 knowledge are theories of UG, using the term loosely to include a number of competing variants, the differences among which we can ignore here. This is regrettable, for although interesting and valuable SLA research can be and is being carried out without an underlying well-articulated property theory, ultimately the question of that underlying theory needs to be addressed. The UG/SLA people – or some subset of them, at least – may turn out to be correct, but we don't know that yet, and it's always beneficial to have competition. At the moment there simply is no well-articulated rival theory of L2 competence against which to measure UG theories.

Now, it might seem that connectionism offers just such a rival, but appearances can be misleading. What one sees, by and large, are connectionist simulations of language acquisition, whose results are (perhaps overoptimistically) interpreted by connectionists as obviating the need for "classical" entities like syntactic rules or principles. But even on the rosiest interpretation of connectionist work on SLA – even, that is, if we were to concede that the simulations are truly successful in "acquiring" the knowledge in question, *and* even if we were to make the much greater concession that the simulations mirror human language learning processes – we still have no explanation of what it is that the learner has acquired. As Sterelny, anything but a foe of connectionism, says, "[T]here is no argument to connectionism as a global theory of the mind from its demonstrated success in dealing with some major portion of it" (Sterelny, 1990, p. 192). Classical theories, including UG theories of language, can explain – whether correctly or incorrectly is another question – such robust phenomena as the systematicity and productivity of language, because classical theories can appeal to rules and principles with causal powers. Connectionist theories are at a disadvantage when trying to explain systematicity and productivity precisely because they reject the concept of non-artifactual rules, without replacing them with anything that can do the job. As McLaughlin and Warfield argue, "connectionists have yet to articulate an alternative to the classical conception of thought, and we think the prospects for its offering an adequate alternative are dim" (1994, p. 374; cf. Gold and Stoljar, 1999; Jackendoff, 1999). And *mutatis mutandis* for language.

6.2.2 "Access to UG"

Among those property theories based on some concept of UG, there is the question of whether or not UG plays an identical role in adult L2 acquisition and in child language acquisition. This question has often been characterized as the question of "access to UG," an unfortunate metaphor that confuses the issue instead of illuminating it.[18] Basically, the question is whether an adult L2 grammar is constrained in exactly the same way as an L1 grammar is constrained by the various principles and parameters of UG. If it is, we would expect, regardless of whatever other "imperfections" or "gaps" there might be in the L2 knowledge representations, to find nothing that violates UG; there should be no "wild" or "rogue" grammars.

The evidence generally seems to indicate an absence of rogue L2 grammars (but see, e.g., Klein, 1995; Thomas, 1991; for detailed discussion, see White, forthcoming, ch. 2). The question, though, is why one would have expected otherwise. That is, under what conception of UG could the "access" question arise in the first place? With earlier characterizations of the access debate, at least – White's (1989) UG-is-dead/UG-is-alive, Gregg's (1996a) theists vs. deists – the assumption seems to have been that UG is a machine to make grammars. Full access would mean that the machine is still in perfect working order; partial access would mean that the machine was in some way impaired and that the final product consequently lacked some parts; and zero access would entail having to build the L2 grammar with different tools. In any case, UG was implicitly being conceived of as separate from any particular grammar.

Now, this is not an incoherent stance to take, but it is inconsistent with most current understandings of UG, where a given grammar (say, the English grammar I carry around in my head) just *is* the set of UG principles, instantiated in a specific way. Without the principles there's no instantiation, which is to say that I am accessing UG every time I open my mouth, and that UG can't die until I do. Of course, on some views of UG there might be UG principles and parameters – and there certainly will be parameter values – that are not relevant to the L1 (subjacency was once one such candidate; cf. Bley-Vroman,

Felix, and Ioup, 1988). One could then argue that the learner has no access to precisely those elements of the L2, while having access to those elements relevant to the L1. This would be a "partial access" theory, I suppose; but it seems hard to distinguish it from "zero access" proposals like Bley-Vroman's Fundamental Difference Hypothesis (1990), at least as far as their claims about the nature of L2 representations go.

In fact, it would seem that the various proposals about access to UG need to be formulated as transition theories if they are to be distinguished one from the other and compared. UG, after all, is a set of constraints, and having full access to UG in effect means being fully constrained by UG (see White, this volume). Thus Epstein et al., for instance, define "access" as follows: "We mean by 'X is accessible' only that 'X constrains the learner's hypothesis space'" (1996, fn. 5). But as several of their commentators point out (Gregg, 1996b; Sprouse, 1996; White, 1996; *inter alia*), this definition leaves open all sorts of unwelcome possibilities. Given, for instance, that every parameter setting there is lies within the hypothesis space defined by UG, "access" is fully consistent with the L2 learner (or the L1 learner, for that matter) setting every single parameter to the wrong value. It would be cold comfort to both learner and theorist if learners merely avoided rogue grammars while failing to process input at all successfully. More to the point, however deviant their L2 grammars may be, learners don't in fact do anything so irrational as ignore input, and that fact cannot be attributed simply to "full access to UG" if that merely means full obedience to grammatical constraints.

I by no means wish to disparage the "no rogue grammars" argument. If, as seems to be the case, L2 learners do not produce rogue grammars, that is a highly significant fact, calling for an explanation. And indeed, the significance of this fact is often devalued by appeals (e.g., Epstein et al., 1996) to the absence of truly weird grammars among L2 learners: grammars violating structure-dependence, for instance. More to the point would be cases where UG bans a grammar, but common sense and the input don't. For instance, Binding Theory allows certain variations in the scope of anaphors: the Japanese equivalent of *John thinks that Bill should introduce himself to Mary* is ambiguous as to whether John or Bill is to be introduced to Mary. To my knowledge, while there are languages like Japanese that permit reference to either the matrix subject or the embedded subject, and languages like English that permit only reference to the embedded subject, there is no language that permits only reference to the matrix subject.[19] If adult learners still have "access to UG," then English natives learning Japanese should never create such a rogue anaphor system, even if every single instance of anaphora in the input happened to make unambiguous reference to the matrix subject. On the other hand, if learners persist in restricting Japanese anaphora to the embedded subject, they are remaining comfortably within the hypothesis space of UG; they simply aren't getting the appropriate UG-constrained message from the input.

The access question, in short, needs to be illuminated by the transition theory if it is to be settled. We need more than an enumeration of the elements of UG which are no longer "accessible" to an adult learner, if there are such elements. To explain those deficits, we also need an account of how input should affect learning if those deficits were not there.

6.2.3 *Variation across final states*

Sooner or later, any SLA theory must deal with the fact that the final state, however characterized by the property theory, varies across learners, and differs from the final state achieved by a native speaker. Different theories will have different answers to these two problems, and may have different difficulties in making their answers stick.

To start with, why don't L2 learners acquire the L2 to the same degree as natives? The obvious answer might seem to be age: there definitely do seem to be robust negative correlations between age of onset of acquisition and final proficiency (Long, 1990b). And there is strongly suggestive evidence, at the least, for a critical period or periods for language acquisition, although there still is a good deal of disagreement among researchers on this question (see the papers in Birdsong, 1999; Hyltenstam and Abrahamsson, this volume). But even on the most favorable interpretation of the evidence, age cannot be the whole story, or we would expect absolutely no L1 influence on L2 development, which is clearly not the case. But again, to claim that Maria's English competence surpasses Keiko's because, say, both English and Spanish are SVO while Japanese is SOV is to beg an important question: why should these cross-linguistic difficulties be insuperable? Granting that the word-order difference might benefit Maria, why should Keiko fail to catch up? (Assuming she does fail, of course, and putting aside the question of Mariko, who can already run rings around Maria.) Unfortunately, it's hard to answer these questions yet, in part because most of the research related to age effects has not been conducted within a well-articulated property theory, but rather has contented itself with an unsatisfactory concept of "proficiency," which, while it can be "operationalized" with elegant accuracy (TOEFL over 600, say), lacks theoretically interesting content.

7 Conclusion

There are, of course, numerous other problems confronting the SLA theorist, but it is in fact an encouraging sign that we can specify them as clearly as we now can. The last two decades of SLA research have seen not only a huge increase in the database, but also a much higher degree of conceptual precision and theoretical sophistication. And this is not only in the property theory, where generative grammatical theories continue to change and develop, but also in the transition theory. One should not be misled by the common empiricist origins of SLA behaviorism and SLA connectionism into overlooking how much better articulated and detailed the latter is, which makes it much easier to locate the problems. And connectionists have gone well beyond the dogmatic handwaving of the behaviorists to actually offer simulations of acquisition (it would be nice to see some UG/SLA computer models). It is hardly surprising, though, that theoretical and methodological problems still abound; SLA is a newly emerging scientific field, and problems come with the territory.

ACKNOWLEDGMENTS

I am happy to acknowledge the very helpful comments of William O'Grady and Lydia White, although I imagine they'll neither of them be that satisfied with how I've made use of them. Thanks also to Mike Long and to two anonymous reviewers.

NOTES

1 "Someone committed to naturalistic inquiry can consistently believe that we learn more of human interest about how people think and feel and act by studying history or reading novels than from all of naturalistic inquiry. Outside of narrow domains, naturalistic inquiry has proven shallow or hopeless" (Chomsky, 1995, p. 28).

2 One needs to distinguish between the scientific study of SLA on the one hand and the academic field of "applied linguistics" on the other. The latter, when it isn't simply the respectable field of foreign language education cloaked in a meretricious nomenclature, does not seem to have an object of study, a research program, or a goal. Indeed, there are frequent earnest discussions as to what in fact applied linguistics is or should be (*Issues in Applied Linguistics*, 1 (2); Kaplan, 1980). The amorphousness of the field of applied linguistics – the seeming lack of any of the theoretical and methodological constraints that one expects in an empirical discipline – has allowed many of its adepts to wander in what Shelley called the "intense inane," issuing pronouncements that range from vacuous to incoherent to downright delusional. Pasteur had it right a hundred years ago: "[T]here does not exist a category of science to which one can give the name applied science. There are science and the applications of science, bound together as the fruit to the tree which bears it" (cited by Leiden, 1999, p. 1215). It perhaps goes without saying that this chapter – indeed, this handbook – is not about applied linguistics.

3 Relativistic research, as Long suggests, is a contradiction in terms. This does not mean, however, that there are no SLA researchers who have espoused relativism in some form or other. Such espousals as have appeared in the literature, though (e.g., Block, 1996; Lantolf, 1996; Schumann, 1983; van Lier, 1994), are simply risible at best. See

Gregg et al. (1997), Gregg (2000), and Long (1998) for discussion.

4 The existence itself of UG, of course, cannot be rejected on the grounds of non-observability, nor does any sensible empiricist make such a rejection. The empiricist argument is not that what we cannot observe does not exist, but merely that we are not warranted in believing in the existence of what we cannot observe; a huge difference.

5 The so-called New Look perceptual psychology of the 1950s and 1960s seemed to show a strong influence of belief on perception. (J. A. Fodor's modularity thesis, 1983, is in part an extended refutation of, and indeed was a major factor in the rejection of, New Look psychology.) Kuhn (who, after all, was trained as a scientist) drew on these results as major empirical support for his conclusions about the theory-ladenness of observation. The irony of relying on theory-guided empirical research to justify a position which, if correct, would undermine any reason to accept the research was apparently lost on Kuhn.

6 Note that realists and relativists both oppose empiricists on the issue of the theory–observation distinction, although of course they draw radically different conclusions from this common opposition. As Kukla puts it, "realists and relativists agree that theoretical and observational hypotheses, if they can be distinguished at all, are in the same epistemic boat. They just differ as to the nature of the boat" (1998, p. 112). For realists, the illegitimacy of the distinction allows for the reality of (some) unobservable entities; for relativists, it leads to the subsumption of all observational results under the merely theoretical.

7 The idea that one must operationalize one's definitions is a relic of pre-war positivism that has survived only in psychology, to the bemusement of philosophers of science (e.g., Greenwood, 1991; Hempel 1966; Hull, 1974, 1988; Klee, 1997).

8 Eubank and Gregg (1995, p. 54) make this very point with reference to language acquisition: "Although we think the increased interest in neurolinguistics shown by SLA researchers is a promising sign of increasing sophistication in our field, the fact remains that little progress can be expected in acquisition theory if researchers fail to take linguistics seriously." In response, Schumann (1995, p. 61) insists that "A neurobiological perspective on language is responsible to language only and not to any particular linguistic characterization of language." An exactly parallel argument, of course, can be made by the astrologist: "An astrological perspective on the heavenly bodies is responsible to the heavenly bodies only and not to any particular astronomical characterization of heavenly bodies."

9 Cummins (1991, p. 114), however, argues that "adopting a connectionist architecture does not force one to abandon the 'classical' idea that cognition is to be understood as the computational manipulation of semantically structured representations." And on the other hand, Ramsey (1997) questions whether one need consider connection weights to be representations at all, structured or not: "there isn't anything about connectionism that demands we think the weights function as representations of stored information" (p. 49). Suffice it to say

that in general, connectionists themselves do consider their representations to reside in the varying connection weights, and that they do take these representations to differ from "classical" representations precisely in being unstructured.

10 "Clark [1993, p. 225] says that we should 'bracket' the problem of systematicity. 'Bracket' is a technical term in philosophy which means *try not to think about*" (J. A. Fodor, 1998a, p. 99).

11 Well, not infallible, of course, or why does language change over time? Still, the idealization to an unerring language acquisition device seems eminently reasonable, given the essentially uniform final states achieved by all unimpaired members of a roughly identifiable speech community.

12 Ellis and Schmidt (1998) tested their model of the acquisition of plural morphology on a nonce noun, and it did quite well in producing the regular plural of their artificial language. (Actually, it wasn't a true nonce word, but rather one that had only been presented in the singular.) Significantly, Ellis and Schmidt did not bother to test their human subjects on the same nonce word, merely suggesting that their test of the model was analogous to doing so. But of course on a rule-based account of plural-learning, one would predict that human subjects who had acquired the rule would not merely do quite well, but would score at or very near 100 percent, and would not benefit from further input.

13 This is, in fact, a problem for a triggering account of language acquisition. In the case of imprinting, there is a definite, albeit statistically minute, chance that the hatchling, say, will first see something other than its mother, and will form an irreparable bond with that "incorrect" stimulus object. What if the first relevant input for a given parameter happens by misadventure to be inappropriate for the target language? If parameter-setting were as deterministic as imprinting, the unfortunate child would presumably be stuck with a deviant grammar.

14 One might be tempted to treat the weakening of a connection due to the absence of strengthening stimuli as a form of indirect negative evidence; this temptation should be resisted. The idea of indirect negative evidence, as proposed by Chomsky (1984), is that "if certain structures or rules fail to be exemplified in relatively simple expressions, *where they would be expected to be found* [emphasis added], then a (possibly marked) option is selected excluding them in the grammar" (p. 9); in effect, a sort of unconscious deduction by *modus tollens*. But connection-weakening has nothing to do with rules, expected or otherwise; the failure of the learner to make a connection between singular nouns and [ba], based on the total absence of input of [ba] immediately after a singular noun in the input, may well serve to keep that learner from acquiring [ba] as the English plural marker; it won't lead the learner to acquire /z/.

15 The similarity of neural network models to neural networks lies more in the eye of the beholder, or rather the modeler, than in reality, connectionist protestations notwithstanding; for discussion see, e.g., J. A. Fodor (1998e); Rey (1997).

16 "To advocate the biological neuroscience thesis . . . is to claim

that eventually we will have explanations of mental phenomena that are couched in the concepts of neurobiology. This view is extremely interesting, but one would need considerable evidence to accept it" (Stoljar and Gold, 1998, p. 111; see Gold and Stoljar, 1999, for detailed discussion).

17 It is often argued that UG is inconsistent with evolutionary theory (see, e.g., Deacon, 1997; Lieberman, 1984, 1991). If this were true, it would be a strong argument against UG theory, given that evolutionary theory is well confirmed, to say the least. But in fact there is no reason to believe that there is any contradiction; see, for example, J. A. Fodor, 1998f, 1998g; Pinker and Bloom, 1990; for arguments from very different perspectives against the argument from evolutionary implausibility.

18 There is a sizeable literature on the "access" question. See, for instance, the papers in Eubank (1991); Epstein, Flynn, and Martohardjono (1996) and the commentaries thereon. There is also a set of papers given at a colloquium on the issue at the 1998 SLRF (by Bley-Vroman, Carroll, Gregg, Meisel, Schwartz, and White), available on the internet: <www.lll.hawaii.edu/nflrc/NetWorks/NW9>.

19 Actually, if Iatridou (1986) is correct, there is at least one such language (Greek). Still, the point remains that there could be UG-banned but plausible – inductively acquirable – IL grammars, grammars that should not, on the "access" account, be attested.

REFERENCES

Aizawa, K. 1997: Explaining systematicity. *Mind and Language*, 12, 115–36.

Ariew, A. 1996: Innateness and canalization. *Philosophy of Science (Proceedings 63)*, S19–S27.

Ariew, A. 1999: Innateness is canalization: in defense of a developmental account of innateness. In V. G. Hardcastle (ed.), *Where Biology Meets Psychology: Philosophical Essays*. Cambridge, MA: MIT Press, 117–38.

Baron-Cohen, S. 1995: *Mindblindness: An Essay on Autism and Theory of Mind*. Cambridge, MA: MIT Press.

Bates, E. and MacWhinney, B. 1988: What is functionalism? *Papers and Reports on Child Language Development*, 27, 137–52.

Beretta, A. 1991: Theory construction in SLA: complementarity and opposition. *Studies in Second Language Acquisition*, 13, 493–511.

Beretta, A. and Crookes, G. 1993: Cognitive and social determinants of discovery in SLA. *Applied Linguistics*, 14, 250–75.

Birdsong, D. (ed.) 1999: *Second Language Acquisition and the Critical Period Hypothesis*. Mahwah, NJ: Lawrence Erlbaum Associates.

Bley-Vroman, R. 1983: The comparative fallacy in interlanguage studies: the case of systematicity. *Language Learning*, 33, 1–17.

Bley-Vroman, R. 1990: The logical problem of foreign language learning. *Linguistic Analysis*, 20, 3–49.

Bley-Vroman, R., Felix, S., and Ioup, G. 1988: The accessibility of Universal Grammar in adult language learning. *Second Language Research*, 4, 1–32.

Block, D. 1996: Not so fast: some thoughts on theory culling, relativism, accepted findings and the heart and soul of SLA. *Applied Linguistics*, 17, 63–83.

Bogen, J. and Woodward, J. 1988: Saving the phenomena. *Philosophical Review*, 97, 303–52.

Boyd, R. 1989: What realism implies and what it does not. *Dialectica*, 43, 5–29.

Broeder, P. and Plunkett, K. 1994: Connectionism and second language acquisition. In N. C. Ellis (ed.), *Implicit and Explicit Learning of Languages*. New York: Academic Press, 421–53.

Brueckner, A. 1998: Conceptual relativism. *Pacific Philosophical Quarterly*, 79, 295–301.

Carroll, S. E. 1995: The hidden dangers of computer modelling: remarks on Sokolik and Smith's connectionist learning model of French gender. *Second Language Research*, 11, 193–205.

Carroll, S. E. 1999: Putting "input" in its proper place. *Second Language Research*, 15, 337–88.

Carroll, S. E. forthcoming: *Input and Evidence: The Raw Material of Second Language Acquisition*. Amsterdam: John Benjamins.

Chomsky, N. 1959: Review of B. F. Skinner, *Verbal Behavior*. *Language*, 35, 26–58. Reprinted in J. Fodor and J. Katz (eds) 1964: *The Structure of Language: Readings in the Philosophy of Language*. Englewood Cliffs, NJ: Prentice-Hall, 547–8.

Chomsky, N. 1980a: *Rules and Representations*. New York: Columbia University Press.

Chomsky, N. 1980b: Some empirical assumptions in modern philosophy of language. In H. Morick (ed.), *Challenges to Empiricism*. Belmont, CA: Wadsworth, 287–318.

Chomsky, N. 1984: *Lectures on Government and Binding*. 3rd revised edition. Dordrecht: Foris.

Chomsky, N. 1986: *Knowledge of Language*. New York: Praeger.

Chomsky, N. 1995: Language and nature. *Mind*, 104, 1–61.

Clark, A. 1993: *Associative Engines*. Cambridge, MA: MIT Press.

Coltheart, M. and Langdon, R. 1998: Autism, modularity and levels of explanation in cognitive science. *Mind and Language*, 13, 138–52.

Cummins, R. 1983: *The Nature of Psychological Explanation*. Cambridge, MA: MIT Press.

Cummins, R. 1991: The role of representation in connectionist explanations of cognitive capacities. In W. Ramsey, S. P. Stich, and D. E. Rumelhart (eds), *Philosophy and Connectionist Theory*. Hillsdale, NJ: Lawrence Erlbaum Associates, 91–114.

Cummins, R. 1996: Systematicity. *Journal of Philosophy*, 93, 591–614.

Dawkins, R. 1986: *The Blind Watchmaker*. New York: Norton.

Deacon, T. 1997: *The Symbolic Species: The Co-Evolution of Language and the Brain*. New York: Norton.

Ellis, N. C. 1999: Cognitive approaches to SLA. *Annual Review of Applied Linguistics*, 19, 22–42.

Ellis, N. C. and Schmidt, R. 1998: Rules or associations in the acquisition of morphology? The frequency by regularity interaction in human and PDP learning of morphosyntax. *Language and Cognitive Processes*, 13, 307–36.

Epstein, S. D., Flynn, S., and Martohardjono, G. 1996: Second language acquisition: theoretical and experimental issues in contemporary research. *Behavioral and Brain Sciences*, 19, 677–758.

Eubank, L. (ed.) 1991: *Point Counterpoint: Universal Grammar in the Second Language*. Amsterdam: John Benjamins.

Eubank, L. and Gregg, K. R. 1995: "*Et in amygdala ego*"? UG, (S)LA, and neurolinguistics. *Studies in Second Language Acquisition*, 17, 35–57.

Eubank, L. and Gregg, K. R. 1999: Critical periods and (second) language acquisition: *divide et impera*. In D. Birdsong (ed.), *Second Language Acquisition and the Critical Period Hypothesis*. Mahwah, NJ: Lawrence Erlbaum Associates, 65–99.

Firth, A. and Wagner, J. 1997: On discourse, communication, and (some) fundamental concepts in SLA research. *Modern Language Journal*, 81, 286–300.

Fodor, J. A. 1983: *The Modularity of Mind*. Cambridge, MA: MIT Press.

Fodor, J. A. 1998a: *Concepts: Where Cognitive Science Went Wrong*. Oxford: Clarendon Press.

Fodor, J. A. 1998b: *In Critical Condition: Polemical Essays on Cognitive Science and the Philosophy of Mind*. Cambridge, MA: MIT Press.

Fodor, J. A. 1998c: Connectionism and the problem of systematicity (continued): why Smolensky's solution *still* doesn't work. In J. A. Fodor, *In Critical Condition: Polemical Essays on Cognitive Science and the Philosophy of Mind*. Cambridge, MA: MIT Press, 113–25.

Fodor, J. A. 1998d: Review of Paul Churchland's *The Engine of Reason, the Seat of the Soul*. In J. A. Fodor, *In Critical Condition: Polemical Essays on Cognitive Science and the Philosophy of Mind*. Cambridge, MA: MIT Press, 83–9.

Fodor, J. A. 1998e: Review of Jeff Elman et al., *Rethinking Innateness*. In J. A. Fodor, *In Critical Condition: Polemical Essays on Cognitive Science and the Philosophy of Mind*. Cambridge, MA: MIT Press, 143–51.

Fodor, J. A. 1998f: Review of Richard Dawkins's *Climbing Mount Improbable*. In J. A. Fodor, *In Critical Condition: Polemical Essays on Cognitive Science and the Philosophy of Mind*. Cambridge, MA: MIT Press, 163–9.

Fodor, J. A. 1998g: Review of Steven Pinker's *How the Mind Works* and Henry Plotkin's *Evolution in Mind*. In J. A. Fodor, *In Critical Condition: Polemical Essays on Cognitive Science and the Philosophy of Mind*. Cambridge, MA: MIT Press, 203–14.

Fodor, J. A. and McLaughlin, B. 1998: Connectionism and the problem of systematicity: why Smolensky's solution doesn't work. In J. A. Fodor, *In Critical Condition: Polemical Essays on Cognitive Science and the Philosophy of Mind*. Cambridge, MA: MIT Press, 91–111.

Fodor, J. A. and Pylyshyn, Z. W. 1988: Connectionism and cognitive architecture. *Cognition*, 28, 3–71.

Fodor, J. D. 1998: Unambiguous triggers. *Linguistic Inquiry*, 29, 1–36.

Gass, S. 1998: Apples and oranges: or, why apples are not orange and don't need to be. *Modern Language Journal*, 82, 83–90.

Gibson, E. and Wexler, K. 1994: Triggers. *Linguistic Inquiry*, 25, 407–54.

Gold, I. and Stoljar, D. 1999: A neuron doctrine in the philosophy of neuroscience. *Behavioral and Brain Sciences*, 22, 809–69.

Greenwood, J. D. 1991: *Relations and Representations: An Introduction to the Philosophy of Social Psychological Science*. London: Routledge.

Gregg, K. R. 1984: Krashen's Monitor and Occam's Razor. *Applied Linguistics*, 5, 79–100.

Gregg, K. R. 1989: Second language acquisition theory: the case for a generative perspective. In S. M. Gass and J. Schachter (eds), *Linguistic Perspectives on Second Language Acquisition*. Cambridge: Cambridge University Press, 15–40.

Gregg, K. R. 1990: The Variable Competence Model of second language acquisition, and why it isn't. *Applied Linguistics*, 11, 364–83.

Gregg, K. R. 1993: Taking explanation seriously; or, let a couple of flowers bloom. *Applied Linguistics*, 14, 276–94.

Gregg, K. R. 1996a: The logical and developmental problems of second language acquisition. In W. C. Ritchie and T. K. Bhatia (eds), *Handbook of Second Language Acquisition*. San Diego: Academic Press, 49–81.

Gregg, K. R. 1996b: UG and SLA: the access question, and how to beg it. *Behavioral and Brain Sciences*, 19, 726–7.

Gregg, K. R. 2000: A theory for every occasion: postmodernism and SLA. *Second Language Research*, 16, 383–99.

Gregg, K. R. 2001: Learnability and second language acquisition theory. In P. Robinson (ed.), *Cognition and Second Language Instruction*. Cambridge: Cambridge University Press, 152–82.

Gregg, K. R., Long, M. H., Jordan, G., and Beretta, A. 1997: Rationality and its discontents in SLA. *Applied Linguistics*, 18, 538–58.

Hacking, I. 1983: *Representing and Intervening*. Cambridge: Cambridge University Press.

Hanson, N. R. 1958: *Patterns of Discovery*. Cambridge: Cambridge University Press.

Hawkins, R. and Chan, C. Y.-H. 1997: The partial availability of Universal Grammar in second language acquisition: the "failed functional features hypothesis." *Second Language Research*, 13, 187–226.

Hempel, C. G. 1966: *Philosophy of Natural Science*. Englewood Cliffs, NJ: Prentice-Hall.

Hull, D. L. 1974: *Philosophy of Biological Science*. Englewood Cliffs, NJ: Prentice-Hall.

Hull, D. L. 1988: *Science as a Process*. Chicago: University of Chicago Press.

Iatridou, S. 1986: An anaphor not bound in its governing category. *Linguistic Inquiry*, 17, 766–72.

Jackendoff, R. 1999: Parallel constraint-based generative theories of language. *Trends in Cognitive Sciences*, 3, 393–400.

Jacobs, B. and Schumann, J. H. 1992: Language acquisition and the neurosciences: towards a more integrative perspective. *Applied Linguistics*, 13, 282–301.

Kanno, K. 1999: Acquisition of verb gapping in Japanese by Mandarin and English speakers. In K. Kanno (ed.), *The Acquisition of Japanese as a Second Language*. Philadelphia: John Benjamins, 159–73.

Kaplan, R. (ed.) 1980: *On the Scope of Applied Linguistics*. Rowley, MA: Newbury House.

Karmiloff-Smith, A. 1992: *Beyond Modularity*. Cambridge, MA: MIT Press.

Kasper, G. 1997: "A" stands for acquisition. *Modern Language Journal*, 81, 307–12.

Klee, R. 1997: *Introduction to the Philosophy of Science: Cutting Nature at its Seams*. Oxford: Oxford University Press.

Klein, E. 1995: Evidence for a "wild" L2 grammar: when PPs rear their empty heads. *Applied Linguistics*, 16, 87–117.

Krashen, S. D. 1981: *Principles and Practice in Second Language Acquisition*. Oxford: Pergamon Press.

Kuhn, T. S. 1970: *The Structure of Scientific Revolutions*. 2nd edition, enlarged. Chicago: University of Chicago Press.

Kukla, A. 1998: *Studies in Scientific Realism*. New York: Oxford University Press.

Lantolf, J. P. 1996: SLA theory building: "Letting all the flowers bloom!" *Language Learning*, 46, 713–49.

Larsen-Freeman, D. and Long, M. H. 1991: *An Introduction to Second Language Acquisition Research*. London: Longman.

Latour, B. 1987: *Science in Action*. Cambridge, MA: Harvard University Press.

Latour, B. and Woolgar, S. 1986: *Laboratory Life: The Construction of Scientific Facts*. 2nd edition. Princeton, NJ: Princeton University Press.

Laudan, L. 1990: *Science and Relativism*. Chicago: University of Chicago Press.

Laudan, L. 1996: *Beyond Positivism and Relativism*. Boulder, CO: Westview Press.

Leiden, J. M. 1999: Gene therapy enters adolescence. *Science*, 285, 1215–16.

Leplin, J. 1997: *A Novel Defense of Realism*. New York: Oxford University Press.

Lieberman, P. 1984: *The Biology and Evolution of Language*. Cambridge, MA: Harvard University Press.

Lieberman, P. 1991: *Uniquely Human: The Evolution of Speech, Thought, and Selfless Behavior*. Cambridge, MA: Harvard University Press.

Long, M. H. 1990a: The least a second language acquisition theory needs to explain. *TESOL Quarterly*, 24, 649–66.

Long, M. H. 1990b: Maturational constraints on language development. *Studies in Second Language Acquisition*, 12, 251–85.

Long, M. H. 1993: Assessment strategies for second language acquisition theories. *Applied Linguistics*, 14, 225–49.

Long, M. H. 1996: The role of the linguistic environment in second language acquisition. In W. C. Ritchie and T. K. Bhatia (eds), *Handbook of Second Language Acquisition*. San Diego: Academic Press, 413–68.

Long, M. H. 1997: Construct validity in SLA research: a response to Firth and Wagner. *Modern Language Journal*, 81, 318–23.

Long, M. H. 1998: SLA: breaking the siege. *University of Hawai'i Working Papers in ESL*, 17 (1), 79–129.

McLaughlin, B. 1987: *Theories of Second-Language Learning*. London: Edward Arnold.

McLaughlin, B. P. and Warfield, T. A. 1994: The allure of connectionism reexamined. *Synthese*, 101, 365–400.

Maxwell, G. 1962: The ontological status of theoretical entities. In H. Feigl and G. Maxwell (eds), *Scientific Explanation, Space and Time*. Minneapolis: University of Minnesota Press.

Morgan, C. L. 1903: *An Introduction to Comparative Psychology*. 2nd edition. London: Walter Scott.

Nagel, T. 1997: *The Last Word*. New York: Oxford University Press.

O'Grady, W. 1996: Language acquisition without Universal Grammar: a general nativist proposal for L2 learning. *Second Language Research*, 12, 374–97.

O'Grady, W. 1997: *Syntactic Development*. Chicago: University of Chicago Press.

O'Grady, W. 1999a: Gapping and coordination in second language acquisition. In K. Kanno (ed.), *The Acquisition of Japanese as a Second Language*. Philadelphia: John Benjamins, 141–58.

O'Grady, W. 1999b: Toward a new nativism. *Studies in Second Language Acquisition*, 21, 621–33.

Pinker, S. and Bloom, P. 1990: Natural language and natural selection. *Behavioral and Brain Sciences*, 13, 707–84.

Ramsey, W. 1997: Do connectionist representations earn their explanatory keep? *Mind and Language*, 12, 34–66.

Ramsey, W. and Stich, S. P. 1991: Connectionism and three levels of nativism. In W. Ramsey, S. P. Stich, and D. E. Rumelhart (eds), *Philosophy and Connectionist Theory*. Hillsdale, NJ: Lawrence Erlbaum Associates, 287–310.

Rey, G. 1997: *Contemporary Philosophy of Mind*. Oxford: Blackwell.

Schachter, J. 1996: Maturation and the issue of Universal Grammar in second language acquisition. In W. C. Ritchie and T. K. Bhatia (eds), *Handbook of*

Second Language Acquisition. San Diego: Academic Press, 159–93.

Schmidt, R. 1994: Implicit learning and the cognitive unconscious: of artificial grammars and SLA. In N. Ellis (ed.), *Implicit and Explicit Learning of Languages*. New York: Academic Press, 165–209.

Schumann, J. H. 1983: Art and science in second language acquisition research. In A. Guiora (ed.), *An Epistemology for the Language Sciences. Language Learning* special issue, 33, 49–75.

Schumann, J. H. 1995: *Ad minorem theoriae gloriam*: a response to Eubank and Gregg. *Studies in Second Language Acquisition*, 17, 59–63.

Schwartz, B. D. 1986: The epistemological status of second language acquisition. *Second Language Research*, 2, 121–59.

Schwartz, B. D. 1998: The second language instinct. *Lingua*, 106, 133–60. Reprinted in A. Sorace, C. Heycock, and R. Shillcock (eds) 1999: *Knowledge Representation and Processing*. Amsterdam: Elsevier, 133–60.

Schwartz, B. D. 1999: Let's make up your mind: "special nativist" perspectives on language, modularity of mind, and nonnative language acquisition. *Studies in Second Language Acquisition*, 21, 635–55.

Smith, N. and Tsimpli, I.-M. 1995: *The Mind of a Savant: Language, Learning, and Modularity*. Oxford: Blackwell.

Smolensky, P. 1987: The constituent structure of mental states: a reply to Fodor and Pylyshyn. *Southern Journal of Philosophy*, 26, 137–60.

Smolensky, P. 1995: Connectionism, constituency, and the language of thought. In C. Macdonald and G. Macdonald (eds), *Connectionism*. Cambridge, MA: Blackwell, 164–98.

Smolensky, P. 1999: Grammar-based connectionist approaches to language. *Cognitive Science*, 23, 589–613.

Sober, E. 1994a: Contrastive empiricism. In E. Sober (ed.), *From a Biological Point of View: Essays in Evolutionary Philosophy*. Cambridge: Cambridge University Press, 114–35.

Sober, E. 1994b: Evolution, population thinking, and essentialism. In E. Sober (ed.), *From a Biological Point of View: Essays in Evolutionary Philosophy*. Cambridge: Cambridge University Press, 201–32.

Sober, E. 1998: Morgan's Canon. In D. D. Cummins and C. Allen (eds), *The Evolution of Mind*. Oxford: Oxford University Press, 224–42.

Sober, E. 1999: Testability. Presidential address to the Central Division of the American Philosophical Association in New Orleans, May. *Proceedings and Addresses of the APA*, 73 (2), 47–76.

Sokolik, M. E. and Smith, M. E. 1992: Assignment of gender to French nouns in primary and secondary language: a connectionist model. *Second Language Research*, 8, 39–58.

Sprouse, R. A. 1996: Appreciating the poverty of the stimulus in second language acquisition. *Behavioral and Brain Sciences*, 19, 742–3.

Sterelny, K. 1990: *The Representational Theory of Mind: An Introduction*. Oxford: Blackwell.

Sterelny, K. and Griffiths, P. E. 1999: *Sex and Death: An Introduction to Philosophy of Biology*. Chicago: University of Chicago Press.

Stoljar, D. and Gold, I. 1998: On biological and cognitive neuroscience. *Mind and Language*, 13, 110–31.

Strozer, J. R. 1994: *Language Acquisition after Puberty*. Washington, DC: Georgetown University Press.

Tarone, E. E. 1994: A summary: research approaches in studying second-language acquisition or "If the shoe fits . . ." In E. E. Tarone, S. M. Gass, and A. D. Cohen (eds), *Research Methodology in Second Language*

Acquisition. Hillsdale, NJ: Lawrence Erlbaum Associates, 323–36.

Thomas, M. 1991: Do second language learners have "rogue" grammars of anaphora? In L. Eubank (ed.), *Point Counterpoint: Universal Grammar in the Second Language*. Amsterdam: John Benjamins, 375–88.

van Lier, L. 1994: Forks and hope: pursuing understanding in different ways. *Applied Linguistics*, 15, 328–46.

White, L. 1987: Against comprehensible input. *Applied Linguistics*, 8, 95–110.

White, L. 1989: *Universal Grammar and Second Language Acquisition*. Amsterdam: John Benjamins.

White, L. 1996: UG, the L1, and questions of evidence. *Behavioral and Brain Sciences*, 19, 745–6.

White, L. forthcoming: *Universal Grammar in the Second Language: From Initial to Steady State*. Cambridge: Cambridge University Press.

Wimsatt, W. C. 1986: Developmental constraints, generative entrenchment, and the innate-acquired distinction. In W. Bechtel (ed.), *Integrating Scientific Disciplines*. Dordrecht: Martinus Nijhoff, 185–208.

Wimsatt, W. C. 1999: Generativity, entrenchment, evolution, and innateness: philosophy, evolutionary biology, and conceptual foundations of science. In V. G. Hardcastle (ed.), *Where Biology Meets Psychology: Philosophical Essays*. Cambridge, MA: MIT Press, 139–79.

Woodward, J. 1989: Data and phenomena. *Synthese*, 79, 393–472.

24 SLA and Cognitive Science

MICHAEL H. LONG AND CATHERINE J. DOUGHTY

Little more than three decades of research since modern SLA emerged as a serious field of inquiry in the late 1960s have brought significant advances in our knowledge of the acquisition process and of typical patterns in final achievement. A neo-behaviorist conception of second language learning as the substitution of one set of language patterns and habits for another through such opaque processes as "overlearning" has been replaced by an awareness that, to the extent that habit formation plays a role at all, it is in the development of skill and fluency, not to be confused with the new underlying L2 knowledge system that makes "skill" and "fluency" possible – and knowledge is a matter of mind, not behavior. A discernible trend, therefore, especially in the 1980s and 1990s, has been for increasing numbers of researchers and theorists, rationalists all, to focus their attention on SLA as an internal, individual, in part innately specified, cognitive process – one that takes place in a social setting, to be sure, and can be influenced by variation in that setting and by other interlocutors, as demonstrated by several chapters in this volume, but a psycholinguistic process, nonetheless, which ultimately resides in the mind-brain, where also lie its secrets.

A discernible trend does not imply consensus or unanimity, however, and there remain identifiable groupings of scholars – socioculturalists, conversation analysts, and action theorists, for example – who persist in seeing external learner behavior, even group behavior, not mental states, as the proper domain of inquiry. More generally (and more vaguely) there are "critical theorists" and an often overlapping group of self-professed epistemological relativists, who express general angst with SLA's cognitive orientation and/or its growing accountability to one or more theories and to empirical findings while offering no alternative but the abyss.

In this light, it is not surprising that indications abound of increasing tensions and fragmentation within the field. More conferences are held which offer platforms primarily or exclusively for papers with one or other theoretical allegiance, journals are born which attempt to do the same, research funding is sought from different government agencies and private foundations depending on the kind of work involved, philosophical assumptions range from rationalist to relativist, an array of qualitative and quantitative research methods is imported from the various disciplines in which SLA scholars were originally trained, and (healthily increasing numbers of) jobs for SLA specialists are offered in a variety of university departments, including linguistics, modern languages, psychology, English, and education. (To our knowledge, there are as yet no departments of first or second language acquisition.) Given such variability and growing diversification, it is becoming less and less clear whether "SLA" is viable as a discipline at all, or where its future lies if it has one. SLA has traditionally hovered on the borders between the humanities and social sciences, yet many scholars (including most authors in this volume) identify themselves increasingly as cognitive, not social, scientists.

Cognitive science is a field whose unifying focus is its principal object of inquiry: the mind. Cognitive scientists accept that study of cognitive phenomena involves use of the notions of representation and computation, and further that successful research will require interdisciplinary collaboration. Cognitive scientists conduct research on such matters as the evolution and nature of human intelligence; intelligence and reasoning in humans, other animals, and machines; novice and expert approaches to problem solving; individual and group (e.g., cultural) differences in cognition; the localization of mental functions in the brain; biological constraints on language development; the neural bases of perception, learning, and memory; the ways language is processed, acquired, stored, accessed, and used; and relationships between innate and learned knowledge. Applications include robotics, information processing, data retrieval, medical diagnoses and treatments, manufacturing, telecommunications, human–computer interaction, treatment of communication disorders, and the design of instruction.

While knowledge, intelligence, reasoning, consciousness, and thought processes in general have occupied philosophers from Aristotle and Plato to the present day, modern cognitive science is generally accepted as dating from three major developments in the late 1950s and early 1960s. The first of these, based on pioneering work by the British mathematician Alan Turing in the 1940s and 1950s, and the building of the first digital computers soon thereafter, was the initiation by Minsky, Newell, Simon, and others in the 1960s of research programs in artificial intelligence, producing such early successes as Newell, Simon, and Shaw's computer program, Logic Theorist. The second development was the dismantling of the behaviorist hegemony in psychology, begun by Miller's work on short-term memory and Chomsky's famous review of Skinner's *Verbal Behavior* in 1959, and its replacement by a pre-eminently cognitive, information-processing approach that holds sway to this day. The third, heralded by the publication of Chomsky's *Syntactic Structures* in 1957, was related work on language and language learnability by

Chomsky, Fodor, and others that replaced the patterns and habits of American structuralism with the rules and modules of the generative tradition, and had a lasting impact on linguistics and on research in first and second language acquisition.

A survey of publications in the journal *Cognitive Science* and presentations at the annual meeting of the Cognitive Science Society from 1977 to 1995 (Schunn, Crowley, and Okada, 1998) found that two disciplines, cognitive psychology and computer science, had dominated both journal and conference during that period, between them accounting for over half the articles and papers. This dominance may soon change, however. The dramatic increase in the accessibility and use of computers in numerous areas of public and private life has given further impetus to the field, simultaneously providing both seemingly endless new applications and the technological means to achieve them. Not unrelated, in neurophysiology, new brain scanning and imaging techniques, notably computer-assisted tomography, positron emission topography, and magnetic resonance imaging, have led to greater understanding of the functions of different cerebral areas, for example, the location of various linguistic abilities and memory, and relationships between cognitive impairments and anatomical damage in different locations, and have made cognitive neuroscience an increasingly central and successful research area.

While the new science is still young, indications of its institutional recognition have grown rapidly over the past 25 years. The journal *Cognitive Science* was founded in 1977, and the Cognitive Science Society in 1979. Cognitive science programs at the undergraduate and graduate levels are offered by over 60 universities in North America, Europe, and Australasia, with new ones announced every year. Conferences devoted to the whole field or to domains within it are ever more numerous.

As is inevitable in the emergence of any new discipline, the first generations of cognitive scientists hail from diverse academic backgrounds and training programs: artificial intelligence, linguistics, anthropology, biology, neuroscience, philosophy, physiology, mathematics, education, speech and hearing, library information science, computer science, electrical engineering, and more. Most hold formal academic qualifications in those fields, not in cognitive science per se, and collectively they employ a large variety of research methods in their work. The formal academic training now available in the new discipline tends to consist not of a lengthy series of courses in "cognitive science" per se, either, but of one or two introductory survey courses, followed by extensive work in one or more of the feeder disciplines, such as psychology or computer science, emphasizing domains inside them that speak to the broader issues and applications of interest outside, in cognitive science.

The huge diversity of the new discipline means that the work of some practitioners is unintelligible or of only marginal interest to others, and that some research which appears in cognitive science books and journals could just as easily appear in publications within the source discipline, and vice versa. It is not surprising, therefore, that questions have been asked both within the field and by outsiders as to whether a discipline of cognitive science distinct from the disciplines on which it draws really exists, or whether "cognitive science" is just an umbrella term for (sometimes very) loosely related work in each of them. Moreover, is it the case that to qualify as cognitive science, particular research programs should be multidisciplinary (this is sometimes referred to as the *localist* conception of multidisciplinarity; Schunn et al., 1998), or, more inclusively, is it enough that multiple disciplines contribute to the field's overall research program (the so-called *holist* conception; Von Eckardt, 2001)?

To the extent that *Cognitive Science* and the Cognitive Science Society reflect tendencies in the field as a whole both inside and outside the USA (and they may not), the evidence suggests that cognitive science is more than just the sum of its parts, that it increasingly has an identity of its own, independent of, albeit closely related to, its source disciplines. Thus, as indicated by departmental affiliations of first authors, collaboration make-up of authors, research methodology used (computer simulation and/or empirical study, or neither), and disciplinary sources of previous theories and results cited, Schunn et al. (1998) noted that despite the steady dominance of psychology and computer science overall (linguistics and philosophy being very minor players thus far), multidisciplinary studies were on the increase, accounting for 30–50 percent of work in the journal in recent years. The same was true of "cognitive science" departments or institutes as authors' primary work affiliation, recently amounting to nearly 20 percent of the papers.

Cognitive science and SLA, it transpires, exhibit many of the same characteristics: youth, interdisciplinarity, theoretical and methodological diversity, and lack of a single clear institutional home. Cognitive science has the immense advantage, however, of the substantive coherence accruing from its common focus of inquiry, the mind and cognition. As reflected in the chapters in this volume, many SLA scholars share that focus: grammatical nativists, general nativists, connectionists, processing researchers, those studying individual differences in such attributes as age, aptitude, intelligence, memory, or cognitive style, and those investigating such processes as implicit, explicit, incidental and intentional learning, and automatization, among others. Underlying all their work is a shared conception of SLA as a cognitive process involving representations and computations on those representations. There is a big difference between that conception and the view prevalent among some applied linguists that would equate "SLA" with almost any research having to do with non-natives when they *use* a second language. Much of the work that would be included under the broader definition is rigorous and valuable, but little of it has anything to do with how people *learn* a second language – or, at least, a connection has yet to be demonstrated.

But a common focus is not enough. For SLA to achieve the stability, stimulation, and research funding to survive as a viable field of inquiry, it needs an intellectual and institutional home that is to some degree autonomous and separate from the disciplines and departments that currently offer shelter. Cognitive science is the logical choice.

REFERENCES

Schunn, C. D., Crowley, K., and Okada, T. 1998: The growth of multidisciplinarity in the Cognitive Science Society. *Cognitive Science*, 22 (1), 107–30.

Von Eckardt, B. 2001: Multidisciplinarity and cognitive science. *Cognitive Science*, 25, 453–70.

Index